Putting asunder

Putting asunder

A history of divorce
in Western society

RODERICK PHILLIPS

Brock University, Ontario

The right of the
University of Cambridge
to print and sell
all manner of books
was granted by
Henry VIII in 1534.
The University has printed
and published continuously
since 1584.

CAMBRIDGE UNIVERSITY PRESS

Cambridge

New York   New Rochelle   Melbourne   Sydney

Published by the Press Syndicate of the University of Cambridge
The Pitt Building, Trumpington Street, Cambridge CB2 1RP
32 East 57th Street, New York, NY 10022, USA
10 Stamford Road, Oakleigh, Melbourne 3166, Australia

First published 1988

Printed in the United States of America

Library of Congress Cataloging-in-Publication Data
Phillips, Roderick.
Putting asunder: a history of divorce in western society /
Roderick Phillips.
p.   cm.
Bibliography: p.
Includes index.
1. Divorce – Europe – History.   2. Divorce – America – History.
3. Divorce – Religious aspects – History.   4. Divorce – Law and legislation – History.
I. Title.
HQ811.P48   1988
306.8′9′09 – dc19   88–10867

British Library Cataloguing-in-Publication Data
Phillips, Roderick
Putting asunder: a history of divorce in western society.
1. Western world. Divorce to 1988
I. Title
306.8′9′091821

ISBN 0 521 32434 3

For Alyssa

Contents

Contents

Contents

Preface

Of the many paradoxes that the modern Western family presents us, the most striking is the simultaneous popularity of marriage and divorce. Generally speaking, marriage is as popular today as it has been at any period in the past. In the nineteenth century and earlier quite significant proportions of men and women could not hope to marry, and never did; today in most Western countries almost everyone marries at some time in her or his lifetime. What John Gillis writes in the introduction to his history of marriage in Britain holds true for the rest of Western society: "We live in a conjugal age, when the couple has become the standard for all intimate relationships...Commerce panders to the conjugal ideal and municipalities zone in its favour. Children play at it; teenagers practice it."[1]

Children might not play at divorce, explicitly at least, nor teenagers practice it very often, but divorce has become the common partner of marriage at the center of the Western family system. Divorce too has never been as widespread as it has become in recent times. Even though divorce rates in some countries, such as the United States, stabilized in the early 1980s, they did so at unprecedented high levels, whereas in many other countries they continued to rise. Precise statistical measurements of divorce, expressed as rates per thousand population or per thousand married women, demonstrate how divorce has increased during the twentieth century and especially from the early 1970s, although more widely understood expressions have entered popular awareness. We are regularly told, depending on where we live, that one in two, three, or four marriages ends in divorce.

The high divorce rates that have become characteristic of modern Western society have provoked various reactions. Some commentators see them as indicative of the decline of marriage and the family; others construe them as part of an emerging marriage pattern in which many, perhaps most, men and women will marry twice or more often during their lifetimes. Divorce is perceived by some as a threat to social stability; others insist that the Western family system can accommodate a high incidence of divorce. Many different reasons have been given for the increase in divorce. Prominent among them are a shift or decline in morality, the decreased influence of religion, the effects of

[1] John R. Gillis, *For Better, For Worse: British Marriages, 1600 to the Present* (New York, 1985), 3.

xi

the women's movement, married women's employment outside the home, and rising expectations of marriage.

Some of these perspectives confuse divorce with marriage breakdown, and there are various understandings of the relationship between the two phenomena. Some see divorces as little more than the death certificates of marriages that have already ended. Others hold the very availability of divorce responsible for a putative tendency on the part of modern couples to terminate their marriages too readily when they experience stress. As for the extent of marriage breakdown, some commentators insist that the rising divorce rate reflects a rising rate of marriage breakdown. Others, however, argue for a redistributive hypothesis: that marriage breakdown has long been widespread, but that in recent times an increasing proportion of broken marriages is dissolved legally. According to this theory, rising divorce rates should really be seen as a more accurate reflection of marriage breakdown, not an accurate reflection of more marriage breakdown.

With its sensitive social and moral implications, divorce research is a minefield where scholars and other commentators must not only crawl through methodological and theoretical entanglements but also pick their way carefully through political issues that can prove explosive. The incidence of marital dissolution in modern society is seldom observed with equanimity or nonchalance. Social conservatives frequently associate divorce with phenomena such as widespread abortion, illegitimacy, and sexual promiscuity in a complex of putative threats to the social and moral stability of Western society. Even by itself, divorce is generally described, by those alarmed at the divorce rates, in the language of natural disaster; divorce is a flood, a rising tide, an avalanche, anything that will sweep away or erode the foundations of society. Liberal analysts, on the other hand, tend to focus on the benefits of divorce, seeing in it the means for women and men to escape from exploitative or simply unhappy marriages. They often point to the high rate of remarriage as a sign that divorce indicates not a rejection of marriage, but rather a determination to form a satisfying marriage. This more optimistic outlook has been increasingly tempered, however, by an awareness of the negative effects of prevailing divorce policies and their application on women and children in particular.

This book is first and foremost a history of divorce, but it necessarily addresses some of the issues raised by divorce in modern times. The question most often asked about divorce – "Why is it so common today?" – is implicitly historical, for any answer to it must address the implied question of why divorce was so uncommon in the past. Similarly we must look to the past for a full appreciation of other aspects of divorce in the modern world. Popular attitudes toward divorce and divorced women and men, the character of divorce law, and prevailing secular and ecclesiastical policies cannot be properly understood without some idea of their evolution over the long or medium term.

Recent historical scholarship has contributed a great deal to our knowledge of the social, economic, demographic, and cultural aspects of family formation and marriage in earlier times. The outpouring of books and articles since the 1960s on the history of the family has thrown much light on marriage patterns in Western societies, and we now appreciate dominant patterns in marriage rates, trends in age at marriage, criteria for choice of spouse, premarital pregnancy rates, and the duration of marriage. Historians have exploited a wide range of statistical and other sources in order to achieve some understanding of such complex questions as the emotional content of marriages – whether husbands and wives in earlier times had affective relationships that were typically warm, cool, or indifferent.

Yet although central facets of the family such as marriage, fertility, household structure, child–parent relationships, economic activity, and sexuality have been subjected to a great deal of investigation, divorce and marriage breakdown have generally remained tangential issues. The major surveys of the history of the Western family, including those by Edward Shorter, Jean-Louis Flandrin, and Michael Mitterauer and Reinhard Sieder,[2] make only passing reference to divorce and to related phenomena such as separations and other manifestations of marriage breakdown. Lawrence Stone's survey of the family in England[3] deals with divorce somewhat more systematically, but even there divorce and associated issues are clearly considered to be minor topics. John Gillis's magisterial study of marriage in Britain deals overwhelmingly with the making, rather than the unmaking, of conjugal matches.[4] Significantly, one book that surveyed the recent historiography of the Western family not only failed to cite any of the recent work on divorce and marriage breakdown, but also did not mention the existence of those phenomena at all.[5]

I am far from intending to berate these historians for neglecting divorce, for their treatment of it reflects two realities. The first is that except for one or two specific periods, such as the revolutionary years in France, divorces were extremely rare in Western society until the late nineteenth century. Second, signs of marriage breakdown apart from the infrequent divorces and separations are generally sparse and inconclusive. There is evidence of desertions (especially by husbands), bigamy, wife sales, and the like, and there is also a great deal of evidence of marital stress and violence that might or might not indicate marriage breakdown. Broadly speaking, however, the quality of the data is frequently not encouraging for firm conclusions and this, together with its treatment in general histories of the family, tends to reinforce the image that

---

[2] Edward Shorter, *The Making of the Modern Family* (New York, 1975); Jean-Louis Flandrin, *Familles. Parenté, maison, sexualité dans l'ancienne société* (Paris, 1976, translated as *Families in Former Times*, Cambridge, 1979); Michael Mitterauer and Reinhard Sieder, *Vom Patriarchat zur Partnerschaft: zum Strukturwandel der Familie* (Munich, 1977, translated as *The European Family*, Oxford, 1982).

[3] Lawrence Stone, *The Family, Sex and Marriage in England, 1500–1800* (London, 1977). Some of Stone's assertions about divorce and marriage are challenged by R. B. Outhwaite, *Marriage and Society: Studies in the Social History of Marriage* (London, 1981), 8–9.

[4] Gillis, *For Better, For Worse.*

[5] Michael Anderson, *Approaches to the History of the Western Family, 1500–1914* (London, 1980). For criticism of the omission see the review by Olwen Hufton in *Social History* 7 (1982), 344–6.

marriages were stable in the past. The same point is generally true of works that have focused on marriage. There the stress has been on the formation and functioning of conjugal relationships, rather than on breakdown and dissolution, and again these emphases are quite appropriate.

Even so, since the 1970s, soon after divorce rates in Western society began to rise dramatically, a body of historical literature has focused specifically on divorce. It has thrown new light on the development of divorce laws and policies, historical attitudes toward divorce, the application and use of the divorce laws, and the characteristics of couples who divorced. Many of the studies have placed divorce firmly within contemporary social, political, and cultural contexts. They have also illuminated the intimate aspects of married life and outlined the causes of stress and manifestations of marriage breakdown in the past. As a body of historical writing, these forays in the history of divorce form part of the current emphases on the social history of women, gender relationships, the law, the family, and demography.

The more recent books and articles are welcome additions to a rather slender tradition of historical divorce research that goes back to the late nineteenth century. George Elliot Howard's magisterial *History of Matrimonial Institutions* (1904) dealt in great detail with the development of the law of marriage and divorce in England and the United States up to the end of the nineteenth century. S. B. Kitchin's *History of Divorce* (1912) focused on divorce in European thought and legislation from classical times. The twin emphases on legal and intellectual history also informed later studies of divorce, such as O. M. McGregor's *Divorce in England* (published in 1957 to mark the centenary of the first English divorce law), and Nelson Blake's stimulating *The Road to Reno* (1962), a survey of divorce in America from colonial times to the 1950s. The same legal and attitudinal interests dominated Ivar Nylander's study of divorce in Sweden from the sixteenth to the nineteenth centuries, *Studier Rörande den Svenska Äktenskapsrättens Historia (Studies in the History of Swedish Marriage Law,* 1961) and William L. O'Neill's *Divorce in the Progressive Era* (1967), which focused on the great divorce debate in America in the late nineteenth and early twentieth centuries.

Research on the history of divorce since the early 1970s broke with this pattern and tended to reflect prevailing trends in historical research by concentrating increasingly on the social aspects of divorce. Historians began to ask who divorced and why, and to probe the relationship between women and divorce, the main causes and signs of stress in dissolved marriages, and the differences between these marriages and those that did not end in divorce. Such questions reflected not only a broadening of historical enquiry, but also current concerns about marriage and divorce, the family, and the status of women in modern society. Answers to them usually demanded intensive investigation of judicial and other legal records, and for this reason much of the recent work on the history of divorce is restricted in terms of location and time frame.

Preface

This is not the place to catalog the many articles, monographs, unpublished papers, and chapters in more general works that make up modern scholarship on the subject. This book draws on them and they are cited in the footnotes and listed in the bibliography, although I have tried to keep both as compact as possible. At this point let me just draw attention to their wide range in terms of location, period, and perspective. They include analyses of divorce in seventeenth-century Norway, eighteenth-century Connecticut, and nineteenth-century New South Wales, Australia. There are demographic studies of divorce in revolutionary France, philological studies of John Milton's divorce tracts in the seventeenth century, and analyses of the relationship of divorce law to married women's property legislation in nineteenth-century England. Certain phases of the history of divorce have commanded particular attention. Notable are the legalization of divorce in Reformation Europe and its implications, the liberal divorce legislation passed during the French Revolution, and the beginnings of mass divorce throughout much of Western society in the late nineteenth century. As the bibliography shows, I have had a great deal of secondary material to work with, and I must acknowledge the labor of earlier and contemporary historians in providing much of the basis of the present work.

In *Putting asunder* I have exploited the existing literature on the history of divorce and marriage, as well as a broad range of other secondary and both printed and unprinted primary sources, in order to present a history of divorce in Western society from the widest perspectives. "Western society" here comprises Western Europe, Great Britain, Scandinavia, North America, and Australasia, although my analysis at times strays beyond these bounds. Spread across half the globe, and disparate in many social, economic, and cultural respects, this Western society drew on common traditions of family law and policy. European, British, and Scandinavian legislation regarding marriage was determined or greatly influenced by Roman Catholic doctrine up to and beyond the sixteenth century, and marriage and divorce policies in America and Australasia drew in turn from European and British models. Such traditions give this broad Western society sufficient unity to enable us to consider it a coherent unit for historical analysis. At the same time there are enough variations and divergences to make this a comparative study within the broader geographical context. The Reformation led to more or less dramatic legal reform in matrimonial matters throughout Europe, although specific social and political developments as diverse as the English Civil War, the French Revolution, and the advent of national socialism in Germany had impacts on the ways divorce was thought about and acted upon.

When discussing trends in doctrines, legislation, and policies with regard to divorce, I have tried to maintain a balance between the general and the specific. Certain tendencies were clearly common to much of Western society; the legalization or liberalization of divorce in the later nineteenth century is an example. In other respects specific countries experienced developments that were peculiar to them. Examples are the failure of the Church of England,

Preface

alone among reformed churches, to abandon the Roman Catholic doctrine of marital indissolubility, and more recently the failure of the Irish Republic to provide for the legalization of divorce, even though other such predominantly Catholic countries as Spain and Italy have done so. My aim, in short, has been to write a history of divorce that appreciates variations among countries and states and recognizes their different chronologies of change, but that does not lose touch with the more general "Western" trends that give the study coherence.

The time span of the book is straightforward. For the most part it covers the period from the Middle Ages to the present. The initial chapter describes the status of divorce in Roman Catholic doctrine, for that is the immediate background of the Western model of divorce. Non-Catholic traditions from Jewish and Roman law, and from Germanic, Anglo-Saxon, and other customary and common laws, are discussed only briefly. Within the broad scope of the study I have not attempted to give equal space to each period because some were more important than others. For example, the sixteenth and the nineteenth centuries were critical in the development of divorce legislation, and the complexity of these periods required somewhat fuller analyses.

I have tried to illuminate the history of divorce from as many angles as possible, but three themes emerge as especially important. The first, which provides the book with a constant point of reference, is the development of divorce legislation. I have tried to avoid a too narrowly narrative account, however, and have placed legislation in the broader context of divorce policy, by which I mean the explicit or implicit intentions of those who enacted divorce codes or applied the legislation. In these respects we should be interested not only in the grounds on which a divorce could be obtained, but also whether divorce was viewed positively or negatively, whether it was facilitated or made difficult, and whether divorce was integral to a broader family or social policy. These questions involve a discussion of doctrines and attitudes to divorce, and the emphasis here is on the various churches and secular institutions that had authority to regulate marriage. Because divorce is a legal event that requires provision in law, and because divorce has always been a sensitive social and political issue, it is not surprising that the history of divorce at the legal and ideological level is closely associated with broad changes of the kind that have taken place in Western society during the last millennium. By avoiding a narrowly institutional approach, we can integrate divorce more fully into the mainstreams of historical change. For example, divorce had an important role in the doctrinal reforms of the Reformation, became entwined in the debate on political legitimacy of the English Civil War period, and was central to the debate on social reform and stability at the end of the nineteenth century.

The second major perspective of this book is the social history of divorce. Although divorces were rare until the later nineteenth century, they did take place, and limited-scale studies allow us to assess the characteristics of those who divorced. Chapter 7, for instance, examines the use of divorce laws in seven-

xvi

teenth- and eighteenth-century America, eighteenth-century France, and eigh-
teenth- and nineteenth-century England. In addition to highlighting the limitations of divorce legislation and revealing the ways in which laws influenced the
divorce rate, these studies tell us a great deal about the respective roles of
women and men within marriage, the family, and society at large. The social
perspective also permits us to investigate the broader influences on divorce
behavior. Divorce rates were influenced not only by the terms of divorce law
and by marital circumstances in the narrowest senses, but also by long- and
short-term social events. In this respect we can examine the impact on marriage of military conflict and of the major social and economic transformations
associated with industrialization and urbanization.

The third perspective introduces the question of marriage breakdown. It is
obvious that divorce and marriage breakdown are closely associated – so much
so that they are frequently treated synonymously – but it is equally clear that
they are different phenomena. The extent of divorce at any given time needs
bear no relationship to the incidence of marriage breakdown as the example of
divorceless societies, such as the Republic of Ireland shows. Nor do rates of
marriage breakdown necessarily influence divorce rates. However, marriage
breakdown is so evidently a necessary precondition of divorce, even if not a
sufficient precondition, that no history of divorce should overlook it. This study
discusses the way marriage breakdown – a very modern term – was defined in
earlier times, and how the definitions resulted not only from expectations of
marriage but also from the gender relationships within marriage and from the
social, economic, and material contexts of the family. The evidence of marriage
breakdown is described and discussed, and an assessment is made of its extent
in traditional society and changes in its extent over time. When placed in
relationship to divorce rates, this part of the study permits us to draw some
conclusions about long-term trends in marriage stability in Western society.

In short, *Putting asunder* seeks a comprehensive view of divorce in Western
society during the past thousand and more years. The main approaches are
religious, ideological, legal, institutional, social, economic, cultural, and demographic. I do not claim that it is exhaustive, however. I have not attempted to
describe all of the legal reforms in the period; to have done so would have been
boring and repetitive, especially in the case of the United States, where divorce
law is a state responsibility. Instead I have generalized and employed illustrative
examples. Nor have I quoted all opinions on divorce, even when they were
expressed by the great and the famous. Not only did Christ, Erasmus, Luther,
Milton, Voltaire, Frederick the Great, Jefferson, Napoleon, Disraeli, Lenin,
Mussolini, and Keynes all have something to say about divorce, but so did
thousands of other men and women. To have listed them in the text would have
made much of the book a mere catalog of opinions, and even dispatching them
to footnotes would have made it unnecessarily long in terms of my objective to
produce a manageable and readable account of what proved to be a subject
whose limits were not easily defined.

Preface

In the end, a book of this sort must be to some extent idiosyncratic. Some episodes more than others in the history of divorce have caught and held my attention, and readers might feel that I have lingered too long over certain periods at the expense of others. Similarly, some will probably be critical of omissions. Traversing, as I have done here, a broad terrain, I would be surprised if I did not encounter some suspicion or criticism when I happen across inhabited territory. I hope, however, that for the most part this enterprise will be received as it is intended, as an attempt to map the contours of a historical dimension whose topography is too little known.

Acknowledgments

This is my third book on the history of divorce, its predecessors having dealt with divorce in France during the revolution and in New Zealand during the nineteenth and twentieth centuries. Because my research for these earlier works laid the basis for this broader study and provided some of the material for it, the acknowledgments I expressed in them extend to the present book.

Beyond this, however, I have incurred a new set of debts, which I happily acknowledge here. Without exception, the personnel of the research libraries and archives I have used were generous with their help. Principal among them are the British Library, London; Bodleian Library, Oxford; Cambridge University Library, Cambridge; Bibliothèque Nationale, Paris; the Uppsala University library; and the Riksarkiv, Oslo. Access to these and other resources was facilitated by support at various times from the University of Auckland, which granted me leaves of absence, the Queen's University Advisory Research Committee, which provided funds for research and the preparation of the typescript, the Swedish Institute, which awarded me a fellowship at Uppsala University, and Brock University, which gave support from funds provided by the Social Sciences and Humanities Research Council of Canada.

Colleagues and friends in various parts of the world were more than hospitable when I arrived in search of divorces. Paul O'Flinn has always made me welcome in Wolvercote whenever I was reading in the Bodleian. Jan Trost was a congenial host in the months I spent in Uppsala, and Sølvi Sogner and Gudmund Sandvik of Oslo University generously offered their assistance during my brief stay in Norway. I also wish to thank Piers Mackesy, my former tutor at Oxford, and the Fellows of Pembroke College for having granted me membership of the Senior Common Room during one of my periods of research in Oxford. This is also an opportunity to salute my former colleagues Michael Graves and Peter O'Connor, without the likes of whom this book could not have been written.

Among the individuals who directly contributed to *Putting asunder*, I wish particularly to thank those who read and commented on parts of the manuscript: Michael Graves and Barry Reay of the University of Auckland, Christopher Greene and John Gilchrist of Trent University, and the readers engaged by Cambridge University Press, who were remarkably efficient in handling a long work. All made pertinent and valuable comments that saved me from making some embarrassing errors of fact and some contradictions, and their conscientious reading has made this a better book than it would otherwise have been. The book has also benefited from the suggestions of its editor at Cambridge University Press, Frank Smith. From the day we first discussed the project he has been enthusiastic and encouraging, not to mention understanding and patient as I failed to meet various deadlines I optimistically set myself. Michael Gnat and Ernestine Franco, who performed the technical tasks of editing, have been nothing but helpful in improving my presentation; readers might not be aware of my editors' contributions, but the absence of their work would certainly be obvious. For all the assistance I have been privileged to receive, however, I am aware of weaknesses and imperfections in the book, and will no doubt be made aware of yet more; I take full responsibility for them.

The many colleagues and friends who have listened to me talk about divorce for the past ten years or more deserve admiration for their stamina and patience in the face of what must have seemed an obsession on my part. They also deserve thanks for most of their suggestions and comments – although my having completed the book shows that I ignored some of the advice I received. I would particularly like to acknowledge the useful criticism, comments, and suggestions of lines of enquiry that invariably followed papers I gave on various aspects of this research. Among those to whom I owe gratitude in this regard are my friends who convene every two years for the stimulating George Rudé Seminars on French history, the members of the Cambridge Group for the History of Population and Social Structure, and the Social History seminar at the University of Essex.

My last acknowledgment is by no means my least. Alyssa Novick, to whom this study is dedicated, has been my best friend and my best critic during the last three years of its preparation. She has shared the highs and lows of research, writing, and proofreading, put up with my pacing and my ubiquitous coffee mugs, advised on style and content, and has given in more tangible and intangible ways than I could possibly describe. Her simply being there was vital, and it is appropriate, if ironic, that we decided to be joined together while I was writing *Putting asunder*.

1

The Roman Catholic background

1.1 Introduction

Roman Catholic doctrine is the inescapable background to the history of divorce in Western society from the Middle Ages onward. This is paradoxical given that the Catholic church's position that marriage is indissoluble, and that divorce is prohibited, was the orthodoxy that informed ideology and legislation regarding marriage and divorce for hundreds of years up to, and in many countries beyond, the sixteenth-century Protestant Reformation. For the most part, the history of divorce since the sixteenth century has been one of movement away from the Roman Catholic doctrines of marriage. This movement has varied in pace and significance over time and place and has not always followed a linear progression. By the late twentieth century the trend has reached a point where civil divorce legislation, popular attitudes toward divorce, and mass practice in respect of divorce owe virtually nothing to the Catholic marriage doctrines that were dominant only five centuries earlier. This is so not only where the Protestant Reformation was successful but also among modern populations that are predominantly Catholic, such as those of France and Belgium and, to a lesser extent, Italy and Spain.

Despite the fact that the history of divorce is, in one sense, a history of the progressive rejection of Roman Catholic marriage doctrines, any account of the development of divorce in Western society must include an appreciation of those very doctrines. The writings of the apologists and proponents of divorce, especially in the sixteenth and seventeenth centuries, must be placed firmly against the Catholic doctrinal background. Their arguments in favor of marital dissolubility by divorce were based on interpretations of biblical texts and of church authorities such as the Latin Fathers, interpretations that were at odds with those adopted by the Catholic church in the centuries preceding the Reformation. Insofar as the Protestant advocates of divorce did not so much adduce new sources and evidence in favor of their position but reinterpreted the old, we must understand the doctrines and practices they were attacking, as well as their positive proposals for change. We must note, too, that not all critics of the Catholic doctrine of marital indissolubility were Protestants; some, like Erasmus and Thomas More, sought to reconcile positions favorable to divorce with acceptance of broader Catholic doctrines.

1 The Roman Catholic background

The debate on divorce from the sixteenth century had two dimensions. One was among those who agreed that divorce should be permitted but disagreed among themselves on the circumstances that might justify dissolving a marriage. The principal distinction within the "dissolubilists"[1] (who would allow divorce) was between conservatives who would allow divorce for only one reason – almost always adultery – and liberals who would permit a greater range of justifying grounds for the dissolution of marriage – usually adultery and desertion or for those two grounds plus cruelty. The other dimension of the divorce debate set the dissolubilists as a group against the indissolubilists, those who insisted that divorce should not be permitted under any circumstances. Far from all of the indissolubilists were Catholics, but the Catholic church was clearly the prime and most influential exponent of the indissolubilist position. To this extent, Catholic marriage doctrine forms an important continuity, albeit a continuity of opposition, in the history of divorce in Western society.

The divorce doctrine that the Roman Catholic church had developed by the late Middle Ages, and that most Protestants were to react against, can be stated with deceptive simplicity and brevity: A validly celebrated Christian marriage was dissoluble only by the death of one of the spouses. It was a corollary of this principle that a married person might not enter into another marriage during the lifetime of his or her first spouse. But we must immediately note two potential exceptions to what was otherwise an absolute bar to divorce, although neither made divorce mandatory. The first concerned unions in which one member was not a Christian. In certain circumstances such a marriage could be dissolved "in favor of the faith" under the terms of what is known as the Pauline Privilege: in 1 Corinthians 15, in the context of a marriage that united a Christian with an unbeliever, Paul is given as saying: "But if the unbelieving [spouse] depart, let him depart. A brother or a sister [i.e., a Christian] is not under bondage in such cases."[2] This was understood as giving the right of remarriage to a Christian who had been deserted by an infidel spouse. The second area of ambivalence within the Catholic rule of marital indissolubility involved the nonconsummation of a marriage. For instance, where there had been no consummation, a marriage might be dissolved to permit one of the parties to enter a religious order. Dissolution was not possible once the mar-

---

[1] The terms "dissolubilist" and "indissolubilist" are used only as a convenient shorthand. They merely isolate the common feature of otherwise often disparate groups and individuals for the purpose of this study and should not obscure the important differentiations within each category. Max Rheinstein refers to the two competing ideals in respect to divorce as the Christian-conservative ideology (that marriage is indissoluble, save by death) and the eudemonistic-liberal ideology (that marriage may be terminated by either partner at any time). All divorce doctrines or codes may be placed either at or between these two poles. See Max Rheinstein, *Marriage Stability, Divorce, and the Law* (Chicago, 1972), 11.

[2] All quotations from the Bible in the text of this book are taken from the King James version, unless otherwise specified. Biblical quotations within direct quotations are given, of course, as rendered in the sources quoted.

riage had been consummated,[3] although one party could still enter a religious order if the other consented.

These two weak points in the Catholic prohibition on divorce (marriage to a non-Christian and nonconsummation) concerned what we should expect to have been rare circumstances in practice. (Generally the church tried to prevent marriage to a non-Christian in the first place.)[4] For most purposes it is adequate to describe the developed Roman Catholic doctrine, as articulated in the thirteenth century, as forbidding the divorce of married persons such that either was able to enter a new marriage while the other was still living.

The doctrine of marital indissolubility, set down in canon law by the Council of Trent in the 1560s, was achieved only after centuries of uncertainty and debate within the church. Before discussing the development of the doctrine itself, however, we should recognize an evolution in the meaning and application of the word "divorce," because the variety of meanings and contexts has caused confusion and misunderstandings as to the history of attitudes and practices in respect of divorce. The words "divorce" and "dissolution" in respect of marriage were used in various senses in theological writings, legal documents, and polemical works, and they continue to be used loosely in the writing of historians. The three most common meanings are what we might call divorce in the strict sense (the total dissolution of a marriage), annulment of marriage, and judicial separation. It is important that each of these be distinguished from the others at an early stage.

"Divorce" in this study will be used in the restricted sense of a total dissolution of a validly contracted or celebrated marriage. It can be referred to as divorce *a vinculo matrimonii* (divorce from the marriage bond).[5] Divorce in this sense is a legal process requiring a judgment by a competent judicial or administrative person or institution; as we shall see, during the past four hundred years in the West, divorces have been granted variously by secular and ecclesiastical courts, legislatures, governors, and kings. A divorce has the effect of dissolving the marriage concerned and enabling the former spouses or one of them to undertake new marriages that are recognized as legal and valid by a competent authority. Although the ability to remarry is at the heart of divorce, the law might, nonetheless, subject remarriage to either temporary or permanent restrictions. As an example of a temporary restriction, many divorce codes in the West have forbidden remarriage by a divorced woman within nine months of her divorce, in case she were pregnant at the time of her divorce. Had she entered into another marriage immediately after her divorce, it was feared, there would be uncertainty whether paternity of her child should be

---

[3] *The Catholic Encyclopedia* (15 vols., New York, 1909), V, 55.
[4] Jo-Ann McNamara and Suzanne F. Wemple, "Marriage and Divorce in the Frankish Kingdom," in Susan Mosher Stuard (ed.), *Women in Medieval Society* (Philadelphia, 1976), 97.
[5] Also known as *divortium plenum* or *divortium perfectum*.

attributed to her current or her previous husband. A form of absolute or permanent bar to remarriage was the commonly found practice of denying the right of remarriage to the spouse whose matrimonial offense, usually adultery, had been the ground for the divorce, while allowing the innocent or aggrieved spouse to remarry. Restrictions on remarriage have also applied to the choice of partner, as in codes that have prohibited the marriage of a man or woman guilty of adultery to his or her accomplice.

The second procedure often referred to as "divorce" in the literature is the annulment or nullification of marriage. An annulment is critically different from divorce in that it presupposes that the marriage concerned did not exist because of certain preexisting circumstances, defects in the form of marriage, or, rarely, postmarital shortcomings. (These are discussed in more detail in Section 1.2.) The important point to note is that an annulment is a judicial declaration that a given marriage does not exist in legal terms. It is quite different from a divorce, which dissolves a marriage that is extant. Perhaps the best example of the confusion between divorce and annulment in historical literature is the action of King Henry VIII against his first wife, Catherine of Aragon. This was an annulment under an interpretation of Roman Catholic canon law of matrimonial impediments, not a divorce in the strict sense.

The third of the three phenomena often referred to as "divorce" is judicial separation, often known as separation *a mensa et thoro* (separation from bed and board).[6] Separation actions arose from the customary, but often legally enforced, obligation of spouses to live together. Should a fault or offense on the part of one spouse make cohabitation impossible or undesirable (this is discussed in more detail in Section 1.4), the couple or the offended spouse had to obtain judicial authorization to live separately. The characteristic of a separation that distinguished it essentially from a divorce is that it did not dissolve the marriage. Even though wife and husband lived in separate dwellings and could lead individual economic lives, they were expected to remain sexually inactive during the separation – inactively faithful to each other – and neither could remarry while the other was still living. When one of the parties did die, the surviving spouse could remarry, but then did so not as a separated person but as a widow or widower.

In its developed form, Catholic doctrine made provision for annulment and separation but not for divorce. Nonetheless, the study of divorce must include an appreciation of the church's doctrines and practices in respect of annulment and separation because they clearly had affinity with divorce, an affinity demonstrated by the use of the word *divortium* to refer to all three types indiscriminately in the church's legal documents. But the affinity goes further than this. In the first place, all three states affected a married couple or, in the case of an annulment, a couple who were putatively married. All three involved

---

[6] Also known as *separatio tori et cohabitationis, divortium imperfectum,* and in France, *séparation de corps et d'habitation.*

a cessation of cohabitation, although a separated couple had the option of resuming married life together in the same dwelling. Finally, divorce and separation had the similarity of generally implying stress or conflict between husband and wife, while annulment and divorce could each have the effect of restoring individuals to a status enabling them to remarry.

1.2 Impediments to marriage

It has often been argued that the church circumvented its own doctrine of marital indissolubility by using annulments as if they were divorces, so that many annulments in name were divorces in intent and effect. In other words, it has been thought that, in the absence of divorce, many spouses who wanted to be freed from their marriages exploited the provisions for annulment. These provisions rested upon the impediments to marriage that were specified by the church at various periods.[7] Not all impediments actually prevented a marriage from being valid: The violation of some, called *impedient* or *obstructive impediments*, resulted in the imposition of spiritual penalties on the parties concerned, yet left the marriage intact. But other impediments, known as *diriment* or *nullifying impediments*, were a bar to valid marriage unless the couple had obtained a dispensation to overcome them. The presence of such an impediment, even if the couple had married unknowingly in violation of it, could render a marriage null and void in the eyes of the church. It is such marriages that might subsequently be subject to a petition for annulment.

The list of diriment impediments recognized by the Catholic church as capable of rendering a marriage null is long and has changed over time. Arguably the best known are those based on consanguinity and affinity – relationship of the married parties by blood and marriage, respectively – although these were rarely invoked as grounds in annulment proceedings. The specific degrees of prohibition were directly drawn from the Bible, notably from the Levitical prohibitions based on consanguinity, but from the sixth century onward the church extended the prohibitons beyond the biblical limits. By the twelfth century, marriage was forbidden as far as the seventh degree according to Germanic computation (to the fourteenth degree according to the Roman form), which meant that marriage was not possible between a man and a woman who were sixth cousins or more closely related. Jean-Louis Flandrin has described the practical meaning of this prohibition thus: If in each generation each couple had married off one boy and one girl, which was lower than the real average in the eleventh and twelfth centuries, then a marriageable youth would be forbidden to marry 2,731 cousins of his own generation, even without counting their ancestors or descendants of marriageable age. "In other words, whether he were a

---

[7] For general treatments of the development of the Catholic church's rules regarding impediments to marriage, see *A Catholic Dictionary of Theology* (3 vols., London, 1962–71), III, 240–9; G. H. Joyce, *Christian Marriage. An Historical and Doctrinal Study* (London, 1948), esp. 507–69.

great lord marrying into his own class, or a peasant bound to the soil, he would be unable to marry all the marriageable girls he could possibly know and a great many more besides."[8]

This situation could have led to either a rise in celibacy, an increase in the number of petitions for dispensation from the impediments, or to many invalid unions. Such unions would have been unstable because they were susceptible to attack as incestuous by third parties or to petition for annulment by one of the married parties. Perhaps because of the inconvenience of the great number of marriages prevented by such rules or because of the number of petitions for dispensation from them, the Fourth Lateran Council (1215) reduced the prohibitions on consanguinity and affinity from seven to four degrees.[9] This prevented marriage between third cousins and those more closely related, although the prohibition could be overcome by a dispensation. It should be noted that, for canonical purposes, affinity (strictly a relationship formed by marriage, such as that between a man and his sister-in-law) was produced also by sexual intercourse. Known as the impediment of *affinitas illegitima*, this prevented a man from marrying the sister, or first, second, or third cousins of any woman with whom he had had a sexual relationship.[10]

Consanguinity and affinity were only two of the extensive list of impediments whose violation could, under Catholic canon law, lead to the annulment of marriage. Even in their more limited form after 1215, their cumulative effect must have put severe limitations on marriage in the context of medieval society. Choice of marriage partner was effectively limited geographically by such banal considerations as transportation. A peasant or farmer could hardly frequent a woman (courting had this sex-specific distinction) who lived further away than he could walk and return in a day. It is hardly surprising that geographical endogamy was characteristic of marriage, as examples from fourteenth- and fifteenth-century England show. Of seventy-eight marriage contracts from fifteenth-century York, thirty-eight (49%) involved a man and a woman from the same parish. Again, half of forty-two cases in Canterbury (1411–20) united spouses from the same parish, while between 1372 and 1375 the proportion had been closer to two-thirds (62%).[11] Where spouses originated from different parishes, they were generally neighboring parishes. Geographical endogamy of this sort persisted in Europe well into the nineteenth century.[12]

---

[8] Jean-Louis Flandrin, *Families in Former Times* (Cambridge, 1979), 24. See also Jack Goody, *The Development of the Family and Marriage in Europe* (Cambridge, 1983).

[9] It is possible that consanguinity in the more remote degrees was defined as an impedient rather than a diriment impediment. McNamara and Wemple, "Marriage and Divorce," 99.

[10] R. H. Helmholz, *Marriage Litigation in Medieval England* (Cambridge, 1974), 78.

[11] Ibid., 80. On endogamy see also Emmanuel Le Roy Ladurie, *Montaillou* (Harmondsworth, 1980), 182–3; and the good example in Judith M. Bennett, "Medieval Peasant Marriage: An Examination of Marriage Licence Fines in the Liber Gersumarum," in J. A. Raftis (ed.), *Pathways to Medieval Peasants* (Toronto, 1981), Appendix 7.2, 219–21.

[12] See, for example, Martine Segalen, *Nuptialité et alliance: Le choix de conjoint dans une commune de l'Eure* (Paris, 1972), 90–1.

1.2 Impediments to marriage

Medieval marriages were subject not only to geographical limitations but also to others of social status, age, and personal compatibility. Marriages generally brought together spouses of the same social and economic position; it was assumed that persons of significant disparity in social rank should not marry. There seems, too, to have been a prevailing conception of an ideal age at marriage and a belief that the husband should be older than his wife by two or three years. Finally, though not necessarily of least importance, there was the question of personal compatibility, the ability not only to achieve a degree of harmony, or even simply an absence of conflict, but also to be able to work cooperatively in the family economy that each marriage established. Although we should not underestimate the importance of affective or emotional criteria in the choice of marriage partner, we must recognize that marriage was first and foremost an economic relationship, rather than one undertaken primarily for anything like emotional fulfillment. Personal characteristics could come into play when selecting a spouse, but only after the overriding social and economic requirements had been satisfied.[13]

These considerations, together with the ecclesiastical impediments of consanguinity and affinity, presented a series of obstacles to marriage, each one reducing the size of a given individual's constituency of potential partners. The obstacles contributed to the high proportion of the population that never married. The relative geographical stability of medieval populations must have meant that with each generation the opportunities of finding a marriage partner beyond the stipulated limits of consanguinity became progressively more difficult.[14] And if this was true for the peasantry who made up the mass of the populations, it must have been even more difficult for the children of the élites. They were far fewer in absolute terms and were probably even more aware and concerned about the gradations of social and economic status in marriage. The élites might have been less constrained geographically in terms of the catchment area from which they might draw marriage partners, but then, regional or local prejudices might have prevented their selecting a partner from too far afield.[15]

---

[13] On medieval marriage in general see Georges Duby, *Medieval Marriage* (Baltimore, 1978) and *The Knight, the Lady and the Priest: The Making of Modern Marriage in Medieval France* (Cambridge, 1983); David Herlihy, "The Making of the Medieval Family: Symmetry, Structure and Sentiment," *Journal of Family History* 8 (1983), 116–30 (plus a very useful bibliography); Goody, *Development of the Family*. James A. Brundage, *Law, Sex, and Christian Society in Medieval Europe* (Chicago, 1987), came to hand as the present book was in press. Brundage's impressive work will undoubtedly become the standard history of the subject.

[14] One historian writes that "in a lax state of morals, a man would be surrounded by a network of relations, secret and avowed, which made lawful marriage almost impossible for him." T. A. Lacey, *Marriage in Church and State* (London, 1947), 129. It is not necessary to bring a "lax state of morals" into the question. Geographical stability over generations, together with endogamous marriage patterns (both of these in relative terms) would produce the same result.

[15] A preference for a partner from the same locality is expressed in French proverbs such as: "He who marries [someone] within his locality sees what he is drinking," and "He who marries at a distance deceives or is deceived." J.-L. Flandrin, *Les amours paysannes* (Paris, 1975), 141.

1 The Roman Catholic background

Certainly there were instances when the legal and social obstacles virtually ruled out marriage, when it was impossible to find a partner who was of the appropriate social status and age and yet within the prescribed limits of consanguinity and affinity. (This is to say nothing of compatibility of temperament.) If a person were not to be forced to remain celibate in such cases, one of the constraints had to be overcome, and in this context the church made provision for a dispensation to be granted under certain conditions. In France, for example, the church could grant a dispensation for marriage within the prohibited degrees of consanguinity because of "the smallness of the place," a recognition that within the area one could reasonably be expected to find a marriage partner, there was no suitable candidate outside the prohibited degrees. In some instances these dispensations permitted marriage between individuals as closely related as niece and uncle.[16]

Such problems in marriage formation were compounded by other impediments. In addition to consanguinity and affinity by marriage and sexual intercourse, the church also recognized relationship by spiritual affinity as an impediment to a valid marriage. This prevented the marriage of a person or one of his parents with his sponsor at baptism or confirmation, and was generally a bar to marriage between any active participants in a given baptism, confirmation, or marriage.[17] An example of this impediment in action was the fourteenth-century York case of a man, a widower, who was unable to marry the woman who had stood godmother to one of his children by his first marriage.[18]

Yet other impediments could stand in the way of a valid marriage. One was precontract: A prior matrimonial engagement to one person prevented an individual from validly marrying another. There were also impediments of age: Marriage could not be undertaken by a girl under the age of twelve or by a boy younger than fourteen years. An impediment of impotency prevented a valid marriage by a person incapable of having sexual relations. And because consent of the marrying parties was an essential element of marriage in Catholic doctrine, lack of consent was a diriment impediment. Such a lack of consent could be formed by the use of duress, force, or abduction to compel one party to marry or through a defect of intellect, such as insanity or simple ignorance of what marriage entailed. Further impediments existed where one of the parties had previously taken religious vows or where one of them had attacked the sanctity of the previous marriage of the other, either by killing his or her partner or by committing adultery with a promise to marry as soon as the accomplice was free to do so. Finally, clandestinity could be a bar to valid marriage, the only impediment based on procedure.[19]

[16] Ibid., 34–5.
[17] *Catholic Dictionary of Theology*, III, 245.
[18] Helmholz, *Marriage Litigation* 78.
[19] A general survey of impediments is the entry by E. Valton, "Empêchements de mariage" in the *Dictionnaire de théologie catholique* (18 vols,. Paris, 1951–70), IV, cols. 2440–99.

1.3 Annulments: Were they used as divorces?

Although such impediments prevented many potential unions from taking place, marriages still occurred where impediments existed and where no dispensation had been granted. Very likely, the spouses in most of these cases did not know of the impediments at the time of marriage. A proportion of these marriages was subsequently the object of petitions for annulment, although of course there is no way of determining the proportion. The questions we must ask are those the Protestant Reformers answered in the affirmative: Did unhappy spouses cynically exploit the provisions for annulment of marriage by seeking out impediments in order to escape from their marriages? In other words, were annulments used to circumvent the prohibition on divorce? And were the ecclesiastical courts accomplices in these circumventions of Catholic doctrine? Until recently, historians have tended to think that these deceptions took place. Frederick Maitland, for example, wrote that "spouses who had quarrelled began to investigate their pedigrees and were unlucky if they could discover no *impedimentum dirimens*."[20] Similarly, a study of divorce in England refers to the "undermining of the indissolubility of marriage by the expediency of annulments" in the Middle Ages, although it cautions against the notion that "the handling of matrimonial causes was marked by large-scale corruption or that ecclesiastical officials were necessarily guilty of bad faith."[21]

More recent research on the actual operations of the church courts and on the disposition of the cases that came before them has tended to reinforce the strength of the last statement. The fine study by R. H. Helmholz of marriage litigation in England from the thirteenth to the fifteenth centuries provides an important corrective to the impressionistic conclusions of earlier works. In the first place, this period provided surprisingly few petitions for the annulment of marriages. Of twenty-three matrimonial cases before the Rochester Consistory Court between April 1437 and April 1440, only five were for annulment. The comparative representation of annulment cases in all matrimonial cases was twelve out of eighty-eight in fifteenth-century York, and ten out of ninety-eight in Canterbury between November 1372 and May 1375.[22] Petitions for annulment seem to have accounted for about 10%–20% of all matrimonial business before the church courts and were consistently outnumbered by cases involving the enforcement of clandestine marriage contracts. The relative paucity of suits for annulment does nothing to enhance the view of the Catholic

---

[20] Quoted in Helmholz, *Marriage Litigation*, 75. There is a hint of this, too, in Stone's reference to the reduction of the prohibited degrees in England after the Reformation. The reform was undertaken, writes Stone, "to block the scandalous divorce proceedings of the pre-Reformation Church." Lawrence Stone, *The Family, Sex and Marriage in England, 1500–1800* (London, 1977), 138–9.

[21] A. R. Winnett, *The Church and Divorce: A Factual Survey* (London, 1968), 3.

[22] Helmholz, *Marriage Litigation*, 74. See also Michael M. Sheehan, "The Formation and Stability of Marriage in Fourteenth-Century England: Evidence of an Ely Register," *Medieval Studies* 33 (1971), 228–63.

ecclesiastical courts as cryptodivorce mills.[23] What is more, the courts demanded rigorous proof before they would declare a marriage null. Where consanguinity was alleged as a ground for nullifying a marriage, the courts required (in the absence of marriage and birth certificates in the Middle Ages) firsthand evidence, and that of more than one witness.

Helmholz cites the petition for annulment of the marriage of one Richard Broke and his wife Joan because a certain Peter Daneys claimed, first, that he was related to Richard in the second degree of consanguinity, and second, that he had had sexual relations with Joan before her marriage to Richard. This relationship of both husband and wife through a third party (by blood and copulation, respectively) would, if proved, have rendered their marriage null. The evidence adduced was that of one witness to the effect that both Peter and Richard "sprang from two sisters," and that it was a matter of public knowledge, though the witness had no firsthand knowledge, that Peter and Joan had had a sexual relationship. In this case the impediment was deemed not proved, and so the marriage was not declared void.[24] On balance, Helmholz concluded that rather than grant annulments easily, the church courts operated on the principle "that it was better to risk allowing consanguineous unions than to risk separating couples God had legitimately joined together."[25]

In other cases, where the existence of a diriment impediment could be clearly demonstrated, there was little hesitation in agreeing to an annulment. We may take the example of Jean Tartrier and Jeannette Bougratte, who were betrothed in Troyes (France) in 1530 and proceeded to have sexual intercourse, thus forming a valid marriage in the eyes of the church. On May 12, 1530 Tartrier's father cited his son before the *officialité* (bishop's court) of Troyes and demanded the "dissolution" (annulment) of the marriage on the ground that it was incestuous: Jean Tartrier's uncle had had sexual relations with Jeanette Bougratte before her marriage, thus establishing an impediment of *affinitas illegitima*. The court, which ordered Tartrier to be imprisoned while it considered the case to prevent contact between him and Jeanette, finally determined that the union should be annulled. The solemnization of the union in church was forbidden under penalty of excommunication, imprisonment, and a fine.[26]

Further evidence of the church courts in action comes from the *officialité* of Paris, the most important ecclesiastical court in France, in the late fourteenth century. In the three years between November 1384 and September 1387, this court heard some 600 family cases, four-fifths of them dealing with betrothals, the status of marriage, and the relationship between married people.[27] As in the

---

[23] Helmholz, *Marriage Litigation*, 111.
[24] Ibid., 83.
[25] Ibid., 82.
[26] This case is dealt with in Flandrin, *Les amours paysannes*, 32–3.
[27] Jean-Philippe Lévy, "L' officialité de Paris et les questions familiales à la fin du XIVe siècle," in *Etudes d'histoire du droit canonique, dédiées à Gabriel Le Bras* (Paris, 1965), 1265–94.

1.3 Annulments: Were they used as divorces?

English studies of the church courts at this time, what is surprising in Paris is the rarity of nullifications of marriage: During the years studied, only ten marriages were annulled, and none of those was justified on the grounds of consanguinity or affinity. Two judgments of nullification were based on the husband's impotence, and eight on the ground of bigamy (where the second marriage was declared null and void). Again, this argues against the notion of the widespread use of annulments as quasi-divorces, although in one curious decision the Paris judges gave an annulment the appearance of a divorce. This was the case of Philippe Noël, who had petitioned for a separation for reason of his wife's adultery. Instead, the court nullified the marriage because of Noël's impotence (which must have been proved during the case, probably as an extenuating circumstance in respect to his wife's adultery). Further, the court levied a fine against the wife for her offense but agreed to lift it provided that she married her accomplice.[28]

The cases before the court of the bishop of Paris confirm the impression of the care with which individuals approached marriage. They were anxious to ensure that their betrothals, and thus their future marriages, should be canonically valid, and the court was often required to rule on them. Only in one case was the validity of a betrothal challenged on the ground of consanguinity, and in two others on a lack of consent. In the great majority of cases the problem at issue, as in the English examples cited, centered on a precontract or on a previous marriage that had not been nullified or dissolved by the death of one of the spouses. In one case, for instance, a woman was required to prove that her first husband had died before the court would confirm the validity of her current betrothal.

Such cases, where an engagement to marry could be extinguished on canonical grounds, were quite distinct from a second category where betrothals were nullified at the joint request of the parties themselves. One might almost think of these actions as being divorces before marriage – the result of reconsideration as to the wisdom or prudence of a marriage before the marriage or sexual intercourse took place, but after the formalities of betrothal. In some of the cases the desire to terminate the betrothal did not simply indicate second thoughts as to the suitability of the parties, but was based on their youthfulness at the time of the betrothal, implying the tendency to commit oneself rashly, or on the lack of true consent in cases where parents had betrothed their children. The desire of some of the couples to escape a betrothal was based on the misconduct of one of them, such as sexual intercourse with a third party.[29] The attitude of the church to requests to have betrothals annulled where there was no clear canonical impediment was ambiguous, but in late-fourteenth-century Paris, at least, a liberal attitude was adopted, and fiancés and fiancées might be

[28] Ibid., 1278 n. 86.
[29] Ibid., 1273–4.

released from their engagements as long as they obtained the approval of the ecclesiastical authorities.[30] In the cases studied, virtually all of the joint petitions were approved by the judges.

All this does not imply that under Catholic law and practice annulments of marriage could not be, and were not, used as if they were divorces. Even the impediment of precontract could be used as a way out of an unsatisfactory marriage if there were sufficient forethought. It is suggested that there were cases in which a nobleman would secretly contract himself to a woman of humble birth but then enter a marriage with a woman of his own social rank. If the marriage proved unsuccessful from the husband's point of view, he had only to invoke the precontract in order to have his marriage annulled.[31] The risk with this sort of proceeding would be that the court could order the man concerned to marry the woman to whom he had claimed precontract, despite the disparity of their ranks. Even if he avoided this, he would be unable to marry anyone else, in view of the acknowledged precontract.

When we consider the possible use of annulments as quasi-divorces, we must bear in mind that the ecclesiastical courts were interested primarily in establishing the existence of an impediment, not the motivation for a petition for annulment. Quite clearly, given the standards of evidence demanded by the church judges, it would be a fortunate wife or husband who wanted a divorce and who could satisfy the demanding standards of evidence required for an annulment. But no doubt both conditions were met in some cases. We might, after all, ponder the motivation of those who sought an annulment, if they did not want to terminate their marriages. Must we conclude, in such cases, that the couple subordinated their marital happiness or contentment to higher considerations, to the belief that in marrying they had violated God's law? The evidence from the church courts in England and France demonstrates the conscientiousness of men and women to avoid marrying when they believed that a certain union attracted impediments, and it is not unreasonable to think that those already married would have treated the issue with equal seriousness.

The main difficulty in identifying annulments used as divorces lies in attributing motivation. No doubt some men and women did decide that annulment was a convenient way out of a marriage, and cynically used it as if it were a divorce. No doubt the ecclesiastical judges can be considered accomplices in these cases. Remarriage a very short time after an annulment might point to a divorce motive, but we should bear in mind that rapid remarriage was common after the death of a spouse too and did not imply murder or even the desire that the deceased should have died. Quite possibly the exploitation of annulments was most common among those of higher social rank. The best known, Henry VIII's annulments, are discussed in Chapter 2, but we can point to others in earlier periods, such as that between Eleanor of Aquitaine and Louis VII. After

---

[30] Ibid., 1272–3.
[31] *Catholic Dictionary of Theology*, III, 240.

many disagreements Eleanor had their marriage annulled on the ground that she and Louis were within the prohibited degrees. The annulment was agreed to by French bishops in March 1152, and Eleanor married Henry Plantagenet (later Henry IV) in May of the same year.[32]

Quite clearly, the voiding of betrothals meant that many defective marriages did not take place, and this ruled out the possibility or need to annul them later. The activity of the church courts in respect of betrothals goes a long way to explaining the rarity of actions to annul marriages in the Middle Ages. But even the cases of marriage annulment lend little support to the view that the church's laws on marriage were regarded as rules to be cynically broken at the time of marriage and then, just as cynically, applied so as to obtain an annulment in order to escape from an unhappy marriage in a society that did not permit divorce.

1.4 Judicial separation

If annulments were not attempts by men and women to free themselves from marital misery and oppression, separations were. The voluntary and unauthorized separation by a married couple was a sin, whether it took place by the will of one party – by desertion or by his or her refusal to live with the other – or whether it took place by the mutual consent of both the spouses. In the twelfth century the possibility of a sentence of separation *a mensa et thoro* was introduced into canon law,[33] and such separations are the second category of matrimonial action often referred to as "divorce." Separations differed from annulments in various important respects. First, they did not declare the marriage bond invalid and void but implicitly upheld the legal existence of the marriage, while reducing its social implications. Second, separations concerned not the relationship of the spouses before marriage, or premarital circumstances like precontracts, but rather the social relationship of the spouses during their marriage.[34] Separations could be granted under circumstances where the principles of true religion were threatened or where the spiritual or physical well-being of one of the partners was at risk. Under these guidelines, canon law admitted three principal grounds for separation: adultery, cruelty, and heresy and apostasy (which were thought of as spiritual fornication).

Separations cannot be considered divorces because they did not dissolve the marriage but simply authorized the husband and wife to live separately. The persistence of the marriage bond was recognized in the continuing obligation

---

[32] See Margaret Labarge, *Women in Medieval Life: A Small Sound of the Trumpet* (London, 1986), 50–1. Repudiation in royal marriages is discussed in Pauline Stafford, *Queens, Concubines and Dowagers: The King's Wife in the Early Middle Ages* (London, 1983), 79–86.

[33] Gabriel Le Bras, "Le mariage dans la théologie et le droit de l'Eglise du XIᵉ au XIIIᵉ siècle," *Cahiers de civilisation médiévale* 11 (1968), 200.

[34] In some circumstances, annulments could take into account postnuptial factors, such as the inability or failure of the couple to consummate the marriage.

of each to remain sexually faithful to the other, while each was freed of the obligation of sexual intercourse (the marital debt in Catholic doctrine). The result was that separated spouses were required to remain sexually inactive while they were separated. But even given these limitations on the effects of separation, the church courts were reluctant to agree to petitions. Helmholz's study of the English courts shows that they attempted to reconcile the couple wherever possible and granted separations only where there was evidence of severe cruelty.[35] It is almost unnecessary to report that the violence in these cases was directed against women by their husbands. The refusal of the courts to consider even apparently serious violence as sufficient justification for a separation must be understood in the context of a general social acceptance, by men, at any rate, that a degree of wife beating was permissible. A husband who, witnesses said, had attacked his wife with a knife and forced her to flee and had, on another occasion, stabbed her in the arm and broken a bone, could describe his actions as reasonable, honest, and done for the purpose of "reducing her from errors." Equally significant was the court's decision that such behavior did not justify a separation. A bond (*cautio*) was imposed on this husband to treat his wife fairly, and the couple were compelled to remain living together.[36]

Such cases might be interpreted as showing the complicity of the ecclesiastical judges in failing to give an abused woman the relief she requested – to live free of the threats and violence of her husband. The judges were above all motivated by the desire to reconcile spouses in conflict. In some cases they had the husband swear to treat his wife thereafter with proper marital affection and the wife swear to obey her husband. This was a way of returning antagonistic spouses to their designated duties and roles. As an added inducement to good behavior, sureties or pledges of goods or money were commonly required of men who had been accused of violence toward their wives.[37]

Still, some separations were permitted by the church courts, when reconciliation or even the possibility of forging a *modus vivendi* between spouses was clearly impossible. Helmholz cites the case of John and Margaret Colwell in 1442. The judge failed in all his attempts to deter the couple from their common desire to live separately: "They said they would prefer death in prison to living together. They claimed they were living in daily fear of their lives as it was."[38] In such cases – though they were few and far between – the courts accepted the reality of marriage breakdown. For the most part, however, the ecclesiastical judges insisted on the obligation of husband and wife to live together and granted exceptions to this rule only in the most pressing and recalcitrant circumstances.

Several local studies of separations *a mensa et thoro* indicate their rarity. In the Belgian city of Ghent there are only sporadic references to them in court records: four in the 1350s, few more in the 1360s and 1370s, then sixteen

[35] Helmholz, *Marriage Litigation*, 100–7.
[36] Ibid., 105.
[37] Ibid., 101–2.
[38] Ibid., 103.

between April 1385 and May 1390. The books of the Keure, one of the benches of the city council of Ghent, however, refer to more: 108 separations between 1349 and 1390, 59 of those in the 1370s alone.[39] These figures indicate an annual average of perhaps three a year overall (six a year in the 1370s), few enough in a city that counted some 12,000 nuclear families.[40] The number of separations was also low in Brussels in the next century, where the officials' courts listed eighty-nine between 1448 and 1459, an average of eight a year. Fourteen of these separations were based on incompatibility alone, although the rest linked incompatibility to some other cause, usually adultery and less often cruelty or impotence.[41] Separations might have been more common in Belgium than elsewhere in Catholic Europe (only more local studies will show this to be so or not), and the Brussels example suggests that more extensive grounds, notably incompatibility, were accepted there.[42] But even so, marriage policy was far from lax. In his study of Ghent, Nicholas notes that the magistrates discouraged separation and much preferred that the spouses resolve their differences amicably and continue to live together.[43] English cases echo these general tendencies. Suits for separation were extremely rare, making up a tiny proportion of matrimonial business before the church courts, and the clergy were "more like marriage counselors trying to arrange amicable settlements, than judges."[44]

1.5 Divorce in Catholic doctrine

Finally we come to divorce in the strict sense, divorce *a vinculo matrimonii*, but because it was not permitted by Catholic doctrine in its developed form, there are no case principles or examples to examine. Yet if we are to appreciate the reaction against Catholic doctrine, we must have some understanding of the evolution of the doctrine, and later canon law, of marital indissolubility. It is neither possible nor desirable, however, to separate completely Catholic doctrine on divorce from other areas of teaching. Divorce must be understood as an integral part of a complex of attitudes linking such important issues as celibacy, marriage, remarriage, and sexuality.

Catholic tradition taught that celibacy was a superior state to marriage, and

---

[39] David Nicholas, *The Domestic Life of a Medieval City: Women, Children, and the Family in Fourteenth-Century Ghent* (Lincoln, Nebraska, 1985), 34–5.
[40] Ibid., 151.
[41] Monique Vleeschouwers-Van Melebeek, "Aperçu typologique des principales sortes de registres produits par l'officialité de Tournai au Moyen Age, avec notes sur le registre de sentences de Bruxelles (1448–1459)," in *Bronnen voor de Geschiedenis van de Instellingen in België* (Brussels, 1977), 430.
[42] It is suggested that the judges in Brussels accepted incompatibility as a ground for separation when they feared that more serious harm would arise if the couple in question were not separated. Ibid., 430–1.
[43] Nicholas, *Domestic Life*, 36.
[44] Barbara A. Hanawalt, *The Ties That Bound: Peasant Families in Medieval England* (New York, 1986), 211.

from the fourth century this doctrine was institutionalized in the celibate priesthood.[45] The Church counseled celibacy and virginity as the goals for which Christians should aim, but marriage was permitted for those who could not remain sexually continent. The key biblical text here is that of 1 Corinthians 7:8–9: "I say therefore to the unmarried and widows, It is good for them if they abide even as I [i.e., celibate]. But if they cannot contain [sexually], let them marry: for it is better to marry than to burn."

In the eyes of the Catholic church marriage became inseparable from sexuality. It was church teaching that marriage was ordained by God, first as the only acceptable context in which children might be conceived and born and second as a remedy against fornication. That is, the stable forum for sexual activity that marriage provided would make fornication (nonmarital sexual intercourse) unnecessary. Yet even within marriage, sexuality was to be restricted to its primary purpose of procreation. This ruled out sexual intercourse when a wife could not conceive (as when she was already pregnant) and certainly ruled out the use of contraceptive techniques and nonprocreative sexual activity like anal or oral intercourse.[46]

Moreover, even within marriage, the exclusive emphasis on the procreative function implied that sexuality was to be restrained and even joyless. It is not difficult to locate in the Bible and among the church fathers, advice on sexuality that is unambiguously negative. Even if we discount the prohibition on extramarital and premarital sex, homosexuality, and on all forms of sexuality unless they took place between a man and woman married to each other and were capable of leading to conception, sex was regarded as a duty to be performed rather than as a pleasure to be enjoyed. It was not even regarded as a duty in which one might take pleasure. Clement of Alexandria advised that a man who married "for the sake of begetting children must practise continence so that it is not desire he feels for his wife, whom he ought to love, and that he may beget children with a chaste and controlled will."[47] For Clement and others, sex was solely for procreation: "For the husband there is only one time when he may sow the field, and just as for the farmer it is only that moment when the seed can be received with the hope of fruition."[48]

Needless to say there were exceptions – theologians who accepted the positive aspects of sexuality – but the overwhelming attitude was negative. One

[45] Willy Rordorf, "Marriage in the New Testament and in the Early Church," *Journal of Ecclesiastical History* 20 (1969), 203.

[46] The best single source in English on Catholic attitudes to sexuality and contraception is John T. Noonan, *Contraception: A History of Its Treatment by the Catholic Theologians and Canonists* (Cambridge, Mass., 1965). See also Jean-Louis Flandrin, *Le sexe et l'Occident* (Paris, 1981); Philippe Ariès and André Béjin (eds.) *Western Sexuality: Practice and Precept in Past and Present Times* (Oxford, 1985); and Vern L. Bullough and James Brundage (eds.), *Sexual Practices and the Medieval Church* (Buffalo, N. Y., 1982).

[47] Quoted in Vern L. Bullough, *Sexual Variance in Society and History* (Chicago, 1976), 185. Bullough deals with early Christian attitudes toward sex on pp. 159–201.

[48] Quoted in Rodorf, "Marriage in the New Testament," 204.

historian of medieval views of sex sums them up this way:

> With few exceptions, patristic writers and theologians throughout the Middle Ages considered all sex impure and degrading. Sexual relations, even between married persons, tainted those involved with the pungent aroma of sin. Without lust there could be no sexual activity, and sexual relations therefore represented in some degree the triumph of concupiscence over virtue, piety, and reason. The medieval Church, in short, loathed sex.[49]

Clearly, the intimate and interdependent relationship of marriage, sex, and conception in Roman Catholic doctrine, together with a negative attitude toward sex, goes a long way in explaining the less than absolute indissolubility of an unconsummated marriage.

One might have thought that because marriage was considered an inferior state by many of the church fathers, divorce might have been welcomed as a sort of return to celibate status as long as it was not followed by remarriage. But not so. The tenor of the biblical texts dealing with divorce was early interpreted by most ecclesiastical authorities as meaning that marriage, once validly contracted, could not be dissolved. There was an apparent conflict between the divorce texts of Mark and Luke, on the one hand, and Matthew on the other, and this led to some ambivalence within the church. According to Mark, Christ asserted that "whosoever shall put away his wife, and marry another, committeth adultery against her. And if a woman shall put away her husband, and be married to another, she committeth adultery" (Mark 10:11–12). Luke's version of this ran: "Whosoever putteth away his wife, and marrieth another, committeth adultery: and whosoever marrieth her that is put away from *her* husband committeth adultery." Both of these texts were unambiguous in their rejection of "putting away" a spouse and then remarrying, but two of the references to divorce in Matthew seemed to allow adultery as an exception to this rule. The first (Matthew 5:32) had Christ say that "Whosoever shall put away his wife, saving for the cause of fornication, causeth her to commit adultery. . . ." The same qualification, "except *it be* for fornication," is found in Matthew 19:9.

Other biblical texts stressed the indissolubility of marriage by divorce. Matthew 19:4–6 has Christ reply thus to the Pharisees' question "Is it lawful for a man to put away his wife for every cause?": "Have ye not read, that he which made *them* at the beginning made them male and female. For this cause shall a man leave father and mother, and shall cleave to his wife: and they twain shall be one flesh? What therefore God hath joined together, let no man put asunder." Matthew, as we have seen, subsequently went on to introduce the apparent exception of adultery, but this was not so in the text of Paul: "A man [shall] leave his father and mother, and shall be joined unto his wife, and they two shall be one flesh" (Ephesians 5:31).

In another text, however, Paul introduced a different exception, the Pauline

---

[49] James A. Brundage, "Let me count the ways: Canonists and theologians contemplate coital positions," *Journal of Medieval History* 10:2 (June 1984), 81.

Privilege cited earlier. Although stressing that a spouse should not be "put away," Paul raised the issue of a marriage uniting a Christian with a non-believer. If the non-Christian wished to continue to live with the Christian partner, the latter should not leave, "for the unbelieving husband is sanctified by the wife, and the unbelieving wife is sanctified by the husband: else were your children unclean; but now are they holy" (1 Corinthians 14). Divorce and remarriage were permitted, however, when the unbelieving spouse deserted the Christian: "But if the unbelieving depart, let him depart. A brother or a sister [i.e., a Christian] is not under bondage in such *cases*" (1 Corinthians 15). The texts of the New Testament on divorce thus emphasized the indissolubility of marriage. The possible exceptions were the Pauline Privilege and Matthew's qualification of adultery. Even then it is not clear whether the latter referred to adultery only by the wife or by either spouse, for Christ's answer in the text of Matthew was framed to respond to the question as to whether it was permissible for a man to put away his wife.

The biblical position of marital indissolubility or, at most, recognizing very restricted grounds for divorce departed from both Roman and Jewish law at the beginning of the Christian Era. In the early Roman Republic the most common form of divorce was by mutual consent, but simple repudiation was enough to end a marriage because marriage required the continuing consent of both parties.[50] In the later republic, the "full logical consequences of freedom of divorce" were accepted, to the extent that one spouse could repudiate the other with or without just cause. Repudiation without just cause, however, was subject to moral and social stigma.[51] One particular form of divorce was the dissolution of a child's marriage by his or her father; this was one effect of *patria potestas*, the lifelong authority of the father over his children.

Restrictions on divorce entered the empire in the Christian period, however, especially under the reigns of Constantine and Justinian. Constantine permitted a husband to divorce his wife who was guilty of adultery, procuring, or poisoning, while a wife could repudiate her husband if he were guilty of homicide, poisoning, or violating graves. A husband or wife could repudiate the other for less serious offenses or for no specified reason at all, but in such cases remarriage was either forbidden or, if permitted, permitted only after a long lapse of time from the date of the repudiation. Where divorce was penalized by the inability to remarry, it became, of course, tantamount to a separation in important respects.

The Roman law of divorce was revised by Justinian. Divorce by mutual consent was forbidden, although repudiation for just cause was retained. Just causes included adultery by the wife, a false accusation of his wife's adultery on the part of the husband, and the husband's taking a concubine. The guilty

---

[50] J. A. C. Thomas, *Textbook of Roman Law* (Amsterdam, 1976), 425. For a full technical introduction to the Roman Law of divorce, see P. E. Corbett, *The Roman Law of Marriage* (Oxford, 1936), 218–48.
[51] Thomas, *Roman Law*, 426.

spouse in such circumstances suffered penalties in addition to being divorced: A woman lost her dowry and was confined for life to a nunnery, and a man was deprived of a third of his estate. Repudiation for good cause, as distinct from just cause, was a separate category, and included a divorce to permit one of the parties to take up a religious vocation or a divorce on presumption of death, as when the husband had been taken prisoner during war. In these cases no penalties were applied.[52]

The frequency of divorce in Rome is not clear. One tradition has it that there was no divorce in Rome for 500 years, until about 230 B.C., but this has been disputed.[53] In the late republican period there seem to have been many divorces, but because they were among the upper classes, where marriage represented political alliances above all, it could be that the divorces reflected political, as much as marital, instability.[54]

Jewish law at the beginning of the Christian Era also admitted divorce.[55] It was, indeed, a point of Catholic interpretation that God had permitted divorce to the Jews because of the "hardness of their hearts," but that divorce was not available to Christians. The principles of Jewish divorce law rested on the patriarchal organization of the family, which placed women in a subordinate position vis-à-vis their husbands: "Thy [the wife's] desire shall be to thy husband, and he shall rule over thee" (Genesis 3:16). The superior position of the husband gave him the exclusive right of initiative as far as divorce was concerned, and no grounds or matrimonial offenses needed to be specified in justification of a man's repudiating his wife. The key text here is that of Deuteronomy 24:1–2:

When a man hath taken a wife, and married her, and it come to pass that she find no favour in his eyes, because he hath found some uncleanness in her: then let him write her a bill of divorcement, and give it in her hand, and send her out of his house. And when she is departed out of his house, she may go and be another man's wife.

Remarriage was permitted to both parties under this law.

[52] Ibid., 426–7.

[53] Corbett, *Roman Law of Marriage*, 218ff.

[54] J. A. Crook, *Law and Life of Rome* (London, 1967),105–6. The high frequency of divorce, especially among the upper classes, is noted in Beryl Rawson, "The Roman Family," in Beryl Rawson (ed.), *The Family in Ancient Rome* (London, 1986), 25, 51. One epitaph of the early imperial period drew attention to the length of the dead person's marriage and added "rara sunt tam diuturna matrimonia, finita morte, non divortio in[terrupta]." Ibid., 51. Note also that divorce was available in classical Athens, with a strong bias in favor of husbands. A man whose wife committed adultery was required by law to divorce her – a rare example of mandatory divorce – but as men did not have to be sexually faithful in marriage, wives did not have equal access to divorce. Women could initiate a divorce, but it seems likely that the husband's consent was necessary before a marriage could be dissolved, producing a sort of divorce by mutual consent. See Douglas M. MacDowell, *The Law in Classical Athens* (London, 1978), 88. A different work suggests that men and women had equal rights of divorce: W. K. Lacey, *The Family in Classical Greece* (London, 1968), 108–9.

[55] The following account is drawn principally from David Werner Amram, *The Jewish Law of Divorce According to Bible and Talmud* (New York, 1968), esp. 54–77. See also Reuven Yaron, "On Divorce in Old Testament Times," *Revue internationale des droits de l'Antiquité* 3ᵉ série, 4 (1957), 117–28.

Infidelity also justified the breaking of betrothals in Jewish law. According to the New Testament book of Matthew, Christ was almost born into a one-parent family, for Joseph contemplated "divorce" when, discovering that she was pregnant even though they had not had sexual intercourse, he quite reasonably assumed that Mary had been unfaithful to him. The text of Matthew 1:18–19 notes of Christ that "when his mother Mary had been betrothed to Joseph, before they came together she was found to be with child of the Holy Spirit; and her husband Joseph, being a just man and unwilling to put her to shame, resolved to divorce her quietly." Joseph (although described as her husband, he was in fact Mary's fiancé at this time) was dissuaded from this "divorce" by an angel who informed him of the circumstances of the conception.

Some limitations were placed on the husband's right to divorce in Jewish law. He could not do so if he had been guilty of maliciously and falsely accusing his wife of premarital fornication. Nor could a man divorce his wife if their marriage had resulted from his having been compelled to marry her; for example, if she had been a virgin whom he had raped. Moreover, under the influence of contemporary Roman law, which gave women rights in divorce, there was a movement toward giving women greater rights under Jewish law. But even here the superiority of the husband was recognized, for the means by which a wife divorced her husband was to have a court compel him, under threat of punishment, to give his wife a bill of divorce. Under Talmudic law, women became entitled to divorce on such grounds as a husband's falsely accusing his wife of premarital fornication, his being impotent or having a disease such as leprosy, his desertion, apostasy, or restricting his wife's liberty.

Quite clearly, the New Testament position on divorce departed dramatically from both Roman and Jewish traditions and social practices. Even so, the texts were not so unambiguous as to permit the rapid development of a consensus in the early church whether marriage was absolutely indissoluble or whether it was indissoluble with the exception of adultery. What is notable is that both positions within the church drew almost exclusively from the Bible, and ignored contemporary Jewish and Roman practices. Early writers who argued for the absolute indissolubility of marriage attempted to reconcile the exception in Matthew by treating it not as permission to divorce but rather as an authority to dismiss an adulterous wife, without dissolving the marriage and without conferring on either spouse the right of remarriage. This doctrine was expressed in the writings of early Fathers such as Hermas, Justin Martyr, Athenagoras, Tertullian, and Clement of Alexandria, and later by Ambrose, Jerome, and Augustine. This nondissolubilist position was also adopted by various church councils, among them those of Arles (314), Mileve (416), and Hereford (673).[56]

Most nondissolubilists agreed that in the case of a serious matrimonial offense, a separation *a mensa et thoro* was permissible. In Augustine's view, a

---

[56] Rordorf, "Marriage in the New Testament," 204–5.

breach of marital fidelity, which occurred when one of the spouses committed adultery, was a ground for separation, but did not permit either spouse to re-marry.[57] Augustine argued against the opinion of his contemporary, Pollentius, that the innocent party in such a situation should be allowed to remarry because the guilty spouse ought to be considered civilly dead.[58] (This interpretation was based on the Mosaic injunction that an adulterous wife should be stoned to death; it was a justification for remarriage after adultery that was invoked by many writers in favor of divorce, as we shall see.) Pollentius also argued that an incurable disease that prevented a couple from having a sexual relationship could also justify separation, followed by the remarriage of the healthy partner – in effect, a divorce. Augustine contested this opinion, too.[59]

Other authorities took a less rigorous position. The Council of Vannes (465) allowed remarriage after divorce for reason of adultery. The Council of Ver-berie (752) also made provision for divorce in effect, but only to the advantage of the husband, when a man had to go abroad but when his wife, through attach-ment to her home or relatives, refused to accompany him. In such circumstances the wife could not enter a new marriage during her husband's lifetime, but if the husband "has no hope of returning to his own country, if he cannot abstain [from sexual activity], he can receive another wife with a penance."[60] Such decisions, although expressed in general terms, give the appearance of being responses to specific cases that came to the notice of the councils.

The confusion of doctrines and conflicts of laws was reflected in the varying approaches of penitentials toward matrimonial offenses, especially adultery.[61] The Penitential of Finnian (sixth century) provided compulsory sexual absti-nence for a husband or wife who committed adultery, as well as other penances according to the specific circumstances. For example, a married man who had intercourse with a vowed virgin and had a child by her was subject to three years' penance, being one year on bread and water and sexually abstinent, and two years without wine and meats and also sexually abstinent. If the offending act of intercourse with a virgin did not result in the birth of a child, the penance was one year on bread and water, but only half a year without wine or meats, though sexual abstinence had to be practiced for the year and a half. Finnian

---

[57] Augustine, *Adulterous Marriages* [*De incompetentibus nuptiis*], in *Treatises on Marriage and Other Subjects* (ed. R. J. Defferrari, New York, 1955), 91–3.

[58] Ibid., 101ff.

[59] Ibid., 128.

[60] *The Catholic Encyclopedia* V, 57.

[61] Penitentials were guides to penances due in the case of specific breaches of the religious discipline of behavior expected of a Christian. They are prescriptive documents, dating mainly from the sixth to ninth centuries, which reflected the austere codes of their authors, not necessarily social attitudes or practice. An introduction to the penitentials is John T. McNeill and Helena M. Gamer, *Medieval Handbooks of Penance* (New York, 1938). The use of the peni-tentials as a source for the history of the family and sexuality is discussed in Raoul Manselli, "Vie familiale et éthique sexuelle dans les pénitentiels," in Georges Duby and Jacques le Goff (eds.), *Famille et parenté dans l'Occident médiéval* (Rome, 1977), 363–78.

made it clear that any separation or sending away by married people could not be followed by remarriage.[62]

Some of the penitentials did provide for de facto divorce, however. For example, the Judgment of Clement (eighth century) noted that legal marriage may not be dissolved unless there were an agreement by both parties to remain unmarried, and specified excommunication for any man who put away his wife and remarried. Even so, Clement made this provision: "If an enemy seizes the wife of anyone, and if he is not able to recover her, after an entire year he may marry another; and if she afterward comes back, she may marry another man."[63] This last provision also appeared in the important Penitential of Theodore (seventh century), but with additional allowances for remarriage, so that "if a woman leaves her husband, despising him, and is unwilling to return and be reconciled to her husband, after five years, with the bishop's consent, he shall be permitted to take another wife."[64] On the other hand, Theodore provided "penance with tribulation" for seven years or a lighter penance for fifteen years for any man who repudiated his wife and then remarried. The penance was only one year if the husband remarried after his wife had deserted him (the offenses here being the speed of remarriage and failure to obtain the bishop's permission).[65] Most important of all, however, Theodore allowed divorce on the ground of adultery:

If the wife of anyone commits fornication, he may put her away and take another; that is, if a man puts away his wife on account of fornication, if she was his first, he is permitted to take another; but if she wishes to do penance for her sins, she may take another husband after five years.[66]

Moreover, the Eastern church allowed divorce for reason of adultery, following a decision of the Council of Trullo in 692 and based on an opinion of Origen. Origen, noting that "even some leaders of the Church" had permitted one spouse to remarry during the lifetime of the other, thought that they "tolerated this weakness to avoid greater evils, despite what has been commanded from the beginning and written in the Scriptures."[67] Adultery – infidelity – was extended to include other forms of conjugal infidelity. We find among them voluntary abortion, the presence of the wife with immoral intentions at certain festivities, or the absence of the wife from her home at night without her husband's consent. Offenses by the husband that fell within the terms of infidelity included his unjustly accusing his wife of adultery or other dishonorable acts in

---

[62] McNeill and Gamer, *Medieval Handbooks*, 94–6.
[63] Ibid., 272–3.
[64] Ibid., 210.
[65] Ibid., 196.
[66] Ibid., 208.
[67] Rordorf, "Marriage in the New Testament," 205. Oliver Rousseau, "Divorce et remariage: Orient et occident," *Concilium* 24 (1967), 59.

the presence of other men and having had open or covert relations with other women.[68]

Returning to the geographical ambit of the Roman Catholic church, however, it is important to note that secular laws up to the eighth century diverged from the principle of marital indissolubility that had been accepted by most ecclesiastical authorities up to that time. Constantine and Justinian, as we have seen, both restricted divorce, but even so made it more freely available than any of the church authorities permitted. Justinian's policies vacillated. For example, in 536 he confirmed the possibility of divorce by mutual consent, declaring that "all that have been joined together by man can be separated by man." Six years later, however, he brought consensual divorce under the same restrictions as repudiation and subjected it to the sample penalties for abuse. Yet by 566 this had proved to be so unpopular that it was repealed by his successor, Justinian II.[69] None of these changes of policy and law altered the fact that divorce, unilateral or by mutual consent, was available within the Roman state after Christianity had become the established religion, its existence protected by successive emperors.

Not only did divorce persist in the law of the declining Roman state but the Germanic codifications of law between the fifth and ninth centuries also tended to allow divorce, either by mutual consent or unilaterally. The terms of the latter generally favored the husband, who was permitted to repudiate his wife if she were guilty of adultery or if she were unable to have children. Frankish law did not permit a wife to initiate a divorce, while Burgundian law provided that a woman who attempted to repudiate her husband should be smothered in mire.[70] Visigothic law permitted a wife to divorce her husband if he were a homosexual or if he forced her to fornicate with another man,[71] both being circumstances that attacked the sexual character of marriage. In Anglo-Saxon law, too, provisions were made for dissolution of marriage. The code of King Æthelberht of Kent (560–616) permitted a marriage, like any other contract, to be broken by mutual consent or by one partner alone. The law set down the financial implications thus: "If [a wife] wishes to depart with her children, she shall have half the goods...If the husband wishes to keep [the children], she shall have a share of the goods equal to a child's."[72]

The Roman Catholic church had as difficult a time in England as anywhere when it sought to impose its doctrine of marital indissolubility on populations

---

[68] St. Pascu and V. Pascu, "Le remariage chez les orthodoxes," in J. Dupâquier et al. (eds.), *Marriage and Remarriage in Populations of the Past* (London, 1981), 62.

[69] Rheinstein, *Marriage Stability*, 16.

[70] Angela M. Lucas, *Women in the Middle Ages: Religion, Marriage and Letters* (New York, 1983), 69. Roman legal codes issued by the Burgundians did permit a wife to divorce her husband on grounds of murder, sorcery, or the violation of graves. See also McNamara and Wemple, "Marriage and Divorce," 98–100.

[71] Lucas, *Women in the Middle Ages*, 70.

[72] Quoted in ibid., 65.

1 *The Roman Catholic background*

that had a tradition of recognizing divorce. Theodor, Archbishop of Canterbury from 668 to 690, was forced to make concessions to local practice. He forbade the abandonment of wives unless they were guilty of adultery and allowed married women to remarry within the lifetime of their husbands in exceptional circumstances: A wife could remarry one year after her husband was condemned to penal slavery and five years after her husband was carried off into "hopeless captivity."[73]

During the eighth century the divergence that had been apparent between secular and ecclesiastical legal codes began to close in favor of the nondissolubilist position. The initiative was not taken by the church, which if anything was moving toward a less rigorous interpretation of the biblical divorce texts. The general shift toward the principle of marital indissolubility was largely the result of Charlemagne's efforts to strengthen marriage law. In 789 the Ninth Synod of Carthage, convoked by Charlemagne, prohibited the remarriage of any person who had been repudiated by his or her spouse.[74] Eight years later the Council of Friuli decreed unequivocally that adultery did not dissolve marriage, although an adulteress could be punished and her husband could obtain a separation *a mensa et thoro* from her. The doctrine of indissolubility encouraged by Charlemagne was, by the beginning of the ninth century, applied by the civil courts throughout the empire. As two historians of the subject write: "For three hundred years, after Augustine had enunciated the absolute indissolubility of marriage, the Church had hesitated on the question, but now a secular law upheld it for all Christians."[75]

The church itself continued to hesitate. In 826 the Roman synod convoked by Pope Eugenius decreed that divorce was permitted in the case of adultery and that the innocent party could remarry.[76] But three years later, under Louis the Pious, an attempt to reach an unequivocal set of regulations on marriage and divorce reversed this decision. Four Frankish councils in 829 decreed that adultery did not dissolve the marriage bond; a man might separate from his adulterous wife, but the councils urged reconciliation. A man who repudiated his wife and remarried would himself be guilty of adultery. In 829 Louis the Pious provided for a public penance by men who repudiated their wives.[77]

In general, a consensus in favor of marital indissolubility formed in both secular and ecclesiastical codes from the ninth century, and one of the first

[73] Ibid., 68. The necessity for the church to continue to insist on its doctrines is reflected in the fact that in the fourteenth century the clergy were instructed to remind their parishioners every quarter about their marital obligations. The manual they used, the *Book of Vices and Virtues*, described marriage as the third branch of chastity, so that spouses "should be of one heart by true love, nor ever separate in heart or body while they live." Ibid., 131.
[74] McNamara and Wemple, "Marriage and Divorce," 103.
[75] Ibid., 104.
[76] Ibid., 103.
[77] Suzanne Wemple, *Women in Frankish Society: Marriage and the Cloister, 500–900* (Philadelphia, 1981), 81.

to experience the new rigor of the church was King Lothar II of Lotharingia.[78] In 857 Lothar had married Teutberga, but the following year he began to seek opportunities to rid himself of her in favor of Waldrada, who had been his concubine. Charges, probably fabricated, were made to the effect that Teutberga had had an incestuous relationship with her brother and had borne him a child. When it was proved that she had been a virgin at marriage, a theory of virgin birth with occult aid was put forward as a way of getting around the inconsistency. A council at Aix-la-Chapelle in 862 permitted Lothar to separate from Teutberga, and after a confession by her, no doubt made under duress, the council declared that Teutberga was not a suitable and legitimate wife, and granted Lothar permission to marry Waldrada.

This sparked a long battle between Lothar and Pope Nicholas I (ruled 858–67), who opposed the repudiation and remarriage as contrary to church law. The conflict between king and pontiff involved, among other events, the deposition of several archbishops who had agreed to Lothar's remarriage, and the invasion of Rome by Emperor Louis II in their support. Despite this and other forms of pressure from secular rulers, the pope held to his position that Lothar must leave Waldrada and take Teutberga back as his wife. Lothar finally agreed to do so in 865, but Waldrada refused to travel to Rome to answer to the pope for her sins and was excommunicated. In late 865 Teutberga petitioned Nicholas to dissolve the marriage to enable her to enter a convent, but the pope demurred on the ground that the petition was probably not voluntary. He answered that he would agree to grant the couple a separation, but only if she and Lothar promised to remain chaste. Nicholas specified that Lothar would never be granted papal permission to marry Waldrada, even if Teutberga died.

The determination of Nicholas I was continued by his successor, Pope Hadrian II, and early in his rule the issue was resolved. Waldrada repented her sins and sought and obtained absolution. Forsaken by her, Lothar traveled to Rome in 869 and was forgiven by the pope, but he was saved from having to fulfill his promise to take Teutberga back as his wife by his death on his way home from Rome. The whole affair demonstrated the determination of the papacy to enforce a marriage, even in the face of strong pressure and even in the case of a secular prince who might have been treated as an exception to the rule of marital indissolubility.[79]

The general and effective application of the doctrine of indissolubility depended, however, on the development of church law and courts and on the ability of the church to enforce its jurisdiction over matrimonial matters.

---

[78] This case is set out in Charles E. Smith, *Papal Enforcement of Some Medieval Marriage Laws* (Baton Rouge, 1940, repr. Port Washington, N. Y., 1972), 54–76. Also in Wemple, *Women in Frankish Society*, 84–6.

[79] An account of other conflicts between the popes and secular rulers over matrimonial issues up to the fifteenth century is given in Michel Lhospice, *Divorce et dynastie* (Paris, 1960), 23–36.

1 The Roman Catholic background

Throughout Europe the church was successful in claiming jurisdiction over marriage, an area of potential litigation that had lain largely outside the civil law. Matrimonial matters were considered to fall principally within the spheres of religion and morality, and, in the beginning at least, there was little dispute between the secular and ecclesiastical powers as to which should have jurisdiction. Although the church's dominance over marriage matters was eventually challenged, this challenge came later, especially between the sixteenth and eighteenth centuries.

With respect to the success of the Catholic church in bringing marriage within its judicial purview, we must also consider the development of the corpus of church law known as canon law. To enforce the principle that a validly contracted marriage could be dissolved only by the death of one of the parties, it was necessary to define a validly contracted marriage. To a large extent marriage had been outside the formal law and had been a matter of private arrangement and public repute, but the aim of the canon law was to bring it within the realm of formal law where it could be regulated by the church courts. The prime ingredient decided upon for marriage, its sine qua non, was consent, under the principle "consensus facit matrimonium." In reaching this rule, the church authorities finally decided the argument whether marriage was made by sexual intercourse or by consent. (The notion of consent here shifted from the consent of the parents to the consent of the parties actually being married.) It meant that the parties had to give their mutual consent to the marriage, free of coercion or fraud. Consent was held to validate a marriage, even if there were no formal ceremony, for a ceremony involving the participation of a priest and witnesses was not required until the sixteenth century.

Stress on the consent of the parties to marriage not only undermined parental control of their children's marriages but also challenged the control of serfs' marriages, which lords of manors had been able to exercise. It had been a principle of Christian Roman law that a serf could not contract a fully valid marriage, and servile unions were treated as little more than liaisons that could be broken by the spouses' master. This principle was recognized as late as the mid-twelfth century by canons of church law, even though the church had campaigned for servile marriages to be treated as full and enforceable. The progressive acceptance of the principle of consent contributed to certainty of the validity of marriages at all social levels.[80]

From the eleventh to the early thirteenth century the canon law of marriage was refined, particularly under the aegis of popes Alexander III and Innocent III. By the end of the latter's reign (1198–1216), the principle of consensuality had triumphed. Whereas it had been an earlier principle that consent began a marriage but intercourse completed it, marriage was, by the early thirteenth

[80] See Paul A. Brand and Paul R. Hyams, "Seigneurial Control of Women's Marriage," *Past and Present* 99 (1983), 128ff. This is a reply to Eleanor Searle, "Seigneurial Control of Women's Marriage: The Antecedents and Function of Merchet in England," *Past and Present* 82 (1979), 3–43.

century, recognized as being completed by consent, although not perfectly completed until consummated.[81] The distinction was an important one because it gave an unconsummated marriage a more stable and certain existence. As we have seen, an unconsummated marriage could be dissolved – an important concession to consensuality itself, for if an unconsummated marriage had not been complete it would have fallen under the rules of annulment rather than dissolution. But the circumstances permitting dissolution of an unconsummated marriage were extremely limited. Pope Alexander III seems to have granted a dispensation for remarriage in the case of a long absence by one spouse in an unconsummated marriage, and he also permitted one party in such a relationship to choose the monastic life, leaving the other party free to enter another marriage. After Alexander III, Pope Urban III apparently permitted the dissolution of an unconsummated marriage where one party was suffering from leprosy. But Pope Innocent III abolished most of these exceptions, apart from the one based on the desire to enter religious orders.[82] This development of the canon law of marriage was crucial for the successful application of the principle of marital indissolubility. Only by the beginning of the thirteenth century, when the variety of laws and customs had been welded into a coherent body of law and uniform definition of marriage, could there be certainty as to what it was that was indissoluble. Even so, the principle of indissolubility itself was made canon law only in 1563 as part of the decrees of the Council of Trent.

Concomitant with the doctrine of indissolubility was the doctrine that marriage was one of the sacraments. This too achieved canonical form only in the sixteenth century, even though it was influential and had been broadly accepted centuries earlier. The key biblical passage bearing on the sacramentality of marriage is that of Ephesians 5:31–32, which says of husband and wife that they "shall be one flesh. This is a great sacrament: but I speak concerning Christ and the Church." Augustine is generally regarded as the earliest authority treating marriage as a sacrament in the sense of a ceremony by which man obtained God's grace. Subsequent commentators, however, pointed to less rigorous meanings of *sacramentum*, as an expression of the sanctity of marriage or as a sign or pledge of indissolubility, but one that did not ipso facto render the dissolution of marriage unlawful. The eleventh-century scholastics, for example, did not subscribe fully to the Augustinian position. Peter Abelard listed marriage among the sacraments but distinguished it from those that conferred grace. Hugo of St. Victor depicted marriage as a sign of the indissoluble relationship between Christ and the Church but did not state that marriage conferred grace, and Peter Lombard denied that marriage had a grace-giving character, describing it, rather, as a remedy against fornication. Thomas Aquinas, however, reverted to Augustine's opinion that marriage was a

---

[81] Le Bras, "Le Mariage dans la théologie," 197–9.
[82] Charles Donahue, Jr., "The Policy of Alexander the Third's Consent Theory of Marriage," in Stephen Kuttner (ed.), *Proceedings of the Fourth International Congress of Medieval Canon Law* (Vatican City, 1976), 252 n. 2.

sacrament and an equal of the other six in conveying grace. It was this doctrine that was finally accepted.[83]

Finally, we should note the intimate connection between divorce and re-marriage in Roman Catholic doctrine. The ability of divorced spouses, or at least one of them, to remarry during the lifetime of the former spouse was what critically distinguished a dissolution of marriage from a mere separation *a mensa et thoro*. Remarriage, though, was a sensitive aspect of Catholic marriage doctrine. There was no unanimous agreement among the authorities that remarriage was possible or advisable even when one spouse had died. If this were so, how unlikely it was that remarriage would have been conceded on the part of an individual when his or her spouse was still living.

Among those who held that remarriage was forbidden was Tertullian, who took the analogy between marriage, on the one hand, and the eternal union of Christ with the Church, on the other, to its extreme conclusion.[84] If the latter union was eternal, he argued, so was the bond between married couples, such that it survived the death of either spouse. Even authorities who did not accept the full implications of this position followed the advice of the apostle Paul to the effect that remarriage in widowhood was permitted but that it was not recommended. This attitude had two bases. The first was the view that in Christian marriage the union of the flesh represented the union of Christ with the Church. This full sacramental meaning of marriage was lacking in a second marriage because "the remarried man had 'divided' his flesh, and his marital union can no longer represent the mystical Union."[85] Second, there was the purpose of marriage, which was viewed by the church as principally for pro-creation and secondarily for the avoidance of fornication. A first marriage made sense in terms of these ends, but a second or subsequent marriage might call into question the reasons for matrimony. A widow who was past the age of child bearing and who remarried could not justify her marriage in terms of producing children. As for the avoidance of fornication, it was thought that having been married once, a widow or widower ought to be sexually satisfied and able to resist carnal temptation more easily than a woman or man who had never been married at all. A second marriage undertaken for sexual reasons was thus far less creditable than a first marriage, which in itself was considered less preferable to celibacy, and for this reason men and women entering second or successive marriages should do penances in compensation. The ninth-century St. Hubert Penitential, for example, provided for three weeks' fasting by a person entering a second or third marriage, and a thirty-three-week fast for anyone contracting marriage for a fourth time.[86] The Penitential of Theodore

---

[83] V. Norskov Olsen, *The New Testament Logia on Divorce* (Tübingen, 1971), 2–6.

[84] Rordorf, "Marriage in the New Testament," 205.

[85] Stephen Kuttner, "Pope Lucius III and the Bigamous Archbishop of Palermo," in J. A. Watt et al., (eds.), *Medieval Studies presented to Aubrey Gwynn S. J.* (Dublin, 1961), 410.

[86] McNeill and Gamer, *Medieval Handbooks*. A total fast for thirty-three weeks would be fatal, and although that might be a useful deterrent to fourth marriages, it is likely that the fast referred to here implied a reduction of the normal amount of food or the omission of one meal a day.

specified a year's penance for a second marriage: "On Wednesdays and Fridays and during the three forty-day periods he shall abstain from flesh; however, he shall not put away his wife." For subsequent marriages, this penance was to last for seven years.[87]

Further evidence of the church's generally negative attitude toward remarriage is the refusal to pronounce the nuptial benediction over widows who remarried. Previously unmarried women received the benediction. It seems, however, that the benediction was extended to widowers who remarried, if they did so to a previously unmarried woman.[88] The emphasis here was clearly on female sexuality, and the general opposition to remarriage by women in particular was a persistent theme in Catholic marriage doctrine. It was also a characteristic of the marriage doctrine of the Eastern church. There, remarriage was permitted, but tolerated only for reason of human weakness. Remarriage had to be preceded by a penance done before the marriage ceremony, and the marriage service for a remarriage was not the same as for a first marriage.[89]

Other restrictions on remarriage that might be noted here had practical, rather than purely doctrinal, justifications. For example, rapid remarriage by widows was prohibited in some places in order to ensure, first, that there was no confusion over paternity should they bear a child that could have been the deceased husband's and, second, to reduce attraction of remarriage as a motive for spouse murder. The Siete Partidas, a Spanish legal code promulgated by Alfonso X in the thirteenth century, reflected these concerns when it banned remarriage by a widow within a year of her husband's death. A woman who remarried sooner than this was "considered as of bad reputation" and lost any inheritance rights from her former husband.[90]

Such attitudes toward remarriage need not have contributed to the general tendency against allowing divorce, with its implied right of remarriage. Divorce was, after all, permitted by the Orthodox church, despite its negative attitude toward remarriage. In the Roman Catholic church, however, the same attitude toward remarriage meshed with the doctrine of marital indissolubility. It gave emphasis to the integrity of a first marriage that, for all that remarriage was actually permitted, was considered not to have been entirely dissolved by the death of one of the spouses.

This brief survey of the development of the Roman Catholic church's doctrines of marriage and divorce has been presented in the most general way and does not allow for the discussion of nuances nor for the complexity of the interrelationships among doctrines of marriage, divorce, and sexuality. (Some of these are taken up in the course of describing the Protestant reaction against the Catholic doctrines.) Yet the overall trend of a consensus against divorce

---

[87] Ibid., 195–6.
[88] Philippe Ariès, "Introduction," in Dupâquier et al. (eds.), *Marriage and Remarriage*, 29.
[89] Pascu and Pascu, "Le remariage," 63.
[90] *Las Siete Partidas* (trans. S. R. Scott, Chicago, 1931), 947, Partida IV, Title X, Law III. Partida IV deals with domestic relations.

emerging from the ninth century and crystallizing in the eleventh and twelfth centuries ought to be evident. This is not to say that there was complete unanimity among church authorities on any major point of doctrine. Rather, a workable and broadly accepted consensus was achieved, which replaced the ambiguity and ambivalence that had characterized Catholic marriage doctrine until the ninth century.

1.6 Marriage and divorce in Catholic populations

Like all generalizations, this one cries out for qualification. What has been described has been primarily the debate on marriage and divorce at the most elevated levels – among theologians, popes, and church councils and synods. Customary practices of marriage can hardly have responded to the subtleties of an evolving doctrine. Strictly speaking, such considerations did not involve divorce, but there is always the possibility that marriages that took place according to customary procedures not recognized by the church were, for that reason, not subject to the rule of indissolubility. It is not clear, for instance, whether concubinage – defined as a stable, sexually exclusive relationship – was considered by theologians to be indissoluble. Some, like Gratian, sought to make concubinage the equivalent of marriage in many respects. What were the implications for dissolution if concubinage were considered (as by Gratian) "a marriage which lacks legal formalities and full legal consequences, but which was nonetheless a true and valid marriage"?[91] Was indissolubility one of the legal consequences that concubinage lacked? If so, and if the relationship were dissoluble by divorce, how could it be considered to be a true and valid marriage? Perhaps more to the point, did those men and women involved in relationships of concubinage regard themselves as being indissolubly linked to each other until death? Among others, the monk Yves of Chartres argued, in the late eleventh century, that if a man treated a concubine as a wife, their union was indissoluble. They could obtain a separation for "carnal reasons," but could not remarry.[92]

Because these relationships did not have a foundation in canon or secular law and were not subject to the church's marriage legislation and courts, there is a lack of documentary evidence that can provide a means for understanding the fuller implications of customary forms of marriage. There might well have been, within the mass of medieval European populations, a culture that enabled individuals to enter into stable monogamous relationships but that also allowed them to separate under certain conditions (or at will) so that the parties could enter into subsequent long-term relationships.

There is abundant evidence of customary rituals of marriage coexisting with

[91] James A. Brundage, "Concubinage and Marriage in Medieval Canon Law," *Journal of Medieval History* 1 (1975), 4.
[92] Georges Duby, *The Knight, the Lady and the Priest: The Making of Modern Marriage in Medieval France* (Cambridge, 1983), 164–5.

the evolving procedures laid down by the Catholic church, including exchanges of consent and symbolic acts such as sharing food and drink. One case, documented by André Burguière, came before the court of the bishop of Troyes in 1483. It involved one Jean Binet and Henriette, the widow Legouge. Binet had asked Legouge to marry him, she had agreed, and her father had given his consent.

Then the father told his daughter to sit at the table beside Jean Binet, then he put some wine in a glass and told Binet to give it to his daughter to drink in the name of marriage. He obeyed without saying a word. That done, Henriette's uncle said to her: "Give it to Jean to drink in the name of marriage, as he gave it to you to drink." Henriette gave the drink to [Binet]...He drank from her hand, then said "I wish you to receive a kiss from me in the name of marriage," and then he kissed her.[93]

This case came before the court in an attempt to compel Binet to fulfill the terms of the engagement. Other cases, with a similar aim, described rituals involving exchanges of symbols and actions, including the case of Pierre Pellart who, before having intercourse with Marguerite, the widow Jacomart, told her: "Marguerite, so that you may not be afraid that I am abusing you, I put my tongue in your mouth, in the name of marriage."[94]

It seems clear that it was a widespread customary practice for betrothal (according to nonecclesiastical forms) to be followed by cohabitation and sexual relations. Marriages were recognized by public repute if a couple shared daily activities – if they acted as a married couple would act. This is the sense of the saying: "To eat, drink and sleep together; these things seem to make a marriage."[95]

In the church's terms, words of marriage *de praesenti* (in the present tense, i.e., "I take you in marriage," rather than *in verbis de futuro*, a promise to marry in the future) followed by sexual intercourse made for a valid marriage. But it is not clear how binding these contracts were in customary terms. It is perhaps an indication that such engagements were taken seriously that there were so many attempts to have them enforced by the church courts, but that evidence is ambiguous, since each case also represented an attempt to evade the engagement. It must remain an open question whether the cases for enforcement reflected the increasing influence of the church's doctrines and the wider availability of the courts as a means of confirming and enforcing betrothals and marriages. There can be no documentary evidence whether community pressure had earlier done the work of the courts in holding reluctant men and women to their engagements. It is possible to read sources like the penitentials as indicating that some sort of popular divorce procedure had earlier done the work of the courts. The Judgment of Clement, for example, provided for ex-

[93] André Burguière, "Le ritual du mariage en France: pratiques ecclésiastiques et pratiques populaires (XVIᵉ–XVIIIᵉ siècle)," *Annales E. S. C.* 33:3 (May–June 1978), 642.
[94] Ibid., 643.
[95] Martine Segalen, *Amours et mariages de l'ancienne France* (Paris, 1981), 11.

communication of a man who "puts away his legal wife and marries another ...even if the former wife consents."[96]

Moreover, there were practices of trial marriages in various parts of Europe, where a betrothed couple had community approval of living together or having regular sexual contact before marriage. To some extent the purpose of these practices was to test the fertility of the union before marriage, which would follow only after the woman had become pregnant. An implication of this was that a union that proved sterile after several years' cohabitation could be terminated. This practice was found among the Basque populations of southern France. In 1612 the Bordeaux magistrate Pierre de Lancre condemned the Basques for "the liberty they take in trying their women for several years before marrying them, and taking them as if on a trial basis."[97] For the study of divorce such examples highlight the difficulty of definition. For the Basques, marriage was completed not by sexual intercourse, but by the marriage ceremony, so that an infertile couple who terminated their relationship before going through a ceremony were not actually dissolving a marriage. But for the church, consummation of the betrothal was tantamount to marriage, so that the Basque custom appeared as a clear form of customary divorce, to be condemned as contrary to the principle of marital indissolubility.

Such practices, with which the Catholic church competed and that it eventually dominated, speak to a secular model of marriage that was different from the ecclesiastical in many respects. As described by Georges Duby, the secular model stressed the role of marriage in maintaining the social order.[98] Marriage united not simply two individuals but also families and houses. To this extent a marriage was of general social interest; it was part of the strategies for survival and promotion of the families that were brought together by the marriage; and it was seen as too important a transaction to be left to the two individuals most directly concerned. This gave the parents and other relatives of marriageable men and women a legitimate claim to influence if not to control marriage, a claim that could go so far as to override the will of the individuals to be married. Needless to say, this tendency conflicted with the consensus of the church that the consent of the parties was essential to a valid marriage.

The secular model had many implications for the formation of marriage, and in some respects it did not conflict with the doctrines developed within the church. Both, for example, agreed that a public ceremony was the most suitable way of solemnizing a marriage. But there were distinct differences when it came to the question of dissolution of marriage. The stress on the social and familial utility of marriage in the secular model led to an acceptance of the view that divorce was not only possible but even desirable under certain circumstances.

---

[96] McNeill and Gamer, *Medieval Handbooks*, 272.
[97] Flandrin, *Amours*, 187. This is not a medieval example, but it seems likely to refer to behavior that was embedded in traditional Basque culture and that became particularly repugnant to the church as a result of the sixteenth-century reformulations of the canon laws of marriage.
[98] On the secular model of marriage, see Duby, *Medieval Marriage*.

1.6 Marriage, divorce in Catholic populations

When a wife did not produce an heir, and it seemed unlikely that she would ever do so, a case could be made for divorce so as to allow the husband to remarry and have children with another woman. It would even be advantageous for a man to dissolve one marriage and enter another if the other served his interests more effectively. Marriage, from this perspective, was a mechanism of achieving certain social and personal ends, and when an individual marriage failed in its purpose, it could be dissolved.[99] This is not to say that divorce could be obtained easily under those secular laws which ran counter to Catholic principles, but however restrictive they were, they were still at odds with the Catholic principle of indissolubility.

Diversity in marriage practices in medieval Europe was influenced by social level and geography. Although the Catholic church was nominally universal, its doctrines and legislation respecting matrimonial matters were only weakly felt by some of its more distant faithful. Iceland is an example. There, the canon law of marriage was received in the thirteenth century but applied much later: The earliest attempt at enforcement dates from 1429.[100] In the twelfth and thirteenth centuries an indigenous law regulated marriage, and it diverged from church law in important respects. Whereas the Catholic church emphasized that a valid marriage required the freely given consent of both spouses, in Icelandic law (*grágás*) the consent of the woman was not necessary. Moreover, divorce was permitted. According to evidence from legal sources, "if at any time either partner desired to separate, the marriage might end with a divorce, the wife retaining the bride-price, dowry and morning-gift as her portion."[101]

Icelandic saga-literature from the thirteenth century confirms that divorce was possible and gives human dimension to what the legal sources describe. Of twelve divorces recounted in the family sagas, nine were obtained by women, the grounds including "a slap, a family feud, incompatibility, an Icelandic variety of nonconsummation, a fatal illness, the wearing of sexually inappropriate dress, and a mocking verse."[102] All five threatened divorces in the sagas were at the initiative of women, and this together with the proportion of women initiating actual divorces, suggests that women dominated divorce in medieval Iceland. Perhaps that was to be expected, given that they might well have been married against their will, though it seems inconsistent that a woman could be coerced into marriage but could not be coerced into staying in it. Divorce under the *grágás* was not too demanding in procedural terms. It had legal effect when

---

[99] There are echoes here of the role of divorce in Rome, where in the higher levels of society marriage secured sociopolitical ends. Marriages and divorces could thus represent the formation and modification of political alliances much more than anything else. See Rawson, "Roman Family," 33. The secular model discussed here, based on Duby's writings, also draws mainly on an élite, the nobility of northern France.

[100] Roberta Frank, "Marriage in the Middle Ages: Marriage in Twelfth- and Thirteenth-Century Iceland," *Viator* 4 (1973), 474. See also Grethe Jacobsen, "Sexual Irregularities in Medieval Scandinavia," in Bullough and Brundage, *Sexual Practices*, 72–85.

[101] Frank, "Marriage," 476.

[102] Ibid., 478.

either the husband or the wife made a declaration of divorce in front of witnesses. The ability to divorce ended, needless to say, with the enforcement of the canon law of marriage in the fifteenth century. But, as we shall see, Iceland warmed to the Reformation in the following century, and divorce was restored there after a break of only 150 years.

Spain provided yet another variation in Catholic Europe, even as the church was consolidating the doctrine of marital indissolubility. The important thirteenth-century legal code, Las Siete Partidas, did not make allowance for divorce in the strict sense[103] but permitted annulments when one spouse wanted to enter holy orders, committed adultery, or committed spiritual fornication "by turning heretic, Moor, or Jew, if he is not willing to make amends for his wickedness."[104] Where there was adultery, then, the innocent spouse could be freed to remarry, making this provision a divorce in all but name.

1.7 The Council of Trent and its Catholic critics

Surveying the development of the doctrine and application of the Roman Catholic doctrine of marital indissolubility, then, we can appreciate its complexity. This is a useful corrective to the too frequent view of the church's doctrine as having been monolithic and unchanging. Within the church there were competing approaches to marriage and divorce up to, and beyond, the twelfth century, when a consensus in favor of marital indissolubility emerged. Yet even so, it was not until the second half of the sixteenth century that that doctrine entered the canon law, when the church, under pressure from within and without, undertook a broad review of its marriage laws. The results were embodied in the final (thirty-fourth) session of the Council of Trent in 1563, and the canons and decrees then established – some simply codifying, others expanding accepted doctrines – defined the church's attitude to marriage and divorce in the following centuries.

Faced with Protestant attacks on Catholic matrimonial doctrine, the Council of Trent reiterated the superiority of celibacy and virginity over marriage: "If anyone saith, that the marriage state is to be placed above the state of virginity, or of celibacy, and that it is not better to remain in virginity, or in celibacy, than to be united in matrimony, let him be anathema."[105] The sacramentality of marriage was asserted dogmatically, and the council condemned those

impious men of this age raging [who] have not only had false notions touching this venerable sacrament, but, introducing according to their wont, under the pretext of the

---

[103] E. N. van Kleffens, *Hispanic Law until the end of the Middle Ages* (Edinburgh, 1968), 199.
[104] *Las Siete Partidas*, 926–7, Partida IV, Title X, Law II. The adaptation of canon law to local circumstances is also clear in the case of the Spanish colonies. See Luis Martín, *Daughters of the Conquistadores: Women of the Viceroyalty of Peru* (Albuquerque, 1983), esp. 128–150.
[105] *Canons and Decrees of the Council of Trent* (trans. J. Waterworth, London, 1948), 195.

1.7 Council of Trent and its Catholic critics

Gospel, a carnal liberty...have by word and writing asserted not without great injury to the faithful of Christ, many things alien from the sentiment of the Catholic Church.[106]

As regards the formation of marriage, the council modified the impediments that prevented marriage or could result in annulment. Although the prohibited degrees of consanguinity and affinity were maintained in the forms set down by the Fourth Lateran Council in the early thirteenth century, the diriment impediment based on *affinitas illegitima* (sexual intercourse) was reduced from four to two degrees. At the same time, the council elaborated on the impediment of clandestinity. Until this time a marriage contracted or celebrated clandestinely or elsewhere than in a church was considered illicit but valid. The Council of Trent decreed, however, that thenceforth a marriage would be invalid unless it were celebrated publicly after the calling of banns and by a priest in the presence of two witnesses. This was an important step because it gave the church a monopoly on the celebration of valid marriages. The culmination of a centuries-long trend in which the church had claimed responsibility for overseeing and authorizing marriage, this impediment of clandestinity was designed to counteract what were perceived as widespread abuses of marriage and bigamy.[107] Moreover, and clearly in response to criticisms of what were considered abuses within the Catholic church itself, the Council of Trent limited dispensations that could be granted to overcome impediments of consanguinity and affinity. It ruled that "either no dispensation at all shall be granted, or rarely, and then for a cause and gratuitously. A dispensation shall never be granted in the second degree, except between great princes, and for a public cause."[108] No dispensation was to be granted after marriage if the impediments had been deliberately violated, but there was provision for retroactive dispensation when an impediment was discovered of which the parties were likely to have been ignorant at the time of their marriage.

But most importantly, for present purposes, the Council of Trent set down in canon law the indissolubility of marriage. The canon decreed erroneous the opinion that marriage could be dissolved for reason of "heresy, or irksome cohabitation, or the affected absence of one of the parties" (Canon V),[109] but declared that an unconsummated marriage might be dissolved by the solemn profession of religion by one of the spouses.[110] The question of divorce for reason of adultery was dealt with in Canon VII:

If any one saith, that the Church has erred, in that she hath taught, and doth teach, in accordance with the evangelical and apostolical doctrine, that the bond of matrimony cannot be dissolved on account of the adultery of one of the married parties; and that both, or even the innocent one who gave not occasion to the adultery, cannot contract

---

[106] Ibid., 193–4.
[107] *Catholic Dictionary of Theology*, III, 240.
[108] *Canons and Decrees*, 201.
[109] Ibid., 194.
[110] Ibid., 195.

35

another marriage, during the lifetime of the other; and, that he is guilty of adultery, who, having put away the adulteress, shall take another wife, also she, who, having put away the adulterer, shall take another husband; let him be anathema.[111]

At the same time, the Council of Trent defended the use of separations *a mensa et thoro* "for many causes... for a determinate or for an indeterminate period."

As we have seen, these decrees and canons largely reflected a consensus that had been achieved centuries before the Protestant attacks on Roman Catholic doctrines and practices. The Council of Trent removed many ambiguities from marriage doctrines (such as the question of divorce on the ground of adultery) and attempted to correct areas of perceived abuse (such as the sale of dispensations from impediments to marriage). But before turning to the criticisms by the Protestants of Catholic doctrines of marital sacramentality and indissolubility, we should note continuing anxieties expressed within the Catholic church itself by humanists such as Erasmus, Thomas More, and Michel de Montaigne. All were Catholics, yet held beliefs regarding marriage and divorce that appeared to be at variance – radically so, not merely in detail or emphasis – with those of their church. At the same time their views were often stated equivocally, no doubt for fear of retaliation by the church's authorities.

Rather than confront church doctrine directly, Erasmus chose to raise important questions of interpretation and to suggest that conclusions other than those reached by the church were possible. For example, he called into question the meaning of Ephesians 5:32 and resuscitated the debate as to whether the reference to *mysterion* in the Greek New Testament should be translated as "sacrament" (as the church, after Augustine, accepted) or whether it was better expressed as "mystery." The distinction was much more than one of semantics in its implications, for on it might rest much of the force of the doctrine of marital indissolubility.

In his first edition of the Greek New Testament (1516), which gave both the Greek text and a Latin translation, Erasmus gave *mysterion* as *mysterium* (mystery). This was a significant break, and so Erasmus was careful to protect himself against criticism. He made it clear that the translation did not necessarily deny the sacramental character of marriage but that the evidence for sacramentality did not lie in the Ephesians passage. Erasmus wrote in the 1519 edition: "Not that I say this, as if calling into doubt whether matrimony is a sacrament, but because from these words of the Apostle it does not easily appear on the surface."[112]

Erasmus applied this same method of undermining unquestioning acceptance of the church's doctrine of divorce, while drawing back from an outright statement of belief. Surveying church authorities who had admitted the

---

[111] Ibid.
[112] Quoted in Norskov Olsen, *New Testament Logia*, 7. Erasmus's views on marriage are also discussed in Pierre Bels, *Le mariage des Protestants français jusqu'en 1685* (Paris, 1968), esp. 27–44, 74–81.

possibility of divorce, Erasmus cited Origen, Tertullian, Pollentius, Chrysostom, and Ambrose. Of the first of these, he wrote that

> it is manifest and open, that Origen was of this mind plainly, that after a man had put away his wife for whoredom, he may marry another wife. But where, as he says, that the bishops did against the doctrine of the gospel, which permitted and gave licence for marriage after divorcement, he doth mean of those men which did put away their wives for other causes.[113]

Tertullian was of the same opinion as Origen, noted Erasmus, and even though he "went away from the Church," "yet in this matter he was not reprehended of the godly learned men, which he should have been, if this opinion had been contrary to the mind and judgement of them that were in the truth."[114]

Despite his recitation of authorities allowing divorce, Erasmus admitted that the weight of church authorities, especially the later authorities, favored the doctrine of marital indissolubility. Even so, he argued that there was no harm in opening up the issue for discussion, although "I intend, and mind in no place thereof, to be the father and bringer up of any new opinion which should breed contention."[115] He went so far as to reassure his Catholic readers that he knew, "and it is a thing among all Christian people most generally received, and agreed upon, that wheresoever matrimony is once celebrated, that it cannot otherwise be dissolved but by the death of one of the two parties which were so joined together."[116] But as he joined himself to church doctrine, Erasmus distanced himself from it. Without specifying what new circumstances had arisen since the doctrine of marital indissolubility had hardened, he suggested that it might be reviewed:

> The godly men have always thought it good to alter and change their opinions, when it is for a better purpose, and is also standing with reason, to make the laws for to serve us after the fashion as we use medicines, according to the nature of the sickness and disease wherewith man is pained: then let us consider, and weigh, whether it be expedient and profitable that the selfsame thing should not be done in this cause of matrimony: and if we do find it expedient and requisite that it should be, then let us see whether it be lawful, yea or nay, that some sort of marriages should be undone, not without a good ground, but for earnest causes...and that the same matrimony should be so dissolved, that both parties might marry again, to whom they please, or that party which was not the cause of the breach of matrimony.[117]

The church's answer to this plea was the dogmatic assertion by the Council of Trent that marriage might not be dissolved for any cause.

---

[113] Desiderius Erasmus, *The Censure and Judgement of the Famous Clark Erasmus of Roterdam: whyther dyvorsement betwene man and wyfe stondeth with the lawe of God...in the Book of his Annotations, upon these wordes of Paule* (trans. Nicholas Lesse, London, ?1550), sig. B IV[R].
[114] Ibid., sig. B VI[R].
[115] Ibid., sig. A III[R].
[116] Ibid., sig. A III[V].
[117] Ibid., sig. A IV[R].

1 The Roman Catholic background

Thomas More chose a different means of calling church doctrine into question, but like Erasmus he avoided stating his views in such an explicit way as might provoke a reaction by the church authorities. More did not refer directly to the divorce texts of the Bible, nor to tradition, but he dealt extensively with the issues of marriage and divorce in his *Utopia* (1516), where they are discussed in the context of an ideal society. More's image of Utopia was realistic enough to include adultery and marital disharmony, and it was upon these grounds, he argued, that divorce ought to be countenanced, though it was not the automatic consequence of them. Of divorce More wrote that

this provision was the more necessary because the Utopians are the only people in those parts of the world who are satisfied with one wife and because matrimony there is seldom broken except by death unless it be for adultery or for intolerable offensiveness of disposition. When husband or wife is thus offended, leave is granted by the senate to take another mate. The other party perpetually leads a life of disgrace as well as of celibacy.[118]

There was also provision for no-fault divorce for reason of incompatibility:

When a married couple agree insufficiently in their dispositions and both find others with whom they hope to live more agreeably, they separate by mutual consent and contract fresh unions, but not without the sanction of the senate. The latter allows no divorce until its members and their wives have carefully gone into the case.[119]

There was thus great caution in granting divorce, and steps were taken to prevent unhappiness or dissatisfaction in marriage from occurring. One custom among More's Utopians was for prospective spouses to be shown to each other, naked, so that they would know before marriage what they would eventually discover afterward. This was done to prevent disappointment since "such foul deformity may be hidden beneath these coverings that it may quite alienate a man's mind from his wife when bodily separation is no longer possible."[120]

Erasmus and More were prepared to voice disquiet indirectly and cautiously about the Catholic church's prohibition on divorce before it entered canon law. Afterward, other Catholic writers expressed misgivings, perhaps sharpened by the realization that divorce laws had been introduced throughout Protestant Europe. In France, Michel de Montaigne pointed to what he thought were the beneficial effects of divorce for marriage:

We thought we had tied the knot of our marriages more firmly by removing all means of dissolving them; but the bond of hearts and affections has become more loose and slack as that of constraint has been drawn closer. And, on the other hand, what made marriages to be so long honoured and so secure in Rome was the liberty to break them off at will. They loved their wives the better as long as there was the chance of loosing

---

[118] Thomas More, *Utopia*, in *The Complete Works of St. Thomas More* (14 vols., New Haven, 1965), IV, 189.
[119] Ibid., IV, 191.
[120] Ibid., IV, 189.

them and, with full liberty of divorce, five hundred years and more passed by before any took advantage of it.[121]

Within the Catholic church, then, there was pressure from the faithful in favor of relaxing the rule of marital indissolubility. But outside the church, opposition to the canon law of marriage and divorce was far more forthright. The Protestant Reformers were neither ambiguous nor subtle and called for the Catholic church not merely to reconsider its matrimonial doctrines but to abandon them forthwith as socially pernicious and contrary to divine law. This challenge, an integral part of the reformation of religious and social doctrines in the sixteenth century, turned the history of divorce in the West in a quite different direction from that which it had followed up to that time.

[121] Michel de Montaigne, *Essays* (2 vols., Oxford, 1927), II, 64.

2

~~~~~~

The Reformers and divorce:
Theory and practice

2.1 Introduction

The first fifteen hundred years of the Christian Era witnessed the progressive removal of divorce from European legal codes. Acceptable in one form or another in Greek, Roman, and Jewish law, and in Scandinavian, Germanic, and Frankish legal codes, divorce had an ambiguous status in the early Christian church before being suppressed entirely. It remained available only in the regions that fell under the influence of the Eastern Orthodox church, and they, by definition, are outside the scope of Western society. But from the sixteenth century onward the acceptability of divorce underwent a renaissance as a result of the Protestant Reformation. Although few of the Reformers went so far as to regard divorce as a good in itself – they looked upon it as the lesser of two evils or as a means to be reluctantly employed to correct an injustice – almost all nonetheless rejected the doctrine of marital indissolubility. The Reformers incorporated divorce into their marriage doctrines, and under their aegis all of the Protestant states of continental Europe and Scandinavia had legalized divorce by the end of the sixteenth century.

In terms of divorce policy, the most important Reformers were Luther and Calvin. Apart from any other considerations, their doctrines had the widest and most enduring influence and application, being translated into legislation throughout central and northern Europe and Scandinavia, and later in America. Other important Reformers included Zwingli, Bucer, Beza, Melanchthon, Bullinger, and, in England, Tyndale, Hooper, Cranmer, and Becon. These men, and others who will be mentioned from time to time, constituted what could be considered the first generation of divorce law exponents in modern Europe. This is not to overlook the development of the doctrines even within the sixteenth century itself, but rather to recognize the Reformers as sharing a common temper and outlook that distinguished them from the seventeenth-century writers on divorce and even more from those of the eighteenth century. For the most part the important sixteenth-century works on divorce were written or published in the period from 1520 to 1550, three decades that saw the Roman Catholic doctrine of marital indissolubility successfully and irrevocably

40

undermined in much of Europe. It is important to bear in mind the shared experiences of the Reformers, principally their closeness to the break with Rome and the common features of their marriage and divorce doctrines, while simultaneously appreciating the differences among them.

Protestant doctrines of divorce did not long remain at the abstract level but were quickly institutionalized in divorce legislation throughout much of Europe. In some cases the Reformers were directly responsible for the implementation of divorce laws: This was so of Calvin in Geneva, Zwingli in Zurich, and Luther in Württemberg. Indirectly, Calvin influenced the shape of divorce legislation in the Netherlands and Scotland, whereas Luther's influence was felt in many parts of Germany and throughout the Nordic countries. These divorce laws, the courts established to apply them, and the divorce policies they reflected are a second focus of this chapter and give us a broader understanding of the impact of Protestant divorce doctrines on sixteenth-century Europe.

2.2 Marriage in Protestant theology

The common point of departure of the Reformers toward divorce was their unanimous rejection of the Catholic view that marriage was inferior to celibacy. Marriage, they contended, was an estate ordained by God and not to be despised as only a second-best option for those who were unable to abstain from sex for life. Calvin criticized the "unrestrained rhapsodic praises of virginity" that had lowered the status of marriage: "Although marriage was not condemned as unclean, still its dignity was so weakened and its holiness so obscured that a man who did not refrain from it seemed not to aspire to perfection with enough strength of purpose."[1] Bucer condemned the attitude of Augustine and other church authorities as a "preposterous admiration of the celibate life."[2]

Their elevation of the status of marriage to equal that of celibacy led the Reformers implicitly to encourage marriage positively, rather than in the negative Catholic sense of enjoining marriage only if celibacy and virginity were not possible. One implication of this different approach was a general attack on the Catholic church's range of impediments to marriage, and the dispensations and annulments they entailed in some cases. The Reformers did not seek to sweep away all impediments to marriage but wanted to restrict them to those they believed were justified by scriptural authority.

In his *Babylonian Captivity of the Church* (1520) Luther condemned the Catholic impediments as they had been listed in a work that was widely used for the guidance of priests. Luther attacked the "sale" of dispensations in the most vigorous and graphic terms:

---

[1] John Calvin, *Institutes of the Christian Religion* (2 vols., Philadelphia, 1960), II, 1252.
[2] Martin Bucer, *De Regno Christi* in *Martini Buceri Opera Latina* (ed. François Wendel, Paris, (1965), XV, 166.

Among endless other monstrosities which are supposed to instruct the confessor, whereas they most mischievously confuse them, there are enumerated in this book eighteen impediments to marriage. If you will examine them with the just and unprejudiced eye of faith, you will see that they belong to those things which the apostle foretold: "There shall be those that give heed to the spirits of demons, speaking lies in hypocrisy, forbidding to marry" [1 Timothy 4:1–3]. What is "forbidding to marry" if it is not this – to invent all those hindrances and set those snares, in order to prevent people from marrying, or, if they are married, to annul their marriage?... Yet I am glad that those shameful laws have at last reached their full measure of glory, which is this: that the Romanists of our day have through them become merchants. What is it they sell? Vulvas and genitals – merchandise indeed most worthy of such merchants, grown together filthy and obscene through greed and godlessness. For there is no impediment nowadays that may not be legalized through the intercession of mammon.[3]

As we have seen, the granting of dispensations from matrimonial impediments was placed under more stringent controls by the Council of Trent, but this came only after Luther and others, like Heinrich Bullinger, had condemned the "trade."[4] Luther urged priests to confirm all marriages when they encountered any impediment from which the pope could grant a dispensation but which was not to be found in the Bible, and added:

If pope, bishop or official should annul any marriage because it was contracted contrary to the laws of men, he is Antichrist, he does Violence to nature, and is guilty of treason against the Divine Majesty, because this word stands: "What God has joined together, let no man put asunder."[5]

Luther nicely turned this text, frequently used by Catholics to justify their antidivorce doctrine, against the church's own practices in respect of marriage annulments.

This did not mean that Luther recognized no impediments to marriage, only that he sought to restrict them to those having clear scriptural foundation. Of these he found three or four: consanguinity to the second degree and affinity to the first degree, sexual impotence, ignorance of what a validly contracted marriage was, and – Luther was unsure about this final one – a preexisting vow of chastity. Elaborating on these impediments, and denying the validity of all the others recognized by the Catholic church, Luther classed impotence as an impediment of error in that one spouse married in ignorance of the other's inability to have sexual intercourse or to procreate. But even in this circumstance Luther did not advocate a precipitate annulment (which he called a "divorce") but suggested that a woman whose husband was impotent should "have inter-

---

[3] Martin Luther, *The Babylonian Captivity of the Church*, in *Luther's Works* (Philadelphia, St. Louis, 1959), XXXVI, 96–7. Luther's target was the *Summa de Casibus Conscientiae* of Angelo Carletti di Chivasso (first published 1456).
[4] See Heinrich Bullinger, *The Christen State of Matrimonye, wherein housbandes and wyfes lerne to kepe house together with loue* (n. p., 1543), 26^V.
[5] Luther, *Babylonian Captivity*, 98.

course with another, say her husband's brother, but keep this marriage [sic] secret and...ascribe the children to the so-called putative father."[6] This entailed no risk to the woman's salvation because she was free through divine law and could not be compelled to remain continent. But if her husband, even though he were impotent, declined to let his wife have intercourse with another man, Luther "would counsel her to contract a marriage with another and flee to a distant unknown place."[7] (This sounds like desperate and impractical advice, but it highlights the preference for bigamy over divorce, which, as we shall see, Luther frequently expressed.) Even though Luther admitted some impediments to marriage, he was reluctant to see them used as grounds for later annulment.

The anger of the Reformers was aroused not just by impediments to marriage in general: Under Catholic doctrine marriage was forbidden to one class of people entirely – the clergy – and the Reformers turned their attention to this institutionalization of the ideal and superiority of celibacy. All of the Protestant denominations abandoned clerical celibacy and allowed their ministers, priests, or pastors to marry. To the Reformers, vows of celibacy were contrary to God's gift of sexuality. Although asserting that some people were able to remain virgins – Luther thought that "only one in several thousands" had this gift[8] – there was agreement that an inability to live a virginal and celibate life entitled an individual to give up a vow of chastity. Luther, who had himself been a monk and had married, wrote in 1525 to a German monk that God

does not wish man to be alone but desires that he should multiply, and so he makes him a helpmeet to be with him and help him so that he may not be alone...Therefore, whoever will live alone undertakes an impossible task and takes it upon himself to run counter to God's Word and the nature that God has given and preserved in him. The outcome is in keeping with the attempt: such persons revel in whoredom and all sorts of uncleanness of the flesh until they are drowned in their own vices and driven to despair. For this reason such a vow against God's Word and against nature, being impossible, is null and void.[9]

Luther extended his doctrine of active sexuality to women, but with a stress on procreation. God made woman's body for natural purposes, which were not only eating, drinking, walking, and sleeping, but also for bearing children within marriage. "No woman," he wrote, "need be ashamed of that for which God has created and fashioned her, and if she feels she does not possess that high and

---

[6] Ibid., 103–4. "Marriage" here seems to mean a sexual relationship undertaken solely for procreation. The point was to use it but to pretend that the children resulted from the legal marriage. It is noteworthy that the sixteenth-century writers on family matters continued to use such terms loosely. "Divorce" was used interchangeably to refer to the dissolution of marriage, separation, and annulment.

[7] Ibid.

[8] Luther, *Letters I*, in *Luther's Works*, XLVIII, 271.

[9] Ibid., 273.

rare gift [of celibacy], she may leave the convent and do that for which she is adapted by nature."[10]

The Reformers also pointed to the moral effects of enforced celibacy on the Catholic clergy. Unable to accept that the gift of lifelong sexual abstinence happened to coincide with religious vocation in so many cases, they accused priests and members of religious orders of hypocrisy and immorality. Bullinger was particularly eloquent in his denunciation of clerical celibacy:

> For if we judge the tree by the fruits, I pray you, what fruits of single life may we recite? What filthiness, what bawdry, what adulteries, what fornications, what ravishings, what incests and heinous copulations may we rehearse? Who at this day liveth more unchaste or dishonest, than the rabble of priests and monks do?[11]

Although raising the status of marriage, the Reformers denied that it was a sacrament that conveyed grace to the married. The sacramental character ascribed to marriage in Catholic doctrine, it will be recalled, was one of the foundations of the doctrine of marital indissolubility. Luther and Calvin were adamant on this issue and generally set the tone of the Protestant position. Both pointed to what they believed was the error the Catholic church had made in translating *mysterion* of the Greek New Testament as "sacrament," a translation, Luther wrote, that "betrays great shallowness and thoughtless reading of Scripture."[12] There was, Luther argued, no scriptural justification whatever for listing marriage among the sacraments. Marriage existed not only among Christians but also among unbelievers, so "there is no reason why it should be called a sacrament of the New Law and of the Church alone." Marriage was a holy thing, but if the church considered it a sacrament for that reason, it could find a hundred sacraments in scripture.[13]

This was a point Calvin took up in his *Institutes of the Christian Religion* (1536), where he insisted that although marriage was a "good and holy ordinance of God," it was not a sacrament.[14] He went on to assail the apparent contradiction between the Roman Catholic doctrines of marriage and sacerdotal celibacy:

> How absurd it is to bar priests from the sacrament! If they say that they do not debar them from the sacrament, but from the lust of copulation, they will not give me the slip. For they teach that copulation itself is a part of the sacrament, and that it alone is the figure of the union which we have with Christ, in conformity to nature; for man and woman are made one flesh only by carnal copulation.[15]

---

[10] Ibid., 271 (Letter "To Three Nuns"). This indicates that Luther no longer considered preexisting vows of chastity a bar to marriage. Luther himself had taken a vow of chastity and later married a woman who had been a nun.

[11] Heinrich Bullinger, *Fiftie Godlie and Learned Sermons, diuided into fiue Decades, conteyning the Chiefe and principall pointes of Christian Religion* (London, 1577), 510. (Hereafter referred to as *Decades*.)

[12] Luther, *Babylonian Captivity*, 93.

[13] Ibid., 92.

[14] Calvin, *Institutes*, II, 1481.

[15] Ibid., 1483.

To this inconsistency, Calvin wrote, the Catholic church had attached a long train of "errors, lies, frauds, and misdeeds," among them allowing minors to contract valid marriages without parental consent, preventing marriages within seven degrees of consanguinity, prohibiting marriage at certain times of the year,[16] and forbidding remarriage to a man who had put away his adulterous wife.

The Reformers' denial of the sacramentality of marriage did not of itself entail a doctrine of marital dissolubility, but it did remove one obstacle to the development of a doctrine allowing divorce in principle. In most cases the Protestants advocated the possibility of divorce under certain circumstances and located the justification for it in the explicit texts of the Bible and in their understanding of their implications. At this point it makes sense to consider the principal Reformers individually because their approaches to divorce varied, sometimes in important matters of content, sometimes in detail, sometimes in tone.

2.3 Divorce in Lutheran thought and practice

In his early work – "when I was timid," as he would sometimes comment later – Luther was ambivalent about divorce. Although he cited the text of Matthew as seeming to allow divorce for reason of adultery, Luther was undecided in the matter. In 1520 he wrote:

As to divorce, it is still a question for debate whether it is allowable. For my part I so greatly detest divorce that I should prefer bigamy to it; but whether it is allowable, I do not venture to decide...although there is nothing I would rather see decided, since nothing at present more grievously perplexes me.[17]

The question of divorce came up the following year in the context of vows in general. Luther was opposed to the view that vows could be nullified if the person having taken them discovered that he could not keep them. To do this, Luther wrote, "you could also make divorce acceptable, if the marriage partners simply cannot get along."[18] As this suggests, Luther rejected the notion of divorce by mutual consent or unilaterally for reason of temperamental or emotional incompatibility. (Of the prominent Reformers, in fact, only Martin Bucer went so far as to accept these as grounds for divorce.) But even by 1522 Luther was becoming more forthright as to the circumstances that might justify a divorce, and in the *Estate of Marriage* he listed three. The first was really a ground for annulling a marriage that he had described earlier in the *Babylonian*

---

[16] Catholic doctrine forbade marriage during times of penance such as Lent and Advent. In Catholic Europe the number of marriages varied dramatically on a monthly basis because of these prohibitions; generally there were few marriages in March and December. See, for example, François Lebrun, *La vie conjugale sous l'Ancien Régime* (Paris, 1975), 37ff.

[17] Luther, *Babylonian Captivity*, 105–6.

[18] Luther, *Letters I*, in *Luther's Works*, XLVIII, 297–8.

Captivity of the Church, namely, one spouse's "bodily or natural deficiency" that prevented sexual intercourse.[19] The second ground – in fact the first for divorce in the strict sense – was adultery, and the last was a refusal "to fulfil the conjugal duty or to live with the other person."[20] In contrast to references to impotence, where his references had the husband as the offending party, Luther wrote of the wife as being the partner who refused to have sexual intercourse.

For example, one finds many a stubborn wife like that who will not give in, and who cares not a whit whether her husband falls into the sin of unchastity ten times over. Here it is time for the husband to say, "if you will not, another will: the maid will come if the wife will not." Only first the husband should admonish and warn his wife two or three times, and let the situation be known to others so that her stubbornness becomes a matter of common knowledge and is rebuked before the congregation. If she still refuses, get rid of her.[21]

It says a great deal about the respective power and status of wife and husband that the procedure Luther suggested differed as between the case of male impotence and that of female refusal of sexual intercourse. Although the husband was ultimately authorized to repudiate his wife, a wife had first to seek her husband's consent before having intercourse with another man in order to become pregnant and if he refused, she was advised to marry again (bigamously) in secret, and then flee from her home. Of course, the circumstances of impotence and refusal of intercourse differed in terms of responsibility and intent, though they had the same effects in terms of procreation.

It is not clear whether, in 1522, Luther intended desertion to be ground for divorce. Desertion would certainly fall within his condition of refusal to live with the other partner, but Luther's elaboration of this ground stressed the sexual implications of noncohabitation. However, he was quite unequivocal in disallowing divorce on the ground of general incompatibility. In such a case it was preferable for the couple to stay together:

Now if one of the parties were endowed with Christian fortitude and could endure the other's ill behaviour, that would doubtless be a wonderful blessed cross and a right way to heaven. For an evil spouse, in a manner of speaking, fulfils the devil's function and sweeps clean him who is able to recognise and bear it.[22]

But if that partner were unable to endure the domestic hell that Luther described, "let him divorce her before he does anything worse, and remain

---

[19] Luther confused annulment and dissolution here. He made the same suggestion with respect to impotence's justifying divorce as he did for annulment: either contract another marriage with the other spouse's consent or enter a new marriage and flee. See Luther, *The Estate of Marriage*, in *Luther's Works*, XLV, 20–1. Presumably, a woman who opted for the latter could be divorced for reason of adultery.

[20] Luther, *Estate of Marriage*, 33.

[21] Ibid., 34.

[22] Ibid., 34–5.

unmarried for the rest of his days."[23] This "divorce" would be tantamount to a separation since there was no possibility of remarriage. The husband would have been able to divorce and remarry only if he had consistently been denied sexual access to his wife.

In his later writings and reported statements, Luther shifted his emphases, if not his actual ground, from his permission to divorce for reason of adultery or refusal of the conjugal duty (sexual intercourse). Adultery, at least, was a constant reference, Luther anchoring his argument in the fictive death of the adulterous spouse. Marriage is dissolved by death (Romans 7:2), and because death by stoning and burning was the punishment for adultery (Deuteronomy 22:20–1), an adulterer was ipso facto divorced by God's word. The injunction of Matthew, that man might not put asunder what God had joined together, did not apply, Luther argued: "Such a divorce does not mean that it is done by men, because it does not take place without the word of God."[24] Luther held that separation *a mensa et thoro*, which the Roman Catholic church permitted in the case of adultery, should allow at least the innocent spouse to remarry: "For what kind of marriage is it to be separated in bed and board, other than a painted or illusory marriage?... there is no commandment of God that would enjoin him [the husband] to remain unmarried or keep the unchaste woman."[25]

Even so, in Luther's mind divorce was not to be undertaken lightly. The guilty party was advised to beg for forgiveness, and the innocent spouse enjoined to forgive. Nor should remarriage take place too soon after divorce. Luther advised a delay between divorce and remarriage of at least six months or a year, "otherwise it would have the evil appearance that he was happy and pleased that his spouse had committed adultery and was joyfully seizing the opportunity to get rid of this one and so practise his wantonness under the cloak of the law."[26]

But although Luther consistently viewed adultery as a ground for divorce, he moved from refusal to fulfill the conjugal obligation to simple desertion as the other justifying circumstance. Where this desertion was willful the deserter "shows his contempt for matrimony... he does not consider his wife his wedded wife."[27] After six months or a year the ecclesiastical or civil authorities should threaten him with banishment and declare his wife free of the marriage if he did not return to her. In the event of his refusal, the marriage should be dissolved, and the abandoned spouse permitted to remarry. Luther also considered the case of a spouse who was justifiably absent, like a merchant or a soldier, but who failed to return home. His solution, that "the other partner shall wait and not marry again until there is certain and trustworthy evidence that the spouse is dead,"[28] did not add to his divorce grounds. Insofar as the

---

[23] Ibid., 35.
[24] Luther, *On Marriage Matters* (1530), in *Luther's Works*, XLVI, 278.
[25] Ibid., 300. This applied whether it was the husband or the wife who was the innocent spouse.
[26] Ibid., 311.
[27] Ibid., 313.
[28] Ibid., 312.

absent spouse's death had to be certain and proved, not simply presumed by the long and unexplained absence, it meant that the remaining spouse remarried as a widow, not as a divorcée. This ruled out simple absence, as distinct from malicious desertion, as a reason for divorce.

If we read Luther's writings in an aggregative rather than a developmental sense, his doctrine of divorce permitted the dissolution of marriage on the grounds of adultery, desertion, and the refusal of sexual intercourse. Evidently Luther arrived at this doctrine reluctantly, for he found matrimonial matters depressing and complex. Recording Luther's table talk, Jerome Weller noted in 1536 that "Dr. Martin sighed and said: 'Good God, what a bother these matrimonial cases are to us! It takes great effort and labour to get couples together. Afterwards it requires even more pains to keep them together.' "[29] Many people treated Luther as a marriage guidance counselor, and priests frequently wrote asking advice on marriage questions that their parishioners had addressed to them. Luther's agonizing over these issues was partly a result of his refusal to draw up strict rules that could be applied in all cases. Although he thought that guidelines could be established, Luther believed that matrimonial problems should be resolved not by laws, "but by the circumstances and according to equity and the judgement of a good man."[30]

Luther was, moreover, reluctant to counsel divorce unless all other alternatives had been tried. To Valentine Hausmann, burgomaster in Feisburg, whose wife was guilty of an unspecified offense, Luther recommended forgiveness, patience, and firmness:

I should suggest that, if she behaves uprightly in the future, you should not cast her off. She will have to submit to you henceforth, and you will commit no sin, for you will have acted in mercy rather than by the letter of the law. On the other hand, if you proceed strictly in terms of the law, much unhappiness may result and you may ultimately regret it, have a sense of guilt, and suffer heartache.[31]

Where there was no possibility of reconciliation, however, as in a case of desertion, divorce was the only remedy. But it was not a quick and easy option, as Luther explained to John Wickmann, a pastor in Priessnitz.

If the situation is such as you report, namely, that the widow's husband deserted her seven years ago and no one knows where he is, you should first ask the neighbours or the village magistrates, if they have any knowledge of the matter, which of the two is the guilty party. If, according to the testimony of neighbours, it appears that the woman is not to blame, let the pastor in Eisenberg post a public notice on the church door and do the same in your village, asking the man (or someone else on his behalf) to appear within four weeks. If he does not appear, announce from the pulpit that the deserter has not

---

[29] Luther, *Letters of Spiritual Counsel* (ed. and trans. Theodore G. Tappest, London, 1955), 283.
[30] Ibid., 286.
[31] Ibid., 285.

appeared and that the woman is therefore free to marry again. Thereupon you may unite her in marriage with another man in God's name.[32]

We should note, apart from the concern to establish the whereabouts of the husband, Luther's wish to determine that the partner who was to benefit from the divorce was not responsible for the other's desertion. This ruled out constructive desertion, where intolerable behavior on the part of one spouse had forced the other to leave. These qualifications aside, and despite Luther's own wish to maintain flexibility in matrimonial matters, his two prime grounds for divorce, adultery and desertion, were to be one of the principal models for Protestant divorce doctrines and early divorce legislation.

One of Luther's principal adherents in divorce doctrine was Philip Melanchthon who, like the other Reformers, stressed the integrity of marriage as willed by God. In ideal terms marriage was indissoluble, an "eternal, inseparable fellowship of one husband and one wife,"[33] and sexuality was chaste within it: "The distinction between chastity and unchastity is revealed in the very beginning in Paradise, when God says, 'The two shall be one in flesh', that is, only a single man and a single woman should be joined together for reproduction, and they should be inseparable."[34] Melanchthon's emphasis on the connection between chastity and marriage was reflected in his interpretation of the divorce texts of the Bible, for he held that the "inseparable" union of wife and husband was indeed separable when one of them committed adultery. In such a case the innocent partner should be permitted to remarry. Melanchthon implied that the guilty party should not be permitted to marry again. Rather, he suggested that the courts either condemn the adulterous spouse to death or banish him or her from society.[35]

The other ground that Melanchthon recognized for divorce was desertion, but, as if he were unsure whether it were a justifying circumstance in its own right, he attempted to link desertion to adultery. He defined a spouse from whom such a divorce might be obtained as one "who out of malice and without just cause leaves the other, and stays away for a long time, as often happens. Very often such are adulterers and adulteresses."[36] Although Melanchthon drew his scriptural justification for divorce on the ground of desertion from the text of Corinthians (the Pauline Privilege), he did not believe that a divorce was justified simply for reason of disparity of religion. Nor did he agree with some of the other Reformers, like Zwingli, that diseases or illnesses such as leprosy should be a sufficient reason for a divorce. A sick person, he argued, should not

---

[32] Ibid., 284. The reference to the wife in this case as a "widow" presumably means that she was a widow before marrying the man who had now deserted her.

[33] Philip Melanchthon, *Melanchthon on Christian Doctrine: Loci Communes 1555* (trans. and ed. Clyde L. Manschriek, New York, 1965), 329.

[34] Ibid., 113.

[35] Philip Melanchthon, *De coniugio*, in *Corpus Reformatorum* (59 vols., Brunswick, 1863–1900), XIV, cols. 1064–5.

[36] Ibid., col. 1064.

be divorced but helped, and, if necessary, a court should prevent the sick spouse's partner from deserting or neglecting him or her.[37]

Divorce laws conforming broadly to the Lutheran model were enacted throughout Protestant Germany in the sixteenth century. In cities and states such as Württemberg, Augsburg, and Nuremberg, divorce was permitted for reason of adultery or willful desertion.[38] Luther's influence on divorce legislation went far beyond the German states, however, to Scandinavia. The earliest divorce law in Sweden, part of the 1572 Church Ordinance, drew heavily on German laws, especially the 1554 and 1556 ecclesiastical ordinances of Pfalz-Neuburg, which in turn were based on the ordinances in force in Württemberg.[39] The intermediary between the German and Swedish laws was Laurentius Petri, archbishop of Uppsala, who in 1561 drew up a draft reform of church law for Sweden. This draft was largely enacted as the 1572 ordinances. Laurentius Petri held the view that matrimonial affairs fell properly within secular jurisdiction, but the 1572 provisions gave the clergy primary responsibility for supervising marriage and related issues. The reason was partly bureaucratic inertia – the ecclesiastical courts had traditionally had competence in marriage law – and partly because marriage litigation often bore directly on questions of conscience, issues seen as the special sphere of the church.[40]

Although the Swedish church recognized divorce, dissolution of marriage was seen as the final resort to be invoked only after all attempts to reconcile the spouses had failed. The clergy were instructed to use their sermons to urge married couples to live in harmony and not to leave each other. Where marital tension or conflict became notorious, the spouses concerned were summoned to appear before a pastor or the cathedral chapter of their diocese, where they were admonished to behave better. If their domestic relations did not improve, they could be handed over to the secular authorities for punishment, which could consist of a fine, a flogging, or a period of imprisonment. However, marital conflict and simple emotional incompatibility were not in themselves sufficient grounds for dissolving a marriage, for the 1572 laws restricted divorce to the principal Lutheran grounds of adultery and willful desertion.

Divorce could be granted for reason of adultery only after attempts to reconcile the spouses had been tried without success. Jurisdiction in this instance was shared between the secular and ecclesiastical authorities. Under a 1538 law it had fallen to the former to try prosecutions for adultery, and this jurisdiction was retained under the 1572 divorce provisions, although

---

[37] Ibid., col. 1070.

[38] On German divorce laws see Steven Ozment, *When Fathers Ruled: Family Life in Reformation Europe* (Cambridge, Mass., 1983), 90–3; Thomas Max Safley, *Let No Man Put Asunder. The Control of Marriage in the German Southwest: A Comparative Study, 1550–1600* (Kirksville, 1984); Hans Christian Dietrich, *Evangelisches Ehescheidungsrecht nach den Bestimmungen der Deutschen Kirchenordnungen des 16. Jahrhunderts* (Erlangen, 1892).

[39] Emil Färnström, *Om Källorna till 1571 års Kyrkoordning* (Stockholm, 1935), 7, 181–9. This source quotes the relevant section of the Church Ordinance that took force in 1572.

[40] Ivar Nylander, *Studier Rörande den Svenska Äktenskapsrättens Historia* (Stockholm, 1961), 14–15.

authority to pass any consequent sentence of divorce was vested in the church courts.[41] There were provisions for remarriage not only by the innocent party but by the guilty spouse as well, a departure from some Protestant divorce laws. But if the guilty party were permitted to remarry (it was not an automatic right, but could be granted by the court), it was a condition that he or she must not reside in the same part of Sweden as the innocent former spouse. The influence in respect of remarriage might well have been the legislation in force in Zurich, which is discussed in Section 2.5.

The second reason for divorce that was established by the 1572 ordinance was willful desertion (*egenvilligt övergivande*), where "one of the spouses, without authority or reason, abandons and leaves the other with the intention that he will never at any time return and live with her."[42] When the absent spouse stayed within Sweden and his whereabouts were known – the terms of the law imply the likelihood that it was the husband, rather than the wife, who would desert – attempts had to be made to persuade him to return to his wife, before she was able to obtain a divorce. In most cases, however, it was expected that the whereabouts of the deserter would be unknown and could not be discovered, and in such circumstances a divorce could proceed, but only after the passage of a certain period of time after the date of the desertion. No precise period was specified in the law, and synodal decisions in these cases varied from three to five and even seven years. In rare instances divorce was permitted after a shorter period, for example, when a soldier had deserted to the enemy and would have been executed if he had returned to Sweden.[43] In such a case the capital punishment would have dissolved the marriage, and there seemed no reason to compel the wife to have to delay her judicial divorce.

The divorce provisions of the 1572 Church Ordinance remained in force in Sweden until 1686 when a church law was passed. This maintained the twin grounds of adultery and desertion, but by the end of the seventeenth century other circumstances, such as incompatibility between married people, and other procedures, such as royal dispensations from the bond of marriage, began to take effect in practice. These developments represented a departure from the divorce principles of the Reformation, and are examined in Section 6.2 in the context of the secularization of the laws and institutions of divorce and the effects of the Enlightenment on matrimonial issues.

Elsewhere in sixteenth-century Scandinavia the history of divorce took a slightly different course. Norway and Iceland were within the Kingdom of Denmark, and this ensured a broad uniformity of legislation among these territories. In 1582 Articles of Marriage were applied in Denmark and Norway, and five years later they were extended to Iceland.[44] The first coherent divorce

---

[41] Ibid., 16.
[42] Quoted in Färnström, *Om Källorna*, 184.
[43] Nylander, *Äktenskapsrättens Historia*, 48.
[44] This account is drawn from Björn Björnsson, *The Lutheran Doctrine of Marriage in Modern Icelandic Society* (Oslo, Reykjavik, 1971), esp. 55ff.

legislation in these countries, the articles allowed three main grounds for divorce: adultery, desertion, and impotence. Divorce was permitted for reason of adultery only where one of the spouses was clearly innocent of the offense, but could not be obtained when the adultery complained of was the result of some hardship caused by the innocent spouse, such as refusal of marital intercourse. In the case of desertion there was a minimum waiting period of three years after the departure of the deserter before the other partner could obtain a divorce, unless there was evidence that the deserter was cohabiting with another person. (In such a case there was a clear presumption of adultery, which alone would have expedited the action for divorce.) When the third recognized ground for divorce, impotence, was at issue, the incapacitated spouse was granted a period of three years to obtain a cure before the other could obtain a divorce. Moreover, the impotence had to date back to the time of the wedding; if it had developed during the course of the marriage, it had to be endured. A similar provision was made for infectious diseases: They were not a ground for divorce unless it could be demonstrated that they were present at the time of marriage, and could be proved that the affected spouse had concealed his or her illness. These provisions indicate that as far as impotence and infectious disease were concerned, the remedy provided by the Articles of Marriage was more an annulment than a dissolution of marriage.

The articles also dealt with remarriage. In contrast to Swedish law, the Norwegian, Danish, and Icelandic codes permitted only the innocent partner to remarry when a divorce was based on adultery. Even then the innocent spouse had to obtain royal consent to the remarriage, and there was a minimum waiting period of three years between divorce and remarriage. During that time the man or woman had to live a moral and Christian life and was required to provide a testimonial to this effect when petitioning for permission to enter another marriage.

As they were elsewhere in Reformation Europe, divorces in Scandinavia were difficult to obtain, not least because of the procedures imposed by the laws. Divorces were anything but frequent: Only five were granted by the cathedral court of Stavanger (Norway) between 1571 and 1583 (when divorces were granted by ordinance), about one every two years on average. In the following thirteen years, under the terms of the 1582 articles, there were sixteen divorces, which represented a doubling of the annual average to a less than staggering one per year.[45]

2.4 Divorce in Calvinist thought and practice

The Scandinavian and German divorce laws of the sixteenth century were broadly based on the doctrines set down by Martin Luther, one of the two most

---

[45] *Stavanger Domkapitels Protokol, 1571–1630* (ed. Andreas Brandrud, 3 vols., Christiania [Oslo], 1897–1901), I, passim.

influential approaches to divorce in the period. The second model for European divorce legislation was that of John Calvin, whose position was in many
respects more straightforward than Luther's. Calvin began with the proposition
that marriage was too sacred an institution to be dissolved at the mere choosing
of men. Although husband and wife came together freely and by mutual consent, "God ties them in an indissoluble knot from which they may not
afterwards freely depart." But there was one exception, namely, fornication,
"for a woman who treacherously violates her marriage, may well be cast out, as
the bond is broken by her fault and the man gains his liberty."[46] To this Calvin
added the important qualification that the right to divorce for reason of adultery
was equal for wife and husband:

We must note that each party has a common and mutual right, just as their obligation of
loyalty is mutual and equal. A man may hold the primacy in other things, but in bed he
and his wife are equal; for he is not the lord of his body. Therefore if he commits
adultery he has defected from marriage and the wife is given freedom.[47]

As far as Calvin was concerned, divorce for reason of adultery was derived
from the Old Testament injunction that an adulterous wife should be put to
death. In modern times (the sixteenth century) divorce was a substitute for that
punishment: "Today it is the perverted indulgence of magistrates that makes it
necessary for men to divorce their impure wives, inasmuch as there is no
punishment for adultery."[48]

Calvin also heavily relied on the divorce text of Matthew and went to lengths
to deny the validity of the grounds that some of the Reformers had held up as
justifying a dissolution of marriage. By defining these other grounds, Calvin
asserted, they "want to be wiser than the heavenly Maker, [and] are rightly to be
rejected."[49] As an example of an error of this kind he cited leprosy, justified as a
ground for divorce by some theologians because it could affect not only a
spouse but the couple's children. Although advising a man not to come into
contact with his wife if she were a leper, Calvin did not permit a divorce simply
because she had that or some other disease or illness. Nor did he think divorce
was justified by the simple dislike of a wife's behavior or appearance, or, on
the wife's part, because she was subjected to "cruelty or too much rough or
inconsiderate treatment" at the hands of her husband.[50]

Calvin also ruled out impotence as a condition that could permit divorce,
even though it could lead the other spouse into extramarital sexual acitivity.
Calvin's advice to sex-deprived husbands and wives was that they "give
themselves up to be guided by the Lord, [and] they will never want [i.e., lack]

---

[46] John Calvin, *A Harmony of the Gospels Matthew, Mark and Luke* (2 vols., Edinburgh, 1972), I, 190.
[47] Ibid., II, 247.
[48] Ibid. Adultery was made a capital offense in Calvin's Geneva and elsewhere in the sixteenth and
    seventeenth centuries.
[49] Ibid., 246.
[50] John Calvin, *The First Epistle of Paul the Apostle to the Corinthians* (Edinburgh, 1960), 146–7.

continence."[51] Calvin pointed out that many circumstances other than simple impotence – emotional antipathy, palsy, apoplexy, or some incurable disease – could lead to the inability to have intercourse. If a man did not want to have intercourse with his wife and thought that he could remarry and thus be licitly sexually active, it would open up the possibility of divorce in an infinite range of circumstances.

As we might expect, Calvin explicitly ruled out the notion of divorce for reason of emotional incompatibility. Unhappiness in marriage, he argued, was a result of original sin and had to be borne like its other effects, however unpleasant they might be. His advice to the miserably married was succinct:

When now a man has a harsh and dreadful wife, whom he cannot manage by any means, let him know, here are the fruits of original sin and also the corruption that is in myself. And the wife on her side must think, there is a good reason that I must receive the payment that comes from my disobedience towards God, because I did not humble myself before him.[52]

This did not mean that married people should simply accept their unhappiness and conflict passively. The husband, according to Calvin, should not be cruel; his role was one of "companionship rather than kingship,"[53] and there was even a suggestion that wife beating was to be avoided. The way to put an end to marital conflict was awareness of the partners' places in God's ordering of things. For the husband should know that "he breaks the whole order of nature if he is not joined in happy concord with his wife," and the wife "likewise, if she does not submit herself peaceably to her husband, acknowledging him to be her head."[54] The solution to conflict, then, was not to divorce but to reorder the marriage according to God's plans: "When they were tempted to divorce one another, or to be incensed against one another, the right way to subdue all wicked passions was to have an eye to the pledge of the spiritual union between our Lord Jesus Christ and us."[55]

Yet despite Calvin's apparent insistence that adultery was the unique offense that justified divorce, and despite his rejection of doctrines that widened the possibilities, his exegetical works admitted the possibility of divorce where there was religious disparity and desertion. Calvin drew primarily on the text of the Pauline Privilege but extended it to cover marriages where both spouses were believers and where one had deserted the other. It is possible that this additional ground for divorce should be seen as really being subordinate to adultery, which Calvin had argued was the only ground for divorce. Like Luther he seemed to suppose that any spouse who left his or her partner would almost

---

[51] Calvin, *A Harmony*, II, 246–7.
[52] John Calvin, *Sermons on the Epistle to the Ephesians* (Edinburgh, 1973), sermon no. 39, 568.
[53] Ibid., 570.
[54] Ibid., no. 42, 605.
[55] Ibid., no. 39, 575.

certainly enter an intimate relationship with another person.[56] If this meant another marriage, then divorce was desirable because it was preferable to polygamy, and besides, the second marriage entailed sexual intercourse, which was a ground for dissolving the first. In such cases desertion might be thought of as aggravated adultery, allowing Calvin to maintain that there was still only one ground for divorce. Desertion might be seen in this light even when it took place not because of a desire for a different sexual partner but because of antipathy toward the current spouse. The Reformers were under no illusions about the ability of men and women to remain sexually inactive (witness their attacks on Catholic doctrines of celibacy and virginity),[57] and certainly a person who deserted his or her spouse could hardly be expected to be "guided by the Lord" so far as to remain chaste.[58]

With respect to Calvin's divorce doctrine, then, we may choose between thinking of it as allowing a single ground for the dissolution of marriage (that is, adultery, with desertion constituting an offense giving rise to a presumption of adultery) or the same two principal grounds as Luther: adultery and desertion. Calvin excluded other grounds not only as justifying divorce but even as justifying de facto separation. In his letters to noblewomen, Calvin insisted that even if a Protestant wife were cruelly beaten by her Catholic husband, she should not leave him unless she were convinced that her life was actually in danger.[59]

Before discussing the practical application of Calvin's divorce doctrines in Geneva and elsewhere, it is useful to look at the opinions of Theodore Beza, who succeeded Calvin to religious and moral preeminence and leadership in that city. In general, Beza emulated Calvin's close attention to the biblical divorce texts and followed his conclusions from them. Beza frequently made the point that adultery was the only circumstance that could give rise to a divorce, and he echoed Calvin in the opinion that divorce was allowed for adultery only because adultery was no longer a capital offense.[60] Beza also defended divorce for reason of desertion, but he linked this ground to adultery more carefully and explicitly than Calvin had done. The desertion should, according to Beza, be demonstrably that of an unbeliever, and he or she should have left out of hatred of the true faith or having tried to force the other partner to commit an intolerable impiety, such as hearing mass.[61] The link with adultery followed the desertion: "What, therefore, if the unbeliever should desert the believer? It will be imputed to the unbeliever (says the apostle [Paul]) that he is an adulterer if

---

[56] V. Norskov Olsen, *The New Testament Logia on Divorce: A Study of Their Interpretation from Erasmus to Milton* (Tübingen, 1971), 101.

[57] Calvin wrote that "marriage has been ordained as a necessary remedy to keep us from plunging into unbridled lust." Calvin, *Institutes*, I, 405.

[58] Calvin, *A Harmony*, II, 246.

[59] Charmarie Jenkins Blaisdell, "Calvin's Letters to Women: The Courting of Ladies in High Places," *Sixteenth Century Journal* 13 (1982), 71.

[60] Theodore Beza, *Tractatio de Polygamia* (Geneva, 1573), 216.

[61] George H. Joyce, *Christian Marriage: An Historical and Doctrinal Study* (London, 1948), 416.

he consorts with another person, though not legitimately divorced."[62] Yet, as with Calvin, there was in Beza a subtle shift in thinking from adultery implied by desertion to desertion per se as a reason for divorce, such that even an unintended absence might justify a dissolution of marriage if a long enough time were allowed to elapse.[63] Despite this, Beza insisted on adultery as the unique justification for divorce and refused to accept doctrines (like Zwingli's) that held that adultery was given in the Bible only as an example of a matrimonial offense upon which divorce might be grounded. Beza wrote:

I say it is false that any crime can be found which is equal to, or worse than, adultery...Anyone can be idolatrous, a heretic, impious, and yet remain a valid husband: but no one can be an adulterer and a husband, that is to be one flesh of two kinds.[64]

The principles of divorce espoused by Calvin and Beza found their practical application in Geneva, where matrimonial law under the Protestant regime was regulated in 1561.[65] Marriage ordinances drafted by Calvin in 1545, and adopted as part of the 1561 *Ordonnances ecclésiastiques*, set out the main lines of divorce in the city-state and allowed for the dissolution of marriage for adultery and desertion.[66] The former applied equally to husband and wife, but a strong emphasis was placed on unilateral guilt, so that neither could obtain a divorce if he or she had in some way contributed to the other's crime (for example, by refusing intercourse) or was also guilty of adultery. In the case of desertion, a distinction was made between absences that were apparently unintended and those that were willful. The former included cases where a merchant, absent for legitimate commercial reasons, simply failed to return. If there were evidence that he was being held prisoner somewhere or was detained against his will under some other circumstance – in other words, that his continuing absent was not willful – then his wife could not divorce and remarry. If, on the other hand, there were no news of him and there were reasonable grounds for presuming him dead, then a woman could divorce, although she was not entitled to contract another marriage until ten years had elapsed from the date of his departure.

Where the desertion in question was plainly malicious, a divorce was much more easily obtained, although the Geneva law could hardly be called permissive. If a man deserted his wife in order to lead a debauched life, she was obliged to attempt to persuade him to return to her. A proclamation was to be

[62] Beza, *Tractatio de Repudiis et Divortiis* (Geneva, 1573), 227.
[63] Ibid., 242.
[64] Ibid., 249.
[65] The 1541 *Ordonnances* contained only two articles on marriage, and specified that jurisdiction should lie with the secular authorities. It seems that the substance of marriage law, at that time, was still that of canon law.
[66] The text of the 1545 *Projet d'ordonnance sur les mariages* is given in *Corpus Reformatorum* XXXVIII, cols. 33–44. For the text of the 1561 *Ordonnances ecclésiastiques*, see ibid., cols. 91–124 (divorce is in cols. 110–114).

made on three Sundays, each a fortnight apart, requesting the husband to return and warning him that if he did not, his wife could divorce him. Should the husband return, the spouses were to be reconciled. If the husband did not return, the woman could proceed to obtain a divorce. She was able to remarry one year after having made serious enquiries as to her husband's whereabouts. If the husband returned but deserted his wife a second time, he was subject to imprisonment on a regime of bread and water. Should he desert her a third time, more severe penalties (which were not specified) would be used, and the wife would be freed from the marriage.

A somewhat different procedure operated when the deserting spouse was the wife, the procedure indicative of the double standard of sexual morality despite the equality and mutuality of sexual obligations specified in Calvin's doctrines and in the Geneva marriage ordinance. A deserted husband was obliged, like a deserted wife, to summon his spouse to return. If she did not, he could obtain a divorce, but if she did return he could still refuse to accept her back if he suspected that she had committed adultery during her absence. In such circumstances, enquiries were to be made in the places she had been to discover what her conduct had been. If these enquiries turned up evidence of adultery, the husband could divorce her for that reason, but if there was no evidence of adultery, the husband was to receive his wife back and resume their marriage.

There was one further qualification in this Geneva ordinance. If a husband made no complaint to the authorities at the time his wife deserted him, yet subsequently petitioned for divorce, the Consistory court was to investigate the possibility of collusion between the spouses in the divorce petition. This was to avoid "voluntary divorces, which is to say, at the pleasure of the parties, without the authority of justice."

The Geneva divorce law reflected the uneasy relationship between adultery and desertion that had existed in Calvin's divorce doctrine. For example, in the case of a woman who deserted her husband, but returned when summoned, enquiries were to be made as to her sexual activity while absent. If she were subsequently divorced, it was presumably because of her adultery, not the initial desertion, although the law dealt with it under the desertion rubric. Moreover, it appears that this sexual association was more rigorously sought in the case of a woman. A husband who deserted could not be divorced if he returned to his wife when summoned, and no provision specified that enquiries should be made into his sexual behavior. This weakens Calvin's insistence that sexual fidelity was owed equally by wife and husband to each other. Yet in the final analysis, divorce was possible for desertion per se when the absent spouse failed to return. In such circumstances there could be no evidence either way as to adultery, though the presumption in favor of it might be strong. The overriding impression, though, is that the Geneva laws did permit divorce on the ground of desertion, independent of adultery, so that Calvin's doctrine, like Luther's, should be thought of as including the two grounds for the dissolution of marriage. This makes sense in the light of the requirement, set down in the

Geneva ordinance that spouses had to cohabit, to the extent that a wife had to follow and live with her husband wherever he decided to live, provided that his motives in moving were honorable.

The final point of the Geneva law dealt with jurisdiction over marriage. Issues related to the personal aspects of marriage, such as domestic disputes, adultery, and divorce, were to be heard in the first instance by the Consistory, which was composed of twelve male elders and the city's pastors. Although generally dominated by laymen, the Consistory had quasi-ecclesiastical powers, such as the authority to excommunicate offenders who came before it.[67] It did not, however, have the authority of a criminal court, and where it thought a sentence of this type was justified, the Consistory sent the party concerned before the secular judges, together with its recommendation as to the disposition of the case.

How did Geneva's divorce law work in practice? Divorce was a remedy of last resort, not only in doctrine but in practical terms. The Consistory gave primary attention to preventing divorces by reconciling couples who were in conflict, even couples who had separated. Punishment of matrimonial offenders, rather than divorce, was far more often resorted to. In the period from 1559 to 1569, some 302 Genevans were excommunicated for marital quarrels and disputes (*mauvais ménages*) of various kinds. Fifty-six percent of the offenders were men.[68] Adultery, too, was subject to punishment other than divorce. A severe law of 1566 provided a period of imprisonment on a regime of bread and water for fornication, banishment in the case of adultery between a married and an unmarried person, and the death penalty for adultery involving two married persons.[69] The difficulties in obtaining divorces in sixteenth-century Geneva kept the number of divorces low, even though the Consistory complained in the early seventeenth century that the Geneva church had a reputation of being easy [*légier*] in the rupture of marriages.[70] Divorces probably numbered no more than one a year on average.[71]

A useful guide to divorce policy in Geneva is the records of the *Compagnie des pasteurs de Genève*, which was dominated successively by Calvin and Beza. Various cases came before the *Compagnie*, some dealing directly with divorce, others with related issues. The general impression was reinforced that divorce could not be granted for any but the most serious reasons, and that it was a

---

[67] On the Consistory, see E. William Monter, "The Consistory of Geneva, 1559–1569," *Bibliothèque d'humanisme et Renaissance* 38 (1976), 467–84; on social aspects, see E. William Monter, "Women in Calvinist Geneva (1550–1800)," *Signs. Journal of Women in Culture and Society* 6 (1980), 189–209.

[68] Monter, "Women," 191. Men also accounted for a majority of those punished for sexual misdemeanors in this period.

[69] Ibid., 192–3. The death penalty had fallen into disuse by the beginning of the seventeenth century.

[70] R. Stauffenegger, "Le mariage à Genève vers 1600," *Société pour l'histoire du droit* 66, fasc. 27 (1966), 327n. 3.

[71] Monter, "Women," 195.

measure of last resort, to be used only when all attempts to reconcile the spouses had failed. Moreover, there was a strong commitment to the concept of matrimonial fault: Divorce was justified only when one spouse was demonstrably guilty and the other was unquestionably innocent. This last point is made clear in the opinion delivered by Calvin on the divorce petition of François Favre in 1546. Noting that there was evidence that both spouses had committed adultery, so that Favre's wife might with equal justification have entered a petition for divorce, Calvin warned the Consistory that there might be collusion in the case, "which would be an undesirable opening to undo many marriages."[72]

Under the direction of Beza the Geneva court seems to have limited its guidelines on divorce. In 1572, eight years after Calvin's death, the court set down an opinion on divorce following a petition from one Jacques Quiblet.[73] Quiblet's wife had been accused of witchcraft and although she had denied the accusation, even under torture, she had been banished from Geneva, on pain of death if she returned, in February 1571. The following year Quiblet sought permission to contract a new marriage, but the council denied his request, saying that he could remarry only when he could prove his wife dead. Despite this ruling, Quiblet became betrothed, and in response the council declared the engagement null and void. Quiblet and his fiancée were sentenced, respectively, to six and three days' imprisonment on a regime of bread and water, and both were banned from holy communion and excommunicated. In October 1572 Quiblet appealed to the Consistory for a ruling on his case, citing Martin Bucer (see Section 2.5) to the effect that divorce could be obtained for the practical effects of witchcraft, such as banishment for life. Beza and his colleagues, however, ruled that adultery was the only ground upon which a divorce might be obtained. The original of the opinion was written by Beza himself:

It would be difficult to divine all the sophistries which might be invented by men against this simple truth [that adultery was the sole ground for divorce], as for all time Satan has tried to break the bond of marriages, either by those who have shown themselves hostile to conjugal chastity, or by those who have thought they were doing good in separating those who they judged could not live together in harmony.[74]

Quiblet's case was a difficult one in terms of the Geneva law. His wife had not willfully deserted him, and yet she was unable to return to him. Had she done

---

[72] *Registres de la Compagnie des Pasteurs de Genève au temps de Calvin* (ed. Robert M. Kingdon and J.-F. Bergier, 5 vols., Geneva, 1962), I, 41. This aversion to collusion went further than divorce. In 1586 the problem of giving public assistance to abandoned women and children became widespread; many were left without support when married men left Geneva to fight in the wars of religion. Even in these cases the Consistory advised the deacons to give assistance only where the conduct of the wife and children had not contributed to the husband's/father's departure and to watch for collusion, which would render them ineligible for assistance. *Registres de la Compagnie*, V, 99.

[73] Ibid., III, 91–2.

[74] Ibid., III, 274.

so, she would have been executed, and while that would have solved Quiblet's matrimonial dilemma, it is understandable that his wife was unwilling to sacrifice herself – literally – in the interests of her husband's marital career. This case is illustrative of the reluctance of Geneva's judges to dissolve marriages even when, as in this instance, it was impossible for the couple to be reconciled and for the marriage to be reconstituted as a social relationship.

Some citizens of Geneva found the demands too much. One was a M. Gales, who in 1586 attempted to divorce his wife on the ground of her adultery. The Consistory court found that there was no convincing evidence of the adultery he alleged and ordered Gales to take back his wife in good faith. His wife was admonished "to behave herself in such a way as to give [her husband]... every occasion to hold her in high esteem." Gales seemed to be reconciled to his wife after this, but only temporarily: Soon afterward he left alone for Bordeaux, leaving her without means of support.[75]

While Luther's divorce doctrines had been influential as far north as Sweden, Iceland, and Norway, Calvin's took hold in Scotland, where the Reformation had an almost immediate effect on matrimonial law. Before the Reformation, marital causes in Scotland, as in England, had been heard by the bishops' courts (officials' courts), which had applied the canon law and Catholic doctrine. But in 1560 the Scottish parliament abolished papal authority in Scotland, destroying not only the spiritual dominance of the Catholic church but also the spiritual claims that the church's courts had had. Almost immediately the kirk sessions of the Reformed Church of Scotland began to exercise jurisdiction – and to grant divorces – until in 1563 the Scottish Commissary Court was established. Thereafter this court had jurisdiction over marriage matters and granted divorces, and the inferior courts had their competence limited to less important matters.[76]

Although divorce was established as a practice in the 1560s in Scotland, there was no Act of Parliament explicitly permitting divorce. Rather, it was assumed to be a common law right and, as one would expect from the exercise of the function by the church courts, it was justified by religious authority. The prime direct authority was John Knox, whose marriage teachings drew heavily on those of Calvin. Once lawfully contracted, wrote Knox, "marriage...may not be dissolved at man's pleasure, as our master Jesus Christ does witness, unless adultery be committed."[77] When adultery was proved to the satisfaction of the civil magistrate, the innocent party should be freed to remarry, whereas the guilty party should be put to death. The adulterer or adulteress whose life was "foolishly" spared by the magistrate should be excommunicated until there was evidence of repentance. In such a case the offender might remarry: "If they

[75] Ibid., V, 136.
[76] On aspects of jurisdiction, see David Baird Smith, "The Reformers and Divorce: A Study on Consistorial Jurisdiction," *Scottish Historical Review* 9 (1911), 10–36; Ronald D. Ireland, "Husband and Wife," in *An Introduction to Scottish Legal History* (Edinburgh, 1958), 82–9.
[77] *The Works of John Knox* (ed. David Laing, Edinburgh, 1848), 248.

cannot live continent, and if the necessity be such as they fear further offence of God, we cannot forbid them the remedy ordained by God."[78] Knox also anticipated the possibility of a reconciliation of two people after they had been divorced. They could remarry within the church without having to go through the formalities of having the banns read in advance.

In the first years, then, divorce was available to the Scottish population for reason of adultery, with men and women placed equally before the law. But in 1573 another ground, willful desertion for four or more years, was added. This amendment was generally influenced by the Calvinist divorce doctrine, but made specifically for the benefit of the Earl of Argyle, Chancellor of Scotland, who was married to but wanted to divorce Jean Steward, half-sister of Mary, Queen of Scots.[79] The procedure for divorce for reason of desertion was very cumbersome and lengthy, however. The deserted spouse had to raise an action of adherence (a demand that the deserter return) as early as a year after the actual desertion, and the guilty spouse was warned by the court and the church to return. If he or she refused to return, the deserting spouse was denounced and excommunicated and if he or she had not returned at the end of four years' absence, the abandoned spouse was permitted to apply to the Commissary court for a divorce.[80]

These two grounds for divorce, adultery and desertion, remained the only grounds recognized in Scotland until 1938. We might note that the Scottish law was less hesitant about making desertion a ground and did not attempt to draw a connection between desertion and adultery; it referred only the need to show "the malicious and obstinate defection of the party offender" during a four-year period.[81] The Church of Scotland did not object to this extension of divorce law, but it did have reservations about other aspects of divorce in the country. In 1596 the General Assembly of the church listed among common corruptions of the realm "adulteries, fornications, incest, unlawful marriages, and divorcements allowed by public laws and judges," an objection directed against the role of secular authorities in dissolving marriages.[82] One further source of tension between church and state in Scotland was the weakening of the principle of fault, which was implied by allowing adulterous spouses to remarry their accomplices after being divorced. The General Assembly declared that "the marriage of convicted adulterers is a great allurement to married persons to commit the crime, thinking thereby to be separate from their own lawful half-marrows, to enjoy the persons with whom they have committed adultery."[83] The Scottish parliament responded equivocally to this, passing a law that

---

[78] Ibid., 248–9.
[79] Charles J. Guthrie, "The History of Divorce in Scotland," *Scottish Historical Review* 8 (1910), 44–5.
[80] See *Ibid.*, 46. An eighteenth-century case of divorce for reason of desertion is quoted at length in F. P. Walton (ed.), *Lord Hermand's Consistorial Decisions, 1684–1777* (Edinburgh, 1940), 71–2.
[81] Quoted in Guthrie, "Divorce in Scotland," 45.
[82] Ibid., 46.
[83] Ibid., 50.

marriages were null and unlawful when they united a person divorced for adultery and the individual named in the divorce decision as their accomplice.[84] It left open the possibility of such remarriages when the sentence of divorce did not specify the name of the adulterer's accomplice.

2.5 Divorce among other Continental Reformers

Calvin's and Luther's were the most influential divorce doctrines in the six-teenth century for the simple reason that legislation based on one or other of them was widespread throughout Europe, mainly in the Protestant states, but also among Reformed populations within Roman Catholic states, as among the Protestants of France until the Revocation of the Edict of Nantes at the end of the seventeenth century.[85] This is not to deny the significance of the other doc-trines and perspectives that made up the corpus of divorce writing during the Reformation. Some of the other reformers, such as Huldreich Zwingli, also had practical importance at the time, albeit geographically more limited. Zwingli's use of the divorce texts of the Bible differed profoundly from both Luther's and Calvin's. They understood the grounds for divorce set out in the Bible (adultery and, with qualifications, desertion) as being exclusive of all others, but Zwingli took them to be little more than exemplary of the sorts of circumstances that could justify dissolving a marriage. For Zwingli the reference in the book of Matthew to adultery's being a reason for divorce did not mean that adultery was the sole ground, but, rather, that adultery was the matrimonial offense of least seriousness that could give rise to a divorce. He assumed that if a divorce could be obtained for reason of adultery, then it could certainly be obtained in more serious circumstances. All that was required was to specify the circumstances or offenses that were more heinous than adultery, and there were certain indi-cations of these in the Bible. The advice in Paul that people should marry rather than burn, a reference to the need for marriage as a forum for legitimate sexual activity, was interpreted by Zwingli as meaning that impotence (the inability to consummate marriage) in one spouse justified the other's seeking a divorce. Similarly, divorce should be permitted when a believer was married to an unbeliever.

The clearest statement of Zwingli's divorce doctrine was a 1525 ordinance concerning marriage that established a marriage tribunal (*Ehegericht*) for Zurich to replace the jurisdiction of the episcopacy of Constance. Divorce in Zurich was primarily to be permitted for adultery, which was the touchstone of Zwingli's principles of divorce. A "pious person, who has given no cause for such an act"

---

[84] *The Acts of the Parliaments of Scotland, 1424–1707* (rev. edn., 12 vols, Edinburgh, 1908), V, 92–3.

[85] On the doctrines and procedures for divorce followed by French Protestants, see Pierre Bels, *Le mariage des Protestants français jusqu'en 1685* (Paris, 1968), esp. 239ff. The patterns were quite familiar, including compulsory attempts at reconciling the spouses and preventing divorce.

could divorce a spouse caught in open adultery, and in order to prevent adultery's becoming attractive as a way of escaping a marriage (the fear expressed by the Church of Scotland), severe punishments were provided for adultery. Adulterers were excommunicated and the civil authorities were empowered to sentence them to corporal punishment and confiscate their property.[86]

Yet despite the seriousness with which adultery was viewed by Zurich's moral police, it did not lead to an automatic or even a speedy divorce. Instead, the spouses were required to "live together as friends for a year, to see if matters might not better themselves by the prayers of themselves and other honest people. If it did not grow better in that time, they shall be separated and allowed to marry elsewhere."[87] What is notable here is not the compulsory attempt at reconciliation, also found in various forms in other divorce laws of the time, but that both parties, the guilty as well as the innocent, were expressly permitted to remarry. The single restriction appears to have been that the remarriages had to take place elsewhere than the place of their former common domicile, an indication of the unease with which divorce was regarded.

If adultery was the prime ground for divorce in Zwingli's ordinance for Zurich, the other and "greater reasons than adultery" were also set out. These were "destroying life, endangering life, being mad or crazy, offending by whorishness, leaving one's spouse without permission, remaining abroad a long time, having leprosy, or such other reasons, of which no rule can be made on account of their dissimilarity."[88] These, then, were only further examples of the grounds that Zwingli thought justified divorce. Faced with petitions seeking divorce for these or other reasons, the judges of the *Ehegericht* were to investigate "and proceed as God and the character of the case shall demand."[89] It should not be thought, though, that divorce became frequent under the regime of this apparently flexible and comparatively liberal marriage code. Between 1525 and 1531 (when Zwingli died) there were eighty petitions for divorce in Zurich, and the judges of the *Ehegericht* agreed to only twenty-eight of them. Moreover, divorced men and women were required to wait for considerable periods after divorce before they were granted permission to remarry.[90]

After Zwingli's early death, the spiritual leadership of Zurich devolved upon Heinrich Bullinger, who broadly followed his predecessor's precepts on divorce. Bullinger underlined the importance of marriage in God's ordering of the world, so as to detract from the Catholic denigration of the married life, and to emphasize that only the most serious circumstances could justify the dissolution of a marriage. Marriage, he wrote, was to be entered into "devoutly, holily,

---

[86] Huldreich Zwingli, "Ordinance and Notice How Matters Concerning Marriage shall be Conducted in the City of Zurich" (1525), in *Selected Works of Huldreich Zwingli (1484–1531), the Reformer of German Switzerland* (ed. Samuel Macauley Jackson, Philadelphia, 1901), 121–2.
[87] Ibid.
[88] Ibid., 102.
[89] Ibid.
[90] Jean Rilliet, *Zwingli: Third Man of the Reformation* (London, 1964), 179.

soberly, wisely, lawfully, and in the face of God,"[91] and the bond of marriage he described as "indissoluble and everlasting, that is to say, such a knot as never can be undone."[92]

But this description represented only an ideal, the intent with which marriage was to be undertaken. In practical terms marriage could be dissolved in grave circumstances, principally when one spouse was guilty of adultery, but like Zwingli, Bullinger took adultery to be a point of reference, the least serious in a range of grounds for divorce. He wrote: "And yet let not any lesse or lighter cause dissolve this knot betwixt man and wife, than fornication is. Otherwise God which in ye Gospel hath permitted the lesse, doth not forbidde the greater to be causes of divorcement."[93] Divorce in such cases was not the sundering by man of marriages made by God, according to Bullinger, for there were "many whome God coupled not together, but carnal lust, mony, good, flattery, dronkennes, a fleshely arm and frendshyppe."[94] Just as marriage was ordained as "a remedy and medicyne unto our feble and weake flesh,"[95] so divorce was the "medicyne of man, and for amendment of wedlok."[96]

Bullinger, like Zwingli before him, was reluctant to set down excessively rigid rules on the grounds for divorce, preferring to leave individual cases to the wisdom of the courts.[97] Indeed, it was the matrimonial court of Zurich, the *Ehegericht*, rather than his divorce doctrines, that was the most influential of Zwingli's reforms in the area of marriage. Composed of six judges (two beneficed clergy and two laymen each from the Small and Great Councils of Zurich), the *Ehegericht* became the model for the Consistory courts of Geneva and Scotland, as well as for courts in St. Gall, Berne, Schaffhausen, and Basel.[98]

In Basel, for example, a marriage court was established in 1529, and its competence and composition set down precisely in 1533, under the guidance of the reformer Johannes Oecolampadius, a close friend of Zwingli.[99] The Basel *Ehgericht* comprised seven judges — five from the city's legislative bodies and two clergy — who were empowered to deal with all matters concerning marriage.

---

[91] Heinrich Bullinger, "The Fifth Decade," in *The Decades of Henry Bullinger* (ed. Thomas Harding, Cambridge, 1852), 510.

[92] Bullinger, *Decades*, 413–4.

[93] Bullinger, *Fiftie Godlie and Learned Sermons*, 227.

[94] Bullinger, *The Golden Boke of Christen Matrimonye* (n.p., 1543), sig.C viii[V].

[95] Bullinger, *Christen state of Matrimonye*, 32[V].

[96] Ibid., 90[R].

[97] Bullinger, *Decades*, 511.

[98] In Zwickau a marital court composed of clergy and lay town councillors was established in 1536. An innovation was the setting up of a committee of respected married women to advise and investigate in cases involving women. They did not have the authority to make decisions. See Susan C. Karant-Nunn "Continuity and Change: Some Effects of the Reformation on the Women of Zwickau," *Sixteenth Century Journal* 13:2 (1982), 31.

[99] The following summary of the working of the Basel *Ehegericht* is drawn from Thomas Max Safley, "To Preserve the Marital State: The Basler Ehegericht, 1550–1592," *Journal of Family History* 7 (1982), 162–79.

2.5 Divorce among other Continental Reformers

Their competence included ruling on the validity of marriages, judging marital disputes (where they could counsel offenders and punish them if necessary), as well as hearing petitions for separation and divorce. Under Basel's *Ehegerichts-ordnung* of 1533, divorce could be granted for reason of adultery, abuse, impotence, and the conviction of one spouse for a capital crime. The innocent party in such circumstances was permitted to remarry after a suitable waiting period (usually one year) after obtaining the consent of the *Ehegericht*. Separation *a mensa et thoro*, which did not confer the right of remarriage, could be had for reason of insanity or infectious disease. These grounds were less extensive than those recognized by Zwingli, but still more liberal than those allowed by Luther, Calvin, and their followers.

Matrimonial cases were relatively rare in Basel, totaling only 1,356 between 1550 and 1592, an average of thirty-four cases each year.[100] Moreover, only 226 of these (17%) were divorce petitions, and 18 (1%) were suits for separation. Half of the divorce petitions were based on adultery (114 cases), and 84 were grounded on repudiation (in effect, a refusal to cohabit), 21 were for various kinds of abuse, and 7 were for reason of impotence. Most of the petitioners (127, or 56%) were women. It is notable, though, that despite the small number of divorce petitions, only about half (125) were agreed to by the *Ehegericht*. Sixty-five were rejected definitively, although in thirty-five cases the spouses were instructed to resolve their differences amicably. Although divorce was provided as a remedy for the breach of marriage, the *Ehegericht* in Basel gives the impression, according to one of its historians, of deliberately attempting to frustrate divorce suits. In contrast, having granted a divorce, the judges gave ready and rapid consent for the innocent party to remarry, often ignoring the provision that a suitable period should be allowed to elapse between divorce and remarriage.[101]

Luther's and Calvin's divorce doctrines represented the attitudes of mainstream Protestants to a large degree, and the justifications they recognized for divorce – adultery and desertion – may be regarded as the classic Protestant grounds for the dissolution of marriage. Within the Continental Reformation, though, there were divergent attitudes, both in more libertarian and more restrictive directions. For a different approach we might well turn to the Radical Reformation, made up for the most part of the Anabaptist churches and sects.[102] One characteristic that distinguished the Radical from the Magisterial Reformation (of Luther and Calvin and their followers) was that the Radicals did not seek or gain the endorsement of the dominant political institutions or personalities of the countries where they were found. The victory of the Cal-

---

[100] To give this figure perspective, Basel had a population of about 10,000 in the second half of the sixteenth century. Ibid., 168n.10.

[101] Ibid., 173.

[102] For a general treatment, see G. H. Williams, *The Radical Reformation* (Philadelphia, 1962); William Echard Keeney, *The Development of Dutch Anabaptist Thought and Practice from 1539–1564* (Nieuwkoop, 1968), 124ff.

vinist and Lutheran churches over the Roman Catholic church was generally due to the support and patronage of princes and magistrates (hence Magisterial Reformation), and these churches became identified as state churches. The Radical Reformers, however, eschewed secular political establishments, and policy on the relationship between church and state was a key distinction between the Radical and Magisterial traditions. Not only this, but the Radicals tended to reject hierarchical structures within the church itself (although the Hutterites did have bishops). Among most Anabaptist sects, pastors were chosen by the congregation, which had greater participation in church government than among the mainstream Protestant confessions.

To be "radical" in this respect need not imply a very different approach to issues such as marriage and divorce, although there is a lot to be said for the argument that "religions espoused by entire countries seldom seek to overturn the social values of those countries."[103] Moreover, the Radicals' unwillingness to accept given secular institutions might well have extended beyond the strictly political to fundamental social institutions such as marriage and the family. An important influence in this regard was the higher status that Anabaptists accorded women. The position of women in Radical Protestantism is a debated issue that admits no unqualified generalizations, yet it is clear that women were given rights of education and participation in the church that were much closer to equality with men than was the case in society at large. We might well expect these features to have produced, among Radical Protestants, doctrines on marriage and divorce that diverged from the classic Protestant positions as represented by Luther and Calvin.

In fact, for the most part the Radical Reformers were more restrictive than the others in the matter of divorce, confining the grounds for dissolution of marriage to adultery and certain circumstances foreseen by the Pauline Privilege. An example is the Hutterite Five Articles of 1547, written by Peter Walpot:

Nothing can break the marriage bond but adultery. Where, however, a brother has an unbelieving wife, and she agrees to live with him, he may not divorce her (nor vice versa). But where she is endangered in her faith or is hindered by the unbelieving husband in the training of her children in the true faith, she may divorce her husband, but must remain unmarried as long as her husband lives.[104]

In strict terms, then, divorce was permitted only for reason of adultery. Even the Pauline Privilege was interpreted as allowing only a separation in effect (because remarriage was ruled out), and this facility was restricted to women's initiative. It might have been perceived that a believing wife would be in more moral danger from an unbelieving husband than would a believing husband from his unbelieving wife. The authority of the male would certainly make a heretical husband more of a threat to the children's upbringing than a heretical wife would be.

[103] Joyce L. Irwin, *Womanhood in Radical Protestantism, 1525–1675* (New York, 1979), xi.
[104] Quoted in Williams, *Radical Reformation*, 517.

2.5 Divorce among other Continental Reformers

Doctrines similar to the Hutterite were espoused by the Dutch Mennonites and Swiss Brethren. An example from the latter, a tract on divorce written in 1527, adhered strictly to the divorce text of Matthew:

We declare that when a man or woman separates except for fornication [adultery], and takes another wife or husband, we consider this as adultery and the participants as not members of the body of Christ, yea, he who marries the separated one we consider a fornicator according to the words of Christ, Matthew 5, 19.[105]

The overall tendency of the Radical Reformation, then, was more restrictive in terms of divorce than that of the Magisterial confessions. The principal reason for this was the Radicals' reliance upon scripture, making them less willing to extrapolate from the biblical divorce texts or to use the biblical grounds (as Zwingli did) as simple examples of matrimonial offenses that might justify divorce. The Radical Protestants also placed a heavy onus on marriage, making it a covenant, a means by which men and women could recover the harmony of Adam and Eve before the Fall. This could well have produced a reaction against Lutheran and Calvinist (not to mention Zwinglian) divorce doctrines that, since they were not grounded exclusively on a literal reading of the Bible, would have been regarded as being conducive to a lax attitude toward the sanctity of marriage.

The Pauline Privilege was more problematic. Radical sects like the Mennonites forbade mixed marriage, but in the case of an existing marriage between a believer and a nonbeliever, divorce was (as in the Hutterite prescription quoted earlier) heavily circumscribed. The 1554 Mennonite Wismar resolution allowed the nonbeliever in such a marriage to separate for reason of the faith but stipulated that the believer should "conduct himself honestly" (that is, chastely) and could not enter a new marriage unless the nonbeliever committed adultery or remarried. Even then, the believer could only remarry "subject to the advice of the elders of the congregation."[106]

Ironically, the Pauline Privilege was turned on the Anabaptists themselves. In 1571 a Württemberg regulation prescribed divorce in cases where a Lutheran spouse was deserted by his or her Anabaptist partner, especially when children had been left behind. Anabaptism was also punishable by banishment and imprisonment, and these had the effect of dividing marriages on a permanent or temporary basis. A 1584 Württemberg ordinance recognized the hardships these punishments imposed on the remaining spouse and children, and "for this reason, and also because of the plaintive requests of husbands, such cases [of heresy] have been dealt with leniently, and such wives have been handed over to their husbands to be chained in the house."[107] But, according

---

[105] Quoted in John C. Wenger (trans. and ed.), "Concerning Divorce: A Swiss Brethren Tract on the Primacy of Loyalty to Christ and the Right to Divorce and Remarriage," *Mennonite Quarterly Review* 21 (1947), 114–19.

[106] Williams, *Radical Reformation*, 516.

[107] Irwin, *Womanhood*, 64.

to the ordinance, husbands had often secretly unchained their wives, and magistrates and officials were enjoined to visit such houses without warning to ensure that Anabaptist women were being kept confined as they had been sentenced. This is a rare example of the state or church intervening in marriages to separate husband and wife. The fact that men were freeing their wives from their chains suggests that they themselves were not too concerned about religious disparity. In defense of the regulations it might be argued that although their short-term effect was to separate wife from husband or to emphasize their religious differences, the ultimate aim was to bring the wife back to doctrinal conformity, both to the church and her husband.

Returning to the Radical Reformation, we find that its theologians approached marriage from somewhat different perspectives from those of the Magisterial Reformers. One result was a more restrictive interpretation of the biblical divorce texts, limiting the grounds for divorce to adultery and a narrow version of the Pauline Privilege. This had been the initial doctrine of Luther and Calvin, and we have seen that it was only reluctantly that they extended the grounds for divorce to include simple desertion, after bringing desertion into a close relationship with adultery. The Radicals did not take this additional step.

One area in which the Radical Reformation diverged more markedly from mainstream Protestants was in the polygamy fostered by several of the sects.[108] The best-known example is the German city of Münster, which in 1534 declared that polygamy was the ideal form of marriage. The justifications for this were given by the city's leader, John of Leyden, as being the example of the patriarchs who had had many wives, and God's injunction that the faithful should increase and multiply. Population would increase if each man had the possibility of impregnating more than one woman, because a single wife could be already pregnant, sterile, or past the age of child bearing. In such cases a man's semen would be wasted, unless he committed adultery or had more than one wife. Adultery was forbidden to the point of being made a capital offense, but from July 1534 polygamy was practiced in Münster, with numbers of men having as many as three or four wives.[109]

The relationship between polygamy and divorce is ambiguous. On the one hand the possibility of marrying a second (or additional) wife could be a response to a man's dissatisfaction with his first. Polygamy would respond to this situation by accretion, where divorce responded by replacement. It is suggested that John of Leyden himself heard the voice of God command him to marry his second wife (and thus to embrace polygamy as an institution) because he was in love with the woman in question but was also already married. Divorce from a fellow believer was not possible, and instead of suppressing his feelings for another woman, he transformed the institution of marriage itself.[110]

---

[108] Williams, *Radical Reformation*, 511–13. A general account of polygamy in the sixteenth century is John Cairncross, *After Polygamy Was Made a Sin* (London, 1974), 1–30.

[109] Ibid., 13.

[110] Ibid., 4.

2.5 Divorce among other Continental Reformers

Although polygamy might be regarded as a divorce substitute in such cases, it was not portrayed as such; polygamy in Münster was made a positive injunction, not a remedy for discontent on the part of men within existing marriages.

Later, the Münsterites did provide for divorce within polygamous marriages. In the men's eagerness to fulfill God's command, many women of the city were forced to marry (as were many young girls), and a decree of January 1535 permitted such women to have their marriages dissolved. Of some 2,000 women married in the preceding five months (after polygamy was declared the ideal), about 200 obtained divorces on the ground of compulsion. Divorce could also be obtained for reason of impotence (which is hardly surprising in light of the emphasis on procreation), and for reason of lack of Anabaptist conviction by husband or wife,[111] an application of the Pauline Privilege.

Generally, though, the Radical Reformation did not provide more radical divorce doctrines than those promulgated by conventional Protestants. For the radical libertarian among divorce reformers in the sixteenth century, we must look to Martin Bucer, the Reformer of Strasbourg. Bucer adopted a doctrine of divorce that permitted the dissolution of marriage under a broad range of circumstances, including matrimonial offenses and mutual consent, and in doing so he placed himself outside the mainstream of Protestant thought on divorce.[112] Little less than a century after Bucer's writing on divorce was published,[113] the English writer John Milton translated it as his own second work on divorce, *The Judgement of Martin Bucer, concerning Divorce* (1644); but then too, in the mid-seventeenth century, Bucer's ideas were unacceptably libertarian. Indeed, the sentiments, if not the letter, of Bucer's divorce doctrine, were not translated into legislation in the West until the late twentieth century.

Bucer tied his attitude to divorce more closely and directly to his doctrine of marriage than did other sixteenth-century Reformers. He explicitly rejected the traditional Catholic teaching on the purposes of marriage, which stressed procreation and the avoidance of nonmarital sex, rather than companionship. If the proper and ultimate end of marriage were copulation for having children, Bucer argued, there would have been no true marriage between Joseph and Mary. Bucer held, contrary to the Catholic church and many of the other Reformers, that "the most proper and highest and main end of marriage is the communication of all duties, both divine and human, with the utmost benevolence."[114] These duties imposed four necessary properties on a marriage. The married couple should live together, unless a divine calling should require otherwise for a time; they should love each other with the greatest benevolence and charity; the husband should be the head and protector of his

---

[111] Ibid., 13.
[112] General discussions of Bucer are Constantin Hopf, *Martin Bucer and the English Reformation* (London, 1946), and Hastings Eells, *Martin Bucer* (New Haven, 1931).
[113] *De Regno Christi* (1557).
[114] Bucer, *De Regno Christi*, ch. XXXVIII, 208. Translations from *De Regno Christi* are mine; Milton's translation is an edited one and is obscured by seventeenth-century formulations.

wife, and she should be a help to him; and finally, they should be sexually faithful to each other. The important point made by Bucer was that these duties
were essential for a true marriage to subsist: "According to the sentence of
God, which all Christians must follow, there is no true marriage, nor should
they be considered husband and wife, who either through obstinacy, or because
they are unable, cannot or will not fulfil these duties."[115]

This statement of the conditions necessary for a valid marriage opened the
way for a wide range of grounds justifying dissolution. In the first place, divorce
should be available in the cases of adultery and for reason of desertion by a nonbeliever (the Pauline Privilege) because these circumstances were unambiguously permitted in the Bible. Desertion per se would be a reason for divorce,
as well, because the deserter failed in the obligation to cohabit with his or her
partner. The obligation of mutual love led Bucer beyond the concept of
matrimonial fault to recognize the breakdown of marriage, and he advocated
the possibility of divorce by mutual consent and by repudiation. There were
qualifications, however. Bucer suggested that divorce by mutual consent ought
to be made more difficult if there were children of the marriage than in the
case of a childless couple. And to prevent abuses of the right of repudiation,
he proposed that, as among the Christian emperors, "a man who wrongly
repudiated his wife [Bucer did not specify the circumstances] should return her
dowry or a quarter of his goods. A similar penalty would be imposed on a wife
who left her husband without just cause."[116]

Bucer went further in his approval of the early Christian emperors' divorce
laws and suggested that the legislation of Theodorus and Valentinian might
be – indeed, ought to be[117] – resurrected by any Christian prince. This
extended the grounds for divorce to include specific offenses by the wife and
husband that, in addition to adultery, included witchcraft, the desecration of
sepulchers, committing sacrilege, favoring thieves, the wife's feasting with
strangers without her husband's knowledge or consent, the husband's frequenting lewd women within his wife's sight, and violence, whether it emanated
from the wife or the husband. In such cases the marriage could be dissolved
and the spouses had the right to remarry (the wife not until a year had elapsed
from the divorce, in case she were pregnant).[118] The offenses Bucer listed as
grounds for divorce had been subject to extreme penalties such as death or
deportation, and Bucer argued that God had never intended that a decent man
or woman should have to remain coupled for life with an infamous partner.
Here was an explicit rejection of the notion that matrimonial faults or shortcomings ought to be borne like a cross, with Christian charity. To Bucer's
mind, this approach rewarded the wicked. If there were a possibility of
repentance on the part of the guilty, he thought it was more likely to be

[115] Ibid., ch. XXXIX, 209.
[116] Ibid., ch. XXXVII, 203–4.
[117] Ibid., ch. XI, 210–15.
[118] Ibid., ch. XXXVII, 203–4.

realized when the offence was punished than when it was condoned or forgiven.

The extension of the grounds for divorce in Bucer's doctrine did not imply a careless attitude toward marriage, however. One chapter of *De Regno Christi* was devoted to the means of keeping marriage holy.[119] Bucer proposed that every church should have "certain grave and devout men" who would oversee marriages to ensure that husbands and wives behaved properly toward each other, the former loving and helping their wives in the fulfillment of their piety and duties, the latter being a true help to their husbands. If the church officials should find marriages that did not conform to God's prescriptions, the couples concerned were to be admonished. If the admonition were ignored, then the couple were to be brought before the civil magistrate, who had the power to punish violations of the code of behavior within marriage.

Bucer did not take marital breakdown or matrimonial offenses lightly, then, and in this sense he was at one with the other Reformers. But his doctrine was much more liberal than theirs, not only because he permitted divorce on a wider range of specific grounds but also because he envisaged the dissolution of marriage by mutual consent and by simple repudiation by either spouse. Under Bucer's principles, in fact, divorce and remarriage were possible under any circumstances, subject to financial penalties for the abuse of repudiation. As the odd man out, Bucer was much criticized for his approach to divorce. John Burcher, for example, wrote that "Bucer is more than licentious on the subject of marriage. I heard him once disputing at table upon this question, when he asserted that a divorce should be allowed for any reason, however trifling. . . ."[120] In letter, this description of Bucer's doctrine is correct. But it overlooks the seriousness with which Bucer regarded marriage and divorce, and the qualification that he imposed on "trifling" reasons, which we may assume came within his category of divorces without just cause. Bucer's main influence on divorce was probably in England. He gave an opinion on the attempt by Henry VIII to annul his marriage to Catherine of Aragon, and posthumously influenced the terms of the *Reformatio Legum Ecclesiasticarum*, a draft reform of English church law produced in the 1550s (see Section 2.7).

2.6 The "divorces" of Henry VIII

If Martin Bucer represented the permissive end of the spectrum of Protestant divorce doctrines, the Church of England represented the restrictive end. England was unique in the sixteenth century as the only country where an established or dominant reformed church did not break with the Roman Catholic doctrine of marital indissolubility. This was an irony given that the catalyst for the Anglican church's break with Rome was the attempt by King Henry VIII to rid himself of his wife, Catherine of Aragon. Henry's action was

---

[119] Ibid., ch. XXI, 164–5.
[120] John Burcher to Henry Bullinger (8 June 1550), quoted in Hopf, *Bucer*, 115n.1.

not a divorce, however; what he sought was an annulment on the ground that his marriage was invalid because of a preexisting impediment. Despite this, it deserves some consideration here because Henry's "divorce" throws light on the state of thinking about marriage and divorce in the early Reformation, both in England and on the Continent.

Most of the facts of the case can be stated in a fairly straightforward manner.[121] In November 1501 Henry VIII's older brother Arthur, then Prince of Wales, married Catherine, who had been brought from Spain for this dynastically advantageous union. But after only five months the marriage was cut short by Arthur's death of consumption. In that period, no child was conceived by the couple and, indeed, the marriage of Arthur and Catherine was never consummated. It was soon decided that Henry, now heir to the English throne, should marry his dead brother's widow, and a treaty was signed in June 1503 to the effect that the marriage should take place when Henry reached the age of fifteen. Because Catherine had been married to Henry's brother, there existed an impediment in the first degree collateral to her remarriage to Henry, and a dispensation was duly obtained from Pope Julius II to overcome the impediment. Henry and Catherine were betrothed and were finally married in June 1509, soon after Henry succeeded his father to the throne.

It is not clear when Henry began seriously to consider the possibility and desirability of divesting himself of Catherine, though Catherine herself was informed of his scruples about the legitimacy of their marriage in June 1527. Nor are the reasons for Henry's intentions and actions perfectly clear, although the overriding consideration was the failure of the marriage to produce a male heir. After twenty years of marriage the net product was one daughter, the future Queen Mary, while Catherine had borne five other children, none of whom had survived, and had had several miscarriages. It is impossible to overestimate the importance that Henry attached to this failure to produce a son and heir, and this must have been uppermost in his mind when he determined to take another wife. At the same time, the appearance on the scene of Anne Boleyn, with whom Henry became infatuated, clearly acted as a catalyst and added impetus and urgency to his desire to get rid of Catherine and to remarry.

It is important to remember that during this first of Henry VIII's series of matrimonial trials, the church in England was Roman Catholic. When Henry sought to divest himself of Catherine, he did not think of divorcing her because that was not possible under church law, and would, in any case, have been an implicit admission that the marriage was valid. It was Henry's contention that the marriage to Catherine was invalid *ab initio* because of the impediment

---

[121] The best general accounts of Henry VIII's matrimonial cases are Henry Ansgar Kelly, *The Matrimonial Trials of Henry VIII* (Stanford, 1976), and J. J. Scarisbrick, *Henry VIII* (Berkeley, 1968), esp. 163–240. I am also grateful to Professor M. A. R. Graves for comments on these issues. The following account is drawn primarily from these sources. A useful collection of documents is Nicholas Pocock, *Records of the Reformation: The Divorce, 1527–1533* (2 vols., Oxford, 1870).

resulting from Catherine's former marriage to Arthur. Henry drew for his argument on the texts of Leviticus: "Thou shalt not uncover the nakedness of thy brother's wife: it is thy brother's nakedness" (Leviticus 18:16), and "If a man shall take his brother's wife, it is an impurity: he hath uncovered his brother's nakedness; they shall be childless" (Leviticus 20:21). (The latter text seemed particularly cogent in view of the sad catalog of Henry and Catherine's children; although they did have a surviving daughter, this counted for little with Henry who wanted a male heir.) Henry argued from the texts that not only was the affinity between himself and Catherine an impediment, but that it was a diriment impediment from which they could be dispensed by God alone, not by the pope. This being so, he held, the dispensation granted by Pope Julius had been to no effect, the impediment stood, the marriage was void, and he was free to marry another woman. It is important to place these concerns – the validity of the marriage and the absence of a male heir – within the context of Henry's preoccupation with the succession to the throne.

It must remain an open question as to whether Henry concocted this argument as a means of getting rid of Catherine or whether he really believed in it. If the former, his would be a perfect example of the Catholic provision for annulment of marriage's being used cynically as a covert divorce in the strict sense. If we are to believe that Henry argued his case sincerely, then we might have to credit him with being so troubled in conscience by his invalid marriage that he was driven to having its invalidity recognized by the Church. This would be more credible if Henry had been exclusively concerned with his marriage to Catherine, whereas it is clear that his attention was as much on Anne Boleyn as his next wife. Very likely the best explanation is a combination of the two possibilities, which are not mutually exclusive in any case. Henry's overriding concern was for the provision of an undisputed male heir, and the fact that his marriage to Catherine was blighted in this respect brought him to the conviction that the union was invalid in the eyes of God, despite the papal dispensation. The appearance of Anne Boleyn at court was arguably more important to the timing of the petition for annulment, not its formulation. The concern for a secure succession also explains Henry's desire to annul the marriage rather than dissolve it. If he had obtained a divorce from Catherine, many of his subjects would not have regarded his second marriage as valid, and this would have made the children of the union illegitimate in their eyes. Only an annulment of the first marriage would eliminate that problem.

In 1529 Henry petitioned Pope Clement to have the marriage declared null and void, but he was met with a refusal. For one thing it was asking a lot for the pope to declare an earlier papal dispensation ineffective, thus implicitly undermining one of his own powers. For another, by 1529 the pope was virtually a prisoner of Emperor Charles V, who was Catherine's nephew. Charles was understandably anxious to protect his aunt's interests in particular, and his dynasty's in general, neither of which was best served by Catherine's removal from the throne of England.

2 Reformers and divorce: Theory and practice

In addition to the political inhibitions to the pope's agreeing to the petition, there were theological arguments against the annulment. Against the Levitical texts adduced by Henry, Catherine's supporters proposed Deuteronomy 25:2: "When brethren dwell together, and one of them dieth without children, the wife of the deceased shall not marry to another; but his brother shall take her, and raise up seed for his brother." On the surface this seemed not simply to enable Henry to marry Arthur's widow, but even positively to enjoin him to do so. This interpretation was upheld by those who took Catherine's side, whereas Henry's supporters argued that this practice of the Jews (the levirate) was abrogated by the coming of Christ. Over a period of several years, both sides to the dispute marshaled texts, canons, precedents, authorities, and opinions in support of their respective positions.

In addition, there were some questions of fact at issue. One concerned the consummation of the marriage between Arthur and Catherine. If the marriage had been consummated, the impediment to the marriage of Henry and Catherine would have been one of affinity, since that impediment arose from sexual union. If, on the other hand, the marriage had not been consummated, the impediment was not one of affinity but a lesser one of "public honesty," which arose from the relationship of two people created by betrothal or marriage where the latter was not consummated. The question of consummation in Arthur and Catherine's brief marriage was at issue between Henry and Catherine. He maintained that she was not a virgin when he married her, and his supporters drew on a reported statement by Arthur "the next Morning after his Marriage, that he had been that Night in the Midst of Spain."[122] Only at the end of the annulment proceedings did Henry finally concede that Catherine had been a virgin at the time of their marriage.

There is no need here to enter the intricacies of the law, nor of the details of the procedure by which Henry annulled his marriage to Catherine and married Anne Boleyn. Suffice it to say that Henry was not divorced in the strict sense. He adopted the view that the marriage was invalid and proceeded to marry Anne Boleyn secretly in January 1533, soon after she was found to be pregnant. As far as he was concerned, this was recognition of the nonexistence of the first marriage, though to his opponents it made him a bigamist. A definitive decision that the marriage to Catherine had been invalid came months after the marriage to Anne Boleyn: In April 1533 the Southern Convocation of the Church of England declared that the earlier marriage had been impeded by divine law and that the papal dispensation had been to no effect.[123]

---

[122] *The History of the Life, Victories, Reign and Death of Henry VIII* (London, 1682), 87.

[123] This was not an autonomous ecclesiastical action, but one made possible by the 1533 Act in Restraint of Appeals that blocked appeals to Rome, made royal jurisdiction and authority final in English law, and, in this particular case, gave Cranmer's court the right to deal definitively with the matter. On these aspects see Mortimer Levine, "Henry VIII's Use of the Spiritual and Temporal Jurisdictions in his Great Causes of Matrimony, Legitimacy, and Succession," *Historical Journal* X (1967), 3–10.

2.6 The "divorces" of Henry VIII

What is interesting, from the point of view of the history of divorce, is that Henry did *not* divorce Catherine. The scholars who were consulted on Henry's case generally gave an opinion against the annulment but did not propose divorce as an alternative. Luther's opinion began:

Even if the king might have sinned by marrying the wife of his deceased brother, and even if the dispensation granted by the Roman pope might not have been valid (I do not debate this now), nevertheless it would be a heavier and more dreadful sin to divorce the woman he had married, and this especially for the reason that then the king, as well as the Queen and the Young Queen [Mary] could forever be charged with, and considered as, incestuous people.[124]

(Almost certainly, Luther used the word "divorce" here to mean annulment, since this was the issue upon which Henry was seeking opinions.)

Zwingli argued that marriage with a sister-in-law was prohibited by natural and divine law, which ruled out the efficacy of a papal dispensation. Henry not only could, but should, escape from Catherine, but Zwingli advised that in order to avoid scandal the king should annul the marriage by judicial decision. Moreover, the annulment should not be retroactive, which was to say that the children born within the marriage should be considered legitimate.[125] Oecolampadius took a contrary view. Although agreeing that the papal dispensation was invalid, he argued that the consummation and ten years of cohabitation had validated the marriage.[126]

One striking feature of the range of opinions given by scholars on Henry's case was that divorce in the strict sense was hardly ever mentioned, even by those who argued that there was no case for an annulment but realized that Henry was determined to take another wife. Only Capiton proposed that Henry should repudiate or divorce Catherine to avoid popular horror at bigamy, which was the alternative many other scholars suggested. Luther, Melanchthon, Bucer, Erasmus, and others all suggested that Henry should take a second wife without annulling his marriage to Catherine.[127] This was preferred to an unjustified annulment. Luther wrote that "before I would approve of such a divorce [annulment] I would rather permit the king to marry still another woman and to have, according to the example of the patriarchs and kings, two women or queens at the same time."[128]

Melanchthon, too, considered that reasons of state weighed heavily enough to justify a second marriage: "It may be done without any peril to the conscience or reputation of anyone by polygamy."[129] He too cited the example of the patriarchs to show that bigamy was not forbidden by the law of nature. The

---

[124] Luther, *Works*, L, 32.
[125] Jacques V. Pollet, *Martin Bucer: Etudes sur la correspondance* (2 vols., Paris, 1958–62), I, 442.
[126] Ibid., 442–3.
[127] Ibid., 444–5.
[128] Luther, *Works*, L, 32.
[129] Preserved Smith, "German Opinion of the Divorce of Henry VIII," *English Historical Review* 27 (1912), 678–81.

opinion of Erasmus was much the same, and it was even suggested by Cardinal Cajetan, who argued that polygamy was not against natural law, that it was not forbidden in the Bible, and that the pope might grant a dispensation for it.[130]

The case of Henry VIII and Catherine, then, sheds some light on prevailing attitudes to divorce, if in a primarily negative way. Divorce was not proposed as an option by Henry himself for reasons already suggested: The arguments in favor of annulment were plausible, if not convincing, and an annulment would provide for a secure succession in a way in which a divorce could not. It is more surprising that theologians such as Luther and Melanchthon, who did permit divorce under some circumstances and recognized that individual cases ought to be considered on their merits, did not deal with divorce as one solution to Henry's case. To such men, the fact that a king and reasons of state were involved could justify bigamy but not divorce, and this is strong evidence of the reluctance with which the Reformers approached the issue of the dissolution of marriage. Later, in 1539, the leading Protestant Reformers were to approve of a bigamous marriage on the part of Philip, the landgrave of Hesse. Philip had separated from his wife but argued that because he could not remain sexually abstinent, failure to contract a second marriage would place him in danger of a mortal sin.[131] Again in this case, bigamy was preferred to divorce, but this is not to say that bigamy was considered good in itself. Luther, who supported Philip's second marriage, later distanced himself from it a little: He wrote in 1540 to the Elector of Saxony that he had hoped that Philip would, instead of remarrying publicly have kept "an honest girl in a house, have her on account of his dire need and for the sake of his conscience in a secret marriage (although, of course, the world would have considered it adultery), and visit her from time to time, as great lords have often done."[132] Unlike Philip of Hesse, however, Henry VIII did not marry bigamously. Henry, despite his popular image and because of his preoccupation with having a male heir, was relatively fastidious in matrimonial matters.

The annulment of Henry's marriage to Catherine was only one of the three annulments Henry obtained, but it was the most intricate and famous. Its result, the marriage to Anne Boleyn, was also annulled (in 1536), and for a similar underlying reason: the failure to produce a male heir. Anne did give birth to one daughter, the future Queen Elizabeth, but thereafter she experienced a series of miscarriages such that again Henry began to despair of his succession. As in the case of Catherine, the motives for the annulment were mixed. Henry seems to have tired of Anne Boleyn, he desperately wanted a son, and he also began to fear divine displeasure at the marriage. In any event, the actual grounds for the annulment are not known, although it was alleged that Anne was already

---

[130] Ibid., 673.

[131] On the case of Philip of Hesse see William Walker Rockwell, *Die Doppelehe des Landgrafen Philipp von Hessen* (Marburg, 1904).

[132] Luther, *Letters of Spiritual Counsel*, 290 (Letter to John Frederick, Elector of Saxony, 10 January 1540).

married when she married Henry, and that she had committed adultery with several men and incestuous adultery with her brother. The charges of adultery were without foundation, but Anne Boleyn, her brother, and the other alleged accomplices in adultery were all executed.[133]

Henry VIII's third annulment voided his fourth marriage, to Anne of Cleves. Once again the motives are unclear, though it is evident that Henry was not enthusiastic about the marriage in the first place. In his deposition to the commission hearing the petition for annulment, Henry cited Anne's lack of beauty, his lack of consent to the marriage, his desire to escape the marriage, and his inability to consummate it. There were suggestions that Anne was not a virgin at the time of the marriage, and Henry argued that her physical appearance was such as to render him impotent. For a third time the Church of England acquiesced in the doctrinal contortions that Henry's matrimonial suits entailed and allowed the rules of annulment to be exploited in precisely the way the Reformers had condemned the Roman Catholic church for doing.[134]

2.7 The Church of England and divorce

In a sense Henry's matrimonial cases can be seen as setting the tone for the development of divorce law in England. Henry broke with Rome in order to obtain the annulment to which he believed he was entitled. He might subsequently have broken with the Catholic doctrine of marital indissolubility; there were, after all, precedents on the Continent by the early 1530s. In fact, the Church of England remained faithful to this aspect of Catholic marriage doctrine, even though it abandoned other elements such as clerical celibacy. But such was the tenacity with which the Anglican church held to indissolubility, and such was the influence of the church, that no divorce legislation was passed in England until the middle of the nineteenth century. To this extent, the sixteenth-century English proponents of divorce who are discussed in the following pages put forth their doctrines and opinions in circumstances quite different from their continental and Scottish counterparts, who did not have to contend with a reformed church hostile to the notion of divorce.

William Tyndale, one of the earliest English reformers, spent his final twelve years on the Continent and formed something of a bridge between his Protestant compatriots and the continental Reformers. For Tyndale, marriage was an estate ordained by God as a remedy against fornication in which men and women mutually served each other. The grounds he admitted for divorce were adultery and desertion, but with certain qualifications. Adultery, which Tyndale consistently referred to in terms of an offense committed by the wife, certainly

[133] This case is described and analyzed in Kelly, *Matrimonial Trials*, 241–60. See also Margery Stone Schauer and Frederick Schauer, "Law as the Engine of State: The Trial of Anne Boleyn," *William and Mary Law Review* 22 (1980), 49–84.
[134] The annulment of the marriage to Anne of Cleves is dealt with in Kelly, *Matrimonial Trials*, 261–78.

broke the marriage, and in a society where an adulterous wife was put to death, the husband was free to contract another marriage. But

> where they [adulterous wives] be let live, there the man (if he see sign of repentance and amendment) may forgive it once. If he may not find in his heart [to forgive]...he is free no doubt to take another, while the law interprets her dead: for her sin ought of no right to bind him.[135]

It is not clear whether Tyndale extended this right of divorce to the wife of an adulterous husband.

On the other hand, Tyndale referred to desertion in terms of its being an offense committed by the husband. If a man left his wife for a year or more, he should be banished, to return only on pain of death. His wife should be free to remarry. Yet it is clear that in Tyndale's mind desertion was closely linked to adultery and might even be thought of as aggravated adultery. Referring to the husband who deserted his wife, Tyndale asked:

> For what right is it that a lewd wretch should take his goods, and run from his wife without a cause, and sit by a whore, yea, and come again after a year or two (as I have known it) and rob his wife of that she hath gotten in the mean time, and go again to his whore?[136]

Tyndale noted that according to the text of Corinthians, a believer who was deserted by her unbelieving spouse was free to enter a new marriage. He related this privilege to the case of a deserting husband who was a believer: "And even so is this man much more to be interpreted for an infidel, that causeless runneth from his wife."[137] Desertion as a ground for divorce was thus brought into a relationship with both the texts explicitly allowing divorce for reason of adultery and for rejection or desertion by an unbelieving spouse. Desertion, it might be noted, was specifically a ground for divorce, whichever spouse was the guilty party, even though Tyndale's examples cited the husband: "In like manner, if the woman depart causeless and will not be reconciled, though she commit none adultery, the man ought of right to be free to marry again."[138] The element of adultery was explicitly removed here, and simple desertion became sufficient justification for the dissolution of a marriage.

Adultery and desertion, sometimes jointly, sometimes individually, were the only grounds Tyndale recognized for divorce: "In all other causes, if they separate themselves of impatience that the one cannot suffer the other's infirmities, they must remain unmarried."[139] Needless to say, Tyndale did not

---

[135] William Tyndale, "An exposition upon the Fifth, Sixth and Seventh Chapters of Matthew," in Henry Walter (ed.), *Expositions and Notes on Sundry Portions of the Holy Scriptures, together with the Practice of Prelates by William Tyndale, martyred*, 1536 (Cambridge, 1849), 51.
[136] Ibid., 54.
[137] Ibid., 54–5.
[138] Ibid., 55.
[139] Ibid.

2.7 The Church of England and divorce

propose divorce as a solution to Henry VIII's marital problem with Catherine of Aragon, and he also opposed the annulment of the marriage. He found no support in scripture or practice for Henry's arguments in favor of annulment, and, moreover, suggested that annulling the marriage might provoke dynastic problems since there was no certainty that a second marriage would be any more successful than the first in producing a male heir to the English throne.[140]

If Tyndale readily interpreted the biblical divorce texts in favor of permitting the dissolution of marriage, Thomas Cranmer (archbishop of Canterbury from 1532 to 1553) was only much later persuaded to abandon the doctrine of marital indissolubility. Cranmer had held to this position even though he had rejected other key parts of Catholic doctrine such as the sacramentality of marriage and the church courts' practices in respect of annulling marriages. It was probably Cranmer's representations to Henry VIII that resulted in a 1540 Act of Parliament forbidding such annulments.[141] In 1540, too, Cranmer was distressed by the bigamous marriage of the landgrave Philip of Hesse, and one of his letters from this time reveals his opposition to divorce. In a letter to Osiander, a Reformer who had defended Philip's second marriage, Cranmer asked: "What can possibly be alleged in your excuse when you allow a man, after a divorce, when both man and woman are living, to contract a fresh marriage?"[142] According to Cranmer, bigamy and divorce *a vinculo matrimonii* were equally indefensible: Both are contrary to the nature of marriage that made one flesh of two, and to the scriptures, which made it clear that a man or woman could not remarry while his or her spouse was alive.[143] Cranmer admitted no exception to this position and explicitly rejected adultery as a reason for dissolving a marriage.[144] In the light of these views it is not difficult to understand why Cranmer eventually agreed to participate in the annulment of Henry VIII's marriage to Catherine and his remarriage to Ann Boleyn, rather than advise (like others cited earlier) that Henry should remarry bigamously.

Yet within a decade of giving his opinion against divorce in the case of Philip of Hesse, Cranmer had altered his views and was prepared to admit divorce in the case of adultery. This change of mind came about by a particular instance of a separation *a mensa et thoro* that became a divorce. The case concerned William Parr, Marquis of Northampton, who in 1542 obtained a separation from the church court on the ground of his wife's adultery. Northampton subsequently sought permission to contract another marriage, even though his wife was still living, and on May 7, 1547, Cranmer, as archbishop of Canterbury, was com-

---

[140] William Tyndale, *The Practice of Prelates*, 323–34. The sections of this work dealing with Henry VIII's "divorce" were suppressed in sixteenth-century editions; the suggestion that Henry's marriage with Catherine was valid called into question the marriage to Anne and by implication the heritage to the throne of England.
[141] Norskov Olsen, *New Testament Logia*, 113.
[142] *The Work of Thomas Cranmer* (ed. G. E. Duffield, Appleford, Berks., 1964), 307.
[143] Ibid., 307–8.
[144] Ibid.

79

missioned "to try whether the Lady Anne [Northampton's separated wife] was not by the Word of God so lawfully divorced, that she was no more his Wife, and whether thereupon he might not marry another Wife."[145]

The very fact that Cranmer was commissioned to investigate the possibility was an important concession by the Church of England. But before Cranmer could report his opinion in the matter, Northampton remarried on January 28, 1548, claiming

that by the Word of God he was discharged of his tye to his former Wife; and the making marriages indissoluble was but a part of the Popish Law, by which it was reckoned a Sacrament [and] that the condition of the Church was very hard, if upon Adulteries, the innocent must either live with the Guilty, or be exposed to temptations to the like sins, if a separation was only allowed, but the bond of marriage continued undissolved.[146]

Northampton posed two challenges to the Anglican church. The first was that the fact of adultery on the part of one spouse was sufficient to justify the dissolution of a marriage, rather than a mere separation. The second, made by word and in his action of remarrying, was that adultery dissolved a marriage "by the Word of God." This implied that adultery per se entailed divorce and that a judicial process and judgment were not required. In the case of Northampton the adultery of his wife had already been proved to the satisfaction of the ecclesiastical court that had granted his separation. But taken to its logical conclusion, Northampton's view of procedure might have placed the right to dissolve a marriage within the hands of the individuals concerned, without any formal legal or judicial oversight.

Neither of Northampton's contentions was immediately accepted, and he and his second wife were ordered to separate until Cranmer's report on the first marriage was presented. When the archbishop did finally report, he vindicated the argument that adultery was a ground for divorce. His important judgment read in part:

Christ condemned all Marriages upon Divorces, except in the case of Adultery; which seemed manifestly to allow them in that Case. And although this is not mentioned by St. Mark, and St. Luke, yet it is enough that St. Matthew has it. Christ also defined the state of Marriage, to be that in which two are one flesh; so that when either of the two hath broken that Union, by becoming one with another Person, then the marriage is dissolved. And it is oft repeated in the Gospel, that married Persons have power over one anothers Bodies and that they are to give due benevolence to each other; which is plainly contrary to this way of separation without dissolving the Bond. St. Paul putting the case of an Unbeliever departing from the Partner in Marriage, says, the Believing Party, whether Brother or Sister, is not under Bondage in such a case: which seems a discharge of the Bond in case of desertion: and certainly Adultery is yet of a higher nature.[147]

[145] Gilbert Burnett, *History of the Reformation* (ed. Nicholas Pocock, 7 vols., London, 1865), II, 275.
[146] Ibid.
[147] Ibid.

2.7 The Church of England and divorce

Not only did Cranmer thus justify divorce for reason of adultery, he also raised the possibility that desertion might be a ground as well.[148]

Cranmer's opinion on the Northampton case was accepted, but there was obvious unwillingness to allow it to stand as a precedent for other men and women to contract second marriages because they were divorced "by the word of God," whether or not they had been separated by a church court. Northampton's second marriage was allowed to stand, but only by a special Act of Parliament that dissolved the first marriage "any decretal canon constitution ecclesiastical law common law statute usage prescription or custom of this realm to the contrary notwithstanding."[149] The act was repealed, however, during the reign of Queen Mary, which saw a revival of Catholicism in England.

The cases of King Henry VIII and the Marquis of Northampton were instrumental in drawing out attitudes toward divorce and, as far as Cranmer was concerned, the latter was significant in compelling him to study the issues to the extent of altering his opinion on the admissibility of divorce. Other English Reformers, however, developed their divorce doctrines independently of specific cases, and two in particular, Thomas Becon and John Hooper, deserve some consideration. Becon, for some time chaplain to Archbishop Cranmer, is especially noteworthy for his tirades against sexual nonconformity, which he described as a rising tide of "adultery, whoredom, fornication, and uncleanness," to which he attributed "a great part of the divorces, which now-a-days be so commonly accustomed and used by men's private authority, to the great displeasure of God, and for the breach of the most holy knot and bond of matrimony."[150] (By "divorces by private authority" Becon was probably referring to de facto or consensual separations.)

Despite these strictures on "divorces" but because of his abhorrence of adultery, Becon did admit that a man could divorce his "harlot wife." He condemned the Catholic doctrine that "if a man shall have an whore to his wife, it shall be lawful to him to be divorced from her, both from bed and board; but he may by no means marry again, live as he may."[151] In addition, Becon admitted divorce for desertion when the offender was not a believer. Again, he condemned the Catholic doctrine that in such a case remarriage was not permitted and the advice that the husband should "take the Whore again if ye will, other wife get ye none."[152] (Once again there is the association of desertion with adultery.)

[148] It is interesting that Cranmer reinforced his claim for adultery to be allowed as a ground for divorce by arguing that it was "certainly of a higher nature" than desertion, which he thought justified divorce in at least some circumstances. This ranking of adultery and desertion differs from that of Reformers like Zwingli.

[149] Cited in Lewis Dibdin and Charles E.H. Chadwyck Healey, *English Church Law and Divorce* (London, 1912), 68.

[150] Thomas Becon, "An Homily Against Whoredom" (1547), in John Ayre (ed.), *The Catechism of Thomas Becon* (Cambridge, 1884), 643.

[151] Thomas Becon, "The Acts of Christ and Antichrist, Concerning both the Life and the Doctrine," in John Ayre (ed.), *Prayers and Other Pieces of Thomas Becon* (Cambridge, 1844), 532.

[152] Ibid.

2 Reformers and divorce: Theory and practice

Becon's quite literal interpretation of the divorce texts of the Bible, and the restrictive doctrine he elicited from them, contrasted with most of the Reformers but closely resembled that of John Hooper, bishop of Gloucester. Hooper began with the proposition that marriage had two purposes, procreation and the avoidance of fornication, and this emphasis on the sexual aspects of marriage goes some way to explaining his restriction of the grounds for divorce to that of adultery. Divorce, he wrote, could be justified only for reason of adultery, "because my book maketh no mention of any other."[153] In the context of Reformed divorce doctrines this in itself was a conservative position, but Hooper went to lengths to justify the equality of wife and husband in relation to adultery and divorce. Many of the sixteenth-century writers did not make it clear whether they considered adultery by the husband to be as serious as adultery by the wife, and we are often left to make what we can of examples that frequently refer only to the wife as the offending party. According to Hooper, many writers held firmly to the double standard of sexual morality in this respect: He referred to "the state of all this controversy between my contraries and me"[154] on the issue. For his own part, Hooper insisted on the equal commitment of each spouse in respect of sexual fidelity: "The man breaketh as well the bonds of matrimony by his giving the use of his body to an harlot, as the woman the use of her body to an adulterer."[155] The arguments of those (unnamed) who claimed sexual privileges for men were denied by Hooper at extraordinary length. Adultery aside, the only ground he would even countenance for divorce was desertion by an unbeliever of a believing spouse, a strict interpretation of the Pauline Privilege.[156]

In either case, adultery or desertion by an unbeliever, Hooper pointed out, the consequent divorce did not infringe the injunction that man could not put asunder those whom God had joined together:

Man dissolveth not the matrimony but the person's self that offendeth; and the magistrate is but a testimony of his or her ill fact, that hath broken and dissolved that that God coupled, and protesteth to the world that they, thus dissolved, may marry again, notwithstanding the former marriage.[157]

Even so, divorce was to be undertaken only as a last resort. Where one of the spouses was guilty of adultery, they should "attempt all manner of means, secretly between them both, to amend the fault." If that did not work they should "solicitate the same by honest arbiters and godly friends; and in the mean time, the innocent party to pray diligently unto God for the party that is in the lapse." Only if these efforts proved unsuccessful should the innocent party

---

[153] John Hooper, "A Declaration of the Ten Holy Commandments of Almighty God" (1548), in Samuel Carr (ed.), *Early Writings of John Hooper, D. D.* (Cambridge, 1843), 382.
[154] Ibid.
[155] Ibid.
[156] Ibid.
[157] Ibid.

appeal to the magistrates to punish the adulterous spouse and set the innocent one free "civilly in the world. . . as the crime and fault hath already sundered them before God."[158]

Although it is clear that not all English Reformers were in favor of permitting divorce, those who were tended to be prominent theologians. In view of this, and of the decision in the case of Northampton, and even allowing for the brief period of Catholic reaction during the reign of Queen Mary, it is still surprising that divorce was not made available from the English secular or ecclesiastical courts in the sixteenth century. Yet it was not for want of trying. In 1543 Henry VIII set up a commission of thirty-two men (eight each being bishops, divines, laymen, and lawyers) to draft a reform of the canon law in light of Anglican doctrine. The commission was renewed in 1550 under King Edward VI and during the 1550s it produced a draft revision of church legislation, the *Reformatio Legum Ecclesiasticarum*. Among the commissioners responsible for the direction of the text of the *Reformatio Legum*, Archbishop Cranmer and Peter Martyr are thought to have been particularly influential.[159]

In the present context the most important section of the *Reformatio Legum Ecclesiasticarum* is that entitled "De Adulteriis et Divortiis," which argued that divorce could be allowed on a number of grounds. It specified that when one spouse was guilty of adultery the innocent party should be allowed to divorce and remarry, but only after a six-month period had elapsed so as to give the couple an opportunity for reconciliation. The adulterous spouse would not be permitted to remarry. Divorce would also be justified for reason of desertion or absence without news, with the qualification that the deserted partner could not remarry for two or three years. If a remarriage did take place but the absent spouse subsequently returned, then the first (dissolved) marriage was to take precedence and the second would be declared null. It is not clear whether this provision would operate in all cases, for the *Reformatio Legum* also prescribed life imprisonment for desertion and for prolonged absence that could not be satisfactorily explained.

These grounds for divorce – adultery and desertion – were a Protestant orthodoxy, as we have seen, so it is interesting to note that the *Reformatio Legum* went even further and permitted divorce where one spouse was the victim of deadly hostility or violent treatment on the part of the other. "Deadly hostility" referred to attempted murder:

If deadly hostility should arise between husband and wife, and become inflamed to such an intensity that one attack the other, either by treacherous means or by poison, and should wish to take his life in some way, either by open violence or by hidden malice, we

---

[158] Ibid.
[159] On the *Reformatio Legum Ecclesiasticarum*, see M. A. R. Graves and R. H. Silcock, *Revolution, Reaction and the Triumph of Conservatism: English History 1558–1700* (Auckland, 1984), 358–9; Norman L. Jones, "An Elizabethan Bill for the Reformation of the Ecclesiastical Law," *Parliamentary History* 4 (1985), 171–87; and Dibdin and Healey, *English Church Law*, 68ff. The following account draws principally on these sources.

ordain that, as soon as so horrible a crime can be proved, such persons should be by law separated by divorce in the courts.[160]

As for ill-treatment, the *Reformatio Legum* specified that "should a man be violent to his wife and display excessive harshness of word and deed in dealing towards her," he should be admonished and cautioned to "treat her as the intimate union of marriage requires." If the husband failed to improve his behavior, the wife should be able to obtain a divorce. This provision did not abrogate the legal authority vested in husbands to administer "moderate correction" to their wives who were "rebellious, obstinate, petulant, scolds and of evil behaviour."[161] (The concept of "moderate correction" and attitudes toward it are discussed in Section 9.3).

None of these grounds for divorce implied the automatic dissolution of marriage (for which Northampton had argued earlier). Divorce and permission to remarry could be granted only by a judge of the ecclesiastical court. In addition, lest there were misunderstandings, the draft reform of church law specified those grounds that did *not* justify divorce: trifling disagreements, incurable disease, adultery by one spouse at the instigation of the other, and instances where both spouses were guilty of adultery. Neither could such grounds be invoked to secure a separation *a mensa et thoro*; separations would be abolished as being contrary to scripture.

Had they been given legal effect, these draft revisions of canon law would have given the Anglican church and England a more liberal divorce policy than any European church or country. Yet despite the efforts of Cranmer, and later of John Foxe, the provisions of the *Reformatio Legum* remained a dead letter. They were discussed briefly in Parliament, but proved to be too liberal to be acceptable. When the first systematic revision of the canon law of the Anglican church was promulgated in 1604, it permitted separations *a mensa et thoro*, but explicitly ruled out the possibility of divorce (see Section 3.3).

2.8 Conclusion: Divorce and Protestantism

This chapter has surveyed the principal Protestant writers on divorce in western and northern Europe during the sixteenth century. It has attempted not only to set down the content of the divorce doctrines of the most important and influential Reformers but also to examine the development of these doctrines and some of the considerations of which they took account. If the account has seemed at times belabored, it is because the Reformers themselves – Luther and Calvin are good examples – worked out their doctrines on divorce only slowly, with difficulty, and, above all, with great reluctance. This chapter has also given attention to the practical aspects of the doctrines, insofar as divorce legislation was put in place in various Protestant states, each influenced by the

---

[160] Quoted in A. R. Winnett, *Divorce and Remarriage in Anglicanism* (London, 1958), 32–3.
[161] Ibid.

2.8 Conclusion: Divorce and Protestantism

divorce policies of its dominant reformer: Calvin in Geneva, and indirectly in Scotland, the Netherlands and France, Zwingli in Zurich, and so on. At this point, having established the basic data on the Reformers, their ideas on divorce and their laws, it should be possible to make some general statements about divorce during the Reformation.

Perhaps the first point to note is that although the major Reformers were at one in rejecting fundamental tenets of Roman Catholic marriage doctrine, they varied, sometimes markedly, when it came to dealing with divorce. They agreed that marriage was not a sacrament, and they unanimously attributed to marriage a higher status than it had had in Catholic doctrine, where it had been subordinated to celibacy. Yet for all this we cannot say that the reformed churches agreed in rejecting the doctrine of the indissolubility of marriage. The Anglican church was the most notable exception to the general rule that the Protestants permitted divorce, although within that church, as we have seen and shall see further in the next chapter, there was a vigorous and important body of opinion in favor of legalizing divorce.

The admissibility of divorce should not be regarded as a logical consequence of the elaboration of Protestant marriage doctrines, for the Reformers rejected the doctrine of marital indissolubility far more hesitantly than they abandoned other key elements of Catholic marriage doctrine. As we have seen, in England Archbishop Cranmer began as a nondissolubilist but was converted to the position of allowing divorce for reason of adultery after his examination of the Northampton case. That he was subsequently influential in drawing up the wide-ranging provisions of the *Reformatio Legum Ecclesiasticarum* suggests that his views were later further liberalized. Cranmer was far from alone in traveling what appeared to be the tortuous road that led from the nondissolubilist to the dissolubilist position. Luther himself began by writing that "as to divorce, it is still a question for debate whether it is allowable,"[162] before deciding that it was. Most of the Reformers, indeed, give the impression of having decided in favor of divorce only with the greatest reluctance. Their strictures against the Catholic doctrine of marital indissolubility were expressed in tones far more subdued than their condemnations of such practices as the annulment of marriages, celibacy, and the sacramentality of marriage. It is not that the Reformers felt themselves to be on doctrinally uncertain ground in advocating the permissibility of divorce, but more, perhaps, that they felt no great pleasure in reaching the dissolubilist stance. Their reluctance in this respect is a point to which we shall return shortly.

Within the broad themes of the divorce doctrines developed by the Protestants there were both common features and significant variations. One shared characteristic was an emphasis on divorce being justified only by matrimonial fault. This was thought of as an offense committed by one spouse, not so much, perhaps, against his or her partner, as against their marriage itself.

---

[162] Luther, *Babylonian Captivity*, 105–6.

2 Reformers and divorce: Theory and practice

Within this general position, there was an emphasis on the crime of adultery, the only ground that was common to all divorce doctrines and legislation. Adultery was the matrimonial offense par excellence. It was not only an offense in its own right but could also be fundamental to, or implied by, other offenses as well. Calvin, Beza, and others brought adultery and desertion into an intimate relationship.

Adultery did not have such a status in Catholic marriage doctrine. Although it was a sin punishable by the church courts, it had no special status as a matrimonial offense. It could, indeed, be invoked to justify a separation *a mensa et thoro*, but in this respect it was only one of several justifying offenses or circumstances, and there was no sense in which it was considered the fundamental ground upon which other grounds might rely for their significance. We must, then, confront the question of why adultery was considered by the Reformers to have been preeminent as an offense, having a unique status in their divorce doctrines.

The most evident explanation is the fact that adultery was the only ground for divorce explicitly and unambiguously admitted by a biblical text. The fact that the reference to divorce in Mark and Luke did not mention the exception of adultery did not matter: As Cranmer noted, "it is enough that St. Matthew has it." The Protestant emphasis on adultery in respect to divorce, then, reflected the greater reliance on scripture, rather than on tradition and authority, that was characteristic of the Protestant theologians. We see this taken further among the Radical Protestants, who refused to go even as far as Luther and Calvin in extrapolating from the Bible.

Another part of the explanation for the stress on adultery must lie with the Reformers' notions as to the ends or purposes of marriage. In general these did not differ from the Catholic position, which attributed to marriage the prime purpose of procreation. The secondary purpose was to provide an acceptable context for sexual activity or, as it was often expressed, marriage was a "remedy for fornication." The third purpose of marriage, generally cited in Protestant writings, referred to the mutual companionship, help, and social obligations that marriage fostered between wife and husband. The conservatism of most of the major Reformers in this respect was clear. Luther and Calvin accepted the conventional ordering of the purposes of marriage, and their doctrines were echoed throughout the Reformation generally. For Melanchthon, wedlock was "the lawfull and perpetual joyning together of one man with one woman, instituted by God to bringe forthe frute, and is ordered to avoyde lustes forboden according to this scripture."[163] Peter Martyr listed the purposes of marriage as "for the increasing of children, for the taking away of whoredome, and that thereby the life of man might have helpes and commodities."[164]

Some of the Reformers did diverge from the conventional ranking of the

[163] Melanchton, *A Very godly defence*, sig. A V[R].
[164] Peter Martyr, *Common Places*, 418.

86

2.8 Conclusion: Divorce and Protestantism

ends of marriage, but they were a minority. Bullinger's views appeared to undergo an evolution. In one work he listed the ends as procreation, the avoidance of fornication and third "to conforte, maintayne, helpe, counsaill, to clense, to further unto good manners, honestie and shamefastnesse, to expell unclennesse, avaunce the honoure of God and the publique welth, and to set up many other vertues more."[165] Yet in a later work, Bullinger altered the ranking: "Ye first cause whie wedlocke was instituted, is mans commoditie, that thereby the life of man might be the pleasaunter and more commodious"; the second cause was "the begetting of children for the preservation of mankind by increase, and the bringing of them uppe in the feare of the Lorde," while the third was avoidance of fornication.[166]

The principal exception among the Protestants, though, was Martin Bucer, whose views were outlined earlier but may be recalled at this point. For him the ends of marriage were neither procreation nor licit copulation, but "the communicating of all duties, both divine and humane, each to other, with utmost benevolence and affection."[167] Bucer's exclusive focus, then, was on the social and affective aspects of marriage, rather than on the sexual.

Bucer aside, Protestant marriage doctrines directly linked the ends of marriage to sexuality – the obligations of procreation and chaste (i.e., marital) sexual intercourse. For this reason, not to mention the scriptural references, adultery was considered as the most serious matrimonial offense in that it struck at the prime and essential quality of marriage. It is quite clear that divorce doctrines should in this way reflect marriage doctrines. Offenses against aspects of marriage that were considered central to it should be more likely to give rise to divorce than offenses against aspects of marriage that were marginal. No doubt it was principally for this reason that the divorce doctrines of the Reformers (Bucer again excepted) did not go so far as to permit divorce in social or emotional circumstances such as temperamental incompatibility. Emotional compatibility, respect, companionship, and love were all considered desirable elements of marriage, but their absence or decline did not threaten the existence of an individual marriage. As we have seen, various Reformers maintained that if spouses in conflict could not reconcile their differences, they should bear their unhappiness as a cross. Again, Martin Bucer provided a contrast with the majority of the Reformers by making friendship and companionship the main purpose of marriage. To this extent incompatibility between spouses undid the very essence of marriage, and Bucer quite logically permitted divorce for this reason. Equally logically, the other Reformers did not.

The Reformers' emphasis on the sexual side of marriage and on adultery in the context of divorce must also be considered as part of the general Protestant attitude toward sexuality. The Protestants were much occupied with the horrors

---

[165] Bullinger, *Christen State of Matrimonye*, 33ᵛ.
[166] Bullinger, *Fiftie Godlie and Learned Sermons*, 224–6.
[167] Bucer, *De Regno Christi*, translated as part of *The Judgement of Martin Bucer*, in *Complete Prose Works of John Milton* (8 vols., New Haven, 1966–82), II, 465.

87

of illicit sexual activity, whether premarital, nonmarital, or extramarital. They were convinced that the corruptions of the Roman Catholic church, by preventing marriages by appeal to impediments, and counseling celibacy for those who possessed the "gift" of lifelong sexual abstinence, had led to a decline in sexual morality. The English theologian Thomas Becon was certainly the most quotable Reformer in his denunciations of illicit sexuality under the regime of the Catholic church, with his fulminations against the "stinking puddle of whoredom," and "the outrageous seas of adultery, whoredom, fornication, and uncleanness, [which] have not only brast in, but have overflowed almost the whole world."[168] Others might have lacked Becon's style, but their sentiments lacked none of his vigor. Bullinger declared adultery to be a "hyghe dishonoure of the ordinance of God, a wickednesse grown out of the devell yvilnesse of the flesh, a shameful unfaithfulness, a wilfull truce breaking and periury."[169] Even so, he regarded simple adultery as less serious than rape, incest, sodomy or "medling with beastes" (they might all be considered aggravated adultery – as later divorce laws would do – when they were committed by a married man), which were to be punished by death in this world and by "fire and stinking brimstone" in the next.[170]

Many of the Reformers explicitly justified divorce for reason of adultery by appeal to the Old Testament injunction that an adulteress should be put to death. Some explicitly included male offenders within the purview of this principle, whereas others seem to have held to the sexually discriminatory form of the original. Whatever the decision on this issue, divorce was to be the sixteenth century's functional substitute for the death penalty, casting the adulterous spouse into the state of being divorced yet unable to remarry, a dangerous limbo between marriage and celibacy. As we have seen, there were expressions of regret in the sixteenth century that the old laws, prescribing death for adultery, had fallen into disuse. Calvin was far from being alone in lamenting "the perverted indulgence of magistrates" that made it necessary for men to divorce their unfaithful wives.[171] Becon's typically extreme view was that "although death of the body seemeth to us a grievous punishment in this world for whoredom, yet it is pain nothing in comparison of the grievous torments which adulterers, fornicators, and all unclean persons shall suffer after this life."[172] It is noteworthy that adultery was made a capital offense for a time in sixteenth-century Geneva, in Münster under the leadership of John of Leyden, and in Scotland.

All of these considerations contributed to the attention given to adultery in the divorce writings of the Protestants: the explicit references to adultery as justifying divorce in the Bible, the continuity of emphasis on the sexual aspects

[168] Becon, *Homily*, 643.
[169] Bullinger, *Christen State of Matrimonye*, 44[R].
[170] Bullinger, *Fiftie Godlie and Learned Sermons*, 235–6.
[171] Calvin, *Commentaries*, II, 247.
[172] Becon, *Homily*, 649.

of marriage within Protestant doctrines, and a strong belief in the corruption of their times and the need for a reaffirmation of the values they believed had been undermined or forgotten by the Roman Catholic church.

To the extent that other obligations and duties were less critical or central than the sexual to the existence of marriage, failure to honor and fulfill them was that much less likely to provide a reason for divorce. The duty of cohabitation was considered important enough for most of the Reformers to allow desertion as a ground for divorce, but only after elaborate efforts had been made to persuade the deserter to return, and after a long time had elapsed from the time of desertion. Even then, men like Calvin seem to have been sufficiently ambivalent about the seriousness of desertion per se that they attempted to bring it into a close relationship with adultery, the prime matrimonial offense, before allowing it as a ground for divorce.

Cruelty of any kind seems to have been ignored by the divorce doctrines that have been discussed, with the notable exception of the English *Reformatio Legum Ecclesiasticarum* (and it was notable partly because it failed to be translated into law). Wife beating, which was doubtless the most widespread form of marital ill-treatment, was rarely condemned, either explicitly or implicitly. Even the *Reformatio Legum Ecclesiasticarum* was careful to specify that the ability of women to divorce would not imply a reduction of men's power of "moderate correction" over their wives. Such neglect of cruelty as a matrimonial offense was quite consistent with the prevailing social attitudes toward the relationship of husband and wife, which specified the latter's inferiority and her duty of obedience. This was the message Martin Luther conveyed to a man whose wife had refused to accompany him when he moved home from Württemburg to Zwickau:

Your lord and mistress has not yet come to see me, and thus her disobedience to you displeases me greatly. Indeed, I am beginning to be somewhat put out with you too, for by your softheartedness you have turned into tyranny that Christian service which you owe her, and you have hitherto so encouraged her that it would seem to be your own fault that she ventures to defy you in everything. Certainly when you saw that the fodder was making the ass indolent (that is, that your wife was becoming unmanageable as a result of your indulgence and submissiveness), you should have remembered that you ought to obey God rather than your wife, and so you should not have allowed her to despise and trample underfoot that authority of the husband which is the glory of God, as Saint Paul teaches.[173]

Heinrich Bullinger referred to corporal punishment of the wife in terms that were certainly not disapproving, even if they did not positively encourage it: "Somtyme yf the husband be displeased, then the wife with spitefull wordes and wanton fashions, provoketh him to more anger. Some had rather have theyr back full of strypes, then to holde theyr tonge and forbeare a little."[174] Martin

---

[173] Luther, *Letters* (April 12, 1528), 277.
[174] Bullinger, *Christen State of Matrimonye*, 69[R].

Bucer included physical violence among the grounds he would admit for divorce, but even then he placed the wife in a subordinate position vis-à-vis her husband and did not condemn wife beating with anything like the explicitness and vigor of, say, Henry Smith at the end of the sixteenth century or of some of the next century's writers on domestic issues (see Section 9.3).[175]

The absence of ill-treatment and emotional incompatibility from the Protestant divorce doctrines should not be read as implying that they gave little or no thought to these matters. They were still considered important enough to be concerns of the spiritual and secular authorities, as is shown by the various regulations giving the authorities the right to oversee domestic relations and, where necessary, intervene to attempt to conciliate between hostile spouses. Discord and violence within marriage were deplored, and attempts were made to correct them, but their presence did not affect the essence of matrimony as it was understood by the Reformers. The existence of adultery and, less unambiguously, desertion, did affect marriage significantly. Hence their status as grounds for divorce in Protestant doctrines.

Much of our understanding of divorce in the sixteenth century must turn upon the way divorce was conceived of at that time. Divorce was not thought of primarily as a remedy for marital breakdown in the modern sense of the term, which concerns itself with the functional aspects of the marriage process. Rather, the sixteenth-century emphasis was principally, though not exclusively, on the behavior of the individual partners. Divorce was not a response to the state of a particular marriage, in this respect, but rather to a matrimonial offense. Only secondarily was it a response to the effect of a matrimonial offense upon the marriage and upon the relationship between husband and wife. Divorce, then, was grounded primarily on the concept of matrimonial fault. As Max Rheinstein has written, "the new institution of divorce [i.e., from the time of the Reformation] was thus started on the path of that principle of marital offense by which it is still dominated in the major part of the United States and in a great many other parts of the world of Christian tradition."[176]

Such was the emphasis on fault in the Protestant doctrines that there was great care to ensure that one spouse, the petitioner for divorce, was demonstrably innocent. Most of the divorce doctrines and legal codes ruled out the possibility of divorce where, for example, both spouses were guilty of adultery. Dissolution of marriage was not thought of as a remedy for marriage breakdown as such but as a punishment for a matrimonial crime and as a relief for the victim of the crime (the innocent spouse). In this view, divorce was clearly inappropriate where both husband and wife were guilty. The issue of remarriage was relevant here, too. Many of the divorce laws permitted remarriage only on the part of the innocent spouse. Where both had been guilty, remarriage of either would have been excluded, and to have divorced two guilty

---

[175] See Bucer in Milton, *Prose Works*, II, 463.
[176] Max Rheinstein, *Marriage Stability, Divorce and the Law* (Chicago, 1972), 23.

spouses in such circumstances would have produced the effect of a separation *a mensa et thoro*, separation without the right of remarriage.

Yet for all their emphasis on matrimonial offense, the focus of the Protestant divorce doctrines was not exclusively on the attribution of fault. There were, in the first place, provisions for divorce where strict fault could not be attributed. An example was the circumstance where one spouse was absent, but where there was no evidence that he or she had maliciously deserted or had willfully remained away from home. Divorces in cases such as these (they have been referred to earlier in this chapter) did not rest necessarily upon deliberate actions on the part of one spouse, although the absent partner might be thought of as the active party in producing the circumstances. In these cases, where we might prefer to talk about "responsibility" rather than "fault," the focus of the divorce provisions seems to have been on the state of the marriage, of its termination in social terms that was the result of one spouse's absence. Divorce in such cases of absence – which could be occasioned by imprisonment in war, shipwreck, or prolonged illness – has more the appearance of being a substitute death certificate for the missing spouse rather than a statement of the marriage's breakdown in a moral sense. In the absence of evidence that the missing person was dead, and yet despite lack of evidence that he or she had maliciously deserted, a divorce decree could be granted, freeing the remaining spouse to enter a new marriage. In such cases there might well have been a presumption that the absent person was indeed dead, and no doubt this was the case quite often; here divorced status took on the appearance of a surrogate widowhood, permitting remarriage. Some divorce codes, such as the Swedish law, provided for the divorce in such circumstances to be voided if the missing spouse did return, as long as he or she could prove that the absence had not been deliberate, and that it had been impossible to get news to the spouse who had been left. If the remaining spouse had remarried following the divorce, then the remarriage was annulled under Swedish law, and the first marriage was reinstated as the legal one.

Simple absence, then, and especially unavoidable absence, cannot be regarded as a matrimonial offense of the same order as adultery and willful desertion. Nor were madness and leprosy, which were admitted as grounds for divorce by Zwingli. Bucer, again, was exceptional: His stress on incompatibility deflected attention from the specific offenses or grievances of one spouse or the other and focused on the state of the conjugal relationship.

Yet even where the emphasis of the divorce doctrines was quite unequivocally on a matrimonial offense such as adultery, attention was also given to the state of the marriage in question. Most of the divorce codes excluded an automatic right to divorce in the face of a demonstrable matrimonial offense. Most provided for attempts at reconciliation, and some for compulsory periods of cohabitation, even when one spouse had been found guilty of adultery. In cases of desertion there were stipulations for attempts to be made to locate the deserter and to persuade him or her to return and make good the marriage.

Only when these attempts at reconciliation had failed might a divorce be granted, and this evidences concern for the condition of the marriage and the ability of the spouses to continue their marital relationship.

Thus, if we look beyond the simple grounds for divorce, to the actual procedures, we see that the Protestant divorce doctrines went further than setting the course of Western divorce on its path of matrimonial fault. Even apart from Martin Bucer's contribution, the mainstream Protestant Reformation doctrines did pay some attention to the ability of a marriage to function, and of husbands and wives to resolve their problems, as well as to the commission of matrimonial offenses. This was true not only in the context of their general attitudes toward marriage but within the divorce provisions themselves. The issue of fault, it is true, triggered the possibility of divorce, and determined which spouse should be the petitioner and which the defendant. But the final disposition of a divorce petition – whether it was granted or refused by the appropriate court – often depended directly not on the simple existence of the offense but on the ability or inability of the couple to achieve a reconciliation and to regain harmony within their marriage. Only where the reconciliation proved impossible, where the offense had produced irreversible stresses within the marriage, was divorce granted. In such circumstances we are, arguably, not as far from the modern concept of divorce as a response to marriage breakdown, as the division of factors between "fault" and "no-fault" might suggest.

This brings us back to an issue raised earlier, namely, the reluctance with which divorce was allowed. This refers not only to the reluctance the Reformers evinced in permitting divorce at all but also to the clear hesitancy of the judges and other officials to grant divorces. The latter has been noted in several studies of the divorce courts of the sixteenth century, and seems evident in the simple statistics of the proportion of divorce petitions that were successful. For example, 28 out of 80 divorce petitions were successful in Zurich between 1525 and 1531, and 125 out of 226 in Basel between 1550 and 1592.[177] These represented success rates (success, that is, from the perspective of the petitioners) of 35% and 55%, respectively. In Zwickau the rate was so low that "divorce was practically as hard to obtain from the Protestant regime as it had been from the Catholic."[178] Nuremberg was yet another example. Although the city was Lutheran in its confessional allegiance, its administrators were afraid of the consequences that might flow from the legalization of divorce. Only after decades of pressure from the Lutheran clergy was divorce (for adultery and desertion) made available to Nuremberg's population.[179]

A reading of the literature gives the very strong, if paradoxical, impression

---

[177] Statistics for Zurich and Basel are from Safley, "To Preserve the Marital State," 172–3. See also Karant-Nunn, "Continuity and Change," 32–3.

[178] Ibid., 32.

[179] Judith W. Harvey, "The Influence of the Reformation on Nuremberg Marriage Laws, 1520–1535," (unpub. Ph.D. dissertation, Ohio State University, 1972), 90–100, cited in Ozment, *When Fathers Ruled*, 92.

that sixteenth-century divorce doctrines and laws did not focus on divorce at all, but on marriage. There were often provisions, within the context of divorce principles, for the supervision of marriages as a precautionary measure, so that dissensions and open conflict between spouses might be dealt with by conciliation or punishment before they became too serious. But even when a divorce petition had been lodged there were, as we have noted, legal mechanisms designed to maximize the possibility of reconciliation, and thus to avert a divorce. Only when these measures had proved unsuccessful was a dissolution of marriage granted. At this point the emphasis switched to the formation of new marriage. The *Ehegericht* of Basel was not alone in making divorce difficult to obtain, but, once having agreed to a divorce, in facilitating and encouraging an early remarriage.

Clearly, the overriding concern of the authorities was to preserve the integrity of individual marriages. If that were not possible, then they sought to preserve the integrity of marriage as an institution, by providing a second as a replacement for that which had been dissolved. In this respect the discontinuity between Roman Catholic and Protestant doctrines of marriage becomes less distinct than the nondissolubilist – dissolubilist dichotomy might suggest. To be sure, there was an important difference in the means employed, but the reluctance of the Catholic church's courts to act in separations *a mensa et thoro* and in annulments of marriages, which has been documented by scholars such as Helmholz, is strongly reminiscent of the policy that the courts of the Protestant states apparently applied in respect of divorce.

The critical difference, arguably, was the greater importance attributed to marriage that was implied by divorce. This is why we might say that divorce doctrines concerned marriage as much as they did divorce per se. The Catholic church was prepared to separate spouses for reasons such as adultery, and to leave them in the ambiguous status of being married in legal terms – so that neither was able to contract another marriage while the other was still alive – yet of being not married in the social sense of sharing social and sexual activities with an exclusive partner. This ambiguity implied by separation *a mensa et thoro* struck the Reformers as being intolerable to the spouses concerned and as dangerous to society. They conceived of marriage as an important weapon in the constant battle of Christians against evil. Marriage, an institution ordained by God, had the ability of containing carnal sins and of being a forum wherein virtues might be practiced. Through marriage, men and women had a real opportunity for salvation. Indeed, marriage was not only an instrument that would reinforce Christian values, it could also be a means of converting Catholics to a true faith. Calvin advised a Protestant woman who was being harassed by her Catholic husband that she should endure persecution bravely and not desert the hostile, unbelieving partner, because there was always the possibility that he would be converted.[180]

---

[180] Blaisdell, "Calvin's Letters to Women," 71.

2 Reformers and divorce: Theory and practice

Outside marriage, on the other hand, single and separated men and women were subject to all of the temptations that marriage could help them to resist, and therein lay the core of the Protestant objection to celibacy, as well. From this perspective, the provision of divorce was a measure of the important role that the Protestant reformers attributed to marriage and the family in the maintenance of the moral and social order. Recognizing that there would inevitably be sin, that some vices practiced within marriage were unredeemable, they believed that the marriages made possible by divorce (remarriages) would contribute more to the totality of morality, just as enforced celibacy and separated men and women detracted from it.

In a broader context, the roles and values prescribed within marriage were linked to general social stability. The writings of men like Erasmus, Vives, Bullinger, and Agrippa in praise of matrimony stressed the value of marriage not only to the individuals and families involved, but also to society. To the Catholic schoolmen marriage had been an ecclesiastical matter, unworldly, and much inferior to celibacy. "For the renaissance humanists, however, matrimony was coming to be a worldly affair that gave spiritual meaning and moral value to the social order."[181] This shift from the Roman Catholic doctrines gave marriage much more significance and a higher value. Both of these qualities were evident in the Protestant writings that led to the acceptance of divorce where God's presciptions for marital behavior were ignored.

We may conclude generally that the Protestant attitudes toward divorce, and the Protestant laws dealing with it, broke significantly with their Roman Catholic precedents, yet were informed by many of the same values and some of the same fundamental moral orientations.[182] This paradoxical character of Protestant divorce reflected the paradox of divorce itself. Divorce has generally been seen as detrimental to the family: nothing seems at first sight more evident that a process that dissolves a marriage is a negative one. To advocate the ability to divorce is easily interpreted as a desire to weaken marriage as an institution. Yet there is an argument to be made that permission to divorce in the Protestant Reformation reflected a higher estimation of marriage, a shift in emphasis away from the forms of marriage to its content, to the quality of the marriage for those involved. This distinction between form and content emerged in starker forms in the eighteenth century and later. In the sixteenth century the Protestants were groping toward a broader conception of marriage than Roman Catholic doctrines and laws had embodied. But they were still too close to the breach with Rome to be able to shed entirely the unease inspired by the conclusions about divorce to which the logic of their social theology drove them.

---

[181] John K. Yost, "The Value of Married Life for the Social Order in the Early English Renaissance," *Societas* 6 (1976), 25–39.

[182] Safley puts it this way: The canons of the Council of Trent and the Protestant divorce reforms "were isolated elements in a far larger marital code, which remained unchanged upon both sides of the religious division of the period." *Let No Man Put Asunder,* 38.

3

Seventeenth-century England: Divorce frustrated

3.1 Introduction

By the beginning of the seventeenth century, what might be thought of as the divorce map of Europe had taken shape. Absent from the Iberian peninsula, France, and Italy, and wherever else the Catholic church remained dominant after the Reformation, divorce was nonetheless available in almost all those states where Protestant confessions had been entrenched, especially in Germany, Switzerland, Scotland, and Scandinavia. The major exception to this pattern was England, where divorce remained unobtainable despite the breach between the English church and Rome (a breach forced, ironically, by a dispute involving Henry VIII's desire to escape his marriage from Catherine of Aragon), and despite the support that divorce had received from important English theologians and ecclesiastical lawyers. This exceptional character makes England in the seventeenth century an especially interesting phase in the history of divorce. Although the divorce debate was settled one way or the other by the end of the sixteenth century in the rest of Europe (though it was to be reopened during the Enlightenment), it continued and even intensified in England in the first half of the seventeenth century, as the advocates of divorce persisted in arguing their case against a reluctant church.

Moreover, the seventeenth century constituted an important period of transition in terms of divorce. It began with the promulgation of canon laws of the Anglican church that ruled out divorce, but by the end of the century a procedure had developed to permit marriages to be dissolved by private Act of Parliament. This was an expensive and restrictive means of divorce that nonetheless continued to be the only means of divorce in England until the middle of the nineteenth century. As unsatisfactory as it was in many respects, legislative divorce was one way out of the impasse created by the refusal of the Anglican church to give up the doctrine of marital indissolubility.

Finally, as well as seeing this limited movement in the availability of divorce in England, the seventeenth century witnessed the spread of European notions of divorce beyond Europe. Ironically it was England, recalcitrant in divorce policy, that was largely responsible for exporting divorce to the New World:

3 Seventeenth-century England

The Puritans who settled the New England colonies legalized divorce there from the 1620s. Thus, although England did not participate in the initial wave of divorce legislation that swept through Protestant Europe in the sixteenth century, its experience in the seventeenth was a significant transitional one that deserves particular attention.

Emphasis on marriage and the family in the seventeenth century is far from inappropriate. The family was one of the great moral, social, and political issues that preoccupied theologians, social critics, and other intellectuals of the time. The evidence of this lies in the hundreds of conduct-books, sermons, tracts, treatises, and theses devoted to all aspects of the family: marriage, divorce, parent – child relations, the status of women, family government, property, sexuality, and the duties of fathers, mothers, husbands, wives, and children.[1] The family was understood to be the basic unit of society, and order within the family was the guarantor of order within the society and government, a point made at the end of the last chapter. The vast literature on the family in the seventeenth century, then, had two thrusts. The first, the immediate one, was to define precisely the roles and relationships of members of the family household: how parents should behave toward children and wives toward husbands; the necessity of obedience and authority; the legitimate and illegitimate use of power. In short, the conduct books laid out a constitution for family government that would ensure that families functioned smoothly, each member knowing his or her place, roles, and duties in respect of other family members and the family as a whole.

The second thrust was indirect and bore upon government in a wider sense. The family was perceived as a little commonwealth, a microcosm of the larger

---

[1] There is an extensive literature on seventeenth-century attitudes toward the family. Much of it has focused on what was for a long time perceived as a peculiarly "Puritan" idelology of marital and familial relationships that stressed companionship and equality as distinct from a "non-Puritan" model of the family in which marriage was dominated by authoritarian and unaffectionate husbands. Works stressing the notion of a Puritan family ethic include C. L. Powell, *English Domestic Relations, 1487–1653* (New York, 1917); Levin L. Schücking, *The Puritan Family: A Social Study from the Literary Sources* (Leipzig, 1929, trans. Brian Battershaw and repr. London, 1969); W. Haller and M. Haller, "The Puritan Art of Love," *Huntington Library Quarterly* 5 (1941–2), 235–72; R. M. Frye, "The Teachings of Classical Puritanism on Conjugal Love," *Studies in the Renaissance* 2 (1955), 148–59. More recently scholars have pointed to the continuity of Puritan ideas with Catholic and early Protestant writing on marriage and the family. See, notably, Kathleen M. Davies, "'The Sacred Condition of Equality' – How Original Were Puritan Doctrines of Marriage?" *Social History* 5 (1977), 563–80, reprinted with revisions as "Continuity and Change in Literary Advice on Marriage," in R. B. Outhwaite (ed.), *Marriage and Society: Studies in the Social History of Marriage* (London, 1981), 58–80. The present study generally supports the view that the English Puritans were not particularly distinctive in their ideologies of marriage, and certainly not in their doctrines of divorce. The only area in which there does seem to have been unprecedented emphasis in the early seventeenth century is opposition to "moderate correction," or legally permitted violence against wives. (On this, see Section 9.3). I leave aside the issue of defining "Puritanism." It is important, however, not to make a sharp distinction between "Puritans" and "Anglicans," and to acknowledge the breadth of doctrinal positions within the Church of England. A useful discussion is J. F. A. New, *Anglican and Puritan. The Basis of their Opposition, 1558–1640* (Stanford, 1964).

society and polity. The patriarchal explanation of government propounded by men such as Richard Hooker and Robert Filmer, indeed, made the family the direct source and model of the political order.[2] Even in the attenuated form, which did not give so much emphasis to the power of the monarchs (and thus of the father in the family), the familial model of government was an attractive one. Individuals were born into families, as they were into political societies; they accepted their status in both, as well as in their rights and duties to govern or to obey. Moreover marriage and the family were ordained by God, so that the legitimation of the political order in familial terms gave the polity divine authority. For these reasons the family was of crucial importance: Upon its stability rested social and political stability; the breakdown of the family had implications far beyond its mundane effects on the women, children, and men concerned.

Integral to these considerations was religion. Marriage was ordained by God, the seventeenth-century writers argued, as were the familial relationships that derived from marriage. Men, women, and children within the family had opportunities on a daily basis to live according to God's commandments – in harmony and according to their place as defined by the constitution that defined their responsibilities and duties within the family. Behavior that ran counter to this – disobedience by wives toward husbands or children toward their parents or the abuse of their authority by husbands or parents – flouted God's commandments, and not only called into question the offender's godliness but also undermined the familial, social, and political order.[3]

3.2 Marriage breakdown in social thought

Given the importance attributed to the smooth functioning of the family, it is hardly surprising that writers on the issue regarded dysfunction, stress, or worse, marriage breakdown, with apprehension and fear. The failure of family members to conform to their ascribed roles was serious enough in any form – for children to disobey their parents or servants their masters. But the collapse of order within marriage was particularly alarming. In the first place, the married couple was the fundamental relationship, the primary dyad, of any given household, since each new household was formed by a marriage: The nuclear family was by far the dominant residential type, as many studies have shown.[4] Second, the relationship between husband and wife was more closely regulated than other relationships because the spouses, by marrying, had entered into a relationship ordained by God. Some writers on the subject, indeed,

---

[2] Robert Filmer, *Patriarcha...and Other Political Works of Sir Robert Filmer* (ed. Peter Laslett, Oxford, 1949); Richard Hooker, *Of the Laws of Ecclesiastical Polity* (2 vols., London, 1969).
[3] On the role of the family as an agent of political socialization in this period, see Gordon J. Schochet, "Patriarchalism and Mass Attitudes in Stuart England," *Historical Journal* 12 (1969), 413–41, and *Patriarchalism and Political Theory* (New York, 1975).
[4] The best collection is Peter Laslett, with Richard Wall, *Household and Family in Past Time* (Cambridge, 1972).

regarded marriage as a triad, uniting God, husband, and wife (in that order) in an indissoluble union. But even when commentators did not go this far, they nonetheless emphasized the special sanctity of marriage. Third, the maintenance of the conjugal order was regarded as especially important because the husband and wife were thought of as exemplars to other members of the family: If they could not order *their* relationship and carry out *their* duties, what hope had the rest?

Once we appreciate the religious, social, and political emphases placed on the family, especially on the married couple, and the attempts to ensure that it functioned smoothly, we can begin to understand why marriage breakdown was regarded with such horror. The failure of wives and husbands to carry out their duties and obligations to each other was one symptom of the chaos that the Fall had brought to the social and political order. Robert Abbot made this clear:

> You know that the first government that ever was in this world was in a family; and in the first disorder that ever was in the world was in a family; and all the disorders that ever fell out since, sprung from Families. If families had been better, Churches and Common-Wealths all along had prospered.[5]

The notions of order and government in marriage related not only to the classic marital obligations of sexual fidelity and cohabitation, but also to the many other duties set out in the conduct-books and other works in the seventeenth century. These can be summarized as the duties of the husband to love, assist, and guide his wife and for the wife to love, comfort, and obey her husband, and generally to be a "helpmeet" for him. Thus marriage failure in seventeenth-century terms included not only adultery and desertion but also such actions and circumstances as mutual or unilateral hatred or emotional indifference, violence, and slander, as well as disobedience on the part of the wife. These were recognized as failings, even by the writers who did not propose that they should be made grounds for divorce.

The concern expressed at the implications of marriage breakdown and domestic disorder was not merely academic. Many seventeenth-century writers, if we take their professions at face value, believed that husbands and wives were, on a grand scale, neglecting their duties and that marriage failure was a widespread and increasing occurrence. We find here, in short, the belief common to most periods that the commentator's age was especially marked by a decline in marriage, the family, and morals. Robert Abbot, subsequently bishop of Salisbury, preached the following in a 1608 wedding sermon:

> Nature, religion, fidelity, civilitie, equitie, all cry it out that the husband and the wife should walke together; and yet the cry of all these availeth not, but that lamentable ruptures and divisions betwixt husband and wife are everywhere to be seene amongst us,

---

[5] Robert Abbot, *A Christian Family Builded by God, Directing all Governours of Families how to act* (London, 1653), sig. A4R.

specially amongst men of higher place, yea so common in many places as if it were a thing out of fashion for great men and their wives to live and walk together.[6]

In midcentury, Daniel Rogers wrote of separations that:

The practice of the greater sort is so rife now adaies, that it grows common, among the inferior sort, and will be a sore incurable. A deserted Lady, or Gentlewoman, is become a common notion. As one sayd, now the dogs bark at the Masters of the family, when they return, as if they were absolute strangers: forgetting them, as they do their wives.[7]

Nor did assessments of the marital state of the nation improve, for later in the century Richard Allestree made the same point, albeit hyperbolically:

We see every day the slightest disgust now adays too strong for the matrimonial love, nay indeed it does of coyese fall off of it self, which is an event so much expected, that 'tis no wonder to see it expire with the first circuit of the moon; but it is every bodies admiration to see it last one of the sun.[8]

Such harking back to an earlier time of matrimonial bliss and stability had a theological foundation. It was not a matter of believing that marriage in the sixteenth century was more satisfactory than in the seventeenth, and certainly not *before* the sixteenth, when marriage was corrupted by popish practices. Rather, discord and unhappiness – "jarres" as they were often referred to – had entered marriage with the Fall and the beginning of sin. There are many echoes of Bucer's sentiments on this theme, which were cited earlier (see Section 2.5). John Sedgewick, for example, prefaced one of Thomas Taylor's works with the observation that "it now adaies falleth out in the corruption of our time of sinne, that the merry estate of marriage is altogether amongst most, marred."[9]

Such general attitudes to conjugal stress and marriage breakdown are clearly relevant to the issue of divorce. To what extent was divorce thought to be socially and theologically acceptable as a remedy for marriage breakdown or as a punishment for matrimonial offenses? If divorce were not permitted, what alternatives were offered? Questions such as these demanded the formulation of an etiology of matrimonial disharmony, analysis of its most common forms, and proposals for their correction or solution. Many works in seventeenth-century literature dealt with these issues, and because they bear directly on divorce, they provide a social and ideological context for a discussion of the divorce doctrines that were elaborated in the period.

Not surprisingly, sexual offenses were regarded as a prime area of moral decline: A preoccupation with illicit sexuality is almost synonymous with the

---

[6] Robert Abbot, *A Wedding Sermon preached at Bentley in Darbyshire, upon Michaelmass day last past Anno Domini 1607* (London, 1608), 49–50. Edmund Bunny also drew attention to marriage breakdown, especially among "the greatest" and "those of some note" in *Of Divorce for Adulterie, and Marrying Againe: That there is no warrant so to do* (Oxford, 1610), preface (no pagination).

[7] Daniel Rogers, *Matrimoniall Honour, or, the Mutuall Crowne and comfort of godly, loyall, and Chaste Marriage* (London, 1642), 218.

[8] Richard Allestree, *The Ladies Calling* (Oxford, 1673), 171–2.

[9] Thomas Taylor, *A Good Husband and a Good Wife* (London, 1625), sig. A2[R].

Puritanism that is often regarded as characteristic of the century, although, as we have seen, it was one of the preoccupations of the sixteenth century as well. Seventeenth-century literature made frequent reference to widespread fornication and lamented the lighthearted way in which it was treated, especially (it was said) by the young.[10] In contemporary terms, fornication often referred to premarital sex (rather than adultery), but it was given a relationship to marriage in two ways. First, too many marriages were said to have been entered for carnal reasons, men marrying women not for reasons of love, respect, and companionship, but primarily out of sexual lust. Second, it was argued that fornication before marriage led to adultery after marriage. As John Dod, a lecturer at Banbury, put it, premarital sex poisons the body and lingers within it, ready to break out into adultery after marriage:

An olde fornicator shall be a new adulterer, I mean by an old fornicator such an one that hath committed fornication before marriage without repentance, for he hath a wilde fire within, that will not keepe within long, but will make him burn in lust as fast as before.[11]

Unlike fornication, which was described as widespread, adultery tended to be condemned in more abstract terms. There is little explicit suggestion that it was a common offence, unless we are expected to deduce this from the causal connection between fornication and adultery. Much attention, however, was given to the consequences of adultery, a sin that merited fire and brimstone in the next world, even if the culprits escaped punishment in the present (and the latter, many commentators complained, was far too likely to be the case). Many writers expressed regret that adultery was not a capital offense and warned that God would punish the whole society that allowed adulterers to pursue their activities with impunity, or that treated adultery too leniently. Such was the complaint of Thomas Cartwright, among others. Adultery, Cartwright wrote,

doth not only waste the familie where it is, but maketh a breach unto the common wealth, whilest the right of inheritance either of landes, or offices, is oftentimes thus translated from the true inheritors: whilest the children which are so begotten, having oftentimes less care, and coste bestowed upon them in their education, become hurtefull members of the common wealth. Whereby all men may clearly see the perpetuall equitie of the lawe of God in the revengement of this sinne by death...for fault of exequuting his Judgement of death, he threateneth the whole common wealth, with mischief to fall upon it.[12]

This was part of the tradition that culminated in the 1650 Adultery Act, which prescribed the death penalty for adultery under certain circumstances (see Section 3.6).

---

[10] See, for example, Arthur Dent, *The Plaine Mans Path-way to Heaven* (16th impr., n. p., 1617), esp. 56ff.

[11] John Dod and Robert Cleaver, *A Treatise or Exposition upon the Ten Commandments* (London, 1603), f.54ᵛ. See also John Downame, *Four Treatises, Tending to Disswade all Christians from four no lesse hainous then common sinnes; namely, the abuses of Swearing, Drunkennesse, Whoredome, and Bribery* (London, 1652), 140.

[12] Thomas Cartwright, *The Second Replie of Thomas Cartwight Against Maister Doctor Whitgiftes second answer, touching the Church Discipline* (London, 1652), 101–2.

3.2 Marriage breakdown in social thought

Adultery was credited with a variety of social and personal results, summarized by John Dod and Robert Cleaver as "a diseased body, a poore estate, a blemished name, and damned soule, and the drawing and murdering of another soule." The diseases – the "French pox" and other venereal diseases – were not described in detail: They were "eating and incurable diseases," a plague "loathsome in the sight of man," "filthie diseases which bring the adulterer. . . to his death."[13] But as far as the majority of commentators were concerned, the most serious effects of adultery were familial rather than corporal: the introduction of bastards into the family. This emphasis reinforced the view that adultery by a married woman was more serious than adultery by a married man, since a child resulting from adulterous intercourse would take its place physically in the woman's household. The effect was that "a Spurious issue that robs the Husband by wholesale of his Estate, of all his own and his Ancestors Acquisition, is brought into his family. The Crime is then a Complication of all the Wickedness in Lust, Breach of Faith and Robbery."[14]

Sexual fidelity was one focus of seventeenth-century commentators on marriage. Companionship, with its associations of affection, consideration, and even love, was another. According to the literature, husbands and wives all too often fell short of the behavior that God expected of them. Robert Crofts was not alone in lauding the beneficial effects of marital love, as he simultaneously lamented its absence among his contemporaries:

Nuptiall Love and society sweetens all our Actions, discourse; all other pleasures, felicities, and even in all respects, Encreases true Joy and happinesse. . . [but] after Marriage it is strange to thinke, what Jealousies, Contentions, Feares, Sorrowes, strange Actions, Gestures, lookes, bitter words, outrages and debates, are between men and their wives for want of true love and discretion.[15]

Nathanial Hardy, too, pointed to the loss of love; most men, he wrote, "do not hate, and yet they do not love their wives, and in this the bare want of love is no small sinne."[16]

Failure to live together as husband and wife, sexual infidelity, lack of love and companionship: These were the main signs of trouble within marriage that the analysts identified. They are readily recognized as separation or desertion, adultery, and incompatibility. The commentators went on to define the fundamental and mediating causes of the stress and breakdown of marriage, ranging from the very general to the highly specific, from the economic to the sexual problems that could come between wife and husband. Together these writings constitute a fascinating body of literature on social pathology, and for this reason alone they deserve attention. But they are especially important here because they bear directly on the question of divorce.

---

[13] Dod and Cleaver, *Treatise or Exposition*, f. 56[R].

[14] *A Letter to a Member of Parliament with Two Discourses enclosed in it. The one shewing the Reason why a Law should pass to punish Adultery with Death* (London, 1675), 5.

[15] Robert Crofts, *The Lover: Or Nuptiall Love* (London, 1638), sigs. A8[V]–B1[R].

[16] Nathaniel Hardy, *Love and Fear. The Inseparable Twins of a Blest Matrimony* (London, 1658), 10.

The most general explanation of domestic discord – one on which all of the writers would have agreed, though many went a good deal further than it in their analyses – was that it was the devil's work. Marriage was, after all, one of God's institutions, and was a prime target for his wrecking rival: "For then did God create the world, first he made thinges, than he macht [matched] them; first hee created, and then he coupled them; of man and woman he made one in marriage . . . but then came the devill upon the stage, and his part was againe to divide what God had united."[17] Before the Fall, marriage could be nothing but harmonious, but "by sinne the case of marriage is much changed, and many cares and encumbrances and distractions are incident to the married estate."[18] Given mankind's propensity to sin, and therefore for marriages to fall short of replicating heavenly bliss on earth, the challenge for writers on marriage was to advise Christians as to what steps they should take to maximize the possibilities of a good marriage. Two approaches were taken: advice to the unmarried on how to select the best spouse and advice to the already married on how to increase harmony and happiness within their families. Both rested upon an understanding of the faults inherent in unsatisfactory marriages.

There emerged a ready consensus on advice to the unmarried. Most of it reflected the active role in courting that was ascribed to the male, and was directed explicitly to young men, describing the qualities to be sought in a wife. Men were first warned to be sure that they were marrying for the right reasons. Although God had provided marriage as a remedy for fornication, men should not marry with sex uppermost in their minds. Sexual needs were well recognized, but warning was given of sexual enticement, "the fruit of that Tree, the kernell of that Apple, which first destroyed us all, faire to sight, but of fatall and dreadful consequence to the taster, rendering him subject to slavery, that was born free, and Her to command, who ought in righter reason to serve and obey."[19] This suspicion of the allurements of female sexuality and its ability to reduce a sovereign male to a vassal of his love's vagina – an attitude so familiar to historians of sexual attitudes – was expressed more succinctly by the same author thus: "I have heard a well-built woman compared in her motion to a ship under saile; yet I would advise no wise man to be her owner, if her Fraught [freight] be nothing but what she carries between wind and water."[20]

Once he had decided to marry, a young man seeking a wife should take care to give greatest consideration to qualities such as piety and personality than to characteristics of appearance, charm, and wealth. "If it [marriage] be built upon beautie, Riches, Wealth and such like vanishing and changeable things, it

[17] Robert Wilkinson, *The Merchant Royall. A Sermon preached at White-hall upon the sixth of Ianuarie 1607. beinge the twelfe day: At the Nuptials of the Right Honourable, the Lord Haye and his Ladie* (London, 1615), sig. F1[R].

[18] Abbot, *Wedding Sermon*, 45.

[19] Francis Osborne, *Advice to a Son: Or Directions for your better Conduct through the various and most important Encounters of this Life* (London, 1656), 42.

[20] Ibid., 59.

cannot endure, but faileth when the foundation is taken away."[21] Another writer noted the same in practical terms:

It being observ'd that our Domestick breaches (now so familiar) generally have their rise from the first visible decay of Husbands in their Estates, and their necessary abridging the superfluity of such Wives: for they are mere Summer-friends, and a sort of legal Concubines; their love depends on their fare, and no Penny, no Pater-noster, is their Principle.[22]

In general, a similarity of age, quality, and wealth was advised. Anything more than a moderate disparity of age, for example, could, by itself, have appalling effects. "An old woman," wrote one author, "is a very unfit and unpleasing companion for a young man, and for an old man to dote upon young wenches is very inseemely hurtful...and commonly much strife, suspicion, jealousy, discontents and miseryes ensue such marriages."[23]

Observance of precepts such as these would, it was thought, minimize the potential for discord within marriage. But it was clear that too many people married unwisely, or, once married, failed to observe the rules of matrimony. In principle, nothing should have been more straightforward than a happy marriage: With conduct-book in hand, the carefully matched couple should have been able to cut a straight path through the most barbed thickets of married life. But in practice the conduct-books were simply not used; husbands and wives neglected their duties, and blundered down the twisting trails of discord to certain disaster.

It was the neglect of duties by women upon which most of the immediate blame for the marriage breakdown was placed. Women were accused of neglecting their obligations in respect of household economy, and there were references to "the very sloth and incapacity of most women now a-days...even to a contempt of Huswifery."[24] A number of commentators went so far as to blame married women for their husbands' perversity. In Robert Snawsel's *A Looking-Glasse for Married Folkes*, written in the form of a dialogue, "well-spoken" Eulalie tells Xantip, "a scold," that she is responsible for her husband's ill-temper and perverse behavior: "I can tell you, Xantip, we wives may doe much either in making or marring our husbands."[25]

Against this tendency to blame women alone or primarily for marital discord, ran another, though less prominent, tendency that made the husband more responsible by virtue of his superior domestic position, which supposedly gave

[21] Robert Pricke, *The Doctrine of Superiority, and of Subjection, contained in the fifth commandment of the holy law of Almighty God* (London, 1609), sigs. 16^V–17^R.
[22] A. B., *A Letter of Advice Concerning Marriage* (London, 1676), 2.
[23] Crofts, *The Lover*, sig. B2^R.
[24] A. B., *A Letter*, 2.
[25] Robert Snawsel, *A Looking-Glasse for Married Folkes, wherein they may plainly see their Deformities: And also how to behave themselves one to another, and both of them towards God* (London, 1631), 40–1.

him the ability to determine the tone of the marriage. Thomas Carter most clearly expressed this point of view.

It is a harts griefe to any good Christian, or well minded man to see and heare the dayly contentions, uproares, quarrelles, and disgreements betwixt husbands and wives in these dayes, and yet who can deny but the world is too full of such, what shall wee say to these thinges? Excuse it who will by laying the fault on the wives, I say still the greatest part is in the Husband, he by his unkind and churlish speeches not fitting a husband to give unto his wife, his unthriftiness in wasting abroad, what all doe labour for at home his drunkenesse, his rash furiousness, these with the rest aforesaid and a number more not here expressed, he (I say) by these occasions is dayly the cause of all these evills.[26]

The suggestion that wives, by being assertive, scolding, disobedient, and materially covetous, were primarily responsible for dissension within marriage, raised the issue of the husband's authority. It was an accepted precept in law and social practice that a husband was accountable for his wife's actions, just as a master was for his servant's. In the context of marriage this principle justified the notion that a husband had a right to punish his wife physically – to beat her – if that course were necessary to prevent her from behaving in an improper way or from committing a wrong for which he would ultimately be held responsible. The right to beat a wife was referred to as the right of "moderate correction" since it was intended to be moderate and a response to an offense on the part of the wife. It was a much-debated right in the seventeenth century, however. Some writers defended it as a necessary adjunct – an instrument of last resort – to the husband's authority within marriage.[27] Others, though, thought that physical violence was totally inappropriate within marriage.[28] (This debate, and its relationship to marriage breakdown, is discussed in Section 9.3.)

Even the opponents of "moderate correction" did not dispute the principle that the husband ought to be the dominant partner in marriage. If the wife should not be beaten, many argued, it was because she should not need to be: She should be obedient to her husband and tolerant of his faults, even when he seemed to exceed or even abuse his legitimate authority as head of the household. Behind much of this writing lurked the specter of Eve. Just as the serpent used Eve's weakness to tempt Adam to sin, so the devil did his work of matrimonial destruction through the wife. The dominant position of the husband and his marital authority were supposed to overcome this evil tendency. The new Adam was presumed to be stronger willed than the old in this respect.

---

[26] Thomas Carter, *Carters Christian Common Wealth: Or Domesticall Dutyes deciphered* (London, 1627), 18–19. Carter calculated that only one husband in a hundred loved his wife as he ought to (p. 15), whereas as for wives loving their husbands, "I thinke we shall scarce find one in five that doth it, no not among ten, I pray God there bee one in 20" (p. 67).

[27] For example, Moses à Vauts, *The Husband's Authority Unvail'd Wherein It is moderately discussed whether it be fit or lawfull for a good Man, to beat his bad wife* (London, 1650).

[28] Those unequivocally opposed to the use of "moderate correction" included Henry Smith (in "A Preparative to Marriage," in *The Sermons of Mr. Henry Smith* [2 vols., London, 1866], I, 22); and Thomas Carter (in *Christian Common Wealth*, 22). But for a more general discussion of the debate on wife beating, see Section 9.3.

One female voice on the subject of uxorial obedience emerged from the late seventeenth century in particularly distressing and poignant circumstances. In 1677 a woman named Sarah Elston killed her husband during a domestic dispute: "He having beat her very severely, she with a pair of sizzars gave him a wound on the left part of his breast, whereof, without speaking one word, he died."[29] According to a broadside dealing with this affair, the couple had lived together for several years "with much Discord and frequent wrangling; of which some would now partly excuse the woman, and alleadge the man as the principal Cause of their Differences by his ill husbandry, cross carriage, ill company and other indulgent provocations."[30] The court was not among those indulgent enough to listen to such excuses; Sarah Elston was convicted of petty treason for murdering her husband and sentenced to be burned to death.[31] Tied to the stake, she devoted her last words to giving advice that, given her imminent fate, was wholly understandable.

Desiring all women to take warning by her, and to live in Love and Peace with their Husbands if it were possible; at least to avoid their Fury by going out of the way for the present, when they are in rage, rather than to stand bandying of words, or teazing them with reproachful Language; which she acknowledged had oft been her own fault: That they should remember that their Husband is their Head; and that the Apostle requires them to be obedient to them in every thing; and this not onely to the kinde and indulgent, but even the peevish and froward ought to have the same obedience.[32]

If this was not a vindication of or apology for male superiority, it was at least advice for survival. When Sarah Elston had finished her homily, the fire was kindled, "and giving two or three lamentable shrieks, she was deprived both of Voice and Life, and was burnt to Ashes according to the Sentence."[33]

3.3 Attitudes toward divorce up to 1640

There is no doubt that seventeenth-century writers were faced with a problem. If there were an inherent propensity (as a result of sin) on the part of married people to disregard the marital duties set down for them, and if they refused to heed the guidance of the conduct-books and the admonitions of the hortatory

---

[29] *A Warning for Bad Wives: Or, the Manner of the Burning of Sarah Elston. Who was Burnt to death at a Stake on Kennington Common neer Southwark, on Wednesday the 24 of April 1678. For Murdering her husband Thomas Elston, the 25th of September last* (London, 1678), 2–3.

[30] Ibid., 2.

[31] Under the 1352 Statute of Treason, petty treason included the slaying of a master by a servant, a husband by a wife, or a prelate by a subject. Such executions of women for killing their husbands continued into the eighteenth century, although by the seventeenth century it was accepted that a woman should be strangled before being burnt rather than being burnt alive. Sarah Elston was apparently not strangled first. On this question see Ruth Campbell, "Sentence of Death by Burning for Women," *Journal of Legal History* 5 (1984), 44–57. There is continuing criticism of the practice in the *Parliamentary History of England* (London, 1818), XXVIII, cols. 782–84 (May 10, 1790).

[32] *Warning for Bad Wives,* 6.

[33] Ibid., 7.

sermons, what was to be done? It was at this point that the question of the dissolution of marriage arose and at which many writers advocated that an innocent spouse should be entitled to a divorce under certain circumstances. But far from all writers approved of divorce, and none (at least, until John Milton in the 1640s) went further than supporting divorce for reasons other than adultery and desertion. If that were the most liberal position – and it was supported by few Anglicans, Puritan or non-Puritan – what was suggested in cases of emotional conflict, hatred, and general incompatibility of temperament? The answer was, in a word, patience. If the causes of discord could not be overcome, an unhappy marriage was to be borne as a cross. Perhaps the least appealing formulation of this doctrine was that of Alexander Niccholes, who likened unhappy spouses to prisoners in jail:

This knot [marriage] can neither bee cut nor loosed, but by death, therefore as wise prisoners inclosed in narrow roomes sute their mindes to their limites, and not, impatient they can go no further augment their paine by knocking their heades against the walles, so should the wisedom both of Husbands and Wives, that have undergone either this curse, or blessing, as the success or use make it unto them, to beare it with patience and content the asswages of all maladies, and misfortunes, and not storme against that which will but the deeper plunge them into their own misery.[34]

For some writers, patience was the final word in marriage stress or breakdown even when it was manifested in adultery. Richard Allestree, for example, recommended "a patient submission" in the face of adultery by a husband, adding that

they are therefore far in the wrong, who in case of this injury pursue their husbands with virulencies and reproches...They are not thunders and earthquakes, but soft gentle rains that close the fissures of the ground; and the breaches of wedlock will never be cemented by storms and loud outcries.[35]

He had no advice to give husbands in the face of their wives' adultery. Other writers, however, suggested that a temporary separation might be permissible, perhaps to allow emotions to cool. Robert Abbot, for example, allowed it "by mutual consent for a time for the good of the family."[36]

Patience and charity on the part of the innocent, repentance on the part of the guilty, the observance by both of their divinely ordained roles and duties: These were the solutions offered to women and men whose marriages were marked by discord, discontent, and "jarres" of an emotional kind. The notion that a marriage might be dissolved on the ground of incompatibility, as proposed by John Milton and by Martin Bucer before him, found no sympathy

---

[34] Alexander Niccholes, *A Discourse of Marriage and Wiving: And of the greatest Mystery therein contained: How to choose a good wife* (London, 1615), sig. G1ᵛ.
[35] Allestree, *Ladies Calling*, 168.
[36] Abbot, *Christian Family*, 36.

among Puritan and non-Puritan theologians. It was not that Puritans were simply slow to adopt this position, as one historian has suggested:[37] They considered it and rejected it definitively. Some writers, indeed, ruled out absolutely the dissolution of marriage by divorce, with the right to remarry. Others would allow it where one of the spouses was guilty of adultery or desertion; others for adultery alone. Most of the remainder of this chapter discusses these divorce doctrines and places them within the context of a general doctrine of marriage formation, practice, and dissolution.

As discussed in Chapter 2, the sixteenth-century Anglican church maintained the Catholic doctrine of marital indissolubility in spite of the opinion of a number of leading English reformers that divorce was allowed by scripture. The *Reformatio Legum Ecclesiasticarum* of the later sixteenth century was clearly out of line even with the thinking of most of those English theologians who favored divorce and was completely abhorrent to those who did not approve of divorce in any circumstances. The liberal character of this draft reform of canon law ensured that it was never enacted, and perhaps it was partly as a reaction to it that no provision whatsoever was made for divorce in English church law. In fact, when reference to divorce was made, in the church canons of 1604, it was expressly to prohibit divorce entirely. The reformed canon law specified that separations *a mensa et thoro* (which it called "divorces" in places) could be granted by an ecclesiastical court, but added the rider that in all such judgments

there shall be a caution and restraint inserted...that the parties so separated shall live chastely and continently; neither shall they, during each other's life, contract matrimony with any other person. And, for the better observation of this last clause, the said sentence of divorce shall not be pronounced until the party or parties requiring the same have given good and sufficient caution and security into the court, that they will not in any way break or transgress the said restraint or prohibition.[38]

Even so, the issue was not settled in absolute terms. When bigamy was made a felony in England for the first time in 1604, the law stipulated that a person who had separated *a mensa et thoro* before contracting a second, but bigamous, marriage, was to be treated more leniently than a bigamist who had not previously obtained a separation from his or her first spouse.[39] The bigamy law responded in part to a case that came before the Court of Star Chamber in 1602 in which Hercules Foljambe was charged with marrying while his first wife, from whom he had obtained a separation *a mensa et thoro*, was still alive. Foljambe's second marriage was voided, even though he argued in his defense

[37] James Turner Johnson, *A Society Ordained by God: English Puritan Marriage Doctrine in the First Half of the Seventeenth Century* (Nashville, N. Y., 1970), 31.
[38] Canon 107. C. H. Davis (ed.), *English Church Canons of 1604* (London, 1869), 97. This was later interpreted to mean that a separated person could remarry, even while his or her spouse was still alive, as long as he or she was willing to forfeit the caution paid at the time of the separation.
[39] A. R. Winnett, *Divorce and Remarriage in Anglicanism* (London, 1958), 53–4.

that "divers divines and civilians of great account and learning" agreed that remarriage was permissible after such a "divorce."[40]

The retention of the doctrine of marital indissolubility by the reformed Church of England was clearly unsatisfactory to many English theologians, and it doubtless accounts for the fact that the divorce debate continued in England with an intensity it had lost elsewhere. Divorce was a highly sensitive issue and there is some evidence that the Anglican hierarchy tried to suppress the controversy by discouraging the publication of works on the subject, whether they were for or against divorce. In the preface to his 1610 antidivorce book, Edmund Bunny recorded that he had written the work in 1595 and had sent the manuscript to the then archbishop of Canterbury, John Whitgift:

> But as touching the publication of it, that he [Whitgift] thought not good so to doe; yet giving no other reason then, but that hee would have as few controversies in the Church as might be; and that others had offered a Treatise of contrary judgement which he had staied.[41]

How serious Whitgift and others were in their attempts to suppress debate, we do not know, but their failure is demonstrated by the appearance of numerous works on divorce. The first two decades of the seventeenth century saw an impressive production of closely argued theological treatises defending the Anglican doctrine that marriage was indissoluble. Their tone was set by John Dove, a vicar of London, who in 1601 preached a sermon against divorce and then, apparently in response to criticisms, published it under the title *Of Divorcement*. The work is mainly an analysis of Matthew 19:9, which advocates of divorce had interpreted as allowing divorce for reason of adultery, but which Dove read to contrary effect in the light of other biblical texts. Dove considered the practicalities of a marriage beset by an adulterous wife but still could not agree that divorce was warranted in such circumstances. In such a case, Dove wrote, a magistrate might order the adulteress to be imprisoned "for her chastisement untill shee shew manifest tokens of ammendment," but he stressed that this was not a dissolution permitting remarriage. To the argument that a wife's adultery placed an unbearable burden on the husband, who might not wish to resume a sexual relationship with her, Dove responded: "if a husband can exercise restraint in the case of his wife's illness, can he not equally do so in the case of her adultery?"[42]

John Dove's defense of marital indissolubility was followed in 1606 by the publication of John Howson's thesis, which had been submitted to the University of Oxford in 1602, against divorce for adultery. Howson, who was successively bishop of Oxford and Durham in later life, painstakingly examined the New Testament divorce texts and concluded that the apparent permission

---

[40] Winnett, *Divorce and Remarriage*, 47.
[41] Bunny, *Of Divorce*, Preface, n. p..
[42] John Dove, *Of Divorcement: A Sermon preached at Paul's Cross the 10 of May 1601* (London, 1601), 29.

of divorce in Matthew was a description of the old law of divorce available to the Jews, while the doctrine of indissolubility represented the new law of the Christian Era.[43]

In 1610 two more antidivorce works appeared. The first was Edmund Bunny's, to which reference has already been made. Bunny argued that the marriage bond united not only the spouses to each other, but each to the other and to God, and that divorce could take place only when all these links had been broken. Adultery broke the conjugal bond only between the spouses, but did not dissolve the complex of ties that constituted marriage.[44] The second work of 1610 was that of Lancelot Andrewes, who was bishop of Ely, and subsequently of Winchester. In a brief treatise, Andrewes argued against remarriage after divorce (and thus against divorce in the strict sense) on three grounds. The first was that adultery did not dissolve the marriage bond because if it did, a reconciliation would require a remarriage, which was unheard of. Second, he argued, the 1604 canons expressly forbade remarriage following a separation granted by the ecclesiastical courts; finally, despite the doctrines of some divines, the evidence of scripture and the weight of tradition were opposed to divorce.[45]

Perhaps it is predictable that the Anglican church's doctrine of marital indissolubility was supported notably by those who held, or were to hold, high ecclesiastical office. The antidivorce sentiments of two bishops have already been noted, and four more can be added to the list: Godfrey Goodman (bishop of Gloucester), John Prideaux (Worcester), Anthony Sparrow (Exeter), and John Fell (Oxford). No bishop or incumbent of other high office in the Church of England in the first half of the seventeenth century supported the legalization of divorce, and this no doubt reflected not only the attitudes of the Church's hierarchy but also the general criteria for election to offices within the church. Men of unorthodox opinions on such sensitive matters as marriage and divorce were surely less likely to be promoted.

At the lower level of clergy and lecturers, the antidivorce position was defended by men of many theological shades, Puritans and non-Puritans alike. An example of a Puritan who did not approve of divorce was Thomas Gataker, rector of Rotherhithe in Surrey and in 1643 named a member of the Westminster Assembly of Divines. Gataker did not discuss divorce and matrimonial faults with great explicitness, and his general affirmations of the desirability for married people to stay together until death should not in themselves be re-

---

[43] John Howson, *Uxore dimissa propter fornicationem aliam non licet superinducere* (Oxford, 1602).
[44] Bunny, *Of Divorce*, 50–2.
[45] Lancelot Andrewes, *Minor Works* (London, 1854), 106–10. Andrewes was a member of a commission appointed to investigate and rule on the 1613 petition by Lady Essex for the nullification of her marriage on the ground of her husband's physical inability for sexual intercourse. In an acrimonious case, Andrewes came out in favor of granting the petition. This was taken by some of his critics as indicating an inconsistency with his position on separation and divorce. The Essex case concerned annulment, however, a quite different matter. See Winnet, *Divorce and Remarriage*, 70–1.

garded as indicative of an inflexible indissolubilist position: Even liberals on divorce (in the seventeenth century and at all other times) regarded marriage as indissoluble in ideal terms, and marriage breakdown as an unfortunate and undesirable departure from God's design. Yet there were more than generous hints that Gataker did not support divorce at all. In one of his works he almost appeared to adopt the view that a woman who fails to perform her wifely duties ceases thereby to be a wife: "Thou are no wife, if thou does not the duties of a Wife."[46] Yet this is clearly not meant to be taken any more literally than his subsequent comment that "shee ceaseth to be a Wife, yea to be a Woman, when she ceaseth to be a good to Man." Gataker condemned separations lightly decided upon for reason of discord, the breaking of "a bond knot by God," and forgetting "the covenant of thy God," adding (his comments are addressed to an innocent husband confronted by a guilty wife):

Yea, but some will say, her behaviour is such as cannot be endured. And we may serve God asunder better than wee can being together...to this I answer: first with the Apostle, Art thou married? seek not to be loosed: abide in the calling God hath called thee in...for if cohabitation be of God, then the contrary unto it is of Satan.[47]

Gataker made a distinction between the obedience owed by a servant to a master and that owed by a wife to her husband. This very distinction was made by various writers in support of their opposition to physical punishment of a wife, but Gataker brought it to bear on divorce:

Thy servant, if he please thee not, thou maist put off againe, upon a quarter, or halfe a yeeres warning at most. But thy Wife there is no casting off againe: She must all thy daies abide by thee, all hers at least, like enough to last as long as thou livest.[48]

The early seventeenth-century works in support of the official Anglican doctrine on divorce make interesting reading from the point of view of exegesis, but they are undeniably repetitive and, defending an established position, tend to fall back on frequently made and well-enunciated arguments. It is, of course, not necessarily a weakness that they should not have advanced new arguments for their doctrine or against their opposition. What is interesting, though, is their almost complete reliance on scriptural interpretation. They contrasted strongly with works by the advocates of divorce, which relied for much of their force on social arguments. This is not to suggest an absolute difference in approach, however. Both sides founded their arguments on theological bases, but the prodivorce writers brought a closer and more explicit relationship to their social philosophies, and their divorce doctrines emerged from a dialectical process drawing on scriptural interpretation and their conceptions of natural

[46] Thomas Gataker, *A Wife in Deed. A Sermon concerning the Matter of Marriage* (London, 1624), 12.
[47] Thomas Gataker, *Marriage Duties Briefly Couched Together; out of Colossians, 3.18, 19* (London, 1620), 39.
[48] Gataker, *Wife in Deed*, 63. Although Gataker could not know it when he wrote this, he was to marry four times and survive all of his wives. *Dictionary of National Biography* VII, 940.

justice and of the right ordering of morality and society. John Milton was to refer to the antidivorce position as "resting on the meere element of the Text," as distinct from the arguments in favor of the legalization of divorce, which he saw as "consulting with charitie, the interpreter and guide of our faith."[49]

Perhaps the first significant contribution to the prodivorce side of the seventeenth-century debate was a 1598 sermon of Henry Smith. Smith, a London preacher, intimately related biblical doctrine with a description of conjugal duties and an injunction to practice patience and charity:

For if any jar do arise, one saith, in no wise divide beds for it, for then the sun goeth down upon their wrath. . .and the means of reconcilement is taken away. Give passions no time; for if some men's anger stand but a night, it turneth to malice, which is incurable.[50]

In what was to become the tradition of seventeenth-century conduct-books, Smith stressed the duties of men and women within marriage. If these duties were performed, he wrote, there would be no need to "speak of divorcement, which is the rod of marriage." In fact even when husbands and wives neglected their duties they could not divorce, and Smith advised them not to be quarrelsome "for this law will hold their noses together, till weariness make them leave struggling; like two spaniels which are coupled in a chain, at last they learn to go together, because they may not go asunder." The only condition that could justify divorce, according to Smith, was adultery, "for marriage is ordained to avoid fornication. . .and therefore if the condition is broken, the obligation is void."[51]

Henry Smith, regarded as a Puritan, thus confined divorce solely to the ground of adultery, a position more conservative than the Protestant mainstream. This limited doctrine (of a unique ground for divorce) was to constitute one of the two principal schools within those English theologians who wrote in favor of divorce. The others held that provision should also be made for divorce on the ground of desertion, the dominant continental Protestant position, but this probably had the support of a small minority in England. Among them was William Perkins, a lecturer at Great St. Andrews, whose commentary on divorce was published posthumously.

Perkins seemed to argue that adultery was the only ground that justified divorce: "the sinne of adulterie is that alone, which breakes the bond, and renounceth the troth plighted in marriage, and is the proper cause of divorce and not Idolatrie or Infidelitie."[52] But despite this, Perkins added that willful desertion by an unbelieving spouse left the deserted and Christian partner free to remarry. There are two points to note here. The first is that according to

---

[49] John Milton, *The Doctrine and Discipline of Divorce* (2nd. edn., London, 1644), 3.
[50] Smith, "Preparative to Marriage," 19.
[51] Ibid., 35.
[52] William Perkins, *Christian Oeconomie: Or, a Short Survey of the Right Manner of erecting and Ordering a Familie, according to the Scriptures*, in Perkins, *The Workes* (3 vols., Cambridge, 1608–9), III, 680. (Perkins means infidelity in the religious sense here.)

Perkins the divorce in such circumstances was effected by the person who deserted, not the spouse left behind:

The malitious and wilfull departing of the unbeleever, doth dissolve the marriage; but that is no cause of giving a bill of divorce; onely adulterie causeth that. Here the beleever is a mere patient, and the divorce is made by the unbeleever, who unjustly forsaketh, and so puts away the other.[53]

This implies an automatic divorce, with the right of remarriage, without the need for a judicial process. Second, anyone who deserted his or her spouse, Perkins wrote, was ipso facto not a Christian, for no true Christian would behave in this manner. In William Perkins's writing, then, the Pauline Privilege was extended to what might be called a "Wilhelmine Warrant," which meant that any person deserted by his or her spouse was thereby considered free to remarry at will. This was a potentially very permissive point of view.

William Ames, who was a student of Perkins, supported this liberal doctrine but held that marriage should not be dissolved at the mere pleasure of the married persons themselves. Ames was more directly liberal than Perkins in his definition of desertion, however. Although insisting that the offending spouse was not entitled to divorce, but that the deserted partner had a fair claim to a divorce "after the triall of all other meanes [of reconciliation] in vain," Ames added that even "a voluntary and spontaneous absence, if it bee beyond the time appointed and confirmed by deceit," was tantamount to desertion.[54]

One of the most interesting supporters of the liberal divorce position in the early seventeenth century was William Whately, a Puritan vicar at Banbury, near Oxford, from 1610 until his death in 1639. In 1617 Whately published *A Bride-Bush*, a sermon "compendiously describing the duties of married Persons, by performing whereof, Marriage shall be to them a great Helpe, which now find it a little Hell." Following the contemporary trend in family treatises, Whately stressed the reciprocity of duties within marriage, but, departing from this trend, he made a critical and explicit distinction between the duties that were "principall" and those that were "less principall." The former he defined as those "by the breach whereof this knot [marriage] is dissolved and quite undone: and which being observed (other small infirmities notwithstanding) the bond remains entire on both sides."[55] The failure to observe the "principal duties" in marriage thus justified divorce, and Whately isolated two of them: mutual chastity and cohabitation.

Of adultery, the violation of the former of these duties, Whately wrote:

The Husband must not dare to give himself to any woman in this world but to his wife; nor the wife to company under heaven besides her owne husband. Against which

---

[53] Ibid. III, 69.

[54] William Ames, *Conscience with the Power and Cases thereof* (n.p., 1639), 209.

[55] William Whately, *A Bride-Bush: Or, a Wedding Sermon: compendiously describing the duties of Married Persons: By performing whereof, Marriage shall be to them a great Helpe, which now finde it a little Hell* (London, 1617), 2.

duty if either of them shall offend, the party so transgressing, hath committed adultery, broken the covenant of God, remooved the yoke from his yoke-fellowes neck, and laid himselfe open (if the Magistrates did as Gods law commands) to the bloody stroke of a violent death.[56]

Similarly, desertion violated the mutual obligation imposed on married people to live together: "They must have the same habitation as one bodie." Whately recognized that private business or public service could require absence, and even a prolonged separation at times,

but a wilfull and angry separation of beds or houses must not be tolerated. And if it so fall out, that either party doe frowardly and perversely withdraw him or herselfe from this matrimoniall society (which fault is termed desertion) the man or woman thus offending, doth so far violate the covenant of marriage, that...the other is loosed from the former bond, and may lawfully (after an orderly proceeding with the Church or Magistrate in that behalfe) ioyne him or her selfe to another.[57]

Desertion justified divorce, Whately wrote, first because it was "a wilful frustrating of the proper purpose and end of matrimony," and second because "unfaithfull desertion is almost never separated from adultery."[58] This perspective echoes that of earlier commentators, such as Calvin, who brought these two matrimonial offenses into a close relationship.

Whately's divorce doctrine placed him among the liberal English proponents of divorce.[59] A Bride-Bush was reprinted in 1619, but the ideas it promoted on divorce were so repugnant to the Anglican church authorities that Whately was summoned to appear before the Court of High Commission to explain himself.[60] He did not actually appear and instead retracted his divorce doctrine in 1621. Nevertheless, when a second edition of A Bride-Bush was published two years later, in 1623, the section on divorce remained as it had appeared in the first edition. An advertisement from the author to the reader was appended to the volume in which Whately admitted the error of his divorce doctrine. The retraction was fairly straightforward, although the reasons Whately gave for it are less than wholly convincing.[61]

---

[56] Ibid. Note here the advocacy of the death penalty for adultery.

[57] Ibid., 3–4.

[58] Ibid., 4.

[59] Winnett, *Divorce and Remarriage*, 79, incorrectly writes that only Andrew Willett and Bishop Cosin among English divines of the later sixteenth and seventeenth centuries approved of divorce for causes other than adultery. (There is no reference to Whately in Winnett's book.)

[60] *Dictionary of National Biography*, XX, 1341–2.

[61] Whately cited an example of adultery that seemed to refute his earlier contention that adultery dissolves marriage: "Who can doubt, but that a man or woman, having secretly sinned in this kind, repenting of the sinne, and keeping his or her own counsell, may lawfully continue to give due benevolence unto his yoke-fellow? Wherefore betwixt man and wife, after the sinne of Adultery committed, the bond of matrimony remaineth undissolved: and therefore the contrary opinion if false." This begs the fundamental question of the difference between an automatic divorce as a result of adultery – which Whately here denied – and the possibility of a court's granting a divorce for reason of adultery, which is not dealt with here. Whately's hypothetical case ruled out the possibility of a judicial divorce because the innocent spouse is presumed not to know of the other's offence. See Whately, *Bride-Bush* (1623 edn.), sigs. Ff3^R–Ff3^V.

It must be an open question as to whether Whately really did change his views or whether he remained at least ambivalent on the issue of divorce. The carelessness and brevity of the printed retraction must raise some doubts, just as we are entitled to question the sincerity of anyone who is "convinced by sound reason"[62] of a position whose contrary was leading him to appear before a court and could conceivably have cost him his living.

Whately's experience in having to retract his views on divorce seems to have influenced his other major work, *A Care-Cloth*, published in 1624.[63] This was a significant book in that it broke with the seventeenth-century tendency of promoting marriages as a God-given opportunity for worldly happiness and spiritual salvation. In *A Care-Cloth* Whately came dangerously close to advocating celibacy (the Catholic doctrine) in order that men and women should avoid the troubles, trials, and burdens that, he seemed to say, were intrinsic to marriage. Perhaps it was as a reaction to the Anglican church's refusal to allow divorce that Whately warned of the dangers of marriage, and warned of them over and over again in the most graphic terms:

Many husbands and wives doe fare almost always, as Job fared, cursing their Wedding-day, as much as he did his Birth-day, and thrusting after divorce as much, as ever he did after death. Whence it is, that many wedded people brooke their wedlocke in none other fashion, then a dog doth his Chaine, at which he never ceaseth snarling and gnawing, that he may break it asunder and set himselfe at libertie.[64]

Whately advised against marriage by the young and by the old. Those who did marry should take care to establish their own households, for living with parents could easily lead to "being tormentors of their parents, or tormented by them."[65] But even if these torments were avoided, there were the spouses themselves. Some husbands are churlish, hard, miserable, niggardly, wasteful, riotous, unclean, and lust after other women; wives, for their part, could be proud, arrogant, sullen, scolding, sluttish, jealous, raging, and extravagant.[66] In case prospective marriage partners looked forward to the joy of children, Whately put them right. Sometimes children die in infancy or childhood, leaving their parents grieving; but worse, children might survive childhood

onely to be their parents tormentors and murderers, by their evil and lewd conditions, so disquieting their hearts, that they would count it an advantage to have been barren, and doe often wish they had laid them in their graves, before ever they had used a tongue to speake.[67]

---

[62] Ibid., sig. Ff3^R.
[63] Whately retracted his views on divorce in this book too, but again his comments are ambiguous; he referred to divorce as "at least a doubtfull, and an hazardous liberty." *A Care-cloth: or a Treatise of the Cumbers and troubles of marriage: Intended to advise them that may, to shun them; that may not, well and patiently to bear them* (London, 1624), sig. A8^V.
[64] Ibid., sigs. A2^V–A3^R.
[65] Ibid., sigs. A6^R–A6^V.
[66] Ibid., 45.
[67] Ibid., 51.

Finally even the death of a spouse, releasing the other from the hell on earth Whately described, was a mixed blessing; a woman contemplating marriage should think that "hee may leave me the mother of some children, and now great with another, and (sending his soule to heaven) give me alone his cold corpse to put into the earth."[68]

It was not an attractive image of married life, and it was scarcely tempered by some token positive statements about marriage at the end of the work. Whately's overall purpose was to advise "widdowes, Maids, Batchelors, Widdowers, if you can. . . to keeps as you be, and not to procure miserie to your selves by a needlesse change of your estates."[69] Curiously, during Whately's tenure at Banbury, the number of marriages in the parish seems to have declined. In the two decades before Whately became the vicar in 1610, there was an average of twenty-three marriages a year, while in the following three decades, marriages averaged eighteen or nineteen.[70] There could have been many reasons for this, of course, but it is at least conceivable that Whately's pre-marital counseling was so rigorous and pessimistic that some of his parishioners decided either not to marry or to be married in another parish by a vicar with a less jaundiced view of matrimony.

William Whately was a Puritan, as were many other writers on marriage and divorce in the seventeenth century. What is significant about the divorce doctrines up to the 1640s is that no peculiarly Puritan doctrine was formulated. There was nothing approaching a consensus on divorce among the Puritans, although it might be argued that the weight of Puritan opinion was toward the liberal position, and the weight of non-Puritan Anglican opinion was concentrated at the conservative end of the spectrum. But the middle ground, which allowed divorce only for reason of adultery, was held by men of varied religious doctrinal positions. Even at their most liberal, when they advocated divorce for adultery or desertion, Puritans and non-Puritans went no further than mainstream Continental Protestants of the preceding century. If the much-celebrated revolution in marriage doctrines, which has often been associated with the Puritans, did take place, it was certainly not manifested in attitudes to divorce.

This point is most clearly seen when we bring divorce doctrines into relationship with notions as to the ends or purposes of marriage and to the nature of the conjugal relationship. We should expect that a matrimonial offense or other circumstances serious enough to warrant divorce should relate closely to the ranking in importance of the characteristics of marriage; once the possibility of divorce is admitted, we should expect it to be granted first in

---

[68] Ibid., 49.
[69] Ibid., 65.
[70] The annual average number of marriages by decade for Banbury were as follows: 1590–9, 20.7; 1600–9, 25.8; 1610–9, 16.6 (Whately's tenure begins in 1610); 1620–9, 16.9; 1630–9, 22.1. Registrations for the following decades of civil war and upheaval are incomplete. Source: Parish registers, Banbury. Bodleian Library MSS D. D. Par. Banbury d. 1.

circumstances where the most important obligations of marriage have been breached. What is implied here is what William Whately made explicit: the distinction between the essential qualities of matrimony (Whately's "principal duties"), whose absence or contravention rendered marriage dissoluble and lesser or nonessential qualities. If these assumptions are valid, the grounds for divorce should have shifted as increasing emphasis was place on the importance of companionship and the reciprocity of duties and obligations of marriage. Indeed, the Puritan divine William Bradshaw would have had his readers believe that Puritans thought it "an injurie...to force a man to maintain one for his wiffe, that either is not a woman, or that refuseth in hir owne person to doe the duties of a wiffe unto him."[71] Bradshaw was wrong. No Puritan before Milton advocated divorce for any reason other than adultery or desertion, the classic Protestant grounds for divorce. As one historian writes, "Despite the Puritan reform movement, during the first half of the seventeenth century the dominant opinion and practice among Puritans and Anglican alike was that divorce could only be granted for adultery...."[72] To this extent, there seems to have been a clear incongruence between any increased emphasis on the companionate aspects of marriage and the continued emphasis on the imperatives of sexual fidelity and cohabitation expressed by the divorce doctrines of the time. In this respect, the Puritans of the first half of the seventeenth century were anything but innovative.

3.4 Marriage and divorce in political debate

The lack of any consensus on divorce among Puritans was highlighted by the proponents of the parliamentarian cause during the 1640s. English parliaments had been in dispute with King Charles I since the 1620s over issues such as the right of the monarch to impose taxes without the consent of Parliament, and Charles actually governed without a parliament from 1629. In 1640, however, he summoned Parliament, but the dispute between it and the monarch proved irreconcilable and in 1642 Parliament rebelled and the English civil war broke out. It is interesting, from the perspective of divorce, that in the political debate preceding and accompanying this civil war protagonists both on the royalist and parliamentarian sides attempted to justify their respective causes by appealing to images of marriage and the family. Both sides agreed that the relationship between a king and his subjects was analogous to the contractual relationship between husband and wife. The question was whether, in the case of a tyrannical husband (the king at the political level), the wife (the kingdom) was permitted to rebel and finally to divorce – to repudiate the husband and dissolve the union between them. At last the constitutional metaphor that had under-

---

[71] William Bradshawe, *English Puritanisme, Containening the maine opinions of the rigidest sort of those that are called Puritanes in the Realme of England* (London, 1605), 20–1.
[72] Mary Lyndon Shanley, "Marriage Contract and Social Contract in Seventeenth-Century English Political Thought," *Western Political Quarterly* 32 (1979), 81.

lain seventeenth-century writing on marriage had an explicit and practical application.

On the royalist side it was argued that the political contract between subject and king was binding and indissoluble, like a marriage. There was a distinction, the royalists allowed, in that individual men and women entered into marriage by their own consent (which was a sine qua non of marriage) whereas all subjects were born into the political arrangement without giving their personal consent. Nonetheless, the argument went, they were bound by the consent of their forbears who first entered the political contract. Although it had been possible for individuals at the beginning of monarchical polity not to enter into a contractual relationship, once they had done so they lost the freedom to alter it or to leave it. The royalist position, then, was based on the principle of contractual indissolubility, the doctrine of the Church of England in relation to marriage. Henry Ferne, bishop of Chester and an apologist of the royalist stance, likened Parliament's rebellion against Charles to divorce in order to demonstrate its illegitimacy and illegality. He argued that the rebellion was

as if, in matrimony (for the King is also *sponsus Regni*, and wedded to the kingdom by a ring at his coronation) the parties should agree, on such and such neglected duties, to part asunder...what our savior said of their light and lawfall occasions of divorse, *non suit ab initio*, it was not so from the beginning, may be said of such a reserved power of resistance [by Parliament], it was not so from the beginning.[73]

Ferne did not make it clear what legal relief was available to the subordinate party in the relationship – whether it be wife or kingdom – when she was confronted by a partner who had become tyrannical and had abused his authority. What is clear, though, is that rebellion by Parliament and divorce by a wife were rejected by the royalists on the same grounds.[74]

The matrimonial metaphor for the political dispute was adequate at a crude level but did not extend to the nuances of separation *a mensa et thoro* or the limitation on the husband's (and, by analogy, the king's) power by the notion of "moderate correction." A wife might prosecute her husband for excess, and even obtain a separation from the church courts in the seventeenth century, but Parliament, it seemed, had no equivalent relief in the constitution. Even more than an abused wife, it seemed, Parliament was to be patient and submissive, and to pray that her master would behave as the constitution intended.

This argument by matrimonial analogy posed a dilemma for the parliamen-

---

[73] Henry Ferne, *Conscience Satisfied: That there is no warrant for the Armes taken up by Subjects* (Oxford, 1643), 12.

[74] "The Husband, also, who is the head of the wife, had the advantage on his part in the poynt of Divorce: He might give the Bill [of divorce] to her upon Jealousies and displeasure, she could not to Him; this Liberty was permitted to good and bad Husbands equally, notwithstanding the occasion, that evill Husbands might take thereby to be unjust and cruel; as it is usually objected against this *Ius Regis*, or advantage of security on the king's part." Henry Ferne, *A Reply unto severall Treatises pleading for the Armes now taken up by Subjects in the pretended defense of Religion and Liberty* (Oxford, 1643), 87–8.

3 Seventeenth-century England

tarians. In order to justify rebellion in the same terms they had first to argue for limitations on the power of king and husband (which they had no trouble doing) but second to justify the rebellion as being as legitimate as divorce. This was much more difficult because of the conservative tendency of divorce doctrines. It was compounded by the fact that Parliament was cast as the woman in the partnership, and this made defense of its initiative against established authority that much less legitimate in matrimonial terms.

The parliamentary propagandists wrestled manfully with the metaphor. Herbert Palmer, for instance, tried to find a middle ground between passive submission in the face of domestic tyranny, and divorce:

A wife is tyed to her Husband by the Covenant of God, (so called, Prov. 2.) and by the Ordinance of God more ancient, and no lesse strong than that of Politick Goverment. She cannot recall wholly her Husbands Authority over her...Yet for her necessity, she may by the Law of God and conscience...secure her Person from his violence by absence (though that ordinarily be against the Law of Marriage, and the end of it) or any other means of necessary defence.[75]

The implication here was that Parliament's rebellion was an act of self-defense but short of divorce. The awkwardness of the argument is indicated by Palmer's suggesting that a tyrannized wife might leave her husband even though that was ordinarily against the law of marriage.

Henry Parker went further to avoid being driven by a metaphor into accepting divorce. He turned the matrimonial analogy upside down, arguing that "if men, for whose sakes women were created, shall not lay hold upon the divine right of wedlock, to the disadvantage of women; much lesse shall Princes who were created for the peoples sake, chalenge any thing from the sanctity of their offices, that may derogate from the people."[76] Here Parker reversed the dominant partner: Women were made for men, but princes for the people. This made parliamentary rebellion not the equivalent of a wife's rejection of her husband's tyranny but a husband's repressing too assertive a wife. This clearly made the parliamentary position much more acceptable, making it analogous to current conceptions of gender relations and avoiding the logic that otherwise led to support of divorce.

Neither Parker, nor Palmer, staunch defenders of the parliamentary position that they were, admitted divorce at the matrimonial level. Resistance to, and rebellion against, the abuse of authority were permitted, and "absence" or separation were countenanced in extreme circumstances, but divorce was not made an explicit relief. (It might be argued that Palmer's "any other measures" could encompass divorce, but it did not do so explicitly.) William Bridge went further than this, arguing that inherent limitations on the monarch's powers were analogous to limitations implied in marriage:

[75] Herbert Palmer, *Scripture and Reason Pleaded for Defensive Armes* (London, 1643), 35–6.
[76] Henry Parker, *Jus Populi* (London, 1644), 4–5.

118

3.5 Milton's divorce doctrines

There is a covenant stricken between a man and a woman at Marriage; when they marry one another it is not verbally expressed in their agreement, that if one commit Adultery, that party shall be divorced; and yet we know that the covenant of Marriage carries the force of such a condition.[77]

Only to a limited extent, then, did the parliamentary apologists take up the argument by analogy with the same force as the royalists. It is, arguably, an indication of the reluctance of the parliamentary propagandists to be compelled, by the logic of political analogy, to adopt a position in favor of divorce that they had not taken when considering divorce in its own terms.[78] This political debate demonstrates the essentially conservative approach to divorce across the spectrum of seventeenth-century English intellectuals.

3.5 Milton's divorce doctrines

The major exception to this generalization was John Milton, who in the early Civil War period, published four tracts on divorce: *The Doctrine and Discipline of Divorce* (1643, with further editions in 1644 and 1645), *The Judgement of Martin Bucer, concerning Divorce* (1644), *Tetrachordon* (1645), and *Colasterion* (1645).[79] The timing of Milton's interest in divorce, so clearly demonstrated by his prolific publication record over a three-year period, was unquestionably related to his own marital experiences. Milton married his first wife, Mary Powell, in 1642. The marriage appears to have been a surprise to everyone; Milton had visited Richard Powell, one of his father's debtors, in order to collect a debt, but returned home instead with Powell's seventeen-year-old daughter as his wife, together with the promise of a thousand-pound dowry (which was never paid). The early weeks of the marriage are as much a mystery to us as are the circumstances of the brief courtship that preceded it, but they were clearly unsatisfactory for Mary Powell, who left Milton after only one or two months, and returned to her family in Oxfordshire. This was intended to be only a temporary absence, but she prolonged it to three years. There can surely be little doubt that Milton was spurred into print on the subject of divorce because

---

[77] William Bridge, *The Wounded Conscience Cured, the Weak One Strengthened, and the Doubting Satisfied* (London, 1642), n.p. This work was ordered to be printed by a committee of the House of Commons as a reply to a work by Henry Ferne who, as we have seen, argued the contrary by analogy to marriage and divorce.

[78] There is no evidence (other than Milton) that "Apologists for resistance to Charles I were forced to take more liberal positions with regard to marriage and divorce than were generally acceptable," Shanley, "Marriage Contract and Social Contract," 85.

[79] There is an extensive literature on Milton's attitudes toward marriage and divorce. Among the most useful works are John Halkett's masterly *Milton and the Idea of Matrimony: A Study of the Divorce Tracts and "Paradise Lost"* (New Haven, 1970); Eivion Owen, "Milton and Selden on Divorce," *Studies in Philology* 43 (1946), 233–57; Christopher Hill, *Milton and the English Revolution* (London, 1977), esp. chapter 9, "Marriage, Divorce and Polygamy"; David Aers and Bob Hodge, "'Rational Burning': Milton on Sex and Marriage," *Milton Studies* 13 (1979), 3–33; John M. Perlette, "Milton, Ascham, and the Rhetoric of the Divorce Controversy," *Milton Studies* 10 (1977), 195–215.

of this experience of being deserted by his wife. Moreover, he stopped writing divorce tracts when Mary Powell returned to him (with her family in tow) in 1645.[80]

To admit this highly personal influence on timing is not to say that the substance of Milton's divorce doctrine was dictated by the specific circumstances of his own marriage. Had it been so, Milton would not have had to go beyond the liberal position of the times, which would have allowed divorce for reason of desertion. But Milton's vision of divorce went further than this, although not as far as some commentators would have us believe. It encompassed not only more grounds for justifying divorce but also made the radical break of shifting from divorce solely as a response to a matrimonial offense to espousing a version of no-fault divorce – divorce in circumstances of incompatibility.

Moreover, Milton went further than other parliamentary supporters in linking constitutional and matrimonial contracts. The second edition of *The Doctrine and Discipline of Divorce* (1644) was dedicated "to the parliament of England with the Assembly," and Milton drew a forceful analogy between political and marital relationships:

He who marries intends as little to conspire his own ruine, as he that swears Allegiance: and as a whole people is in proportion to an ill Government, so is one man to an ill marriage. If they against any authority, Covnant, or Statute, may by the sovereign edict of Charity, save not only their lives but honest liberties from unworthy bondage as well may he against any private Covnant, which hee never enter'd to his mischief, redeem himself from unsupportable disturbances to honest peace and just contentment. . . For no effect of tyranny can sit more heavy on the Common-wealth, then this household unhappiness on the family. And farewell all hope of true Reformation in the state, while such an evill as this lies undiscern'd or unregarded in the house.[81]

It is evident that the parallels Milton drew between politics and the family were far clearer and firm than those (quoted earlier) of Palmer and Parker. The simple reason was that Milton supported divorce, whereas they did not; the constitutional – matrimonial analogy worked for him, whereas it embarrassed them.

Milton based his ideas on divorce upon his conception of the nature of marriage. Rejecting the doctrine of the Roman Catholic church that celibacy was preferable to marriage, and the doctrine of the Catholic and most Protestant churches that marriage was primarily for procreation and the avoidance of fornication, Milton argued that marriage was designed to provide men and women – but above all, men – with companionship and comfort. God ordained marriage, he wrote, "for the apt and cheerful conversation of man with woman, to comfort and refresh him against the evill of solitary life."[82] As

---

[80] For biographical details see James Holly Hanford, *John Milton, Englishman* (New York, 1949); Halkett, *Milton and the Idea of Matrimony*, 2–3.
[81] Milton, *Doctrine and Discipline*, sig. A3^V–A4^R.
[82] Ibid., 2.

he wrote this, Milton was living the solitary life, for his wife had left him and there was no certainty that she would return. This situation must have brought him to the realization that, for lack of divorce, he was bound to his absent wife until she died. There is a note of despair in Milton's description of the plight of married couples who found their marriages intolerable, but inescapable:

> Yet now. . . let them find themselves never so mistak'n in their dispositions through any error, concealment, or misadventure, that through their different tempers, thoughts, and constitutions, they can neither be to one another a remedy against loneliness, nor live in any union or contentment all their dayes, yet they shall. . . be made, spight of antipathy to fadge together, and combine as they may to their unspeakable wearisomnes and despaire of all sociable delight in the ordinance which God establisht to that very end.[83]

In a marriage where a man could not obtain that "meet and happy conversation [that] is the chiefest and the noblest end of marriage," Milton insisted that a husband was driven to immorality, "by visiting the stews [brothels], or stepping to his neighbours bed."[84] Although this seems to place an inappropriate (for Milton) stress on the sexual aspects of marriage, there is a nice reversal here of Catholic and mainstream Protestant doctrines. They held that one of the ends of marriage (conventionally the second, after procreation) was as a prevention against fornication. Milton argued that divorce also had this end, by permitting an unhappy spouse to remarry, rather than be forced into fornication and adultery: "The reasons which now move him to divorce, are equall to the best of those that could first warrant him to marry."[85]

This statement did not commit Milton to giving priority to the carnal aspects of marriage, however. He insisted on placing sexuality within the broader social context of marriage. Marriage merely to avoid the burning of lust was no marriage at all unless the spouses enjoyed each other as companions: "All ingenuous men will see that the dignity and blessing of marriage is plac't rather in the mutual enjoyment of that which the wanting and needfully seeks, then of that which the plenteous body would joyfully give away."[86] Milton's view was that to place adultery above all other breaches of the marriage contract, and make it the sole or principal ground for divorce (the dominant trend in contemporary divorce doctrines) "affirms the bed to be the highest [end] of mariage, which is in truth a grosse and borish opinion, how common soever."[87] This notwithstanding, adultery was, in his eyes, one of the grounds that could justify a divorce by either wife or husband.

Milton argued against the limitation of divorce to one particular set of circumstances, however, by recognizing individuality and by relating marriage breakdown directly to marriage. One passage of the *Doctrine and Discipline of Divorce* in particular shows Milton's argument in this respect:

[83] Ibid., 2–3.
[84] Ibid., 8.
[85] Ibid., 13.
[86] Ibid., 12.
[87] Ibid., 22.

Among Christian Writers touching matrimony, there be three Chiefe ends thereof agreed on; Godly society, next civill, and thirdly, that of the marriage-bed...but if the particular of each person be consider'd, then of those three ends which God appointed, that to him is greatest which is most necessary: and mariage is then most brok'n to him, when he utterly wants the fruition of that which he most sought therin, whether it were religious, civill, or corporall society.[88]

Milton would not, however, leave it to individuals to decide on their priorities of marriage so as to allow them to determine when they might divorce. He accepted that marriage was indissoluble when the spouses had been joined by God, but he did not relate this to the mere marriage ceremony. The consent of the parties and their friends did not imply God's work because the consent "may concurre to lewdest ends." The church ceremonies were not necessarily God's work either, "for the efficacy of those depends upon the presupposed fitnesse of either party." Nor did sexual intercourse represent God's joining the spouses: "Least of all; for that may joyn persons whom neither law nor nature dares ioyn." Rather, God's adhesive work in marriage takes place "when the minds are fitly dispos'd, and enabl'd to maintain a cheerfull conversation, to the solace and love of each other, according as God intended and promis'd in the very first foundation of matrimony."[89] If these conditions did not exist, spouses were not joined by God and "there [is] no power above their own consent to hinder them from unioyninge...Neither can it be said properly that such twain were even divorc't, but onely parted from each other, as two persons unconiunctive and marriable together."[90] A divorce (Milton uses the term despite his denial that it is really a divorce) in such a case is undoubtedly a lesser evil than "a hatefull hardhearted and destructive continuance of marriage."[91]

This leads us to an important point and qualification about Milton's divorce doctrine. Although *The Doctrine and Discipline of Divorce* was subtitled "Restor'd to the good of both sexes," it gave primacy of action in divorce to the husband. Milton never tired of repeating that woman was made for man, and it was this principle that gave the husband jurisdiction over the marriage:

For even the freedome and eminence of mans creation given him to be a law in this matter to himselfe, being the head of the other sex which was made for him: whom therefore though he ought not to injure, yet neither should he be forc't to retain in society to his own overthrow, nor to hear any judge therin above himself.[92]

The implication of Milton's view of the subordinate status of women went further than the procedure for divorce to the very grounds that could justify the absolute parting of spouses. He admitted, first, that either wife or husband could obtain a divorce for reason of adultery or heresy but implied that adultery,

[88] Ibid.
[89] Ibid., 63.
[90] Ibid.
[91] Ibid.
[92] Ibid.

at least, was an offense of relatively little significance – a not unusual popular attitude for this period, as we shall see (Section 9.4), though one rarely stated in the literature of the time. Milton described adultery as "but a transient injury" and an act "soon repented, soon amended."[93] But the principal reason for divorce as far as he was concerned was a sort of incompatibility – a mismatch of unmeet minds – and this could be interpreted as being a recognition of de facto marriage breakdown without the attribution of fault to either spouse in particular. Milton wrote of the grounds that void marriage:

> Which if anything in the world doth, unfitnes doth, and contrariety of minde; yea, more then adultery, for that makes not the mariage void, nor much more unfit, but for the time, if the offended party forgive; but unfitnes and contrariety frustrates and nullifies for ever, unless it bee a rare chance, all the good and peace of wedded conversation.[94]

Milton's emphasis on the subordinate role of women made it the particular duty of the wife to ensure compatibility in marriage by making herself compatible. Women, we noted earlier (Section 3.2), were generally held responsible for problems within marriage, and, incompatibility was thus the result of the wife's failure to perform her most important duty: to mold herself to her husband's needs. Incompatibility should be seen, then, less as a form of no-fault divorce and more as a covert matrimonial offense that could be committed only by the wife. As Milton wrote of the unhappily married man: "Is it not most likely that God in his Law had more pitty towards man thus wedlockt, then towards the woman that was created for another."[95] From this perspective, Milton's radicalism in bringing the ends of marriage into direct relation with divorce can be seen as the result of taking to its extreme implications one of the most firmly entrenched of contemporary social attitudes, the belief that women were the inferior of men.[96]

Although these conclusions and interpretations can be drawn from *The Doctrine and Discipline of Divorce*, Milton also supported the doctrine of Martin Bucer, the translation of whose work constituted Milton's second tract on divorce, *The Judgement of Martin Bucer, concerning Divorce*. In the preface Milton wrote that he learned of Bucer's opinions on divorce only after the second edition of the *Doctrine and Discipline* had been published and that "I soon perceav'd, but not without amazement, in the same opinion, confirm'd with the same reasons which in that publisht book without the help or imitation of any precedent Writer, I had labour'd out and laid together."[97] Yet although there were indeed striking similarities, there were also notable divergences between Milton's and Bucer's views regarding the grounds for divorce, the respective

---

[93] *Complete Prose Works of John Milton* (8 vols., New Haven, 1966–82), III, 331–3, 591.
[94] John Milton, *Colasterion* (London, 1645), 9.
[95] Milton, *Doctrine and Discipline*, 60.
[96] Christopher Hill attempts to correct the image of Milton as a mysogynist in *Milton and the English Revolution*, 117ff.
[97] John Milton, *The Judgement of Martin Bucer, concerning Divorce* (London, 1644), sig. B2^v.

roles and status of women and men in matrimony, and the procedures for obtaining divorce.

Milton, as we have seen, grounded divorce in the lack of the proper relationship ordained by God to exist in a Christian marriage. He did not discuss specific matrimonial offenses, other than adultery, or the symptoms that betrayed the effective absence of marriage. Milton preferred to leave the determination of these to the spouses jointly or to the husband alone. Bucer, on the other hand, listed a host of conditions that could justify divorce. A husband might divorce his wife who was guilty of such offenses as adultery, witchcraft, murder, favoring robbers and thieves, feasting with strangers without her husband's knowledge, committing sacrilege, frequenting theaters without her husband's consent, or plotting against the state. A wife might divorce a husband guilty of these offenses or of frequenting lewd women in the sight of his wife or of beating her.[98] Either could be divorced for desertion.[99] Such specific grounds for divorce fell within the context of the purpose of marriage, which was "the communicating of all duties, both divine and humane, each to other, with utmost benevolence and affection,"[100] such that if it did not exist, then the covenant of marriage did not exist either.

Although it might be argued that the circumstances justifying divorce in *The Judgement of Martin Bucer* could also fall within the general doctrine of marriage expressed in *The Doctrine and Discipline of Divorce*, the emphasis on the equality of obligations of men and women in marriage was far stronger in the former. Bucer accepted that the husband was the head of the family and preserver of the wife and that the wife was the helpmeet to her husband, but he stressed the mutuality of duties and concluded that either could divorce the other where the duties were not performed.

To the differences in attitude to women, we must add difference in approach to divorce procedure between Bucer's work and Milton's first essay. Milton, we have seen, wrote specifically that divorce "is not to be try'd by Law, but by conscience, as many other sins are."[101] Bucer argued the contrary. Marriage was a civil contract and laws were required so that men might "rightly contract, inviolably keep, and not without extreme necessitie dissolv mariage."[102] Without just and Christian laws, consciences (to which alone Milton had appealed) became "entangl'd, afflicted, and in danger."[103]

In his other works on divorce, *Colasterion* and *Tetrachordon*, Milton reverted to the tone of *The Doctrine and Discipline of Divorce*, stressing the primacy of incompatibility as a ground for divorce. But even if the contradictions between his and Bucer's doctrines seemed irreconcilable at times or coexisted uneasily

[98] Ibid., 15.
[99] Ibid., 20.
[100] Ibid., 17.
[101] Milton, *Doctrine and Discipline*, 74.
[102] Milton, *Judgement of Martin Bucer*, 1.
[103] Ibid.

3.5 Milton's divorce doctrines

at others, Milton's attitudes to divorce represented a radical departure from the trend of thinking among English writers in the first half of the seventeenth century, just as Bucer's had done in the sixteenth century. Above all, Milton's extension of the right to divorce and his firm linking of the ends of marriage to the acceptable grounds for divorce demonstrated, in sheer contrast, the essential conservatism of the doctrines of the seventeenth-century English proponents of divorce.

At the very time that Milton was preparing his tracts on divorce, his contemporary John Selden was also turning to study the question of divorce in Jewish and Christian doctrines. Selden's views were published in his *Uxor Ebraica* (1646) and tended to support the position that divorce could be justified by a number of offenses. There was an important qualification: Only the husband was entitled to divorce, for only the wife's offenses were serious enough to rupture the marriage bond.[104] Selden grounded this conclusion in his detailed study of a doctrinal conflict within Judaism at the beginning of the Christian Era as to what grounds could justify dissolving a marriage. The rabbinical school of Schammai argued for a restrictive form of divorce, allowing a husband to divorce his wife only when she was guilty of a serious offense. The other school, of Hillel, adopted a more liberal or permissive position that divorce was lawful if a wife did anything at all to displease her husband.[105]

Selden interpreted Christ's words on divorce, as recorded by Matthew, Mark, and Luke, not as an isolated response to a question but rather within the context of this rabbinical dispute over divorce. He wrote that Christ denounced the school of thought that advocated the complete liberty of divorce by the husband and decreed that

henceforth among his followers, who were to include all the Jews and all other races, divorce must by no means be allowed...for any sort of cause or at the mere caprice of the husband or, in fact, saving for the cause of fornication or except for fornication. But when there was fornication, then divorce could duly be and had universally been allowed from the beginning of things.[106]

The remaining problem was to define "fornication," a question to which Selden devoted many pages. His conclusion was that the Greek word used in the Bible was the translation of a Hebrew or Syriac word that went beyond meaning simple sexual infidelity and encompassed disgraceful or criminal acts generally.[107] Selden's divorce doctrine remained frustratingly vague in the end, however. Certainly he thought divorce permissible by divine and natural law but only to a husband whose wife was guilty of an offense. The offense should be a relatively serious one, however, for Selden interpreted Christ as ruling out dis-

---

[104] See the discussion in Eivion Owen, "Milton and Selden on Divorce," *Studies in Philology* 43 (1946), 233–57.
[105] Kitchin, *History of Divorce*, 133–4.
[106] Owen, "Milton and Selden," 248–9.
[107] Ibid., 249.

solution of marriage for any cause whatsoever or at the mere whim of the husband. Selden's doctrine had the potential to go further than the dominant Anglican dissolubilist position, though not to go as far as Milton's. But in the end it was framed too generally to allow us to locate him precisely on the spectrum.

3.6 Popular and official attitudes to divorce after 1640

Even though the debate on divorce in England up to the Civil War period generally had a very limited scope, we can assume that there were men and women who believed that more liberal, or even radical, doctrines on divorce could be justified. Part of the explanation of their apparent silence, in documentary form at least, must lie in their reluctance to expose themselves to official censure or general criticism. They had before them, after all, the example of William Whately, summoned to explain his liberal stand on divorce, and the desire of the Anglican church hierarchy to suppress the debate on the subject might also have been a factor. The reaction to Milton's works, discussed later in this section, would make other matrimonial dissidents think twice before expressing their views publicly. Moreover, in realistic terms, advocates of divorce might have judged any literary effort in favor of liberal divorce legislation to be futile, given that the church was set against divorce in any, even the most limited, form. The conservative attitude of the English church must have been the more galling to those would-be divorce reformers who knew that divorce had been legalized in some of the American colonies by men who called themselves Puritans (see Chapter 4).

Many of the constraints against expression and dissent dissolved during the turbulence of the Civil War and revolution, however. In this "time of reformation,...of free speaking, free writing,"[108] not only was authority in the state and church challenged but so were commonly accepted institutions and moral beliefs. The family, and codes of behavior associated with the family – marriage, divorce, sexuality, and sex roles among them – proved no more immune to questioning, and even outright attack, than other elements of the social order.[109] The principal deviates from conventional doctrines and practices were the religious sects that proliferated during the Civil War, sects such as the Baptists, Quakers, Ranters, and Muggletonians, but when examining the divorce doctrines of the sects, we must be careful not to make assumptions by association. For example, acceptance of marriage as a civil contract or by public declaration does not imply that divorce was permitted. Gerrard Winstanley advocated the "full liberty" of women and men to marry "whom they love, if they can obtain the love and liking of the party whom they would marry," and

---

[108] John Milton, *The Judgement of Martin Bucer*, in *Complete Prose Works*, II, 479.
[109] See Christopher Hill, *The World Turned Upside Down* (London, 1972), esp. chapter 15; Keith Thomas, "Women and the Civil War Sects," *Past and Present* 13 (1958), 42–62; Leo Miller, *John Milton Among the Polygamophiles* (New York, 1974).

proposed marriage by declaration by local officials and neighbors. But he did not explicitly allow the possibility of divorce.[110] Neither did the acceptance of adultery by some of the more radical religious sects necessarily imply the right to divorce – indeed, it made acceptable what had been, until that time, the most commonly accepted matrimonial offense.

We must also treat cautiously the descriptions of the sectarians' moral doctrines and practices by hostile commentators. Critics of unorthodox religious and political groups, especially groups that cut themselves off physically or morally from society in general, have historically alleged moral, and specifically sexual, misdemeanors by members as a means of calling into question their religious, political, or other beliefs. Such methods were frequently used by opponents of monasticism. Divorce could easily be included among a group's alleged offenses against the social order not only because divorce was forbidden but because it was easily associated with sexual promiscuity – men and women exchanging their spouses for new sexual partners. Some pamphleteers attacked women preachers in the 1640s on the ground that they advocated lax marriage practices. It was alleged that one preacher in Kent "preached that if husbands crossed their wives' wille they might legally be forsaken."[111]

This is not to say that some of the mid-seventeenth-century sects and religious leaders did not pronounce in favor of divorce. Indeed, divorce could be the logical implication of the separatist character of sectarianism, whereby each sect believed that its membership included only the spiritually regenerated and that women and men who were not members were simply not Christians. To this exclusivist doctrine was applied the Pauline Privilege, the right of a believer to divorce a spouse who was not a believer, and as a result marriage was limited to unions involving men and women who were members of the same sect. The justification for the divorce of a nonbeliever by a Christian was, as we have seen, generally supported by Protestants in the sixteenth century in circumstances of desertion. The difference between these early proponents of the privilege and the seventeenth-century sectarians lay in the breadth of their definition of believer and nonbeliever: Some sectarians permitted themselves to divorce members of other sects as well as members of the established church. An example was Mrs. Attoway, a sectarian preacher, who put away her "unsanctified husband, that did not walk in the way of Sion, nor speak the language of Canaan."[112] Mrs. Attoway subsequently coupled herself with (though it is not clear that she married) one William Jenney, who had earlier put away his wife because she was not a member of his sect. Ranters and extreme sects were the most experimental, some doing away entirely with marriage and practicing "stand-away divorces" and free love. Such rare cases apart, there is in fact little evidence (and divorce by declaration would leave no documentary

---

[110] *The Works of Gerrard Winstanley* (ed. G. Sabine, New York, 1965), 599.
[111] Roger Thompson, *Unfit for Modest Ears* (Totowa, N. J., 1979), 47.
[112] T. Edwards, *Gangraena* (2nd edn., London, 1646), II, 10–11, quoted in Thomas, "Civil War Sects," 50.

evidence) that divorce was much practiced or advocated even during the social upheaval of the Civil War period.[113] Mrs. Attoway argued for it, as did the Anabaptist preacher, Hugh Peter,[114] but overall one is tempted to conclude that divorce played a more significant role as a polemical weapon against the sects than it did in the social life of the sectarians themselves.

That there was no great outpouring of sentiment in favor of radical ideas about marriage and divorce during the English revolution is shown by the response to Milton's *Doctrine and Discipline of Divorce*. Mrs. Attoway might have commended Milton's arguments as worthy of serious study, and the first printing of *The Doctrine and Discipline* sold fast enough to warrant another printing within six months, but the overwhelming reaction we are able to recover was negative.[115] Many of the criticisms and attacks were little more than casual references in works that focused on broader subjects. Ephraim Pagitt, for instance, listed "a tractate of divorce in which the bonds are let loose to inordinate lust" as an example of current "hereticall opinions".[116] Criticisms in these terms could not have been unexpected, but others carried the threat of action against the works or against Milton himself. Herbert Palmer, the exponent of Parliament's right of rebellion (see Section 3.4) preached a sermon to Parliament in which he referred to *The Doctrine and Discipline of Divorce* as "a wicked booke...and *uncensured*, though *deserving to be burnt*."[117] The Stationers' Company petitioned the House of Commons (Milton's first work on divorce was unlicensed) and as a result the Commons' Committee for Printing was instructed "dilligently to inquire out the Authors, Printers, and Publishers of the Pamphlet against the Immortality of the Soul, and concerning Divorce."[118] For his part, William Prynne urged Parliament to suppress "*many Anabaptisticall, Antinomian, Hereticall, Atheisicall opinions, as of the souls mortality, divorce at pleasure &c.*"[119] These were only some of the many hostile references to Milton's divorce works, especially *The Doctrine and Discipline*, in the 1640s. They provoked the writing of *Colasterion* and *Tetrachordon*, and the rumors of prosecutions forthcoming against *The Doctrine and Discipline of Divorce* were the background to Milton's *Areopagitica* (1644), a call for the liberty of unlicensed printing.

The confusion of the issue of freedom of the press and the contentiousness

---

[113] Hill writes that divorce was defended and practiced in public during the revolution. *World Turned Upside Down*, 251.

[114] Hugh Peter, *Good Work for a Good Magistrate* (London, 1651), 117.

[115] See Ernest Sirluck's introduction to the divorce tracts in Milton, *Complete Prose Works*, II, 137–45, and William R. Parker, *Milton's Contemporary Reputation* (Columbus, 1940), esp. 17–22.

[116] Ephraim Pagitt, *Heresiography: Or, a Description of the Heretickes and Sectaries of these latter times* (London, 1651), sig. A3ᵛ, quoted in Parker, *Milton's Contemporary Reputation*, 74–5.

[117] Herbert Palmer, *The Glasse of Gods Providence Towards His Faithful Ones* (London, 1644), 57 (italics in original).

[118] Quoted in *Complete Prose Works*, II, 142.

[119] William Prynne, *Twelve Considerable Serious Questions touching Church Government* (London, 1644), 7 (italics in original).

of Milton's contribution to the debate on divorce was compounded in the only sustained response to any of Milton's divorce tracts. The anonymous *An Answer to a Book, Intituled, The Doctrine and Discipline of Divorce* (1644), was not only licensed by Joseph Caryl but endorsed by him:

To preserve the strength of the Marriage-bond and the Honour of that estate, against those sad breaches and dangerous abuses of it, which common discontents (on this side Adultery) are likely to make in unstaied mindes and men given to change, by taking in or grounding themselves upon the opinion answered, and with good reason confuted in this Treatise, I have approved the printing and publishing of it.[120]

This rejoinder to Milton's work was unimpressive. It was characteristic of *The Doctrine and Discipline of Divorce* to have dispensed with the commonly accepted definitions and associations of key concepts such as marriage and divorce. Divorce, for Milton, was a positive notion, as much (to the extent that it was justified by conditions that were ordinarily thought to justify marriage) an institution ordained by God as was marriage. Marriage, too, meant something special to Milton; it was not merely a legal contract or a covenant but the existence of spiritual harmony between husband and wife.[121] The author of *An Answer to a Book*, however, argued in conventional terms. Divorce was treated as an institution foreign to the social and moral order, rather than integral to it and marriage was discussed in conventional seventeenth-century terms. Milton's redefinition of marriage as a harmony of minds and spirits was dismissed thus:

The consent of the minde ought to be had in marriage, or else it will hardly become a human societie: but that after marriage the mindes of the Husband and Wife must in all things agree, or else the marriage becomes no humane societie, is a new principle unheard of till now, and so I leave it.[122]

One can hardly blame the anonymous critic for failing to come to grips with Milton's doctrine. To have dealt adequately with the argument would have required accepting the premises and definitions, but to have accepted these would have meant accepting the argument, so logically did it proceed from its premises.

The attacks on Milton and other supposed advocates of permissive divorce reflected the dominant view, which was that marriage was indissoluble. On this it seems that the Anglican church and Oliver Cromwell's secular government were at one, for no divorce law was enacted in the Civil War period and interregnum. Only in one respect, and it was an oblique one, might Cromwell's Puritans be said to have responded to the pressure in favor of divorce, and that was by passing the 1650 Adultery Act.

Hostility to adultery is, needless to say, part of the Christian sexual code, and

---

[120] *An Answer to a Book, Intituled, The Doctrine and Discipline of Divorce* (London, 1644), n.p.
[121] A provocative analysis of Milton's polemical method is Lana Cable, "Coupling Logic and Milton's Doctrine of Divorce," *Milton Studies* 15 (1981), 143–59.
[122] *An Answer*, 43.

not peculiarly Puritan. But the Puritans did go further than their predecessors and put into action the frequently expressed wish that adultery be made a capital offense by passing the 1650 Adultery Act.[123] It might be argued that this act, "for the suppressing of the abominable and crying sins of Incest, Adultery, Fornication, wherewith this Land is much defiled and Almighty God highly displeased," responded in some way to contemporary divorce doctrines as much as to attitudes on sexuality per se. The act embodied a double standard insofar as it provided the death penalty for a married woman convicted of adultery, and for her accomplice. Thus a married man who committed adultery would be executed only if he did so with a married woman. If his adultery involved an unmarried partner (or, the act specified, a woman whom he *believed* to be unmarried – a useful defense for a man), the punishment was a comparatively very lenient three months' imprisonment plus a bond of good behavior for the following year. There is a clear connection between the 1650 act and divorce: The terms of the act made punishment for adultery a functional substitute for divorce, since death dissolved a marriage in any case, and it was immaterial (though not for the individual involved) whether death supervened by natural causes or whether it was accelerated by the judicial process. It had long been an argument of the advocates of divorce that divorce for adultery was justified because the law no longer treated adultery as a capital offense, as it had done in earlier times.[124] In theory, the 1650 act should have satisfied advocates of divorce for this reason and should have made a divorce law unnecessary, at least in respect of adultery by married women.

The only other potentially fruitful move in the direction of divorce at this time was Cromwell's 1653 Marriage Act, which provided for civil marriage in England.[125] This piece of legislation was the culmination of a century of argument by reforming Protestants that jurisdiction over matrimonial issues belonged properly to the secular courts, not to the ecclesiastical judiciary as the English religious settlement had provided. The 1653 act made a civil marriage ceremony before a justice of the peace obligatory, after the publication of banns of marriage either in the church or marketplace. The age of majority for marriage was set at twenty-one years for both men and women, and evidence of parental consent was required before minors could be married. The forms set down were to constitute the only form of legally recognized marriage in England.

---

[123] The best single work on this act is Keith Thomas, "The Puritans and Adultery. The Act of 1650 Reconsidered," in Donald Pennington and Keith Thomas (eds.), *Puritans and Revolutionaries. Essays in Seventeenth-Century History Presented to Christopher Hill* (Oxford, 1978), 257–82. Thomas sets out the ideological context of the act.

[124] These are surveyed in ibid. The author of one legal treatise wanted it both ways, calling for the death penalty for all adulterers, "Buggerers, Sodomites, Ravishers, and professed or common Whores," as well as divorce for reason of adultery. *Examen Legum Anglicae* (London, 1656), sigs. Z1^V–Z3^V.

[125] Aspects of this legislation are discussed in Dorothy McLaren, "The Marriage Act of 1653: Its Influence on the Parish Registers," *Population Studies* 28 (1974), 319–27.

Divorce was not introduced under Cromwell's regime, however, even though there was a proposal to admit it in the case that "either the Husband or Wife had committed the detestable Sin of Adultery." Under the terms of the proposal the evidence of one or more "credible Witness" would suffice, and divorces would be dealt with by a panel of three justices of the peace.[126] But although justices of the peace were given jurisdiction over all other legal aspects of marriage, divorce was excluded, and this is indicative of the prevailing opposition to its being legalized. Indeed, the acceptance of divorce in Jewish law was one of the arguments put forward in 1654 against Jews' being permitted to reside in England. The divines consulted by Cromwell on the issue argued, in part, "that their [Jews'] Customs and Practices concerning Marriage and Divorce, are unlawful and will be of very evil Example amongst us."[127] Both the 1653 Marriage Act and 1650 Adultery Act lapsed with the restoration of the English monarchy under King Charles II in 1660.

With the transition in constitution and politics, marriage seemed to undergo some changes as well. Among the upper strata of English society a period of sexual permissiveness set in, marked by open adultery and the flagrant disregard of the church's moral teachings.[128] There was also a shift in the terms of the continuing debate on marriage and divorce. Before the Civil War the debate had been framed almost entirely in theological terms. It was a battle of biblical quotations, a war over the Word. This was quite appropriate if we consider the general controversies within the Church of England – not just over divorce, but over the gamut of issues touching doctrine and ecclesiastical organization – as a continuation of the Reformation. The Anglican church had retained more of the doctrine and form of the Roman Catholic church than any other Reformed church, and the critics within wanted to purify it, to bring it closer to the mainstream confessions of the continent, particularly those influenced by Calvinism. It should not be surprising, then, that the changes they sought in the Anglican canon law of marriage were essentially those that the European Protestants had embraced in the sixteenth century. To the extent that Puritans took up these doctrines – and not all did, as we have seen – they were not the super-Protestants that they have sometimes been made to seem, but partners in the dominant Protestant tradition, if anything on its conservative wing in terms of divorce. And we must remember, too, that their position on this issue was shared by many non-Puritan Anglicans.

Yet the pressure to allow divorce achieved nothing in the end. The Anglican church resisted divorce and the secular government that ruled in the 1640s and 1650s was scarcely more receptive to it, despite innovation in the laws of marriage and adultery. From the late seventeenth century the pressure in favor of divorce took on new perspectives. The cause of divorce was taken up by men

---

[126] *Parliamentary or Constitutional History of England* (24 vols., London, 1751–62), XX, 214–18, quoted in Ivan Roots, *The Great Rebellion, 1642–1660* (London, 1966), 168, 289.
[127] Joseph Grove, *A Reply to the Famous Jew Question* (London, n.d. [1654]), 67.
[128] See Section 9.4.

and women outside the churches, and the debate took on a more secular tone. Writers such as John Locke invoked the Bible, to be sure, but placed more weight on contract and natural rights' theories to justify divorce. This was part of a more general secularization of marriage and divorce, not only in doctrinal terms but also in respect of the institutions that regulated matrimonial matters.

In England alone the shift from the religious to the secular was stark. For a hundred years the advocates of divorce had presented their arguments to the Anglican church in theological terms. Their aim had been to reform the canon law so as to allow divorce, and they envisaged that divorces would be judged by the ecclesiastical courts, just as separations, annulments, and other marital litigation were. As we have seen, this was to no avail. As if to acknowledge the intransigence of the Anglican church in this respect, a secular body stepped in. In 1670, at the request of Lord Roos, Parliament passed a private act dissolving his marriage and authorizing him to remarry. Lord Roos's wife had committed adultery years earlier and before introducing his private bill to the House of Lords he had obtained a separation *a mensa et thoro* from a church court, as well as an Act of Parliament declaring his wife's children to be illegitimate and therefore incapable of inheriting his title and property. The act dissolving his marriage and permitting him to remarry was thus the last in a series of legal measures Lord Roos had taken.[129]

The passage of Lord Roos's divorce bill was helped by the interest shown in it by King Charles II. The king's marriage to Catherine of Braganza had produced no heir, although Charles had fathered many illegitimate children. In the late 1660s consideration was given to obtaining a royal divorce so that Charles could remarry and have an heir, and Lord Roos's application to Parliament for a divorce was seen as a potentially useful precedent. The king himself demonstrated his interest in the matter by regularly attending the House of Lords when the divorce bill was debated, not an arduous duty, apparently, for he described the often lively proceedings as "better than going to a Play."[130] However, despite the success of Lord Roos's bill and some preparations for the introduction of a royal divorce bill to the House of Lords, Charles finally declined to divorce. The royal interest in the Roos divorce was widely recognized, however, and was no doubt advantageous to this, the first of hundreds of parliamentary divorces.

Lord Roos's divorce also highlighted the active role of Parliament in marriage matters in the face of the refusal of the Church of England to act. To the extent that the dissolution of marriage by private Act of Parliament became the means of divorce for almost two centuries after 1670, the debate on divorce during the sixteenth and two-thirds of the seventeenth centuries, focusing as it did on theological issues, proved to be largely irrelevant to the history of divorce

[129] On Lord Roos's divorce see Antonia Fraser, *The Weaker Vessel: Woman's Lot in Seventeenth-Century England* (London, 1984), 337–49; Winnett, *Divorce and Remarriage*, 109–17.
[130] *Cobbett's Parliamentary History of England* (London 1808) IV, col. 447.

in England. Parliament had sidestepped the religious problems and adopted a pragmatic solution. As far as divorce is concerned, the Reformation had passed England by; it was to have effects not in Old England, where the Anglican Church proved to be an insuperable obstacle, but across the Atlantic, in the colonies of New England.

❀◈◈◈❀

Divorce in the American world:
Seventeenth and eighteenth centuries

4.1 Divorce in the New England colonies

European divorce policies and legislation arrived in North America in the mid-seventeenth century in the baggage of the Puritan settlers. As we have seen, acceptance of divorce was not peculiar to Puritan Anglicans, nor was it acceptable to all of them, and we cannot explain the legalization of divorce in the New England colonies simply by appeal to Puritanism, without some qualification. It is likely, however, that those Puritans who migrated to America were those men and women most discontented with the early seventeenth-century settlement in England. Although we do not know the religious doctrines of all those who set the tone of New England's moral and social climate, it is reasonable to suggest that their attitudes to issues such as divorce were more likely to be at odds with those of the Anglicans than were those of the Puritans who did not emigrate. Significantly, the group of Puritans who first landed at Plymouth in 1621 to found Plymouth Colony had left England in 1607 for Holland. Clearly they expected that the Dutch Calvinist society, where divorce had been legalized, would be more congenial than their own country under what they considered its inadequately reformed church. In short, the American Puritans were more likely to occupy the prodivorce end of the spectrum of attitudes than they were to span it completely, as did English Puritans as a whole. But we must also avoid the temptation to create an alternative, but equally misleading, homogeneity for Puritanism in America, for there were clear dissensions within the New England Puritan community over issues relating to the family, marriage, and divorce.

Fundamental to the marriage doctrine that predominated and informed law and practice in the New England colonies was the principle that marriage was a civil contract. This was a characteristic Protestant principle implied by the denial that marriage was a sacrament. The American Puritans took the application of the contractual principle further than the Church of England and even many of the Continental reformed churches had, however, to encompass the legal and procedural aspects of marriage. Without detracting from the religious significance of marriage, regulations in New England specified that only civil

4.1 Divorce in the New England colonies

magistrates, not ministers of the church, could solemnize marriages. William Bradford, governor of Plymouth Colony during most of the years from 1621 to 1656, wrote that in the colony marriage "was thought most requisite to be performed by the magistrate, as being a civill thing, upon which many questions aboute inheritances doe depende."[1] This was apparently acceptable to most of the New England population, but inevitably there were dissenters. Some, perhaps believing that if a minister were not necessary to celebrate a marriage, then anyone could do it, did it themselves, and ran afoul of the law. In 1678 the General Court at Plymouth fined Edward Wanton ten pounds for "disorderly joyning himselfe in marriage."[2] Others, not only less wanton but more traditional, seem to have yearned for the old English ways. In 1647 some Bostonians wanted a Hingham preacher, Peter Hobart, to come and preach at a wedding. The Boston magistrates forbade it, however, for fear that it could lead to lobbying in favor of the introduction of clerical marriage; Hobart, they noted, was "averse to our ecclesiastical and civil government, and a bold speaker."[3]

In fact from 1686, when the charters of the various colonies were revoked and royal government was extended for a time throughout New England, ministers of religion were empowered to perform marriages. Even then there were limitations: Ministers could perform marriages only for inhabitants of their own towns, and such marriages had to be recorded with the civil authorities. The changes made little difference to the essentially secular administration of matrimonial and family law and litigation. After charter government was restored to the colonies, marriages continued to be performed by ministers and magistrates alike, but this change had no effect on other facets of family law and procedure, such as divorce. The treatment of marriage as a civil contract and the denial of its sacramental nature by the Puritans did not necessarily entail a belief that dissolution of marriage by divorce was permissible. As we shall see, the southern colonies of America also instituted civil marriage, yet they did not legalize divorce until the late eighteenth and even the nineteenth centuries. The secular contractual approach to marriage law was, however, an indispensable precondition of divorce, and the two went hand in hand in the New England colonies as they did in Protestant Europe.

Divorce provisions and laws – some of the colonies made ad hoc facilities for divorce in the early years of settlement, but did not pass statutes in respect of divorce until later in the seventeenth century – drew on both Continental divorce laws and on the English canon law relating to separations *a mensa et*

[1] William Bradford, *Bradford's History of Plymouth Plantation, 1606–1646* (ed. William T. Davis, New York, 1908, repr. 1964), 116. See also John Demos, *A Little Commonwealth: Family Life in Plymouth Colony* (London, 1970), 162; Lynne Carol Halem, *Divorce Reform. Changing Legal and Social Perspectives* (New York, 1980), 12–13.
[2] *Records of the Colony of New Plymouth, in New England* (ed. N. B. Shurtleff and D. Pulsifer (12 vols., Boston, 1855–61), V, 263.
[3] Quoted in John A. Goodwin, *The Pilgrim Republic: An Historical Review of the Colony of New Plymouth* (Boston, 1920, repr. New York, 1970), 596.

thoro. In most of the colonies, divorce was permitted on the grounds of adultery or desertion, but there were important qualifications and variations. In Plymouth Colony, the settlers were directly influenced by the Calvinist practices in Holland, where they had sojourned for thirteen years between leaving England and arriving in America, and divorce was permitted for reason of adultery or desertion. There was no double standard inherent in this legislation; either husband or wife could obtain a divorce for reason of simple adultery.[4] In this respect divorce law diverged from general morality legislation in the colony; for example, in the first decades of the colony's existence adultery was a capital offense, but married men were subject to execution only when they committed adultery with a woman who was married or betrothed to be married. Married women who were adulterous could be sentenced to death by hanging, irrespective of the status of the man with whom they committed the offense.

It might be noted that although the settlers of Plymouth Colony were separatists, refusing common membership with the Church of England, there is only indirect evidence that some of their number believed in, or practiced, divorce in the case of marriage uniting one member of the congregation with an outsider. (Perhaps such marriages simply did not take place.) One reference to this doctrine, which was espoused by some of the Civil War sects in England (see Section 3.6), concerned Roger Williams, a minister in Plymouth who moved to the church at Salem in Massachusetts. Williams's separatist tendencies were manifested in his refusal to join in communion with the church at Boston because the members of that church would not repent their having been members of the Anglican church when they had lived in England. Williams transferred his exclusivism to the church of Salem, but because of its members' refusal to separate from all other churches, he separated from them, isolating himself entirely as a one-man church. What is significant, in respect of divorce, is that "to make compleat work of it, he separated from his own wife, and would neither ask a blessing nor give thanks at his meals if his wife was present, because she attended the publick worship in the Church of Salem."[5] It is unclear, however, whether this separation was permanent or whether either Williams or his wife later resumed cohabitation.

Limited additional legal relief, outside the restrictive grounds for divorce, was provided in Plymouth Colony by the ability of men and women to obtain a separation *a mensa et thoro*. Many couples whose relationship failed to accord with the ideals of tranquility and harmony encouraged by the Puritan authorities found themselves in court. The priority of the courts in these cases was to attempt to reconcile the spouses, but it was not always possible. For example, in 1665 John Williams, Jr., was charged with "abusive and harsh carriages" against his wife, as well as having accused her of being a whore; he had alleged

---

[4] Bigamy was also a ground for terminating a marriage in Plymouth Colony.
[5] Thomas Hutchinson, *The History of the Colony and Province of Massachusetts Bay* (L. S. Mayo, ed., Cambridge, Mass., 1936, repr. New York, 1970), I, 35.

that he was not the father of the child she had recently borne. The court tried to reconcile the couple over a period of two years, but eventually gave up when Williams not only persisted in his violence toward his wife but also admitted his impotence, his "insufficiency for converse with weomen."[6] The court granted the couple a separation, though it must be noted that if Williams was indeed impotent, his wife must have committed adultery in order to have become pregnant.

In Massachusetts Bay Colony divorce could be obtained from 1629 from the secular Court of Assistants, and the first divorce was granted ten years later. The grounds for divorce were not codified, and the circumstances that were actually considered sufficient to justify dissolution of a marriage can best be ascertained from the successful actions for divorce (see Chapter 7). According to Massachusetts's first governor, Thomas Hutchinson, who presided over the court for many years, divorce could be obtained for reason of the wife's adultery (but not the husband's), "desertion for a year or two, where there was evidence of a determined design not to return," and "the cruel usage of the husband."[7] According to Hutchinson the double standard in respect of adultery was introduced only after some debate and after the elders of the colony had been consulted. The double standard was applied consistently, and it was not until the second half of the eighteenth century that a woman in Massachusetts obtained a divorce for reason of adultery alone, although others earlier included adultery in a composite suit against their husbands. As for divorce on the ground of "cruel usage," this must have been intended to refer only to severe violence. The degree of violence generally referred to by contemporary laws as "moderate" was not accepted in Massachusetts as it was in Europe when exercised by a husband against his wife. Both men and women were subject to a fine of ten pounds or to corporal punishment on conviction for assault on a spouse.

Although divorces were granted in Massachusetts from 1639, the grounds and procedures did not take statute form until 1660, when they did little more than codify existing practice. In the early 1690s the Cambridge Association, composed of the colony's most influential ministers, argued for a liberalization of divorce. They proposed that marriages could be dissolved for bigamy, for adultery – when "any married person be convicted of such *criminal uncleanesses* as render them one *flesh* with another object than that unto which their marriage has united them" – and for malicious desertion and lengthy absence.[8] Desertion, they argued, followed from the Pauline Privilege, whereas in cases of absence "the government may state what *length of time*... may give presumption of *death* in the person abroad, as may reckon a second marriage free from

---

[6] *Plymouth Colony Records*, IV, 93, 125.
[7] Hutchinson, *Massachusetts Bay*, I, 375.
[8] Edmund S. Morgan, *The Puritan Family: Religion and Domestic Relations in Seventeenth-Century New England* (Boston, 1944, repr. New York, 1966), 35. For the earlier period, see Barbara Aronstein Black, "The Judicial Power and the General Court in Early Massachusetts (1634–1686)," (Ph.D. Dissertation, Yale University, 1975), 195.

scandal."[9] The ministers wrote that once divorced, only the innocent party might remarry. They also argued for the annulment of marriage in cases of *"natural incapacities*, and *insufficiencies*, which utterly disappoint the confessed ends of marriage" – a reminder of the traditional view of the purpose of marriage that these Puritans held – and incest, by which they probably meant consanguinity.[10]

Massachusetts law was not liberalized, however, and neither was the double standard in respect of adultery removed. The principal legal changes relating to divorce during the seventeenth century were 1695 and 1698 provisions for remarriage when an absent spouse could be presumed lost at sea. The 1698 act provided that

> if any married person, Man or Woman, [who] has lately or shall hereafter go to Sea in a Ship or other Vessell bound from one Port to another where the Passage is usually made in three months time, and such ship or other vessel has not been or shall be heard of within the space of Three full Years, [then the remaining spouse could petition the Governor and council and shall] be esteemed single and unmarried; and...may lawfully marry again.[11]

This represented a reduction of the waiting period of seven years set down in 1695. Although confined to persons missing at sea, which was probably a not uncommon occurrence in the seventeenth century, this divorce provision responded to the proposal of Cambridge ministers, cited earlier, that argued for divorce where there was a presumption of death.

Massachusetts law broke self-consciously from English precedent in providing divorce and from a secular court, though it should be noted that the grounds of adultery, desertion, and cruelty were just those that could justify a separation *a mensa et thoro* from the ecclesiastical courts in England. Governor Hutchinson, however, wrote that the colonists

> left the rules of the [English] canon law out of the question, with respect to some of them prudently enough. I never heard of a separation, under the first charter, *a mensa et thoro*. Where it is practised, the innocent party often suffers more than the guilty.[12]

The citizens of Massachusetts did not trample one another to get divorced. During the seventeenth century (1636–98) there were fifty-four petitions for divorce and annulment, of which forty-four are known to have been successful.[13] This was still many more than the two known divorce petitions in New Hampshire (one of which was referred to Maine jurisdiction). New

[9] Ibid.
[10] Ibid.
[11] Nelson Blake, *The Road to Reno: A History of Divorce in the United States* (New York, 1962) 38.
[12] Hutchinson, *Massachusetts Bay*, I, 375.
[13] Lyle S. Koehler, *A Search for Power: The "Weaker Sex" in Seventeenth-Century New England* (Urbana, Ill., 1980), 453–6.

Hampshire had legalized divorce on substantially identical bases to the law in effect in Massachusetts.[14] In contrast, Rhode Island followed an independent line. A 1650 law stated that "no bill of divorce shall stand legall...butt that which is sued for, by the party grieved" and not "for any other case but that of Adulterie."[15] However there was a gradual liberalization. In 1655 the possibility that grounds other than adultery might be accepted was implied by a decision that "in all other cases of separation or divorce between man and wife, all persons shall addresse themselves for release to ye Generall Court of Commissioners."[16] In practice this permitted men and women at least to petition for divorce for reason of desertion. In 1655 one Thomas Jennings sued for divorce from his wife because of her desertion, but the disposition of the action is not known.[17] In 1685 absence for five years and neglect were explicitly added to the list of grounds justifying divorce.[18] Still, divorces in Rhode Island remained rare: There are records of sixteen petitions between 1644 and 1697, of which twelve are known to have been successful.[19]

Of all the New England colonies, Connecticut arguably had the most liberal and systematic provisions for divorce. An early (1640) law dealing with the banns of marriage evinced concern for the state of matrimony and the care that men and women should take before entering wedlock: "Many persons intangle themselves by rash and inconsiderate contracts for their future joining in Marriage Covenant, to the great trouble and grief of themselves and their friends."[20] Despite such strictures, some couples married unwisely, and the General Court, which had legislative power, assumed the authority of granting divorces in the towns of Windsor, Hartford, and Wethersfield, which made up the early colony. At this time divorce procedure was informal. There was no established legal mechanism and no specified grounds, and the court had to attempt to prevent divorces by reconciling the parties. For example when in 1665 Rebecca Smith complained to the court that her husband Samuel had deserted her, three members of the court sent him a message stating that he must return to his wife and resume his conjugal duties. They warned that if he refused to return, he would commit an offense against God, and concluded: "We must tell you that some friends have advised your wife to sue for a release or divorce from you and if you do not suddenly return it will be seriously considered."[21] In this instance the reconciliation seems to have worked, despite evidence of serious problems in the marriage: The year before, Samuel Smith had unsuccessfully

---

[14] Blake, *Road to Reno*, 40.
[15] Ibid., 39.
[16] George E. Howard, *A History of Matrimonial Institutions* (3 vols., Chicago, 1904), II, 360–6.
[17] Koehler, *Search for Power*, 459.
[18] Halem, *Divorce Reform*, 5; Howard, *Matrimonial Institutions*, II, 360–6.
[19] Koehler, *Search for Power*, 459.
[20] Quoted in Henry S. Cohn, "Connecticut's Divorce Mechanism: 1636–1969," *American Journal of Legal History* 14 (1980), 37.
[21] Ibid., 38.

sought a divorce from Rebecca on the grounds of alleged desertion and adultery.[22] Their reconciliation of 1665 was short-lived, however; in 1667 Rebecca was granted a divorce because Samuel had again deserted her and this time refused to return.[23] Other divorces were granted in Connecticut between 1655 and 1667 for such reasons as impotence, desertion, adultery, and refusal to have intercourse.

Divorce was also possible in the town of New Haven before it subsequently merged into Connecticut. From 1655 New Haven law allowed dissolution of marriage when one spouse had been found guilty of adultery and had fled to evade punishment, when a husband failed in his conjugal duties to his wife, or when one spouse had willfully deserted the other.[24] In 1663 these grounds for divorce were expanded by the addition of seven years' absence. These consolidated grounds formed the basis of Connecticut's divorce law after the union of New Haven and the rest of the colony in 1665. A Court of Assistants, later to become the Superior Court, was established in 1666 and given jurisdiction over divorces when they were justified by the grounds set down by law, namely adultery, desertion, fraudulent contract, or seven years' absence. It remained possible to obtain divorce in other circumstances, but such divorces were considered on an individual basis by the General Assembly, the colony's legislature. Apart from some annulments for reason of impotence, however, the only divorce in Connecticut based on any single ground other than those set down by statute was a successful 1677 action in which Elizabeth Rogers divorced her husband John because of his heretical opinions and "hard usage".[25] Other successful divorce petitions included complaints of cruelty, but only in conjunction with adultery and desertion.

Among the New England colonies, only Massachusetts and Connecticut produced significant numbers of divorces in the seventeenth century. Forty-four marriages were dissolved or annulled in Massachusetts between 1636 and 1698, and forty in Connecticut, including New Haven, between 1655 and 1699.[26] (The use of divorce laws in the American colonies is discussed in more detail in Chapter 7). These were few enough in absolute numbers and highlight the fact that in the colonies, as in Europe, formal divorce was a rarity. Yet the simple existence of divorces demonstrates the difference between New England and the other American colonies. The middle colonies (New York, New Jersey, Pennsylvania, and Delaware) made more restrictive provisions for the dissolution of marriage in the seventeenth century, whereas the southern colonies (Virginia, North Carolina, South Carolina, Georgia and Maryland) made none.

---

[22] Koehler, *Search for Power*, 457.
[23] Ibid.
[24] Cohn, "Connecticut's Divorce Mechanism," 38.
[25] Koehler, *Search for Power* 457.
[26] Ibid., 453–8. It is impossible to distinguish divorces from annulments with complete certainty from these lists.

4.2 Divorce in the middle and southern colonies

The development of divorce in New York differed from that in other colonies in that it was originally a Dutch settlement that passed to English control in 1664. While the Dutch ruled New York (then called New Netherlands), the divorce law of Holland, based on Calvinist principles, was applied. There are three known cases of divorce under Dutch jurisdiction, all between 1655 and 1664. When the colony came under English control the Duke of York, brother of Charles II, was granted a charter to govern by laws "not contrary to but as near as conveniently may be agreeable to the laws, statutes and government of this our realm of England."[27] In 1665 a codification of legislation known as the Duke's Laws was passed, and although it did not refer explicitly to divorce, it did set out the circumstances under which "it shall not be punishable to re-marry." These circumstances obtained when one spouse was convicted of falsifying his or her oath to the justices of the peace, if one could be proved to have died away from New York, or if one spouse had traveled to any "forraigne parts" and had not been heard of for five years. Anyone who remarried in contravention of these provisions was subject to prosecution for adultery or forni-cation, and any children born of such a marriage "shall be reputed bastards, and the parents suffer such paines and penalties by fines or punishment as they have deserved."[28]

It is noteworthy that the second and third of these circumstances rested on the known or presumed death of one spouse; indeed the second circumstance did no more than permit a widow or widower to remarrry. The reference to a falsified oath presumably referred to an oath at the time of marriage, and was intended to apply to bigamous marriages. Insofar as the Duke's Laws referred to death, presumed death, and bigamy, then, they did not envisage divorce in the strict sense. As if to emphasize this, a 1665 amendment to them stated that "in all cases of adultery, all proceedings shall be according to the laws of En-gland, which was by divorce from bed and board [i.e., separation *a mensa et thoro*] if sued, corporal punishment, and fine or imprisonment."[29]

Despite these provisions, the English governors of New York did authorize a few divorces between 1664 and 1675, some of them for reason of adultery by a married woman. For example, in 1672 Thomas Pettit obtained a divorce from his wife for "defiling the marriage bed and committing adultery with several persons."[30] Governor Francis Lovelace, who granted the divorce, stated that the judgment conformed to the "Lawes of the Government as well as the practice of the civill law, and the lawes of our nation of England." Had Lovelace done

---

[27] Matteo Spalleta, "Divorce in Colonial New York," *New York Historical Society Quarterly* 39 (1955), 425.
[28] Quoted in ibid., 426.
[29] Ibid.
[30] Quoted in ibid., 428.

no more than separate the couple, he would have been on safe legal ground, but Thomas Pettit was "discharged and acquitted from the Matrimoniall Contract" by what was termed this "absolute and Authentick Bill of Divorce."[31] Governor Lovelace was not alone in his wholly mistaken belief that he had the power to grant a divorce. The case in question had been referred to him by the Court of Assizes, which had punished Sarah Pettit for adultery and declared it "reasonable" that her husband should have a divorce, "the which the Cort doth recommend to ye Governor."[32]

It is possible that the court and governors believed that the granting of divorces by the previous Dutch administration had established precedent and common law in the colony, the English charter and Duke's Laws notwithstanding. It has been noted that Dutch legal terms, personnel, and procedures persisted in New York until 1680,[33] and it is conceivable that divorces continued to be granted as part of this institutional continuity. If New York's governors granted divorces in this belief, they were almost certainly mistaken in doing so. Divorce was clearly contrary to the Duke of York's charter – though no more so than divorces in the New England colonies – and the disappearance of divorce from New York for more than a century after 1675 suggests that the governors realized, or were reminded, that they did not have the authority to dissolve marriages.

British law and practice with respect to divorce also impinged directly on Pennsylvania's divorce legislation, just as it had done on New York's. From 1664 the Duke's Laws applied to Pennsylvania as well as to New York, but it seems that in Pennsylvania the law was applied strictly, and no divorces were granted while the legislation was in force. Nor were any separations granted, even though they were permitted for reason of adultery. In 1682, however, divorce was provided for by William Penn's Great Law, the sole ground being adultery. Either husband or wife could petition, but any suit for divorce had to be lodged within a year of the other's conviction for adultery. In 1700 divorce was extended to cover other sexual offenses, when a law dealing with sodomy and bestiality specified that if an offender "be a married man, he shall also suffer castration, and the injured wife [sic!] shall have a divorce if required."[34] If a married woman were found guilty of these offenses, her husband was eligible for a divorce. Another law, also passed in 1700, provided life imprisonment with hard labor upon conviction of bigamy and permitted the first wife or husband of a bigamist to obtain a divorce if it were desired.[35]

However, these 1700 Pennsylvania laws were disallowed by the British government as being both cruel and contrary to English law. They were replaced

---

[31] Ibid., 428–9.
[32] Ibid., 429.
[33] Lawrence M. Friedman, *A History of American Law* (New York, 1973), 39.
[34] Thomas Meehan, "'Not Made Out of Levity': Evolution of Divorce in Early Pennsylvania," *Pennsylvania Magazine of History and Biography* 92 (1968), 442.
[35] Ibid.

in 1705 by four statutes relating to marriage and divorce. The first specified the degrees of consanguinity and affinity within which marriage was forbidden and permitted the governor to "divorce" (we might say "annul") marriages in violation of them. The second law provided punishments of whipping, imprisonment with hard labor, and fines for adultery, the punishments increasing in severity for subsequent offenses, and allowed the innocent spouse to obtain a separation *a mensa et thoro*. A law dealing with bigamy provided for punishments of a whipping and imprisonment with hard labor and permitted the first spouse to obtain a separation. Similarly, the final law of this quartet, relating to buggery and sodomy, allowed the innocent spouse to obtain a separation from the guilty partner, who was also subject to imprisonment with hard labor, together with a whipping of up to thirty-nine lashes every three months during the first year after conviction.[36] The net effect of these legal developments was to make divorce available in Pennsylvania only after 1682 and then only for reason of adultery. The colony did not ignore the prohibitions of the Duke's Laws, as the governors of New York had done for ten years, and when, in 1700, attempts were made to allow divorce for other sexual offenses, they were disallowed by the British government and replacement laws specified separation instead of divorce as matrimonial relief.

The history of divorce in New Jersey is unclear. At first the governors of the colony assumed the power to dissolve marriages, rather as they did in New York, and even divorces by mutual consent were given legal recognition. For example, Marmaduke and Mary Potter had their divorce recognized in 1676, as did Thomas and Margaret Davies in 1683.[37] There is no record of divorces having been granted in Delaware Colony in the seventeenth century.

Yet even with these limited divorce provisions, the middle colonies went further than the southern colonies, which generally followed the English church's position of allowing nothing more than separation as a response to a matrimonial offense. Maryland was a special case in that the domination of the colony's administration by Roman Catholics was enough to ensure that divorce was not legal. In this instance the direct precedent might well have been Anglican, but the fundamental doctrinal influence was Catholic. However, the southern colonies did diverge from English practice in important respects. For instance marriage was a civil, not a religious matter, and the county courts were given jurisdiction over separation agreements.[38] Even so, divorce was not permitted. South Carolina did not legalize divorce until 1868 (and then only to abolish it in 1895, before making it legal again in 1949) while the other colonies in the South permitted divorce rather sooner after achieving statehood: North Carolina in 1814, Maryland from 1790, Virginia from 1803, and Georgia from 1798. (They are discussed in Chapter 11.)

---

[36] Ibid., 442–3.
[37] Blake, *Road to Reno*, 42.
[38] Wesley F. Craven, *The Southern Colonies in the Seventeenth Century, 1607–1689* (Baton Rouge, La., 1949), 274–5.

4.3 Marriage and divorce in early American law

In the seventeenth century, then, the New World was a patchwork as far as divorce is concerned. This heterogeneity of divorce laws among the colonies is not surprising given the fact that each took responsibility for regulating marriage formation, annulment, and dissolution. This was not the intention of the British in granting charters to the American colonists, however. The colonies' charters, which stipulated the limits of authority of the colonial administrations, all contained clauses to the effect that laws should not be enacted that varied significantly from contemporary English legislation or that were repugnant to it. Yet in a number of the colonies, notably those of New England, divorce was available from the courts or legislative bodies, and we must enquire as to why these colonies chose so readily to reject the English model of prohibiting divorce, whereas others opted to emulate it. Two broad areas of analysis seem likely to produce answers to this question: the social context of the colonial family and the religious and moral ideologies predominant in the various colonies.

One attempt to explain the discrepancy between the southern and northern colonies in respect of divorce has been made by William O'Neill, who focused on the degree of cohesion in colonial family types and on the importance attributed to the family as a source of social stability. As a general principle O'Neill suggested that

> when families are large and loose, arouse few expectations, and make few demands, there is no need for divorce. But when families become the centre of social organization, their intimacy can become suffocating, their demands unbearable, and their expectations too high to become easily realizable. Divorce then becomes the safety valve that makes the system workable. Those who are frustrated or oppressed can escape their families, and those who fail at what is regarded as the most important human activity can gain a second chance. Divorce is, therefore, not an anomaly or a flaw in the system, but an essential feature of it.[39]

O'Neill's hypothesis makes sense in terms of modern divorce legislation that allows dissolution of marriage when there is evidence of marriage breakdown or irremediable incompatibility or physical or mental cruelty. It makes far less sense in the context of colonial America where, with the rarest exceptions, divorce was available only for reason of clear matrimonial offenses such as adultery and desertion. Seventeenth-century divorce laws simply did not permit men and women who were "frustrated or oppressed" to "escape their family." They might desert their family or seek sexual solace elsewhere through adultery, but having paid the penalty for these offenses and after being divorced as a bonus, they were then, as the guilty spouse, forbidden the opportunity of gaining "a second chance" at marriage. The only spouse who had a second chance

---

[39] William L. O'Neill, *Divorce in the Progressive Era* (New York, 1977), 6–7.

was the innocent one, and he or she had to wait for the other to commit a matrimonial crime.

Even so, there is something to be salvaged from O'Neill's proposed explanation of the different approaches to divorce taken by northerners and southerners. The family systems of these two broad regions differed significantly, at least in the early phases of settlement. Migration to the southern colonies was first by single males, and only later by women and children. Virginia was the most extreme example of this tendency: A census of 1624 showed that of the 1,253 whites in the colony, fully 983 (78%) were adult males. (This overwhelming preponderance of adult males declined until they accounted for only 16% of the white population by 1703.)[40] Moreover there is a general impression that family life was informal in the South. Common-law marriages outnumbered legal ones in some areas, and intimate sociability extended well beyond the bounds of the recognized conjugal family unit.[41] Finally, the immigrant populations of the southern colonies were predominantly mainstream Anglicans who did not share the extreme family-focused piety characteristic of their Puritan brethren.[42]

The New England colonies offered a stark contrast to their southern counterparts. Settlement was largely by family groups, as witness Hingham, Massachusetts: Of 206 people who settled in the town between 1633 and 1639, only ten came by themselves, as single men and women.[43] This was a pattern of migration that reflected the Puritans' emphasis on familial integrity, and the importance attributed to family government as the basis of social and political order.[44] Moreover, the portrayal of the New England family as a tightly knit unit is reinforced by what is known of the material conditions of life. Houses were small and cramped, and almost "all important daytime activities were sustained *in one room*, by groups comprising six, eight, ten, and even a dozen persons."[45]

Social and demographic factors such as these might well have played a role in influencing the legalization of divorce in the northern colonies, especially those of New England. Yet ideological considerations seem to have been of overwhelming importance. In the first place, it was not simply coincidental that the New England colonies were settled by family units. It was, rather, a deliberate policy or strategy of settlement and social organization. Puritan ideology placed the family at the center of social stability and made the family the first level of

---

[40] Robert V. Wells, *Population of the British Colonies in America before 1776: A Survey of Census Data* (Princeton, N. J., 1975), 162–4.
[41] O'Neill, *Divorce in the Progressive Era*, 8–10.
[42] Ibid., 9.
[43] Morgan, *Puritan Family*, 145n.40.
[44] Demos, *Little Commonwealth*, 60ff; Wells, *Population*, 331–2. So important was family life that solitary living was forbidden. See David H. Flaherty, *Privacy in Colonial New England* (Charlottesville, 1972), 175–9.
[45] John Demos, "Demography and Psychology in the Historical Study of Family-Life: A Personal Report," in Peter Laslett and Richard Wall (eds.), *Household and Family in Past Time* (Cambridge, 1972), 563.

social control and government. It was for this reason that solitary living was forbidden in the New England colonies: Men and women who lived alone, outside familial contexts, escaped the positive moral influence of the family, were free of its controls, and were thus at risk of corruption by the forces of evil. Many men and women were convicted of the offense of solitary living, like Henry Jackman, charged before the Suffolk County Court "for living from under family Government."[46] The fear of the Puritans was well expressed in the conviction of John Littleale in Essex County because he "lay in a house by himself contrary to the law of the country, whereby he is subject to much sin and iniquity, which ordinarily are the consequences of a solitary life." Littleale was given six weeks to "settle in some orderly family in the town, and be subject to the orderly rules of family government."[47]

Such laws against living alone – the original "solitary vice" – were passed in colonies such as Massachusetts, Plymouth, and Connecticut, but they were not enacted in the South, nor, as far as can be ascertained, in the middle colonies. To this extent, then, the patterns of migration and the familial composition of the colonies were not simply a result of chance or local economic conditions that might have favored work by individuals or by family units. The family-based character of the colonies of New England was, rather, the result of deliberate policies that reflected the importance of the family unit.

For the Puritans, marriage bore two main benefits. On the social level, marriage was the basis of the family, and the family was the basis of the social order and continuity. To this extent the soundness of marriages, the ability of husbands and wives to live in harmony according to God's laws, was of critical social importance. The second benefit was conferred by marriage on the individual. Marriage was a forum within which a man and a woman could practice virtue, not only toward each other but toward their children and any others who came under the moral umbrella of "family government." Marriage also protected the spouses from the carnal temptations of the world by providing a context for approved and clearly delimited sexual activity. The integrity or completeness of the marriage was in these senses a fundamental part of the Puritan moral and social world. Anything that detracted from this integrity, anything that undermined matrimony was to be resisted; anything that promoted it was to be approved.

It is clear that divorce, as conceived by the Puritans, was a remedy for marriage disintegration in two ways. In the first place, divorce was provided where a marriage had been socially dissolved by absence or desertion. Divorce in the case of absence, generally after a period of about seven years, was intended to free the remaining spouse to contract another marriage. Divorce in the case of desertion had the same purpose, although in this circumstance there

---

[46] *Records of the Suffolk County Court, 1671–1680* (2 vols., Boston, 1933), I, 232.
[47] *Records and Files of the Quarterly Courts of Essex County, Massachusetts* (8 vols., Salem, Mass., 1911–21). V, 104. See also Morgan, *Puritan Family*, 145–6.

was also an element of punishment. Desertion was an offense against marriage, and the deserting spouse, if he or she refused to return, was effectively cast into the wilderness by divorce. Forbidden to remarry, the guilty ex-wife or ex-husband was condemned to live outside marriage, that forum that God had provided for the sanctification of men and women, and within which they could live virtuously, protected from evil. These risks to the soul, implied by exclusion from marriage – a sort of excommunication from marriage – were the real punishment that divorce inflicted on the matrimonial offender.

Adultery, the matrimonial offense accepted by all divorce laws as justifying divorce, was a special case. When one of the spouses committed adultery, the effect on marriage was not at all the same as when one deserted or left and did not return. It was possible for a marriage to continue in the face of adultery if the innocent spouse were prepared to forgive. In seventeenth-century Massachusetts, eighty-one men and sixty-six women were convicted of adultery, and yet only eleven women and four men obtained divorces on grounds that included adultery; in Connecticut fifty-six men and women were convicted of adultery, yet only twelve of the divorces granted included reference to that offense.[48] Divorce was not mandatory when one spouse committed adultery, but the offense was considered so heinous that the innocent spouse was entitled to a divorce if he or she could not forgive the adulterous partner. It is noteworthy, though, that only a minority of the spouses of the men and women convicted of adultery chose to seek a divorce; in Massachusetts only 10% of convicted adulterers suffered divorce in addition to other punishments, while in Connecticut 21% did so.

Husbands and wives might have been prepared to forgive adultery, but the civil authorities were not so lenient. The special status given to adultery as a matrimonial offense was reflected in the harsh penalties it attracted in the New England colonies. Massachusetts, Connecticut, Plymouth, and New Haven made adultery with a married or betrothed woman a capital crime, and at least three people were hanged for the offense. Capital punishment, although rarely applied, remained on the law books until the 1670s, when less severe, but still harsh penalties, including branding, were put in place. The mere provision of execution for adultery, even if it were rarely used, indicates the seriousness with which adultery was regarded; it placed adultery in the same category as murder, rape, bestiality, and treason, which were also capital crimes.[49] Such a rigorous approach to adultery was not peculiar to the Puritan colonies. As we have seen, adultery was a capital crime in Calvin's Geneva, which directly inspired the Puritans' doctrines, and in England under the 1650 morality legislation. All of these laws were based on the Old Testament injunction that adulterers should be put to death. The fact that the authorities were reluctant to apply the penalty in all cases did not mean their horror at the crime was any the

---

[48] Koehler, *Search for Power*, 149, Chart 5.1 (adultery) and 453–8 (divorce).
[49] Ibid., 11.

less, and divorce was provided as a substitute for death. The adulterous spouse, although allowed to live, could be considered legally dead as far as the marriage was concerned. To make the point, the ritual of execution was played out even in noncapital penalties for adultery, by having convicted adulterers wear a noose around their necks. An example was the punishment meted out to Joshua Rice. Convicted in Massachusetts in 1683, Rice was ordered

> to be taken out of the prison and with a rope about your neck Conveyed through the Town to the Gallows and there to be set on a ladder and stand on a full hour with your Rope turned over the Gallows and then to be taken down and Conveyed to the beginning of the street entering the Town to be stripped and tied to the Carts Tail and be severly whipped with thirty stripes through the streets to the Gaol and there left till you discharge the Charge of your trial, prison and court fees, which when done to be released from prison.[50]

His accomplice received the same punishment.

Adultery was also a serious offense in the northern colonies outside Puritan New England. Under the Duke's Laws, we have noted, it could provoke a separation, corporal punishment, a fine, or imprisonment – the penalties applied in England at the time. In Pennsylvania the ill-fated legislation of 1700, which was disallowed by the British government, specified for a first offense "twenty-one lashes well laid on, at the common whipping post," together with either a fine of fifty pounds or imprisonment at hard labor for one year; for a second conviction, an adulterer was given twenty-one lashes and could elect to pay a fine of one hundred pounds or suffer seven years imprisonment; for a third and subsequent offenses, prison and the fine were supplemented by branding the letter *A* on the forehead.[51] Significantly, adultery was the one ground favored for dissolution in all these colonies, even though both New York and Pennsylvania suffered direct interference in their provision for divorce by the British colonial authorities.

Variations in the provision of divorce among the British American colonies in the seventeenth century resist any easy explanation. To some extent we must put aside the differences of detail and concentrate on the major variation between the absence of divorce in the South and the relatively liberal divorce laws put into effect in the New England colonies. The middle colonies, which attempted briefly to apply restrictive divorce provisions – in New York and Pennsylvania for adultery only – form a sort of middle ground. Unlike the southern colonies, they did at least attempt to provide for the dissolution of marriage. In that their laws or procedures conflicted with English practice to which they bowed, they ended up closer to the southern colonies in their absence of divorce facilities. Although it is clear that there were differences in social and familial structures between north and south, these were largely a re-

---

[50] *Records of the Court of Assistants of the Colony of the Massachusetts Bay, 1603–1692* (ed. John Noble, Boston, 1901), I, 240.
[51] Meehan, " 'Not Made Out of Levity'," 442–3.

flection of prevailing family ideology, especially in the case of New England, where settlement was focused on the family unit.

In the final analysis the provision of divorce rested on ideology. The New England authorities (theologians and law administrators) held classic Protestant views about marriage and the family and believed that divorce should be legal. Their counterparts in the South held more traditionally Anglican views and did not believe in divorce. The middle colonies were mixed; some, like New York and Pennsylvania, might well have allowed divorce in restrictive ways had not the British government interfered. But there is an important point to note in this respect, too, and that is that divorce was strictly beyond the legal authority of the courts and legislatures of all the colonies because all were bound by their charters to observe English laws and practices when establishing their own. By persisting with their divorce facilities, the New England colonies displayed much more determination and independence than, say, the government of Pennsylvania. Again, the motivation was ideological, and this must be the explanation for the varying status of divorce among the American colonies. Ideology alone might not be a popular explanation among historians now that we so fully appreciate the significance of cultural, economic, and social factors in the development of law, but it seems appropriate in the case of divorce. It was, after all, appropriate in Europe, where the legalization of divorce in the sixteenth century ignored patterns of social structure, urbanization, and economic development, and varied simply according to the established religion in each jurisdiction.

4.4 The American challenge to English divorce policy

The mixed pattern of divorce policies among the American colonies in the seventeenth century persisted throughout most of the eighteenth. Only after independence was wrested from Britain was divorce legalized more widely in what was by then the United States, and then the reason for its more widespread availability was not solely the removal of the British constitutional obstacles, but also the evolution of more tolerant attitudes. This shift in attitudes not only to divorce itself but toward the right of the British to control such areas of law, was shown in a number of challenges that some colonies presented to the British government before the outbreak of the war of independence, specifically over the right of the colonies to dissolve marriages. Divorce, then, was one of the issues – a minor one, to be sure – that provoked dissatisfaction in colonial America at its continuing subservient status. It should be noted at the outset, however, that the New England colonies had, from the beginning, disobeyed British practice and colonial mandates with respect to divorce. They ignored the restrictions implied in their charters of foundation and ignored subsequent explicit instructions. In 1773, for example, the British government sent royal instructions to colonial governors in America and

Canada expressing the king's

expressed will and Pleasure that you do not upon any pretence whatsoever give your assent to any Bill or Bills that may have been or shall hereafter have been passed by the Council and Assembly of the Province under your Government for the naturalization of Aliens nor for the divorce of persons joined together in Holy Marriage.[52]

Instructions such as these were ignored by the governor of Massachusetts, where divorces continued to be granted at an increasing rate through the eighteenth century (see Chapter 7). It is possible that Massachusetts was able to ignore the British instruction as there was no new divorce legislation in the eighteenth century to which the governor might refuse his assent. Moreover, divorces were granted by the courts, so that bills for the dissolution of individual marriages were not considered by the colony's legislature. Connecticut, too, continued to dissolve marriages during the eighteenth century, even more than Massachusetts, and it was not impeded by British instructions. In fact the royal instructions of 1773, addressed to the governors of the American colonies, did not include Connecticut or some other colonies, such as Rhode Island, in which divorce had been legalized in the seventeenth century. This was ironic; in Connecticut both the Superior Court and the General Assembly (the colony's legislature) had the right to dissolve marriages, and these bills were ratified by the governor. One such legislative divorce, obtained by Sarah Wolcott against her husband Jeremiah, was passed in 1773.[53]

As we have seen, Pennsylvania's divorce law of 1700 was disallowed by the British authorities, and in the middle of the eighteenth century one of the Canadian colonies, Nova Scotia, also encountered problems when it tried to legalize divorce. In 1750, a year after the colony was founded, the governor of Nova Scotia and his council, composed of army officers, agreed to a petition from a lieutenant for a divorce on the ground of his wife's adultery. The husband was given permission to remarry, but the wife was forbidden to do so during his lifetime, and in addition she was ordered to leave the colony within ten days.[54] The British authorities quickly intervened in what seemed like an exercise of ad hoc justice. The executive divorce was disallowed, but the Nova Scotia authorities persisted in their determination to have provision for the dissolution of marriage. In 1758 the colony moved to government by assembly, and promptly passed an act "Concerning Marriage, and Divorce, and for Punishing Incest and adultery, and Declaring Polygamy a Felony." This law would have allowed divorce on the grounds of impotence, marriage within the prohibited degrees, adultery, and desertion while withholding maintenance for three years.

---

[52] Leonard Woods Labaree (ed.), *Royal Instructions to British Colonial Governors, 1670–1776* (New York, 1935, repr. 1967), 154–5.

[53] Cohn, "Connecticut's Divorce Mechanism," 42.

[54] Kimberley Smith, "Divorce in Nova Scotia, 1750–1890," in J. Phillips and P. Girard (eds.), *Essays in the History of Canadian Law, Volume 3: The Nova Scotian Experience* (Toronto, 1988). Smith kindly agreed to let me see her essay in typescript before publication. References to it in this book omit pagination. See also Constance Backhouse, "'Pure Patriarchy': Nineteenth-Century Canadian Marriage," *McGill Law Journal* 13 (1986), 267.

4.4 American challenge to English policy

The British government disallowed this legislation in turn, in 1761, because it was at odds with prevailing English law, but then quite inconsistently approved a law allowing divorce on the grounds of impotence, precontract, adultery, and cruelty. The last two of these grounds were recognized as reasons for a separation *a mensa et thoro* in England, and it is difficult to understand why the authorities in London should have approved the 1761 provisions when they had disallowed the 1758 act. The earlier law, which had included the classic Protestant grounds of adultery and desertion (aggravated desertion in the abortive Nova Scotia law) should, in principle, have been more acceptable than the latter version that stressed adultery and cruelty. Yet the 1761 law was approved and remained the basis of the colony's (later the province's) divorce law until the twentieth century.[55]

The legislative precociousness of Nova Scotia among the Canadian colonies in terms of divorce was in part influenced by its Scottish Calvinist character, and in part a reflection of the influence of the New England colonies to the south. The Canadian maritime colonies had more commercial and cultural links with New England than with the other Canadian colonies to the west. Many of Nova Scotia's settlers came from Massachusetts, as did the colony's chief justice, Belcher, who drafted many of its earliest statutes.[56] Perhaps the determination of Nova Scotia to provide for divorce, despite the British rebuffs of 1750 and 1758, reflected the experience of Massachusetts that throughout the seventeenth and eighteenth centuries ignored the constitutional prohibitions on divorce legislation.

Other American colonies were less persistent, although they did sporadically attempt to dissolve marriage, as we have seen. The British reaction in 1773, in the form of a circular warning governors against assenting to divorce laws, seems to have been provoked specifically by attempts to dissolve marriages by several colonial legislatures between 1769 and 1773. The British aim at this time appears to have been less to stamp out divorce laws and procedures where they already existed and had become part of some colonies' legal and social institutions and more to prevent their spread to colonies where there were no legal or other provisions for divorce.

The first of the acts to which the British took particular exception was passed by the Pennsylvania General Assembly, dissolving the marriage of Curtis and Anne Grubb for reason of her adultery and subsequent bigamous remarriage, and permitting the husband to remarry. The bill was passed and given assent by the governor, then submitted to the Board of Trade and Plantations in London for royal approval.[57] The board in turn referred the bill to a prominent London barrister, Richard Jackson. His opinion was that Grubb's divorce was not

---

[55] The explanatory note issued with the 1761 law only confused the issues, making inconsistent distinctions among divorce, separation, and annulment. See Backhouse, " 'Pure Patriarchy'," 268–269, n. 10.
[56] Smith, "Divorce in Nova Scotia."
[57] Meehan, " 'Not Made Out of Levity'," 443.

repugnant to the laws of England, perhaps because it seemed similar in substance and form to divorces then allowed in England; it was a dissolution of marriage granted by a legislature to a husband for reason of his wife's adultery, just as English divorces by private Act of Parliament were (see Chapter 7). Even so, the barrister urged the attorney-general and solicitor-general to review the Pennsylvania act "as the exercise of this power might frequently affect other parts of [the] Dominions...and [as] very important Consequences might be drawn from [its] allowance."[58] It appears, though, that the British officials accepted that the Pennsylvania law was not repugnant to British law, and King George III gave his assent to the dissolution of Curtis Grubb's marriage.

Grubb's success seems to have encouraged other Pennsylvanians, and in 1772 and 1773 there were four petitions to the General Assembly for dissolutions of marriage. In two of these the assembly took no action. In the third case, which involved a marriage between a woman of "insane Mind and Understanding" and a man "almost an Idiot," the assembly agreed to a dissolution, but the governor, on the advice of the provincial council, declined to approve it. The probable reason was that the ground for divorce varied from English practice, which limited divorces to a woman's adultery. Perhaps it was because it did conform to English practice that the fourth Pennsylvania divorce bill, lodged in 1772 by George Keehmle against his wife for adultery, had more success. It was passed by the General Assembly, given assent by the governor, and referred to London for royal approval. There, however, Keehmle's divorce died. The Board of Trade submitted the bill to the Privy Council

to the end that if it shall be thought that the [colonial] Acts of Divorce...are either Improper or Unconstitutional...[it] may be advised to give such Directions as shall have the effect to prevent the Laws passed by the Legislature of Pennsylvania becoming a Precedent and an Example for the Exercise of the like powers in other colonies.[59]

The principal concern of the Board of Trade was that Pennsylvania's method of dissolving marriages involved only the legislature, not, as English practice required, a prior separation *a mensa et thoro* from an ecclesiastical court and a successful civil action for damages for criminal conversation against the wife's accomplice in adultery. This opinion ignored the fact that the American colonies had made matrimonial law a matter of civil jurisdiction, and it was a sign of the hardening attitude of the British authorities that the Privy Council "disallowed, revoked and rendered null and void" Keehmle's divorce. Six months later the British government issued its instruction to colonial governors, requiring them to refuse assent to any divorce bills.

In the preceding few years, divorce bills from other American colonies had been disallowed by the British government. A 1772 act of the New Jersey legislature, dissolving the marriage of David and Margaret Baxter was disallowed the following year.[60] Similarly, two New Hampshire divorce bills, one

[58] Quoted in ibid., 445.
[59] Quoted in ibid., 446; see also Blake, *Road to Reno*, 47.
[60] Blake, *Road to Reno*, 45, 47.

from 1771 and the other from 1773, were disallowed in the latter year. As Nelson Blake comments: "What embarrassments were thus caused by upsetting divorces two or three years after the event, we can only imagine."[61]

The refusal of the British to give their approval to divorce bills in three of the American colonies, together with the blanket instruction to governors to deny approval to such legislation, must have contributed to the resentment the colonists felt against British rule. The first specific grievance cited by Thomas Jefferson against King George III was that he "has refused his Assent to Laws, the most wholesome and necessary for the public good."[62] Even the historian of divorce, tempted to find divorce at the center of all intellectual change and social trends, would be straining the evidence to make the issue central to the outbreak of the American Revolution, but it was clearly one complaint.

It is noteworthy that Jefferson, a member of the Virginia legislature, did address the question of divorce directly in the period 1771–2, just when the Pennsylvania, New Jersey, and New Hampshire legislatures were passing acts to dissolve individual marriages. Jefferson's interest in divorce arose from his work as a lawyer and representative involved in the marital problems of Dr. James Blair, of Williamsburg, and his wife. The Blairs married in 1771, but did not consummate the marriage, and separated definitively after nineteen months of what appears to have been continuous misery relieved only by several periods of brief separation. In late 1772 Jefferson undertook to prepare a divorce bill for Dr. Blair, but the bill was never put before the legislature because Blair died in December of that year. Nonetheless, Jefferson's notes for the bill (under the title "Blair v. Blair. On a bill of Divorce to propose during the General Assembly") show that he had read widely in seventeenth- and eighteenth-century works on the subject, particularly those of Pufendorf, Locke, Hume, and Montesquieu.[63] Jefferson's notes were composed overwhelmingly of arguments in favor of divorce, as they were bound to, given his sources. Although there were also some counterarguments, it can safely be assumed, from the very fact that he was marshaling support for a divorce bill, that Jefferson believed that divorce should be possible not only in cases of adultery but also when marriages were struck by incompatibility. This was the circumstance in the Blairs' marriage; although Dr. Blair had accused the governor of Virginia, Lord Dunmore, of committing adultery with his wife, he withdrew the allegation,[64] leaving only incompatibility, or some equivalent word or phrase, as the possible justification for dissolving the marriage.[65]

---

[61] Ibid., 47.
[62] Quoted in ibid.
[63] Frank L. Dewey, "Thomas Jefferson's Notes on Divorce," *William and Mary Quarterly* 3rd. ser., 39 (1982), 214.
[64] Ibid., 214n.8.
[65] We can assume that this was a divorce, not an annulment on the ground of nonconsummation. Had it been the latter, there would have been no need for Jefferson's research and the marshaling of authorities in favor of divorce.

4.5 Independence and the spread of divorce

Clearly, the British prohibition on divorce bills had kept a lid on what was growing pressure for a broader availability of divorce. With the outbreak of the American war of independence and the effective end of British interference in American legislation, petitions for dissolutions of marriage and legislative divorces began to increase. Pennsylvania led the way, perhaps appropriately because it was the Pennsylvania divorce bill of 1773 whose disallowance by the British government had been the reason for the blanket rejection of all colonial divorce bills referred to London for royal approval. Unsuccessful in 1773 because of British opposition, the Pennsylvania legislature was able to act without constraint after 1776. Between 1777 and 1785 thirty-five petitions for divorce were made to the state's General Assembly, and eleven of them were successful.[66] Of the remainder only seven were rejected, while seventeen lapsed or died in the full assembly or in the committee that was delegated to investigate and determine the facts of each individual case. Most of the successful petitions were based on adultery,[67] the ground that had been accepted in earlier Pennsylvania law. The legislators clung to the principle of fault, quickly rejecting a joint request by Dolly and Graft Gosse "praying that their marriage...be dissolved," on the ground that there was collusion.[68] One petition of particular interest was that of George Keehmle, the legislative dissolution of whose marriage was rejected by the Privy Council in 1773. Ten years after her husband's landmark failure, Elizabeth Keehmle petitioned to have the colonial legislature's bill given legal effect. Just as she seemed on the verge of success, however, George Keehmle, not knowing when to leave well enough alone, intervened to have his wife's petition dismissed so that he could apply in his own name for the colonial bill to be made operative. The General Assembly declined his request and refused to take any further action in the case.[69] After all their trouble, the Keehmles' marriage remained intact until dissolved not by divorce but by the death of one of them.

Movement in divorce legislation was by no means confined to Pennsylvania. If we consider together those states that either began to dissolve marriages by acts of their legislatures or passed legislation making divorces available from the state courts, the list is impressive. In addition to the beginning of legislative divorce in Pennsylvania in 1777, it included Pennsylvania (new statute, 1785), Massachusetts (1786), New York (1787), Maryland (1790), New Hampshire (1791), New Jersey (1794), North Carolina (1794), Georgia (1798), Vermont (1798), Rhode Island (1798), and Tennessee (1799). More states enacted divorce laws or introduced divorce in some other form during the first decade of the nineteenth century (see Section 11.8).

---

[66] Meehan, "'Not Made Out of Levity'," 446.
[67] Ibid., 448.
[68] Ibid., 447.
[69] Ibid., 448.

4.5 Independence and the spread of divorce

This surge in divorce-related legislative activity and the spread of divorce throughout almost all of the United States at the end of the eighteenth century took various forms. It was not consistently progressive, as witness the Massachusetts statute of 1786 that allowed the state's supreme court to grant divorces on the grounds of bigamy, impotence, or adultery and to permit separations where there was evidence of "extreme cruelty." As such, the statute was regressive compared to the seventeenth-century legislation that had permitted divorce for reason of desertion, in addition to the grounds specified in the 1786 law. It was not until 1811 that desertion was again made a matrimonial offense, and then it attracted only separation, not divorce, as its remedy.

With this exception, however, the northeastern states enacted legislation in the 1790s permitting divorce either on the grounds that had been accepted during the colonial period or in more liberal forms.[70] Adultery and desertion continued to be regarded as sufficiently serious offenses to warrant divorce, and the individual states added further grounds as they considered them appropriate. New Hampshire's 1791 legislation recognized impotence, adultery, extreme cruelty, and three years' absence as grounds for either husbands or wives to file for divorce, and wives could also seek a divorce on the ground of abandonment and failure to provide over a period of three years. The 1798 Vermont law recognized impotence, adultery, intolerable cruelty, three years' malicious desertion, and long absence with a presumption of death. In Rhode Island the grounds for divorce were similar, together with a general authority for the courts to grant divorces in cases of "gross misbehaviour and wickedness in either of the parties, repugnant to and in violation of the marriage covenant."[71] What was significant about these divorce laws was not only their codification of existing practice and principle, and in some cases their liberalization, but also their shift in jurisdiction. They tended toward giving the power to dissolve marriages to the highest level of state courts, thus removing divorce by legislative act from New England.

This trend toward judicial divorce was also evident in the middle colonies. Pennsylvania was one case in point. After the end of British control, the General Assembly had been struck by what must have seemed a veritable deluge of divorce petitions (thirty-five between 1777 and 1785), occupying the time of the legislators to an unprecedented, and no doubt unwanted, extent. Each divorce bill had two readings in the full assembly before being referred to a committee composed typically of three representatives from the petitioner's county. The committee acted as a court, hearing witnesses, determining the facts of the case, and finally recommending a decision. This decision was advertised in newspapers to ensure public knowledge of the divorce, and then, in the form of a bill, went through three more readings in the General Assembly before becoming law.[72] This unwieldy procedure rivaled that of the English

---

[70] See Blake, *Road to Reno*, 48–63.
[71] Ibid., 50.
[72] Meehan, " 'Not Made Out of Levity'," 450.

155

parliamentary divorces, but because Pennsylvania divorces were not expensive, the General Assembly was faced with more divorce bills than it wanted to handle. They cut so deeply into legislative time that in 1783 a committee was appointed to look into "the most just and proper mode of regulating divorces in this state".[73]

The result of this investigation was Pennsylvania's divorce law of 1785. It gave jurisdiction over divorce to the state supreme court, with the right of appeal to the High Court of Errors and Appeals. Moreover, the law expanded the grounds for divorce from adultery alone to adultery, bigamy, desertion for four years, and, in the case of second marriages, foreknowledge of impotence or sterility. A further provision added an unusual ground for dissolution: If a husband or wife, "upon false rumour in appearance well founded, of the death of the other," contracted a second marriage, then the first spouse, if he or she returned, could choose either to have the original marriage restored or could elect to have it dissolved, leaving the other spouse's second marriage intact.[74] In addition to these grounds for divorce, the 1785 Pennsylvania statute permitted separation *a mensa et thoro* for adultery, bigamy, desertion, or if a husband should "turn his wife out of doors, or by cruel and barbarous treatment endanger her life or offer such indignities to her person as to render her condition intolerable...and thereby force her to withdraw from his house and family."[75]

This act placed Pennsylvania's divorce provisions among the most liberal in the American states and in practice they went even further. Although the law gave jurisdiction over divorce to the supreme court, the General Assembly reserved the right to dissolve marriages by legislative act when they did not fall into the circumstances specified by the law. Between 1795 and 1874 the legislature approved 291 divorces by this means.[76] The 1785 law also contained two other provisions that began to appear frequently in divorce legislation. The first was a residency requirement, the necessity for petitioners for divorce to have lived a specified time in the state where they were seeking divorce, before filing a petition. In the case of Pennsylvania the residency requirement was one year. The purpose of such clauses was to prevent states with liberal divorce laws from becoming "divorce havens" for the citizens of states where divorce was restrictive. Out-of-state divorce petitioners could not only clog up the courts of liberal states, but the movement of citizens from one jurisdiction to another for the purpose of divorce could create problems of the recognition of divorces that might be acceptable in one state but not in others. The second innovation of the 1785 law was the provision of alimony, though it was restricted to women who obtained separations. In such cases the court could grant alimony depending on

[73] Ibid., 453.
[74] Ibid.
[75] Ibid.
[76] Ibid., 453n.1. Legislative divorces were terminated by the state constitution of 1874.

the husband's financial circumstances, but in no case could it exceed a third of his annual profits, income, or wages.[77]

In general, the transfer of authority to dissolve marriages from legislature to regular courts went together with a liberal approach to divorce. Most of the laws providing for judicial divorce allowed a wide range of justifying grounds, whereas those that entrusted divorce to the legislatures tended to be restrictive in terms of grounds. Judicial divorce was far less cumbersome and opened the way for many more divorces than could be managed by legislators in full assembly or committee, hearing and attempting to assess evidence in matrimonial matters, as well as dealing with the myriad other areas of legislation and concerns of government. It was finally the sheer bulk of divorce petitions that drove many state legislatures to surrender the power of divorce to the judiciary. New York's first divorce law, passed in 1787, demonstrated the two aspects of restrictive legislation. Divorce was available only for adultery, and the guilty spouse was forbidden to remarry. Petitions for divorce were filed with the chancellor of the state, who had the power to authorize divorce, although he could provide for a lower court to hear the facts of each case.[78]

It was in the southern states that legislative divorce was retained more systematically, indicative of their continuing conservatism in marriage law, even after they had made divorce available. In Maryland, as we have noted, the legislature granted a divorce in 1790 to a man whose wife had committed adultery and borne a mulatto child. Full jurisdiction over divorce was not given to the Maryland courts until 1842, and the legislature of the state retained the authority to dissolve marriages until 1851. The Georgia constitution of 1798 provided for the superior court of the state to hear petitions for divorce and to issue decrees, but they had no legal force until each house of the legislature had approved them by a two-thirds vote. Between 1798 and 1835 the legislature approved 291 divorces in this way.[79] In North Carolina the first divorce was granted by legislative act in 1794, and from then until 1814 only the legislature could dissolve marriages. After that date both the courts and legislature granted divorces, and it was only in 1835 that legislative divorces were terminated.[80] In Virginia the first divorce, by an act of the legislature, was decreed in 1803. Legislative divorces on the sole ground of adultery were granted in the state until 1848, although in 1827 the Virginia Court of Chancery was empowered to annul marriages because of impotence, idiocy, or bigamy and to grant separations for reason of adultery or cruelty.[81]

---

[77] Ibid., 455.
[78] Blake, *Road to Reno*, 65; Henry H. Foster and Doris J. Freed, *Dissolution of the Family Unit* (New York, 1972), 256–8.
[79] Friedman, *A History of American Law*, 182.
[80] Joseph S. Ferrell, "Early Statutory and Common Law of Divorce in North Carolina," *North Carolina Law Review* 41 (1963), 609–10.
[81] Blake, *Road to Reno*, 52.

4 Divorce in the American world

It would be repetitious and tedious to set out the developments in divorce law in every one of the American states in the first decades of independence. But the pattern is clear enough: the codification of practice into statute law in the New England colonies and the spread of divorce to more of the middle colonies and to the South. The enduring conservatism and caution with regard to divorce was manifested in the restrictions imposed by the legislative procedures. In such states the legislators, fearing a deluge and wanting to keep direct control of the floodgates, monitored the rate of divorces, either by keeping the whole procedure within the legislature or at least by reserving the right to give assent to divorce decrees issued by the courts. The conservatism of South Carolina in these matters went even further to a refusal to allow any kind of divorce in the state until 1868, and then only temporarily.

The essential point about divorce in this period was its dramatic geographical spread throughout the American states. It was not merely fortuitous. It is clear that the constitutional impediment to the legalization of divorce – British opposition – was destroyed when the American colonies achieved their independence. Even so, the end of British rule did no more than make divorce possible. It explains why the Pennsylvania legislature almost immediately began to grant divorces, but it does not explain why those states that had never legalized divorce or shown any eagerness to, participated in what appears to have been a feverish bout of divorce legislating in the 1780s and 1790s. It could well have been that these colonies had bowed silently to the requirements of their charters and accepted that the authority to dissolve marriages was beyond their authority. On the other hand it is also clear that several colonies, in particular the southern ones, were led by men who shared the Church of England's opposition to divorce. In these cases we must look to changing attitudes toward divorce and an increased readiness to accept it as a remedy in certain circumstances for explanations of the spread and liberalization of divorce policies in America.

5

•••

Eighteenth-century France:
Enlightenment and legislation

5.1 Marriage and divorce in the Old Regime

The development of divorce in France was irrevocably altered by the French Revolution. A divorce law enacted in 1792 gave France one of the most liberal and permissive divorce policies that have ever been applied on a national basis in Western society; it is rivaled in these characteristics only by modern Swedish divorce law. What is particularly striking is that the French revolutionary law was not the culmination of an evolution of divorce legislation in an increasingly liberal direction but that it came into effect in a country where, until 1792, divorce had not been available at all. This French divorce law, then, represented a truly radical break with French legal tradition and continuity, and it had long-term implications for the development of divorce in France in the nineteenth and twentieth centuries.

The doctrine of marital indissolubility was enforced in Old Regime France not only by the Catholic church but also by the state, which took an increasing interest in family law. Although the decrees of the Council of Trent were not officially received in France, the Tridentine doctrines on marriage passed into French law through the Edit de Blois, issued by Henry III in 1580.[1] Secular and ecclesiastical laws did not permit the dissolution of marriage, then, although judicial separations – *séparations de corps et d'habitation* – were provided for. Jurisdiction over separations changed over time. In the Middle Ages the church courts had authority over matrimonial matters in France for the most part, but by the eighteenth century there was general agreement that because separations almost invariably entailed issues involving property, the secular courts had a claim to jurisdiction over them.[2]

The grounds for judicial separation varied somewhat according to region and jurisdiction, but they almost always involved a matrimonial offense on the part of the husband. Describing the state of the law in the middle of the eighteenth

---

[1] This edict was part of the French monarchy's attempt to take authority over marriage and family legislation from the church. These efforts of the monarchy to control the validity of marriages are described in Chapter 6.

[2] David Houard, *Dictionnaire analytique, historique, étymologique, critique et interpretatif de la Coutume de Normandie* (4 vols., Rouen, 1780–2), II, 275.

century, the *Encyclopédie* set out six broad grounds upon which a *séparation de corps* might be obtained. These were the husband's violence or ill-treatment, but only when it was considerable; his falsely accusing his wife of adultery or other dishonorable acts; the conviction of the husband for attempting to murder his wife; his insanity, where there was reason to fear for his wife's life; and his conceiving a deadly hatred (*haine capitale*) of her.[3]

The *Encyclopédie* made the important point that, except for rare occasions, it was the wife who sought a *séparation de corps* because, being under the authority of her husband, she could not legally leave him unless granted permission to do so by a court.[4] This explains why the grounds for separation cited were all framed in terms of a matrimonial offense on the part of a husband: When faced by a wife guilty of an offense, whether it be the equivalent of those listed or an informal one such as disobedience, a husband was presumed to have other means at his disposal to remedy the situation. By virtue of his superior legal and social position he could, in the first place, order his wife to change her ways, and he could apply a certain degree of physical force to this end. Physical force was known as *correction modérée* ("moderate correction") and, as elsewhere where husbands were given this power, the law did not define "moderation."[5] If such methods failed, other means were available to the husband: "The wife who behaves badly towards her husband must not, for that reason, be released from his authority, but he may obtain an order for her to be confined in a convent."[6] As an example, we can cite the case of one Sieur Delaître, who in 1774 applied to have his wife committed to a convent in Evreux (Normandy) "in order to restrain her from her habits of drunkenness."[7]

Married men, then, had a variety of informal and formal remedies when faced with behavior on the part of their wives that they considered unacceptable. Women lacked the equivalent legal, social, and even physical standing, and the law provided *séparations de corps* as some compensation. Separations in Old Regime France should be seen, though, not as remedies for marriage breakdown, nor even as punishments for matrimonial offenses by the husband, but rather as a means of protecting the wife physically and morally from her husband's depredations. The terms under which the customary law of Normandy allowed *séparation de corps* are revealing in this respect. For example, adultery by the husband was a ground for a separation only when he committed it in the marital dwelling; when a man committed adultery other than at home, he could do so with impunity, and his wife had simply to be patient. But "when her husband becomes her oppressor and forces her to witness his immorality, then public decency demands that the unfortunate woman be helped." It was not the husband's adultery per se that was the offense, but the form of it that

---

[3] *Encyclopédie, ou dictionnaire raisonné des arts et des métiers* (17 vols., Paris, 1785), XV, 60.
[4] Ibid.
[5] The concept of "moderate correction" is discussed in Section 9.3.
[6] *Encyclopédie*, XV, 60.
[7] Archives départementales de la Seine-Maritime, C 25 (Parlement de Normandie), 1774.

directly offended the wife's honor and sensitivity. Similarly, a *séparation de corps* protected the wife's physical well-being when she was subject to her husband's ill-treatment, but only if it was severe (beyond "moderation") and "capable of endangering the wife's life." A third motive was public defamation of his wife by the husband.[8]

This general rule, that *séparations de corps* were solely at the disposal of a morally or physically endangered married woman, was especially applied by the civil law regulating separations. Ecclesiastical legislation was more balanced and aimed at dealing with the marital relationship itself, as well as with the well-being of the wife. Under church law there were four broad grounds that could justify a separation: adultery, heresy, ill-treatment, and the mutual consent of the spouses when one of them wished to take up a religious vocation. Although there was probably discrimination in practice, in principle either wife or husband could petition for a separation on any of these grounds. For example, a wife could obtain a separation from her adulterous husband (as long as she was innocent of the same offense),[9] but it should be noted that while imprisonment in a convent was provided in ecclesiastical law for an adulterous woman, there was no such penalty for a husband who was convicted of adultery.

Generally, then, whether we are referring to civil or ecclesiastical legislation, the terms of legislation regulating *séparations de corps et d'habitation* were very limited. The costs of proceedings added to the restrictive character of the institution, and we should expect the number of separations to have been small.

The limitations of separations as a means of dealing with marital problems are shown in a study of *séparations de corps* in the diocese of Cambrai, which included parts of northeastern France and of the Austrian Netherlands.[10] Separations there were dealt with by judges of the *officialité* (bishop's court), who applied canon law. We may compare this situation with Rouen, in Normandy, where petitions for separations were judged by secular magistrates of the civil chamber of the Bailliage court, applying not canon law but the customary law of Normandy.[11] In fact, both of these legal codes recognized similar grounds for separation, although there were some differences between them. For example, canon law did not permit separation for reason of insanity, whereas Norman customary law did; in 1782 one woman from Rouen was separated from her husband who had claimed to have seen the Holy Spirit in the form of a butterfly and to have been chosen by God to convert the Jews to Christianity. The husband in question, evidently well-to-do, had gone to Paris, dressed in a suit of white silk, where he distributed money to understandably willing converts. More recently, he had been seen back in Rouen wearing "a sheet on his back, a

---

[8] Houard, *Dictionnaire*, II, 275.

[9] Louis de Héricourt, *Les loix ecclésiatiques de France dans leur ordre naturel et une analyse des livres du droit canonique conférés avec les usages de l'Eglise gallicane* (2 vols., Paris, 1748), II, 107, sec. xxix.

[10] Alain Lottin, *La désunion du couple sous l'Ancien Régime: L'exemple du Nord* (Lille; Paris, 1975), is the source for the following data on the diocese of Cambrai.

[11] The following information on Rouen is from Roderick Phillips, *Family Breakdown in Late Eighteenth-Century France: Divorces in Rouen, 1792–1803* (Oxford, 1980), 6ff.

towel on his head, one black and one white stocking, a haversack on his back, a doll and a rabbit in his arms."[12]

There were also differences between the two jurisdictions in terms of the incidence of separations, but in neither case could they be described as common. There is no long-term study of separations in Rouen, but there appear to have been only thirty-three petitions during the decade 1780–9, and of these, a mere four appear to have been successful. In the diocese of Cambrai there were more than 593 separations (the records are incomplete) in the period from 1710 to 1791, an average of 7 annually for a population considerably larger than that of Rouen; Rouen had a population of about 85,000 at the end of the eighteenth century, while at midcentury the diocese of Cambrai comprised some 400,000 inhabitants. Within the eighteenth century, separations were more common in the second half than the first: In Cambrai diocese there was an annual average of 5.4 separations from 1710 to 1736, increasing to 8.7 between 1737 and 1774 (when the records cease to be reliable), although we should note that population increased appreciably in the period, too.

All of the separations in Rouen were obtained (and all of the petitions lodged) by women because customary law made separation accessible only to wives. The canon law, however, enabled either spouse to petition, and we find separations in Cambrai being obtained by men. Between 1710 and 1736, women initiated 71% of separations, men 24%, and 5% were joint petitions. By the period 1737–74, the proportion of petitions lodged by women had increased to 76%, those by men had fallen to 13%, and joint requests for a separation had increased to 11% of the total. It is interesting to note that his range of 71–76% of petitions by women coincided with the proportion of wife-initiated divorce petitions almost everywhere in France after divorce was legalized in 1792 (see Section 7.4).

Not only were separations rare, but they were largely confined to the relatively well-off social groups. In Cambrai, more than half those involved in separation proceedings emanated from the urban middle classes (bourgeois, professionals, and those with private incomes), a quarter from the social élite (nobles and notables), and a fifth from the lower strata, such as artisans. Only 6% of separations in this region involved men and women in agricultural work, a clear indication of the urban association with separations and divorces.[13]

Judging from regional studies, separations were rare in eighteenth-century France – as rare as divorces were in those parts of Europe where divorce had been legalized. It might be argued that the infrequency of separations indicated widespread happiness, satisfaction, or resignation to the married state, but the much higher rate of divorces after the legalization of divorce in 1792 suggests that separations were a less attractive remedy than divorce for marriage breakdown. After 1792, divorce was often used to terminate marriages that had

---

[12] Ibid., 156.
[13] Alain Lottin, "Vie et mort du couple: Difficultiés conjugales et divorces dans le Nord de la France aux XVII\ee{}et XVIII\e{} siècles," *XVII\ee{} siècle* 102–3 (1974), 66.

effectively ended by desertion or informal separation many years earlier. Divorced spouses were thus enabled to remarry and put de facto relationships on a legal footing. Separation did not imply these advantages, and separated women in particular were left in an ambiguous social position, neither in a functioning marriage nor able to form a new marriage, yet expected to live the socially and sexually restricted life of a married woman.

5.2 Critics of Old Regime marriage law

Séparations de corps were unpopular not only with those who might possibly have used them but also among social commentators and critics, and from the sixteenth century there was a current of criticism hostile to the doctrine of marital indissolubility and in favor of the legalization of divorce. One of the first reactions against the Tridentine affirmation of the doctrine of indissolubility was that of Michel de Montaigne, for it was included in the second book of his *Essays*, published in 1580, the very year that the Edict of Blois affirmed the doctrine in France. Writing to the proposition "that our devices are increased by difficulty," Montaigne noted "we thought to tie the bond of our marriages the faster, by removing all means to dissolve them; but by how much faster, that of constraint has been tied, so much worse has that of our own will and affection been slackened and loosened." In Ancient Rome, he wrote, it was the liberty of divorce that had held marriage together; "they kept their wives the better, because they might leave them; and when divorce might freely be had, there passed five hundred years and more, before any man would ever make use of them."[14] There were other, sporadic, references to divorce during the seventeenth century, but it was not comparable in vigor and extent with the debate that went on in England at the same time.

At the end of the seventeenth century the annexation of Alsace brought divorce within the frontiers of France, for the majority of the province's population was Lutheran, and divorce had been permitted there since the sixteenth century. After annexation, the Consistory courts of Alsace continued to grant divorces for reason of adultery, but in 1692 a French royal order forbade the practice.[15] The order was provoked by protests on the part of the minority Catholic population of Strasbourg against the granting of a divorce to a man in 1690 on the ground of his wife's adultery. Representations were made, and in 1692 the Praetor (royal governor) of Strasbourg ordered the city authorities:

You will advise the magistrates of Strasbourg that it is not the King's pleasure that they render any future decisions permitting inhabitants of the city who are separated on grounds of adultery to remarry, and that if, having been informed of the will of His Majesty, they should fail to observe it, whoever presided over the deliberations will be put into prison and all his belongings confiscated.[16]

[14] Michel de Montaigne, *Essais* (3 vols., Paris, 1972), Book II, Chapter 15.
[15] Jean-Baptiste Denisart, *Collection de décisions nouvelles et de notions relatives à la jurisprudence* (9 vols., Paris, 1783–8), VI, 569.
[16] Franklin L. Ford, *Strasbourg in Transition, 1648–1789* (New York, 1966), 92.

5 Eighteenth-century France

We might note, too, that Jews, the other main non-Catholic population in France that allowed divorce, also encountered problems with French law. In the eighteenth century there were some 50,000 Jews living in France, concentrated (by law) in Alsace, Lorraine, Paris, Avignon, the Comtat-Venaisson, Bordeaux, and Bayonne. The difficulties faced by Jews, whose religion permitted divorce, in a Catholic country that did not, was exemplified by two notable cases. In the first, Joseph Jean-François-Elie (Borach) Lévy, a Jew married according to Jewish law, converted to Catholicism and was baptized, but his wife refused to abjure her religion. Lévy was led to believe that his baptism had dissolved his first, non-Christian, marriage, and tried to marry a Catholic woman, only to have the priest refuse to call the banns on the ground that Lévy was already married. The case, Lévy versus the bishop of Soissons, came before the Parlement of Paris in 1758, where Lévy argued that although marriage was indissoluble, there were exceptional cases such as his own. He cited the example of Jews in Germany (where, he said, baptism in the Catholic faith required Jewish couples to remarry as Catholics), and he also invoked the Pauline Privilege, a variety of church authorities who admitted divorce, and even precedents in France. For all this, the Paris Parlement rejected his suit and reaffirmed, in the most uncompromising terms, the doctrine of marital indissolubility.[17]

Yet in the second case involving a Jew, the French judicial authorities seemed prepared to countenance the possibility of recognizing a Jewish divorce. This was the suit involving Samuel Péixotto and Sara Mendes, who had been married in London. Péixotto argued that he should be allowed to divorce because various royal edicts had given the Portuguese Jewish community, of which he was a member, the right to live in France according to their own customs. Jewish custom, he held, provided for the dissolution of marriage, so he should be permitted to divorce despite the Catholic doctrine of marital indissolubility. The Parlement of Paris, to whose jurisdiction this case fell on appeal in 1777, went so far as to refer the matter to the sephardic community in Bordeaux to see whether or not Péixotto would be entitled to a divorce under Jewish law. This case was not resolved (Péixotto left France to live in Spain), and we cannot know whether the divorce would have been allowed had the Jewish authorities sanctioned it according to their law. Yet it is noteworthy that the Parlement did not dismiss the petition summarily and was prepared to consider it seriously.[18]

The more flexible attitude of the Parlement of Paris in the 1770s reflected a

---

[17] The case is set out in Denisart, *Collection de décisions*, VI, 569–86. It is also summarized in James F. Traer, *Marriage and the Family in Eighteenth-Century France* (Ithaca, 1980), 61–3.

[18] See Denisart, *Collection de décisions*, VI, 586–8; and Traer, *Marriage and the Family*, 63–4. Venette, *De la génération de l'homme ou tableau de l'Amour Conjugal* (Paris, 1716), provides the decree of a Jewish unilateral divorce that appears to date from the seventeenth century, but it emanated not from France but from the Jewish community in Venice.

relaxation in the universal application of Catholic principles in respect of family issues that seems to have begun about the middle of the eighteenth century. One sign of this was the greater willingness of French courts to uphold the provisions made in wills drawn up by Protestants; earlier in the century, Protestants had had their property confiscated at death because they had not been married according to Catholic rites and the courts had deemed their children to be illegitimate.[19] The modest culmination of this more tolerant trend was the 1787 Edict of Toleration that gave formal recognition of the validity of non-Catholic marriages and provided for registers of vital events to be kept for non-Catholics, parallelling the parish registers for Catholics. The Catholic doctrine of marital indissolubility, however, was maintained for Catholics and non-Catholics alike.

Pressure to reform French family law and its underlying principles was exerted throughout the eighteenth century. As we shall see in Chapter 6, there were criticisms of the dominance of the church and of church doctrine over marriage and family law in the seventeenth century by Erastian proponents of state dominance and by advocates of contract theory. But it remained for the intellectual ferment of the next century, the century of the Enlightenment, to take the issue up in a more sustained and vigorous manner. All aspects of the family were analyzed and criticized in the light of rationalism, natural law, liberty, and natural rights: marriage, inheritance, paternal authority, marital authority, the role of religion, and divorce. These writings – and the emphasis here will be on those dealing with marriage and divorce – represented a significant theme in the social criticism of the Enlightenment, and they take on even greater importance when considered as the background to the radical reform of French family law in the 1790s.

Among the writers in favor of legalizing divorce in eighteenth-century France, we may distinguish two broad groups. The first comprised many of the better-known *philosophes*, such as Montesquieu, Condorcet, Voltaire, Diderot, Helvétius, d'Holbach, and Morelly. Yet apart from Montesquieu and Morelly, they dealt with divorce in a cursory and often frustratingly vague way, and we need to turn to a corpus of literature by minor writers to find a careful consideration of the issues. Among those works were a great number devoted solely to the advocacy of divorce, and other writers placed divorce firmly in the context of other social issues.

One of the prime lines of argument in favor of divorce was that the doctrine of marital indissolubility was contrary to nature. Humans, it was argued, were too fickle to be able successfully to engage themselves in perpetuity in an indissoluble relationship. Wrote Lavie:

Natural law gives man the right to flee from unhappiness and to free himself of it. Civil societies were established to provide man with more happy and peaceful days; their

[19] David Bien, "Catholic Magistrates and Protestant Marriage in the French Enlightenment," *French Historical Studies* 2 (1962), 409–29.

purpose was never to make of his life a perpetual torment: the perpetuity of marriage is thus contrary to the intention of nature, and to the principle of association among men.[20]

Morelly went so far as to construct the rules of society according to nature in his *Code de la Nature* (1755). As far as matrimony was concerned, Morelly specified that every citizen had to marry after reaching puberty, unless there were physical reasons making marriage impossible or undesirable, and that celibacy was permitted only to those over the age of forty. He proposed allowing divorce either by mutual consent or unilaterally, but only after a marriage had lasted at least ten years. Divorce was not to be undertaken for trivial reasons, and the couple or spouse petitioning had to set out their reasons before their tribe (in Morelly's utopia, families were to be organized into tribes). The heads of families were obliged to try to reconcile the spouses, but it appears that they could not refuse to grant a divorce. Once the divorce had been decreed the spouses could not remarry each other for six months, during which time they lived with their respective families and were forbidden to communicate with each other directly, although they could engage common friends to negotiate a reconciliation. Divorced persons could marry a different spouse only after a year had elapsed from their divorce, but they were prohibited from marrying anyone younger than themselves or younger than the spouse from whom they were divorced. Finally, Morelly's law provided that the children of a divorced couple would be entrusted to the care of the father.[21]

Other writers of the time, equally convinced that indissoluble marriage was contrary to human nature, looked to recently discovered societies as examples of natural law in practice. In his *Supplément au voyage de Bougainville*, Diderot portrayed the distinction between his own society and the "natural" society of Tahiti in a fictional dialogue between a French priest and Orou, a Tahitian who represents natural man. Orou is shaken to learn that in civilized Catholic countries men and women were united in marriage until death, and exclaims:

These strange precepts I find opposed to nature, contrary to reason...In fact, does anything seem to you more senseless than a precept which denies the change which is within us; which commands a constancy which cannot be there, and which violates the nature and freedom of male and female, in chaining them for ever, one to the other...[22]

The attempt to discover natural law through the study of supposedly natural societies combined a philosophic prejudice and anthropology, but the latter was generally fictional or wishful. Most of the eighteenth-century writers who brought the light of comparative institutions and laws to bear on the issue of divorce in France chose their examples not from primitive non-European societies but from the classical world and contemporary Europe. The model was perhaps the article on divorce in the *Encyclopédie*, written by Boucher d'Argis. It began by stating the Catholic doctrine that "divorce is certainly con-

---

[20] Jean Charles Lavie, *Des corps politiques et de leurs gouvernments* (2 vols., Lyons, 1764), I, 66.
[21] This is a summary of Morelly, *Code de la Nature* (Paris, 1950), 310–13.
[22] Denis Diderot, *Supplément au voyage de Bougainville* in *Oeuvres philosophiques* (Paris, 1964), 480.

trary to the first institution of marriage, which by its nature is indissoluble,"[23] but then proceeded to demonstrate that divorce had been allowed by the Jews, the Romans, and during the early French monarchy. This historical approach was adopted in many works, and there developed an almost obligatory introductory genuflexion in prodivorce works to the wisdom of Justinian, the Romans, the Visigoths, Franks, and the various church councils and authorities that had approved of divorce.

As repetitious and selective as this evidence was, it served several purposes. First, it reminded readers that although divorce was contrary to orthodox Catholic doctrine, it had not always been so. The apparently neutral history of divorce that Boucher d'Argis wrote for the *Encyclopédie* made the implicit point that this "divine" indissolubility of marriage was of quite recent origin. Secondly, it was argued that the examples of earlier societies showed that divorce did not necessarily have disastrous social consequences. Lavie pointed out, contrary to later interpretations of classical history, that the availability of divorce in Ancient Rome had not had the effect of corrupting minds or weakening marriage and other family relationships and had not brought the empire to its knees.[24]

Yet although historical and anthropological perspectives served their purpose in highlighting the discontinuity of church doctrines of marriage and divorce and the relatively recent origins of the rule of indissolubility, most emphasis in the prodivorce literature focused on the contemporary world. Attention was drawn to the fact that divorce was permitted in the Protestant states of Europe. In 1784 the duc de la Rochefoucauld noted that "English husbands have an advantage over us of which they sometimes avail themselves, namely divorce."[25] This was a reference to divorce by private Act of Parliament. By 1784 there had been only eighty such divorces in England, making it a very limited advantage but still one that French men did not have. The comparative perspective took on a nationalist tone in one work that expressed concern that the English had access to such a beneficial institution of which the French were denied: "The English have adopted divorce, but in a defective form: our glory is not only to imitate but to surpass them."[26] The general sense of grievance that the French were deprived of the ability to divorce that everyone else enjoyed was neatly encapsulated in the title of one treatise that called for the legalization of divorce "in conformity with the laws of the primitive Church, with current practice in the Catholic Kingdom of Poland, and that of all the people of the earth who exist or have existed, except us."[27]

But many commentators went beyond the bland recitation of countries and

---

[23] *Encyclopédie*, IV, 1983.
[24] Lavie, *Des corps politiques*, I, 71–2.
[25] François, duc de la Rochefoucauld, *Mélanges sur l'Angleterre*, quoted in John Hajnal, "European Marriage Patterns in Perspective," in D. V. Glass and D. E. C. Eversley (eds.), *Population in History* (London, 1965), 115.
[26] A. J. U. Hennet, *Du Divorce* (Paris, 1789), xi.
[27] Cerfvol, *Cri d'une honnête femme qui réclame le divorce conformément aux loix de la primitive Eglise, à*

societies that had allowed or did allow divorce and addressed themselves to the crucial question of why France should emulate them? Was it simply that divorce was an ancient right of the French that the medieval church had suppressed and that cried out to be restored on principle? This was the implication of some works, but most went much further to construct arguments for the social and political utility of divorce. In this respect, divorce was portrayed as conferring three major benefits on society: It would increase population, regenerate morality, and enhance happiness and harmony within families.

The demographic argument for divorce was put forward early in the eighteenth century by Montesquieu, who noted that Christian populations had a generally lower birthrate than non-Christians, and suggested that this was the effect of the prohibition of divorce among the former.[28] Montesquieu's concern about population might have been provoked by the stagnation of the French population in the late seventeenth and early eighteenth centuries. But although the population of France began to increase markedly and at an accelerating pace from the 1730s, there was a widespread belief until the 1770s that the country's population was actually declining. The prospect of depopulation was alarming because of the prevailing belief that the economic, political, and military strength of nations depended on their having robust and increasing populations. It is interesting for present purposes that the legalization of divorce was seen as one method of promoting demographic growth, and for this reason divorce was prominent in the works of the "depopulationist" demographers – those who believed that the French population was declining.

Perhaps the most imaginative scenario of depopulation was drawn by Cerfvol (almost certainly a pseudonym) whose rate of divorce-tract production equaled that of John Milton: Cerfvol published five works on divorce between 1768 and 1770.[29] The most important of these, *Mémoire sur la population* (its second edition was published under the title *Utilité civile et politique du divorce*), presented a pessimistic image of France's demographic future.[30]

Cerfvol held that between the reign of Charles IX (1560–74) and 1700 the number of French people had fallen from 24 million to fewer than 18.7 million.

(footnote 27, cont.)
l'usage actuel du Royaume catholique de Pologne, et à celui de tous les peuples de la terre qui existent ou qui ont existé, excepté nous (London, 1770).
[28] Charles-Louis de Secondat, Baron de Montesquieu, *Lettres persanes* (Paris, 1960), Letter 116. Unlike Lavie, Montesquieu made no distinction in this respect between Catholic and Protestant populations.
[29] It has been suggested that Cerfvol was the pseudonym of a jurisconsult charged by a group of high French governing officials (including Chancellor Maupéou) to demonstrate the validity of divorce in order to allow Louis XV to dissolve his marriage in order to marry Mme. Dubarry. Alfred Sauvy, "Quelques démographes ignorés du XVIIIᵉ siècle," annexed to Joseph Spengler, *Economie et population: Les doctrines françaises avant 1800* (Paris, 1954), 371n.30.
[30] The following account of Cerfvol's demographic calculations is from his *Mémoire sur la population* (London [sic], 1768), parts II and III. His initial estimate of the population of France in the sixteenth century is much higher than recent studies have shown it to have been, at about 18 millions. See, for instance, Marcel Reinhard and André Armengaud, *Histoire générale de la population mondiale* (Paris, 1961), 88.

He maintained that on average a married couple had four children, but that as one of these did not survive its first year and another died before reaching the age of eighteen, spouses did no more than replace themselves, by producing two children who reached adulthood.

However – and this was the crucial qualification – not every man produced a child. Cerfvol estimated that of the 1700 population, some 1,020,000 males were not productive of children; 300,000 of these men were celibate clergy, 120,000 were celibate soldiers, and there were 600,000 miscellaneous bachelors. If there had been that many more men than women, the number of non-reproductive males would not have affected the birthrate provided every woman mated, but because France had men and women in equal numbers, the 1,020,000 nonreproductive men rendered an equal number of women "useless." Thus, the French population failed to reproduce itself.

This scenario was bad enough, but it was made worse by Cerfvol's calculation that celibacy increased by about 2% each generation (every twenty-three years). More and more males were rendered nonreproductive by wars, colonization, emigration, illness, exile, punishment, employment in the merchant marine, or as celibate valets or clergy. Others would choose to remain unmarried. The progressive decline in the number of men (and therefore women) able and willing to produce children would mean that from the 16,660,000 productive people in 1700, France would move to 14,320,000 in 1723, 11,973,000 in 1746, and 9,548,000 in 1769, the year after the *Mémoire* was published.

The principal way to arrest this galloping celibacy and its disastrous effects was, according to Cerfvol, the reintroduction of divorce.[31] There were various factors causing France's depopulation: incontinence, unequal and excessive taxation, the use of wet nurses, too readily available education, and the use of corsets (which affected women's ability to bear children). But these factors, he held, were no more than the effects of immorality, and immorality flowed from the unique source of all evil, the indissolubility of marriage: "Let us seek the true cause of our depopulation nowhere else than in the indissolubility of marriage. All the other causes are derived from this."[32] It was because men knew that they could never escape from a marriage that they chose to remain bachelors. The legalization of divorce would, ironically, encourage marriage, cure all immorality, and give France a large and vigorous population.

The demographic argument for divorce was a powerful one, and it was fundamental to what was without doubt the most influential divorce work of the century, Hennet's *Du Divorce* (1789).[33] Hennet's emphasis was less on total population numbers and more on the increasing rate of illegitimate births.

---

[31] Like so many writers in favor of divorce, Cerfvol referred to the "reintroduction" of divorce, arguing that what they sought was simply the revival of an ancient right, not an innovation.

[32] Cerfvol, *Mémoire*, 27.

[33] This work was influential in the sense that it sold widely and foreshadowed many specific provisions of the 1792 divorce law.

5 Eighteenth-century France

Again there was the argument that indissolubility of marriage was a deterrent to marriage, leading to immorality and increased illegitimacy because unmarried men frequented prostitutes and committed other immoral acts, notably fornication and adultery. Moreover, once married and unable to divorce, unhappy spouses continued to live together but ceased to share the same bed, thereby further depressing the legitimate birthrate. Unhappily married and involuntary sexually abstinent men also frequented prostitutes, and thus added to the illegitimacy produced by men who were afraid to marry in the first place. Had unhappy spouses been able to divorce, they might have contracted new, blissful unions, and produced happy children, thereby increasing both legitimate births and the nation's population.

The issue of divorce was raised in most of the French depopulationist literature of the eighteenth century, including the works of Grimm, Linguet, and Lavie.[34] It was not as popular among the later demographers who realized that the French population was not declining, but, in fact, increasing. For example, Moheau thought that divorce would simply weaken marital and family bonds; he could see that the population was rapidly increasing despite the absence of divorce.[35] Du Buat-Nançay answered the arguments of the pro-divorce depopulationists head-on. Even if the population were declining, he wrote, allowing divorce would not favor natality for if a man left his wife for another woman and they had children, they would do no more than compensate for the children the first wife would have had had her husband not left her.[36]

The regeneration of morals was scarcely less important than the regeneration of the population for many eighteenth-century French social critics. The evidence of immorality could be seen in what they imagined was increasing celibacy and the certainly increasing number of illegitimate and abandoned children.[37] Condorcet and Helvétius were among those who believed that divorce would relieve these problems, and both argued that the lack of divorce was the main reason for adultery and illegitimacy. Helvétius held that divorce was a particularly appropriate remedy in the case of adultery – hardly an original thought – and that adultery should not be the subject of criminal legislation.[38]

---

[34] On Grimm and Linguet see Spengler, *Economie et population*, 223n.120, and 312. For Lavie, see *Des corps politiques*, I, 75, to the effect that the population of Protestant northern Europe was growing and that of Catholic southern Europe declining because of their respective provisions for divorce.

[35] Spengler, *Economie et population*, 105.

[36] Ibid., 144.

[37] See, for example, Jacques Depauw, "Amour illégitime et société à Nantes au XVIIIᵉ siècle," *Annales. Economies Sociétés Civilisations* 27 (1972), 1155–81; Jean-Pierre Bardet, "Enfants abandonnés et enfants assistés à Rouen dans la seconde moitié du XVIIIᵉ siècle," *Sur la population française aux XVIIIᵉ et XIXᵉ siècles* (Paris, 1973), 19–47.

[38] Marie Jean Antoine Nicolas Caritat, Marquis de Condorcet, *Esquisse d'un tableau historique des progrès de l'esprit humaine*, in *Oeuvres de Condorcet* (12 vols., Paris, 1847–9), VI, 523. Claude Adrien Helvétius, *Réflexions morales*, in *Oeuvres complètes d'Helvétius* (14 vols., Paris, AnIII/1795), XIV, 194.

5.2 Critics of Old Regime marriage law

Quite clearly, the incidence of immorality described in these works, and manifested in such forms as illegitimacy, celibacy, and child abandonment, was considered the principal cause of the depopulation that was believed to be occurring.[39] Divorce, by remedying this one problem, would thereby solve the others. As if this were not enough, divorce was credited with even more curative effects on the illnesses that afflicted the body social. It would not only give relief to unhappily married men and women, by freeing them to engage in new marriages, but in many instances the availability of divorce would make existing marriages more happy and harmonious. Montesquieu drew on historical example to make the point. Among pagans, he wrote,

nothing contributed more to mutual affection than the ability to divorce; a husband and wife were led patiently to tolerate domestic difficulties, knowing that they were able to put an end to them, and they often held this power in their hands all their lives without using it, for the single reason that they were free to do so.[40]

This was the other side of the argument that men and women were reluctant to enter marriage because it was indissoluble; Montesquieu was arguing that men and women were more likely to stay in marriage when it was dissoluble.

A subtheme within that of the promotion of domestic happiness focused on the relationship of divorce to women. Many writers argued that the ability of women to divorce would be a useful counterweight to male authority and would result in husbands being more considerate and less tyrannical. Montesquieu proposed giving the right of repudiation (unilateral divorce) only to women; to confer it on the husband, the master of the house, would be to give him only another means of abusing his power. "But a wife who repudiates only makes use of a dreadful kind of remedy. It is always a great misfortune for her to have to go in search of a second husband, when she has lost the greatest part of her attractions with another."[41] This was echoed by d'Holbach, who thought that divorce would enable a wife to

rebel against tyranny, ill-treatment, tiresome emotions, against the continued bad-temper of a spouse, life together with whom had become intolerable. This tyrant should lose the rights which he has so badly abused; the law should wrench his authority away from him; the spouses should be separated for ever.[42]

The appeal of divorce as a means to better the position of women in marriage, by providing them with a counter to *puissance maritale* (the husband's

---

[39] Lavie pointed out that for the purpose of population strength it could not be argued that a child was a child whether it were legitimate or illegitimate, since illegitimate and abandoned children had a much higher mortality rate than legitimate children. He had seen (he wrote) registers of *enfants trouvés* that showed that only one in fifty survived to puberty. Lavie, *Des corps politiques*, I, 70. Mortality rates like these were approached only in Rouen: See Bardet, "Enfants abandonnés," 27–8.

[40] Montesquieu, *Lettres persanes*, Letter 116.

[41] Montesquieu, *De l'esprit des lois*, Book XVI, Chapter 15.

[42] Paul Henri Thiry, Baron d'Holbach, *Ethocratie, ou le gouvernement fondé sur la morale* (Amsterdam, 1776), 208.

authority over his wife), was a powerful one. It was repeated in petitions to the legislatures in the early years of the French Revolution and, not surprisingly, was taken up by the feminist movement in late eighteenth-century France. Furthermore, prognostications as to the benefits of divorce to women in particular seemed to be borne out by their predominance among divorce petitioners when divorce was finally legalized in 1792 (see Chapter 7). Still, the impression one gets from the writing on divorce is that it should be available to both spouses. It is difficult to be certain because although many writers approved of the principle of divorce not all went into details as to the grounds they thought would justify divorce.

For all this, the writers who were in favor of divorce should not, for that reason, be considered hostile to marriage. In seeking to give women divorce, the aim was to give them a weapon against marital oppression, a far more satisfactory weapon than *séparation de corps* could ever be. It was specific marriages, not marriage in general, that needed to be reformed. As the writings on depopulation and morality show, each divorce was seen as nothing so much as a prelude to another marriage. It was, as Lavie pointed out, that

marriage offers the most sweet and the most bitter fruits; when tenderness, which is less impetuous than love but deeper than friendship, unites the two spouses, it is the source of the most pleasant and most constant happiness. On the other hand there is no hatred as strong as that which takes root in an indissoluble marriage.[43]

Divorce, from this point of view, was a remedy for marriage breakdown and incompatibility between spouses: "People always marry with the intention of spending their whole lives in the exclusive company of one spouse. Divorce can only be considered, at most, as a violent remedy which is applied to even more violent ills."[44]

The writing on divorce in France before the revolution was thus disparate and fairly general in its approaches to the problem. At issue were the broad questions whether it should remain prohibited or be legalized. For this reason, perhaps, the arguments were understandably general and did not, for the most part, penetrate the more detailed issues, such as the grounds for which divorce might be granted. The principle of fault seemed uppermost, however, since many of the authors used the words "*divorce*" and "*répudiation*" interchangeably; this seemed to rule out the possibility of the consensual dissolution of marriage. It is difficult to assess the influence and impact of this body of writing, although it is tempting to see it as the background to the 1792 divorce law in the sense of its representing a welling-up of opinion in favor of divorce. Yet for the most part the divorce literature was imprecise and disparate and, like so many themes studied in historical perspective, seems to become coherent only under the pen of the historian.

---

[43] Lavie, *Des corps politiques*, I, 66.
[44] Cerfvol, *La Gamologie, ou de l'éducation des filles destinées au mariage* (Paris, 1772), 20–1.

5.2 Critics of Old Regime marriage law

Even so, it would be surprising if the cumulative pressure for the reform of marriage law had had absolutely no effect. It was, after all, an integral part of the literature of social criticism that dissected, analyzed, and pronounced on the various organs and members of Old Regime society, diagnosing the ills and proposing remedies. (The medical metaphor was a popular one among writers on divorce, who often saw divorce as a miracle elixir for national rejuvenation.) The reforms of the revolutionary period must be understood in light of these criticisms, even if we avoid the crude causal arguments that try to relate specific laws and policies to specific intellectual currents. In fact, if we are to link pro-divorce opinion to the legalization of divorce in September 1792, it is likely that the works and petitions from 1789 to 1792 were more effective than the whole *corpus* of literature published up to 1789.

The single most influential work of this time, Hennet's *Du Divorce*, was published in late 1789, soon after the formation of the Constituent Assembly. Hennet's work was the first in France to put forward a detailed plan for divorce legislation – Morelly's divorce code was designed for a utopian society, not contemporary France – and he suggested that there were twelve circumstances that ought incontestably to justify divorce:

1. condemnation to death,
2. sentence to a degrading punishment (*peine infamante*), or
3. sentence to a long term of imprisonment;
4. captivity when no release could be foreseen;
5. the exile or disappearance of one of the spouses;
6. sterility for a specified period;
7. incurable illness;
8. insanity;
9. any crime;
10. adultery;
11. extreme dissoluteness; and
12. incompatibility of temperament.[45]

The first nine of these matrimonial offenses could be proved (Hennet referred to them as *divorces déterminés*) and they should be obtained by a regular judicial process. The final three (*divorces indéterminés*) should be approved by an assembly of relatives convoked by the plaintiff. This family assembly would communicate its decision to a judge who would then inform the defendant, and the latter could appeal against it, although only on procedural grounds. Three months after the family assembly's decision had been rendered, a second assembly would be held, after which a provisional divorce would be decreed. Following the elapse of a further three months the judge would declare a definitive divorce. Hennet's plan thus proposed a procedure of more than six months' duration for a *divorce indéterminé*. Divorced spouses would have the

[45] Hennet, *Du Divorce*, 122–3.

status of widowed persons, they would be forbidden to remarry each other, and the better-off spouse would be required to help the other financially.

Hennet stressed the interests of the children, which he held to be more important than the wishes of the parents. In certain cases, such as divorces based on exile or imprisonment, there would be no dispute over custody, but when both parents were capable of looking after the children of the marriage and when no custody arrangement could be reached amicably, the father should take the eldest children, the mother the youngest. If there were an odd number of children, the middle one in age would stay with the mother until the age of seven, and thereafter a daughter would remain with her, while a son would go to the father. This gender principle was to apply, as well, in the case of an only child. In general, though, the distribution of children between their parents would depend on the parents' circumstances and their ability and wish to look after them.

Hennet's proposed legislation was in many respects so similar to the law on divorce passed in 1792 that there can be no doubt that *Du Divorce* was an influential work. It was also popular; on January 1, 1790, the Paris newspaper *Le Moniteur universel* enthusiastically reviewed the second edition of the book and pointed out that "the first edition of this work disappeared immediately; nothing better demonstrates the interest which the question of divorce inspires." Further evidence of the growing interest in divorce in 1789 came in the publication of several more pamphlets, at least two of them designed for the electoral assemblies drawing up *cahiers de doléances* for the meeting of the Estates-General in May,[46] and in the adoption of the divorce cause by some women's newspapers.[47]

Such manifestations of opinion in favor of the legalization of divorce occurred too late to have any effect on the *cahiers de doléances*, the lists of grievances and proposed reforms drawn up for the meeting of the Estates-General in 1789. Only three of the more than 600 general *cahiers* presented to the king at Versailles raised the issue of divorce at all, and all three opposed its legalization. These were the *cahiers* of the Third Estate (Commons) of Marseilles,[48] of the Clergy of Orange (Grenoble), and the Clergy of Soule (Auch). The Clergy of Orange held divorce to be "contrary to divine law and good morals,"[49] whereas their brothers at Soule sought to have their customary law

---

[46] Hilaire Joseph Hubert de Matigny, *Traité philosophique, théologique et politique de la loi du divorce, demandée aux Etats-Généraux par S.A.S. Mgr Louis Philippe Joseph d'Orléans, premier Prince du Sang, où l'on traite la question du célibat des deux sexes, et des causes morales de l'adultère* (Paris, 1789); Simon Nicolas Henri Linguet, *Légitimé du divorce, justifiée par les Saintes Ecritures, par les Pères, par les Conciles, etc. aux Etats-généraux de 1789* (Bruxelles, 1789).

[47] Evelyne Sullerot, *Histoire de la presse féminine en France des origines à 1848* (Paris, 1966), 39–40, 42ff.

[48] Beatrice F., Hyslop, *A Guide to the General Cahiers of 1789* (New York, 1936, repr. 1967), 59. Hyslop writes that this was the only general *cahier* to mention divorce.

[49] *Archives parlementaires*, Ière série, IV, 267.

purged of the article that permitted repudiation.[50] The low priority given to divorce in the general *cahiers* was reflected in the preliminary *cahiers*, for of the more than 25,000 drafted in 1789,[51] only 4 are known to have mentioned divorce, of which 2 were in favor and 2 were opposed.[52] The Third Estate of the District of l'Eglise des Théatins (Paris) advocated divorce "because an indissoluble contract is contrary to the changing character of man."[53] The Third Estate of the Prévôté de Fleury-Mérogis (Oise) also called for divorce and specified that divorces should be granted by an assembly of relatives of the spouses, held before a royal judge, that would consider the rights of any children of the marriage and also decide on the division of property should the divorce be granted.[54] On the other hand the inhabitants of the parish of Stains (near Paris) enjoined their representative at the Estates-General to oppose any demand that might arise for divorce,[55] while the parish of Aulnay-lès-Bondis (also close to Paris) seized on the moral consequences of divorce: "It would be the greatest danger to admit divorce, which would cause general turmoil in France and would be the cause of the greatest scandal."[56]

There was, then, no evidence in the *cahiers de doléances*, which are generally considered the best index of French public opinion on the eve of the revolution, of a ground swell in favor of the legalization of divorce. In fact in simple numerical terms opinion was opposed to divorce, which suggests that the effect of propaganda in favor of divorce had, if anything, done more to provoke fear and opposition to divorce than to rally support to the cause. Even so, it is clear that divorce was a negligible issue compared to the other problems, such as constitutional and fiscal reform, that confronted France in 1789. These problems, together with the sensational events that occurred in 1789, kept serious consideration of the divorce question out of the French legislatures during the first three years of the revolution, and within that period the occasional parliamentary references to divorce were the result of extraparliamentary events or pressure.

5.3 Divorce and the French Revolution

Divorce was first mentioned in the National Constituent Assembly on April 8, 1790, when Hubert de Matigny presented the assembly with a copy of his *Traité*

---

[50] Ibid., V, 775.

[51] Hyslop, *General Cahiers*, ix–x.

[52] Cruppi reported that several of the special *cahiers* of Dauphiné and Provence requested divorce legislation, but that they were all inspired by the king's cousin, the duke of Orleans, who was an advocate of divorce (Marcel Cruppi, *Le divorce pendant la Révolution* [Thèse de droit, Paris, 1909], 21n.2). The duke published a model *cahier* that included approval of divorce, but Hyslop (*General Cahiers*, 57–61) rejects the notion that the assemblies that drafted the *cahiers* allowed themselves to be dictated to by prominent individuals such as the duke.

[53] *Archives parlementaires*, lère série, V, 316.

[54] Ibid., IV, 549.

[55] Ibid., V, 124.

[56] Ibid., IV, 326.

philosophique, which advocated a divorce law, but the first call for the legalization of divorce from a member of the assembly came only in August 1790. The deputy Pierre-François Gossin, speaking in the debate on the establishment of the family courts *(tribunaux de famille)*, told his fellow legislators that

after having made man again free and happy in public life, it remains for you to assure his liberty and happiness in private life. . . the *tribunal de famille* which is proposed to you, Messieurs, is going to destroy for ever these trials for a *séparation de corps*. . . but when you destroy, Messieurs, one of the disadvantages of this gothic custom called *séparation de corps*, why do you do your work imperfectly?. . .*Séparation de corps* was also unjust and unwise in its results: after having half-separated the spouses, without distinguishing the innocent from the guilty, it left the two parties in a situation which was cruel to them, and dangerous for society.[57]

Gossin suggested that spouses who had obtained a *séparation de corps* should be allowed to contract another marriage – a facility that would have transformed these separations into a restricted form of divorce available primarily to women – but his proposal was not acted upon.

In the course of 1791 several petitions on the subject of divorce were presented to the National Constituent and Legislative Assemblies,[58] but the most important development in that year was the declaration made in the constitution of 1791 that "the law considers marriage to be only a civil contract."[59] This provision struck at the sacramental basis of Catholic marriage and was interpreted by some couples as meaning that marriages could be dissolved like any other contract. A number of couples obtained divorces on the basis of this declaration in the 1791 constitution, even before the legalization of divorce in 1792.

It is likely that this reference to marriage in the constitution, which was approved in September 1791, inspired the petitions in favor of divorce at the end of that year and at the beginning of the next, for between January and March of 1792 there were a further six petitions to the legislature calling for divorce. On February 13, 1792, the deputy Aubert-Dubayet, who was to become a leading proponent of divorce in the assembly, presented a letter on behalf of "several men and women citizens" of Paris seeking provisional legislation on divorce.[60] The letter was referred to the Legislative Committee of the Assembly. On February 17 came what may be interpreted as the first sign of a general sympathy for divorce within the Legislative Assembly. On that day Hennet presented the deputies with a copy of the latest (the third) edition of his *Du Divorce* and some deputies, apparently hostile to the work's sentiments, called for the assembly to return to the day's agenda without giving Hennet's work the

---

[57] Ibid., XVII, 617.
[58] The National Constituent Assembly was replaced by the newly elected Legislative Assembly on October 1, 1791.
[59] Constitution of 1791, Title II, Article 7.
[60] *Archives parlementaires*, 1ère série, XXXVIII, 466.

customary acknowledgment, a *mention honourable*. They were opposed by the deputy Roux who stated: "The question of divorce is not yet on the agenda but I hope that it will be. In the meantime I demand *la mention honourable* be accorded to the honour done to the Assembly."[61] Roux's motion was accepted by the assembly. There was a similar scene of apparent support for divorce on March 19, 1792, when a letter was read from the English lawyer William William in favor of divorce; it was granted a *mention honourable* over the protests of several deputies.[62] On April 1, 1792, a petition was presented that called for a broad range of reforms in favor of women since "men are finally free, and women are slaves to a thousand prejudices." Among the specific reforms requested were equality in political rights and the legalization of divorce.[63]

These and other petitions were only the most visible signs of opinion in favor of divorce that developed after 1789 and that was stimulated by the laicization of marriage in the 1791 constitution. Further pressure came from mayors, justices of the peace, and municipal councils in various parts of France, who had performed marriage and divorce ceremonies as a result of the declaration in the constitution that marriage was simply a civil contract. They wrote to the assembly, telling the legislators what they had done, and requesting approval. The ambiguity created by the constitution and the rash of divorces that resulted from it were important pressures for an unequivocal decision as to whether or not divorce was permissible. As for the other currents of opinion, they are almost impossible to recapture. There are references to prodivorce songs among the laundrywomen of Paris.[64] By March 1792 a Paris newspaper commented: "From all sides there are demands for a divorce law, and the National Assembly appears to be on the verge of considering it."[65]

Under the pressure of petitions and other manifestations of support for the introduction of divorce, the Legislative Assembly moved toward considering legislation. What proved to be a catalyst occurred on August 20, 1792, when a letter from a Sieur Gremion, calling for divorce, was read to the assembly. An anonymous deputy successfully moved that the letter be sent to the Legislative Committee and that the committee be instructed to report within three days, after which time any deputy might present a draft divorce law.[66] We can only speculate as to the reason for the suddenly receptive attitude of the assembly toward Sieur Gremion's letter. Perhaps the resistance of the deputies to taking positive action had finally been eroded by the nagging of the propagandists. In addition, we cannot ignore the fact that the assembly took its first step toward legalizing divorce only ten days after the *journée* of August 10, when a crowd of

---

[61] Ibid., XXXIX, 127.
[62] Ibid., XL, 138–9.
[63] Ibid., XLI, 63–4.
[64] Cruppi, *Divorce pendant la Révolution*, 21. Cruppi, who was generally hostile toward revolutionary divorce, thought that divorce was popular among the people of Paris, but not elsewhere in France.
[65] *Le Moniteur universel*, March 21, 1792.
[66] *Archives parlementaires*, 1ère série, XLVII, 40.

5 Eighteenth-century France

Parisians had invaded the Tuileries and forced the suspension of the monarchy. As an immediate consequence of this action many monarchist deputies left the Legislative Assembly and returned to the provinces, and this left the assembly effectively in the control of the liberal Girondins. With the exception of those who took part in the divorce debate, we have no information on the opinions of individual deputies, but it seems likely that attitudes toward divorce fitted general political and social attitudes and that the departure of so many monarchists from the assembly removed an influential bloc of opposition to divorce legislation. Still, divorce was not seen as a great priority, and on September 6 Aubert-Dubayet reminded the assembly that the Legislative Committee, charged with drafting a law on August 20, had not reported. This was rectified the following day when a draft law was presented, and it was this bill, debated and amended between September 13 and 20, 1792 (the last day of the Legislative Assembly's existence), that became France's first divorce law. The final form of the legislation was essentially that of the draft except that the assembly, reflecting the turbulent times (France was at war and the French defeated the Prussians at Valmy the very day the divorce law was passed), insisted on politicizing divorce. The draft presented by the Legislative Committee had confined the grounds of divorce to strictly matrimonial offenses, but the deputy Jean-Baptiste Mailhe proposed adding to them the crimes of emigration and lack of patriotism. After noting that emigration was a ground for divorce in Prussia, the assembly added it to the specified grounds for divorce (*causes déterminées*) proposed in the draft but rejected lack of patriotism as sufficient cause for dissolving a marriage.[67]

In brief, the divorce law of September 20, 1792, specified that marriage was dissoluble by divorce and that *séparations de corps*, described in the debate as "gothic" and "barbarous," were abolished. The law recognized the principles both of the breakdown of marriage, without the attribution of responsibility, and of matrimonial fault. In the first category, both spouses could petition jointly for a divorce by mutual consent or one spouse could apply unilaterally for a divorce on the ground of incompatibility of temperament (*incompatibilité d'humeur et de caractère*). A divorce for reason of incompatibility required no proof and was designed to avoid a petitioner's being embarrassed by having to detail the intimate and shameful aspects of her or his marriage. In order to prevent abuse of this type of divorce, which was tantamount to repudiation, a long (minimum six-month) procedure was demanded in order to prevent hasty decisions and to provide ample time and opportunities for reconsideration and reconciliation. The second category of divorce, based on matrimonial fault, allowed either spouse to obtain a divorce, on one or more specific grounds, namely, madness, condemnation to certain degrading forms of punishment,[68]

[67] Ibid., XLIX, 643–4.
[68] Defined as long terms of imprisonment or humiliating punishments such as being pilloried or placed in stocks.

178

5.3 Divorce and the French Revolution

cruelty or ill-treatment, notoriously dissolute morals, desertion for at least two years, absence without news for at least five years, and emigration. The law also dealt with divorce procedures and the effects of divorce on the spouses, their children, and their property.[69]

This first French divorce law underwent several modifications before its repeal and replacement in 1803, but most were of a procedural nature, such as varying the delay that had to be observed between divorce and remarriage. There was, however, one amendment of substance, when on 4 Floréal Year II (April 23, 1794) divorce was permitted on the basis of *de facto* separation for six months or longer. This amendment, which liberalized even more an already liberal law, responded to requests to the Convention for divorce to be made more accessible. On August 27, 1793, for example, a Sieur Noé, controller of customs at Longwy, complained that the procedures for divorce were too complicated and long and called for "a speedier form of divorce, more beneficial to oppressed spouses."[70] On 20 Ventôse Year II (March 20, 1794) a *citoyen* Sentix similarly sought a more rapid form of divorce, and it was this petition that inspired the *décret* of 4 Floréal Year II.[71] The *décret* remained controversial, however, and it was suspended only fifteen months after its introduction on the ground that it was being exploited to abuse the intent of the divorce law. Many women, it was said, were taking advantage of it to divorce their husbands who were away from home on military service.

Yet even without the short-lived addition of the *décret* of 4 Floréal, the 1792 divorce law was an extremely liberal piece of legislation that made divorce available for any reason whatsoever. Divorce was not prevented under any circumstances, but temporary procedural impediments were designed to deter too hasty a recourse to divorce, and the potential for abuse of the respective grounds for divorce correlated with procedural difficulty. Thus a divorce on the ground of incompatibility of temperament took at least six months to obtain, whereas divorce for one of the specific matrimonial offenses, such as ill-treatment and adultery – which had to be proved – could be obtained within a matter of days, depending on the speed with which a *tribunal de famille* could convene and render a judgment. Herein lay the objections to the *décret* of 4 Floréal Year II, which allowed divorce for reason of six months' *de facto* separation: It was susceptible to abuse; it could be obtained within days since the only proof required was the fact of separation.

As for the arguments by which the legislators justified the introduction of divorce, they were more restricted than the considerations put forth by most of the proponents of divorce earlier in the eighteenth century. Divorce was finally

---

[69] The 1792 law is reprinted in J. H. Stewart (ed.), *A Documentary Survey of the French Revolution* (New York, 1951), 333–40.

[70] Gérard Thibault-Laurent, *La première introduction du divorce en France sous la Révolution et l'Empire* (Thèse de droit, Montpellier, 1938), 115.

[71] François Olivier-Martin, *La crise du mariage dans la législation intermédiaire (1789–1804)* (Thèse de droit, Paris, 1900), 223.

introduced almost solely for the ideological reason that the facility to dissolve a marriage was an indispensable element of the freedom the revolution was bestowing upon the French people. Despite the feminist arguments that divorce was needed particularly by women, only the deputy Aubert-Dubayet, who had been one of the staunchest supporters of divorce, advanced such an argument: "It is time husbands bowed themselves to universal justice."[72]

As we have seen, pressure in favor of divorce developed and intensified in the first years of the French Revolution, even though divorce was insignificant as an issue in the *cahiers de doléances*. But neither the growth of popular pressure nor the fact of revolution alone explain why divorce was introduced in 1792, because the legislators neither acceded to all requests put forth in petitions nor overturned all the principles and laws of the Old Regime. In order to fully understand why divorce was legalized it is necessary to consider divorce in the broader context of changed attitudes toward the family that were embodied in revolutionary legislation and in terms of the general revolutionary conception of the family. An important point to note is that divorce was only one aspect of a thorough revision of family law undertaken in the first years of the French Revolution. The 1792 divorce law was itself only part of a multifaceted reform of legislation that simultaneously revised the law of marriage and secularized the registration of vital statistics. It swept away the church's responsibility of recording baptisms, marriages, and burials, and from late 1792 the state, through a civil registrar, would record births, marriages, divorces, and deaths. Thus the reduction of religious and ecclesiastical influence over family law was one of the key themes in the legislative revision. It went further than removing the functions of registrar from parish priests: because marriage was secularized, groups such as actors – who had been forbidden marriage by the Catholic church – and Jews were able to marry and have their marriages recognized by the state.

Divorce, too, must be seen in the context of this loosening of the church's grip on family legislation, and the introduction of divorce is an indication of the progress of secularization. As well, it was an indication of the extent to which the church had been neutralized by 1792 as a body opposed to the revolution that legislation so abhorrent to its doctrines could be so easily introduced. By 1792 the clergy were under attack as counter revolutionaries and subject to deportation. The abolition of *séparations de corps*, which accompanied the legalization of divorce, is further evidence of the law's anti-Catholic bias; under the 1792 law, Catholics had no remedy for marriage breakdown but divorce.

The second principal theme that runs through revolutionary family legislation is an emphasis on individualism. The family was no longer thought of as a corporative unit to which the interests of the individual members had to be subordinated but more as a union of individuals whose separate interests were considered important in themselves. The corporativeness of the family unit was not completely abandoned, just as individual rights had never been completely

---

[72] *Archives parlementaires*, 1ère série, XLIX, 117.

obliterated under the family law of the Old Regime, but the emphasis had changed, and individualism and egalitarianism informed the revolutionary reforms in family law. In legislation governing inheritance, for instance, laws that discriminated against children on the basis of their age or sex or that permitted parents to favor one child over the others were suppressed and equal inheritance by all children was made mandatory. Parental control over children was relaxed in other respects as well. The age of majority of women and men was reduced from the customary 25 or 30 years of the Old Regime to 21 years. The infamous *lettres de cachet*, which had enabled parents to imprison wayward or disobedient children and husbands to incarcerate their wives (see Section 8.7), were abolished in 1789. Even illegitimate children were briefly given equal rights of succession during the Jacobin period of the revolution, by the law of 12 Brumaire Year II (November 2, 1793).[73]

An important characteristic of the individualism injected into family law was that it applied equally to women and to men. This area of legal reform thus differed from other spheres of revolutionary change where women remained the social and legal inferiors of men; women did not gain equality of political rights, for example. Within the family, however, daughters were given the same rights of succession as their brothers and were freed from paternal authority at the same age. Married women were liberated from the restrictions placed upon them by the legal codes of the Old Regime. They could enter into contracts without their husbands' consent and were given control over the property they brought to the marriage. In this respect divorce must be considered an important facility for women in that it broke down the unitary concept of the couple and gave men and women the opportunity to escape from a marriage that had become intolerable. In the absence of change in the relationships between wives and husbands at the level of social behavior – the changes that have been outlined were merely prescriptive–divorce gave women at least a limited legal counterweight to the social dominance that men could exercise.

By emphasizing individualism as a guiding principle for the reform of family law, the revolutionary legislators did not seek to destroy the family unit. The attention given to the family, associated as it was with the appropriation by the state of powers until then exercised by the church, has earned the revolution the undeserved reputation of attempting to destroy the family, and this period of family legislation is often referred to as the *"crise du mariage."* Opponents of the reforms in family law refused to believe that a family system not based firmly on canonical precepts, was a family at all. For the legislators of 1789–92, however, it was not a matter of destroying the family but of modifying it to fit the new social order. The architects of the new society recognized the importance of transforming not only the major political and social institutions of France but also the fundamental relationships among individuals and their attitudes toward one another. In the cause of equality all Frenchmen became *citoyens* and women

[73] See Phillips, *Family Breakdown*; Michel Garaud, *La Révolution française et la famille* (Paris, 1973).

became *citoyennes*, and in the cause of fraternity even strangers would *tutoyer* one another. There were limits to the changes that could be effected by legislative prescription and proscription, and moral exhortation had often to take the place of laws. The conjugal relationship – the most fundamental, immediate, and enduring for most adults, and whose varieties were as many as the number of married couples – fell into this category. No law could prescribe the behavior of a woman toward her husband or of a man toward his wife, and harmony between wife and husband could not be decreed. It is not surprising, then, to find among the national festivals of the French Republic a Festival of Marriage (*fête des époux*) that would extoll the virtues of family life, marital fidelity, and filial piety. This cult of the family was intended to rid France of the corruption within the family that had been engendered by the Old Regime. The Bureau of Fine Arts and National Festivals enjoined citizens to "consign to scorn and public censure, bad morals, seduction, debauchery, the neglect of duties, all those vices born in the corruption of monarchy, and which Republican virtue must proscribe and destroy."[74]

At the *fête des époux* celebrated in Rouen in Year VI of the republic the president of the administration of the *département* told the assembled citizens that

it is morality that constitutes the strength of states, and it is domestic virtues, it is happy marriages, that principally constitute good morals. The festival of virtuous spouses. . . is thus one of the most important national festivals in its object; it is, perhaps, the most essentially republican of all our festivals.[75]

Such sentiments did not indicate a burning desire to destroy the family but rather the wish to remould it in the shape of the new society. Reflecting its contemporary social and political environment, the family of the Old Regime had bestowed upon the *paterfamilias* the status of a monarch in a domestic realm. The coming of the revolution meant that these household Capets had to be stripped of the despotic aspects of their power.

But if it was impossible to prescribe conjugal behavior, the law could at least provide a remedy for the victims of unhappy marriages. The main remedy in case of marital breakdown was divorce, which, it was hoped, would be a deterrent against conjugal conflict: It was a "necessary remedy, whose existence prevents that of the evil which it must cure, regarding which Montaigne said so well: 'Never were marriages more holy and more sacred than when it was possible to dissolve them'."[76]

Divorce was thus an integral and crucial part of the family legislation and policy of the revolution, which set out to destroy the corporate nature of the family that, under the Old Regime, had suppressed the rights of all but selected members of the family and that had perpetuated inequalities among the members of the family that led to resentment and conflict. By making the distri-

[74] Archives départementales de la Seine-Maritime, L 359 (*Fêtes des époux*).
[75] Ibid.
[76] Ibid.

bution of rights more equal, the revolutionary legislators intended to make the family a more harmonious unit. Where harmony could not be achieved between spouses, divorce was provided as a last resort.

Although divorce was hailed by some legislators, politicians, and patriots as a liberty finally restored to the French people, it was not greeted with universal enthusiasm. The Catholic church, which ought to have been unanimously opposed to it, was divided on the issue, as it was on so many issues during the revolution. Part of the division is explicable by sheer confusion, for many priests were clearly uncertain as to what their attitude ought to be toward the new matrimonial legislation. In the diocese of Rouen many priests – a "crowd" of them – wrote to their bishop for advice on the matter. In reply he reiterated the orthodox Catholic doctrine of indissolubility, but added:

But this is far from condemning or disapproving of the conduct of legislators who judge it appropriate to permit divorce. It [the church] knows that they are often obliged to tolerate a lesser evil in order to avoid a greater one...We must tell married people that they are forbidden to remarry during the lifetime of their first spouses.[77]

In effect this advice suggested that Catholics might use the divorce law as a means of obtaining the same effect as a *séparation de corps*, which had been abolished by the law on divorce. Divorce would enable Catholic spouses to live separately and to regulate their finances appropriately, but as long as they did not remarry while their spouses were alive, they would not offend Catholic doctrine.

But even this moderate response and the explicit recognition that remarriage during the other's lifetime was forbidden were too much for some clerics. In Rouen the *abbé* Guillaume Baston, a canon of the Cathedral chapter, denounced divorce, whether or not it was followed by remarriage, as absolutely incompatible with Christianity.[78] The debate between Baston and his bishop very likely reflected the state of many of the clergy, torn between outright hostility toward divorce and a sort of reluctant accommodation with the civil law while maintaining Catholic doctrine as far as the two were compatible. Some clergy did, in fact, approve of divorce in word or deed. Priests appeared in Rouen's divorce records as witnesses to their relatives' divorce registrations and as witnesses before the divorce courts. Those who abandoned their church's doctrine of marital indissolubility entirely were probably a very small minority, just as a minority abandoned their vows of clerical celibacy and married during the revolution.

As for the mass of the population, their attitudes toward divorce must have covered the spectrum from utter hostility to the most positive approval whether (in either case) for personal reasons or reasons of principle. There is no way of

---

[77] Jean-Baptiste Guillaume Gratien, *Lettre circulaire de J.-B. Gratien, évêque de Rouen, au clergé de son diocèse, sur l'administration des sacremens de baptême et de mariage* (Paris, n.d. [October 19, 1792]).
[78] Guillaume-André-René Baston, *M. Gratien invité à revoir ses assertions sur le mariage* (Rouen, 1792).

gauging public opinion, except to note that divorce did take hold in French urban society at least. If we consider divorces undertaken but not completed, as well as those completed, the number of people in the city of Rouen who were involved in divorce in some capacity or other – as spouses, witnesses, lawyers, arbiters, members of family assemblies, and cosignatories to divorce registrations – must have amounted to more than 10,000 over a period of 10 years, out of an average annual population of about 85,000. A significant proportion of the adult population had participated in some way in divorce cases, and few people in the city can have been unaffected in some respect by divorce during the revolutionary years.[79]

Theatrical portrayal of divorce in the period, however, tended to be negative. In Demoustier's play *Le Divorce*, the ease of having a marriage dissolved under the 1792 law was satirized thus:

> What a fine institution this divorce is!
> Couples take each other, leave each other
> and take each other again when they like.
> Just like contracts, or sales, or exchanges...[80]

A report of the Bureau Central de Police in Paris noted on 28 Ventôse Year V (March 18, 1797) that "the public has greeted with prolonged applause what the characters of the play *La Mère Coupable* had to say sensitively and satirically against the institution of divorce." It is possible that public opinion, like opinion within the legislatures, had swung away from divorce later in the revolution.[81]

In general, it seems that criticism of divorce was muted during the early years of the law's application, but that by Year III (1794–5) there were petitions attacking various aspects of the divorce legislation. The first three years of divorce saw a large number of divorces decreed in France and this appeared to confirm the belief of conservatives that divorce could be obtained too easily. Evidence of the reaction against too liberal divorce came in the form of the suspension on 15 Thermidor Year III (August 2, 1795) of the law of 4 Floréal Year II that had allowed divorce on the ground of six months' separation. A Jacobin addition to the 1792 law, this provision was unacceptable to the men of Thermidor. The main target of those who sought to restrict the availability of divorce, however, was the ground of incompatibility of temperament. In the legislature the attack was led by the deputy Reynaud who, while admitting the general usefulness of divorce, condemned the abuses of the ground of incompatibility: "Well! Tell me, what is more immoral than to let a man change his wife as he changes his coat, and a woman to change her husband as she changes her hat."[82] To demonstrate the abuse of this mode of divorce, one *citoyen*

[79] See Phillips, *Family Breakdown*, passim.
[80] Charles Albert Demoustier, *Le Divorce: Comédie en deux actes, en vers* (Paris, An III). See also Desfontaines de la Vallée, *Le Divorce: Comédie en un acte* (Paris, An II).
[81] Cruppi, *Divorce pendant la Révolution*, 100n.1.
[82] *Le Moniteur universel*, 24 Brumaire Year V/November 14, 1796.

Bertrand, a captain of dragoons, told the Council of 500, the lower chamber of the legislature after 1795, that just as he was about to leave for Italy his wife, the mother of four children, "initiated against him a petition for divorce based on the frivolous pretext of incompatibility of temperament, but in reality in order to appropriate for herself part of his possessions."[83] Immediately after this petition the council set up a commission to report on the possibility of suspending the availability of divorce for reason of incompatibility, but although the commission reported in favor of suspension, the council agreed with the deputy Lecointe that if the law on divorce were to be revised it should be done as a whole, not piecemeal.[84] The question of divorce was taken up later the same year, after the royalist gains in the elections of Year V, but the only concession the council made to conservative opinion was to prolong (from six months to a year) the minimum time in which a divorce for reason of incompatibility could be obtained. The reaction against divorce that developed in the period of the Directory was largely unsuccessful. The debate in this period was closely interrelated with the turn of events in France – liberal republicans defending divorce, royalists attacking it. The issue was not resolved until the seizure of power by Napoleon who undertook the codification of French civil law and who imposed upon family law a conception of the family that was significantly different from that of the early revolutionary period.

5.4 Napoleonic divorce law

The Napoleonic law on divorce (30 Ventôse Year XI/March 21, 1803) restricted divorce to far fewer grounds than had been allowed in the 1792 law. Divorce for reason of incompatibility of temperament was suppressed. Divorce by mutual consent was retained, but the grounds justifying a unilateral divorce were confined to cruelty, adultery, and condemnation to certain degrading forms of punishment.[85] A marriage could not be dissolved by mutual consent unless it had lasted for more than two years, and neither could divorce by mutual consent be obtained in the case of a marriage that had lasted more than twenty years or in which the wife was more than 45 years old. The 1803 law also introduced discriminatory provisions by stipulating that a man could divorce his wife for reason of her adultery but that a woman could divorce her husband for adultery only if the adulterous act was committed in the marital dwelling.[86] Not only was Napoleonic divorce law more restrictive in its justifying grounds, but the procedures were made more difficult and longer. The overall effect of the new law was to make divorce less easily obtained, especially by women.[87]

---

[83] Ibid., 5 Nivôse Year V/December 25, 1796.
[84] Ibid., 20 Nivôse Year V/January 25, 1797.
[85] Code Napoléon, Articles 229–33.
[86] This provision echoed elements of Old Regime law (see Section 5.1).
[87] See Julien Bonnecase, *La philosophite du Code Napoléon appliquée au droit de la famille* (Paris, 1928).

5 Eighteenth-century France

This legislation reflected a changed orientation of attitudes toward the family. The emphasis was no longer on the individual within the family, but again on the corporate nature of the family unit. This did not entail a wholesale reversal to the assumptions of the Old Regime in respect of family law, for divorce was maintained (even though restricted), and equality of inheritance was provided for in the Civil Code, as was adoption. Nor was ecclesiastical influence over the family restored, and the registration of vital statistics remained securely in secular hands. In a general sense the Napoleonic family legislation drew from the laws of the Old Regime and the revolution, but its bias was toward the former; in many spheres of family life it restored prerevolutionary lines of authority, especially male authority, within the family. The authority of parents was strengthened to the extent of giving them the right to refuse their children, no matter how old, the required permission to divorce. Similarly the authority of the husband over his wife was restored; the code specified that a wife owed obedience to her husband, a husband protection to his wife, and that the wife was obliged by law to live with her husband and to follow him wherever he judged it convenient to live.[88]

This legislation had implications beyond France, for the Napoleonic code was extended, though sometimes in amended form, to the states making up the French Empire in Europe created during the revolutionary and Napoleonic wars. In Italy, for instance, divorce was introduced in the *Codice Civile* of 1806, which was little more than a translation of the Code Napoléon, while in Belgium the divorce provisions came into effect in 1807. In Spain, however, Napoleonic divorce was not introduced, perhaps, as one historian has suggested, to avoid antagonizing the Spanish population by introducing a practice so inimical to established custom.[89] (Spanish law did not even allow for judicial separations until 1875.) Yet sensitivity to national customs was not a hallmark of the French Empire: In Italy Napoleon refused to accept a suggested compromise that divorce should be available only to non-Catholics, as it had been under Austrian law in Lombardy-Venezia, and insisted that the law had to be applied uniformly throughout the population.[90]

Of the hundreds of divorces granted under the 1803 French divorce legislation, the most famous was that of Napoleon himself and the Empress Josephine. Yet for all that Napoleon found divorce essential for his personal and dynastic purposes, it is unlikely that he retained it in the Code Napoléon in order to profit from it himself. For one thing, it appears that he did not begin seriously to consider divorcing Josephine until 1805, and for another, a statute of 1806 actually forbade divorce within the imperial family. In fact, although Napoleon and Josephine's divorce seemed to conform to prevailing law, it actu-

<hr/>

[88] Code Napoléon, Articles 213–14.
[89] Ricardo Lezcarno, *El Divorcio en la Segunda República* (Madrid, 1979), 26–7.
[90] Maria Graziella Lulli, "Il problema del divorzio in Italia dal sec. XVIII al codice de 1865," *Il Diritto de Familia e delle Persone* III (1974), 1233.

186

ally overrode it. Like many other monarchs and emperors before him, Napoleon subordinated matrimonial law to broader political goals.

The direct motivation for Napoleon's decision to terminate his marriage was reminiscent of Henry VIII's: the desire to have an heir. In 1796 Napoleon had married Josephine de Beauharnais, a widow with children from her first marriage, but by 1805 no more children had been born, and the fact that Josephine had reached the age of 42 made it most unlikely that she would again conceive a child. Napoleon's concern for his dynasty was clear:

If only I at least had a child by her! It is my life's torment not to have a child; I well understand that my position will be secure only when I have one. If I happened to disappear, none of my brothers is capable of replacing me; everything has begun, nothing has been completed. God knows what will happen.[91]

Like Henry VIII, Napoleon considered a range of solutions to this matrimonial problem. One was that he should adopt one of his brother Louis's sons. Another, more extraordinary, was that Napoleon should impregnate another woman, that Josephine should feign a pregnancy, and that Napoleon's personal physician should lend credence to the deception by agreeing to be present when Josephine "gave birth." The plan might well have been put into effect, but the physician balked at the idea.[92]

In the end, however, Napoleon had fewer scruples than Henry VIII about dissolving his marriage. Even though divorce had earned a poor reputation during the French Revolution, it was widely recognized as acceptable and justified in certain circumstances. There was no real fear, as there had been in sixteenth-century England, that an heir born within a remarriage made possible by divorce would be considered illegitimate. Although the French church did not approve of divorce, a concordat with the papacy had given Napoleon's regime an apparent imprimatur of approval. This assessment of the impact of a divorce, together with the growing belief that his empire needed an heir to give it stability, led Napoleon to decide on a divorce by the end of 1809. Josephine was devastated by the decision, but agreed to a divorce by mutual consent.[93] In accordance with the law, an assembly of relatives was convoked to hear the determination to divorce and, as an additional measure, the divorce was approved by the Senate.

Apart from the obvious characteristics that set this divorce apart from others that took place in France under the Civil Code, there were several legal irregularities. First, the divorce breached the imperial law of 1806 that had forbidden divorces within the imperial family. Second, the divorce law of 1803 forbade divorce by mutual consent where the wife was forty-five years old or older, and by 1809 Josephine was forty-six years old. Even though she had

---

[91] Michel Lhospice, *Divorce et dynastie* (Paris, 1960), 191–2.
[92] Ibid., 192.
[93] Frances Mossiker, *Napoleon and Josephine. The Biography of a Marriage* (New York, 1964), 339.

understated her age by four years at the time of her marriage to him in 1796, Napoleon must have known her real age. Third, Napoleon ignored the stipulation that in divorces by mutual consent the spouses could not remarry within three years of the divorce; he remarried within three months. In these respects, Napoleon placed himself above the law.

Although the divorce dissolved the civil marriage of 1796, there remained a problem in that Napoleon and Josephine had gone through another marriage ceremony, a religious one this time, in 1804. By 1809 there was little possibility that the pope, Pius VII, would agree to annul the marriage so as to clear the way for Napoleon to enter a valid marriage with a Roman Catholic. In the few years before the divorce, Napoleon had alienated the pope by overriding papal protests and insisting that divorce should be included in the Italian Civil Code. Pius VII had excommunicated Napoleon, and by 1809 the pope was a prisoner of the French. Nevertheless, an annulment was essential if Napoleon was to marry, as he planned, a member of one of the royal families of Europe, specifically a daughter of the Austrian imperial family. The solution to Napoleon's dilemma was to ignore the pope entirely and to place the petition for annulment before the court of the bishop of Paris. Napoleon alleged that the 1804 marriage was canonically invalid because his and Josephine's own priest was absent from the marriage ceremony, the required witnesses were lacking, and because he himself did not truly consent to the marriage. In the end the annulment petition was approved on the single ground that the bride and groom's own priest was not present at the marriage.[94] The pope protested against the decision, but it was a mild objection that focused on the issue of jurisdiction rather than on the substance of the case.[95]

The dissolution of the civil marriage and the annulment of the religious one cleared the way for Napoleon to remarry. This he quickly did to the Austrian Archduchess Marie-Louise, in March and April 1810, in Vienna and Paris, respectively. Not only was the remarriage rapid – it took place only two months after the annulment had been approved – but so were the desired results: a son was born to Marie-Louise in March 1811, so that Napoleon achieved his aim less than fifteen months after he divorced. It was one of history's ironies that all these matrimonial efforts were to prove wasted; Napoleon's son died in 1832, and when a Bonaparte did return to power in France it was a son of Napoleon's brother, Louis. Napoleon might just as well have adopted him in the first place.

The general use of divorce under the terms of the Code Napoléon is discussed elsewhere.[96] For the present it is enough to note that in France the number of divorces fell dramatically when the 1792 law was repealed. In Rouen, for instance, the number fell from an average of sixty-seven a year between 1796 and 1803, not very many for a population of 85,000 in any case, to an average of only six a year under the Napoleonic law.

[94] The annulment is analyzed in Lhospice, *Divorce et dynastie*, 213–32.
[95] Ibid., 238–9.
[96] See Section 7.4.

5.5 Abolition of divorce

Even so, any divorce law at all and any divorces at all were repugnant to the legislators of the Bourbon Restoration after the fall of Napoleon, and on May 8, 1816, King Louis XVIII issued a decree abolishing divorce "in the interest of religion, of morality, of the monarchy, of families."[97] The campaign against divorce had been championed by the Vicomte de Bonald, the apologist of Catholic and monarchist political and social doctrines. Bonald argued that as well as being anathema to Catholic teaching, divorce was inconsistent with the sanctity of the family, and that it was especially harmful to women and children. In a conjugal society, he told the Chamber of Deputies in 1815, "the situations are not equal: the man deploys his strength there, the woman her weakness." In the event of divorce, the husband could withdraw from the marriage with his independence intact, while the wife was bereft of all her "virginal purity, youth, beauty, fecundity, esteem," and rescued only her money from the ruins of her marriage.[98] Such an image of the ravages wrought on women by marriage was hardly an advertisement for matrimony.

Bonald and some of his fellow conservative deputies also pointed out the deleterious effect of divorce on the authority of the *paterfamilias*. The Baron de Trinquelague argued that "the head of the household is more respected when his authority is permanent."[99] Bonald gave the point a broader political perspective. Just as political democracy "allows the people, the weak part of political society, to rise against the established authority," so divorce, "veritable domestic democracy," allows the wife "the weak part, to rebel against marital authority." Thus "in order to keep the state out of the hands of the people, it is necessary to keep the family out of the hands of wives and children."[100] Other considerations reinforced the monarchist arguments against divorce. Divorce was contrary to their conception of Christian principles for one thing, and it was perceived as an anti-Catholic innovation of the revolution. These arguments apart, however, it can be seen that the Restoration attitude to divorce was predicated on an authoritarian, corporative image of the family, even more so than the Napoleonic image and was thus even further removed from the conception of the family embodied in the legislation of the early period of the revolution.

The introduction of divorce in 1792 can be explained in various ways, each contributing something to an overall understanding of the phenomenon, which was a truly revolutionary departure not only from French law but from European law generally. It was the culmination of a trend in social thought and criticism that went back far into the Old Regime, and it was an implication of secularization and of antichurch sentiment among the revolutionaries who were dominant by 1792. It represented the strict application of the principles of

---

[97] *Bulletin des Lois du Royaume de France*, 7ᶜ série, II (Paris, 1816), 687–8.
[98] *Archives parlementaires*, 2ᶜ série, XV, 611.
[99] Ibid., XVI, 195.
[100] Ibid., XVI, 612.

contract to the family and the embodiment of individualism within marriage and the family. Whatever the explanation for it, the French divorce law clearly responded to social and intellectual trends within society, as we shall see further in Chapter 7. Like the revolution itself, however, divorce seems to have outstripped the evolutionary development of these trends and brought upon itself a reaction. It might be unhistorical to refer to an innovation as having been in advance of its time, but in the context of the history of divorce in Western society, the French divorce law of 1792 certainly was that. We cannot but be struck by the modernity of that law. Its liberal terms, its provisions for alimony and custody of children, are only now, two centuries later, being matched by national divorce policies and legislation in the Western world.

6

⦾⦾⦾

The secularization of divorce, 1600–1800

6.1 Introduction

In the period covered by this survey of divorce, from the Middle Ages to the present, Western society was transformed. In simple geographical terms it expanded as Europeans extended their political, economic, and cultural hegemony across the Atlantic Ocean and then across the North American continent and, even further, to the antipodes. Western society also underwent an immense and far-reaching structural evolution as it experienced urbanization, industrialization, and the other changes summed up in the concept "modernization."[1] As we shall see, the individual areas of change impinged on marriage and the family in various ways, and in so doing affected divorce. Urbanization and industrialization, for instance, modified the traditional family economy, the interdependent economic relationships of husband and wife, and enhanced the potential for marriage breakdown. (Issues such as these are taken up in Chapters 11–13.)

This chapter focuses on religion, one of the most important areas of change in the evolution of Western society and one that had clearly discernible effects on marriage and divorce. It is evident that one of the most stark differences between perspectives on marriage in the Middle Ages and those in the modern world lies in their religious content. Theories and doctrines of marriage have surrendered their almost exclusively theological foundations to secular emphases based on social and personal considerations. At the institutional level, marriage is no longer regulated by church law enforced by church courts but is governed by the civil law, and litigation and enforcement proceed in the civil courts.

This is not to deny the continuing role of religion in modern marriage, where individuals may be guided by their religious beliefs to a greater or lesser extent, where religious considerations might inhibit the use of divorce, and where the spiritual courts still play a role in matrimonial matters, albeit peripheral-

---

[1] There is a large literature on the concept of modernization in Europe. For an illuminating discussion see E. A. Wrigley, "The Process of Modernization and the Industrial Revolution in England," *Journal of Interdisciplinary History* 2 (1972), 225–59.

ly.[2] Despite the residual roles of religion with respect to the institutions and ideology of marriage, however, the decline of religion as an influence has been dramatic over the long term, and at these levels secularization was the principal motor of modernization. Only by breaking out of the religious models and discarding the theological assumptions were legislators able to broaden their conceptions of marriage and, by implication, of divorce as well. To this extent, secularization was the bridge between the first generation of divorce laws of the sixteenth century and the second generation of the nineteenth century. As this chronology suggests, the period from 1600 to 1800 was a critical phase of transition, and it is these 200 years on which the present chapter concentrates.

Secularization refers to the decline of formal and informal religious or spiritual influences on political, social, and personal life and their replacement by secular influences.[3] As such, it is a relatively straightforward concept, but it is impossible to pin the process down to a single chronology. Secularization was a long-term development that must be thought of in relative, not absolute terms; in Western history the religious and the secular have been so intimately intertwined that we must ask which of the two influences was dominant, rather than expect one of them to obliterate the other entirely. Secularization also varied from place to place and among social classes, although its progress was generally faster among men than within the female population. Neither should we think of it as unilinear, moving steadily and inexorably forward like some demolition machine, a Whig at the controls, cutting a swathe through religious structures and strewing spiritual debris in its wake. At times secularization stagnated, at other times it went into remission for a period. Despite all of these qualifications, however, the clear tendency was for Western society to become more secular over time, and marriage and divorce were not insulated from its effects.

It is important to recognize that secularization took various forms, of which two are important to us here. The first is institutional secularization, the transfer of social functions from religious institutions, usually the established church in a given state, to secular or lay bodies. Over the long term we can appreciate that social, political, and economic tasks that used to be carried out by the churches and their agencies have progressively been taken over by the secular state and its agencies. Fundamental functions, such as making law, staffing the judiciary, providing education, health services and poor relief, and the keeping of vital records, were in the past wholly or principally the responsibility of the church. If we take France as an example, we can see that in the sixteenth century the Catholic church exercised many of the functions we now associate with the state. The church kept parish registers, the only

---

[2] Within the Roman Catholic church diocesan and other tribunals deal with petitions for annulments of marriage and and for marriage dispensations.

[3] A concise account of secularization is Peter Burke, "Religion and Secularization," in *The New Modern Cambridge History* (14 vols., Cambridge, 1964–9), XIII, 293–317.

6.1 Introduction

contemporary records of vital events, that recorded baptisms, marriages, and burials. Ecclesiastical legislation dealt with many areas of law, not only those relating to church discipline and faith but also morality, the family, and the law of persons. The laws were enforced by ecclesiastical courts that not only dealt with criminal matters but also heard litigation in matrimonial and other civil cases. The church, through the regular clergy, operated schools, hospitals, foundling homes, charities, workhouses, and in Paris religious orders ran the capital's fire-fighting service until the 1770s.[4]

In many of these enterprises the church worked in a partnership with the state, even though their relationship was often uneasy. Ecclesiastical law coexisted with laws deriving from the monarchy, from the customary codes of northern France, and from the Roman law tradition of the south. The parish registers kept by the priests were maintained at the behest and under the supervision of the state, and the secular authorities also took a role in education and social welfare. Over time the secular partner asserted its dominance over the church, and gradually stripped it of most of its functions, such as its being the official registrar of vital events. Those formal institutional functions that the church retained, in education for example, were regulated by the state. Where the church did retain its freedom of action, as in charitable works, the overall importance of its role diminished as the state extended its influence. In these terms, institutional secularization – not only in France, but generally – saw the churches and their agencies gradually lose their independence and their influence. It was the mirror image of the process by which the secular state extended its authority over society, economy, and culture, for although institutional control was unprecedented in many respects, in others the state's enhanced authority derived from its taking jurisdiction from the religious authorities.

The second important facet of secularization relates to ideology. Political, social, and legal theories have progressively shed their religious points of reference in favor of secular considerations based on social, moral, or individualistic criteria. Again, there was generally an intermingling of the secular and the religious, particularly in the seventeenth and eighteenth centuries, but even during this period there was a discernible change of emphasis in favor of the secular. Insofar as the writers we shall examine here were Christian, they continued to regard marriage as ordained by God. But as far as determining the constitution of marriage and the relationship between husband and wife, they referred less and less to the Bible and more and more to the notions of contract in civil law and to the principles of natural law (which themselves were shorn of religious elements).

Coexisting with élite ideologies were popular ideologies, or *mentalités* as they are commonly known in much historiography. *Mentalités* were less likely to be articulated in explicit verbal forms or to be recorded in documents; they

[4] Jacques Godechot, *The Taking of the Bastille* (London, 1970), 72.

193

emanated from the mass of the population, which was either illiterate or barely literate. Because *mentalités* were not the product of conscious reasoning but emerged from the exigencies and imperatives of social and material life, they can often be recovered only by the examination of individual and collective behavior. As a crude example, we might look for evidence of secularization within a peasant or working-class population not in letters and theological treatises or in the often-skewed accounts of lower-class life by middle-class commentators but in changes in behavior. Did people attend church with the same regularity and conscientiousness over time? Did they observe church regulations and injunctions relating to personal and marital behavior? Given the choice between secular and religious forms of marriage or other events, which did they choose?

In this chapter these various aspects of secularization – institutional, ideological, and attitudinal – will be brought to bear on various facets of marriage and divorce. Between 1600 and 1800, we shall see, there were significant changes in the perspectives commonly invoked by those who wrote about marriage and its dissolution. There were also dramatic changes in the institutions of marriage and divorce. Bearing in mind that there were many other forces at work in this period, which was a turning point in Western history in many respects, secularization can nonetheless be taken as one of the critical forces that established the foundation for the modernization of divorce in the nineteenth and twentieth centuries.

6.2 Secularization of institutions

The clearest form of secularization was the increased involvement of essentially secular institutions in legislation and judicial disposition concerning divorce. In the Middle Ages these functions had been effectively monopolized by the Roman Catholic church: Catholic doctrine and canon law regulated marriage and related questions such as divorce, separation, annulment, and bigamy, whereas the spiritual courts, notably the bishops' or officials' courts, had immediate jurisdiction over matrimonial law. We should recall that this situation had resulted from a process that might be called desecularization, in which the church had challenged, then progressively superseded, secular laws on marriage and divorce that were based on Frankish, Anglo-Saxon, and other customary codes, and on the heritage of Roman law. Although popular marriage practices in many parts of Europe testified to the persistence of secular marriage traditions, the ecclesiastical and lay élites had, by the thirteenth century, reached a consensus that the church would regulate marriage and that its doctrines and laws would be enforced by the church courts.

This view, that the spiritual power should have a monopoly in matters of matrimonial law in the widest sense, attracted critics throughout the period of its consolidation, but it was challenged effectively only by the sixteenth-century Reformers. Luther, Calvin, and their contemporaries were unanimous that marriage was not a sacrament and that the ecclesiastical courts had no special claim to jurisdiction over it. Although they agreed that marriage was ordained by God and that it had God's blessing, the Reformers expressed a much more secular vision of it than the Catholic church could begin to countenance. Marriage was not a sacrament, Calvin argued; rather it was a civil contract, and jurisdiction concerning it fell properly to the lay authorities. Luther described matrimony as a "worldly thing" and insisted that it was the duty of the secular government to establish laws to regulate marriage and divorce.[5] In Sweden, Laurentius Petri's introduction to the Västerås ordinance, the basic reforming document of the Swedish church, specified that marriage was a matter for the secular law to deal with.[6]

It might have been expected that these doctrines would lead to the establishment of purely secular marriage legislation and of civil courts with matrimonial jurisdiction in Protestant states, but they did not. In most of them, marriage and divorce legislation derived, as we have seen in Chapter 2, from the Reformers themselves, and was issued in the form of church ordinances; this was so in Germany, Switzerland, Scandinavia, and the Netherlands. Although this arrangement conflicted with a strict interpretation of the Protestant doctrines that marriage was a secular matter, it was not without justification in practical terms. It was expected that marriage law, when determined by the secular authorities, would be in accord with God's law, and it was the role of the churches to describe that law by interpreting the Bible. In theory, then, the civil law of marriage and divorce would have been no different from church law, and it is therefore understandable that the civil authorities felt no particular urgency to duplicate an existing law. In these cases we must also assume that the secular authorities in each state approved of their churches' marriage regulations, at least in the short term, for they could have intervened if they had not. For example, in Nuremberg for some decades the secular government had resisted pressure by the clergy to permit divorce.[7] This exceptional case highlights the general pattern of secular acquiescence in the churches' legislating on marriage and divorce.

If marriage laws in Protestant Europe continued to emanate from the spiritual authorities (as they had done before the Reformation), there was at least a change in respect of the judiciaries enforcing them. For the most part the marriage tribunals in Reformed states were composed of clerical and lay members, but the latter predominated. The *Ehegericht* of Basel had five members drawn from the city's legislative bodies and two members drawn from the clergy,[8] and the marriage court of Zurich comprised four lay and two clerical

---

[5] See Björnsson, *The Lutheran Doctrine of Marriage in Modern Icelandic Society* (Oslo, Reykjavik, 1971), 22.
[6] Ivar Nylander, *Studier Rörande den Svenska Äktenskapsrättens Historia* (Uppsala, 1961), 112.
[7] See Section 2.8.
[8] Thomas Max Safley, "To Preserve the Marital State: The Basler Ehegericht, 1550–1592," *Journal of Family History* 7 (1982), 162–79.

judges.[9] In Scandinavia ecclesiastical and lay tribunals remained discrete but worked cooperatively, and here too the secular authorities had the final decision. In Sweden, for example, the church tribunals acted in marriage matters as courts of first instance, hearing matrimonial disputes. They were forums where the clergy could exert their moral authority in attempts to reconcile husbands and wives in conflict. If these attempts were unsuccessful and it was decided that the couple should be punished or their marriage dissolved, the secular court accepted jurisdiction over the case and was empowered to dispose of it.[10]

To some extent the persistence of ecclesiastical jurisdiction in these states resulted from the circumstances of transition from Catholic to Reformed confessions: Often, the institutions of the Catholic church were abolished before new institutions were devised to replace them. In regions influenced by Lutheranism, for instance, there was a period of uncertainty after the bishops' courts were dissolved. Matrimonial cases and litigation, often affecting the status of spouses and children, could be urgent, and in the judicial vacuum created by the abolition of the Catholic church's courts, they were referred to parish priests, jurists, and theologians for help. Often they were referred directly to Luther himself (see Section 2.3), the final authority in these matters. Thus in the earliest phase of the Reformation the churches retained the traditional spiritual jurisdiction over marriage for quite practical reasons, despite doctrinal affirmations as to the worldliness of marriage. When consistorial courts were established – starting with the court in Württemberg in 1539 – the participation of the clergy with lay judges provided a continuity not only with the practices of the transitional phase but also with the preceding Catholic period.[11]

Similar patterns were evident elsewhere. In Scotland the Officials' courts were suppressed in 1560, but it was not until 1563 that the Church of Scotland's judicial system was properly organized. In the interim the individual kirk sessions took over jurisdiction in order to provide judicial services for the faithful.[12] In Iceland the basic Reformatory Church Order, which reformed the Icelandic church, was issued in 1539 but not applied in the southern diocese until 1541 and in the rest of the island until 1551. This order gave the clergy the right to perform marriages but specified no further control over them. The reform of marriage law followed much later, with a partial law of 1564 and a more comprehensive marriage code in 1587.[13] It was inevitable that there should have been delays in consulting authorities and drafting legislation (and

[9] See Section 2.9.
[10] Nylander, *Äktenskapsrättens Historia*, 73ff.
[11] George E. Howard, *A History of Matrimonial Institutions* (3 vols., Chicago, 1904) II, 69–71.
[12] David Baird Smith, "The Reformers and Divorce: A Study on Consistorial Jurisdiction," *Scottish Historical Review* 9 (1911), 15–18; Ronald D. Ireland, "Husband and wife: Divorce, Nullity of Marriage and Separation," in *An Introduction to Scottish Legal History* (Edinburgh, 1958), 82.
[13] Björnsson, *Lutheran Doctrine of Marriage*, 47, 52–5.

no doubt they were compounded by Iceland's isolation), and almost inevitably the new church officials stepped in to provide continuity, rather than leave a hiatus of decades during which no matrimonial issues could be adjudicated or resolved. Thus it was that in Iceland, despite the limitations implicitly placed on their authority by the 1539 church order, the bishops continued to provide jurisdiction in marriage cases, although many decisions were apparently made by "half-courts," tribunals composed equally of ecclesiastical and secular judges, all sitting under the presidency of a bishop.[14]

England was, in this question of jurisdiction, a special case in that the institutional reformation of the church there broke less decisively than the continental and Scottish churches with Catholic practices. Marriage law continued to come within the scope of the church courts, and the fundamental law applied was the canon law – from 1604 the reformed canon law of the Church of England. However, in the sixteenth century, there were harbingers of the secular involvement that would increase in the next century. It will be recalled that when Henry VIII established a commission to revise the canon law of his church, he specified a combination of lay and clerical members: The commission comprised eight bishops, eight divines, eight lawyers, and eight laymen.[15]

The net effect of the Reformation on European matrimonial legislation and jurisdiction was to undermine the exclusivity of the church without, however, giving the secular authorities complete control. There emerged a close partnership between churches and states, and in most cases the result was that predominantly secular courts applied church laws. For a short time at least, there seems to have been an identity of views. As we have seen, the religious conceptions of divorce were generally extremely restrictive, and similarly the laymen who dominated the marriage tribunals were, to judge from the success rates of divorce petitions in the sixteenth century, anything but anxious to interpret the marriage ordinances in a permissive way.[16]

The partnership between clerical and lay bodies and institutions in regulating divorce marked the beginning of secularization in these matters. In the course of the seventeenth century the process continued, not so much by the state's taking over the roles of the church in legislation and jurisdiction as by the development of parallel institutions and practices that provided exclusively secular alternatives to the religious or mixed clerical – lay institutions. The effect of this increased secular influence was to reduce the significance of the church's role in the overall pattern of divorce law and judicial practice.

Sweden is one example of this practice at work. Divorce law there was regulated by the Swedish Lutheran church, first by the 1572 church ordinance and later by the 1686 church law, both of which limited divorce to the classic

---

[14] Ibid., 48–9.
[15] Lewis Dibdin and Charles E. H. Chadwyck Healey, *English Church Law and Divorce* (London, 1912), 68.
[16] See Section 2.8.

Lutheran grounds of adultery and desertion. From the 1630s, however, a practice developed by which the king could dissolve marriages by royal dispensation, that is, a dispensation that freed successful petitioners from the constraints of church law.[17] In the earliest dispensations the king acted rather as an adjunct, giving flexibility to existing law, amplifying it but not altering its essence. These cases generally involved marriages where one spouse had almost certainly committed adultery, but where the evidence, although compelling, was defective in terms of the requirements of the law.[18] In this early phase of royal dispensations, the king's actions could be interpreted as falling within the spirit of church law and as being a complementary source of jurisdiction where divorce petitions might be judged less by strict application of the law but rather with a broader sense of equity. This in itself is testimony as to the rigor of the courts in Sweden in their application of divorce legislation.

Gradually, however, royal dispensations were extended to include cases of extreme hardship, which were not recognized by Lutheran doctrine, and in this way the monarchy began to create, in practice, a more liberal divorce policy than that envisaged by the church. By creating a body of case law and precedent, the king established, in effect, royal legislation on divorce that was no longer complementary to church law but increasingly in competition with it.

The grounds the Swedish kings began to accept as justifying divorce included not only specific matrimonial offenses such as ill-treatment and, from the eighteenth century, drunkenness but also circumstances such as "hatred and bitterness between the spouses." This formula, which could be tantamount to incompatibility of temperament, represented a movement toward no-fault divorce. There was a limitation to this concept, however, in that if both spouses were deemed equally guilty of creating the disharmony that existed between them, neither was permitted to enter into a new marriage while the other was still alive.[19] In this way the principle of guilt was both removed and maintained. Divorce on this ground could be approved where one spouse was not demonstrably innocent and one demonstrably guilty. In contrast, ecclesiastical codes required clear-cut cases of guilt and innocence before they would approve of divorce, which was why they clung to a limited range of offenses. Yet this apparently no-fault form of divorce by royal dispensation in Sweden retained the implication of fault by denying the reward of divorce – remarriage – to the guilty. In these cases, both were guilty, so neither could remarry. It is important to note, though, that despite the prohibition on remarriage, these royal acts dissolved the marriages concerned and did not merely separate the spouses *a mensa et thoro.*

Royal dispensations to dissolve marriages for reason of incompatibility were rarely granted; there were only about two a year[20] during the eighteenth

---

[17] Nylander, *Äktenskapsrättens Historia,* 112.
[18] Max Rheinstein, *Marriage Stability, Divorce and the Law* (Chicago, 1972), 132.
[19] Nylander, *Äktenskapsrättens Historia,* 131.
[20] Ibid., 158.

century, on average. Nonetheless they are significant as reflecting a shift in jurisdiction and an extension of the range of grounds recognized in Sweden as justifying divorce. (As we shall see, the broadening of divorce grounds was in itself an aspect of secularization in that it denoted the abandonment of the primarily scriptural grounds for divorce.) The use of royal dispensations also circumvented existing church law. The 1686 church law had specified that where there was domestic discord, the parish authorities should intervene and attempt conciliation. If that failed, the couple in question should be turned over to the secular authorities to be dealt with, if necessary by imprisonment for a short time. If that had no salutary effect on their relationship, the case could be transferred to the church court, which could order a separation *a mensa et thoro*.[21] Dissolution of the marriage in such circumstances was not envisaged by the law, however, and discord became a ground for divorce only when granted by royal dispensation.

In addition to incompatibility, divorces by royal decree were granted when one spouse had been imprisoned for a serious crime, or when one was suffering from a serious illness such as leprosy, mental illness, or incurable insanity.[22] Again, royal practice in this respect extended the concept of divorce beyond the Lutheran form, but again the number of divorces in these categories was small. Nylander suggests that during the eighteenth century (from 1724 to 1810) the kings granted only two or three dispensations annually for reason of imprisonment,[23] and perhaps twice that number on the grounds of various kinds of illness.[24] In total it appears that during the eighteenth century some ten or twelve divorces a year were granted by royal dispensations.

In 1734 the Swedish monarch stepped into the regulation of divorce in a more systematic way, with the promulgation of a civil code, the *Sveriges Rikes Lag*, the first such legal codification in modern Europe. Despite the fact that the kings' dispensations were progressively extending the grounds for divorce, the 1734 code maintained adultery and desertion as the only grounds acceptable for a judicial dissolution of marriage in Sweden. However a multistage procedure for divorce in circumstances of incompatibility was established. In such cases the couple would initially be warned to behave more correctly toward each other, but if they failed to heed two such warnings, and having been punished twice (by fines) for having failed to do so, they could be granted a separation. The separation could in turn be converted to divorce by royal act.[25] This

---

21 Ibid., 76.
22 Ibid., 159–84 (punishment) and 185–200 (illness).
23 Ibid., 184.
24 Ibid., 193ff. A contemporary English work on Sweden noted that "domestick Quarrels rarely happen, and more seldom become Publicke; the Husbands being as apt to keep the Authority in their own hands, as the Wives by Nature, Custom, or Necessity, are inclin'd to be Obedient: Divorces, and other Separations between Man and wife, scarce ever happen, but among the inferior Sort, when the innocent Party is allowed to Marry again." *An Account of Sweden* (London, n.d. [?1700]), 70–1.
25 Johan Thorsten Sellin, *Marriage and Divorce Legislation in Sweden* (pub. Ph. D. diss., University of Pennsylvania, 1922), 35–6.

procedure put on a formal basis an existing practice, but there was no formalization of the other various grounds for divorce that royal dispensations had recognized, and the dual judicial – executive forms of divorce continued after the 1734 code was promulgated. Other grounds for divorce by judicial decree were not legalized until 1810, when a new divorce law was enacted.

The Swedish monarchy was not alone in intervening directly in the regulation of marriage and divorce in the seventeenth and eighteenth centuries. In Denmark the king also granted dispensations from the restrictive church laws. In the 1790s, a watershed period in the divorce history of Denmark, divorces began to be granted by royal decree after the spouses had lived separate for a determinate period of time, fixed in 1796 at three years.[26]

In early eighteenth-century Prussia, too, King Frederick William I took the authority to grant divorces by personal decree in circumstances not recognized by prevailing church law. The ability of the Prussian monarch to participate in the judicial process in this way was guaranteed by the principle of *Machtsprüche*, an irregular measure exercised by royal authority where a court judgment should properly have been rendered.[27] Under Frederick William I this power was exercised in a wide range of civil and criminal matters, not only in matrimonial causes. But his son and successor, Frederick II ("the Great") took a rather different view of the royal authority over such matters as divorce. In 1751 he issued a rescript that permitted the Prussian courts to dissolve marriages that were affected by "deadly and notorious hostility" (*inimicitiae capitales et notoriae*).[28] This additional ground moved divorce in Prussia away from the principle of strict fault and from some of the limitations placed on divorce by the Reformation codes.

The 1751 rescript not only secularized divorce to the extent of making it the subject of civil law, but it also made divorce available from the civil courts. Moreover, it put divorce on a more secure basis, removing it from the largely arbitrary influence of the monarchy, for the rescript entailed the abandonment of the practice of *Machtsprüche*. In his 1752 political testament, Frederick II wrote: "I have decided never to interfere in the course of legal proceedings, for in the courts of law the laws must speak and the ruler must remain silent."[29] It was a principle he practiced. When a citizen of Breslau petitioned for a royal order to permit him to divorce his wife, Frederick advised him to take his case to the regular courts, for "the king never grants *Machtsprüche*, either in judicial or matrimonial matters."[30] He did, however, reserve to himself the power to be

---

[26] Nylander, *Äktenskapsrättens Historia*, 111.
[27] The exercise of *Machtsprüche* was justified as a response to widespread abuse in the Prussian courts. See Herman Weill, *Frederick the Great and Samuel von Cocceji: A Study in the Reform of the Prussian Judicial Administration, 1740–1755* (Madison, 1961), 31–2.
[28] Heinrich Dernburg, *Familienrecht und Erbrecht des Privatrechts Preussens und des Reichs* (n.p., 1896), 56.
[29] Quoted in Weill, *Frederick the Great*, 61.
[30] Ibid.

the final court of review and to supervise the activities and decisions of the courts.

By the middle of the eighteenth century, under the influence of natural law jurists such as the Prussian Chancellor Samuel Cocceji (see Section 6.4), Prussian divorce law was liberalized and modernized. It was available from the civil courts and although the practice of direct royal intervention in individual cases ended, Frederick II's rescript gave the courts more discretion in disposing of cases. In 1794, a few years after Frederick's death, the first comprehensive codification of Prussian law, the *Allgemeines Landrecht für die Preussischen Staaten*, put prevailing practices on a statutory basis. Under the code divorce could be granted not only on the Lutheran grounds of adultery and desertion but also by mutual consent when there were no children of the marriage or at the unilateral request of one of the spouses. In the last case the courts needed proof that there was, within the marriage, such a violent and deeply rooted aversion that there were no longer any possibilities that the spouses could be reconciled or that the ends of marriage could be achieved.[31]

With two specific grounds for divorce, as well as divorce by mutual consent and a version of incompatibility, the 1794 Prussian code reflected the liberalizing tendency of the late eighteenth century, a tendency that took its fullest form in the French divorce law, which preceded it by two years (see Chapter 5). The Prussian code was generally more reserved, however. There were difficult procedural obstacles to surmount before a divorce could be obtained, and in the case of incompatibility there was a residual notion of fault, as in contemporary Swedish law. Rather than considering the character and behavior of the spouses when deciding the question of custody in divorces based on incompatibility, the Prussian courts were required to deny custody to the partner who had actually petitioned for the divorce.[32] To this extent divorce – and those who resorted to it – was clearly stigmatized.

Another enlightened ruler, Emperor Joseph II of Austria, a thoroughgoing secularizer whose treatment of the Catholic church in his realm provided precedents for the nationalization of the French church during the revolution, also undermined ecclesiastical authority over the family. Under Joseph the civil authorities were given competence to hear petitions for separations and to deal with annulments of marriage that were based on nonreligious impediments. In 1781 he went so far as to introduce civil marriage into Austria's Italian territories of Lombardy and Venice, and to permit non-Catholics there to divorce.[33] In 1784 the non-Catholic inhabitants of the Austrian Netherlands (later to become Belgium) were granted access to divorce as long as it was

---

[31] Rheinstein, *Marriage Stability*, 25–6.
[32] Ibid. and Richard J. Evans, *The Feminist Movement in Germany, 1894–1933* (London, 1976), 13–14.
[33] Maria Graziella Lulli, "Il problema del divorzio in Italia dal sec. XVIII al codice de 1865," *Il Diritto di Famiglia e delle Persone* 3 (1974), 1232.

preceded by a separation *a mensa et thoro*.[34] Joseph II's edict of September 28, 1784, could not have been a clearer statement of the contemporary secular claim to jurisdiction over matrimonial issues of all kinds. It forbade the church courts to have jurisdiction over any matter concerning the validity of marriage, legitimacy of children, promises of marriage, engagements, or any other matter touching marriage. The preamble to the edict referred to "the importance that matrimonial commitments have to both the well-being of individual families and to the general good," and the first article unambiguously defined marriage as a civil matter in all respects:

Marriage is considered to be a civil contract, and the civil rights and relationships which it implies derive their existence, their form and their definition entirely and uniquely from the civil power; jurisdiction over and disposition of litigation relative to these and associated matters, belong exclusively to the civil courts; whereby We forbid any ecclesiastical judge, under pain of absolute nullity, to take jurisdiction [over any matrimonial case].[35]

6.3 Secularization of divorce policies

The intervention of the Swedish, Danish, Prussian, and Austrian monarchs in marriage and divorce law, both on a personal basis and by edicts and statutes, not only added to the secular element in legislation and jurisdiction but also extended divorce policies significantly. The grounds for divorce that were recognized, including incompatibility, discord, insanity, incurable illness, and imprisonment, went well beyond the doctrinal perspectives of the dominant Lutheran churches in Scandinavia and Prussia. In the case of Austria, Joseph II overrode Catholic doctrine in order to extend divorce to some of his outlying Protestant populations. In these instances it was not only the form of legislation and jurisdiction that was secularized but the very understanding of the nature of marriage and divorce. The new conceptions of these institutions, we shall see, owed more to theories of natural law than to the Bible.

In the same period changes also took place within the judicial bodies established to deal with divorce in the sixteenth century. A striking example was the consistorial court at Württemberg, the well-spring of the Lutheran Reformation. By the middle of the eighteenth century this court had adopted a much more permissive attitude toward divorce than Luther's church ordinances had allowed, and judges were exercising wide discretion when disposing of divorce petitions. This did not necessarily conflict with Luther's doctrines; he had been reluctant to define too narrowly or precisely the acceptable grounds for divorce. But when it came to legislation, the Württemberg church ordinances had confined divorce to the grounds of adultery and desertion.[36] Two

[34] Henni le Page, *Traité élémentaire de droit civil belge* (3rd edn., Brussels, 1962), I, 961n.2.
[35] Quoted in John Gilissen, *Introduction historique du droit* (Brussels, 1979), 523–4.
[36] See Section 2.3 on Luther's reluctance to sanction divorce and the gradual development of his divorce doctrine.

hundred years later, however, the consistorial court was dissolving marriages not only on these grounds but also in such circumstances as long absence, excessive cruelty, incurable diseases (such as leprosy), insanity, impotence, and banishment or imprisonment for life. Some of these grounds, such as long absence, were justified under the rubric of desertion, whereas the others were permitted by appeal to equity and natural law. To a large extent the liberalization of the perspectives of the Württemberg court resulted from the influence of Leyser, who was its president for many years in the first half of the eighteenth century. For all that he extended the grounds for divorce, however, it is notable that Leyser did not move beyond the principle of matrimonial fault and refused to permit divorce where the spouses were simply incompatible.[37]

In other parts of Europe the courts established during the Reformation to oversee divorce were gradually secularized. In Iceland the civil courts won increasing jurisdiction over marriage law. The mixed clerical – lay "half-courts" gradually disappeared during the second half of the seventeenth century until divorce fell exclusively under the control of the secular judges.[38] In Geneva, too, lay influence grew. From the end of the sixteenth century civil officials replaced the mixed courts, giving secular authorities control over marriage, divorce, and questions of morality.[39]

In England the progress of secularization was also discernible, even though ecclesiastical courts maintained control over matrimonial justice until well into the nineteenth century and applied the canon law of the Church of England. Still, the state stepped in with increasing effect. In 1548, we have seen, Parliament dissolved the marriage of the Marquis of Northampton, and in 1604 bigamy was made a criminal offense, not only an offense against the church law. State intervention in marriage law went further under Cromwell, first with the 1650 Adultery Act, then, and more importantly, with the 1653 act that provided for civil marriage. These two measures lapsed by the Restoration, but the enduring effect of secularization on marriage and divorce law in England began with the practice of parliamentary dissolutions of marriage in 1670 and Lord Hardwicke's Marriage Act of 1753.

Divorce by private Act of Parliament was significant because it represented a secular body's taking the initiative on divorce against the refusal of the Anglican church to modify its doctrine of marital indissolubility. It not only meant that a divorce policy, no matter how restrictive, was put into operation that was contrary to that of the established church but that jurisdiction over an issue that had been assumed to belong to the church was seized by the secular legislature acting in its judicial capacity.[40] Similarly the 1753 marriage legis-

---

[37] S. B. Kitchin, *A History of Divorce* (London, 1912), 138–9.
[38] Björnsson, *Lutheran Doctrine of Marriage*, 70.
[39] E. William Monter, "Women in Calvinist Geneva (1500–1800)," *Signs: Journal of Women in Culture and Society* 6 (1980), 207.
[40] Because bishops sit in the House of Lords, it might conceivably be argued that it was a mixed secular–religious tribunal.

lation, which set out the procedures and preconditions for a valid marriage in England, represented an incursion into an area of law that had been regulated until that time by the church. The primary aim of the act was to put a halt to clandestine marriages, celebrated in scandalous numbers by the clergy in certain parts of England.[41]

We should note, however, that in both of these examples the Church of England was given a role. As far as divorce was concerned, any petitioner for divorce by private Act of Parliament had first to obtain a separation *a mensa et thoro* from a church court to demonstrate that his wife was guilty of adultery or, in the rare cases where a woman petitioned for divorce, that her husband was guilty of aggravated adultery.[42] The necessity of a prior separation gave the church a role in the divorce process, even though being a party to the dissolution of a marriage was anathema to the Anglican church. It did, however, remove some of the illegitimacy from Parliament's action in allowing the remarriage of persons divorced by parliamentary act; as noted earlier, bigamy was mitigated if the offender had been separated judicially before contracting the second marriage. For its part, the 1753 Marriage Act specified the form of a valid marriage, but left the solemnization of marriage in the hands of the clergy. The option of a civil marriage was not provided in England until 1837.

In Scotland the parliament intervened earlier in marriage law, determining the form of marriage in a series of acts between 1641 and 1698. This body of legislation, which regulated marriage procedure in Scotland until the nineteenth century, continued the tradition of religious marriage and gave exclusive authority to celebrate marriages to the clergy of the Church of Scotland. In practice, however, irregular marriages, usually solemnized by the clergy of other churches, were accepted as valid provided that it could be shown that the parties had freely consented.[43]

The overall tendency that emerges from these various examples from Scandinavia, Germany, Austria, Scotland, and England is of secularization at several levels. One was the intervention of secular institutions such as Parliament or the monarchy in both legislation and jurisdiction; legislative, executive, and judicial functions often mingled happily in these cases. Second, the role of the church courts in dealing with the dissolution of marriage was curtailed. Third, the content of divorce policies was extended beyond the grounds theologically approved in the sixteenth century to include circumstances and offenses justified by essentially secular notions of contract law, natural law, and equity. (This last point is discussed more fully later in this

---

[41] See Roger Lee Brown, "The Rise and Fall of Fleet Marriages," in R. B. Outhwaite (ed.), *Marriage and Society: Studies in the Social History of Marriage* (London, 1981), 117–36; and Christopher Lasch, "The Suppression of Clandestine Marriage in England: The Marriage Act of 1753," *Salmagundi* 26 (1974), 90–109.

[42] The procedure for obtaining a divorce by private Act of Parliament is discussed in Section 7.2.

[43] T. C. Smout, "Scottish Marriage, Regular and Irregular, 1500–1940," in Outhwaite (ed.), *Marriage and Society*, 205ff.

chapter.) These developments were not peculiar to matrimonial law but were an integral part of a broad process by which the European states arrogated functions that their churches had been accustomed to performing.

In France, for example, the seventeenth and eighteenth centuries witnessed a continuous struggle between state and church over a range of issues over which each claimed primary authority. Marriage law was one of the most sensitive of these issues,[44] and over the long term ecclesiastical jurisdiction in the matter was steadily eroded by the monarchy, which exploited various legal and political means. The royal courts developed an action known as the *appel comme d'abus*, based on the notion that an ecclesiastical court hearing a case was acting beyond its authority, and that its decision in a case infringed on the authority of the secular power. The French monarchy used the *appel comme d'abus* from the late sixteenth century in order to gain control over the gamut of matrimonial law: the marriage of minor children, bigamy, impediments to marriage, opposition to marriages filed by relatives, broken engagements, as well as all property questions affecting spouses, children, and parents.[45] Although the church courts were not deprived of all jurisdiction in marriage matters, they were, in effect, forced to apply royal law or at least laws not repugnant to royal law. If they did not, the crown could use the *appel comme d'abus* to nullify a judgment and transfer the case to a secular court for disposition.[46]

By the late eighteenth century legislative control over marriage in France had effectively passed from the church to the monarchy. Jurisdiction in matrimonial matters was in the hands of the royal courts, which applied royal law, or in the hands of other secular courts applying equally secular law. In Normandy, for example, petitions for separations were dealt with by the *bailliage* court, which disposed of them according to the terms of the customary law of Normandy.[47] Where the church courts did exercise functions in these respects, they did so effectively on the sufferance of the government.[48] The church had not passively abdicated authority over marriage; the authority had been wrested from it by the increasingly powerful state. However we should not conceive of royal and ecclesiastical legislation as being different or at odds in all respects. There were critical areas of difference to be sure, such as the necessity of parental consent

---

[44] The conflict between church and state over control of mariage is ably described in James F. Traer, *Marriage and the Family in Eighteenth-Century France* (Ithaca, N. Y., 1980), esp. 31–47. See also J. Gaudemet, "Législation canonique et attidues séculières à l'égard du lien matrimonial au XVII° siècle," *XVII° siècle* 102–103 (1974), 15–30.

[45] Traer, *Marriage and the Family*, 38.

[46] Ibid.

[47] Roderick Phillips, *Family Breakdown in Late Eighteenth-Century France: Divorces in Rouen, 1792–1803* (Oxford, 1980), 5–8; on the way in which the *parlements* (sovereign courts) intervened in marriages, see Jacques Ghestin, "L'Action des parlements contre les 'mésalliances' aux XVII° et XVIII° siècles," *Revue historique de droit français et étranger*, 4th sér., 34 (1956), 74–224.

[48] In the diocese of Cambrai, petitions for *séparations de corps* were heard by the ecclesiastical courts. Alain Lottin, *La Désunion du couple sous l'Ancien Régime: L'exemple du Nord* (Lille, Paris, 1975), 22–5.

to marriage: The monarchy was anxious to ensure that children (up to the age of twenty-five or thirty years) did not marry against the wishes of their parents, whereas the Catholic church was, in the final analysis, more concerned about the consent of the two spouses involved than about their parents'.[49] Still, on many issues there was agreement between church and state, and the indissolubility of marriage was one of them. The ability of French Protestants to divorce was terminated by Louis XIV's revocation of the Edict of Nantes in 1685, and in 1692 he had ordered the Lutheran magistrates of Alsace, which had been annexed to France, to end their practice of granting divorces.[50] The secularization of marriage institutions in France in the seventeenth and eighteenth centuries, then, focused on the source of legislation and jurisdiction rather than on the content of the law. The French monarch's action in suppressing divorce by Protestants was quite the contrary of the policy of tolerance pursued by the Austrian emperor. Nonetheless, the secularization that did take place in French marriage institutions was extensive and provided the foundation, if one were needed, for the laicization of family law during the French Revolution.

The American colonies in the seventeenth and eighteenth centuries posed different problems with respect to secularization, for matrimonial institutions there – legislation and the judiciary – were never dominated by a church as they had been in Europe until the Reformation. The founders of the New England colonies brought the secular notions of marriage and divorce with them, not from England, where the Anglican church continued to have jurisdiction over marriage, but from the Netherlands, where civil authority over marriage had been entrenched on Calvinist principles, if not Calvinist practice. Plymouth Colony's first marriage, in 1621, was a civil one, as William Bradford emphasized, no doubt to stress the break with English practice:

May 12 [1621] was the first marriage in this place which, according to the laudable custom of the Low Countries, in which they had lived, was thought most requisite to be performed by the magistrate, as being a civil thing, upon which many questions of inheritance depend, with other things most proper to their cognizance and consonant to the Scriptures (Ruth iv) nowhere found in the Gospel to be laid on the ministers a part of their office.[51]

The secularization of marriage obviously went much further in the American colonies than in England, and the colonial authorities and the Anglican church were unhappy about it. When Edward Winslow, a magistrate and the groom in this first marriage, was in England in 1634, he was accused by Archbishop Laud of preaching in church and performing marriages – practices the archbishop found anything but laudable. Winslow admitted that he had

[49] Traer, *Marriage and the Family*, 33–4.
[50] Pierre Bels, *Le Mariage des Protestants français jusqu'en 1685* (Paris, 1968), 399ff.
[51] William Bradford, *Of Plymouth Plantation, 1620–1647* (ed. S. E. Morrison, New York, 1952), 86.

6.3 Secularization of divorce policies

performed several marriages and defended himself by saying that "marriage was a civil thing and he found nowhere in the Word of God that it was tied to the ministry." He added that "it was no new-thing, for he had been married himself in Holland by the magistrates in their Statt house."[52] It was a brave affirmation of the secular view, but a costly one, for Laud had Winslow imprisoned in the Fleet prison for seventeen weeks.[53]

The secular approach to matrimonial issues, including divorce where it was permitted, was initially common to the New England colonies generally. Massachusetts prescribed marriage by magistrates in 1646, New Haven in 1648, while Plymouth enacted its first statute to this effect in 1671, and Connecticut in 1650.[54] In Rhode Island, on the other hand, Quaker and Anglican clergy as well as civil magistrates were licensed to perform marriages,[55] and this optional lay – clerical approach was gradually extended throughout the New England colonies as the rigorous Calvinism of the earliest settlers was eroded. In 1686, during the "usurpation" period, Joseph Dudley, president of New England, issued an order in council empowering clergymen to solemnize marriages, and they began to do so throughout the area.[56] Massachusetts permitted clerical marriage (by "settled ministers" in the towns where they lived) from 1692, and Connecticut from 1694.[57]

In these respects the northern colonies of America shifted from their purely secular matrimonial forms, although in all cases divorces continued to be granted by the civil courts. Ministers could celebrate marriages, but they could not dissolve them, and ecclesiastical courts were never established.

In other parts of colonial America the course of secularization was different. Rather than beginning with civil marriage and extending practice to alternative religious forms, the southern and middle colonies began with religious conceptions for the most part and gradually permitted secular forms as options. Some of the colonies moved in this direction in the seventeenth century; others delayed much longer: Virginia, for instance, did not allow civil marriage until 1794, and then only in exceptional circumstances.[58] But even though matrimony fell within the authority of the church – generally the Anglican church – in the southern and middle colonies, it was more secular there than in contemporary England. For one thing, there were no bishops and no ecclesiastical courts, so that the separations allowed by Anglican canon law had to be heard by secular courts. The jurisdiction thus granted to these courts over some matrimonial issues would be a means by which they would later be authorized to deal with divorces.

[52] Ibid., 274
[53] Howard, *Matrimonial Institutions*, II, 132.
[54] Ibid., II, 133–5.
[55] Ibid., II, 134–5.
[56] Ibid., II, 135.
[57] Ibid., II, 138.
[58] Ibid., II, 228.

6 *The secularization of divorce, 1600–1800*

Maryland, the only American colony settled by a predominantly Roman Catholic population, was exceptional in marriage law in many respects.[59] In the seventeenth century provision was made for marriage by either civil or religious ceremony. Under Catholic regulation this policy of toleration prevailed but after the "Glorious Revolution" in England in 1688, royal government was established in Maryland, and in 1692 the Church of England was elevated to the status of being the established church of the colony. For the next century there were progressive inroads on secular marriage. In 1692 members of the Anglican church were prohibited to marry other than according to the rites of their church, and in 1702 and 1717 the rules were tightened to ensure that all marriages, even those of non-Anglicans who could be married by their respective clergy, conformed to Anglican rules such as those governing consanguinity and affinity. Finally in 1777, just as other states were beginning to secularize marriage further and to legalize divorce, a statute was passed in Maryland that banned civil marriage entirely. This was the one case in America in which civil marriage was ever abrogated once it had been permitted.

The patterns of secular and religious influence in marriage legislation and jurisdiction in America were more complex than those in Europe. The colonies were founded at a time of transition in Europe, the individual states' experiences derived from the character and circumstances of their settlements, and, in the background, the possibility of intervention by the colonial authorities in London might well have skewed the organic development of matrimonial institutions. It is notable that with independence from Great Britain the secular legislatures took rapid action in almost every state to make divorce available either from the regular courts or by legislative act (see Chapter 4). Had it not been for the peculiar circumstances of legislative dependence in these matters, the American colonies might well have taken these steps earlier throughout the eighteenth century, and thus resembled more closely the secularizing tendency within Europe itself.

With regard to Europe, we should note a distorting effect on the progress of secularization due to the influence of the French Revolution. As we have observed, the most dramatic example of secularization was the institutional changes in France from 1789. Not only was the Catholic church brought clearly under the control of the state in all but doctrinal matters (and they too came under attack with the short-lived policy of de-Christianization),[60] but church properties were nationalized and confiscated, and the church's functions in law, the judiciary, education, and social services were taken over by the state. In some respects, such as poor relief and education, the immediate results were far from impressive.[61] In terms of legal reform, however, there was considerable success in promulgating new codes of civil and criminal law, and in reorgan-

[59] The development of marriage law in Maryland is described in ibid., II, 239–47.
[60] See John McManners, *The French Revolution and the Church* (London, 1969), esp. 86–97.
[61] See, for example, Alan Forrest, *The French Revolution and the Poor* (Oxford, 1977).

6.3 Secularization of divorce policies

izing the judicial system. As far as marriage was concerned, the results were dramatic: Marriage was formally made a civil contract, and ceremonies had to be performed by an official registrar in order to be valid. Divorce was legalized, and the whole of matrimonial law was brought under secular control. Jurisdiction was given to the civil courts, either regular courts or the informal tribunals established to render quick, speedy, and cheap justice in litigation involving family members.[62] The content of these legal reforms represented a radical break with the French tradition of marriage law, although the secularization of jurisdiction had its precedent, as we have seen, in the seizure of jurisdiction by the state during the preceding two centuries.

With the expansion of France's borders during the revolutionary wars, and later with the spread of the French imperium during the Napoleonic period (discussed in Chapter 11), the secular approach to marriage was implanted throughout Europe. The Netherlands, Belgium, Switzerland, parts of Germany, and Italy all had their matrimonial laws secularized as part of the package of benefits the French conferred upon defeated populations. This process tended to distort the national development of marriage legislation for some time, and it created a quite artificial uniformity, or near uniformity, among states that had had until then quite different legal and institutional traditions.

Apart from the direct imposition of French legislation and institutions on territories within the empire, France also influenced by example. Despite the fact that Prussia and France were at war and at odds in political systems and ideology, the Prussian legal reforms in the civil code of 1794 were clearly influenced by French innovations as well as developing earlier Prussian legislation.[63] Swedish law, specifically the 1810 divorce legislation, was influenced by the French Revolution through the person of Bernadotte (see Section 11.2), and in Norway in 1797 the influence of French family tribunals was reflected in the establishment of committees to mediate in marital disputes.[64]

The French Revolution might have accelerated secularization in France and elsewhere, but it did not alter the direction of movement. Quite clearly, throughout Western society in the seventeenth and eighteenth centuries, the balance of secular and religious authority over marriage and divorce had shifted, often dramatically, in favor of the secular. This was part of a broader process. Between 1600 and 1800 the European monarchies were generally successful in extending their authority geographically, bringing outlying provinces under more effective central control and reducing particularism somewhat. They also curtailed the authority of the churches, which they saw as

---

[62] A general study is Marcel Garaud, *La Révolution française et la famille* (Paris, 1978). See also Traer, *Marriage and the Family*, esp. 79–165.
[63] Rheinstein, *Marriage Stability*, 25–7; Hans Dolle, *Familienrecht. Darstellung des Deutschen Familienrechts mit Rechtsvergleichenden Hinweisen* (Karlsruhe, 1964), 57–8.
[64] Information from Professor Gudmund Sandvik, Faculty of Law, Oslo University. See Gudmund Sandvik, *Landesbericht Norwegen* (mimeo, n.p. [Oslo], 1978), esp. 15–17.

209

rivals to the authority of the state. Church – state relations became a prominent theme in political writing of the period, partly because the Reformation had produced two models of the way in which a church might stand constitutionally in relation to a state. The first was the Roman Catholic church, a universal church with its head in Rome, and that by these very characteristics represented a challenge to any state that sought to increase its power within its borders. The second model was that of the Protestant churches, founded under the aegis of secular rulers and taking the form of state or national confessions. In practice the monarchies tended to opt for an Erastian solution to the problems of church – state relations, meaning that the church should be subordinated to the state and that what had been ecclesiastical functions, such as legislation, justice, and punishment, should be taken over by the secular powers. Changes in the legislation and jurisdiction of marriage and divorce were an integral part of this much broader process.[65]

6.4 Secularization of ideologies and doctrines

In addition to this long-term trend of secularization in terms of the institutionalization of divorce, there was also a secularization of attitudes and doctrines. In most cases we discern the association of secular jurisdiction and an expansion of the divorce policies to take in circumstances not envisaged by the sixteenth-century Reformers. The points of reference of divorce had been secularized as well; legislators, legal commentators, and theorists looked for inspiration and guidance not to the Bible and ecclesiastical tradition but to other, generally secular, sources of law. In the seventeenth and eighteenth centuries two sources were particularly prominent in legal, social, and political theory: natural law and the theory of contract. The elaboration of divorce doctrines based on natural law and contract principles, associated with the secular institutions of marriage and divorce, opened the way for a new phase in the development of the idea of divorce in Western history.

Although we cannot go into detail here on the origins and development of natural law theory, we may note that from the early seventeenth century political and legal philosophies gradually shook off the theological assumptions they had carried over from the medieval period.[66] There were various reasons for this facet of secularization. With the notable exception of the Thirty Years' War, religious controversies had receded somewhat as the Reformation settlement had stabilized in Europe. At the level of intellectual trends the study of ancient

---

[65] For a general account of the development of European states in this period, see Eugen Weber, *A Modern History of Europe* (New York, 1971).

[66] On the development of natural law see George H. Sabine, *A History of Political Theory* (3rd edn., New York, 1961), 415–34; Heinrich A. Rommen, *The Natural Law: A Study in Legal and Social History and Philosophy* (trans. Thomas R. Hanley, St. Louis, 1947, repr. 1964); Richard Tucker, *Natural Rights Theories: Their Origin and Development* (Cambridge, 1981).

history had increased in popularity, classicism spread throughout northern and western Europe, and there was a renewed interest in the principles of Roman law. Progress in mathematics and the physical sciences led social, political, and legal philosophers to think of society, the polity, and the law as natural occurrences, susceptible to study and analysis by a logical, scientific method.

The natural law philosophers generally sought to discover a legal code that was grounded in criteria more general and enduring than the mere practical needs of mankind. This law, they believed, could be discovered by the application of reason. Hugo Grotius, a founder of modern natural law theory, put it this way:

> The law of nature is a dictate of right reason, which points out that an act, according as it is or is not in conformity with rational nature, has in it a quality of moral baseness or moral necessity; and that, in consequence, such an act is either forbidden or enjoined by the author of nature, God.[67]

But Grotius insisted that the law of nature was not contingent on God's existence; it would be the same if God did not exist. One element that was common to most natural law theories reinforced this secular implication, and that was the principle of contract. Most natural law theorists held that in order to be really binding, an obligation must have been entered into freely by the parties bound to it. This notion was readily brought to bear upon marriage to strengthen the principle that marriage was essentially a civil contract.

The practical effect of natural law theory lay in its putting forward a code of law, apparently based on nature and reason, against which prevailing positive (or statute) law could be compared and measured. The discovery of the natural law of marriage, then, provided a basis for assessing contemporary European marriage legislation and the platform from which could be launched a wide-ranging criticism of laws, including those governing the dissolution of marriage.

We should not expect all natural law and contract theorists to have shared identical views on divorce, any more than theologians drawing on their particular sources reached the same conclusions. There was, moreover, evolution within the schools of natural law that must be taken into account, notably a trend toward an increasingly secular approach to problems. The earlier theorists of modern natural law, such as Grotius, attempted to bring divine and natural law into a working combination, interpreting the one in terms of the other. Grotius had no difficulty in concluding that divorce was permitted in natural law, and focused his efforts on reconciling this with the Biblical texts, which seemed to prohibit divorce except in cases of adultery. He brought the two sources of law into some sort of working harmony by arguing, as others had done before him, that "adultery" was a generic term encompassing a broad range of offenses that effectively ruptured the marriage bond. "Adultery" in

---

[67] Hugo Grotius, *De jure belli et pacis*, quoted in Sabine, *Political Theory*, 424.

this sense included not only sexual infidelity but also threats of death, apparent adultery, and infanticide.[68] Grotius originally conceived of the purpose of marriage as being procreation, but he subsequently included social ends, such as mutual assistance and comfort. This development of his thought provided a bridge for Grotius to move to a more secular perspective. In another context the evolution of Grotius's thinking has been described thus:

He explained what God wants in terms of man's innate sociability, to which all further natural laws were to be related, and in that explanation we can see the first indications of what was to be his eventual untheistic theory, with man's sociability becoming his sole premiss.[69]

Samuel Pufendorf went further than Grotius in articulating the place of divorce in natural law. Pufendorf left to his readers the final decision as to what grounds might justify divorce in practical terms, but he suggested that they could include violation of the marriage contract, sterility, crimes against nature, incompatibility of temperament, and even mutual consent.[70] In his *De Jure Naturae et Gentium*, Pufendorf discussed marriage and related issues in the context of a broad discussion of law: "We must,...before treating of civil government, consider matrimony, which is the source of families and furnishes, as it were, the material for the establishment of governments and states."[71] Pufendorf, like Grotius before him, believed that the prime purpose of marriage was procreation, but instead of seeing in this nothing more than a divine injunction, he explained it as part of the pact made between a man and a woman at the time of their marriage. Proceeding from this, Pufendorf held that a marriage could be dissolved in cases where the conduct of one spouse made the performance of the terms of the contract unattainable. This implied that divorce was permitted in cases of adultery by the wife, because "marriage is contracted so that a person may obtain, not adulterine or suppositious offspring, but his own." Similarly, malicious desertion or obstinate and voluntary refusal of sexual intercourse frustrated the principal end of marriage, and could for this reason justify divorce.[72]

Yet although Pufendorf took into account God's law when determining the ends of marriage, he explicitly focused on natural law and the nature of contracts when determining the criteria against which the legitimacy of divorce was to be measured. Regarding the Lutheran doctrine of divorce prevailing in

[68] Albert Dufour, *Le Mariage dans l'école allemande du droit naturel moderne au XVIIIe siècle* (Paris, 1972), 246.
[69] Tucker, *Natural Rights Theories*, 59–60.
[70] Dufour, *Mariage dans l'école allemande*, 246–7. This broad range of divorce grounds was specified in one of Pufendorf's earlier works. His later thoughts on the subject were less liberal. On Pufendorf's doctrines more generally, see Horst Denzer, *Moralphilosophie und Naturrecht bei Samuel Pufendorf* (Munich, 1972).
[71] Samuel Pufendorf, *The Law of Nature and Nations: Eight Books* (trans. C. H. Oldfather and W. A. Oldfather, 2 vols., Oxford, 1934), II, 859. Marriage is dealt with in 36 sections in this work (Book VI, chapter I, 839–909).
[72] Ibid., II, 859.

his native Saxony, Pufendorf argued that the reason why adultery and desertion were recorded in the Bible as being sufficient causes for divorce

is not due to a special positive law of God, as though those were the two exceptions added to the absolute stability [indissolubility] of marriage, but to the fact that the common nature of pacts is such that when one party does not abide by the agreements, the other is no longer bound by them. So much so that not only is the injured party no longer required to cohabit with such a perfidious consort, but he or she may marry again.[73]

Pufendorf went on to discuss whether divorce might be permissible when the husband was "unreasonably" severe and did not accord his wife due respect or when the wife was rebellious or "of unbearable disposition, who will not brook correction." He concluded that such incompatibilities or difficulties might have to be tolerated since they did not necessarily prevent "the performance of the dues which pertain to the bringing forth of issue," and suggested that while procreation was an essential part of the marriage pact, pleasure in cohabitation might be thought of as only additional. (There is a resonance here of William Whately's distinction between "principal" and "less principal" duties; see Section 3.3). But Pufendorf left the question of divorce on such grounds open, contenting himself with the observation that separation *a mensa et thoro* in such cases was repugnant to natural law because it punished not only the guilty party but also the innocent, the latter "being forced to pay for another's sin and compelled to a life of celibacy, perhaps highly inconvenient or intolerable."[74]

Finally, Pufendorf took a swipe at Milton's *Doctrine and Discipline of Divorce*, which proposed that divorce was permissible for broadly and self-defined incompatibility between wife and husband (see Section 3.5). Pufendorf's was a sharp attack, beginning with an *ad hominem* reference to Milton's being concerned with divorce "perhaps because irritated by his own domestic infelicity," and including a fine, if unfair, parody of Milton's ideal of marriage. Pufendorf's fundamental objection was that Milton had ranked the social or "conversational" aspects of marriage first among the divinely ordained ends of marriage and had placed procreation in a secondary position. This, wrote Pufendorf, denied the importance of sexuality within marriage; emphasis on the merely social aspects of marriage to the exclusion of the end of procreation might just as well result in marriage between individuals of the same sex. Having dismissed the foundation of Milton's divorce doctrine, Pufendorf concluded, predictably, that "of Milton's arguments in general it is to be observed that they prove nothing at all."[75]

The other major seventeenth-century exponent of natural law and contract theory who focused on divorce was John Locke. In his *Second Treatise of*

[73] Ibid.
[74] Ibid., II, 879–81.
[75] Ibid., II, 885.

Government Locke argued for divorce by analogy to the nonhuman natural world. Among animals, he wrote, mating lasts only as long as it is necessary for the offspring to achieve independent survival. Among herbivorous creatures mating lasts only as long as copulation because the young are first suckled by the mother and after weaning feed on grass; the male parent contributes nothing to their sustenance. Among beasts of prey and among birds, mating lasts until the young can fend for themselves. The longer period of dependence of human offspring requires a longer period of dual parentage, especially when the woman is likely to conceive again before her most recent child reaches the age of independence. But, Locke asked, once the general well-being of children had been taken care of, why should marriages not be permitted to end? Marriages could be "made determinable, either by consent, or at a certain time, or upon certain conditions, as well as any other voluntary compacts, there being no necessity in the nature of the thing, nor to the ends of it, that it should always be for life."[76]

The suggestion here was that divorce would be contingent upon either the couple's having no children or upon their having provided for their children's well-being (Locke here referred specifically to education and inheritance), or upon the marriage's having lasted long enough for the children to have become independent of their parents' care. But Locke did not specify the grounds upon which divorce might be justified, although he does mention "different wills" and "controversies" between wife and husband. In such circumstances Locke suggested that the wife had in many cases a right to separate from her husband "where natural Right, or their Contract allows it, whether that Contract be made by themselves in the state of Nature, or by the Customs or Laws of the Countrey they live in." The custody of children would also be determined by the terms of the marriage contract.[77] It is quite clear that Locke's notion of divorce and its implications owed little or nothing to the Christian tradition as we have described it and everything to the principles of contract and nature.

During the eighteenth century natural rights theorists continued to give a great deal of attention to marriage and divorce. As Albert Dufour has demonstrated in his work on the treatment of marriage by the German natural rights schools of the eighteenth century, divorce figured prominently as a lively issue, often within the wider context of polygamy.[78] The rigorously logical method of many of the German scholars led them to articulate divorce doctrines that were libertarian, even though others pursued more restrictive lines of argument and some, a small minority, argued for the indissolubility of marriage by appeal to natural law.

An example of the first school was Johann Heineccius, an influential professor of philosophy who was led to conclude that both divorce and polygamy were legitimate in natural law. He wrote:

[76] John Locke, *Two Treatises on Government* (ed. Peter Laslett, Cambridge, 1963), 339.
[77] Ibid.
[78] Dufour, *Mariage dans l'école allemande*, 299.

6.4 Secularization of ideologies, doctrines

Because marriage is the union of a man and a woman concluded for the procreation and education of offspring, it follows 1. that whatever has been concluded by mutual consent may by its nature be dissolved by a mutual dissent; 2. that the inability of one of the spouses to procreate or to educate, or the presence of certain character defects which make life in common impossible, are sufficient grounds to permit the dissolution of the marriage.[79]

Among other writers who adopted similarly liberal positions on divorce was Henri Cocceji, one of the leading lights of late seventeenth- and early eighteenth-century German juridical thought. Cocceji argued for divorce from the consensual nature of the marriage contract and from the natural right of every person to dispose freely of his own property and rights.[80] These views were taken up and extended by Cocceji's son Samuel. The latter argued for divorce by mutual consent in order to stress that "it belongs to no one to intervene and force spouses to live together against their will."[81] As for specific circumstances that would justify one spouse's seeking a unilateral divorce, Cocceji suggested grounds such as adultery, malicious desertion, deadly hatred, and one spouse's having a venereal disease.[82]

Samuel Cocceji's views on divorce were influential in practical terms because he held positions in the Prussian state that gave him the opportunity to press for reforms of the law of marriage and divorce. In 1731 he was appointed president of the High Court in Berlin, in 1738 he became minister of justice to King Frederick II, and in 1747 he was appointed chancellor of Prussia. As minister of justice and then chancellor, Cocceji undertook judicial and legislative reforms. He began the first codification of Prussian law in 1749, but it remained unfinished when he died in 1755. Despite this, there is no doubt that the liberalization of Prussian divorce policy in 1751 (when the courts were authorized to dissolve marriages where there was deadly hatred between the spouses) reflected Cocceji's influence.[83]

Cocceji and other natural law critics of prevailing divorce legislation grounded their arguments explicitly in terms of the dissolubility of a freely entered contract, but some worked variations on the theme. Most theorists of the genre held that marriage was a contract undertaken in perpetuity, but that it could be formally dissolved by one of the spouses if the other did not or could not fulfill the conditions implied. This approach to the marriage contract meant that at the time the marriage was undertaken, it was understood by both spouses that it would last until dissolved by the death of the first of them.[84] To this

---

[79] Quoted in ibid., 300. Pufendorf believed that polygamy was contrary to natural law; see his *De Officio Hominis et Civis Juxta Legem Naturalem* (trans. Frank Gardner Moore, New York, 1964), 95.

[80] Dufour, *Mariage dans l'école allemande*, 300–1.

[81] Ibid., 301.

[82] Ibid., 300–1.

[83] Ibid., 206–207n.539; Weill, *Frederick the Great*, passim.

[84] Some Catholic theologians, as we have noted, believed that the marriage union continued even beyond death and discouraged remarriage by widows and widowers as quasi-bigamous. See Section 1.5.

215

extent, contract theory did not differ in its forms from Christian doctrines of marriage and divorce, although the natural law theorists generally recognized a wider range of grounds than the dissolubilists of the Christian tradition.

Other contract theorists, however, insisted that marriage should be even more like contracts in economic life, and undertaken not in perpetuity but for pre-determined periods. At the end of the contract period it would be dissolved, giving the spouses the opportunity to renew it for another period or of con-tracting marriage with different partners.[85] German commentators such as the theologian Immanuel Weber and the philosopher Gottlieb Treuer advocated this policy. This notion of the dissolution of marriage after the expiration of a fixed-term contract is far removed from the ordinary concept of divorce. The dissolution of the marriage by termination of the contract would have no bearing on the relationship between husband and wife. In such a matrimonial system we should be less interested, as students of divorce, in the dissolution of each marriage and more interested to know whether the former spouses de-cided to renew their contract or whether, dissatisfied with each other, they contracted marriages with new partners or remained unmarried.

Theories and policies such as these verged toward the extreme fringes of seventeenth- and eighteenth-century commentaries on marriage. At this time there was a burst of publications advocating not just civil marriage and liberal divorce but also polygamy. The idea of fixed-term marriages can be thought of as successive polygamy, but other commentators promoted polygamy in the ordinary sense of a man's having two wives simultaneously. Advocates of polygamy were not necessarily secular in their outlook (though most were), for they were able to draw support for their ideas from the practices of the kings and the patriarchs described in the Bible. John Milton was one of the earliest exponents of polygamy in this period, writing that "polygamy is allowed by the law of God."[86]

It is indicative of the complexity of issues that just as polygamy could be justified by appeal to secular and religious arguments alike, so divorce could be supported or rejected by both. Although the general tendency was for the natural law theorists to argue for the legitimacy of divorce on quite liberal grounds, there were some who used natural law and contract principles to support the view that marriage was indissoluble. Perhaps the least equivocal proponent of this view was Johann von Waldkirch, a Swiss professor of public law. Von Waldkirch stressed that marriage was undertaken in perpetuity and was indissoluble in the lifetimes of the spouses and that these qualities were required by the obligation to give children a good education and also by the implications of property ownership. He based his doctrine of indissolubility partly on the view that if natural law permitted divorce it would have to be

---

[85] See Dufour, *Mariage dans l'école allemande*, 302–3.
[86] John Cairncross, *After Polygamy Was Made a Sin* (London, 1974), 129. On Milton's views, see ibid., 126ff.

conceded equally to both spouses, but that the freedom of divorce would lead to social disorder.[87]

Others shared von Waldkirch's views but argued from different premises. His contemporary, Eberhard Otto, also a professor of law, held that if we start with the principle that every human has the right in natural law to dispose of his goods and rights, then nothing would conform to natural law more closely than the right to put an end to a freely undertaken contract by mutual consent. But although this principle from natural law and contract worked perfectly well in respect of commerce and politics, it did not apply to such a sensitive relationship as marriage.[88] Others in the German natural rights school also adopted the indissolubilist position on divorce or argued that divorce should be allowed only in the most limited circumstances, such as adultery.

But such commentators ran against the trend of natural law writing, which was to find divorce permissible in relatively liberal terms. Christian Thomasius, one of the most prominent of the German theorists, found divorce allowed on grounds of adultery, desertion, refusal of sexual intercourse, sterility, ill-treatment, and in cases where the spouses were incompatible.[89] Thomasius held more tightly than most to strict contract principle in some circumstances, however. Adultery, for example, would be a ground for divorce only if the husband had agreed with his wife that she would not present him with adulterine children or that she would not have extramarital relationships. Similarly, incompatibility and ill-treatment would justify divorce only if the spouses had stipulated at the time of the marriage that they intended to maintain a friendly and considerate relationship.[90] By insisting that these terms, considered by most writers to be implied within the marriage contract, should be explicit, Thomasius took the notion of contract further and applied it more rigorously to marriage than any of his contemporaries.

The other dominant figure in German natural law theory, Christian Wolff, also applied contract principles carefully, but in a different way from Thomasius.[91] For Wolff, as for many theorists of his time, the primary purpose of marriage was the education of children, and divorce had to be considered within this context. It meant that childless couples had more freedom of divorce, and Wolff would permit spouses in these cases to divorce by mutual consent, a straightforward application of the principle of consensual contract. Couples without children might also divorce for reason of certain specific offenses that could also justify divorce when there were children in a marriage. The grounds included adultery, willful desertion, the obstinate refusal of sexual intercourse, and irreconcilable hostility between the spouses. As far as Wolff was concerned, the first three of these were violations of the essential conditions of the marriage

---

[87] Dufour, *Mariage dans l'école allemande*, 303.
[88] Ibid.
[89] Ibid., 338ff.
[90] *"Familiarem et amicam conversationem"*; ibid., 341.
[91] Ibid., 399ff.

contract. Irreconcilable hostility was recognized as a ground for divorce because under such circumstances the couple could not but compromise the good education of their children; the latter's education and unbringing would be better assured if the parents were divorced than if they were not. Wolff even suggested that it was their effects on children, by perturbing family life, that justified making the other offenses grounds for divorce, as much as their being violations of marriage in themselves. The other major principle of Wolff's divorce doctrine was the equality of spouses before the law. Either could use the grounds for divorce that he recognized; neither could terminate a marriage unilaterally without just cause.

Although theories of natural law were particularly influential in Germany, the Netherlands, and Switzerland, they also attracted followings elsewhere.[92] Jean Barbeyrac's translation of Pufendorf contributed to awareness of the latter's work in France in the eighteenth centuy. Barbeyrac, himself a jurist and the son of an émigré Calvinist pastor, wrote in favor of divorce in terms similar to those of Christian Wolff, John Locke, and others who stressed the rearing and education of children as the principal purpose of marriage. Once these functions had been completed, Barbeyrac wrote, there was no reason why a marriage should not be terminated. Indeed, because marriage was a contract, the parties should be able to specify before marrying whether they intended their union to last for life or whether it should end after a determinate period.[93]

The emphasis on children in some of the important seventeenth- and eighteenth-century works on divorce is worth noting for it was a new development. Earlier works on divorce, with their theological bases, had included children in the purposes of marriage in a relatively impersonal, even abstract, manner. Marriage had been described as for the purpose of procreation, and the stress was on the production of children for the glory of God, in the light of the scriptural injunction that the faithful should go forth and multiply. Among the natural law treatments of divorce, however, the social obligations incurred by parenthood were given at least as much, and often more, emphasis than the biological fact of procreation. It was not enough to have children; they needed to be cared for and educated as well. This is a further example of the development of consciousness of childhood in this period, a phenomenon noted by many historians.[94]

We might also note the secularization of the religious injunction to procreate. In the seventeenth and eighteenth centuries procreation became regarded not only as a purpose of marriage but as a reason for legalizing or liberalizing

[92] Natural law principles were introduced to Swedish legal theory by the jurist David Nehrman, especially in his *Inledning til then Swenska Jurisprudentiam Civilem af Naturens Lagh och Sweriges Rikes aldre och nnare stadgar uthdragen och upsatt* (Lund, 1729).
[93] Cited in Traer, *Marriage and the Family*, 50n.4.
[94] See, for example, J. H. Plumb, "The New World of Children in Eighteenth-Century England;" *Past and Present* 67 (1975), 64–95.

divorce. This populationist tendency has already been noted in the context of the debate on divorce during the French Enlightenment, but it is to be found elsewhere. In 1783 Frederick William II issued a cabinet order to judges specifying that "in matters of divorce one ought not to be so easy going as to further abase; but one should not be too difficult either, because that would impede population."[95] Similarly, it is suggested that a pronatalist aim lay behind Joseph II's permission for Protestants in the Austrian Netherlands to divorce.[96] These concerns were expressed, ironically, as the population of Europe was beginning to increase dramatically and rapidly after centuries of virtual stagnation. In eighteenth-century America, too, divorce and population growth were linked. In 1769 the lieutenant-governor of New York noted that divorce could be obtained in neighboring colonies "more easily. . . than perhaps in any other Christian country," and went on to ask whether divorce might not be advantageous for the new land: "It is certain that the natural increase of people in New England has been very great, perhaps more than in any of the other English colonies."[97]

During the eighteenth century the exhortation to multiply had been thoroughly secularized. It now emanated not from the churches, expressing God's will, but from secular rulers who believed that a growing and robust population would make for strong states. By making remarriage possible, divorce would thus help to strengthen the state, not to weaken it, as detractors of divorce had argued. Where divorce could not be legalized for doctrinal reasons, more drastic measures could be taken. One unusual example resulted from the peculiar demographic circumstances that followed the devastating Thirty Years' War in Germany from 1618 to 1648. The male population had been so reduced by the conflict that in 1650 the Regional Council of Catholic Franconia decided not only to limit the admission of young men to monasteries and to encourage priests to marry but also to authorize laymen to take two wives each during the following ten years.[98] This law, which had the approval of the region's Catholic archbishops and Protestant leaders, was not intended as a substitute for divorce. Nor is it known how it worked in practice. The pro-bigamy law is, however, significant as an early example of the use of marriage law for populationist objectives. Although this 1650 example was undertaken in particularly urgent circumstances, from the late eighteenth century population and family policies took on a more coherent form.

Yet we must not think of the secular approach to marriage and divorce as

[95] Quoted in Rheinstein, *Marriage Stability*, 25n.56.
[96] Walter W. Davis, *Joseph II: An Imperial Reformer for the Austrian Netherlands* (The Hague, 1974), 102–3.
[97] Quoted in Alden Chester (ed.), *Legal and Judicial History of New York* (New York, 1911), I, 318–19. See also Kimberly Smith, "Divorce in Nova Scotia, 1750–1890," in J. Phillips and P. Girard (eds.), *Essays in the History of Canadian Law, Volume 3: The Nova Scotian Experience* (Toronto, in press).
[98] Cairncross, *After Polygamy was Made a Sin*, 74.

6 The secularization of divorce, 1600–1800

having taken over completely from the religious. Many predominantly secular theorists referred to theological criteria as well – no doubt because it was politic to do so in many cases. And whereas the tendency of eighteenth-century French writers in favor of divorce focused on reason, social utility, nature, and the rights of man, others invoked the Bible and church tradition in their arguments for or against divorce. In Britain the same duality persisted through the eighteenth century. David Hume was one who dealt with divorce in purely secular terms. There were, as far as he was concerned, three "unanswerable objections" to freely available divorce. The first was the effects of divorce upon children; the second was that marriages would be happier if divorce were not available, because spouses would resign themselves to their lots; and the third was that if society were to join people closely, as in marriage, then the union must be "entire and total," because the least possibility of separate interests would inevitably entail "endless quarrels and suspicions."[99] Contemporaries of Hume, however, drew upon religious arguments. Daniel Defoe insisted that although marriage was not a sacrament, it was still a sacred thing, and he argued against the notion that it was essentially a civil contract.[100] Defoe wrote at length about the trials and troubles of marriage in terms reminiscent of William Whately in the preceding century, and his image of discord in marriage was graphic: A couple bound in an unhappy marriage, he wrote, was "like the way of punishing Malefactors in Persia, viz. tying the living Body to a dead corpse, till the rotting Carcass poisoned the living, and then they rotted together."[101] But Defoe did not refer to divorce and throughout his work wrote of marriage as if it were an indissoluble union.

Caleb Fleming also held to religious principles and attacked those who argued from secular grounds. Fleming's position was that divorce should be permitted only for reason of adultery, and he criticized those who supported more liberal policies. Milton's views, he wrote, meant that "unless the wife be found affable and courteous, every way suitable to their [husbands'] genius and disposition, she is to be discarded."[102] As for Locke, Fleming wrote that "the best apology I am able to make for that excellent man, is, *he was a batchelor, and had no adequate ideas of the subject he wrote upon*; otherwise, he would have known, that the conjugal society will bear no manner of comparison with the brutal couplings!"[103] More to the point, Fleming rejected the notion that marriage was essentially a contract. As far as divorce was concerned, the analogy from bilateral contracts should have no bearing because marriage

---

[99] David Hume, *Essays* (London 1741), Essay xviii, "Of Polygamy and Divorce."
[100] Daniel Defoe, *A Treatise Concerning the Use and Abuse of the Marriage Bed* (London, 1727), 22.
[101] Ibid., 216.
[102] Caleb Fleming, *The Oeconomy of the Sexes: Or the Doctrine of Divorce, the Plurality of Wives, and the Vow of Celibacy Freely Examined* (London, 1751), 1–2.
[103] Ibid., 25.

220

6.4 Secularization of ideologies, doctrines

"relates to persons, and their inseparable union, which are not things in commerce."[104]

Nonetheless, despite the continued coexistence of both the religious and the secular traditions of argument in the debate on divorce, and despite the persistence of ecclesiastical jurisdiction in marriage in parts of Western society, the clear trend between 1600 and 1800 was in favor of secularization. This process would culminate in the nineteenth century, when all but a few jurisdictions made provision for civil marriage and divorce, and when secular perspectives on marriage were unequivocally more important than religion in the law and practice of marriage.

As for the practice of marriage before the nineteenth century, it is rather more difficult to assess the progress of secularization within Western populations or to assess the extent to which notions of marriage had lost their religious content. Historians debate the meaning and significance of social secularization and the difficulty of distinguishing it from other variables. If we take what must be the most crude indicator of secularization – attendance at church on particularly important occasions, such as Easter – we can appreciate that it is influenced not only by the level of religious conviction in a community but can also be affected by other, apparently extraneous factors. A decline in church attendance might reflect the personality of the priest or minister and his relations with his parishioners, disputes that set the church against the community,[105] a period of prosperity that reduced the importance of the church's social services, or a change in the social composition of the community. To the extent that such factors can affect church attendance they might be thought of as contaminating influences that distort the true image of devoutness. On the other hand, devoutness, as an intellectual and spiritual orientation, does not exist independent of its social and material context. If a community ignored its church's rules when there was no advantage in observing them, it is likely that it observed them out of self-interest, not a pure or abstract devoutness. It would be unreasonable, then, to argue that secularization should be monodimensional, a change only in *mentalité*, not related to changes in the social and economic spheres.

If we think of devoutness as encompassing not only spiritual piety but also an outward, behavioral conformity to the precepts of the church, then there is good evidence of secularization in many Western populations, particularly in the

---

[104] Ibid., 27. This kind of argument, that marriage was a contract unlike any other, was rejected by most contract theorists. Few, however, were as explicit as the author of a pamphlet advocating divorce, who insisted that marriage was just like any agreement, such as one between two men over the sale and purchase of a horse; it could be broken by their common accord. *The Counsellor's Plea for the Divorce of Sir G. D. and Mrs. F.* (London, 1715), 8.
[105] In many parts of eighteenth-century England the Church of England was involved in litigation against the people over issues such as enclosures of common lands and tithes. See Eric J. Evans, "Some Reasons for the Growth of English Rural Anti-Clericalism, c. 1750–c.1850," *Past and Present* 66 (1975), 84–109.

eighteenth century. At the very basic level of participation in church activities, there are shifts to be noted. Church attendance declined in many parts of Europe, recruitment to the regular and secular clergy fell off, and pilgrimages and other religious activities attracted fewer participants.[106] Religion seemed to play less of a role in the most sensitive and intimate aspects of personal life: sexuality, birth, and death. The eighteenth century saw widespread neglect of the churches' prohibitions on premarital sexual activity, and rates of illegitimacy and premarital conception soared almost everywhere.[107] There is considerable debate as to whether these changes represented a revolution in sexual attitudes or the breakdown of traditional courting and marriage practices, with illegitimacy resulting from the failure of couples to marry after having pursued a courtship involving sexual relations.[108] But whether it was sexual or marital or both, the change represented behavior quite at odds with the teaching of all churches on marriage and sexuality. To this extent they reflect indifference to religious morality, even if they also reflect a heightened sexual drive or occupational mobility.

It is difficult to discover, for the eighteenth century, direct evidence of secularization in popular attitudes toward marriage. In states where the church or churches had a monopoly over the celebration of marriage, as they did in England until 1837, France until 1792, and in Italy until 1806, all valid marriages had to be celebrated according to religious rites, no matter what the religious convictions or spiritual orientations of the women and men concerned. Only when a choice of civil or religious marriage was offered are we able to gauge popular preferences. The attraction of civil marriage might well have been very small in eighteenth-century England, for even by 1844 only 3% of all marriages were civil, and the proportion had increased to only 18% by 1904.[109] In Scotland "irregular marriages," which can be treated as equivalent to civil marriages, were even less popular, running at less than 1% of all marriages in the 1860s and 1870s, and reaching 6% by 1904.[110] In these respects there was

---

[106] On the decline of religion, see Burke, "Religion and Secularization"; Michel Vovelle, "Le tournant des mentalités en France, 1750–1789: la 'sensibilité' pré-révolutionnaire," *Social History* 5 (1977), 605–29.

[107] See the statistics brought together in Michael W. Flinn, *The European Demographic System, 1500–1820* (Brighton, 1981), 118–23, Tables 5 and 6 (illegitimacy and premarital conception).

[108] Edward Shorter has argued for the existence of a sexual revolution in a number of works, including *The Making of the Modern Family* (New York, 1975). Prominent among Shorter's critics were Louise A. Tilly, Joan W. Scott, and Miriam Cohen, "Women's Work and European Fertility Patterns," *Journal of Interdisciplinary History* 6 (1976), 447–76.

[109] Olive Anderson, "The Incidence of Civil Marriage in Victorian England," *Past and Present* 69 (1975), 55, Table I.

[110] T. C. Smout, "Scottish Marriage, Regular and Irregular, 1500–1940," in R. B. Outhwaite (ed.), *Marriage and Society: Studies in the Social History of Marriage* (London, 1981), 223, Table II. In the eighteenth century as much as one-third of marriages were irregular according to one contemporary source. At this time irregular marriages were celebrated by clergy of churches other than the Church of Scotland, and represent religious nonconformity rather than secularization. Ibid., 218.

evidence of slow secularization in the late nineteenth century, and we should expect to find even less a century earlier.

One case study is provided by the revolutionary and Napoleonic periods in France. In 1792, as we have seen, a civil ceremony became the obligatory and only form of marriage recognized by law in France. Despite this and the persecution of the church that various French governments practiced, priests in some areas of the country continued to carry out their pastoral duties clandestinely, baptizing children, marrying the faithful, and holding burial services. The surviving registers kept by these clandestine priests enable us to assess the attitudes within the communities to which they ministered, for their parishioners effectively had a choice of religious and civil forms that was denied to the mass of the French population. One clandestine parish register from Montaut (Ariège) showed that between 1793 and 1815, 69% of the marriages in the community were performed in both secular and religious forms, 13% were solemnized only by the civil officials, and 18% of marriages were exclusively religious.[111] For the most part, when couples went through the two ceremonies, they went to the priest first and to the civil registrar of marriages later (usually within a day or two, but in some instances as long as two years later). Quite clearly the faithful Catholic members of French communities were caught between marrying according to the civil law, which was the only kind of marriage that would give the union legal force (and was therefore important where property and inheritance issues were concerned), and marrying according to the law of the church, and thus in the eyes of God. The clandestine priests were rigorous in their rejection of civil marriage, however. Some of the registers show that couples who had married civilly were required to repent before they were married by a priest. Registrations of clandestine marriages in Bayeux in 1796 referred to the spouses "having asked God and the Church for pardon for having committed the crime of marrying in defiance of all the rules of the Church and State," whereas in others there was a briefer notation that the couple "having had the misfortune to have been married solely by the municipality...sincerely repent their error."[112] The tendency in these cases to maintain the religious forms of marriage either exclusively or in order of precedence, need not tell us much more than that a clandestine priest was more likely to survive and carry out his pastoral activities in a devout area. They are, however, a valuable corrective to the impression that the secularization of marriage by the state was passively accepted everywhere.

Against these signs of continuing obedience to the church's marriage laws there was evidence of their neglect. An example is the monthly distribution of marriages throughout the year. The Catholic church prohibited the celebration

---

[111] Suzanne Grezaud, "Un cas de registres paroissiaux tenus par un prêtre réfractaire," *Annales historiques de la Révolution française* 200 (1970), 348.

[112] Paul Longuet, "Une source pour l'étude de l'activité sacerdotale des prêtres réfractaires dans le Calvados: les actes des baptêmes et des mariages clandestins," *Annales historiques de la Révolution française* 200 (1970), 344.

of marriage during times of penance, notably during Advent and Lent, and this ban characteristically produced a low number of marriages in the months of December and March.[113] The contiguous months (November, January, and February) generally had above-average numbers of marriages to compensate for the periods when marriage was not permitted. This uneven distribution of marriages throughout the year was maintained as long as the church was responsible for marriage, but with the advent of secular marriage, it is clear that church rules were widely ignored and people married when they wanted to, whether or not it was a time of penance. As Table 6.1 shows, the monthly distribution of marriages rapidly lost its religious character. Only a shadow of the religious calendar of marriage remained in the third period. Marriages were not distributed perfectly even throughout the year (they never are), but the range was reduced dramatically from 11–213 in the first period and 19–217 in the second to an impressive 69–140 after the secularization of marriage procedures.

It would be a mistake to push this kind of evidence, compelling though it might seem, too far. Although we can assemble a great deal of evidence of secularization, there was also evidence of devoutness and religious revival, especially in the Napoleonic period. In marriage, tradition seems to have been of overriding importance. John Gillis has pointed to the continuity of cultural forms and procedures among the British working class, and there is no doubt that they persisted throughout Europe as well.[114] In Scotland the custom of hand-fasting (betrothal) continued to be a popular practice and was conjoined to the marriage rites of the Church of Scotland.[115]

As far as divorce is concerned there is little evidence of popular attitudes in the seventeenth and eighteenth centuries. We may hypothesize that the more secular populations became, the more distanced from religious and ecclesiastical doctrines, which placed restrictions on divorce, the more likely they were to rally to it. French urban populations rapidly accommodated to divorce after 1792, even though it had been completely forbidden by the religion to which most of them professed to adhere. Not only did thousands of couples divorce, but many more thousands of their friends and relatives took part in the institutions and procedures of divorce, as arbiters and witnesses on the family courts and assemblies, as witnesses to the facts, and as witnesses when divorces were registered.[116] In these ways they demonstrated a general acceptance of divorce. In other jurisdictions, however, laws remained restrictive, divorces were rare, and there is no evidence either way as to popular attitudes toward it.

If the later nineteenth century witnessed what might be called a divorce revolution – the widespread legalization of divorce and liberalization of existing

---

[113] See François Lebrun, *La vie conjugale sous l'Ancien Régime* (Paris, 1975), 37–38.
[114] John Gillis, *For Better, For Worse: British Marriages, 1600 to the Present* (New York, 1985), passim.
[115] Smout, "Scottish Marriage," 210–12.
[116] Phillips, *Family Breakdown*, passim.

6.4 Secularization of ideologies, doctrines

Table 6.1. *Monthly distribution of marriages, Caen 1740–9, 1780–9, and 1796–1805 (monthly average = 100)*

	1740–9	1780–9	1796–1805
January	142	140	112
February	213	217	140
March	11	19	69
April	69	80	80
May	102	83	109
June	85	94	101
July	117	96	99
August	97	75	103
September	88	103	93
October	100	115	116
November	156	158	100
December	20	20	78

Source: Jean-Claude Perrot, *Genèse d'une ville moderne. Caen au XVIIIe siècle* (2 vols., Paris, 1975), II, 824. These figures are expressed graphically in ibid., 818. The same effect is to be found in other studies of French nuptiality from the 1790s. See, for example, Marcel Lachiver, *La population de Meulan du XVIIe au XIXe siècle (vers 1600– vers 1870). Etude de démographie historique* (Paris, 1969), 86.

divorce laws, together with a dramatic increase in the number of divorces – then the seventeenth and eighteenth centuries set the foundations for it. State regulation of marriage had its institutional foundations in this period, which culminated in the radical reforms undertaken by the French Revolution. Ideologies and doctrines of divorce shook off the restrictions imposed by theological reasoning, and although some doctrines simply replaced these with secular shackles, the dominant trend was toward far more permissive ideas about divorce. Divorces also increased in the period although, with the exception of France, they remained rare in absolute terms. As we shall see in the following chapter, there was a steady increase in divorces in Massachusetts and Connecticut, the two American colonies (later, states) that had the highest rates of divorce. Divorces by private Act of Parliament increased from the middle of the eighteenth century, as did divorces in Geneva, and separations *a mensa et thoro* in England and France.

We cannot, however, attribute these increases solely or even primarily to the progress of secularization. The later eighteenth century was a time of transition in many respects. It was a period of early industrialization, urbanization, of revolutionary sentiment, and international warfare. These and other factors, which are discussed in the final chapters of this book, must have contributed to increased marital instability, but the mechanisms are complex. The secularization of popular attitudes must have played an important role in weakening inhibitions against using divorce facilities, but that role was to come into play in the later nineteenth and twentieth centuries. The achievement of the secularization process in this earlier period lay in establishing the institutional framework for the subsequent revolution in divorce law and behavior.

7

The use of the early divorce laws: England, America, and France

7.1 Introduction

In the preceding chapters there have been references to divorce legislation from the sixteenth to the eighteenth centuries and to the use made of divorce in various countries at various times. For the most part these have been used to illustrate aspects of divorce doctrines, and in most cases the numbers of divorces have been too small, in any case, to allow a systematic study of the divorced populations. In the present chapter three approximately contemporaneous sets of legislation are studied in rather more depth in order to focus on the use of the divorce laws and to illustrate the varieties and similarities of practices in respect of divorce in different jurisdictions.

The first case study deals with dissolutions of marriage in England by private Act of Parliament between 1670 and 1857, but with emphasis on the period from 1770 to 1850. Such divorces were rare, but they are of interest because they throw light on aspects of marriage within some social élites and because they were the only legal divorces in England until the mid-nineteenth century. The second case study deals with divorce in the American colonies, especially the New England colonies, in the seventeenth and eighteenth centuries. Most of the information here is drawn from secondary sources. Finally there is consideration of divorces in France during the revolution and empire. Divorce was legalized in France in 1792 and abolished in 1816, and this period provided a unique opportunity in European history for the study of a phenomenon that approached mass divorce. Much of the material here is drawn from local studies of divorce, especially from my own work on divorce and marriage breakdown in the Norman city of Rouen.

7.2 England: Divorces by Act of Parliament, 1670–1857

The dissolution of individual marriages in England by private Act of Parliament was the means by which the Anglican church's opposition to divorce was circumvented (see Section 3.6). Despite the fact that these parliamentary divorces involved a cumbersome, long, and expensive procedure, they were the

227

only means of dissolving marriages legally in England until 1858, when England's first divorce law came into force.[1] As the practice of parliamentary divorce developed, a petitioner for divorce was generally required to fulfill two preconditions in law. The first was a successful civil action against the accomplice in adultery, adultery being the sole ground for a divorce. Such actions were generally known as actions for "criminal conversation," although terms such as "adulterous conversation," "adulterous connexion," and "unlawful familiarity" were also used. These actions could only be brought by a husband against his wife's lover because the wife was considered, in legal terms, to be virtually the property of her husband. These suits were, then, actions for trespass, the corespondent's violation of the husband's exclusive rights in his wife.[2] A wife had no property rights in her husband, by contrast, and therefore she had no grounds for suing any woman with whom he had sexual intercourse.

A successful action for criminal conversation would reward the plaintiff with monetary damages and the costs of the action. Under some circumstances, however, a prosecution was not possible, notably when the name of the wife's accomplice was not known to the husband, when he was abroad and beyond English jurisdiction, or when he was dead. In 1792, for instance, one James McGauley found himself unable to lodge a suit against the "one or more men to him wholly unknown" with whom his wife had been adulterous. Similarly, in 1839 the Reverend Dionysius Lardner was cheated of damages by the death of his wife's lover, one Samuel Murphy. It was one of life's injustices that when, in 1845, Dionysius Lardner was himself the defendant in a suit for criminal conversation, damages of £8,000 were awarded against him.[3] Damages for criminal conversation in divorces obtained between 1770 and 1850 ranged from the nominal sum of one farthing to £20,000 plus court and other legal expenses. The statutes give precise damages in 143 cases, in about a half of which (53%) the award was for £1,000 or more. The sums most commonly awarded by the courts were £500 (nineteen cases), £2,000 (eighteen cases), and £1,000 (seventeen cases). At the upper end of the scale there were seven awards of £10,000 and £20,000, whereas at the lower end, five judgments gave nominal damages of less than £5.

[1] At the time this section was prepared, there were no general studies of parliamentary divorces. Since then, two studies have appeared that add detail to the findings here but do not give reason to change their basic thrust. One important conclusion reached by Stuart Anderson is that divorce acts were less expensive than often reported; instead of costing almost a thousand pounds typically, many cost only £200 or £300. This placed divorce within the financial grasp of a larger group than earlier supposed, though it was still inaccessible to ordinary people. See Stuart Anderson, "Legislative Divorce – Law for the Aristocracy?" in G. R. Rubin and David Sugarman (eds.), *Law, Economy and Society: Essays in the History of English Law, 1750–1914* (London, 1984), 412–44; Sybil Wolfram, "Divorce in England 1700–1857," *Oxford Journal of Legal Studies* 5 (1985), 155–86. Further references are O. M. McGregor, *Divorce in England* (London, 1957); Randolph Trumbach, *The Rise of the Egalitarian Family* (New York, 1978), 155–60.
[2] See Leonore Davidoff, "Mastered for Life: Servant and Wife in Victorian and Edwardian England," *Journal of Social History* 7 (1974), 406–28.
[3] 2 & 3 Vict. cap. 53; 8 & 9 Vict. cap. 36. The private Acts of Parliament dissolving marriages are to be found in the *Statutes at Large of Great Britain*.

The amount of damages awarded depended on various considerations. Not least of these was an assessment by the court of the amount of honor the husband had lost as a result of his wife's adultery, and this depended on how much he was judged to have had initially. The happiness of the couple before the adultery was also taken into account; the happier they had been, the greater the loss brought about by the wife's infidelity, and the greater the damages her accomplice had to pay.[4] Nominal damages were often awarded when, although the fact of adultery had been proved, it was clear that the husband had contributed to it by neglecting his wife or by placing her in compromising situations.

The amount of damages sought by the plaintiff also had an influence. In some cases the damages were clearly beyond the means of the defendant to afford, like the £10,000 given against a military bandsman. On the other hand, some awards seem to have been assessed with the social status and income of the defendant in mind, such as the £50 against a steward of estates and the same sum against a private in the army.[5] In yet other cases the damages were purely nominal, the purpose of the action being simply to obtain a judgment of guilt so that a subsequent divorce petition might be lodged. There was, of course, no guarantee that the damages could or would be paid, no matter what the size of the award. Some men avoided payment by leaving England; others simply could not afford to pay; at least one was imprisoned for nonpayment of damages in a criminal conversation action. In a few cases, indeed, the likelihood of default in payment was such that a husband could be excused from bringing an action for monetary damages in the first place. One Thomas Darby did not sue the two men with whom his wife had been adulterous – they were a miller and soap-boiler, respectively – because they were "persons in exceedingly indigent circumstances, and, in respect of their Poverty, unable to have paid [him]...any Damages which might have been recovered against them, and in Regard [he]...must have been at considerable Expense in prosecuting any Suit or Suits against them."[6]

An action for criminal conversation was, however, usually a precondition of a divorce petition by private Act of Parliament. The second precondition, one which was obligatory in all cases, was a decree of separation *a mensa et thoro* granted by an ecclesiastical court for reason of adultery. Such a decree did not of itself dissolve the marriage, of course, but the action placed part of the onus of convicting the guilty spouse on the judges of the church courts. We might note that dissolution of marriage by Act of Parliament overrode the prohibition

---

[4] Susan Staves, "Money for Honor: Damages for Criminal Conversation," *Studies in Eighteenth-Century Culture* (1982), 279–97.

[5] An eighteenth-century commentary on the law noted that "a jury in a case of such atrocious guilt as that of violating the marriage bed, generally allots large damages. But the condition of the person sued is always considered, and the quantum of damages ascertained by his fortune and rank." *The Laws Respecting Women, As they regard their Natural Rights, or their Connections and Conduct* (London, 1777), 317.

[6] 18 Geo. III cap. 103.

on remarriage after a separation *a mensa et thoro* that had been made by the canon laws of 1604.

Divorce by Act of Parliament was, then, a three-stage process: an action for criminal conversation against the wife's accomplice in adultery, a separation from the ecclesiastical court for reason of the adultery, and finally dissolution of the marriage with the right to remarry. This procedure, together with the single matrimonial offense justifying divorce, made divorces extremely difficult to obtain. It was even more difficult for women, who had to prove their husbands guilty not simply of adultery but of aggravated adultery – that is, adultery aggravated by some circumstance such as bigamy, incest, or sodomy. Moreover, the procedure made divorce very expensive, although an award and payment of generous damages for criminal conversation could well offset the expense of the whole proceedings, which ran to hundreds of pounds in the nineteenth century.

Under these procedures, divorce was a privilege of the wealthy, and especially of wealthy men. The effect of costs as a deterrent to divorce was cited in the 1840 divorce bill of Jonathon Warr, a slate merchant from Bolton in Lancashire. Married in 1819, Warr and his wife separated in 1827. In 1829 she gave birth to a child and was later married bigamously. As a result she was imprisoned for a year. Warr wrote in his 1840 petition that when he first discovered his wife's adultery he was only a journeyman slater and flagger "and was not in circumstances of sufficient affluence to enable him to bear the expense of any legal proceedings, but [he]...has since that time by industry and frugality improved his circumstances and condition in life, and did so [i.e., lodged a petition for divorce] as soon as he was enabled to do so...."[7] The restrictive character of divorce in England (it was relaxed only in the middle of the nineteenth century) should not be surprising; divorce was literally a privilege in a society characterized by privilege. Those who were advantaged in society, well-to-do males, were the very same advantaged by the divorce provisions as they evolved in practice. Indeed, the divorce procedure by Act of Parliament gave members of the English ruling class close control over this sensitive area of domestic life, and ensured that divorce was kept out of the hands of the lower classes, where it might have been used irresponsibly.

In fact, if one of the purposes of allowing divorce only by Act of Parliament was to limit the number of divorces in England, then it was successful. During the whole period 1670–1857, when the procedure was in effect, only 325 divorces were granted, an average of between one and two a year. Of the total 325, a mere four divorces were obtained by women, reflecting not only informal social and economic constraints, such as the financial dependence of married women on their husbands and the double standard of sexual morality, but also the institutional inhibitions of the divorce procedure, especially the more serious matrimonial offense (aggravated adultery), which women had to prove their husbands guilty of in order to obtain a divorce. Not only was the vast

---

[7] 3 & 4 Vict. cap. 50.

7.2 England: Divorces by Act of Parliament

Table 7.1. *Divorce Acts of Parliament, England, 1670–1857*

Period	Divorce acts	Period	Divorce acts
(1670, 1698)	2	1780–9	12
1700–9	3	1790–9	42
1710–9	2	1800–9	23
1720–9	3	1810–9	27
1730–9	2	1820–9	25
1740–9	4	1830–9	35
1750–9	15	1840–9	54
1760–9	13	1850–7	29
1770–9	34		

majority (99%) of divorces obtained by men, but the earliest examples made divorce seem a positively aristocratic prerogative. After the first divorce act dissolving the marriage of Lord Roos in 1670, the next successful petitioners were the Earl of Macclesfield (1698) and the Duke of Norfolk (1700). The aristocratic tone of these early divorce proceedings was soon lowered by the intrusion of commoners, however, although there was no early rush to Westminster by men seeking divorces. By 1750 only sixteen Acts of Parliament dissolving marriages had been passed, and it was not until the second half of the eighteenth century that divorces became more common. Even then the absolute numbers of divorces was never great, as the decennial totals in Table 7.1 indicate.[8]

Other divorce bills were introduced, only to be subsequently withdrawn or rejected. For example, there are records of six rejected bills between 1714 and 1779, and ten in the period 1780–1819.[9] In these two periods there were 71 and 104 divorce acts, respectively, indicating rejection rates of 8% and 9%.

Divorces, then, were infrequent, and they drew from a limited social range, as we should expect, even though they were far from being confined to the aristocracy alone. Of the 242 petitioners for divorce between 1770 and 1850 whose rank or occupation is given in the statutes, only 16 (7%) were peers. Twelve others had titles of some sort (ten were baronets), but even if we add all these titled divorced men together, they account for only 12% of the total. The largest single group, accounting for 40% of men who divorced by Act of Parliament, were described as "gentlemen" or "esquires," a designation that

---

[8] Figures taken from the statutes for each year. There is a "Return of the Number of Acts of Parliament since the Reformation to the Present Time, for Dissolving Marriages and enabling the Parties to Marry again" (tabled in 1857) reprinted in *Parliamentary Papers: Marriage and Divorce* (3 vols., Shannon, 1971), III, 117. It lists 315 such divorces between 1670 and 1856 but is somewhat suspect. Other tables in the same source (*Parliamentary Papers*) cite some annual numbers of acts that are at variance with those in the "Return."

[9] *Journals of the House of Lords*, volumes for 1 Geo. I to 19 Geo. III and 20–60 Geo. III.

masks their specific occupation or source of income. Other groups also made significant contributions to the divorce lists. Military men, especially majors, lieutenant-colonels, and captains, were prominent, and all ranks in the army and navy provided more than a fifth (21%) of divorced men. Seventeen clergymen contributed a further 7%, a surprisingly high representation given the Church of England's doctrine of marital indissolubility. The remaining 20% of the husbands who obtained an Act of Parliament dissolving their marriages between 1770 and 1850 were primarily men in the professions, commerce, or white-collar occupations, notably fifteen merchants and nine doctors or surgeons, but also including civil servants, a banker, chemist, and a civil engineer. A final group of six men had occupations as a coach founder, trimming maker, riding master, butcher, piano maker, and flour factor.

The social spectrum of men obtaining divorces was thus a limited one. The concentration in the upper strata of society reflected the expense of proceedings under the parliamentary regime. Of the four women who were granted dissolutions of marriage by Act of Parliament in the period 1770–1857, little is revealed in the statutes, except that in one case the husband was a merchant and in another a gentleman.

It is interesting to compare the social position of the divorce petitioners with that of corespondents in individual cases. With what sort of men did the wives concerned commit adultery? In broad terms, and to the extent that information on the corespondents is given in the statutes, the social profile of aggrieved husbands and their wives' lovers were similar, although the corespondents were somewhat more diverse and exotic. Among them we find twenty-five men with titles, including an Italian count, a Spanish marquis, an Austrian prince, and a son of the ex-Caliph of Constantina. Titled men accounted for 15% of identifiable corespondents, a slightly higher proportion than among the men who actually obtained the divorces. Gentlemen, on the other hand, had a reduced representation as corespondents, where they accounted for only 23%. Clergymen, too, were less common as illicit lovers than as cuckolded husbands (5% as against 7%).

On the other hand, men in the professions, especially doctors, lawyers, merchants, and civil servants, were comparatively more frequently represented, at 20%, as were men in the military. The latter contributed 29% of corespondents, compared to their 21% of petitioners. The vagueness and overlapping of social ranks and occupations – a military officer or a professional man might also be described as a "gentleman" – makes an accurate comparison of the two sets of men very difficult. We cannot say whether adultery was, overall, a means of upward or downward mobility for married women.[10]

When we move from the general social profile to individual cases, we find interesting patterns in the relationship between the occupation of women's husbands and their partners in adultery. One was for a woman to have a sexual

---

[10] An occupational profile is given in Wolfram, "Divorce in England," 169–73.

liaison with a man in the same occupation as her husband (excluding, here, the cases where rank was given only as a "gentleman," which is too general to be useful). The wife of a civil engineer, for instance, eloped with another civil engineer, the wife of a chemist committed adultery with another chemist, and the wife of a surgeon did the same with another surgeon. These relationships, like the others that will be examined, reflected the relatively restricted limits of sociability with males that we should expect married women to have experienced in the late eighteenth and nineteenth centuries, especially women of the social classes represented in the divorce lists.

As well as meeting their husbands' colleagues and associates, married women of these strata also had contact – intimate contact sometimes, as the evidence shows – with their social inferiors. It is well recognized that sexual relationships between men and their female servants or employees were not uncommon in the past and that the phenomenon was closely linked to the economic dependence and social vulnerability of the women concerned in this sort of sexual exploitation. The evidence from the English divorce cases is, of course, biased almost wholly toward adultery committed by married women, but it does show evidence of sexual relationships between women and household employees or employees of their husbands. In 1774, for example, the wife of a merchant eloped with her husband's servant, who was also his clerk; in 1778 the wife of an attorney committed adultery with her husband's clerk; in 1791 the wife of a gentleman eloped to France with one of their servants; and in 1811 a woman committed adultery with the steward of her husband's estates. These cases are far from numerous (there are six documented in all), but they reveal a little of the social reality of this phenomenon, which has been frequently celebrated in literature.[11]

A far more striking pattern in the divorces between 1770 and 1850 was the Indian connection: Nearly one in five (18%) of divorces had some association with India or, in one case, Ceylon. The recurrent pattern was of a couple marrying in England, and soon afterward moving to India, generally because the husband had been transferred there as a civilian or military employee of the East India Company or the United Company of Merchants Trading to the East Indies. In many of these cases the wife returned to England after a few years, either to recover from ill-health brought on by living in India or to accompany her children who were being sent back to England for their education. En route to England, or once there, the wife committed adultery. In due course this was discovered by the husband who was still in India, he petitioned for divorce, and in many cases witnesses had to travel to Westminster to give evidence.

---

[11] It is debatable whether this kind of relationship was less exploitative than that between a male employer and a female servant or employee. Presumably a male employee who had a sexual relationship with his employer's wife was, if discovered, in no more secure a position than a female servant who had a sexual liaison with her master: Less so, perhaps, for married women might be forced to turn a blind eye to their husbands' extramarital sexual activities, but married men were unlikely to tolerate their wives' infidelity.

7 The use of the early divorce laws

Several examples illustrate this pattern. In 1787 Thomas Weston, a major in the 96th Regiment of Foot, married Frances Lenn in England. The next year he was ordered to the East Indies, where the couple lived until April 1794, when Frances Weston returned to England for reasons of health. There, from 1796, she lived with Hector Weir, an officer in the South Devon Militia, and had two children by him.[12] In another case, William Simpson and Sarah Torriano were actually married in Bombay in 1792, but she left alone for England in 1802. En route she committed adultery with a fellow passenger, Robert Richards, and became pregnant.[13] A third example saw James Allardyce marry his wife Dorothy in 1813, and subsequently move – with their four children – to Madras, where he was a surgeon with the 34th Regiment of Infantry. In 1820 Dorothy Allardyce and the children left India for England – partly for her health, partly for the children's education – and she committed adultery on board ship with Alexander Johnson, a soldier with the East India Company. When the divorce was decreed in 1823, the two were living in France.[14]

The association of divorce with India became increasingly strong in the first half of the nineteenth century, when more than a quarter (46 of the 168 divorces on which the statutes give sufficiently detailed information) had this connection. Such was the trend that in 1820 an Act of Parliament was passed permitting witnesses in English divorce cases to be examined in India and Ceylon, so as to avoid the necessity of their traveling to Westminster to give evidence at the bar of the House of Lords.[15]

Clearly, mobility and independence were prime factors in the adultery of married women who left their husbands – with the supposed intention of returning to them or of being joined by them later in England – in India. The same conditions of independence existed when a husband left his wife to go on military service abroad. Henry Sheridan's absence in North America, where he was a major in the Regiment of New York Volunteers from 1776, gave his wife an opportunity to elope to France with one Francis Newman. Admiral Sir Hyde Parker's command of H. M. S. Victory in the Mediterranean from 1793 allowed his wife the chance to commit adultery with an army major and to give birth to "a base-born child."[16] As a final example, the wife of the Honorable Pownoll Bastard Pellew matched his military service in her own way; she committed adultery with an army officer (but did not become pregnant), while her husband was at sea in command of H. M. S. Impregnable.[17]

Military service, then, impinged on conjugal life in the late eighteenth and

---

[12] 45 Geo. III cap. 76.
[13] 46 Geo. III cap. 75.
[14] 4 Geo. IV cap. 32.
[15] 1 Geo. IV cap. 101: "An Act to enable the Examination of witnesses to be taken in India in support of Bills of Divorce on account of adultery committed in India."
[16] 39 Geo. III cap. 102.
[17] 1 Geo. IV cap. 66.

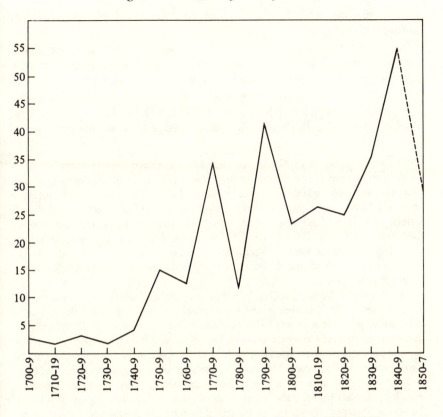

Figure 7.1 Divorces by Act of Parliament in England, 1700–1857.

early nineteenth centuries as the British fought in North America and in the Napoleonic Wars. This, together with the seemingly divorce-prone servants of the empire in India, accounts for the increase in divorces in the later eighteenth century (see Figure 7.1) and for the high representation of military men among the divorced. It is not that war brought about social instability and thus family instability, but rather that the military conflicts separated husbands and wives for prolonged periods and provided opportunities for adultery.[18] As in other instances of this kind, the adultery of the spouse who stayed at home – the wife – was far easier to prove than the adultery or other sexual activity of men abroad on active service.[19] To this extent we must recognize that the women's adultery described in the English divorces under the jurisdiction of Parliament repre-

---

[18] Other references to the effects of war on marriage and divorce are scattered throughout this study, but see especially Section 13.2.
[19] Presumably, homosexual activity was not regarded as adultery, so the divorce lists do not reveal such relationships within the military. Records of courts-martial do, however: See Arthur N. Gilbert, "Buggery in the British Navy, 1700–1861," *Journal of Social History* 19 (1976), 72–98.

sented only the adulteries susceptible to legal relief by dissolution of marriage at that time.

Commerce, as much as military service, also demanded that men absent themselves from their wives, and there were several cases of adultery in such circumstances. In one case, James McGauley, a ship's master, was away from his Liverpool home on trading voyages to the coast of Africa from December 1786 to March 1789 and from August 1791 to June 1792. During these absences his wife, Elizabeth McGauley, engaged in a different sort of commerce.

During your said Subject's Absence on such first-mentioned Voyage [his wife] had an adulterous Commerce; and committed the Crime of Adultery; with One or more Man or Men to your Subject wholly unknown, insomuch that she became pregnant; and on or about the Month of February [1789]...being one Month before your said Subject's Return to England; and upwards of Two Years after his Departure and Absence therefrom, was delivered of a Female Child at Liverpool aforesaid; and that your Subject never knew or was informed of such adulterous Commerce with your said Subject's Wife, or of the birth of such Child, until after his Return from his Second Voyage as hereinafter-mentioned:

That the said Elizabeth McGauley, during your Subject's Absence on such Second Voyage; carried on a further adulterous Commerce; and committed the Crime of Adultery, with the same or other Man or Men to your said Subject wholly unknown, so that on your Subject's return from such last-mentioned Voyage to Liverpool...your Subject having been absent from England...for the Space of Ten Months and Twenty-Two Days, the said Elizabeth McGauley had become and was again pregnant, and being afraid of Detection on account of such her Condition, or being otherwise desirous of avoiding your said Subject; she left and eloped from the Dwelling-House of your said Subject at Liverpool shortly before his return thereto; and afterwards, in or about the Month of August...[1792], being Two Months after such Elopement, was delivered of another Child....[20]

The marriage was dissolved, and Elizabeth McGauley's two children were "deemed, taken, and declared to be Bastards by Authority of Parliament."

In such cases of adultery during geographical separation, there is no explicit evidence of marital unhappiness before the adultery, although we might, with benefit of hindsight, assume that the marriages in question were not totally blissful. The lack of evidence of such circumstances as emotional incompatibility or ill-treatment is not surprising, for the only evidence that was relevant to the divorce petitions related to adultery. In other instances, however, the adultery that formed the basis of the petition for divorce was preceded by a mutually agreed separation. Henry Farrer, for example, wrote that when he returned to England in 1787 after a two-year absence as commander of the East Indiaman *True Briton*, he "discovered that his said Wife was a Woman of a loose, abandoned, and vicious Disposition; and that she carried on an adulterous Intercourse or Connexion with One or more strange Man or

---

[20] 37 Geo. III cap. 97.

Men."[21] Farrer and his wife separated by mutual agreement, but he did not apply for a separation *a mensa et thoro* from the ecclesiastical court until 1792, and for a dissolution of marriage by Act of Parliament until 1796. Other cases of separation by mutual accord were based on simple incompatibility ("differences and disputes having arisen between them")[22] or because of antipathy by the wife; John Hartley agreed to separate after his wife "began to evince a distaste for her home, and an indifference to [his]...society...to the great neglect of her household duties and diminution of [his]...comfort and happiness."[23]

Illness on the part of the wife preceded adultery in a number of cases apart from those associated with India described earlier. Rosa Todhunter, for example, was "afflicted with a long and dangerous illness, which caused her life to be despaired of." In 1839 in the interest of her health she went to Naples, then Rome, where she committed adultery with one Signor Leuci.[24] In a different case Jemima Hall was "attacked by a pulmonary complaint [and]... advised that she should pass the winter months in a warm climate." In October 1837 she embarked for Madeira "on board a yacht furnished and fitted out for her convenience" by her husband. Despite the latter's instructions that she should return, she stayed abroad, and in January 1839 had a child.[25] Was the illness in such cases a symptom of marital stress or was the adultery a result of the independence that travel conferred on women?

In two divorces, we might note, the youthfulness of the husband at marriage played a part in the separation. In the first, Herbert Morgan married in 1837 at the age of sixteen. Whether he had parental consent to the marriage is not clear, but four days after being married "in consequence of [his]...extreme Youth, and his Education being unfinished, he was removed by his Father...placed at Frankfurt in Germany, and afterwards at Tours in France, for the Purpose of carrying on his studies" (and, no doubt, for the purpose of keeping his wife at a good distance). By 1840, at the age of nineteen, Morgan was in India as a lieutenant in the Dragoons, where he discovered that his wife, whom he had not seen for three years, had committed adultery. The following year a separation was obtained and later a dissolution of the marriage.[26] In the second case, Edward Cripps married in 1842 as an "infant" – he was nineteen – and without his father's knowledge or consent. Cripps was allowed seventeen days' cohabitation with his wife before being convinced by his elder brother that his wife was "a person of immoral habits." This marriage, too, was eventually dissolved by Act of Parliament.[27]

Of the four parliamentary divorces obtained by women – all between 1801

21 36 Geo. III cap. 104.
22 38 Geo. III cap. 57.
23 13 & 14 Vict. cap. 19.
24 6 & 7 Vict. cap. 19.
25 4 & 5 Vict. cap. 57.
26 6 & 7 Vict. cap. 39.
27 12 & 13 Vict. cap. 32.

and 1850 – two involved incestuous adultery between a husband and his wife's sister and two were justified by adultery aggravated by bigamy. In the first of the incestuous adultery cases, the husband of Jane Campbell committed adultery with his sister-in-law while her husband, apothecary-general to the East India Company, was absent in Calcutta.[28] The latter in turn divorced his wife in the same year because of the adulterous relationship. The second case of incestuous adultery involved a wife's sister who was not married and, as there was no husband to complain of criminal conversation, the wife was persuaded to remain with her husband for ten years after the offense "to avoid the scandal and disgrace that must have befallen the family. . . from the public exposure of a crime so atrocious and to spare the feelings of her aged parents."[29]

In one of the cases of bigamous adultery, there were clearly severe problems before the offense. Ann Battersby noted that she and her husband had lived together from the date of their marriage, June 15, 1826, only until the thirteenth of the following month.

> Within a few Days of the said Marriage the said Arthur Battersby began to treat [her]. . .with Neglect and Harshness, and frequently left her at Night and went abroad and was and remained until late Hours in the company of common Prostitutes, and with the said Prostitutes carried on an adulterous Intercourse and Connexion.

Arthur Battersby not only had his marriage dissolved because of his subsequent bigamous marriage but was also sentenced to seven years' transportation.[30] In the final divorce obtained by a woman by Act of Parliament, Georgina Hall married her husband in September 1848, but without her parents' knowledge or consent. She returned to her parents directly after the marriage, which was never consummated. In January of the next year her husband committed adultery and in March married in Brussels, no doubt in an attempt to avoid detection.[31]

Beyond the specific grievances in individual cases, it has been suggested that divorces by Act of Parliament served a more general purpose, allowing men, peers in particular, to divorce women who had not borne them male heirs and to remarry younger women, who might produce a son.[32] Of the twenty-three peers and baronets who were divorced and on whom information is readily available, eight definitely had sons living at the time of the divorce, and a further

---

[28] 41 Geo. III cap. 102.
[29] 1 & 2 Will. IV cap. 35.
[30] 3 & 4 Vict. cap. 48.
[31] 13 & 14 Vict. cap. 48.
[32] See, for instance, Lawrence Stone, *The Family, Marriage and Sex in England, 1500–1800* (London, 1977), 38. The Roos case of 1670, the parliamentary divorce that set a precedent for the eighteenth- and nineteenth-century divorces, *was* undertaken for the clear purpose of enabling Lord Roos to produce an heir. His wife had committed adultery and borne two illegitimate children and remarriage was the only recourse left to Lord Roos if he were to father a son who could inherit his title. Lord Roos did remarry after his divorce, but this second wife died in childbirth. Remarried a third time, on this occasion as a widower, Lord Roos did eventually have the heir he sought. An account is in Antonia Fraser, *The Weaker Vessel: Woman's Lot in Seventeenth-Century England* (London, 1984), 337–51.

three might have; they admitted to having children, without specifying their sex. Three of the remaining twelve had daughters only, four declared that there were "no issue" of their marriages, and in four cases there was no mention of children at all. The desire to produce a male heir might well have motivated some petitions for divorce, although adultery by the wife still had to be proved, but it would be rash to extend it to an all-embracing explanation.

The 325 dissolutions of marriage by Parliament in England between 1670 and 1857 must have represented only a tiny fraction of marriage breakdowns during that period. They were heavily biased by the restrictive terms of the divorce provisions – there is little evidence of matrimonial offenses other than adultery – and by the expense, which concentrated divorce into a narrow social range. Women, and women's grievances, especially desertion and severe ill-treatment, were virtually excluded. Despite these qualifications there are patterns to be observed, such as the association of adultery and mobility, and the social range of married women's sexual contacts. More to the point, perhaps, is that the study of this form of divorce demonstrates how the terms of divorce influence perceptions of marriage breakdown. If we took this source at face value and isolated it from its context, we might believe that marriage breakdown was rare and that women were almost always responsible for it.

Divorce by Act of Parliament was an unsatisfactory compromise between a rule of marital indissolubility and provision for divorce by judicial process. It was unsatisfactory not only for those married people to whom divorce was effectively unavailable but also to many members of the Houses of Parliament: There were pressures within Parliament both to restrict and liberalize divorce in the late eighteenth and early nineteenth centuries, and these are discussed in Chapter 11. But what of those husbands and wives prevented from divorcing? Many, of course, remained married and lived together, whereas others separated informally or obtained separations from the church courts. For yet others – still the better-off – one possibility was to seek a divorce in Scotland where, as we have seen, divorce had been available since the sixteenth century on the grounds of adultery or desertion. Moreover, Scottish divorce laws gave equal access to divorce to women.

The flight to Scotland and recourse to Gretna Green marriages by English men and women seeking to avoid the restrictive procedures of the English marriage law after 1753 are well known. Not as well known is the use, or attempted use, of Scotland as a divorce haven in the face of restrictive English divorce provisions. In modern terms, eighteenth- and nineteenth-century Scotland hardly qualifies as a Reno or Mexico, but until 1858, when divorce became available from the English courts, it did offer a divorce facility far more accessible, in principle, than England.

Scottish judges did not always welcome divorce petitioners from south of the border, however, and often insisted on a significant Scottish connection before they would accept jurisdiction over a divorce petition. They were mindful that the dissolution in Scotland of a marriage contracted in England might not be recognized by English law. One decision of the Scottish court noted that

the Courts of one country ought not to be converted into engines for either eluding the laws of another, or determining matters foreign to their territory, and that decrees of divorce, pronounced by incompetent courts, cannot, effectually and securely, either loose the bonds, or dissolve the marriage, or fix the status of the parties thereto, but might become cause or snares to involve other persons, as well as the parties and their children, in deep distress.[33]

Some petitions to dissolve marriages not contracted in Scotland were rejected by the Scottish courts, but others were granted, where one or both of the parties had been born or had been domiciled in Scotland for a reasonable time or where the adultery that constituted the matrimonial offense had been committed in Scotland. What is of particular interest is some connections between the English and Scottish divorces. One involved Henry William, Lord Paget, who was named as corespondent in an 1812 parliamentary divorce. He had committed adultery with one Margaret Guard, whose husband had subsequently been awarded damages of £20,000 for criminal conversation. In England, Lady Paget had no recourse in law against her husband's adultery, but in Scotland she did, and in the same year, she obtained a divorce from the Consistorial Court of Scotland on the ground of simple adultery.[34] Another couple who appeared in cases in both jurisdictions was Elizabeth and Frederick Tewsh, who were divorced in Scotland in 1811. It seems likely that they were the same couple mentioned in the House of Lords in 1805, where the name was spelled Teush. At that time the divorce bill introduced on behalf of the husband was not passed, although the reason was not stated. In 1811, however, Elizabeth Tewsh obtained a Scottish divorce because, although they had been married in England, her husband had deserted her and was, at the time of her divorce petition, cohabiting with a woman in Scotland.[35]

Scotland, then, was the nearest thing to a divorce haven for the English, even given the severe limitations placed on divorce by the Scottish courts. It is possible that France, where an extremely liberal divorce law was in force from 1792 to 1803, might have attracted the maritally miserable English had the two countries not been at war during almost the entire period. One English parliamentary divorce did deal with a marriage that had already been dissolved in France, but this simply demonstrated the problem of international recognition of divorce decrees. In this case James Woodmason divorced his wife Mary Magdelain [sic] Gaville, who was French born and had returned to France in August 1789, just after the revolution broke out. She lived in Paris with her father, and, "taking Advantage of the Laws, Decrees, or Regulations made in France, did, on or about the Fourteenth Day of June [1796] . . . procure

[33] An 1811 decision, quoted in James Fergusson, *Reports of some recent decisions of the Consistorial Court of Scotland, in Actions of Divorce, concluding for Dissolution of marriages celebrated under the English Law* (Edinburgh, 1817), 41.
[34] Ibid., 23ff.
[35] Ibid.

there...a certain pretended Divorce." In April 1797 she "contracted, or pretended to contract, a Marriage." The next year, Woodmason secured his own divorce by Act of Parliament.[36]

Divorce by Act of Parliament provided a limited access to divorce in England and represented a long transitional phase between a divorceless society and the eventual legalization of divorce in the middle of the nineteenth century. From almost every point of view it was an unsatisfactory compromise. It probably lasted so long because the members of the House of Lords and the House of Commons – the very men who would have had to pass a divorce law – were faced with an increasing number of divorce bills, each accompanied by what they considered appalling evidence of immorality on the part of married women. Their fear that legalizing divorce would increase immorality and marriage breakdown – a commonly expressed apprehension – must have contributed to the cautious approach English legislators took for so long with respect to divorce policy.

7.3 Divorces in the American colonies, seventeenth and eighteenth centuries

As we have seen, many of the English men and women who emigrated to the British colonies in America had much better access to divorce than those who stayed in the home country; although several of the colonies legalized divorce in the seventeenth century, and more states did so after the American Revolution, the English remained confined to restrictive legislative divorce (by private Act of Parliament) from 1670 until England's first divorce law was passed in 1857.

This is not to say that attitudes to marriage and divorce in America were very lax, an allegation that was to be made by Europeans in the nineteenth century. Not all the colonies – nor, later, all the states – legalized divorce quickly, and neither were the grounds for divorce in the seventeenth and eighteenth centuries very liberal; they were for the most part limited to adultery and desertion, as contemporary European Protestant states had provided. In general terms, the American experience fell somewhere in the vast middle range that separated the very limited English divorce facilities and the libertarian law of revolutionary France.

Appropriately, the number of divorces in America in this period fell between those in England and France. Eighteenth-century England produced some 130 parliamentary divorces, whereas in France more than 20,000 marriages were dissolved by divorce between 1792 and 1803. Providing a middle range, the two American colonies of Massachusetts and Connecticut together produced more than 800 divorces in the second half of the eighteenth century.[37] Like the

---

[36] 38 Geo. III cap. 59.

[37] Nancy Cott, "Divorce and the Changing Status of Women in Eighteenth-Century Massachusetts," *William and Mary Quarterly* 3rd. Ser., 33 (1976), 586–614; Sheldon S. Cohen, "'To Parts of the World Unknown': The Circumstances of Divorce in Connecticut, 1750–1797," *Canadian Review of American Studies* 11 (1980), 275–93.

development of the divorce laws there, trends in divorcing in the American colonies appear to have fallen into three broad phases. The first was the period of early settlement up to the middle of the eighteenth century, when the laws were at their most restrictive and divorces were the fewest. In the second phase, from the mid-eighteenth century to the American Revolution, some laws and procedures were reformed, and there were significant increases in the use of divorce in Massachusetts and Connecticut. The third phase, the revolutionary and immediate postrevolutionary periods, saw a further boost in divorces in those states that as colonies had earlier legalized divorce, as well as the spread of divorce to states that had not provided for divorce before the revolution. This linkage of legal change and divorce behavior is not intended to suggest that the increasing number of divorces was simply a product of legislative reform, however. The following discussion will examine the use of divorce in America in the seventeenth and eighteenth centuries in the light of social as well as legal changes.

Even though the New England colonies provided facilities for divorce that were denied to the English in the seventeenth century, divorces were far from common. Moreover, the disparate jurisdictions and variety of divorce-granting institutions (courts, governors, councils, and legislatures, depending on the practice in each colony) make access to the cases problematic, and we cannot be certain that all divorces and divorce petitions have been retrieved. In his 1904 work *A History of Matrimonial Institutions*, George E. Howard listed 40 petitions for divorce and annulment in seventeenth-century New England, but Lyle Koehler, researching more systematically for *A Search for Power* (1980), has enumerated 128 petitions for divorce, separation, and annulment of marriages, from a wide range of sources. It is this latter list that provides much of our data on the early colonial divorces.[38]

The 128 petitions, lodged between 1620 and 1699, were not all for dissolution of marriage in the strict sense, but included some requests for marriages to be annulled and yet others for separation. In addition there were idiosyncratic petitions described as "self-divorce" and "common-law marriage split up." The distinction between divorce and annulment is blurred because some of the colonies' laws provided for divorce on grounds such as impotence, bigamy, and fraudulent contract, which traditionally justified annulment rather than the dissolution of marriage. To this extent, it is rather more difficult to define, and therefore to quantify, divorces in seventeenth-century New England.

The exclusion of twenty-five petitions that can most properly be thought of as relating to annulments – petitions based solely on affinity, impotence, bigamy, or fraudulent contract – reduces the total list from 128 to 103 petitions. They

---

[38] Lyle S. Koehler, *A Search for Power: The "Weaker Sex" in Seventeenth-Century New England* (Urbana, Ill., 1980), Appendix 1: "Petitions for Divorce in New England, 1620–1699," not paginated but equivalent to pp. 453–9.

7.3 Divorces in the American colonies

Table 7.2. *Petitions for separation and divorce, New England, 1620–99*

	Mass.	Plym.	N. Hamp.	Conn.	N. Hav.	Rh. Is.	Totals
Women's petitions							
Adultery	4	1		3			8
Desertion	10	1	1	19		2	33
Adultery and desertion	7		1	4			12
Adultery and cruelty	2					1	3
Cruelty	1						1
Desertion and incest	1						1
Absence	2						2
Heretical opinions					1		1
"Oppression of spirit"						1	1
Threats to life						1	1
Unknown	3					1	4
(Subtotals)	30	2	2	27		6	(67)
Men's petitions							
Adultery	3	2		2		2	9
Desertion	2	1		3		1	7
Adultery and desertion	1	2		4			7
Adultery and cruelty	1						1
Incest		1					1
Refusal of intercourse				1			1
Refusal to accompany				1			1
Unknown	2					2	4
(Subtotals)	9	6		11		5	(31)
Mutual consent	1					4	5
Totals	40	8	2	38		15	103

are set out by colony, sex of petitioner, and ground for petition in Table 7.2.
Women were petitioners in almost two-thirds (65%) of the cases, men in 30%,
and both spouses petitioned jointly in 5%. This sex ratio is little different from
that in the total 128 petitions listed, where women – or parents on their behalf
– petitioned in 67% of cases, men petitioned in 27%, and both spouses
petitioned jointly in 5%.

Of the total number of divorces and legal separations in seventeenth-century
New England, little need be said. There were few enough overall, and certainly
not enough to warrant drawing refined conclusions from the number of petitions in the individual states. Massachusetts Bay and Connecticut, easily the
most populous colonies, had by far the largest number of divorce petitions, but
there was no close relationship between population size and the number of
petitions. In 1690, for example, Massachusetts (including Plymouth Colony)

243

had 57,000 inhabitants, whereas Connecticut had only 16,000. Connecticut's population almost doubled, to 30,000, by 1700, and Massachusetts's increased by a quarter to 70,000 inhabitants,[39] yet there was, if anything, a reverse proportional relationship in divorce petitioning: Between 1690 and 1699 there were four petitions in Massachusetts and seven in Connecticut. The figures involved are too small to permit any worthwhile analysis of this sort, although we might note that divorce legislation was more liberal and divorce itself apparently more socially acceptable in Connecticut. It is also notable that New Haven colony produced no divorce petitions at all, although there were two for annulment, partly because the colony had an independent existence only until 1665, when it united with Connecticut.

An examination of the grounds for the petitions offers more scope for analysis. Although there were variations among the divorce law provisions in the colonies – and the restrictions these imposed must have influenced the number of petitions – all allowed for divorce for reason of adultery or desertion. These two grounds, individually and jointly, comprised 77% of all unilateral divorce petitions (79% of women's, 73% of men's). But women were more likely to invoke a husband's desertion than his adultery. Simple desertion accounted for 49% of women's petitions, and desertion was an element in 11% more (a total of 60%). Men alleged simple desertion in 23% of their petitions, and as an element in a further 23% (a total of 46%). Men, on the other hand, more often alleged adultery. This ground alone justified 29% of their petitions, as against only 13% of women's. Women were more likely to make adultery one of a pair of joint grounds (especially linked to desertion), giving the appearance of its being aggravated adultery, which was more likely than simple adultery to justify a petition by a woman. These characteristics – women petitioning predominantly for reason of desertion and men for adultery – are familiar ones where the law provides them as grounds for divorce or separation. They reflect, on the one hand, the greater mobility of men and need for deserted married women to regularize their status (often to remarry), and, on the other hand, the greater emphasis given to adultery committed by a married woman than by a married man.

The apparent tendency for women to commit adultery more frequently than men, which a superficial reading of the divorce figures might suggest, is contradicted by convictions for adultery by the New England courts. Of 308 such convictions during the seventeenth century, 174 (56.5%) were of men, and 134 (43.5%) were of women. Only in Maine did men comprise fewer than half of the convicted adulterers, and then they were a scant minority (thirty out of sixty-one). In the other colonies men accounted for between 55% and 100% of convicted adulterers.[40] New England laws generally provided the same penalties for adultery by either wife or husband (including hanging in the early

[39] *Historical Statistics of the United States: Colonial Times to 1957* (Washington, D.C., 1957), 756, Series Z1–19.
[40] Drawn from Koehler, *Search for Power*, 149, Chart 5.1.

seventeenth century), but paradoxically this equal-handed treatment concealed the especial harshness for women because with respect to most other offenses they were subject to more lenient punishments than men. Petitions for divorce must be seen in this context, too. Unilateral divorce was viewed not as a remedy for marriage breakdown but as a severe punishment for a matrimonial crime. The greater propensity for women to be divorced because of their adultery enhances the image of the double standard at work in the social attitudes of the period. How else are we to explain why the sex ratio of adulterers in divorce suits did not reflect the sex ratio of convicted adulterers, except by appeal to the greater tolerance by married women (and social attitudes generally) of their husband's offenses than vice versa? (This should be understood as a tolerance forced by financial dependence or by the social embarrassment that could result from publicity, not necessarily as a voluntary tolerance; this point is discussed in Section 9.4).

As a final point on this issue, we can note that among divorce petitions based solely on adultery, men and women had the same rate of success: seven out of eight succeeded in obtaining such divorces, and the final outcome of the remaining petition is unknown. Seven successful petitions out of eight filed (88%) represented a favorable rate of success for men, but an unfavorable rate for women: Where the disposition of all divorce petitions is considered, women had a success rate of 98%, and that of men's petitions was only 81%. The merging of success rates in petitions based solely on adultery reflected the fact that women's adultery was considered far more serious than men's, a perspective embodied in the morality legislation of the New England colonies. For example, the early laws of Massachusetts, Connecticut, Plymouth, and New Haven all provided the death penalty for adultery when it involved a betrothed or married woman, whereas a married man who committed adultery with an unmarried woman was subject only to imprisonment and other lesser penalties. (These laws prefigured the adultery act in force in England from 1650 to 1660). Capital and sexually discriminatory punishments for adultery were repealed in the colonies in the 1670s, but even then the equality of treatment contrasted with the more lenient approach to women, as compared to men, who were guilty of other kinds of offenses. Even then, the reduced, noncapital penalities were far from lenient: They included whippings (in practice, between twenty and thirty-nine lashes), wearing the letters AD sewn onto the convicted adulterer's clothes, time on the gallows, and substantial fines.

It could well have been that the more tolerant attitude toward adultery, reflected in the repeal of capital punishment provisions, evolved because officials "believed that adultery was so commonplace that it was unrealistic to prosecute offenders to the full extent of the law."[41] Even so, adultery, as a

---

[41] R. W. Roetger, "The Transformation of Sexual Morality in 'Puritan' New England: Evidence from New Haven Court Records, 1639–1698," *Canadian Review of American Studies* 15 (1984), 246.

serious crime against marriage and society, remained a highly charged emotional issue so that prosecutions must have been filed by spouses with the
greatest reluctance, and convictions must have been brought down in a way that
reflected differential attitudes toward male and female offenders. Both of these
considerations are reflected in the profile of adultery in New England divorce
petitions, but in no sense can the picture of adultery in them be thought of as
representative of the extent of adultery in society at large, nor as necessarily
indicative of the actual ratio of male to female offenders.

With regard to this issue of the representativeness of the behavior that
constituted the basis of divore petitions, it is likely that desertion reflected
actual behavior more sensitively than did adultery. Many more women than
men cited desertion as a sole or joint ground for divorce, indicative of the fact
that men have traditionally been more mobile and historically more disposed to
abandon their spouses (and often their children as well) than women have been.
Greater economic independence on the part of men, their involvement in
military forces, specific mobile occupations (such as seafaring and migratory
labor), together with social attitudes more tolerant of solitary males, combined
to enable men to be more peripatetic than women. The socialization of women
into less flexible and more confined roles of family responsibility and the
limitation on female nondomestic paid occupations in preindustrial society had
the reverse effect on women. These were not absolute differences between men
and women, needless to say. But the evidence of the greater predisposition of
men to desert their families, to turn temporary absences into permanent ones or
simply to go missing, is incontestable.

Desertion – by men and women – was not particularly different in New
England from elsewhere, although it might have been facilitated by the close
geographical proximity of a number of colonies with distinct jurisdictions over
marriage. This was to be a feature of divorce patterns in the nineteenth and
twentieth centuries, when individuals could migrate to states where divorce was
most readily obtainable, but in the seventeenth century the legal patchwork
enabled men and women to desert a spouse in one colony and flee to another
from where they could not easily be repatriated against their will. Some
subsequently remarried without bothering to divorce, although many bigamous
marriages were voided by the New England courts. In Massachusetts alone
between 1639 and 1698, six women had marriages annulled because of their
husbands' bigamy, and another four women and one man obtained divorces on
the joint grounds of bigamy and desertion. For example, in 1674 Mary Sanders
obtained a divorce because her husband William had deserted her and had
remarried in London (England), and in 1682 Elija Street was similarly divorced
from her husband Robert, who had remarried in Jamaica.[42] Bigamy was,
indeed, almost an implication of the conception of divorce as a punitive
measure that did not enable the guilty party to remarry. A woman or man so

---

[42] *Records of the Court of Assistants of the Colony of Massachusetts Bay, 1630–1692*, I, 30, 227.

driven by marital unhappiness to desert was, as the guilty party, unable to petition for divorce and could not remarry even if her or his spouse obtained a divorce. The deserter's principal choices were to live alone (which was viewed with disfavor and was even illegal in some colonies), to cohabit without marriage (which was also socially condemned, and in some colonies was subject to the same penalties as fornication), or to marry bigamously, which was a criminal offense.

Although it is possible to draw some conclusions about adultery and desertion from the petitions for divorce and separation, other forms of marital stress and breakdown are concealed by the limited grounds upon which a petition might be founded. Only five petitions mentioned or referred to cruelty, for example, although we can be certain that domestic violence, and the physical ill-treatment of women in particular, was widespread. Between 1630 and 1699, 128 men and 57 women were prosecuted in New England for physically abusing their spouses. Five men killed their wives.[43] Despite the severe penalties (lashings and heavy fines) that the law specified for marital assault, in practice the courts dealt leniently with the guilty.[44]

Of the other circumstances that could give rise to divorce, little need be said in the New England context. But the variety of doctrines and the fluidity of legislation, especially in Rhode Island, did raise the issue of self-help marriage (common-law marriages) and divorces; one Rhode Island divorce ended a common-law marriage; another was a "self-divorce." Many other "self-divorces" of self-married couples must never have come – indeed, need never have come – to the notice of the authorities. As with divorce statistics relating to other places and other times, those from seventeenth-century New England reveal much about the texture of familial and social life, provide hints of other trends, yet positively conceal the social extent of behavior and circumstances that might give rise to a petition for dissolution of marriage or separation. In seventeenth-century New England, 693 marriages were involved in court processes for violence, adultery, refusal to cohabit, murder or attempted murder, refusal to have intercourse, and petitions for divorce or separation. Of these, 103 (15%) showed as petitions for divorce or separation.[45]

Not all of the matrimonial offenses could have been translated into divorces, even if the aggrieved spouses had wanted to, since the grounds for divorce were far from all-encompassing. All the other factors that can inhibit the use of divorce must also have come into play: financial dependence, religious scruples, social pressure, and the individual decision that a specific offense was not so severe as to warrant a divorce. Among the Puritans of New England divorce was permitted, but it was still regarded with disfavor, as a shameful act, particularly in colonies such as Massachusetts and Plymouth. On one occasion a divorced woman and her new husband complained to authorities that some people had

---

[43] Koehler, *Search for Power*, 139.
[44] Ibid.
[45] Statistics taken from various sections of Koehler, *Search for Power*.

insulted them "in most reviling speeches" (including the accusation of adultery) because of the divorced status of the woman. And divorce was regarded by the Massachusetts judiciary as such a weighty action and serious recourse that the reconciliation of divorced spouses could not be countenanced. In 1677 Philip Wharton had divorced his wife Mary on the ground of "adulterous carriage."[46] But in April of the following year the Suffolk (Massachusetts) County Court was faced with the case of "Phillip [sic] Wharton and Mary Gridley formerly his wife, being bound over to this Court to answer for theire disorderly and offensive cohabiting together having sued out a divorce." The couple admitted that they were living together, and were ordered "to refrain the Company of each other," under a bond of twenty pounds each.[47]

In Connecticut attitudes toward divorce seemed to be more tolerant. Sarah Knight, a commentator on American society at the opening of the eighteenth century, wrote of Indians in Connecticut that "they marry many wives and at pleasure put them away, and on ye least dislike or fickle humor, on either side, saying stand away to one another is a sufficient divorce." It is not clear whether Sarah Knight was blaming Indian influences for divorces among the colonists of Connecticut, when she added: "And indeed those uncomely Stand aways are too much in Vogue among the English in this Indulgent Colony as their Records plentifully prove." Knight was accurate enough in pointing to the high number of divorces in Connecticut (thirty-eight as compared to forty in Massachusetts, although Connecticut's population was less than half that of Massachusetts). On the other hand, Sarah Knight was not a flawless observer. She noted that in Connecticut women "the foolish sex, have had too large a share" in obtaining divorces.[48] In fact, as can be seen from Table 7.2, women sought 71% of the unilateral divorces in Connecticut, compared to 77% in Massachusetts, and 75%, 100%, and 55%, respectively, in Plymouth Colony, New Hampshire, and Rhode Island. If it were not more tolerant social attitudes, some other factor, such as a more flexible judiciary, produced the higher divorce rate in Connecticut Colony.[49] As with the rest of the New England colonies in the seventeenth century, however, the number of divorces is simply too small to permit any refined analysis.

Little is known of the use of divorce in the colonies outside New England, but given the more restrictive character of divorce provisions in the middle colonies and total absence of divorce laws from the south, we should expect divorces to have been rare. In New York there are records of only eight divorce decrees during the seventeenth century, and none at all during the eighteenth

---

[46] Ibid., 454, divorce 27.

[47] *Records of the Suffolk County Court 1671–1680* (Boston, 1933), II, 914.

[48] Ibid., 153.

[49] One factor that must have facilitated access to divorce in Connecticut is that judges in that colony rode circuit, hearing actions in county seats. Petitioners for divorce in Massachusetts had to attend court in Boston. Alison Duncan Hirsch, "The Thrall Divorce Case: A Family Crisis in Eighteenth-Century Connecticut," *Women and History* 4 (1982), 70–1n.4.

century up to 1787.[50] Of the seventeenth-century divorces, three were granted under Dutch jurisdiction, the first in 1655 by a husband on the ground of his wife's desertion and remarriage nine years earlier. Two years later one Joris Baldingh (or Balden) obtained a divorce from his wife for reason of her adultery, and in 1664 Anneke Adriaens successfully petitioned for divorce because her husband had married again in Amsterdam. He in turn suffered not only divorce but was condemned to be flogged, branded, and banished from New Netherlands for the offense. A further five divorces were granted in New York under English jurisdiction, all between 1669 and 1675. Three were obtained by men on the ground of their wives' adultery, and two women obtained divorces for reason of adultery and an aggravating circumstance (bigamy in one case, rape and incest in the other).[51]

The division of time into centuries is a construct that social behavior ignores. There was little change in the number of divorce petitions from the seventeenth century through the first third or half of the eighteenth, and what change there was, was not necessarily in the form of an increase. In Massachusetts, for example, there were fifty-one petitions for divorce in the fifty-seven-year period from 1636 to 1692, an annual average of almost one petition. But in the forty-three-year period from 1692 to 1734, there were only twenty-seven petitions, a reduced annual average.[52] The number of petitions by intervals is shown in Table 7.3, which demonstrates that there was generally little change in the absolute numbers of divorce petitions in the first hundred years of divorce in Massachusetts. All but one of the ten-year periods produced between four and nine petitions, the exception being the period from 1675 to 1684, when nineteen women and three men filed for divorce. (Nineteen of the twenty-two petitions succeeded.) This number of petitions represented a remarkable aberration from the normal range of numbers, but there is no ready explanation for it. The grounds for divorce were principally desertion (cited in ten cases) and adultery or "adulterous carriage," a less specific sexual offense (cited in seven petitions). Apart from this abnormally high number of divorces between 1675 and 1684, the number of petitions was fairly stable in absolute numbers between the 1630s and 1730s. When demographic increase over the period is taken into account – the number of inhabitants of Massachusetts rose fivefold between 1690 and 1780[53] – the rate of petitioning in relation to population must actually have fallen quite dramatically during the first thirty or forty years of the eighteenth century.

Beginning in the 1730s, however, there were marked changes in the number

[50] Matteo Spalleta, "Divorce in Colonial New York," *New York Historical Society Quarterly* 39 (1955) 422–40, passim.
[51] Ibid.
[52] On Massachusetts divorces, see Nancy Cott, "Divorce," and "Eighteenth-Century Family and Social Life Revealed in Massachusetts Divorce Records," *Journal of Social History* (1976), 20–43.
[53] Cott, "Divorce," 592n.19.

7 The use of the early divorce laws

Table 7.3. *Petitions for divorce, separation, and annulment:*
Massachusetts 1636–1786

	Petitions by		
	Women	Men	Total
1636–44	4 (3)	0	4
1645–54	4 (4)	1 (1)	5 (5)
1655–64	7 (7)	1 (0)	9 (8)
1665–74	3 (3)	1 (0)	4 (3)
1675–84	19 (16)	3 (2)	22 (18)
1685–92	3 (2)	2 (2)	7 (6)
1692–1704	4 (3)	3 (2)	7 (5)
1705–14	3 (2)	3 (3)	6 (5)
1715–24	4 (1)	1 (1)	5 (2)
1725–34	4 (1)	5 (3)	9 (4)
1735–44	8 (4)	15 (11)	23 (15)
1745–54	12 (6)	9 (5)	21 (11)
1755–64	12 (7)	14 (9)	26 (16)
1765–74	28 (13)	18 (11)	46 (24)
1775–86	53 (37)	33 (24)	86 (61)
Total	168 (109)	109 (74)	280 (183)

Note: Known successful petitions are shown in parentheses. Totals greater than the sum of men's and women's petitions include petitions filed jointly by the two spouses.
Sources: 1636–92, Lyle S. Koehler, *A Search for Power: The "Weaker Sex" in Seventeenth-Century New England* (Urbana, Ill., 1980), 453–6; 1692–1734, Nancy Cott, "Divorce and the Changing Status of Women in Eighteenth-Century Massachusetts," *William and Mary Quarterly* 3rd. Ser., 33 (1976), 592, Table I.

of petitions filed and divorces granted in Massachusetts, as Table 7.3 indicates. From an average seven per decade between 1692 and 1734, petitions increased to twenty-nine per decade between 1735 and 1774, and there were eighty-six in the ten years from 1775, the period of the American war of independence. (Successful petitions, as distinct from all petitions, increased in proportion, from four per decade 1692–1732 to seventeen per decade 1735–74 to sixty-one in the ten years from 1775.) Expressed another way, more than half the divorce petitions filed in this period of almost a hundred years dated from the final two decades, and more than one-third were filed in the last decade alone. Such an increase outstripped the growth in the population of Massachusetts in the second half of the eighteenth century, although demographic growth would explain part of the increase in divorce petitions, assuming a constant rate of petitions in relation to population. The other obvious explanation for a rise in divorce petitions, a liberalization in the formal terms of the legislation in force, did not occur. The grounds for divorce in Massachusetts remained limited to adultery, desertion, and severe cruelty, either individually or in combinations.

Connecticut, the other colony that produced a significant number of divorces in the seventeenth century, also experienced an increase in the eighteenth. Unlike Massachusetts, however, Connecticut petitions did not decline in the first half of the century. Seventeenth-century Connecticut produced on average one petition a year (45 petitions between 1655 and 1699).[54] In the first half of the eighteenth century divorce petitions averaged 2.5 per year (123 petitions),[55] but this increased to an astonishing 17 each year in the second half of the century (839 petitions filed between 1750 and 1797).[56]

Again, population growth can account for some of the increase in petitions but far from all of it: The population of Connecticut rose from 30,000 in 1701 to 130,000 in 1756 to 250,000 by 1800. The real increase in divorce actions is shown when petitions are expressed in relation to population. From 1750 to 1762 there was an annual average of 0.062 petitions per thousand inhabitants of Connecticut, and this rose to 0.081 (1762–74) and dropped slightly to 0.075 (1775–85), before rising dramatically to 0.17 between 1786 and 1797. In Connecticut, then, the sudden increase in divorce actions seems to have taken place a decade later, after 1786 rather than after 1775. And again, as in Massachusetts, the divorce legislation applied in eighteenth-century Connecticut did not change; the law continued to dissolve marriages on the grounds of desertion, adultery, fraudulent contract, and lengthy absence.

Massachusetts and Connecticut were the only American colonies to produce more than a few divorces in the eighteenth century. The other colonies either had no provision for divorces or ran afoul of the colonial government in Britain and had divorce legislation or divorces granted by legislatures disallowed. But the number of divorces in Massachusetts and Connecticut – more than a thousand petitions in the second half of the eighteenth century – permits us to analyze the characteristics the colonies shared with respect to divorce behavior as well as to appreciate the differences between them.

Unlike England, where the parliamentary procedure limited the privilege of divorce to the wealthy few, divorces in these two American colonies spanned the social spectrum. Sheldon Cohen's study of Connecticut divorces is not specific about the social origins of the divorced but does point out that they ranged from Colonel Henry Beekman Livingston, a member of a prominent New York family, to "James, a Norwich slave who sought separation from his wife Grace, a mulatto servant."[57] Each divorced his wife for reason of desertion. As for the Massachusetts divorces, whose social origins are provided by Nancy Cott, they derived mainly from the "middling classes". One-third of the

---

[54] Koehler, *Search for Power*, 457–8.
[55] Sheldon S. Cohen, " 'To Parts of the World Unknown'," 277. One of these was the Thrall case, analyzed in rich detail in Alison Duncan Hirsch, "The Thrall Divorce Case."
[56] Cohen, " 'To Parts of the World Unknown'," 275.
[57] Ibid., 275–6.

husbands involved as petitioners or defendants in divorce suits were artisans or traders, 22% were husbandmen or yeomen, another 22% were mariners or fishermen, and 17% were more prestigious, being gentlemen, merchants, professionals, ships' captains, or officers in the militia. The remaining 7% occupied the lower end of the occupational and social scale: laborers, truckmen, and servants. As a general conclusion "whether or not they were a representative sample, the group included all varieties of the Massachusetts population, urban and rural dwellers, rich and poor."[58]

There seem to have been differences between Massachusetts and Connecticut in the sex ratio of divorce petitioners. Over the whole period 1692–1780, women sought 56% of Massachusetts divorces, separations, and annulments (see Table 7.3) and obtained 52% of them. The female preponderance increased as the century progressed: 61% of the petitions and 54% of those successful from 1765 to 1774; 62%, and 61%, respectively, from 1775 to 1786. In the Connecticut study the sex ratio is not stated. Extrapolation from the given statistics suggests that over the period 1750–97 a majority of petitions was filed by women,[59] but that, unlike the Massachusetts case, their preponderance did not increase consistently over time. Women accounted for 74% of petitions for 1750–62, 73% for 1763–74, 91% for 1775–85, and 69% for 1786–97.[60]

There were important differences, too, in the distribution of matrimonial offenses that formed the basis of divorce actions in the two colonies. In 457 (54%) of the Connecticut suits, desertion was the sole ground. In contrast, desertion alone was the basis of only 18 (8%) of Massachusetts actions. A further 22 Massachusetts divorce petitions were based on desertion followed by remarriage, but these cases were construed more as adultery preceded by desertion rather than as cases of desertion as the prime offense, aggravated by adultery. It is clear that one key to understanding the different numbers and rates of divorces between the two colonies lies in the lesser significance given to desertion, as a matrimonial fault, in Massachusetts divorce law. It could well be that given the fluidity of colonial society, the high rates of mobility and the closeness of jurisdictions that provided havens for deserters, desertion was, in terms of social reality, the most common of the matrimonial offenses: It was not only alleged as a sole ground in more than half the Connecticut petitions but was included as a joint ground in many more. Desertion, as well as being the only ground in eighteen of the Massachusetts actions, was mentioned in seventy-six more in conjunction with adultery, cohabitation with another person, or remarriage. It thus played a part, albeit usually a contingent one, in ninety-four (41%) of the Massachusetts divorces.

[58] Cott, "Divorce," 588. Husbands' occupations were far more frequently stated in the divorce documents than wives'.
[59] Cohen states that five-sixths of petitions based on desertion were filed by women, as were 40% of those based on adultery. Cohen, "'To Parts of the World Unknown'," 277.
[60] Calculated from Ibid., 278.

In cases that included desertion, women clearly dominated the lists of petitioners. Women sought five-sixths of the Connecticut divorces based on desertion alone.[61] In Massachusetts sixteen wives, but only ten husbands, alleged desertion and adulterous cohabitation; nineteen wives, but only three husbands, alleged desertion and remarriage, and ten wives, but eight husbands, alleged desertion alone.[62] These cases, together with the legal action against bigamy – also dominated by women petitioners – indicate that the mobility afforded by the colonial context was exploited more by married men than by married women.

Examples of desertion figure prominently in the records of divorces, and often relate to women left destitute by their husbands. Mary Dewey, of Colchester in Connecticut, reported in 1764 that her husband Elias left her and remarried in Rhode Island, forcing her to go "begging from house to house for support for her and her infant child."[63] Ruth Crary, married in 1785, stated that in 1788 her husband "did Absent himself from the Family and Friendship of your Petitioner and hath gone some parts of the world unknown to the Petitioner, leaving her wholly Destitute of Support...."[64] There are relatively few examples of women deserting (men sought only one in six divorces on the ground of desertion). One involved Mary Parsons who deserted her husband Luke in 1755 and refused to return, allegedly telling one woman (a witness in the divorce case) that "She had rather be a captive in Canady" than live with her husband.[65]

The other familial circumstances that provoked divorce – adultery and cruelty for the most part – are familiar in the history of divorce. Men took advantage of their geographical mobility not only to desert but to commit adultery, and on occasion they were punished for it by being divorced. One Jedediah Beckwith, captain of a trading schooner, was divorced by his wife after a witness testified that Beckwith had had sexual relationships in four separate New York ports on a recent voyage.[66] Women, on the other hand, took similar advantage of their husbands' absences: One had a child while her husband was away on a three-year voyage.[67] Men could be brazen in telling of their adultery, perhaps believing they were immune from punishment and that their wives would not divorce them. One example was the husband of Jane Lamphear, who boasted that since he had left his wife "he had Carnal knowledge of more than two hundred women."[68] In another case, Olive Seaton versus her husband Rufus, a neighbor reported that

---

[61] Ibid., 278.
[62] Cott, "Divorce," 599.
[63] Cohen, "'To Parts of the World Unknown'," 279.
[64] Ibid., 275.
[65] Ibid., 278.
[66] Ibid., 280.
[67] Ibid., 281.
[68] Ibid., 279.

often times when said Rufus had been absent and Return'd home, his wife would ask him where he had been. I have more than once heard said Rufus answer his said Wife, and tell her that he had been after other women which he loved better than he did her: his wife asked him where the woman lived? he said (in my hearing) that it was old Peter Hoffmans Daughter, and he had *humped* her often, and that she might help herself if she could; and furthermore I the Deponent saw the said Rufus pull out his *Penis*, and shewed it to his said Wife and said there it is, Olive, *it* has been in old Peter Hoffmans Daughter the night before last; and that if he lives, said Hoffmans Daughter should have *it* again before Saturday night.[69]

The circumstances revealed by divorce records in Connecticut and Massachusetts run the gamut of those familiar to the historian of divorce. They are skewed by the grounds that were acceptable as justifying divorce, so that there is much evidence of adultery and desertion, less of cruelty and simple incompatibility. Cruelty alone was the basis of twenty-three petitions by women in Massachusetts, but it never justified a divorce. Fifteen of the twenty-three women who alleged cruelty sought only a separation *a mensa et thoro* with maintenance, but six of these had their petitions rejected. Of all twenty-three petitions based on cruelty, in fact, nine obtained separations, three were settled by separations by mutual consent, six were dismissed, and five unresolved. Not one divorce was granted for the single reason of cruelty.[70] In Connecticut it was not much different. More than 10% of women's petitions cited verbal and physical violence, but only one woman in that colony obtained a divorce on the ground of cruelty. The unique instance was a particularly tragic case in which the husband not only assaulted his wife but also killed his own infant son as well as the wife and child of a neighbor who were visiting at the time.[71]

Over time, there seem to have been shifts in patterns of divorce petitioning that may throw light on broader social changes that help to explain the increases in divorce and predominance of women among the petitioners. In Massachusetts there was a marked increase in women's petitions from 1765, and the proportion of their petitions that included adultery charges rose dramatically. Between 1692 and 1764, 78% of men's petitions referred to adultery but only 40% of women's petitions did so. Between 1765 and 1774 these proportions rose to 94 and 50%, respectively, but in the period 1775–86, the proportion of men's petitions including adultery charges fell slightly to 91%, and women's petitions alleging adultery (alone or with other offenses) rose to 79%. The gap between men's and women's petitions in this respect thus moved from thirty-eight to forty-four and then narrowed to twelve points over these three periods. This can be interpreted as indicating a lowering of women's tolerance of their husbands' infidelity. Moreover, women had increasing success with their adultery-inclusive divorce petitions. Between 1692 and 1774, men's petitions

[69] Quoted in ibid., 280.
[70] Cott, "Divorce," 608.
[71] Cohen, " 'To Parts of the World Unknown'," 286.

were successful in 66% of cases, women's in only 49%, but from 1775 to 1786 men succeeded in 73% and women in 70%. In other words, from a position of disadvantage in respect to divorce for reason of adultery before the 1770s, women achieved in the revolutionary period a status of something approaching even-handed treatment from the divorce courts of Massachusetts.[72]

In her study of the Massachusetts divorces, Nancy Cott proposes a connection between political ideologies current in the era of the American Revolution and a more egalitarian notion of sexual justice. The rejection of British "vice" and "corruption" implied a moral regeneration and a "critique of the traditionally loose sexual standards for men of the British ruling class."[73] Such a transfer between political ideology and rhetoric on the one hand and attitudes to sexuality and the application of morality legislation on the other must remain where Cott left it, at the level of hypothesis. But there is more interesting supporting evidence from the Connecticut divorces. Cohen writes that women "imbibed the revolutionary doctrines of national rights, liberty and equality from newspapers, pamphlets, town meetings and sermons."[74] The word "tyranny," applied to marital rather than colonial oppression, appeared in some wartime and postwar petitions filed by women, and in one case, a 1788 petition by Abigail Strong, was the clearest example one could wish to find: She applied for divorce "being fully convinced that she is under no obligation to live with him [her husband] any longer or submit to his cruelty, for even Kings may forfeit or discharge the allegiance of their Subjects."[75]

The American colonies in the seventeenth and eighteenth centuries offered a divorce structure that can be described easily enough but that proves intractable to detailed analysis and explanation. The primary problem lies in the rarity of divorces outside Connecticut and Massachusetts; even in the latter colony the number of divorces in the eighteenth century is too small to make trends significant until the very end of the eighteenth century. There is little point in attempting to calculate divorce rates in any meaningful way. Even so the colonial divorces illustrate trends such as the importance of women in the population petitioning for divorces, the way in which specific grounds for divorce were used primarily by men (adultery) or women (desertion), and the increased appeal of divorce in the revolutionary and immediate postrevolutionary periods. We should note, however, that this increase took hold in Massachusetts a decade before it did in Connecticut. It could well have been that marital and sexual attitudes were affected by political ideas, but the explanation for the rise in divorces could be more banal. As the case study of English parliamentary divorces demonstrated, and as the following section on divorce during the French Revolution will also show, the mobility and family

---

[72] Cott, "Divorce," 605.
[73] Ibid., 606.
[74] Cohen, "'To Parts of the World Unknown'," 289.
[75] Ibid.

disruption brought about by war and revolution frequently provide the grounds for divorce. Under such conditions there is, to put it simply, greater scope and more occasion for absence, desertion, and adultery. Where divorce can be obtained on these grounds, it is likely that the number of divorce petitions and divorces will increase without any additional assertiveness or consciousness of rights on the part of women. For all the limitations imposed by the small number of divorces, the American colonies in the seventeenth and especially the eighteenth century provide a further example of divorce in early modern society, but they take on fuller significance not when analyzed in isolation but rather when they are placed in relation to other studies of divorce elsewhere in Western society.

7.4 France: Divorce under revolution and empire, 1792–1816

Divorce was legalized for the first time in France on September 20, 1792, during the French Revolution. As we have seen in Chapter 5, this divorce law was the culmination of a long campaign in favor of divorce that had accelerated and intensified from 1789, when all of France's traditional institutions were scrutinized and called to account. Even then, the legislators of the early period of revolution were in no hurry to legalize divorce, and it was not until the liberal Girondin phase of the revolution that divorce legislation was seriously considered. When the law was passed, within days of the proclamation of the First French Republic, it was a self-consciously revolutionary piece of legislation. Indeed, it was seen as revolutionary in the strict sense: Supporters of divorce argued that divorce was an ancient right of the French people that had been corrupted and suppressed by the medieval papacy; by legalizing divorce, the French were merely recouping another lost right.

The deliberations of the Legislative Assembly on divorce during 1792 and the passage of the law were widely reported in France. There is every reason to believe that divorce was a lively issue of discussion even before it was legalized, despite the fact that it competed for public attention with far more sensational events such as the suspension of the monarchy in August, the massacres of priests and other inmates in the prisons of Paris in September, and the Battle of Valmy, which took place the very day the divorce law was passed.[76] In fact, numbers of men and women divorced irregularly in anticipation of the law in the months before its final enactment.[77]

The possibility of divorce, then, was not an evolutionary process of legal precedents, as divorce by Act of Parliament became in England. Nor was it a

[76] On popular reactions to divorce, see James F. Traer, *Marriage and the Family in Eighteenth-Century France* (Ithaca, 1980), 123ff.
[77] There is evidence of six such illegal divorces, all of which were subsequently given legal force by the legislative assembly.

facility provided by the law yet regarded as a desperate recourse attended by shame, as divorce was elsewhere, as in Massachusetts Colony. In France the legalization of divorce was heralded by extensive advance publicity and described as a revolutionary innovation that would help to regenerate the national morality that had been corrupted during the Old Regime. The provisional *Commissaire* of le Havre described the divorce law as having been "awaited for so long by many of our fellow-citizens."[78] If the French people were not actually encouraged to divorce, neither were they discouraged. As we shall see, the divorce procedure aimed to prevent embarrassment on the part of those who wished to divorce and to facilitate divorce when it was sought in good faith and for good cause.

All of this goes far in explaining the early acceptance and ready use of divorce in France, especially during the first few years of its availability. The positive reaction, especially in the cities, might otherwise seem surprising in a country where the Catholic church had for so long been intimately integrated into all facets of social life and ideology, though less than astounding given the progress of secularization during the eighteenth century. There are no statistics on the total number of divorces granted in France under the terms of the 1792 legislation, the eleven years between September 1792 and March 1803 (when a new law was put in place). It is likely, though, that in the nine largest cities, where divorces were concentrated, there were almost 20,000 divorces over that period. Paris was by far the most significant, with some 13,200 divorces; in Lyon there were 1,049, and in Rouen 1,046 divorces under the 1792 divorce law. There were 795 divorces in Marseilles, 617 in Strasbourg, and 567 in Bordeaux.[79]

Twenty thousand divorces over a period of eleven years in nine cities with a combined population of more than a million does not seem impressive from the perspective of the late twentieth century, but in the late eighteenth century it was a fantastic figure. One has only to compare the number of divorces in England or the American colonies in the same period to appreciate this. It seems even more significant when divorces are expressed as a ratio of marriages contracted in the same period. In Paris there was one divorce for every four marriages, in Rouen one for every eight, and in Marseilles, Lyon, and Toulouse

[78] Philippe Manneville, "Les Premiers divorces au Havre," 1. Paper presented to the Société d'Etudes Normandes, 1982. M. Manneville kindly provided me with a copy of this paper.
[79] Statistics on divorce in most French cities are given in Gérard Thibault-Laurent, *La Première introduction du divorce en France sous la Révolution et l'Empire* (Montpellier, 1938), 156–7, but they must be considered only approximate. Divorce numbers given here are corrected for Paris, Rouen, and Lyon, using, respectively, Elaine Kuehn, "Emancipation or survival? Parisian women and Divorce: 1792–1804," (Paper presented to the Eighth Annual Conference, Western Society for French History, University of Oregon, Eugene, Oregon, 1980), 2; Roderick Phillips, *Family Breakdown in Late Eighteenth-Century France: Divorces in Rouen, 1792–1803* (Oxford, 1980), 44–5; and Dominique Dessertine, *Divorcer à Lyon sous la Révolution et l'Empire* (Lyon, 1981), 95.

one divorce for every ten to thirteen marriages.[80] (These are not divorce rates, it should be noted.)

Divorces were not distributed evenly throughout the period 1792–1803. With few exceptions, all localities where divorce has been studied showed a concentration of divorces in the first two or three years, with a lower level of divorce in subsequent years. In Rouen, for example, the first three twelve-month periods saw 108, 185, and 191 divorces granted, respectively, an annual average of 161 divorces. But from 1795 to 1803 the average fell to 67 a year. Divorces in the first triennium accounted for almost half of all divorces granted during the eleven-year life span of the 1792 legislation, and the same effect has been noted elsewhere.[81] In Le Havre more than half of the divorces decreed during the revolutionary period were obtained during these first years.[82] The major exception was Lyon, where the number of divorces declined from 180 in the first twelve-month period (September 1792–September 1793) to 83 in the second. This was surely a result of the siege of Lyon in 1793; it has been estimated that by May 1794 the combined effects of war and migration had cost Lyon one-fifth of its population of 120,000.[83] The conditions of military conflict and political and social chaos must have disrupted this and other aspects of personal and social behavior.

The trend in divorces in several French cities and towns is shown in Figure 7.2, which clearly demonstrates the high numbers of divorces in the first years and their subsequent decline. The early peak in the graph of divorces in France did not, however, represent the sudden collapse of existing marriages under the impact of revolutionary upheaval. Nor did it represent the influence of radical revolutionary ideologies hostile to marriage and the family, although a persistent line of argument in reactionary historiography has associated the high levels of divorce with the social disruptions of the Jacobin regime, and the decline in the number of divorces with the putative social and political stability of the Thermidoreans and Directories from 1794 onward.[84] Rather than divorces reflecting changes in dominant political groupings and administrations, they obeyed a dynamic that reflected the discontinuity of divorce legislation in France. The surge in divorces in the early years represented the release of a reservoir of potential divorces that had, of course, been prevented from being realized until divorce was made legal. Nothing more graphically illustrated the inadequacy of *séparations de corps et d'habitation* of the Old Regime than the flood of divorces after 1792 that replaced the mere trickle of separations up to that year: In Rouen, for instance, there were 5 separations in

---

[80] See marriage statistics in Phillips, *Family Breakdown*, 4. Ratios of divorces: marriages give only a rough comparative guide and do not constitute a divorce rate in any meaningful sense since those forming and those dissolving marriages draw on distinct constituencies.

[81] Phillips, *Family Breakdown*, 44–51.

[82] Manneville, "Les Premiers divorces au Havre," 3.

[83] Renée Fuoc, *La Réaction thermidorienne à Lyon (1795)* (Lyon, 1957), 23.

[84] See, for example, Marcel Cruppi, *Le Divorce pendant la Révolution, 1792–1804* (Paris, 1909), 66.

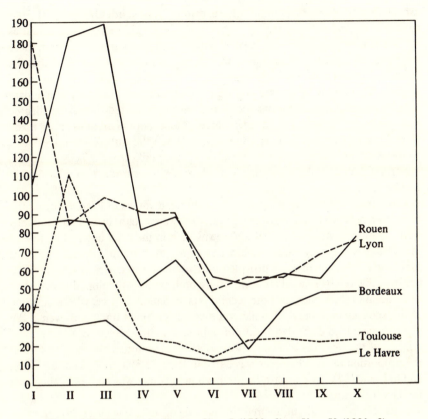

Figure 7.2 Divorces in France, Year I (1792–3) to Year X (1801–2).

1791, 3 in 1792 (January to September), but 108 divorces in the twelve months from September 1792. Significantly many of the early divorces were granted for reason of desertion or absence going well back into the Old Regime. In Rouen, Marie Piedeleu, a sixty-six-year-old woman, divorced her husband in December 1792: He had left home to go on military service more than thirty years earlier during the Seven Years' War. Sixteen days after her divorce, Marie Piedeleu married a man who was living at the same address as she.[85] Her divorce and remarriage evidently put on a legal footing an arrangement that might itself have predated her divorce by decades. No doubt many of the early divorces in France from 1792 served a similar purpose.

Once the initial backlog of potential divorces had been transformed into legal dissolutions, though, the number of divorces declined. It is in this sense that the rise and fall in divorce numbers reflected a dynamic peculiar to the discontinuity of divorce law. A sudden surge in divorces is what we might

[85] Phillips, *Family Breakdown*, 48.

259

expect in any Western country where divorce was suddenly legalized after having been prohibited, especially when the initial legislation was as liberal as the French law of 1792. In the case of France in the revolutionary period, there were peculiar social and ideological factors at play too. It could well be that the campaign of dechristianization pursued by the Jacobin government lowered religious inhibitions to divorce and that the socially and politically reactionary policies of the Thermidoreans and Directories contributed to making divorce less popular. (Procedural changes under these administrations also made divorce more expensive.) It is impossible to trace the diffuse effects of such factors with any precision, but overall, the sociopolitical influences were less important than the inherent dynamic produced by the introduction of divorce in 1792.

Apart from the uneven distribution over time, divorces in France during the revolution had two prime characteristics: Most were sought by women, and they were far more common in cities and towns than in the rural areas. The first of these traits emerges from an examination of the most frequently used grounds for divorce. The law of 1792 provided for two broad categories of divorce. The first was divorce by mutual consent, where both spouses petitioned jointly for a dissolution of their marriage; the second was unilateral divorce, where only one of the spouses petitioned. A unilateral divorce remained unilateral even if the other spouse (the defendant) did not oppose the divorce action. Generally, a quarter of the divorces in France were obtained by mutual consent. In Rouen the proportion of such divorces was 24%, in Paris 25.5%, in Le Havre 23.5%, and in Lyon 22%. By contrast, the proportion in Nancy was only 14% (between January 1793 and 1795).[86]

Little can be said about divorces by mutual consent. The cases did not come before a court but before a private family assembly that had the obligation of attempting to reconcile the couple concerned. In most divorces by mutual consent the spouses were living apart at the time the petition was filed, indicative that these divorces were primarily means of giving existing de facto separations a legal form. One Rouen example indicated the nonchalance with which this type of divorce might be undertaken. Edme Herard, a war invalid, and his wife Anne Barrouin, appeared before the civil registrar in April 1793 and explained that "having been apart from each other for ten years or thereabouts, having no fixed abode, and having met by chance in this town, they have filed a petition with the District Court of this town to authorize them to lodge a petition for a divorce by mutual consent."[87]

Even in these cases, where both spouses petitioned jointly for divorce, there

[86] Rouen: Phillips, *Family Breakdown*, 55–6; Paris: Kuehn, "Emancipation or Survival?" 6; Le Havre: Manneville, "Les Premiers divorces," 5; Lyon: Dominique Dessertine, *Divorcer à Lyon*, 160; Nancy: Geneviève Ducrocq-Mathieu, "Le Divorce dans le district de Nancy de 1792 à l'an III," *Annales de l'Est* 3 (1955), 211.

[87] Archives départementales de la Seine-Maritime (hereafter ADS-M), Etat-civil (divers): Actes préliminaires de divorces, Division 1, April 9, 1793.

is evidence that women were more likely than their husbands to have taken the initiative in pressing for divorce.[88] But it is among the unilateral divorce actions that the dominance of women as petitioners is unambiguous. Women consistently petitioned for two-thirds to three-quarters of divorces in French cities and towns. In Paris the petitions for divorce filed by women accounted for 74% of the unilateral petitions. In Rouen the figure was 71%, in Metz 73%, in Toulouse 64%, in Nancy (1793–95) 71%, and in Le Havre 72%. Toulouse apart, the consistent concentration of proportions between 70 and 75% is quite remarkable.[89]

The predominance of women among the divorce petitioners is most notable in particular categories of divorce. Tables 7.4 and 7.5 present the figures for Rouen. Table 7.4 gives the distribution by sex of petitioner among the various types of unilateral divorce; Table 7.5 provides a breakdown according to the seven specific grounds for divorce under the 1792 legislation.

Although women dominated almost all of the individual categories of divorce in both tables, they were markedly more prominent in those founded upon matrimonial offenses such as ill-treatment and desertion or absence. The only category where men outnumbered women was in divorces based on "notorious immorality," where fourteen men and twelve women initiated petitions. The same general effect of women being a majority of petitioners, and especially in cases of specific grievances such as ill-treatment and absence, is found in other local studies. And similarly, divorces for reason of immorality were the main exception elsewhere too: In Paris such divorces were equally sought by men and women, although the numbers involved were very small – there were only 8 such divorces among 495 reconstructed unilateral divorces in the capital.[90]

It is not difficult to explain the preponderance of women petitioners for divorce. In eighteenth-century society men were more mobile and more likely to desert or to be absent, leaving their wives at home to fend for themselves and their children. When divorce was legalized, it was these women who were able to take advantage of it and have their status put on a formal basis. Even when there was no desertion or absence and a couple lived together, it was the wife

---

[88] In Rouen, for example, when a unilateral divorce was converted to a petition by mutual consent, it was the wife who more often had lodged the original petition. In this sense the husband was the secondary petitioner, following his wife's initiative. Similarly, in instances where one of the spouses withdrew from a joint petition, it was more often the husband, showing the wife to be more determined to obtain a divorce. See Phillips, *Family Breakdown*, 57.

[89] Paris: Kuehn, "Emancipation or Survival?" 3; Rouen: Phillips, *Family Breakdown*, 56; Metz: Jean Lhote, "Le divorce à Metz sous la Révolution et l'Empire," *Annales de l'Est* 5ᵉ serie, 3 (1952), 175; Toulouse: Simone Maraval, "L'Introduction du divorce en Haute-Garonne (1792–1816): étude de moeurs révolutionnaires," (Mémoire de Diplôme d'Etudes Supérieures, Toulouse, 1951), 70; Nancy: calculated from Ducrocq-Mathieu, "Le Divorce dans le district de Nancy," 221; Le Havre: calculated from Manneville, "Les Premiers divorces," 10.

[90] Elaine Kuehn kindly provided me with the provisional results of her reconstruction of the Paris divorce records. Of 962 divorces for which some records exist, there is adequate information for analysis of 677. Of these, 182 were by mutual consent, 369 were petitions by women and 126 by men.

7 The use of the early divorce laws

Table 7.4. *Sex of petitioning spouses in unilateral divorces (1792 law)*

Grounds for divorce	Women	Men	Total
Incompatibility	210 (69%)	95 (31%)	305
Specific Grounds	234 (77%)	71 (23%)	305
Décret 4 Floréal Year II	113 (68%)	54 (32%)	167
(6 months separation)			
Converted *séparation de corps*	8 (57%)	6 (43%)	14
Totals	565 (71%)	226 (29%)	791

Source: Roderick Phillips, *Family Breakdown in Late Eighteenth-Century France: Divorces in Rouen, 1792–1803* (Oxford, 1980), 56.

Table 7.5. *Sex of petitioning spouses: Divorces on specific grounds (1792 law)*

Grounds for divorce	Women	Men	Total
Insanity	1	2	3
Conviction	21	6	27
Ill-treatment	64	3	67
Immorality	12	14	26
Desertion (2 years)	36	25	61
Absence (5 years)	71	16	87
Emigration	13	—	13
Other (more than one ground or ground unknown)	16	5	21
Totals	234	71	305

Source: Phillips, *Family Breakdown*, 57.

who was the more likely to be dissatisfied with the marriage. Women were placed, legally, socially, and economically, in a subordinate position, often dependent on their husbands. Married women were subject to violence in the form of "moderate correction" (*correction modérée*) by their husbands. Insofar as this "correction" was viewed as an obligation on the husband to punish his wife for a misdemeanor or to guide her back to her marital duties, women had little or no recourse in law against ill-treatment during the Old Regime unless it was tantamount to attempted murder.

During the revolution assault on a woman was made a criminal offense subject to severe penalties – a maximum of a fine of a thousand *livres* (the average working-man's daily wage was one *livre*) and a year in prison, double the punishment applied in cases where it was a man who had been assaulted. But the courts were reluctant to proceed on a married woman's complaint against her husband's violent behavior. In a 1796 case in Rouen, for instance, a woman was told by the *Tribunal de Police Correctionnelle* that as she "is under the authority [*puissance*] of her husband, is not divorced and has not started divorce proceedings" she was unable to prosecute her husband for beating her.[91] The woman in this case lodged a divorce petition within a week, and the example is not only illustrative of the limited range of options available to abused women but also indicates why women, in particular, benefited from the ability to obtain a divorce. It goes far in explaining why women dominated the lists of divorce petitioners throughout urban France.

The divorce court records of the revolutionary period provide a unique window on domestic life and marital stresses in the eighteenth century. They allow us to draw some conclusions about the familial and social pressures on married couples, although we must constantly bear in mind that the evidence is, by the nature of its provenance, skewed in the direction of stress, tension, and conflict.

The fact of male superiority within marriage, even if it is banal, is an important theme that can be considered universal, present in marriages other than those that faced the scrutiny of the divorce courts. The dominance of the husband in the home took many forms, of which physical violence was only the least subtle and most visible and audible. The case of Marie Vasse is exemplary of the ill-treatment described in evidence before the divorce courts of the French Revolution. In May 1793 her husband

without reason or excuse...seized the fire shovel which was by the chimney, and dealt his said wife three blows with it, hurled himself upon her like a madman, dealt her various blows to the head and to the body, threw her to the ground, and tore at her hair while she was on the ground, while threatening to break her arm or leg if she should have the misfortune to cry out.[92]

More subtle forms of male dominance – now referred to as mental or emotional cruelty – included controlling a wife's physical movements by forbidding her to see or make contact with her family, by locking her in her home, or by the contrary action of evicting her from the house, leaving her to find such refuge as she could with neighbors, friends, or family. Men displayed their domestic superiority by destroying their wives' property or by selling it to finance gambling or drinking. It is indicative of the husband's overall control of the family's economy and material goods that women, leaving home because of ill-treatment or being evicted, would make a public demonstration that they were taking nothing with them. One witness in a Rouen divorce case testified of Marie Causse, ordered by her husband to leave home, that "when leaving the house she turned out her pockets to show that she was taking nothing from her husband's

[91] Phillips, *Family Breakdown*, 111.
[92] ADS-M, LP 7098, Tribunaux de famille (June 4, 1793). The complete text of this petition and judgment is given in Phillips, *Family Breakdown*, 204–6.

house."[93] Women who left home, whether voluntarily or involuntarily, had to petition the courts in order to retrieve such basic personal possessions as their clothes and bedding. Obviously not all marital relationships were characterized by conflict of these kinds. But when they were, it is clear that women, in a position of legal, economic, social – and in the most direct sense, physical – inferiority were more likely than men to be the victims of violence and oppression, and were therefore more likely to take the decision to dissolve the marriage by divorce.

This aspect of male–female relations within the family provides a sort of historical continuity. So does the greater mobility of men and their predisposition to desert their wives, although this form of behavior tends to be more sensitive than masculine violence to prevailing social and economic conditions. For example, the desertions and absences recorded in divorces in Rouen reflected the depression that struck the Norman textile industry from the mid-1780s. The Parlement of Normandy estimated that by 1788 some 2,000 unemployed men had left the region in search of work, many of them no doubt married.[94] Some of those who stayed demonstrated in front of the city hall in 1788, demanding "work or bread for themselves, their wives, and their children."[95] In other towns, local economic conditions were similarly reflected in absence and desertion. In the English Channel port of Le Havre more than half the men who were described as "absent" in divorce petitions had occupations linked to the navy or merchant marine: ships' captains, sailors, and ships' carpenters, for example. An illustrative case was that of Marie Viard, whose husband

embarked at this port as a sailor on board the ship *le Double Louis*, with Colombel as her captain, destined for the island of Port au Prince and the coast of Santo Domingo, and he disembarked at the said place of Port au Prince on the 3 September 1773, and that since that time he has not reappeared in this town.[96]

The specific conditions of the French Revolution also impinged on marriage in various ways. It is often speculated that major social upheavals, such as revolution and war, produce instability in the family. This can be discussed at a general social level but it is impossible to verify the impact of diffuse social phenomena at the level of the individual marriage. The wars between France and the other European powers, which broke out in early 1792, did have a discernable impact on marriages, but it was not the wars themselves or social disruption that accounted for the marital stresses that led to divorce. Rather it was primarily the fact that war gave men an opportunity to leave home, in effect to

---

[93] Ibid., 139.
[94] G. Panel (ed.), *Documents concernant les pauvres de Rouen* (3 vols., Paris, Rouen, 1917), II, 242–3.
[95] Letter of December 13, 1788, from the municipality of Rouen to Jacques Necker, Director-General of Finance, quoted in Panel, *Documents*, II, 260.
[96] Manneville, "Les Premiers divorces," 6.

desert their wives and families, and provided both husbands and wives the opportunities to commit adultery. It was, then, the mobility associated with war that was the crucial variable, as was seen in the case of English parliamentary divorces earlier, with their disproportionately high representation of military men among the petitioners.

When military conscription was introduced in France in 1793, it affected only unmarried men, but even so it is clear that many married men did answer the call to arms, and that in some cases they did so as much in order to leave home and family as to serve the republic. In Rouen one Louis Poussolle jumped the gun and volunteered in 1792: "citizen Poussolle...without telling [his wife]...left her, two days passed and, making enquiries as to what had happened to him, she learned that he had signed up to go on military service on the frontiers."[97]

On the other hand, some divorces were provoked by adultery committed by women while their husbands were on active service. (This is the French side of the English phenomenon discussed earlier.) In the twentieth century there was a similar effect after each world war and then, as in revolutionary France, it was the women who were generally the defendants in divorce cases, as men's adultery while away was far less readily demonstrable. In some instances in the French case, pregnancy was the evidence of sexual infidelity, such as the case of one Marie Gruchy who bore two children while her husband was away for two years in the army, and was pregnant with a third at the time of his return home. The husband sued for divorce. During the trial, the neighborhood baker testified that he had asked Gruchy who was responsible for her pregnancies, and that she had replied "it is my husband who is away serving the Republic; he sends them to me in a letter."[98]

Adultery, desertion, and absence happen at any time, provoked by personal whims, crises, and marital difficulties; this is clear from divorce material in disparate localities over time. But it is also evident that the circumstances of revolution and war provided more opportunities for them, even if it is unlikely that they increased any predisposition toward their occurrence. Divorces in late eighteenth-century France, in fact, dealt with universal domestic circumstances. There were few exceptions. One was a divorce in Rouen that revealed that a former noble (a widow), fearing arrest during the Terror, had married a man she described as "a decent commoner citizen" to demonstrate her civic mindedness and adherence to the egalitarian principles of the revolution. Once the Terror was over, she divorced him, "seeing in him only a commoner whom she regretted having married."[99]

The major category of divorces that had an explicit link to the French

---

[97] ADS-M, LP 7098, Tribunaux de famille (July 1, 1793), cited in Phillips, *Family Breakdown*, 151.
[98] ADS-M, LP 6760, Tribunaux de famille (15 vendémiaire Year 1V/October 7, 1795), quoted in Phillips, *Family Breakdown*, 130.
[99] Ibid., 2–3.

Revolution were those justified by emigration, which was a political crime carrying a mandatory death penalty. Just as a former noblewoman might demonstrate her political reliability by marrying a commoner, so might the wife of an émigré by divorcing her husband. And there were additional benefits in such cases. Ex-noblewomen divorced from émigrés were spared the penalties normally imposed on ex-nobles. Divorce was also a means to preserve family property. The land and possessions of émigrés were subject to confiscation and sale by the state, but a woman who divorced an émigré could retain the property as her own as part of the divorce settlement. It is clear that many divorces involving émigrés were fictive, devices designed to preserve aristocratic patrimonies, and in some cases the divorced spouses remarried each other after the revolution when it was safe for the émigré to return to France. Remarriages of this sort reunited six out of thirteen émigré couples in Metz, but only two of the fourteen in Rouen.[100] By no means, then, should all divorces of émigré husbands be regarded merely as ways of salvaging life and property from the revolution; many, it is clear from the evidence, were justified by circumstances of marital unhappiness.

Truly revolutionary divorces, those with direct connections to the political and social conditions of the revolution, were few. The great majority of divorces in France between 1792 and 1803 were rooted in definably domestic contexts that were probably little different from those in contemporary England and America. The different incidence of divorce might well have been influenced by the secularizing and dechristianizing policies of revolutionary regimes, but it is likely that the far greater incidence of divorce in France can be accounted for by the much more liberal divorce legislation in force from 1792.

There were, in fact, practically no institutional barriers to divorce in France. Not only was the range of justifying grounds all-inclusive, but the procedure in all cases was inexpensive and relatively informal, and men and women were placed on the same footing with respect to divorce. The procedure varied according to the motive for divorce. In the case of petitions based on a matrimonial offense, the spouses had to put together a family court (*tribunal de famille*) composed of their relatives or, if relatives were not available, of neighbors or friends.[101] Each spouse was required to nominate two family arbitrators (*arbitres de famille*), but if one of the spouses (the defendant) refused to cooperate, then a judge of the local district court would name arbitrators for him or her. The arbitrators established themselves as a court, listened to the spouses and questioned them, and also took evidence from any witnesses the spouses wanted to call. Finally the *arbitres de famille* brought down a verdict as to whether the petitioner had proved the matrimonial offense alleged, and on this

---

[100] Lhote, "Le Divorce à Metz," 176; Phillips, *Family Breakdown*, 85–6.
[101] On the *tribunaux de famille* and their operation see James F. Traer, "The French Family Court," *History* 196 (1974), 211–28; Phillips, *Family Breakdown*, 17–34; and Roderick Phillips, "Tribunaux de famille et assemblées de famille à Rouen sous la Révolution," *Revue historique de droit français et étranger* 58:1 (1980), 69–79.

basis the petition was granted or refused. The judgment of the family court had to be countersigned by a district court judge to ensure that it conformed to the terms of the law; the family arbitrators were, after all, not professional judges or legally trained men, but nominated because they were related to the parties in the divorce suit, or were their friends. If the family court agreed that the petition was justified and it was countersigned by a judge, then the successful petitioner had only to take the judgment to the municipal official who recorded births, marriages, divorces, and deaths, to have the divorce registered. The entire procedure could take as little as a week, though the actual time depended on the speed of the arbitrators in dealing with the case, the number of witnesses to be heard, and the extent of the defendant spouse's cooperation: There was provision for an appeal against the judgment of a family court.

The aim of the French legislators in setting up the family courts was to provide cheap, rapid, and intimate justice in family matters. (They were established in 1790, before divorce was legalized, and had been given competence in disputes among family members, guardians and wards, and others having a familial relationship; most disputes heard by them dealt with successions.) It had been intended that these courts should exclude professional lawyers, but in practice such men were often appointed as "friends," probably because the parties in disputes thought that a lawyer would be more effective in representing their position and interests than a relative untrained in the law. Even so, the family courts carried out their functions conscientiously and proved anything but a barrier to divorce. One of their obligations was to reconcile the spouses who appointed them, and although in none of the cases in Rouen was conciliation successful, at least the attempts were made. In some cases the family courts postponed their proceedings in order to give the couple a chance to resolve their differences.

Such was the procedure in divorces based on matrimonial fault, where there were accusations, defenses, and evidence to be evaluated. When a divorce petition was lodged jointly by the wife and husband (that is, a divorce by mutual consent), a family assembly (*assemblée de famille*) was convoked. Each spouse nominated three members (called *témoins*), who could be their relatives, friends, or neighbors.[102] The couple and their *témoins* met in assembly, where attempts were made at reconciliation. The law prescribed that the two spouses would declare that they wished to divorce and that "the relatives or friends assembled would make the observations and representations to them which they thought appropriate."[103] If the attempt at reconciliation failed, the family assembly would draw up a declaration to this effect. After a delay of at least one month, the couple had simply to present this declaration to the registrar of births, marriages, divorces, and deaths, who entered the divorce in his register and declared the couple divorced.

---

[102] On *assemblées de famille* see Phillips, *Family Breakdown*, 34–42, and Phillips, "Tribunaux de famille."

[103] Divorce law of September 20, 1792, Titre II, article 4.

7 The use of the early divorce laws

In the case of divorce for reason of incompatibility of temperament, the procedure was essentially the same, but differed with respect to the length of the procedure. Because this type of divorce was unilateral, and could be a simple repudiation in that no evidence needed to be produced and no matrimonial offenses proved, the procedure was made more demanding than in cases where the two spouses were agreed on the desirability of a divorce. When a divorce was based on alleged incompatibility, the petitioner had to convoke a family assembly not just once, but three times, during a six-month period. The members of the assembly were required to try to dissuade the petitioner from his or her intention, and the longer time scale was designed to give greater opportunity for a change of mind. If the petitioner persisted, however, and three declarations of the assembly's failure to conciliate were drawn up, then the divorce was granted. In no case did a family assembly have the power to prevent a divorce.

Family courts and family assemblies were the divorce institutions of the first years of the 1792 divorce law in France. (The family courts were abolished in 1796, after which time divorces grounded on matrimonial offenses were heard by the regular courts.) Their purpose was not to prevent divorces: Both had to attempt to conciliate, but in the final analysis the assemblies could not stop a divorce, and the courts, which could, did not turn down a single divorce petition, at least in Rouen. The French system of divorcing was a libertarian one. There were no barriers to divorce in terms of the justifying circumstances since the divorce for reason of incompatibility of temperament, which required no proof, covered every conceivable circumstance from serious matrimonial offense to a whim on the part of the petitioner: It was a catchall category intended to protect men and women from having to describe events and circumstances in their marriages they found embarrassing. The financial obstacles to divorce, such as lawyers' fees and court costs, were minimal since the assemblies and courts were to be composed of relatives and friends. Even the inhibiting effect of formal court proceedings was reduced: The assemblies met in the municipal buildings, but family courts convened in private dwellings and in inns for the most part. The principal checks on divorce under the 1792 law were suspensive, not prohibitive: the compulsory attempts at conciliation and the length of the divorce procedure, which could be a test of the petitioner's determination to have his or her marriage dissolved.

This liberal and permissive approach should have made divorce available to a wide spectrum of the French population. Taking again the example of Rouen, a textile-manufacturing city at the end of the eighteenth century, we find that all sections of society had recourse to divorce.[104] The social spectrum of divorce petitions ranged from noblewomen to the wife of a man described as a beggar. Even so, there was a clear concentration within this spectrum. Of the female divorce petitioners whose occupations are known, almost three-quarters (72%)

---

[104] On the social range of divorced people in Rouen see Phillips, *Family Breakdown*, 89–92.

were working women, notably in the textile and ancillary occupations: spinners, some weavers, degreasers of wool, wool carders, seamstresses, and linen makers. Combined, they accounted for almost half of all women who obtained unilateral divorces. Other occupations represented at this social level were laundry women, vinegar makers, domestic servants, and day laborers.

Of the remaining 28% of women petitioners for divorce, 8% were small retail merchants of all kinds, such as fish sellers, merchant bonnet makers, or simply described as merchants (*marchandes*). Another 15% had private means (*vivant de leur revenu*), which could encompass a broad range of wealth. The number of this group was inflated by the inclusion of all the women who had divorced their aristocratic husbands on the ground of their emigration from France. The remaining few women petitioners had an assortment of occupations such as teacher and midwife.

The occupation profile of male petitioners for divorce was similar to that of the women, with a preponderance (69%) of working men among them. Occupations in the textile industries were somewhat less common, though there was an abundance of weavers, fabric printers, dyers, and stocking makers. But on the whole, the men concerned had a broader range of manual occupations than the women petitioners. The most common nontextile occupations represented were shoemakers, carpenters, and daylaborers. Men also had a greater range of nonmanual occupations, and we find not only small merchants of various kinds but also men in the higher ranks of commerce and the professions: barristers, solicitors, wholesale merchants, and entrepreneurs.

As we should expect, occupational profiles varied with the economic character of the town. Just as Rouen's divorce list was characterized by a heavy representation of textile workers, so coastal towns produced a significant representation of men and women in maritime and related occupations. In the Channel port of Le Havre they accounted for more than one-third (34%) of divorced men whose occupation can be defined: sailors, naval carpenters, captains, bureaucrats, and the like.[105] As noted earlier, more than half the men divorced in this town for reason of absence or desertion were employed in seagoing occupations.

There was a difference between those who divorced unilaterally and those who divorced by mutual consent with respect to social position measured by occupation. (We can refer only to the male occupation in joint husband – wife petitions for divorce because of a male bias in the registration that left the women's occupations seriously underrecorded.) Men involved in divorces by mutual consent included relatively few in manual occupations (57%), and those in the "small merchant" category comprised 14%. But the representation of the middle classes was substantial. Fully 21% had private means, were professionals (especially lawyers, architects, and doctors), or were engaged in substantial commercial enterprises. They were mainly manufacturers, entre-

---

[105] Manneville, "Les Premiers divorces," 11–12.

preneurs, and wholesale merchants. (In Le Havre those seeking divorce by mutual consent were generally better educated than those involved in other kinds of divorces.)[106] Perhaps mutual consent divorce was more attractive for the better-off social groups in Rouen because it avoided any hint of scandal, which might be suggested by a unilateral divorce, especially one founded on a matrimonial offense. If that were so, it suggests that divorce had a negative connotation, perhaps of shame and failure, despite the nonjudgmental way it was treated by the legislators and ideologists of the early revolution.

A simple assessment of the social groups that used divorce in Rouen, let alone France generally, is not possible. Compared to a sample of married people who did not divorce, the divorced population seemed generally representative. Neither groups captured the poorest elements of the population, who presumably coupled and uncoupled without bothering to alert the civil authorities. The overall impression is that whereas men seeking divorce had broadly the same socioeconomic profile as married men who did not divorce, the women who petitioned contained a larger proportion from the middle class and above. This result derived partly from the inclusion of wives of émigrés, but that is only part of the explanation. It is probably more important that middle-class women, women with private means or small businesses, had the financial independence to sustain the autonomous lives they might lead after divorce if they did not remarry. (We might note at this point that about one-quarter of men and women remarried after divorce; this is discussed in greater depth later in this section.)

There were criteria for independence other than finance, however. The divorced population of Rouen seems to have been predominantly child free. The existence of children in dissolved marriages can be ascertained only in cases of divorce by mutual consent because the procedure differed slightly when there were minor children who would be affected by the divorce of their parents. In such cases the one-month waiting period between a family assembly and having the divorce registered was extended to two months in order to give greater opportunity for the couple to change their minds and reconcile. Of 255 divorces by mutual consent in Rouen, 163 couples (64%) had no children, an extraordinarily high proportion.[107] (The absence of children cannot be explained by the brevity of the marriages involved; they averaged ten years in duration from marriage to dissolution, although the period of actual cohabitation might have been considerably shorter.) Of the remainder, 38 (15%) had one child, 50 (20%) had two or more children, and in 4 cases the wife was pregnant at the time of the divorce. The absence of children in divorcing couples in Le Havre was even more striking. Of thirteen couples for which information is available, twelve had no children and one couple had two.[108] The conclusion is ines-

---

[106] Ibid., 7.
[107] Phillips, *Family Breakdown*, 77–80.
[108] Manneville, "Les Premiers divorces," 10.

capable that the presence of children in a marriage acted as a powerful deterrent to divorce. (It is impossible to say whether children acted as an emotional adhesive or whether the simple presence of children and the difficulty – or impossibility – of maintaining them on a single income, deterred women who were mothers in particular from starting divorce proceedings.)

It is rather more difficult to penetrate the other factors associated with divorce in revolutionary France. The immediate circumstances such as desertion, violence, and adultery were set out graphically in the evidence recorded by the family courts and, later, the district courts. Financial independence and the absence of children clearly facilitated the use of divorce, and divorce was arguably an easy enough option (not to say a perfectly logical one) when the marriage concerned had already terminated in social terms, whether or not the spouses were living together. The search for predisposing circumstances leads to one further major finding, the association between youthfulness at marriage and subsequent divorce. In Rouen, a comparison between those divorcing and a sample of marriages that did not end by divorce indicated that men and women who eventually divorced were generally younger at marriage. Men who divorced were on average twenty-seven years old at marriage, compared to an average of thirty years among those who did not divorce. For women the ages at marriage were twenty-four years among the divorced and twenty-seven years among those not divorced. The critical difference lay among those who were married at very young ages. Fully 40% of women who were later divorced had married before reaching the age of twenty-one, a percentage twice that of women in the married but not divorced group. This association of youthfulness at marriage and divorce is often found in studies of modern divorce, and it is interesting to find it as far back as the end of the eighteenth century. (The question is further discussed in general terms in Section 14.2.)

It was noted earlier that divorce in revolutionary France had two characteristics: It was dominated by women (which has been discussed) and it was concentrated in the cities and towns of France. This urban trait is unambiguous. In the *département* of Haute-Garonne, for example, Toulouse had 374 divorces between 1792 and 1803, and the number of divorces decreased the further one went from the city, until the outlying districts of Revel and Muret each had only two divorces in the whole period.[109] It was not simply a question of the number of divorces varying according to population. In the Moselle, the city of Metz (with a population of 35,000) had 257 divorces, whereas the 8 next important towns, with a combined population of 25,000, had a total of only 80 divorces.[110] In another region, the *département* of Seine-Inférieure, the largest town, Rouen, easily had the largest number of divorces. Although it is difficult to translate absolute numbers of divorces into precise divorce rates (since the basic information of the number of married couples in the population is often not avail-

[109] Maraval, "L'Introduction du divorce," 47.
[110] Lhote, "Le Divorce à Metz," 182.

able), it seems that the divorce rate in Rouen was more than four times greater than that in the eleven communes immediately surrounding the city. In the rural areas further from the towns of Seine-Inférieure, divorce was even more rare.[111]

An explanation of the apparently greater readiness of the town and city dwellers to use divorce leads us to some of the broader questions associated with changing divorce rates, which are discussed in greater detail in the final chapter of this book. For the present it is sufficient to draw attention to the considerations that might be taken into account by a man or woman contemplating lodging a petition for divorce. He or she would have to consider the means of survival outside the marital unit. In most cases divorce would entail having to locate a new dwelling and, where the husband and wife constituted an economic unit (which was common in agricultural and artisanal enterprises), divorce would disrupt the couple's occupational pattern. Both of these concerns were more likely to affect women, since a divorced man would be more likely to remain in what had been the marital dwelling, and he would be in a better position to continue his normal occupation.

The material needs of the divorced person, and especially the divorced woman, would have been more easily satisfied in the city than in the countryside, although in neither instance should we underestimate the difficulties. But the late eighteenth-century urban economy did at least have a labor market that offered casual employment not available in the rural areas. Moreover, the city provided a far wider range of rental accommodation in tenement buildings, *chambres garnies* and *pensions*. From this perspective, it is hardly surprising to find that divorce was a less attractive proposition in the rural areas than in the towns, nor that the divorce rate should increase in proportion to the proximity of urban centers of employment and accommodation. Moreover, it is significant that where divorce did take place in the rural areas, it lost the characteristic of being dominated by women, which was so marked in the towns and cities. In Rouen some 71% of unilateral divorces were obtained by women, but only 42% of such divorces were initiated by women in the communes around the city. Such distinctions between town and country are stark reminders that all the sexually egalitarian traits of the 1792 French divorce law meant little when confronted by the social and economic dependence in which married women found themselves in their everyday lives.

The divorce law reduced this dependence by providing for alimony and child-support payments. Alimony could be granted to the financially worse-off of the divorced spouses, but it depended on the ability of the other to pay. In Rouen, alimony awards were generally in the range of two to three hundred *livres* a year, about the annual income of a manual worker, although in one case, where the former husband's assets were estimated to be 60,000 *livres*, a woman

---

[111] Urban–rural differences are discussed in Phillips, *Family Breakdown*, 92–104.

7.4 France: Under revolution and empire

was granted 3,000 *livres* a year.[112] This was considerably more than other divorced women received, but still a good deal less than the 10,000 *livres* she had requested. It is not clear how often alimony was sought and granted. It made no sense in cases where one spouse had deserted or was absent, his or her whereabouts unknown. In Rouen there are records of alimony judgments in only fourteen divorces. Two of them involved payments to men, both of which were well above the range normally awarded to women: One man was granted 775 *livres* a year, the other 2,248 *livres*. The disparity between men's and women's alimony awards reflected the inferior wage levels of women in the eighteenth century.

Payments for the maintenance and support of children were generally half the adult scale. In seven of the ten maintenance orders in Rouen, the sum was 150 *livres*, the others being for 100, 200, and 300 *livres*, respectively. Child support could depend on the age of dependent children, and was subject to time limits. For instance one father was ordered to contribute 100 *livres* a year to his daughter's education and support until she reached the age of fourteen.

The law also stipulated that the parents themselves should decide on who had custody of the children. In cases where the parents could not reach a mutually satisfactory agreement, the law provided for a division of children according to gender: The father would have custody of any sons, the mother custody of any daughters. Children under the age of seven would be looked after by the mother, but on reaching seven, sons would be turned over to their father's care.

In some cases there was conflict over custody, as one parent argued that the other was unfit to look after a child or children. An example was a court bailiff, Nicolas Bernard, who declared that he should be granted custody of his daughters and agreed to "give them all the care a father owes his children." When this was contested by his wife, who wanted custody of the two youngest children, Bernard objected that

the little care that his wife has had until now for her children by letting them go to bed without undressing, by neglecting to comb their hair or dress them properly, is the main reason for his opposition to her having responsibility for any of the children.[113]

(Sentiments such as these throw a contrary light on the common historical view that parents had a callous attitude toward their children.) In the end the family court gave Bernard's wife custody of their six-year-old daughter, but Bernard

---

[112] Alimony, child support, and custody arrangements are dealt with in ibid., 165–75.

[113] Quoted in ibid., 172. It is possible that the division of children by gender specified by the 1792 law – that sons should live with their father, daughters with their mother – reflected practice with respect to orphaned children. It has been noted that when Robespierre's mother died the children were farmed out among their relatives, the girls going to their aunts, the boys (Maximilien and Augustin) going to their grandfather. Joseph I. Shulim, "The Youthful Robespierre and His Ambivalence toward the Ancien Régime," *Eighteenth Century Studies* 5 (1971–2), 399.

secured the right to see her every week and to supervise her education and upbringing. No consistent general rules seem to have been applied in cases where custody was at issue. The fitness and ability of each parent was considered, although some courts maintained that a young child needed maternal care – an assumption implicit in the divorce law's provisions. In most cases of divorce, as we have seen, there were no children involved, and even when there were, in circumstances of desertion or absence there was no debate over custody. Apart from the few examples of contested custody, parents either agreed voluntarily to acceptable arrangements or applied the gender formula specified by the law.

Arrangements for custody and child support, together with provisions for alimony, must have facilitated divorce and for women in particular lowered the barrier to divorce that economic dependence could be. It was a measure of the relative economic independence of men and women divorced in France that few of them remarried. They seem not to have been subject to the economic pressures that would compel them rapidly to reconstitute a married unit. In Rouen slightly more than one-quarter (28%) of divorced men and one-quarter (25%) of women had married again in the city by 1820. (Divorced between 1792 and 1803, they would have had between twenty-eight and seventeen years to remarry by 1820.) In Le Havre remarriage rate was even lower: 9% of divorced men and 6% of divorced women.[114] These are minimal rates since people divorced in Rouen might have remarried elsewhere in France: The marriage registers of Rouen from 1793 onward include divorcé(e)s from Paris, Lyon, and Avignon, as well as elsewhere in Normandy. Despite these qualifications the rates of remarriage of divorced men and women in revolutionary France were far lower than modern rates of remarriage and, significantly, lower than the contemporary remarriage rates for widows and widowers. One might expect divorced men and women to have been more likely to remarry, if only because they were younger: On average, men were about thirty-nine, women about thirty-six years old at the time of divorce. Apart from this, divorcé(e)s were less likely to feel certain pressures to contract another marriage. As we have seen, they were characteristically without children, and even when there were children, the provision for alimony and maintenance payments would have lightened the financial burden and thus reduced the need to remarry. It is possible, too, that divorced people were reluctant to enter a new marriage simply because of their experience of the first. But the fact that this deters only a small percentage of modern divorcé(e)s from remarriage should indicate that this is not a very important factor.

Finally, there is the possibility that divorce without remarriage was a compromise by the French that made divorce acceptable within a Catholic context. When the bishop of Rouen was asked in 1792 about the church's attitude to divorce, he replied that the legalization of divorce should not in itself be con-

[114] Manneville, "Les Premiers divorces," 15–16, 18.

demned, but that priests should advise the faithful who divorced not to remarry in the lifetime of their former spouse.[115] It is possible, then, that Catholics used divorce as a kind of separation (separations had been abolished by the law that legalized divorce) in order to regularize their marital status and property ownership, in a manner not wholly repugnant to the Catholic church. Such hopes were in vain, for the French Catholic church took a rigorous view of civil marriages and divorces obtained during the revolutionary period.

But the liberal 1792 divorce law was objectionable not only to the church; its permissiveness and the flood of divorces it was blamed for provoking were unacceptable to secular politicians as well. Even so, years of parliamentary debate from 1794 onward failed to produce anything more than some changes in procedure, and it was not until 1803 that a new divorce law replaced that of 1792. The new legislation, part of the general revision of French law that resulted in the great Napoleonic Code, made divorce much more difficult to obtain. The number of specific grounds for divorce was reduced from seven to three (certain serious criminal convictions, adultery, and ill-treatment). Divorce by mutual consent was maintained, but the ground of incompatibility was suppressed. Divorce was made more difficult in procedural terms, more expensive, and a double standard of sexual morality was introduced: Women could be divorced for simple adultery; men could be divorced only when they had committed adultery in the marital dwelling.

The result of the legal changes was a dramatic decline in the number of divorces. In Rouen the annual average fell from sixty-seven divorces in the period 1795–1803, to six divorces under the Napoleonic divorce law. In Lyon, divorces averaged eighty-seven annually in the revolutionary period, but only seven during the empire.[116] Despite the sexual inequality of the Napoleonic law, women continued to dominate the divorce lists, however, notably in those actions based on criminal conviction and ill-treatment. But they were well outnumbered in divorces based on adultery. The figures for Rouen are given in Table 7.6.

Women, it will be noted, petitioned for 71% of divorces under the 1803 law, precisely the same percentage as under the 1792 divorce legislation. But if the proportion of women's petitions remained constant, the total number of divorces plummeted dramatically. The restrictions imposed by the Napoleonic law effectively deprived sixty men and women in Rouen and eighty in Lyon of divorce annually. These were not staggering numbers in absolute terms, but they were significant enough in relation to the prevailing divorce rates. Napoleonic legislation reduced divorce, as a remedy to marriage breakdown or as a response to a matrimonial offense, to a pale shadow of the facility afforded by the revolutionary law of 1792. Even this pale shadow faded entirely, however, when in 1816 the restored monarchy suppressed divorce (see Chapter 11).

[115] See Phillips, *Family Breakdown*, 197.
[116] Dessertine, *Divorcer à Lyon*, 95.

275

Table 7.6. *Sex of petitioners in divorces on specific grounds (1803 law):*
Rouen 1803–16

Grounds	Women	Men	Total
Ill-treatment	26	3	29
Conviction	24	1	25
Adultery	1	13	14
Unstated	4	5	9
Totals	55 (71%)	22 (29%)	77 (100%)

Thereafter, marriage breakdown in France was once again translated only into judicial separations, rather than into divorce, until 1884, when divorce was once again legalized.

7.5 Conclusion

We can draw several broad conclusions from these case studies of the use of divorce in three different jurisdictions (treating the American colonies as one, for the present purpose). The most striking characteristic must surely be the importance of divorce legislation in heavily influencing, if not determining, the contours of divorce behavior. The limitations that laws imposed on the grounds that could justify a dissolution of marriage, the restrictions of costs, and complexity of procedures, all had their impact on the simple number of divorces. This is clear when we compare the case of England with those of America and France. There were fewer divorces in England (with a population of 9 million in 1800) between 1670 and 1857 than there were in Connecticut (population 250,000 in 1800) in the second half of the eighteenth century or in Toulouse (population 50,000 in 1800) during the ten years of the French Revolution. Strictly speaking, the divorce rates in the three places are not comparable because of the different age and marital distributions of their populations, yet it is incontrovertible that the divorce rates in Connecticut and Toulouse were far higher than in England. It would be absurd to suggest that the English were so much happier in their marriages than the citizens of Connecticut or revolutionary France; and it is doubtful that the incidence of marriage breakdown (as distinct from divorce or legal separation) varied much from one area to another. Indeed, if it is true that family stress and breakdown increases with urbanization, then England, far more urbanized than Connecticut or France in the eighteenth century, should have experienced a higher incidence of marriage breakdown. It seems almost self-evident that the divorce legislation in effect in each place was the most important variable in limiting the number and rate of divorces. This can be seen comparatively not only over space but also over time, in the decline of divorces in France following the introduction of restrictive legislation in 1803 to replace the liberal 1792 divorce law.

7.5 Conclusion

The sex ratio of petitioners for divorce was similarly dependent on the terms of legislation. The nondiscriminatory law of the French Revolution gave women equal access to divorce, and the predominance of women in initiating divorce actions reflected this. We should add to this factor the likelihood that women had more reason to be unhappy in marriage or (having been abandoned) to want a divorce in order to remarry. By contrast, English divorces by Act of Parliament effectively excluded women from divorcing their husbands until the nineteenth century, and even then, only 4 women, compared with 321 men, obtained divorces. The American colonies provided a middle course, discriminating against women (for example, by making it more difficult for a wife to divorce her husband for adultery than vice versa) but less emphatically than English divorce practice did.

Variables other than legislation did, needless to say, come into play. In both France and the American colonies the divorced were concentrated in urban areas rather than the countryside. This is very clear in France, less so in America because of the smaller number of divorces overall, but it is significant that more than one-quarter of Massachusetts divorce petitioners lived in Boston, even though the city contained only 6% of the colony's population.[117] Social pressure, reflecting prevalent attitudes toward divorce, must also have played a role in encouraging or deterring men and women from filing for divorce. The official attitude to divorce in France – that the divorce law was integral to the regeneration of morals and the nation after the corruption of the Old Regime – might not have encouraged divorce, but it certainly would not have inhibited it either. A more positive attitude to divorce in Connecticut has been proposed as part of the explanation for the greater incidence of divorce there than in Massachusetts, but such variations in social attitudes are difficult to verify. The key to the larger number of divorces in Connecticut seems to have been the acceptance there of simple desertion (rather than desertion as an offense aggravating adultery) as a ground for divorce. It could be argued, of course, that the more liberal divorce provisions in Connecticut, compared to Massachusetts, reflected more tolerant attitudes in the former colony. But in the final analysis, factors such as public opinion or social attitudes remain less certain, less susceptible of proof and analysis, than variables such as the terms of divorce legislation and its application.

Apart from these more general issues, the three case studies throw light on some common aspects of marriage and divorce.[118] One was the impact of social

---

[117] The fact that divorce actions in Massachusetts had to be filed and prosecuted in Boston gave Bostonians an advantage over inhabitants of other parts of the colony. No doubt it contributed to the overrepresentation of Boston marriages before the divorce court.

[118] After this chapter was completed and in press, a study of divorces in seventeenth-century Bergen diocese (Norway) was brought to my attention by Sølvi Sogner. The profile of divorces bore a striking resemblance to those in revolutionary France and colonial Massachusetts and Connecticut. In Bergen there were some 256 divorces between 1604 and 1708, producing an annual average crude rate of about 0.25 per thousand population. Women dominated as divorce petitioners; some 72% of divorces were sought by wives. More than half the cases (142, or

disruptions like war and revolution on marriage and the family. In all three cases, the impact of mobility associated with war was translated into an increased use of divorce. This effect is perceptible elsewhere and at other times, such as following both world wars. There are also interesting common characteristics, such as the duration of marriages dissolved by divorce. Marriages dissolved by divorce in Rouen during the revolution had lasted on average 11.2 years. In Massachusetts, dissolved marriages had lasted on average 11.65 years where actions were filed by women and 10.69 years where the divorce was initiated by men. In England the 88 marriages dissolved by Act of Parliament between 1770 and 1800 had lasted on average 11.7 years. It remains to be seen whether these similar mean durations (calculated as the time between date of marriage and date of divorce) are anything more than fortuitous.

These three studies provide a fascinating insight into the use of divorce in three jurisdictions in roughly the same period and permit us to move beyond the level of legal, ideological, and institutional analysis. Unfortunately, the data in the three cases are uneven so that we are unable to make all of the comparisons we should like. It would be interesting to know whether youthfulness at marriage and relative childlessness, both characteristics of divorced men and women in France, were also traits of divorced couples in England and America. There are difficulties inherent in the analysis of divorce in earlier times, however, and paucity of data is one. The most important problem, however, is the paucity of divorces themselves (which does not imply its unimportance). Even the more than 20,000 divorces in revolutionary France pales in comparison to later nineteenth and twentieth century figures. Divorce rates, where they are worth calculating, were low. The highest divorce rate calculable in Rouen occurred in 1793: 6.2% of marriages contracted in the first nine months of that year were dissolved by divorce. In the years II and III (September 1793 to September 1795), the rates were 4.8% and 4.9% respectively. These rates, like those of Connecticut, were relatively low, but they tell us about the limitations placed on divorce by the law, by attitudes, by variables such as financial dependence, and by expectations of marriage. These factors are analyzed in greater depth in Chapters 9, 10, and 14, but these case studies provide us with an entrée to social realities of marriage and marriage dissolution that were sometimes discussed by theologians, social engineers, and legislators, but often (like the social and economic subordination of married women) overlooked by them as they debated and devised facilities for divorce.

55%) involved desertion, 70 (27%) adultery, 6 (2%) impotence, and another 38 (15%) were based on the "informal" ground of cruelty. Divorce in the diocese was concentrated in Bergen itself; 61% of the couples involved in divorce actions lived in the city. Divorce petitions generally emanated from the lower social strata. Hanne Marie Johansen, " 'At blive den tyran qvit': En studie av skilsmissesakene ved kapittelretten i Bergen, 1604–1708," *Bergens Historiske Forening Skrifter* 83–4 (1985), 7–43. Ms. Johansen very kindly sent me a copy of her article.

8

∞∞∞∞∞∞∞∞∞∞∞∞∞∞∞∞∞∞∞∞∞∞∞∞∞∞∞∞∞∞∞∞∞∞∞∞∞∞

The alternatives to divorce

8.1 Introduction

Divorce laws and policies in early modern Europe were extremely restrictive, and their general inaccessibility to the majority of people contributed to the rarity of divorces. When divorce provisions were sexually discriminatory, women were usually disadvantaged. This was most clearly the case in England, where divorce by private Act of Parliament could be obtained by men far more easily than by women: Hence of 325 divorces between 1670 and 1857, only four were obtained at the request of wives. The grounds justifying divorce could be equally inhibiting to both men and women or to one sex in particular. The classic Protestant grounds for divorce, adultery and desertion, did not make allowance for a woman to obtain legal relief when she was faced with persistent physical, emotional, or mental cruelty, nor did they provide any relief for a couple who found life together intolerable for any of a range of reasons. The notable exception was the legislation of the French Revolution, which provided for divorce based on matrimonial fault, simple incompatibility, or by the mutual consent of both spouses.

There were also material inhibitions to the use of divorce, the most obvious and immediate being the cost of proceedings. Perhaps the most extreme example was the use of private Acts of Parliament in England: The most straightforward uncontested divorce cost hundreds of pounds in the mid-nineteenth century, and more complicated actions could cost thousands of pounds. The cost of divorce in other jurisdictions cannot always be ascertained, but as the examples discussed in Section 14.3 show, even relatively modest legal and court costs often placed divorce beyond the means of most people. In contrast, the divorce provisions enacted in France in 1792 had the effect of making divorce widely accessible: The use of nonprofessional institutions such as the *tribunaux de famille* and *assemblées de famille* reduced the cost of divorce to minimal proportions.

A less tangible, but no less important, inhibition was the ability or preparedness of individuals to petition for divorce, even when they were financially able to and where their domestic circumstances fell within the purview of the prevailing divorce provisions. It is likely that in early modern society the great mass of the population distrusted the law, its institutions, and its personnel, be they the police, lawyers, or judges. Ordinary people must have perceived the law primarily as an agent of oppression and social control from above rather than as an agency toward which they might turn in times of trouble and need. There is, of course, no way of verifying such a hypothesis: The relative absence of ordinary people among petitioners and the initiators of litigation might be understood in this way, or might be explained otherwise. In the same way, the rarity of legal divorces in early modern society might be held up either as proof that divorce was difficult to obtain or that marriages were, with the most rare exceptions, perceived as satisfactory by those involved.

Common sense tells us that there must be a "dark figure" of marriage dissolution behind the legal divorces and separations, just as there is a dark figure, a hidden extent of criminality, beneath the prosecutions and convictions that judicial records reveal. It must be recognized at the very outset that the full extent of such a figure can never be ascertained, but this should not deter us from trying to penetrate the more obscure and noninstitutionalized forms of any behavior. By doing so we not only demonstrate that the legal forms constituted only one dimension of the phenomenon under discussion, but we are also made aware of the variety within a phenomenon to which institutionalization can often give an appearance of homogeneity.

This chapter examines the range of extralegal, informal means of dissolving or ending marriages in practical terms. It does not deal with the forms, catalysts, and symptoms of marital stress and breakdown, however. Informal dissolution of marriage should have some of the characteristics of divorce, notably the ending of cohabitation (ideally on a permanent basis), though it need not entail a remarriage or subsequent de facto coupling by either or both of the spouses. Under the rubric of informal divorces, then, we look at phenomena such as wife sale, mutually agreed separations, desertion, bigamy, and spouse murder.

The existence of marital stress is quite a different matter from de facto dissolution, just as marriage breakdown differs from divorce. Too often the two are confused because particular symptoms of stress may be grounds for divorce. For example, the desertion of a spouse entails the social termination of marriage, and, under many jurisdictions, it justified a legal dissolution of the marriage. Adultery, too, could justify a divorce (more commonly than desertion, in fact), but adultery in itself cannot necessarily be regarded as a form of de facto dissolution, since most marriages survive adultery by one or both spouses. Confusion in this respect probably arises because adultery, and other symptoms of stress or incompatibility, have constituted grounds for divorce. As we shall see, there are particular problems involved in defining the symptoms of marriage stress and even marriage breakdown. They are discussed in Chapter 9 in the light of such phenomena as adultery and marital violence.

Two further points should be made. First, the geographical and temporal scopes of this study present some difficulties. It is not possible to give appropriate attention to all of the phenomena in every region in order to make comparative judgments. In each case we are dependent on the existence and survival of documentary evidence for de facto dissolution, as we are for legal divorce. Variations in definition, jursidiction, enforcement, and the importance attributed to events such as desertion and the failure or refusal of spouses to live together have inevitably resulted in uneven coverage in judicial and other kinds of records. In this field, as in others, the scope of our knowledge is heavily influenced, if not dictated, by the type and content of records dating from particular periods and places.

The second point is perhaps obvious: De facto dissolution of marriage does not occur only when legal divorce is not available. Even in modern times, when divorce is far easier and far more common than ever before, some spouses choose to desert, to commit bigamy, or to kill their partners rather than have their marriages dissolved by the courts. But for the most part the kinds of behavior we shall examine here took place in societies that were effectively divorceless and before the liberalization of many divorce policies in the late nineteenth century. If divorce were available at all it was, as we have seen, on extremely restrictive terms: Grounds for divorce were limited, divorce could be expensive, and the courts were reluctant to accede to petitions. The present chapter indicates the alternatives to divorce that married men and women might take at any time, but that they were probably more likely to resort to in the period when legal divorce was effectively beyond the reach of the mass of the population.

Faced with the reality that divorce was either not available or available only at great cost or in circumstances that were not appropriate to their particular situation, what were married women and men to do when their marriages broke down or became intolerable? There are several examples from seventeenth-century England that present us with the range of options. One was the case of Mary Hobry, described as "a French midwife," who killed her husband in January 1688. The evidence she gave at her trial (published as a broadside) set out her perception of the background to the murder, and outlined the escalating remedies available in cases of marital unhappiness. Her husband, she was reported as saying, had beaten and abused her for years, and she had tried to find a solution to their difficulties:

She chose to make Tryal if she could prevail upon him to agree to a Final Separation, and pressed it upon him several times with great Earnestness; but he still refused it with Outrages of Language and Actions...finding herself without Remedy, in a Distraction of Thoughts, and under the Affliction of Bodily Distempers, contracted by her said Husband's dissolute Course of Life, her Frailty was no longer able to resist the Temptations of dangerous Thoughts; sometimes [she]...was thinking to go into some other Part of the world and leave him; and other while she was tempted to think of Extremities either upon her Husband or upon her Self; and often told her Husband plainly, That *she would kill him if he followed that course.*[1]

---

[1] *A Hellish Murder Committed by a French Midwife, On the Body of her Husband, January 27. 1687/8* (London, 1688), 31. In the same vein, see *A True Relation of Four most Barbarous Murders Committed in Leicester-shire by Elizabeth Ridgway* (London, 1684). Elizabeth Ridgway was burned for killing her mother, a fellow servant, her "sweet-heart," and her husband.

8 The alternatives to divorce

One night Mary Hobry's husband came home drunk and beat and abused her. When he was asleep, she strangled him, and later cut off his head, arms, legs, and thighs and tried to dispose secretly of the dismembered body. Her attempt to conceal the crime was unsuccessful, and Mary Hobry was tried and executed.

Killing her husband was a desperate act, the ultimate and most extreme of the remedies that she herself had outlined, namely, mutually agreed separation (which her husband had refused), desertion, suicide, and murder. Although by 1688, when this crime took place, Lord Roos had obtained the divorce by private Act of Parliament that was to be the precedent for hundreds more in the next century and a half, men and women of the Hobrys' social rank were excluded from its benefits, and had to have recourse to less formal, but often more desperate, measures to free themselves from marital misery.

A less sensational scenario was sketched in a work, also from the seventeenth century, that dealt with the question of whether polygamy was consistent with Christian doctrine. The issue was presented in the form of a debate between Telypoligamous and Ochinus, in which the former explained his marital dilemma thus:

I have a Wife not suitable to my minde, so that I cannot love her, and as far as I can perceive, she is both barren and unhealthful; and I finde my selfe so disposed, that I cannot Want [i.e., do without] the Company of a Woman: also I desire to have Children both for Posterities sake, and that I may instruct them in the fear of Gode. I could indeed keep a Concubine or two, but my Conscience will not suffer me: also I could falsly charge my wife with Adultery, so to put her away; but in so doing I should both offend God, and blemish mine own, and my wives reputation, which I will not do. I could also poyson her, which is a thing I abhorre. But a thought is come into my minde, to take another Wife, so as to keep her that I have already, notwithstanding....[2]

Polygamy as proposed here was to be legal, institutionalized, and open. It was not to be confused with a married man's keeping "a Concubine or two," as the text makes clear, nor was it to be confused with clandestine bigamy. The latter was condemned in the same work as

that base practise of certain impudent, sharking rogues, whose manner it is, to marry a Wife in one City or town, and devour her Substance, and abuse her Body, and then run away to some far distant place, and marry another leaving the first, with poverty, shame, and, it may be, a great Belly to boot...[3]

Yet the author gave no hope even for the respectable polygamy proposed by Telypoligamous. It was declared incompatible with Christianity, and in an attached work, *A Dialogue for Divorce*, even dissolution of marriage was ruled out except on the ground of adultery.

[2] Bernadino Ochino, *A Dialogue of Polygamy* (London 1657), 1–2.
[3] Ibid., sig. A7^R–A8^R.

8.2 *Informal separation*

Before examining the individual forms of informal divorce, we might note that the range of options was canvassed by Henry VIII who, for quite different reasons from the majority of married men and women, could not divorce. In the end, Henry availed himself of annulments and executions, either jointly or individually, and his third wife, Jane Seymour, obliged him by dying before Henry had to resort to other means of disposing of her.

8.2 Informal separation

In many respects, the most straightforward method of terminating a marriage socially was for the husband and wife to separate, to live in different dwellings and to lead their own lives, free of any mutual social, economic, or sexual obligations. Wives and husbands who were at least able to agree to separate informally might well have continued to live in the same or neighboring communities, something that distinguished separations from desertion where one spouse, usually the husband, left the other, often for parts unknown. Informal or de facto separation circumvented having to petition for a separation before a civil or ecclesiastical court, which had the power to refuse to let them separate. In all but the rarest cases, the secular and canon laws governing separations rested on the principle of matrimonial fault and did not encompass those marriages where the spouses were simply incompatible and could not bear each other's company.

Separation by mutual consent was not always simply a matter that concerned only the husband and wife involved, however. As with marriage, separation was a social concern and was regulated by the authorities. Separations, being informal, did not of themselves leave any written record, but fortunately for the historian, if not for the unfortunate couples in question, many legal codes required married people to live together. This obligation was enforced by the courts when infractions came to light, and prosecutions for separation or failure to cohabit indicate the existence and forms, if not the true extent, of informal separations.

In sixteenth- and seventeenth-century England, for example, the Anglican church was keen to ensure conformity in marriage matters. Only validly married couples should live together, and once married they should live together, not separately or illicitly with other partners. Local ecclesiastical authorities were encouraged to seek out offenders, and the terms of the offenses were set down in the visitation articles that accompanied the periodic examinations of individual dioceses. For instance the articles issued when John Whitgift, archbishop of Canterbury, visited the Diocese of Chichester in 1585 required the authorities to discover "whether have anie married within the forbidden degrees, consanguinitie or affinitie; any separated in that respect, do keep company still together; any lawfully married, which offensively live asunder, or which have married elsewhere; any man which has two wives, or woman two husbands. . . ."[4] Similarly the visitation articles issued when Cardinal Pole visited the diocese of Canterbury in 1557 included: "Item. Whether any have put away their wives, being not lawfully divorced?"[5]

To judge from the results of these investigations, the English were an obedient people, for although matrimonial irregularities were discovered, they were far from common. One of the better catches of marital offenses, when a visitation dragged its net through a community, was the cases presented to Bishop Redman during his examination of Norwich in 1597. There, fourteen cases were presented where the authorities alleged that individual husbands and wives refused to live together. For example, William Matthew and his wife Agnes were presented because "they kepe not together, and he have absented himselfe from her companie theis iij or iiij years last past."[6] William and Agnes were clearly unwilling to resume living together, for both were excommunicated. Another married man, Robert Crickner, was charged "for that he hath not kepte with Anne his wife by the space of theis foure yeares past, beinge lawfullie married to her." In his defense, Crickner replied "that he have not kept with her for feare of his life," but despite this, the two were ordered to resume cohabitation.[7] In a third case, the judgment in which was deferred, Richard Banye and his wife Margaret were presented on the ground that "they being married lyve asonder without divorceiment for anie thinge they know."[8] A final example is the prosecution of Thomas Draper "for that he kepeth not with his wife but remayneth with his mother, and so have contynewed a quarter of a yeare now last past."[9] Such cases are only exemplary, for we cannot know how diligent the church officials were in attempting to bring all transgressors to book. Among presentments before several late sixteenth- and early seventeenth-century visitations of deaneries in Yorkshire, Cheshire, Suffolk, and Somerset, one study found 48 cases of noncohabitation between husband and wife.[10] They constituted only a tiny proportion (2%) of the total 2,544 individual presentments analyzed, a proportion that pales against the 778 (31%) presentments for sexual immorality.

Cases of failure to cohabit were also brought before the courts in New England. In seventeenth-century Massachusetts it was an offense for a husband and wife not to live together, and the injunction was enforced in what appeared to be the most recalcitrant of cases. For example, in November 1676 Mary and Hugh Drury were brought before the Suffolk County Court where Mary was

[4] Quoted in Edward Cardwell (ed.), *Documentary Annals of the Reformed Church of England* (2 vols., London, 1844), II, 27.
[5] Ibid., I, 207 (article 27). This visitation took place during the brief revival of Catholicism in the reign of Queen Mary. "Divorced" here means "separated *a mensa et thoro*."
[6] J. F. Williams (ed.), *Diocese of Norwich: Bishop Redman's Visitation, 1597. Presentments in the Archdeaconries of Norwich, Norfolk and Suffolk* (Norwich, 1946), 52.
[7] Ibid., 43.
[8] Ibid., 52. "Divorceiment" presumably refers to separation *a mensa et thoro*.
[9] Ibid., 69.
[10] Ronald A. Marchant, *The Church Under the Law* (Cambridge, 1969), 219, Table 32.

charged with "leaving the fellowship of her husband." Each alleged that the other had been guilty of matrimonial misdemeanors, and the justices fined each of them fifty shillings and placed them under a thirty-pound bond of good behavior.[11] The following year, in July 1677, Mary Drury was again in court charged with failing to live with her husband. Although she argued that she found life with him intolerable – among other things, she alleged that he had not been able to consummate the marriage – Mary Drury was fined five pounds (double the earlier fine) and ordered to resume living with Hugh.[12] Later that year, she petitioned to the Massachusetts superior court for a divorce. But despite the evidence of incompatibility that their former convictions revealed, her petition was turned down and the court "enjoyne[d] them both to live together according to the ordinance of God as man and wife."[13]

The same court did, however, recognize mutually acceptable separations in other instances. In the case of Henry and Ellen Seawall, for example, the court recognized their "consent and desire" to order "that his saide wife shalbe att her owne disposeall, for the place of her habitacion and that her saide husband shall allowe her, her weareing app[ar]ell and...[twenty-one pounds annually] to be paide quarterly, as also a bedd with furniture to it."[14]

8.3 Desertion

The distinction between separation and desertion is frequently blurred. Just as there is a difference between a mutually agreed upon arrangement that wife and husband will live separately, so there is between one spouse's moving out of their common dwelling into a nearby house, and his or her deserting without warning to some distant place, thereby abandoning his family and responsibilities. Many of the references in court, poor law, and other records do not make it clear what sort of separation, absence, or desertion is at issue. The prosecutions for failure to cohabit cited clearly involved men and women living in the same community or in neighboring communities. It would be absurd, not to say unjust, to haul a woman into court and indict her for not living with her husband when he had deserted her and had left no forwarding address.

The simple absence of one spouse must have been a potentially quite common phenomenon. Men's occupations, in particular, led to their absenting themselves from home, often at long distances and for extended periods. Hawkers or pedlars, ships' crews, soldiers, coachmen, men involved in large-scale commerce, or those engaged in seasonal work necessitating seasonal migration, all might be absent from their homes and families for months at a

[11] *Records of the Suffolk County Court, 1671–1680* (2 vols, Boston, 1933), II, 754 (November 6, 1676).
[12] Ibid., II, 837 (July 31, 1677).
[13] *Records of the Court of Assistants of the Colony of Massachusetts Bay, 1630–1692* (ed. John Noble, Boston, 1901–28), I, 91.
[14] Ibid., II, 60.

time. For example, a traveling sieve salesman in Normandy, seeking a marriage dispensation in 1788, declared that his business required him to be absent from home eight months of the year.[15] Of those who did not return, no doubt many died while away, and the lack of systematic methods of identification meant that their families were never informed. The loss of a ship at sea might be notified only by its being long overdue. In yet other cases, however, the failure to return must have been deliberate, as a married man – it would normally have been a man – turned an intended temporary absence into a permanent one. Jewish law from the Middle Ages to World War I sought to protect women in such circumstances by a conditional divorce granted when husbands left for extended periods of time on business or military service. If the husband did not return within a specified period of time, the divorce took effect.[16] It is often impossible to distinguish between desertion and absence in such cases, and the perception of the spouse who was left behind might provide evidence only as to the absent spouse's motivation at the time of departure.

One source for evidence of desertion or absence is marriage registers that give the address of the parents of the woman and man being married. By definition such parents had been married long enough to have had a child old enough to be married, often, in fact, long enough for one of the spouses to have died. Yet there might also be reference to absence or desertion. The *état-civil* (registers of birth, marriage and divorce, and death) of revolutionary France is an example. An examination of the domiciles of parents in the marriage registers of Rouen in two sample years, Year II (September 1793 to September 1794) and Year XII (September 1803 to September 1804), showed that of the cases where both parents were still alive, a small percentage were not cohabiting. In Year II, 2%, and Year XII, 7% of couples were separated. Some spouses were living at different but known addresses in or away from Rouen, but in most of the cases of noncohabitation one of the spouses was absent, his or her address unknown. In Year XII, for example, six husbands and one wife (fathers and mothers, respectively, of women and men being married that year) were absent, their whereabouts a mystery. Notations generally took the form "absent for ten years, address unknown" or, more simply, "absent for several years."[17]

Examples such as these provide an entrée to an understanding of the extent and character of marriage termination in real terms, but they should properly be regarded as minimal. There were cases where one spouse was absent and one dead, where it was possible to ascertain that the absence of the one predated the

---

[15] Jean-Marie Gouesse, "Parenté, famille et mariage en Normandie aux XVIIᵉ et XVIIIᵉ siècles. Présentation d'une source et d'une enquête," *Annales. Economies Sociétés Civilisations* 27 (1972), 1154. On seasonal migration, see Olwen Hufton, *The Poor of Eighteenth Century France, 1750–1789* (Oxford, 1974), 69ff.

[16] Menachem M. Brayer, "The Role of Jewish Law Pertaining to the Jewish Family, Jewish Marriage and Divorce," in Jacob Fried (ed.), *Jews and Divorce* (New York, 1968), 21.

[17] Archives départementales de la Seine-Maritime, état-civil (Rouen), An II and An XII.

8.3 Desertion

decease of the other. The most striking characteristic – which was also reflected in divorces based on desertion or absence – is that men were more likely than women to be absent. Year III (1794–5) in Rouen provides a further example of this: Seven husbands were absent, two having left before the date of their wives' death, compared with one wife who had left her husband living in the city. Information on such cases is too sparse to permit any generalizations about the circumstances surrounding or provoking the absences. The men involved were drawn from occupational categories as diverse as clothier, doctor, and soldier.

The connection between absence or desertion and military service is, in fact, a strong one, and we should expect it to be so particularly in times of war. In revolutionary Rouen several of the absent husbands had gone on active service and never returned, like the man who "left this town in the tenth Seine-Inferieure battalion in October 1793,"[18] and had not returned by the time his daughter married in late 1803. No doubt some of these men were killed in action, and at least one was a prisoner of war.[19] But others doubtless chose the army as their means of escaping an unsatisfactory marriage. As we have seen, the military connection is to be found in relation to legal divorces in revolutionary France, in Geneva during the religious wars of the sixteenth century, and in England during the American and European wars of the late eighteenth and early nineteenth centuries.

Censuses, too, produce evidence of desertion, particularly among the poor. The 1570 Norwich (England) census of the poor showed that 8% of married poor women in their thirties had been deserted by their husbands; many of these women had children.[20] The information gathered by the census enumerators in two of the cases may be quoted as examples.

Jone, the wyf of a William Cayn, paynter, that was nott with hyr this 2 yeres, which Jone is of 40 yere, and spyn while warpe, and 3 childerne, 2 of them spyn, the other a yong son, and have dwelt here ever.

Elizabeth, the wyf of John Skyven, dier, of the age of 30 yeris, from whom hyr husband have ben awaye 4 yeris, and she withoute helpe of hym, and a daughter of 6 yer that go to skole, that have dwelt her ever.[21]

There was a similar finding in the 1587 census of Warwick. Of eighty-four households that were defined as poor, eleven were headed by widows, and twelve (14%) by women who had been abandoned by their husbands.[22]

Yet another source of information on desertion, this time predominantly by women, is provided by newspaper advertisements announcing that one spouse had abandoned the other. Often the purpose of these announcements was

---

[18] Ibid., Year XII, marriage 205.
[19] Ibid., Year III, marriage 129.
[20] John F. Pound (ed.), *The Norwich Census of the Poor, 1570* (Norwich, 1971), 18.
[21] Ibid.
[22] A. L. Beier, "The Social Problems of an Elizabethan Country Town: Warwick, 1580–90," in Peter Clark (ed.), *Country Towns in Pre-Industrial England* (Leicester, 1981), 60–1.

to make it clear that because a married woman had left her husband he would no longer assume responsibility for any debts she might contract. Some advertisements went so far as to detail the circumstances of the desertion:

Catherine Treen, the wife of the subscriber [advertiser] having, in violation of her solemn vow, behaved herself in the most disgraceful manner, by leaving her own place of abode, and living in a criminal state with a certain *William Collins*, a plaisterer...her much injured husband, therefore, in justice to himself, thinks it absolutely necessary to forewarn all persons from trusting her on his account, being determined, after such flagrant proof of her prostitution, to pay no debts of her contracting.[23]

A study by Herman Lantz of such advertisements announcing desertion or the renunciation of responsibility for debts, located almost 3,500 examples from a survey of eighteenth-century American newspapers.[24] The survey included only about half of the newspapers being published at that time, and Lantz suggests that one could project a total of about 7,500 such advertisements in the eighteenth century. For crude statistical purposes he treated these advertisements as if they were divorces and calculated an "index of marital incompatibility" by expressing the number of advertisements found in each colony or state in terms of its population. Lantz found, for example, that there were 994 advertisements (and slightly more again projected) in Pennsylvania, giving a rate of 0.09 per thousand of population. The rates varied from a high of 0.15 advertisements per thousand of population in Ohio, to none per thousand in Virginia (where only 31 advertisements were located in the period from 1770 to 1799).[25]

The value of such statistics, particularly comparative statistics among states, is as debatable as comparative divorce rates. Divorce rates vary according to various criteria, but especially according to the character of divorce provisions, such as ease of access and the degree of restrictiveness of grounds for divorce. The use of advertisements such as those analyzed by Lantz depended, similarly, on such factors as the degree of social acceptance of separation and whether or not shame was attached to marriage breakdown – and hence the likelihood of advertisement by aggrieved spouses – the availability of newspapers, and their editors' willingness to accept such advertisements. It is possible that colonies or states that had liberal divorce provisions or where divorce was relatively frequently resorted to possessed a social climate less condemnatory of marriage breakdown, which would have been less inhibiting in respect to such advertising. Indeed, Lantz demonstrates that those regions with high marital incompatibility rates (calculated from the advertisements) in the eighteenth century also had

[23] Quoted in Herman R. Lantz, *Marital Incompatibility and Social Change in Early America* (Beverly Hills, 1976), 14.
[24] Ibid.
[25] This sort of calculation is very crude and is subject to many qualifications that cannot be set out here. Some are noted in ibid., 17–22.

high divorce rates in the late nineteenth.[26] It is risky to draw associations between the two time periods because of the immense social changes that took place between them, but it is nonetheless possible that a high incompatibility rate in the eighteenth century and a high divorce rate in the late nineteenth both reflect the same phenomenon – a regional tradition of relative permissiveness in respect to marriage breakdown and dissolution.

Yet even granted the questionable assumptions lying behind some of Lantz's calculations, the study of advertisements announcing desertions is valuable in that it provides a body of evidence for the breakdown of marriage below the level of official divorce statistics. The advertisements shrink the "dark figure" of marital breakdown, but by what proportion we cannot, of course, determine.

8.4 Wife sale

Of the extralegal forms of divorce that can be identified, the English practice of wife sale was arguably the most socially formalized. Wife sale involved the effective termination of an existing marriage by the sale of a woman by her husband to another man, so that her transfer from the one to the other can be regarded as marking the dissolution of one partnership and the formation of another. As a form of popular divorce (that is, divorce available to the mass of the people), wife sale had its limitations. For a start, it seemed to rely on the initiative of the male, and the examples of wives selling their husbands are very rare. It was no different in this respect from the sexually discriminatory divorces by private Act of Parliament. In the second place the transaction involved not only a dissolution of one marriage but the formation of another couple, and the success of the transaction depended on the first husband's being able to find a buyer for his wife. Given the marital disharmony that must have provoked the sale, we should have expected potential purchasers to be very wary of buying a woman who could be a potential problem.

One impressionistic study throws some light on the practice of wife sale and its function as a means of divorce for those unable or unwilling to avail themselves of other means.[27] The first firmly recorded example of a wife sale

---

[26] Ibid., 24–7. Lantz ranked sixteen states by their rates of marital incompatibility for the period 1790–1800 (it should be 1790–9) and compared their ranking in terms of divorces per thousand of population in 1870. The results are given in his work, 25, Table 6. Of the sixteen states, four of the six with the highest marital incompatibility rates were among the six states with the highest divorce rates. Of the six states with the lowest rates of marital incompatibility, four were among those having the lowest divorce rates. The tendency toward a general correlation is clear from this.

[27] Samuel Pyeatt Menefee, *Wives for Sale* (Oxford, 1981). This is the only general study of wife selling, but it is profoundly unsatisfactory in many respects, notably in the imprecision of its statistical content, its crude use of social theory, and lack of chronological awareness. Its redeeming virtue lies mainly in its bringing together examples of wife sale, and I have drawn on it for this section. A brief but interesting discussion of wife sale is John R. Gillis, *For Better, For Worse: British Marriages, 1600 to the Present* (New York, 1985), 211–19. Edward Thompson includes a chapter on wife sale in his forthcoming book on popular culture.

occurred in 1553, but references to specific cases did not appear on a regular basis until the eighteenth century. There are only 7 references (almost all sources of information are newspaper articles) in the seventeenth century, 83 in the eighteenth, and 268 in the nineteenth. The earliest reference seems to have been to a wife sale in Scotland or Ireland in 1073, and there are references for England even as late as the 1970s. The bulk of the references to wife sale fall between the mid-eighteenth and mid-nineteenth centuries, a period that saw 278 (72%) of the 387 known references.[28] Wife selling does not appear, from such figures, to have been a common happening, but even so, there are reports of as many wife sales as there were divorces by private Act of Parliament over the same period. Moreover, the references were for the most part newspaper reports, which must have covered only a proportion of actual instances, depending on the editor's assessment as to the newsworthiness of the sale, and indeed, on the sheer existence of the provincial press and journalists.

One nineteenth-century French commentator, anxious to highlight the immorality of the heretical English, gleefully wrote of wife sales as if they were common events. Go to a marketplace in London or any other town in England, he wrote, and you will see

in the midst of a crowd which gives vent to the most crude and insulting expressions, unfortunate women, with their eyes lowered and looking hopeless, wearing around their necks a rope, held by a man. These are wives whose husbands have tired of them, and who are trying to sell them. Would you not believe you were in some town in Egypt, China, or Turkey? The government has tried hard to abolish this barbarous practice, but its efforts have been to no avail. Such is the result of schismatic and heretical doctrines of marriage, and this is proved by the fact that in Catholic Ireland, which is ruled by the same government, and under the same civil law as Great Britain, such revolting sales have never been witnessed.[29]

As far as the geographical distribution of wife sales is concerned, the practice appears to have existed not only in England but also sporadically in Ireland, Scotland, and Wales, in parts of western France, and even in Canada.[30] The majority of references, however, relate to England. By the end of the eighteenth century they had been located in all parts of the country, although their distribution contracted during the nineteenth century. By the late 1880s they were largely confined to the industrialized north of England, particularly to Yorkshire.[31]

Wife sale was accompanied by a high degree of ritual, tending to stress the

[28] Menefee cites 387 cases and references in *Wives for Sale*, Appendix, 211–59.
[29] Quoted in Alexandre Dumas fils, *La Question du divorce* (Paris, 1880), 140. Similarly, Charles Fourier took aim at the English: "Even in nations that are bloated with philosophy, such as England, a man has the right to take his woman to the market, with a rope around her neck, and sell her like a beast of burden, to anyone who can pay his asking price." Quoted in J. Beecher and R. Bienvenu (eds.), *The Utopian Vision of Charles Fourier* (London, 1972), 178.
[30] Kimberley Smith, "Divorce in Nova Scotia, 1750–1890," in J. Phillips and P. Girard (eds.), *Essays in the History of Canadian Law, Volume 3: The Nova Scotian Experience* (Toronto, in press).
[31] Menefee, *Wives for Sale*, 31.

social and contractual characters of the transaction. Its social character was guaranteed by the sale's taking place in a public place, witnessed by a large number of onlookers, so that it was open to surveillance by the community. In the late eighteenth and nineteenth centuries, most wife sales took place in markets or fairs, but these locales gradually gave way to inns as preferred places during the nineteenth century.[32] The use of a market or fair was particularly symbolic in view of the fact that wife sales were presented as economic transactions. Typically the wife to be sold was led to the place of sale in a halter, as if she were livestock, and there is reason to believe that the transfer of the halter from vendor to purchaser marked the transfer of responsibility for the woman from the one to the other.[33]

The actual sale took the form of an auction, but as pointed out, it is clear that in many cases the purchaser was determined in advance with the consent of the wife. Some of these cases were connected with the wife's adultery, her lover apparently buying her as the price for his offense.[34] The halter might well have been significant in this respect: Punishments for adultery in the seventeenth century included not only whipping and branding with the letters A or AD but also being forced to wear a halter or noose around the neck.[35] This was to remind the adulterer – and the public, since part of the punishment could involve standing under a gallows – that adultery had been a crime punishable by the death penalty. Placing a rope around the neck of a woman subject to a wife sale could well have been a symbolic reference to her adulterous behavior, especially if women involved in these sales were generally sold to men with whom they had had a sexual relationship.

Menefee cites the example of a London shopkeeper who discovered a stranger in his wife's bedchamber: "After some altercation on the subject of this *rencontre*, the gallant proposed to purchase the wife, if she was offered for sale, in due form, in Smithfield market. To this the husband readily agreed..."[36] In other instances the auction appears to have been a genuine one, with the wife being sold to the highest bidder, such that the purchaser could not have been decided beforehand. This was clearly the case, too, where no acceptable bids were made. The prices paid for wives must have depended largely on such considerations. Some were high, such as one instance of a hundred guineas paid in a Yorkshire sale, whereas many were token sums of one or two shillings, or a leg of mutton, or a combination of cash and a specified quantity of ale or

---

[32] Ibid., 34.
[33] Ibid., 70–1. See the reproduction of a nineteenth-century illustration of a wife sale in Gillis, *For Better, For Worse*, 212.
[34] One commentator observed that "in nineteen cases out of twenty the purchaser was a former lover, or a secret paramour, whose readiness to relieve the husband of his wife was known to him." G. T. Lawley, "Wife Selling in Staffordshire," *Midland Weekly News*, 6 and 13 January 1894, quoted in Gillis, *For Better, For Worse*, 214.
[35] This is mentioned in various contemporary judgments, and in R. W. Roetger, "The Transformation of Sexual Morality in 'Puritan' New England: Evidence from New Haven Court Records, 1639–1698," *Canadian Review of American Studies* 15 (1984), 246.
[36] Menefee, *Wives for Sale*, 78.

punch.[37] Such payments, when made to a husband by his wife's lover, might be seen as the poor man's equivalent of damages for criminal conversation.

In general, women seem to have acquiesced in their sales – some, in fact, appear to have been more anxious to be sold than their husbands were to sell them. This raises the questions of initiative in the proceedings and of the circumstances that gave rise to the sale. At the level of the marital relationship various reasons for terminating the union can be discerned. Simple incompatibility underlay some of the instances, as in the case of the husband who declared: "It is her wish as well as mine to part for ever. She has been to me only a bosom serpent. I took her for my comfort and the good of my house, but she has become my tormentor, a domestic curse, a night invasion, and a daily devil. . ."[38] In most cases, however, the circumstance apparently provoking the sale was adultery by the wife, often involving the future purchaser as the accomplice. An example has already been cited, and others may be deduced from the wife's position as a housekeeper to her eventual purchaser before the sale.

The more general social influences on wife sale are difficult to determine, partly because it cannot be shown whether the distribution of references to wife sale over time reflected the distribution of the actual practice, that is, having a concentration between the mid-eighteenth and mid-nineteenth centuries. It is not clear that the incidence of wife sale was in any way related to the beginnings of secularization in England, nor with changes in public morality. Nor can the institution be wholly explained in terms of the absence of any other means of divorce because wife sales seem to have gone into decline before the passage of the 1857 English divorce legislation. In any case that legislation, although bringing divorce within reach of a greater proportion of the English population than parliamentary divorce had done, still kept divorce inaccessible to the mass of the people (see Section 14.3).

The institution of wife sale has, indeed, a curious status in English social behavior. There is no doubt that it forms a tradition at one level of the social structure, initially the artisans and subsequently the industrial workers. But there is no evidence that it was anything but rarely resorted to, and there is ambiguous evidence as to its social acceptability. That sales took place in public, before witnesses, indicates popular – perhaps especially male – acquiescence at the very least. In one 1815 Derbyshire case the witnesses attacked some constables who had been sent to arrest the parties to a wife auction in progress.[39] But in other examples, the crowd reaction was equivocal (a London sale took place amid "the disgust of some and the laughter of others"),[40] and in still others there was a hostile social reaction, especially by women. In Manchester

---

[37] Ibid., 160, Table 3.
[38] Ibid., 62.
[39] Ibid., 121.
[40] Ibid., 122.

the female part of the crowd, apprehensive of the dangerous effects of such a precedent and urged on by a proper feeling of the indignity offered them, determined upon a protest against so indecent a proceeding, and in the absence of pen, ink and parchment, they recorded, with ample heaps of mud upon the faces of the *cattle dealers*, the burden of their indignant sentiments.[41]

There is an impression that hostility toward wife sales was more common in the later eighteenth and in the nineteenth centuries, than earlier. In the 1820s and 1830s especially, organized groups of women disrupted wife sales.[42] A growth of antipathy might in itself explain the gradual decline of the practice from the middle of the nineteenth century.

It remains to be shown how effective a form of divorce wife sales were. In order to assess them, we must appreciate the variety within the institution itself. They were not, as we have seen, simply the sale of a married woman, by her husband and at his will alone, to a random stranger who made the highest bid at an auction. In many cases the purchaser was determined in advance, and the wife appears to have consented to the sale, which allowed her to live with the man with whom she already had a sexual relationship, and with whom, indeed, she might have been living for some time before her sale to him. In such cases the wife sale did not mark the transfer of the woman in social terms but rather was a public declaration of an existing marital dissolution and a new partnership. Legal divorces can serve this function, too.

The legal status of the relationship between a sold woman and her purchaser depended on the status of her previous relationship with the vendor. If the earlier union had not been a marriage recognized in law, then she might marry the man who bought her. But if the first union were a legal marriage, a subsequent marriage was not possible until the first husband died. This point might have been lost on some couples at the time of the sale. "A Bodmin pair, refused permission to marry because the wife's husband still lived, went away apparently much disappointed."[43] Such were the limitations of wife sale as a form of popular divorce, when compared to the potential effects of a legal divorce that dissolved a marriage and freed both spouses to undertake new marriages.

In the final analysis, wife sale must be seen as an institution that had a variety of functions in traditional English society. It could be, in the first place, a means of publicly announcing a rearrangement of cohabitation, a ceremony drawing the community's attention to a de facto "divorce" and "remarriage." The living metaphor of a sale of livestock, with attention to the market and the role of the halter, might seem out of place to twentieth-century eyes (and clearly became so to nineteenth-century eyes, too), but it no doubt made sense within rituals that had derived from an agricultural society. The growth of hostility to, and the progressive decline of, the practice might reflect the decline of rural social

[41] Ibid., 123–4.
[42] Ibid., 124.
[43] Ibid., 117.

forms as much as the development of more enlightened notions of the rights of women.

Wife sale might also have been a popular means of dealing with adultery. Putting an adulterous relationship on a socially recognized footing might save the corespondent from an action for criminal conversation (although such legal suits were rare among the poorer classes), and might well have been a face-saving measure for the cuckolded husband. In this respect the sale of an adulterous wife to her lover could serve the same function as the forced marriage ("shotgun marriage") of an unmarried daughter and her lover when intercourse had taken place.

It might be argued that either of these two broad considerations motivated the institution of wife sale and that sales under these circumstances represented the institution in its ideal form. The existence of the practice could easily have given rise to abuse and to bastardized forms, such as the recorded instances of a husband deciding to sell his wife on impulse. For example, there is a report of a Northamptonshire shoemaker who sold his wife in order to finance his drinking.[44] Wife sale shares this variety with legal divorce, which has ideal forms, either as punishment for a matrimonial offense or as a remedy for marriage breakdown, but which may be abused by one of the parties in a manner not envisaged by the law or by the institution.

Wife sale might well have been an important institution in parts of England, as a popular form of divorce. It must be recognized that until Lord Hardwicke's marriage legislation of 1753 a large proportion of marriages continued to be given legitimacy in customary terms. What mattered was not whether the church celebrated, approved, or recognized marriages, but how they were received by the community. An example is "rough music," the English form of charivari, by which a community could show its displeasure at a marriage (for example, if it brought together a couple of widely disparate ages), regardless of whether they had been validly married in church.[45] If regional or local customs could influence or regulate a union, by giving legitimacy to a couple who shared living activities, then they could also legitimate the dissolution of a union. Wife sale could well have served the purpose not only of altering living arrangements and relationships, but also of doing so in a public manner that parallelled the publicity of marriage.

8.5 Customary divorce

Wife sale was one among many forms of customary divorce. Perhaps it is the most notorious and scandalous because it seemed to reduce the wife so dramat-

---

[44] Ibid., 74.
[45] See E. P. Thompson, "Rough Music': le charivari anglais," *Annales. Economies Sociétés Civilisations* 27 (1972), 285–312. See also Martin Ingram, "Ridings, Rough Music and the 'Reformation of Popular Culture' in Early Modern England," *Past and Present* 105 (1984), 79–113.

8.5 Customary divorce

ically to the status of a commodity to be bought and sold on the open market, although, as we have seen, it only rarely took this form. Other kinds of informal divorce, sanctioned by custom in various regions, involved not contractual representations but rituals denoting the undoing of marriage, in some the reversal of the marriage ceremony. One form was the "besom divorce," a reversal of the "besom marriage" found in parts of Wales, England, and in America. A besom, or broom, made of branches was placed aslant in the doorway of a house and, in the presence of witnesses, the couple intending to marry jumped over it. If both did so successfully, without touching the broom or dislodging it – thus overcoming an obstacle and entering the house together (the husband first) – they were deemed to be married.[46]

The same custom allowed for the marriage to be dissolved by the mutual agreement of both spouses within a year if they found themselves unable to have children or temperamentally incompatible. One account of the divorce procedure runs as follows:

By jumping backwards over the besom the marriage was broken. The wife had the right to jump back, too. But this step had to be taken by either within the first year. Both of them, afterward, were free to marry again. If there was a child the father was responsible for its upkeep. In jumping backwards to break a marriage, as well as in jumping forward to make a marriage, if any part of the body touched the besom or the door post the effort was in vain. There were witnesses there to watch.[47]

Appropriately, it is more difficult to negotiate a besom backward than it is forward; the custom thus reflected the historical reality that it is easier to enter matrimony than to exit from it.

Other communally recognized forms of divorce also involved reversals of marriage. In parts of England and Wales there was a belief that "if a husband failed to maintain his wife, she might give him back the wedding ring and then she would be free to marry again."[48] As important as this kind of symbolism and ritual was, it was primarily a means of publicizing the event and focusing the attention of the community on it. For a couple to separate so as to be able to form new cohabiting relationships with others, and yet to remain in the same locality where they had lived together, they needed to have social approval, or at the very least social recognition of their separation. To have ignored or blatantly transgressed community norms in these matters would have made life difficult, if not intolerable. These considerations could be ignored only by men and women who simply left their spouses and traveled to new parts in order to establish another relationship. Community standards might also be ignored by the transient and peripatetic, whose very manner of existence freed them from the constant surveillance and potential censure of any community.

---

[46] Gillis, *For Better, For Worse*, 198.
[47] William Rhys Jones, "A Besom Wedding in the Ceiriog Valley," *Folk-Lore* 39 (1928), 155. Quoted in Gillis, *For Better, For Worse*. 198–9.
[48] Quoted in Gillis, *For Better, For Worse*, 204.

8 The alternatives to divorce

Once we leave the ritualized forms of coupling and uncoupling, however, we enter the world of consensual marriage and divorce, what are called in French *unions libres* (and, presumably, *désunions libres*). There is any number of examples of men and women living together in short- or long-term stable relationships, many coming to light only when they were prosecuted in the ecclesiastical courts. References in these cases tend to be curt and restricted to the essential facts of the case, and they provide no evidence of ritual or community approval. Shorn of this context they tend to appear somewhat patternless, random, and idiosyncratic, and the phenomenon fades off into the obscurity of the dark figure of cohabitation and separation that lies behind the statistics of legal marriage and divorce, as well as behind more formalized traditions such as besom marriage and divorce and wife selling.

8.6 Bigamy

Next to wife sale, the form of extralegal behavior that most closely resembled divorce was bigamy. In most jurisdictions bigamy was a civil or criminal offense, but it was not subject to the severe penalties we now associate with it. (We might recall that in the sixteenth century, theologians were willing to recommend bigamy to both King Henry VIII of England and the Landgrave Philip of Hesse, rather than see them divorce.) Under church law in England, bigamy was punished only by excommunication, the same punishment meted out to those who failed consistently to attend church, and to married men and women who refused to live together. The 1604 canon law of the Church of England made bigamy a felony, but it was mitigated if the guilty person's first spouse had been absent for seven years or more, if the first marriage had taken place before the parties had reached puberty, or if the spouses had been separated *a mensa et thoro*. In other words, there was this provision for a kind of pseudodivorce in England – separation by the church courts, followed by remarriage – provided that the parties involved were prepared to forfeit the bond they paid at the time of the separation, and to suffer some further penalty set by the church courts, such as excommunication, which could be commuted by payment of a fine. This lenient view was reflected in the first English bigamy law, in 1604.[49]

Bigamy closely resembled divorce in its effects, namely, the social termination of one marriage (the cessation of cohabitation, sexual relations, and the sharing of daily activities and economic benefits) and its replacement by another. Generally we should expect the termination of the first union to have been the result of desertion, whereas the second marriage was usually entered into under the deception that the deserter was either unmarried or a widower (most bigamists were men). Bigamy thus includes one legal element (a remarriage), which

---

[49] Not all jurisdictions were as lenient. A Pennsylvania act of 1705 made bigamy a criminal offense punishable by whipping and imprisonment for life. The second (bigamous) marriage was annulled. Michael Grossberg, *Governing the Hearth: Law and the Family in Nineteenth-Century America* (Chapel Hill, 1985), 121.

8.6 Bigamy

distinguishes it from situations in which a man or a woman cohabits with a succession of partners in a series of de facto relationships or common-law marriages.

Bigamy might well have been a common occurrence in traditional societies where there was no centralized system of registration of vital events and no ready access to marriage registers from distant parts of each country. Lawrence Stone suggests that bigamy "seems to have been both easy and common."[50] Brian Outhwaite, however, challenges this assessment: "It is true that deserted wives are commonly encountered in the Poor Law records of the period, but can this support the notion that bigamy was therefore easy? Does the relative absence of prosecutions for bigamy also betoken its ease?"[51] The truth is that we shall never have any notion of the true extent of bigamy in past time. The paucity of prosecutions for bigamy might well "betoken its ease," that is, the ease for bigamists of escaping detection and punishment, or it might just as convincingly betoken its rarity. Public attitudes toward bigamy would be an important variable in bringing the guilty to trial, for where marriage was regarded as a fairly loose contract it is likely that bigamy would be tolerated and bigamists accepted within the community. In the period before systematic records were kept, it is probable that bigamy came to light only when it caused offense to the bigamist's legitimate spouse or to the community at large.

Whatever the actual incidence of bigamy in traditional Western society, the offense rarely appeared in judicial records. During Bishop Redman's visitation of Norwich in 1597 there were five presentations for bigamy, and a sixth man, John Kente, was brought into court as being "suspected to have two wives."[52] The bigamy cases were fairly straightforward. Nicholas Beckingham was presented because "he married about 5 years past one Isabel Burne, wif of [blank] Burne who is now liveinge and returned home to her, by which meanes the said Isabel hath ij [two] husbands at this time liveinge."[53] Isabel herself was presented for reason of bigamy, but it is interesting to note that her husband was considered equally responsible even though he was not, strictly speaking, the bigamous spouse. (His conviction suggests that he must have known of the earlier marriage.) Both Nicholas Beckingham and Isabel Burne were convicted and excommunicated for this offense. Another of the Norwich cases involved bigamy and desertion: The woman who was charged had married two men but refused to live with either of them.

Yet bigamy was not simply defined as remarriage by a man or woman during the lifetime of his or her spouse. As we have seen, the canon and civil laws of

---

[50] Lawrence Stone, *The Family, Sex and Marriage in England, 1500–1800* (London, 1977), 40.
[51] R. B. Outhwaite, "Introduction: Problems and Perspectives in the History of Marriage," in R. B. Outhwaite (ed.), *Marriage and Society: Studies in the Social History of Marriage* (London, 1981), 8–9.
[52] Williams, *Diocese of Norwich*, 48.
[53] Ibid., 66. It appears that the second marriage took place while Isabel Burne's first husband was absent and presumed dead.

seventeenth-century England made allowance for mitigating circumstances. This was apparently the argument in mitigation of one of the women presented for bigamy in the Norwich visitation of 1597. Anne Dawbney was charged with having remarried "being devorsed from Mr. Dawbney."[54] This "devorse" could only have been a separation *a mensa et thoro* (called *divortium a mensa et thoro* in church law). In eighteenth-century England more or less permanent desertion could be regarded as morally dissolving the marriage. Lawrence Stone cites two cases that illustrate this point. The first concerned the sister of Francis Place, England's first birth control propagandist. When her husband was transported to the colonies for life in the 1790s for robbery, she quickly married a former suitor, "apparently without any qualms or objections on the grounds that she already had a husband who was presumably still alive."[55] As she was not prosecuted for bigamy, it seems that the authorities, too, either had no objections or were not aware of the circumstances. In the second case cited by Stone, a Somerset rector agreed in 1807 to call the banns for the second marriage of a woman whose husband had left to do military service in the East Indies seven years earlier and had not been heard of since that time.[56] Here was an instance of the clergy accepting that a remarriage could take place where the first had effectively ended, even though both spouses were still alive.

The seven-year absence of the soldier-husband in this case probably represented the earliest that his wife could remarry. In many places there was either a custom, common law, or statute that recognized the right of remarriage when one spouse had been absent without news for seven years.[57] One woman in Ravenstone, charged with marrying while her husband was still living, defended herself before a church court by pointing out that he had left her seven years earlier.[58] The seven-year criterion also came into play in the custom of "leasing," in which a man and a woman lived in a marital relationship even though they both had living spouses.[59] The underlying assumptions in most of these provisions based on seven years' absence was that the absent spouse was dead, enabling the remaining spouse to remarry, in effect, as a widow or widower. Where divorce could be obtained in such circumstances, it was tantamount to a death certificate in the absence of a body. Indeed, a divorce in Metz in 1796 exemplifies this perfectly: Wishing to remarry, but unable to because she could not prove that her husband was dead (even though rumor had it that

---

[54] Ibid., 39.
[55] Stone, *Family, Sex and Marriage*, 40.
[56] Ibid. A similar case of a church marriage involving a woman whose husband was still alive, although sentenced to life transportation to the colonies for life, is given in Section 10.2.
[57] We have here an inversion of the notion of the "seven-year itch," that husbands or wives often want to separate or form extramarital relationships after about seven years of marriage. In these earlier cases, solitary husbands and wives wanted the opposite, to remarry. Both, of course, indicate a wish for a new relationship.
[58] Gillis, *For Better, For Worse*, 99.
[59] Ibid., 210. In these cases the husband or wife "leased" his or her spouse to another partner, thus giving approval to the new "marital" arrangement.

he had died), one Catherine Maxant obtained a divorce, "the remedy the law specifies in the absence of a certificate of death."[60]

But permission to remarry when a spouse was absent did not in all cases imply an absolute and irrevocable dissolution of the first marriage. The dissolution of the marriage by death was assumed, but it was given a provisional character in recognition that the absent spouse might not only be alive but might return. (The example of Francis Place's sister is quite a different case: Her husband, having been transported to a penal colony for life, was clearly alive when she remarried, but the character of his sentence meant that he could never return to her.) The provisional form of dissolution in cases of absence is made clear in Scandinavian divorce laws, which recognized that the absent spouse might have been held a prisoner, shipwrecked, or have been prevented by some other reasons from communicating with the apparently abandoned partner. If he (it was usually the husband) did return home to find his wife remarried, he could resume married life with her, and she would have to end her marriage with her second husband.[61] Needless to say, this could have complex and agonizing repercussions not only for all three spouses, but also for children of either or both marriages, not to mention implications for property disposition.

In the Somerset case referred to earlier, things did not work out as custom intended. The husband, who had been absent as a soldier in the East Indies, did finally return home to find his wife remarried and proceeded to reclaim her. But when she, instead of embracing him as her proper husband, continued to frequent her second husband, the first one deserted her again and was said soon to have remarried.[62] Technically his remarriage was improper, even in terms of the custom, although it seems perfectly reasonable in light of the fact that his wife had remarried and apparently had no intention of returning to him. Such cases reveal the potential complexity of marital and quasi-marital relationships when they are not regulated by marriage and divorce laws, which confer certainty of matrimonial status.

Apart from varying circumstances that might make a bigamous marriage less culpable or not at all culpable, there were also social distinctions in the acceptance of second marriages within the lifetime of first spouses. Some prominent public men, such as Sir Ralph Sadler in the middle of the sixteenth century, were able to obtain private Acts of Parliament that confirmed the legality of second marriages that had all the characteristics of being bigamous.[63]

The imprecision of the law of bigamy in England explains in part the rarity of

---

[60] Jean Lhote, "Le divorce à Metz sous la Révolution et l'Empire," *Annales de l'Est* 5ᵉ série, 3 (1952), 178.

[61] Johan Thorsten Sellin, *Marriage and Divorce Legislation in Sweden* (pub. Ph.D. diss., University of Pennsylvania, 1922), 36.

[62] Stone, *Family, Sex and Marriage*, 40.

[63] Arthur J. Slavin, *Politics and Profit: A Study of Sir Ralph Sadler, 1507–1547* (Cambridge, 1966), 216–18.

prosecutions for bigamy. Apart from circumstances (such as lengthy absence) that might permit a married man or woman to remarry with impunity, the incidence of prosecutions was clearly influenced by such factors as public sympathy and the diligence and discretion of local civil and ecclesiastical officials. It could well be that couples or individuals obtained what were effectively "divorces" by exploiting the loophole in the laws: obtaining a separation, then remarrying in defiance of the law and suffering, if the bigamy were discovered, the relatively light penalties set down in the 1604 canon law. It is significant that a study of the English county of Wiltshire turned up seven prosecutions for bigamy between 1586 and 1599, two between 1600 and 1604, but only one between 1605 and 1640.[64] It seems likely that the virtual disappearance of bigamy from the church courts after 1604 reflected the low ranking among offenses that it was accorded in the canon law from that year, and perhaps the tendency for remarriage to be preceded more often by a separation.

Yet if bigamy ceased being regarded as a serious crime in seventeenth-century England, it began to be viewed as a problem in the American colonies. There were, as we have seen, numerous cases of men leaving their wives in one colony and remarrying in another, examples of the ease of mobility and the facility with which a bigamous marriage might be contracted, even if some of them were detected afterward. In 1680, for instance, Elizabeth Stevens divorced her husband in Plymouth Colony after he was shown to have three wives in addition to her. One lived in Boston, another in Barbados, and the third lived in an unspecified town in England.[65] The phenomenon of married men (and some women) moving from colony to colony, leaving their spouses and married status behind them, was a chronic problem the courts and churches in the American colonies had to face. Another related problem was posed by the number of married men who arrived in the colonies and attempted to pass themselves off as single. Prosecutions in the Suffolk (Massachusetts) County court tell two of these stories. In the first John Tipping, a cordwainer, was prosecuted "for making sute to some maids or women in order to marriage, hee having a wife in London."[66] Tipping admitted being married but denied having courted or proposed marriage to anyone in Massachusetts. Nonetheless the justices ordered him "to depart to his wife by the next opportunity of Shipping" under penalty of twenty pounds if he failed to leave. In another case, Henry Jackman was presented to the court "for lying in saying hee was a single man and attempting marriage with severall, who hath since confessed hee had a wife in England..."[67]

The Englishmen and women who found themselves in court for committing or attempting bigamy may evoke some sympathetic understanding. They were

[64] Martin Ingram, "Ecclesiastical Justice in Wiltshire, 1600–1640, with special reference to cases concerning sex and marriage," (D.Phil. thesis, University of Oxford, 1976), 149.
[65] John Demos, *A Little Commonwealth: Family Life in Plymouth Colony* (London, 1970), 93.
[66] *Records of the Suffolk County Court*, II, 943.
[67] Ibid., I, 232.

unable to obtain divorces under the prevailing law in England, and they might well have seen a bigamous marriage as their only alternative to remaining in an unacceptable marriage or living alone. Moreover, the latter was not always a viable alternative anyway: Henry Jackman, prosecuted for lying about his marital status, was also charged with "living from under family Government." Bigamy was surely to be expected in such circumstances where mobility and anonymity (through lack of centralized personal records) coexisted with the inability to obtain a divorce, or when divorce was provided only in a very restricted form.

But the easy availability of divorce does not necessarily lead to the disappearance of bigamy, even though it would seem to rule out the necessity of committing the offense in order to remarry. There were, for example, continuing examples of bigamy in France during the revolution, despite the fact that divorce could be obtained anywhere, equally easily by men and women, for any reason, and at minimal cost. Three cases of bigamy were prosecuted in Rouen in Year VIII (1799–1800) alone.[68] In two of the cases the defendants (both men) claimed that they had remarried in the belief that their first wives were dead. One of the men, Pierre Fabulet, a tailor who had left Rouen to fight in the revolutionary wars (even though, as a married man, he would not have been conscripted) remarried in Lille, where he was garrisoned. When he and his second wife returned to Rouen, he promptly started divorce proceedings against his first wife, but was arrested for committing bigamy. Fabulet argued in his defense that at the time he had remarried he had not had news of his wife for five years, that she was notorious for running after soldiers and sailors, and that when his mother had informed him that a woman of loose morals who frequented military men had been found drowned in the harbor at Le Havre, he had assumed that it was his wife. Fabulet was found guilty of the fact of bigamy, but not of having guilty intent.

The third case of bigamy in Rouen in Year VIII bore directly on the relationship between bigamy and divorce. Marie Grenier, a trader in brandy and cotton in the nearby town of Yvetot, married Jean Menu in 1787 and Pierre Ventras in 1797. The circumstances were outlined by Menu, who told the court that he had left Grenier after learning that she had committed adultery, but had later returned to ask her to join him. She had agreed, and the couple had lived in Rouen for a year. Grenier, however, persisted in her extramarital sexual life, and Menu left her a second time. After divorce was legalized in 1792, Menu twice visited her to ask her to agree to dissolve their marriage, but she refused. When Menu visited her a third time "to ask his wife either to agree to a divorce or to return and live with him, he was surprised to find her married to Ventras for almost two years, and that Menu's appearance in Yvetot, where he was well-known, had aroused the interest of the authorities."[69] In her defense, Grenier

---

[68] The following cases are detailed in Roderick Phillips, *Family Breakdown in Late Eighteenth-Century France: Divorces in Rouen, 1792–1803* (Oxford, 1980), 163–5.
[69] Quoted in Ibid., 164.

alleged that she had received a copy of Menu's death certificate from a young man she had never seen before and had not seen since. The prosecution, however, insisted that the certificate was a forgery, and commented:

> This crime is all the more reprehensible in that this woman had only to agree to the divorce which her husband had constantly asked for. But as she knew that his intention was to remarry, she refused out of pure perversity, knowing that her husband, who lived far away, could not leave his business to come to Yvetot to satisfy the formalities stipulated by the divorce law.[70]

(Divorce petitions were to be lodged in the domicile of the defendant.) Grenier was found guilty of forgery and of bigamy with criminal intent and was imprisoned.

8.7 Lettres de cachet

In the eighteenth century the French produced an institution that could in some instances be an alternative to divorce or judicial separation. This was the *lettre de cachet de famille*, or arrest warrant, by which one family member could have another imprisoned for a period of time or by which a family group could have one of its members incarcerated. *Lettres de cachet de famille* were particular types of *lettre de cachet*, orginally arrest warrants issued by the king as a means of dealing with troublesome nobles or other disobedient subjects. Many were imprisoned in the Bastille, giving that establishment the reputation that justified its destruction in 1789. Gradually the application of *lettres de cachet* was broadened to enable institutions such as the church and army to put dissident members out of public circulation. Although there are no precise global figures on their use, one study has suggested that between 1741 and 1785, about 24,000 *lettres de cachet* were issued, about one-quarter of them affecting members of the clergy, the remainder involving sanctions against lay men and women.[71] Not all such orders in themselves necessarily entailed imprisonment; some confirmed or increased punishments ordered by the regular courts. But the effect of a *lettre de cachet* was always to remove an individual from the political scene or from an institution for a specified or indeterminate period.

The family was one such institution. *Lettres de cachet* provided a means by which a father might have his wastrel son or immoral daughter imprisoned, either to put a brake on the offending behavior, to provide a deterrent, or as a simple punishment. A family group might seek collectively to remove a father whose behavior threatened to dissipate the family wealth. But, more to the present point, a husband or wife might have his or her spouse put away for any number of reasons. In all such cases, acceptable grounds had to be demon-

---

[70] Ibid., 164–5.

[71] Henri Debord, *Contribution à l'histoire des ordres du Roi au XVIIIe siècle* (Paris, 1938), cited in Arlette Farge and Michel Foucault, *Le désordre des familles. Lettres de cachet des Archives de la Bastille* (Paris, 1982), 14.

strated before the arrest warrant would be issued. Although *lettres de cachet* were criticized as being issued arbitrarily (and in this sense became regarded as symptomatic of the corruption of the Old Regime), the evidence suggests that they were issued only after careful enquiries had been made to ensure that the allegations made in the *placet* (petition) were true, and that imprisonment was justified.[72]

The procedure for obtaining a *lettre de cachet de famille* varied according to region and class. In Paris, in the late seventeenth century, *placets* affecting important families were addressed directly to the king or his ministers. The decision was made within the royal council, giving the king effective control. Petitions affecting families of less exalted social rank were made to the *lieutenant général de police*, who also directed the investigation and made a recommendation to the royal minister of state, who would in turn issue the *lettre de cachet*. In the eighteenth century the procedure was often modified in practice, and *lieutenants-généraux* sometimes issued arrest warrants without the approval of the royal ministry.[73]

Although it was long thought that *lettres de cachet* were used above all by members of the highest social groups, it is clear that they were employed throughout society. Arlette Farge and Michel Foucault suggest that between one-half and two-thirds of Paris cases involved families in modest circumstances.[74] In Provence, however, there was a clear tendency for those interned by *lettres de cachet* to emanate from the higher echelons of society. The solid middle class of bourgeois, merchants, court officials, and professionals accounted for almost one-half the prisoners, and nobles (real or purported) contributed 14%. The working and lower middle classes – domestics, artisans, street traders, small shopkeepers – who made up most of the population, accounted for only one-quarter of the detainees.[75]

Not all of the family matters referred to in requests for *lettres de cachet* related to marriage problems. In Paris, petitions to have a spouse imprisoned accounted for about one-third of all family-based requests.[76] In Provence, however, they were less common. Out of 613 petitions between 1745 and 1789 where one or more members of a family sought to have another member of the family incarcerated, 56 husbands and 13 wives requested the imprisonment of their spouses, so that such cases contributed 11% of the total.[77] In Caen only 5% of problems revealed in the *placets* involved conflicts between wives and husbands.[78] Marital problems thus accounted for only a low percentage of the family-

---

[72] F.-X. Emmanuelli, "'Ordres du Roi' et lettres de cachet en Provence à la fin de l'Ancien Régime. Contribution à l'histoire du climat social et politique," *Revue Historique* 252 (1974), 357–92.
[73] Farge and Foucault, *Désordre des familles*, 15–16.
[74] Ibid., 9, 364n.6.
[75] Emmanuelli, "'Ordres du Roi'," 376.
[76] Farge and Foucault, *Désordre des familles*, 23.
[77] Emmanuelli, "'Ordres du Roi'," 373.
[78] Jean-Claude Perrot, *Genèse d'une ville moderne. Caen au XVIIIᵉ siècle* (2 vols., Paris, 1975), II, 837.

centered petitions for *lettres de cachet*, and we might note that husbands had their wives imprisoned four times more frequently than wives their husbands.

As for the number of *lettres de cachet de famille*, it is not known for France generally. For those relating to internments in the Bastille, there were few in the period before 1720, when imprisonments were generally politically motivated; and documents relating to familial cases after 1760 have been destroyed, lost, or dispersed. Between 1728 and 1758, however, there is documentation relating to about 2,000 cases: In 1728 there were 168 requests for internment; in 1758, 78 requests.[79] Elsewhere in France the numbers were smaller: In the Norman city of Caen there were 83 applications for *lettres de cachet de famille* in the period 1750 to 1769, and 131 between 1770 and 1789.[80]

The affinity of *lettres de cachet* to divorce is evident from a reading of the circumstances that provoked applications. We might well be reading divorce court records, with their allegations and evidences of immoral behavior, violence, and the disregard of marital duties. Similar to petitioning for divorce in most jurisdictions, seeking a *lettre de cachet* was a very serious undertaking, not likely to be initiated for frivolous reasons. If the circumstances were less than serious, there was little chance that the application would succeed. As in divorce petitions there is no typical application for *lettres de cachet*, but several *placets* will serve as examples.

In 1728 Marie Marguerite Fournier, wife of Louis Duplessis, petitioned that

she had the misfortune to have married thirty years ago or thereabouts the said Duplessis, with whom she has experienced utter misery and ill-treatment; the said Duplessis by his ill conduct and debauchery has been confined three times in the Bicêtre, and the petitioner, his wife, is in daily fear that some terrible event will happen, because he threatens every day to kill her, having ill-treated her this day the 18 July 1728, as a result of which she is seriously injured.[81]

A surgeon testified that her terrible injuries (described in detail) placed her in danger of dying, and a priest, who had administered the last rites, supported the petition (lodged, one supposes, in case she survived). Other women also complained of violence in their petitions. Madeline Dessessart wrote that

in thirteen years of marriage she has received nothing but ill-treatment at her husband's hands, he being a most deranged man who takes wine every day, which leads him to the extremities of madness, that she is not safe with him, and that several times she had only just missed being killed by his blows...[82]

Other women's petitions described their husbands' immorality and financial dissipations. Jeanne Catry wrote that her husband of forty-six years, Antoine Chevalier,

[79] Farge and Foucault, *Désordres des familles*, 18–19.
[80] Perrot, *Genèse d'une ville*, II, 836.
[81] Quoted in Farge and Foucault, *Désordre des familles*, 101.
[82] Ibid., 112.

always spent at the tavern everything he earned, without any concern for his family, constantly sold his wife's and even his own clothes so that he could drink...Often returned home at all hours of the night, quite naked, without his hat, clothes, even without his shoes, which he left at the tavern as payment.[83]

Men had similar complaints. Charles Bourin, a grave digger, described his wife's sale of their furniture and clothes so that she could buy alcohol.[84] Other husbands complained of their wives' extramarital sexual activities. One Flamand wrote that "his legitimate wife has for six months led a most scandalous life, she frequents a certain apprentice wig maker...,"[85] and Michel Corneille's petition was based on "the ill conduct and considerable disorderliness of Anne Doisteau his wife which led not only to prostitution, even to behave in a manner quite out of keeping with decency..."[86]

Violence, financial dissipation, alcoholism, notorious immorality: All – singly or in combinations – made married life intolerable for women and men who sought to have their spouses interned. Indeed, the complaints in the *placets* for *lettres de cachet* read much like the evidence produced before the French divorce courts of the revolutionary period. A crude breakdown of grounds for *lettres de cachet* in the Bastille for the years 1728, 1756, 1758, and 1760 suggests that two-thirds of the petitions included complaints about economic behavior (dissipation of wages, sale of furniture to finance drinking, and the like), and one-third referred only to personal misconduct without mention of economic matters. Not surprisingly women's petitions most often cited physical ill-treatment: Three-quarters of wives' petitions fell into this category, compared to only eight of seventy husbands' petitions.[87]

Overall, the Bastille records for the sample years suggest that men were about as likely as women to be sentenced to confinement by *lettre de cachet*. Taking not only husbands and wives, but also parents, those imprisoned were 195 men and 181 women.[88] In this there lies a difference from the use of the divorce law at the end of the eighteenth century when women clearly pre-dominated as successful petitioners. Yet there was one similarity between *lettres de cachet* of the Bastille and the effect of the 1792 divorce law: the length of time that elapsed between marriage and one spouse's taking legal action against the behavior of the other. In Rouen the duration of marriage until divorce was between eleven and twelve years.[89] In Paris the time lapse between marriage and lodging a *placet* for *lettre de cachet* was twelve years.[90]

The broad circumstances that might well be described as marriage break-

[83] Ibid., 95.
[84] Ibid., 49.
[85] Ibid., 86.
[86] Ibid., 74.
[87] Ibid., 28.
[88] Ibid., 364n.11.
[89] Phillips, *Family Breakdown*, 72–5.
[90] Farge and Foucault, *Désordre des familles*, 24.

down, the specific grievances that were made in the *placets*, even some of the characteristics of the petitioners, all draw attention to the similarities of confinement by *lettre de cachet de famille* and divorce. Of course they did not have the same effects as divorce, for imprisonment in no way affected the validity of the marriage. Nor was confinement permanent. In Provence the average length of imprisonment ranged from thirty-one months (1750–4) to sixty-four months (1765–9).[91] The *lettre de cachet de famille* was not a form of divorce, then, but it was some sort of remedy, even if only a temporary respite from marital oppression or misery, in a matrimonial system that did not permit dissolution of marriage.

Lettres de cachet were unusual because they permitted one spouse – with cause, but not necessarily criminal cause – to have the other incarcerated. Not many societies have provided this kind of personalized prison service. But there were other sorts of institutions to which husbands and wives could be dispatched at the request of their spouses under extreme circumstances. Asylums for the insane, for example, might accept private patients at the request of their families. A study of two Oxfordshire asylums (Hook Norton and Witney) in the first half of the nineteenth century shows that of those admissions where information on marital status is known (358), some 170 (47%) were married.[92] These patients need not have been detained for the rest of their lives, but the ability to commit a spouse to a private asylum did remove him or her for a time from active participation in marriage. In the cases where the detention was a long-term one, or where the spouse died in the asylum, committal did perform to some extent the function of divorce on the ground of insanity (which was not legalized in England until 1937).

8.8 Spouse murder

One of the most drastic forms of informal divorce was spouse murder, the killing of a wife by her husband or a husband by his wife. It might be argued that the phenomenon was more akin to voluntary widowhood than to divorce. But be that as it may, it can hardly be disputed that murdering one's spouse was an extremely effective means of terminating a marriage, and reflected a high degree of dissatisfaction with married life. One seventeenth-century example of a wife's killing her husband was cited at the beginning of this chapter; it was the last in a series of actions Mary Hobry considered taking (and the one she eventually took) against her husband. Mary Hobry was detected and executed, but there was always the possibility – even if it were slight – that a husband or wife who murdered his or her partner might escape detection or, if convicted, might survive punishment and even remarry. Of eighteen men convicted of

[91] Emmanuelli, " 'Ordres du Roi'," 381, Table 2.
[92] William Ll. Parry-Jones, *The Trade in Lunacy. A Study of Private Madhouses in England in the Eighteenth and Nineteenth Centuries* (London, 1972), 163, Table 23.

8.8 Spouse murder

murdering members of their families in seventeenth-century Essex, twelve were executed, five were branded, and one suffered another (unspecified) penalty; of ten women similarly convicted, six were hanged and four were punished otherwise.[93] In eighteenth-century Toulouse, in the south of France, the great majority of men and women convicted of spouse murder were executed, generally by hanging, although women were burned. A small number were sentenced to life on the galleys or to be banished from the region.[94]

As such statistics indicate, the murder of husbands and wives was anything but a common phenomenon. We can draw this inference from homicide prosecutions and convictions with more certainty than would be appropriate for statistics relating to crimes and offenses such as adultery, failure to cohabit, violence, and bigamy. Murder was, in the first place, a serious crime, unlikely to be overlooked or ignored by policing authorities who could use their discretion in prosecuting other offenses. Moreover, discovery of the crime was almost certain in cases of homicide. Even in a relatively mobile society, it would be difficult to conceal the sudden disappearance of an individual, particularly of a family member. Nor was it easy to dispose of the victim's body.

Few as they might be, family homicides – murders in which the culprit and victim were related – account for a significant proportion of homicides in modern Western society, currently more than 50% in England and Wales, for example. There is a historical continuity here, although there are also important variations in the proportions, depending on time and place. In the English county of Essex in the late sixteenth and the seventeenth centuries, only 14% of homicides were familial, although a further 10% involved individuals in master–servant relationships (which contemporaries would have considered familial, but which we do not).[95] In the city and area around Toulouse, however, a much higher proportion of homicides in the eighteenth century related to family members. Between 1663 and 1750, culprit and victim were related in 63% of homicides, and between 1750 and 1775 the proportion was 46%. Homicides involving married couples accounted for 41 and 16% of all family homicides in the two periods, respectively.[96] This meant that spouse murder in this region represented between 7 and 26% of all murders.

It would not be surprising to find that wives were more frequently guilty of spouse murder than husbands. Men had many more options other than murder when faced with oppression, provocation, or simple incompatibility; husbands could more easily leave, evict their wives from the house, or force some sort of compliance by sheer physical strength. On the other hand it is also likely that the violence commonly exercised by husbands against their wives often resulted, unintentionally, in death. This is not to excuse the violence in any way,

---

[93] J. A. Sharpe, "Domestic Homicide in Early Modern England," *The Historical Journal* 24 (1981), 39, Table 3.
[94] Nicole Castan, *Justice et répression en Languedoc à l'Epoque des Lumières* (Paris, 1980), 32.
[95] Sharpe, "Domestic Homicide," 34.
[96] Castan, *Justice et répression*, 26.

but rather to make the important distinction between wife battering and wife murder. It is significant that English law made this distinction in respect of physical "correction" against a wife, although it did not against other categories of dependent persons. The eighteenth-century English legal commentator William Blackstone, for example, held that when an act of physical correction on an offspring (by a parent), a servant (by a master) or a schoolchild (by a teacher) resulted in death, the verdict should not be murder but "death by misadventure."[97] Married women were excluded from this lenient approach. On the other hand, women who murdered their husbands were certainly not treated leniently. The act was not only a homicide but was aggravated because the victim was an individual in a position of authority. In such circumstances women were often charged with petty treason rather than simple murder.

Despite the reasons for thinking that women might kill more often within the family context, men predominated. They were, for example, responsible for 69% of domestic homicides in thirteenth-century England and 58% of killings of relatives in seventeenth-century Essex.[98] However, women were much more likely to be involved in family homicides than in nondomestic murders. In Essex, again, women were responsible for only 7% of nondomestic murders, but 42% of murders of relatives, and 41% of murders of servants.[99] Their greater involvement in family homicide no doubt reflected the limited social ambit of women. Simply and crudely expressed, people beat and murder victims from among people they confront, and women were more likely to have their relationships within the household. Hence the greater likelihood that they would be involved in murders within the households, their main social reference, where they dealt with their husbands, children, and servants. Men, with a much wider range of social contacts, beat and murdered on a broader social and geographical spectrum, although it should be noted that murders involving brothers as culprit and victim ranked high in family homicide lists.[100] This reflected the often-noted male sibling rivalry, particularly resentment by younger brothers against the eldest because law and practice in early modern society frequently favored elder brothers in respect to inheritance.[101]

This tendency for males to dominate violence carried through to spouse murder. In a study of some courts in thirteenth-century England, women victims of conjugal homicide outnumbered men by two to one: Thirty-two men fell victim to their wives, whereas sixty-four women were killed by their husbands.[102] In fourteenth-century England women were victims in almost all such kill-

---

[97] William Blackstone, *Commentaries on the Laws of England* (4 vols., London, 1771), IV, 182.
[98] Sharpe, "Domestic Homicide," 36, Table 2.
[99] Ibid.
[100] James B. Given, *Society and Homicide in Thirteenth-Century England* (Palo Alto, Calif., 1977), 57, Table 6. Brothers were the second highest category of victims, after husbands and wives.
[101] See Joan Thirsk, "Younger Sons in the Seventeenth Century," *History* New ser., 54 (1969), 358–77.
[102] Given, *Society and Homicide*, 56, Table 6.

ings,[103] and women accounted for most victims in seventeenth-century Essex as well.[104] In eighteenth-century Toulouse, however, three-quarters of spouse murders in rural areas were carried out by women, although in the city men reasserted their dominance in these sad statistics by being responsible for 60% of deaths.[105] In the second half of the eighteenth century, women in Paris were three times as likely as men to fall victim to a spouse.[106]

What circumstances brought about this ultimate response? In some cases the motive was money. In 1738 Gill Smith, a Kentish apothecary, murdered his wife for her insurance money.[107] In eighteenth-century Toulouse, the father of Suzanne Dayral was unwilling or unable to pay the dowry he had promised when his daughter married. As punishment, her husband made her work all day at weaving hemp but denied her food so that she was forced to go begging. Suzanne Dayral's married life dragged on this way until the day she was found, her body lacerated and her stomach split open, drowned in the millpond.[108] But most cases of spouse murder appear to have been motivated by adultery: Eighty-three percent of cases fell into this category in the region around Toulouse.[109] The extensive literature on spouse murder that was published in England in the seventeenth century also focused on sexual issues – incompatibility, jealousy, infidelity – as background. This might have been journalistic sensationalism as much as anything, but it might also have reflected evidence that came before the courts dealing with the murder cases.

Spouse murder was not commonly resorted to as a means of informal or surrogate divorce. In the early seventeenth century the social commentator William Gouge wrote that "the nearer and dearer any persons be, the more violent will be that hatred which is fastened on them."[110] If it is true that emotional intensity in early modern society was low, that companionship and friendship, rather than romantic love, characterized marriage, then the kind of hatred that would result in murder should, following Gouge's reasoning, have been rare. But insofar as murder is frequently a crime of passion, impulsive and spontaneous rather than premeditated, prolonged emotional attachment need not be an important issue. It could well be that "since divorce was virtually impossible and annulment rare in ecclesiastical courts, the tensions of marriage could be prolonged and therefore increase the potential for murderous solution to marital difficulties."[111] But this is to overlook the many other alternatives to

[103] Barbara A. Hanawalt, *Crime and Conflict in English Communities, 1300–1348* (Cambridge, Mass., 1979), 160.
[104] Sharpe, "Domestic Homicide," 36.
[105] Castan, *Justice et répression*, 32.
[106] Ibid.
[107] Sharpe, "Domestic Homicide," 41.
[108] Castan, *Justice et répression*, 32.
[109] Ibid.
[110] Quoted in Sharpe, "Domestic Homicide," 35.
[111] Hanawalt, *Crime and Conflict*, 165.

8 The alternatives to divorce

divorce other than murder. As we have noted, desertion, bigamy, and separation were more common responses to dissatisfaction with marriage.

Even so, the association of divorce and spouse murder is compelling as a
partnership of alternatives. Each dissolved marriage in its own way, and advocates of divorce law liberalization in the nineteenth century particularly were
fond of pointing out that such murders (thought to be increasing) were among
the fruits of restrictive divorce policies. An American feminist magazine
editorialized in 1868 that in the absence of divorce

> there is no hope for two people shackled in the manacles of an unhappy marriage, but a
> release by death; and no wonder each desires deliverance, and longs for the death of the
> other...That the number of people who find marriage intolerable is not small, the
> annals of crime prove. Wife murders are so common that one can scarcely take up a
> newspaper without finding one or more instances of this worst of all sins; and none but
> God can know how many men and women are murderers at heart.[112]

The same point was made by proponents of the relegalization of divorce in
France in the 1880s. One senator argued that if divorce had been available,
crimes such as that committed by Marie Lafarge would not have occurred, a
reference to a notorious 1840 case in which a woman was convicted of poisoning
her husband with arsenic.[113]

8.9 Suicide

As a response to marital unhappiness, suicide was arguably even more desperate than killing one's spouse. There was always the possibility that in the
case of spouse murder, detection might be avoided, that provocation might be
successfully pleaded in mitigation, that in some way there might be life after the
other's death. But not so with suicide, which must be seen as the ultimate in
desperation. Apart from the obvious result of losing one's life, in traditional
Western society there were additional consequences for men and women who
committed suicide. Bodies of suicides could not be buried in consecrated
ground; in England until 1823, suicides were generally buried at the crossroads
with a stake through the heart, and all their goods were forfeited to the Crown.
In France, royal edicts provided that the corpse of a suicide should be prosecuted in court by secular judges and, when convicted, should be dragged
through the streets, exposed by being hung up by the feet, then either buried in
an unmarked grave or burned and the ashes thrown to the winds.[114] In Brittany
as recently as the early twentieth century, there were special cemeteries reserved
for suicides, where the coffin was passed over a wall that had no opening.[115]

112 *The Revolution*, quoted in Ann Jones, *Women Who Kill* (New York, 1980), 114–15.
113 This case is analyzed in Mary S. Hartmann, *Victorian Murderesses* (London, 1977), 10–50, a
rich work that very effectively places case studies of husband murder in nineteenth-century
France and England in their social context.
114 John McManners, *Death and the Enlightenment* (Oxford, 1981). 409.
115 Philippe Ariès, *The Hour of Our Death* (New York, 1982), 44.

310

Such consequences must surely have made suicide the least attractive of all responses to unhappiness in marriage. It certainly put an end to the misery of mundane life, but for the faithful it placed the soul in the greatest jeopardy.

It is, of course, impossible to ascertain how many suicides were motivated wholly or primarily by an inability to tolerate a marriage any longer. Too often the circumstances and catalysts of suicide are unclear and certainly unstated. Suicide notes are a rarity, and we cannot assume that the suicide of a married person was the result of marital conditions. For example, one-third of suicides fished out of the Seine at Paris at the end of the eighteenth century were married, but there is insufficient information on their lives to warrant drawing any conclusions about the quality of their marriages.[116]

A study of suicides reported in some eighteenth- and early nineteenth-century English periodicals throws some light on the family circumstances that could give rise to such acts of desperation. Of more than 1,500 suicides reported between the early 1730s and 1823 (when the law relating to suicide was amended), some 240 (about 15%) explicitly suggested that family difficulties were significant as motivations.[117] The circumstances involved here concerned not only difficulties in marriage but also parent–child problems, master–servant relationships, the effects of bereavement, and disappointment in courtship. Unambiguously marital problems accounted for 68 suicides, 41 of them by men and 27 by women. Of all 1,500 reported suicides, then, only 4 or 5% were likely to have been motivated by marriage problems.

The precise background varied, as we should expect. Women appeared to be driven to suicide mainly by desertion, an unwanted separation, by jealousy, or by a quarrel. For instance in 1809 a Mrs. Gooch of Anthorpe tried to drown herself in "a fit of jealousy" concerning her husband.[118] Although rescued from the water, she soon afterward secured her own demise by taking two ounces of sublimate. Husbands' suicides were the result of desertion or deception by their wives. In 1790 a London pork butcher sent his wife and a friend on a day trip to the country, but they took the opportunity to elope. When the husband learned of it, he drowned himself in a tub.[119]

8.10 Prayer

Suicide, murder, and desertion were all, to varying degrees, desperate responses to unhappiness in marriage. Prayer for deliverance from a brutal or oppressive spouse was another kind of desperation, and it too had its place in history. This response belonged to women only, probably for two principal reasons. First, women were more likely than men to be devout enough to

---

[116] Richard Cobb, *Death in Paris* (Oxford, 1978), 9.
[117] Donna T. Andrew (University of Guelph, Ontario, Canada), "Suicide and the Family in Eighteenth-Century English Periodicals" (unpublished paper).
[118] *Examiner*, October 29, 1809, cited in Andrew, "Suicide," 7.
[119] *Times* (London), July 30, 1790, cited in ibid.

believe in the efficacy of prayer (even if the saint whose intercession they invoked is held to be spurious, as we shall see). Second, wives had fewer realistic options open to them than did their husbands, when faced with an unsatisfactory marriage; they were, for example, less mobile and therefore less able simply to leave.

Under these general circumstances, it is hardly surprising to find a saint who could be called upon to free women of their unwanted husbands. A cult of St. Wilgefortis seems to have originated in fourteenth-century Flanders, and from there spread across Europe.[120] In England, Wilgefortis was known as Saint Uncumber and in France as Ste. Livrade (from the Latin *Liberata* – the liberated woman). The story of Wilgefortis is that she was the daughter of a king of Portugal, and was betrothed by her father to marry the king of Sicily. But because Wilgefortis had taken a vow of virginity, she prayed to become unattractive, and as a result grew a moustache and beard. When the king of Sicily refused to take her as his wife in this hirsute condition, Wilgefortis was crucified by her father to punish her for her disobedience. While she was on the cross, she prayed that all those who remembered her suffering should be liberated from all encumbrances (hence Uncumber). It became customary for women who wanted to be freed from their husbands to offer oats to her. Thomas More, deriding the practice, suggested the reason:

Whereof I cannot perceive the reason, but if it be because she should provide a horse for an evil husband to ride to the devil upon, for that is the thing that she is so sought for, as they say. Insomuch as women have therefore changed her name and instead of Saint Wilgeforte call her Saint Uncumber, because they reckon that for a peck of oats she will not fail to uncumber them of their husbands.[121]

8.11 Conclusion

This chapter really has no conclusion. Its aim has been to delve beyond the legal forms of divorce to discern what steps husbands and wives might take, individually or jointly, when they wanted to terminate their marriages (and perhaps enter another) but could not do so legally. Thus expressed, the problem is biased in favor of legal divorce, and we should take care not to think of all of the alternatives outlined in these pages as being unsatisfactory actions undertaken *faute de mieux*. It is certainly true that some men and women, those who had to flee from their homes or who were driven to kill themselves or their spouses, would rather have separated or divorced legally. For them the absence of accessible divorce was a hardship. For others, however, the informal action they took was the most appropriate for their situation. We can include in this category the besom divorces and others who dissolved their marriages by means acceptable

---

[120] On Wilgefortis, see David Hugh Farmer, *The Oxford Dictionary of the Saints* (Oxford, 1978), 403–4, and Gillian Edwards, *Uncumber and Pantaloon* (London, 1968), 75–82.
[121] Quoted in Farmer, *Dictionary of the Saints*, 404.

8.11 Conclusion

to their communities. Attended as they often were by arrangements regarding property and children, they were surely as satisfactory to the individuals concerned and to the community as legal divorce would be. It might even be suggested that they were more satisfactory from some points of view; these terminations of marriage had social approval and did not attract the stigma that was attached to divorce until very recently.

One point this chapter has brought out clearly is the continuing difficulty of defining marriage and divorce. We have noted that marriage was defined precisely in canon and statute law late in Western society. The Roman Catholic and Protestant churches specified the procedures for a valid and legally recognized marriage only in the sixteenth century; in England the first law regulating marriage forms effectively was passed as recently as 1753 (Lord Hardwicke's act). But the lawmakers and those others who wished to give certainty to marital status for legal and administrative purposes were in fierce competition with traditions and customs that died hard and died slowly, with populations that persisted in marrying and divorcing in their own ways. Examinations of the marital and dwelling arrangements of parishioners and the prosecution of bigamists by the secular courts represented continuing attempts to bring marriage and divorce within the framework of the law. Until these attempts were successful – and that was probably not until the twentieth century in some parts of Western society – we must be aware that there are dimensions to marriage and divorce other than the purely legal.

9

The meaning of marriage breakdown
in the past

9.1 Introduction

So far, this book has concentrated on a limited range of facets of divorce in the history of Western society: the evolution of attitudes toward divorce, the development of divorce policies and legislation, and the general trends in the use of divorce, the last particularly up to the beginning of the nineteenth century. Throughout, the main point of reference has been legislation: The law has been treated as reflecting the attitudes and doctrines of the dominant social and political groups, and law has – implicitly and explicitly – been regarded as an important influence on the incidence of divorce at any given time. Although the remaining chapters will explore the range of other influences on the divorce rate, the role of legislation is beyond question. In the most banal sense, there is no divorce where there is no provision in law for the dissolution of marriage; that is, there is no divorce as defined in this study as a legally sanctioned dissolution of a valid marriage, enabling one or both of the former spouses to enter a new marriage whose validity was recognized by law. In these terms there were no divorces in France until 1792, and none between its abolition in 1816 and its relegalization in 1884; there were no divorces in South Carolina between 1878 and 1949; none in Italy until 1970; and none in Spain until 1981.

This point is easily granted; given the definitions, it is necessarily true. But the association between divorce law and the divorce rate has often been taken further. It has frequently been argued that the liberalization of divorce law leads to more divorce. This is, in fact, almost universally so, as the study of trends in divorce has shown. Whenever divorce law has been liberalized, the divorce rate has increased, sometimes dramatically, as marriages that had not qualified for dissolution under the terms of the earlier law began to fall within the more liberal criteria for dissolution. An example is the reform of English divorce law in 1937, which permitted divorce on more grounds than simply adultery. From 1938 onward, marriages affected by desertion, cruelty, or insanity were embraced by the terms of the law, and the number of marriages at risk of divorce thereby increased. From 1937 to 1939 the number of divorces rose from 5,044 to 8,248 (an increase of 64%), and the divorce rate rose from 0.12 to 0.19 per thousand population.[1] Conversely, reforms of divorce law in a more restrictive direction (which have historically been much less common than liberalizing reforms) have tended to depress the number of divorces. The repeal of the permissive French 1792 legislation and its replacement by the 1803 Napoleonic divorce law had just this effect throughout France (see Section 7.4).

That legislation has influenced divorce rates over the short- and longer-terms is incontestable, although it is impossible to make universally applicable generalizations about the effects. Certainly the magnitude of legal influence has varied markedly. The legalization of divorce in a previously divorceless society need not provoke a stampede to the divorce courts as the experience of Italy showed: In the eight years during which divorce was available under the terms of the 1806 Codice Civile, fewer marriages were dissolved in the whole country than there were divorces in one large French city under similar legislation. Moreover, a jurisdiction with a restrictive divorce law can have a higher divorce rate than one with more liberal divorce provisions. Although important in making divorce possible and in defining the range of conditions that can give rise to the legal dissolution of a marriage, the formal terms of legislation constitute only one of the many influences on the incidence of divorce in a society. The other factors involved are institutional, social, economic, ideological, and demographic, and the final chapter seeks to integrate them into a general account and explanation of divorce in Western society during the past century and a half.

What are we trying to account for when attempting to explain trends in divorce? Regarded over the long term, divorce on any significant scale must be treated as a recent phenomenon, a characteristic of little more than the past century. In the United States, even in those areas that had permitted divorce during the colonial period, divorce can scarcely be measured as a rate before the end of the nineteenth century. Late-eighteenth-century Massachusetts is an example. In the period 1775–86 there was a total of sixty-one divorces, separations, and annulments (most of them divorces), an average of five a year. Using the colony's population of about 270,000 in 1780 as a base, the crude annual divorce rate would be at most 0.04 per thousand inhabitants.[2] Connecticut's rate was higher than this throughout the eighteenth century: From 1750 to 1762 the colony's divorce rate was about 0.05 per thousand, and from 1786 to 1797 (after independence) it rose to about 0.14 per thousand.[3]

---

[1] *Royal Commission, Report, 1951–1955*, 359, Table 2; *United Nations Demographic Yearbook* 1958, 470, Table 25.

[2] Divorce statistics: Nancy Cott, "Divorce and the Changing Status of Women in Eighteenth-Century Massachusetts," *William and Many Quarterly* 3rd ser., 33 (1976), 592, Table 1. The population of Massachusetts in 1780 is estimated at 268,627. *Historical Statistics of the United States: Colonial Times to 1957* (Washington, D.C., 1960), 756, Series Z1-19.

[3] These rates are calculated from Cohen, " 'To Parts of the World Unknown': The Circumstances of Divorce in Connecticut, 1750–1797," *Canadian Review of American Studies* 11 (1980) 287. Cohen gives crude rates of divorce actions as 0.062 per thousand population in the period 1750–62, and 0.17 per thousand for 1786–97, but they must be reduced by 22% and 19%, respectively, to allow for petitions that failed.

These two colonies had the highest rates of divorce in America in the eighteenth century, and most of the other colonies produced so few divorces that they are not worth calculating as rates. Similarly, in those parts of Europe that had legalized divorce in the sixteenth century, it was three hundred years and more before any line of divorce could be distinguished from the horizontal axis of a graphic depiction of divorce rates. To take the by now familiar example of revolutionary France – the only example of anything approaching widespread divorce before the late nineteenth century – there were perhaps 25,000 (a maximum estimate) over eleven years in a country with a population of about 28 million. Averaged over eleven years, there were about 2,250 divorces a year, or a rate of 0.08 per thousand population. The rate in the peak years 1793–4 could have been twice that, and Paris, which accounted for half the divorces, had a remarkably higher rate.[4] The fact that divorce has historically been concentrated in cities means that urban divorce rates have consistently been much higher than national divorce rates.

With the notable exception of the revolutionary period in France, a case that was exceptional in so many respects, the incidence of divorce in Western society has been very low until recent times. We must guard, however, against judging earlier divorce rates anachronistically and too rigidly from the perspective of the late twentieth century, a time when we are accustomed to, though by no means universally reconciled to, divorces in the tens and hundreds of thousands a year, and national annual divorce rates in the range of two to five or more per thousand population. We must recognize the legitimacy of the anxiety and alarm of contemporary commentators in seventeenth-century Massachusetts, eighteenth-century England, or mid-nineteenth-century America when they were confronted by divorce rates that astonished them, even if these now seem negligible over the long-term historical perspective. Yet even though appreciating that these low rates were measured and evaluated against the even lower rates (or nonexistent rates) that had preceded them, we must also benefit from our ability to take this longer-term view and recognize that divorce is a recent development as a socially and statistically significant phenomenon. At most it has a historical depth of one century. The emotion that divorce generated for hundreds of years was quite disproportionate to its incidence and reflected the fears of earlier generations about the future more than about their own times.

Questions provoked by the increasing extent of divorce have generally, and quite logically, laid stress on the increase itself. Contemporaries, as well as later scholars who have adopted a historical view, described the trends of increase as best they could in statistical or impressionistic terms and posed the question:

---

[4] The peak divorce rate in Rouen during the revolutionary period (September 1794–September 1795) was about 2.2 per thousand population (191 divorces in a population of about 85,000). Roderick Phillips. *Family Breakdown in Late Eighteenth-Century France: Divorces in Rouen, 1792–1803* (Oxford, 1980), 44ff.

9.1 Introduction

Why have divorce rates risen? This is a perfectly appropriate question, needless to say, but familiarity with long-term trends and the virtual absence of divorce from Western society for so many years, even during the centuries when divorce legislation was in place, surely provokes another question: Why was there so little divorce until the past hundred years? To be sure, the two questions are related, but the point is that both questions must be asked and answered if we are to understand the course of divorce in early modern and modern history. It could be that the answer to each question is the reverse of the other: The conditions that led to low rates of divorce from the sixteenth to the nineteenth centuries were absent in the late nineteenth and twentieth centuries; and the conditions that produced the recent high divorce rates are of recent origin. We shall see, however, that the factors involved, and their relationships to one another, are more complex, that some factors that have helped to produce the high divorce rates and the characteristics of divorce in modern times prevailed in earlier times as well. In such cases the major shift has been in the relationships among factors rather than changes in the factors themselves.

Divorce is not an isolated event, unrelated to other personal, familial, and social events and actions, but is, rather, the final stage of a marital process. In crude and schematic terms the main stages in this process are marriage, marriage breakdown, the decision on the part of one or both spouses to terminate the marriage, and finally its legal dissolution by divorce. Needless to say, far from all marriages complete the process; only a minority do so, as the divorce statistics attest. Some, however, might go to the point of marriage breakdown without going so far as to manifest it in social or legal terms. Yet other broken marriages are terminated socially, the spouses living apart and quite independently of each other, without any legal formalization such as separation or divorce. At each stage in the process, then, a proportion of the total population of marriages goes no further. Many marriages never break down (the concept of marriage breakdown is discussed later) and last until one of the spouses dies; others break down but show no public evidence of it. Some spouses who wish to terminate their marriages find that for legal, economic, social, or other reasons they cannot do so legally, and instead end their marriages de facto, by deserting or by separating by mutual agreement. Finally others – those who contribute to the divorce rate – experience breakdown, decide to terminate their marriages, and can, and eventually do, divorce.

It is clear that divorces reflect only a proportion of the marriages that break down, and that marriage breakdown and divorce, although intimately related, must be treated quite distinctly. For one thing they draw on quite different marriage populations. All marriages have the potential to break down, but only broken-down marriages have the possibility of being dissolved by divorce. (We can exclude divorces of convenience, those rare divorces undertaken for political, economic, or other motives than for reasons to do with the quality of the marital relationship.)[5] Yet the distinction between marriage breakdown and divorce has not always been clearly made, and there has often been an assumption that a rising divorce rate is indicative of an increasing incidence of marriage breakdown. Such an assumption ignores the fact that marriage breakdown and divorce are subject to different sets of influences. Proponents of this view have frequently expressed it as an argument against liberalizing divorce law, that the more divorces that would result would not draw on an existing reservoir of broken marriages – marriages awaiting the legal facility of divorce – but that a liberalization of a divorce law would actually encourage the breakdown of more marriages.[6]

Two crude models of the relationship between marriage, marriage breakdown, and divorce are implied by much of the writing on divorce. They are set out graphically in Figure 9.1. In the first of these models both marriage breakdown and divorce are depicted as rising over time, so that divorce trends reflect trends in marriage breakdown. This was the model favored by the late-nineteenth-century conservatives who interpreted the rising divorce rate as meaning that marriage breakdown was increasing. In the second model the incidence of marriage breakdown is viewed as stationary and the divorce rate rises over time, with the effect that the divorce rate more and more closely resembles the rate of marriage breakdown in society. This is a more recent perspective, which generally assumes that factors such as more accessible divorce, greater economic independence on the part of women, and the provision of social welfare have permitted more and more broken marriages to be dissolved by divorce. This perspective implies that modern divorce rates more accurately reflect the extent of marriage breakdown than did the low divorce rates of the past. One work on marriage breakdown, for example, suggests that "it may be that, with the greater ease with which divorce could be obtained in the 1960s, the [divorce] figures during this period are a closer approximation to the actual numbers of marriages which broke down than they were formerly."[7] Variations on these two models are possible, perhaps the most plausible being a hybrid: an increase in both rates, with the divorce rate increasing more rapidly than the rate of marriage breakdown.

The difficulty with these models is that although the divorce rates can be

---

[5] An example of divorces of convenience was the group of divorces involving émigrés during the French Revolution. A woman who divorced her émigré husband could thereby protect herself from prosecution as the wife of an enemy of France, as well as protect the matrimonial property from confiscation by the state (see Section 7.4). In more recent times divorce may confer financial benefits where taxation policies weigh heavier on incomes considered jointly rather than separately. Divorces of convenience also undo marriages of convenience, such as those undertaken for political or immigration purposes. Among prominent figures who have thus married and divorced in order to secure someone from political persecution are the German socialist Rosa Luxembourg and former Swedish prime minister Olaf Palme.

[6] There is probably something to be said for this view, even though the effect is not as great as its proponents often believe. The effects of divorce law reform on divorce behavior are discussed in more detail in Chapter 14.

[7] John Eekelaar, *Family Security and Family Breakdown* (Harmondsworth, 1971), 35.

318

9.1 Introduction

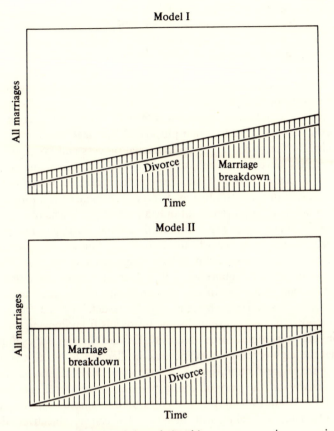

Figure 9.1 Competing models of the relationships among marriage, marriage breakdown, and divorce over time.

plotted with certainty, the extent of marriage breakdown at any point in time, and thus changes in its incidence over time, cannot. It would be convenient if marriage breakdowns could be determined like other sociodemographic variables such as fertility. Using records of vital statistics, parish registers, declarations of pregnancy, and the like, historians have been able to plot, with a high degree of reliability, various rates of fertility – the fertility of the married, illegitimate fertility, and premarital fertility.[8] In these cases the event – a birth – was recorded either by legal requirement or by custom and social pressure (such as baptisms before registrations of birth became mandatory). Giving birth was and is both a personal and social event, but it had to be recorded formally and so became a legal or quasi-legal event as well. It was not and is not so in the case of marriage breakdown. True, some manifestations of marriage break-

---

[8] See, for example, the articles in Peter Laslett, Karla Oosterveen, and Richard M. Smith (eds.), *Bastardy and its Comparative History* (London, 1980).

319

down, such as bigamy, desertion, or the refusal of one or both spouses to cohabit, were offenses under ecclesiastical law in England, America, and elsewhere (see Chapter 8). But the decision to prosecute offenders, and hence the likelihood of the cases' being recorded, depended on the discretion and zeal of the community, local officials, and judges of the civil and church courts. For the rest, marriage breakdown generally appears in court and other records only when one or both spouses decided to bring it to the attention of ecclesiastical or secular officials. (A prominent exception is cases of desertion that come to light in censuses or surveys taken for other purposes.) Marriage breakdown, then, is like childbirth in that it is a social and personal process and event, but unlike it in that it has never been subject to the same requirements of official notification. In fact a more accurate analogy for marriage breakdown is not fertility but sexual intercourse. Just as divorces represent only a proportion of broken marriages, so births represent only a proportion of acts of intercourse. And just as there are stages separating divorce from marriage breakdown, so there are stages separating birth from intercourse: The use of contraception, the likelihood of conception from an act of intercourse, the possibilities of spontaneous or procured abortions, all reduce the proportion that births represent of all completed acts of sexual intercourse between men and women.

The quite understandable absence of records detailing the frequency of sexual intercourse has not prevented some historians from drawing speculative conclusions about it from records of fertility. Edward Shorter, for example, has argued that the eighteenth-century increase in illegitimate births was brought about by a sexual revolution, one of whose characteristics was an increase in sexual activity on the part of young working women.[9] As successful or unsuccessful as historical enterprises such as Shorter's have been, they at least have the advantage of dealing with behavior that can be objectively defined, sexual intercourse. It is in this issue, definition, that lies the principal obstacle to our measuring or assessing the extent of marriage breakdown in the past and, indeed, in the present as well: For the most part marriage breakdown is not a matter of objectively defined conditions, circumstances, or behavior that can be determined by the outsider, whether a contemporary or a later historian. Rather, the decision as to whether an individual marriage has broken down is made directly by one or both of the spouses involved.

There are, it is true, some conditions and circumstances that we can reasonably argue implied marriage breakdown, independently of the perception of the spouses involved. The most important of these have been discussed, with examples, in Chapter 8, where forms of informal divorce were surveyed. Some of these, such as desertion and de facto separation at the agreement of both parties were surely indicative of marriage breakdown, if the term is to have any meaning at all. Forms of popular divorce such as wife sale, to take another

[9] Edward Shorter, "Illegitimacy, Sexual Revolution, and Social Change in Modern Europe," *Journal of Interdisciplinary History* 2 (1971), 237–72; "Female Emancipation, Birth Control, and Fertility in European History," *American Historical Review* 77 (1973), 605–40.

example, hardly suggest that the vendor and the object of the transaction had been closely bound together by the silken ropes of matrimonial bliss prior to the sale. Little more need be said of the remedies of desperation – spouse murder and suicide – as a response to the conditions of marriage. Whether they were carefully premeditated acts and the culmination of years of misery or the impulsive and impassioned reaction to a particular situation in a marriage, they reflected the will and determination to terminate the intolerable. Such manifestations of marriage breakdown were the more observable and were more likely than others to find their way into the historical record. Desertions and refusal to share a dwelling with one's spouse could lead to arraignment in court, as we have seen, and suicides and murders, the least common responses to marriage breakdown, were, in the perverse way of the historical record, the most likely to be documented by the authorities.

Apart from these signs of marriage breakdown there were many others, some of which are familiar as grounds for divorce. The most common of these were physical violence and adultery, but we may also include failure to provide the means of support, drunkenness, and emotional or mental cruelty. These circumstances involve a degree of fault or at least responsibility on the part of either husband or wife, but other conditions, such as the insanity of one spouse, need not. Finally there is incompatibility, a category of marriage breakdown in which it is difficult, if not completely impossible, to attribute fault wholly to one spouse or the other, or even to distribute proportional responsibility between them. Divorce legislation has generally qualified the incompatibility as "of character" or "of temperament." As a category it includes marital relationships that are not necessarily characterized by violence or even hatred (although the latter might well be present), but where the depth of emotional commitment is less than the spouses – or one of them – consider appropriate to marriage. These individual perceptions and expectations of marriage are of critical importance, and must be taken into account when we assess the extent of marriage breakdown in societies past or present.

9.2 Expectations of marriage

As a concept, marriage breakdown can be thought of as a condition or behavior on the part of one spouse, which one or both spouses regard as wholly inappropriate to their marriage. More formally we might describe it as an irremediable incongruence between the marital expectations of one or both spouses and the perceived state of the marriage. At any given time there have been individual and social views as to what kind of behavior was appropriate between husband and wife, and where the limits of a marital relationship should be drawn. Often these views are implicit and are expressed only when one spouse behaves in an inappropriate manner. In evidence before the divorce courts of revolutionary France women frequently complained that their husbands did not act toward them *maritalement*, a word that is best translated by

321

the phrase "in a manner appropriate between married persons." Husbands in some cases, seeking to dissuade their wives from divorce, promised to behave *maritalement*. It is unlikely that these women had, prior to the behavior – violence, adultery, eviction, mental cruelty – to which they took exception, explicit notions as to what was proper behavior within a marriage. But that they did have inherent notions is demonstrated by their divorce actions, which can be seen as statements that certain kinds and degrees of oppressive and abusive behavior were not acceptable to them.[10]

Some appreciation of expectations of marriage is clearly essential to an understanding of why some behavior was acceptable and some not. In principle, behavior or a relationship that failed to meet the individual or joint expectations of a couple could be seen as indicating marriage breakdown. But we must take into account the perceived gravity, the frequency, and context of the offensive behavior. A husband coming home drunk, having spent his wages on alcohol, or a wife's failing to do her allotted domestic chores, might well have fallen outside the marriage expectations of women and men in the eighteenth or any other century. But isolated occurrences of this kind might well have been overlooked, or punished and then forgiven, forgotten, or absorbed, as might befit a minor infrequent offense. Persistent repetition of minor offenses might not have been as easily accommodated. On the other hand, a single occurrence of a more serious offense, such as adultery or a severe physical assault, might have been enough to convince some men and women that their marriages were intolerable. We must also take into account changes in expectations of marriage over time, not only over the historical *longue durée*, but over the duration of marriage. Men and women might well have raised or lowered their expectations in the light of experience as reality overwhelmed their abstract notions of married life or because economic and social conditions gave them no alternative but to tolerate behavior or a relationship that they might, before entering it, have thought intolerable under any circumstances.

As we shall see, expectations at and of marriage have varied, not only over time but also according to social class and gender, and finally, from individual to individual. Even so, it is possible to break expectations of marriage in Western society into a few broad categories, although the following order does not necessarily indicate their relative importance.

> *Standard of living*: This might be an expectation of no more than maintaining the initial standard of living (in terms of habitation, diet, and clothing), though it might include an expectation of improvement. It would rarely comprise an expectation of a decline of living standards.
> *Sexuality*: Predominant is the expectation of sexual exclusivity by the spouses, together with a certain frequency of

---

[10] See Roderick Phillips, "Women and Family Breakdown in Eighteenth-Century France: Rouen 1780–1800," *Social History*, 2 (1976), 197–218.

sexual activity (elevated to the level of a conjugal "duty" or "obligation" in some religious and secular doctrines). A certain extent of adultery on the part of the husband might be expected.

Affective: An expectation of a minimal degree of emotional compatibility, considerate behavior, friendship, affection, or love. It would include an expectation that violent behavior should be moderate if present at all.

Domestic obligations: Within this category fall variable expectations as to the division of labor and responsibilities within marriage and the household, income earning, and child care.

Other family members: Implicitly or explicitly there are expectations that the couple will or will not have children. An important issue in this category relates to expectations regarding relationships between the spouses and other family members such as parents and parents-in-law.

Although expectations of marriage can vary widely from individual to individual, there are general expectations that are widespread. Widely shared social expectations of marriage must, however, be regarded developmentally, not as static over the duration of individual marriages nor as unvarying according to other geographical, class, and gender criteria. To take the example of sexual fidelity, it might well have been that the English aristocracy was much more tolerant of adultery in the late seventeenth century than was the contemporary middle class, and it is certainly true that women have historically been more tolerant of adultery by their husbands than husbands have of adultery by their wives. Expectations with respect to sexuality, then, are not fixed and universally shared, and to this extent neither are definitions of marriage breakdown. The challenge to the historian of this aspect of marriage is to define patterns and trends. These can help us to determine whether, in terms of expectations alone, the risks of marriage breakdown have remained constant, have increased, or have decreased over time. In the following sections three principal areas of marriage will be examined: violence, adultery, and emotional content. All three figured prominently in those cases of marriage breakdown that were transformed into divorces, and from this and other evidence we should expect them to have been particularly problematic aspects of marital relationships in the past. The question is whether they can be considered to be indicative of marriage breakdown.

9.3 Marital violence and "moderate correction"

Marital violence is a good example of the difficulties we face when seeking to generalize about marriage breakdown. Historically, most physical violence within marriage has been directed by the husband against the wife, and may simply be called wife beating or wife battering. The historical evidence shows that wife beating was far from uncommon and that, at least to a certain degree, it was widely recognized as being acceptable and even normal within marriage. To this extent it could be encompassed within prevailing expectations of marital behavior, and its presence would not be regarded as incompatible with a functioning and tolerable marriage. But there are important qualifications to be made. Wife beating varied from couple to couple in terms of severity, frequency, and quality, and these variations influenced its acceptability. Moreover, this was male violence, and although it might have been acceptable and normal to men – those who administered it, male witnesses, male judges, and male commentators on the subject – it was no doubt often less acceptable, and sometimes not at all acceptable, to women. In this issue, as in so many others, women did not fully share the attitudes of their male counterparts. Finally, when we consider whether wife beating was indicative of marriage breakdown we need to take into account differences among social classes in relation to such violence.

The questions of the extent of wife beating in the past and of its social acceptability are, we might note at the beginning of this discussion, issues over which historians disagree. Keith Wrightson, for example, concluded that in seventeenth-century England "wife-battering was certainly known...but this is not something which can be held to demonstrate that physical violence was an accepted feature of lower-class marriages."[11] On the other side, Edward Shorter generalized that "the average husband in small towns and villages would beat his wife...As a practical matter, wife-beating was universal."[12] In this question all historians work with incomplete and impressionistic evidence, no matter what the place or period from which it derives. Is it possible to reach any conclusions about the extent of wife beating and its place in marriage?

The ability of husbands to beat their wives without attracting legal sanctions or consequences was enshrined in Western common and statute law. It was one facet of men's legal and social superiority over women in general and of the husband's superiority over his wife in particular. The principle entered Western law directly from Roman law, which had originally given the husband the right to kill his wife if she committed certain offenses, notably adultery.[13] By medieval and early modern times, however, this right had been considerably attenuated. A husband no longer had the right to kill his wife,[14] but his position as her superior did endow him with the right, indeed the duty, to chastise or punish her using physical means. In part this right was justified in terms of the legal obligations borne by the husband to answer for his wife's actions; because he was thus personally responsible for her misdeeds, it was considered rea-

[11] Keith Wrightson, *English Society, 1580–1680* (London, 1983), 99.
[12] Edward Shorter, *A History of Women's Bodies* (Harmondsworth, 1984), 5.
[13] P. E. Corbett, *The Roman Law of Marriage* (Oxford, 1930), 128–9. A father could also kill his married daughter under certain circumstances. Ibid. 137–8.
[14] Some legal codes permitted a husband to kill his wife with impunity if he did so on discovering her in the act of adultery. This was enshrined in French law until it was repealed, after a public campaign against it, in 1907.

sonable that he should have the right to control her behavior and to repress her when necessary. To this extent the right to chastise a wife physically was integral to the legal relationship that existed between husband and wife.

It is important to note, though, that violence was to be used only as a response to a wrong committed by the wife, and there was also the expectation on the part of the law that it would be a last resort, not a first reaction. Friar Cherubino of Ciena (ca. 1450–81) advised that when a wife committed an offense, her husband should correct her lovingly and pleasantly. "But," he went on,

> if your wife is of a servile disposition and has a crude and shifty spirit, so that pleasant words have no effect, scold her sharply, bully and terrify her. And if this still does not work...take up a stick and beat her soundly, for it is better to punish the body and correct the soul than to damage the soul and correct the body...You should beat her ...only when she commits a serious wrong... Then readily beat her, not in rage but out of charity and concern for her soul, so that the beating would redound to your merit and her good.[15]

There were guidelines not only as to the motivation for beating a wife but also as to the degree of violence that might be employed. A husband no longer had the right to kill his wife, and neither did he have the right to beat her with such violence as would result in serious or permanent injury. The notion of "moderate correction" developed, permitting a husband to beat or otherwise physically chastise his wife "moderately," as distinct from excessively. Lethal weapons were ruled out, and a rule developed to the effect that if a stick or rod were used, that it should be no thicker than a man's thumb. (This is the origin of the term "rule of thumb.") There is a recognition of this guideline in the promise of a German husband in the fifteenth century that he would beat his wife only with switches (rather than anything more substantial, presumably) "as was fitting and consistent with the fidelity and honour of a worthy man."[16] It was, needless to say, impossible to distinguish precisely those circumstances or actions that were moderate from those that were excessive. A thin rod can be wielded more or less harshly, more or less frequently. One seventeenth-century English commentary on the law relating to women noted that just as a man might beat an outlaw, a pagan, or a traitor with impunity, so a husband might beat his wife, but only as long as he did not do "any bodily damage, otherwise than appertaines to the office of a Husband for lawfull and reasonable correction." But, the commentator conceded, "how farre that extendeth I cannot tell...."[17] In the next century a legal text also recognized the husband's legal

---

[15] Quoted in William J. Hawser, *Differences in Relative Resources, Familial Power and Spouse Abuse* (Palo Alto, 1982), 8.

[16] Rudolf Huebner, *A History of Germanic Private Law* (Boston, 1918), 618.

[17] *Lawes Resolutions of Women's Rights* (London, 1639), 128–29. The anonymous author of this work noted that it was because of their special responsibility for the original sin that "women have no voyce in Parliament, they make no Lawes, they consent to none, they abrogate none. All of them are understood either married and their decisions...subject to their husbands...." (Ibid., 6).

power over his wife but qualified the right of physical correction: It should not be "violent or cruel" or "outrageous," and if a husband did go beyond these limits, he could be bound over to keep the peace or his wife could sue for a separation.[18]

The right of a husband to beat his wife was recognized by canon law and by ancient customary laws in medieval Europe.[19] For example, the thirteenth-century customary law of the Beauvaisis held that "it is licit for the man to beat his wife, without bringing about death or disablement, when she refuses her husband anything."[20] The 1404 edition of the customary law of the Barrèges valley stated that "every master and head of household may chastise his wife and family without anyone placing any impediment in his way."[21] As we shall see, these general principles were echoed by legal codes, statutes, and common law throughout Western society until quite recently, and it is clear that wife beating in moderate form was permitted, acceptable, and even recommended. The limitations lay in the severity, which was not to be excessive, and the motivation, which was to be chastisement, so that the character of approved wife beating was expressed in the very term "moderate correction."

Even though this tradition was for the most part retained until the nineteenth century in terms of the laws, and beyond in terms of social attitudes and practice, it became questioned and even attacked from the sixteenth and seventeenth centuries, especially the latter. Reformed church pastors instructed husbands not to be tyrants in their homes; they should govern their wives with love and intelligence rather than with force, "repeated grumbling, insults, curses and blows to a poor, defenseless, weak woman."[22] In the late sixteenth century the Anglican vicar Henry Smith rejected outright any violence as wholly inappropriate to marriage: "In all [the husband's]...offices is found no office to fight. If he cannot reform his wife without beating, he is worthy to be beaten for choosing no better."[23] (It is noteworthy that Smith rejected wife beating but advocated legalizing divorce, which he called "the rod of marriage.") In the next century, which saw a much more systematic campaign against wife beating, the theologian William Ames argued that a husband "may and ought to restrain her [his wife] by such meanes as are not repugnant to conjugall society, as by admonitions, reprehensions, and the deniall of some priviledges which are due to a godly and obedient wife. But it is by no means the part of any Husband,

[18] Matthew Bacon, *A New Abridgement of the Law* (5 vols., London, 1778), I, 285. Bacon did not explain how a husband was to beat his wife nonviolently.
[19] E. William Monter, "The Pedestal and the Stake: Courtly Love and Witchcraft," in Renate Bridenthal and Claudia Koontz (eds.), *Becoming Visible: Women in European History* (Boston, 1977), 124.
[20] Jean-Louis Flandrin, *Families in Former Times* (Cambridge, 1979), 123.
[21] Ibid.
[22] Justus Menius, quoted in Steven Ozment, *When Fathers Ruled: Family Life in Reformation Europe* (Cambridge, Mass., 1983), 51.
[23] Henry Smith, "Preparative to Marriage," in *The Sermons of Mr. Henry Smith* (2 vols., London, 1866), I, 22.

9.3 Marital violence and "moderate correction"

to correct his Wife with blowes. . . ." Ames based his argument against marital violence on various considerations, both utilitarian and moral. "Experience teacheth," he wrote, "that this is not the way, either to the amending of the Wife, or the peace of the Family."[24] Moral objections were more important, though: For Ames, violence was a manifestation of bitterness and cruelty – neither of which had a place within a marriage – it was repugnant to the "quiet and peaceable society of wedlocke," and it destroyed the affection between husband and wife when the latter was treated no differently from a servant.[25]

We should note that the opponents of moderate correction did not challenge the principle of the husband's superiority over his wife, but rather its enforcement by physical violence. Other seventeenth-century English commentators shared this general opinion: Robert Abbot, who denied the right of the husband to treat his wife like a slave ("even the very heathen man accounting it to a point of sacriledge for a man to strike his wife");[26] Robert Allestree, who held that husbands should love their wives as their own bodies "and therefore to do nothing, that may be hurtful, and grievous to them, no more than they would cut, and gash their own flesh";[27] Nathaniel Hardy, who argued that "surely we may account them besotted in their minds, or possessed with a divel who lay violent hands upon their wives";[28] Thomas Taylor, who pointed out that authority in the home "will not be kept by force of armes or violence; but by religious examples, and shewing your selfe the best and most godly"; [29] John Wing, who prescribed "servile correction by blowes" as appropriate for children from parents, servants from masters, slaves from tyrants, and beasts from owners, but as something "which the hart of a husband should abhorre, and the nature of this love will not beare";[30] and "R. C." who wrote that a husband should follow three rules when dealing with his wife's faults: "often to admonish; seldome to reprove; and never to smite her."[31]

Against the opponents of moderate correction rallied its defenders. One, Moses à Vauts – who briskly wrote off detractors of physical chastisement as "(no doubt) the spurious issue or products of Adulterous Parents, Pride and

---

[24] William Ames, *Conscience with the Power and Cases thereof* (n.p., 1639), 207.
[25] Ibid.
[26] Robert Abbot, *A Wedding Sermon preached at Bentley in Darbyshire, upon Michaelmas day last past Anno Domini 1607* (London, 1608), 58.
[27] Richard Allestree, *The Practice of Christian Graces, or the Whole Duty of Man Laid Down in a Plaine and Familiar Way for the Use of All, but especially the Meanest Reader* (London, 1658), 315.
[28] Nathaniel Hardy, *Love and Fear: The Inescapable Twins of a Blest Matrimony* (London, 1658), 16.
[29] Thomas Taylor, *A Good Husband and A Good Wife* (London, 1625), 25.
[30] John Wing, *The Crowne Conjugall or, The Spouse Royall* (Middleburgh, 1620), 48.
[31] Quoted in Wrightson, *English Society*, 98. Kathleen Davies underestimates this movement when she notes that "if there was any kind of movement towards equality of treatment between husband and wife, it seems to have found no expression in the lessening of violent behaviour as described in the marriage manuals." Kathleen M. Davies, "Continuity and Change in Literary Advice on Marriage," in R. B. Outhwaite (ed.), *Marriage and Society: Studies in the Social History of Marriage* (London, 1981), 68. Richard L. Greaves writes that Puritan authors were more opposed than non-Puritan Anglicans to wife beating. Greaves, *Society and Religion in Elizabethan England* (Minneapolis, 1981), 739.

atheism" – devoted a treatise to the prejudiced question of "whether it be fit or lawfull for a *good Man*, to beat his *bad Wife.*" Vauts proposed that faults should first be corrected by "many familiar compellations in a loving way," but that continual and serious challenges to a husband's authority demanded corporal correction, "the last and worst of remedies." Such challenges included disobedience, habitually interfering with his "Personall-domestick Quiet" by "customary scolding, railing and Clamors," by impugning her husband's reputation, or by threatening his financial security by wastefulness and luxury.[32] Beatings in such cases constituted a favor to the wife, bringing her back to her divinely ordained duties of obedience, respect, and reverence for her husband. Moderate correction did not indicate hatred but was consistent with the greatest affection, as the "most pious, tender hearted Husband" prevented his wife from falling deeper into the sins of self-assertion and disobedience. Vauts did not specify the kind of violence he recommended, but in an autobiographical note rare in such writings, he described the one instance when he had struck his own wife:

When, after mild Admonition, she would not forbear Swearing; but let fly 2 or 3 bloudy, horrid Oaths to my Face, I bestowed so many Flaps with my bare hand alone on her mouth, the part offending. . . Neither did I offer this, but on the same Terms I will gladly accept the Like, from any Christian other than my Wife, whatever.[33]

Other writers shared the view that wife beating was permissible under certain conditions. John Dod and Robert Cleaver counted it a part of the husband's duty to instruct his wife: "If she be of a gentle spirit, he may use gentle meanes which will then doe most good, but if she be of a more hard nature, rougher meanes must be used, and she must be dealt withall after a more round manner."[34] Yet others only reluctantly approved of violence as a last resort. William Perkins opposed correction by "stripes or strokes" and advised admonition and persuasion, and even taking a wife before a magistrate to have her punished for serious misdemeanors. Even so, Perkins was prepared to be understanding in the case of a provoked husband who, confronted by a "stubborne and peevish" wife, lost his patience and struck her: "He may in some sort be pardoned and pitied, but he is not wholly to be excused."[35] Women's attitudes toward wife beating are less extensively recorded than men's in published form, but women writers did not ignore the issue. The author of *An Exact Picture of a Bad Husband* included among the genre's characteristics this one: He "picks a causeless quarrel, gives her [his wife] a Remembrance with a Bed-Staff, that she is forc'd to wear the Northumberland

---

[32] Moses à Vauts, *The Husband's Authority Unvail'd; wherein It is moderately discussed whether it be fit or lawfull for a good Man, to beat his bad Wife* (London, 1650), 75–8.

[33] Ibid., 84.

[34] John Dod and Robert Cleaver, *A Godlie Forme of Householde Government* (London, 1612) f. 23ᵛ.

[35] William Perkins, *Christian Oeconomie: or, a Short Survey of the Right Manner of ordering a Familie, according to the Scriptures*, in Perkins, *The Workes* (3 vols., Cambridge, 1608–9), I, 692–3.

9.3 Marital violence and "moderate correction"

Arms a week after; which the good-natur'd Soul must excuse, by pretending an unlucky fall, or blaming an innocent Door-latch for the injury."[36] Lady Mary Chudleigh also contested wife beating, even though she accepted women's inferior status within marriage. Women, she wrote, should not challenge their husbands' "reasonable authority," "yet that's no reason why they should be their most obedient Slaves and Vassals." She wrote this in response to one supporter of physical correction whom, she said, she would like to meet as long as he had "his hands ty'd behind him, and his Cane secur'd (that he might not use that method of Conviction which he thinks proper for a Woman)."[37]

This theme of opposition to moderate correction does seem to have represented a break with earlier attitudes toward the principle and practice. But the campaign (if it can be called that) against wife beating had relatively little impact on law, although there were some reforms in the sixteenth and seventeenth centuries. In Calvin's Geneva spouse beating was made a crime, and between 1564 and 1569 some sixty-one men and two women were convicted and excommunicated for the offense.[38] (No doubt the example of Geneva reinforced opposition to wife beating in certain circles in seventeenth-century England, just as Geneva provided a model for those who wanted to make adultery a capital offense.) The same position was adopted in Puritan Massachusetts in the seventeenth century, where the first code of law (1641) emancipated married women from having to put up with "bodily correction or stripes by her husband, unless it be [given] in his owne defence upon her assault." In 1650 punishments of a fine of up to ten pounds or a whipping were specified for a husband who struck his wife or for a wife who struck her husband.[39] But despite these examples we should not too readily associate opposition to wife beating with Puritanism. The association – part of the putative Puritan stress on companionship and equality within marriage – is by no means consistent. Non-Puritan Anglicans opposed corporal punishment of wives, and some identifiable Puritans found the status quo more than satisfactory. Among the Puritan colonies of New England only Massachusetts went so far as to make marital violence a criminal offense, although the others did "lightly penalize husbands who abused their wives too readily."[40] We should note again, too, that criminalizing wife beating did not imply a belief that wife and husband were equals; in Massachusetts, for example, women

---

[36] *A Scourge for Poor Robin: or, the Exact Picture of a Bad Husband* (London, 1678), 8.
[37] Mary Chudleigh [Eugenia, pseud.], *The Female Preacher: Being an Answer to a late Rude and Scandalous Wedding-Sermon by Mr. John Sprint* (London, n.d.), 10–12.
[38] E. William Monter, "The Consistory of Geneva, 1559–1569," *Bibliothèque d'Humanisme et Renaissance* 38 (1976), 479–80.
[39] Lyle S. Koehler, *A Search for Power: The "Weaker Sex" in Seventeenth-Century New England* (Urbana, Ill., 1980), 49; Arthur W. Calhoun, *A Social History of the American Family from Colonial Times to the Present* (3 vols., Cleveland, 1919), I, 144ff.
[40] Koehler, *Search for Power*, 49. In contrast to this, the Plymouth General Court in 1655 authorized a husband to chastise his wife at home after she had attacked him physically and cursed him. Ibid., 46.

continued to be subordinates, and married women continued to need their husbands' consent for a wide range of activities.

The right of moderate correction, which in practice could be invoked to justify a broad spectrum of violent acts, was, we can see, deeply entrenched in legal codes and social attitudes. From the seventeenth century in particular there seems to have developed a reaction against it, based on the notion that although a wife was her husband's inferior, she was an inferior different from children and servants and should not be subject to the physical punishments that could be administered to them. This questioning of moderate correction was, however, the merest beginning, and we should not assume that it had rapid effects. It was a long time before these new attitudes were widely expressed in legislation, and even longer before they began to be shared by significant sections of the population. It is possible to locate popular expressions of opposition to wife beating, such as the sixteenth-century German proverb: "To strike a woman brings little honour to a man."[41] But against this we can pit popular adages in favor of beating a wife, such as the proverb from Languedoc: "Don't expect any good from an ass, a nut or a woman unless you have a stick in your hand,"[42] or the Provençal saying that "good or bad, the horse gets the spur. Good or bad, the wife gets the stick."[43]

It was not until the late eighteenth century that Continental legal codes began to undermine the traditional rights of moderate correction. The 1794 Prussian Allgemeines Landrecht significantly did not mention the right of moderate correction, although it did not make assault by a husband punishable under all circumstances. In contrast the Bavarian and other regional legal codes in Germany continued explicitly to recognize the right of correction.[44] In 1790 French law was reformed to provide heavier penalties for an assault on a woman than for assault on a man. Violence against a man could be punished by a fine of up to 500 *livres* and imprisonment for six months, but the penalties for assault on a woman were twice as severe.[45] And despite the reassertion of the husband's authority in many respects by the Code Napoléon, the principle of *correction modérée* was not reestablished after the French Revolution. But wife beating continued to be treated leniently; in late-nineteenth-century France "beating one's wife might cost as little as five francs, beating a strange woman four times as much."[46]

Only in the nineteenth century did legislation and case law systematically begin to forbid the physical correction of married women or at least to admit that beaten women might obtain some kind of relief or redress through the criminal or civil law. Marital violence was the subject of a series of laws in

[41] Ozment, *When Fathers Ruled*, 203n.14.
[42] Martine Segalen, "Le mariage et la femme dans les proverbes du sud de la France," *Annales du Midi* 87 (1975), 285.
[43] Shorter, *Women's Bodies*, 6.
[44] Huebner, *Germanic Private Law*, 620.
[45] Phillips, *Family Breakdown*, 110ff.
[46] Eugen Weber, *Peasants into Frenchmen: The Modernization of Rural France* (London, 1979), 62.

9.3 Marital violence and "moderate correction"

England, such as the 1853 Act for the Prevention and Punishment of Aggravated Assaults on Women, which gave justices of the peace or police magistrates the power to punish a convicted husband with a fine of up to twenty pounds or imprisonment for up to six months with hard labor.[47] In 1868 this act was amended to provide for a maximum sentence of one year, and in 1882 the Wife Beaters Act gave police magistrates the power to order convicted men to be flogged and exposed on a public pillory. This act was passed over the objections of those who believed that harsh punishments would only exacerbate the problem. For example, the social critic Frances Power Cobbe, who campaigned vigorously against marital violence, objected that "after they had undergone such chastisement...the ruffians would inevitably return more brutalized and infuriated than ever, and again have their wives at their mercy."[48] In 1878 aggravated assault was made a ground for judicial separation (but it was not until 1937 that it became a ground for divorce in English law). Yet despite these legal reforms, the right of moderate correction was abolished in England only in 1891. At that time senior law officers doubted whether it had ever existed as a husband's right: The Master of the Rolls expressed doubt whether moderate correction "ever was the law," and the Lord Chancellor referred to the right as "quaint and absurd *dicta*."[49] A course in English legal and social history might have rewarded them with some surprising insights.

In the United States, too, the nineteenth century saw challenges to the husband's right to beat his wife. An 1824 Mississippi judgment limited a husband to only "moderate chastisement in cases of emergency" (it did not specify what constituted a matrimonial "emergency"), but by the end of the century even this restricted form of correction had been discarded.[50] North Carolina law saw a similar transformation. In 1867 a state court had acquitted a man who had struck his wife with a switch "smaller than his thumb," and declared that the courts should "not interfere with family government in trifling cases." But soon afterward, in 1874, the North Carolina supreme court issued a declaration to the effect that a husband had no right to chastise his wife physically under any circumstances. However, the court added, in a tone of solid Victorian domesticity, that "if no permanent injury has been inflicted, nor

---

47 This legal overview is from Nancy Tomes, "'A Torrent of Abuse': Crimes of Violence between Working-class Men and Women in London, 1840–1875," *Journal of Social History* II (1978), 340.

48 Francis Power Cobbe, *Wife Torture* (London, 1878), quoted in Michael D. Freeman, "The Phenomenon of Marital Violence and the Legal and Social Response in England," in John M. Eekelaar and Sanford N. Katz (eds.), *Family Violence. An International and Interdisciplinary Study* (Toronto, 1978), 73–4. On the campaign against wife beating in the late nineteenth century see the two articles by Carol Bauer and Lawrence Ritt: "'A Husband is a beating animal' – Frances Power Cobbe Confronts the Wife-Abuse Problem in Victorian England," and "Wife-Abuse, Late Victorian English Feminists, and the Legacy of Frances Power Cobbe," in *International Journal of Women's Studies* 6 (1983), 99–118 and 195–207, respectively.

49 Freeman, "Marital Violence," 79. Freeman cites decisions upholding husbands' rights to moderate correction in Great Britain as recently as 1975. Ibid.

50 Del Martin, *Battered Wives* (San Francisco, 1976), 31.

malice, cruelty, nor dangerous violence shown by the husband, it is better to shut out the public gaze, and leave the parties to forget and forgive."[51]

The North Carolina judges were at least ambivalent about wife beating. Further north their Canadian counterparts were more traditional, emphasizing throughout the nineteenth century that wives should be submissive and subservient, and defending the right of husbands to correct their wives physically. Although more liberal judges were prepared to admit that the law should intervene when violence was extreme, they argued that a wife had to tolerate "the necessity of bearing some indignities, and even some violence, before [the court would] sanction her leaving her husband's roof."[52] For the most part, however, Canadian judges were reluctant to face the need to intervene in what they saw as private marriage matters, despite the physical and emotional consequences to the wife that this policy might entail. In a Nova Scotia case judges insisted that cruelty could not be acted against unless it were "so aggravated as to render it impossible that the Duties of the married life could be discharged ... It is the duty of the courts to keep the rule extremely strict."[53]

In spite of examples such as these, the general trend of law and judicial interpretation was to provide penalties for wife beating, a trend that indicates a decreasing tolerance of the practice among the élites; wife beating was more and more treated as reprehensible by those who made the laws, and we should expect them to have reflected the ideas of the higher social groups. But legal change need tell us nothing of the reality of marital violence, of the attitudes of the mass of the population, or even of the practices of the élites, as distinct from their public affirmations. Nor do the terms of laws against such violence indicate how they were administered. Was it easy for women to lodge complaints against their husbands, and how receptive to these complaints were the police and judges? Because of the traditional Western legal principle that husband and wife are one person in law, litigation setting one spouse against the other – circumstances when the fiction of identity cannot be maintained – has long been considered problematic. This was merely one obstacle that judges had to confront when a married woman wanted to prosecute her husband for assault. Beyond this there was a residual attitude that, despite legal enactments to the contrary, men had authority to beat their wives under certain circumstances. (One aspect of this belief is male solidarity – a judge siding with a husband against his wife; this issue is dealt with in more detail later in this section.)

Examples of the difficulty women had in obtaining redress against their husbands emerged from France in the 1790s, after the civil law had provided

---

[51] Ibid., 31–2.
[52] Chancellor Spragge (1873), quoted in Constance Backhouse, "'Pure Patriarchy': Nineteenth-Century Canadian Marriage," *McGill Law Journal* 13 (1986), 307.
[53] Kimberley Smith, "Divorce in Nova Scotia, 1750–1890," in J. Phillips and P. Girard (eds.), *Essays in the History of Canadian Law, Vol. 3: The Nova Scotian Experience* (Toronto, in press).

stiffer penalties for assaults on women. In one instance the appropriate court in Rouen refused to hear a woman's complaint of being beaten because it was "only a matter of an altercation between a husband and wife."[54] In another case the judge declared that because the wife – who had complained of being assaulted – "is under the authority of her husband, because she is not divorced and has not begun divorce proceedings, the court declares her action against her husband void."[55] Not only do these and similar cases exemplify a historically common reluctance on the part of the courts to intervene in matrimonial problems – in many ways an understandable reluctance, but one that generally worked to the disadvantage of women – but they also show that legal reforms could look fine on paper but have little or no practical effect. Despite the 1790 law, these Rouen judges insisted on viewing marriage in terms that gave husbands the right to beat their wives. Many complainants, like the woman in the second case cited here, simply abandoned their actions for assault and sought divorces instead.

It was similar almost a century later in England, where the disposition of wife assault cases by the courts often depended on the attitudes of individual judges and magistrates. Some shared the notions of Edward Cox, a judge who also wrote on problems of crime and punishment. According to Cox, few cases of wife beating were unprovoked and therefore most were justified.[56] This view was echoed at the 1887 Yorkshire winter assizes where a man was charged with knocking his wife down and then striking her about the head with a poker so that blood flowed from her ears. Her offense had been to go to "some amusement" without first getting her husband's permission, and his reaction certainly went beyond the accepted limits of moderate correction. Yet the judge trying the case held that the violence involved was within the limits of "reasonable chastisement" and stated that it was a "waste of time to bring these cases before the jury." Needless to say, the husband was acquitted.[57] Other judges, though, were more critical of wife beating, calling it "barbaric," describing the assailants as "brutes," "tyrants," and "monsters," and regarding violence by a man against a woman as, in principle, unmanly and cowardly.[58] Given this range of opinion on the bench, it should not be surprising that the success or failure of a prosecution for wife beating could depend less on the law and the evidence and more on the prejudices of the presiding judge.

The rarity of wife beating cases before the courts until and beyond the late nineteenth century resulted to some extent from the state of the law and its administration. Either married men were able to assault their wives with impunity because there was no law to punish them or the law was applied, if it was applied at all, with such reluctance and leniency that women were deterred

---

[54] Phillips, *Family Breakdown*, 111.
[55] Ibid.
[56] Tomes, "'A Torrent of Abuse'," 339.
[57] Bauer and Ritt, "Wife Abuse," 198.
[58] Tomes, "'A Torrent of Abuse'," 339.

from attempting to use it. (We must recognize the plight of a woman who had to return home after a prosecution to face the probable wrath of her husband for having been brought before the court.) Even in the late nineteenth century, when the English law against wife beating had been strengthened, the proportion of assaults actually reported was very small.[59] Deficiencies in the law were pointed out in 1875, and in 1898 the Home Office produced a report showing that in the preceding year some 8,075 men had been charged with assaults on women in the larger cities and towns of England, Scotland, and Wales. Of these, fifty-three had been sentenced to punishments of more than two years in prison, and there was evidence that magistrates tended to sympathize not with the victims in these cases but with the perpetrators. Crimes against property were punished more heavily than crimes against wives: In two cases before one magistrate, a man who vandalized public seats was fined two pounds, whereas a man who kicked his wife and drew blood was fined one pound.[60]

There are no ways of calculating the extent of marital violence on the local level, let alone the more general level, but there are ways of gauging the attitudes of the popular classes, as distinct from those of middle- and upper-class men who staffed the courts, wrote the laws, and published their views. Popular reactions to marital violence manifested themselves in various ways. One form was the charivari, a ritualized form of sanction toward individuals who had breached certain rules of the community. Charivaris, known as "rough music" in England, often involved a crowd's making a public spectacle of the victim by taunts, rough treatment, symbolic reenactment of the offense that was objected to, and by ritualized humiliation. A relevant example is the treatment frequently meted out to husbands who were beaten by their wives. Significantly, such men – unlike their female equivalents – were not treated as the victims of injustice but were dealt with almost as if they were accomplices in the offense by failing to maintain proper masculine authority within marriage. In England, France, and elsewhere such husbands were often forced to ride through the community, facing backward, on an ass. In a description of the treatment directed at beaten husbands in Lyon, France, in 1566, it is clear that the humiliations were ritualized representations of the way men were ill-treated by their wives: They were beaten with tripe, sticks, knives, frying pans, and other domestic items, had their beards pulled, and were kicked in the genitals.[61] Charivaris more commonly focused on men who beat their wives; there were many more of these offenders. But there was an important difference between the community response to husband and wife beating. The former was con-

---

[59] Ibid., 330.
[60] Bauer and Ritt, "Wife Abuse," 197.
[61] Natalie Zemon Davis, *Society and Culture in Early Modern France* (Stanford, 1975), 100, 140. See also Flandrin, *Families in Former Times*, 124–25; John R. Gillis, *For Better, For Worse: British Marriages, 1600 to the Present* (New York, 1985), 80, 133–4; Edward Shorter, *The Making of the Modern Family* (New York, 1975), 222–3.

9.3 Marital violence and "moderate correction"

sidered socially reprehensible not because of the violence itself but because
it represented a reversal of what was held to be the "natural" relationship
between wife and husband. Reversal was the theme of the charivaris against
beaten husbands. Quite clearly these charivaris did not challenge male superiority but, on the contrary, upheld it; nor did they condemn the marital
violence per se but rather gave emphasis to the sex roles in violence. This leads
us to believe that when wife beaters were the targets of community sanction it
was not the violence itself that was held up to popular condemnation but more
likely the circumstances – its degree, frequency, or appropriateness.

The employment of charivaris against wife beaters is well documented,
especially in France and England. In a survey of 250 reported examples of
"rough music" in England in the eighteenth and nineteenth centuries, wife
beating was the provocation in 49, one-fifth of them.[62] It seems likely that wife
beating became increasingly prominent in English charivaris during the nineteenth century, which could indicate an increasing popular distaste for the
practice, an increased incidence of wife beating, or the decline of antagonism
toward remarriage, which had been the single most common target of charivaris.[63] Charivaris against wife beaters took various forms. One example from
Surrey in the 1840s involved a crowd's surrounding the offender's dwelling and
treating him to a deafening cacophony with whistles, horns, cowbells, rattles,
pans and gongs. (This was the "rough music.") At a signal the noise ceased and
an orator declaimed a number of salutary verses, including:

> There is a man in this place.
> Has beat his wife! (*forte. A pause.*)
> He beat his wife!! (*fortissimo*)
> It is a very great shame and disgrace
> To all who in this place
> It is indeed upon my life!!

The crowd then opened up again with its rough music and danced crazily
around a bonfire before departing with an admonition to the subject of their
attention that he should conduct himself better in future.[64]

Charivaris against wife beaters seem to have been common in Britain and
Europe and a reminiscent practice is reported from colonial America. In the
1750s a group of men in Elizabethtown, New Jersey, went about at night with
painted faces and in women's clothes and flogged men who were reported to
have beaten their wives.[65]

---

[62] Violet Alford, "Rough Music or Charivari," *Folklore* 70 (1959), 505–18, cited in E. P.
Thompson, "'Rough Music': le charivari anglais," *Annales. Economies Sociétés Civilisations* 27
(1972), 290. The most common objects of charivaris in this group were second marriages (77
cases) and adultery (35 cases).
[63] Thompson, "'Rough Music'," 300, refers to an increase in the proportion of wife beaters
among the targets of charivaris.
[64] Shorter, *Modern Family*, 224–5; Gillis, *For Better, For Worse*, 132.
[65] J. E. Cutler, *Lynch-Law* (London, 1905), 46–7, cited in Davis, *Society and Culture*, 315n.45.

9 Marriage breakdown in the past

Informal, if ritualized, sanctions against wife beating complemented at the popular level the anxiety about the practice that was expressed by religious and lay social commentators. It had the advantage of enforcing community norms when statute or other law made no provision for punishing offenders, and the humiliation of being the target of a charivari might well have deterred some would-be wife beaters. The English poet Andrew Marvell evidently thought that young men might profit from the example:

> Prudent Antiquity, that knew by Shame,
> Better than Law, domestick Crimes to tame,
> And taught Youth by Spectacle innocent![66]

Even so, there are qualifications to be made before we conclude that charivaris necessarily indicated widespread popular hostility to wife beating. As noted earlier, issues of frequency, degree, and the appropriateness of the violence were probably taken into consideration by the populace, just as they were by the judges who dealt with wife beaters in court. It has been noted that although wife beating was illegal in parts of New England, it was at least tacitly condoned by the community, and when a case reached the courts, the judges were interested in the appropriateness of the violence, not the violence per se. "Presented with evidence of a bruised limb or a broken head, the court tended to ask... Did the wife provoke the husband?"[67] All of the Quarter Courts of New England prosecuted wife beaters, but if there was evidence of provocation by the wife, they tended to be lenient.[68] A certain lenience crept into the treatment of wife beaters by charivaris, too: In the hierarchy of severity, wife beating ranked lower than certain other offenses, such as sexual transgressions.[69] An even more stark qualification must be made in respect of charivaris against wife beaters in France. In some parts of the country action against wife beating was limited to the month of May, a special month for women during which they were entitled to be treated without violence.[70] The clear implication is that husbands could beat their wives (moderately, of course) with impunity during the other eleven months.

It is impossible to recapture the precise circumstances that, on the one hand, led to one wife beater's being paraded through town to the cries and taunts of local men and women and those that, on the other hand, allowed another wife beater to escape his community's attention. Notoriety for serious or frequent violence probably came into play, whereas sporadic or less injurious assaults

---

[66] Andrew Marvell, "The Last Instructions to a Painter," quoted in Davis, *Society and Culture*, 303n.45.

[67] Laurel Thatcher Ulrich, *Good Wives: Image and Reality in the Lives of Women in Northern New England, 1650–1750* (New York, 1982), 187.

[68] Ibid., 269n.7.

[69] Thompson, "'Rough Music'," 290. These sexual transgressions were not specified, but probably included homosexuality and cases of adultery involving two married people, rather than a married man or woman with an unmarried accomplice.

[70] Davis, *Culture and Society*, 100, 118; Shorter, *Modern Family*, 223.

were overlooked. The documentation suggests that such acts were so widespread and common that no community could possibly have allocated the time and resources to give each incident of marital violence the full ritual treatment.

No doubt some of these other examples, apparently ignored by charivaris, were also subject to social sanction, but on a less elaborate scale. Evidence presented to courts at various times and places shows that neighbors, friends, and relatives often intervened when there was violence between wife and husband. Here too, however, we must make qualifications, for far from all wife beating was considered reprehensible by the whole community. In Rouen during the 1780s and 1790s, for example, the likelihood of outside intervention rose with the severity of violence, and women were more likely than men to intervene to try to stop the violence. Although it is impossible to measure the degree of the violence in each case presented to the courts, there is a strong impression that men intervened only when it had reached a point at which the wife might be seriously injured. One illustrative case involved two men who, invited to dinner at a friend's house, stood by while their host swore at his wife, beat her about the arms and breast, and grabbed her by the throat. Their sole recorded sign of disapproval was to the effect that it was not proper to ill-treat one's wife in front of friends. They seem to have been more offended by the timing than by the violence itself, and it was not until the husband seized a knife and threatened to kill his wife that they restrained him.[71] Other cases, too, showed men standing by, and intervening to stop a husband's violence only when he was on the verge of using a knife, sword, pistol, or other potentially lethal weapon. Women – generally neighbors – on the other hand, seem to have intervened at a lower level of violence and even when there was no more than a threat that a husband might begin to assault his wife. Similarly, male employees were reluctant to involve themselves in disputes between their married employers whereas female workers and domestics appear readily to have come to the aid of their mistresses against their masters.[72]

Gender-specific variations in responses to wife beating are not surprising. Even supposing that women accepted the principle that they should be subjected to physical chastisement as part of the husband's overall authority, we would expect them to accept it only within the limitations implied by the term "moderate correction": The degree of violence should not be excessive, and the violence should be provoked by a wrong they had committed. As far as the degree of violence is concerned, we should expect men and women – perpetrators and victims, respectively – to have defined "moderation" differently, such that women had a lower level of tolerance when it came to assessing the the violence they were receiving than did men of the same violence they were inflicting. As far as the responses of outsiders were con-

[71] Roderick Phillips, "Gender Solidarities in Late Eighteenth-Century Urban France. The Example of Rouen," *Histoire sociale/Social History* 13 (1980), 331–2.
[72] Ibid., passim.

cerned, we can appreciate that men might well have shared the assessment of the husband involved, women the assessment of the wife. Put more directly, male observers of an incident of wife beating were unwilling, as the Rouen evidence suggests, to challenge another man's (and by implication their own) right to administer *correction modérée*, and were thus willing to grant greater latitude in their definition of *modérée*.[73] As we have seen, moderation appeared to end when assault with a lethal weapon began, a reaction noted a century later in working-class London; there, there was a basic belief that a husband could beat his wife but not to the point of drawing blood or using a weapon.[74]

Gender-differentiated reactions to wife beating extended further, to giving refuge and medical assistance to a battered wife. Women neighbors almost invariably opened their doors, even though by doing so they risked becoming additional victims of a husband's anger. Men, however, were less likely to admit a beleaguered woman without first getting the consent of her husband, thus respecting even a violent husband's right to control his wife's movements. Women relatives, too, were more likely to help a wife in distress. Although it is difficult to quantify, the impression from the excellent Rouen records is that the wife's parents, especially her mother, were likely to come to her assistance when she was beaten or threatened by her husband. One reason for this was the statistical probability that of all the couple's parents, the wife's mother was, at any time, more likely to be alive.[75] But there was also a compelling social reason: When a married woman needed help, it was more likely to come from her mother – a woman who could empathize with her plight, and who might well have experienced violence in her own marriage – than from her father, a man who might have been reluctant to challenge another man's authority in his household, even if it was being exercised brutally over his own daughter. From this perspective, the archetypal mother-in-law (from the husband's perspective) should be considered not as an interfering busybody to be scorned and made fun of but as an important element in a process that sought to ensure that the exercise of power within marriage did not become tyrannical and, at its worst, fatal.

Again, however, we must qualify any impression that wife beating was not accepted under any circumstances by outsiders. The circumstances of marital violence are by no means clearly recorded, but it is evident that in most cases the objections were to the manner or degree of violence or its circumstances, not to the violence itself. Male and female neighbors alike complained that men beat their wives at night (and thereby disturbed their neighbors' sleep), or that they beat them "thus" (with a weapon, for example), rather than that the beatings took place at all.[76]

---

[73] Solidarities among men and women in relation to marital violence and other crises are the central theme of Phillips, "Gender Solidarities."
[74] Tomes, "'A Torrent of Abuse'," 336.
[75] Phillips, "Gender Solidarities," 335, Table 1.
[76] Phillips, *Family Breakdown*, 180ff.

9.3 Marital violence and "moderate correction"

Having briefly surveyed the range of attitudes to physical punishment that was expressed in legislation, by social commentators, by community action, relatives, and outsiders up to the nineteenth century, we come to the couple themselves. What do we know of the attitudes of wife beaters and their wives? Court records of convictions for such assaults are often disappointing for the silence they impose on the protagonists; rarely do they reveal more than the most sketchy details of the offense and the terms of the punishment. Where evidence of witnesses is preserved, however, we are sometimes allowed an entrée to personal feelings and, as we should expect, attitudes varied. The most forthright claim to the right of correction among the Rouen cases was made by one Jean Savary. In response to a charge that he had ill-treated his wife, he replied that "it was true that he had ill-treated her several times, but that he had the right to punish her when she did wrong."[77] Other men defended their violent behavior not in principle but in terms of specific grievances; a wife had failed to look after the children, had failed to cook a meal, had failed to perform some other duty. The clear implication was that violence was a justifiable reaction when a wife was derelict in her domestic duties. Yet other husbands, faced with divorce because of their violent behavior, were contrite. One husband "admitted his wrongs, hopes that his wife will forget them and that she will withdraw her divorce petition."[78]

Women, the victims of the violence, shared a similar range of reactions. Those who insisted on prosecuting their husbands showed that they did not consider the violence they had experienced as being appropriate for their marriage. Those who abandoned their divorce and other actions either reconsidered or were compelled by other circumstances (such as financial dependence, which are discussed in Chapter 10) to tolerate ill-treatment. The evidence from wife beating cases in nineteenth-century London shows that many women refused to appear in court to give evidence against their husbands and that some 10% of prosecutions were dismissed for this reason.[79] Judge Edward Cox complained that too often a wife later "denies all that she has stated to the magistrate... The wound was caused not by any blow from [her husband]...she fell by accident against the knife; the black eye was caused by the bed-post."[80] (The same tendency to pretend that injuries were not caused by domestic violence was noted earlier for the seventeenth century.)[81] Another theme that runs through the various sources was for women to accept responsibility for some or all of the violence they suffered. Women in the London cases studied by Tomes blamed themselves, saying "it serves me right."[82] Women in Rouen complained of being beaten "without cause or pretext," implying that violence was other-

---

[77] Ibid., 110.
[78] Ibid., 161.
[79] Tomes, "'A Torrent of Abuse'," 333.
[80] Quoted in ibid.
[81] See Chapter 3.
[82] Tomes, "'A Torrent of Abuse'," 334.

wise justified. To this extent women and men could share a fundamental belief in the appropriateness of physical correction, even if they agreed less often as to what limits should be placed on "moderation."

Bearing in mind that wife beating covers a wide spectrum of violence, from a single and relatively mild slap to persistent assaults causing serious injury and sometimes death, the overall image of the phenomenon is complex. It is impossible to draw a comprehensive picture of attitudes and behavior, but it is possible to sketch the outlines and to indicate the perimeters of the subject. They reveal men who defended the principle of moderate correction and men who condemned it outright in all circumstances. Social disapprobation, in the form of charivaris, revealed community feelings toward some wife beaters, but it is clear that many were ignored. Women who were beaten – and those who were not – variously tolerated violence to some degree or did not. There is little sense of change over time, of variations from place to place or among classes, for at each point we encounter wife beating and its punishment, its supporters and its detractors. There is a suggestion that wife beating became less acceptable in the nineteenth century in England (charivaris focused on it more, and there was a series of laws aimed at reducing it) and that it even declined: By 1889 the number of reported aggravated assaults in London (about 200) was only one-quarter the number reported in 1853. Yet it is possible that wife beating had simply been driven into the private recesses of the Victorian household, where it was less open to social surveillance.[83] The increased severity of punishments for wife beating – by 1882 police magistrates could have a husband flogged and exposed in a public pillory – might well have deterred women from reporting their husbands' violence more than it deterred men from committing the violence in the first place. Just as adultery "disappeared" in England after the severe 1650 law was passed, so might wife beating have "declined" in the face of harsher penalties during the nineteenth century.

Judges in Canada at this time were noticeably reluctant to punish husbands for beating their wives, even when the assaults were severe, and more than one judge voiced a preference that these cases should not be brought into the public forum. In one case a woman was repeatedly beaten and assaulted until on one occasion she was forced to flee from her home, bleeding badly and severely bruised between hip and abdomen. She was pregnant at the time and subsequently had a miscarriage. Despite the evidence of neighbors, friends, and even the couple's son, the judge urged them to reconcile and remarked: "Happily, transactions of this sort are for the most part screened from the public gaze."[84] The privatization of family life might well go a long way to

---

[83] Phillips, "Gender Solidarities," 335–7, notes the way in which husbands tried to prevent their neighbors from hearing assaults on wives and the latter's cries for help. The attitude of violent husbands in this period is perfectly expressed in the title of Erin Pizzey's ground-breaking book on wife abuse in England: *Scream Quietly or the Neighbours Will Hear* (Harmondsworth, 1973).
[84] Backhouse, " 'Pure Patriarchy'," 304.

explaining a number of apparent changes in married life during the nineteenth century, the decline of wife beating among them.

One further question begs an answer: Were there class differences in attitudes toward wife beating? The evidence, sparse at the best of times, is unclear on this point. Certainly much of the Puritan and other religious writing that stressed companionate marriage and that opposed marital violence in principle is thought to have been written for a middle-class readership. Legislation against wife beating reflected élite opinion (as did legal and judicial tolerance of it), whereas in the nineteenth century middle-class reformers were active in campaigning against wife beaters. John Stuart Mill, for example, wrote that it was of the nature of marriage that the "vilest malefactor" had "some wretched woman tied to him, against whom he [could] commit any atrocity except killing her, and, if tolerably cautious, [could] do that without much danger of the legal penalty."[85] The Society for the Protection of Women strove for legal reform to permit women to obtain a judicial separation on the ground of aggravated assault, that is, assault with a dangerous or deadly weapon. Their campaign was successful in 1878. It is not clear, however, whether élite opposition to wife beating is simply better recorded or whether it was more general. It is certainly not clear whether wife beating itself was more or less common among the middle and upper classes than among the mass of working people in town and country. The élites did believe that wife beating was more common, and was probably endemic, among the "dangerous classes," and that although the violence was a shame, it was nonetheless to be expected of the poor and uneducated. They supposed, too, that ordinary people were somewhat inured to physical hardship of all kinds, and that working-class wives could easily tolerate being knocked about by their husbands. In the eighteenth century the great *Encyclopédie* noted in the context of separations that verbal abuse or insults were as serious to women of a superior social position as physical ill-treatment was for "ordinary people."[86] A similar point has been noted in the United States in nineteenth-century judicial decisions in the South when the sensitivity of "ladies" to verbal abuse was likened to the results of physical assault on women of the lower classes.[87] Finally, an Australian legal text made the point this way:

> Some people can endure far more than others and, therefore, the social status, ages, character, education, physical condition and mental capacity of the parties must be borne in mind; for instance, slight blows, abuse and indignities have far greater effect on the mind of a person of refinement than on that of a person in a lower station of life, who may treat them as practically matters of course.[88]

---

[85] John Stuart Mill, *The Subjection of Women* (London, 1869), 35.
[86] *Encyclopédie* XV, 60.
[87] See Jane Turner Censer, "'Smiling Through Her Tears': Ante-Bellum Southern Women and Divorce," *American Journal of Legal History* 25 (1981), 24–47.
[88] P. E. Joske, *The Law of Marriage and Divorce* (Sydney, 1925), 75, quoted in Hilary Golder, *Divorce in 19th-Century New South Wales* (Kensington, N.S.W., 1985), 178.

341

9 Marriage breakdown in the past

Until quite recently it was commonplace that domestic violence was characteristic of the working class but rare in the middle classes and above. This assumption has been exploded for modern society by recent research and experience. Historically the relative incidence of wife beating among the social classes is unclear. The ethic of domestic or familial privacy entered the higher classes first and then filtered down, and privacy was indispensable for keeping marital violence from the eyes and ears of the community and thereby from official records. Middle- and upper-class women would also have been more reluctant than their working-class counterparts to publicize their husbands' violent behavior. We should certainly not assume that middle-class men who condemned the violent character of marriage among the lower orders did not know violence in their own marriages; they also condemned adultery.

Wife beating persisted relentlessly in the face of opposition whether the opposition, which was by no means unanimous or unambiguous, emanated from the élites (social commentators, theologians, and the law itself) or from the popular classes in collective or individual form. Male physical superiority and the virtually unchallenged principle of the husband's social and legal superiority were all too often partners in the exercise of physical coercion and violence. To be sure, there were social sanctions, judicial punishments, and some exhortations against matrimonial violence, but we cannot know their collective effect on behavior. As Steven Ozment has noted in the context of sixteenth-century condemnations of wife beating, "the historian can never know for sure the degree to which such advice was regularly translated into practice. . . ." But Ozment's next point is more debatable, that "it would defy experience to believe that an age which wrote and taught so much about companionable marriage and the sharing of domestic responsibility utterly failed to practice what it preached."[89] Even admitting that it is impossible to quantify violence over time and that we are left with patchy statistics and impressionistic evidence, it is difficult to discern change. Despite the pressure of law and opinion in colonial New England, wife beating is described as "tacitly condoned."[90] In eighteenth-century Languedoc it is reported that "it is common enough to hear wives express the just fear they have of being chastised and beaten by their husbands. Among those of low and modest condition it seems that such apprehensions were accepted without suggesting abnormal brutality."[91] In late-nineteenth-century London wife beating is described as "normal" when it served a disciplinary function.[92] Some industrial districts of England and Scotland were known as "kicking districts" after the incidence of husbands' assaults on their wives.[93] In Ireland in the early twentieth century childlessness was customarily blamed on the wife and entitled the husband to

---

[89] Ozment, *When Fathers Ruled*, 55.
[90] Ulrich, *Good Wives*, 187.
[91] Yves Castan, *Honnêteté et relations sociales en Languedoc, 1715–1780* (Paris, 1974), 172.
[92] Tomes, "'A Torrent of Abuse'," 338.
[93] Bauer and Ritt, "Wife Abuse," 109.

9.3 Marital violence and "moderate correction"

"bounce a boot off her now and then for it."[94] Obstetrical literature often mentioned in passing that women miscarried because of being beaten. "The doctors were not particularly distressed by wife-beating, but mentioned it casually along with other medical details."[95] Wife beating seems simply to have been a constant in Western society, sometimes criticized, perhaps more so with the passage of time, but always present.

To insist on the normalcy of wife beating is not to condone it, even historically, but rather to describe the continuous presence of this coarse thread of behavior in the fabric of married life. It is at this point that we can return to the question posed some pages earlier, the question of whether violence in marriage, of which wife beating was the most common form, betokened marriage breakdown. There is no universally applicable answer, but the evidence leads one to conclude that generally it did not, although sometimes it did. Violence per se did not fall outside the expectations of married men and women. Given the prevalence of wife beating and the openness of family life until recent times, women must surely have anticipated being struck at some time, more likely some times, during marriage. It was, then, only when the degree or frequency of violence was significantly greater than expected, less tolerable than anticipated, that we can begin to think of it as indicating marriage breakdown. Even then we must allow for changes in expectations as women adapted to more violent marriages than they had expected or when considerations such as financial dependence, dependent children, or other factors simply gave women no alternatives but to put up with behavior within marriage that, before marriage, they would have thought insupportable. We cannot enter the minds of women who put up with constant abuse or who refused to prosecute their husbands; women like Elizabeth Ela who fled from her husband's assaults but then declared in court that if she had "spoke Agenste him: Abowghte his barbarose usage toward me," she had done so only in the heat of passion, and that now, in court, "I have nothinge Agenst my husband to charge him with."[96] At the individual level we can seldom know what forces – emotional, social, economic, or other – produced an acceptance or rejection of violence as appropriate behavior within marriage, and thus contributed to the definition of marriage breakdown in particular cases. But we can be sure that the simple existence of violence did not indicate marriage breakdown. It might well have revealed tensions, stresses, and deeper conflicts within the relationship between husband and wife, but not always its breakdown. Although we might be able to generalize to some extent, we must accept that marriage breakdown is, in the final analysis, a matter of individual as much as social definition. It is little short of arrogant for a historian to deem marriages broken

---

[94] David Fitzpatrick, "Divorce and Separation in Modern Irish History," *Past and Present* 114 (1987), 178.

[95] Shorter, *Women's Bodies*, 6.

[96] Ulrich, *Good Wives*, 188.

down because they possessed some characteristic or another, when the couple concerned, in their personal and social context, were able to integrate those characteristics into their conception of an acceptable and functioning marriage.

9.4 Adultery and the double standard

The second example of behavior that can be related to marriage breakdown, adultery, provokes many of the same issues of evidence and interpretation that marital violence brought into focus. Attitudes are often difficult to pin down, and we must take into account the possibilities of variation over time, place, and by gender and social class. With adultery, though, we are dealing with a form of behavior that seems to strike more directly and less ambiguously than violence at the character of marriage in the Western tradition: the breach of sexual exclusivity. Because adultery relates to the sexual relationship that was central to marriage, it has been dealt with explicitly and implicitly in various respects throughout this study. At this point, however, we shall briefly recapitulate the legal status of adultery before attempting to plumb social attitudes and the possible role of adultery in marriage breakdown.

The control of sexuality has long been one of the objectives of both ecclesiastical and secular legal codes, which have generally defined sexual activity as licit or illicit according to two criteria. The first relates to the potential for conception, such that sexual relationships or acts that were not procreative, such as masturbation, homosexuality, oral and anal sex, and sexual intercourse with contraception, were treated as illicit.[97] The second criterion was the relationship of sexuality to marriage, such that sexual intercourse was licit only when it involved two married persons – married to each other, that is. This second criterion hardened over time as marriage itself became more formally defined, and from the late Middle Ages the law could be more precise in making premarital sex (fornication) and extramarital sex (adultery) the subject of legal sanctions. The actual penalties for adultery have varied considerably among jurisdictions and over time, as has the rigor of the application of these laws, but in general terms until very recently the only kind of sexual activity that has not been actionable by law – secular or ecclesiastical, criminal or civil – has been genital intercourse within marriage.

In the hierarchy of sexual offences adultery has generally been allotted a middle-ranking position. Crimes "against nature," such as sodomy and bestiality and sometimes homosexuality, have frequently been capital offenses.[98] In France until the revolution of 1789 sodomy was punishable by burning, and this penalty was carried out at least three times between 1750 and 1789.[99] Sodomy was a capital offense in seventeenth-century New England, too, and

[97] General works in the history of sexuality are Vern L. Bullough, *Sexual Variance in Society and History* (Chicago, 1976); Jean-Louis Flandrin, *Le Sexe et l'Occident* (Paris, 1981).
[98] Bullough, *Sexual Variance*, 564.
[99] Ibid.

executions were far from uncommon.[100] In England, even after the penal reforms of the 1820s, when the death penalty was abolished for more than a hundred offenses, it was retained for buggery, rape, and carnal knowledge of a girl under the age of consent.[101] Against this tendency, some illicit sexual activity was treated as a misdemeanor and dealt with leniently. Fornication, intercourse between an unmarried man and woman, attracted penalties from the church courts in particular, but they rarely went beyond temporary excommunication, public penance, and social humiliation.

Adultery usually fell between the extremes of illicit sexual activity. It was not an offense against nature itself, but it was readily viewed as an offense against the nature of marriage, and it was this that made adultery more serious an offense than premarital sex. With fornication there was not necessarily any victim or deception, and it could even be a preliminary to marriage; in many cultures sexual intercourse was socially acceptable after betrothal but before marriage.[102] Adultery was quite a different matter in that it usually involved deception and that it had a victim: the adulterer's spouse. Moreover it necessarily involved a breach of the contract of sexual exclusivity that marriage entailed.

Historically the penalties for adultery have sometimes belied its moderate seriousness. In Roman law, we have seen, a husband who surprised his wife *in flagrante delicto* could kill her and her accomplice on the spot, without fear of retribution from the law.[103] In ancient Jewish law the penalty for adultery was death by stoning, but the crime was defined exclusively in terms of an offense committed by a married woman.[104] In the first millenium and a half of the Christian period adultery was usually classified as a less serious offense than in the Judeo-Roman traditions, perhaps because of the relatively low status marriage had in Christian theology,[105] but the former rigor was restored by some regimes in the sixteenth and seventeenth centuries, especially those influenced by Calvinist moral theology. Adultery was made a capital offense in Calvin's Geneva, in Scotland, and briefly in England under Cromwell's 1650 adultery legislation.[106] The New England colonies also made adultery a crime

---

[100] Bert F. Oaks, "'Things Fearful to Name': Sodomy and Buggery in Seventeenth-Century New England," *Journal of Social History* 12 (1978), 268–81.

[101] The best survey of attitudes toward homosexuality is John Boswell, *Christianity, Social Tolerance and Homosexuality* (Chicago, 1980). This work also touches on many other aspects of sexuality.

[102] On these practices in England, see Gillis, *For Better, For Worse.*

[103] Rawson, "Roman Family," esp. 33ff; Marilyn Arthur, "'Liberated Women': The Classical Era," in Bridenthal and Koontz, *Becoming Visible,* 82–3.

[104] Bullough, *Sexual Variance,* 81.

[105] James A. Brundage, "Adultery and Fornication: A Study in Legal Theology," in Vern L. Bullough and James A. Brundage (eds.), *Sexual Practice and the Medieval Church* (Buffalo, N.Y., 1982), 132.

[106] In Scotland only a few convicted adulterers were executed. Others were banished from Scotland, but most seem to have suffered considerably lighter penalties involving long penances (of twenty-six to fifty-two weeks) and fines. See Norah Smith, "Sexual mores and attitudes in Enlightenment Scotland," in Paul-Gabriel Boucé (ed.), *Sexuality in Eighteenth-Century Britain* (Manchester, 1982), 53ff.

punishable by execution, and it is suggested that it was regarded there as even more serious than the traditional crimes against nature. For example, in a 1646 New Haven case a married man convicted of sodomy and of corrupting youth "by masterbations" was sentenced to death, but it seems that the corruption of youth and "frustrating the ordinance of marriage" (that is, adultery) weighed more with the magistrate.[107]

These were exceptionally harsh penalties for adultery, however, and for the most part punishments were a good deal lighter. In sixteenth-century England the penalty for adultery, administered by the church courts, centered on shame and humiliation. The guilty parties were compelled to stand in white sheets in the town marketplace on market day or in church in front of the full congregation, on two or three consecutive Sundays.[108] The consequences could be more severe if the adulterous relationship had resulted in pregnancy. Then the father, if he could be identified, was forced to support the child, and the mother was often whipped, half-naked, through the streets of the community and then imprisoned for up to a year. The severity in such cases, though, was a response not to the adulterous relationship in itself, but to the woman's producing an illegitimate child that could become a financial burden on the community.[109] French ecclesiastical law generally treated adultery more seriously than its English equivalent, giving rise to a belief that the English were peculiarly indulgent toward the offense. A French woman convicted of adultery (and judicially separated from her husband for that reason) could be confined to a convent for two years.[110] A husband who did not want to separate judicially from his wife could have her arrested and imprisoned by private warrant (*lettre de cachet*) at his own expense, a facility provided by the monarchy that could avoid the embarrassment of more public proceedings.[111] These penalties were abolished during the French Revolution (which contributed to the revolution's gaining a reputation for being lax where marriage and morality were concerned),[112] but reappeared in the patriarchal Code Napoléon, which specified that if a woman were divorced for reason of adultery, she "shall be condemned...to confinement in a house of correction, for a determinate period, which shall not be less than three months, nor exceed two years."[113]

---

[107] This and other similar cases are cited by Oaks, "'Things Fearful to Name," 273.

[108] Stone, *Family, Sex and Marriage*, 519. See also Greaves, *Society and Religion*, 234. Penalties in Scotland were more rigorous; see note 106.

[109] Alan Macfarlane, *Marriage and Love in England, 1300–1840* (Oxford, 1986), 241.

[110] Phillips, *Family Breakdown*, 5.

[111] See Section 8.7 on *lettres de cachet*.

[112] The suggestion that the French Revolution promoted immorality by its liberal family legislation is made not only in conservative historiography, but also in literature. In *The Importance of Being Earnest* Lady Bracknell, learning that her daughter's suitor does not know who his parents are and was found as an infant in a bag in the cloakroom at Victoria Station, retorts: "To be born, or at any rate bred, in a hand-bag...seems to me to display a contempt for the ordinary decencies of family life that reminds one of the worst excesses of the French Revolution." Oscar Wilde, *The Importance of Being Earnest* (London, 1899, repr. 1936), 47.

[113] Code Napoléon, Book I, Title VI, Article 298.

9.4 Adultery and the double standard

In addition to these and other similar criminal punishments for adultery, the offense was actionable by law in a number of ways. As we have noted throughout this book, adultery, the only exception to the ban on divorce explicitly made in the New Testament, was the only matrimonial offense common to all laws of separation and divorce. It was the sole matrimonial offense that was accepted by all as justifying some degree of legal relief for the innocent spouse. In some jurisdictions there were provisions for the innocent spouse to obtain other kinds of relief as well. In England a husband whose wife had committed adultery could sue her accomplice for criminal conversation and thereby obtain either nominal or substantial monetary damages.[114]

There is, then, this continuity and universality in the attention paid by legislators to adultery. If it was not a criminal offense, it was actionable at civil law; if the state did not prosecute, the aggrieved spouse could; and although many other sexual offenses, such as premarital intercourse and homosexuality, have disappeared from many codes of criminal and civil law, adultery has held on most tenaciously in matrimonial law as an offense that can justify separation or divorce. Adultery, then, retains its status as the foremost crime against marriage. Only very recently have some revisions of family law abandoned explicit reference to adultery as they rejected the principle of fault and moved to defining the sole ground for divorce as the irretrievable or irremediable breakdown of marriage as evidenced by a failure to cohabit over a fixed period of time.[115]

The endurance of this legal status of adultery might lead us to assume that an act of adultery was almost necessarily a symptom of marriage breakdown. In the sixteenth century it alone had been paired with desertion (which did clearly terminate a marriage in all but legal terms) as an act that signified a breach of the essential nature of marriage,[116] and the strength of the legal tradition gives the appearance of continuously reinforcing this view. However, divorce and legal separation have rarely been mandatory when one of the spouses was guilty of adultery.[117] On the contrary, we have noted that for the most part policy has been to attempt to dissuade petitioners from divorce whenever possible, by providing cooling-off periods and conciliation. There was, then, an expectation that although adultery could not be reconciled with the abstract notion of marriage, it could be accommodated within individual marriages. We know that there were many more reported acts of adultery than there have been proceedings for separation or divorce, and reported acts must have represented

---

[114] On criminal conversation, see Section 7.2, and Susan Staves, "Money for Honor: Damages for Criminal Conversation," *Studies in Eighteenth-Century Culture* 11 (1982), 279–97.

[115] The development of no-fault divorce legislation based on the notion of the breakdown of marriage, is discussed in Chapter 13.

[116] See Sections 2.2 and 2.3.

[117] One exception was Rome, where the morals legislation of Augustus in 18 B.C. required a husband to divorce his wife if he caught her in the act of adultery. Rawson, "Roman Family," 33–4.

only a fraction of known instances. We must ask whether this disparity, this tendency not to take action to divorce or separate in cases of adultery, arose from social, economic, or other inhibitions against legal proceedings or whether adultery was simply not considered a serious enough offense to convince the innocent spouse that the marriage had broken down. How are we to explain the apparent incongruence between the consistently punitive approach toward adultery by the law and dominant ideologies of most periods and the evident toleration of adultery within so many marriages?

First, the status of adultery in law was severely qualified in terms of the gender of the offender. Most of the laws focused solely or primarily on adultery by married women, reflecting the double standard of sexual morality that treated offenses by women more severely than the equivalent acts committed by men. As far as adultery was concerned, a wife's was thought to be more dangerous because of the risk of pregnancy and the possibility that the paternity of a child borne by the woman would be uncertain. A woman who committed adultery thus threatened her family with the intrusion of a spurious child. There were other, less explicit, reasons for more severe attitudes toward adultery by married women. Wives were regarded by law as the virtual property of their husbands. To this extent they had no right to give or lend themselves to another man. Where their accomplices in adultery could be prosecuted by aggrieved husbands, the actions were usually equivalent to actions for theft or trespass.[118] Whatever the explicit and implicit rationales, the existence and endurance of the double standard of sexual morality in respect to adultery is beyond question. In theoretical terms Christian theologians required sexual fidelity of both spouses, but in practice the church courts prosecuted women more diligently. There were some exceptions to the double standard, such as the New England adultery laws that adopted a more or less even-handed approach, but for the most part women's adultery was more severely dealt with. The 1650 English adultery law, as we have seen, provided hanging for an adulterous married woman, but a married man was subject to execution only if his accomplice was married. Likewise, provisions for imprisonment in French laws applied only to adulterous women. Civil and ecclesiastical legislation that recognized the culpability of adultery by either spouse as a ground for divorce or separation often required that a husband prove only simply adultery, whereas a wife had to prove her husband guilty of notorious or aggravated adultery, such as adultery within the home. Finally, an aggrieved husband might seek damages or other forms of redress or revenge from his adulterous wife's accomplice, but no law gave the innocent wife the power to obtain compensation from her adulterous husband's accomplice.

Even within this difference between the treatment of men's and women's adultery, there was room for discretion. Women, we have noted, were treated

---

[118] See Keith Thomas, "The Double Standard," *Journal of the History of Ideas* 20 (1959), 210ff.

more harshly when their adultery resulted in pregnancy: Here was a definite incentive for women in extramarital relationships to practice some kind of contraception (thus compounding their offense, but at the same time reducing the risk of detection).[119] Second, notoriety seems to have provoked a more vigorous reaction against adultery. Needless to say, discreet adultery, known of only to the couple involved, was for this very reason safe from prosecution or community sanction. It was also at less risk when knowledge of it was confined to the offenders and their spouse or spouses. Even adultery that was the subject of local rumor or suspicion might also escape too much attention from the authorities, as officials generally demanded direct and firm evidence, and were rarely prepared to proceed on the basis of hearsay.[120] But blatant and public adultery, the flaunting of an intimate relationship between a married person and another not his or her spouse, was perceived as a direct affront, perhaps a challenge, to community standards. It was likely that such a challenge would be taken up. Gillis notes that adultery was usually tolerated among the popular classes of sixteenth- and seventeenth-century England, but only if it were "sufficiently discreet and caused no public scandal,"[121] whereas Smith observes that in late-eighteenth- and nineteenth-century Nova Scotia it was "community shock" at their husbands' adultery, rather than the adultery per se, that "provided the motivation for a resort to the court."[122] The principle of scandal was incorporated in the 1792 French divorce law that allowed divorce for "notorious" immorality – including adultery – rather than for simple adultery.[123]

The acceptability of adultery within individual marriages varied a great deal, as the range of reactions displayed in court cases (the most important single source of evidence) shows. In the divorce courts of Rouen during the revolution a number of women related their husbands' careers of adultery that went back many years. In one exemplary case a wife lived in the same house for five years together with her husband, his mistress, and their children.[124] She could have obtained a separation because the customary law of Normandy regarded a husband's adultery within the marital dwelling as an adequate ground for one, but on this occasion the wife delayed taking action for a number of years.

[119] In the seventeenth century the French theologian Abbé de Brantôme suggested that high-born ladies who committed adultery took care to practice coitus interruptus to avoid conception. Jean-Louis Flandrin, *Le Sexe et l'Occident*, 121–2.
[120] G. R. Quaife, *Wanton Wenches and Wayward Wives* (London, 1979), 138, gives the example of a churchwarden who refused to present a case before the ecclesiastical court even though the husband, who laid the complaint, had found his wife in bed with another man. The churchwarden wanted an absolute undertaking from the husband that he "saw the thing in the thing."
[121] Gillis, *For Better, For Worse*, 78–9. This point is implied also by Wrightson, *English Society*, 99: "Blatant or 'scandalous' adultery in village communities was liable to lead to the presentment of offenders of either sex in the church courts."
[122] Smith, "Divorce in Nova Scotia."
[123] "*Dérèglement de moeurs notoire.*" Law of September 20, 1792.
[124] Phillips, *Family Breakdown*, 126.

Indeed, in more than half the cases where a husband was divorced for reason of adultery, he had lived with the two women – his wife and his accomplice – simultaneously during a considerable period.[125] Although such cases indicate a toleration of adultery, the very fact that our evidence comes from the divorce court shows that the toleration was finite. How many other cases did not come to court, we do not know, but there is some impression of the disparity between the incidence of adultery and divorce action in seventeenth-century New England. There, 308 men and women were convicted of adultery or "adulterous carriage" (the latter including behavior such as attempted seduction by a married man or woman). In the same period only 40 divorces were obtained on these grounds.[126] This means that some 268 men and women, whose spouses were not only guilty, but judicially convicted of adultery, did not seek divorce. Were these innocent spouses eventually able to reconcile their guilty partners' behavior with an acceptable marriage?

The range of individual reactions to adultery by a spouse is well exemplified in Quaife's study of peasant marriages in seventeenth-century Somerset. Some husbands attacked their wives' lovers with knives and other weapons; others banished the offending accomplice from their houses. Some men beat their adulterous wives, others evicted them, or brought them (or tried to bring them) before the church court. Others, however, did nothing at all or evinced little more than a mild irritation. One man, "finding his workmate attempting his wife could only respond with annoyance – 'this is no good for you to call me forth to go to work and then come back to misuse my wife.' The two men then left for work."[127] So lax were some husbands in taking formal action against their adulterous wives that the community did it for them. Many of the cases of adultery brought before the courts in Quaife's study "stemmed from a desire of the parishioners to protect or discipline wives whose husbands had done nothing to control the situation."[128] In such cases we are a long way from the image of the husband as the jealous defender of his proprietorship of his wife's body. It is of the nature of historical evidence that the past is usually more silent about acquiescence than it is about opposition, but the data from these sources show that adultery was far from universally regarded as a serious matrimonial offense, let alone necessarily a symptom of marriage breakdown.

Not only that, but when adultery was a focus for community disapproval, it was often less because of the physical act itself and more because of its social implications. When a wife's adultery was the target of charivaris, it was the husband who bore the brunt of the criticism because of his putative failure to

---

[125] Ibid., 127.

[126] Koehler, *Search for Power*, 149, Chart 5.1; 453–9. Women were the petitioners in twenty-three divorce actions, men in seventeen. This means that only 13% of men and the same proportion of women who were convicted of adultery were the subject of divorce actions. There is no evidence here of a double standard of tolerance of adultery.

[127] Quaife, *Wanton Wenches*, 139, and see 124–42 generally on adultery.

[128] Ibid., 139.

control his wife's behavior and to maintain his position of authority within the household. (His wife's committing adultery was as effective an affront to her husband's authority as if she had beaten him, and we have noted that the beaten husband, not the husband-beating wife, was the object of ridicule and censure by collective action.) The rare cases in which unfaithful wives were the target of charivaris were those where the adultery had produced a child that had to be raised at the community's expense.

Were there distinctions by social class in attitudes toward adultery? It is commonplace that from the early modern period the European élites were particularly permissive about extramarital sexual activity. Richard T. Vann writes that although lower-class women gained some sexual freedom before marriage, "after marriage, such freedom was chiefly indulged in by members of the aristocracy among whom adultery was common."[129] Contemporary opinion noted adultery by both men and women of the higher social groups. Lady Mary Wortley Montagu held that it was so common that "the appellation of rake is as genteel in a woman as a man of quality."[130] Although historians vary in their assessments of the attitudes toward adultery committed by husbands and wives respectively, there is an agreement that a sexual libertinism set in within the upper social strata. It had been foreshadowed in the Middle Ages and Renaissance by the idea of "courtly love," a literary tradition that celebrated the romantic – and either potentially or actually adulterous – relationship between an aristocratic married woman and a knight.

By the later seventeenth century, however, overt adultery within the upper classes had made the leap from the book to the bed.[131] Their role models, if they needed any, were kings such as Charles II of England, "who kept mistresses and spawned bastards in ostentatious profusion." Adultery, according to most assessments, became a normal fact of life in the court aristocracy, then in rural élite society.[132] As if to put distance between this behavior and the adultery that as recently as the 1650s had been a capital offense, English practitioners of the adulterous arts adopted the euphemism "gallantry" to describe their activities, in itself an indicator of a more permissive, even an approving attitude toward extramarital sexual relationships.

Elsewhere there were signs of increasing lenience toward adultery, as its status as a capital offense declined. In New England less draconian penalties were dispensed from the end of the seventeenth century.[133] In France a more lax judicial attitude was noted. The *Encyclopédie*, for instance, compared the harsh penalties that had been inflicted on adulterers in the past in various

---

[129] Richard T. Vann, "Toward a New Lifestyle: Women in Preindustrial Capitalism," in Bridenthal and Koontz, *Becoming Visible*, 200.
[130] Quoted in Stone, *Family, Sex and Marriage*, 533. See Stone's section on "Aristocratic Adultery," 529–34.
[131] Evidence for the earlier seventeenth century is given in Antonia Fraser, *The Weaker Vessel: Woman's Lot in Seventeenth-Century England* (London, 1984), 17–19.
[132] Stone, *Family, Sex and Marriage*, 530.
[133] Roetger, "Transformation of Morals," esp. 244–7.

countries with the lenience in contemporary France; men were not prosecuted at all, it was noted, and women were at most deprived of their dowry and other matrimonial rights, and dispatched to nunneries. Women were not even whipped any longer, for fear that the public degradation it entailed would deter a husband from taking his wife back.[134] In eighteenth-century Scotland, too, there were complaints that the church was taking a more lenient attitude toward adultery: Even though it remained a capital crime by statute, offenders were being let off with relatively light sentences of imprisonment or banishment and transportation to the plantations for life.[135]

In time there was a reaction against what appeared to be an excessively tolerant attitude toward adultery. In England there were persistent attempts to tighten up the already restrictive provisions of parliamentary divorce by preventing adulterers from being "rewarded" by remarriage.[136] Attempts to criminalize adultery failed, but adultery became the sole matrimonial offense recognized by the first English divorce law in 1857. In France the indulgent attitude of revolutionary law ended with Napoleon who provided imprisonment for an adulterous wife and her accomplice (who could be fined as well), and a fine of between 100 and 2,000 francs for a husband who was guilty of aggravated adultery.[137] Moreover, Article 324 of the Napoleonic Penal Code specified that the murder by a man of his wife and her accomplice, when he had caught them in the act of adultery, was excusable in law.[138] A more rigorous attitude toward a wife's adultery was also evident in Spain. Under an early law of the seventh century, a husband was entitled to kill his adulterous wife and her accomplice, but in the thirteenth century the sole right of punishment in these circumstances was transferred to the courts. In 1805, however, a new code restored the right to the husband but with an important qualification: He could legally kill both his wife and her accomplice, but not only one of the pair.[139]

Viewed from the legal perspective, we find that in the nineteenth century the trend was against the easier tolerance of adultery, just as nineteenth-century law had shifted against wife beating. Again, however, this tells us nothing about practice. There is no reason to believe that adultery increased or diminished as social and legal tolerance rose and fell. The apparent change in incidence might just as well reflect more or less open discussion of the subject, shifts in the vigilence or exercise of discretion by prosecutors and judges, or trends in literary fashion, as much as it reflected actual social behavior. In these cases there really is no way of separating the levels of evidence and of extricating ourselves from its contradictions and circular explanations. When it comes to

---

[134] *Encyclopédie*, I, 151. Note the implication here that adultery by the wife need not lead to the termination of the marriage.
[135] Smith, "Enlightenment Scotland," 54.
[136] See Section 11.3.
[137] John Lough, *The Philosophes and Post-Revolutionary France* (Oxford, 1982), 212.
[138] Ibid.
[139] Lucy A. Sponsler, "The Status of Married Women under the Legal System of Spain," *Journal of Legal History* 3 (1982), 142–3.

assessments of the incidence of adultery, we can always find some commentator of the opinion that adultery had never before been so common. In the 1550s a delegation to the Geneva Consistory complained that the standards of sexual morality set down were impossibly stringent and that if the court continued to insist on such purity of behavior "they feared that their wives might all be tied in weighted sacks and thrown into the river (the punishment for flagrant adultery)."[140] A century later, Cromwell responded to complaints that adultery and fornication were rampant in the land by making adultery by married women a capital offense. In the next century a doctor in France commented that "adultery is very frequent in the countryside,"[141] and at the end of the eighteenth century Lord Auckland pointed to an epidemic of adultery in England.[142] An administrator in early-nineteenth-century Bavaria stated that "almost every peasant has a sweetheart alongside his spouse, and the peasant woman evens things up with one of the servant lads,"[143] and at midcentury Dr. William Acton, a frequent commentator on sex and morality, wrote that no one acquainted with rural life would deny that seduction was "a sport and a habit with vast numbers of men, married...and single, placed above the ranks of labour."[144]

But contemporary observers are by no means renowned for the accuracy of their observations, and in the end we must fall back on conclusions based not only on them but on other incomplete and impressionistic evidence, as unsatisfactory as that procedure is. My feeling is that adultery was by no means universal, but that it certainly affected a considerable minority of marriages, a minority whose magnitude must have varied significantly. It is not difficult to believe that the great majority of aristocratic men in the late seventeenth and eighteenth centuries committed adultery, nor that it was uncommon among peasant populations, particularly when committed by men. For the most part it seems that adultery was incorporated within the expectations of marriage or was tolerated when it occurred, or was discovered, on an ad hoc basis. Women in particular might well have been prepared for their husbands' adultery. The first Marquis of Halifax wrote to his daughter at the end of the seventeenth century that

you live at a time which hath rendered some kind of frailties so habitual, that they lay claim to large grains of allowance...Remember, that next to the danger of committing the fault [adultery] yourself, the greatest is that of seeing it in your husband. Do not seem to look or hear that way: If he is a man of sense, he will reclaim himself...if he is

---

140 Sherrin Marshall Wintjes, "Women in the Reformation Era," in Bridenthal and Koontz, *Becoming Visible*, 172–3. The Consistory scolded the members of the delegation for being flippant, and had its leader imprisoned.
141 Dr. Jean-Emmanuel Gilibert, quoted in Shorter, *Modern Family*, 247.
142 See Section 11.3.
143 Joseph Hazzi, quoted in Shorter, *Modern Family*, 247.
144 William Acton, *Prostitution, Considered in its Moral, Social, and Sanitary Aspects* (London, 1857), 75.

not so, he will be provok'd, but not reform'd...Such an undecent complaint makes a wife much more ridiculous than the injury that provoketh her to it.[145]

The message was clear: A wife should expect her husband to be unfaithful, and she should overlook his infidelity; adultery did not affect a marriage.

At many levels of society, and not only in England, wives acted according to this advice, as did many husbands who were faced with their wives' adultery. Many fell short of the equanimity suggested, reacting with violence or other informal sanctions. Yet others, a small minority we should expect, took their grievances to the authorities, where we encounter them as criminal suits, petitions for divorce and separation, actions for criminal conversation, requests for *lettres de cachet*, and the like.

The relationship of adultery to marriage breakdown is at many points similar to that of marital violence. Either *could* indicate that a marriage had broken down, but neither necessarily did so. For personal reasons, because of emotional, economic, social, or other factors, some husbands and wives manifested a lower level of tolerance than others of these forms of behavior. What is clear from both of these examples is that it is impossible to deal with such matrimonial offenses in absolute terms. Contemporaries, whether they were the spouses involved or outsiders, did not deal in absolutes, such that any violence or any adultery would be held necessarily to signify the collapse of marriage. The law might have referred only to "adultery," especially when it referred to women's adultery; in practice, however, men and women treated these matrimonial offenses, if they regarded them as such, in situational terms, taking into consideration the broader social and familial contexts, the character of the offense, its explanation, its frequency, and its degree. Such a situation makes it extremely hazardous to generalize about marriage breakdown in the past and serves to emphasize the role of the individual in the definition and application of socially accepted norms of behavior.

9.5 Emotional expectations and romantic love

The third aspect of marital relationships to examine in respect of marriage breakdown is their emotional content, the intensity of passion, love, affection, friendship, coolness, antipathy, hatred, or sheer indifference that characterized the daily relations and social transactions between husband and wife. It is an assumption about marriages in modern Western society that they are founded on love as well as other criteria, but that the endurance of love is of such overriding importance that a qualitative change in it threatens the survival of a marriage, no matter how satisfactory it might be in financial, social, or other respects. This emphasis on romantic love as a precondition of marriage, and as a necessary condition for the endurance of a marriage, is a relatively recent

[145] *Miscellanies by the Right Noble Lord, The Late Marquess of Halifax* (London, 1700), 17–18, quoted in Thomas, "Double Standard," 196.

development. One implication of this is that intensely emotional relationships were less important to married couples in the past, that expectations of what today is called "emotional fulfillment" were minimal, and that the emotional content of marriage had, in itself, as little to do with marriage breakdown as it had with marriage formation.

A number of important historical works have pointed to key indicators of change in marital emotions, notably the process by which men and women chose their partners in marriage, and the criteria that came into play during that process. Over time there have been two principal lines of change in these respects. First, the responsibility of choosing a spouse gradually shifted more and more to the individuals concerned, while the participation of others, notably parents or other family members, correspondingly declined. Second, the criteria upon which spouses have been chosen have focused increasingly on the personal qualities of the prospective partner and the likelihood of emotional compatibility, and less on "interest" factors such as wealth, economic prospects, and social rank.

Within these general trends, historians have pointed to varying chronologies and to different social classes as being the purveyors of changed attitudes and practices. Edward Shorter, for example, sees the romantic revolution as part of a more general transformation in attitudes, perceptions, and behavior, of which the sexual revolution was also an integral part. Shorter located the origins of this revolution within the younger cohorts of the eighteenth-century working classes, who, he argued, were freed from the traditional constraints of family and community by increased geographical mobility and by the opportunities and individualistic ethos offered by the capitalist market system. From the lower classes these attitudes, including a stress on affection and love within relationships, courtships, and marriages, percolated upward until they became generalized in the nineteenth and twentieth centuries.[146]

Lawrence Stone's account of the rise of romantic love in England, and its fulfillment in companionate marriage, also stressed the eighteenth century, particularly the final two decades of it, as a critical period of transition from marriages based primarily on interest to those based on affection. Stone recognized the important point that the transformation was not a question of abandoning one set of criteria in favor of another but of shifts in the relative emphasis of criteria within a broad range.[147] Marriages continued to be endogamous in many respects: Men married women of similar social and economic rank, age, and appropriate cultural and educational level, so that marriage continued to serve its traditional socioeconomic purposes. But within these implicit limits there was increased stress on affective factors going beyond the minimal desire for compatibility to the search for positive emotional

---

[146] Shorter, *Modern Family*, esp. 15, 120–67, 259–60. See also Edward Shorter, "Différences de classe et de sentiment depuis 1750: l'exemple de la France," *Annales. Economies Sociétés Civilisations* 24 (1974), 1034–57.

[147] Stone, *Family, Sex and Marriage*, esp. 282–324.

attraction. Stone is inconclusive as to the social class that adopted the romantic ideal first but indicates the early status of the gentry and the squirarchy as "accept[ing] the need for affection" within marriage.[148]

Shorter and Stone are only two of a number of historians who have concluded that romantic love assumed unprecedented importance within marriage during the eighteenth century. Randolph Trumbach pointed to its evolution within the English aristocracy.[149] Jean-Louis Flandrin has seen its development in France, in part in emulation of supposed English practices, in the late eighteenth century. He noted that only six books published in France between 1723 and 1789 bore the words "married love" (*amour conjugal*) in their title, but that five of the six appeared after 1770.[150] Similar trends toward greater individual initiative and freedom in spouse selection, and a decline of the importance of interest factors, have been suggested by Daniel Smith's analysis of marriage patterns in late-eighteenth- and early-nineteenth-century Massachusetts.[151] Finally, Carl Degler has pointed to the same period as important for a generalized and "growing acceptance of affection as the primary ground for family formation."[152]

These and many other similar findings and their interpretations have their detractors, some of whom point to the continuity of attitudes and behavior before and after the eighteenth century in order to undermine notions of its significance as a period of transition in the rise of romantic love within marriage. Michael MacDonald, for example, discovered that almost 40% of the men and women who consulted the astrologer Richard Napier in England in the seventeenth century complained of their frustrations in courtship and married life, and many of Napier's clients who suffered stresses in courtship attributed them to problems arising from love. Another forty clients mentioned that they had been in love before they were married (presumably with the same person). MacDonald concluded from his fascinating evidence that the clients' accounts "make nonsense of historians' confident assertions that romantic love was rare in seventeenth-century England or that it was unimportant in choosing marital partners."[153] Alan Macfarlane, too, has taken issue with the notion that romantic love originated in England in the eighteenth century.[154]

In many respects the debate on the rise of romantic love has often been misconceived, misstated, and misrepresented. Like many long-term evolutions of ideas or behavior (capitalism, urbanization, and secularization are examples),

[148] Ibid., 288.
[149] Randolph Trumbach, *The Rise of the Egalitarian Family* (New York, 1978), esp. 113–17, 157–60.
[150] Flandrin, *Families in Former Times*, 169–70.
[151] D. S. Smith, "Parental Power and Marriage Patterns: An Analysis of Historical Trends in Hingham, Mass.," *Journal of Marriage and the Family* 35 (1973), 419–28.
[152] Carl Degler, *At Odds: Women and the Family in America* (New York, 1980), 18.
[153] Michael MacDonald, *Mystical Bedlam. Madness, anxiety and healing in seventeenth-century England* (Cambridge, 1981), 88–9, but see 72–111 on the family.
[154] Macfarlane, *Marriage and Love*, 148–208, esp. 205–8.

the increase in conjugal sentiment should be considered not in terms of the complete or absolute replacement of one set of criteria, attitudes, or practices by a different set but rather a shift on the relative balance within a spectrum of variables. It is evident that there need be no mutual exclusivity or contradiction between affective and interest criteria for marriage, to take the issue at point. The process by which men and women choose marriage partners is neither random nor wholly calculated, but subject to a subtle process, conscious and unconscious, of selection and rejection, in which various factors – social, economic, sexual, and emotional – interact with one another. To this extent the dichotomy often made between interest and affective considerations is a false one.

Even if interest factors weighed very heavily, even if they weighed most heavily – as seems to have been the case – in the making and survival of marriages in traditional society, this is no reason to suppose that emotional considerations had no role. It is more likely that interest criteria – social position, economic prospects in the broadest sense, and age differentials – were the means by which an individual defined the constituency of potential marriage partners appropriate to him or her, and that affective criteria determined which of the candidates was chosen from within that constituency.[155] The apparent rise of conjugal love, placed within this context, suggests that over time in those strata where there is evidence of more widespread appeal to affective criteria, either the interest factors became less important, which would have enlarged the potential marriage constituency, or that they continued to come into play with the same force but in a less explicit manner. In either case we should expect to find fewer references to social rank or economic utility of a proposed match. In neither case would the interest criteria be extinguished entirely, but in both cases there would be an increased propensity to justify or explain a marriage in terms of affection or love.

To the extent to which this is true, the accumulation of quotations and examples of marriages based on love and of lovesick young men and women before the eighteenth century, or of marriages based primarily on economic utility in the twentieth,[156] proves nothing except that motives for marriage and the affective content of marriages varied from marriage to marriage at any given time.[157] In light of the vicissitudes that decide the survival of historical evidence, these examples often do not give us much to go on when we seek to define change and to locate it socially and temporally.

More useful for these purposes are some series of continuous data or evi-

---

[155] There is a very intelligent discussion of these issues in Wrightson, *English Society*, 79–88.
[156] See Section 10.2 for examples of twentieth-century marriages based on economic interests.
[157] A broad survey is Herman R. Lantz, "Romantic Love in the Pre-Modern Period: A Sociological Commentary," *Journal of Social History* 15 (1982), 349–70. Lantz concludes that "although romantic love was present far back in western history, the rapid spread of romantic love in Europe and America was influenced by economic, political and social variables, which were part of the process of modernization. This is especially the case in the eighteenth century in Europe and the nineteenth century in America" (p. 365).

dence over time (as distinct from the sporadic and isolated references in letters, diaries, literature, and the like), and several examples apply to eighteenth-century France. One has already been noted, the increased (but still tiny number of) references to married love in the titles of published works.[158] A second and more substantial source lies in the petitions for dispensations from the Roman Catholic church's impediments to marriage. Men and women who wanted to marry within the prohibited degrees of consanguinity or affinity were required to explain why they wished or needed to marry their chosen partner rather than another person to whom a marriage would not conflict with the church's rules. Among petitions in two dioceses in Normandy from the late seventeenth to late eighteenth centuries there was a shift in emphasis toward the end of the period: "At the end of the Old Regime, the hope of salvation [which was expressed as a reason for marriage] was no longer only the intention of living as a Christian, and in many declarations there is particular evidence of a search for pleasure [within marriage], the desire to live happily."[159] A similar tendency was found in petitions for dispensations lodged with the diocese of Montauban in southwestern France in the eighteenth century. Before 1770 only 9% of petitions mentioned emotional attachment as a reason for marriage; after 1770, 41% did so. What is notable about this study is that it shows that the trend was shared across the social spectrum, from peasants and workers through the bourgeoisie to the aristocracy. Moreover, there is clear evidence of the persistence of interest criteria alongside the more frequent appeal to affective reasons for marriage.[160]

We cannot go into the details of the debate on the rise of romantic love and its enhanced importance relative to the range of considerations that determined the choice of spouse. There is general agreement that it took place, and that the late eighteenth century is a more likely candidate than most as being the main period of transition, although we should not expect to find a single chronology that is universally applicable: It might have occurred first in England, then in Europe, and later in America. As for the social strata that first manifested an emphasis on affection and love, all social classes, from the working classes through the middle classes to the aristocracy, have been proposed.[161]

It is the fact, character, and implications of the change toward stressing love that are of greatest interest in our consideration of the definitions of marriage breakdown. We must admit first of all that the evidence is sketchy and difficult

---

[158] Flandrin, *Families in Former Times*, 169–70.

[159] Jean-Marie Gouesse, "Parenté, famille et mariage en Normandie aux XVIIe et XVIIIe siécles. Présentation d'une source et d'une enquête," *Annales. Economies Sociétés Civilisations* 27 (1972), 1139–54.

[160] Margaret H. Darrow, "Popular Concepts of Marital Choice in Eighteenth-Century France," *Journal of Social History* 18 (1985), 261–72. It could be that the arguments were framed to appeal to the judges hearing these petitions, and in that case we should have to assume that the petitioners believed that applications based on affective reasons would be sympathetically considered.

[161] The debate is surveyed in Lawrence Stone, "Family History in the 1980s. Past Achievements and Future Trends," *Journal of Interdisciplinary History* 12 (1981), esp. 71–8.

to interpret, but it does suggest that emotional incompatibility or indifference were in themselves seldom a reason for marriage breakdown before the nineteenth century. One difficulty in reaching any firm conclusion is that emotional states were translated into actions that could provoke marriage breakdown in some contexts. Violence could be a symptom of hatred, and adultery might reflect antipathy toward a spouse. When marriages broke down in such circumstances we can never be certain as to whether they did so because of the violence or adultery themselves, or whether these actions were catalysts, provoking a separation that was essentially grounded on an underlying emotional relationship that had become intolerable. Clearly, emotional conditions had to take some physical, verbal, or behavioral form such as quarreling, fighting, scolding, desertion, cruelty, or adultery. It is a pointless task to attempt to distinguish the emotion from its expression as provocative of marriage breakdown. There are few examples of broken marriages in the absence of an offense that was either the catalyst of separation or its substantive cause. The historical record indicates that although quarreling couples were often admonished to get along better, there was no assumption that such marriages had broken down because of the lack of affection between the spouses.

This is what we should expect from a marriage system that was pluralist when it came to criteria for choosing a spouse and in its expectations of marriage. Marriage in traditional society fulfilled many functions. It was, as we shall see in the following chapter, an economic partnership, but it also had functions in terms of reproduction, socialization, education, and welfare, as well as providing a legitimate forum for sexual activity and emotional companionship. As befitted such marriages that were so varied in the functions they performed, expectations were also varied. A spouse had to satisfy a broad range of needs – economic, social, sexual, and personal. Emotional satisfaction, then, was an expectation of marriage, but only one expectation among many. If this expectation were not met, the marriage could survive as long as it continued to satisfy the other needs well enough. To this extent, traditional marriages might have been far more flexible in emotional terms because there were compensations for the failure of emotional expectations. This scenario changed over time as the affective aspects of marriage took on a proportionately greater significance. Put crudely, the more important affection or love was to marriage formation, the more significant its role in marriage breakdown when it declined or disappeared. The logical progress of this trend in modern Western society, where love is conceived of as being the single most important consideration in the choice of spouse and in the relationship between husband and wife, is that the loss of sentiments of love on the part of one spouse toward the other (or mutually) is more likely than ever to be perceived by them as indicative of the breakdown of their marriage. In traditional society emotions simply had a lower profile in the making and unmaking of marriages.

Sentiments within marriage, the emotional relationship between husband

and wife, tend thus to parallel violence and adultery in their roles in marriage breakdown in the past. It is impossible to enter the minds and share the feelings of men and women in earlier times, just as it is often impossible to understand what motivates our contemporaries to enter, continue, or terminate their marriages. What is most striking about husbands and wives in traditional society is the flexibility and adaptability of their expectations of marriage. These qualities seem to have enabled them to accommodate a wide range of conditions and behavior within their definitions of marriage, so that they defined marriage breakdown in a very restrictive manner, women even more restrictively than men. These characteristics of flexibility and adaptability, mediated through definitions of marriage breakdown, produced a high degree of stability in marriages in traditional Western society.

10

~~~~~~

The social context of marriage breakdown

10.1 Introduction

The image of marital relationships that emerges from the previous chapter is anything but homogeneous. No universally applicable picture of marital behavior and attitudes is to be discovered. Although patterns, regularities, and trends can very likely be located and defined, we must finally admit the diversity of attitudes and behavior in the past, just as we do for the present. Too many historians have overambitiously pursued the chimera of a dominant model of marital relationships, and too often we have been treated to a war of quotations and examples as a caring husband is pitted against a callous one, a romantic relationship is squared off against an indifferent one, and an egalitarian marriage is contrasted with an authoritarian one. There has no doubt been an evolution in affective content and expression over the past four centuries, but the diversity of examples that historians have adduced reflects the historical reality: jealous wives and indifferent wives, abusive husbands and affectionate husbands, relationships that were emotionally warm and those that were emotionally void. Not only were there variations among couples, but individual relationships themselves changed over time. These are hardly ground-breaking conclusions, but the diversity we must insist on has been too often obscured by the search for universal models and ideal types.[1]

The fact that these vastly disparate conditions – affection, indifference, hatred, caring, abuse – could all exist within what were, to all appearances, functioning marriages, tells us that expectations of marriage in the past could be very low. There is no evidence of marriages breaking down for trifling reasons: Husbands did not leave their wives, wives did not leave their husbands, be-

---

[1] The most ambitious example is Lawrence Stone's *The Family, Sex and Marriage in England, 1500–1800* (London, 1977), in which Stone defined a number of family types such as "The Restricted Patriarchal Nuclear Family, 1550–1700," and "The Closed Domesticated Nuclear Family, 1640–1800." This book, rich in detail and insight, but often overambitious in terms of theories and typologies, has stimulated much work on the history of the family. Its search for models and theories provoked a number of hostile reactions, such as Alan Macfarlane's review in *History and Theory* 18 (1979).

cause of an isolated incident of violence, an abusive word or two, or because the relationship was other than ideal. Just the opposite: In fact, husbands and wives, especially wives, tolerated a great deal of abuse, oppression, and exploitation within marriage, taking no effective counteraction even when they were faced with extreme brutality, blatant and habitual sexual infidelity, and all manner of exploitation and oppression. The evidence speaks for expectations of marriage that were flexible and potentially very low. A key word, in this respect, is "potentially," for what is suggested here is not that marriages necessarily plumbed the limits of these low expectations but that expectations were sufficiently flexible that they could accommodate a broad spectrum of behavior. The other side of these potentially low expectations was a potentially high tolerance of what we should consider negative conditions and behavior. It was precisely a sense of this tolerance that emerged from the preceding chapter, particularly tolerance on the part of married women. Clearly the marriages in which we can observe the tolerance at work were those where there were tensions and conflicts within marriage: These are the cases that interest us for the history of marriage breakdown.

It is difficult to locate the origins of these attitudes that permitted women and men to put up with far from ideal conditions within marriage. Socialization and emulation, the experiences of family life both through participation and observation were important, more important to the mass of the population than were treatises, conduct-books, and legal commentaries. But apart from experience and ideology, a complex of material and other influences made the de facto dissolution of marriage (desertion or the mutual agreement to separate) unthinkable – simply inconceivable for most men and women in traditional European society. The economic interdependence or dependence of husbands and wives, the difficulties involved with making a living outside marriage, the presence of children – these and other variables could effectively lock husbands and wives into marriage. We shall see that they impinged particularly strongly upon married women, the spouses more likely to be oppressed within marriage and more likely to want to escape. Whereas there might have been some avenues of escape open to men, women had access to many fewer options, their scope of initiative limited by their very social, legal, and physical inferiority within marriage and society generally.

The consequences and implications of breaking up a marriage, as they will be outlined in this chapter, would have made life so difficult for men and especially women that spouses accommodated themselves to conditions and behavior within marriage that, in recent times, have proved to be less and less tolerable. What is suggested here is that the economic, social, demographic, and ideological conditions, which combined to make it so difficult for couples to end their marriages, produced a generally pragmatic attitude toward marriage. Within this attitude, expectations were low and flexible, and there was a correspondingly high tolerance of what we might think of as negative behavior. Physical violence, mental cruelty, sexual infidelity, emotional indifference, all appear to have been widely tolerated to the point of being thoug█ and not particularly abnormal, even though some of them might █ recognized as being far from ideal. Resignation to these kinds of co█ within marriage was probably a result of there being effectively no alternati█ continued married life. Men and women might have entered marriage with l█ expectations as to the lives they would live and their spouses' behavior, or they might have begun with high expectations, only to adjust them to the reality of marriage. But what is clear from the study of individual marriages in traditional society, is that a surprisingly high degree of tolerance of what we should consider oppressive or offensive behavior was widespread. Wives put up with violence; husbands and wives seem not to have regarded extramarital sexual activity too severely; both accepted emotional indifference and hostility. In all cases, the qualification should be made that women proved themselves more tolerant than their husbands. It could be argued, quite validly, that such behavior is not uncommon in modern marriages as well. The point is, however, that in modern times the high divorce rate attests to the widespread intolerance of negative behavior and emotionally unsatisfactory relationships. In traditional Western society there was neither a significant rate of divorce or formal separation; nor is there any evidence that the informal dissolution of marriages was widespread or common.

We cannot enter deeply into the relationships between husbands and wives in the past. We know that they rarely divorced or separated formally or informally, but we cannot infer from this that they necessarily resigned themselves to unsatisfactory marriages. Might they not have chafed continuously at the socioeconomic chains that bound them together, and lived out their lives in marriages that alternated between cold war and outright conflict until one of them released the other from the torment by dying? No doubt many of them did live their lives in chronically conflict-ridden marriages, but it is more likely that most couples made whatever adjustment was necessary to the conditions they experienced within marriage. As we shall see, marriage was a cooperative enterprise, not simply or predominantly an emotional relationship, and constant conflict and aggression would have weakened it and rendered it less efficient, something that was in the best interests of neither spouse nor of the family as a whole.

Acceptance of the reality of marriage, no matter how unpleasant, was the frequent advice given to husbands and wives – especially wives. As we have seen, seventeenth-century conduct-books recommended patience, forbearance, and forgiveness, not resistance and thought of escape or separation, in the face of oppression, abuse, and incompatibility. Early in that century Alexander Niccholes advised husbands and wives that, because marriage was a permanent relationship,

therefore as wise prisoners inclosed in narrow roomes sute their mindes to their limites, and not, impatient they can go no further augment their paine by knocking their heades

ould the wisedom both of Husbands and Wives...beare
d content ... and not storme against that which will but the
heir own misery.[2]

to be a particularly attractive metaphor for marriage,
opriate, and the advice was clear: Since they could not
on into which they had voluntarily committed them-
ves should reconcile themselves to whatever their
vas not a formula for high expectations of marriage,
... ...d pragmatic approach, with the potential for very low
expectations. It is the argument of this chapter that these were the prevailing
attitudes to and expectations of marriage, not because husbands and wives en
masse were convinced by conduct-books, but because the advice reflected the
realities of married life and the economic and social demands of it. There is this
important distinction to make, however. Niccholes and his fellow marriage
counselors thought of the permanence and indissolubility of marriage in
ideological, legal, and religious terms; marriage could not be dissolved legally,
and separation was contrary to God's law, they wrote, so rather than think about
escaping from marriage, husbands and wives should reconcile themselves
to each other for life. This was fine as far as it went, but there were other,
more tangible deterrents to terminating a marriage. These were the material
conditions and social context of marriage, and it is to these that we must now
turn.

The practical consequences of separation in traditional society were both
dramatic and traumatic, much more so than in modern times, and we must
understand them in order to appreciate how they influenced the decision to
terminate a marriage. The most obvious aspect of separation was physical, the
departure of one spouse from the common dwelling, followed by his or her
establishment of a new household or joining an already existing one. In some
cases separation could mean a domiciliary relocation on the part of both
spouses. It was difficult enough for a solitary person to create or join a
household in traditional society, but additional consequences flowed from the
elementary fact of separation.

10.2 The family economy

There were, first of all, economic dislocations. For the mass of the population
in traditional Western society, marriage was at base an economic partnership,
the nucleus of the family economy that linked all members of a family in a
network of economic and social relationships in addition to their kinship ties.
The family economy is one of the most important concepts for an understand-

[2] Alexander Niccholes, *A Discourse of Marriage and Wiving: And of the greatest Mystery therein contained: How to choose a good Wife* (London, 1615), sig. G1^V.

10.2 The family economy

ing of the family in traditional society.[3] In crude terms it was a small-scale economy, generally based on the family household, in which the family – usually the wife, husband, and their children – worked cooperatively as a unit of production. The most simple form was the agricultural family, specifically the family farm, where all members of the family were expected to carry out specific production tasks. All members of the family, regardless of gender and with little regard to age, were expected to work, but specific tasks were generally allotted on the basis of gender and age. Adult males, for example, were likely to take responsibility for jobs that required the greatest physical strength, such as plowing. Adult women's work was centered on the household and its immediate environs, and included specific tasks such as brewing, baking, and milking. Children were allotted work within their physical and intellectual capacities. Only at certain times, such as during the harvest, when the maximum labor was required, might all members of the family participate in the same work.[4]

The precise forms and content of the family economy and the division of labor within it varied from economy to economy. The family farm is perhaps the clearest and most readily understood example because it endured longest in Western society. The family economy extended, however, to most other areas of productivity. In fishing communities there was a division of labor that might see both husband and wife fish, the husband market the catch, and the wife care for the household whenever her husband was away.[5] The essence of the couple's cooperation was captured in a Scandinavian proverb: "No man can be a fisherman without a wife."[6]

Domestic textile production was another clear example of the family economy at work, as women, men, and children prepared the raw materials (such as carding wool), spun the yarn, and wove the cloth, all as a cooperative effort. The role of the family as a unit of economic production was recognized during the early phase of industrialization, when factories employed not individuals but entire families. Families – parents and children – were quite appropriately seen as units of labor having their own intrinsic relationships and rhythms of work, as well as established patterns of authority and discipline.[7]

---

[3] An illuminating analysis is Hans Medick, "The proto-industrial family economy," in Peter Kriedte, Hans Medick, and Jürgen Schlumbohm, *Industrialization before Industrialization* (Cambridge, 1981), 38–73, esp. 41ff.

[4] There are many descriptions of the family economy. See Medick, "Proto-industrial family economy"; Martine Segalen, *Mari et femme dans la société paysanne* (Paris, 1980), esp. 87–121; Louise A. Tilly, Joan W. Scott, and Miriam Cohen, "Women's Work and European Fertility Patterns," *Journal of Interdisciplinary History* 6 (1976), 452ff.

[5] See the testimony by Norman fishermen as to the role of the wife, quoted in Jean-Marie Gouesse, "Parenté, famille et mariage en Normandie aux XVIIᵉ et XVIIIᵉ siècles," *Annales. Economies Sociétés Civilisations* 27 (1972), 1154.

[6] David Gaunt and Orvar Lofgren, "Remarriage in the Nordic Countries: The Cultural and Socio-economic Background," in Jacques Dupâquier, et al., *Marriage and Remarriage in Populations of the Past* (London, 1981), 54.

[7] Ann Oakley, *Woman's Work: The Housewife, Past and Present* (New York, 1974), 37–8; Eric Richards, "Women in the British Economy since about 1700: An Interpretation," *History* 59 (1974), 337–57.

Only in the later phases of industrialization was this pattern of familial production undermined and finally destroyed.

It is not essential to detail the various kinds of family economy here, for they are the subject of a large and sophisticated literature.[8] For our present analysis of the effects of the family economy on marriage breakdown, one feature of the system was paramount, and that is the position of economic interdependence that it implied for members of the family, above all for the husband and wife. The different but complementary work roles performed by the spouses highlight the economic bases of marriage in the past, and this state of mutual dependence was enhanced by other features typical of the preindustrial family economy. In the first place it was frequently not a wage economy. Individuals within the family economy did not earn an individual wage or other identifiably individual return for their labor because work was not individualized. Although each task had particular bounds and definitions – carding wool was distinct from spinning, which in turn was distinct from weaving – it had no discrete purpose in itself. Instead, each task was integral to, and derived its meaning from, the broader labor process that was the family's economic enterprise. This was as true of farming and fishing as it was of domestic industry.

Moreover the prevalence of the family economy, particularly in rural areas but also, if to a lesser extent, in the towns, meant that workers were often locked into their family's economy. In the virtual absence of any significant wage labor market, skills and labor were not easily transferable or portable from one place of work to another. In an economic system based on domestic and family production, a textile worker, to take one example, could not easily pick up, leave his or her family, and readily find employment elsewhere. Families did take in hired help at various times in the family cycle when children were too young to work or when the family was below the optimum size for its production base,[9] but such opportunities were limited and anything but certain. Similarly, artisans took on apprentices, but the number of vacancies at any given time was extremely limited.

As far as the married couple was concerned, the general effect of the family economy was to highlight the mutuality of their partnership. We should perhaps think specifically of a conjugal economy that made it very difficult – not impossible, but very difficult – for either spouse to transfer his or her labor to another forum of production, and was therefore a powerful deterrent to separation. To make these points is not to say that marriage or the family generally was nothing more than a set of economic relationships. Families

---

[8] See, for example, Medick, "Proto-industrial family economy"; Olwen Hufton, "Women and the Family Economy in Eighteenth-Century France," *French Historical Studies* 9 (1975), 1–22; Richard Wall, "Work, Welfare and the Family: An Illustration of the Adaptive Family Economy," in Lloyd M. Bonfield, Richard M. Smith, and Keith Wrightson (eds.), *The World We Have Gained: Histories of Population and Social Structure* (Oxford, 1986), 261–94.

[9] Lutz K. Berkner, "The Stem Family and the Developmental Cycle of the Peasant Household: An Eighteenth-Century Austrian Example," *American Historical Review* 77 (1972), 415ff.

performed many other functions as well, such as socialization, we
education, and they were bonded by emotional ties of varying int
Nonetheless, in traditional society the economic relationships were func.
mental, for on them the family as a unit and its members as individuals
depended for their sheer survival. In these respects the interests of the
individual members of the family were identical to those of the family as a
corporate entity.

What evidence is there that the conjugal economy inhibited separation or the
voluntary dissolution of marriages? The actual social, economic, and intellectual
mechanisms were, of course, not explicit, but there is convincing indirect and
negative evidence. One form of indirect evidence lies in the parallels between
the effects of separation or voluntary dissolution of marriage on the individual
spouses and the effects of the death of a spouse on the family economy. Death,
it is clear, not only dissolved a marriage as a legal entity but also the economic
partnership of husband and wife, and the latter had far-reaching consequences.
Olwen Hufton writes that "the loss of either party in a marriage would almost
certainly wreck the entire fabric of the family economy."[10] Peter Laslett's
assessment of the same event is a little more qualified: "The breaking up of a
marriage by the death of the husband threatened an end to the familial undertaking almost as surely as the beginning of marriage meant its foundation."[11]
(Laslett goes on to argue that in simple economic terms a wife could be more
easily replaced than a husband.)

This point has been made in many studies of the popular family, that the
death of the husband or wife – perhaps it *was* more so in the case of the
husband – brought about a severe dislocation in the functioning of the family
economy, and often destroyed it entirely. An analogy might be the removal of a
key worker from an assembly line in a modern factory. The economic impact of
the death of a spouse required an economic response and solution, and in
traditional society this meant the rapid replacement of the dead spouse by
means of remarriage. In what might seem to be crass terms, remarriage by a
widow or widower was the common way of taking on a new economic partner so
as to enable the family economy to operate efficiently again.

The need to restore the family economy quickly can be discerned in the hasty
remarriages that were characteristic of traditional Western society. From a vast
number of local studies of remarriage patterns, a few examples will indicate the
range of possibilities. In the English community of Earls Colne from the
sixteenth to the eighteenth centuries, 60% of widowers who remarried had
done so within a year of their wives' deaths, and on average these men waited
only five months before remarrying. Widows in the community remarried with
less rapidity.[12] In the French peasant community of Thézels-Saint-Sernin in

---

[10] Hufton, "Women and the Family Economy," 17.
[11] Peter Laslett, *The World We Have Lost further explored* (London, 1983), 115.
[12] Alan Macfarlane, *Marriage and Love in England, 1300–1840* (Oxford, 1986), 235. The period
studied ran from 1580 to 1740.

y (1700–92), almost a half of the widowers (fifteen out of
arried did so within seven months of their wives' deaths.
ied less rapidly, but more than one-third of them (five out
married within a year and a half of being widowed.[13] As a
may take nineteenth-century Etne, a rural community in
There the median lapse of time between the death of one
rriage by the survivor was twelve months for men, twenty-three
en.[14]

Su... lays between the death of one spouse and remarriage to another
might strike the modern observer as callous, and indicative of a low level of
emotion that grief could apparently be overcome so quickly. But they are
perfectly understandable as expressions of the need to reconstitute the family
economy rapidly so as to ensure the continued well-being of the survivors.
Widowers needed to remarry in order to provide for the work carried out by the
wife, the duties centering on the household, caring for children, and for the
multitude of other tasks that were the traditional province of the married
woman. Martine Segalen makes the point that although women might readily
have taken on what was normally a man's work, men were reluctant to perform
tasks that were defined as women's.[15] Of course, a widower had the option of
hiring help to compensate for the loss of labor created by the death of his wife,
but this option had disadvantages. It was more expensive to hire a partner than
to marry her; employing help introduced the notion of an individualized return
for work into an economy that might not recognize it; and finally marriage
implied other benefits, such as sexual partnership and companionship that were
not guaranteed in an employer–employee relationship. Needless to say, the
tendency to marry rather than hire labor had the effect of keeping the
wage labor market minimal, which in turn reduced the availability of work
for women who separated; being still married, they were unable to enter the
marriage-cum-labor market.

When it was the husband who died, leaving a widow in need of a new partner,
some of the same considerations came into play. In such cases remarriage was
less frequent and less rapid, as the case studies cited earlier showed.[16] Widows,

---

[13] Pierre Valmary, *Familles paysannes au XVIII⁻ siècle en Bas-Quercy* (Paris, 1965), 102–3. For other examples in France, see Jean-Louis Flandrin, *Families in Former Times* (Cambridge, 1979), 115–16, and Micheline Baulant, "The Scattered Family: Another Aspect of Seventeenth-Century Demography," in Robert Forster and Orest Ranum (eds.), *Family and Society* (Baltimore, 1976), 104–5.

[14] Figures are for widowers and widows under fifty years of age in the period 1801–44. Stale Dyrvik, "Gagne-pain ou sentiments? Trait du remariage en Norvège au dix-neuvième siècle," in Duâquier, *Marriage and Remarriage*, 301.

[15] Segalen, *Mari et femme*, 87ff.

[16] Often there were constraints on remarriage by a widow. Some legal codes forbade remarriage before the elapse of a certain period to ensure that the widow was not pregnant by her deceased husband. The 1686 Swedish church law, for instance, prohibited a widow from marrying within a year of her husband's death. Gaunt and Lofgren, "Remarriage in the Nordic Countries," 56–7.

10.2 The family economy

particularly when they had young children, were apparently less attractive than widowers as marriage prospects.[17] In all cases of remarriage, whether it was of widowers or widows, various factors must have been important: their age, the number and ages of their children, and the size, character, and prosperity of their economic enterprises. Eilert Sundt noted of Norway in the late eighteenth century that few widows who held land had difficulty in finding husbands.[18] The economic basis of remarriage is also clear in a category of remarriage in which the parties had had an economic relationship antedating the death of the spouse of one of them. A study of the London marriage market showed a recurrent pattern of widowers marrying women who had been their servants. Their new wives would thus "have accumulated considerable experience in caring for children and in household affairs."[19]

In various ways, then, remarriage patterns in traditional society reflected the economic importance of the conjugal partnership. Choice of spouses in first marriages was also heavily influenced by economic considerations, as men and women sought out partners who were not only emotionally congenial but who would contribute to the formation of a family economy. In the case of remarriages, though, the economic imperatives seemed to take on a greater urgency.[20] Perhaps it is the speed with which widowers in particular remarried that leads us to think that emotional criteria were given little thought, and were almost completely subordinated to economic needs. Certainly the urgency to remarry, when there was work to be done and perhaps children to be cared for, was greater than at the time of first marriage, when there was no established family economy and no children.[21]

When we consider the conjugal and family economies from these various perspectives we can see that they bear on the question of marriage breakdown and separation in two ways: self-interest and altruism. From the point of view of the wife or husband so dissatisfied with marriage that she or he contemplated leaving, there were inhibitions deriving from simple self-interest. The labor

[17] Macfarlane, *Marriage and Love*, 235, observes that in Earls Colne widows with no children married more rapidly than widows with children.
[18] Michael Drake, *Population and Society in Norway 1735–1865* (Cambridge, 1969), 136.
[19] Vivien Brodsky Elliot, "Single Women and the London Marriage Market: Age, Status and Mobility, 1598–1619," in R. B. Outhwaite (ed.), *Marriage and Society: Studies in the Social History of Marriage* (London, 1981), 88–89. A similar principle is noted for a later period in Leonore Davidoff, "Mastered for Life: Servant and Wife in Victorian and Edwardian England," *Journal of Social History* 7 (1974), 406–28.
[20] Macfarlane points out that social pressures, such as the consent of parents and kin, decreased over time. The fact that, in the case of remarriages, greater freedom should coexist with primarily economic criteria in the choice of spouse, makes it clear that there is no necessary pairing of marriages into "free choice/affective" and "restricted choice/interest" matches, as much writing has tended to assume.
[21] Rapid remarriages echoed the brief courtships that preceded first marriages, however, at least in Britain. There couples seem to have married within six months and long courtships were frowned upon. John R. Gillis, *For Better, For Worse: British Marriages, 1600 to the Present* (New York, 1985), 43, 57f. The crucial difference between marriages and remarriages, though, was that widowers and widows spent less time searching out a partner before the brief courtship.

market was extremely limited, especially in rural areas, and there was no certainty at all that a solitary person could find any kind of security outside the family. At the altruistic level of decision making there must have been the recognition that separation or desertion would be an economic hardship, if not a disaster, for the family members who were left behind. Desertion by a husband or wife was, in fact, even more serious than his or her death. A widow or widower could at least reconstitute a disrupted family economy eventually by means of remarriage. In the case of a deserted spouse this was generally impossible, and even where it was possible, in those rare cases where remarriage was permitted on presumption of death after seven years' absence without news, or where the community seemed tacitly to approve of a bigamous remarriage,[22] the waiting periods imposed hardships that widows and widowers did not have to confront. Speed of remarriage was, as we have seen, of the essence. Even short-term absence by one spouse created difficulties for the family's economy. The effects of absence, indeed, must have been a powerful deterrent against one spouse's reporting the other to the authorities for committing an offense, such as adultery by the wife, that might lead to imprisonment. It is conceivable that what appeared to have been passivity by some men and women in the face of adultery by their spouses were in fact examples of tolerance produced by economic necessity. Against the satisfaction a husband might gain from seeing his unfaithful wife's illicit ardor cooled by a period in jail, he had to weigh the difficulties and disruptions her absence would cause in domestic and other productive work.

Clearly there was a mixture of selfish and altruistic considerations that could prevent a man from abandoning his family. If we consider the potentially disastrous effects on their wives and children as factors militating against husbands deserting, we are attributing a degree of altruism – why not call it affection? – which overrode the personal interests that desertion might serve. On the other hand, a husband who abandoned his home and family gave up his economic base, however poor it might be, and took with him only his labor to offer on an uncertain market. We should expect that desertion by men was more frequent among the landless poor, those who had no material interests or possessions to bind them, than among men who owned or otherwise held land, and who thus lost tangibly by abandoning it. There are no hard rules to be discovered in these cases, but patterns of lesser and greater likelihood. Each man would decide in his own way; all men experienced some constraints of economic, social, or affective kinds, but they reacted to them individually.

---

[22] There are occasional examples of what appear to have been socially approved bigamous marriages. In the village of Freswell, Nottinghamshire, in 1826 the marriage was celebrated of George Bell, a bachelor, and Mary Hunt, whose husband John Hunt, the church register noted, "was transported for Life [to Australia] having received a Reprieve from 'sentence of death' passed on him at Lincoln for stealing a Mare." There was no secrecy about this remarriage, performed after the banns had been called, in a small community of about 200 people, by the same vicar who had married Mary and John Hunt in 1821. The case is reported in Freda M. Wilkins-Jones, "A bigamous marriage," letter in *Local Population Studies* 22 (1972), 61.

10.2 The family economy

Poverty, it has been noted, could test marital and familial bonds to breaking point and beyond. Olwen Hufton has eloquently observed that "poverty is an acid: it corrodes and dissolves human relationships."[23] The evidence lies in the frequent association of poverty and families where one spouse, almost invariably the husband, had deserted or was permanently absent. Many men, faced with unemployment and impoverishment, left home in search of work, probably intending to return but never doing so. Others simply abandoned their families to fend as best they could. These were men who were not deterred by economic considerations because there were none: no family economy and no property to give up.[24] Nor were these men apparently inhibited by the thought of what would happen to their wives and children, although it is conceivable that some of the men calculated that their families would stand a better chance of obtaining charity if they themselves were absent. There is an analogy here to the abandonment of infants and children in times of economic hardship. In many cases these abandonments indicated not callous disregard for the welfare of the children but the opposite, a belief or hope that they would have a better chance of survival in a foundling hospital than in an impoverished household.[25]

Material deterrents to desertion did not deter men from deserting when the deterrents had weakened or did not apply for some reason. Poverty – the absence of material constraints and the equal lack of viable alternatives both inside and outside the family – is a good example. Poverty was poverty no matter whether one experienced it inside or outside the family. In other cases men were able to abandon their families by timing their desertions to the most propitious periods. In southeastern England in the eighteenth and nineteenth centuries, for example, desertion was most common in September and the harvesttime. "Such seasonality owed more to favourable weather and the high wages of summer and harvest (the latter paid in September) which helped allow the man to desert."[26] The harvest period provided a short-term labor market in the rural economy, and evidently it could act as a financial bridge to permit some men to free themselves from the constraints of the family economy.

The role of the family economy and its implications in inhibiting separation must remain somewhat schematic and speculative. Certainly there are qualifications and nuances to be made to the generalized conclusions advanced here. One must be that women felt the inhibitions more keenly than men. We should expect women generally to have been more anxious than their husbands to exit from marriage, but the family economy bore more heavily on them. A solitary woman was in a far more ambiguous and vulnerable social position

---

[23] Olwen Hufton, *The Poor of Eighteenth-Century France, 1750–1789* (Oxford, 1974), 114.

[24] Ibid., 115–16.

[25] Some parents of abandoned children placed identifying tokens such as ribbons, on them, to facilitate identification when they came to collect their children. Others attached notes to their children's clothing, saying that they would take them back when times improved. See Jean-Pierre Bardet, "Enfants abandonnés et enfants assistés à Rouen dans la seconde moitié du XVIIIᵉ siècle," *Sur la population française aux XVIIIᵉ et XIXᵉ siècles* (Paris, 1973), 37–8.

[26] K. D. M. Snell, *Annals of the Labouring Poor* (Cambridge, 1985), 361.

than a solitary man. The wages she could expect to earn, if she could find employment, would barely support her alone and would certainly not support children as well. For a glimpse of her future as a sole parent with dependent children, a married woman had only to look about her, at the poverty-stricken widows and deserted wives of traditional Western society. Women, it is clear, had much more compunction than men about abandoning their children. There are, it is true, many documented examples of mothers deserting their families, but they are only a small percentage of total desertions. There are other indicators that mothers felt stronger bonds than fathers to their children, and that men, given an opportunity, more readily deserted their families in the most dire circumstances.[27]

Men certainly had more opportunities. For all that married men were locked into marriage by the family economy, they had a variety of external options. Men had the possibility of being geographically more mobile, and were less vulnerable as solitaries. They had access to occupations that gave them a wider geographical field of initiative. As we noted in Chapter 8, men could migrate in search of work, take up employment in maritime occupations, emigrate to other towns, regions, and countries, or join the army. Although we should not exaggerate the attractiveness or ease of solitary life and work for men outside marriage and the family, there is no doubt that men found it on the whole less problematic than women.

Another important qualification to be made about the role of the family economy in decisions to terminate a marriage is that it was strongest in rural areas. Towns and cities offered something like a labor market where both men and women could take up employment in a variety of manual, skilled, or service occupations, and the family economy was weaker there than in the countryside. There were significant differences between town and country in various forms of behavior that indicated that the imperatives of the family economy were weaker in the former. For example, because wage labor was more common, the need for widows and widowers to remarry rapidly was reduced. Although it is true that the death of either spouse, especially the husband, meant the loss of essential income, it did not imply the disruption of the labor unit in quite the same way. The departure of a weaver husband would leave a family economy based on textile manufacture incomplete and render the other tasks, such as spinning, purposeless; the family, paid for the production of finished textiles, would receive no income. On the other hand the departure of a husband who was employed outside the family as a weaver would result in a decline in his family's income; it would not stop his wife, employed as a spinner, from continuing in gainful employment. Where there was no integrated family productivity, then, the departure (or death) of a spouse imposed less of a hardship on the remaining (or surviving) family members. If this were so, we should expect

---

[27] Snell notes that the deserted spouse was "almost always the wife." Ibid., 360. See also Hufton, *Poor of Eighteenth-Century France*, 115.

there to have been less drive to remarry when one spouse died, and indeed some studies have indicated that remarriage rates were lower in urban than in rural areas. In eighteenth-century Caen, for example, remarriages involving widows and widowers formed a smaller proportion of all marriages than in contemporary rural Normandy.[28] As we shall see, a decline in remarriage rates can be indicative of a general decline of the family economy over time.[29]

There is more direct evidence of the effects of the family economy from Rouen at the end of the eighteenth century. As we have already seen, the divorce rate in that city was much higher than in the surrounding rural areas, and it is clear that the integrated domestic economy played a much reduced role in the city by the time of the French Revolution. Only a few of the couples who divorced in Rouen under the law of 1792 had complementary occupations indicative of the traditional family economy. One couple was composed of a *chandelière* and a *chandelier* (candlemakers), another of a *cabaretière* and a *cabaretier* (innkeepers). Another divorce was contested on explicit economic grounds, the husband arguing that the dissolution of the marriage "would inevitably bring about the ruin of both husband and wife by destroying their small business."[30] The fact that these cases of economic interdependence were exceptional among the hundreds of divorces in Rouen highlights the shift away from the occupational identity or complementarity of the married couple. If the traditional family economy persisted in the city, it was noticeably absent from the divorce records, which is equally significant. The reasons why husbands and wives who were economically interdependent might have shied away from divorce is made only too clear by the effects of divorce on the exceptional cases in Rouen. The women in these marriages were forced to change not only their place of dwelling after the divorce but also their occupations: Both eventually obtained work in Rouen's textile industry. These cases, few as they were, illustrate the effects of separation on a women in a marriage that was an economic partnership. In contrast, the husbands in these cases remained in what had been the matrimonial home and maintained the occupations they had had before their divorces. We should note that the very scarcity of the evidence of this sort helps to bear the hypothesis out: If there had been many cases, they would have undermined the notion that is suggested here, that the traditional family economy, with its interlocking economic roles, deterred marital dissolution, formal or informal. We should also note that the remarriage rate

---

[28] Jean-Claude Perrot, *Genèse d'une ville moderne. Caen au XVIIIᵉ siècle* (2 vols., Paris, 1975), II, 822.

[29] There are, however, problems with the comparison of rural and urban remarriage rates, for the widowed population of cities was inflated by the migration of widowers and widows to the cities in search of subsistence and the larger urban marriage market. This generally pushed up urban rates of remarriage, just as migration also inflated urban rates of illegitimacy. See the survey of literature on widowhood and remarriage in Guy Cabourdin, "Le remariage," *Annales de Démographie Historique* 1978, 305–32, esp. 306–8.

[30] Roderick Phillips, *Family Breakdown in Late Eighteenth-Century France: Divorces in Rouen, 1792–1803* (Oxford, 1980), 98.

among divorced men and women was low, again indicative of reduced imperatives to remarry. Only about one-quarter of men and women divorced in Rouen are known to have remarried afterward. The speed of remarriage by divorced people cannot be compared to that by widows and widowers. Many of the remarriages on the part of divorced men and women simply regularized cohabiting relationships that antedated the divorce, a phenomenon that did not apply in the case of remarriages by widows and widowers, and in addition the divorce law specified certain delays that had to be observed between divorce and remarriage.[31]

The essential characteristic of the rural family economy was that it endured for lack of alternatives. Quite clearly the towns, with their growing wage labor markets, did provide some alternatives to work within the family. For women who lived in the country but close enough to a large town, the pressure of the family economy might well have been weaker than for women in more isolated communities. Taking the region around Rouen as an example again, it is notable that most women who divorced left the community where they had lived while married. Of twenty women who divorced in the communities surrounding Rouen, eight moved to Rouen itself, and another four went to neighboring textile-manufacturing towns such as Elbeuf. Of the eight who remained in their communities, two had been deserted already, the husband of one was in prison, and a fourth was living with her mother, all of these circumstances making it unnecessary for the women to migrate, either to find accommodation or work, or to avoid their former husbands. In contrast with this clear tendency for women to have to move after divorce, nineteen out of the twenty-one men divorced in these communities stayed in the same places where they had lived while married.[32] Again, the implications of marriage dissolution were much more severe for women than they were for men, and that would also be so in the case of marriage breakdown. The uncertainties and dislocations that were the result of separation cannot but have been strong inhibitions against ending a marriage, and these inhibitions acted on women particularly.

Not only would a woman living apart from her husband have problems finding accommodation and employment on which to subsist, but she was by no means assured of being able to own any property in her own right. Under most legal codes in Western society women could own no property while they were married. At marriage any property they did own, in addition to their dowry, was transferred in title or trust to their husbands for the duration of marriage. In France, for instance, a married woman's property was administered by her husband under the Old Regime, a situation remedied by legal reform during the French Revolution, when the rights of married women to own property and to enter into property and business contracts in their own right were recognized. In England, too, married women had virtually no property owner-

---

[31] On remarriage, see Section 7.4.
[32] Phillips, *Family Breakdown*, 92–104.

ship rights until the passage of a series of Married Women's Property Acts toward the end of the nineteenth century.[33]

Widows were provided for by inheritance at their husbands' death, and alimony and other financial arrangements were made for the wife in cases of judicial separation and divorce. But a woman who left her husband, or whose husband left her, or who simply lived separately from him, remained married to him in the eyes of the law. And although that law had given her husband ownership or control of her property, it often made no provision to compel him to support his wife. In England the husband's responsibility to support his wife was recognized only in 1834, when the new poor law legislation specified that any relief given to a married woman by the poor law guardians should be considered as a loan that they could recover from her husband.[34] The parlous position of the married woman in respect to property and financial security is highlighted by the fact that the husband retained control over her property, including wages she might earn, even after he had deserted her. We should expect that in practical terms this made little difference to a deserted wife, particularly if her husband had abandoned her entirely and left the district. But even so, we can appreciate that the deprivation of property and the state of economic dependence into which the law thrust women until the late nineteenth century was yet another disincentive to women's initiating a separation.

So far this discussion of the constraints imposed by the family economy has focused on property and the difficulty of finding work outside the family. Habitation was no less pressing a need – it was, in fact, the most immediate requirement after separation – but it was no more easily found, particularly in rural areas. Although the cities did offer rooms in private houses, furnished apartments, tenements, *pensions*, and inns (all at a cost),[35] the familial character of the countryside did not provide for casual accommodation. Again, this represented a hardship for women in particular. A husband who could afford to do without his wife could evict her from their home; generally it was the husband who had legal title or lease to it. The difficulty of finding somewhere to live was exemplified by a divorce in Bondeville, a village to the north of Rouen, where one Catherine Joret reported the apparently amicable agreement that her former (divorced) husband would "leave her the cow-shed in his field until next St. Jean-Baptiste day, for her to live in and keep her belongings in, she being at present unable to procure any other lodgings."[36] Casual accommo-

---

[33] The best single work is Lee Holcombe, *Wives and Property: Reform of the Married Women's Property Law in Nineteenth-Century England* (Toronto, 1983).

[34] Ibid., 31.

[35] In eighteenth-century London the main type of housing of this kind was rented furnished rooms, "an arrangement which shaded off into the 1d. [one penny] per night common lodging house." Leonore Davidoff, "The Separation of Home and Work? Landladies and Lodgers in Nineteenth- and Twentieth-Century England," in S. Burman (ed.) *Fit Work for Women* (London, 1979), 68.

[36] Phillips, *Family Breakdown*, 100.

dation, probably never readily available in rural areas, became utterly unobtainable in the later eighteenth century as population increased rapidly and placed pressure on all resources, including housing. Arthur Young, a perceptive observer of such matters in this period, noted that in England a scarcity of housing ("no cottage is empty") led to difficulties and postponements of marriages,[37] as couples could not establish their own households. Paradoxically, it would just as much lead to difficulties in ending marriages.

If the family economy locked men and women into marriage and deterred them from separating or deserting, as has been proposed, then we should expect these inhibitions to have weakened as the family economy declined as a response to the transformations in the technologies and organization of production. In this respect we should note again the important differences between town and country. The family economy was quite different in urban areas. Although members of the family might pool their resources and contribute to a combined budget, there was a greater likelihood that work would be individualized, that it would be performed outside the home, and that it would be rewarded with individual wages. The individual character of work in itself reduced the interdependence imposed by labor conditions in the traditional family economy. Although it is impossible to measure marriage breakdown, manifestations of it, such as desertion, seem to have been more common in larger towns and cities, as were judicial separations and divorces later, and it is likely that the weaker economic constraints on husbands and wives played an important role in producing this rural–urban dichotomy.

The tightly knit family economy weakened not only in urban areas but everywhere over time. To some extent this amounted to the same thing, as urbanization progressed from the late eighteenth century and intensified during the nineteenth. But the family economy declined for the most part under the impact of industrialization and the penetration of the wage economy to all sectors of the economy, and to rural as well as urban areas.[38] The critical implication of this development was that individual family members, by gaining an individual income, won an increasing degree of potential independence. The incomes, especially women's, might have been meager, and in no way should we exaggerate the liberating effects of industrial or other employment for women, men, or children. On the other hand, neither should we underestimate them. There were frequent complaints of the self-assertion and independent behavior on the part of young people in nineteenth-century England – it was perceived by their elders as rebelliousness – as a direct result of their beginning to earn an

---

[37] Quoted in Macfarlane, *Marriage and Love*, 94.
[38] The decline of the family economy varied over time. A relatively late example was the nailmaking industry in the English Midlands. Even in the middle of the nineteenth century it represented a classic example of production by the family unit, but it declined from the 1860s under the impact of mechanization, the inroads on children's labor by the Workshops Acts and Education Acts, and finally by the depression of the 1880s. Eric Hopkins, "The Decline of the Family Work Unit in Black Country Nailing," *International Review of Social History* 22 (1977), 184–97.

income over which they had control, rather than having it subsumed within the family's corporate revenues. One witness giving evidence before a commission of enquiry into industrial and social conditions noted that children of sixteen to eighteen years were often earning as much as they ever would, and that "this premature independence too often induces them to quit their parents' houses, that they may be at liberty to follow their own inclinations."[39] Another commentator wrote that "the result of this precocious independence is, of course, the utter relaxation of all bonds of domestic. . . control. Within. . . recollection, a spinner working in the mill, often with his family about him, received their wages, and kept them under proper control."[40] Although these complaints focused on the moral aspects of family behavior, it is evident that it was not the moral authority of the father that kept the family in line, but the conditions of financial independence. Once the financial restriction was removed, if we are to take this evidence at face value, the children left home or did as they wanted, regardless of their fathers' wishes.[41]

This same loosening of family ties must also have affected married men and women and their relationships. The spread of wage labor, the labor market, and easier geographical mobility, all gave husbands and wives greater opportunities to consider breaking up their marriages, deserting, or separating amicably, even allowing, again, that we should not minimize the remaining economic, social, and ideological constraints, the effects of low wages, and sense of obligation to the family. There was no certainty, either, that married women would have had access to their wages, even though their children were apparently able to use theirs as they liked. Still, there were constant complaints from the middle classes in the nineteenth century about the instability of working-class marriages and families.[42] Complaints and observations from these sources are hardly conclusive evidence. In fact it is possible that although desertion by husbands might well have increased, the increased opportunities for wives to terminate their marriages were in part counteracted by other social and economic developments.

There was, first, a shift in marriage patterns. Economic change and increased geographical mobility appear to have thwarted many marriages. Courtships began between young working-class men and women in the industrial cities in the early nineteenth century, and, in the customary manner, they were consummated sexually. But in a great many cases the anticipated marriages did not take place because the young men involved left the locality in search of employment. This left many young women not only jilted but pregnant, women

---

[39] Quoted in Michael Anderson, *Family Structure in Nineteenth-Century Lancashire* (Cambridge, 1971), 124.
[40] Ibid.
[41] This aspect of parent–child relations is discussed in ibid., 68–78 and 124–32.
[42] See, for example, Louis Chevalier, *Labouring Classes and Dangerous Classes in Paris During the First Half of the Nineteenth Century* (London, 1973). Friedrich Engels pointed to the dissolution of family ties – an effect of industrialization, he argued – in *The Condition of the Working Class in England* (Oxford, 1958), 160–6.

who would customarily have married the fathers of their children, but who were now abandoned and left to give birth out of wedlock. The result was a contribution to the rapidly rising rates of illegitimacy across the Western world, which peaked in the middle of the nineteenth century.[43] These were not cases of marriage breakdown or marital desertion, but they shared certain common characteristics. Within traditional courtship patterns these couples would almost certainly have been considered betrothed and would have established a cohabiting relationship, forming a de facto couple, even if they were not formally married. The fact that men left their pregnant partners in sufficient numbers as to push up the illegitimacy rates is evidence of a number of things, callousness among them. But it also attests to the fact that the material context of these relationships had altered. Men and women were no longer locked into these quasi-conjugal relationships, either, and the mobility and employment patterns of industrial society facilitated separation – again, this was especially true of men. These frustrated marriages, as David Levine has called them,[44] might well be seen as premarital breakdown or betrothal breakdown. Although there is no direct evidence we can draw on, we might expect the effects of industrialization on marriages to have been similar.

The nineteenth century also saw changes in other areas of society and economy. The development of factory industrialization, changes in employment patterns in favor of men, and the growth of the ideals of femininity and domesticity, meant that women were progressively excluded from employment in the paid work force. Traditionally female-intensive sectors of the economy, such as textiles, went into relative decline, and areas that experienced growth, especially domestic service, tended to employ young, unmarried women. In countries such as Germany only about 10% of married women were recorded as being formally employed throughout most of the nineteenth century.[45] In England there was a net decline in married women's employment outside the home as the broader economic and social changes were reinforced by a series of protective statutes that limited the scope of work women and children could be employed to perform. A result was that of married women with husbands alive, one in four was employed in the mid-nineteenth century, but by the eve of World War I (the 1911 census) the proportion had fallen to one in ten.[46] In the United States, too, married women were rarely employed outside the home. There, as elsewhere in Western society, the great mass of paid women workers were young and unmarried, so that in working-class neighborhoods in Chicago and New York at the end of the nineteenth century no more than 5% of married women were employed in paid work outside the home.[47] Carl Degler

---

[43] Tilly, Scott and Cohen, "Women's Work," 465ff.
[44] David Levine, *Family Formation in an Age of Nascent Capitalism* (New York, 1977), 127ff.
[45] Patricia Branca, *Women in Europe since 1750* (London, 1978), 32–3.
[46] Oakley, *Woman's Work*, 44.
[47] Robert Smuts, *Women and Work in America* (New York, 1959), 56; see also Carl Degler, *At Odds: Women and the Family in America* (New York, 1980), 375–6.

10.2 The family economy

quotes the telling comment of a working woman about another woman her age: "She must be married, because she don't work."[48]

There are many reasons why most married women did not take paid employment outside the home in the nineteenth century. Trade unions and male workers were often opposed to female employment, protective legislation placed restrictions on the kinds of labor women could do and the hours they could work, women were barred from employment in many of the professions, and above all the ethic of domesticity stressed that women should be in the home, caring for house and children, not out earning a living or contributing directly to the household income.[49] As economically irrational as it was, most women ceased nondomestic employment at marriage, and the family's income was thus largely limited to that which the husband could provide. This single income was supplemented in many working-class families by domestic work on the part of wives who took in laundry and piecework such as making match-boxes or who performed services such as child minding. A major source of additional income was derived from lodgers or boarders, and it fell to the wife to provide for their needs.[50]

As far as the potential for marriage breakdown and separation is concerned, such changes in work and employment patterns must have had two somewhat contradictory effects. On the one hand, married women were effectively denied access to the paid employment that could have given them a measure of self-sufficiency, the financial base from which to launch an independent life if they had wanted to. Instead of being employed and bringing in their own wages that, although often low, would at least have been something, married women found themselves as firmly as ever locked into marriage by economic constraints. Under the regimes of industry and domesticity these constraints were of a different order from those produced by the traditional family economy, but they were effective constraints nonetheless. Women continued to contribute, by child rearing and other domestic work, to the overall productivity of the husband, freeing him of domestic concerns,[51] but their contribution was re-garded as secondary – it involved no marketable skill except as domestic servants, where employers preferred young unmarried women, in any case. Women were effectively demoted from the status of partner in the family economy to the rank of subordinate.[52]

---

[48] Degler, *At Odds*, 385.
[49] Peter N. Stearns, *Lives of Labour* (London, 1975), 275–6; Oakley, *Women's Work*, 43–52.
[50] Davidoff, "Separation of Home and Work?" 65 and passim. Tilly, Scott, and Cohen, "Women's Work," 463, note that in England in the 1880s most employed married women worked at home.
[51] The ideal wife was supposed to shield her husband from knowledge and involvement with the practicalities of running a household. See Davidoff, "Mastered for Life."
[52] The wife's status of partner in the traditional family economy should not be overestimated. Women might have had primary responsibility for running the household, and might have participated fully in the family economy in many ways, but this objective partnership was not necessarily translated into partnership status. The husband retained overall authority in all matters, and his authority could be enforced physically if necessary.

On the other hand, industrialization had created a labor market and an extensive wage economy, and Western society was increasingly urbanized. (During the nineteenth century the distribution of population shifted so that in most countries the majority of people lived in areas designated as urban.) Changes such as these made for much wider opportunities for employment and habitation if a married woman did decide to leave home. It is not that *no* married women worked, after all; there were employment possibilities, even if they were more limited for married women than for single women and for men. On balance it is likely that the sheer existence of alternatives outside marriage and the family, alternatives that had not existed to such an extent in traditional society, enhanced somewhat the possibilities of married women's taking the initiative to terminate their marriages. As we shall see, other nineteenth-century developments, especially in law, complemented the economic changes discussed here. As far as married men were concerned there is no doubt that their potential for escape from marriage was increased. Social and economic changes had given them far greater independence within the family as well as outside marriage, in the industrial work force.

Changes in remarriage rates indicate that marriage was no longer the kind of economic partnership it had been in traditional society. Remarriages declined as a proportion of all marriages but more significantly, age-specific rates of remarriage fell.[53] In addition, the rapidity of remarriage declined dramatically. A study of German villages shows that in the eighteenth century of those widowers who had remarried within ten years, 42% had in fact done so within six months. In contrast, by the first quarter of the twentieth century the rate had fallen to 16%. For widows the decline was even more dramatic, from almost 50% to 3% during the same period.[54] There are many reasons for the decline of remarriage. For instance, higher life expectancies meant that men and women were generally older at widowhood and were therefore less likely to remarry. But the fact that age-specific remarriage rates declined indicates a fall-off in the phenomenon due to other factors. One of these was the decline of the family economy. If we explain the characteristics of remarriage in traditional society – rapid and frequent – in terms of the need for a widower or widow to reconstitute the economy after the death of a spouse, then the decline of these characteristics must be evidence of the decline of those economic imperatives, no matter what other factors also came into play. The declining popularity of remarriage, then, reflected, among other changes, a loosening of the economically associative relationships that had bound husband and wife together so tightly in the family economy.[55]

---

[53] See Cabourdin, "Le remariage," esp. 311–15; and the articles in Dupâquier, *Marriage and Remarriage.*

[54] John Knodel and Katherine A. Lynch, "The Decline of Remarriage: Evidence from German Village Populations in the Eighteenth and Nineteenth Centuries," *Journal of Family History* 10 (1985), 34–59. This study encompasses fourteen villages in five different regions of Germany.

[55] This is formulated in terms of the productive family unit in Michael Mitterauer and Reinhard Sieder, *The European Family* (Oxford, 1982), 40.

10.2 The family economy

The foregoing discussion of the family economy, its decline, and the effects on potential marriage breakdown has been general and in many respects crude. It has glossed over distinctions by region and class (the stress has been on the peasantry and working class), and much of it has been hypothetical, as the recurrent use of phrases such as "could have been," "must have been," and "was very likely" indicates. However unsatisfying the lack of precision and direct evidence is, it is the nature of broad historical explanations that the evidence is rarely explicit. There are, alas, no written records by married women to the effect that

my great-grandmother, who spun wool at home, had nowhere but her husband and family to look to for survival, so never thought of leaving, despite being beaten; but thanks to industrialization and urbanization, I was able to travel to an industrial city and get work in the mill when my own husband's violence became unbearable.

In place of hard data, we must be satisfied with formulating the most plausible hypothesis, backed by appropriate direct and indirect evidence when it is available. But it is important not to push the explanations or conclusions beyond reasonable levels of refinement, and for this reason the account of the family economy and its effects has been general and broadly based.

The conclusions drawn from it are correspondingly broad and may be recapitulated at this point. Under the traditional family economy, economic relationships within the family locked married men and especially women into marriage. These intrafamilial forces were reinforced by a lack of alternatives for work and living outside the family context. Industrialization and urbanization provided opportunities for employment and accommodation outside the family, and this, together with the separation of home and work and the spread of wage labor, weakened the economic bonds that bound husband and wife together in marriage. The importance of remarriage in traditional society and its decline from the end of the eighteenth century testify to the changes in the economic impact of the death of a spouse and, by analogy, of the impact that marriage breakdown or separation might have had. If we want one eloquent example of the way in which husbands and wives were interdependent in the traditional conjugal or family economy, it is perhaps that of Jean Plicque, a vinegrower in Villenoy (near Meaux) and his wife Catherine Girardin. They were separated by judgment of an ecclesiastical court in September 1694 for reason of incompatibility, but seven months later reappeared before the court to request that the separation be annulled because it would be "not only more praise-worthy [a sop to the clerical judges here?] but much more advantageous and useful [for them] to be united in marriage again than to remain separated."[56]

What is suggested then, is two ideal types: a family economy in which the members were bound together by economic ties of mutual dependence and an economy that allowed individuals to work and earn as individuals. The progress

---

[56] Quoted in Baulant, "Scattered Family," 106.

from one to the other denoted increased possibilities of marriage breakdown. It must be recognized that there were important variations among social classes, between town and country, that men and women were affected differently, and that no single chronology of change can be defined. The traditional family economy persisted in many rural areas with variations that did not greatly affect the strength of its economic constraints. Eugen Weber has described its endurance and strength in the French countryside in the late nineteenth century and beyond. Married men and women, he writes, "complemented each other in a working partnership."[57] The family economy might even have experienced a resurgence in rural colonial societies just at the time it was beginning to decline in the more urbanized and industrialized parts of the West. In early twentieth-century New Zealand, matrimonial advertisements stressed the economic aspects of marriage. One 1907 example read: "A Respectable Man, 39, about to purchase a respectable little farm, would like to meet a Respectable Protestant woman, with view to Matrimony; an experienced country woman with a little means preferred." Another advertisement made a similar point: "Young gentleman in business wishes to meet Lady with £500 to £1,000, view Partnership and Matrimony."[58]

10.3 Other pressures against separation

The family economy might well be seen as the most important single economic force that bound husband and wife together in traditional society. But there were other social and economic constraints that directly or indirectly had inhibiting effects on the likelihood that either husband or wife would seriously consider ending a marriage and starting life as a solitary. Conditions of high mortality produced a large number of widows and widowers in traditional society although, as we have seen, they tended to remarry in large numbers and rapidly, so as to replace their dead partners as efficiently as possible. The position of the separated spouse, again, was in this respect worse than that of the widow or widower. Husbands and wives who contemplated abandoning their marriages, then, could glimpse their extramarital future in the lot of widows and widowers who did not remarry.

For women in particular, the future it indicated was often far from attractive. To be sure, some widows who did not remarry were well-off in their own right or inherited substantial or adequate property from their husbands, and others took over ownership and operation of their husbands' trades and businesses. Widows in such circumstances were not impelled to remarry. A woman who simply left her husband and family, however, could expect to take nothing with her, and was in the position of the widow left without resources. Such women,

---

[57] Eugen Weber, *Peasants into Frenchmen: The Modernization of Rural France, 1870–1914* (London, 1979), 172.

[58] *New Zealand Herald*, December 2, 1907, and November 2, 1909, respectively, quoted in Roderick Phillips, *Divorce in New Zealand: A Social History* (Auckland, 1981), 79.

no matter how well they had survived in marriage, fell rapidly into the most dire poverty. Widows, especially those with dependent children, formed a distinct group within the population of the poor and destitute, and often ended up on the very margins of society, as criminals, vagrants, and prostitutes.[59]

There were sources of assistance for potentially impoverished widows in some regions. In Scandinavia there were some customary provisions for what were, in effect, pensions. In fishing communities, for example, where the rate of widowhood was high because of the loss of fishermen at sea, a fisherman's widow and her children were entitled to a share of the catch from other fishermen, usually from the crew of which her husband had formed a part.[60] This contribution would at least tide her over the first period of widowhood, and stave off the desperate plight into which she might otherwise have been plunged by her husband's death. Widows' and orphans' pension funds were established in Denmark early in the eighteenth century, and thereafter spread progressively throughout Scandinavia.[61] All were recognition of the need to provide alternatives to remarriage in the nonlandowning classes. But such pensions were for widows, not women who left their husbands, even though their conditions might be equally desperate. Abandoned women might get the same kind of charitable relief as widows,[62] but it would not be extended to a woman who left her husband; no matter what appalling conditions within marriage she might have fled, she would be seen by the authorities as having brought her poverty-stricken plight upon herself. In seventeenth-century New England poor widows were often quite well looked after, but other needy women sometimes received no assistance until they had reached the depths of poverty, having to wear rags, sleep on straw, and eat seaweed.[63] In England well into the nineteenth century a deserted or solitary woman was assumed to be the responsibility of her husband, and could not be sure of obtaining poor relief: "The Poor Law guardians might not grant her request for aid or might not apply to the magistrates for an order requiring her husband to contribute to her support, so that she was left without recourse."[64]

Not only was charitable assistance everywhere extremely limited and wholly

---

[59] Hufton, *Poor of Eighteenth-Century France*, esp. 115ff; Olwen Hufton, "Women Without Men: Widows and Spinsters in Britain and France in the Eighteenth Century," *Journal of Family History* 9 (1984), 355–76. As we shall see in Chapter 14, there is a continuity here in that mass divorce in the late twentieth century created a new category of poor: divorced women and their dependent children.

[60] Gaunt and Lofgren, "Remarriage in the Nordic Countries," 54–5.

[61] Ibid., 55–6.

[62] Hufton, *Poor of Eighteenth-Century France*, 115–17: "The old, the young, the widowed, the abandoned mother and her brood fit emphatically into the category of the deserving poor."

[63] Koehler, *Search for Power*, 127.

[64] Holcombe, *Wives and Property*, 33. Women simply could not, it seems, count on their relatives for assistance. Richard Wall notes among the inmates of a workhouse in Cardington, Bedfordshire, in 1782, "a few elderly widows, some younger widows with children, a couple of mothers with bastard children." He adds that although they were inmates it was "unlikely that they were entirely bereft of relatives in the surrounding community." Richard Wall, "The responsibilities of kin," note in *Local Population Studies* 19 (1977), 58.

inadequate to cope with the needs of the poor, but a woman who deliberately left her husband would, in all likelihood, not qualify for aid at all. Such a woman would almost certainly leave not only her husband but her community, and it was even more unlikely that she would be adopted as a recipient of charity elsewhere. In New England local authorities sometimes refused to let solitary women take up residence out of fear that they would become a public charge. Poor women who might need charity were warned out of town in the same way that "sharp-tongued and immoral" women were.[65] The precise conditions of poor women varied, but in almost all cases the position of a solitary, still-married woman would have been more desperate than that of a widow, which itself was often bad enough. We must wonder at the circumstances under which any woman would opt for such a future, one whose outlines must have been apparent as she considered her unhappiness within her marriage. Widows were not responsible for the plight their husbands' deaths cast them into, but married women at least had the alternative of continuing married life. It would have to have been utterly appalling for them to exchange it for a precarious extramarital existence of grinding poverty and social rejection.

There was an additional potential consequence for women who might consider leaving their husbands and living alone. At certain times, especially in the sixteenth and seventeenth centuries, solitary women were the focus of witch-hunts. Study after study of witchcraft trials has borne out the association of the witch with the "lonely old widowed woman."[66] In the French town of Toul 29 of the 53 women (55%) tried as witches between 1584 and 1623 were widows, and 12 (23%) were unmarried.[67] In Geneva between 1537 and 1662, of the 235 women tried as witches, 81 (35%) were widows, 104 (44%) were married, and 50 (21%) were unmarried.[68] One sample of women accused of witchcraft in England in this general period showed that more than 40% were widows.[69] In general widows and unmarried women were disproportionately highly represented among the accused, whereas married women, even though sometimes a majority, were underrepresented in terms of their proportion of the adult female population. Old age was undoubtedly an important element in the popular image of the witch that led to allegations of witchcraft, but living alone, outside the authority of a household and especially outside the authority of a husband, was at least as important a consideration. Men and women who lived alone were thought to be easy targets for the devil. We have already noted the intense social suspicion of the solitary, and the fact that in some areas, such as Puritan New England, solitary living was forbidden on the ground that it led to a disordered life. For women there were other considerations. Popular male

---

[65] Koehler, *Search for Power*, 127.
[66] Peter Laslett, *The World We Have Lost* (London, 1965), 95.
[67] E. William Monter, *Witchcraft in France and Switzerland: The Borderlands during the Reformation* (Ithaca, 1976), 80.
[68] Ibid., 121, Table 8.
[69] Alan Macfarlane, *Witchcraft in Tudor and Stuart England* (New York, 1970), 164.

suspicion and fear of female sexuality made it unthinkable that a woman could live without a sexual partner; hence the image of the seducing widow. But if the solitary woman, whether she were married, unmarried, or widowed, did not have an identifiable sexual partner, there was the possibility that her lover might be the devil himself.

The witch craze of the sixteenth and seventeenth centuries obviously had close associations with perceptions of religious heresy, but the identification of individuals as witches was enhanced in the cases of women who lived beyond the marital pale. This is not to say that the association of solitary living and an accusation of witchcraft was made either consciously or unconsciously by women who lived in unhappy marriages or that they were deterred from leaving their husbands for fear of ending up being burned as witches. The phenomenon does, however, highlight the social importance attached to marriage, and it certainly illuminates from another angle the precarious social status of the woman who lived alone.

As sensational and exceptional as it was, the witch craze drew for some of its force on prevalent social conceptions of solitary women, representing a sharpened form of hostility in traditional society toward men or women who lived alone. The social pressure – not to mention the economic pressure – against solitary life is evident in patterns of household structure in traditional Western society. One of the principal characteristics of the Western marriage system was that, in relation to Eastern and Mediterranean Europe and most of the rest of the world, a high proportion of men and women never married. Celibacy rates of 10% or 15% were not uncommon,[70] and in some places at certain times they could be much higher. More than 20% of the population of both sexes did not marry in England in the mid-seventeenth century.[71]

Social anxiety and hostility were directed not so much at celibacy itself, however, but at solitary residence.[72] Celibates could be tolerated if they lived within the framework of a household, and it is striking, given the number of unmarried persons in traditional society, that so few actually lived alone. In Peter Laslett's study of a hundred English communities between 1574 and 1821, fewer than 6% of households consisted of a single person.[73] When we consider what proportion of the adult population had never married and add the more than 6% of the total population that was widowed at any given time,[74] the

[70] John Hajnal, "European Marriage Patterns in Perspective," in D. V. Glass and D. E. C. Eversley (eds.), *Population in History: Essays in Historical Demography* (London, 1974), 101–6.
[71] E. A. Wrigley and Roger Schofield, *Population History of England* (London, 1981), 260, Table 7.28.
[72] At times celibacy itself has come under attack. The unmarried were sometimes regarded as either unproductive in terms of fertility and thus responsible for sluggish population growth (see, for instance, Cerfvol's criticisms in Chapter 5), or productive of illegitimate children who were a burden on the state or community. But even here the stress was less on marital status alone, and more on the sexual implication of not being married (if the two issues can be separated).
[73] Peter Laslett, "Mean Household Size in England since the Sixteenth Century," in Peter Laslett and Richard Wall (eds.), *Household and Family in Past Time* (Cambridge, 1972), 142, Table 4.6.
[74] Of Laslett's population 6.2% was widowed. Ibid., 145, Table 4.6.

proportion of adults who might have lived alone was a great deal higher than the 1% who actually did so.[75] The effects of the economic and social pressures that militated in favor of familial coresidence are clear here. Perhaps they were also clear to women and men who contemplated quitting marriage.

There must also have been community pressure against marital dissolution, against a husband and wife separating. In traditional society marriage rested upon the decision and consent of the two partners, but it was something that concerned the whole community, a point made vividly by John Gillis throughout his work on marriage in Britain.[76] Not only did the community have an interest and positive role in courtship and the actual wedding, but we have seen that neighbors and other outsiders intervened in the course of marriage, particularly at times of crisis, such as extreme violence, transgressions of sexual codes, and the breakdown of authority. On occasions the intervention was formalized in the charivari, or "rough music." It is unlikely, then, that the community would adopt a disinterested stance when a couple was on the verge of separation or when they actually separated. Some charivaris, such as those directed against wife beating, notorious adultery or "scolding," could well have been expressions of serious community concern that a marriage was at a critical point of breakdown. If there are no recorded examples of popular demonstrations directed at couples because they had separated, it could be for several reasons. If the separation were the result of the husband's desertion, there would be no reason to hold a charivari: The target would have been absent. In other cases it is possible – we can only speculate – that a separation might have been socially approved, for example, when one of the spouses seemed to be physically or morally endangered by the other's behavior.

Men and women who did overcome these various deterrents to separation still faced the problem of finding a new residence yet avoiding the option of living alone. They could do as others without conjugal attachments – bachelors, spinsters, widows, and widowers – did when faced with the prospect of a solitary life (which, we recall, was an economic hardship as well as a socially ambiguous position). They could, for example, move in as lodgers with existing families.[77] It is not clear, though, how welcome a married woman would be as a

---

[75] Peter Laslett, *Family Life and Illicit Love in Earlier Generations* (Cambridge, 1977), 199. The point is also illustrated in 1820 Indiana, a frontier state peopled by newcomers. Only 2.7% of households were composed of one person. John Modell and Tamara K. Hareven, "Urbanization and the Malleable Household: An Examination of Boarding and Lodging in American Families," in Tamara K. Hareven (ed.), *Family and Kin in Urban Communities, 1700–1930* (New York, 1977), 165.

[76] Gillis, *For Better, For Worse*, passim. There was a telling case of community interest in a marriage in the village of Terling, Essex, in 1617. A poor man arraigned for sexual incontinence (he had lived with a woman out of wedlock for a year) claimed that he would have married but that "the parishe would not suffer them to marry." Cited in Keith Wrightson and David Levine, *Poverty and Piety in an English Village. Terling 1525–1700* (New York, 1979), 133.

[77] Lodging in historical perspective is discussed for England by Davidoff, "Separation of Home and Work?" and for America by Modell and Hareven, "Urbanization and the Malleable Household."

lodger, and it seems likely that few families would be willing to take in a woman who had left her husband. Alternatively a woman might turn to her family, perhaps return to her parents' dwelling; but there were also obstacles to her taking that step. In the first place, many parents had died by the time their children married. (This was the combined effect of late age at marriage and child bearing together with low life expectancy.) Only 62% of the women married in the parish of St. Gilles in Caen in the late eighteenth century had mothers alive at the time of the marriage, and 48% had fathers alive at the time.[78] In early-seventeenth-century London the situation was similar: Nearly half of the fathers of London-born women had died by the time their daughters married.[79]

The percentage of parents surviving declined the longer their children's marriages lasted, needless to say, thereby reducing the probability of returning to a parent in the event of a separation. But even if a married woman did want to leave her husband and did have a parent to whom she could turn for accommodation, there was no certainty that she would be welcomed. The evidence from Rouen suggests a strong ambivalence as to whether a married child should be allowed to return to the parental home. Mothers tended to receive their daughters more willingly than did their fathers, but overall the primary assistance women received when they were forced to leave their matrimonial homes in emergency conditions, such as extreme violence or eviction by the husband, came from their neighbors and friends, not from parents or other relatives.[80] Male relatives in particular were very unhelpful when it came to the formal procedures of divorce, giving the impression that they wanted nothing to do with the breakdown or dissolution of the marriage.[81]

It is possible that the very neolocal character of marriage in Western society led to a rupture in the ties between parents and their married children that proved difficult to repair. Writing of the problems facing the separated woman in England, Alan Macfarlane puts it this way: "There was no kin group to return to: no brothers, parents or more distant kin had any responsibility to shelter and maintain her and her children. Marriage had cut the last strong links, and she was alone."[82] Married children found themselves, in fact, in a situation analogous to that of widowed parents who frequently discovered that they could not count on their children to support them.[83] It would be unwise, however, to overstate the degree of the rupture caused by marriage and the abandonment of the married child by parents and other relatives; it is too

---

[78] Figures relate to 1775–89 and are taken from Perrot, *Genèse d'une ville moderne*, I, 314. Comparative statistics for Rouen are slightly higher, at 65 and 56%, respectively. See Roderick Phillips, "Gender Solidarities in Late Eighteenth-Century Urban France: The example of Rouen," *Histoire sociale-Social History* 13 (1980), 335, Table 1.
[79] Elliot, "London Marriage Market," 97.
[80] Phillips, "Gender Solidarities," passim.
[81] Phillips, *Family Breakdown*, 34–42.
[82] Macfarlane, *Marriage and Love*, 228.
[83] Laslett, *Family Life*, 59–60.

reminiscent of the notion of the "isolated nuclear family."[84] But the thrust of Macfarlane's description is valid enough and is borne out by studies such as that focusing on Rouen – married children could not assume that their parents and other members of their biological family would hasten to their assistance at times of matrimonial crisis.[85]

Further possibilities of postseparation accommodation were open to a married woman. One was for her to establish a relationship with another man, such that she could leave her husband and move directly into another partnership, albeit an illicit one. Laslett speculates that "consensual unions between partners indissolubly married to other persons may well have been fairly common" in earlier times,[86] but there are few direct unambiguous examples of occurrences, let alone a pattern.[87] Visitation records, as we have noted, occasionally made reference to married couples living apart, some of whom might have entered cohabiting consensual relationships, and to cases of bigamy. But the examples were sparse. Moreover, the mechanism of such a procedure was a risky one. The wife would have to establish a sufficiently serious relationship, presumably including sexual intercourse – adultery – with a man who would receive her if and when she decided to leave her husband. In all likelihood, he would have to be a bachelor or widower. If the relationship were sufficiently discreet, she might get away with it, but the overall success of such an enterprise would depend on such variables as the community's response (for practical reasons, we should expect the new couple to live in the same area as the wife had lived in with her husband), and the husband's willingness to let his wife leave, or to leave her unmolested after she had left him. It is possible that some wife sales were a variant on this phenomenon, for some of the wives who were "sold" and their "purchasers" had had a sexual relationship before the formalized transfer of the wife from her husband's control. Wife sales might well have been a ritualized form of a more widely spread but discreet practice that, by its very nature, has escaped the historical record.

It was not only that there were economic and other advantages to be gained from moving directly from marriage to another cohabiting relationship; more often than not it would have been a sheer necessity. But what about those cases where a woman was able to live alone, such as occasions where a husband deserted his family and left his wife with a comfortable living or with work she could continue without his help? Even then, it seems, there were strong imperatives to form a relationship, to establish, perhaps, a consensual union. We can only speculate here again as to the influences at work, but they probably

---

[84] The notion that the modern urban nuclear family is cut off from wider kin networks. The classic rebuttal of this is P. Willmott and M. Young, *Family and Class in a London Suburb* (London, 1960).

[85] See Phillips, "Gender Solidarities."

[86] Laslett, *Family Life*, 121.

[87] See Chapter 8. Gillis, *For Better, For Worse*, 167, writes that when couples lived together without marrying, "this appears to have been the result mainly of a failed previous marriage," but he gives no examples.

included the desires for companionship and for a sexual relationship. It is arguable that the solitary life was more difficult for those who had lived in a marriage than for those who had never done so, for the simple reason that they had become accustomed to companionship. Whether women who had escaped an intolerable marriage were less likely to want to enter another union, albeit consensual, it is impossible to say. It is possible that what one historian has called "the climate of insecurity that made solitude difficult to bear" was overwhelming in many cases.[88] Widowers whose motives for remarriage are recorded cited a range of reasons, but included loneliness and the need for friendship and companionship of the kinds to which they had become accustomed in marriage.[89] Some men and women, however, were happier to have been released from marriage, and we should expect those who had escaped an intolerably oppressive marriage to have figured prominently among them, and to have thought long and hard, if they had the luxury to do so, before entering another union, licit or illicit.

This discussion of the great difficulties that faced married people trying to readjust after separation has focused on women. As far as men were concerned the situation might have been worse in some specific respects, but overall it was undoubtedly more favorable. Men might have been even less enthusiastically received by their parents or other relatives after a separation, in the rare cases where it was the husband who was forced to find accommodation. Husbands were less likely to have had parents alive at any given time than their wives, as well.[90] To balance these problems, however, husbands were far less likely than their wives to have to leave home in the event of separation, and even though they could no more marry again than their wives while both spouses were alive, they could cope better with a fractured family economy. Moreover, men had many more opportunities for employment and they had control over their own (and their wives') property and income. As a last resort they could go to sea or join the army, even though these were avenues of employment of the most desperate kind. Hufton notes that "any married woman whose husband joined the army was as good as abandoned... [In the Auvergne] priests equated the enlistment of the married with the pressures of poverty and the anxiety of the male to be quit of his obligations."[91] The point has been made before, but bears repeating: When a married person decided, for whatever reason, to break up the marriage and leave, it was almost always the husband who did so. This in itself attests simultaneously to the strength of the various constraints on women and their relatively weak effect on men.

---

[88] Baulant, "Scattered Family," 106.
[89] Macfarlane, *Marriage and Love*, 237, citing and quoting diaries and autobiographies on this point.
[90] See the comparison of survival rates of parents of brides and grooms in Phillips, "Gender Solidarities," 335, Table 1.
[91] Hufton, *Poor of Eighteenth-Century France*, 115. Snell makes a similar point in respect of the English poor: "Enlistment was the institutionally accepted form of family desertion." Snell, *Annals of the Labouring Poor*, 362.

Husbands themselves were a constraint on their wives' ability to take the initiative to leave home. The Western legal tradition placed many limitations on a married woman's freedom of action, and one of them was on her simple freedom to move about at will. Married couples were required to live together and their place of dwelling was decided by the husband. The Code Napoléon, the archetypal codification of male authority, but one that expressed many of the principles of Western law in respect to the relationship between husband and wife, specified that "the wife is obliged to live with her husband, and to follow him to every place where he may judge it convenient to reside."[92] Such principles were translated into practice by husbands' controlling their wives' residence in various ways. As far as her ability to leave is concerned, she could be prevented from doing so by being forcibly confined to the house or, if she tried to leave, by being compelled, physically, to return. There is documentary evidence of both sorts of behavior.[93]

Then there were children. How likely is it that the presence of children, especially young children, was a deterrent to separation? A great body of modern literature on children and on parental attitudes has failed to produce a clear image of historical parent–child relationships. Although some studies have suggested that parents were indifferent, emotionally cool, or even harmfully negligent in their attitudes toward their offspring, others have concluded that they were warm and caring.[94] There is possibly little more to be said about the role of children in marriage breakdown than that they would be a consideration, a potential deterrent to separation or desertion when they were loved, but not when they were not. There were those who believed that children could be the cement that could hold a couple together through times of crisis. One draft plan for a divorce code in eighteenth-century France envisaged a role for children in a conciliation procedure. Children under the age of seven were to pass from the arms of their mother and father alternately, to bring home to them in a tangible way the bonds that united them. Children would have "the right to speak every time they wanted to in order to remind [their parents] . . . of sentiments of harmony."[95]

Such a plan is evidence of a belief in the unifying influence of children. But in practice there is evidence both for and against this notion. In one divorce in Rouen there was a hint that the presence of a child dissuaded a woman from

---

[92] Code Napoléon, Book I, Title V, Chapter VI, Article 214.
[93] See, for example, Phillips, *Family Breakdown*, 136ff.
[94] The classic work is Philippe Ariès, *L'enfant et la vie familiale sous l'Ancien Régime* (Paris, 1960), translated as *Centuries of Childhood* (London, 1962). Parental neglect is stressed by historians such as Edward Shorter, *The Making of the Modern Family* (New York, 1975), and by some of the articles in Lloyd de Mause (ed.), *The History of Childhood* (New York, 1974). A more positive view of child rearing is presented by historians such as Steven Ozment, *When Fathers Ruled: Family Life in Reformation Europe* (Cambridge, Mass., 1983).
[95] Cited in François Olivier-Martin, *La crise du mariage dans la législation intermédiaire (1789–1804)* (*Thèse de droit*, Paris, 1900), 244.

pursuing her divorce action.[96] In contrast, men deserted their children as well as their wives. The 1597 census of the poor in Norwich showed that most of the deserted wives had dependent children,[97] and this was also true of the abandoned women in southeastern England in the eighteenth and nineteenth centuries.[98] The implication of this evidence, sketchy though it is, is that fathers were far less likely than mothers to be deterred by children from quitting their marriages.

Bearing in mind the caveats made earlier about the level of abstraction of this discussion of marriage breakdown, the image of the traditional family that emerges is quite clearly one that reduced to a minimum the potential for separation. As far as women were concerned, there were virtually no alternatives to married life once they had married. They were locked firmly into a conjugal economy and the options for life and work outside were negligible. Social, community, and familial pressures against separation, the low status and discrimination that solitary women faced, the affective bonds that alone might prevent a woman from leaving her husband and children, all of these considerations bound women to marriage. It is not to say that all or even most women would gladly have left their husbands if they had been given the opportunity. No doubt many, even most, marriages were more than satisfactory. Other women and men stayed together, even though they were not happy, when the security offered by marriage outweighed its emotional costs. But these forces must have constrained those wives who found themselves in oppressive and abusive marriages, too. These are the women of greatest interest in this study. Yet even they, it is suggested here, did not chafe continuously against their bonds. Rather, their flexible expectations of marriage enabled them to accommodate themselves to a wide range of violent and exploitative behavior on the part of their husbands. David Hume commented that marriages would be happier if divorce were not possible. The heart of man, he wrote, "naturally submits to necessity, and soon loses an inclination, when there appears an absolute impossibility of gratifying it."[99] We can modify Hume's point by stressing not the legal impossibility of divorce, but the social and economic factors that prevented married women in particular from defining their marriages as broken, and from taking action to escape from them.

Men, we should note again, were subject to the same forces but to a lesser degree. Although they shared the mutual dependence of husband and wife in the conjugal economy, they had more options outside the family and more initiative within it, as the sex ratio of deserting spouses shows. Moreover, it seems that men's emotional attachments to spouse and children were weaker than women's.

---

[96] Phillips, *Family Breakdown*, 79.
[97] John F. Pound (ed.), *The Norwich Census of the Poor, 1570* (Norwich, 1971), 18, Table VII.
[98] Snell, *Annals of the Labouring Poor*, 360–1.
[99] David Hume, *Essays, Literary, Moral and Political* (London, 1741), Essay VIII.

10.4 How common was marriage breakdown?

It is impossible to begin to estimate the incidence of informal marital separation by unilateral desertion or by mutual agreement in traditional society. Olwen Hufton writes of the eighteenth-century poor of France that "the broken home was a common phenomenon," almost always because the husband and father had left the family.[100] Lawrence Stone comments that desertion "must have been a not infrequent occurrence among the poor."[101] Several studies have produced statistics of abandonment. As noted earlier, surveys of marriage registers in late-eighteenth- and early-nineteenth-century Rouen indicated that between 2% and 6% of marriages were broken by desertion.[102] In Metz the 1806 census revealed 132 abandoned wives out of approximately 6,565 married women, or about 2%.[103] In the southeastern counties of England in the eighteenth century, 4% or 5% of wives in the poor strata had been deserted by their husbands.[104] The 8% of poor wives deserted in late-sixteenth-century Norwich represented a markedly higher rate.[105] Perhaps these figures indicate the kind of incidence we should expect to find generally, although because these marriages affected by desertion were either poor or were located in periods of social turmoil and military conflict, they might have had higher rates than those that occurred in the better-off sections of society or at times of relative social and political tranquility.

Aside from the strictly familial and related socioeconomic constraints that inhibited marriage breakdown and separation, other broad demographic, social, and cultural changes took place in Western society that had a bearing on marriage breakdown. One of the most commonly reiterated explanations of the high rates of divorce in modern society, compared to the past, is that in earlier times marriages were soon dissolved by the death of one of the spouses. Divorce, it is argued, fulfills the same function in modern society as death did in the past. Lawrence Stone expressed the notion this way:

> ...it looks very much as if modern divorce is little more than a functional substitute for death. The decline of the adult mortality rate after the late eighteenth century, by prolonging the expected duration of marriage to unprecedented lengths, eventually forced Western society to adopt the institutional escape-hatch of divorce.[106]

To be fair, none of the proponents of this thesis put it forward as the sole or even the major explanation of the relative absence of divorce in the past or the

---

[100] Hufton, *Poor of Eighteenth-Century France*, 115.
[101] Stone, *Family, Sex and Marriage*, 38.
[102] See Section 8.3.
[103] Jean Lhote, "La femme seule à Metz en 1806," in Jean Lhote, *Une anticipation sociale: le divorce à Metz et en Moselle sous la Révolution et l'Empire* (Metz, 1981), 40–1.
[104] Snell, *Annals of the Labouring Poor*, 361, Table 7.8. Percentages varied: 4.4%, 1700–50; 4.0%, 1751–80; 6.5%, 1781–1800; 5.1%, 1801–34. The increase after 1781 was a result of men leaving their wives to enlist in the army.
[105] Pound, *Norwich Census*, 95.
[106] Stone, *Family, Sex and Marriage*, 56.

10.4 How common was marriage breakdown?

frequency of divorce in the present. Yet although the idea of divorce as a death substitute has its merits, it also raises some problems and implications that cannot be accepted uncritically.

The evidence as to the relative brevity of many marriages in the past is quite overwhelming, although it must be qualified. In general the age at first marriage was high and life expectancy was low, so that the duration of marriage was that relatively short period between marriage and the death of one of the spouses. A study of parishes in late-eighteenth-century Sweden showed that for peasant wives the duration of marriage averaged less than fifteen years, and for wives of landless workers less than thirteen years.[107] In Crulai (a village in Normandy) in the eighteenth century, more than half the marriages (52%) lasted less than fifteen years, and 37% lasted less than ten years.[108] The duration of marriages in preindustrial England was about twenty years.[109] Again, the examples are prolific and demonstrate how the period of marriage was often squeezed between late marriage, often in the mid-twenties for women and the late twenties for men, and relatively early death.[110] Frequently, married women died in childbirth, although the extent of maternal mortality might not be as great as has often been thought.[111]

But whatever the causes of death of either spouse, the higher mortality rates in traditional society contributed to a foreshortening of married life. Over time not only have mortality rates fallen, but the age at marriage has tended to decline, the net result being a progressive elongation of the potential and real duration of marriages not interrupted by divorce. In crude terms the average duration of marriage increased from about fifteen or twenty years in preindustrial Europe to about thirty-five years in 1900, and then to almost fifty years today, when marriage occurs in the early twenties and life expectancy in most Western countries is higher than seventy years.[112] In other words, by 1900 marriages had the potential to last twice as long as eighteenth-century marriages, and modern marriages can last more than three times longer than those entered into two centuries ago and earlier.

---

[107] Michael W. Flinn, *The European Demographic System, 1500–1820* (Brighton, 1981), 29–30.

[108] Louis Henry and Etienne Gautier, *La Population de Crulai, paroisse normande, étude historique* (Paris, 1958), 112.

[109] Laslett, *Family Life*, 184.

[110] Even so, we should not overlook the fact that many marriages lasted longer than these mean statistics suggest. In Meulan, a village on the Seine, an equal proportion (34%) of marriages in the period 1660–1739 lasted less than fifteen years and thirty or more years, respectively. Marcel Lachiver, *La population de Meulan du XVIIe au XIXe siècle (vers 1600–1870): Etude de démographie historique* (Paris, 1969), 169, Table 45. In Aldenham, Hertfordshire, between 1580 and 1810, the mean duration of marriages was 28.8 years, the median was 25 years, and 37% lasted 35 years or more. Peter Laslett, "Philippe Ariès and 'la famille'," *Encounter* 66 (March 1976), 80–3.

[111] See Roger Schofield, "Did Mothers Really Die?" in Bonfield, Smith and Wrightson, *The World We Have Gained*, 231–60. There are statistics on maternal mortality from the fifteenth to nineteenth centuries in Edward Shorter, *A History of Women's Bodies* (Harmondsworth, 1983), esp. 97–102.

[112] Michael Anderson, *Approaches to the History of the Western Family, 1500–1914* (London, 1980), 20.

Simple demographic changes – we need not go into the reasons for the changing age at marriage or the decline in mortality rates here – have thus placed an unprecedented burden of longevity on modern marriages. Insofar as any marriage is at risk of breakdown, marriages in more recent times have, therefore, been at risk over a significantly longer period. On the other hand, marriages in the eighteenth century and earlier, being relatively short, were at risk of breakdown over a shorter period, no matter what other inhibiting factors came into play. The argument for increased marriage breakdown over time as a result of the lengthening of marital duration (at least, from the late eighteenth century) thus relies on probabilities. In concrete terms we should note that duration of marriage need not be a determining influence on the incidence of separation because marriages can break down in the first few years of married life. In the eighteenth- and nineteenth-century marriages studied by Snell, for example, the average period between marriage and the husband's desertion was less than seven years.[113] It might well have been true of marriage break-down in the past as it is of divorce in the twentieth century, that it occurs far more frequently in the first decade of marriage than in later years, but even so it is logical to expect that the longer marriages last, more of them rather than fewer, will break down. The relative brevity of marriages in traditional society should have reduced the incidence of marriage breakdown and separation to some extent, then, even though we cannot be more precise than that.

A number of general conclusions may be drawn from this survey of marriage breakdown. The most important is that there is little direct evidence of de facto separation or desertion in traditional Western society. If marriages did break down on any significant scale, they did not manifest it in physical terms that have been captured by the historical record. The reported examples of separa-tions and desertions are remarkable either for their absence or their rarity. It could be that the paucity of examples of marriage breakdown reflects a deficiency in the historical record, that records were simply not kept that would throw light on this phenomenon, just as there are few recorded examples of events such as wife-beating, which we assume to have been common. It is striking, however, that the kinds of sources where we should expect deserted or separated spouses to have been noted simply do not provide us with examples, or, if they do, do so very infrequently. Census-type documents seldom mention the phenomenon, even those, such as visitation records, generated by the ecclesiastical authorities who were usually sensitive and alert to departures from normal household or approved marital forms. Moreover, some apparent ref-erences to husbands or wives who were living alone or in illicit relationships are quite ambiguous. Peter Laslett writes that in a society such as England, where divorce was a privilege of the wealthy, the only choice open to those whose marriages broke down was to live in consensual unions. The example he

---

[113] Snell, *Annals of the Labouring Poor*, 361, Table 7.8. This figure is obtained by subtracting from the average elapse of time between marriage and the date of examination (10 years), the average time elapsed since the husband had left (3.2 years).

provides consists of two successive listings from the parish of Llanelian in Denbighshire, Wales. The first (from 1685) makes the following reference: "Edward Parry keepeth his concubine"; the second (from 1686) states: "Edward Parry who liveth still with his concubine unmarried." Although it is true, as Laslett notes, that the couple seemed to be living in a "stable consensual partnership" (it had lasted at least a year), there is no evidence here that either of the couple was married to another person.[114] In other cases apparently deserted wives might not have been so. A clerical listing in Eccleshall (Cheshire) during the 1690s "with obvious scepticism, described some of the women heading households as *claiming* to be married to a husband then absent."[115] In an age before systematic record taking and centralized record keeping, it was at best difficult to verify or disprove such claims, which might have been made so as to conceal the illegitimacy of children or to make a stronger case for charitable assistance. The point is that even what appear to have been broken marriages might well not have been.

Our direct knowledge of the extent of marriage breakdown in traditional society – that it was rare – is reinforced by what we should expect to have been the case. There is no incongruence between what we find in the historical sources and what we should expect to find, given the social and economic contexts of marriage. Traditional society was above all familial and conjugal. This might seem paradoxical in light of the high rates of celibacy we have noted, but it is not so. Those who failed to marry did so not because they rejected marriage but because they could not fulfill the demanding preconditions of marriage in the Western tradition, primarily the economic ability to establish a new household.[116]

To the basic economic constraint that the family economy represented to separation must be added more social and cultural deterrents. Women's initiatives in almost all respects were controlled and restricted by their husbands. There were probably strong communal pressures against separation, which was a threat to the social stability that rested so firmly on the family unit. The presence of children might (or might not) have acted as a deterrent to desertion; it probably deterred women more than men from abandoning their families. Broader influences also came into play. The relative brevity of marriage under the demographic regime of late marriage and early death meant that marriages were at risk of breakdown over a relatively short time. In addition, the ideology of unity within marriage, even within a marriage of inequality and oppression, which was disseminated by secular and religious authorities, could not easily be ignored. The opinion of the clergy could be particularly important when the church carried out important functions such as dispensing charity. Under the pressure of this complex of economic, social, demographic, legal, and cultural forces, it would be surprising, to say the least,

---

[114] Laslett, *Family Life*, 121–2, where the actual entries in the parish listing are reproduced.
[115] Ibid., 122n.16.
[116] See Hajnal, "European Marriage Patterns," 132–33.

to discover that there was widespread separation and desertion in traditional Western society. The point is that the historical record does not give us cause for surprise.

As for marriage breakdown that was not manifested in desertion or separation, we can say little. The evidence examined in Chapter 9 suggests that marriages could survive in the face of violence, sexual infidelity, mental cruelty, and indifferent emotional relationships. The evidence is of tremendous flexibility in expectations of marriage, an ability to adjust expectations to prevailing conditions, and of potentially very low expectations. It is suggested here that the economic, social, and other forces that, combined, all but prevented separation, were largely responsible for this pragmatic approach to marriage. This is not to say that wives or husbands passively accepted brutality, adultery, or other kinds of offensive and exploitative behavior. There is plenty of evidence of attempts to reason and reform, to resist or escape from the immediate dangers, though there is little evidence of attempts to leave the marriage on a permanent basis.

Physically or emotionally abusive behavior was surely recognized as such, and we can assume that neither husbands nor wives wished to be subjected to it. We can assume that despite their flexible and potentially low expectations, they did possess implicit or explicit notions as to conditions or behavior that were ideal within marriage. What is significant about wives and husbands in these traditional marriages, and what distinguishes them from those in modern marriages, was that they rarely traveled the distance that separates the recognition of unacceptable behavior and undesirable conditions in marriage on the one hand and the definition of these conditions as indicative of marriage breakdown on the other. Definitions of marriage breakdown, in short, do not emerge from a socioeconomic vacuum, but result from the interaction of the social, economic, ideological, and cultural characteristics and context of marriage. In traditional society, let us say up to the beginning of the nineteenth century, husbands and wives could simply not afford to let their marriages break down, and definitions of breakdown reflected this reality. David Hume, already quoted earlier, came very close to stating this interpretation in his essay on divorce. Observing that "the heart of man naturally submits to necessity, and soon loses an inclination, when there appears an absolute impossibility of gratifying it," Hume went on to distinguish between "passion," which was "restless and impatient...full of caprices and variations," and which was not appropriate within marriage, and "friendship," which was a proper sentiment between spouses. The notion of friendship and its context, as described by Hume, echoes in a somewhat idealized way the description of conjugal relations and marriage breakdown proposed in this chapter:

Friendship is a calm and sedate affection, conducted by reason and cemented by habit; springing from long acquaintance and mutual obligations, without jealousies or fears, and without those feverish fits of heat or cold, which cause such and agreeable torment in the amorous passion. So sober an affection, therefore, as friendship, rather thrives under constraint, and never rises to such a height, as when any strong interest or necessity binds two persons together, and gives them some common object of pursuit. We need not, therefore, be afraid of drawing the marriage knot, which chiefly subsists by friendship, the closest possible. The amity between the persons, where it is solid and sincere, will rather gain by it: and where it is wavering and uncertain, that is the best expedient for fixing it. How many frivolous quarrels and disgusts are there, which people of common prudence endeavour to forget, when they lie under a necessity of passing their lives together; but which would soon be inflamed into the most deadly hatred, were they pursued to the utmost, under the prospect of an easy separation?[117]

Hume's description of the intellectual and emotional accommodation of spouses to the social and economic limitations imposed by the traditional marriage system was designed as an argument against the legalization of easy divorce. But it was more than that, in that it captured the essential reason for the absence of marriage breakdown in earlier generations. We should want to differ from Hume in a number of respects, the most important being that a simple alteration of the law to allow divorce would not have made much difference to most married men and women; they stayed in their marriages not just because of legal requirements but because of a number of social and economic deterrents to separation, and they probably rarely thought of leaving their spouses, so desperate was that course of action.

Within these general principles of constraints producing tolerance, it is likely that women's expectations of marriage were in many respects different from men's. They were more likely to encompass violence and adultery, for example, and they were generally lower. Once married, women were more securely locked into the family economy, they had fewer alternatives to marriage, and in addition they had to tolerate more in global terms. The evidence is quite unambiguous on this last point especially: Women were more oppressed and exploited within marriage. Men's behavior speaks to a generally different set of reactions to tensions or problems within marriage. Married men were able to take action when faced with behavior they considered inappropriate within marriage. When a wife failed to carry out her duties or behaved improperly by scolding or disobeying, the husband was as likely as not to correct her, physically if he wanted to. If the sexual relationship between him and his wife was unsatisfactory, he was more likely than she to look outside marriage for a sexual partner. But even so, there is little evidence of marriages ending for reasons directly related to the circumstances of the marriage or their wives' behavior. We cannot be certain precisely what motivated husbands to desert when they did desert, but the circumstances suggest broader social or economic reasons, such as unemployment or a slide into poverty, rather than specific grievances against the wife or dissatisfaction with their marital relationship. A married man might, in conditions of indigence, decide to slough off his familial

---

[117] Hume, *Essays* (London, 1906), 138–9.

responsibilities and join the army or emigrate to the antipodes (both desperate reactions), but these were not familial motivations in the same sense as conditions of violence or mental cruelty that most often motivated women to define their marriages as broken down, and to flee from them. Such differences between men and women in relation to marriage breakdown are important, but they tended to apply mainly in terms of the informal dissolution of marriage. Whereas men took the initiative most frequently in dissolving marriages by desertion, when it came to initiating divorces and judicial separations women were generally to the fore. This shift in the gender ratio of initiatives suggests that women were not ready to define their marriages as broken, and to take action to separate or to dissolve them, until there were institutional means to guarantee some sort of security after separation, in the forms of alimony, custody of children, and a property settlement that provided the means for an independent life. (These points are discussed further in Chapter 14.)

This image of the family economy and other pressures that militated so strongly against marriage breakdown and separation is, quite evidently, a crude and somewhat static one. The individual aspects of the complex of constraints varied in their intensity according to gender, as we have seen, and over place and time. Only studies at the local level will indicate the range of combinations, but it is expected that they will fall within the parameters of the image presented here.

Our representation of change must be equally schematic. First, the system of constraints has been located within what has been called traditional society and the traditional family. In general this might be thought of as referring to preindustrial society and family systems, insofar as many of the changes that broke down the traditional family economy were associated with industrialization in its various stages. The undermining of the family as a labor cooperative and the individualization of work is the most striking example. But the strength of other factors that have been discussed here ebbed without any necessary direct impact of industrialization. The duration of marriages, for example, increased everywhere in Western society, in the industrial cities and in the rural areas where the agricultural economy remained dominant.

We should not conceive of these changes in terms that are too stark, dramatic, and uniform. They took place slowly, more rapidly in some areas than in others, and their impact bore variably on populations according to social class, occupational distribution, and gender. It was an evolutionary process of adaptation followed by change. For example the family economy did not break down immediately with the introduction of individualized employment outside the home. Instead, in the decadent form of the traditional family economy the individual family members pooled their wages, just as they had earlier pooled their labor resources. Only in subsequent stages did individuals begin to regard their incomes as their own, and capable of giving them the potential to assert their individuality, to follow their own inclinations over the corporate interests of the family group. This area of change lay at the heart of a complex of changes that greatly weakened the earlier constraints and correspondingly enlarged the possibilities for separation. If we accept that expectations of marriage were low and tolerance of oppressive behavior high under the traditional family system, then we should predict that expectations would rise and tolerance fall as escape routes from marriages became more numerous and accessible. The evidence of rising expectations lies in the lower tolerance of adultery, wife beating, and in the middle-class notions of moderation in relationships, and of the respectable woman and the way she should be treated.

In many respects what we call Victorianism represented these elevated ideals of marriage and their higher expectations. The nineteenth-century middle-class ideals of marriage echoed, in a different world, the marriage doctrines of the seventeenth-century writers of conduct-books and treatises on marriage and the family. They themselves were persons of the middling sort and wrote for a middle-class readership. There were similar emphases on moderation in marriage relationships (and suspicion of passionate love), the same stress on sexual fidelity, and on the need for considerate and respectful behavior toward one's spouse. All of these prescriptions fell within the context of an authoritarian and patriarchal family.[118] In the two hundred years that separated the seventeenth and nineteenth centuries, however, the bourgeoisie had become a much stronger force in society and the economy. Whereas in the seventeenth century its family morality had made little discernible impact on the ungovernable masses, or for that matter on the unruly gentry, the nineteenth century became the bourgeois century. The middle class rose to economic preeminence and increased its social standing to the point that middle-class ideals of behavior percolated upward and filtered downward through the social strata, until they colored the social expectations of the whole society. This is not to assume an automatic impact on social behavior, but middle-class notions of social relationships did modify ideals and expectations. Moreover, the institutions and legislation of the nineteenth century, which impinged upon areas of social life until then little touched by the state, were informed by bourgeois ideals, not least in respect of the family.

If we want an example of the adoption of middle-class notions of domesticity by the working class, it is the idea of the "idle" wife, the wife who did not go out to work, but stayed at home, occupied herself with household tasks and children, and was supported financially by her husband's labor and income.[119] As we have seen, women were pushed out of the labor force by various pressures, including protective legislation and union antagonism toward female employment, but working-class men also wanted their wives to stay at home and become housewives. In this particular case a middle-class attitude coincided

---

[118] "Puritanism" and "Victorianism" are often used interchangeably in reference to nineteenth-century moral codes. This should not be taken to mean the seventeenth-century moral writings on the family were specifically Puritan, however. (See Chapter 3.)

[119] See Patricia Branca, "Image and Reality: The Myth of the Idle Victorian Woman," in Mary Hartmann and Lois W. Banner (eds.), Clio's Consciousness Raised (New York, 1974), 179–91.

with popular notions as to the more passive domestic roles of women, as distinct from the active, exterior roles of men. The effect was to be seen in the declining employment of married women in the paid work force. Working-class husbands were so adamant that their wives should not work that they took in boarders to supplement their income, preferring to surrender some domestic privacy to achieve the status that an idle wife could confer.[120] We see in this example the transfer of a bourgeois practice and its adoption – better, its adaption – by the working class. In the middle-class home the idle wife could coexist with domestic privacy; in many working-class homes the two could not be achieved simultaneously, and it was the marital ideal that won out. There was also a contradiction in the evolution of the working-class marriage toward the middle-class model. Women had traditionally played a full role in the family economy, but the gender division of roles had allocated wives a domestic role, one limited for the most part to the environment of the home.[121] The separation of work and home made this impossible, and faced with the options of having a wife in paid employment away from home, or out of paid employment but in the home, working-class men opted for the latter.

The mechanisms by which middle-class ideals spread through society were complex and varied. Increased literacy, better communications, and the creation of a mass market for consumer goods and services tended to homogenize societies, to undermine and break down the divisions between popular and élite cultures. As far as the family is concerned the changes in attitudes, the higher expectations of marriage and marital behavior were expressed by the great wave of legislating activity relating to marriage, separation, and divorce that took place during the nineteenth century, particularly from the middle of the century. The legalization of divorce where it had not been legal before, and the liberalization of existing divorce laws, together with changes in laws affecting such intimately related matters as married women's property and the custody of children, all pointed to a willingness to relax the legal bonds that had treated the marriage as a corporate unit that could subsume the individual members within it. These legal changes complemented the social, economic, demographic, and cultural changes that had been underway from the late eighteenth century, changes that had weakened the variety of constraints preventing separation and marriage breakdown. We should regard these various levels of change – the socioeconomic, the ideological, and the legal – as integral parts of a general and major shift that produced the increased potential for marriages to break down and for the spouses to separate.

Seen in this light the Victorian period – in Europe, America, and Australasia, as well as in Britain – should be viewed as a period of transformation as far as marriage is concerned. The beginnings of mass divorce are located in the nineteenth century, and it is argued here that marriage breakdown on a

---

[120] Davidoff, "Separation of Home and Work?"; Modell and Hareven, "Urbanization and the Malleable Household," 166ff.
[121] Gouesse, "Parenté, famille et mariage," 1148–9; Segalen, *Mari et femme*, 87–121.

significant scale began in this period as well, as the traditional constraints against it began to fall away. There was, then, this contradiction in nineteenth-century marriage, that the rising expectations that were encouraged entailed a higher risk that the expectations would be disappointed and that marriages would break down. These expectations, we should note, focused more and more on the affective aspects of marriage, now that the productive functions of marriage had declined. But the greater the emphasis on marriage as an institution, on companionship within marriage, and on marital stability, and the more these ideals became adopted as expectations of marriage, the greater the probabilities of marriage breakdown. This kind of contradiction is not such an unfamiliar one in Western society. Under the traditional marriage pattern such a strong emphasis was placed on marriage as an economic relationship, one that individuals could enter into only after satisfying rigorous economic precondi-tions, that many men and women – 10%, 15%, and more – never married at all. From the nineteenth century and especially during the twentieth, a greater proportion of men and women married than ever before in Western society,[122] but now a greater proportion than before exited from marriage, informally by separation or desertion or, more and more commonly, by judicial separation or divorce. (Perhaps modern divorce should be seen as the modern functional substitute not for death in earlier times, but for celibacy!) These questions are taken up in Chapter 14, which examines the reasons for the rise of divorce rates from the later nineteenth century, a phenomenon made possible not only by more liberal divorce policies but by the unprecedented pool of broken marriages that were a result of the evolution of Western society from the late eighteenth century.

As for the evidence of increasing marriage breakdown from this time, it must remain for the most part oblique – the mixture of negative and indirect data presented in this chapter – and it is to be hoped that in the present case logic has not outrun the data to create an account that is beyond credibility. Of its very nature the direct evidence is sparse. Historians have cited an increase in desertion from the late eighteenth century,[123] but one of the few in-depth studies, by Keith Snell, might be read as locating the increase more firmly in the nineteenth century. Among 4,961 poor families in the southeastern counties of England between 1700 and 1880, Snell found 289 cases of desertion, representing 5.8% overall. But although the rate of desertion was fairly stable from 1700 to 1834, varying between 4.0% and 6.5%, it shot up to 10.5% in the

---

[122] See, for example, Rosalind Mitchison, *British Population Change Since 1860* (London, 1977), 74 Table 9. Between 1861 and 1971 the percentage of women "ever-married" at ages forty to forty-four rose from 86% to 93% in England, and from 78% to 90% in Scotland. The same holds for the rest of Western society.

[123] One historian noted that "as the eighteenth century proceeds one is struck by the increasing frequency with which men fall under the ban of the Vagrancy law for the offence of running away and leaving their families chargeable to the parish. The ties of family life had been loosened at all points." E. M. Hampson, *The Treatment of Poverty in Cambridgeshire, 1597–1834* (Cambridge, 1934), 140.

period from 1835 to 1880.[124] This might reflect an increase in desertion, although it could also be nothing more than the effect of the introduction of the new Poor Law in 1834. Further possible evidence of increased breakdown lies in changes in family structure in some areas, particularly in the increase of households headed by women, wives described as having been deserted by their husbands. In the west Cornwall mining community of St. Just, for example, the households headed by women increased from 15% of all households in 1851 to 26% in 1871. Most of the increase was accounted for by women left to head their families after their husbands had abandoned them when copper mining went into a recession. The full extent of the increased desertion was actually concealed by those abandoned women who moved into other households.[125]

Poverty, economic recession, the onset of war with its opportunities for desertion, all seem to have sparked increases in the incidence of desertion and separation. But behind the particular cases, exemplified by the effects of economic recession in the Cornish mining communities, there seems to have been a generalized increase in desertion and other signs of marriage breakdown from the late eighteenth century. They are rarely susceptible to precise quantification, but they have been noted by historians in various contexts.

Marriage breakdown might, then, join the list of other sociodemographic phenomena that began to shift in the later eighteenth century. Rates of illegitimacy and premarital pregnancy, intergenerational tension, divorces, and separations, all began to increase.[126] But whereas some of these trends (such as illegitimacy) rose, peaked, and then fell in the next century, marriage breakdown and its formal consequences in judicial separation and divorce, continued to increase. As for the period before the later eighteenth century, our conclusion must be that marriage breakdown was extremely rare. Desertion was uncommon, informal separation even more so, and we have noted the infrequency of divorce and judicial separation. Marriages in the past, beyond the middle of the eighteenth century, were stable. Husbands and wives stayed together, even if only for the fifteen or twenty years on average before one of them died. What is important is that the marriages lasted not necessarily because the spouses were morally superior to later cohorts of husbands and wives, nor because they loved each other more deeply or cared more for their children, nor because they worked harder at their marriages and were less fickle than their descendants, but simply because there was nothing else they could do, and they accommodated themselves to that reality.

---

[124] Snell, *Annals of the Labouring Poor*, 359–64.
[125] Mark Brayshay, "Depopulation and Changing Household Structure in the Mining Communities of West Cornwall, 1851–71," *Local Population Studies* 25 (1980), esp. 34–8.
[126] A good synthesis of these trends in France is Michel Vovelle, "Le tournant des mentalités en France 1750–1789: la 'sensibilité' pré-révolutionnaire," *Social History* 5 (1977), 605–29.

11

Nineteenth-century divorce laws:
Liberalization and reaction, 1815–1914

11.1 Introduction

In many respects, divorce was transformed during the nineteenth century. For one thing, it spread geographically so that by 1900 only a few Catholic states, notably Spain, Portugal, Italy, and Ireland did not have provision for divorce, and they, with the exception of Portugal, held out until the late twentieth century. In other parts of Europe that had predominantly Catholic populations, such as Belgium and the southern states of Germany, divorce laws were instituted during the century; in the case of France, divorce was abolished in 1816 but reintroduced in 1884. Moreover, divorce in the European tradition spread beyond the Western society of the Atlantic world. Divorce legislation was put in place in the American states of the Midwest and West and in British colonies in Australasia, the West Indies, Africa and Asia. By the end of the century, the Western form of divorce had global dimensions, as seemed appropriate to a period that saw a surge of European imperialism.

The progress toward making divorce more widely accessible geographically was matched by progress making divorce more widely available in social terms. By the end of the nineteenth century, wherever divorce was available, it was almost always available from the courts, either the regular civil courts or from specially established divorce tribunals. In 1857, for instance, divorce by private Act of Parliament in England came to an end, and the first English divorce law placed divorce within the jurisdiction of a new Court for Divorce and Matrimonial Causes. Similarly the governors, councils, and legislatures of the American states progressively surrendered their authority over divorce to the regular courts. There was no reason why the judiciary should have had control of divorce, particularly when there was no controversy, as when a divorce petition was uncontested. Scandinavian practice throughout the century, indeed, tended to maintain both judicial and executive (royal) divorce.[1] But once

---

[1] Max Rheinstein makes the point that "the reason why courts have been charged with jurisdiction to grant freedom of remarriage is an accident of history." "Divorce Law in Sweden," in Paul

removed from the control of kings, governors, councils, and legislatures, divorce became more accessible to the population at large. Judicial divorce was generally less expensive, less demanding in procedural terms, and probably less daunting to potential petitioners than executive and legislative divorces had been. Moreover, there was a general liberalization of divorce legislation through the nineteenth century. As the secular authorities more and more took responsibility for regulating marriage and divorce, divorce provisions increasingly diverged from the limitations traditionally imposed by church doctrine. One influence on liberalization was the nineteenth-century ideology of domesticity and femininity, which added matrimonial offenses stressing the obligations of husband and wife: to provide and to serve, respectively (see Chapter 12). There was, too, growing pressure in favor of giving women the same access to divorce that men had and of removing the double standard of sexual morality from divorce laws. In some jurisdictions greater sexual equality before the divorce courts served to double the constituency of potential divorce petitioners, as women were legally enabled to divorce their husbands on the same grounds as husbands could divorce their wives.

The net effect of these changes, combined with more general social and economic developments in the nineteenth century, was a rapid increase in the number of divorces sought and obtained. Even though the numbers of divorces in the early 1900s seem almost insignificant in late-twentieth-century terms, they represented staggering increases during a few decades. For example, there were almost 10,000 divorces in the United States in 1867, but by 1906 there were more than 72,000, a sevenfold increase.[2] There were 5 divorces in England in 1857, the last year in which divorces were granted by Parliament; by 1870–4 an average of 215 divorce decrees were issued each year; by 1900–4 the annual average had risen to 590.[3] Such increases reflected, among other things, a changing climate of opinion in favor of accepting divorce, at least in limited circumstances. But the increases also reinforced opposition, and provoked a reaction against liberal divorce laws on the part of those who saw in the growing use of divorce the destruction of the family and the weakening of the fabric of society. The transformation of divorce, indeed, emerged from the clash of a number of contradictory forces that tended at once to social conservatism and to social change. At times during the century these forces – ideological, economic, and social – seemed finely balanced, and at other times

(footnote 1, cont.)

Bohanan (ed.), *Divorce and After* (New York, 1970), 137. This is surely an overstatement. Ecclesiastical courts had had jurisdiction over marriage matters such as separations and annulments before the legalization of divorce. Moreover, actions for divorce frequently involve conflicts of evidence and require the determination of facts. It is notable that in recent years, when simple de facto separation for a specified period has been deemed sufficient to justify a divorce in some legal codes, judicial processes have given way to dissolution of marriage by administrative act.

[2] James P. Lichtenberger, *Divorce: A Study in Social Causation* (New York, 1909), 11.

[3] Griselda Rowntree and Norman H. Carrier, "The Resort to Divorce in England and Wales, 1858–1957," *Population Studies* 11 (1957), 201, Table 2.

it appeared that the reaction against divorce liberalization would prevail. In the end, however, divorce legislation and use continued to expand, establishing a trend for the following century.

11.2 Revolutionary, Napoleonic, and Restoration Europe

On the European continent, the development of divorce legislation became inextricably intertwined with general political developments, beginning with the legacies of the French Revolution and Empire. As we have seen, until the revolution the distribution of divorce laws in Europe was relatively straightforward. Divorce had been introduced into all of the Protestant states in some form or other, but remained unavailable wherever the Reformation had not taken hold. In 1783 and 1784 divorce had been extended to the non-Catholic populations of Austria and Austrian territories, notably the Austrian Netherlands (later Belgium) and Lombardy and Venetia in northern Italy. The expansion of French legal institutions, first by conquest during the revolution and subsequently under the French Empire (1804–14), wrought havoc with this pattern that had emerged from the religious and social development of the individual European states. As territories were annexed to France (such as Luxembourg, which became the Département des Forêts) or were turned into sister republics (such as the Netherlands and Switzerland, which became the Batavian and Helvetic Republics, respectively), reforms were imposed upon their legal and social institutions so as to bring them into harmony with the universal principles that the French revolutionary leaders believed underlay their own reforms. Part of this reform was the application of the liberal 1792 law in the conquered territories. In Belgium, for instance, the dual system established by Joseph II, giving Catholics access to separations and non-Catholics access to divorce, was replaced by the French solution that deprived devout Catholics of a remedy for matrimonial offenses or breakdown: Divorce was available to all, separations to none.

Divorce *à la française*, in its more restrictive Napoleonic form, spread even further through Europe after the promulgation of the Civil Code. One of the benefits conferred upon the annexed and associated states of the First French Empire was the Civil Code and its divorce provisions. These permitted men and women to divorce by mutual consent or unilaterally. Husbands could divorce their wives for reason of simple adultery, and wives who could prove that their husbands had committed adultery in the marital dwelling could also obtain a divorce. Either spouse could divorce the other on the ground of conviction for certain shameful crimes or for insanity. This divorce law was applied in substantially identical form throughout the French Empire – about three-quarters of continental Europe – with the notable exception of Spain. In this one case the civil law recognized that traditions and practices were opposed to the legalization of divorce. Elsewhere, however, the spread of French hegemony brought about a standardization of divorce law (and other areas of civil legislation), replacing the organic diversity that individual national histories had produced.

The short- and long-term effects of French legal imperialism were varied, but divorce was not widely used in the empire except where it had been legal before the French conquest. Italy is an example. Divorce had been available to non-Catholics in the Hapsburg territories from 1784, and the gradual annexation of Italian territories had spread divorce on the model of the French law of 1792. A divorce law was enacted in the Piedmont in 1796, for example. With the amalgamation of the various Italian provinces into a more unified Italian state and the application of Napoleonic divorce law in the Codice Civile of 1806, divorce was for the first time available throughout Italy, to Catholics as well as to non-Catholics. As we should expect, the Roman Catholic church opposed the law and attempted to obtain a compromise on the earlier Hapsburg model of confining access to divorce to non-Catholics, but the French regime insisted on uniform application of the law throughout Italy and its populations.[4]

The Italians, unappreciative of the liberty imposed upon them, were either hostile to divorce in principle, hostile to it because of its association with the French conquerors, or simply indifferent because divorce did not fall within the Italian legal and social tradition. Between 1809 and 1815 there were only nineteen divorces in all of Italy.[5] There was, as might be expected from such a statistic, little opposition when divorce was abolished by the regimes that were restored after the French Empire ebbed in 1813 and 1814, and Italy was again divided into a series of independent states. In the Duchy of Modena a new law of 1814 gave non-Catholics the right to marry according to their rites, but forbade divorce to all citizens. Ferdinand IV, the restored Bourbon king of Naples (there had been three divorces in Naples between 1809 and 1815), decreed in 1815 that "the provisions of the Codice Civile which permit divorce no longer have effect," and gave matrimonial jurisdiction back to the Catholic church.[6] Divorce was, in fact, retained only in those parts of Italy where it had been allowed before the French Revolution: Lombardy and Venetia, returned to Austrian control in 1815, fell within the 1811 Austrian General Civil Code that allowed non-Catholics to divorce. Under the terms of this code, divorce petitions were heard by a civil court, could be based only on serious grounds (*per gravi motivi*) and entailed a slow and difficult procedure in which the judge was to act as the "defender of marriage,"[7] predisposed to deny rather than to grant a divorce.

In the remainder of the nineteenth century, divorce made little progress in

[4] Maria Graziella Lulli, "Il problema del divorzio in Italia dal sec. XVIII al codice de 1865," *Il Diritto di Famiglia e delle Persone* 3 (1974), 1237. A general account of the development of divorce in Italy is Annamaria Galoppini, "Profilo storico del divorzio in Italia," *Il Diritto di Famiglia e delle Persone* 9 (1980), 594–666.
[5] Lulli, "Divorzio in Italia," 1238.
[6] Decree of June 1, 1815. Ibid., 1241.
[7] Ibid., 1242.

Italy. In the 1830s the reforming regime of King Carlo Alberto of the Piedmont promulgated a civil code (the Codice Albertino) that extended the right of divorce to non-Catholics within the Piedmontese population. The unification of Italy under the leadership of the Piedmont, a process that took place between 1859 and 1870, might well have entrenched divorce in the law of a united Italy. However, Carlo Alberto, the sponsor of liberal reforms, abdicated in 1849 in favor of his son, the more conservative Victor Emmanuel II. In 1852 divorce was completely abolished in the Piedmont, even for non-Catholics, and this nondissolubilist approach to marriage doctrine was applied as the Kingdom of Italy was extended throughout the peninsula. In 1865 a new Italian civil code recognized civil marriage because it was in accord with "the unconquerable trend of our time towards the strengthening of secular institutions."[8] The code did not provide for divorce, however, and explicitly stressed that marriage was to be indissoluble. This did not, it might be noted, mollify the papacy, which remained hostile to the creation of a unified Italian state, especially after 1870 when the papal territories were incorporated into it.

Divorce, in fact, was not legalized in Italy for more than a century after the 1865 code, but it remained a live issue during the nineteenth century. Between 1878 and 1892 five divorce bills, ranging from the liberal to the restrictive, were introduced into the Italian parliament. An 1878 bill, for instance, proposed that divorce should be available for reason of the intolerable temperament of one spouse or for reason of incompatibility, whereas an 1880 bill proposed a different pair of grounds: life imprisonment of one spouse or six years' separation.[9] Liberal or restrictive, however, the bills failed, even though an 1884 draft divorce law had been approved by the legislative commission of parliament.[10] The failure of attempts to introduce divorce into Italian law was to some extent a reaction against Napoleonic civil law, in other respects a desire to conform to Catholic doctrine. Although this was not surprising in the case of the regimes restored in the immediate post-Napoleonic period, it is more surprising that liberal nationalists, such as Camillo Cavour (who was married to a Swiss Protestant), did not exercise more influence in favor of divorce. Cavour was very influential as Victor Emmanuel II's premier from 1852, the year in which Piedmontese non-Catholics were deprived of the right to divorce. It could well have been, though, that the unpopularity of divorce had been demonstrated by its rarity during the Napoleonic period, and that divorce was kept out of Italian legislation in the unified Italian state partly so as to remove one source of hostility on the part of devout Catholics and the clergy, when there were no evident political benefits to compensate for it.

It was not only Italy whose divorce history was distorted by French influence;

---

[8] Giovanni B. Sgritta and Paolo Tufari, "Italy," in Robert Chester (ed.), *Divorce in Europe* (Leiden, 1977), 256.
[9] Ibid., 256–7.
[10] Ibid.

11 Nineteenth-century divorce laws

Belgium and the Netherlands were also caught up in the legal contortions that surrounded the revolution and the empire. Both countries had provided for divorce before the French Revolution, Belgian non-Catholics having been given the right to divorce in 1784, and the Netherlands having legalized divorce in the sixteenth century. Both territories were invaded by French forces during the period of revolutionary expansion – Belgium in 1793, the Netherlands in 1795 when it was transformed into the Batavian Republic – and the prevailing French divorce law of 1792 was given effect. In 1807 Napoleonic divorce law was made operational in Belgium by the Civil Code, which was thenceforth the basis of Belgian civil law, and in the Netherlands in 1810, when that country was incorporated into the French Empire. In 1815, after the defeat of the empire, the two countries were combined by the Congress of Vienna into a strengthened Holland, and the terms of the Napoleonic divorce law were retained.

Almost immediately there was an attempt to liberalize the law, probably to bring it more into line with Dutch practice before the 1790s. But it was unsuccessful. In 1816 the parliament defeated a bill to make divorce available on grounds of adultery, long-term desertion, unnatural immorality, the attempted murder of one spouse by the other, or the attempted murder or injury to the other spouse, or his or her children or parents.[11] A second attempt to liberalize divorce in 1820 also failed, despite an accompanying "explanatory memorandum" emphasizing that the divorce bill reflected "the spirit of the people," that it recognized "the holiness of marriage," and that because the bill's sponsors were

convinced that nothing furthers more frivolity in contracting marriages than the easiness of dissolving the marriage bond, we believe that divorce by mutual consent should be completely rejected; while the reasons for a request for marital dissolution should be limited to such an extent that it will be difficult for the parties to conspire.[12]

Only in the 1830s were there legal developments, however. The first was forced by the secession of Belgium and its establishment as an independent state in 1830. Despite its predominantly Catholic character and population, Belgium legalized divorce in the very year of independence, using the Napoleonic Code as its model. Divorces there remained rare: There were four in 1830, twenty-six in 1840, twenty-nine in 1850, fifty-five in 1860, and eighty-one in 1870, a steady increase but few enough in absolute terms.[13] As for the Netherlands, divorce law was recodified as part of the 1838 Burgerlijk Wetboek, the grounds being adultery, desertion, imprisonment, and serious physical cruelty. Dutch couples could also obtain a divorce by mutual consent using a two-stage procedure of first obtaining a separation and then converting it to divorce after a

[11] Gerrit Kooy, "The Netherlands," in Chester, *Divorce in Europe*, 103.
[12] Ibid.
[13] Wilfred Dumon, "Belgium," in Chester, *Divorce in Europe*, 130.

408

five-year waiting period. The 1838 law regulated divorce in the Netherlands for fifty years and resulted in few divorces. Attempts to liberalize the law in the 1880s failed, but the practice of consensual divorce developed, whereby a divorce could be granted if one spouse alleged adultery and the other admitted it.[14]

In quite a different manner the French Revolution also had a longer-term effect on Swedish divorce law. Although legalized in the relatively restrictive Lutheran terms in the sixteenth century, divorce was gradually liberalized in Sweden by the 1734 Sveriges Rikes Lag and by the wider range of grounds that were recognized by royal dispensations. In the period of the regency after the assassination of King Gustavus III in 1792 there was an even more liberal approach to divorce, which reflected the influence of the revolution in Europe, but a reaction set in when King Gustavus IV ascended the Swedish throne in 1796.[15] During his reign, divorce was generally more difficult to obtain, but this rigorous policy ended when Gustavus IV was deposed in 1809 and Jean-Baptiste Bernadotte became crown prince. Bernadotte was one of the success stories of the French Revolution. A native of Gascony, he had enlisted in the French army in 1780 and was promoted to the rank of general in 1793. He was later minister of war and made a marshal under Napoleon, but in 1810 he was elected by the Swedish Diet as crown prince of Sweden, partly as a result of his release of Swedish prisoners of war in 1806. From this time Bernadotte's loyalty was to Sweden, and he joined the anti-French alliance in 1812.

It was a supreme irony that a revolution identified with the establishment of a republic and the regicide of Louis XVI should have catapulted a French soldier to one of the European thrones; Bernadotte, as King Karl Johann, ruled Sweden from 1828 to 1844. But if he abandoned his republicanism, he did not as readily give up the zeal for legal reform so characteristic of the French Revolution. As crown prince, Bernadotte quickly had a body of jurists draft a new marriage law for Sweden, and in 1810 it was approved by all the houses of the Diet, including that of the clergy.[16] The law declared that marriage was a union founded on the mutual respect of the spouses and that marriage ceased to exist in their consciences once the mutual respect had vanished. That being so, divorce would be permitted on a wide range of grounds, including those recognized in the 1734 law, adultery and desertion, as well as those that had most often been permitted by royal dispensation. These included banishment, attempted murder, life imprisonment, and incurable insanity dating back at least three years. The law specified that other grounds could be recognized by royal dispensation and gave as examples a death sentence, loss of honor, wasteful management of property, alcoholism, cruel temperament, and situations where mutual hostility between the spouses had turned into aversion and hatred. This

---

[14] Kooy, "Netherlands," 103–4.
[15] Gerhard Hafstrom, *Den svenska familjerättens historia* (Lund, 1975), 80.
[16] The following account of the 1810 law is from Ivar Nylander, *Studier Rörande den Äktenskapsrättens Historia* (Stockholm, 1961), 209–19.

11 Nineteenth-century divorce laws

legislation, allowing for both judicial and executive divorce on a flexible range of·
grounds, regulated divorce in Sweden until the early twentieth century.

Sweden, however, was a peculiar example of French influence on divorce
legislation. There the influence filtered through the person of Bernadotte and
led to the codification of a more liberal divorce law. Elsewhere in Europe the
pattern was different. Divorce laws – first liberal, then restrictive – were implanted in Europe by the French armies as the revolution, then the empire,
flowed forth. As the imperial tide ebbed, so did divorce legislation. It was a
pattern that occurred in France itself, where divorce was abolished in 1816
after a vote by the two chambers of the French parliament.[17] There had been
opposition to divorce in France throughout the revolution, and there were many
attempts in the legislatures in the later 1790s to abolish it. There had been
doubt as to whether it would be retained in the new civil code drawn up under
the guidance of Napoleon Bonaparte. Even the restrictive Napoleonic law drew
opposition, however, and it was not surprising that, with the Restoration, this
aspect of marriage law was brought into harmony with Catholic doctrine.

Divorce was portrayed, in the French legislature in 1816, as harmful to
society, to religion, to women, and to children. Bonald, the apologist of Catholic
political and social doctrine, led the attack on divorce. He argued that, when a
divorce was granted, the husband could leave the marriage with his independence intact, but the wife had lost all her "virginal purity, youth, beauty, fecundity, esteem," and rescued only her money from the ruins of the marriage.[18]
(Bonald's picture of the ravages wrought on a woman was hardly an advertisement for marriage.) Divorce, he went on, implied the primacy of love over utility
and interest in marriage, and even provoked dissension within marriages.
Divorce weakened the authority of the father in the family and also weakened
fertility and thus undermined French population.[19] Underlying the social arguments, however, was the Roman Catholic prohibition of divorce. The argument
for social stability was a strong one after the unpheavals of the revolution and
the empire, but the fundamental motivation for the abolition of divorce was the
clear desire to return to family laws based firmly on Catholic church doctrine.
This is not to say that French legislation after Napoleon reverted wholesale to
its prerevolutionary forms. Civil marriage was maintained as obligatory, although an optional religious ceremony was permitted. But the maintenance of
divorce was quite a different matter, and in 1816 France once again became,
after twenty-four years of experience with divorce, a divorceless society. For the
unhappily married only *séparations de corps* could be obtained, and they became
increasingly popular during the nineteenth century until divorce was again
legalized in France in 1884.

During the early decades of the nineteenth century, as we can see, divorce

---

[17] Law of May 8, 1816.
[18] *Archives parlementaires*, 2ᵉ série (Paris, 1869), XV, 611.
[19] The debate is well summarized in Raymond Deniel, *Une image de la famille et de la société sous la Restauration* (Paris, 1965), 97–102.

legislation first expanded geographically and then contracted in tandem with French imperialism on the Continent. It is significant that, although other reforms imposed by the French, such as the abolition of serfdom, were retained after 1814 in the states that had made up the French Empire, divorce was abolished wherever it had not been permitted before the French conquest. It is not difficult to understand why divorce was suppressed in Catholic states, where it had been imposed against the will of the secular and religious authorities and in the face of legal and social tradition. It is also not difficult to understand that divorce conflicted with the general social and political perspectives of the regimes that assumed power in 1814 and 1815, perspectives that were conservative when they were not reactionary. To such men as were restored to their thrones and ministries, divorce would have been anathema, symptomatic of a liberalizing and secularizing society in which the traditional lines of political and familial authority had broken down. They probably shared the sentiments of Bonald, the apologist of the French Restoration who had published a work against divorce in 1800.[20] In 1816 he gave the antidivorce stance a social and political perspective. Just as political democracy "allows the people, the weak part of political society, to rise against the established authorities," Bonald argued, so divorce, which reflected "veritable domestic democracy," allowed the wife, "the weak part, to rebel against marital authority." Thus, he concluded, "in order to keep the state out of the hands of the people, it is necessary to keep the family out of the hands of wives and children."[21] Clearly, the suppression of divorce was seen as a major contribution to this end. Despite the facts that Napoleonic divorce law was much less liberal than the legislation it replaced, and that the Napoleonic regime could hardly have been termed liberal in any meaningful sense, even this restrictive divorce facility was considered by the reactionaries of Restoration Europe as excessive and dangerous to social and political order.

The contraction of divorce legislation was temporary, however. In 1875 divorce was extended beyond the Protestant states of northern Germany to the Catholic states of the south of the empire. In 1857 England's first divorce law was passed, and in 1884 divorce was reintroduced in France. Soon after the turn of the century, in 1910, Portugal enacted divorce legislation for the first time. These developments, together with the passage or liberalization of divorce laws in America and the British colonies around the world, made the second half of the nineteenth century a remarkable period of legislative activity. If the sixteenth century represented the first generation of divorce laws in Western society, the later nineteenth century surely witnessed the second.

This chapter focuses on the development of divorce legislation and on other legal changes that affected divorce. There are general patterns to be discerned throughout Western society: a broad trend of liberal legislation, the generation

---

[20] Louis Gabriel Ambroise de Bonald, *Du Divorce* (Paris, 1800).
[21] *Archives parlementaires*, 2ᶜ série (Paris, 1869), XV, 612.

of a conservative reaction, the further progress of secularization of institutions and law, movements toward divorce law harmonization, and the regulation of conflicts of law arising from disparate divorce legislation. At the same time, divorce was frequently caught up in political, religious, and social developments within each country. In the following pages the history of divorce will be discussed from national, thematic, and broader Western perspectives.

11.3 The first English divorce law

One of the more important legislative developments in Europe in the nine-teenth century was the passage of the first divorce law in England in 1857. It marked a legal breakthrough in the sense that there had been pressure for such legislation during the preceding three centuries; it took that long for English matrimonial law to fall into line with that of the other Protestant states of Europe. (It might be noted, though, that by the nineteenth century the division between Protestant and Catholic states in respect to divorce law was by no means as marked as it had been in the sixteenth century.) The removal of the English anomaly did not reflect a shift in the marriage doctrine of the Anglican church, which maintained that marriage was indissoluble. To this extent the passage of the 1857 law marked an important stage in the secularization of English marriage legislation. Moreover, this law not only made divorce available to the residents of England and Wales, but it had global implications. The 1857 legislation became the model for laws throughout the British Empire, as col-onies in the West Indies, Australia, and New Zealand introduced their own divorce legislation. The irony is that in itself the 1857 English law was as conservative as could be imagined – anything but a great leap forward in the concept or formal terms of divorce law. Its domestic and global implications, however, endowed it with importance quite out of proportion to its intrinsic significance.

As we have seen, the pressure in favor of legalizing divorce in England had tended to dissipate after Parliament took the initiative long rejected by the Anglican church and began to dissolve individual marriages by private acts. Even though this facility made divorce a privilege reserved for the benefit of wealthy men, it seemed to satisfy many of those who were opposed to the principle of the indissolubility of marriage, and for a hundred years from the late seventeenth century there is relatively little evidence of pressure to liber-alize divorce. When the issue did enter the arena of public debate again, it was not because divorce was difficult to obtain but rather because it was perceived as becoming too common and as promoting immorality. Although parliamentary divorces were few enough in absolute terms, they began to in-crease markedly from about 1770, and there were twice as many in the last three decades of the eighteenth century as there had been in the first seven. This increase was noted and deplored both inside and outside Parliament. One Member of Parliament, Herbert Makworth, referred to the "evil of divorce daily increasing,"[22] and the archbishop of Canterbury lamented in 1809 that divorce had spread so widely that there was "hardly a pedigree that was not stained and broken by this sad frequency of crime."[23]

The fact that acts dissolving marriages continued to pass through Parliament in increasing numbers shows that the majority of members of the Lords and Commons at least accepted the principle of divorce. Even so, there were attempts to make divorce less attractive. A number of bills were introduced into the House of Lords from 1770 onward, having as their purpose preventing marriages between a woman divorced for reason of adultery and her accomplice. The supporters of these bills argued that parliamentary divorce, instead of being a means for cuckolded husbands to obtain legal redress, was being used by women in order to change spouses. The bishop of London argued that the prevailing system rewarded, rather than punished, the adulterous wife: "At present, she received a reward for her misconduct: she got quit of a husband whom she disliked, and became the wife of the man whom she adored."[24] It was argued further that the provision of divorce in these cases actually served to increase the incidence of adultery; seducers were able to have their way with married women by pleading that, if the infidelity were discovered and divorce action taken, they would marry the women in question and restore their honor. Considerations such as these gave rise to the bills aimed at prohibiting marriages of divorced women with the men named as corespondents in their divorces. Two bills, introduced in 1770 and 1779, successfully passed through the House of Lords but were defeated in the House of Commons, although by narrow margins (twenty and nine votes, respectively). A third bill, the "Adultery Prevention Bill, for the more effectual Prevention of the Crime of Adultery," which was provoked by "scandalously frequent" divorces, according to its sponsor, Lord Auckland,[25] was abandoned during one of its readings and replaced by an even more stringent proposal. This new draft law, "for the Punishment and more effectual prevention of the Crime of Adultery," would not only have prohibited the marriage together of the adulterous couple, but would also have made adultery a crime, punishable by a fine and imprisonment. Had it succeeded, this proposal would have restored adultery to the criminal status it had had under Cromwell's 1650 law on adultery. As usual, there was vigorous support for the bill by most of the lords, all of whom claimed no personal knowledge of the subject under discussion.

Within the House of Lords, however, there was some opposition to these attempts to restrict the remarriage of divorced women. The Duke of Clarence argued that remarriage was the only hope a divorced woman had of salvaging her reputation. He pointed out that because divorce was limited to persons of

[22] *Parliamentary Debates* (Commons), XVII, 382 (March 11, 1772).
[23] Ibid., XIV, 326 (May 2, 1809).
[24] Ibid., XXV, 274 (May 16, 1800).
[25] Ibid., XXV, 225 (April 2, 1800).

property and rank, divorced women were expelled from society and deprived of the usual means of earning a livelihood. "They could not work as menial servants: they were not instructed in any line of business: they could not beg. And what other line of providing the means of life was left open to them, but abandoning themselves to prostitution?"[26] Clarence perceptively noted that the increase in divorces was not due to increased adultery necessarily but to the wars that kept men from their wives over extended periods. Once the war was over, Clarence predicted (less perceptively this time), there was "no doubt that applications for divorce bills would diminish."[27]

It was opposition in the House of Commons to these putative antiadultery bills that led to their regular defeat, but Lord Auckland, the indefatigable scourge of seducers, was not deterred. Nine years (and twenty-three parliamentary divorces) later he revived the issue and had more success. Although he still regretted that the "assassins of domestic happiness" were not subject to criminal prosecution – he spoke of the salutary effect of solitary confinement for two or three years – Auckland was able to obtain a Standing Order of the House of Lords to the effect that future divorce statutes should contain a clause expressly forbidding remarriage of a guilty wife and her accomplice in adultery. Making the provision a Standing Order of the Lords neatly sidestepped the need for the Commons to agree. The order was not applied universally, however; some divorce acts passed after 1810 carried the prohibition clause, but others did not. In one case the House of Commons challenged the inclusion of the clause because the wife in question had committed adultery with her deceased sister's husband: It would have been legally impossible for the two to marry because of their relationship of affinity.[28]

In general, then, legislative activity on divorce in England in the early nineteenth century aimed at reducing the already low incidence of divorce. It is difficult to see how the dissolution of marriage by Act of Parliament, with its long and expensive procedure and unique ground for divorce, could have been made more restrictive unless divorce were abolished altogether, and so it was that the problem was attacked obliquely. Divorces would decline when adultery declined, the reasoning went, and adultery would decline when it was no longer rewarded by remarriage. We should note that the proposed restrictions were aimed specifically at women. Under the rules guiding parliamentary divorce, men had to be proved guilty of aggravated adultery, and in most cases this involved incestuous adultery. In those circumstances, of course, there was no question of remarriage involving the husband and the corespondent.

In 1820 a sensational divorce case came before the British Parliament: a Bill of Pains and Penalties was introduced in the House of Lords to dissolve the marriage of King George IV and Queen Caroline.[29] George and Caroline had

[26] Ibid., XXV, 228 (April 2, 1800).
[27] Ibid., XXV, 229 (April 2, 1800).
[28] See Allen Horstman, *Victorian Divorce* (London, 1985), 15–16.
[29] On the case between George IV and Queen Caroline see ibid. 24–6; and Thomas W. Laqueur,

11.3 The first English divorce law

long been unhappy in marriage – they had separated a year after their marriage in 1795 – but it was not until he ascended the throne that George took action to divorce. Even then he did so against the advice of his ministers, who quite properly feared the consequences should the divorce bill succeed and George decide to remarry. England would, in such circumstances, have been faced with the spectacle of a king, head of the Anglican church, divorcing and remarrying in the face of his church's doctrine of marital indissolubility. The church would have strenuously opposed any remarriage, and there would certainly have been doubts as to the legitimacy of any children that might have been born of a second marriage. A royal divorce, then, could have set off a train of events that would have culminated in a dynastic and constitutional crisis.

George, probably motivated by extreme hatred of Caroline, was at first undeterred by these considerations and pressed on with the divorce bill, which was based on the alleged adultery of his queen. An earlier attempt in 1806 to investigate Caroline's intimate behavior had proved nothing conclusive,[30] but by 1820 her comportment had become far less ambiguous. Caroline had by then forsaken England in order to tour the Continent, her entourage managed by a reputedly handsome Italian, Bartolomeo Pergami, described in Parliament as "a foreigner of low station." (It is not clear which of these qualities was the more objectionable.) The royal divorce bill specified that Caroline had behaved toward Pergami "with indecent and offensive familiarity and freedom, and carried on a licentious, disgraceful and adulterous intercourse... by which conduct of her royal highness, a great scandal and dishonour have been brought upon your majesty's family and this kingdom."[31] The bill was presented, then, as dealing with a matter of state as much as with a state of matrimony.

The bill passed two readings in the House of Lords, and the sessions proved sensational. Witnesses testified to such matters as the sleeping arrangements on Caroline's ship during sultry nights in the Mediterranean, the sartorial inadequacies at Italian masked balls, and a maid even testified about stained bedsheets in a hotel. The evidence in Parliament was relayed to the public through cartoons and broadsheets that provided a brief period of intense activity for Grub Street.[32] In the end, however, the government cut off the supply of salacious news by withdrawing the bill. Despite the apparently compelling evidence of Caroline's adultery, there was little sympathy for George, whose own commitment to marital fidelity was, to say the least, imperfect. Caroline, portrayed as the pilloried victim of an unpopular king, became a popular heroine, and opposition by the Whigs to George made it increasingly unlikely that the divorce bill would be supported by the House of Commons. It

"The Queen Caroline Affair: Politics as Art in the Reign of George IV," *Journal of Modern History* 54 (1982), 417–66.

[30] Horstman, *Victorian Divorce*, 25.
[31] *Parliamentary Debates* III (1820), 1727.
[32] The publicity surrounding the divorce bill is analyzed in Laqueur, "Queen Caroline Affair." The debates are in *Parliamentary Debates*.

was doubtless a national embarrassment and scandal to have the queen of England floating around the Mediterranean, sleeping with a nondescript Italian – and being none too discreet about it, given the number of witnesses who gave evidence. In this divorce case, however, dynastic implications, constitutional considerations, and political complications overrode the evidence and even the will of the king, and the bill, which was certainly misconceived from the beginning, was withdrawn.

In the 1830s divorce once again flared up as a prominent issue of political and social debate in England. The debate did not take place in a vacuum; this was, as we shall see, a period of profound social and economic change that affected marriage and the family. There was renewed concern about parliamentary divorces, and we cannot disagree with the author of a contemporary pamphlet on divorce who wrote that "all parties are agreed that the proceedings connected with divorce in this country are most imperfect; all agree that our system is neither good in itself, nor beneficial in its operation."[33] The pamphlet set out many of the objections to the prevailing system: It encouraged hypocrisy, compelling a man to get a separation from an ecclesiastical court and pledge himself not to remarry, "while he is resolved the next moment to lay the case before the House of Lords, and to marry again as soon as he can obtain his freedom";[34] it was unjust to women; and it discriminated against all who could not afford the expense. The author went on to deny that wider access to divorce would necessarily lead to more immorality. Divorce was available in Scotland, but that "is not the place where we read of constant infidelity among married persons... but, on the contrary, it is there that the moral feeling of the whole population is of the highest cast... that the matrimonial vow is observed with the most scrupulous reverence."[35] In contrast stood France and Italy, where divorce was prohibited. In these countries "the faithlessness of married persons is proverbial. The woman too often looks to the day of her marriage as the period for her commencing a life of intrigue... The husband connives at his own shame, and equally with his partner revels in vice."[36]

Pressure for a reform of divorce also came from the judiciary. The best-known example is an often-quoted judgment of Mr. Justice Maule in 1845 at the Warwick Assizes, dealing with the case of Thomas Hall, a laborer accused and convicted of bigamy. Maule's judgment, a prolonged exercise in irony that effectively highlighted the deficiencies of statutory divorce, is worth quoting in full.

Prisoner at the bar, you have been convicted before me of what the law regards as a very grave and serious offence: that of going through the marriage ceremony a second time

---

[33] *Plea for an Alteration of the Divorce Laws* (London, 1831), 1.
[34] Ibid., 5.
[35] Ibid., 11.
[36] Ibid., 12.

while your wife was still alive. You plead in mitigation of your conduct that she was given to dissipation and drunkenness, that she proved herself a curse to your household while she remained mistress of it, and that she had latterly deserted you; but I am not permitted to recognise any such plea. You had entered into a solemn engagement to take her for better, for worse, and if you infinitely got more of the latter, as you appear to have done, it was your duty patiently to submit. You say you took another person to become your wife because you were left with several young children who required the care and protection of someone who might act as a substitute for the parent who had deserted them; but the law makes no allowance for bigamists with large families. Had you taken the other female to live with you as a concubine you would never have been interfered with by the law. But your crime consists in having – to use your own language – preferred to make an honest woman of her. Another of your irrational excuses is that your wife had committed adultery, and so you thought you were relieved from treating her with any further consideration – but you were mistaken. The law in its wisdom points out a means by which you might rid yourself from further association with a woman who had dishonoured you; but you did not think proper to adopt it. I will tell you what that process is. You ought first to have brought an action against your wife's seducer if you could have discovered him; that might have cost you money, and you say you are a poor working man, but that is not the fault of the law. You would then be obliged to prove by evidence your wife's criminality in a Court of Justice, and thus obtain a verdict with damages against the defendant, who was not unlikely to turn out a pauper. But so jealous is the law (which you ought to be aware is the perfection of reason) of the sanctity of the marriage tie, that in accomplishing all this you would only have fulfilled the lighter portion of your duty. You must then have gone, with your verdict in your hand, and petitioned the House of Lords for a divorce. It would cost you perhaps five or six hundred pounds and you do not seem to be worth as many pence. But it is the boast of the law that it is impartial, and makes no difference between the rich and the poor. The wealthiest man in the kingdom would have had to pay no less than that sum for the same luxury; so that you would have no reason to complain. You would, of course, have to prove your case over again, and at the end of a year, or possibly two, you might obtain a divorce which would enable you legally to do what you have thought proper to do without it. You have thus wilfully rejected the boon the legislature offered you, and it is my duty to pass upon you such sentence as I think your offence deserves, and that sentence is, that you be imprisoned for one day; and in as much as the present assizes are three days old, the result is that you will be immediately discharged.[37]

Parliament itself generated pressure to have the system of divorce overhauled. Within the House of Lords in particular there was growing dissatisfaction with the amount of parliamentary time consumed by each bill to dissolve a marriage. Lawyers for both prosecution and defense pleaded their cases, and witnesses were heard, all at the bar of the House of Lords. The pressure on time had been reduced somewhat in 1820 by the law that enabled witnesses in divorce bills emanating from India to be examined in the colony, but even so, divorce bills detracted significantly from the time the House of Lords could devote to other parliamentary business. Finally, in 1840, a select committee of

---

[37] Quoted in O. M. McGregor, *Divorce in England* (London, 1957), 15–17.

nine members of the House of Lords was established to examine evidence in divorce bills, although the bills had still to be voted upon by the full House of Lords and subsequently by the House of Commons.

In response to the growing criticism of the English mode of divorce, a royal commission was set up to report on the divorce law in 1850. The report of this commission, published in 1853, became the basis of the 1857 legislation. The report adopted a cautious approach, arguing that ease of divorce would conflict with the institution of marriage, which was intended chiefly to protect children from their parents' inconstancy and women from their husbands'. The commissioners took a great deal of evidence, including information on the working of the prevailing system, and descriptions and assessments of divorce legislation in other countries. It found that separations *a mensa et thoro* (which were called "divorces" in the commission's report) granted by the Consistory Court of London between 1845 and 1850 generally cost between three and five hundred pounds, and that there had been fifty-four during the six-year period under review,[38] an average of nine a year. This showed that the separation was the most expensive part of getting divorced in England: The actual parliamentary process cost between two and three hundred pounds.[39]

In contrast stood Scotland, where divorces on average cost about thirty pounds, but where an unopposed suit cost as little as twenty pounds. In the five-year period from November 1836 to November 1841, the Court of Sessions in Edinburgh had granted ninety-five divorces (an average of nineteen a year). Forty percent had been sought by women, and the divorces involved mainly "the humbler classes," such as servants, laborers, bakers, tailors, soldiers, butchers, shoemakers, carpenters, and weavers.[40]

The recommendations of the royal commission on divorce in England were essentially for a transfer of jurisdiction in matrimonial cases from Parliament and the church courts to the civil courts. Divorce should be available from the courts on the ground of adultery (when sought by a man) or aggravated adultery (when sought by a woman). There would be no need for a prior separation by an ecclesiastical court, and in fact ecclesiastical separations *a mensa et thoro* should be replaced by civil form of judicial separation. The commission proposed that adultery, gross cruelty, or desertion should be grounds for separation and that men and women should have equal access to this remedy, unlike divorce.[41] As conservative as these proposals were – they did not extend the grounds for divorce or separation – it took four years before a divorce bill successfully passed through Parliament.

As we should expect, reaction to the proposals of the royal commission

---

[38] *First Report of the Commissioners...into the Law of Divorce* (London, 1853), 28–31. Anderson, however, calculates that 80% of these "divorces" cost less than £175. Stuart Anderson, "Legislative Divorce – Law for the Arrstocracy?" in G. R. Rubin and David Sugarman (eds.), *Law, Economy and Society: Essays in the History of English Law, 1750–1914* (London, 1984), 440.

[39] *First Report...into the Law of Divorce*, 32–4.

[40] Ibid.

[41] Ibid., 21–2.

covered a wide spectrum of opinion, from those who thought that Parliament should seize the opportunity to abolish divorce entirely to those who wanted divorce made available well beyond the limits that had been recommended. Among areas of criticism of the divorce bills that were introduced after the commission's report were the court and legal costs that divorce would entail. One pseudonymous author pointed out that "the poor man has rights, has feelings, as well as the rich," and asked, "Is the rich man, with his thousands a year, is he alone to enjoy the privilege of buying release from a tie which has become degrading?"[42] Other critics focused on the need for women to have equal access to divorce. One wrote of "the thousands of noble-hearted English wives, the mothers of our great and good, the mothers of many a Crimean hero. . .whose life-long existence is passed in worse than widowhood – in that utter desolation of spirit which follows the wreck of earthly happiness."[43]

Against such writers who supported the extension of divorce were ranged those who opposed it entirely. Prominent were both the Roman Catholic and Anglican churches; their doctrines did not allow divorce, and they were driven to the position of advocating the suppression of divorce entirely. One clergyman, writing against the 1857 divorce bill, pointed out that parliamentary divorces began to be passed in the reign of, and through the influence of, "that not particularly chaste and virtuous monarch, Charles the Second."[44] He went on to argue that the bill was unfair to the poor, but instead of supporting a more democratic form of divorce, he proposed that divorce in any form would only increase evil by encouraging "inconsiderate and ill-assorted marriages," permitting men freely to "gratify their passions," and allowing men to get rid of their wives when they were tired of them, by tempting them to commit adultery and then divorcing them. Moreover, remarriage was not the boon it was portrayed as: "The married life of persons who have been divorced, is seldom, if ever, a really happy one. There is a shadow, if not a blight, that seems to rest on such marriages."[45]

The issue of remarriage was especially problematic to the clergy since it raised the question of whether divorced persons might remarry in church. Since 1837 it had been possible to celebrate marriages in England and Wales according to either secular or religious forms in any building licensed for weddings, so the Anglican church, which until 1837 had had a monopoly on celebrating marriages, was not in the position of being compelled to marry divorced men and women. But it was clear that some Anglicans would divorce and want to celebrate their subsequent marriages in church, a notion almost certainly opposed by the majority of Anglican priests as well as the church's

[42] Presbyter Anglicanus, *A Few Words upon the Marriage and Divorce Question* (London, 1857), 4. The debate in England in the decades before the 1857 law is discussed in Horstman, *Victorian Divorce*, 20–84.
[43] A Wife and A Mother, *What Will the Commons do with the Divorce Bill?* (London, 1857), 6–7.
[44] A Clergyman, *Why Should We Petition Against the New Divorce Bill?* (London, 1857), 4.
[45] Ibid., 5–6.

11 Nineteenth-century divorce laws

hierarchy. The 1857 divorce law specified that, if a priest refused to celebrate the marriage of a divorced person, then another priest in the diocese could officiate in the church of the priest who had refused. The prospect of intruder priests celebrating such marriages prompted the Oxford Clerical Association to consider ways of dissuading the divorced from remarrying in church. The clergymen of the association considered withholding the keys of the church and the parish registers from any priest who might want to use a colleague's church for such a marriage. One member of the association suggested that when a divorced person made known his or her intention to remarry in church, the clergyman should exercise his right to preach on the subject at the time of the marriage. "The prospect of such an exposure would in most cases effectually deter applicants." When an intending couple was "ready to dare it, and fight the matter out," the clergyman should start proceedings to have the "divorced adulterers" excommunicated.[46] Later the association circulated a petition against the remarriage of divorced persons by the Church of England.[47]

It was against this range of opinions within which the historian can discern no ready consensus, that the British Parliament legalized divorce in 1857. From the first day of the following year, divorce was available from the Court of Divorce for reason of adultery (or aggravated adultery, depending on the sex of the defendant), and judicial separations replaced those that until then had been granted by the ecclesiastical courts. In its formal respects the legalization of divorce was carried out timidly. The grounds for divorce were no more liberal than had been established by parliamentary procedure in the late seventeenth century, and they were not liberalized until well into the twentieth century. (From 1923 women could obtain divorce for reason of simple adultery, but grounds other than adultery were not added until 1937.) In strict terms, then, the 1857 act did little more than transfer jurisdiction over divorce from Parliament to a special court. There were limitations in this respect, too, for although the divorce court was empowered to sit outside London, it did not do so,[48] and this presented an obstacle to divorce for petitioners who lived outside the capital. In addition to legal and court expenses, they had to pay for the costs of transportation and accommodation for themselves and their witnesses. In such respects the 1857 law represented a very conservative approach to divorce reform in England.

Conservative or not, however, it was achieved only after a great deal of parliamentary debate and discussion, far more and far more intense than one would expect of such a limited objective. The actual process of dissolving marriages had, after all, been in effect for almost two centuries. The vigor of the debates in Parliament, then, indicate how sensitive an issue divorce was at this period.

[46] Minutes of the Oxford Clerical Association, vol. VIII, Meeting of September 14, 1857. Bodleian Library MS Top. Oxon.e.29.
[47] Ibid., Meeting of October 12, 1857.
[48] McGregor, *Divorce in England*, 18.

11.3 The first English divorce law

During the 1850s there had been four divorce acts annually on average, but from 1858, the number rose to between two and three hundred a year. Although England's divorce rate in the nineteenth century was one of the lowest in the West (probably because of the restrictive legislation and still prohibitive costs, despite the reductions) and the number of divorces in any single year did not exceed a thousand until 1918, the increased use of divorce as a result of the 1857 legislation is quite evident. The costs of divorce under the new system were in the range of forty to sixty pounds, a significant amount for workers, but a dramatic reduction from the hundreds of pounds that a relatively uncomplicated parliamentary divorce had cost. In addition, the prospect of initiating a parliamentary divorce preceded by a separation from an ecclesiastical court and a suit for criminal conversation must have deterred many of the wealthy few who could afford it. On balance the 1857 provisions scarcely opened the floodgates to a tide of immorality that swept away the English family, as the opponents of divorce had predicted, but the new law did make divorce accessible to the well-off middle classes, especially those in London.[49] Of a sample of 101 cases of divorce reported in the London *Times* between 1860 and 1919 the occupational groups most commonly represented by husbands were the military, trade (such as shopkeepers), workers (butlers, sailors), professionals, clerks, and men of independent means. Working men were represented, but disproportionately infrequently, accounting for only about one-sixth of the husbands whose occupation was reported.[50]

Within the limited extension of divorce, women benefited the most. As we have noted, women succeeded in obtaining only 4 of the 325 parliamentary divorces between 1670 and 1857, but between 1859 and 1909, women were petitioners in 7,525 of the 17,952 divorces granted, or 42% of the total. Women's petitions had a slightly better chance of succeeding than men's: The annual range of success varied from 63% to 84% for men but from 65% to 94% for women.[51] In general the use of divorce by women under the 1857 law is quite phenomenal, given that their husbands had to be proved guilty not only of adultery but also bigamy, incest, sodomy, desertion, cruelty, rape, or bestiality. Women were also placed at a disadvantage informally. They were more likely to be financially dependent and could only be sure of recouping the costs of a divorce action if it were successful. They were under great social pressure to conform to the middle-class model of the domesticated wife, subordinate to her husband and infinitely tolerant and suffering of his matrimonial offenses. There was a further inhibition; women often lost custody of children after a divorce,[52] for until the twentieth century it was a working principle on

---

[49] Gail L. Savage, "The Operation of the 1857 Divorce Act, 1860–1910. A Research Note," *Journal of Social History* 16 (1983), 104.
[50] Ibid., 106. There were nine workers among the fifty-eight husbands whose occupations were reported in the *Times*. The social profile of those divorced in 1871 is discussed in Chapter 14.
[51] Ibid., 105.
[52] Ibid., 106.

the part of the judiciary that children belonged to their father – a precept enshrined in law that had only begun to be challenged in the 1830s (see Section 14.3). In view of these disincentives, it is remarkable that such a high proportion of nineteenth-century divorces – more than two-thirds of them – were sought by women.

11.4 Restoring divorce to France

Divorce was legalized (or, more correctly, relegalized) in France in 1884 in circumstances quite different from those that produced the first English divorce law. France had a history of stark contrasts and discontinuity in providing for divorce; it was not permitted up to 1792 or after 1816, but in between fell the revolutionary phase (1792–1803) when divorce law was more liberal than any national divorce legislation before or since. The trauma of France's divorce experience during the revolution, and its misleading association with immorality and social and national degeneration, hung over the question of divorce throughout the nineteenth century, just as the specter of the revolution itself haunted French politics. Yet there were several occasions before 1884 when it seemed that the time had arrived for divorce to be restored to the French civil code, each time coinciding with a new regime and the promise or expectation of reform.

In the early years of the July Monarchy (1830–48), for example, there was renewed interest in divorce legislation as more liberal institutions replaced the reactionary policies of King Charles X. Bills to legalize divorce, on the lines of Napoleonic law, passed successfully through the Chamber of Deputies in the four years between 1831 and 1834, but all failed to gain enough support in the Chamber of Peers.[53] The revolution of 1848 also seemed to offer hope for the restoration of divorce, but the Second Republic, which it founded, was too deeply riven with ideological tensions, and the liberal measures that inaugurated the republic soon gave way to political conservatism. The republic's minister of justice, Adolphe Crémieux, attempted to have divorce legalized, but failed.[54] The only legal reform bearing on marriage during the brief life of the republic was the provision of legal aid for husbands and wives who wanted to sue for a judicial separation.[55]

---

[53] For the debates in 1831–2 see *Archives parlementaires*, 2ᵉ série, vols. 69, 72, 76–8.

[54] The 1848 divorce bill is reprinted in Alexandre Dumas *fils*, *La question du divorce* (Paris, 1880), 186–7. It is placed in the context of women's rights in Claire Goldberg Moses, *French Feminism in the 19th Century* (Albany, N. Y., 1984), 141–2. See also Theodore Zeldin, *France, 1848–1945* (vol. I, Oxford, 1973), 358.

[55] The law of January 22–30, 1851, permitted indigent litigants to have the costs of legal actions paid for in advance by the state. If they won their cases, the other party repaid the advance; if they lost, the state attempted to recover the advance – by definition with little likelihood of success. One study suggests that this legal aid scheme had virtually no effect on litigation in the nineteenth century except for actions to obtain *séparations de corps*, which increased appreciably for a brief period from 1852 to 1854. See Bernard Schnapper, "La séparation de corps de 1837 à 1914. Essai de sociologie juridique," *Revue historique* 259 (1978), 457.

11.4 Restoring divorce to France

Finally, it seemed possible that Emperor Louis Napoleon might restore divorce to France during the Second Empire (1852–70). In his political testament, *Napoleonic Ideas*, Louis Napoleon intimated that divorce would be legalized when he came to power.[56] Yet divorce was not legalized, perhaps because the emperor was anxious not to alienate the Catholic church in France. We should recall that it was partly to win the support of the church that Louis Napoleon sent French troops to Rome to protect the reactionary Pope Pius IX against Italian nationalist forces, and thus held up the completion of the unification of the country. Only after the fall of the Second Empire did the Bonapartists return to the advocacy of divorce. In 1879 Jérôme Napoleon, the cousin of the former emperor, became leader of the Bonapartist party, which in the 1881 elections adopted a program that included the legalization of divorce.[57] By that time, however, Bonapartism was a spent force.

It remained, in fact, for the successor of the empire, the Third Republic, to make provision for divorce once again in French law. The defeat of France in the Franco-Prussian war, which brought the republic into being, did actually result in the legalization of divorce in one part of France. Alsace-Lorraine, a territory in chronic contention between France and Germany, was annexed to the new German Empire after the French defeat in 1871. In 1873 divorce was restored to the territory on the Lutheran principles that had governed marriage and divorce there until Alsace and Lorraine had been incorporated into France in the late seventeenth century.[58] Unhappily married men and women in the rest of France had to wait longer, however. Bills to legalize divorce were introduced into the French parliament from 1876 onward, but it was not until 1884 that one was successful, and the French were able to divorce once again.

The question of restoring divorce to French law raised the question of the principles that should be accepted. The politicians of the Third Republic could look back, as they often did, to the revolution of 1789 as their inspiration, or they could legalize divorce on Napoleonic terms, which were more restrictive. The first time a divorce bill was introduced into the Chamber of Deputies of the Third Republic, in 1876, it aimed quite simply to revive the liberal legislation of 1792. The bill's sponsor was Alfred Naquet, a former professor of chemistry who was to become the moving force behind the campaign for divorce until he finally succeeded in 1884. Naquet began his parliamentary career (he was first a deputy, then from 1883 a senator) as a socialist with radical ideas about the family. In a book published in 1869 he had advocated the abolition of marriage as a step toward the destruction of bourgeois society.[59] It is not clear whether Naquet believed the reactionary mythology that insisted that the family

---

[56] Louis Napoleon called for the legalization of divorce to "secure the morality of families" in "Idées napoléoniennes" (1839), translated in *The Political and Historical Works of Louis Napoleon Bonaparte* (2 vols., London, 1852), I, 319.
[57] Zeldin, *France, 1848–1945*, I, 567.
[58] Alfred Naquet, *Le Divorce* (2nd. edn., Paris, 1881), 63ff.
[59] Alfred Naquet, *Religion, Propriété, Famille* (Paris, 1869). Naquet was jailed after this book was judged to be an attack on religion and morality.

had been imperiled during the revolution by the hammer blows of divorce and other legislation, and hoped that the revival of the 1792 law would finish the job it had obviously failed to do almost a century earlier.

Naquet's attempt to legalize divorce on revolutionary lines failed in 1876, however, as did a similar effort in 1878. By 1881 he had either moderated his views or faced political realities.[60] In that year he proposed that divorce should be legalized on the more restrictive Napoleonic principles: by the mutual consent of the two spouses or for a limited range of matrimonial offenses. This bill was passed by the Chamber of Deputies by the healthy margin of 331 votes to 138 in 1882, which indicated that it was the terms of the bill, not the principle of divorce per se, that had held up passage of earlier draft legislation. The same bill was passed by the Senate, after considerable procedural delays, in 1884. The Senate was more cautious, however. It removed the article permitting divorce by mutual consent and passed the more restrictive bill by a margin of 153 to 116 votes.[61] This amended bill was in turn accepted by the lower chamber, and the whole process indicated that the legislators of the 1880s wanted to distance themselves from the revolutionary tradition of divorce. Alfred Naquet himself condemned the results of divorce during the revolution in his long contributions to the 1884 debate in the Senate, and in this respect he was at one with all the speakers in the debate, whether they supported the divorce bill or opposed it.[62] For example, Baron Lafond de Saint Mür, who argued that divorce, wisely legalized, did not harm the stability of the family, pointed out that the 1792 divorce law inspired in him the same horror as it did in the adversaries of divorce. In 1792, he said "divorce entered our laws with excesses and violence, accompanied by an ease which profoundly harmed the interests of society. In this law of 1792 there were many of the most dangerous conditions favouring caprice, the emotions, and the impulses to which human nature is prone." The result had been thousands of frivolous divorces, 3,000 in Paris in one year alone.[63]

The divorce law that came into effect in July 1884, then, restored the fault clauses of Napoleon's legislation to the civil code. Divorce would be available on the grounds of the wife's adultery, the husband's adultery if it were committed in the marital dwelling, either spouse's "outrageous conduct, ill-usage, or grievous injuries," or the condemnation of either spouse to an infamous

[60] In a much later work Naquet wrote that he had never changed his principles, but that he had moderated his public position for pragmatic political purposes.

[61] The debates on the divorce bill in 1884 are in the *Journal officiel*, the record of proceedings in the Chamber of Deputies and the Senate. The issues are also discussed in Esther Kanipe, "The Family, Private Property and the State in France, 1870–1914," (Ph.D. dissertation, University of Wisconsin, Madison, 1976), 103–49.

[62] One interesting side effect of the debate on divorce in France in the 1880s was that a number of books, articles, and theses were written on the history of marriage and the family in France, especially during the revolutionary period. Some are listed in the bibliography in Roderick Phillips, *Family Breakdown in Late Eighteenth-Century France: Divorces in Rouen, 1792–1803* (Oxford, 1980), 235–41.

[63] *Journal officiel*, Sénat, 1er trimestre 1884, 960 (May 26, 1884).

punishment. This was not, it should be noted, a piece of legal reform sponsored by the government, although the minister of justice did declare the government's support for the measure. The law was above all the success of the campaign led by Alfred Naquet, and in recognition of his crucial role, the 1884 divorce law became widely known as "the Naquet law."

The decision to legalize divorce again in France revolved around several issues. There was the question of whether divorce was harmful of beneficial to women in particular. Proponents of divorce argued that women could only benefit; as one of them put it, "rather than being the victim of divorce, the wife will only benefit from it. And under the rule of *séparations de corps* the fate of children is more to be deplored than it is under the rule of divorce."[64] Opponents of divorce, on the other hand, held that, if marriage protects women, then divorce must make them vulnerable. To shouts of "Very good! Very good!" from the right of the chamber, Senator Jules Simon stated that the wife,

unable to defend herself on her own, defends herself with the force of the law, with the sacred institution of marriage. She is, without doubt, our equal, but she does not appear to be our equal and she exercises her equal rights only thanks to the virtue of this indissoluble marriage.[65]

The issue of divorce also involved the religious question, the question as to whether divorce should be legalized in a country such as France that had an overwhelmingly Roman Catholic population. This highlighted the issue of church–state relations, which were a chronic problem during the Third Republic. In the early 1880s the government went a long way toward reducing the church's influence in education, for example by abolishing the catechism in schools, suppressing Catholic universities, and setting up training colleges for women primary school teachers to replace nuns.[66] This secularizing trend carried over to the divorce law as well. As they did elsewhere, supporters of divorce law in France argued that Catholicism was not the only religion in the country, that to deny divorce to Protestants, Jews, deists, and freethinkers was to violate their rights and freedoms, and that anyway, Catholics would not be forced to use the divorce law if they found it repugnant to their faith. Alfred Naquet went further and pointed to inconsistencies in the history of Catholic attitudes toward divorce. Roman Catholics in Belgium did not protest against divorce there any more than French Catholics protested against civil marriage; Pope Pius IX had signed a concordat with Austria that had allowed the Protestant partner in mixed-faith marriages to divorce and remarry, even though the Catholic spouse could only separate and was forbidden to remarry; and the

---

[64] Ibid.
[65] Ibid., 81 (May 27, 1884).
[66] The secularization policies of the Third Republic are discussed in Evelyn Acomb, *The French Laic Laws (1879–1889)* (New York, 1941, repr. 1967). Acomb deals with divorce on 193–201 of this work and concludes that religion was less important a consideration than morality, the effects of divorce on women and children, and the implications of divorce for social stability.

divorce of Napoleon and Josephine had been approved by the bishop of Paris. It was necessary, Naquet insisted, to distinguish between "militant" Catholics and "ordinary" Catholics.[67] The latter had already shown their support for divorce: In 1881 the Chamber of Deputies had rejected a divorce bill by thirty-two votes to thirty, and in the elections later that year all but one of the pro-divorce deputies had been reelected by the predominantly Catholic electorate, whereas many of those who had voted against divorce had been defeated.[68]

The overriding issue, however, was whether legalizing divorce would actually increase marriage and family breakdown in France and undermine public morality. (French politicians generally had a higher opinion of the nation's morality than did foreign critics of France's divorceless state.) Opinion on the matter was, predictably, divided. It was pointed out that the degenerate condition of cities like Glasgow and London showed the effect that divorce could have on morals, and that elsewhere where divorce had been legalized, the number of marriages had gone into decline. Of all nations, one senator argued, the Belgians should have resisted divorce; they were a Catholic people "with solid morals, a cool and serious character [which] seems to protect them against emotional impulses." Yet even in Belgium, he pointed out, the number of divorces had risen alarmingly, from 4 in 1830 to 151 in 1879.[69] Other opponents of divorce insisted that it would break up families that had so far been held together by the all-embracing tolerance of married women. Marcel Barthe described the patience of the typical worker's wife: "When she has children, she endures everything, she puts up with violence, ill-treatment, terrible insults, she even forgives adultery" as long as the husband continues to support his family. If divorce were available, it would lead to the dissolution of these families.[70]

Beneath these predictions of social breakdown lay the perennial French fear of depopulation. This fear seemed justified in the 1880s; the French population had stagnated at the 36 million level in the 1860s and 1870s, and the French defeat by the Prussians in 1871 was widely attributed to population weakness. National strength was generally viewed as a function of population strength, and one reason why the prospect of divorce and marriage breakdown inspired such alarm in some quarters was not only that they implied social decline but also that divorce would interrupt the fertility cycle of French marriages. The debates on the 1884 law show that divorce and other measures considered at the same period, such as the reform of inheritance laws, explicitly aimed at the growth of national population.[71]

Against the views of their opponents, Naquet and his fellow supporters of divorce legislation held that the availability of divorce would not in itself lead to

[67] *Journal officiel*, Sénat, 1er trimestre 1884, 975–7 (May 27, 1884).
[68] Ibid., 963 (May 27, 1884).
[69] Ibid., 1108 (May 27, 1884).
[70] Ibid.
[71] See Acomb, *French Laic Laws*, 198–9.

an increase in marriage breakdown. Naquet suggested, indeed, that the rate of divorces could well be lower than the prevailing rate of separations. To illustrate the rate of formalized marriage breakdown in France without divorce, Naquet pointed out that the ratio of separations to marriages celebrated in any given year in France was consistently one-third higher than the ratio of divorces to marriages in Belgium. In 1881, for example, there were 117 *séparations de corps* per thousand marriages celebrated in France, compared with 81 separations or divorces per thousand marriages celebrated in Belgium. Comparing two similar regions, the three Flemish *départements* of Belgium and the *département* of Nord in France, Naquet showed 1 separation or divorce per 691 marriages in Flanders, but 1 separation per 193 marriages in the Nord. Such examples showed, Naquet insisted, that divorce did not necessarily increase marriage breakdown, and the same weak influence of legislation on behavior could be shown over time within France itself: In 1802, under the divorce law of 1792, there was 1 divorce for every 2,000 marriages, while in 1882, when divorce was not available, there were 22 separations for every 2,000 marriages.[72] The level of marriage breakdown and its formalization, then, was not a result of the mere availability of divorce, but resulted from factors such as religion (Catholics divorce less than Protestants); race (populations such as Bretons and Flemings divorce less than others); socioeconomic status (city dwellers and professionals were more likely than others to divorce); and time (marriage breakdown increases as "civilization develops").[73]

It was not divorce that was to be feared, Naquet argued, but the consequences of not being able to get a divorce. In 1881 the courts had granted 2,870 separations, which had the effect of releasing more than 5,700 men and women from some of their matrimonial obligations, such as cohabitation, without permitting them to remarry. Forbidden to form new legitimate unions, Naquet said, separated people nonetheless fell in love and were forced to form "illegitimate families." Naquet was clearly not seeking the separated vote, for he somewhat broadly and unflatteringly characterized these separated men and women as "5600 agents of corruption and of moral and social disorder."[74] Divorce, needless to say, would reduce this danger by permitting remarriage. Other speakers in favor of divorce pointed to additional social benefits. In a reference to the notorious murder case in 1840 in which Marie Lafarge was convicted of poisoning her husband with arsenic, Baron Lafond de Saint Mür insisted that Madame Lefarge would not have had to commit the crime if divorce had provided her an escape from marriage.[75] "Let the civil code liberate the wife," the baron exclaimed. "She will seek the protection of the law instead of taking vengeance with arsenic, sulphuric acid or a revolver."[76]

[72] *Journal officiel*, Sénat, 1er trimestre 1884, 965 (May 27, 1884).
[73] Ibid., 965–6 (May 27, 1884).
[74] Ibid., 967 (May 27, 1884).
[75] On the Lafarge case see Mary S. Hartmann, *Victorian Murderesses* (London, 1977), 10–50.
[76] *Journal officiel*, Sénat, 1er trimestre 1884, 962 (May 26, 1884).

The success of the 1884 divorce bill was hardly inevitable, but in the context of other social legislation passed in the same period, the passage of the divorce law is not too surprising. A great deal of liberalizing and secularizing legislation was passed in the 1880s in France, including the education reforms referred to earlier, and the divorce law of 1884 must be seen in this context. It is also likely that, the opposition of the Catholic church notwithstanding, many French men and women were prepared to support the reintroduction of divorce. Naquet argued that the French press (with the exception of clerical news-papers) favored a divorce law, and there was also the evidence, slight and circumstantial as it might have been, that politicians who supported divorce continued to be elected. Divorce was popularized in plays and novels, and soon after its legalization it was embedded in French social behavior. As we shall see when we consider the use of divorce laws in the nineteenth century, within a few years of the passage of the 1884 law the annual number of divorces ex-ceeded 7,000, twice the annual number of separations in France in the early 1880s. The popularity of divorce confounded the predictions of Alfred Naquet and others and served to intensify, even if it did not spread, opposition to divorce. The French were not about to abolish divorce yet again, however, and for the most part the increasing number of divorces – more than 15,000 a year on the eve of World War I – was accepted by the French, despite the continuing opposition of the Catholic church and other conservative elements within French society and politics.

11.5 Prussian and German divorce law

Just as the history of divorce in nineteenth-century France was associated with political and constitutional developments, so it was in Germany, where the evolution of divorce legislation was closely linked to the formation and con-solidation of the German Empire. With the exception of a brief period of legal standardization during the French Empire, when hundreds of German states and principalities were bonded into the Confederation of the Rhine, the provi-sion of divorce in Germany had followed religious divisions: The Lutheran states, concentrated in the north and dominated by Prussia, had allowed divorce since the Reformation, whereas the Catholic states had resisted it. Over time, as we have seen, divorce laws had expanded well beyond their Lutheran terms so that by the mid-nineteenth century Prussian law (as an example) provided eleven broad grounds for divorce:

1. adultery or unnatural vices;
2. desertion;
3. refusal of sexual intercourse;
4. impotence;
5. raging insanity or madness;
6. violence, attempted murder, or repeated and unfounded de-famatory accusations;

7. acts of felony or pursuing a disreputable occupation;
8. leading a disorderly life;
9. continued refusal by the husband to maintain his wife;
10. giving up the Christian religion; and
11. insurmountable aversion or the mutual consent to separate, where there were no children of the marriage (or, in exceptional circumstances, where there were children).[77]

The progressive expansion of the grounds for divorce in Prussia was not greeted with universal enthusiasm, however. In the 1840s there was an attempt, led by the jurist Friedrich Karl von Savigny, to restrict Prussian divorce law.[78] The attempt, which failed, was a reaction against the current tendency toward drawing up laws with universal applicability. Savigny and others held that laws developed historically from the spirit of the people (*Volksgeist*), and they upheld custom and tradition against legal innovation and uniformity. In the late 1850s there was yet another attempt to make Prussia's divorce law less liberal. In 1857 a bill was introduced in the Prussian *Landstag* that would have abolished divorce for refusal of intercourse, insanity, insurmountable aversion, and by mutual consent and would have placed certain limitations on some of the grounds that would have been retained under reformed legislation. Critics of the existing law pointed to the general decline of principles and morals in the eighteenth century especially those "which eventually brought in the French Revolution [and] reduced the law of marriage to the low state in which it is now found among us."[79] A British Member of Parliament, in his introduction to the English translation of a speech in the Prussian assembly (published in London as the British Parliament was debating the 1857 divorce bill) added his view that, because divorce law was so liberal in Prussia, "in point of fact there is no such thing as marriage in Prussia, nor is the bond so binding as it has been and is in many heathen countries."[80]

In this published speech, Baron von Gerlach attacked the ease of divorce and stressed the importance of keeping divorce from the lower classes in particular. "The upper classes are able to help themselves in some measure, through their higher cultivation," but for the lower classes, as soon as "the sacredness of this primitive institution [marriage] is depreciated, there remains nothing but an irremediable demoralization." The baron's paternalism extended to women, as well: "I claim...your especial sympathy on behalf of the female sex...The women are the chief sufferers from the laws facilitating divorce."[81] The full horror of divorce was illustrated by the number of divorces in Prussia, running at a rate of about 3,000 a year and by the circulation of common sayings that

---

[77] *The Speech of Baron von Gerlach, in the Prussian Chamber, on the Marriage Law* (London, 1857), 3–4.
[78] Rudolf Huebner, *A History of Germanic Private Law* (Boston, 1918), 616.
[79] *Speech of Baron von Gerlach*, 9.
[80] Ibid., 4.
[81] Ibid., 6–7.

revealed the way in which divorce had devalued marriage: "Married together is not bound together," "One is more cautious about buying a pig or a cow for fattening than about taking a wife," and "It is easier and costs less to get quit of a bad wife than of an unprofitable head of cattle."[82]

This attempt to reduce the scope of divorce law in Prussia also failed, however, and the failure held important implications for the law in Germany. In 1871, as an indirect result of the Prussian victory over France, Germany was unified in an empire, but it was by no means a federation of states on an equal footing. Rather, Prussia dominated the empire: The Prussian king became the emperor and Prussian institutions and personnel dominated the imperial system. This pattern applied in respect to divorce as well when an imperial divorce law was passed as part of the Personal Status Act of 1875. This law abolished separations and extended divorce to all German states, including Catholic states such as Bavaria and Saxony. In such territories divorce was made available on the grounds that had, up to that time, justified a separation. For most of the German states, however, divorce was based on the Prussian model and allowed divorce for

1. unnatural vices (with the condition that a woman could petition for a divorce on this ground only if she were not also guilty);
2. desertion;
3. obstinate and permanent refusal to perform conjugal duties;
4. impotence;
5. "loathsome and incurable diseases of the sexual organs";
6. madness or insanity lasting at least a year and judged incurable;
7. imperiling the life of the other spouse, which included defamation of character and restrictions on freedom;
8. conviction for a felony;
9. refusal of maintenance; and
10. a disorderly mode of life, including drunkenness and extravagance.

Divorce by mutual consent, which the Prussian code provided, was not recognized by all the German states, but many of them made allowance for their respective regents to dissolve individual marriages, a type of executive divorce not available in Prussia.[83]

The passage of an imperial divorce law in Germany in 1875 reflected two current trends in particular. One was the development of imperial institutions. Even if the law was not standardized throughout the German Empire and the legal traditions of individual states were respected, the continuation of those traditions was now dependent on the imperial legislature. Within twenty-five

---

[82] Ibid., 16–17.
[83] *British Parliamentary Papers*, "Marriage and Divorce," vol. III (Shannon, 1971), 478–80.

years, in fact, divorce law was standardized throughout the empire. The divorce law, then, was one minor aspect of the consolidation of the unified German nation. Second, the divorce law was passed in 1875, the highest point of the *Kulturkampf*, Chancellor Bismarck's campaign against the Roman Catholic church in Germany.[84] The purpose of the *Kulturkampf* was to reduce the influence of the church in matters such as education and to undermine the rival claim that the church had on the loyalty of Germans. The consolidation of divorce by imperial legislation and the abolition of separations can easily be interpreted as a slap in the face of Catholics (particularly as Pope Pius IX had expressly condemned divorce as recently as 1864) and a support of the Protestant tradition of tolerance for divorce.

As the *Kulturkampf* ran its course and the support of the church was needed in the new struggle between Bismarck and the social democrats and liberals, the 1875 imperial divorce legislation was modified to accommodate Catholic doctrine somewhat. A kind of separation order (called a "dissolution of the conjugal community") was established. It had the effects of a separation and did not dissolve the marriage, but it could be converted to a divorce at the request of either party.[85]

It makes more sense to see the 1875 German divorce law in the context of Bismarck's religious policy, rather than as the liberal measure that it was in countries such as France and England. German nationalists were not renowned for their liberalism, and for this reason it is not surprising that when the imperial legislature dealt again with divorce, it was to restrict its availability. In 1900 a new divorce code for Germany was promulgated within the Bürgerliches Gesetzbuch (civil code). This law restricted divorce and made it especially difficult for women to have their marriages dissolved. The possibility of obtaining a divorce for reason of "insurmountable aversion" or by mutual consent was abolished, and all grounds for divorce were limited to circumstances where a matrimonial fault could be shown. Some grounds, considered "absolute," including infidelity, bigamy, desertion, and "unnatural" intercourse, justified divorce when they were proved. Other grounds, considered "relative," including dishonorable and immoral conduct, serious neglect of marital duties, and serious maltreatment, could justify divorce at the discretion of the court. The court could dissolve a marriage in these latter circumstances if it were satisfied that the guilty party had "caused such a deep disruption of the marriage that the plaintiff cannot reasonably be expected to continue it."[86]

In the sense that its divorce law was reformed in a restrictive direction in 1900, Germany ran counter to the general Western trend of liberalization in the later nineteenth century. On the other hand, the 1900 imperial divorce law provided Germany's first standardized national divorce code, replacing regional

---

[84] W. M. Simon, *Germany in the Age of Bismarck* (London, 1968), 54 (and 48–58 on the *Kulturkampf* generally).
[85] Ernest J. Schuster, *The Principles of German Civil Law* (Oxford, 1907), 524.
[86] Ibid., 525.

and confessional variations in divorce laws that had existed before unification and that had been recognized by the 1875 divorce legislation. This did not imply a liberal attitude, however. The restrictive tendency of German divorce legislation reflected well enough the essentially paternalistic and conservative tenor of the German imperial administration. The extension of a uniform divorce law to all of Germany, including states with overwhelming Roman Catholic populations, reflected the continuing dominance of Lutheran Prussia, and the desire to strengthen the empire at the expense of its constituent states.

11.6 Divorce elsewhere in Europe

The tensions between the pressure to liberalize divorce policy and the conservative objections to divorce, so evident in France and Germany in the last decades of the nineteenth century, persisted throughout Europe up to World War I. Austria provided another example. In the first half of the century divorce was permitted to non-Catholics under the terms of the 1811 General Civil Code, but the restoration of a conservative monarchy after the revolution of 1848 led to a reaction against liberal ideas and policies. In 1855 a concordat was signed that transferred control of marriage to the Catholic church, thus effectively eliminating the possibility of divorce for all Austrians, regardless of their religious affiliation. This retreat from the Erastian policies implemented a century earlier provoked such a reaction, however, that the clauses dealing with marriage in the 1855 concordat were abrogated in 1868.[87] In 1870 the grounds for divorce, which remained formally denied to Austrian Catholics until the Nazi divorce law of 1938, included adultery, condemnation for certain crimes, willful desertion, having an infectious disease, ill-treatment, and threats. Divorce was also permitted when there was an "irremediable aversion" between the spouses, but only after there had been a period of separation.[88]

In neighboring Switzerland there was also a reform of divorce law in this period, with the promulgation of the first federal legislation in 1874 to replace the regional codes that had regulated divorce. The federal law recognized divorce on a number of specific grounds: adultery, willful desertion, insanity, and being sentenced to a degrading punishment. In comparative terms this Swiss law was quite restrictive, and this was enhanced by the limitations it placed on remarriage. A divorced woman could not marry within 300 days of her divorce, and the guilty party – husband or wife – had to wait twelve months, a period that could be extended to a maximum of three years in cases of especially serious matrimonial offenses.[89]

Perhaps one of the most striking pieces of legislation before World War I was the legalization of divorce in Portugal in 1910. The Portuguese Civil Code of

[87] Max Haller, "Austria," in Chester, *Divorce in Europe*, 212.
[88] *British Parliamentary Papers*, "Marriage and Divorce," III, 427.
[89] Ibid., 555–6. The Swiss law of 1874 also provoked religious conflict; see Wieland, "Switzerland," in Chester, *Divorce in Europe*.

1867 had ruled out the possibility of divorce by declaring marriage to be a "perpetual contract," and bills aiming to legalize divorce were regularly defeated, right up to 1910.[90] In that year, however, the monarchy of King Manoel II was overthrown and a republic was proclaimed, drawing much of its inspiration from the French Revolution of 1789. One of the first legal reforms of the new regime was an extremely liberal law that allowed divorce by mutual consent, converted separation, and on any of ten specific grounds, including adultery, absence, desertion, ill-treatment, and addiction to gambling.[91] Like the French revolutionary legislation that was a model for the Portuguese republicans, the 1910 law also made husbands and wives equal in all respects before the law, made civil marriage obligatory, and created a "Day of the Family," its importance in the republican scheme indicated by its being designated on December 25.[92]

Even where divorce was not legalized in this period, we might note that significant changes were made (or attempted) in marriage law. In Spain, for example, an 1870 law transferred control of marriage from the ecclesiastical to the secular authorities, but the tension between church and state, and between conservative and liberal tendencies quickly became apparent. The secularization of marriage created such a reaction that in 1875 it was repealed and obligatory religious marriage reinstated; only Spaniards who could prove that they were not Roman Catholics were permitted to go through a civil marriage ceremony. Even so, divorce was not possible for non-Catholics, the nation's leaders being convinced that the great majority of the Spanish people were opposed to it.[93] However, separation *a mensa et thoro* was legalized by the 1889 civil code, a modest advance for Spain's unhappily married couples at the time when divorce was becoming more widely available elsewhere in Europe and the West generally.[94]

11.7 Divorce law in the British Empire

By extending divorce throughout Europe, nineteenth-century reforms indirectly disseminated the European model of divorce around the world. The principal mechanism was the British Empire that, by 1857, even before the final paroxysm of European imperialism at the end of the century, comprised territories in Canada, the West Indies, Australia, New Zealand, Asia, and

---

[90] Gabriel Le Bras (ed.), *Divorce et séparation de corps dans le monde contemporaine* (Paris, 1952), 247.
[91] The full list of grounds established in 1910 was adultery by either spouse; condemnation to prison, deportation or banishment for at least fifteen years; violence or insults harmful to the reputation; desertion for three years; absence for four years; incurable insanity; agreed separation for ten years; addiction to gambling; and certain contagious or incurable diseases. Ibid., 250–1.
[92] A. H. De Oliveira Marques, *A History of Portugal* (2 vols., New York, 1976), II, 135.
[93] Ines Alberdi, *Historia y sociologia del divorcio en España* (Madrid, 1979) 83.
[94] Lucy A. Sponsler, "The Status of Married Women under the Legal System of Spain," *Journal of Legal History* 3 (1982), 140.

11 Nineteenth-century divorce laws

Africa. British colonies had been forbidden to enact legislation that would be repugnant to English law and legal practice, and the necessity of royal consent for colonial laws acted, in principle at least, as a guarantee that legislative harmony between the colonies and the mother country was observed. In reality, as we have seen, the principle was breached. Several of the American colonies, notably Massachusetts and Connecticut, provided divorce facilities during the seventeenth and eighteenth centuries, and others emulated them in this respect after they had won independence from Great Britain. But it was not only the future states of the United States of America that had ignored colonial office instructions not to allow divorce. Three future provinces of Canada did so as well: Nova Scotia, New Brunswick, and Prince Edward Island, all maritime (Atlantic) provinces that were closely associated with the northern American colonies and that were probably influenced by the relatively liberal approaches to divorce there. In 1761 Nova Scotia enacted legislation recognizing adultery and cruelty as matrimonial crimes justifying divorce, and in 1791 New Brunswick legalized divorce for reason of adultery.[95] Much later, but still well before the English divorce law of 1857 was passed, another of the Canadian Atlantic colonies provided access to divorce: A law of 1837 in Prince Edward Island made divorce and annulment available from a court consisting of the lieutenant-governor and his council on precisely the same grounds as had been set out in the 1791 New Brunswick law.[96]

Beyond the North Atlantic coast of America, however, the British colonies had generally complied with the prohibition on permitting divorces. Inhabitants of colonies without divorce facilities were allowed to petition for dissolution of marriage by Act of Parliament in Westminster, and as we have seen (Chapter 7) many British soldiers and civil servants stationed in India did so. But no parliamentary divorces were sought by colonists outside the subcontinent, although one man who petitioned for a statutory divorce in 1843 had lived in Australia and cited the impossibility of obtaining a divorce there.[97] No doubt the difficulties of transportation, the time involved, and the costs of traveling to London (with witnesses) made parliamentary divorce a rather abstract privilege for colonists. What was worse, church courts had not been established in many of the colonies, so separations *a mensa et thoro* could not be obtained, as they could in England. Even though these courts were facing growing opposition in England because they were expensive and the remedies they offered unsatisfactory, they would have provided some redress for unhappily married colonials. Instead, ad hoc regulations were put in place to provide for cases of marriage breakdown such as desertion. An example is an 1846 New Zealand "Ordinance for the support of destitute families and illegitimate children," which made it an offense for a man to "unlawfully, and without cause for doing

---

[95] Julian D. Payne, *The Law and Practice Relating to Divorce and Other Matrimonial Causes in Canada* (2nd edn., Calgary, 1964), 8.
[96] Ibid., 9–10.
[97] Hilary Golder, *Divorce in 19th-Century New South Wales* (Kensington, N.S.W., 1985), 52.

434

so desert his wife or...children under the age of 14 years and...leave them without means of support."[98] Justices could require a man convicted under the ordinance to pay up to a pound a week to support his family. Similar legislation had been passed earlier in the Australian colonies of Tasmania and New South Wales, but the provisions gave only limited relief to abandoned women and their children. One New South Wales court awarded most successful petitioners for support only eleven shillings a week in maintenance, less than the lowest paid domestic servant.[99]

With the establishment of a divorce court in England in 1857, the situation in the colonies changed. Divorce was no longer repugnant to English law, and colonial legislators were not only permitted to enact divorce laws, but actually encouraged to do so. In 1858 the secretary of state for the colonies, Lord Stanley, sent a copy of the English divorce act to colonial governors and suggested that they recommend similar legislation to the colonial legislators. Some colonies acted with breathtaking haste. In South Australia divorce legislation on the English model was in place within seven months of receipt of Lord Stanley's memorandum. Others waited longer; for example, New Zealand's first divorce law was passed in 1867, New South Wales's in 1873, and Jamaica's in 1879.

The arguments for and against divorce in the colonies generally echoed the debate that had taken place in England. Opponents insisted that divorce was not only contrary to Christian doctrine, whether Catholic or Anglican versions, but that it would lead to the collapse of the family and the social order. This was a fate that might well have seemed more likely in the newly established colonial societies than in Europe, where the family had survived centuries of social and economic upheaval (although to contemporary commentators there, the disruptions associated with industrialization seemed unprecedented in their effects on the family). But those promoting divorce in the colonies had one powerful argument on their side: The British Parliament, the mother of parliaments, had, in its wisdom, legalized divorce. Moreover, there was no evidence of immediate social or moral breakdown in England as a result. The argument from British example gave the prodivorce lobbies in the colonies a lever that British proponents of divorce had not had, because arguments based on "foreign" (non-British) legislation were by no means as convincing. It was pointed out in the parliamentary debate on divorce in New Zealand that in Prussia and France "they formerly went to the extreme in allowing the most trivial pretext for divorce,"[100] and that in Chicago, "when the great American

---

[98] Roderick Phillips, *Divorce in New Zealand: A Social History* (Auckland, 1981), 130n.4.

[99] Golder, *Divorce in 19th-Century N.S.W.*, 37. In Canada, Ontario was the only province to make such a provision; the 1888 Deserted Wives Maintenance Act enabled the courts to order a husband to pay up to five dollars a week to support his wife. James G. Snell, " 'The White Life for Two': The Defence of Marriage and Sexual Morality in Canada, 1890–1914," *Histoire sociale-Social History* 16 (1983), 122.

[100] *New Zealand Parliamentary Debates* (hereafter *N.Z.P.D.*), IV, 1043 (September 23, 1867).

railway stopped, they could hear shouted out: 'there's ten minutes allowed for divorce, and twenty minutes for refreshments'."[101] That such countries allowed divorce was not an argument for its legalization but simply further evidence of the weakness of their morality and national character.

Otherwise the objections to divorce and their rebuttals in the colonial debates traversed now familiar ground. Divorce would be disastrous for women, who would be abandoned by their husbands at the least whim; conversely, divorce would give women some measure of protection against their husbands' crimes and offenses. Children would suffer; children would benefit. Divorce would destroy marriage; divorce would correct the most flagrant abuses within marriage. There were familiar configurations of opposition and support, too. The Catholic church everywhere fought against the introduction of divorce, and in some instances Catholic Members of Parliament were able to determine the outcome of attempts to legalize divorce by holding the balance of power. Against the Catholics, Presbyterians, drawing on the Scottish Calvinist tradition of divorce, were often in the fore in promoting divorce legislation.[102]

Throughout the British Empire the result was the same as it had been in England: Divorce was legalized so as to give men and women access to divorce on the grounds of adultery and aggravated adultery, respectively. Although encouraging the passage of divorce laws in the colonies, the British government was anxious that they should continue to conform to English law and practice. To have had widely varying provisions for divorce could have produced problems of recognition of divorce decrees from one jurisdiction to another. As one New Zealand politician, arguing against divorce liberalization, put it, if divorce laws varied, "a woman may be a lawful wife in one part of the Empire, and be living in immorality in another."[103] Yet despite such warnings, and in the face of the known wishes of the Colonial Office in London, many of the British colonies liberalized their divorce laws before the English law was reformed. In New Zealand, for example, a reformed law of 1898 enabled women as well as men to obtain divorce for reason of simple adultery, rather than aggravated adultery, and added new grounds for divorce, namely, desertion for five or more years; drunkenness on the part of the husband, coupled with a failure to maintain his wife; drunkenness on the part of the wife, coupled with a failure to carry out her domestic duties; and the conviction of one spouse for attempting to murder the other.[104] These reforms anticipated their English equivalents by several decades: Women were given equal access to divorce in England in 1923, and the grounds for divorce were extended in 1937.

[101] Ibid. XII, 261 (August 2, 1872).
[102] For two studies of the parliamentary and nonparliamentary debate on divorce in British colonies, see Phillips, *Divorce in New Zealand*, 17–34, and Golder, *Divorce in 19th-Century N.S.W.*, 17–99.
[103] *N.Z.P.D.* LVIII, 453 (November 17, 1887).
[104] Divorce Act, 1898. See Phillips, *Divorce in New Zealand*, 146.

11.7 Divorce law in the British Empire

The Canadian colonies remained apart from the trend of emulating, then surpassing, English divorce law, which was evident in Australia and New Zealand in the later nineteenth century. As we have noted, three of the Canadian Atlantic colonies had introduced divorce provisions in advance of the British legislation, but their fellows had faltered. A bill to legalize divorce was introduced into the Legislative Assembly of Upper Canada (Ontario) in 1833 but was dropped before its second reading.[105] Six years later, however, the Legislative Assembly of Lower Canada (Quebec) bypassed divorce legislation proper, and granted a divorce by statute, Canada's first. This act dissolved the marriage of one John Stuart, whose wife had committed adultery, then eloped with her accomplice. The legislative council of the colony (its upper chamber) defeated a motion to reject this statutory divorce (by thirty votes to ten), and there were four more such divorces up to 1867, when legislative authority over marriage passed to the newly established federal parliament. Despite sporadic pressure for the enactment of a proper divorce law in Quebec, such as an 1860 petition by residents of Quebec City for a law on the model of the 1857 English act, no action was taken.[106]

The limited autonomy of the Canadian colonies in matters such as divorce was lost when they confederated to form the Dominion of Canada in 1867. The British North America Act, which defined the respective areas of jurisdiction of the federal and provincial governments, gave authority over matrimonial legislation to the dominion (federal) parliament. Because the act specified that laws in force in the colonies at the time of confederation should stand, divorce continued to be available in Nova Scotia, New Brunswick, and Prince Edward Island on the terms they had already established. For the inhabitants of the other provinces, however, the sole means of obtaining a divorce during the rest of the nineteenth century was by individual Act of Parliament. The Canadian parliament entered the marriage dissolution business, then, ten years after the British Parliament had ended the practice. As in England, Canadian statutory divorces were quite rare (sixty-nine between 1867 and 1900, or three a year).[107] The sole ground for divorce that was recognized was adultery, but the Canadian practice did not recognize a double standard of morality: Men and women could obtain divorces for the reason of simple adultery. To this extent Canadian statutory divorce retained the form of the earlier English system but improved on the terms of both it and the succeeding judicial form of divorce.

There was pressure for parliament to exercise its authority to establish divorce courts, but it came to nothing, and the first Canadian federal divorce legislation came into effect as late as 1968. Bills aiming to establish provincial courts with jurisdiction over divorce were defeated in 1875, 1879, and 1888. In

---

[105] John A. Gemmill, *The Practice of the Parliament of Canada upon Bills of Divorce* (Toronto, 1889), 17.
[106] Ibid., 17–20.
[107] Constance Backhouse, " 'Pure Patriarchy': Nineteenth-Century Canadian Marriage," *McGill Law Journal* 13 (1986) 276.

1879, for example, a bill to enable the Court of Chancery in Ontario to dissolve marriages was rejected before it could have a second reading.[108] There was even a threat to the continued existence of the divorce courts in the three provinces that had divorce laws. In 1870 the government introduced a bill to modify some aspects of the divorce court of New Brunswick, but quickly withdrew it when there were calls for the federal government to abolish the court entirely. For lack of satisfactory remedies at home, some Canadians went south to the United States to have their marriages dissolved, just as Americans would eventually seek a divorce haven in Mexico.[109] It is not clear how many Canadians resorted to the divorce courts of amenable American states, but the Canadian government was not readily disposed toward accepting foreign divorce decrees at face value. The issue came to the surface in 1887 when a woman sought a parliamentary divorce on the ground that her husband had obtained a divorce in Boston and subsequently remarried in Ontario. Parliament was loathe to declare the divorce invalid, as it would have made the remarriage bigamous, the second wife a "concubine" and her children "illegitimate." It was equally unwilling simply to accept that a Massachusetts court's divorce decree had automatic validity in Canada, and finally decided on a compromise; it implicitly accepted the Boston divorce so as to validate the husband's second marriage, but also agreed to the petition for a parliamentary divorce as a way of claiming its own right to jurisdiction.[110] The couple in this case appear to have been divorced twice, each by a different tribunal, and the case highlighted the problem of interjurisdictional recognition of divorces, an issue that would be dealt with eventually by international convention.

Canada's reluctance to legislate on divorce as readily as other British colonies in the nineteenth century arose from several considerations. There were, in the first place, inconsistencies in the matter of jurisdiction, in that the authority to pass divorce legislation was vested in the federal parliament whereas the operation of the divorce courts themselves was to be a provincial responsibility. Thus it was that the Atlantic provinces of Canada were able to maintain their individual courts even in the absence of a federal divorce law. The refusal of the federal legislators to move on the divorce issue was no doubt due in large part to their apprehension that, if divorce laws were passed piecemeal, on a province-by-province basis according to the wishes and terms set down by each one, legislation across Canada would not be uniform. By 1867 divorce provisions differed between New Brunswick and Nova Scotia. More to the point, perhaps, there was the example of the United States, where divorce laws ranged from the nonexistent through the restrictive to the very liberal, and where, in the later nineteenth century, there was a vigorous reaction against the putative ease of divorce in some states. Canadians had no wish to emulate this heterogeneous

---

[108] *Debates of the House of Commons of Canada* VII (1879), 1697.
[109] On migratory divorce from Canada, see also Backhouse, "'Pure Patriarchy'," 275–6.
[110] *Debates of the House of Commons of Canada* XXIV (1887), 1017ff.

pattern of legislation, with its potential for problems in the recognition of divorce decrees among the various provinces. Finally, there was one particular obstacle to the enactment of uniform divorce provisions across Canada: the province of Quebec, with its predominantly French Catholic population, more resistant to secularizing legislation such as divorce than other parts of Canada.[111] The progress of divorce faltered in Canada from 1867, then, largely because it was caught up in the wider political and constitutional issues provoked by the establishment of the new nation.[112]

11.8 The United States

The United States of America assumes particular importance in the history of divorce in the nineteenth century. Between 1850 and 1900 American divorces began to increase rapidly, to the point that divorce rates in America surpassed those in Europe, a position they have maintained ever since. One result was that America gained notoriety as a country of unstable institutions and declining morals, a reputation that was noted in debates on divorce in other countries. Distinctions within the United States itself were also important, however, and in the nineteenth century the legal and other foundations were laid for what would become the especially high divorce rates in the Midwest and West of the nation, initially in states such as Indiana and South Dakota, later in Nevada and California. Although it is important to place the United States within the more general context of divorce in Western society, it is important first to appreciate the development of divorce laws and policies in the nation itself. This is complicated by the fact that marriage and divorce legislation fell within the jurisdiction of the states. An account of the progress of divorce in each state individually would be long and tedious,[113] however, and for the purpose of the following discussion the United States is divided into three large regions: the Northeast, the South, and the Midwest and West. Generally this division works as a way of making some sense out of a situation that approached legal chaos, but there will no doubt be objections that such a broad treatment of a complex issue fails to do justice to exceptions, nuances, and peculiarities. Taking such objections into account where possible, ignoring them where not, this discussion deals primarily with the legal policies vis-à-vis divorce in nineteenth-century America, and with some major issues of attitudes. The social basis of divorce in America and elsewhere at this time is dealt with in Chapter 14.

As we noted in Chapter 4, many of the northeastern states of the United

---

[111] Quebec's Code Civil of 1854 was modeled on the French civil code, but generally omitted the secular elements of family law, and permitted separations but not divorces.
[112] I am grateful to Professor Donald Swainson of Queen's University for discussing some of these issues with me.
[113] George E. Howard, *A History of Matrimonial Institutions* (3 vols., Chicago, 1904) is an invaluable detailed survey of the development of marriage law in the United States up to the end of the nineteenth century.

11 Nineteenth-century divorce laws

States proceeded to pass divorce legislation soon after independence, in the 1780s and 1790s. In the following half century all consolidated their laws, some states sorted out the residual confusion between legislative and judicial divorce, and most of the states liberalized their divorce legislation. Pennsylvania is one example of a state that went through these phases. After a brief period of providing only for legislative divorce, of which there were eleven between 1776 and 1785, the state's legislature, the General Assembly, passed a law in 1785 permitting divorce for reason of bigamy, adultery, or malicious desertion for four years. Wives who could prove extreme cruelty or other misconduct on the part of their husbands were entitled to a separation. Beginning in 1815 this law was gradually liberalized. In that year the period of desertion was reduced to two years and two further grounds for divorce were recognized: cruel treatment by the husband such that the wife's life was endangered, and indignities offered to the wife that made her condition intolerable and forced her to leave home.[114] (The latter is known as "constructive desertion.") In 1843 a wife's insanity was added to the grounds for divorce, and in 1854 two further grounds extended the list; the imprisonment of either spouse for a felony, and the wife's extreme cruelty toward her husband. The expansion of grounds for divorce was gradual, sometimes incomprehensible (why was a wife's insanity a ground for divorce but not a husband's insanity?), but steady. In addition, Pennsylvania's legislature surrendered the power of dissolving marriages in 1838, giving sole jurisdiction to the regular courts.[115]

Connecticut followed the path of divorce liberalization even more rapidly. As we have seen, Connecticut provided quite liberal divorce laws in the seventeenth and eighteenth centuries, and divorces there had outnumbered those elsewhere in colonial America. This law, which allowed divorce for adultery, fraudulent contract, desertion for three years, or prolonged absence with a presumption of death, apparently functioned well. Judge Zephaniah Swift described it in 1795 as preferable "to the practice of all other nations" and as favoring "the virtue and happiness of mankind,"[116] and the colonial law continued without modification through to the early republican period. Swift's appreciation of Connecticut divorce was not universally shared, however, and two voices in particular were raised against the state's law. In 1788 a New Haven Congregationalist pastor, Benjamin Trumbull, inveighed against all divorces allowed for any reason but adultery, and called upon the clergy to put pressure on the legislature to limit divorce to this sole ground permitted by the Bible.[117] Trumbull's call motivated the general assembly of the church to protest to the state assembly about the "numerous instances of divorce which

---

[114] Nelson Blake, *The Road to Reno: A History of Divorce in the United States* (New York, 1962), 57.
[115] Blake (in ibid., 56) states that legislative divorce in Pennsylvania ended in 1838, but that there were more than a hundred such divorces between 1817 and 1849.
[116] Quoted in ibid., 57.
[117] Benjamin Trumbull, *An Appeal to the Public, Especially to the Learned, with Respect to the Unlawfulness of Divorces* (New Haven, 1788).

have taken place in this state, especially of late years" and to call for divorce to be restricted to cases of adultery.[118]

The other dissident, the more prominent Timothy Dwight, president of Yale University, attacked Connecticut's divorce law in an 1816 sermon given in the presence of the state governor and many legislators. Dwight condemned all but scriptural divorce (for adultery only) and fulminated against the effects of the prevailing laws. The evil of divorce had been contained in earlier times by religion, he asserted, but "at the present time, the progress of this evil is alarming and terrible": In New Haven alone there had been 50 divorces in the preceding five years and more than 400 in the whole state. Dwight dwelt on the horrors that divorce had provoked in France during the revolution (by coincidence, divorce was abolished in France in the year of Dwight's sermon), and predicted a similar fate for Connecticut:

> ...It is clearly evident, that the progress of divorce, though different in different countries will in all be dreadful beyond conception. Within a moderate period, the whole community will be thrown, by laws made in open opposition to the Laws of God, into a general prostitution... Over such a country, a virtuous man, if such an one be found, will search in vain to find a virtuous wife. Wherever he wanders, nothing will meet his eye, but stalking bare-faced pollution. The realm around him has become one vast Brothel; one great province of the world of Perdition.[119]

Connecticut's governor and legislators might have had no choice but to listen to such forceful representations, but they did not act on them. At the same time, there was no great desire to see Connecticut become a divorce haven (especially after New York had enacted a very restrictive divorce law in 1787) and in 1797 a three-year residency requirement had been added to the state's divorce provisions. The law itself was not limited as Trumbull and Dwight had demanded, however, and when it was finally reformed, in 1843, it was in a liberal direction by the addition of two more grounds for divorce: habitual drunkenness and intolerable cruelty.

The number of divorces in Connecticut at this period is not known, although its frequency might be indicated by the fact that by the 1820s printed petition and judgment forms were in use.[120] Divorces were often fast – an undefended action seldom took longer than two months – and procedures were streamlined. Such measures no doubt reflected the growing demand for divorce and in turn facilitated recourse to the courts. Throughout the period, too, the Connecticut legislature also dissolved marriages by legislative act, usually where cases did not comply with the circumstances envisaged by the law. Curiously, the divorce activity of the legislature increased in the 1840s, just as the law itself was

---

[118] Quoted in Henry S. Cohn, "Connecticut's Divorce Mechanism: 1636–1969," *American Journal of Legal History* 14 (1980), 44.

[119] Timothy Dwight, *Theology Explained and Defended in a Series of Sermons* (3 vols., London, 1827), III, 268.

[120] Cohn, "Connecticut's Divorce Mechanism," 45.

liberalized. In 1849 the committee of the legislature that tried divorce petitions dealt with more than forty cases, and advised divorce in fourteen of them. The circumstances alleged in these petitions included offensive behavior, cruelty, eviction, and failure to provide.

The number of cases the legislators tried in 1849 tried their patience in turn, however, and that very year a bill was introduced to give sole responsibility for divorce to the courts. Opponents of the bill argued that under the judiciary control over divorce would become lax, even though its supporters insisted that legislative divorce was too arbitrary. One assemblyman pointed out that the success or failure of divorce bills in the legislature often depended on which members happened to be attending at the time.[121] The 1849 bill was passed, ending legislative divorce in Connecticut.[122] In addition, the grounds for divorce were extended even further, to include life imprisonment, any infamous crime involving a violation of the conjugal duty, and – most important – "any such misconduct as permanently destroys the happiness of the petitioner and defeats the purpose of the marriage relation."[123] This last ground, known as an "omnibus clause," gave the courts wide discretion and was clearly designed to compensate for the loss of the discretionary element that legislative divorce had provided. The overall result of the 1849 legislation was to give Connecticut one of the most liberal divorce laws in the United States at that time, although it was protected against an invasion by out-of-state petitioners by the three-year residency requirement.

Yet not all states pursued consistently more liberal divorce policies after independence. Massachusetts, the state that, with Connecticut, had produced a large number of divorces during the colonial period, had in 1786 enacted a law that was less liberal than the provisions that had been in force in the seventeenth and eighteenth centuries. Perhaps as a result of a more conservative trend of thought within the state's Congregational church, desertion was excluded as a ground for divorce.[124] The grounds recognized for divorce were impotence, bigamy, and adultery, although a separation could be obtained for reason of cruelty. From this reactionary position, however, Massachusetts gradually moved to liberalize divorce. In 1811 the grounds for separation were extended to include cases where a husband deserted his wife or neglected her and refused to provide for her maintenance.[125] Later in the century, additional grounds were added to divorce: a sentence to seven years' imprisonment at hard labor (1835); malicious desertion by either spouse for five years (1838); and either spouse's leaving the other for three years or more to belong to a religious

---

[121] Blake, *Road to Reno*, 59–60.
[122] Cohn, "Connecticut's Divorce Mechanism," 48, states that the state legislature continued to dissolve marriages, though in smaller numbers, even after 1849.
[123] Howard, *Matrimonial Institutions*, III, 13.
[124] Blake, *Road to Reno*, 50.
[125] Ibid., 61.

sect that believed that the sexual relationship between a husband and wife was unlawful (1850).[126]

As these examples indicate, the tendency in the northeastern states of the United States was toward the liberalization of divorce law and the abandonment of the practice of dissolution of marriage by the legislature. It is evident that the two processes were linked. Legislative divorce had provided a facility for divorce beyond the limits specified by the statute law and introduced an element of flexibility to divorce facilities. (In this respect state legislators performed the same function as some European monarchs – in Sweden and Prussia, for instance – in granting divorce by dispensation where the law was thought to be inadequate.) Legislative divorce might well have been arbitrary, but the least that can be said in favor of it is that it benefited those who benefited from it, whereas those who were denied a divorce from the legislature would have been no more successful had they applied to the courts. The decline of legislative divorce must be seen as underlying the growth of omnibus clauses in divorce laws in some states. By permitting judges to develop case law by defining such terms as "intolerable hardship" and "offenses against marriage," the legislators gave to the courts the discretion that had been exercised by legislatures when they dissolved marriages for reasons not foreseen by divorce laws. From this point of view, the shift of jurisdiction from legislature to the judiciary should not in itself be regarded as a liberalization of divorce. Without a corresponding expansion of the grounds for divorce to be applied by the courts, the abolition of legislative divorce generally entailed a contraction of the accessibility of divorce. Omnibus clauses in divorce laws, however, made discretionary divorce more widely available than it had been before and represented a real liberalization of the laws.

Other northeastern states pursued more or less liberal policies. Rhode Island, New Hampshire, and Vermont had passed divorce laws in the 1790s that recognized adultery, cruelty, and desertion among other grounds for divorce. Rhode Island's also included one of the earliest omnibus clauses, allowing divorce where there was "gross misbehaviour and wickedness in either of the parties, repugnant to and in violation of the marriage covenant."[127] This state in particular might have left its divorce legislation alone and still have been among the most liberal states in respect of divorce at midcentury, but Rhode Island's legislators persisted in expanding the grounds for divorce. In 1844 habitual drunkenness was added, and in 1851 desertion for a period of less than five years could be accepted at the court's discretion.[128]

The most striking exception to the liberal and liberalizing approaches to divorce law and policy in the Northeast was New York State. It was striking

---

[126] Ibid. This final ground was aimed at the Shakers, a religious sect that believed that marriage and sexual intercourse were contrary to divine law.

[127] Howard, *Matrimonial Institutions*, III, 14.

[128] Ibid.

because it diverged markedly in a conservative direction and because the restrictive divorce law enacted there in the late eighteenth century remained substantially unchanged for almost two centuries.[129] This 1787 law specified adultery as the sole ground for divorce and gives the impression of being legislation designed to deal with adultery rather than with marriage per se. The preamble to this first New York statute permitting divorce referred not to its need in light of the absence of legal provision for the dissolution of marriage but stated that "the laws at present respecting adultery are very defective"[130] and that it was appropriate for the legislature to provide relief to the husbands and wives who were victims of their spouses' infidelity. The strongly punitive tenor of the law was reflected in its absolute prohibition of remarriage on the part of the guilty partner.

The history of New York divorce legislation from 1787 until the Civil War and beyond is little more than a catalog of unsuccessful attempts to liberalize the law. It is true that there were reforms in related areas, such as separation. An 1813 law gave women the right to obtain a separation for reason of a husband's cruel and inhuman treatment, his conduct if it made cohabitation with him unsafe and improper for the wife, or if he had abandoned her and refused to provide for her. And in 1824 the law of separation was reformed so as to give men equal access to it. But the law of divorce, with adultery as its sole ground, remained unchanged. Despite pressure for liberalization, especially in the 1840s and 1850s, the state's legislators refused to budge and fended off attempts to introduce as grounds for divorce such offenses as drunkenness, desertion, cruel and inhuman treatment, and desertion to join an antimarriage sect such as the Shakers.

Unlike other states with limited divorce laws, New York did not provide ready access to legislative divorce in this period. Although many petitions for divorce were filed with the state legislature, the majority of them were rejected, and the few legislative divorces that were passed in New York attest to the determination of the petitioners more than to the preparedness of the legislators to exercise the power to dissolve marriages. One successful petition for a legislative divorce, involving a husband's cruelty, violence, and accusation that his wife had committed adultery with several men, was filed in 1809 and succeeded only after two years. Another, lodged by a woman whose husband joined a Shaker community and had taken their children with him, was filed in February 1815 and was finally passed in March 1818. Some divorce bills passed one house of the legislature but failed in the other, and other bills did not survive even the first legislative hurdle.

---

[129] The following discussion of New York's divorce law draws primarily on Blake, *Road to Reno*, 64–79. A further source is Henry H. Foster and Doris J. Freed, *Dissolution of the Family Unit* (New York, 1972), 256–71.

[130] Quoted in Blake, *Road to Reno*, 64. Beyond the restrictive terms of the divorce law, New York also recognized traditional grounds for the annulment of marriage, such as fraud, impotence, and coercion.

The net result was that New Yorkers had more limited access to divorce than the inhabitants of almost all other states during the nineteenth century. Only the unhappily married inhabitants of South Carolina, where there was no provision at all for divorce, might have looked enviously at New York. New York's matrimonial discontents looked in turn to states with more liberal divorce laws than their own. By the mid-nineteenth century migratory divorce was being discouraged in many states by the imposition of minimum residency requirements, although New York's Chancellor James Kent concluded that the severity of his state's divorce law was inducing those who wanted to divorce to seek one elsewhere.[131] Such divorces could be obtained in those parts of the Northeast that had more liberal laws. The fact that divorce migration should have taken place within the region testifies to the variety of legislation that persisted there from the colonial period through the nineteenth century.

The south of the United States met independence with a more homogeneous but quite different legal tradition from that of the northeastern states. Unlike their middle and northern counterparts, the southern colonies had failed to enact divorce legislation under British rule or to make other provision for the dissolution of marriages. Soon after independence, however, some southern states began to make divorce available by legislative act: Maryland granted its first legislative divorce in 1790[132] and North Carolina in 1794,[133] and the 1798 Georgia constitution allowed the legislature to dissolve marriages after a court had authorized divorce "upon legal principles."[134] From 1799 divorce laws began to be passed in the South. Tennessee led the way with a 1799 law, and it was followed by divorce legislation in Georgia (1802), Alabama Territories, which included Alabama and Mississippi (1803), Arkansas (1807), Kentucky (1809), North Carolina (1814), Florida (1827), Virginia (1827), Louisiana (1827), and Texas (1841).[135] South Carolina did not legalize divorce until 1872, and then only briefly: The law was repealed in 1878.[136] In most of the southern states the legislatures continued to play a role in dissolving marriages even after divorce laws were enacted. In some cases divorce actions were heard in a regular court, then sent to the legislature for confirmation and the actual decree of dissolution. In other states the legislature was specifically empowered to grant divorces in circumstances or on grounds not recognized by the divorce legislation it had passed. Gradually, however, the southern states sloughed off their legislative participation in divorce, and constitutional amendments forbidding legislative divorce were passed in Tennessee (1834), North Carolina

---

[131] Quoted in Foster and Freed, *Family Unit*, 258n.13.
[132] Blake, *Road to Reno*, 51.
[133] Joseph S. Ferrell, "Early Statutory and Common Law of Divorce in North Carolina," *North Carolina Law Review* 41 (1963), 604.
[134] Blake, *Road to Reno*, 52.
[135] Ibid., 50–6. See also Jane Turner Censer, "'Smiling Through Her Tears': Ante-Bellum Southern Women and Divorce," *American Journal of Legal History* 25 (1981), 24–47.
[136] Blake, *Road to Reno*, 234.

(1835), Arkansas (1836), Florida (1838), Louisiana (1845), Texas (1845), and Virginia (1850).[137]

Compared with the northeastern states, the South was tardy in making provision for divorce, but it would be wrong to see the region as having particularly restrictive divorce policies once they had legalized it. The southern states liberalized their divorce laws during the nineteenth century, and, even in the early decades, when the laws were not notably generous, some states provided access to legislative divorce as a supplementary recourse, allowing a more liberal divorce facility than that envisaged by statute alone. The preindependence tradition of the southern colonies in not providing for divorce, the striking example of South Carolina in resisting divorce through most of the nineteenth century and half of the twentieth, together with a general association of the South with conservative social policies have tended to produce an image of legal retardation with respect to divorce.[138] In fact the picture is much more complex and conflicting liberal and conservative pressures produced a generally liberalizing trend in divorce law and policy.

The development of North Carolina's divorce law is not typical of the South as a whole, but it is an example of the way one southern state's legislators wrestled with the divorce question. Divorce was unknown in North Carolina in the colonial period, and it was not until 1779 that there was a petition to the legislature for a dissolution of marriage. The first legislative divorce was not granted until 1794, however, and up to 1800 there were a further nine. North Carolina law did provide some surrogate relief for women who had fled from intolerable marriages, by passing acts granting alimony even though there was no divorce or even a judicial separation *a mensa et thoro*. For example, a court decision of 1796 determined that one Margaret Spiller had been forced to leave her husband's home on account of his cruel treatment. The court ordered the husband to pay his wife £100 a year for the rest of her life, as well as £200 to cover her living expenses between the dates of her leaving home and the court's decision.[139] Such judgments, although not affecting the legal status of the marriage concerned, at least permitted a wife to live independently of her husband.

From the 1790s, however, there was pressure for a more consistent response to such circumstances in the form of a general divorce law. In 1808 a bill was introduced that would have allowed divorce for reason of impotence, adultery, and cruelty on the part of the husband. The bill was published to permit public discussion, and provoked a predictable range of responses. One correspondent in the *Raleigh Register* in 1809 argued for judicial divorce over legislative divorce because the latter "employ a very considerable part of the time of the Legislature and of course consume a considerable part of the taxes which are

[137] Censer, "'Smiling Through Her Tears'," 26n.8.
[138] A general discussion is in Catherine Clinton, *The Plantation Mistress: Woman's World in the Old South* (New York, 1982), 80–5.
[139] Ferrell, "Law of Divorce in North Carolina," 620.

paid every year by the people."[140] Against arguments for the financial efficiency and general social utility of a divorce law, opponents raised the specter of social disintegration: A divorce law would "loosen the bands of Society and turn mankind upon each other like brutes."[141] Scenarios such as this helped to defeat the bill, which gained twenty-five votes to the thirty-five cast against it in the legislature.

When North Carolina's first divorce law was eventually passed, in 1814, it drew on the principles of the 1808 bill, but was more restrictive than had been envisaged at that time. It gave the courts the power to grant either a separation *a mensa et thoro* or a divorce, as they saw fit, for reason of natural impotence or adultery. A separation might also be obtained by a woman on grounds of desertion, cruel treatment, "such indignities to her person as to render her condition intolerable or life burthensome," or being evicted from the home.[142] Despite these relatively generous and flexible grounds for a separation at the request of a woman, divorce remained very restrictive, and the whole procedure for obtaining either kind of decree was surrounded by obstacles. In order to discourage hasty divorces sought in the heat of emotion, the legislators specified that any offenses alleged in a divorce action had to have existed for at least six months before the petition was filed. The final decree dissolving a marriage could not be issued until twelve months had elapsed from the time of the judgment. Finally, the court's decision had to be confirmed by the legislature before it became effective. If the petitioner survived this procedure (which might have necessitated a woman's tolerating her husband's being adulterous for six months, then living separate and perhaps without resources for twelve), then she (or he) was rewarded with a divorce that conferred the right of remarriage only on the innocent party.[143]

For seven years after the 1814 law made divorce available from the state courts, the North Carolina legislature did not dissolve any marriages (except to confirm divorces already granted by the courts, and that requirement of legislative confirmation was repealed in 1818). Even so, petitions continued to be lodged with the General Assembly by men and women who wanted divorces but whose circumstances were not covered by existing legislation. In 1821 the assembly resumed the practice of granting divorces by statute and had passed fifteen by 1827 when a law attempted to halt them. The preamble of this act complained that applications for divorces to the General Assembly "consume a considerable portion of time in their examination, and consequently retard the investigation of more important subjects of legislation." Having the courts alone deal with divorce would be less expensive for the state and provide more

[140] Quoted in Guion G. Johnson, *Ante-Bellum North Carolina: A Social History* (Chapel Hill, 1937), 217.
[141] Letter in *Raleigh Register*, June 8, 1809, quoted in ibid., 218.
[142] Ferrell, "Law of Divorce in North Carolina," 611. The following discussion of North Carolina's law draws on this useful article except where otherwise indicated.
[143] *North Carolina Session Laws*, 1814.

impartial justice to individuals.[144] Moreover, the 1827 act seemed to broaden the grounds for divorce by empowering the courts to dissolve marriages "whenever they may be satisfied...of the justice of such application."[145] This clause seemed to transfer the discretion, until then exercised by the legislature, to the courts, but North Carolina's judges took a restrictive view of the law and continued to limit divorce to the terms of the 1814 legislation. The state's chief justice, Thomas Ruffin, opposed the use of discretion, commenting, "I can not suppose...that the discretion conferred is a mere personal one, whether wild or sober, but must...be confined to those cases for which provision was before made by law."[146]

It was no doubt because of the judiciary's reluctance to apply a more liberal divorce code that legislative divorce began to appear again. Under continuing pressure from constituents who could not satisfy the narrow requirements of the law (or rather, the courts' narrow interpretation of the law), the General Assembly began to grant divorces once more in 1832. Only in 1835 (in which session alone fifteen marriages were dissolved) was a constitutional amendment passed that once and for all abolished the power of the state legislature to grant statutory divorces.

The development of North Carolina's divorce policy clearly had restrictive facets. The 1814 legislation was very limited in its scope, the procedure was difficult and demanding, and the principle of fault was more rigorously applied than in many other states. In North Carolina the guilty spouse could not remarry during the lifetime of the innocent one (but could do so once a widow or widower), and the 1827 act restated that principle more forcefully be specifying that a man or woman who remarried in contravention of this stipulation was guilty of bigamy, a crime that carried the death penalty. On the other hand legislative divorces provided a recourse for those men and women who could not prove their spouses naturally impotent or adulterous and yet who seemed deserving of a divorce. One study of legislative divorces in the state showed that they were granted most commonly on the grounds of desertion, "cohabitation with a Negro," adultery, separation, cruelty, prostitution, and wasting property, and yet other cases involved incompatibility, drunkenness, ill-temper, and indecent conduct. Even so, there were relatively few such divorces and the success rate of petitions was low. In twenty-six years between 1800 and 1835 (the records for ten years are missing), 266 divorce petitions were presented to the General Assembly, but only 52 (20%) were successful.[147] In all there were only about 62 legislative divorces between 1794, when they began, and 1835, when they were abolished.[148] The two methods of divorce – restrictive judicial and discretionary legislative – might have been inconvenient and might have

[144] Ferrell, "Law of Divorce in North Carolina," 610.
[145] Ibid., 612.
[146] Quoted in Censer, "'Smiling Through Her Tears'," 28.
[147] Johnson, *Ante-Bellum North Carolina*, 217ff., esp. 221.
[148] Ferrell, "Law of Divorce in North Carolina," 609.

permitted arbitrary decisions, but together they offered a more liberal divorce facility than some of the northern states. Moreover the 1827 law seemed designed to give the courts sole jurisdiction to exercise discretion to allow divorces in circumstances recognized by previous legislative dissolutions of marriage, a very wide range of grounds indeed. The courts declined this invitation and virtually forced the General Assembly back into the divorce business in 1832; if it had not resumed granting extralegal divorces at that time, divorce would have been more restrictive in practice than it had been since 1814.

As individual as North Carolina's early-nineteenth-century divorce history was, it shared certain characteristics with that of other southern states. Most abolished legislative divorce in the period from 1834 to the early 1850s, and from 1830 until the Civil War there was a general liberalization of divorce laws in the South. In many states this was done by accepting as grounds for divorce the generally more widely embracing grounds that had justified only a separation. Between 1835 and 1842 the grounds for divorce had been extended in this manner in Florida, Arkansas, Tennessee, and Mississippi. An 1826 Louisiana law allowed separations to be converted into divorces after a waiting period of two years (from 1857, after one year).[149] In North Carolina from the mid-1830s the courts finally began to use the omnibus clause of the 1827 law. In Virginia from 1853 the courts were empowered to grant divorces on such grounds as imprisonment, adultery, impotence, desertion for three years, conviction of an infamous offense before marriage without the knowledge of the other partner, and evidence that the wife had been pregnant by another man at the time of marriage or that she had been a prostitute.[150]

The process of divorce law liberalization was not always linear and smooth, as the example of North Carolina demonstrated and as the examples of Georgia and Missouri confirm. The 1798 Georgia constitution had provided for a two-stage divorce procedure: a court trial to authorize a divorce "on legal principles" (which were not specified) followed by an act, dissolving the marriage, passed by the legislature. Between 1798 and 1835, 291 such divorce acts had been passed, an average of 8 a year.[151] A constitutional amendment of 1835 permitted the courts alone to grant divorce when the parties had obtained concurrent verdicts from two special juries that they were entitled to divorce "on legal principles." But the whole process was thrown into doubt when in 1847 a justice of the Georgia supreme court ruled that the sole grounds for divorce in the state were those of the common law (old English ecclesiastical law). This allowed only annulment and separation, not divorce, and threatened to invalidate any marriages that had taken place as a result of divorces decreed in Georgia. The state legislature acted quickly to avert matrimonial chaos. In 1849 it passed an act validating all remarriages resulting from divorces in

---

[149] Censer, " 'Smiling Through Her Tears'," 26n.9.
[150] Howard, *Matrimonial Institutions*, III, 52.
[151] Blake, *Road to Reno*, 53.

Georgia, and the next year legalized divorce on eight grounds, including adultery, willful desertion for three years, and imprisonment for two or more years for a morals offense.[152]

In Missouri there was a battle for jurisdiction over divorce between the judiciary and the legislature, with dozens of unhappily married couples temporarily held hostage. The state had a divorce law, but, as in North Carolina, men and women continued to seek matrimonial relief from the legislature in order to circumvent the restrictions imposed by judicial divorce. In 1833 Governor Daniel Dunklin vetoed a legislative divorce bill, arguing that such bills were not only contrary to the state constitution but also that legislative divorces might not be recognized outside the state.[153] The legislature passed the divorce bill over the governor's veto, but undeterred, Governor Dunklin then vetoed a collective bill dissolving thirty-seven marriages. This too was passed over his veto, and so the process went on until forty-nine divorces had been dissolved in that one session, although the governor had assented to only two of them.[154] In the short term this jurisdictional struggle must have caused anguish to the couples involved, who were either married or divorced depending on whether it was the governor or the legislature that had had the last word, but over the longer term it produced a more liberal law. In 1835 the courts were permitted to grant divorces not only for adultery and desertion but also for habitual drunkenness and extreme cruelty. In addition, the law abolished separations and relaxed the prohibition on remarriage by the guilty partner in a divorce: As of 1835 he or she could remarry after a five-year probationary period.[155]

Divorce law liberalization was not always an easy road, then, but it was a road traveled by almost all of the southern states. Apart from South Carolina, all of the states that would later form the Confederacy had by 1860 included adultery, cruelty, and desertion among the grounds justifying divorce. Moreover, as Jane Turner Censer has shown, the liberalization of divorce policy in the South should be judged not simply by the terms of divorce legislation but also by court decisions. This was especially important in the definition of "cruelty" that was to be accepted in divorce actions. Although "adultery" and "desertion" could be defined and recognized in a relatively straightforward way, "cruelty" encompassed a wide spectrum of offenses. In its strict construction, cruelty was restricted to physical violence that went beyond the limits of moderate correction and actually threatened the life or health of the victim. In the divorce courts of the South this limited definition was progressively eroded and discarded. Verbal violence and threats began to be included, as were general

---

[152] Ibid., 53–4.
[153] Chancellor James Kent of New York had suggested that legislative divorces might not be valid outside the state where they had been obtained because such divorces were, in effect, statutes. For one to have effect in another state would give the appearance of one state's dictating law to another. James Kent, *Commentaries on American Law* (2nd edn., New York, 1832), II, 117.
[154] Blake, *Road to Reno*, 55–6.
[155] Ibid., 56.

insults and imputations of immorality. An 1836 Louisiana court ruled that "a series of studied vexations and provocations on the part of the husband, without even resorting to personal violence might constitute that degree of cruel treatment and outrages..."[156] An 1849 Arkansas court ruling listed the following acts as constituting a personal indignity: rudeness, vulgarity, unmerited reproach, contumely and studied neglect, intentional incivility, injury, manifest disdain, abusive language, malignant ridicule, "and every other plain manifestation of settled hate, alienation and estrangement, both of word and action."[157] When such indignities were "habitual, continuous and permanent," they could justify a divorce.

The notable exception to the expanding definition of cruelty was Mississippi, where an 1856 ruling held that "mere intemperance in a man's habits, harshness of manner and...indecency of conduct are not sufficient. The cruelty must be something more than mere injuries to a person's sensibility or sense of delicacy."[158] It was just this sense of injury to sensibility and delicacy that lay beneath the liberalization of divorce policy in the South. Petitioners for divorce in the southern states were, above all, women from well-to-do families,[159] and their status produced a lowering of the threshold of tolerable behavior. Whereas women of the lower classes might be expected to put up with domestic violence and crude language, one judge argued, "between persons of education, refinement and delicacy, the slightest blow in anger might be cruelty."[160]

The overall image of divorce in the South in the first half of the nineteenth century is far more complex than a broad survey indicates. It is clear, however, that even though the southern colonies did not permit divorce, and although the South started legalizing divorce more slowly after independence than the northeastern states, there was still a comparable trend of liberalization of law and policy and a transfer of jurisdiction from legislatures to courts. By the outbreak of the Civil War, in fact, the southern states had adopted policies about as liberal as those in force in the Northeast. South Carolina was recalcitrant, but it was no more typical of the South than the restrictive divorce law of New York was representative of the laws of its neighboring states in the North.

If the South had a reputation (little deserved) for conservatism in policies related to divorce, it was balanced by the association of the West with matrimonial libertarianism. As the American West opened up during the nineteenth century, the territories, then the states that were formed from them, quickly gained notoriety for divorce laws that were wide-ranging in their grounds, lax in their operation, and whose minimal residency requirements

---

[156] Quoted in Censer, "'Smiling Through Her Tears'," 33.
[157] Quoted in ibid., 29.
[158] Ibid., 34.
[159] Ibid., 37n.44.
[160] Judge George Goldthwaite, quoted in ibid., 35.

seemed to invite migratory divorce. Was this reputation, like that of the South, a result of association with other social values? "The West" surely conjured up an image of a rough, violent, transient society of men and horses, hardly conducive to the formation and survival of stable marriages and families. This popular image of the "wild" West, however, has misrepresented the essentially traditional character of social structure and relationships in the western states, where, as elsewhere, marriage and the family were important fundamental institutions. For example, one study shows that nine out of ten women who traveled west in the mid-nineteenth century had married by the age of twenty-five, and eight out of ten men had done so by the age of thirty.[161] Gunsmoke from the clashes of independent men has too often obscured the dominant reality of family life in the little house on the prairie, in the hills, and on the Pacific coast. But if the image of society has been distorted, the association of the West with very liberal divorce policies has not. As in the Northeast and the South, there was no uniformity in divorce legislation in the Midwest and West, but even so the divorce laws were generally more liberal than elsewhere. This fact, together with other social factors, combined to produce the particularly high divorce rates in the western United States in the later nineteenth and twentieth centuries.

One reason for the rapid installation of liberal divorce laws in the West was the simple fact that these states entered the union at a time when divorce policy was being liberalized in the older established parts of the country. The legislators of the new states, drawing on their experience and knowledge of the East and looking there for precedent or guidance in developing civil and constitutional law, would surely have noted the trend toward divorce law reform. They might well have adopted liberal divorce policies more readily than their eastern counterparts, many of whom had to deal with legal traditions set firmly against liberal divorce, as the examples of North Carolina and New York showed. Developing law from first principles and without precedent is surely easier than reversing established legal tendencies and traditions. What is certain is that the western states wasted little time in legalizing divorce. Ohio, for example, gained statehood in 1802 and passed a divorce law in 1804; Illinois became a state in 1818 and legalized divorce the following year; whereas Michigan took a little longer, passing its first divorce law in 1812, seven years after entering the union.[162] This common readiness to enact divorce laws apart, though, the individual states followed their own paths of legal and institutional development in respect of divorce.

Ohio's 1804 law recognized four grounds for divorce – bigamy, adultery, extreme cruelty, and willful absence for five years – and these terms were progressively extended. In 1822 the period of absence was reduced to three years and two new grounds were added: physical incompetence for intercourse

---

[161] John Mack Faragher, *Women and Men on the Overland Trail* (New Haven, 1979), 144–6. See also Sandra L. Myres, *Westering Women and the Frontier Experience* (Albuquerque, 1982), 173ff.
[162] Howard, *Matrimonial Institutions*, III, 113–15.

at the time of marriage and imprisonment for a crime. In 1853 the grounds were again extended, this time to encompass fraudulant contract (in marriage), gross neglect of duty, habitual drunkenness, and cases where one spouse had been divorced before and had married in violation of a prohibition on remarriage imposed by the divorce law of another state.[163] Two points might be noted here. The first is that there was a blurring of grounds for dissolution and for annulment: The act made no distinction. Second, the last ground reflected awareness, probably resulting from specific cases, of the problems that arose from differing state laws on marriage and divorce. These legal variations permitted men and women, banned from marriage in one state, to travel to another and marry there. It is interesting that Ohio, which permitted both divorced spouses – petitioner and defendant, innocent and guilty – to remarry, should have enacted a law upholding the more restrictive provisions in force in certain other states.

By midcentury, Ohio law recognized ten grounds for divorce, but Indiana had gone even further. Indiana's territorial legislature had begun to dissolve marriages as early as 1807, and did so on 104 occasions between 1807 and 1846,[164] and a general divorce law was passed in 1824. It encompassed matrimonial offenses such as inhuman treatment, adultery, and abandonment, but also included an omnibus clause allowing for divorce "in all cases where the court in its discretion thinks it just and reasonable."[165] This law was confirmed without substantial changes in 1831 and 1843, and in 1852 new legislation set down seven grounds for divorce: adultery, impotence, abandonment for one year, cruel treatment, habitual drunkenness or the husband's failure to provide, conviction of an infamous crime, or– this was the omnibus clause rephrased – "any other cause for which the court shall deem it proper that the divorce shall be granted."[166] These provisions were liberal enough, but access to divorce in Indiana was made even easier by minimal residency requirements. The 1824 law required nothing more than residence in the county where the divorce petition was lodged, at the time it was lodged. In 1831 and 1843 the period of residence was increased to twelve and twenty-four months, respectively, but a study of Indiana divorce suggests that these requirements were not enforced, and the state's 1852 divorce act reflected this reality by specifying no minimum period of residence. Thenceforth a divorce petitioner had to be a bona fide resident of the county which the petition was filed, but the petitioner's own affidavit sufficed and no additional evidence was demanded.[167] This lax policy provided the basis for Indiana's reputation as a divorce haven and for the phenomenon of "Indiana divorces," analogous to later Mexican divorces or Reno divorces.

[163] Ibid., III, 113–15.
[164] Richard Wires, *The Divorce Issue and Reform in Nineteenth-Century Indiana* (Muncie, 1967), 3.
[165] Howard, *Matrimonial Institutions*, III, 115.
[166] Wires, *Divorce Issue*, 11.
[167] Ibid., 14.

Other western states went through similar stages of development, setting out specific grounds for divorce, then moving to omnibus clauses. Illinois, for example, provided three grounds in 1819, expanded them to six in 1827, and added an omnibus clause in 1832, before extending the grounds further in 1845.[168] This example highlights a characteristic of western states' divorce laws: the continual tinkering with legislation so that successive statutes were enacted, amended, and repealed in constant succession. We may take Iowa as a further example of this tendency. The first state law on divorce was passed in 1838. It was repealed the following year and replaced by a new statute, which in turn was replaced three years later, in 1842. In 1846 an omnibus clause was added to allow divorce "when it shall be made fully apparent to the satisfaction of the court, that the parties cannot live in peace and happiness together."[169] Five years later, in 1851, this law was amended, and in 1855 provision for separation was added. In 1858, as a final act before the Civil War provided an intermission in this ongoing legislative drama, Iowa's legislators revived the terms of the 1851 statute with a few modifications. Such a process ensured that the subject of divorce was constantly before the lawmakers and reveals the sensitivity of divorce as an area of legislation.

There were significant variations among the divorce laws of the midwestern and western states, but their liberal tendency is quite clear. Omnibus clauses giving the courts broad discretion and creating the potential for a progressive and even radical lessening in the seriousness of offenses that could justify a divorce, were widely enacted. There were important exceptions to this, however. California's first divorce law (1851) provided only specified grounds for divorce (impotence, adultery, extreme cruelty, desertion or neglect, habitual intemperance, fraud, and conviction for a felony). This was an especially influential law because it was used as a model for other western states such as Montana, Idaho, the Dakotas, and Nevada. This influence says something for the coherence of the 1851 California legislation, as does the fact that, unlike their counterparts elsewhere, California lawmakers did not fiddle ceaselessly with the legislation. Formal liberalization did little more than reduce the periods of intemperance, desertion, or neglect that had to be proved, from three years to two (1870) and then to one (1872). The courts, too, liberalized divorce provisions by extending the definitions of existing grounds, just as judges in the South had done. One 1857 California decision, for example, ruled that "women's finer sensibilities deserved respect and that imprecation as to her sexual conduct constituted cruelty."[170] The judge in this case explicitly rejected the traditional legal notion that cruelty necessarily involved physical violence. Similarly an 1863 decision recognized mental cruelty, and contributed to a redefinition of cruelty in the

[168] Howard, *Matrimonial Institutions*, III, 119.
[169] Ibid., III, 125–6.
[170] Robert L. Griswold, *Family and Divorce in California, 1850–1890* (Albany, N.Y., 1982), 19.

454

1870 statute.[171] The example serves to emphasize the point that it is necessary to go beyond the formal terms of divorce legislation in order to understand the trends in overall divorce policy.

Not only was western divorce liberal in terms of the law and its application, but these states generally required shorter periods of residence to qualify for filing a petition. The maximum residence requirement was three years, but most were set at one year. Others, however, were less: Nebraska, Idaho, and Nevada demanded only six months' residence, and South Dakota's was set at ninety days.[172] Utah went even further in a liberal direction and specified that a divorce petitioner had to demonstrate that he or she was "a resident or wishes to become one."[173] This section of Utah's 1852 divorce law, combined with specified grounds for divorce and an omnibus clause allowing judicial discretion, gained Utah instant notoriety among Americans concerned about the decline of marriage and the family.[174]

Interest in the state of marriage in Utah was heightened by the practice of polygamy by the Mormons who had settled there. Polygamy was an integral part of Mormon theology that virtually placed an obligation on men in the church to produce many children, a duty enhanced by plural marriage.[175] This policy attracted a campaign of opposition that culminated in action by the federal government. Even though a federal law against bigamy had been passed in 1862, it was not made effective until 1882 when an act outlawing polygamy denied the vote and the right to hold office to those guilty of "unlawful cohabitation." Polygamous Mormons were prosecuted and jailed, and in 1889 a bill proposed the disenfranchisement of all Mormons on the ground that simple belief in polygamy was sufficient to exclude an individual from voting rights. In 1890 the Mormons' leaders issued a manifesto advising them "to refrain from contracting any marriage forbidden by the law of this land."[176] Specific issues such as this kept the more general question of marriage and the family in the public mind, and divorce was a constant point of reference.

It was not only liberal divorce policies that began to ring alarm bells in the minds of conservatives but also a belief that the laws were being used, that large numbers of marriages were being dissolved, and that many marriages were breaking down on account of the easy availability of divorce. Unfortunately there are few reliable statistics for divorce until the last third of the nineteenth

---

[171] Ibid., 20. On this trend specifically, see Griswold's interesting article "The Evolution of the Doctrine of Mental Cruelty in Victorian American Divorce, 1790–1900," *Journal of Social History* 19 (1986), 127–48.
[172] Howard, *Matrimonial Institutions*, III. 157.
[173] Ibid., III, 131.
[174] Ibid., III, 131–32.
[175] For concise accounts of polygamy in Mormon theology, see Klaus J. Hansen, *Mormonism and the American Experience* (Chicago, 1981), esp. 80–1, 147–78; John Cairncross, *After Polygamy was Made a Sin* (London, 1974), 166–97.
[176] Hansen, *Mormonism*, 145.

century because the states did not make provision for the collection and publication of such data until the very end of that century or the beginning of the twentieth.[177] Tardiness in this respect is all the more surprising given the growing concern at the number of divorces after the Civil War. There are indications as to the number of legislative divorces in various states, however. For example the Ohio legislature had granted more than a hundred divorces by 1850, and the Kansas legislature had dissolved one marriage in 1857, three in 1858, eight in 1859, and forty-three in 1860.[178] The dramatic rise was no doubt the result of an amendment banning legislative divorce, passed in 1859 to come into effect later in 1860; clearly many men and women rushed to divorce before the legislative avenue was blocked. By the end of the Civil War, though, legislative divorce had ceased to be significant; by 1867 thirty-three of the then-existing thirty-seven states had prohibited the practice.[179]

The first major tremors of anxiety over the divorce rate in the United States were provoked by the number of divorces granted in some of the midwestern states, particularly in Indiana, Ohio, South Dakota, and Illinois. In the mid-nineteenth century the high divorce rates in these states were attributed to the liberal character of their laws. In Indiana, the relative ease of divorce in statutory terms was compounded by procedural laxity, and although there was a two-year residence requirement it was seldom enforced.[180] Indiana's 1851 constitution prohibited legislative divorce (there had been forty-one of them in 1846 alone), but the 1852 divorce law promised to allow even more divorces in that it recognized seven grounds for divorce and effectively abandoned any residence requirement.[181]

Concern at the divorce rates current in the Midwest was expressed by prominent social and political commentators and the editor of the *New York Tribune*, Horace Greeley. In 1852 and 1853 the *Tribune* had published a series of articles on marriage and divorce by Henry James (father of Henry James the novelist) and by Stephen Pearl Andrews, a former minister who had converted to the ideology of free love.[182] Early in life, Greeley had been attracted to Fourier's ideas, but opposed his sexual and marriage doctrines, and by the 1850s he had marked out his own position of firm opposition to divorce. Greeley favored indissoluble marriage, although he reluctantly admitted that Christ's words appeared to allow divorce for reason of adultery. His prognostication of the results of allowing divorce was dire:

Marriage indissoluble may be an imperfect test of honorable and pure affection – as all things human are imperfect – but it is the best man can devise, and its overthrow would

[177] Howard, *Matrimonial Institutions*, III, 30, 95, 160.
[178] Ibid., III, 98.
[179] Blake, *Road to Reno*, 56.
[180] Wires, *Divorce Issue*, 13–14.
[181] Ibid., 11–14.
[182] For a synopsis, see Blake, *Road to Reno*, 82–7.

result in a general profligacy and corruption such as this country has never known, and few of our people can adequately imagine.[183]

In 1860, prompted by yet another attempt to have New York's divorce law liberalized, Greeley returned to the subject: "Our Legislature is again importuned to try its hand at increasing the facilities of Divorce. We trust it will ponder long and carefully before it consents."[184] Greeley was more fortunate than earlier opponents of divorce in that he did not have to go back to the decay of Rome or the chaos of the French Revolution for apparent evidence of the social disintegration wrought by divorce. To the West lay Indiana, which Greeley characterized as "the paradise of free-lovers" where men and women could "get unmarried nearly at pleasure." He attributed this deplorable state to the "lax principles of Robert Dale Owen,"[185] a member of the Indiana legislature and son of the Utopian socialist reformer Robert Owen, whose divorce doctrines are discussed in Section 12.2. Greeley's famous dictum "Go West young man" was evidently not directed to unhappily married men looking for a divorce haven.

Greeley's attack on Indiana's divorce laws, the rate of divorce there, and on Owen specifically provoked a long series of exchanges between the two men in the *New York Tribune*. Greeley must have thought that he came out ahead, for he later published the correspondence in full in his memoirs.[186] The debate was, in fact, more productive of heat than light. Owen argued that he was not solely responsible for Indiana's divorce policy (he had sponsored an amendment making habitual drunkenness a ground for divorce), but he defended his state's laws as more likely than New York's to produce morality. In New York, he wrote, "you have elopements, adultery, which your law virtually encourages; you have free-love, and that most terrible of all social evils, prostitution."[187] Owen argued vigorously against the limited Christian view of divorce for adultery only, against separations ("of all the various kinds of divorce...the most immoral in its tendency"),[188] and against the idea that procreation was the main end of marriage. The chief end, he countered, was to produce "all that is best and purest in the inner nature of man, love in the broadest acceptation of that much profaned word."[189] According to Owen, it was not enough to say that a marriage *might* be dissolved if the ends of marriage were frustrated or it were "defiled by evil passions"; in such cases "for the sake of virtue and for the good of mankind...[the marriage] *ought* to cease."[190]

---

[183] *New York Tribune* (hereafter referred to as *Tribune*), December 18, 1852, quoted in Blake, *Road to Reno*, 84. Subsequent quotations from the *Tribune* are from ibid., 84–92.
[184] *Tribune*, March 1, 1860.
[185] Ibid.
[186] Horace Greeley, *Recollections of a Busy Life* (New York, 1869), 570–618.
[187] *Tribune*, March 5, 1860.
[188] Ibid., March 12, 1860.
[189] Ibid., March 17, 1860.
[190] Ibid., March 28, 1860.

In his own contributions to the debate Greeley repeated the doctrine of marital indissolubility and its religious justifications. But he went further and considered the social implications of divorce. Marriage, he insisted, was divinely designed for parentage, for the continuation of the human race, and for this purpose a stable marriage was indispensable: "That each child should enjoy protection, nurture, sustenance, at the hands of a mother not only but a father also. In other words, the parents should be so attached, so devoted to each other, that they shall be practically separable but by death."[191] In Greeley's eyes there were two advantages to restricting, or better still abolishing, divorce. First, restrictive divorce laws would act as a deterrent against hasty marriages or marriages for the wrong reasons: "To the libertine, the egotist, the selfish, sensual seeker of personal and present enjoyment at whatever cost to others, the Indissolubility of Marriage is an obstacle, a restraint, a terror; and God forbid that it should ever cease to be."[192] The second point was that lax divorce laws encouraged ill-assorted unions, then encouraged their collapse. Greeley did not impugn the morality of the inhabitants of Indiana; most of them were moral, he said, because they came from states where marriage was indissoluble – an odd assertion because only South Carolina held to this principle. But he argued that in time, and under the influence of Owenite divorce policy, Indiana would follow the example of Rome, "which under the sway of easy divorce, rotted away and perished, – blasted by the mildew of unchaste mothers and dissolute homes."[193]

The debate on divorce was itself blasted from the pages of the *New York Tribune* and American popular awareness generally by the outbreak of the Civil War in 1861. After the war, however, the concerns at the divorce rates, which had arisen in the 1850s, developed into a full-scale reaction against divorce. Again the provocation was a rise in the number of divorces. It is likely that divorces decreased somewhat between 1861 and 1865 while the war was in progress, but like most military conflicts, the Civil War was followed by a marked, if short-lived, increase in divorces. Statistics for this period are not wholly reliable, but one calculation suggests that the combined numbers of divorces, separations, and annulments in the United States were as shown in Table 11.1. The few available state-based divorce statistics generally confirm this tendency of decline during the war years or increase in the immediate post-war period. The annual number of divorces in three New England states between 1860 and 1870 is given in Table 11.2.

We should want much more detail on these divorces before making precise statements as to the reasons in the annual changes in the number of divorces, but several explanations, based on the study of divorce in other times of military conflict, suggest themselves. Any decline in the number of divorce petitions during the war probably reflected the separation of wives and husbands as

---

[191] Ibid., March 17, 1860.
[192] Ibid., April 7, 1860.
[193] Ibid., March 5, 1860.

11.8 The United States

Table 11.1. *Divorces, separations, and annulments by year: United States, 1860–70*

Year	Number	Rate per 1,000 population	Rate per 1,000 existing marriages
1860	7,380	0.3	1.2
1861	6,540	0.2	1.1
1862	6,230	0.2	1.0
1863	6,760	0.2	1.1
1864	8,940	0.2	1.4
1865	10,090	0.3	1.6
1866	11,530	0.3	1.8
1867	9,937	0.3	1.5
1868	10,150	0.3	1.5
1869	10,939	0.3	1.6
1870	10,962	0.3	1.5

Note: The base population excludes slaves to 1865.
Source: Richard Wires, *The Divorce Issue and Reform in Nineteenth-Century Indiana* (Muncie, 1967), 7.

Table 11.2. *Divorces by year: Massachusetts, Vermont, and Connecticut, 1860–70*

Year	Massachusetts	Vermont	Connecticut
1860	243	95	282
1861	234	66	275
1862	196	94	257
1863	207	102	291
1864	270	98	426
1865	333	122	404
1866	392	155	488
1867	282	159	459
1868	339	167	478
1869	339	148	491
1870	379	164	408

Source: Nathan Allen, "Divorces in New England," *North American Review* 130 (1880), 549.

the latter were away on military service. In the most banal sense, separation removed temporarily the sources of marital tension and unhappiness, and in fact the massive death toll during the Civil War must have dissolved some marriages that would otherwise have ended in the divorce courts.[194] But if absence

---

[194] The death toll in the American Civil War, about 365,000 in all, was more than three times the number of Americans killed in World War I and almost as many as in World War II.

on military service ameliorated some marriages for a short time, demobilization and the return to married life from 1864 and 1865 was evidently accompanied by a rise in the number of divorces. No doubt some were based on adultery that had taken place while the spouses were separated, whereas others reflected the difficulties of readjustment to marriage after a year or more of separation. It is important to note that the shifts in the number of divorces were small in absolute terms, but the increase in divorce in postbellum America was relatively significant. From Table 11.1 it appears that between 1861 and 1865 (the war years) there was an annual average of 6,510 separations, divorces, and annulments of marriage, whereas between 1865 and 1867 the average was 10,519, representing an increase of 60%. The increase between these periods in Massachusetts, Vermont, and Connecticut (Table 11.2) show the same tendency: Divorces rose between 58% and 67% between the wartime and postwar periods. However, the rate, calculated in terms of population or marriages, changed very little as Table 11.1 indicates.

It was enough that the number was increasing however, and the impression of spreading marital destruction in a period of national reconstruction brought a quick response from the social saviors of the time. The president of Yale University, Theodore Woolsey, following in the footsteps of his predecessor Timothy Dwight, published a series of articles in 1867 on the history of divorce. He drew a warning from history (specifically from Rome, of course) that America was showing signs of increasing vice, materialism, and "corruption in the family, as manifested by connubial unfaithfulness and divorce." Making a more contemporary reference Woolsey concluded

We have got rid of one of [Rome's] curses, slavery, and that is a great ground of hope for the future. But whether we are to be a thoroughly Christian nation, or are destined to decay and loss of our present political forms, depends upon our ability to keep family life pure and simple.[195]

Nor was Woolsey's a lone voice. Among others, a Connecticut pastor criticized divorce as leading to bigamy and polygamy, and the rector of Trinity College argued that divorce led to the breakdown of the family and ultimately to communism.[196]

The pressure by Woolsey and other opponents of divorce in Connecticut in the postbellum period had immediate and far-reaching effects. The immediate impact was on his state's divorce legislation. Connecticut's legislature set up a committee to investigate the divorce rates, and the rising number of divorces revealed by the study, together with lobbying by Woolsey and other clergymen for restrictions on divorce, led the legislators in 1878 to repeal the 1849 amendment that had permitted divorce for the discretionary reason of "misconduct which permanently destroys the happiness of the petitioner and

---

[195] Quoted in Nathan Allen, "Divorces in New England," *North American Review* 130 (1880), 563n.

[196] Cohn, "Connecticut's Divorce Mechanism," 48.

defeats the purpose of the marriage relation."[197] Two years later a mandatory waiting period of ninety days was introduced between the lodging and hearing of an uncontested petition for divorce. Encouraged by these successes, Woolsey and Samuel Dike, a Congregational minister from Vermont, founded the New England Divorce Reform League in 1881. This organization, which underwent several changes of name – it became the National Divorce Reform League in 1885 and the National League for the Protection of the Family in 1897 – was the first organized opposition to liberal divorce policies and the rising divorce rate. Its creation reflected the unease that was spreading throughout America and Western society generally.

11.9 The rise of divorce and the conservative reaction

During the last decades of the nineteenth century, a period of general social conservatism throughout the world, divorce became a major issue of social debate; it became, as William O'Neill put it, "one of the first aspects of what we call the Revolution in Morals to become a matter of public controversy."[198] Many issues were drawn into the vortex of the debate, and although divorce was generally dealt with in moral terms – that is, in terms of its effects on individual and social morality – it was also approached from many other perspectives. Ironically for a period that was apparently secularizing, the dominant tendency was for the disputants to assert and reassert the religious bases for the various divorce policies they advocated. But the secular interests were well represented, too, by those who argued that marriage and divorce should not be determined by religious considerations at all, let alone by one particular religious point of view. The emerging social scientists had their input as well, and attempted to promote an understanding of the rising divorce rate in social, economic, and environmental terms, rather than as an indicator of increasing moral laxness. Finally, divorce became caught up in other moral and social issues that exercised conservative and even not-so-conservative minds: sexuality (especially venereal disease and prostitution); the continuing pressure of the women's rights movements, and its implications for family life; abuse of alcohol (reflected in the temperance movement); and the control of mental defectiveness (which provoked the eugenics movement). Because the reaction against divorce and divorces took root most firmly first in the United States, our consideration of the divorce debates and their implications will start there. But it is important to realise that the reactionary current flowed through Western society generally, and the following pages deal with it internationally.

We should begin by asking what the conservative reaction was reacting against: Were increasing marriage breakdown and divorce merely a perception,

---

[197] Lynne Carol Halem, *Divorce Reform: Changing Legal and Social Perspectives* (New York, 1980), 34; Blake, *Road to Reno*, 131. This legal change is not mentioned in Cohn, "Connecticut's Divorce Mechanism."

[198] William L. O'Neill, *Divorce in the Progressive Era* (New York, 1963), vii.

or were they established facts? Initially the divorce reform (that is, antidivorce) movement in America had few reliable statistics on divorce, although the number of divorces in four New England states had been published by Nathan Allen in 1880 to prove that the "evils of divorce" were spreading.[199] These statistics and Allen's conclusions contributed to the formation of the New England Divorce Reform League in the following year, and the league subsequently petitioned Congress for an official study of divorce on a national basis. The lobbying was successful, and in 1889 the Department of Labor published a report on marriage and divorce in the United States from 1867 to 1886.[200] This report, as faulty as it was in its data collection,[201] demonstrated that what the conservatives had claimed and feared was true, that the numbers of divorces in the United States had risen dramatically during this twenty-year period; in 1867 there had been 9,937 divorces, but in 1886 there had been 25,535, a more than 150% increase. Part, but only part, of the increase could be explained by the growth of population; between 1870 and 1880 the population had grown by 30%, but annual divorces had increased by almost 80%.[202] Even so, the absolute number of divorces was fairly small in relation to population, as is indicated by the fact that between 1867 and 1886 the divorce rate scarcely moved: it rose from 0.3 to 0.4 divorces per thousand population.[203]

The 1870s and 1880s were only a prelude, however. From that time divorces took off to levels that were not only unprecedented but also unanticipated except in the worst-case scenarios projected by opponents of divorce. The number of divorces and divorce rates are given in Table 11.3, which indicates the progress of divorce in the United States. Such increases easily outstripped population growth. Between 1880 and 1890 divorces increased by 70%, population by 26%; between 1890 and 1900 the increases were of the order 67% and 21%, respectively.[204]

The United States was not atypical. Elsewhere in Western society divorces increased during the long nineteenth century (that is, up to the outbreak of World War I). In France, where divorce had been legalized in 1884, the number of divorces rose from 4,227 in 1885 to 6,751 ten years later, and then to 14,261 by 1910.[205] In other countries divorces were fewer in absolute terms, yet showed even more significant increases. Annual divorces in England and Wales increased more than fivefold between 1867 and 1910 (there were 119

[199] Allen, "Divorce in New England," 547. Statistics on divorces, marriages, and divorce: marriage ratios are given in this source, 549–50.
[200] Carroll D. Wright, *A Report on Marriage and Divorce in the United States, 1867 to 1886* (Washington, D. C., 1889).
[201] See Blake, *Road to Reno*, 134.
[202] Wright, *Report*, 139–40.
[203] *Historical Statistics of the United States, 1789–1945: A Supplement to the Statistical Abstract of the United States* (Washingtion, D. C. 1949), 49.
[204] Griswold, *Family and Divorce*, 1.
[205] Wesley D. Camp, *Marriage and the Family in France Since the Revolution* (New York, 1961), 80–1, Table 24.

Table 11.3. *Divorces and divorce rates by decade: United States, 1860–1910*

Year	Divorces	Rate per 1,000 population	Rate per 1,000 existing marriages
1860	7,380	0.2	1.2
1870	10,962	0.3	1.2
1880	19,663	0.4	2.2
1890	33,461	0.5	3.0
1900	55,751	0.7	4.0
1910	83,045	0.9	4.5

Sources: Paul H. Jacobson and Pauline F. Jacobson, *American Marriage and Divorce* (New York, 1959), 90; *Historical Statistics of the United States, 1789–1945*, 49.

and 588 divorce petitions in those years, respectively),[206] and divorces in Belgium rose from 55 in 1860, to 373 in 1890, and then to 1,089 in 1910.[207] Figure 11.1 shows the number of divorces in five jurisdictions between 1860 and 1910 and gives an idea of the general pace of increase as well as of the differences among them in terms of absolute numbers. This figure graphically shows how easily the number of divorces in the United States outstripped those in Europe by the beginning of the twentieth century. To make the point a little more precisely, we can put it this way: In 1910 there were 83,045 divorces in the United States compared to a combined total of 20,329 in England, Scotland, France (which alone contributed 14,261 of the total), Belgium, the Netherlands, Switzerland, Norway, Denmark, and Sweden.[208]

With the exception of the United States, the simple number of divorces involved was hardly striking by late-twentieth-century standards, as divorce rates show. Expressed as a crude rate per thousand population, divorces in the United States grew from 0.3 in 1870 to 0.7 in 1900 and then to 0.9 on the eve of World War I.[209] That represented the West's highest divorce rate at the time: In 1910 no European country registered a divorce rate above 0.5 per thousand population (Switzerland's was 0.41, France's 0.36), and most fell below 0.2 divorces per thousand.[210] But to contemporaries the thought that these statistics of divorce might pale into insignificance by later standards was

[206] *Royal Commission, Report 1951–1955*, 358, Table 2.
[207] Wilfred Dumon, "Belgium," in Chester, *Divorce in Europe*, 135, Table 1.
[208] Statistics are drawn from *Royal Commission, Report 1951–1955*, 368, Table 5. Comparative populations in 1910 were as follows: United States, 92 million; European countries, 108 million.
[209] Paul H. Jacobson and Pauline F. Jacobson, *American Marriage and Divorce* (New York, 1959), 90, Table 42.
[210] Crude divorce rates in 1910 were as follows: England, 0.02; Scotland, 0.05; France, 0.36; Belgium, 0.15; Netherland, 0.15; Switzerland, 0.41; Norway, 0.17; Denmark, 0.30; Sweden, 0.11; Canada, 0.01; New Zealand, 0.16; Australia, 0.11. Source: *Royal Commission, Report 1951–1955*, 368, Table 5. World wide, the U. S. rate was exceeded only by Japan's.

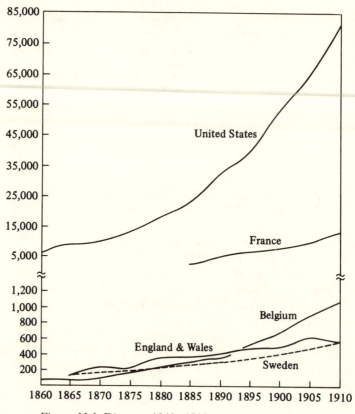

Figure 11.1 Divorces 1860–1910 in selected countries.

hardly a consolation. On the contrary, it was the very belief that divorces, if unchecked would grow to appalling proportions, that reinforced the concerted reaction against the tide of divorce. America was a constant point of reference. Conservatives and reactionaries in the United States, needless to say, concentrated on the divorce problems there: the rise of divorce havens in some states, the general ease of divorce law throughout the nation, and their increased use. Conservatives in other countries, for their part, held America up as an example of what the future held for them if they did not contain divorce quickly. Arguing against divorce liberalization, politicians in New Zealand, a far-off British colony, regularly flayed America for its "general carelessness with regard to the marriage tie." One Member of Parliament attributed the high divorce rate in the United States to the fact that "large numbers of families. . . live in hotels," and others, less given to generalization, distinguished states with easy divorce from those with restrictive legislation; New England states were described as permitting "successive polygamy," whereas it was argued that in New York and South Carolina "where marriages are almost indissoluble, the people are better in their social life and altogether of a better character."[211] The constant fear was that New Zealand – and it was a fear echoed in other countries – would eventually suffer the same moral decline as the United States was undergoing.

It is likely that the country most concerned with American states' liberalism in divorce policy was Canada, where divorce law generally lagged behind Western trends. This fact heightened the contrast between Canada and its neighbors to the south and was exploited by Canadians anxious to define a national identity and character distinct from that of America. Divorce was frequently cited by Canadian commentators, who pointed to the rarity of divorce in their own country with the excesses in some American states. Between 1867 and 1907 there were 431 divorces in Canada, compared with 1,274,341 in the United States. Even allowing for different population bases, divorce was 230 times more common in America than in Canada.[212] Canadian observers tended to overlook the fact that divorce was available from the courts in the United States, whereas in Ontario and many other provinces divorce could be obtained only by special Act of Parliament, a time-consuming and expensive process. Instead of recognizing the effect of legal and institutional differences, Canadians drew moral conclusions, seeing in the higher American divorce rate evidence of a moral inferiority. In 1880, for example, the *Canadian Methodist Magazine* commented that "we are free from many of the social cancers which are empoisoning the national life of our neighbours. We have no polygamous Mormondom; no Ku-Klux terrorism; no Oneida communism; no Illinois divorce system; no cruel Indian massacres."[213] In 1910 the chancellor of McGill University in Montreal drew the social contexts of divorce even more clearly. The causes of the high divorce rates included the nervous irritability of leading life at high pressure and the economic independence of women, but most of all the absence of social restraint among Americans; "the same spirit which, carried to the extreme length, is manifested in lynchings and murders finds a milder expression in the intolerance of control in the family."[214]

Organized religion was to the fore everywhere in the fight against divorce. This marked a change because although individual clergymen had been prominent critics of divorce, the churches had generally not played a major and consistent role in the divorce debate. The notable exception was the Roman Catholic church, which constituted a permanent and continuous opposition to divorce, but even this opposition intensified in the second half of the nineteenth century. The Syllabus of Errors promulgated by Pope Pius IX in 1864 devoted ten of its eighty articles to the family and denounced civil marriage and divorce

---

[211] Quoted in Phillips, *Divorce in New Zealand*, 19, 30–1.
[212] Carl Berger, *The Sense of Power: Studies in the Ideas of Canadian Imperialism, 1867–1914* (Toronto, 1967), 160. See also Backhouse, "'Pure Patriarchy'," 274–5.
[213] *Canadian Methodist Magazine*, 11 (February 1880), 188, quoted in Berger, *Sense of Power*, 155.
[214] F. P. Walton, "Divorce in Canada and the United States: A Contrast," *University Magazine*, 9 (December 1910), 579–96, quoted in Berger, *Sense of Power*, 160.

as two of the errors of the modern age. The papacy returned to divorce in 1880 when Pope Leo XIII published his encyclical *Arcanum* (see Section 12.3).

The churches were interested in divorce for moral, social, and other practical reasons. First each religious denomination wanted divorce laws that reflected its own divorce doctrine. The Roman Catholic church and the Anglican church in England and throughout the British Empire held to the rule of the indissolubility of marriage, and argued for the suppression of divorce because it was forbidden by God's law. Among Protestant churches, some argued that divorce should be limited, on scriptural authority, to adultery, whereas others, following Calvinist, Lutheran, or other doctrines, were prepared to countenance wider grounds for divorce. No mainstream Christian denomination, however, accepted the open-ended or discretionary approach to divorce that had become policy in some states of America and that advocates of easier divorce were seeking elsewhere. To this extent, even though they differed in their divorce doctrines, the major churches had enough in common to enable them all to participate in the reaction against divorce liberalization in the late nineteenth century. The second reason for ecclesiastical interest in divorce flowed from the first. Each church insisted that social disintegration would follow from the application of any divorce law more liberal than its own particular doctrine permitted. For example, the Reformed Church of America, which opposed divorce outright, referred in 1889 to "the deplorable evils growing out of the existing methods for procuring easy divorce," and called upon its members to work to "diminish if not suppress the evil practice and correspondingly elevate the character of public and private morality."[215]

One issue that justified the churches' interest in divorce was the immediate and practical one of remarriages. Men and women resorted to divorce in spite of the doctrines of the faiths to which they confessed adherence. But many of them, having divorced and wishing to remarry, then expected to have their second marriages celebrated in church. As long as the civil courts regulated divorce, the churches could not control who divorced or why, but they did have control over the celebration of second marriages according to religious rites. This was an important question in doctrinal, social, and personal terms. In all good faith the churches were unable to celebrate remarriages of divorced men and women whose divorces they did not recognize; to have done so would have implicated the churches in bigamous marriages according to their own understanding of marriage. The refusal of religious marriage became less important in the nineteenth century, when the alternative, civil marriage, became more widely available, but it could still remain a personal problem for the devout, even if they did ignore their churches' teachings on divorce. Yet the refusal of remarriage in church could also be a political weapon in the fight against divorce. A clear warning to the faithful that if they flouted the law of

---

[215] Minutes of the General Synod of the Reformed Church of America, 1899, quoted in Halem, *Divorce Reform*, 33.

their church on divorce they could not hope to remarry within it was one way of dissuading men and women from resorting to the divorce courts.

Faced with an increasing number of divorces, and thus of divorced men and women who wanted to remarry, the various churches considered the issues in the late nineteenth century. In general they adopted a rigorous, apparently punitive approach: Those who divorced contrary to God's law, as interpreted by each individual church, had to live with the consequences of remarrying civilly or remaining unmarried. In the eyes of the churches, those who divorced against church doctrine remained married to the first spouse. In America the Episcopal church acted as early as 1863, when ministers were forbidden to celebrate any marriage involving a divorced person, unless he or she had been the innocent party in a divorce for reason of adultery.[216] By 1907 this restrictive rule was tightened to provide that even the innocent party in such a divorce should not be allowed to remarry in church until at least a year after the divorce. The church was given authority to investigate divorce court records to confirm the innocence of the party, and even then a minister of the Episcopal church could, if he wanted, refuse to celebrate the marriage of a divorced man or woman.[217] Other major Protestant churches in America, such as the Presbyterian, Methodist Episcopal, and Reformed churches, followed the lead of the Episcopalians in placing restrictions on church marriages by the divorced. From 1884, for instance, the Methodist Episcopal church allowed its ministers to solemnize the marriages of divorcés only when they were the innocent parties in adultery suits or in the case of two divorced former spouses remarrying each other.[218]

These attitudes reflected the divorce doctrines of the churches involved, as we should expect. In line with this, the Lutheran church's policy on remarriage was a good deal more liberal and indicated changes within Lutheran doctrine since the sixteenth century. In 1907 the General Synod of the Evangelical Lutheran Church in America passed a resolution to the effect that Lutherans had, since the Reformation, recognized adultery and willful desertion as grounds for divorce and that many Lutheran theologians had also recognized other grounds as legitimate, including impotence, extreme cruelty, conspiracy against life, and habitual drunkenness. The synod proceeded to recommend that the innocent party to a divorce on legitimate grounds should be able to remarry in church after twelve months had elapsed from the date of the divorce.[219]

In England the Anglican church wrestled with the problems raised by the remarriage of divorced people. This church, however, was divided on policy.[220]

[216] James P. Lichtenberger, *Divorce. A Study in Social Causation* (New York, 1909), 121.
[217] Ibid., 124.
[218] Ibid., 129.
[219] Ibid., 133–38.
[220] The doctrines and policies of the Anglican church on remarriage are discussed in A. R. Winnett, *Divorce and Remarriage in Anglicanism* (London, 1958), esp. 161–2.

11 Nineteenth-century divorce laws

Draft changes to Anglican canon law proposed in 1873 reaffirmed the principle that marriage could be dissolved only by death and advised the clergy not to celebrate second marriages that had been made possible by any form of dissolution other than death. In 1885, however, a committee of bishops advocated a more liberal stance, recommending that divorced people should not remarry but that if the innocent party did so, the church should be prepared to solemnize it. This committee recommended in addition that even a repentant guilty party might remarry in church if the bishop thought it "most consonant with the teaching of Holy Scripture and the mind and practice of the Primitive Church."[221] Among many other Anglican statements on the issue was the resolution of the 1888 Lambeth conference, an international conference of Anglican bishops, that stated that the guilty party should not be permitted to remarry in church, but as far as the innocent party was concerned, the clergy should not be instructed to refuse a religious celebration of a second marriage.[222] The practice of the Anglican church was as varied as its attitudes. An 1895 survey showed that of the thirty-four dioceses in England and Wales eleven (32%) refused to issue marriage licenses to any divorced person, innocent or guilty, while sixteen (47%) issued licenses only to the innocent party. Another six (18%), including the important and populous diocese of London, had no fixed rule against the issue of a marriage license to a divorced person.[223]

However, the churches were not content to confine their interest in divorce to those aspects of the issue that directly involved them and their faithful in a practical way. Reflecting the traditional role of the church as a supervisor of public and private morality, many churches became self-appointed missionaries for the purification or elimination of secular divorce laws. In America twenty-five Protestant denominations formed an Inter-Church Conference on Marriage and Divorce in 1903. Although the conference was unable to formulate a common policy on remarriage, it was at least initially more successful when it turned to campaigning for uniform divorce laws in America. The pressure for uniform laws was one aspect of the reaction against divorce, the main purpose being to end very liberal policies of some of the midwestern states, even though it was recognized that, in theory, uniformity could require states with restrictive divorce laws or no legislation on divorce, such as New York and South Carolina, respectively, to liberalize their divorce policies. In fact the first attempt to obtain uniformity in marriage and divorce legislation was sponsored by the governor of New York in 1889, and a commission of states' representatives agreed on a model divorce bill in 1901. This would have allowed divorce on the grounds of adultery, extreme cruelty, habitual drunkenness, and desertion,[224] but only two states went so far as to enact legislation on these lines.

[221] Ibid., 181.
[222] Ibid., 177.
[223] Ibid., 189–90. One diocese did not reply to the survey.
[224] Halem, *Divorce Reform*, 36.

11.9 Rise of divorce – conservative reaction

In the light of this failure by states to achieve legal uniformity, the Inter-Church Conference on Marriage and Divorce collaborated with the National League for the Protection of the Family to lobby the federal government to encourage more uniformity in matrimonial legislation. President Theodore Roosevelt, who shared the reformers' alarm at the rising divorce rates and their social implications, readily cooperated. In 1905 he sent a message to Congress calling for funds to be made available for the compilation of reliable marriage and divorce statistics that would aid the movement for law reform. Roosevelt's message stated that

there is a widespread conviction that the divorce laws are dangerously lax and indifferently administered in some of the States, resulting in a diminishing regard for the sanctity of the marriage relation. The hope is entertained that cooperation among the several States can be secured to the end that there may be enacted upon the subject of marriage and divorce uniform laws, containing all possible safeguards for the security of the family.[225]

As a response to this new phase of activity a National Congress on Uniform Divorce Laws, with representation from forty-two states and territories, met in Washington in 1906. The delegates agreed on some principles – for example, that a federal divorce law was not feasible – but found it impossible to agree on a single divorce code that was acceptable to all the states. At its first session the Congress adopted a resolution that the acceptable grounds for divorce were adultery, bigamy, conviction of some crimes, intolerable cruelty, desertion for two years, and habitual drunkenness. These grounds were common to many of the states' laws, and the Congress recommended that no grounds other than these should be recognized in any state. To the reactionary tenor of this resolution was added the conservative qualification that any state that currently offered a more restricted range of grounds should continue to do so.[226] As far as this Congress was concerned, then, uniformity did not mean that each state would have the same divorce law: It meant no more than restricting the availability of divorce in the states with the most liberal divorce policies. Nine months later in the second session of the Congress, however, their conservative position lost ground. The same six grounds for divorce were listed, but the Congress resolved that "each state is at liberty to reduce or increase the same as its citizens may deem advisable."[227] This was effectively an admission that uniform divorce legislation was impossible in the United States. The congress did agree on the desirability of uniformity in certain matters of procedure, and a model statute was also agreed upon that would have limited migratory divorce. The model specified that if any inhabitant of one state went to another state to obtain a divorce on a ground that was not recognized in his or her own state,

---

[225] Quoted in ibid., 37.
[226] Lichtenberger, *Divorce. A Study in Social Causation*, 116; the congress is discussed generally on pp. 114–20.
[227] Halem, *Divorce Reform*, 38.

then the divorce would have no legal effect there.[228] Yet although this model statute was approved unanimously, only New Jersey, Delaware, and Wisconsin passed legislation based on it.[229] The supporters of divorce law uniformity, however, tried to achieve their aims through an amendment to the Constitution that would have given the federal government jurisdiction over divorce. This goal, pursued over the years, never received anything like the support it needed to be accepted by Congress.

Just as the churches had spearheaded the campaign to restrict divorce legislation in the United States, so they did elsewhere. In England a royal commission was established in 1909 to investigate the law of divorce, but the division of opinion within the Anglican church prevented it from speaking with one voice. Some Anglican bishops who gave evidence defended the doctrine of indissolubility, whereas others argued in favor of allowing divorce for adultery and other grounds. Canon Hensley Henson of Westminster, for example, attacked the indissolubilist position as based on ignorance of scripture and history and argued that divorce should certainly be permitted for adultery, cruelty, and desertion, and should probably also be allowed in cases of incurable insanity and long-term imprisonment.[230] For the most part, however, the Anglican church and its representatives continued to oppose divorce in the abstract and to argue strongly against any liberalization of the restrictive 1857 legislation. The opposition of the church was undoubtedly an important factor in the slow development of English divorce policy.

In the Australian colony of New South Wales divorce was liberalized in 1892 to include adultery, desertion, drunkenness, assault, and long-term imprisonment,[231] a reform that was the culmination of almost a decade of legislative activity that saw various churches react in different ways. The Catholic church took surprisingly little interest in the liberalization issue, perhaps because it had lost the most important battle when divorce was first legalized in the colony in 1873. The Protestant churches divided over liberalization, and the Presbyterians were internally split. The law of Scotland, following Calvin and Knox, permitted divorce for reason of adultery and desertion, but the Presbyterian Synod of Eastern Australia declared itself in 1887 against the extension of the grounds for divorce beyond adultery, although individual Presbyterians were in favor of liberalization. The Anglican Synod in Australia, however, achieved a degree of unanimity that the English Anglicans lacked, and repeatedly condemned divorce law liberalization. But it might not have represented the feelings of ordinary Australian Anglicans; a great petition campaign was organized to demonstrate the extent of lay Anglican opposition to divorce liberalization, but it attracted fewer than 7,000 signatures. Even so, if the

[228] Lichtenberger, *Divorce. A Study in Social Causation*, 118.
[229] Halem, *Divorce Reform*, 39.
[230] Winnett, *Divorce and Remarriage*, 197–8.
[231] Golder, *Divorce in 19th-Century N.S.W.*, 219. The following section on the colony's divorce law is from 219–21.

11.9 Rise of divorce – conservative reaction

Anglican church in New South Wales was finally unsuccessful in stopping reform of divorce law, it was able to delay it by five years. In 1887 the colonial legislature passed a divorce extension bill, and when it was reserved for royal assent Anglican bishops petitioned Queen Victoria to withhold her approval.[232] It was not until 1892 that assent was given and the reforms became law.

This temporary victory was one of the successes scored by those who wanted to turn back the clock of social and legal history by restricting divorce. The reaction against liberal divorce had more notable successes in America, where a number of state legislatures were persuaded to remove omnibus clauses from their divorce legislation. Such a move in Connecticut in 1878 has already been noted, and in the 1880s other states followed suit. In 1883 Maine's omnibus provision allowing divorce when the supreme court judged it "reasonable and proper, conducive to domestic harmony, and consistent with the peace and morality of society," was abolished and replaced by seven specific grounds for divorce, namely, adultery, impotence, extreme cruelty, desertion, intoxication, cruel or abusive treatment, and refusal to maintain.[233] The guilty spouse in such cases was required to wait two years before he or she could remarry (no such restrictions on remarriage had been specified before 1883), and residence requirements were tightened.[234] Other New England states – New Hampshire, Vermont, and Massachusetts – under pressure from the New England Divorce Reform League from 1881, also restricted divorce in the 1880s. But the main targets, the midwestern and western states that provided divorce havens, were scarcely touched by the movement of reactionary reform. Indeed, if it were true, as the opponents of the reaction argued, that it was not so much the liberal divorce policies of these states that attracted divorce migrants but the restrictive divorce laws elsewhere that forced them to migrate to the divorce havens, then the limitation of divorce in the eastern states should have done nothing but increase the incidence of migratory divorces.

Implicit in the reaction against liberal divorce laws was the assumption that the demonstrably rising divorce rates resulted from permissive legislation. It is, of course, true that more liberal divorce laws can produce more divorces. There can be no divorces where divorce is not provided for in law, and the more grounds for divorce recognized by the law, the broader the range of marital circumstances susceptible to dissolution, and the more marriages at risk of divorce. (We must distinguish carefully here between marriage breakdown and divorce.) Yet there are many factors, other than the legal, at play in producing the divorce rate. As the final chapter of this book shows, divorce rates are produced by the complex interplay of economic, social, demographic, institutional, and legal factors, mediated through social and personal attitudes toward marriage. But in the late nineteenth century the established fact of

---

[232] One Australian bishop, who was in London, made personal representations against the divorce law's being given approval.

[233] Howard, *Matrimonial Institutions*, III, 17–18.

[234] Ibid., III, 20–5.

consistently high divorce rates in states that had liberal divorce laws was a seductive argument for the determining influence of law on behavior, and this explains the emphasis of the conservatives and reactionaries on legal reform. The attempt to make remarriage more difficult was justified in different terms: It was intended to prevent divorce by making the reward – remarriage to a new partner – impossible for the guilty (a deterrent to would-be adulterers and other matrimonial offenders) and difficult for the innocent (a deterrent to divorce and encouragement for spouses to resolve their problems without recourse to the divorce court).

For most conservatives on the divorce issue, the upwardly spiralling divorce rate could be explained quite simply. Too many married men and women were behaving immorally; their innocent spouses were resorting too quickly to divorce rather than attempting to solve their difficulties in such a way as to save the marriage; and legislators and policymakers were accomplices in these deeds by providing divorce facilities whose ease of access was irresistible. The way to halt the divorce evil in its tracks was to revive traditional – generally this meant "Christian" – morality and to make divorce almost impossible, if not wholly impossible, to obtain by reforming the laws. Against this moral-legal approach there arose a wider perspective on the divorce question, one that focused less on the legal act of divorce and more on the social aspects of marriage break-down. Proponents of this view – the new social scientists of the late nineteenth century – sought to explain the divorce rate in social and economic terms. Marriage breakdown and de facto divorce had taken place and would continue to occur despite the state of the law, they argued. This critical point, the distinction between marriage breakdown and divorce, and the need to understand both more clearly, was recognized by Caroll Wright, the United States commissioner of labor who oversaw the compilation of the first collections of American divorce statistics. "Law does not create divorce," Wright wrote; "divorce occurs when the husband and wife are estranged. Law steps in and defines the status of divorced parties, but does not create it."[235]

The social scientists and their analyses of divorce and marriage breakdown are described elsewhere in this book. What is important to note here is that they not only shifted the focus of attention to environmental factors, and made the almost exclusive emphasis on divorce legislation seem misplaced, if not irrelevant, but they also tended to support the liberal view on divorce. Although social scientists continued to support and uphold marriage and the family as fundamental social institutions, most were not appalled by the rising divorce rates, nor did they view them as certain harbingers of social disintegration and moral collapse. Rather, they represented repressive divorce laws, not divorce per se, as the evil. George Elliot Howard, a University of Chicago professor whose pioneering *A History of Matrimonial Institutions* (1904) has been an invaluable source for the present study, made the point that many marriages were

[235] Wright, *Report*, 176.

472

bound to be failures because of the characters of those involved and their motives for marrying. "On the face of it," Howard noted, "is it not grotesque to call such unions holy or to demand that they shall be indissoluble?" Dissolution of these unions was to be preferred to their continuation, not least for the sake of the children: "In sanctioning divorce the welfare of the children may well cause the state anxiety; but are there not thousands of so-called 'homes' from whose corrupting and blighting shadow the sooner a child escapes the better for both it and society?"[236] Howard's analysis stressed the need for moral regeneration, but his methodology was heavily influenced by the social sciences. Like social scientists generally he was driven to a position of deploring divorces because they were symptomatic of problems in human relationships. Divorce was unpleasant and painful to those involved, but it was necessary in the prevailing state of society. In conventional terms this made Howard a liberal on the divorce issue, as it made most social scientists. To judge from papers given at the third annual meeting of the American Sociological Association (in 1908), most professional sociologists could be counted as liberals on divorce.[237] Divorce was the first major social issue confronted by the nascent social sciences, and no doubt the liberal perspectives to which their studies drove them were instrumental in producing the suspicion and hostility with which conservatives have viewed sociologists ever since.

11.10 Migratory divorce and international law

As this account of the development of divorce policies in the nineteenth century has shown, there was a wide variation in divorce legislation, procedures, and prerequisites such as residency requirements. By the end of the century some countries had liberal divorce policies, others had more restrictive policies, and still others did not allow for divorce at all. The United States, with more constituent states than there were sovereign nations in the Western world as a whole, was a large microcosm, and reflected Western society's heterogeneity in divorce policies.

Such variations need not have been especially problematic, but for the greater ease of geographical mobility that the period ushered in. The scale of population movements across national and state borders and across the oceans in the second half of the century was unprecedented. Much of it, of course, was accounted for by permanent migrants, as millions of Europeans sought the prospects offered by the new worlds in the Americas and Australasia. Within this process we must also include the westward movement of population across North America. But there were also temporary migrations. The transport revolution, especially the development of railroads and steamships, made travel

---

[236] Howard, *Matrimonial Institutions*, III, 255.
[237] William L. O'Neill, "Divorce as a Moral Issue: A Hundred Years of Controversy," in Carol V. R. George (ed.), *"Remember the Ladies": New Perspectives on Women in American History* (Syracuse, N. Y., 1975), 135.

for leisure and tourism accessible to the growing middle class. It also facilitated their more utilitarian journeying to states or countries where divorce could be obtained more easily and with less publicity than in their home states.

The extent of migratory divorce – of men and women obtaining divorces elsewhere than in their usual places of domicile – is not known for the nineteenth century. Conservative commentators, horrified at the lax divorce policies in some jurisdictions, were convinced that divorce migration was common and increasing in the second half of the century. Canadians, for instance, were said to head in large numbers for the United States, despite uncertainty as to whether the divorces they obtained there would be recognized in Canada.[238] An apparent influx of Ontario residents to upper New York state divorce courts was noted at the turn of the century, and in 1905 one judge refused a divorce to a Canadian who had obtained legal residence in Niagara Falls (on the Canada – United States border) a year earlier, but was still doing business in Toronto. The judge commented:

For some time I have been watching closely divorce cases in which the principals were married in Canada and formerly resided there...I have reached the conclusion that a noticeable percentage of the divorce cases before this department are brought by Canadians, who establish a residence here mainly that they may sue for divorce.[239]

Greater concern about migratory divorce was expressed in the United States than elsewhere, and no doubt the phenomenon was much more extensive there; it was far easier in all respects for an American to travel from one state to another and take up temporary residence there in order to obtain a divorce than it was to take up residence in another country. The distinction of being the most popular divorce haven was shared by several midwestern and western states at different times. In the 1850s Indiana's omnibus divorce clause and virtually nonexistent residence requirements attracted many out-of-state petitioners. According to one source more than two-thirds of divorce actions pending in Marion County in 1858 were filed by nonresidents.[240] The attraction of Indiana to out-of-state petitioners was not unanimously reciprocated, however. The *Indiana Daily Journal* wrote, in metaphorical confusion, that the state was being "overrun by a flock of ill-used, and ill-using, petulant, libidinous, extravagant, ill-fitting husbands and wives as a sink is overrun with the foul water of the whole house."[241] The reaction against this tide (or flock) produced more rigorous residence regulations, and the declining attraction of Indiana in the wake of these legal changes was reflected in the state's standing in the national

---

[238] Gemmill, *Practice of the Parliament of Canada*, 26–27.
[239] Samuel E. Moffett, *Americanization of Canada* (Toronto, 1970), 111.
[240] More than fifty of seventy divorce petitions were filed by out-of-state residents, according to the *Indiana Daily Journal*. See Val Nolan Jr., "Indiana: Birthplace of Migratory Divorce," *Indiana Law Journal* 26 (1951), 517–20.
[241] Ibid., 522.

11.10 Migratory divorce and international law

divorce rate league. Between 1867 and 1871 Indiana had the highest divorce rate of any state, but it slipped rapidly to seventh place by 1877–81.[242]

In the following decades other states gained notoriety as meccas for pilgrims in search of divorce. Illinois, Utah, and South Dakota each had its turn in the limelight. In the 1890s the divorce issue, and a proposal to extend the term of residence to a year, were debated hotly in Sioux Falls, South Dakota. Businessmen and hoteliers who benefited financially from the divorce traffic defended the status quo, but in 1893 a conservative lobby led by clergymen was successful in having deterrent residence requirements imposed.[243] In the last years of the nineteenth century North Dakota and Wyoming attracted out-of-state divorce applicants because of their short residence requirements, but in both states the facility was closed down by the imposition of longer residence rules.

This pattern, of divorce havens rising to public awareness before declining under conservative pressure, was broken by Nevada. Like other states, Nevada had accommodated its earlier transient population by demanding only short residence (in this case, six months) before granting citizenship and voting rights. This same requirement was extended, quite logically, to divorce, but unlike their counterparts in other states, Nevada's legislators resisted conservative opposition to their state's becoming a divorce colony. It was not that the divorce business in Nevada was any less blatant than it had been earlier in other states. Cashing in on Nevada's growing reputation for easy divorce, a New York lawyer set up office in Reno and widely advertised the state's facilities and his own services. His advertisements in New York, Washington, and San Francisco newspapers included one that read in part:

Divorce Laws of Nevada
Have You Domestic Trouble?
Are You Seeking DIVORCE?
Do You Want Quick and Reliable Service?
Send for My Booklet
Contains Complete Information[244]

Nevada's status as a divorce haven was a source of bitter and protracted controversy from the early years of the twentieth century, but the opposition to it and attempts to pass laws restricting migratory divorce had little success. In 1913 the state legislature gave in when the assembly chamber was virtually invaded by antidivorce campaigners, and imposed a one-year residency requirement, but two years later, pressure from businessmen and lawyers led to the restoration of the former six-month requirement. Nevada, in fact, has retained its status as a divorce haven throughout the twentieth century and is able to draw upon its reputation and tradition to attract out-of-state divorces,

---

[242] Ibid., 515–16.
[243] Blake, *Road to Reno*, 123–9.
[244] Ibid., 154.

even though other states now have equally short or shorter residence requirements.[245]

How widespread migratory divorce was, we do not know, but that it was a pattern of behavior is incontestable. The phenomenon raised a number of serious legal and social questions, the most immediate being the recognition of divorce decrees outside the state where they were granted. In one notorious case Earl Russell, an English peer, divorced his wife in Nevada and remarried, only to have the divorce declared invalid in England. Russell was tried for bigamy by the House of Lords and imprisoned.[246] Apart from the personal consequences of the refusal of reciprocal recognition of divorce decrees, there were social implications. Migratory divorce was a way by which a state's population could circumvent the restrictions imposed by law, and this was no trivial matter to legislators and social critics who conceived of restrictive divorce policies as a means of maintaining moral standards and social stability.

In the late nineteenth century concern about migratory divorce produced two responses. The first was attempts to bring divorce laws into harmony or greater uniformity. Success in this endeavor would reduce the range of variation and thereby reduce or eliminate the advantage of divorce migration. The failure of the movement for divorce law uniformity in the United States has already been described, although it should be understood more as part of a drive to restrict divorce in all respects than as an interest in divorce law uniformity in its own right. The movement for legal harmonization had more success in Scandinavia, however. Beginning in the first decade of the twentieth century there was consultation and cooperation among Sweden, Norway, and Denmark (and later Finland and Iceland) in a wide range of legislation. One result was that during or just after World War I, new and broadly uniform divorce laws were enacted in these countries.[247]

Overall, however, progress toward divorce law harmonization was minimal in the Western world. Its success in Scandinavia was facilitated by a similar (often a common) legal tradition since the sixteenth century, but it was quickly apparent in the United States that the individual states would not surrender their legislative independence to a standardized approach to the issue. There was little thought, and even less hope, that the nations of Europe, with their disparate religious, legal, and social traditions, would standardize legislation in this or any other area.

There remained the problem of interjurisdictional recognition. Should a divorce granted in Indiana to a New York resident be recognized in New York?

---

[245] In 1985 Nevada law required six weeks' residence, but South Dakota, having revived its liberal tradition in divorce policy, required only physical presence in the state, together with the intention to reside there.

[246] On Lord Russell's divorce and its effects in England see Duncan Crow, *The Edwardian Woman* (London, 1978), 174–9.

[247] Rheinstein, "Divorce Law in Sweden," 138–141. This movement of legal harmonization took place at a time of growing consciousness of Scandinavian unity.

11.10 Migratory divorce and international law

Should a divorce granted in France to a national of Spain be recognized in Spain? These were not simply legal questions, for the recognition of divorce decrees determined important social and personal issues such as the possibility of remarriage and the legitimacy or illegitimacy of children of second marriages. Some of the American states passed legislation in an attempt to stop their own citizens from circumventing their divorce restrictions by having their marriages dissolved in states with more permissive policies. At the same time they were careful to respect the divorces granted in other states to residents of those states. An example was a 1902 Massachusetts law that specified that a divorce granted in another state or country had force in Massachusetts, but that if an inhabitant of Massachusetts went elsewhere for a divorce on grounds that occurred in Massachusetts or that were not recognized as grounds for divorce in Massachusetts law, then the divorce would have no force or effect in Massachusetts.[248] This law, and similar provisions in some other states, was challenged under that section of the United States Constitution that bound each state to give "full faith and credit" to the public acts, records, and judicial proceedings of every other state.[249] The restrictive provisions in respect of recognition of out-of-state divorces were upheld, however, as not being unconstitutional. These laws did not challenge the legitimacy of divorces granted to citizens of the states where they were decreed.

In the United States the main issue in migratory divorces was domicile: whether a state had the right to jurisdiction over a marriage in cases where the spouses were living in another state, even though they might have established fictive residence elsewhere. This issue gave rise to the residence requirements that were designed to ensure that petitioners for divorce were more than transient. The minimal residence requirements of some states and their lax enforcement, however, tended to undermine the effectiveness of these guarantees. Outside the United States the legal issue was more often one of nationality than of domicile. Migratory divorce was not a matter of an American citizen living in one state and seeking divorce in another, but of citizens of one country seeking divorce in another. International case law is full of examples of Italian citizens, unable to divorce in Italy, seeking divorce in France; of Spanish nationals, similarly deprived of divorce, trying to dissolve their marriages elsewhere; and of British couples, unable to satisfy the restrictive 1857 law, introducing actions to divorce courts on the Continent. In many instances courts refused to accept jurisdiction, even when a foreigner had taken out citizenship of the country where the divorce was sought. In 1897, for example, a French court declared that it did not have competence to dissolve the marriage of two Italians, even though one of them had obtained French citizenship.[250]

Confusion over national divorce laws and their applicability to nationals of

---

[248] Blake, *Road to Reno*, 178.
[249] Constitution of the United States of America, Section I, Article IV.
[250] *Journal du Droit international privé* 24 (1897), 333–4.

other states, together with concern as to the recognition of foreign divorce decrees, resulted in an international convention signed in The Hague in 1902 by major European powers (France, Germany, Austria-Hungary, Spain, Italy, Portugal, Switzerland, Sweden, Norway, Luxembourg, and also Romania).[251] The aims of the convention were to ensure that some states did not become divorce havens for the nationals of others, thus introducing uncertainty into European marriages, and to establish rules for jurisdiction over divorce actions and for the recognition of divorce decrees. In essence the terms of the 1902 Hague convention meant that there would be no advantage to seeking divorce in another country. A divorce in one country involving citizens of another would be valid only if the laws of *both* countries recognized the pertinent circumstances as grounds for divorce. Thus a German couple might obtain a divorce in France for reason of adultery, and the decree would be recognized in both France and Germany because both states included adultery as a ground for divorce. But an Italian couple could not do likewise because Italian law did not recognize adultery (or any ground) as justifying divorce. There were, needless to say, questions of interpretation of the terms of the convention, but for our purposes the technical operation of the agreement is less important than its sheer existence.[252] The necessity for an international convention governing divorce testifies to the spread and growing legal complexity of divorce in the later nineteenth century, the diversity of divorce policies, and the issues raised by men and women who were determined to dissolve their marriages even when their own state or national laws did not permit it.

[251] The convention on divorce was one of several resulting from a number of conferences in The Hague, starting in 1893, with the aim of harmonizing rules for the conflict of laws. A survey is in *The Progress of Continental Law in the Nineteenth Century* (Boston, 1918), 470–500. The text of the Hague Convention, signed June 12, 1902, on conflicts of law and jurisdiction in divorce and separation, is reprinted in the *Journal du Droit international privé* 31 (1904), 755ff.

[252] See the criticisms of the 1902 convention by Friedrich Meili, Swiss delegate to The Hague conferences, in *Progress of Continental Law*, 483–6. On other issues raised by the convention see P. Arminjou, *Précis de droit international privé* (3 vols., Paris, 1947), III, 38–50.

12

●●∿∿∿∿∿∿∿∿∿∿∿∿∿∿∿∿∿∿∿∿∿∿∿∿∿∿∿∿∿∿∿∿●●

Divorce as a social issue, 1850–1914

12.1 Introduction

Although it is possible to isolate divorce as a theme in Western history, it is obvious that attitudes and policies regarding divorce are anything but autonomous. They can be understood and explained only in relation to attitudes toward such questions as sexuality, the nature of marriage and the family, and the social relation of men and women and in the context of prevailing social, economic, and demographic conditions and the way they are perceived. These points are seldom more evident than during the nineteenth century, when there was, as we have seen, a wave of legislative and judicial activity related to divorce across Western society. In the preceding chapter the outlines of this activity were drawn, but we no more than hinted at the associated social issues. The following pages seek to place divorce within a wider political, social, and ideological context in order to explain why divorce became such an important social issue in the period up to the outbreak of World War I.

As we know, the nineteenth century was a period of rapid social and economic transformation in Western society. Although the long phase of political revolutions that began in the mid-eighteenth century effectively ended with the wave of revolutions that swept across Europe in 1848, the other revolutions persisted. Industrialization intensified as rural industrialization gave way to the growth of the new industrial cities, and as new technologies and sources of energy were applied to new kinds of industry. Urbanization accelerated, so that by the end of the nineteenth century the populations of many countries were predominantly urban. Economic changes produced new classes and class relationships, with the growth of the industrial working and middle classes and with heightened class consciousness. Population, which had begun to increase in the early eighteenth century, continued to do so at accelerating rates during the nineteenth in almost all Western countries. Finally there were unprecedented movements of population, particularly from Great Britain and Europe to North America, Australasia, and Africa, and westward across the North American continent.[1]

---

[1] For general accounts of social, economic, and cultural changes in the nineteenth century see Peter Stearns, *European Society in Upheaval: Social History Since 1750* (New York, 1975), Parts

12 Divorce as a social issue, 1850–1914

It is true that there were many continuities threaded through the complex of changes. Rural regions of Europe, such as the southern half of Italy, appeared little touched by the great structural changes that were underway;[2] France, which remained relatively rural in population distribution and agricultural in economic activity, maintained many features of traditional society longer than countries such as England and Germany.[3] Popular traditions, customs, and attitudes often persisted everywhere in the face of change.[4] Even many quite fundamental economic and social relationships retained their traditional forms longer than we might have expected.[5] Yet for all this, change was the order of the century, and the dramatic shifts in the social and economic structure of Western society highlighted new ideological alignments and social issues, many of which either focused on marriage and divorce or dealt with them obliquely. Among the major political ideologies of the period were socialism, liberalism, and conservatism; among the specific social issues that attracted attention from the middle of the nineteenth century were women's rights and social purity, temperance, illicit sexuality, and the cults of femininity and domesticity.

Although we cannot go into these issues in any great depth here, we should note that one issue of concern to all social commentators, no matter what their political position, was the role of the family in the social order. Progressives and conservatives alike recognized that marriage and the family were fundamental social institutions, and that social change or the maintenance of the prevailing social order could not be achieved without taking account of the family. Many progressives saw the family as so pivotal an institution that they believed that social change would begin with the transformation of familial relationships. Others saw the family as less fundamental but no less integral, and demonstrated that change in economic and familial relationships must occur in tandem. Conservatives agreed with these assessments as to the critical role of the family in the social order, but in line with their objectives they sought to prevent significant changes within it so as to guarantee minimal social change on a wider scale. For many reactionaries, who wanted to roll back what they perceived as the destructive forces of industry, class conflict, and city life, the restoration of "traditional" family values and relationships (generally the patriarchal family model) was a vital first step. In short, marriage and the family lay at the heart of plans and descriptions of both social transformation and social conservatism, and it is not surprising that divorce was a critical issue in these varying and often contradictory calculations. Ease of divorce was

---

(*footnote 1, cont.*)

4 and 5; Eugen Weber, *Europe Since 1715: A Modern History* (New York, 1972), esp. Chapters 9 and 10.
[2] See Denis Mack Smith, *Italy: A Modern History* (Ann Arbor, 1969), esp. 230–42.
[3] Eugen Weber, *Peasants into Frenchmen* (London, 1979), passim.
[4] On the persistence of traditions regarding marriage in Britain, see John R. Gillis, *For Better, For Worse: British Marriages, 1600 to the Present* (New York, 1985), Parts II and III.
[5] Arno J. Mayer, *The Persistence of the Old Regime* (New York, 1981), passim.

associated with lax family policies, and both were endowed with far-reaching political and social implications. In this way, divorce became a common theme in the broad social and political debates of the nineteenth century, as the following survey of the spectrum shows.

12.2 The family in progressive social and political thought

Of particular interest are the social commentators and activists known collectively as the utopian socialists. Although they were a disparate group that included prominent men such as Robert Owen, Charles Fourier, and Etienne Cabet whose specific doctrines and critiques of society differed widely, the utopian socialists shared certain characteristics. For one thing, they were alarmed at the social effects of industrialization, urbanization, and capitalism, and devised plans for the regeneration of society and morality. Many of the utopians, realizing that change could take place, initially at any rate, only on a small scale, planned model communities or envisaged future societies made up of small communities. Fourier, for example, proposed a system in which the population would live in "phalansteries," communities of up to a thousand inhabitants. Some of the utopians, such as Robert Owen, actually tried to put their ideas into practice, and in the 1830s and 1840s utopian communities sprang up in many places, particularly in the United States where there were more than a hundred by 1870.[6] If the originators of these models did not themselves found communities, as Owen did at New Harmony in Indiana, they at least inspired others to do so.

Without exception, the utopian socialists gave a good deal of attention to the character of marriage and the family in contemporary society (what Owen called "the old immoral world") and to their status in the regenerated society of the future ("the new moral world").[7] The family was generally considered problematic. It was undeniably a basic institution of society, but for many utopians it embodied the worst in social practices. Owen, for one, saw the prevailing system of marriage as a fundamentally divisive influence in society, even more divisive than social classes. Marriage, he believed, provided a façade for much crime, vice, tyranny, and oppression – particularly of women – which led to widespread misery as well as insanity and suicides. Moreover, and this was a criticism shared by other socialists, the loyalty demanded by family relationships tended to reinforce individualism and division within society at large, and to militate against a spirit of broader social cohesion and cooperation.

---

[6] Joan Harvey Baker, "Women in Utopia: The Nineteenth-Century Experience," in Gairdner B. Moment and Otto F. Kraushaar (eds.), *Utopians: The American Experience* (Metuchen, N. Y., 1980), 57.

[7] Earlier utopian thinkers also paid attention to marriage, divorce, and the organization of the family. See, for example, Thomas More's *Utopia*, referred to in Section 1.7, and the references in J. C. Davis, *Utopia and the Ideal Society: A Study of English Utopian Writing, 1500–1700* (Cambridge, 1981), and Marie Louise Berneri, *Journey Through Utopia* (London, 1950).

Owen did not advocate celibacy, which he regarded as unnatural, as a remedy for the evils of marriage. Rather he urged a radical transformation of attitudes, social practices, and legislation relating to the family. Marriage should be removed from the control of the churches and their regulations, and this would eliminate "the cause of the vice and misery now created by impediments to marriage, by inducements to form marriages from monetary motives, by proceedings tending to destroy mutual confidence and affection, and by hindrance of the dissolution of marriages which prove unhappy."[8] In the society that Owen envisaged, "marriages will be formed, as the laws of God unequivocally direct, at a proper period of life [i.e., not too early], under such arrangements as will be the most likely to prevent ill-assorted unions, and to insure the greatest permanency of the first natural inclinations between the parties."[9] Affection was the sole criterion for continuing a marriage, according to Owen, and when it had dissipated the marriage had ended. It should be as acceptable to dissolve a marriage "when the esteem and affection cannot be retained for each other, and when the union promises to produce more misery than happiness," as it was to form the marriage in the first place.[10]

Owen placed only two qualifications on the right of divorce: that women had equality and that the education and well-being of children were not compromised. However, divorce should not be hastily pursued and should be permitted only after the spouses had waited long enough to have had the opportunity to recapture the love they had felt for each other. But if, after three publications of their mutual desire to separate, the publications at intervals of three months, the couple had not reconciled, their marriage could be dissolved and they would be free to remarry.[11] For all this Owen, like other utopians, believed that marriage breakdown was a result of a corrupt marriage system. In the regenerated society he planned, where women and men would be equal in rights and education, where those intending to marry would know each other's thoughts and feelings intimately, and where marriage would be based on love and not social or material considerations, "it is most likely that marriages so formed would be more permanent than they have ever yet been."[12]

Perhaps the most libertarian of the utopians in respect of marriage was Charles Fourier. Fourier provided for the retention of family units within his planned communities but believed that they would wane as individuals developed a broader sense of social loyalties. The family reinforced selfish sentiments, and in a natural state men, women, and children tended to break

---

[8] Robert Owen, *The Revolution in the Mind and Practice of the Human Race, or the Coming Change from Irrationality to Rationality* (London, 1849), v.

[9] Ibid., 84.

[10] Robert Owen, "Oration, Containing a Declaration of Mental Independence, Delivered in the Public Hall, at New Harmony, Indiana ... 4 July, 1826," in Oakley C. Johnson (ed.), *Robert Owen in the United States* (New York, 1970), 72.

[11] Raymond Lee Muncy, *Sex and Marriage in Utopian Communities in Nineteenth-Century America* (Bloomington, 1973), 59.

[12] Owen, "Oration," 72.

away from the family group to join other social formations, such as peer groups. While marriage existed, however, divorce would be readily available; in the free society of the future, characterized by looser social bonds and no sexual exclusivity, marriage, and therefore divorce, would be anachronistic.[13] Similarly the followers of the utopian Henri, Comte de Saint-Simon, doubted the permanence of family ties in a naturally ordered society. One, Abel Transon, rejected the Christian doctrine that a man and a woman should find "straightaway, without prior experience, that man or woman among all mankind who will be able to make him happy for the remainder of his life." Transon firmly denied that "the *exclusive love* of any one man for one woman lasting their whole lives is a law or even a *universal* tendency of mankind."[14]

Against Fourier and the other libertarians who planned for the disappearance of orthodox family relationships stood some utopian socialists who upheld marriage and the family. Etienne Cabet, whose ideas inspired several communities in America, stressed the benefits of matrimony for women in particular: "Yes, Marriage and the Family are, for the woman, the source of a thousand moral pleasures far superior to other pleasures. Yes, it is the woman especially who ought to desire the conservation of Marriage and the Family, purged of all their vices.[15] Cabet recognized that women were oppressed in the contemporary family, but saw this not as a necessary effect of marriage per se, but of vices such as an emphasis on money in choosing marriage partners. There was room, however, for divorce in Cabet's thoughts, and in his *Voyage in Icaria*, a fictional utopia, he allowed for divorce as long as the families of the couple concerned gave their approval.[16]

The American communities modeled on Cabet's Icarian vision stressed marriage but allowed limited access to divorce. In the California commune of Icaria Speranza (1881–6), for example, voluntary celibacy was prohibited, and the inhabitants were obliged to marry. Divorce was permitted, but rapid remarriage was encouraged.[17] Divorce was also allowed in the communities based on Owenite principles. In Nashoba (Tennessee) the inhabitants were urged to marry, and although the ideal of permanence was upheld, there was recognition that "it will not outlive the affections: from the moment the heart has ceased to love, the connection will be dissolved."[18] In the community at Skaneateles, New York, which drew on both Fourier's and Owen's doctrines, divorce was

---

[13] See J. Beecher and R. Bienvenu (eds.), *The Utopian Vision of Charles Fourier* (London, 1972) and Louis Devance, "Les théories de la famille et de la population chez Fourier et Proudhon," paper presented at the Congrès des Sociétés Savantes, Besançon, 1974. M. Devance kindly sent me a copy of this paper.
[14] Abel Transon, *Affranchissement des femmes* (1832), quoted in Frank E. Manuel and Fritzie P. Manuel (eds.), *French Utopias* (New York, 1966), 293.
[15] Etienne Cabet, *Douze Lettres*, quoted in Christopher H. Johnson, *Utopian Communism in France. Cabet and the Icarians* (Ithaca, 1974), 91.
[16] Leo Loubere, *Utopian Socialism: Its History Since 1800* (Cambridge, Mass., 1974), 48.
[17] Robert V. Hine, *California's Utopian Colonies* (New York, 1953), 70.
[18] Arthur John Booth, *Robert Owen, the Founder of Socialism in England* (London, 1869), 118–19.

positively encouraged when the husband and wife no longer contributed to each other's happiness.[19]

Provision for divorce in the utopian communities did not, however, necessarily mean that the utopian socialists supported easy access to divorce in society at large. The divorce they contemplated in the abstract or practiced within their communities was divorce in the context of egalitarian marriage systems. For the most part the utopian socialists were enthusiastic only about the total regeneration of morals and social relations, and were not interested in reforms that merely tinkered with the prevailing system so as to reduce the effects of its most obvious corruptions; that role they left to conservatives, as we shall see. There was, then, some recognition that although divorce played a proper and beneficial role in a regenerated marriage system based on equality and love, it could only ever be little more than a means of exploitation while marriage was a tool of oppression in the hands of men.[20] Unregenerated men, it was thought, would divorce their wives too readily for the wrong reasons, leaving them and their children without financial or social support. In contrast, under the moral codes of the utopians, divorce would simply be a recognition that love or affection, the basis of marriage, had waned. Women – equal in education and rights – and children – as much the responsibility of the community as of their parents – would not be adversely affected when a marriage was dissolved.[21]

To this extent, and because their followings were limited, it is not clear what impact the utopians might have had on more mainstream attitudes toward marriage and divorce. As a group they tended to fall within the libertarian trend of social criticism of the period, and it is likely that their radicalism provoked opposition to social and legal change as much as support for it. One reason for this was the sexual extremism that many utopians espoused as they abandoned notions such as the desirability of virginity until marriage and sexual exclusivity within marriage. These sexual doctrines implied loose marriage ties and thus easy access to divorce, and although they were intended to be understood in utopian terms – in the context of a reformed society – they were readily interpreted by opponents as doctrines for sexual promiscuity, adultery, and incest. Robert Owen's teachings in particular touched off a vigorous debate in England in the 1830s and 1840s on the range of issues related to marriage and divorce, and Owenites complained that "it is scarcely possible to travel anywhere...or enter into any mixed company, without hearing this subject broached, and the most licentious, vicious and brutalizing opinion ascribed to the Socialists."[22] One critic, for example, charged the Owenites with trying

---

[19] Ibid., 114.
[20] This echoed a point made by Montesquieu and others that divorce by men in the context of a male-dominated family system could only be harmful to women. See Charles Secondat, Baron de Montesquieu, *The Spirit of the Laws* (trans. T. Nugent, New York, 1949), Book XVI, Chapter 15, p. 260.
[21] Muncy, *Sex and Marriage*, 55.
[22] *New Moral World* (Owenite newspaper), April 4, 1840, quoted in Barbara Taylor, *Eve and the New Jerusalem: Socialism and Feminism in the Nineteenth Century* (London, 1983), 183.

12.2 The family in progressive thought

"to break up house, to tear asunder our household ties, and put to death the strongest and dearest affects of our hearts...to throw our wives and children into one common stock...."[23]

The criticisms of the socialists' views on marriage and divorce were satirized by one writer. Among the "wicked, unchaste, disgusting, and beastly" opinions of the Owenites, the author noted their beliefs that marriage was a civil contract;

that the holy state of matrimony had been designed to increase the happiness of the parties who think fit to adopt it;...[and that] whenever extraordinary circumstances happen to destroy that affection upon which the married parties may have come together, and more misery than happiness is produced in consequence, that the divorce should be as easily obtained by the poor man as it is now by the rich.[24]

The author of this pamphlet added that, faced with the argument that easily procured divorce would lead to "cases without number, and children innumerable...thrown upon society for support," the Owenites point to the United States, Switzerland, and other states where a system of liberal divorce had produced "much good, but not evil."[25]

Public debates on marriage and divorce, which pitted socialists against their critics, attracted huge crowds: More than 5,000 tickets were sold for one 1840 match between Robert Owen and his arch-opponent John Brindley in Bristol. Although the issue of sex was more sensational and commanded more attention, divorce was a prominent issue in its own right. One result of their participation in the public debate on marriage and divorce reform was that the Owenites began to express their views not only in utopian terms but also in terms of the contemporary discussion of legal reform. For example, they supported the English marriage legislation of 1837 that allowed for civil marriage and for the licensing of any building for weddings. Under the new law, Owenites could celebrate marriages according to their own rites, and despite accusations to the contrary, these were conventional marriages in intent, stressing mutual love and the ideal of indissolubility. An Owenite "social hymn" of marriage ran as follows:

> United by love then alone
> In goodness, in truth and in heart
> They both are so perfectly one
> Their bonds they never can part.
> Their union has love for its ground
> The love of a man and his bride;

---

[23] Joseph Barker, *The Overthrow of the Infidel Socialism* (1840), quoted in Taylor, *Eve and the New Jerusalem*, 184.
[24] *A Full and Complete Exposure of the Atrocious and Horrible Doctrines of the Owenites* (London, n.d.), 5. The last reference is to the limitations of divorce by private Act of Parliament.
[25] Ibid.

And hence in affection they're bound
So close they can never divide.[26]

On occasion, however, even Owenite love waned, and "divorces" took place within the movement even before divorce was legalized in England. In 1842 three Cheltenham socialists contracted a "divorce" and "remarriage," in which Amelia and James Vaughn agreed that they would separate and that Amelia would marry William Stanbury. The contract stipulated that Stanbury would be responsible for Amelia Vaughn's debts, while James Vaughn agreed that, as far as her relationship with him was concerned, Amelia was "as free... as though she had never been married."[27] This proceeding was much more sedate than the wife sales that were taking place at the same time in England, but it had the same legal force as they did: none. It did, however, reflect the tendency of this group to practice its marriage doctrines in a utopian manner, though in a less overtly separatist form than the utopian communities in America did. Further evidence of the Owenites' concern for nonutopian reform was their rallying to the support of divorce law reform at their 1840 congress. To this extent some of the utopian socialists played a part in generating pressure for more conventional piecemeal reforms of marriage law. Whether the utopian communities and their marriage practices had any impact on their surrounding society is not clear, but it is unlikely that the uncommitted took them very seriously as models worthy of emulation.

The marriage doctrines of the utopians and their notions of the role of the family in social change were challenged within the socialist movement itself. Many of the utopians believed that broad social change could be sparked by the example of the small-scale communities they established, and because of the scale of these experiments they were driven to giving the family an enhanced role in fomenting change. The family was the basic cell of society, and the reform of family relationships would necessarily influence other social relationships and institutions. This was the early view of Alfred Naquet, the prime mover of marriage law reform in France from the 1860s to the early twentieth century. As a social revolutionary in the 1860s Naquet believed that the transformation of society would begin with the family and then spread to economic relationships, a view not inconsistent with that of many other utopians. But Naquet later moved to the position that the economic revolution would come first and that "the freedom of the family, instead of being its origin, will be its result."[28] This view was more akin to that of the scientific socialists who saw the family less as an agent of social and economic change and more as part of the superstructure of society that would be transformed as the economic relations

---

[26] Quoted in Taylor, *Eve and the New Jerusalem*, 209.
[27] Ibid., 198. On Owenites and marriage see also Gillis, *For Better, For Worse*, 224–8.
[28] Alfred Naquet, *La loi du divorce* (Paris, 1903), vi. This was the view of the Marxist socialist Jules Guesde who called for a revolution in the relation between the sexes but specified that "it can only follow the economic and social revolution." See Charles Sowerwine, *Les femmes et le socialisme* (Paris, 1978), 49.

underwent change. The classic formulations were those of Marx and Engels in *The Communist Manifesto* (1848) and Engels in *The Origin of the Family, Private Property and the State* (1884). These are discussed in Chapter 13 in the context of the 1917 Soviet marriage law, but we should note here that the Marxists of the nineteenth century were less involved in the contemporary debate on marriage and sexual relations because they believed that to focus on them was to begin at the wrong end of the social revolution. After the socialist revolution relationships would be regulated by the couple concerned, and the characteristics marriage derived from its origin in property relations – the supremacy of the man and indissolubility – would disappear. But the economic revolution must occur before the marriage revolution: "Full freedom of marriage can therefore only be generally established [after]...the abolition of capitalist production and of the property relations created by it...."[29] This did not, of course, prevent all socialists from writing on marriage and divorce, and many did so, particularly in the context of women's rights[30] (see Section 12.5). But for the most part, socialists in the Marxist tradition regarded this area of social reform as secondary to the primary goal of the transformation of fundamental economic relationships.

Besides the more radical progressive critiques of nineteenth-century society, the current of liberalism eddied around the questions of marriage and divorce. Liberalism, like other broad tendencies, was varied and multifaceted, but its exponents shared a general concern for the achievement of individual happiness and a common aversion to external interference in matters of personal life. Such beliefs easily and logically led liberals to support marriage and divorce policies that maximized individual freedom, and they approached social issues from the perspectives of the individuals directly concerned rather than with the social impact uppermost in their minds. According to liberal lights, men and women should not be imprisoned for life in unsatisfactory marriages that brought them more misery than happiness, and in general liberals advocated the deregulation of marriage and divorce. This is not to say that liberals sought the abolition of marriage or looked forward, like the Marxists, to its eventual disappearance. Nor did they argue for a system in which men and women might live together as long as it suited them and then separate at will to form new partnerships regardless of the consequences for themselves, their partners, their children, or society at large. Rather, the liberal position permitted the maximum degree of personal freedom within a context of minimal regulation and the recognition of the individual responsibilities that marriage and divorce implied.

---

[29] Friedrich Engels, *The Origin of the Family, Private Property and the State* (New York, 1942), 145. In some writings, however, Engels suggested an autonomous role for the family's development; see Ann J. Lane, "Women in Society: A critique of Frederick Engels," in Berenice A. Carroll (ed.), *Liberating Women's History: Theoretical and Critical Essays* (Urbana, 1976), 4–25.

[30] See, for example, August Bebel, *Woman in the Past, Present, and Future* (London, 1885), esp. 55ff. on divorce.

There were, needless to say, variations within this liberal approach to marriage and divorce. The libertarian end was represented by John Stuart Mill and his wife Harriet Taylor, each of whom wrote an essay on marriage and divorce in 1832. The essays themselves could not have been influential at the time, for they were first published in 1951,[31] but they do indicate two liberal perspectives on these issues. Both essays were couched in the context of women's status in marriage and society, a common focus of much nineteenth-century literature on divorce. Mill argued that while women had been highly dependent on men, it was as well for marriage to be indissoluble: It anchored men, who would otherwise tend to be wayward, to their responsibilities. But, Mill insisted optimistically, women were no longer in a condition of inequality and dependence, and marital indissolubility had become a hardship; divorce, therefore, should be permitted. It is noteworthy that at no point in his essay did Mill suggest that divorce should be limited by law. In pure liberal terms he implied that men and women should regulate their own status: "Were divorce ever so free, it would be resorted to under the same sense of moral responsibility and under the same restraints from opinion, as any other of the acts of our lives."[32] Social attitudes and pressure would prevent men and women from changing partners frequently or for trivial reasons. In Mill's view, couples would stay together, especially if they had children, except in two cases: where there was "such uncongeniality of disposition as rendered it positively uncomfortable to one or both of the parties to live together" or when one of them conceived "a strong passion" for a third person.[33] These were the grounds that Mill implicitly accepted as justifying divorce, although it was not for legislation to specify them and to exclude any other reasons for terminating a marriage.

In her essay on divorce, Harriet Taylor did envisage limits on the right to divorce. Although she specified no particular grounds or justifications, Taylor proposed a lengthy waiting period – she suggested a minimum of two years – before a divorce was finalized and either party could remarry. Evidently this waiting period was designed to give the spouses a chance to reconcile, for a divorce suit could be withdrawn during the period. The sole criterion for marriage was personal happiness, and Taylor thought that divorce would be the natural recourse of unhappily married men and women: "Who on earth would wish another to remain with them against their inclination – I should think no one...."[34] This took care of the possibility that one of the spouses might object to being divorced and Taylor equally briskly dismissed the problem of children: "All the difficulties about divorce seem to be in the consideration for the children – but on this plan it would be the woman's *interest* not to have children."[35]

[31] John Stuart Mill's and Harriet Taylor Mill's essays are published in *Essays on Sex Equality* (ed. Alice S. Rossi, Chicago, 1970), 67–87.
[32] Ibid., 82.
[33] Ibid.
[34] Ibid., 86.
[35] Ibid.

Truly, it is hardly possible to describe the magnitude of evils that flow from divorce. Matrimonial contracts are by it made variable, mutual kindness is weakened, deplorable inducements to unfaithfulness are supplied, harm is done to the education and training of children, occasion is afforded for the breaking up of homes, the seeds of dissension are sown among families, the dignity of womanhood is lessened and brought low, and women run the risk of being deserted after having ministered to the pleasures of men. Since, then, nothing has such power to lay waste families and destroy the mainstay of kingdoms as the corruption of morals, it is easily seen that divorces are in the highest degree hostile to the prosperity of families and States, springing as they do from the depraved morals of the people, and, as experience shows us, opening out a way to every kind of evil-doing in public as well as in private life.[37]

The voice of the Roman Catholic church was heard across Western society, as bishops condemned divorce, priests denounced it in sermons, and the Catholic press editorialized vigorously against it. Other reactionary groups contributed to create a chorus of opposition to what they perceived as the collapse of marriage. Some of these groups and individuals have been mentioned already in the context of the reactionary movement at the end of the nineteenth century (see Section 11.9). Much earlier than this, however, the libertarian notions and practices of the utopian socialists had produced a reaction within the broader communitarian movement. For example, the Hopedale Community, established in 1839 in Mendon, Massachusetts, was an independent Christian community that upheld what it believed was the traditional Christian view of marriage. Divorce was permitted, it is true, but only for reason of adultery, and only when the offense was conclusively proved.[38] Hopedale set itself firmly against libertarian doctrines that proposed the removal of conventional constraints, "especially in the matter of marriage, and [granted]... to each and everyone the privilege of forming connubial alliances and dissolving them at will, as inclination, pleasure, convenience, or whatever else, might dictate."[39] The community's principles of chastity, monogamy, and fidelity were challenged by a case of adultery in 1853, but the couple was forgiven after performing a penance. However, when they repeated the offense they were evicted from Hopedale and moved to another, presumably more liberal, community. This case of marital infidelity, occurring at a time when "the most lax, corrupting and dangerous sentiments concerning [marriage]... were bruited abroad and extolled throughout the general community," led Hopedale to issue a resolution in 1853 explicitly repudiating free love and upholding traditional Christian family values and practices.[40]

Not only within the broader utopian movement, but within the ranks of their own adherents, the utopian socialists in England encountered opposition specifically to their libertarian doctrines of marriage and sexuality. Barbara

---

[37] Leo XIII, *Arcanum Divinae Sapientiae*, February 10, 1880, in Joseph Husslein (comp.), *Social Wellsprings* (2 vols., Milwaukee, 1940–2), I, 38–9.
[38] Muncy, *Sex and Marriage*, 94.
[39] Adin Ballou, *History of the Hopedale Community* (Lowell, Mass., 1897), 246–7.
[40] Ibid., 248.

12.3 Conservative and reactionary approaches

Taylor's excellent book on socialism and feminism in the nineteenth century points to opposition toward greater laxness in marriage, particularly on the part of women.[41] The early decades of the nineteenth century were a period of transition in marriage patterns and ideology, and the frequent result was to make the status of working women more precarious than ever. An imbalance in the sex ratio produced a larger number of women than men in the prime marriage age groups, and to aggravate this men began to marry at later ages. At the same time women were pressed, ideologically and economically, to marry. In ideological terms the image of the Victorian woman, limiting her work to marriage and motherhood, began to filter down to the working classes. In economic terms, the limitations of women's employment and the lower wages women earned, placed them in a position of economic dependence. The result of these pressures was probably an increase in common-law marriages or simple cohabitation. This tendency, interpreted as a sign of the innate immorality of the lower orders, partly because of its effect in raising the illegitimacy rates, was noted by middle-class observers throughout the nineteenth century. Other factors militated against marriage as well. In England the cost of a marriage license and fees was about twelve shillings,[42] up to a week's wages for a poorer artisan, and many couples did not marry simply because they could not afford to.

In these circumstances of increased vulnerability, it is not surprising that many women were in favor of more stable and permanent marriage arrangements and the more rigorous enforcement of matrimonial obligations, especially when there were children to be supported. Taylor notes that the City Missionaries, who sought to improve the morals of the working classes, were frequently welcomed by women who lived in de facto marriages, and that they combined to urge the men in these relationships to put them on a legal basis.[43] To this extent, notions of loose sexual relationships, ill-defined marriages that had no more permanence than emotional passion, and vaguely phrased responsibilities for children must have sounded less than ideal to many women. It must have seemed that they already inhabited this particular utopia, and that they would rather be rescued from it than be condemned to it for life.

For many intellectuals, too, utopia lay not in a future of sexual and matrimonial libertarianism but in a past characterized by well-defined stable family responsibilities, uxorial obedience, and marital indissolubility. This was the image of the traditional family that was promoted by a number of reactionary theorists who sought to regain this lost familial paradise and restore it to the modern world in the second half of the nineteenth century. The regeneration of the family was an integral part of their yearning for a time when

---

[41] Taylor, *Eve and the New Jerusalem*. I have drawn here on Taylor's discussion of sex and marriage in the nineteenth century, esp. 192–205.

[42] Olive Anderson, "The Incidence of Civil Marriage in Victorian England and Wales," *Past and Present* 69 (1975), 65.

[43] Taylor, *Eve and the New Jerusalem*, 205.

involved. The motivations and the meaning of the liberalization of divorce policies are complex, not least because they involved a number of paradoxes. The trend of liberalization in divorce legislation has frequently been portrayed as indicative of changing attitudes toward the family, in particular an increasing acceptance of the equal rights of women and of individuality over the legal forms of marriage. Historians of the family from Arthur Calhoun to Carl Degler have emphasized the significance of divorce reform in the nineteenth century as reflecting more sympathetic attitudes toward women's rights.[49]

However, if we look closely at the reasons that legislators put forward to justify divorce law reform and at the substance of the reforms themselves, we can see that they were designed to achieve essentially conservative results. If they often give the appearance of aiming to change the character of the family, it is mainly for two reasons. First, we conventionally describe the reforms as "liberalization," thus appearing to distinguish them from conservative objectives and associating them with liberalism, even though they had little or nothing to do with liberal doctrines in any meaningful sense. Although the extension of the grounds for divorce allowed for the dissolution of the most unsatisfactory marriages, divorce remained very restrictive and highly regulated. "Divorce extension" might be a better term than "divorce liberalization," but the latter is more familiar. Second, divorce laws were reformed in the face of opposition that was conservative in the most strict sense of wishing to maintain the status quo. What we should recognize, however, is that for the most part those responsible for the reform of divorce laws shared the conservative ideals of marriage and the family, but differed on the means to achieve their realization. The reforms in marriage law might well be thought of as having been a more realistic and pragmatic approach to social conservatism.

These and other conclusions emerge from a consideration of the way in which divorce was liberalized from the middle of the nineteenth century up to the outbreak of World War I. Liberalization in this period consisted principally of the gradual accretion of specific matrimonial offenses or conditions, the most common being adultery, desertion, ill-treatment, cruelty, drunkenness, long-term imprisonment, and the failure to support a family. When omnibus clauses recognized such vaguely worded conditions as "incompatibility" or "intolerable circumstances," it was left to the judiciary to determine whether a specific case warranted a divorce. In all cases the definition of what was acceptable and what was not acceptable in marriage was made by a precise statutory provision or by judicial interpretation. As we should expect of nineteenth-century legislators and judges, the thrust of legal reform was thus to define as unacceptable those actions or conditions that were incompatible with a conventional middle-class image of the family. Adultery contradicted the ideal of sexual fidelity; desertion negated the duties of a spouse in all respects; wife beating contradicted the

---

[49] Arthur W. Calhoun, *A Social History of the American Family from Colonial Times to the Present* (3 vols., Cleveland, 1919), III, 271; Carl Degler, *At Odds: Women and the Family in America* (New York, 1980), 172.

ideals of marital harmony and of respect for women; drunkenness was anathema to the ideal of moderation and sobriety in all matters. If we needed a picture of the traits that made up the nineteenth-century middle-class ideal of marriage, we would find it in the mirror image of the grounds for divorce, for divorce was designed to reinforce the conventional family, not to change it.

Neither was it intended that divorce reform should be a vehicle for women's emancipation. For the most part, as we have seen, divorce was provided as a means of last resort in the worst cases of abuse and oppression within marriage. With the exception of adultery, which was a special case, the most commonly recognized grounds for divorce – desertion, cruelty, long-term imprisonment, and drunkenness – were assumed to be principally male offenses that involved women only as victims. To this extent the divorce laws fitted into the pattern of paternalistic social legislation of the nineteenth century that sought to protect women from the most harmful implications of their inferior status without attempting to change that status significantly.

Apart from the actual content of the divorce legislation enacted in this period, there are several other considerations that suggest that it was essentially conservative in its objectives. One was the fact that the reforms were carried out by men who were anything but radical, and often not even liberal, in their approaches to social issues. As unaccustomed and unwilling as we might be to accept politicians' affirmations at face value, we should believe the nineteenth-century legislators when they claimed to be interested only in ensuring the stability of the family and the permanence of marriages. Some, such as Alfred Naquet in France, might well have had a secret agenda and have sympathized with ideologies that looked to the eventual disappearance of conventional family forms, but they were few. Most saw limited divorce law reform as the most effective means of dealing with what they believed were the rare cases of abuse and exploitation, without affecting the great majority of marriages in any way. The second body of evidence in favor of the conservatism of divorce law reforms lies in the way in which the questions of marriage and divorce became intertwined with a number of social and moral issues during the nineteenth century. The objectives of the movements that focused on them and reactions to them throw additional light on the meaning of divorce reform, as a brief survey of the most common forms of divorce policy reform will show.

12.5 Divorce, social purity, and women's rights

From the middle of the nineteenth century drunkenness, habitual drunkenness, or drunkenness associated with other matrimonial offenses was added to the grounds for divorce in many American and Australian states, New Zealand, Germany, and Scandinavia, while elsewhere, such as in Scotland and England, drunkenness was made a ground for separation. This new emphasis reflected a growing and unprecedented concern at the social effects of alcohol consumption; even during the gin binge in eighteenth-century England, when alcohol

than men. Husbands, for their part, were expected to be active outside the home. They should work and support their families financially; the public world was their sphere of activity. As we have noted, many of the nineteenth-century reform movements, such as those that focused on temperance, drew their leadership and the bulk of their support from women, but this did not breach the division between the male and female spheres. Participation in these movements was seen as an extension of women's moral guardianship – extended, that is, beyond the confines of the home to society at large. It was recognized that corruption in the family had roots that extended deep into the social subsoil. To attack them at their source was a logical and necessary task for women to undertake, and one that enhanced, rather than contradicted, the essentially moral and nurturing roles that were ascribed to them.

The notion of separate spheres was not a description of how wives and husbands actually functioned in nineteenth-century marriages, but it was a powerful ideological prescription. It described the ideal marital relationship in which wives and husbands had complementary but different roles. Nothing could be more logical than that a consistent failure to practice the ideal should be a reason for terminating the marriage, and so it was that divorce codes began to express the principles bound up in the doctrine of separate spheres. As we have noted, Australasian divorce laws provided for the dissolution of marriage when either husband or wife failed to perform the specific domestic roles allotted to them: support and service, respectively. This trend is observable in American divorce laws, too. In 1883, for example, Maine included among the grounds for divorce "gross, cruel, and wanton neglect or refusal by the husband, being able, to provide for the wife." Kentucky divorce law cast a somewhat wider net and coupled domestic responsibility to alcohol abuse; divorce could be obtained by a married woman when her husband had had a confirmed habit of drunkenness for at least a year and it was "accompanied with a wasting of his estate, and without any suitable provision for the maintenance of his wife and children."[58] In many American states, however, the tendency was less toward statutory reform along these lines and more for the judiciary to extend the concept of cruelty to accommodate offenses such as extravagance, failure to support adequately, and negligence in caring for the household.[59]

The essence of the doctrine of separate spheres was the difference between men and women, but although it was stoutly defended by many social reformers, other areas where law and social practice had enshrined gender distinctions were vigorously assailed. Perhaps the most important of these was the double standard of sexual morality that had traditionally given men more

---

[58] Howard, *Matrimonial Institutions*, III, 18, 54.

[59] The issues involved in divorces for reason of failure to fulfill financial and material obligations are discussed in Elaine Tyler May, "The Pressure to Provide. Class, Consumerism, and Divorce in Urban America, 1880–1920," *Journal of Social History* 12 (1978), 180–93.

latitude than women in terms of sexual activity and initiative.[60] During the nineteenth century medical and scientific evidence was adduced to support long-standing social beliefs that men were more sexually active than women, less modest, more sexually motivated.[61] Women, on the other hand, were assumed to be naturally modest, to have at most a moderate sex drive, and to have an innate propensity toward chastity that men might only envy. In the later nineteenth century, however, the double standard came under a concerted attack led by the social purity movement that saw it as one of the fundamental causes of many of the most appalling vices rampant in society: prostitution, seduction, adultery, illegitimacy, and the spread of venereal diseases. One speaker to the first American National Purity Congress in 1895 pointed out that "the only true way to deal with prostitution is, first, to diminish the demand upon which it is based by stamping vice with public reprobation in men as well as in women."[62] She rejected the notion that prostitution protected family values by permitting men to satiate their sexual appetites without subjecting their wives to frequent or immoderate intercourse:

That wives and mothers should be pure, another class of women must have the whole balance of evil poured out upon them. The higher sense of mankind says that the family is the essential unit of the State. Our practice says the family plus prostitution is the essential unit.[63]

In England and the British colonies opponents of the double standard attacked the Contagious Diseases Acts, regulations that required prostitutes, or women suspected of being prostitutes, to submit to physical examinations for venereal disease but that did not require their male clients to do likewise.[64]

For our purposes the important common element in the various moral campaigns was their rejection of the double standard of sexual morality, particularly as it bore on adultery. The argument was prominent in social purity and other reform literature that illicit sexual behavior should not be treated more leniently when committed by men that when committed by women. Men, it was argued, should be educated and socialized to follow the rules of modesty and moderation that most women already observed. "Equality of moral obligation," one speaker told the 1895 Moral Purity Congress, "is the one idea

---

[60] See Keith Thomas, "The Double Standard," *Journal of the History of Ideas* 20 (1959), 195–216 for a survey of the principle.

[61] See Jill Conway, "Stereotypes of Femininity in a Theory of Sexual Evolution," in Martha Vicinus (ed.) *Suffer and Be Still: Women in the Victorian Age* (Bloomington, 1973), 140–54. Degler discusses theories of women's sexuality in *At Odds*, 249–78.

[62] Emily Blackwell, "The Responsibility of Women in Regard to Questions Concerning Public Morality," in *National Purity Congress*, 79.

[63] Ibid., 74.

[64] Paul McHugh, *Prostitution and Victorian Social Reform* (London, 1980); Judith R. Walkowitz and Daniel J. Walkowitz, " 'We are not beasts of the field': Prostitution and the Poor in Plymouth and Southampton under the Contagious Diseases Acts," in Mary Hartmann and Lois W. Banner (eds.), *Clio's Consciousness Raised* (New York, 1974), 192–225.

moved to strike Stanton's resolution from the minutes on the ground that divorce concerned men as well and was therefore not an appropriate issue to be discussed at a conference devoted to women's rights. This move was defeated and the draft resolution was recorded, but the convention refused to adopt it.[73]

The confusion over divorce at Seneca Falls was indicative of the division on opinion within the American women's rights movement that persisted throughout the nineteenth century and beyond. Prominent advocates of women's rights such as Stanton, Amelia Bloomer, and Susan B. Anthony insisted that liberal divorce policies were beneficial to women, but Stanton pursued the divorce reform cause more assiduously and openly than the others, making it a fundamental part of her feminist philosophy; the marriage question, she argued, "lies at the very foundation of all progress."[74] At the 1852 Women's State Temperance Society conference Stanton (who was the society's president) called for habitual drunkenness to be a ground for divorce ("let no woman remain in the relation of wife with the confirmed drunkard"),[75] and a letter from her to the 1856 women's rights convention shocked the audience by its radical proposals for divorce law reform.[76]

Stanton clearly expressed her liberal views in her speech to the 1860 convention. Marriage and divorce, she insisted, were private matters that should not be regulated by secular or church law. Marriage should be a simple contract, and if legislators wanted to interfere with it they should do so by making divorce easier and marriage more difficult by raising the minimum age for marriage and imposing mandatory waiting periods to prevent hasty marriages. As for the specific grounds for divorce, Stanton proposed drunkenness, insanity, desertion, cruel and brutal treatment, adultery, and simple incompatibility.[77]

Not only were these views not influential in New York state, which had one of the most restrictive divorce laws in the United States until the 1960s, but they were not shared within the women's rights movement. The 1860 convention, like its predecessors, failed to adopt the resolution calling for more liberal divorce legislation. Some prominent feminists, such as Susan B. Anthony, feared that a too liberal approach to divorce would frighten away many potential converts to the movement, and Lucy Stone lumped divorce, abortion, and infanticide together as subjects too sensitive to be discussed.[78] Yet others were simply opposed to the policy of more liberal divorce, seeing it as a threat to the institutions of marriage and the family, and by extension to the social order. The conservative approach of the women's rights movement to marriage and

---

[73] Ibid., 204.
[74] Elisabeth Griffith, *In Her Own Right: The Life of Elizabeth Cady Stanton* (New York, 1984), 104–5.
[75] Ibid., 76, 101. See also Ross Evans Paulson, *Women's Suffrage and Prohibition: A Comparative Study of Equality and Social Control* (Glenview, Ill., 1973), 70.
[76] Griffith, *In Her Own Right*, 102.
[77] On Stanton and divorce, see ibid., 86–107.
[78] Ibid., 102.

divorce reform is particularly revealing. As Carl Degler has pointed out, most American women did not rally to the cause of women's suffage mainly because it was perceived as a threat to the family.[79] Women's suffrage was predicated on the individuality of women and their right to assert their own self-interests, notions quite at variance with the role that was prescribed for women in the nineteenth-century family. The apprehension that the women's rights movement threatened to destroy the family lay behind the movement – dominated by women – that campaigned against women's suffrage from the 1890s.[80] In terms of divorce, we find that there was, if anything, a consensus between the suffragists and the antisuffragists. Despite the existence of a group within the women's rights movement that did seek to change marriage and the family, both movements shared a commitment to the maintenance of prevailing family values. Where they differed was on their respective assessments of the impact of women's legal and political equality on the family; many of the women's rights advocates held that the reforms they sought would only strengthen the family, whereas the antisuffragists saw women's equality as a negation of its very essence.

The fundamentally conservative objectives of many reforms in women's status extended to many aspects of divorce law reform. As we have noted, one area of reform in many jurisdictions was the removal of the double standard of sexual morality and the extension to women of the same access as men to divorce. A case in point was New Zealand, which had legalized divorce in 1867 on English principles (for reason of the wife's adultery or the husband's aggravated adultery), and which in 1893 was the first country to give women the vote in national elections. The granting of women's suffrage, together with other improvements in women's rights to education and employment, reinforced feminist arguments in favor of equality in family law. Prominent women's organizations, such as the Women's Christian Temperance Union and the National Council of Women agitated for women to be put on an equal footing in divorce law, and in 1895 alone fourteen petitions on these lines were presented to parliament by women's organizations.[81] Liberalization was far less attractive than equalization, however, as a paper read to the 1898 conference of the National Council of Women suggests, warning of "the very free divorce laws in force in the United States of America [that] did not lead to satisfactory results."[82]

Despite the mixed attitudes of New Zealand feminists toward divorce law reform in the 1880s and 1890s, it was perceived as a feminist issue and attacked

---

[79] Degler, *At Odds*, 342ff.
[80] Ibid., 349.
[81] Phillips, *Divorce in New Zealand*, 32–3. American temperance advocates also urged equality, even though they did not favor the liberalization of divorce laws. See Ruth Bordin, *Women and Temperance: The Quest for Power and Liberty* (Philadelphia, 1981), 14.
[82] *The National Council of the Women of New Zealand. Third Session, April 20–28, 1898* (Wanganui, 1898), 61.

tions. The status of women within marriage and the family was immeasurably improved, but women were denied political rights; in 1913 women were specifically excluded from the suffrage, and it was not won until 1945, and even then there were restrictions. In this respect, Portugal reversed the order of political and family law reforms that were enacted in most other parts of Western society at this time. The reason seems simply to have been that this was the way the French republicans had done things at the end of the eighteenth century.

The Portuguese example highlights the limited scope of divorce liberalization elsewhere. Even though divorce reform was urged by proponents of radical social change, we should not think that the reforms that took place responded to anything but conservative objectives. As we have seen, they reflected some of the most prominent social issues of the day, such as the social effects of alcohol, the decline of morality, and notions such as domesticity, femininity, and the doctrine of separate spheres for women and for men. Few if any of the reforms satisfied the demands of the progressives who wanted to equalize the status of wife and husband, for the grounds introduced into divorce codes everywhere were based on the principles that women were subordinate within marriage and that they needed not equality but simply protection from the worst moral and physical effects of their subordination.

This is certainly not to say that those who fought for social purity, temperance, and general social reform necessarily approved of divorce even in these limited cases. Most of the speakers at the 1895 National Purity Congress who referred to divorce condemned it without qualification. They were uncompromising in their commitment to the integrity of marriage and the family and saw their task as that of purifying morals and behavior, not surrendering to immorality, as liberalizing divorce appeared to them to do. One speaker condemned the divorce laws that had been enacted in the United States, and cited them as examples of the rule that "all trifling with fundamental and approved institutions of society means mischief, social disorder, social danger, social sin and inevitable corruption."[91] The temperance movement was no more inclined to urge divorce for habitual drunkenness than the social purity advocates were to advocate it where one spouse was impure. In 1886 the *Union Signal*, the newspaper of the Women's Christian Temperance Union in the United States, had proposed that divorce should be accepted in cases of habitual drunkenness, but in the early 1890s there was a vigorous debate on the policy that the union ought to adopt on divorce.[92] One 1895 letter to the *Union Signal* from a member nicely expressed the conservative view.

[91] J. B. Welty, "The Need of White Cross Work," *National Purity Congress*, 241. The view seems to have been shared by Canadian moral reformers: see Snell, "Defence of Marriage."

[92] Barbara Leslie Epstein, *The Politics of Domesticity, Women, Evangelism, and Temperance in Nineteenth-Century America* (Middletown, Conn., 1981), 135. The leader of the American temperance movement, Frances Willard, believed that women were enslaved within marriage, but could not bring herself to support divorce. See Bordin, *Women and Temperance*, 114.

12.6 Divorce and the eugenics movement

I cannot think of anything more dangerous to home and to society [than divorce]...
Whatever breaks down the home, hurts woman most, because she is most dependent
upon home affections for her happiness...There are no true friends of the real ad-
vancement of woman who would attempt to loosen the bond of marriage or to make it
anything less than the life long union of one man and one woman.[93]

The editorial board of the newspaper, caught within the debate, tried to
compromise by suggesting that drunkenness should justify a separation. This
would be a legal remedy but would not, they hoped, offend the conservatives;
"indeed," they pointed out anxiously, "a legal separation, which forbids the
marrying again of either party during the lifetime of the other, tends rather to
emphasize its indissolubility."[94]

Apart from the common areas of divorce law reform that have been discussed
so far in this chapter, some legislators used divorce policy to respond to specific
issues as they arose. In the early nineteenth century, for example, a number of
American states permitted divorce when one spouse joined a religious sect that
rejected marriage or sexual intercourse. These clauses were provoked by the
attraction of the Shaker movement, which taught that human misery derived
from the sexual sins of Adam and Eve. Shakers rejected marriage and espoused
celibacy; it was not necessary to procreate, they believed, because after the
millennium life would be eternal.[95] Many of the adherents to the Shaker
philosophy were married, so that their religious commitment entailed
suspension of the social effects of their marital status. (The founder of the
Shakers, Ann Lee, had been deserted by her husband.) To the extent that
acceptance of Shaker principles entailed a rejection of marriage, divorce of a
Shaker spouse seemed a reasonable reform that appealed to many American
states.[96]

12.6 Divorce and the eugenics movement

A final but major area of divorce reform whose roots were firmly implanted in
the late nineteenth century centered on insanity. The influence here was the
eugenics movement, which intersected at vital points with the broader concerns
with social purity and that was a specific reaction to the perceived decline and
degeneration of Western populations. Eugenics was based on pseudoscientific
principles predicated on the belief that a wide range of physical, medical, and
moral conditions, from syphilis to alcoholism to criminality, were biologically
inherited. Eugenics theories purported to explain racial degeneration, and
eugenicists put forward suggestions for policies and legislation they believed

---

[93] Epstein, *Politics of Domesticity*, 134.
[94] Ibid.
[95] On divorce issues related to the Shakers see Nelson Blake, *The Road to Reno: A History of Divorce in the United States* (New York, 1962), 69–77.
[96] For example in 1830 Massachusetts extended divorce to cases where one spouse joined a sect which rejected marriage. Howard, *Matrimonial Institutions*, III, 18.

hand, he argued, divorce was often provoked by men who wanted to marry another woman who "had aroused sexual desires." In this sense divorce increased the field of choice for mating, and because divorced men tended to marry women who were younger than their first wives, the result would be increased fertility. This would counteract the fertility decline that so concerned eugenicists. The critical question for Darwin, however, was not simply whether the number of children was increased, but whether the quality of the race was raised or lowered by divorce. Like tended to marry like, he suggested, and it was probable that divorced people were below average in terms of what he called "civic worth." Although he conceded that this was "not a matter on which a decision can be given with perfect confidence," Darwin pointed out that an incapacity to live in harmony with one's spouse indicated "some serious defect in character and qualities." He went on to argue that it was generally the less desirable partner who remarried and that because most divorces were obtained on the ground of adultery, remarriages would produce children with an inherited predisposition toward adultery. The overall conclusion of this work was that for eugenic reasons divorce should be regulated very carefully, and Darwin proposed that only one ground should be recognized, namely, an unbroken seven-year period of noncohabitation.

The effects of the eugenicist arguments on divorce legislation varied from place to place, but the most common form was the progressive inclusion of insanity among the grounds for divorce. It is true that insanity had been recognized as a ground in earlier divorce codes – by royal dispensation in Sweden from the seventeenth century, under the 1792 French divorce law, and in the 1843 Pennsylvania legislation (the wife's insanity only) – but the reasons had not been eugenic. Rather than manifesting concern at the social consequences of inherited insanity, these earlier provisions were designed to free married men and women from partners who were unable to perform the functions normally required in a marriage. In the early twentieth century, however, the eugenic arguments led legislators in many countries and states to add insanity to the grounds for divorce. One of the first examples of eugenic influence was a 1907 New Zealand law allowing divorce where one spouse had been confined to an asylum for ten of the twelve years preceding the divorce petition and where there was little hope of recovery. A number of considerations lay behind this legal reform, one being that it was unfair to compel a man or a woman to remain married to an incapable spouse, but the eugenic justification was dominant. One Member of Parliament argued forcefully that

we have got to guard this colony against the fertility of the unfit. It is the question of the procreation of children that we have to consider...What is to become of the future peoples of this dominion if we allow either a man or a woman who has been certified to as a lunatic to come back and resume cohabitation, resulting in the breeding of a race which...would be unfortunate in every sense of the word.[108]

108 Phillips, *Divorce in New Zealand*, 37.

12.6 Divorce and the eugenics movement

Taken to its logical conclusion this position might have led to mandatory divorce, but the legislation did not go that far.

In making insanity a ground for divorce for eugenic reasons New Zealand, then a progressive nation in terms of its social policies, was well in the lead of most other jurisdictions that hesitated when confronted by the moral dilemmas that insanity presented. There was no shortage of advocates that insanity should be a ground for divorce for reasons of eugenic advantage and individual interest. One American doctor wrote that mental disease alters or abolishes the normal personality and that divorce of the insane was "a measure of defense for the sane and of preservation of society against procreation of the mentally abnormal."[109] Against this view was posed the traditional and Christian argument that it was immoral for one partner to repudiate the other when the latter was suffering a mental illness or disease: "The constancy of husband and wife to one another in sickness or health, in accordance with the marriage vow, is the crown of matrimony, and rebellious passion is too mean a flame to burn by its side."[110] Supporters of this perspective argued that the spouse of an insane person should not think of divorce, but should be prepared to stand by the side of the afflicted party in the hope of an eventual recovery. Even some eugenicists opposed divorce in such circumstances. Leonard Darwin, a relative conservative in these matters as we have noted, held that a "high-minded" person would not divorce his or her insane spouse, but would loyally await recovery, while taking great care to avoid parenthood.[111]

Only a few countries quickly followed New Zealand in invoking eugenic reasons for making insanity a ground for divorce. The Scandinavian nations, also socially progressive, were among them. Insanity had not been recognized as a ground for divorce by statute in Sweden, but marriages had been dissolved in such circumstances by royal dispensation. Of the total 4,735 divorces by judicial decree or royal fiat granted in Sweden between 1901 and 1910, only 132 (2.8%) were for reason of insanity.[112] When the Swedish Law Commission was charged in 1910 with the task of drafting a revision of the country's code of family law, which envisaged the abolition of divorce by royal dispensation, insanity was shifted to the list of specified grounds for judicial divorce. The eugenic argument was recognized by the commission, which noted the "increasingly strong demands...for legislation which shall safeguard the future generations and improve the human race...[legislation that would] prevent the marriage of those who are, from a eugenic point of view, unfit and also provide means for the dissolution of such marriages."[113] The commission

---

[109] Quoted in Chester G. Vernier, *American Family Laws* (5 vols., Stanford, 1932), II, 59.
[110] Ibid.
[111] Darwin, *Eugenic Reform*, 474–5.
[112] Johan Thorsten Sellin, *Marriage and Divorce Legislation in Sweden* (Ph.D. diss., University of Pennsylvania, 1922), 85. The percentage of divorces granted for reason of insanity did not change after the 1915 law, making insanity a ground for judicial divorce, came into effect.
[113] Ibid., 59.

family were translated into law (see Chapter 13). For the most part the real debate throughout Western society – in the sense of the debate that resulted in law and policy – excluded the radicals, the extreme reactionaries and social progressives, the libertarians, and the liberals. The debate that gave birth to nineteenth- and early-twentieth-century divorce reform took place between two kinds of conservatives: those who believed that the conventional family was best protected by prohibiting divorce and those who thought that the same objective was more effectively achieved by allowing restrictive divorce. The divorce reformers were liberals only in terms of this narrow spectrum, for they held to the primacy of marriage over the wishes and happiness of the spouses. Divorce by mutual consent or for reason of incompatibility was rejected almost everywhere, and divorce was closely controlled by expensive and rigorous procedures, just as marriage itself was increasingly regulated.[124] The outcry at the exceptions, notably the American divorce colonies, by men who were liberals on the divorce issue in their home states, demonstrates their own relative conservatism. Divorce was to be no more than an escape valve, designed to release spouses, especially wives who needed the assistance and protection of the law, when the pressure of marital oppression reached intolerable levels.

One of the clearest statements of the compatibility of limited divorce with the maintenance of traditional relationships within the family was a survey conducted by the Women's Cooperative Guild in Great Britain and presented to the 1909 royal commission on the English divorce law. The guild was an organization of some 27,000 working-class women, almost all of whom were married and had ceased work outside the home after marriage. Their brief to the commission described them thus:

They have the strict tradition of an old civilization in their view of the duty of a housewife and mother. Neglect of the home is not tolerated, and there is no disposition to be hard on husbands, or to look lightly on drunkenness, uncleanliness, thriftlessness, or other faults in women. They are not of the class which readily takes the law of marital relations into its own hands.[125]

Within these views the members of the guild were able to accommodate demands for an extension of the grounds for divorce, almost all matching those issues discussed in this chapter. The double standard of morality was rejected unanimously, one respondent to the survey writing that "a woman has the right to expect from a man the same purity that he demands from her."[126] The proposed grounds for divorce that received most support were, in descending order of popularity, cruelty (including the communicating of diseases, especially

---

[124] See Michael Grossberg, "Guarding the Altar: Physiological Restrictions and the Rise of State Intervention in Matrimony," *American Journal of Legal History* 26 (1982), 197–226.
[125] *Working Women and Divorce: An Account of Evidence Given on Behalf of the Women's Co-operative Guild before the Royal Commission on Divorce* (London, 1911), 2–3.
[126] Ibid., 5.

venereal diseases); insanity (for both personal reasons and "to benefit the future race"); desertion; and the husband's persistent refusal to support his wife and family.[127] The respondents to the guild's questionnaire also favored allowing divorce by mutual consent or where there was serious incompatibility, but the main thrust of their recommendations for divorce law reform, together with the very language they employed, reflected the moral and social principles that characterized writing on the family in this period.

The use of divorce as a tool by social engineers from the middle of the nineteenth century to the end of World War I involved many contradictions. There was the problem of reconciling equality of women and men before the law with conventional morality. There was the contradiction inherent between the belief that for the most part the behavior defined as matrimonial offenses worthy of divorce – drunkenness, imprisonment, adultery, failure to support a family – were assumed to be concentrated in the working class, and the fact that the costs of divorce placed it beyond the reach of most working-class wives.[128] Yet such contradictions, paradoxes, and tensions were, it seems, inherent in any conservative treatment of divorce; to have denied women the protection of the law would have produced only a different set of them. Under the conflicting pressures to conserve and to modify, but with an eye constantly to social stability, legislators and judges in this period sanctioned divorce in a way they hoped would ensure that divorces were rare and that marriage was fundamentally unaffected. When the number and rates of divorce began to rise in the last decades of the nineteenth century, they did so despite the divorce reforms, not because of them.

[127] Ibid., 13ff.
[128] Canada was one country where this contradiction did not apply. Divorce law was not reformed in this period and the high costs of divorce ensured that it was available only to the very well-off. Snell, "Defence of Marriage," 129.

13 The twentieth century: Rise of mass divorce

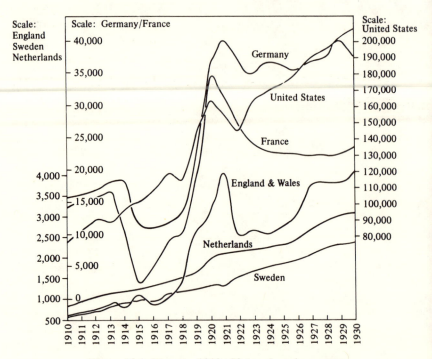

Figure 13.1 Divorces 1910–30 in selected countries.

predispose them toward breakdown and their dissolution by divorce.[7] There appear to be four principal circumstances that largely explain why marital relationships might be, and are, weakened by wartime conditions. First, many marriages are contracted during the war after the couple have known each other for only a short time, certainly a shorter time than the couple would normally – that is, in peacetime – have waited before contemplating marriage. War, specifically the expectation that the male partner might soon leave on active service, has in this sense an accelerating effect on courtship that is not neutralized by the possibility that the new bride might just as rapidly become a young widow. Arthur Marwick writes of morality that "the safest generalization about the First World War would be that it was a time of powerfully heightened emotional activity and responses."[8] This "emotional activity" found one formal shape in marriage, as evidenced by the increased number of marriages in the early phases of the war, before the young men left for battle. In England marriages had numbered 288,000 annually between 1912 and 1914, but in 1915 they leapt to 361,000, a 25% increase. In the later war years, when the number of marriageable men was reduced, the marriage rate fell below the

[7] For a general discussion of divorce and World War I see Jacobson and Jacobson, *American Marriage and Divorce*, 91–2, and Rowntree and Carrier, "Resort to Divorce," 203–5.

[8] Arthur Marwick, *The Deluge: British Society and the First World War* (Harmondsworth, 1967), 118.

prewar levels.[9] The effect of the war on the American marriage rate can be plotted more precisely. The United States entered World War I in April 1917, and marriages immediately increased. From a monthly average of 74,000 in the first three months of 1917, marriages rose to 112,000 in April, 93,000 in May, and 130,000 in June, giving a monthly average of 112,000, a 50% increase overall.[10]

The link between the increase in marriages at the outbreak of war (1914 for England, 1917 for the United States) and the increase in divorce after the war lies in the assumption that many wartime marriages, more than in peacetime, at any rate, united men and women who were ill-matched. The assumption is that had it not been for the war many of these couples would not have married, that the marriages were for this reason fragile to begin with and were certainly not strong enough to survive the hardships of years of separation that the war could impose. This explanation appeals to common sense, and no doubt many marriages that contributed to the early wartime marriage boom also contributed to the postwar divorce bulge in countries such as the United States and England. But it does not help to explain the increased divorce rates of Germany and France after the war: These two countries experienced not an increase but a decline in marriages in the early war period. Marriages in France fell from 299,000 in 1913 to 205,000 in 1914, before plummeting to 86,000 in 1915. They recovered only from 1918 onward.[11] In Germany marriages declined from 513,000 in 1913 to 461,000 in 1914 and then more dramatically to 278,000 in 1915.[12] Yet despite the apparent absence of wartime marriages following a rapid courtship, the divorce rates in France and Germany shot up after the war. Clearly, although wartime marriages might have contributed to the postwar rise in divorce in some countries, they cannot be invoked as a factor in all cases.

There are three other broad explanations for the increased divorce rates after World War I. One is that the enforced separation of husbands from wives weakened not only recent marriages but also many marriages of comparatively long-standing. This factor should have had less effect in the United States since there was only a year and a half between the departure of American troops for the European battlefields and the end of hostilities. It was potentially far more important an influence on French, German, British, and colonial marriage and divorce rates. Again, we can only generalize about the social, personal, and other factors at work here. One profitable area of investigation lies in the differing wartime experiences of a husband who was absent from home on military service and a wife who stayed at home. Their divergent experiences of the war must have affected them in different ways such that they developed

[9] B. R. Mitchell, *European Historical Statistics 1750–1975* (2nd rev. edn. London, 1980), 106.
[10] Jacobson and Jacobson, *American Marriage and Divorce*, 25, Table 3. To some extent the impressive number of marriages in June 1917 reflected a social preference for June weddings. More marriages normally took place in June than in any other single month.
[11] Mitchell, *European Historical Statistics*, 101.
[12] Ibid., 102.

13.2 World War I and the 1920s

It was the same for married women who remained at home during the war: Although most probably remained faithful, many equally certainly did not. Some men returned home to find children or pregnancies for which they themselves could not possibly have been responsible. In his impressionistic account of life in Salford in northern England at this time, Robert Roberts writes of the married women who had gone to London during the war and had a good time with soldiers who were on leave: "Some returned to home and husband with a very dented reputation," whereas others turned permanently to prostitution.[17] Indeed, some married women might have turned to that profession for financial reasons during their husbands' absence. For a variety of reasons, it should be noted, women's adultery was more susceptible than men's of discovery. Like men, women risked contracting a sexually transmitted disease, but unlike men they also risked becoming pregnant. Even without such misfortunes, married women living at home lived under the surveillance of neighbors and community. Gossip must surely have reached the ears of demobilized soldiers, and some neighbors are known to have been thoughtful enough to send men on military service anonymous letters detailing their wives' indiscretions. In crude terms, an English wife's adultery at home, her comings and goings and associations with a man or men, were far more likely to be observed and reported than, let us say, her husband's visits to a brothel in France or Egypt. Apart from the relative anonymity that war can provide, there must also have been a tacit and mutually beneficial consensus that soldiers did not report their colleagues' sexual activities.

Some effects of wartime marital infidelity were quite evident in England, where adultery was the sole ground for divorce. Up to 1915 women had consistently filed more than 40% of divorce petitions (for reason of their husbands' aggravated adultery), but in the five years from 1916 to 1920 the proportion of women's petitions fell, running at 33, 27, 23, 20, and 29%, respectively, each year. Only in 1921 did the percentage of women's petitions return to the prewar levels.[18] This shift in the sex ratio of divorce petitioners, occurring in the years of an increased divorce rate, meant simply that many more husbands divorced their wives on the ground of adultery in the later-war and postwar years. In 1919 and 1920 alone, a total of 7,387 men divorced their adulterous wives, more than all the divorces in England in the war years combined.

A further partial explanation of the increased number of divorces after the war is that they compensated for the decline in divorces and divorce rates during the war period. In most countries involved in the war divorces and rates decreased during the time of actual military engagement, whether this was of three or four years (as in England, France, and Germany) or one year (as in the case of the United States, where divorces dipped in 1918). Given the trends in divorce from the late nineteenth century to World War I, divorce rates might

[17] Roberts, *Classic Slum*, 230.
[18] Statistics from Carrier and Rowntree, "Resort to Divorce," 204, Table 4.

521

well have been expected to increase steadily. In fact the circumstances of war produced a period of decline, a deficit compared to what might have been anticipated had the war not occurred. The increased resort to divorce after the war can be seen in part as compensation for that deficit. This explanation cannot be confirmed at the level of individual marriages. We can speculate that some divorces, which would have taken place between 1914 and 1918 had there been no war, were postponed until the war was over. The separation of husbands and wives by war made divorce proceedings more complex, and, moreover, the very fact of separation would have made the need to dissolve a marriage that much less urgent. Such suggestions must be speculative, although it is important to acknowledge, at a more general level, the compensatory effect of postwar divorces for the wartime decline in the use of divorce.

The increased use of divorce was not wholly the result of war conditions in every country, however, and in England it is clear that procedural changes made divorce more widely available. In June 1914, just before the outbreak of hostilities, a Poor Persons' Procedure gave the less well-off better access to divorce. Until 1914 divorce proceedings for the poor (*in forma pauperis*) made volunteer solicitors and barristers available free of charge (though incidental costs such as traveling expenses had to be borne by the petitioner), but this service was available only to those owning property valued at less than twenty-five pounds. This limit effectively excluded most wage earners, so that "pauper divorces" were rare, estimated at only about fifteen a year.[19] From June 1914, however, the property ownership level was raised to a hundred pounds, and the divorce actions thereby made possible under the pauper rules contributed to the overall increase in divorces in England. One study suggests, in fact, that this change of procedure was responsible for as much as 40% of the increase in divorces between 1914 and 1922, that the war and its consequences accounted for 33%, and that a normal trend of increase explains 17%.[20] A glance at Figure 13.1, however, shows that the movement of divorces in England and Wales followed a pattern similar to that in countries such as France, Germany, and the United States, where there were no equivalent procedural changes just before or during the war. It is possible, then, that had the Poor Persons' Procedure not been introduced, the divorce trend in England might have looked more like the Netherlands or Sweden than the other countries.

The dramatic rise in the level of divorces after World I had several other dimensions. Although it is easy enough to understand that stresses and conflicts might have occurred in more marriages as a result of the war, there is no ready explanation as to why so many of these marriages were dissolved. We should like to know why men and women – more men than women in this period – were apparently so ready to file for divorce than to opt for alternatives, such as living together unhappily or simply ceasing to live together without

[19] Ibid., 193.
[20] Ibid., 204–5.

going through a legal formality. We must, in short, distinguish between marriage breakdown and divorce here. There is no way of calculating the proportion of socially or emotionally dissolved marriages that do not end in divorce at any given time but the argument that appeals to increased breakdown due to war rests on the assumption that the couples involved were predisposed to end their marriages definitively. The assumption could be valid. It could well be that the end of war and the outbreak of peace produced a sentiment that sought to shed or reject the past and look to the future. The question of one's marriage could have been part and parcel of this sentiment. Put crudely, many men and women, having survived the trenches and the rigors of war at home, might have had little wish to participate in a peacetime marriage that meant stress or outright conflict. Looked at from their point of view, as part of a desire to start life anew after the war, divorce can be seen as a facet of the process of sloughing off the conflict-ridden past – a sort of matrimonial demobilization.

A second important point about divorces in the postwar period is that they ushered in a period in which the level of divorce was much higher than it had been before the war. As Figure 13.1 shows, after the phases of greatly increased divorce, the number and rate of divorces generally settled at significantly elevated levels. Divorces in prewar Germany had fallen in the range 15,000 to 20,000 a year, but in the 1920s averaged between 35,000 and 40,000. Before the war there had never been more than 1,000 divorces in England in any year, but in the 1920s the annual range was between 2,500 and 4,000. To some extent the increased use of divorce in the 1920s might have been spurred by the familiarity with divorce that the postwar boom engendered; divorce must have lost some of its mystery and even some of its taboo qualities at this time (shifts in attitudes and their implications are discussed more fully in Section 14.5). It is apparent that among legislators in the West there was a new liberal attitude toward divorce, and the 1920s saw a fresh burst of legislative activity, extending the grounds for divorce and making access to divorce easier for more sections of the population, especially women. This liberalization of divorce laws was itself a significant manifestation of more liberal attitudes, and it in turn facilitated an increase in the number of divorces.

In the 1920s people in Europe, North America, and Australasia seemed to breathe a collective sigh of relief. The great and long-expected war had finally come and gone, and had catalyzed international and social tensions; there was a feeling that the potential existed for the world to start afresh, almost from first principles. Such expectations proved to be as misplaced as the notion that the recent conflict had been the war to end all wars, but they nonetheless injected a sense of freedom and optimism into Western society. The Russian Revolution gave a boost to socialists and others who wanted to believe that paradise might yet be regained, morals and manners seemed to undergo a phase of liberalization, and young middle-class women in particular made a vivid social impact. The economic and social problems that followed the world war in Europe especially have not detracted from the images of the "gay," "roaring," and "swinging" twenties.

Changes in social and moral attitudes, together with increasing prosperity later in the decade, almost inevitably had an impact on marriage. In most countries the crude marriage rate increased between 1920 and 1930, and divorced men and women made up an increased proportion of grooms and brides. In the United States the proportion of the divorced among those married in the 1920s was twice that among those married before the war.[21] The flood of divorces immediately after the war raised the profile of divorce not only on the marriage market but in society generally. It cannot but have increased the direct exposure and daily contact of millions of men and women to divorce, and in doing so influenced attitudes toward divorce.

In an impressionistic contemporary account of the 1920s in America, Frederick Lewis Allen wrote of the "decline in the amount of disgrace accompanying divorce," and gave his opinion that in the cities at least, divorced men and women were socially accepted without question. Indeed, he went on,

there was often about the divorced person just enough of an air of unconventionality, just enough of a touch of scarlet, to be considered rather dashing and desirable. Many young women probably felt as did the young New York girl who said, toward the end of the decade, that she was thinking of marrying Henry, although she didn't care very much for him, because even if they didn't get along she could get a divorce and "it would be much more exciting to be a divorcee than to be an old maid."[22]

Probably not a widely shared sentiment, it might nevertheless have been indicative of change. Certainly the divorce rate was considerably higher in the 1920s than it had been before the war, and it seemed to attest to the persistent effect of the postwar divorce boom.

But it would, of course, place too much weight on attitudes to explain increased postwar divorce solely in terms of them. The 1920s witnessed dramatic changes in other aspects of social and political life. The status of women rose somewhat with the extension of women's suffrage during or after the war. Before 1914 women had been granted the vote only in New Zealand (1893), Australia (1902), Finland (1907), Norway (1913), and in eleven of the western states of the United States. In 1920 American women were granted the vote nationally, and after the war it was gained in Britain, Sweden, Germany, and in many other European and Western countries. The interwar period also saw an extension of social welfare and related programs, shifts in the composition of the labor force that had implications for separation and divorce, and changing expectations of marriage. Many of these questions are taken up in Chapter 14,

---

[21] In 1910, 3% of grooms and 4% of brides had been divorced; in 1925 the respective proportions were 7 and 8%. Calculated from Jacobson and Jacobson, *American Marriage and Divorce*, 168, Table A15.

[22] Frederick Lewis Allen, *Only Yesterday: An Informal History of the 1920's* (New York, 1931, repr. 1964), 95.

and for the rest of this chapter we shall be concerned primarily with describing the trends of divorce from the 1920s to the 1980s, and the influences on them of legislation, family policy, and political change.

13.3 Reform in Britain, the empire, and the United States

England is a prime example of the liberalization of divorce law. At the end of World War I divorce was still available in England only on the very restrictive terms of the first (1857) divorce legislation, which enabled men to divorce their wives for reason of simple adultery, but which required women to prove aggravated adultery in order to obtain a divorce. As early as 1912 a royal commission on divorce, which had been set up in 1909, recommended extending the grounds and removing discrimination against women, but these proposals had been out of line with the prevailing conservative attitudes. Despite attempts to have the commission's recommendations enacted in 1913 and again in 1921, it was not until 1923 that any changes were made. Even then the reform was limited: Women were given equal access to divorce for reason of adultery, but adultery remained the only ground recognized as justifying the dissolution of marriage.[23]

This was a significant reform, but in comparative legal terms a modest one, and although it became law it was attacked on all sides. Some politicians who wanted divorce law reform to go much further were afraid that such piecemeal and limited amendments would delay a much-needed general revision of divorce law. Others, however, argued against the egalitarian character of the 1923 reform and in favor of retaining the double standard, claiming that a woman's adultery was a far more heinous offense than a man's. Praising the superior virtue of women, which was the basis of the double standard of morality, Sir Henry Craik exclaimed in the House of Commons that

chastity in women is a star that has guided human nature since the world began, and that points to far higher and teaches us of the other sex things which we could not otherwise know. We bow in humble reverence to that high star of chastity, and we celebrate it in song and poetry.

But, Sir Henry added, "I do not think that any mere man would thank us for enshrining him in such a halo."[24] The implication was that because men were by nature less prone than women to marital fidelity, it was unfair to subject them to the same laws relating to adultery. Such arguments were clearly out of step with the sentiments of most Members of Parliament, however. Major Entwistle, the sponsor of the 1923 bill, which was not sponsored by the government, called sexual inequality an "anachronism and an indefensible anomaly." He pointed out that from the married women's property acts of the

---

[23] Matrimonial Causes Act, 1923.
[24] *Parliamentary Debates* (Commons), 5th series, vol. 160, col. 2374 (March 2, 1923).

1870s onward there had been a succession of laws in favor of women, including the granting of suffrage in 1919, and that the time had come for the divorce law to be purged of its most blatant injustice.[25]

The coming into force of the 1923 act had immediate effects on divorce in England. The number of petitions filed by women rose so that for the first time women sought a majority of divorces; between 1923 and 1939 women's petitions accounted annually for between 50% and 60% of all divorces.[26] Moreover, because the 1923 legislation did not affect men's access to divorce, but simply improved women's, the result of increased petitioning by women was a general increase in the number and rate of divorce petitions as a whole. It is difficult to calculate precisely the effect of the 1923 reform on divorce because it followed hard on the heels of the surge in divorces of the immediate postwar period. But by 1922 that surge had ebbed somewhat, and we can no doubt discern the effects of the legal reform on the number and rate of divorce petitions, which increased steadily from 1923.[27] Expressed as a proportion per 10,000 married women (aged fifteen to forty-nine) the divorce petitioning rate had exceeded five only in the three postwar years from 1919 to 1921, but it did so again in 1923 and continued upward thereafter, exceeding six in 1926, seven in 1927, eight from 1934, and nine from 1936, the year before the first major revision of English divorce law. These compare with annual rates of only one or two divorce petitions per 10,000 married women before World War I, so that from the prewar base the divorce petitioning rate had effectively risen three- or fourfold in the 1920s and four- or fivefold in the 1930s. Part of the increase can be attributed to the general trend of increase that was independent of specific legal changes, but one study estimates that the 1923 act alone was responsible for between one-fifth and one-quarter of the increase in the divorce rate.[28]

Liberalization of divorce policy in England proved to be a painfully slow process. After the 1923 measure there was some improvement in the Poor Persons' Procedure in 1926, but it was not until 1937 – eighty years after the country's first divorce legislation – that a general revision of divorce law took place. The 1937 reform extended the grounds for divorce beyond adultery for the first time, to include three years' desertion, cruelty, and prolonged and incurable insanity. Women were also enabled to obtain divorce from husbands guilty of rape, sodomy, or bestiality. With the exception of insanity these had been the grounds for divorce recommended by the royal commission in 1912. (Nor were desertion and cruelty entirely new to English divorce law, for they had figured among the circumstances that could "aggravate" adultery so as to

---

25 Ibid., col. 2356.

26 Rowntree and Carrier, "Resort to Divorce," 201, Table 2; *Royal Commission, Report 1951–1955*, 356–7, Table 1. In 1924, the first year of the new act, women filed more than 60% of the petitions.

27 Figure 13.1 shows a decline from 1923 to 1924, then an increase from 1925 onward. The lower number of divorce decrees reflected the failure of the courts to clear the backlog of petitions filed in the previous year.

28 Rowntree and Carrier, "Resort to Divorce," 206–7.

justify a divorce by a wife before the 1923 reform came into effect.) These extensions to divorce in 1937 were accompanied by some new restrictions, notably the stipulation that, except in cases of extreme hardship, no petition for divorce could be filed during the first three years of marriage. It was a provision clearly designed to prevent the hasty divorce of recently married couples and to give them time to solve their problems or reconcile their differences before having recourse to the divorce court.

The liberalization of English divorce law in 1937 was accepted with relative ease, although it was opposed by the perennial opponents of divorce such as the Roman Catholic and Anglican churches.[29] Various arguments were put forth to justify a reform of the law, among them that the single ground for divorce encouraged those wishing to dissolve their marriages to commit either adultery or perjury. In the parliamentary debate on the bill one proreform member had described a "well-known" way of circumventing the law: "The thing can be done by the wife writing a letter to the husband asking him to come back, and then the husband writes a letter refusing and sends his wife the address of some hotel where she can obtain evidence sufficient to obtain a divorce."[30] Above all there was a sense that divorce law reform was long overdue, a sentiment expressed by one Member of Parliament who described the existing divorce law as being "like some architectural monstrosity which stands upon a hill and offends the eye of all beholders year after year, and yet, because it is so familiar, if anybody tries to pull it down, there arises a great outcry."[31] Such outcry as there was at the repeal of the old divorce law proved ineffective, however, and the liberalized legislation went into effect in 1938.

It was ironic that the liberalization of divorce in England was accomplished with such apparent ease, for soon after the 1937 act had survived its second reading in Parliament, in November 1936, the nation was faced with a constitutional crisis that centered on divorce. The issue involved King Edward VIII, who had succeeded to the throne in January 1936 and who was involved in a romantic relationship with an American woman, Wallis Simpson. The prospect of a marriage between the king and her was complicated by virtue of her being an American and a commoner, but it was made critical by the fact that she was divorced – and not only divorced, but twice divorced, the more recent one having taken place in October 1936.[32] In early December 1936 the British prime minister, Stanley Baldwin, discussed the question and its implications with the king and pointed out that the marriage Edward was contemplating

---

[29] On the response of the Anglican church see A. R. N. Winnett, *Divorce and Remarriage in Anglicanism* (London, 1958), 230–4. For an account of the passage of the 1937 divorce act by its sponsor, see A. P. Herbert, *The Ayes Have It: The Story of the Marriage Bill* (London, 1937).

[30] *Parliamentary Debates* (Commons), 5th series, vol. 160, col. 2366 (March 2, 1923).

[31] Ibid., vol. 317, col. 2093 (November 20, 1936).

[32] For a general account of the affair involving Edward VIII and Mrs. Wallis Simpson, see Brian Inglis, *Abdication* (London, 1966). Personal correspondence also sheds light on the divorce and constitutional crises: Michael Bloch (ed.) *Wallis and Edward: Letters 1931–1937. The Intimate Correspondence of the Duke and Duchess of Windsor* (London, 1986), esp. 191–223.

would not "receive the approbation of the country."[33] It seems that Edward canvassed the possibility of Parliament's passing legislation permitting him a morganatic marriage (such that his wife would not become queen), but Baldwin refused to entertain the idea. Finally, accepting that his alternatives were to remain king and give up Mrs. Simpson or to marry Mrs. Simpson and give up his throne, Edward abdicated in favor of his brother and left for France. He and Mrs. Simpson were married there in June 1937 and remained in virtual exile in France, as the Duke and Duchess of Windsor, until their deaths.

The abdication crisis brought into focus a number of issues related to divorce. It served, first, as a reminder that although divorce was becoming increasingly acceptable – even though it was far from respectable – for ordinary people, it was unthinkable that a king of England should choose as his wife a woman who had two husbands living. There were also the questions of the Church of England's acceptance of divorce, the status of a royal marriage involving a divorced woman, and, inevitably, the legitimacy of any children the couple might have and their rights of succession, although Mrs. Simpson's age – she was forty-two in 1936 – made this issue less problematic. Apart from English popular opinion, which the prime minister represented as being opposed to the marriage, there was fear that a marriage with Mrs. Simpson would weaken the British Empire. Canadian sentiment was said to be particularly set against the marriage; it was reported to the British government that "Canada is the most puritanical part of the Empire, and cherishes very much the Victorian standards in private life... Canadian pride has been deeply wounded by the tattle in the American press, which she feels an intolerable impertinence."[34] Clearly, Canadians were embarrassed by American press coverage of the relationship between Edward and Mrs. Simpson, which seemed to suggest that the royal family, the epitome of imperial virtue and respectability, was enmeshed in the type of scandal that Canadians had long enjoyed portraying as peculiar to America.

In fact the American connection itself was important to the whole issue. The term "American divorcée," which aptly described Mrs. Simpson, was loaded with connotations for non-Americans, suggesting a woman of loose morals.[35] It made no difference that Mrs. Simpson had been the petitioner, and thus the innocent party, in her two divorces. The point had frequently been made in the

[33] *Parliamentary Debates* (Commons), 5th series, vol. 318, cols. 2180–1 (December 10, 1936).
[34] Quoted in Inglis, *Abdication*, 276. Mail to the Canadian prime minister about Edward VIII seems to have been slight and mixed. One Saskatchewan resident wrote that "a vast majority" of Canadians would not care whether Edward married a woman who had been divorced once or more; what "the nation at large cannot very well tolerate," he continued, was that the king "solicited the affection of another man's wife; fell in love with her and proposed marriage to her before she was divorced." M. L. M. King Papers (Correspondence), Public Archives of Canada (Ottawa), MG 26 J1, vol. 214, pp. 184362–4.
[35] The wife of the prime minister's private secretary described Wallis Simpson as "a twice-divorced person of low birth, with an intermittent career of coquetry behind her." *Toronto Star*, December 11, 1986, A18.

debate on divorce, which was going on just as the scandal became public, that many divorces involved collusion, and that men were wont to do the honorable thing by letting their wives divorce them, even if it was they, the wives, who had been guilty of adultery. For these various reasons, all connected with divorce, Mrs. Simpson was unacceptable to Parliament, to the representatives of the British Empire, to the English establishment, to the press, and probably to the English people too, although there was a wave of popular sympathy and support for Edward, evoked by the image of a king giving up his crown for the woman he loved.[36] But that was not enough; divorce was still too scandalous. As one Member of Parliament observed, "I could have wished that the king had been able to live here married, happy, and king, but he has wished otherwise. A thousand years hence, perhaps, we shall be liberal enough to allow such a thing; but it is too early now."[37]

Although it could not permit divorce to stain the reputation of the royal family, Parliament enacted the 1937 divorce law reform, which took effect at the beginning of 1938. It had an immediate practical effect in the form of a doubling of the number of divorce petitions, which rose from 5,903 in 1937 to 10,233 in 1938.[38] Actual divorces (decrees) also rose, though less dramatically: from 5,044 in 1937 to 7,621 in 1938 and then to 8,248 in 1939. The annual average of 7,935 divorces in 1938 and 1939 was 60% higher than the average 4,956 in the preceding two years, but it is difficult to calculate the longer-term effects of the 1937 law on divorces in England because of the disruptive effects of World War II, which broke out in the second year of the act's life. Two characteristics of 1938 and 1939 divorces might be noted, however. The first is that the marriages dissolved in these years were generally of quite long duration. In both years more than 68% of divorces dissolved marriages that had lasted ten years or more, compared to the 53 and 55% that such marriages had contributed to the divorces decreed in 1936 and 1937.[39] Whatever the longer-term effects, it seems that new provisions gave some men and women the opportunity to dissolve marriages that had effectively ended years earlier, but where there had been no adultery. We can speculate that one category of divorce here comprised those men and women who had been deserted years earlier but who had been unable to divorce until desertion was added to the grounds for divorce in 1937. The second characteristic of the post-1937 divorces might bear on this. It is that the number of divorces for reason of adultery did not change markedly before and after the new legislation came into effect. Adultery had been the ground for 4,864 divorces in 1936 and 5,042 in 1937, and with the addition of new grounds from this time, adultery remained the ground for 5,349 divorces in 1938 and 4,439 in 1939. Put another way, the increase in divorces from 1938

---

[36] See Inglis, *Abdication*, 166ff. on reaction to the issues.
[37] *Parliamentary Debates* (Commons), 5th series, vol. 318, col. 2193 (December 10, 1936). The speaker was Col. Wedgewood.
[38] Rowntree and Carrier, "Resort to Divorce," 201, Table 2.
[39] Calculated from ibid., 208n.1., unnumbered table.

was accounted for by men and women using the new grounds of desertion and, to a much lesser extent, cruelty and insanity.[40] As noted later, however, the dramatic increase in divorces based on adultery, which followed World War II, interferes with any attempt to understand the specific longer-term effects of the 1937 act.

Divorce policies elsewhere were also expanded in the interwar period. In Scotland the substance of the sixteenth-century divorce law had scarcely been changed for almost 400 years. (The snaillike progress of English divorce law reform would look rash and precipitate in comparison, were it not for the fact that the 1937 English law was only a little more liberal, in terms of grounds, than the Scottish Reformation law.) Procedural changes were made in Scotland's divorce law during the nineteenth and early twentieth centuries, and there were echoes of the contemporary trends in divorce policies elsewhere. For example, habitual drunkenness, increasingly recognized as a ground for divorce in the United States, Europe, and Australasia, was made a ground for separation in Scotland in 1903. But only in 1938 were cruelty and habitual drunkenness included among the grounds for dissolution of marriage.[41]

An even more cautious approach to divorce reform was evident in Canada. A bill that would have established a uniform divorce law for the whole country except Quebec passed successfully through the Senate in 1920, but failed in the House of Commons. In 1925 a modest reform, modeled on the principles of the 1923 English law, gave women equal access to divorce wherever it was available in Canada. In 1930, however, there was a breakthrough in Canadian terms when parliament passed legislation giving the inhabitants of Ontario, the nation's most populous province, the right to obtain a divorce from a provincial court, rather than by means of an individual Act of Parliament.[42]

By contrast New Zealand, another British colony at the beginning of the interwar period, pushed ahead with progressively more generous terms in respect to divorce. In 1919 a statute reduced the period of desertion justifying divorce from five to three years when the defendant in question was a person "of enemy origin" – doubtless a legislative response to a specific case or cases, which ignored the fact that the war was over. In 1920 a further reform made divorce for reason of insanity easier to obtain, gave the courts discretionary powers to grant a divorce when a couple had been legally separated for at least three years, and added as a new ground for divorce the conviction of one of the spouses for wounding the other or his or her child. By 1920 the cumulative effect of divorce law reforms in New Zealand had produced eight distinct grounds for divorce, some divided into subsidiary grounds.[43]

As usual, the United States presented a rather more complicated picture of

---

[40] *Royal Commission, Report 1951–1955*, 359, Table 2.
[41] Divorce (Scotland) Act, 1938. See also the *Royal Commission, Report 1951–1955*, 5–6.
[42] D. C. McKie, B. Prentice, and P. Reed, *Divorce: Law and the Family in Canada* (Ottawa, 1983), 46–7.
[43] Roderick Phillips, *Divorce in New Zealand: A Social History* (Auckland, 1981) 41–4, 146–7.

divorce legislation, but the general trend of liberalization continued there as well. Soon after World War I a veritable divorce trade war broke out among states such as Nevada, Idaho, and Arkansas, each vying for out-of-state clients for its divorce courts. In 1927 Nevada reduced its residence requirement from six to three months, but in 1931, when Idaho and Arkansas appeared to be on the verge of matching this period, Nevada legislators lowered their state's requirement even more, this time to six weeks.[44] The competition among these few states was not for the distinction of having America's most lax divorce policy, but more directly for the revenue that such divorce policies produced for the state, which was especially welcome during the Depression. Legal fees, court costs, travel, accommodation, and subsistence, all brought in millions of dollars annually for the state governments and local lawyers and businesses. The magnitude of the divorce industry and the advantages of minimal residence requirements are indicated by the number of divorces decreed in Nevada. In 1926 there had been 1,021, but after the residency requirement was lowered to three months in 1927, divorces almost doubled to 1,953 in that year and to 2,595 in 1928. Between 1930 and 1931, when the residence requirement was again lowered (to six weeks) divorces again doubled, rising from 2,609 to 5,260.[45] By 1940 Nevada accounted for only one in fifty of the divorces decreed in the United States, but on a population basis its divorce rate was by far the highest of all states: at 49 divorces annually per 1,000 resident population, it was followed at some distance by Florida's rate of 5.8 divorces.[46] Quite clearly, the bulk of Nevada's divorces were obtained by men and women who traveled to the state and took up residence just long enough to enable them to dissolve their marriages.

Although we should not overestimate the statistical importance of migratory divorce, it seems that in the interwar period especially, Americans were inveterate seekers of out-of-state divorce. It is true that some important and populous states, such as New York, continued to have very restrictive divorce policies, and that many couples or spouses preferred to avoid committing perjury to obtain a divorce – perjury, in the case of New York, which would have required one of the spouses to confess to adultery. These reasons in themselves would account for migratory divorce, and it is also likely that others migrated in order to avoid local publicity and scandal. Were it simply a matter of a New Yorker's obtaining a divorce, there would have been no reason to look further afield than the nearest American divorce haven, yet thousands of Americans traveled to France in the 1920s in order to divorce. Apart from the undoubted gastronomic and cultural advantages that Paris had over Reno and Miami, the wealthy found in France a publicity-free divorce facility, for the 1884 French divorce law forbade the reporting of divorce cases in the press.

---

[44] Nelson Blake, *The Road to Reno: A History of Divorce in the United States* (New York, 1962), 156–8.
[45] Jacobson and Jacobson, *American Marriage and Divorce*, 103–4.
[46] Ibid., 100, Table 48; 171, Table A19.

Moreover, there were no effective residence requirements to satisfy before a divorce could be obtained from a French divorce court, and lawyers in Paris advertised *"divorces rapides"* for foreigners, especially Americans.[47] Travel and other costs inevitably limited France to the wealthiest, and it is estimated that in the peak year 1926, some 300 American couples had their marriages dissolved in Paris alone. It is significant that the number dropped (to 100 by 1928) after American newspapers, which were not subject to the French restrictions on reporting divorce cases, began to publish the names of Americans divorced in the French capital.[48]

Americans sought equally exotic, but less distant and expensive, divorces in the Virgin Islands, Cuba, and especially in Mexico, where divorce was legalized by the 1917 constitution. As in the United States, divorce law in Mexico fell to the jurisdiction of the individual states and, also as in the United States, this arrangement resulted in a marked variation of divorce policies within the republic. Soon after divorce was legalized, some Mexican states recognized the economic and fiscal benefits that could flow from the migrant divorce business. In 1918 Yucatan State set minimal residence requirements in the hope of attracting Americans, and permissive divorce policies were soon adopted by other states competing for clients. The ease of divorce was exemplified by the state of Morelos, where there was no residence requirement at all; the state's jurisdiction over divorce was established simply by having notice of the petition posted on the wall of the courthouse or published in the official gazette. If the defendant spouse did not answer the petition within three days (which was likely if he or she lived in New York – or in fact anywhere but Cuernavaca, capital city of Morelos – at the time the petition was filed), then a divorce could be granted within twenty-four hours.[49] In some states, such as Morelos, the law allowed divorce for reason of incompatibility of character, and in others a wide range of grounds was defined. In Sonora, the state with a common border with Arizona, divorce could be obtained for reason of adultery, a wife's bearing an illegitimate child, immoral conduct, desertion for six months, syphilis, insanity, having an infectious or incurable disease, being unable to fulfill conjugal duties, cruelty, threats or mistreatment, false accusation of a serious crime, imprisonment or banishment for more than ten years, habitual intemperance, and separation for six months or more.[50] The most popular Mexican state for Americans seeking divorce, however, was Chihuahua, which shares a border with Texas. Chihuahua's divorce law provided for residence to be established by registration on arrival and for divorce for reason of incompatibility.[51]

The popularity of Mexico as a divorce haven grew during the interwar

---

[47] *South African Law Journal* 43 (1926), 440–1.
[48] Jacobson and Jacobson, *American Marriage and Divorce*, 105.
[49] Ibid., 107–8.
[50] *Divorce Law of Sonora, Mexico* (trans. and commentary by Antonio D. Melgarejo Randolph, New York, 1929), 15–7.
[51] Jacobson and Jacobson, *American Marriage and Divorce*, 108.

period. It is estimated that in 1926 230 divorces (24% of Mexico's total) dissolved marriages in which one or both spouses was born in the United States. Between 1933 and 1937 the number of American marriages dissolved in Mexico rose to an annual average of 1,612, representing 37% of all the divorces in Mexico in that period.[52] In all it appears that at least 13,500 Mexican divorces involved Americans between 1926 and 1940. Matrimonial transients from the north no doubt injected useful funds into local economies and government coffers. In Sonora the state levied a tax on divorces of between 100 and 500 pesos (U.S.$50 to $250 at 1925 rates of exchange), and the federal government imposed an additional 25% tax.[53]

Migratory divorce, whether within the United States or, less frequently, outside, testified to the continuing variation in state divorce policies in America; no other nation produced the phenomenon on anything approaching the same scale. Italians might well have sought divorce outside Italy, and discontented English men and women might have looked to the Continental or American divorce laws for solutions to their matrimonial problems, but none had the same connotations as were attached to American divorce. The reports of thousands of Americans traveling abroad to divorce did nothing to lessen the reputation of America as a country of weak marriages and questionable morals. Mrs. Wallis Simpson was far from unique, though her divorces were by far the most publicized of the 1930s, and acted as a focal point for the expression of attitudes long held about Americans and their marital behavior. But as sensationalized as it was, the extent of migratory divorce outside the United States is easily overstated. Mexico was the most popular foreign destination for Americans in search of divorce, but the 13,500 or so divorces granted to Americans there from 1926 to 1940 pale against the more than 3 million marriages dissolved in the United States itself in that same period.

13.4 Political ideology and divorce between the wars

Apart from these developments in patterns and policies, divorce was given an explicit political dimension in Europe between the two world wars. We have noted political associations of divorce at earlier times, suggesting that attitudes to divorce correlated with general political orientations. During the French Revolution, for example, more radical republicans favored a libertarian divorce policy, moderate republicans a more restrictive divorce law, and royalists totally opposed divorce. In this instance political orientations also largely correlated with religious convictions that, in the case of royalists at least, who were for the most part devout Catholics, determined attitudes to marriage and divorce.

---

[52] Ibid., 108, Table 51. This is a minimum estimate of the number of American divorces in Mexico. By using place of birth as the criterion, the Mexican statistics do not take into account Americans born outside the United States.

[53] The total costs of a divorce in Sonora state in the 1920s were about $575, making them very expensive.

13 The twentieth century: Rise of mass divorce

Later, in the nineteenth century, liberals and socialists tended to favor easy access to divorce, whereas political conservatives were either opposed to divorce or were prepared to tolerate it only in a very restrictive form. These are generalizations, and it is easy enough to point to exceptions, even if they can be explained in terms of exceptional circumstances, such as Bismarck's promoting divorce not so much as a good in itself but as a weapon against the Catholic church. In general, though, the associations of political liberalism with positive attitudes toward divorce, and of political conservatism with negative attitudes toward divorce, are a useful rule of thumb. The interwar years provide an interesting testing ground for this association. The period was marked by a polarization of political ideologies in continental Europe and was characterized by the coming to power of fascist regimes in Italy, Germany, and Spain and by semifascist administrations in Portugal and in Vichy France after 1940. Against these regimes, which stressed the corporative character of society, were movements of the left, often inspired by the example of the Soviet Union. The divorce policies adopted by these various regimes should indicate the strength of the political correlation.

Although not part of the Western world, the Soviet state formed as a result of the 1917 revolution had an immediate and enduring impact on social and political thought in Western Europe. Revolutionary and even nonrevolutionary political movements and parties were inspired by or modeled on the Soviet example, such as the short-lived "Red Republic" in Bavaria in 1918–19. Many Western intellectuals traveled to the Soviet Union after the revolution, especially in the 1920s, to see for themselves what was hailed as the workers' paradise. Many of them were disillusioned by what they found, but among the Soviet innovations that they found less disheartening was a family policy radically different from what they were accustomed to in Western society. Abortion was not only legalized but made available at no cost in public hospitals; there were no restrictions on the dissemination of birth control information or the availability of contraceptives; marriage was secularized; and women were given formal equality with men in all aspects of family law. This new Soviet family policy represented a rejection of traditional notions of the family. It was based on the belief that history had made the family a bourgeois institution that tended to oppress women and children in particular and that definitely promoted and reinforced bourgeois social values. This attitude toward the family derived from a number of sources, but particularly from the joint and individual writings of Karl Marx and Friedrich Engels, who predicted the disappearance of the bourgeois family as part of the fundamental transformation of society. In the *Communist Manifesto* they had written that "the bourgeois family will vanish as a matter of course when its complement vanishes, and both will vanish with the vanishing of capital."[54] A communist society, Engels anticipated, would

---

[54] Karl Marx and Friedrich Engels, *The Communist Manifesto* (New York, 1933), 77.

promote the freedom of individuals from family constraints: communism transforms the relation between the sexes into a purely private matter which concerns only the persons involved and into which society has no occasion to intervene. It can do this since it does away with private property and educates children on a communal basis and in this way removes the two bases of traditional marriage, the dependence, rooted in private property, of woman on the man and of the children on the parents.[55]

It was this theory of the family that was quickly translated into law by the new Soviet government in 1917 and 1918.[56] The aim was clearly to reduce the legal barriers to freedom within the family so as to allow the forces of historical change to do the work that would ultimately lead to the disappearance of the family as it was known in bourgeois society. Divorce was a keystone of the code of family law since it suppressed the compulsion implied by the indissolubility of marriage. Engels had foreseen the need for divorce as arising from the nature of human relationships. Partnerships of men and women should endure only as long as the love between the couple endured, he wrote, and "the intense emotion of individual sex-love varies very much in duration from one individual to another, especially among men."[57] Closer to the Bolshevik revolution – a year before it, in fact – Lenin wrote of divorce that "one cannot be a democrat and a socialist without demanding full freedom of divorce, for the absence of such freedom is an additional burden on the oppressed sex, woman...."[58]

The actual law on divorce that was decreed in principle in November 1917, then promulgated in detail in 1918, was a brief one of thirteen articles.[59] It specified that a marriage could be dissolved by divorce, and that the "grounds" were the mutual desire of the husband and wife, or of only one of them, for a divorce. The questions of fault or even of no fault were, therefore, of no concern to the law; the wish to divorce was enough. Procedure was minimal. The divorce petition could be delivered orally or in writing to the local court and the defendant spouse, if there was one and if his or her address were known, was to be summoned to appear. Since the law recognized no concept of fault, however, there was no defense against the petition. Provision was made for an appeal against a divorce decree to the Court of Appeal, but it is not clear what grounds might be invoked. The law also provided for regulation of the spouses' names after divorce, and the local court judge was to decide on issues relating to the custody, maintenance, and upbringing of any children the couple

---

[55] Friedrich Engels, *Principles of Communism* (New York, 1952), 18.

[56] There is an extensive literature on the development of Soviet family law and policy, but see in particular H. Kent Geiger, *The Family in Soviet Russia* (Cambridge, Mass., 1968). For a collection of translated laws and commentaries on the family in the Soviet Union from 1917 to 1944, see Rudolf Schlesinger (ed.), *The Family in the U. S. S. R.* (London, 1949).

[57] Engels, *Principles of Communism*, 73.

[58] V. I. Lenin, *A Caricature of Marxism* (1916), quoted in *Women and Communism. Selections from the Writings of Marx, Engels, Lenin and Stalin* (London, 1950), 78. Lenin added that "the recognition of the *right* of women to leave their husbands is not an *invitation* to all wives to do so!" Ibid.

[59] An edited translation of the 1918 family law is in Schlesinger, *Family in the U. S. S. R.*, 33–41.

had. According to one commentator, judges tended to grant custody to the parent with the greatest "proletarian sympathies."[60]

Divorce in the early years of Soviet law was thus easy, speedy, and inexpensive. It was actually easier to divorce than to marry: A marriage required the consent of two people, a divorce the consent of only one.[61] Precise statistics on the use of divorce are difficult to obtain, but the number of divorces seems to have been high. There were ten divorces for every twenty-two marriages in the urban population of the European USSR in the 1920s, and ten divorces for thirteen marriages in the city of Moscow. These are especially impressive in light of the fact that the marriage rate had increased after the revolution in European Russia (from 8.3 per thousand population to 11.4 per thousand between 1913 and 1924). A survey of students in Odessa in the 1920s indicated that 11% of male students and 16% of female students had been married and divorced.[62]

By the later 1920s and in the 1930s there was increasing concern over the ease of divorce, over abuses of the law, and over the effects of the existing family policy generally. Peasant men, needing help during the harvest, were alleged to marry at the beginning of the harvest and divorce when it was over, using their temporary wives as unpaid labor.[63] A delegation of women, opposing the family law in the 1920s, argued that it was women who suffered when men married, divorced, and remarried in succession. One delegate remarked that it was possible, as things stood, to get married and divorce at the same table in a government office.[64] By the mid-1930s the government began to share these qualms and imposed financial sanctions that cut dramatically into the divorce rate. At the same time (1935–6) other legal reforms reflected an abandonment of the libertarian family policies that had been introduced from 1917.[65]

The eventual rejection of the early Soviet family law was unforeseen, of course, and the early laws were praised not only by the Soviet leaders as the foundation of a new society but also by many Western observers, who found the policy fascinating and exciting. A letter from a German visitor to Moscow in 1920 noted that "the marriages in present-day Russia are interesting... Divorce is as easy as marriage. [It takes five minutes]."[66] Lancelot Lawton, an English commentator and newspaper correspondent who visited the Soviet

[60] Lancelot Lawton, *The Russian Revolution (1917–1926)* (London, 1927), 221. Lawton visited the Soviet Union in 1924.

[61] Geiger, *Family in Soviet Russia*, 254.

[62] Sheila Fitzpatrick, "Sex and Revolution: An Examination of the Literary and Statistical Data on the Mores of Soviet Students in the 1920s," *Journal of Modern History* 50 (1978), 261, 258.

[63] Lawton, *Russian Revolution*, vi.

[64] Ibid., 224. On the effects of the marriage laws on women see Bernice Glatzer Rosenthal, "Love on the Tractor: Women in the Russian Revolution and After," in Renate Bridenthal and Claudia Koontz, (eds.), *Becoming Visible: Women in European History* (Boston, 1977), 383–5.

[65] Later reforms of Soviet law, including restrictions on divorce, are discussed in Geiger, *Family in Soviet Russia*, 93ff.

[66] Quoted in Stanley W. Page (ed.), *Russia in Revolution* (Princeton, N. J., 1965).

Union in 1924, commented favorably on the new marriage code as reflecting "intelligent Russian opinion."[67] Bertrand Russell, who traveled to the Soviet Union in 1920 and was greatly disillusioned by what he saw, later wrote more favorably about marriage and the family there. Attacking the traditional bases of marriage, Russell noted that

there is no country in the world and there has been no age in the world's history where sexual ethics and sexual institutions [including marriage] have been determined by rational considerations, with the exception of Soviet Russia. I do not mean that the institutions in Soviet Russia are in this respect perfect; I mean only that they are not the outcome of superstition and tradition....[68]

Other commentators, as we should expect, were hostile to the changes in the family encouraged by the early Soviet policy. One wrote of the communists' aim of destroying the family and of the new Soviet laws on marriage and the family leaving both institutions floating "on little else than the unstable element of sexual affinity and satisfaction." Divorce, he wrote, was very easy to obtain; "men and women so minded stand in line before the proper officers as compunctionless as those in bread queues."[69]

Ironically, strictures and hostility to Soviet divorce law in the early years were made at a time when divorce rates in America and Europe were soaring after World War I. Continuing criticism of Soviet family policy in the 1920s was made against a background of continuing high rates of divorce, and a spread of anxiety and questioning of marriage and morals, in Western society. Perhaps it was this conjunction that reinforced conservative alarm, a fear that the Soviet experience represented the future of the West if socialist political and social ideologies were to prevail there too. Certainly, many Western socialists found Soviet family policy a useful model. A publication of the socialist Independent Labour Party in England pointed out that, although the Bolshevik system might be tyrannical in some respects, in terms of marriage and divorce "it would seem to have worked on the side of freedom [and]...has purified the relation of men and women."[70] George Bernard Shaw also praised Soviet divorce law in *The Intelligent Woman's Guide to Socialism and Capitalism*:

when once it becomes feasible for a wife to leave her husband...without any intention of returning, there must be prompt and almost automatic divorce. At present a deserted wife or husband, by simply refusing to sue for divorce, can in mere revenge or jealousy, or on Church grounds, prevent the deserter from marrying again. We should have to follow the good example of Russia in refusing to tolerate such situations.[71]

---

[67] Lawton, *Russian Revolution*, 225.
[68] Bertrand Russell, *Marriage and Morals* (London, 1929), 10.
[69] Ethan T. Colton, *The XYZ of Communism* (New York, 1931). The anti-Soviet press tended to dwell on the new laws and practice in respect of women in particular. See Christopher Lasch, *The American Liberals and the Russian Revolution* (New York, 1962), 121–2.
[70] H. M. Swanwick, *Women in the Socialist State* (Manchester, 1921).
[71] Bernard Shaw, *The Intelligent Woman's Guide to Socialism and Capitalism* (London, 1928), 408–9.

13 The twentieth century: Rise of mass divorce

Soviet family policy, and divorce policy specifically, found support – qualified and unqualified – across the liberal and socialist spectrum in Europe and America. It responded to liberal and socialist hostility to the oppressive character of bourgeois marriage, and complemented the socialist feminist critiques of Western family institutions and practices. In this sense the Soviet experiment, even though it was later greatly modified, reinforced the individualist tendencies of the Left's analysis of the family, and contributed to the polarization of family ideologies in the interwar period. The parties and critics of the political Right generally adopted a corporative approach to the family, stressing its integrity and coherence, and elevating the interests of the family group above the interests of its individual members. For the most part the Right stressed the necessity, for the maintenance of social and political order and stability, of well-ordered family life. Although they did not unanimously oppose divorce outright, they stressed the dangers of it, especially in the hands of women, and insisted on the importance of maintaining strong lines of authority within the family: Husbands were to control wives, fathers were to control children. The dichotomy between Left and Right was expressed in the family policies, and particularly in the divorce laws, which were advocated and put in place by regimes of Left and Right in the 1920s and 1930s.

Divorce was a contentious social and political issue in Spain during the turbulent decade of the 1930s. The republican government that came to power in 1931 pursued left-liberal policies and quickly enacted extensive reforms designed to reduce the influence of the Catholic church. The constitution of 1931 separated church and state, prepared for the dissolution of religious orders and forbade the orders to teach. Article 43 of the constitution claimed jurisdiction over the family for the state: It declared marriage to be founded on the equality of rights of both sexes and specified that it might be dissolved "for mutual discord or at the request of either of the spouses, with evidence of just causes in each instance."[72] This statement of broad principle was soon followed by the passage of specific divorce legislation. A draft law was hotly debated in the Cortes in February 1932 and was easily approved by a margin of 260 votes to 23.[73] The division between supporters and opponents of the divorce law parallelled the division that would become all too familiar during the civil war. Divorce was opposed by the Nationalist Bloc of monarchist and Roman Catholic deputies, especially those from rural areas, but was supported by liberals, republicans, and socialists. The principal focus of the parliamentary debate was on the religious implications of legalizing divorce, as we might expect in a country where the Catholic church's control over marriage was extensive. Antidivorce deputies portrayed the proposed divorce law as one more insult to the church, although defenders of the law took the liberal attitude that

---

[72] Ines Alberdi, *Historia y sociologia del divorcio en España* (Madrid, 1979), 87–8.
[73] The government had an overwhelming majority in the Cortes and could generally count on more than 350 votes against an opposition having about 60. Hugh Thomas, *The Spanish Civil War* (London, 1961), 71.

divorce was a civil right that Catholics would not be forced to use if they found it repugnant to their faith.[74] The opposition also pointed to the putatively catastrophic effects of divorce on Spain. One Basque nationalist deputy cited statistics purporting to prove that the crime rate among divorced and widowed Germans was twice the average rate. Divorce, he argued, led to increased crime, juvenile delinquency, and suicide, and legalizing divorce in Spain would result in an additional 4,500 deaths a year in the country.[75]

Objections to divorce in 1932 were based not simply on the introduction per se of divorce into Spanish law but also on the fact that the proposed legislation was very liberal. In its final form the 1932 Spanish divorce law was, in fact, the most liberal divorce code in contemporary Europe. First, it permitted divorce by mutual consent, provided that both spouses had reached the age of majority and that the marriage had lasted more than two years. Second, the law set out a range of thirteen specific grounds for a unilateral divorce:

1. adultery by either spouse;
2. bigamy;
3. an attempt by the husband to prostitute his wife or by either spouse to corrupt their sons' morals or to prostitute their daughters;
4. the disappearance of either spouse;
5. desertion for one year;
6. absence for two years;
7. one spouse's attempt to murder the other or their children, or ill-treatment or serious insults;
8. a violation of conjugal obligations or immoral behavior that made life in common impossible;
9. contagious and serious sexual diseases;
10. serious illnesses that made fulfillment of the conjugal duties impossible;
11. loss of liberty (imprisonment) for more than ten years;
12. *de facto* voluntary separation for three years; and
13. incurable mental illness.[76]

The law also retained judicial separation (*separatión de bienes y persones*), an important facility for Roman Catholics, giving them an alternative to remaining fully married or being divorced. Separation, too, could be obtained by mutual consent, on any of the grounds recognized for divorce, but also in cases where a marriage was disturbed by a difference in behavior, mentality, or religion.

[74] The debate in the Cortes is described and analyzed in R. Lezcarno, *El divorcio en la Segunda República* (Madrid, 1979), 73–106; and in Richard A. H. Robinson, *The Origins of Franco's Spain* (Newton Abbot, 1970), 65–70.
[75] Robinson, *Franco's Spain*, 70. Contemporary articles and comments on the divorce law in the early 1930s are reprinted in Mary Nash, *Mujer, Familia y Trabajo en España 1875–1936* (Barcelona, 1983), 197–223.
[76] The law is reprinted in ibid., 234–48; see also Alberdi, *Divorcio en España*, 91–2.

This part of the law, enabling couples to separate for emotional or personal incompatibility without having to attribute guilt, made the provision for separation even more liberal and advanced than provisions for the dissolution of marriage. A separation could, however, be converted into a divorce after three years, so divorce was actually available in these circumstances too, albeit in an indirect and slow form.[77]

The only reliable statistics on divorces and separations in Spain under the 1932 law relate to the relatively stable period from March 1932 to December 1933. During these twenty-two months there were 7,059 petitions for divorce and 832 for separation, of which 4,920 (62%) resulted in an actual decree of divorce or separation. Calculated on an annual basis, there would have been 2,382 divorces at this time, giving Spain one of the lowest divorce rates in Europe in terms of population.[78] The bulk of the divorces emanated from the two largest cities, Madrid and Barcelona. In Madrid there were 1,936 petitions (one-quarter of the total), in Barcelona 1,747 (22%). The next highest concentration was in Valencia, which produced only 417 petitions, or 5% of the national total. The urban concentration is quite clear from this and also from the occupations of men involved in divorce actions. Spain was predominantly rural and agricultural, yet urban workers, the main supporters of the Republic, were involved in 31% of divorces, whereas agricultural workers contributed only 8%. Significantly the urban dwellers tended overall to opt for divorce, whereas rural workers preferred to file for separations. This reflected not only the greater religiosity in the rural areas but also, and possibly more importantly, the limitations placed on dissolutions of marriage by material conditions in these rural areas.

Divorce had long been claimed by its supporters in Spain, as elsewhere, as a benefit for women in particular, and it is interesting to note that women petitioned more often than men for divorce. Of unilateral divorce petitions filed 56% were by wives, against 44% by husbands, but when it came to separation actions the percentage initiated by women rose to 81%. Religion, in the form of the greater religiosity of women, was certainly a factor here, as was the material and economic dependence that effectively disabled many women from seeking a total dissolution of marriage.

Divorce trends in Spain after 1933 are unclear. It has been suggested that the number of divorces increased in republican-dominated areas, particularly as procedures were simplified when the legal system broke down under the impact of the civil war. Although little is known of divorces in this period, it is clear that more than a little laxness crept into attitudes and practices relating to marriage. Hugh Thomas writes that "marriages were celebrated with the greatest ease at [republican] militia headquarters, and the partners shortly afterwards with

[77] Ibid., 93–4.
[78] Statistics are from ibid., 95, Cuadro I. There were 4,367 divorces between March 1932 and December 1933. Statistics on divorce in the following paragraphs are from the same source, 95–105, Cuadros I–VIII.

equal facility forgot them."[79] The republican government later validated any marriage involving a militiaman that had been celebrated before a war committee or an officer, and in 1937 the government also instituted a form of "marriage by usage." This meant that a man and a woman were considered legally married if they lived together for ten months or if the woman became pregnant. This decree was later repealed because it had led to a large number of bigamous marriages when married men or women took up long-term cohabitation without having first gone through the process of obtaining a divorce from their spouses.[80]

The fascist government of General Franco, which took power in Spain in 1938, had close links with the Roman Catholic church and would certainly have abolished divorce even if it had been legalized and practiced in a very restrictive way. Faced with what appeared to be matrimonial anarchy in the former republican zones of Spain, Franco's regime moved quickly to restore order on ecclesiastical principles. Legislation of March 1938 suppressed civil marriage, suspended the divorce law, and reactivated the 1889 civil code as an interim measure. In September 1939 the 1932 divorce legislation was repealed with the express purpose of returning to Spanish laws "the traditional value, which is the Catholic one."[81] Divorces that had been decreed were declared void, a move that implied the possibility of nullifying any civil marriage that had been contracted following the dissolution of a canonical one. The fascist solution thus placed in jeopardy the validity of many marriages, but this was seen as a short-term problem; it was certainly considered the lesser of two evils, the greater being divorce. Spaniards were protected from the dangers of divorce throughout Franco's rule, and even well after his death in 1975; not until 1981 was divorce relegalized in Spain.

The principal influence on the Spanish fascists' marriage policy was clearly the Catholic church. Franco was a member of Opus Dei, an influential religious confraternity, but apart from this the Catholic ban on divorce was an integral part of the legal tradition of Spain, and fascist ideology drew heavily on the importance of traditional institutions. The ideologists of fascism in Spain also stressed the importance of the family unit as the foundation of the state. José Antonio Primo de Rivera, the founder of Falange Española (the fascist movement coopted by Franco) insisted that the genuine Spanish state would be based on the "authentic realities of life," of which the first was the family.[82]

Strengthening marriage and reinforcing the integrity of the family might have been common to fascist social ideology, but hostility to divorce to the extent of abolishing it was not necessarily so. In Portugal, for example, Oliveira Salazar, the premier who ruled as a semifascist dictator from 1932 to 1974, did

[79] Thomas, *Spanish Civil War*, 244.
[80] Ibid. and n.3.
[81] Alberdi, *Divorcio en España*, 107.
[82] José Antonio Primo de Rivera, *Selected Writings* (ed. Hugh Thomas, London, 1972), 62–3.

not repeal the liberal divorce law that had been enacted by republicans in 1910. According to one commentator, divorce was well received in Portugal from the time of its legalization, and this alone might well explain why it was retained by the right-wing and Catholic regime that came to power in the 1920s and was eventually dominated by Salazar.[83] Salazar himself was certainly not in favor of divorce. His attitudes toward women and the family were traditional ones, stressing the importance and permanence of marriage and the role of the wife within the home.[84] The corporatist character of the family and its importance in what Salazar called the "New State" was expressed in the 1933 political consitution: "The State shall ensure the constitution and protection of the family as the source of preservation and development of the race, as the first basis of education, discipline and social harmony."[85]

A general current of hostility toward divorce in fascist Portugal was evident, however. In 1935 and 1936 there were unsuccessful attempts to repeal the divorce law, but the most effective inroads on divorce were made by the 1940 concordat between the Portuguese government and the Vatican. This effectively deprived the predominantly Catholic population of the right to divorce by requiring Catholics, at the time of marriage, to renounce their right of access to the divorce law.[86] A further limitation on divorce was imposed in 1942 when the supreme court of Portugal decided that adultery by a husband, which until then had been an unqualified ground for divorce, could justify a dissolution of marriage only when the adultery was clear evidence that conjugal love had disappeared from the marriage.[87] An adulterous husband could thus prevent his wife from obtaining a divorce by insisting that he loved her, despite his infidelity. Yet in spite of the banning of divorce for Catholics who married in church, and the undermining of the sexual equality that had characterized the 1910 divorce law, divorce was reaffirmed in a new Portuguese civil code of 1944. The new law provided for divorce by mutual consent, unilaterally, and for the conversion of separations into divorce after a specified period. The explanation for the retention of divorce by the country's conservative and Catholic regime might well have been its popularity again. Between 1930 and

---

[83] Gabriel Le Bras (ed.), *Divorce et séparation de corps dans le monde contemporaine* (Paris, 1952), 250–5. See also Maria Manuela Rama and Carlos Plantier, *Divórcio: da Concordata à Revolução* (Lisbon, 1975), esp. 22–9.

[84] Antonio de Oliveira Salazar, *Doctrine and Action. Internal and Foreign Policy in the New Portugal, 1928–1939* (London, n.d.), 162. On women and the family see ibid., 101–2, 152, 161–4, 290.

[85] Political Constitution of the Portuguese Republic, Article 12, Chapter III, quoted in Charles F. Delzell, *Mediterranean Fascism, 1919–1945* (New York, 1970), 340.

[86] F. Brandão Ferreira Pinto, *Causas do Divórcio: Doutrina, Legislação, Jurisprudência: Portugal e Brasil* (Coimbra, 1980), 10–11 and notes. It appears that Roman Catholics in Portugal did not use divorce very frequently, because after the 1940 restrictions were imposed (on August 1, 1940) the number of divorces declined only marginally. There were an average 800 divorces annually between 1937 and 1939, and 694 between 1940 and 1942. After that decline, the number of divorces rose to an annual average of 1,037 from 1943 to 1950. *United Nations Demographic Yearbook* 1951, Table 26.

[87] Le Bras, *Divorce et séparation de corps*, 250.

1946 divorces in Portugal averaged 868 a year, a relatively high rate in terms of population. Statistics indicate that the most common grounds in this period were adultery by the wife (26% of divorces), ill-treatment (24%), desertion (20%), and adultery by the husband (19%). Divorces by mutual consent accounted for only 6% of the total.[88]

The ideological and legal status of the family and divorce in Portugal was reminiscent of that in France between 1940 and 1944. In 1940, following the German invasion, a semifascist government headed by Marshal Pétain was established in the south of France. Under the slogan *"Travail, Famille, Patrie"* ("Work, Family, Motherland") this Vichy government (named after the town where it was based) adopted a program ostensibly designed to strengthen the family. In 1941 a *Commissariat général de la famille* was set up, employing regional inspectors whose tasks including overseeing the application of family law and promoting "a programme of propaganda in favour of the family and family ideas."[89] Family law itself was geared to encouraging fertility, a policy that responded to deeply entrenched French fears of depopulation. Stiffer penalties were provided for infanticide, abortion was prohibited, and fiscal and other benefits were granted to mothers and to heads of families with more than three children.[90]

The reform of divorce legislation fell within this context. The Vichy government was faced with the prospect of administering the existing divorce law, which had been liberalized during the 1920s and 1930s and which by 1938, on the eve of World War II, had permitted the dissolution of 26,300 marriages. In 1941 divorce was restricted by legal reforms. The clauses allowing divorce on the grounds of adultery or condemnation to a degrading punishment were retained, but spouses – in practice, women – were permitted to divorce for reason of ill-treatment only if the violence constituted "a serious or continual violation of the obligations of marriage and render the maintenance of married life intolerable." Other restrictions on divorce introduced by the Vichy regime included a provision that no divorce petition could be filed within the first three years of a marriage and an increase to three years of the delay that had to be observed before a separation could be converted into a divorce.[91] The aim of these reforms was clearly to reduce the number of divorces, which was seen as threatening to social stability and the legitimate birthrate. An apologist of the regime argued that Marshal Pétain's administration sought to restore "the great French family which makes up the nation," and asked, rhetorically, how it could be possible to establish a family "when on each marriage registration there appeared, superimposed, a registration of divorce."[92]

The effect of the new legislation on divorce in France is difficult to gauge.

[88] Ibid., 257.
[89] *Les Institutions de la France Nouvelle*, Supplement, vol. II (Paris, n.d.), 403.
[90] Ibid., vol. II (Paris, 1941), 111–29.
[91] Ibid., 112.
[92] Jean Thouvenin, *Pétain tient la barre* (Paris, 1941), 13.

13 The twentieth century: Rise of mass divorce

Divorces declined from 26,300 in 1938 to 21,188 in 1939, but then plummeted to 11,070 in 1940. The decline thus began before the Vichy government's restrictions on divorce, and even before the German invasion, which led to the loss of territory in eastern France, and thereby some divorce registration districts, to Germany. The drastic decline in divorces in 1940 must be attributed to the effects of the outbreak of war and the defeat of the French forces. The new Vichy divorce provisions came into force in April 1941, and if anything the number of divorces recovered from that time from its low point in 1940: There were between 14,000 and 15,000 divorces a year in 1941 and 1942, and between 17,000 and 18,000 in 1943 and 1944. By 1945, after the liberation of France, divorces had reached the prewar level and exceeded it (there were 51,946 divorces that year), and in 1946 and 1947 France shared the general Western increase in divorces of the postwar period. To some extent these later divorces must have represented a compensation for the relatively small number of divorces during the war itself, but as we shall see there were other factors involved.[93] In the general confusion of influences during the war, however, it is impossible to isolate the particular importance of the 1941 divorce law changes on divorce use. It is quite possible that they were minimal and that the low level of divorce during the Vichy period resulted from conditions of war, as did the generally reduced rate of divorce in other war-affected countries.

Italy produced yet another example of fascist divorce policy, one that demonstrated clearly the primacy of national tradition and political considerations over purely ideological principles. Divorce, as has been noted earlier in this study, was not available in Italy, despite continual attempts to have it legalized during the nineteenth century and in the twentieth century up to World War I. However, the postwar settlement, which gave Italy territories that had been part of the Austrian Empire, introduced divorce into Italy; in the annexed territories of Alto Adige, Venezia Giulia, Trentino, and the city of Fiume, non-Catholics were permitted by imperial law to divorce, and the Italian prohibition on divorce was not imposed on them for some time (in 1924 in Fiume and in 1928 in the other regions).[94] Fascist policy clearly favored the standardization of law, a consideration that alone would have led to the suppression of divorce within the new parts of Italy. An even more important factor, however, was Mussolini's wish to attract the support of the Catholic church to his regime, which governed Italy from 1922. Divorce played a minor, yet significant, role in the Fascist regime's religious policy.

[93] Divorces in France numbered as follows:

1938	26,300	1941	14,519	1944	17,300
1939	21,188	1942	14,273	1945	20,068
1940	11,070	1943	17,563	1946	51,946

Some of the annual variation is accounted for by changes in the number of *départements* (administrative districts) considered. Some parts of France were annexed to Germany in 1940. Wesley D. Camp, *Marriage and the Family in France since the Revolution* (New York, 1961), 81–2.

[94] Giovanni B. Sgritta and Paolo Tufari, "Italy," in Robert Chester (ed.), *Divorce in Europe* (Leiden, 1977), 258.

The specter of divorce in Italy had haunted the Catholic church since the creation of the unified Italian state in 1870, and the Catholic political party, the Popolari, and the Vatican had vigorously combatted any divorce bills introduced into the Italian legislature. There was recognition that the continued policy of the indissolubility of marriage coexisted more than a little uneasily with the fact that, from the civil code of 1865 onward, marriage in Italy had been regarded as being a civil contract. A religious celebration was optional (after the civil ceremony), but alone it possessed no legal validity. It must have seemed to the church – as it did to many liberal and socialist politicians – that the legalization of divorce was a logical step from the existing status of marriage, and that it was only a matter of time before a divorce bill was successful. Mussolini himself, although not advocating that divorce should be available, favored civil marriage in his socialist days. At the Socialist Party's 1910 conference at Forlì he moved for a resolution calling for socialists, under threat of explusion from the party, to avoid religious marriage.[95] In 1916, still adhering to this principle, though not to the Socialist Party, Mussolini married in a civil ceremony.

However, when Mussolini was on the verge of gaining power, and wished to court the Catholic church, he modified his attitudes. Throughout the 1920s he pressed consistently for reforms in family law that were more palatable to the Vatican than the existing provisions of the civil code. In his very first speech to the Chamber of Deputies in June 1921 Mussolini announced his position on divorce: "Fundamentally I am not in favour of divorce because I believe that problems of a sentimental nature cannot be solved with judicial formulas." Yet, pragmatist that he was, he kept his options open by adding: "But I ask the *Popolari* to consider whether it is just that the rich may divorce by going to Hungary whereas some poor devil is obliged to carry a chain around his neck for a lifetime."[96] The implication of this comment seemed to be either that divorce should be available to all Italians, not only the rich, or that steps should be taken to prevent the recognition of foreign divorce decrees in Italy. The reference to Hungary as a divorce haven for well-off Italians was a recognition of the continuing availability of divorce under the former Austro-Hungarian law in Trieste and Fiume.[97]

As fascist policy developed, however, it was clearly opposed to the democratization of divorce by legalizing it in Italy. Two years after Mussolini's initial and somewhat equivocal reference to divorce – and by this time, 1923, the fascists were in power and entering preliminary negotiations with the Vatican for a concordat – the minister of justice, Alfredo Rocco, stated that the Fascist

---

[95] D. A. Binchy, *Church and State in Fascist Italy* (Oxford, 1941), 392.

[96] Quoted in Shepard B. Clough and Salvatore Saladino, *A History of Modern Italy* (New York, 1968), 396–7.

[97] Sgritta and Tufari, "Italy," 258. While Fiume was occupied in 1919–20 by Italian irregulars under D'Annunzio, divorce was provided for Italians who cared to avail themselves of it. Among other things it was a means of raising revenues for D'Annunzio's government. Denis Mack Smith, *Italy: A Modern History* (Ann Arbor, 1969), 336.

Party shared the Italian people's "profound and general repugnance to the institution of divorce."[98] The regime undertook a number of measures designed to appease the church, including giving it more influence in education, the suppression of divorce in the regions acquired after the war, and even Mussolini's going through a religious marriage ceremony in 1925 with the same woman he had married civilly in 1916. The culmination of this process of finding an accommodation between the Catholic church and the fascist state was the Concordat and Lateran Accords of 1929. These agreements represented the first official recognition by the Vatican of the secular Italian state and embodied compromises, concessions, and gains by both church and state across a wide range of issues, including territorial administration, the status of Rome, education, political activity, and, as we should expect, marriage law.

There is much debate as to which side "won" most from the Concordat and Lateran Accords, but as far as marriage and divorce were concerned it is clear that the state made major concessions to the church. Article 34 of the concordat provided that "the Italian State, willing to restore to the institution of marriage, foundation of the family, a dignity consonant with the Catholic traditions of its people, recognizes civil effects in the sacrament of marriage ruled by the canon law."[99] This concession, giving legal force to marriages celebrated solely by the church, was a reversal of Italian policy that since 1865 had insisted on civil marriage as having sole claim to legal recognition. This article in the concordat was made law by a hastily passed statute of May 27, 1929, which one historian describes as "the most chaotic and anomalous marriage law that could possibly be imagined."[100] Although it allowed Italians to choose to be married in church or by the state, jurisdiction over all marriage questions, such as separations and annulments, which had previously been held by the civil courts, was transferred to the ecclesiastical courts. This, together with the recognition of the sacramental character of marriage, ruled out the possibility of legalizing divorce while the concordat remained in force. Apart from anything else, the church courts could certainly not be expected to apply a divorce law.

In many respects Italian fascist divorce policy paralleled that of the fascists in Spain. In both cases divorce was opposed outright for reasons that were religious at base, regardless of whether the religious issue was one of principle or political expediency. In these respects Italy and Spain diverged from Portugal and Vichy France. Mussolini's government did pursue a corporatist policy toward the family and mounted a pronatalist program, and opposition to divorce must be placed within this context too. Marriage was glorified to the level of a patriotic duty, and on a more mundane level was rewarded in tangible ways. Celibacy, on the other hand, was penalized: In 1927 a special tax was levied on bachelors between the ages of twenty-five and sixty-five years, and in 1929 it

---

[98] Binchy, *Church and State*, 399.
[99] John T. Noonan, Jr., *Power to Dissolve: Lawyers and Marriages in the Courts of the Roman Curia* (Cambridge, Mass., 1972), 441n.160.
[100] A. C. Jemolo, *Church and State in Italy, 1850–1950* (Oxford, 1960), 239.

was decreed that single men would no longer qualify for preferment in the civil service. Arguing that Italy needed a population of 60 million, about 20 million more than its population in 1930, Mussolini declared a *battaglia per la natalità* (battle for births): The dissemination of birth-control information was punished, large families were granted tax exemptions, and even illegitimate children were given legal equality with legitimate children.[101] However, the battle for births was abortive; if anything, the birthrate declined from 1925 onward.[102] Significantly for our purposes, Mussolini did not believe in the demographic advantages of divorce (unlike Hitler, as discussed later). Yet even if the fascists had perceived some advantages in this respect from divorce, it is likely that the number of divorces would have been low[103] and that the benefits would have been slight and more than offset by the hostility that legalization would have provoked on the part of the Catholic church. It seems clear that in the case of Mussolini and the Italian fascists, for whom few principles seemed fixed for long, pragmatic political considerations lay at the heart of their refusal to legalize divorce.

The status and role of marriage and divorce in Nazi society were determined by the contribution they were believed to make to the regime's overriding aims of achieving population growth and racial purity. In *Mein Kampf* Adolf Hitler was quite unequivocal as to the purpose of marriage: "Marriage is not an end in itself, but must serve the greater end, which is that of increasing and maintaining the human species and the race. This is its only meaning and purpose."[104] Such a belief might well be construed as a reformulation of the traditional Christian doctrine that the chief end of marriage was procreation. We have noted that this doctrine was secularized by pronatalists in the eighteenth and nineteenth centuries, and from Hitler's pen it reappeared in *völkisch* religious and racial terms:

A folk-State should in the first place raise matrimony from the level of being a constant scandal to the race. The State consecrates it as an institution which is called upon to produce creatures made in the likeness of the Lord and not create monsters that are a mixture of man and ape.[105]

Nazi ideology as expressed by Hitler placed a high value on marriage but only insofar as it was the means to propagate what was referred to as the "Aryan race." By carefully regulating marriage and by attempting to prevent nonmarital

---

[101] On the battle for births see William Elwin, *Fascism at Work* (London, 1934), 164–71.
[102] Between 1925 and 1932 the crude birth rate in Italy (number of births per 1,000 population) ran as follows: 28.3, 27.2, 27.4, 26.2, 25.6, 26.7, 24.9, 23.6, Elwin, *Fascism at Work*, 171. The number of births exceeded a million per annum throughout the 1920s, fell below a million from 1932 to 1937, rallied slightly in the period 1938–40, then declined again. Mitchell, *European Historical Statistics*, 103.
[103] After the concordat, which gave Italians the choice of marrying according to religious rites or civilly, the great majority chose religious ceremonies.
[104] Adolf Hitler, *Mein Kampf* (London, 1939), 213.
[105] Ibid., 337.

fertility, the Nazis sought to produce successive and progressively larger and purer generations of Aryans.

It is scarcely surprising, then, that one of the early concerns of the national socialist government was family legislation, so that in September and October 1935 laws were passed that forbade marriage and sexual intercourse between specified racially defined categories of people. The September marriage legislation, part of the "Nuremberg Laws," was targeted specifically against Jews, and forbade the marriage of a Jew to an Aryan, as well as sexual intercourse between them. The aim was, quite unambiguously, to prevent any further dilution of the purity of the Aryan race. In October 1935 a Marriage Health Law was passed with the aim of preventing marriage where either partner was suffering from any mental or physical illness or disease that might adversely affect the other partner or their potential children. Under this law men and women who wished to marry were required to obtain a medical certificate to the effect that they were fit (as defined by law) for marriage.[106]

The purpose of the 1935 measures was to prevent the marriage of those defined as undesirable, but other policies were put in place to encourage marriage and child bearing by those considered fit and proper: healthy Aryans. As early as 1933 a system of marriage loans was established to provide incentives for young Germans to marry. These loans, in the form of vouchers of up to a thousand marks to be used for the purchase of furniture and other household goods, were granted to couples judged healthy and racially suitable. They were interest free and were to be repaid at a rate of 1% a month, but with each child the couple had the loan was reduced by 25% and repayments were suspended for a year. There was therefore some financial incentive to having children, and having them in rapid succession. The loans were funded by a special tax on unmarried adults, itself an encouragement to marry.[107] The loans had a decided effect on marriage in Germany. In 1932, before the loan scheme was in place, there had been 517,000 marriages, but in 1933 there were 639,000, and 37% of the marriages contracted between October and December 1933 were aided by the loans.[108] In 1934 the number of marriages rose to 740,000, and from then on the annual number of marriages was generally a good deal higher (averaging 660,000 a year between 1935 and 1939) than before the marriage-loans scheme was introduced (marriages averaged 552,000 a year between 1929 and 1932).[109] Seven hundred thousand loans, averaging 600 marks, were made between August 1933 and June 1937,[110] and they clearly contributed to the higher marriage rate. Marriages in many countries increased during the 1930s

[106] On Nazi marriage laws see Jill Stephenson, *Women in Nazi Society* (London, 1975), 37–56; Lucy S. Dawidowicz, *The War Against the Jews, 1933–1945* (New York, 1981), 84–7.
[107] See Clifford Kirkpatrick, *Nazi Germany: Its Women and Family Life* (Indianapolis, 1938), 130; also Franz Neumann, *Behemoth: The Structure and Practice of National Socialism, 1933–1944* (New York, 1942, repr. 1966), 148–9.
[108] Stephenson, *Women in Nazi Society*, 46.
[109] Mitchell, *European Historical Statistics*, 102.
[110] Kirkpatrick, *Nazi Germany*, 131.

as their economies moved out of the depression into a more prosperous phase, but no major nation achieved a rate of increase comparable to that of Nazi Germany. The notable exception was Austria, where marriages leapt after *Anschluss* (incorporation into the German Reich) in March 1938. In 1937 there had been 46,000 marriages in Austria, but in 1938 there were 89,000 and in 1939, 117,000.[111] In both Germany and Austria there were also significant increases in fertility, a result of the greater number of new marriages and also of the Nazi pronatalist policies of closing birth-control centers, banning the advertising of contraceptives, and more restrictive attitudes toward abortion.

It was in this campaign to promote the Aryan population that divorce was given a role to play. The national socialist government inherited the divorce provisions of the 1900 civil code, but as early as 1934 there were plans to reform divorce law in order to bring it into line with the principles of marriage espoused by the new regime. Yet it was not until 1938, when Austria, whose law prohibited divorce for Catholics, was incorporated into the Greater Germany, that a new marriage code, including a revised divorce law, was promulgated.[112] The new divorce law was conventional in appearance in some respects, but bore the unmistakable stamp of the Nazi preoccupation with population growth and racial purity. Refusal to have children was made a ground for divorce, quite logically in light of the doctrine that the purpose of marriage was procreation. In fact some divorces had been granted for this reason even before the new law was enacted. In 1935, for example, one county court dissolved a marriage for reason of the wife's refusal to have children, basing its decision on the argument that the refusal contravened the state's view of the nature of marriage.[113] Under the terms of the 1938 law a divorce could also be granted if either spouse used illegal means to prevent a birth, a ground evidently aimed against abortion. Marriage could also be dissolved when one of the spouses was suffering from premature infertility or from a mental or physical disorder. This included short-term emotional disturbances, mental illness, and diseases that were either contagious or repugnant to the other spouse. Again, the clear rationale underlying these grounds was the desire to restrict marriage to the mentally and physically fit so as to produce a robust and healthy Aryan population.[114] A further ground, this one retained from the 1900 divorce code, was adultery, but

---

[111] Mitchell, *European Historical Statistics*, 100. The popularity of divorce supports the view that the secular laws on education, marriage, and divorce introduced to Austria by the Nazis were widely supported throughout the country: Radomir Luza, *Austro-German Relations in the Anschluss Era* (Princeton, 1975), 185.

[112] The law is printed in the *Reichsgezetzblatt* 106 (Berlin, July 8, 1938), 807–22. There is a commentary in G. W. Dietz, "La nouvelle législation allemande sur le mariage," *Journal du Droit International* 66 (1939), 52–7.

[113] Stephenson, *Women in Nazi Society*, 42.

[114] The compulsory euthanasia program, which was introduced in 1939 and resulted in about 70,000 deaths by August 1941 when it was stopped, also dissolved many marriages. Most of those who were killed were diagnosed as mentally deficient or incurably insane, but many of them had suffered no more than nervous breakdowns. Guenter Lewy, *The Catholic Church and Nazi Germany* (New York, 1964), 264.

even this might be construed, in terms of national socialist ideology, as a means of ensuring that the care taken to ensure that children were produced only by fit and approved married parents was not nullified by irregular and unregulated extramarital relationships.

Apart from these grounds for divorce, all based on the notions of fault or unfitness (in Nazi terms) for marriage, the 1938 law was innovative in providing for no-fault divorce. Divorce was permitted when the couple had lived separately for three or more years and when there was no longer any hope that married life could be resumed. No blame had to be attributed to either spouse in such circumstances, although one spouse could block a divorce on this ground if it could be shown that the petitioner was primarily responsible for the separation in the first place. No-fault provisions in divorce legislation in other Western legal codes were generally justified in terms of the well-being, interests, and happiness of the spouses, but in Germany the justification was again demographic. Spouses who were living separately and who did not intend to take up married life together again were most unlikely to have a sexual relationship with each other, and they thereby depressed the potential birthrate. The aim of the no-fault section of the divorce law was to permit these barren marriages to be dissolved so that the spouses could remarry and produce children for the Reich. In 1939 the law was amended so that there was no defense in divorces sought on the ground of three years' separation. Approval of this amendment was expressed by the Nazi newspaper, *Völkischer Beobachter*, which commented that such marriages were unprofitable and "deprive the partners of any opportunity to make full use of their energies for the benefit of the community."[115]

It is evident that the dominant interest served by the 1938 German divorce law was that of the state. There was far less concern for the effects of particular marital circumstances on the individuals most concerned, the spouses. This was the explicit intention of the divorce law in national socialist eyes.

The value of this new law consists in the fact that the liberal thesis which looked upon marriage as a private contract has been done away with, whereas the interests of the national community have been given due prominence. Useless and barren marriages, and those whose continuation is morally unjustified, are to be dissolved.[116]

From such a perspective, de facto separation was important only insofar as it adversely affected the birthrate, and the risk of physical handicap was less important to the individual than as a threat to racial purity. Indeed, it is notable that of the traditional matrimonial offenses, such as adultery, cruelty, and desertion, only adultery was retained. Its context leads one to believe that for Nazi divorce law adultery was less important in traditional moral terms than for the

---

[115] *Völkischer Beobachter*, March 29, 1939, quoted in *The Persecution of the Catholic Church in the Third Reich: Facts and Documents translated from the German* (London, 1942), 463.
[116] *Schwarze Korps*, July 28, 1938, quoted in ibid., 461.

risks to progeny that were implied by sexual relationships that were not approved in advance by the state, as marriages were. The various breeding projects sponsored by the Nazi regime to propagate an Aryan race indicate a less than fastidious attitude toward sexuality, and certainly no great concern that fertility be confined within marriage. The overriding concern was that sexuality should be regulated by the state and not left to the whims of individuals.[117]

Yet for all that divorce served the political and demographic policies of the regime, rather than the happiness of individuals, we should expect that personal considerations were uppermost in the minds of German men and women who divorced, even if, indirectly and from the broader perspective, their divorces and remarriages satisfied official purposes. It is surely probable that adultery was viewed in quite traditional ways, as a breach of fidelity and the sexual exclusivity of the marriage contract rather than as an act that risked producing children unworthy to live in the Reich. It is equally probable that the other grounds for divorce were usually invoked for selfish personal reasons rather than an overwhelming desire to remarry and breed workers for Hitler. Yet there were explicitly political divorces as well, some apparently based on criteria established by Nazi judges on an ad hoc basis. One county court agreed to a man's petition for a divorce on the ground that his wife patronized Jewish stores: "If the wife of a National Socialist, especially of a National Socialist official, makes purchases at Jewish stores and shops, in spite of the explicit veto of her husband, he cannot be blamed for growing cold in his matrimonial feelings."[118] The county court at Halberstadt granted a woman a divorce because her husband kept "incessantly sneering at her being a member of the Union of National Socialist Women," and expressed indignation at his son's giving the Nazi salute "Heil Hitler."[119] A decision of the German supreme court ruled that "disparagement of the Führer by a wife entitles the husband to claim a divorce."[120] Such explicitly political divorces were very likely rare, and it is probable that most divorces reflected personal dissatisfaction with marriage.

Whatever the motivations for divorce, though, the 1938 law proved popular. The number of divorces in Germany had generally increased during the 1930s: Between 1930 and 1938 there was an annual average of 46,243 divorces, an increase of more than 25% over the annual average of 36,471 divorces granted between 1925 and 1929. In 1939, however, after the new law came into effect, divorces in Germany (excluding the territories annexed in 1938 and 1939), rose markedly to 61,848, more than 12,000 (and 25%) more than the number in the

---

[117] Although quite traditional in appearance, the Nazi ideology of the family was anything but. Traditional values related to women's roles, paternal authority, and family virtues were distorted by Nazi precepts of racial purity, militarization, and the destruction of family bonds so as to bring the individual into a direct relationship with the state.

[118] *Schwarze Korps*, July 28, 1938, quoted in *Persecution of the Catholic Church*, 462.

[119] Ibid.

[120] Ibid., 463.

preceding year.[121] Such divorces might have been well received by those who benefited from them, and by the state that saw in each divorce a remarriage and more children, but others were less than thrilled. The Vatican protested against the Nazi divorce law, which was as repugnant to Catholic doctrine as the rest of Nazi legislation on marriage and the family was.[122] The 1933 concordat between the Catholic church and Germany had accepted the long-standing church demand for a revision of matrimonial law;[123] the bases of German marriage law had been set down in the 1870s during Bismarck's *Kulturkampf* against the Catholic church. But the national socialist legal reforms were clearly not what the church had in mind when it called for reform. Rather, the new laws removed jurisdiction over the family from the control of any authority but the state and represented a radical departure from European Christian (and indeed secular) notions of marriage and divorce.[124]

Clearly, this survey shows that any simple correlation between political orientations and divorce policy is simplistic. It might generally be true that there is a predisposition on the part of conservatives to prefer restrictive divorce policies, and of liberals to opt for more permissive policies. But in concrete historical terms family policy, of which divorce legislation (or its absence) is an integral part, is the product not only of ideology but of specific social, economic, and demographic conditions. The libertarian family policies adopted by the Soviet Union after the 1917 revolution proved to be so demographically and socially disastrous that they were abandoned within two decades. As for the fascist states, Franco's regime in Spain was inherently conservative in social policy and adhered to the family doctrines of the Catholic church; Mussolini's regime was ideologically flexible but clearly saw political advantage in a policy that was in tune with Italian tradition and with Catholic doctrine; and in Germany under Nazi government, family policy marched to the beat of Hitler's racial and population goals. Although we can dismiss easy generalizations about the relationship between political ideology and family policy, the integral role of family policies within broader sociopolitical aims is clear in all of these examples.

Aside from the influences that variations in divorce law and policy had on the rate and patterns of divorce, the more general economic climate also played a discernible role at specific times. It has become accepted that divorces tend to increase in times of prosperity,[125] and there is an assumption that the depres-

---

[121] In 1939 there were 71,950 divorces in the German Reich, but 8,226 of these were granted in Austria and 1,876 in the Sudetenland, both annexed territories. *Statistisches Jahrbuch für das Deutsche Reich*, 1942.

[122] Stephenson, *Women in Nazi Society*, 44.

[123] Lewy, *Catholic Church*, 83.

[124] Article 26 of the 1933 concordat made the concession that in certain emergency situations a church wedding might precede the civil marriage ceremony. Later this was exploited by some priests to celebrate marriages that were forbidden under the Nuremberg Laws. Ibid.

[125] See, for example, Ira L. Weiss, *The Family System in America* (New York, 1971), 284: "Divorce is associated with economic conditions in part; and during good times the overall divorce rate increases." That this generalization does not always apply is shown by the experience of the United States during the 1950s; see Section 14.4.

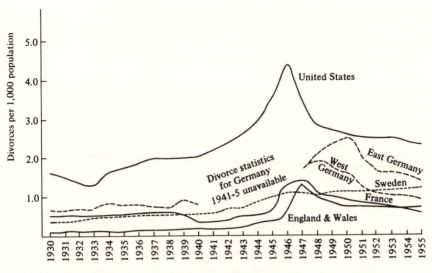

Figure 13.2 Crude divorce rates 1930–55 in selected countries.

sion that struck Western economies from 1929 onward also depressed divorce rates. A glance at Figure 13.2, however, shows that with the exception of the United States, the effects of the depression were either nonexistent or negligible. In England the divorce petitioning rate dipped slightly in 1929, but quickly recovered, and although there was only moderate growth in the rate until 1935, there was certainly no decline.[126] In Germany there was a slight decline in 1931 but there, too, recovery was quick.[127] In both of these countries, which were severely affected by the depression, we can detect little more than a brief hesitation in the divorce trend, and this is generally true of most of the countries we are concerned with; at most the depression produced a one-year decline or a short period when there was little or no increase in the divorce rates. No other country was affected as much as the United States, where the divorce rate peaked in 1929 and then declined for four years, until the number of divorces in 1932 and 1933 was 20% lower than the 1929 level. The decline in the American divorce rate between 1930 and 1933 effectively meant that there was a deficit of between 100,000 and 150,000 in the number of divorces that would have been granted had the divorce rate continued to rise.[128]

Several explanations can be advanced for the decline of divorces during the depression, but it is difficult to understand why they should have had such a great effect in the United States and not elsewhere. The most immediate result

[126] Rowntree and Carrier, "Resort to Divorce," 201, Table 2.
[127] Divorces in Germany numbered 40,722 (1930), 39,971 (1931), and 42,202 (1932). *Statistisches Jahrbuch*, 1932–4. There was also a decline in German divorces in 1923, when inflation shot up, the mark lost its value, and many middle-class families were financially ruined.
[128] See statistics in Jacobson and Jacobson, *American Marriage and Divorce*, 90, Table 42.

of unemployment and economic hardship should have been to make divorce too expensive; divorce should have been relegated to a low priority in terms of expenditures. Another explanation, which bears more directly on separation, is that although financial stresses might have predisposed couples toward breakdown, countervailing forces were more powerful. In the United States and elsewhere, welfare assistance was given more readily to families than to individuals, and employment on relief projects was given first to men with dependents.[129] Despite the lack of real evidence that the depression deterred couples from separating, some commentators have suggested that in this period families were drawn closer together by the need to face common problems. A corollary of this notion of pragmatic family fusion is that the rapid rise in the American divorce rate after 1933 represented divorces postponed during the depression years. The Jacobsons comment that the high divorce rates from 1934 "make it evident that the apparent cohesiveness [of families] often concealed a host of disillusionment, friction and bitterness."[130]

Another result of the depression that must surely have affected the likelihood of separation was the growth of unemployment among women, for we have linked the rise of separation and divorce to the ability of women to support themselves in the work force. In the United States and elsewhere during the depression, married women who were employed were often fired if their husbands were working, and married women who sought employment were often denied jobs. Several states and many municipalities prohibited work by married women on the ground that in a period of unemployment men more than women needed work. In 1932 the federal government required one spouse to be fired if both worked for the government, and almost invariably it was the wife who lost her job.[131] This was a sensible application of an unjust rule since men earned more. But when we consider that in the United States more than two-thirds of divorces were sought by women, and that employment or the possibility of it was an essential practical precondition for separating or divorcing, then it is not difficult to understand how the depression cut into the rate of marriage breakdown and dissolution.

A further factor that must have influenced the divorce rate during the depression was remarriage. Many couples who separate do not divorce until one of the spouses plans to remarry, so that the timing of divorces is often influenced by the potential for remarriage. The difficult economic conditions of the early 1930s were a deterrent to marriage, as the declining nuptiality rates in many Western countries show. But the economic depression seems to have affected the marriage rate more dramatically in the United States than in most other countries. Like the divorce rate, the American marriage rate peaked in 1929 then slumped during the following four years. The average annual number of marriages between 1930 and 1933 was some 13% lower than the

[129] Ibid., 95.
[130] Ibid., 96.
[131] Carl Degler, *At Odds: Women and the Family in America* (New York, 1980), 413–14.

number of marriages in 1929.[132] In comparison, the deficit in marriages in Germany (where the number fell between 1930 and 1932) was 10%, and in England the marriage rate was scarcely affected by the depression.[133] The relatively severe effect of the depression on American marriage patterns might well explain why it had a greater impact on divorce rates there than elsewhere. Marriage, which implied the ability to house and support a family, was clearly a more difficult proposition during the depression, and this applied not only to first marriages, but equally to remarriages that divorced men and women might undertake. The need to postpone remarriage might well have led to the postponement of many divorces until the more prosperous years later in the decade, an explanation that fits the trends of the American divorce rate in the 1930s.

As we can see, it is impossible to generalize about the effects of the depression on divorce, for the impact varied widely. For the most part, however, the effects were remarkably moderate for a phenomenon that so severely affected economic prosperity and other facets of social life. In Germany and England, both of which suffered massive unemployment, there was a slight and short-lived interruption in the divorce trend. The same is true of 1933 and 1934 in France, where the impact of the depression was felt later and less severely.[134] Only in the United States did the divorce rates accompany the indices of industrial performance as they fell from 1929, and it is difficult to isolate the factors involved in this one case that did not apply elsewhere.

13.5 World War II and the 1950s

World War II wrought various effects on the divorce rates of those countries enmeshed in it, as Figure 13.2 (showing crude divorce rates, 1930–55) indicates. In general, wartime divorce increased after phases of relative stability during the later 1930s, although toward the end of the war in 1945 and especially in the two or three years immediately following it, divorce rates reached levels that were not only without precedent but that would not be equalled again for another twenty years. However, we cannot attribute these trends solely to the effects of military conflict in all cases; legal reforms enacted just prior to the war and during it also had their influence. In France the restrictive divorce law passed by the Vichy administration should have depressed the divorce rate, but we have noted that the rate had already begun to decline in 1939, the year before the German invasion of France. There appears to be no way of separating the influences of military conflict from those of legal change and social upheaval. In England, the sequence was reversed, for the outbreak of war came hard on the heels of divorce law reform. The new divorce legislation, which went into effect in 1938, produced a sudden increase in the number of divorces and the higher divorce rate was sustained during the war years; from

[132] Calculated from Jacobson and Jacobson, *American Marriage and Divorce*, 21, Table 2.
[133] Mitchell, *European Historical Statistics*, 102.
[134] Colin Dyer, *Population and Society in Twentieth-Century France* (London 1978), esp 62–3, 67–8.

a crude rate of 0.12 divorces in 1937 (before the revised law went into effect), there was a rise to an average 0.22 divorces per thousand population during the war years. Again, however, it is impossible to specify precisely how much of the increase was a result of war-related conditions.[135]

The case of Germany is at once more complex and more straightforward. First, there are no statistics on divorce in Germany from 1941 to 1946 inclusive. Second, until 1941 the Nazi divorce law of 1938 and the territorial expansion of the Reich from the same year continued to influence the divorce rate, which did not have time to stabilize before the onset of war. Third, after 1945 it is necessary to deal not with one Germany, but separately with the Federal and Democratic republics. Each of these states formulated its own divorce legislation and policy and, as Figure 13.2 shows, each produced its own distinct divorce rate. For these reasons it is difficult to say much coherently about the effects of the war itself on divorce in Germany, and we must acknowledge that it is impossible to plot continuities of divorce trends in Germany from the 1930s through to the 1950s and beyond. It is as though Germany began its divorce history anew after the war although there were, as we shall see, some continuities in terms of legislation.

For a combination of reasons, in the countries whose divorce rates are plotted on Figure 13.2 (and in most of those not plotted, as well), there was a general increase in the divorce rate, an increase most marked in the case of the United States. The most remarkable common feature, however, was a short phase of very rapid increase that peaked, depending on individual countries, between 1945 and 1947. (The different peak years reflected factors such as the timing and duration of postwar demobilization and the varying lengths of time it took the huge number of divorce petitions to work their way through the courts.)[136] If we need evidence as to the effects of war on divorces, we need only to look at neutral or nonbelligerent countries such as Sweden, Switzerland, and Portugal. Divorce was not available in Spain or Ireland, the other main European countries that did not participate militarily in the war. As Figure 13.2 shows, the divorce rate in Sweden rose steadily over the period, and although there was a slight acceleration during the war years, there was no hint of a divorce boom in the immediate postwar period. In Portugal there was a slight increase in the number of divorces in 1946, but nothing to compare with those in countries such as the United States, France, and England.[137] In Switzerland,

---

[135] Rowntree and Carrier, "Resort to Divorce," 210, hypothesize about the weighting that should be given to the various influences on divorce: normal rate of increase, war, legal reform, and legal aid.

[136] Peak years for divorce are as follows: 1946 – the United States, Denmark, Netherlands, Scotland, and New Zealand; 1947 – France, England and Wales, Canada, Belgium, Iceland, Luxembourg, and Australia. In other countries, especially in Eastern Europe, the divorce rates peaked later: in 1948 in Austria, West Germany, and Yugoslavia; 1949 in Hungary and Norway; 1950 in East Germany, Czechoslovakia, and Roumania. Source: *U.N. Demographic Yearbook*, 1958, 464–71, Table 25.

[137] See note 86.

which is not shown on the graph, the divorce rate increased slightly at the end of the war, but instead of then falling to form a peak retrospectively, the rate generally settled at a higher level during the 1950s.[138]

It is likely that the same kinds of influences and conditions that resulted in the higher divorce rates at the end of World War I were operative again at the end of World War II. Immediate postwar divorce was a response to wartime adultery, the effects of separation during the war, and the difficulties of adjustment to married life, and the apparently inherent weakness of marriages contracted, many in haste and the passion of crisis, just before or during the war. Evidence of the first of these factors lies in the increased proportion of divorces based on adultery.[139] In England, for example, adultery was the ground of 56% of all divorces granted in 1940, but this percentage rose until by 1947, when the divorce rate peaked, adultery was the ground in 71% of all divorces. At the same time the proportion of divorces sought by husbands rose, as it had at the end of World War I. Although women had consistently filed between 50% and 60% of all divorce petitions in England from 1923 to 1939, their representation fell to between 40% and 50% from 1940 to 1945, before declining even further, to 37% and 39% in 1946 and 1947, respectively. Only thereafter did the proportion of women's petitions recover to exceed 50%.[140] This was a pattern replicated in many countries and reflected the tendency for postwar divorces to be based on the adultery of married women during the war. As we noted of the same phenomenon after World War I, this does not mean that married women were more likely to have committed adultery but that their behavior was more susceptible of evidence than that of married men on active service abroad.

The increased divorce rate after the war was also fuelled by the instability of marriages contracted during the war itself. In the United States in 1946 alone, one in every 28 (3.6%) of marriages celebrated in the preceding four years was dissolved by divorce, and these recent marriages (of four completed years of duration or less) proved especially prone to divorce in the peak divorce period from 1945 to 1947.[141] This effect was also found in England, where marriages contracted between 1940 and 1945 were not only dissolved by divorce at a greater rate than earlier and later marriages, but were dissolved more rapidly. For example, eleven out of every thousand marriages contracted between mid-1942 and mid-1943 ended in divorce within five years, compared to only two per thousand for 1939–40 marriages and three per thousand for 1946–7

---

[138] The crude divorce rate in Switzerland fell in the range 0.70–0.74 from 1939 to 1944, rose to 0.84 in 1945, 0.96 in 1946, 0.95 in 1947, and 0.94 in 1948. Thereafter it fluctuated around 0.94 until the end of the 1950s. *U.N. Demographic Yearbook*, 1958.

[139] As in World War I the spread of sexually transmitted diseases testified to sexual activity, including extramarital sexual activity. On the reaction within the Canadian armed forces see Ruth Roach Pierson, *"They're Still Women After All": The Second World War and Canadian Womanhood* (Toronto, 1986), 188–214.

[140] Rowntree and Carrier, "Resort to Divorce," 201–2, Table 2.

[141] Jacobson and Jacobson, *American Marriage and Divorce*, 93, Table 44.

marriages. In general, English marriages contracted between mid-1940 and mid-1944 proved to be at greatest risk of early divorce: After seven years, more than 2% of them had been dissolved.[142]

Again, it is difficult to specify the precise conditions that provoked the high rate of dissolution of wartime marriages throughout Western society.[143] Wartime adultery was the declared reason for most of the divorces in some countries, but where the law was sufficiently broad to allow spouses to base their divorces on other, less embarrassing grounds, they probably did so. In New Zealand, for instance, adultery-grounded divorces increased their representation by about 50% between 1942 and 1946, but the greatest increase lay in those divorces based on the refusal of the defendant to obey an order for the restitution of conjugal rights (essentially a court injunction to a deserter to return to his or her spouse).[144] Other divorces affecting wartime marriages must have dissolved unions involving soldiers only temporarily stationed in foreign countries. Although many war brides and war grooms were reunited at the end of hostilities, many were not. In New Zealand such marriages between local women and American military personnel were common enough to give rise to a special piece of legislation, passed in 1947, that facilitated divorce; many women, it was pointed out in parliament, had married "sailors belonging to the [United States] Fleet, and when the Fleet sailed away that was the last the girls heard of their husbands."[145]

In short World War II had dramatic short-term effects on the divorce rates of those countries involved, pushing them temporarily to unprecedented heights. In absolute figures there were more than 3 million divorces in the United States between 1942 and 1948, compared to about 1.75 million in the previous seven-year period. At their peak in 1946, the 628,760 divorces dissolved, in a single year, one in every fifty-five existing marriages in the United States.[146] In England the figures were less spectacular, but still impressive and without precedent; in 1947, petitions were filed for the dissolution of 1 in every 150 existing marriages.[147] The war, then, had a ravaging effect on marriage in Western society, for in addition to those unions terminated by divorce, hundreds of thousands of others were dissolved by the deaths of men on active service, and by the deaths of civilians as a result of military actions and the Holocaust.

[142] Rowntree and Carrier, "Resort to Divorce," 216, Table 10. Marriage-years in these cases refer to midyear points in each calendar year (e.g., 1941–2 marriages are those contracted between July 1, 1941, and June 30, 1942).

[143] These issues are discussed in Lord Horder, et al. *Rebuilding Family Life in the Post-War World* (London, n.d.).

[144] Phillips, *Divorce in New Zealand*, 71–4. These divorces were often consensual: The spouses separated, one of them applied for an order for restitution of conjugal rights, the other refused to comply, and the petitioner was free to seek a divorce.

[145] Ibid., 138n.14.

[146] Jacobson and Jacobson, *American Marriage and Divorce*, 90, Table 42.

[147] There were 48,501 petitions for divorce, a rate of 68 per 10,000 married women aged 15 to 49. Rowntree and Carrier, "Resort to Divorce," 202, Table 2.

13.5 World War II and the 1950s

The postwar divorce boom dissipated as rapidly as it had swelled, and the immediate aftermath was reminiscent of the effects of World War I. Just as they had in the 1920s, so in the 1950s the divorce rates stabilized at rates higher than those attained in the prewar period. In some cases this effect can be accounted for in terms of the natural trend of increase. In the United States, for example, the crude divorce rate ranged between 2.1 and 2.5 annually in the early 1950s, a level not greatly higher than the rates of 1.8 and 1.9 of the late 1930s.[148] In England, however, the divorce rate in the 1950s was four or five times that of the mid-1930s, but in this case we must take into account two legal changes. The first was the 1938 divorce law that boosted divorce in the wartime years. The second development was the passage in 1949 of the legal assistance act, which from 1950 greatly extended the accessibility of divorce. Because of this the divorce rate, which had begun to decline after the postwar boom, shot up again. When divorces finally stabilized after 1952, they did so in the range 25,000 to 30,000 a year, a massive increase compared to the three or four thousand divorces that England and Wales had produced annually in the mid-1930s.[149]

Patterns of divorce in other countries also owed their characteristics to legal change. In Germany and Austria there were political complications because of the Nazi marriage and divorce legislation introduced in 1938. For the most part both Austria and West Germany maintained the 1938 legislation, but in a form modified so as to remove the racist and eugenic elements. For example, the provision for divorce in cases of infertility was repealed.[150] It is also important to recognize that those parts of the 1938 law that were retained, making divorce available for reason of marriage breakdown or matrimonial offense, were applied in the context of quite different social and family policies than those in which they had been introduced in the Nazi period.

The reform of Austrian divorce law after the war entailed a major liberalization of divorce policy in that country. Before 1938 and the application of the Nazi divorce legislation throughout the Greater Reich, Austria's Catholics – the great majority of the nation's inhabitants – had been denied access to divorce. The effects of extending divorce to the Catholic population were immediate: Divorces rose from about 700 a year before 1938 to more than 8,000 in 1939 and never less than 6,000 a year during the war. From 1946 to 1949 they exceeded 12,000 annually (peaking at 14,162 in 1948), and in the 1950s they settled at between eight and nine thousand a year.[151] As in the case of England, legal change must be considered directly responsible for the change in the divorce rate in Austria.

Apart from individual cases where the war marked a transition in the level of divorce, the most striking characteristic of the 1950s was the stability of divorce

[148] Jacobson and Jacobson, *American Marriage and Divorce*, 90, Table 42.
[149] *U.N. Demographic Yearbook*, 1951, 1957.
[150] Renate Kunzel, "Germany," in Chester, *Divorce in Europe*, 178.
[151] *U.N. Demographic Yearbook*, 1951, Table 26.

559

13 The twentieth century: Rise of mass divorce

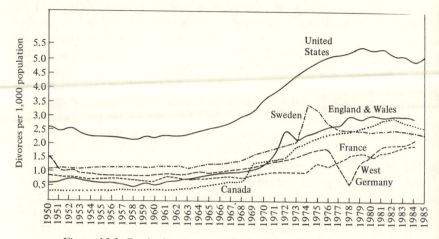

Figure 13.3 Crude divorce rates 1950–85 in selected countries.

rates. This was true whatever the relationship of these rates to prewar levels. In virtually all the countries of the West with which we are concerned, divorce rates remained stationary for a ten-year period beginning around 1950. This was a stark contrast with the preceding decades when, despite the volatility of divorce rates, a clear trend of increase can be detected. Figure 13.3 indicates the stability of the divorce rates in several countries, but their number can easily be multiplied. In Canada the rate ranged from 0.37 to 0.41 from 1952 to 1961; in Portugal it fell between 0.08 and 0.12 (744 and 1,068 divorces) in the same period; in the Netherlands divorce rates of between 0.47 and 0.56 were recorded. In none of these countries, we should note, was there a trend of increase; the rates fluctuated within these narrow limits according to no particular pattern.[152]

Such a near-universal stability in divorce rates was unprecedented in the West since divorce rates had begun to rise appreciably in the 1870s and 1880s, and several explanations are possible. One must be the relative absence of major legal changes in this period; with few exceptions, legislators took a respite from their continual tinkering with divorce legislation, and there were certainly fewer innovations significant enough to produce even the brief surge of divorces usually characteristic of legal reform. Other reasons for the stationary divorce rates in the 1950s are discussed in more detail (Section 14.4) in the broader context of divorce trends throughout the twentieth century. At this point we might note that they include a phase of conservatism in social attitudes during the 1950s, a higher estimation of marriage and the family by those married in the postwar period, a period of economic prosperity, and the hypothesis that the stabilization of divorce rates was a statistical effect resulting from the postwar divorce boom. Whatever the explanations for it, the stabilization of divorce did

[152] Ibid.

560

not last; divorce rates seemed in the 1950s to *reculer pour mieux sauter*, and in the 1960s they entered a new growth phase.

13.6 The 1960s to 1980s: No-fault divorce

The 1960s was a decade of change in many aspects of social life in Western society. After the political and social conservatism of the 1950s, the paroxysms of the following ten years seemed to betoken a widespread breakdown of traditional values and behavior. There were many more people in the youthful age groups because of the postwar fertility rise, and they were restive. There was a sexual revolution of sorts, with more open discussion of sexuality and more permissive attitudes and practices. In the United States and elsewhere, the war in Vietnam generated widespread opposition among young people, especially university students. In Europe the student movement focused on the reform of educational policies, and made its presence felt in Italy, Spain, Germany, and to a lesser extent, Britain. In France the alliance between students and workers in 1968 almost brought down the government of Charles de Gaulle. Authorities of all kinds were challenged from without and within. Stresses were created within the major churches as reformers battled with conservatives; the reforms within the Roman Catholic church, which resulted from the Ecumenical Council (Vatican II), represented the victory of progressive forces. The traditional social and political dominance of men was challenged by a new feminist movement, which would flourish in the 1970s. In the United States the civil rights movement challenged racial discrimination in politics, housing, and other areas.[153]

In general, institutions, authorities, and governments at most levels responded sympathetically, and social policies went through a phase of liberalization. Censorship was relaxed, sex education was extended in more educational systems, and birth control, stimulated by the commercial production of the contraceptive pill, became more widely and freely available. A growing awareness of the social roots of poverty and crime encouraged improvements in social welfare and correctional policies so as to stress rehabilitation rather than retribution. Needless to say, these pressures and reforms were far from uniform throughout Western society. They went further in Scandinavia, especially Denmark and Sweden, and in some of the states of the United States, but countries such as Spain and the Republic of Ireland lagged behind the trends elsewhere.

The more liberal attitudes toward authority and institutions were reflected in family law reform as well, and in no part of it was this more true than in terms of divorce law. What began in the 1960s was a reevaluation of marriage and divorce in the light of more liberal attitudes and its translation into legislation

[153] A succinct account of the gamut of change in Europe in the 1960s is found in Walter Laqueur, *Europe Since Hitler: The Rebirth of Europe* (rev. edn., London, 1982), esp. Part 3, 279–377.

13 The twentieth century: Rise of mass divorce

Table 13.1. *Divorce law reform, 1961–81*

Year of legislation	Country or state	General description
1961	West Germany	Major reform
1963	New Zealand	Complete revision
1967	New York State	Complete revision
1968	Canada	First federal divorce law
1969	England and Wales	Complete revision
1969	Denmark	Major reform
1969	Finland	Major reform
1969	Norway	Major reform
1969	California	Complete revision
1970	Italy	Divorce legalized
1971	Netherlands	Complete revision
1973	Sweden	Complete revision
1974	Belgium	Major reform
1975	Australia	Complete revision
1975	Portugal	Divorce legalized for Roman Catholics
1975	France	Complete revision
1975	Italy	Major reform
1976	Scotland	Complete revision
1976	West Germany	Complete revision
1977	Portugal	Complete revision
1978	Austria	Major reform
1980	Luxembourg	Major reform
1980	New Zealand	Complete revision
1981	Spain	Divorce legalized

and social policy. Between 1960 and 1986 divorce policy in almost all the countries of the West was either completely revised or substantially reformed. Table 13.1 indicates the dates of these legal changes, most of which were preceded by years of study by official commissions. (Apart from California and New York, the American states are omitted: legal reforms in the United States are discussed later in this section.)

There were many more pieces of legislation dealing with divorce than this list of major reform acts indicates. After pausing in the 1950s, legislators again turned their attention to amending divorce legislation, fine-tuning it in response to judicial and public criticisms and to particular cases where existing law

562

13.6 The 1960s to 1980s: No-fault divorce

appeared to produce inequities or hardship. In Belgium, for instance, legislation dealing with divorce was passed in 1962, 1967, 1969, 1972, 1974 (two acts), and 1975. These acts amended divorce law in such ways as to remove the need for parents to consent to divorce (1962) and repealed the section of the law, dating from the Napoleonic Code, that specified that a wife over the age of forty-five could not be divorced (1969).[154] The detailed changes brought about by the many divorce and divorce-related laws passed in Western countries since the 1960s need not concern us here, however. What is important is the general direction of change and the common patterns that may be discerned.

Perhaps the most important element in any divorce policy is the grounds recognized as justifying divorce. Procedures, costs, and provisions for financial settlements, alimony, and the custody of children are vital to an appreciation of overall policy, but discussions of divorce law usually focus on the grounds for divorce, and this will be the emphasis here. (The other facets are discussed in the next chapter.) The first generalization that can be made about this aspect of divorce law reform since 1960 is that the grounds have shifted so as to encompass more and more matrimonial conditions. In this single sense, divorce has become increasingly accessible to Western populations. We have noted that this trend of liberalization occurred in many countries and states from the nineteenth century onward, but from the 1960s there was an important new development, the shift to no-fault divorce.

Earlier divorce law liberalization had tended to be little more than the steady accumulation of specific grounds, often specific matrimonial offenses or conditions. Divorce laws had begun by recognizing adultery and desertion, and had gradually added others such as ill-treatment, absence, drunkenness, and insanity. Divorce legislation accommodated more couples simply by adding more grounds, and in some instances this process began to become unwieldy. By 1915, for example, Swedish divorce law recognized nine principal grounds for divorce (prolonged and severe discord, desertion, bigamy, adultery, venereal disease, assault, imprisonment, drug or alcohol addiction, and insanity)[155] and in addition the judiciary had broadened their interpretation of grounds such as discord and assault.

The process of simple accretion of grounds for divorce stopped in the 1960s. In part there was a realization that the process had to be halted; either legislation would become absurdly complicated or the determination of the grounds for divorce would fall increasingly to the discretion of the courts. It was also clear that many couples who wanted to divorce did not qualify, even though their marriages had effectively terminated in all but legal terms. Rather than liberalize divorce by extending the number of grounds, qualitative changes

---

[154] Jacques Commaille, et al., *Le divorce en Europe occidentale. La loi et le nombre* (Paris, 1983), 31.
[155] Jan Trost, "Sweden," in Chester, *Divorce in Europe*, 35.

were made that essentially permitted couples to determine their own grounds for divorce. This was no-fault divorce, a concept that revolutionized divorce law in Western society, and marked a distinct break from its history up to that time.

No-fault divorce laws, as the name clearly indicates, recognize circumstances for divorce where no fault, reponsibility, or offense is attributed by the law to either spouse. The principle was not a new one in the 1960s and 1970s, but in those decades it was more widely implemented than at any other time. There were examples of no-fault provisions (such as divorce by mutual agreement or for reason of incompatibility) in earlier divorce laws; they occurred in such divergent codes as the French revolutionary legislation, in various American state laws in the nineteenth century, and in the 1938 Nazi divorce law. Other specific grounds for divorce that had long been recognized also give the appearance of being essentially no-fault provisions. Insanity, impotence, and unavoidable absence were not offenses in the same sense as cruelty, adultery, and desertion. Yet these grounds for divorce did place responsibility on one of the spouses, even if they did not attribute fault in the sense of blame. Such grounds are generally referred to as remedial because divorce in these cases is thought of as a remedy for a pathological condition within marriage. Insofar as they placed responsibility for the condition on one of the spouses they were not, strictly speaking, no-fault provisions. Neither, we should note, were the omnibus or discretionary clauses that were inserted in some codes, especially in America in the nineteenth century. Most of these clauses gave judges discretion to recognize or not to recognize particular acts or behavior as sufficiently offensive or cruel as to warrant dissolving the marriage, and in this way fault was attributed to one spouse.

The essence of no-fault divorce law is that it does not attribute fault and does not require one of the spouses to be considered innocent and the other guilty. Rather, it recognizes the breakdown of the marriage, that is, that the relationship between the spouses is such that they can no longer function as a married couple. This condition is defined as terminal, and the various laws employ words such as "irremediable," "irreconcilable," and "irretrievable" to qualify breakdown.

In such laws divorce does not rest on the precise circumstances that produced the breakdown of the marriage but simply on the fact of the breakdown. As an objective criterion of breakdown, most no-fault divorce laws specify a period during which a couple must have lived separately, the assumption being that by living apart for a minimum specified period, the spouses have indicated that as far as they are concerned, the marriage has ceased to have practical meaning. The divorce decree in these cases becomes little more than putting a de facto divorce on a legal basis. The qualifying period for the establishment of marriage breakdown varies among the different laws, and the variations are a measure of the rigor or ease of the respective divorce policies in effect. One of the most restrictive of recent laws in this respect was the 1974 Belgian law that required couples to have lived apart for ten years in order to demonstrate that their marriages had broken down. The English divorce law of 1969 required five years' separate dwelling in the case of a contested divorce, but only two years' when both spouses agreed to have the marriage dissolved. Many laws have set the minimum period at two years, but others, such as the 1986 Canadian divorce law, specify only one year.[156] It is to be expected that the liberalization of divorce in the near future will take the form of the progressive diminution of the period of separation required to prove irremediable marriage breakdown, although it seems unlikely that it will drop below one year.

One important effect of the introduction of no-fault provisions in modern divorce legislation has been to shift the responsibility for defining what the law should recognize as marriage breakdown. In codes that set out specific matrimonial offenses, the acceptable parameters of marriage breakdown were established by statute and interpreted by the courts. As the grounds for divorce were extended on a piecemeal basis, other specific offenses or conditions were added, but others remained excluded. At every point the judiciary had discretionary powers of interpretation, particularly when legislation placed an obligation on judges to attempt to reconcile spouses before dissolving their marriages, even when a specific matrimonial offense had been committed. The advent of no-fault divorce, where breakdown was normally determined by a specified period of noncohabitation, shifted much of the onus of defining breakdown to the spouses themselves. Under no-fault provisions a couple could decide to separate for any reason whatsoever: A wife might leave her husband, or a husband his wife, because of violence, adultery, financial irresponsibility, sexual incompatibility, jealousy, a forgotten anniversary, or any other reason, serious or apparently trivial. The courts take no cognizance at all of the circumstances that provoked the separation and are concerned only that the separation should have lasted the minimum required period.[157]

To this extent no-fault divorce provisions have overthrown the centuries-long principle that divorce must be closely regulated by the church or state. By allowing spouses the right to divorce, in effect for any reason whatsoever, the recent laws have transferred the responsibility of defining the criteria for a satisfactory marriage directly to the spouses themselves.

The progressive adoption of no-fault divorce provisions by legislators across Western society was the result of a long debate about the character of marriage and the functions of marriage law, and was a response to specific practical

---

[156] The terms of European divorce legislation at the beginning of the 1980s are set out country by country in Commaille, *Divorce en Europe*, passim.

[157] Most laws allow the couple to resume cohabitation for short periods in order to attempt reconciliation, without detriment to the duration of noncohabitation required to prove irretrievable breakdown of marriage.

issues that arose in the 1960s.[158] The enhancement of a social scientific approach to divorce and other social "problems" from the later nineteenth century had shifted emphasis away from individual responsibility for actions or behavior to analysis of causal or predisposing conditions in society at large. The growing influence of sociological theory deprived men and women of complete responsibility for their behavior, and provided a model for the analysis and official response to many social phenomena such as criminality, poverty, and divorce. Instead of the moralistic and retributive approaches that had underlain the dominant theological and secular conceptions of marriage and divorce, social scientists stressed the social, economic, and other environmental factors involved and discovered that age at marriage, family background, socioeconomic status, religious, and other factors might play a role in the tendency to divorce.

In fact the issues of individual guilt and innocence had never been as clearly defined in divorce policies as they might appear to have been. Various divorce laws had recognized the principle of constructive desertion, where responsibility was placed not on the spouse who deserted but on the spouse whose behavior had forced the other to leave. There was a similar concept of constructive adultery, where it was clear that adultery by one spouse could be an understandable, if not wholly excusable, response to behavior by the other, such as his or her having venereal disease or obstinately refusing to have sexual intercourse over a long period of time. The principle of fault had historically been qualified in these ways, but nonetheless fault was the undisputed touchstone of divorce policy.[159] Herein lay the significance of the divorce law reforms of the late 1960s and 1970s, that the no-fault principle became the rule. As Homer Clark, Jr. put it, sociologists and psychologists argued

that such activities as adultery, cruelty and desertion were merely symptoms, not causes, of marital failure...that fault itself was out of place in divorce, and that marriages broke up in a context of conflicts in attitude, personality, or other difficulty on both sides, rather than as a result of fault by one spouse and innocence by the other.[160]

This argument was a critical one but it was not new in the 1960s; what was new was the sympathetic hearing it received. Not only were legislators everywhere prepared to translate these principles into law, but other bodies, such as mainstream churches, also rallied to them. One of the most startling changes in attitude took place within the Church of England, which historically had been doctrinally opposed to the dissolubility of marriage. In 1966, however, a church

---

[158] More detailed discussions of the principles of no-fault divorce are in Lynne Carol Halem, *Divorce Reform: Changing Legal and Social Perspectives* (New York, 1980), 233–83; Max Rheinstein, *Marriage Stability, Divorce and the Law* (Chicago, 1972) 317–405, passim; and Lenore J. Weitzman, *The Divorce Revolution: The Unexpected Social and Economic Consequences for Women and Children in America* (New York, 1985), esp. 15–28.

[159] It was disputed by individuals such as Bucer and Milton and by some legal codes that recognized divorce by mutual consent and for reason of incompatibility. But they were exceptions to the trend of Western divorce policies.

[160] Homer H. Clark, Jr., *Cases and Problems on Domestic Relations* (2nd edn., St. Paul, Minn., 1974), 9.

commission established to investigate marriage recommended that divorce should be allowed on the principle of breakdown.[161] This was a breakthrough, and together with a report of the law commission in the same year, it prepared the ground for the English no-fault legislation of 1969. In turn, the English law reform influenced the development of divorce legislation in other countries; legislators did not blindly emulate reforms elsewhere, but in all cases there was a keen awareness of the state of international divorce legislation and the effects of its application, not least because of the issues of reciprocal recognition that arise from great disparities among laws of contiguous states or countries.

The reform of legislation everywhere not only reflected a shift of attitudes toward divorce but also responded to changes in patterns of marriage and divorce in the 1960s. After stabilizing in the 1950s following the postwar boom, divorce rates throughout Western society began to increase steadily. In figures rounded to the nearest thousand, divorces in England and Wales rose from 25,000 in 1960 to 34,000 in 1964 and then to 45,000 in 1968, the year before the divorce law was overhauled.[162] In short, the number of divorces almost doubled in eight years, as did the divorce rate, which moved from 0.52 divorces per thousand population in 1960 to 0.92 in 1968.[163] As Figure 13.1 shows, divorce rates in the United States and other countries broke out of the 1950s doldrums in about 1960 and began what was to become an unprecedented increase.

What is significant is that the initial increase was not generated or even facilitated by changes in divorce legislation. Although the legal reforms might have been responsible for an acceleration of the divorce rates later, an underlying trend of increase was already in place when the laws were reformed, and to some extent the changes in the law were a reaction to it. The legislative response by no means reflected complacency in increasing divorce, and it certainly did not indicate a desire to boost the number of divorces even more. Indeed in many places the legal review and reform was sparked by alarm at what was perceived as rampant marriage breakdown. In California, which in the 1960s was earning a reputation as a state of permissive morals and marital instability, the governor asked a committee of the state assembly to investigate what he called the "festering problem" of divorce. The terms employed by the governor were more evocative of the nineteenth century than of the liberalism we associate with California in the 1960s. Divorce statistics, he said, "seem to show clearly how divorce erodes the very foundation of our society – the family ... [and] tell of an erosion of our precepts and institutions, which are dependent on the endurance, stability and sanctity of the home."[164] A special

---

[161] This report, *Putting Asunder: A Divorce Law for Contemporary Society*, was prepared by a commission of churchmen, lawyers, a psychiatrist and others, chaired by the Bishop of Exeter.
[162] Commaille, *Divorce en Europe*, 91, Table III.
[163] Calculated from *Le Divorce en Europe occidentale* (Paris, 1975), 47, Table 1, and Commaille, *Divorce en Europe*, 91, Table III.
[164] Governor Edmund Brown, quoted in Rheinstein, *Marriage Stability*, 374.

Commission on the Family was set up in 1965, its brief (expressed in the military terms common in American government in the 1960s) being to make a "concerted assault on the high incidence of divorce...and its often tragic consequences."[165] Of the extent of divorce in California there seemed little doubt. In 1960 the ratio of divorces to marriages in the United States was 26 : 100; in California it was 47 : 100, and it reached 69 : 100 in the city of Sacramento and 73 : 100 in Napa County (north of San Francisco).[166]

Fear of increasing the divorce rate even more led California legislators to shy away from simple no-fault legislation, and the law they passed in 1969 sought a compromise between no-fault principles and the maintenance of judicial control and discretion. Under the new law the courts could grant divorce or separation on one of two grounds: incurable insanity or "irreconcilable differences...which have caused the breakdown of marriage." Evidence of the differences was to be weighed by the courts, which could either agree to the divorce or, if there seemed hope of reconciliation, stay proceedings for thirty days. In practice, however, it appears that the judiciary interpreted these terms as liberally as they had earlier treated the term "cruelty." Certainly the divorce rate in California was scarcely affected by the 1969 law; although it fell slightly in 1971, the year after the new law came into effect, it quickly rebounded and reached record levels in the later 1970s.[167]

On the other side of the United States, in New York State, the 1960s also witnessed increasing pressure for a reform of divorce policy. It is indicative of the universality of this sentiment that it should have been manifested in such different social and legal contexts: whereas California already had a liberal divorce policy by the 1960s, thanks largely to judicial interpretation, New York's remained astonishingly restrictive. The sole ground for divorce, adultery, had been defined in the state's first divorce law in 1787, and the only significant reform since that time had been the 1879 repeal of the prohibition of remarriage by the guilty spouse.

Unlike California, New York had a low divorce rate, and it was not so much fear of the divorce rate as awareness of the inadequacies and abuses of New York's divorce law that led to its reform. Collusion and perjury were perceived as widespread, the typical case involving a prearranged "discovery" of the husband in an act of adultery. The judiciary demanded less and less rigorous proof of adultery, until it was enough for a spouse to be found in bed with an accomplice, even if both were fully clothed. A weakening of the law in practice, together with evident abuses of it – individual women appeared in multiple divorces as corespondents – had attracted criticism for many years; in 1949 the New York State Council of Churches had condemned the law as "an occasion

[165] Ibid., 239.
[166] Ibid., 373. Such ratios are not always useful guides to divorce rates, since they can reflect changes in the marriage rates quite independently of movements in divorce patterns.
[167] The crude divorce rate in California fell from 5.7 in 1970 to 5.4 in 1971, but rose to 5.7 again in 1973 and 6.2 in 1976. Halem, *Divorce Reform*, 251.

for evasion and hypocrisy."[168] But in the 1960s pressure for reform became irresistible. It was fueled by two events that highlighted the disadvantages the state's citizens had to endure. In 1962 New York's governor, Nelson Rockefeller, obtained a divorce in Nevada, an act that showed that the wealthy could divorce despite the law. The second event was a decision by the New York Court of Appeal ordering the state to recognize divorces obtained in Mexico.

Pressure for legal reform finally produced a divorce law that came into effect in 1967 and combined fault and no-fault principles. Adultery was maintained as a ground but expanded to include "deviate sexual intercourse," and other offenses were added: cruel and inhuman treatment, desertion for two or more years, and imprisonment for three or more consecutive years. The no-fault clause allowed divorce when the spouses had lived apart for two years (one year from 1972) following a separation decree or a written agreement filed with the state authorities. Even so, the element of fault was retained indirectly because a separation decree could be obtained only where there was a matrimonial offense. In other respects, too, the 1967 New York law attempted to regulate divorce closely. The costs of proceedings were high, and couples had to go through at least one conciliation conference. Despite these restrictions, the legal reforms clearly answered the needs of many couples, and the number of divorces in New York State tripled between 1967 and 1969, rising from 7,136 to 21,184.[169]

California and New York are only examples of the way in which the reform of divorce policy in the 1960s and 1970s resulted from the interplay of existing trends, changed perceptions of marriage and divorce, and various liberal and conservative political forces. Legal reform in each jurisdiction, whether it was national or state, responded to peculiar traditions and situations, but the tendency toward the spread of no-fault divorce is clear. Most U.S. states had introduced no-fault provisions by the late 1970s, and by 1985 some form of no-fault principle underlay divorce law in almost all of them. Thirty-six states specified the irretrievable breakdown of marriage as justifying divorce, another six allowed divorce after a couple had lived apart for a specified time, and others recognized mutual consent, incompatibility, or judicial separation. Many states mixed fault and no-fault grounds, but only one recognized only fault; South Dakota, the state excoriated in the nineteenth century for its lax divorce policies, clung to the grounds of adultery, alcoholism, desertion, conviction of a felony, and extreme cruelty.[170] One effect of the steady liberalization of American divorce laws in the 1970s was the decline of migratory divorce. Apart from the convenience of combining a vacation, gambling, and sun-tanning with a divorce, there were fewer and fewer reasons to travel out of state to have a

[168] Ibid., 257.
[169] Ibid., 268.
[170] Doris Freed and Timothy Walker, "Family Law in the Fifty States: an Overview," *Family Law Quarterly* 18 (1985), 380–1, Table 3.

marriage dissolved, and the gap between Nevada's and other states' divorce rates began to narrow appreciably.[171]

Despite the spread of no-fault divorce laws throughout the United States, there have remained significant variations. The beginnings of legislative activity in the 1960s renewed interest in uniform marriage and divorce laws throughout the country, just as it did at the end of the nineteenth century. A 1970 report of the National Conference of Commissioners on Uniform State Laws recommended that divorce laws should allow for the dissolution of marriage where there was irretrievable breakdown of marriage. No specific criteria for assessing breakdown were suggested, and it was proposed that a divorce petition on this basis should be accepted at face value unless one of the spouses argued that the marriage had not broken down.[172] If implemented this would have introduced divorce by mutual consent across the United States, for more than 90% of American divorce petitions are not contested.[173] After opposition from the American Bar Association, however, this proposal was amended in a more conservative direction. Residency requirements of 90 days would be demanded, evidence of breakdown would have to be furnished (de facto separation for 180 days or "serious marital discord"), and no divorce decree would be issued until matters concerning property and children had been settled. Like other recommended uniform laws, this one has been ignored by state legislators who remain faithful to the tradition of independence and divorce law heterogeneity that began in the seventeenth century.

Variation among divorce laws is not peculiar to the United States, but it is more marked there, partly because of the large number of jurisdictions, their different legal and social traditions, and paces of change. In Europe the movement toward uniformity is more evident. Some European countries have retained fault grounds in their divorce laws along with no-fault provisions, but the trend from 1960 onward has clearly been to replace fault with no-fault clauses specifying marriage breakdown or mutual consent. In 1960 fault-based divorce existed in the thirteen nations of Western Europe with established divorce policies,[174] no-fault divorce (marriage breakdown) in seven, and mutual consent divorce in six.[175] By 1981 fault grounds had been retained in eight, and no-fault divorce had extended to twelve, as had mutual consent divorce.[176] In

---

[171] Nevada's crude divorce rate fell from 24.0 in 1969 to 18.7 in 1970, a decline largely attributable to the implementation of the reformed divorce law in California in 1970. By 1983 Nevada's divorce rate had slumped to 12.8. This was still the highest divorce rate in the United States (the next highest was Alaska, which produced a rate of 8.1 without a migrant contribution), but the range of state divorce rates has shrunk dramatically.

[172] Rheinstein, *Marriage Stability*, 385; Halem, *Divorce Reform*, 270–2.

[173] Halem, *Divorce Reform*, 271.

[174] The following thirteen West European countries are monitored by the Groupe International de Recherche sur le Divorce: West Germany, Austria, Belgium, Denmark, Finland, France, Luxembourg, Norway, the Netherlands, England, Scotland, Sweden, and Switzerland.

[175] The exception is Sweden, which in 1973 moved to a different form of divorce, as discussed later.

[176] The exception is Switzerland, which retains only fault-based divorce.

two decades, then, Western European divorce law had shifted dramatically; in 1960 fault divorce was common to all divorce codes, whereas by 1981 no-fault provisions united all but one.[177] This trend was echoed in major divorce laws outside Europe, in Australia (1975), New Zealand (1980), and Canada (1986).

One country, Sweden, broke with the trend toward divorce law uniformity in Western Europe by adopting such a permissive policy that even the other Nordic countries proved reluctant to emulate it. A Swedish law of 1973 provided no-fault divorce at the request of either or both spouses, without any requirement of a minimum period of de facto separation. The only qualification to immediate divorce is in cases of unilateral petitions or where there are children under the age of sixteen years. In such cases there is a delay of six months between the petition and the divorce decree in order to give the petitioner a chance to reconsider. Where a couple without young children agree to divorce, however, their petition is automatically and immediately approved.[178]

This extremely permissive Swedish law notwithstanding, we can see that since the 1960s divorce law and policy in Western society have been radically reformed. This period constitutes a third generation of divorce legislation, following the Protestant laws of the sixteenth century (the first generation) and the widespread legalization and liberalization of divorce in the latter half of the nineteenth century (the second). But whereas the second generation of divorce laws tended to reform legislation quantitatively, the reforms and revisions since the late 1960s have marked a qualitative shift. For the first time, divorce policies en masse began to discard moralistic and fault-based precepts and the notion that marriage breakdown was a recipe that required equal parts of guilt and innocence. Reform was motivated, too, by a growing awareness of, and objection to, the gap between appearance and reality, by the perception that restrictive laws forced wives, husbands, witnesses, lawyers, and judges into a network of collusion, perjury, and hypocrisy, and that laws could be circumvented by migration.

In the final analysis it is impossible to say precisely what influences were at work right across Western society to produce such a generalized legislative response. The pressure of divorce itself, as divorce rates began to rise anew, must have been a factor. Both behavior and legal reform reflected changed attitudes, however, for given the delay between proposals for legal reform and the passage of the new laws, it seems that the idea of reforming divorce laws became current just as the divorce rates started to rise. Although these attitudes might have derived from the particular conditions of marriage in the 1960s (this is discussed in the next chapter), we should also see more permissive or liberal conceptions of marriage and the family as part of the wide-sweeping liberal-

---

[177] For a discussion of these trends in legislation, see Pierre Guibentif, "L'évolution du droit du divorce de 1960 à 1981. Essai d'analyse des discours législatifs," in Commaille, *Divorce en Europe*, esp. 190ff.

[178] Jan Trost, "Sweden," in Robert Chester (ed.) *Divorce in Europe* (Leiden, 1977), 36–7; Commaille, *Divorce en Europe*, 97.

ization of attitudes toward many institutions and forms of behavior that was characteristic of the 1960s and 1970s.

13.7 Politics and divorce reform in Italy, Portugal, Spain, and Ireland

It is an indication of the strength of the divorce movement after 1960 that the issue was taken up in parts of Europe where the Roman Catholic church has historically been especially influential in shaping family law: Italy, Portugal, Spain, and the Republic of Ireland. Of these four countries only Portugal had provision for divorce before 1970, and there, under the terms of a concordat with the Vatican, it was permitted only to couples who had not married according to Catholic rites. By 1981, however, divorce was available to all married couples in Italy, Portugal, and Spain, leaving Ireland the distinction of being the only European state without divorce legislation.

The first of these three countries to legalize divorce was Italy, where divorce had been resisted throughout the nineteenth century (after the brief period of imposed divorce law in the Napoleonic period) and most of the twentieth. It was not until the 1960s that the question of introducing divorce was taken up seriously by the Italian parliament. Attempts to pass very restrictive divorce legislation (known as *piccolo divorzio*, or little divorce) in the mid-1950s had failed, even though the proposed law would have allowed divorce only in cases of extreme hardship such as one spouse's being sentenced to fifteen years or more in prison, the attempted murder by one of the spouses, desertion for five years, incurable insanity, or separation for five years.[179] Public opinion at this time was anything but favorable to the legalization of divorce; a survey of attitudes in 1955 showed that 34% of Italians were in favor of allowing divorce and 56% were opposed, and four years later the proportion opposed had increased to 61%.[180] Not only was there no political advantage to supporting the introduction of divorce in the 1950s, but there was also recognition that a "little divorce" would be only the thin edge of the wedge; that once divorce was legalized in any form, even in the most restrictive terms, there would be pressure to have it progressively liberalized. The most effective way of preventing mass divorce in Italy was to prohibit divorce entirely.

In the 1960s, however, the drive to legalize divorce became more forceful and more effective. It was not that public opinion swung in favor of divorce; on the contrary, the percentage of Italians opposed to divorce actually increased during the 1950s and later, until by 1962, 69% were opposed to the legalization of divorce and only 22% were in favor of it. In that year, however, the decline in

---

[179] Francisco Narbona, *El Divorcio Viaja a España* (Madrid, 1974), 75. (This is a study of divorce in Italy, presented as a lesson for Spain.)

[180] The 1955 survey showed that 20% were "definitely" and 14% "probably" in favor of divorce, and 41% were "definitely" and 15% "probably" opposed to its legalization. Ten percent gave no opinion. Ibid., 109.

support for divorce stopped and an increasing proportion of Italians – though still far from a majority – began to support its legalization. By 1968, 31% were in favor and 62% were opposed.[181] This more positive view of divorce, particularly among Italian women,[182] even if it did little more than recoup the support lost after 1950, coincided with the increased use of divorce in other parts of Europe, and was a manifestation of the general shift in attitudes toward marriage and the family in Western society.

What brought divorce to the fore in Italy in the 1960s was not the increase in popular support for it but changes in the composition of the government. From the end of World War II the Italian parliament had been dominated by the conservative Christian Democratic Party, a party with close links to the Roman Catholic church and one quite opposed to the reform of family law in favor of divorce. Divorce seemed to be ruled out, in any case, under the terms of Mussolini's 1929 concordat with the Vatican, which had been confirmed by parliament in 1946.

In 1962, however, the Christian Democratic dominance of parliament was broken and a coalition, including the Italian Socialist Party, was formed. The Italian socialists had long advocated the legalization of divorce, and in 1965 the socialist deputy Loris Fortuna introduced a divorce bill. It was not passed when parliament was dissolved and new elections held in 1968, but Fortuna reintroduced it after the elections, and set off the first major debate, inside and outside parliament, on the divorce issue.

The battle in favor of legalizing divorce was led by the Liga Italiana de Divorzio (Italian Divorce League), which was supported by political groupings and parties such as the Socialists, liberals, and Communists. The opposition was led notably by the Catholic church, the Christian Democrats, and various groupings to the political Right. Despite the fact that opinion polls showed that most Italians were *anti-divorzisti*, the Justice Committee of the Chamber of Deputies approved the divorce bill by a large majority, and in November 1969 the chamber itself decided to lead rather than follow public opinion, and accepted the bill by 325 votes to 283.[183] The Senate in turn approved the bill by the narrow margin of 164 votes to 150, but because it amended the bill (in a more restrictive direction), the Chamber of Deputies was required to vote on it again. On December 1, 1970, the deputies voted to accept the Senate's revisions,[184] and on the same day the president of the republic signed the bill into law. It went into effect soon after, on December 18, 1970.

Italy's first national divorce law was complex and reflected the compromises that had been made to incorporate legal and social traditions, political realities,

---

[181] Ibid.

[182] Dominique Memmi, "Le divorce et l'italienne: partis, opinion féminine et referendum du 12 mai 1974," *Revue d'histoire moderne et contemporaine* 30 (1983), 501, Graphique 4.

[183] The progress of the legislation from 1968 to 1970 is chronicled in Narbona, *Divorcio*, 103–20.

[184] The Chamber of Deputies voted 322 : 278 and 321 : 277 in favor of the two amendments made by the Senate.

and contemporary trends in European matrimonial law.[185] There were several specific fault grounds for divorce, some of which had been put forth in the "little divorce" proposals in the 1950s. The grounds set out in 1970 were a prison sentence of more than fifteen years, certain crimes of violence, sexual abuse or fraud committed against a spouse or child, failure to support the family, one spouse's getting divorced and remarried abroad, and failure to consummate a marriage. The other form of divorce provided in 1970 was conversion of a judicial or formalized separation. As of 1970 separations could be obtained only where there was a matrimonial offense such as adultery (the husband's adultery had to be shown to be a "serious injury to the wife"), desertion, cruelty, long-term imprisonment, or the husband's failure or refusal to establish a home appropriate to his means and circumstances. Under the 1970 legislation, a separation obtained for any of these reasons could be converted into divorce at the request of either spouse, but only after a fixed period had passed. If both spouses agreed to the conversion into divorce, it could be obtained five years after the separation; if the conversion were sought by the same spouse who had sought the separation (that is, the innocent spouse), but was contested by the other, the minimum delay was six years; finally, if the divorce petitioner were the spouse who had been declared guilty in the separation judgment and the divorce was opposed by the other, the mandatory delay was seven years.

Divorce in Italy, then, combined fault and no-fault principles: It could be obtained on strictly fault grounds or on the basis of a separation that could be obtained on strictly fault grounds. Its no-fault character lay in its availability to either spouse, regardless of guilt or innocence, after a separation, even though the minimum waiting periods were determined by the relationship of the divorce petitioner to the offense that had occasioned the separation. Essentially, however, the principle of fault lay at the core of the 1970 legislation, so that although the very fact that divorce was legalized reflected broader Western trends, the substance of the law did not.

Ironically, the battle over divorce in Italy seemed to begin, rather than end, with the passage of the 1970 law. Convinced that the votes in parliament were out of line with Italian public sentiment – a conviction borne out by opinion polls – the Christian Democrats and their allies pressed for a referendum on the issue. At first this demand was opposed by the Socialists and other parties, presumably because they also believed that a referendum would result in the overturning of the divorce legislation, but eventually an agreement was reached on a referendum to be held in May 1974. It was a sign of the importance attributed to divorce, for this was the first popular referendum on a non-constitutional issue, the only other referendum having been the 1946 poll on whether Italy should be a monarchy or a republic.

---

[185] The substance of the 1970 legislation is given in *Divorce en Europe occidentale. La loi et le nombre* (Paris, 1983), 65–6.

13.7 Reform in Italy, Portugal, Spain, Ireland

The unofficial struggle for the divorce referendum started well before the official month-long campaign period began, and soon Italy was divided between *divorzisti* and *anti-divorzisti*. (Perversely, those in favor of maintenance of the law had to vote "No" to the proposal to repeal the law, and those against divorce had to vote "Yes.") The forces on each side of the issue were largely as might be predicted: the Catholic church, Christian Democrats and the right-wing MSI (Italian Social Movement) in favor of abrogating the divorce law; the parties to the left of the Christian Democrats (liberals, Socialists, and Communists) in favor of keeping it. Other influential forces also weighed in. The secular press was almost unanimous in its support of the divorce law, the Italian feminist movement rallied behind it, and even within the Catholic church factions and prominent spokesmen emerged advising either absten-tion from the referendum or a vote against repeal of the law. The divorce referendum, indeed, drew on all sections of the Italian population and has been credited with realigning Italian politics. Although the proposition to abrogate the divorce law had been widely expected to win the support of the majority of voters, it gained only 41% of the valid votes cast, and represented an apparent desertion on the part of those who otherwise supported the Christian Democrats and their *anti-divorzio* allies.[186]

The three-year delay between the legalization of divorce in December 1970 and the referendum in May 1974 was crucial in enabling the *divorzisti* to win a majority of the votes. During that period there was time for divorce to be practiced and studied, and for many apprehensions to be put to rest. Contrary to the dire predictions of opponents of divorce, some of whom had forecast a million divorces in the first few years of the law, there was no great rush to divorce. In 1971, the first full year of the divorce law, some 17,134 divorces were granted. In 1972 the number rose dramatically to 32,627, but in the following year, the last complete year for which statistics were available before the referendum, it fell, equally dramatically, to 18,172.[187] These were remark-ably low numbers. Divorces could have been expected to be high in the first years of the law's being applied, and there could well have been a rush to divorce in 1973 when it seemed probable that the divorce law would be repealed. One factor militating against an initial surge of divorce, on the other hand, is that most divorces would be granted on the basis of an existing formal separation, and many Italian couples had separated without going through any formal or judicial procedures. A side effect of the legalization of divorce, then, was an increase in the number of separations. They had increased steadily during the 1960s, just as divorces had increased elsewhere in Europe, but there

---

[186] In all but two regions of Italy, the percentage of votes in favor of retaining divorce in 1974 was greater than the share of the votes received in the 1972 election by those parties that supported the divorce law during the referendum; *La Stampa* (Turin), May 14, 1974, page 1. The best concise treatment of the divorce referendum is Memmi, "Divorce et l'italienne," but see also Narbona, *Divorcio*, 139–220.

[187] *U.N. Demographic Yearbook*, 1975, 429, Table 19.

was a marked acceleration in 1970. Petitions for separations had averaged 14,256 annually between 1966 and 1969, but they rose to an average 22,766 a year (a 60% increase) between 1970 and 1973 inclusive.[188] Formal separation was an essential precondition for most divorces, and it is likely that the increase was made up of couples who had been living separately, but who from 1970 proceeded to put their separation on a legal footing as a prelude to divorce. The growing number of separations could thus be explained to Italians not as an increase in marriage breakdown brought about by the legalization of divorce, but as the regularizing of existing broken marriages.

The delay between the introduction of divorce and the referendum also gave the press – which was in favor of maintaining divorce – the opportunity to explain the implications and terms of the law, and to divest it of some of the demonological characteristics attributed to it. There was stress on the justice of allowing divorce in cases of hardship, and on the protection afforded by the law against abuse of divorce at the expense of women and children. These positions were contested by the "Yes" campaign, which was directed particularly at women and that stressed the harm divorce would do to the family unit and especially to women and children.

Opinion in favor of divorce, which had constituted a minority right up to the referendum campaign, was evidently swung during the campaign itself, although it is possible that the success of the "No" side was ensured not so much by a shift of votes from one position to the other, as by abstentions on the part of Italians who had abandoned the antidivorce position without feeling able to vote in favor of divorce. Whatever the reasons, the divorce law survived the referendum, and the success encouraged Italy's legislators to liberalize the law. As early as 1975 the law relating to separations was revised and the list of specific grounds replaced by a general clause allowing separations in cases where married life appeared to be intolerable or where it would have seriously harmful effects on the education of the children.[189] In this way the notion of no-fault separation and, by implication, no-fault divorce was introduced into Italian law. This reform of marriage legislation led to a slight increase in the number of separations, which rose from 16,451 in 1974, to 19,132 in 1975, and to 21,225 in 1976.[190] Overall, however, Italian divorce law remained relatively restrictive in European terms, resting on a two-stage process and lengthy delays before separations could be converted into divorces. These legal restrictions must go some way toward explaining the consistently small number of divorces in Italy. Between 1976 and 1984, divorces fluctuated between 11,000 and 15,000 annually, and the divorce rate of between 0.21 and 0.26 per thousand population was one of the lowest in Europe.[191]

The legalization of divorce in Italy gave impetus to the reform of marriage

---

[188] Calculated from Sgritta and Tufari, "Italy," 265, Table 2.
[189] Commaille, *Divorce en Europe*, 65–6.
[190] Ibid., 67, Table III.
[191] *U.N. Demographic Yearbooks*, 1980, 1984.

law in Portugal and Spain, two other countries with overwhelmingly Roman Catholic populations. In both countries, however, a critical factor in the legal reforms was political, the end of fascist or semifascist regimes. In Portugal divorce had been introduced in 1910, soon after the republic had been proclaimed, but the 1940 Salazar concordat with the Vatican ruled out the right of divorce for those Catholics who married according to Catholic rites. This dual divorce law was maintained while Salazar was in power, but made even more restrictive in 1966. In that year the Portuguese civil code, running against contemporary trends in family law, suppressed the ability of non-Catholics to obtain mutual-consent divorces and retained only fault-based grounds.[192] The overthrow of Salazar's administration in 1974, however, brought a swift change in family policy. The military regime that took power placed divorce law reform high on the list of its legislative priorities, and within a year of the revolution the critical article of the concordat was modified. Thereafter a series of legal reforms culminated in a complete revision of Portugal's divorce law in November 1977.

The new law recognized three forms of divorce.[193] First, couples could divorce by mutual agreement if they had been married for at least three years. Second, divorce was made available in a number of fault and no-fault circumstances: where one of the spouses violated his or her marital duties in a repeated and serious manner, so as to make life in common impossible; where life in common had been broken by de facto separation of at least six years; the disappearance of either spouse for at least four years; or mental illness, lasting at least six years, which made life together intolerable. The third form of divorce recognized by the 1977 law was conversion of a separation to a dissolution after a minimum delay of two years.

Portuguese law was thus more liberal than its Italian equivalent, but showed the same tendency of mixing fault and no-fault provisions. On the whole it was more in line with prevailing European trends, but the divorce rate remained low. The annual number of divorces had ranged between 509 and 616 between 1970 and 1973, but in 1974, the year of the military coup, there were 777, and in 1975 after some legal changes facilitating divorce, the number rose to 1,552. This effectively doubled the crude divorce rate to 0.16.[194]

In Spain, too, the demise of a regime that had close links with the Roman Catholic church had a direct influence on divorce policy. Divorce had been legalized in Spain in 1932 under the Second Republic, but was abolished in 1939 by the fascist regime of Francisco Franco, which adhered to Roman Catholic precepts in formulating its family policy. After Franco's death in 1975 there was a progressive liberalization in social and political policies that included, in 1981, the legalization of divorce. The renewal of the debate on divorce in the late 1970s provided a focus for continuing political antagonisms

[192] Pinto, *Causas do Divorcio*, 11.
[193] See Commaille, *Divorce en Europe*, 81–183.
[194] *U.N. Demographic Yearbook*, 1978.

that had their origins in the 1930s. In 1980 and 1981, for example, meetings called to lobby for the legalization of divorce were bombed, and the daughter of Pablo Picasso refused to allow the return of his painting *Guernica* to Spain as a protest against the slow progress of social and political reform after the death of General Franco. She cited the absence of a divorce law as an example of the shortcomings of the new regime.[195]

Like the 1970 Italian law, the Spanish legislation of 1981 made judicial separation the precondition of a divorce action in many foreseeable cases. Among the wide range of grounds recognized as justifying divorce was desertion, infidelity, harmful conduct that violates the conjugal relationship, imprisonment for more than six years, alcoholism, drug addiction or insanity rendering life in common impossible, formal separation by mutual consent for six months, and de facto separation for three years. Divorce could be obtained a year after a separation based on mutual consent, two years after formal separation in other circumstances, after five years de facto separation, or when one spouse was convicted of attempting to murder the other or one or more of the other's relatives.[196] As such, Spanish law recognized both fault and no-fault principles. More than in Italy, however, Spanish divorce law seems to have been influenced by European legal trends rather than by national tradition, which was brusquely ignored by the 1981 legislation.

In Ireland, in contrast, tradition continued to be upheld in the face of worldwide trends. The persistence of Roman Catholicism as the dominant confession prevented the legalization of divorce there during the Reformation, and even the country's dependence on England for centuries did not lead to the introduction of divorce. The 1857 English legislation did not extend to Ireland, and those who wished to dissolve their marriages were forced to petition Parliament. With the transfer of legislative power to the assemblies in Protestant-dominated Northern Ireland and the predominantly Roman Catholic Irish Free State in 1921, the Irish tradition divided. Northern Ireland adopted first legislative divorce and later, in 1939, a divorce law that was fundamentally the same as the 1937 English legislation. In the Irish Free State, however, even though divorce remained technically legal – attempts to prohibit divorce bills failed – there was sufficient public awareness of the hostility of the legislators to divorce that no bills to dissolve marriages were introduced into the Dáil or Seanad (the Irish houses of parliament) between 1925 and 1937.[197]

In 1937, just as the divorce law of England and Wales was being liberalized, the long-standing Irish antipathy to divorce was formalized. The constitution of that year specified that "no law shall be enacted providing for the grant of a

---

[195] *Times* (London), January 21, 1981, p. 5.
[196] Commaille, *Divorce en Europe*, 45–6. A full discussion of the law is in M. Lopez Alarcon, *El nuevo sistema matrimonial español* (Madrid, 1983), 198–228.
[197] David Fitzpatrick, "Divorce and Separation in Modern Irish History," *Past and Present* 114 (1987), 174.

dissolution of marriage."[198] The constitution also ruled out migratory divorce by providing that no foreign divorce decree would be recognized in Ireland.

These prohibitions on divorce were part of a broader policy to maintain what were thought of as traditional social and family values, and there was particular stress on preserving the distinctions between male and female social roles. Articles in the same constitution specified that

the State recognizes that by her life within the home, woman gives to the State a support without which the common good cannot be achieved, [and that] the State shall, therefore, endeavour to ensure that mothers shall not be obliged by economic necessity to engage in labour to the neglect of their duties in the home.[199]

The ban on divorce follows these articles in the constitution and should be seen largely as a measure to protect women and the family.[200]

In the absence of divorce, other forms of legal relief were provided. Separation *a mensa et thoro* is available from the civil courts, but it is expensive and procedurally difficult. Between 1968 and 1977 there were only 332 petitions, an average of 33 a year. Throughout the 1970s many couples and spouses applied to the ecclesiastical tribunals to have their marriages annulled, and by the end of 1977 there was a backlog of more than 1,300 applications awaiting consideration. Other measures indicative of marriage breakdown, such as maintenance orders and social welfare payments to deserted wives, increased during the 1970s. By 1978 there were more than a thousand applications annually for maintenance to the Dublin County courts, and by 1976 almost 5,000 deserted wives were receiving allowances and benefits.[201]

From the 1960s Irish family law came under increasing criticism from law associations, the feminist movement, and from pressure groups devoted to the legalization of divorce. Divorce remained a sensitive and recalcitrant issue, however, largely because of the importance of the Church in Irish society. In 1979 Pope John Paul II, visiting Ireland, added his voice to the resistance by praising the country's devotion to the "sanctity and indissolubility of the marriage bond."[202] It was not until 1986 that any government chose to face the issue squarely; in that year the prime minister, Gareth FitzGerald, called a referendum on a proposal to amend the constitution so as to allow a divorce law to be enacted.

The debate and the groups on each side in the referendum campaign in

---

[198] Constitution of Ireland, Article 41.3.2.
[199] Ibid., Articles 41.2.1 and 41.2.2. See Jenny Beale, *Women in Ireland* (London, 1986), 6–7.
[200] Other measures passed in the 1930s that indicated a similar aim, as well as the strong influence of the Catholic church, included a 1935 law that prohibited the sale, advertising, or importation of contraceptives into Ireland. The part of the law relating to importation was declared unconstitutional by the supreme court in 1973.
[201] Statistics from William Duncan, *The Case for Divorce in the Irish Republic* (rev. edn., Dublin, 1982), 77–8.
[202] Homily at Limerick, October 1, 1979, quoted in José Guerra Campos, *La ley de divorcio y el episcopade español (1976–1981)* (Madrid, 1981), 14.

Ireland were reminiscent of those in Italy twelve years earlier. The Catholic church fought vigorously against divorce, and antidivorce campaigners raised the specters of widespread family breakdown leading to social disintegration and the breakup of farms, and of abandoned families and ruined women. Their point was made graphically by one of the women who led the struggle against the constitutional reform: "A woman voting for divorce is like a turkey voting for Christmas."[203] Against this campaign lined up a heterogeneous coalition of liberal politicians, women's and civil liberties organizations, and a few priests who dissented from the church's stand. But if the campaign and debate on divorce in Ireland in 1986 seemed to echo the Italian referendum of 1974, it did so only until the votes were counted. The proposal to allow a divorce law to be introduced in Ireland was defeated, attracting only 34% of the votes cast, as against 66% to retain the constitutional ban on a divorce law.[204]

The passage of a divorce law in Ireland would have completed the extension of divorce legislation throughout Europe, and would have been an appropriate symbol with which to end the narrative history of divorce in Western society.[205] As it is, Ireland must stand instead as a continuity – the resistance of the Catholic church to divorce. Even though social and economic arguments were made against legalizing divorce in Ireland during the referendum, at base the objections were religious, and the movement in favor of a divorce law foundered on the Catholic doctrine of the indissolubility of marriage. This is a doctrine that the church adheres to firmly, even though it (and other social doctrines dealing with priestly celibacy, abortion, contraception, and the ordination of women) are challenged within the church itself. Yet the fidelity of the Irish population to the Catholic doctrine of marriage should not be allowed to mask the changes that have taken place in Roman Catholic policy on marriage and divorce. The church no longer claims to have sole authority to determine the validity of marriage, nor does it dispute the right of the secular state to dissolve marriages. Although the church deplores divorce and divorces, it has reconciled itself to the legalization of divorce in Italy (a new concordat recognizing divorce there was signed in 1983), throughout Europe, and in Central and South America, where most of the world's Catholics now live.[206] In addition, the church has responded to the reality of divorce by providing annulments for some divorced Catholics, enabling them to marry within the

---

[203] Quoted in *Newsweek*, July 7, 1986, 20.
[204] Ibid.
[205] In continental Europe, there is still no provision for divorce in three small territories: the Vatican State, Andorra, and San Marino.
[206] Even so, Pope John Paul II condemned divorce during his 1987 visit to Argentina, where divorce was on the verge of being legalized. At a mass in Córdoba the pope insisted that the legalization of divorce would undermine society, loosen morals, and encourage disrespect for the law: "We should not be surprised," he said, "that the spread of divorce in a society brings with it the loosening of public morals in all sectors. Why, in this hypothesis, would one continue to demand that man be loyal to his country, to labour commitments, to the fulfilment of laws and contracts?" *Toronto Star*, April 9, 1987, A3.

church.[207] The Roman Catholic doctrine of marital indissolubility is a continuity in the history of divorce in Western society, but its policy on secular divorce has evolved in tune with divorce itself.

[207] The widening of the grounds for annulment by the church courts was invoked as an argument in favor of the legalization of divorce in Italy and Ireland; it was alleged that annulments had effectively become treated as divorces, so that in this respect the reputation of the church began to echo that it had had before the Reformation. The best survey of the church's doctrine and practice in these matters is John T. Noonan, Jr., *The Power to Dissolve*.

14

~~~~~~

Explaining the rise of divorce, 1870s–1980s

14.1 Introduction

The steady rise in divorce rates throughout Western society from the end of the nineteenth century and their acceleration since the 1960s have provoked much serious research, analysis, and comment, as well as a lot of silly and superficial speculation. Responding to the awareness that quite fundamental changes in marriage patterns were occurring, and sometimes spurred by apprehension about the social and personal effects of widespread divorce, researchers and commentators have put forth a vast number of hypotheses and explanations of the divorce phenomenon. With varying success they have defined and described many of its putative correlates and causes. In the late nineteenth century the spectacular increase in the American divorce rate in relation to that of other Western countries was widely attributed to deficiencies in the morality and "character" of Americans, and when divorce rates began to climb in some European countries, national and religious characteristics were invoked to explain them. Opponents of the legalization of divorce in France, for example, insisted that the cool, rational temperament of Belgians had enabled them to withstand the moral and social corruption usually brought about by divorce, but they feared the consequences of putting divorce in the hands of their passionate compatriots. When French divorce rates shot up and quickly surpassed those of Belgium, the doomsayers expressed grim satisfaction at the accuracy of their predictions and explanations.

As scientific analyses of divorce – or analyses couched in the language of the social sciences – emerged, marriage dissolution was discussed in psychological and social terms. Divorce was often treated as a form of social pathology: Divorce rates were compared with suicide rates, and the psychological profiles and supposed emotional defects of divorced men and women were explored. There was also an increasing recognition of the effects that broad social and economic changes had on marriage and the family. Divorce was seen as an unfortunate but almost inevitable result of industrialization, urbanization, the decline of religious adherence, changes in morality, and the easing of divorce legislation. The role of women in divorce – most divorces were sought by

14.1 Introduction

women – was given particular attention, and the divorce rate was frequently explained, as we have seen, in terms of women's emancipation generally and of the expansion of women's employment in particular.[1]

More recently, research on the causes of divorce has swelled in tandem with divorce itself. Since the 1960s thousands of popular and scholarly books, articles in mass circulation magazines and academic journals, radio and television documentaries, together with government, university, and private research reports and papers have focused on divorce, its causes and consequences. Researchers have drawn on a wide array of sources and have employed a variety of methods and theoretical perspectives. Census reports, statistical series of all kinds, judicial and other legal records, questionnaires and personal interviews have all been exploited to shed light on divorce and on the process of which divorce is a part. Findings have referred to global and continental trends, to national and state populations, to samples representative of large urban populations, and to relatively small groups of divorced men and women that permit intensive personal interviewing and assessment.

Again, a multiplicity of factors, correlates and causes has been summoned up to explain divorces and their characteristics. Some factors, such as the employment of women and changes in divorce law are still popular. Others are new or have been given greater emphasis as a result of more recent research; among them are the characteristics of dissolved marriages, such as the ages of the spouses at marriage; changing expectations of marriage; the life experience of divorcing couples; changed attitudes toward divorce; and the feedback effects of an increasing divorce rate.

Ironically, however, despite the wealth of plausible explanations and causes that have been offered to us for consideration, we seem almost as poor in our understanding of divorce as earlier generations were. Their simplistic and often monocausal explanations of divorce gave some degree of certainty, even if it was wholly misplaced and based on illusions. More sophisticated recent research has destroyed the credibility of the earlier work and has confronted the complexity of divorce by recognizing that it is not a single event with predominantly moral connotations but a multifaceted process that is integrated into other social, economic, demographic, and cultural processes. Not only does the range of factors create problems of management, but even when correlates of divorce can be defined with some certainty, it is not clear in which direction the primary causal influence runs. These difficulties of interpretation of data are compounded when we seek to generalize using case studies at any level, from small group to national, that differ in the quality and character of their data, employ different methodologies or criteria of evaluation, and that produce divergent conclusions.

[1] Lynne Carol Halem, *Divorce Reform: Changing Legal and Social Perspectives* (New York, 1980) provides the best single description and analysis of changes in the explanations of marriage breakdown and divorce.

14 Explaining the rise of divorce, 1870s–1980s

This chapter attempts a particularly high level of abstraction and generalization by focusing on the character and incidence of divorce in Western society during the past hundred years or so. The single common characteristic that gives this subject coherence is the fact that in all Western countries where divorce is permitted, divorce rates have risen steadily over the period, have fluctuated following each of the world wars, and have accelerated from sometime in the 1960s or early 1970s until the early 1980s. In contrast to this common trait of Western divorce rates, differences at national and other levels abound. Actual divorce rates, and the magnitude and timing of change have varied. Moreover the contexts vary as well, as countries and regions differ from one another in terms of their demographic structures, cultural traditions, and social and economic characters. Nonetheless the common shape of changes in the divorce rates throughout Western society makes it a compelling and fascinating subject for investigation. To a large extent the rise of divorce, like earlier rises of illegitimacy and declines of mortality, seems to have been a phenomenon that has overridden variations in economic structure, cultural climate, and demographic structure, even if these variations have had their impact on the distinctively national and regional differences in the timing and nuances of change.

For the purpose of the present discussion, the recent divorce history of Western society will be divided into three periods according to the phases of growth discernible in Figure 14.1, which shows the divorce rates, from the late nineteenth century to the present, in several countries chosen to provide geographical distribution and variations in social, economic, and cultural characteristics. The first phase was one of gradual take off during the late nineteenth century until World War I. Divorce rates were not high by modern standards, but growth had begun, and the rates were becoming statistically worth measuring. The second phase, running from the end of World War I to about 1960 was one of overall increase but containing marked fluctuations associated with wars and the economic depression of the 1930s. The third and most recent phase, from 1960 to the present, was a period of rapid increase. It is an open question whether this phase of growth in the divorce rates should be considered a fluctuation in the underlying trend of increase or whether it represented a transformation of marriage patterns in Western society.

14.2 Modern divorce research

In seeking the explanations of these changes in the divorce rates we should recognize at the outset that there are several sets of "causes" of divorce, depending on what "divorce" we are attempting to explain. One set of causes lies in the account that a spouse or couple provide of their marriage breakdown and divorce. A study of divorces in Cleveland, Ohio, found that wives tended to cite as reasons for their divorces physical violence, verbal abuse, financial problems, mental cruelty, excessive drinking, neglect of home and children,

584

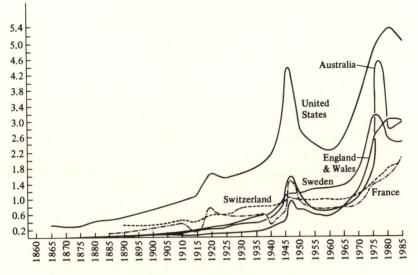

Figure 14.1 Crude divorce rates 1860–1985 in selected countries.

and lack of love in marriage. Men, on the other hand, most commonly cited problems with their parents-in-law and sexual incompatibility.[2] Such causes of divorce are the perceptions of the spouses involved and, as we might expect, spouses frequently give quite divergent accounts of the same marriage. Frequently these causes of divorce are expressed as grounds in divorce actions, but we should be aware that grounds alleged in court are often chosen to conform to the terms of the divorce law or highlighted as part of a litigation strategy by lawyers.

Such causes of divorce as perceived by the couples are generally considered by social scientists as secondary, as symptomatic of more fundamental causes. The manifestations of marriage instability – violence, adultery, incompatibility, emotional indifference, and the like – and their definition as marriage breakdown emerge from the interplay of the personal and social characteristics of the spouses and the context of their marriage. These various conditions and antecedents of marriage are a second set of causes to which divorce can be attributed, when they are shown to correlate highly with divorce. For example it has been widely observed that couples who marry when they are very young (under twenty years of age) are more likely to divorce than those who marry at older ages. Youthfulness at marriage, then, is correlated with divorce and might be considered a cause of divorce in the sense of a factor that predisposes a marriage toward breakdown and dissolution. Other variables that have been correlated with divorce in this way in many countries are low socioeconomic

---

[2] G. Levinger, "Sources of Marital Dissatisfaction among Applicants for Divorce," *American Journal of Orthopsychiatry* 36 (1966), 803–7.

status; marriages of blacks in the United States; premarital pregnancy; differences between husband and wife in social or educational background; marriages without children; employment by the wife or unemployment by the husband; and family histories of divorce.[3]

In each case hypotheses have been developed to link the variable causally with divorce. For example, various reasons have been suggested to explain why youthful marriages more frequently end in divorce. Such marriages are at risk of divorce longer, although the importance of this is generally discounted.[4] More significantly, younger men and women – and here we focus on those under twenty at the time of marriage – are less emotionally mature than men and women who marry at older ages, and such spouses are more likely to develop in different directions and at different rates after marriage.[5] Some studies have suggested that marriages by the young are more often motivated by a desire to escape personal problems and to find a substitute relationship for security, rather than by exclusive attraction to the other partner.[6] Similarly the relationship between childlessness and divorce has been explained in terms of the stresses on marriage caused by infertility. Involuntary childlessness might make the spouses doubt their sexuality and thwart expectations of having a family, and childlessness for any reason might cause stress arising from social pressure to have children. Alternatively, childless marriages might be dissolved more frequently because divorces without custody issues are less complicated. Against this, one persuasive article suggests that the correlation of childlessness and divorce rests on a complete misunderstanding of the data.[7]

But the enumeration of factors that correlate with divorce – and that might therefore be called causes of divorce – and the elaboration of linking hypotheses are of limited use. In the first place, some of the correlates are mutually exclusive. It is difficult to reconcile premarital pregnancy, which assumes a hasty, ill-considered marriage to protect the reputation of the woman or to ensure that the child is born within wedlock, on the one hand, and childless marriage on the other. Similarly, couples of low socioeconomic status have been found to be at high risk of divorce, but certain high-status occupations (such as authors, social scientists, university faculty, lawyers, and judges) have divorce rates higher than some lower-status occupations. Moreover the divorce rate in the higher socioeconomic groups in the United States and some other countries

---

[3] General surveys of these correlates and of much of the recent divorce research literature are: Barbara Thornes and Jean Collard, *Who Divorces?* (London, 1979); Stan L. Albrecht, Howard M. Bahr, and Kristen L. Goodman, *Divorce and Remarriage: Problems, Adaptations and Adjustments* (Westport, Conn., 1983), esp. 29–92; Gay C. Kitson and Helen J. Raschke, "Divorce Research: What We Know; What We Need to Know," *Journal of Divorce* 4 (1981), 1–37.

[4] See, for example, T. P. Monahan, "Does Age Matter in Divorce?" *Social Forces* 32 (1953), 81–7.

[5] See, for example, John Eekelaar, *Family Security and Family Breakdown* (Harmondsworth, 1971), 39–40.

[6] J. Dominian, *Marital Breakdown* (Harmondsworth, 1974), 131–2.

[7] Robert Chester, "Is There a Relationship Between Childlessness and Marriage Breakdown?" in E. Pleck and J. Senderowitz (eds.), *Pronatalism: The Myth of Mom and Apple Pie* (New York, 1974), 114–26.

is increasing much more rapidly than the rate among the lower social strata.[8]

A further complication is that some factors that seem to correlate with divorce have turned out, on closer analysis, to be surrogate factors, disguising more fundamental and influential variables. For example, many studies of divorce in America have reported that blacks are more likely than whites to separate and divorce. In addition, whites were more likely to remarry, and the overall result was to inflate the proportion of blacks reported divorced at any point in time. Various studies attributed the higher divorce rate of blacks to cultural features of the black family, such as the stress on the mother as the prime resource and strength of the family, and to extraneous influences such as racial discrimination that interfered with blacks' employment, educational, and housing possibilities.[9] More recent research, however, has not only nuanced these findings – noting, for example, that on average blacks who divorce do so after being married longer than whites who divorce – but have also suggested that there is no great difference between blacks and whites in terms of their divorce behavior as it had been formulated. A 1975 study indicated that when factors such as income level, home ownership, and family size are taken into account – these are factors that correlate with race in the United States – the separation and divorce rates of blacks were about 6% lower than those of whites.[10]

Similar difficulties arise with the determination of the significance of age at marriage for divorce. Although there are credible hypotheses suggesting why marriages by the young might prove especially prone to breakdown, other variables interfere with our ability to draw definite conclusions. Some studies have shown that two other factors also strongly associated with divorce – premarital pregnancy and unskilled manual occupations – are overrepresented in teenage marriages.[11] A disproportionately high presence of these factors in any marriages, no matter how old the spouses, would be expected to increase their proneness to divorce, so that it is difficult to isolate the importance of individual factors such as age at marriage.

Nor is the direction of causality always very clear. Divorced women generally have a higher labor force employment rate, but we do not always know whether they were employed while married or whether they entered the labor force after divorce. The distinction is vital if we are to theorize as to whether employment by married women predisposes their marriages to breakdown. Similarly, most divorced women are located in the lower socioeconomic groups, but this distribution could well be not so much a factor in the probability of divorce as a

---

[8] A. J. Norton and Paul C. Glick, "Marital Instability in America: Past, Present and Future," in G. Levinger and O. C. Moles (eds.), *Divorce and Separation: Contexts, Causes and Consequences* (New York, 1979), 14.

[9] D. P. Moynihan, "The Negro Family: The Case for National Action," in L. Rainwater and W. L. Yancey (eds.), *The Moynihan Report and the Politics of Controversy* (Cambridge, Mass., 1967).

[10] Kitson and Raschke, "Divorce Research," 12.

[11] See, for example, Thornes and Collard, *Who Divorces?*, 72.

result of divorce; divorced women and their children generally suffer economic decline after the separation, whereas divorced men usually experience an improvement in their economic position.[12]

The plethora of social, economic, ethnic, cultural, religious, and demographic correlates of divorce that research has produced is overwhelming and difficult to manage. Results vary – slightly or radically – from study to study, suggesting that no single universally applicable and comprehensive explanation is appropriate, and some of the suggested explanations are, as we have seen, quite contradictory. Perhaps the most disturbing aspect of divorce research is that none of the suggested causes or correlative factors, whether they are considered individually, collectively or in combinations, appears to be either necessary or sufficient. Thus youthfulness at marriage might be a cause of divorce in some cases but not in others, low level of educational achievement in some but not others, premarital pregnancy in some cases but not others. Some studies indicate that marriages with no children are prone to divorce, and others suggest a higher frequency of divorce among couples with children.[13] The upshot of these findings, considered as a body of research rather than as individual, discrete studies, is that by defining so many causes they have defined none. With the possible exception of youthfulness at marriage – and even this is contaminated by other variables – we would be rash to predict the likelihood of divorce from any one or combination of characteristics of a given married population. Couples seem prone to divorce if the wife is pregnant at marriage or if she is not, if the couple is of low socioeconomic status or one of a range of high-status occupations, if the couple has no children or some children, if the spouses are white or black. Although we should not be unrealistically demanding of generalized conclusions from social research, its application to divorce is disappointing. The many studies have usefully contributed to understanding the divorces that provide their data, but we are still far from being able to formulate conclusions as to the causes of divorce as a more general phenomenon.[14]

Beyond the analyses of the correlates of divorce, which seek to determine what differentiates couples who divorce from those who do not, lies another area of divorce research. Its aim is not to establish the differences between the divorced and nondivorced populations so as to draw conclusions as to the causes of or proneness to divorce, but rather to explain the quantitative and qualitative variations and changes in the incidence of divorce. Two dimensions are significant here, the geographical and the historical.

[12] Lenore J. Weitzman, *The Divorce Revolution: The Unexpected Social and Economic Consequences for Women and Children in America* (New York, 1985) 323ff.

[13] Chester, "Childlessness and Marriage Breakdown," passim.

[14] A very useful overview of the methodological, theoretical, and practical problems involved in divorce research is Kitson and Raschke, "Divorce Research." The most successful attempt to predict divorce is a study reported in D. M. C. Fergusson, L. J. Horwood, and F. T. Shannon, "A Proportional Hazards Model of Family Breakdown," *Journal of Marriage and the Family* 46 (1984), 539–49.

14.2 Modern divorce research

Geographical variations in the divorce rate have long exercised researchers and social commentators who have attempted to explain why the divorce rate is higher in some countries and states than in others, higher in some regions than others within the same country, and higher in cities than in rural areas. Divergences of these kinds can, of course, result from variations in the representation of the apparent correlates of divorce. For example, a greater tendency toward early marriage in one country, or a higher rate of premarital pregnancy among young women in another, could well be expected to contribute to higher divorce rates there. Differences in divorce legislation and policy are frequently proposed as being influential on divorce rates. More permissive divorce laws, it has often been argued, allow a higher rate of divorce, a proposition confirmed by some studies and contradicted by others.[15] As for the urban–rural differences in divorce rates, the distinction is more than a geographical one. International or interstate variations in divorce can be seen to persist even when the regions of comparison are similar in social, economic, and demographic structure. Urban–rural comparisons, however, necessarily deal with quite different social, economic, and cultural contexts, and the variations in the divorce rate must be explained in these terms.[16]

Finally we come to the historical perspective, which is the primary focus of this chapter. The purpose here is to explain the variations and changes in the divorce rate and the composition of the divorce populations over time, specifically during the past hundred years. To some extent the factors that have been suggested as important in explaining geographical variations overlap with those associated with historical change. For example, the higher divorce rates characteristic of urban areas bear on the historical perspective, given the trend toward urbanization in Western society in the past two and a half centuries. Other factors often invoked to explain the rise of divorce during the past hundred years are the erosion of traditional family relationships, progressively more liberal divorce laws, the employment of married women, the decline of religion, major shifts in moral and social values, demographic changes such as the decline of mortality rates and the fall of ages at marriage, the women's movement, rising expectations of marriage, improvements in education and social welfare, increasing tolerance of divorce, and an inherent dynamic of growth within divorce rates. Behind many of these explanations, implicitly or explicitly, lurks industrialization, which is almost always linked directly or indirectly with rising divorce rates.[17]

Such factors are macrosocial, dealing with large-scale social and economic movements, and the historical analysis of divorce rates at this level requires us

---

[15] Kitson and Raschke, "Divorce Research," 8; Albrecht, Bahr, and Goodman, *Divorce and Remarriage*, 49–50.
[16] See, for example, Hugh Carter and Paul C. Glick, *Marriage and Divorce: A Social and Economic Study* (rev. edn., Cambridge, Mass., 1976), 55.
[17] See the discussion in William J. Goode, *World Revolution and Family Patterns* (New York, 1970), esp. 1–6.

to formulate generalizations in which the nuances of the divorce rates and characteristics of divorce are easily lost in the search for broad explanations with wide applicability. Clearly the tendency to lose sight of nuances and exceptions to general rules should be avoided as much as possible. The aim in the following pages is not to propose a single, neat explanation or set of explanations for the rise of divorce, but it does try to draw some coherence from the range of factors that have been suggested as important. In doing so it will try to balance generalization with an appreciation of the breadth of experience and comparative variations. Second, it aims to discuss the factors historically, relating them clearly to their historical context and not treating them as constants possessing implications and consequences that are unchanging over time. Nor should we assume that the factors associated with the increase in divorce have remained the same since the rise in divorce rates began. One set of conditions might have set the increase in motion, and others might have sustained it through subsequent phases. It is also important to go beyond the simple curve line of divorce rates to examine some of the major characteristics of the divorced population – the sex ratio of petitioners and their socioeconomic status, for example – and to see divorce not as a single event but as part of a process of marriage formation, dissolution and, increasingly, re-formation.

Finally we should try to integrate the various sets of causes of divorce: those described by the spouses in terms of the events and behavior of their marriages; the microsocial causes that focus on the correlates of divorce; and the macrosocial causes that describe broad social changes and their impact on marriage. Although these sets of explanations, correlates and causes reflect different perspectives, bodies of data, areas of investigation – they are, quite often, answers to different questions – they ultimately deal with the same phenomenon. Admittedly, the explanations are not always mutually satisfying. A wife who thinks her marriage broke down because of her husband's violence is unlikely to be convinced that the real reason was their social status and age at marriage. Nor will she necessarily find it very useful to be told that her marriage would not have broken down if, instead of living in a city on the west coast of the United States in the early 1980s, she and her husband had lived in rural America in the early nineteenth century. Yet all of these might be considered useful statements, at different levels, about the cause of the divorce. Although the principal aim of this chapter is to focus on historical change, there is an attempt to integrate the other areas of research so as to bridge the gaps that different perspectives have created among divorce researchers.

14.3 Phase one: Up to World War I

Although there is no direct evidence of changes in the extent of marriage breakdown over time, we should conclude that it increased from the end of the eighteenth century and that the rate of increase accelerated from the second half of the nineteenth. Indirect and oblique evidence lies in the decline of those constraints that had locked wives and husbands into marriage, and in rising expectations of marriage; the two go hand in hand, as explained in Chapters 9 and 10 and further analyzed here. Even though there is no explicit documentary evidence of the considerable increase in marriage breakdown, sceptics should bear in mind that in many modern Western countries the likelihood of recent marriages ending in divorce lies between 30% and 50%, and others are terminated informally or go through forms of separation. No historian has ventured to suggest that marriage breakdown before the twentieth century has ever approached these levels. The increase in marriage breakdown during the past 200 years must be accepted, even if its precise magnitude, causes, and timing are subject to debate.

One of the most important factors in the increase of marriage breakdown has been the decline of the economic constraints that in earlier times bound spouses to each other until one of them died. The traditional family or conjugal economy was the foremost expression of this relationship of mutual dependence and, as we have seen (Chapter 10) it declined in the face of broad economic changes. From the late nineteenth century this process continued until the traditional form of the family economy – where spouses had complementary work roles – all but disappeared. A new form did emerge, with the evolution of housewifery as the full-time occupation of most married women during the second half of the nineteenth century.[18] A decreasing proportion of married women worked in paid employment outside (and inside) the home, and they devoted themselves to what became thought of as the "woman's sphere": care of the household, the preparation of meals, and responsibility for caring for children. In providing these services, even though they were unpaid and deprived of social status, women performed tasks that complemented their husbands' paid work outside the home. Men were relieved of the need to spend the time and energy that domestic matters demanded. They could leave for work refreshed and restored, and return home to the security and resources offered by the wife and family, to all of the benefits implied by the notion of the family as a haven. This complementarity of wives' and husbands' tasks created the mutual obligations that were enshrined in so many nineteenth-century laws: the duty of the husband to maintain and provide for his family and the duty of the wife to perform her domestic tasks. So important were these respective gender-specific obligations that, as we have seen, failure to fulfill them was in many jurisdictions a ground for separation or divorce.[19]

Yet although a marriage in which the wife was a housewife and the husband was employed in the labor force was a new form of the family economy, it was much more than a variant from the traditional family economy. The husband's employment was independent of the home, giving him more freedom of

---

[18] On the emergence of housewifery as a full-time occupation, see Ann Oakley, *Woman's Work: The Housewife, Past and Present* (New York, 1974).

[19] See Section 12.5.

initiative, and although the housewife was bound to her home by her work and dependent on her husband's income, the social and economic context had changed dramatically so as to increase her potential for independence. The labor market had expanded and changed so that it was increasingly possible, even if far from easy, for women to obtain employment in the service and manufacturing sectors. At the end of the nineteenth century women quickly dominated growth areas of employment such as teachers, nurses, secretaries, domestics, and retail sales assistants.[20]

The extension of employment opportunities for women in the later nineteenth century has been proposed by a number of historians as an important factor in the increase of marriage breakdown and divorce. Carl Degler, for one, refers to the widening opportunities for women to earn a livelihood outside the home as "a necessary but not sufficient condition to explain the increase in divorces" around the turn of the century.[21] This is undoubtedly right. The availability of work did not cause marriages to break down, but it did enable women to survive outside marriage, and it thereby enabled them to leave their husbands informally or to file for separations or divorces.

As if to confirm the significance of this factor, the majority of divorce petitions in many jurisdictions were filed by women. In the United States more than two-thirds of all divorces from the 1880s to World War I were granted to women, and there was a general increase over time.[22] This figure is echoed by a California rate of 69%.[23] In France women's petitions accounted for between 55% and 65% of all divorces between 1885 and 1914,[24] and in New South Wales in the 1890s, 68% of the divorces were obtained by women.[25] In many places, however, divorce legislation discriminated against women and kept their petitions to a minority. In England and in places where divorce laws were influenced by the English example, wives had to prove their husbands guilty of more serious offenses than husbands their wives (aggravated adultery rather than simple adultery) and this reduced the representation of women among divorce petitioners. In England women filed for between 40% and 45% of divorces from the 1860s, an impressive proportion in view of the legal obstacles women had to overcome.[26] In Canada, divorces by private Act of Parliament were dominated by men, who obtained forty-two (61%) of the sixty-nine

---

[20] Statistics for the United States in 1890 are given in Linda J. Waite, "U.S. Women at Work," *Population Bulletin 36* (Washington, D.C., 1981), 27, Table 8.

[21] Carl Degler, *At Odds: Women and the Family in America* (New York, 1980), 172.

[22] *Marriage and Divorce, 1922* (U.S. Department of Commerce, Bureau of the Census, Washington, D.C., 1925), 14, Table 6. Women filed for 66.6% of divorces between 1887 and 1906, 67.5% in 1906, and 68.9% in 1916.

[23] Robert L. Griswold, *Family and Divorce in California, 1850–1890* (Albany, N.Y., 1982), 29–30.

[24] Boigeol, Commaille, and Roussel, "France," in Robert Chester (ed.), *Divorce in Europe* (Leiden, 1977), 164, Fig. 6.

[25] Hilary Golder, *Divorce in 19th-Century N.S.W.* (Kensington, N.S.W., 1985), 246, Table 13.

[26] *Royal Commission, Report 1951–1955*, 355–7, Table 1. Almost all of the judicial separations (which were less common) were sought by women: in the 1890s, women filed for 95% of them.

divorces between 1867 and 1900.[27] In Nova Scotia, however, where judicial divorce was available, 55% of the divorces (twenty-six of forty-seven) were obtained by women.[28]

When formal discrimination against women was removed, however, petitions by women quickly rose to form a majority. After the equalization reform of English divorce law in 1923, women's petitions increased to constitute between 50% and 60% of all divorce actions.[29] A further example of the same effect is New Zealand, where there had been similar discrimination against women in divorce until 1898. The proportion of divorce petitions filed by women there increased during the nineteenth century (from 19% in 1868–78 to 30% in 1879–88, and to 39% in 1889–98), but when the divorce law was reformed, the effect was immediate. In 1899 and 1900 women initiated 52% and 63% of the divorces, respectively, and thereafter the majority of divorces in most years were sought by women.[30]

Statistics such as these indicate the ability of these women at least to survive outside marriage, so that the rising divorce rate, with women dominant as petitioners, can be read as indicative of better employment opportunities for women, among other things. It is assumed that most women would rather remain married if the alternative were nothing better than a fragile and impoverished future outside marriage. (This is the assumption underlying our earlier conclusion as to the rarity of desertion and separation initiated by wives in traditional society.) Even divorce petitions filed by husbands might be read as indicative of changes in women's circumstances and resulting attitudes. More than 80% of the grounds cited by husbands in American divorces in the 1870s indicated that their wives refused "to live up to the ideal of a submissive subordinate."[31] Desertion and adultery were the main grounds, behavior that did not fit the image of the Victorian wife. The same might be said of other countries, where women were divorced for similar offenses as well as for cruelty, drunkenness, and their failure to perform their domestic duties.[32] Such women need not have been particularly assertive, however. Certainly they did not initiate the divorces, and there is no evidence that they felt confident about their lives after divorce. In terms of divorce being a statement of married women's autonomy and individuality, there is really no comparison between a woman who files for divorce and a woman divorced by her husband.

But the preponderance of divorce and other matrimonial actions initiated by

[27] Constance Backhouse, "'Pure Patriarchy', Nineteenth-Century Canadian Marriage," *McGill Law Journal* 13 (1986), 285.
[28] Kimberley Smith, "Divorce in Nova Scotia, 1750–1890," in J. Phillips and P. Girard (eds.), *Essays in the History of Canadian Law, Volume 3: The Nova Scotian Experience* (Toronto, in press).
[29] *Royal Commission, Report 1951–1955*, 355–7, Table 1.
[30] Roderick Phillips, *Divorce in New Zealand: A Social History* (Auckland, 1981), 65–7.
[31] Degler, *At Odds*, 169.
[32] In New Zealand in 1899 and 1900, 77% of men's petitions alleged adultery, 19% desertion, and 4% drunkenness. Phillips, *Divorce in New Zealand*, 64, Table 3.2. See Griswold, *Family and Divorce*, 79, Table 19, for statistics on nineteenth-century California.

women and the increasing rate over time, indicate changes in women's circumstances and attitudes. There is, of course, a paradox in citing expanding employment opportunities as a factor in women's turning in increasing numbers to divorce, and that is that the proportion of married women in the labor force was in decline as the divorce rate was rising. In the United States by 1900 less than 4% of white married women worked outside the home, and even though that percentage rose during the early twentieth century, it was only about 7% by 1920 and 12% by 1940.[33] Elsewhere the situation was similar.

The apparent contradiction between rising divorce rates at women's initiative and declining or stationary employment by married women need not weaken the point that divorce reflected improved opportunities for women. The least it could imply in this context is that those married women who were in the labor force, no matter how small their numbers, were in a position to countenance divorce, and that changes in the rate of married women's employment might change the base population from which divorces initiated by women might derive. Studies of divorces in the nineteenth century are ambiguous about its correlation with women's work. In Robert Griswold's study of divorces in California in the second half of the century, there is evidence in only 80 of 401 cases that the wife was employed.[34] A 20% rate of employment such as this implies was four or five times the national rate and could indicate that divorce was more likely in marriages where the wife was gainfully employed. What is uncertain, however, is the extent to which women's occupations were underrecorded in the divorce documents,[35] and whether these wives were employed before their divorces or took up employment afterward out of necessity. In any case, even though the known rate of employment in Griswold's study is high, it left four-fifths of the women in these cases apparently without paid work, suggesting that women's employment could not have been a factor in the great majority of divorces. The issue of underregistration is crucial to our understanding of the relationship between employment and divorce.

In Elaine Tyler May's study of divorces in Los Angeles and New Jersey in the 1880s and in 1920, the relationship between women's work and divorce is somewhat less ambiguous. In the 1880s some 33% of wives in Los Angeles divorce cases were employed, compared to only 23% of all women, married and single, in the city. In the 1920 divorces the differences were even greater. In Los Angeles 41% of divorcing or divorced women were employed, compared to 28% of all women at large, and in New Jersey 42% of women in divorce

---

[33] Degler, *At Odds*, 384. Although many women, especially in the working class, had domestic occupations to supplement their husbands' income, they could not necessarily continue them after separation or divorce. Some occupations, such as keeping lodgers, required a house, and others, such as child minding, brought in an income that alone was inadequate for a woman's support.

[34] Griswold, *Family and Divorce*, 82.

[35] Underrecording of women's occupations is common in marriage records where it is considered either peripheral or secondary.

cases were employed, compared to 24% of all women in the state.[36] The discrepancies are enhanced when we take into account the universally higher employment rates by unmarried women, which would have depressed the rate by married women well below the overall proportion of all women employed. May comments on the clear overrepresentation of employed women in the divorces that "financial independence might have made it easier for a woman to go through with a divorce."[37]

Work was arguably the most important single resource required by women who wanted to separate or divorce, but there were other dimensions to economic autonomy, and they were also improved. The last three or four decades of the nineteenth century saw legislation enacted in many countries to give women the right to control and benefit from their own property and income, rather than have them owned or administered by their husbands. It was one of the disincentives to desertion or separation by women among the property-owning strata that such an action effectively entailed their abandoning the economic resources necessary for an independent existence. Similarly a working woman had had no right to keep the wages she earned as long as she remained married. This situation, beneficial to men but detrimental to women, was remedied by married women's property legislation in many countries. In some places the first such provisions were passed as integral parts of divorce legislation, regulating the financial effects of the dissolution of marriage. Needless to say, such provisions made divorce a more feasible alternative to marriage. Elsewhere, however, women's property legislation was extended to all women, married, separated, or divorced, whether or not they lived with their husbands.

Married women first received guarantees of property rights in England under the 1857 divorce legislation. Thereafter a series of laws (1870, 1874, and 1882) gave married women a legal right (often tempered in practice by the realities of marriage) to their property and income.[38] In France the situation was somewhat different because women were able to draw up marriage contracts to protect the property they brought to marriage. Even so, protection did not extend to their salaries and other revenues, and the right of married women in France to manage their property was circumscribed. A series of laws from 1881 to 1907 gradually extended their financial independence within marriage: In 1881 married women were permitted their own savings accounts in banks, in 1893 they were granted the right to control their property free of their husbands' interference, and finally in 1907 married women were given complete control of

---

[36] Elaine Tyler May, *Great Expectations: Marriage and Divorce in Post-Victorian America* (Chicago, 1980), 170, Table 6.

[37] Ibid., 120.

[38] Lee Holcombe, *Wives and Property: Reform of the Married Women's Property Law in Nineteenth-Century England* (Toronto, 1983), passim; Mary Lyndon Shanley, "'One Must Ride Behind': Married Women's Rights and the Divorce Act of 1857," *Victorian Studies* 25 (1982), 355–76.

their own wages.[39] Married women in Sweden gained the right to control their property and income in 1874.[40] In the United States the movement began in Mississippi in 1839, but took off later. Between 1869 and 1887 thirty-three states and the District of Columbia gave married women control over their property and earnings.[41] In short, the movement toward giving married women economic independence in legal terms was general throughout Western society, and an integral part of the improvement of women's legal status that took place at this time.

Factors such as improved opportunities for work and rights of ownership of property and income contributed to creating the material conditions in which an increasing number of women could divorce or separate, but they did not cause divorce. The important variable in this respect seems to have been a change in expectations of marriage, more specifically a rise in these expectations. As suggested in the earlier discussion of marriage breakdown, rising expectations and changing definitions of marriage breakdown – that is, a lower tolerance of unsatisfactory behavior or conditions – result from the interaction of social attitudes, individual perceptions, and the material context of marriage. We should expect that improved economic opportunities for married women would lead them to consider separation or divorce – and even desertion – as increasingly viable alternatives to an unsatisfactory marriage, and to be less tolerant of oppressive behavior or simple incompatibility.

There is ample evidence of rising marital expectations in the later nineteenth century and through the twentieth. Some writers have pointed to the increase in divorces itself as evidence that husbands and wives were increasingly demanding of marriage, but this produces a circular line of reasoning: Divorces are said to increase because of rising expectations of marriage, and the evidence of increasing expectations is found in the rising divorce rate. Nevertheless, expectations of marriage did rise, even though there might well have been different rates of change among the various social classes.[42]

There is, first of all, the evidence of legal reform itself. The grounds or circumstances recognized by divorce and separation laws are an index to the kinds of behavior that men and women are not expected to tolerate; they give, so to speak, a mirror image of marital expectations. When the grounds for divorce or separation are extended, the range of behavior that spouses are required to tolerate without legal remedy contracts, and they are permitted to hold correspondingly higher expectations of their marriages. To this extent the liberalization of divorce laws from the later nineteenth century and the legalization of divorce where it had not been available earlier, together with the pressure to liberalize them even further, are indicative of rising expectations of

---

[39] Patricia Branca, *Women in Europe Since 1750* (London, 1977), 168–9.
[40] Ibid.
[41] Degler, *At Odds*, 332ff.
[42] Gillis suggests that the British working classes' acceptance of the middle-class romantic view of marriage was limited, in *For Better, For Worse*, 301–2.

marriage. Although wives and husbands in many places in the eighteenth century and earlier might have had to tolerate everything but adultery and desertion, legal reforms extended the list of actions and conditions against which they could take legal action; depending on individual laws, they included drunkenness, cruelty, insanity, violence, the husband's failure to provide for his family, and the wife's failure to perform her domestic duties. To this tendency was added the lower tolerance of wife beating in many laws, which was discussed in Chapter 9.

Rising expectations of marriage and correspondingly diminishing tolerance were expressed not only by the progressive accumulation of grounds recognized as meriting the intervention of the law but also by the reinterpretation of specific grounds to include an ever-widening range of circumstances. The notion of matrimonial cruelty is a prime example. Definitions of cruelty within marriage were restricted to physical violence until the middle of the nineteenth century, but from that time the notion of mental cruelty was increasingly accepted. This evolution involved no widespread rewriting of the laws, but reinterpretations by the judiciary. Indeed, by the early 1930s the divorce laws of only seven American states recognized mental cruelty as an explicit ground, but in practice most of the state courts accepted it.[43] The key period in this widening of definitions was the 1880s and 1890s, when various American states' courts accepted as grounds for divorce conditions such as "grievous mental suffering" (Kentucky, 1883), a husband's neglect and insensitivity to his wife during her eight pregnancies (Kentucky, 1894), and a wife's telling obscene stories in the presence of friends and neighbors (North Dakota, 1907).[44] This process took place not only in America but also in Europe. In France, for example, article 231 of the 1884 divorce law, allowing divorce for serious ill-treatment or cruelty, was gradually extended by the judiciary. The trend was attacked by one professor of law who argued that the definition of ill-treatment had become so general and trivialized that divorce could be obtained as if by mutual consent.[45]

Robert Griswold's comment on the American judiciary's expansion of the definition of cruelty probably holds for the liberalized divorce policies almost everywhere:

The increasingly affectionate, expressive and psychologically demanding nature of marital relations in the nineteenth century virtually guaranteed that definitions of unacceptable matrimonial behaviour would expand. Mid-to-late-nineteenth-century couples would not tolerate behaviour earlier generations had endured, for when a spouse

---

[43] Chester G. Vernier, *American Family Laws*, (5 vols., Stanford, 1932), II, 24.

[44] Robert L. Griswold, "The Evolution of the Doctrine of Mental Cruelty in Victorian American Divorce, 1790–1900," *Journal of Social History*, 19 (1986), 135–9; Max Rheinstein, *Marriage Stability, Divorce and the Law* (Chicago, 1972), 102–4.

[45] Paul Luche, "La suppression du divorce," in *Le problème de population* (Lyon, 1923), 302. Luche was a professor in the Faculty of Law at Grenoble.

expected love and mutual respect and instead received insults and gratuitous slights, divorce became a logical option.[46]

It might quite properly be objected that the views of a handful of male judges were not representative of social attitudes generally. We must recognize, however, that the restrictive definitions of cruelty were gradually rolled back not at the whim or initiative of the judges concerned but under pressure from wives and husbands who claimed that the conditions of their marriages were such as they should not have to tolerate. These statements, indicative of rising expectations of marriage, came from the mouths of husbands and wives themselves, and in increasing numbers. In this way the law responded to changing attitudes among the clients of the divorce courts.[47] We cannot compare their expectations with those of couples who did not divorce, but it is reasonable to suppose that they represented the leading edge of a more generalized shift in attitudes. Some, we should note, failed to convince the courts that their spouses' behavior was so awful as to warrant divorce, and to this extent the limits of change marked by the decisions in cruelty cases did not represent the highest expectations of marriage at any given time.[48] This, together with the conservatism and caution generally characteristic of the judiciary, might lead us to believe that the levels of marital expectations expressed in divorce judgments in the late nineteenth and early twentieth centuries were roughly congruent with general social attitudes.

It was not only in emotional terms that expectations of marriage rose in this period. There were also higher expectations of the material standards of life as a mass market for consumer goods and services developed.[49] Married men in particular came under increasing pressure to provide not only the necessities of life, but also the outward signs of financial and social success, signs that varied from class to class. By 1920 financial disputes were significant in many cases of divorce: They were cited in 33% of divorces in New Jersey and in 28% of those in Los Angeles in that year.[50] Just as the definition of cruelty proved elastic enough to include the expanding emotional expectations of marriage, so did the meanings of "provide" and "support" to encompass increasing material expectations. As May writes, in the 1880s "there was no controversy over what constituted the necessities of life. Either a man provided for his family, or he did

---

[46] Griswold, "Doctrine of Mental Cruelty," 139.

[47] A fictional account of the process is given by Arnold Bennett, writing on a divorce action in England where cruelty was an aggravating circumstance that, if proved, could enable a woman to divorce her husband for reason of adultery. Bennett writes of his fictional divorce case that for the petitioner to win her action, "the legal significance of the word 'cruelty' would have to be somewhat broadened," and he shows how the lawyer persuaded the judge of his case. Arnold Bennett, *Whom God Hath Joined* (1906, repr. Gloucester, 1985), 224–5.

[48] It has been noted that the Canadian judiciary was particularly reluctant to accept notions of companionate marriages and held to definitions of cruelty and marriage breakdown that ensured the dominance of the husband over the wife. Backhouse, "'Pure Patriarchy'," 291–312.

[49] See W. Hamish Fraser, *The Coming of the Mass Market, 1850–1914* (London, 1981).

[50] Calculated from May, *Great Expectations*, 176–7, Tables 17–19.

not. By 1920, however, it was no longer clear what constituted adequate support on the part of a husband."[51] It is a cliché that one generation's luxuries are the necessities of the next, and the divorce documents used by May bear it out. The cases included wives accused of being extravagant and spendthrift in their urge for material acquisition, men accused of being miserly, and disputes among the less well-off where the difficulties stemmed simply from lack of money. In most of the cases women initiated the divorces, claiming that they were forced to live at levels of material comfort lower than that which their husbands could afford. In one exemplary case a woman condemned her husband for working for $12 a week when he had had the chance of getting a job that paid $21 and that would permit him and his family to enjoy a higher standard of living.[52]

The decline of the traditional family economy, the expansion of employment opportunities, and rising expectations of marriage can all be associated with the increase in divorce rates in the three or four decades before World War I. But the way they impinged upon women was more important than their effects on men. Divorce reflected, above all, improved opportunities for women to live and work outside marriage and rising expectations of marriage on the part of women. In a sense women's expectations were brought to a level approximating those of their husbands. For centuries men had had expectations of marriage and their wives that were higher than those women had of marriage and their husbands. The tendency of men to beat their wives and to desert their families were statements, as eloquent as divorce could be, that their wives and their marriages were not satisfactory to them. Violence and desertion, no matter how much we deplore them, were men's responses to unfulfilled expectations. Women, locked into marriages and with much less scope for initiative, could not afford to hold such high expectations of their spouses and of married life. It was not until the economic context changed, and divorce and separation became realistic alternatives, that women's expectations in these respects could rise, and the gap between their husbands' and their own expectations narrowed.

Men, it seems, persisted in their traditional behavior by deserting rather than by resorting to divorce. This was evidence that men continued to have greater freedom of initiative and that they acted as freer agents, abandoning their families with much less compunction than their wives would do. Thus it was that in almost every jurisdiction where desertion was a ground for divorce, many were sought by wives for reason of their husbands' desertion.[53] This fact highlights an important association between women and divorce. In traditional

---

[51] Ibid. See also Elaine Tyler May, "The Pressure to Provide: Class, Consumerism, and Divorce in Urban America, 1880–1920," *Journal of Social History* 12 (1978), 180–93.

[52] May, *Great Expectations*, 147.

[53] An exception was California where 64% of men's petitions for divorce cited desertion as the ground, and only 40% of women's petitions did so. Women focused on cruelty and failure to support, grounds that involved desertion in many cases. Griswold, *Family and Divorce*, 79, Tables 19 and 20.

society and even into the twentieth century, men tended to react to marriage breakdown by informal means, by violence and desertion. Women, with less social and domestic power, had to turn to an external agency, the law, for assistance. It is not surprising, in this light, to find women constituting the majority of petitioners for divorce, separation, and other matrimonial remedies throughout Western society.

To some extent this conclusion blurs the distinction between marriage breakdown and divorce. Although rising expectations of marriage were more likely than lower expectations to be disappointed, and although economic and legal changes facilitated separation, we still need to explain why the divorce rate began its rise. It was, after all, possible for husbands and wives to separate informally or to desert – as many did – without going through the procedures and expense of having their marriages formally dissolved. The answer is that divorce implied many advantages that did not accrue from informal or even judicial separation. Divorce allowed for a distribution of matrimonial property, alimony, arrangements for the custody of children, and the possibility of remarriage. Divorce thus offered more solutions to some of the most pressing problems that faced men and women, but especially women, when they contemplated leaving their marriages: how they would survive independently, what resources they would have, and what would happen to their children.

Maintenance or alimony could be particularly important for divorced women. It was critically important for women who were unemployed or without resources, but also valuable to women with a job because women's wages were usually low. So it was that the financial provisions of the 1857 English divorce law could make divorce that much more feasible. Under this law the court could order a husband to pay his wife maintenance, the amount to be determined in light of the woman's own wealth, the husband's ability to pay, and the conduct of both parties during the marriage.[54] Divorce in nineteenth-century England was firmly based on the principle of fault, and this principle also underlay maintenance orders: there was a clear reluctance to give support to an adulterous wife. This principle was challenged, however, and by the beginning of the twentieth century it was accepted that even a woman who had been divorced for reason of adultery should not be left destitute. As far as actual property was concerned, the English divorce law provided that after separation or divorce a woman was to have the same property rights as she would were she unmarried: She could own and dispose of property freely during her lifetime and bequeath it by will, and could sue and enter into contracts.

Similar provisions were integral to divorce legislation elsewhere. Divorce laws in the British colonies followed the English model. Those in America varied, but made it possible for divorced women to control their own property and income, and also provided for the discretionary allotment of alimony.

---

[54] For a general discussion of this aspect of the 1857 English act, see Holcombe, *Wives and Property*, 88–109.

Curiously, permanent alimony was rarely sought. It was requested in only 13% of American divorces between 1887 and 1906, and was granted in about 70% of these cases, meaning that awards were made in less than 10% of all divorce cases.[55] The proportion of divorces with permanent alimony awards tended to increase over time, but it reached only 15% by 1916. These national statistics are supported by local studies. In Los Angeles only 9% of divorces in the 1880s had alimony awards, but this rose to 21% in 1920.[56]

What is especially surprising about these statistics is the small proportion of women who sought alimony in the first place. It was low even when we take into account that in many cases, where the defendant husband had deserted and his whereabouts were unknown, there was simply no point in seeking alimony. That such a small percentage of women did request financial support could reflect realistic assessments of the ability of their husbands to pay any award, or it could be indicative of the financial status of the women who resorted to divorce, that they were by and large financially independent or could fall back on other resources. A breakdown of the sources of support cited by women in the California divorces studied by Griswold revealed that three-quarters of them earned enough to support themselves partly or completely.[57]

In addition to alimony, the nineteenth-century divorce laws made provision for the custody of children, and in this area there were significant developments that might well have made divorce a more attractive option for married women with children. Under most Western legal codes until the nineteenth century, the father was deemed to have primary rights over his children. English common law, for example, regarded children as the virtual property of their father, so in the event of a separation mothers effectively had to give up their children. The fathers' rights in these circumstances were so nearly absolute that even the courts could not grant a mother access to her children if their father did not agree. In the course of the nineteenth century there were some reforms, such as the 1839 Infant Custody Act, which allowed the courts to give mothers custody of children until they reached the age of seven, and which also made provision for mothers to visit their children at arranged times. But the principle of fault worked here, too, and separated women who had been guilty of adultery were generally denied custody of their children or access to them.[58] Under the 1857 divorce legislation the reform went further. The divorce court was empowered to exercise discretion and could make arrangements for the custody, support, and education of children as it saw fit under the specific circum-

---

[55] Paul H. Jacobson and Pauline F. Jacobson, *American Marriage and Divorce* (New York, 1959), 127–8.

[56] In contrast, only 5% of women divorced in New Jersey in 1920 obtained alimony. May, *Great Expectations*, 177, Table 20.

[57] Seventy-five percent of women who described their sources of support mentioned themselves either alone or in conjunction with other sources (usually friends or neighbors, parents, or other relatives). Griswold, *Family and Divorce*, 82–3.

[58] Social and legal issues relating to custody in English law are discussed in Ivy Pinchbeck and Margaret Hewitt, *Children in English Society* (2 vols., London, 1973), II, 362–86.

stances of each case.[59] From this time, women could file for divorce not with any certainty that they would get custody of their children (assuming they wanted it), but at least in the knowledge that they would not automatically lose all contact with them. In 1873 women's rights to custody were extended even further,[60] and later, in the twentieth century, it became a principle that custody of the children in cases of divorce was vested in the wife unless there were compelling reasons why it should be otherwise. Beginning in the second half of the nineteenth century, then, the principles of child custody in English law were completely transformed.

In America, too, the progressive reform of divorce legislation was associated with the gradual undermining of the principle that the father had a natural right to the custody of his children. The main criterion for custody arrangements became the best interests of the child or children, and these interests were generally interpreted in terms of fault. It was assumed that the spouse who had performed poorly in marriage – by committing the offenses leading to the divorce – would be likely to behave no better as a parent, so that custody tended to be awarded to the innocent spouse, the divorce petitioner.[61] As we have seen, most divorces (about two-thirds) in late-nineteenth-century America were sought by women, and so it is hardly surprising to find that women most often won custody of their children. This effect was enhanced by an increasingly clear preference on the part of the judges to place children in the care of their mothers. Child care was, in their eyes, an important role women played within their special "sphere". In California, 91% of women who sought custody of their children were granted it, but this was true of only 37% of men.[62] The same imbalance was true of Los Angeles and New Jersey divorces, where custody was almost always granted to the mother, even if she were the defendant, an indication that the principle of motherhood had begun to override the principle of fault. In New Jersey in 1920, for example, women were given custody in 72% of all cases, and in Los Angeles divorces of the same year, women won custody in 84%.[63] Throughout Western society, in fact, divorce provided a means by which women were increasingly likely to be assured of keeping their children. In New South Wales a law of 1873 gave judges discretion in custody decisions, but almost all awards were made to mothers rather than fathers.[64] In Canada, the law and practice of child custody underwent a similar development.[65]

---

[59] Ibid., 363; Holcombe, *Wives and Property*, 102.
[60] Pinchbeck and Hewitt, *Children*, 377.
[61] The best survey of the evolution of custody law in nineteenth-century America is Michael Grossberg, *Governing the Hearth: Law and the Family in Nineteenth-Century America* (Chapel Hill, 1985), 234–85, but esp. 250–3.
[62] Griswold, *Family and Divorce*, 153, Table 26.
[63] May, *Great Expectations*, 173, Table 11.
[64] In New South Wales almost all custody awards went to women. Golder, *Divorce in 19th-Century N.S.W.*, 191.
[65] Constance B. Backhouse, "Shifting Patterns in Nineteenth-Century Canadian Custody Law," in David H. Flaherty (ed.), *Essays in the History of Canadian Law* (Toronto, 1981), 212–48.

14.3 Phase one: Up to World War I

Trends in this area of family law and their interpretation by the judiciary increasingly in favor of mothers reflected changing ideas about the family. The principles of property and authority that underlay paternal prerogatives in custody issues gradually made way for an emphasis on education and moral guardianship, which placed children firmly within women's sphere of influence. Not only were divorce laws important media by which the legal relationship between mother and child was reformed in the nineteenth century, but the custody provisions were an additional attraction of divorce in comparison with other responses to marriage breakdown, other than enduring an unhappy married life.

There were also provisions for custody arrangements and property ownership in legislation regulating judicial separation, but divorce offered two additional benefits that no other legal remedy could match. The first was the complete dissolution of marriage. For centuries separations *a mensa et thoro* had been condemned by advocates of divorce as at best half-solutions to marriage breakdown, which left husbands and wives in a state of matrimonial limbo between the hell of marriage and the paradise of divorce, legally bound to spouses with whom they had no emotional or social ties, yet prevented from forming new marriages. The debates on divorce legalization and reform in the nineteenth century were filled with denunciations of the iniquity and inequities of separation and endorsements of the right of married men and women to sever their ties completely once their marriages had broken down.[66] Apart from any other advantages, divorce offered husbands and wives the psychological and emotional relief of a total dissolution of the marriage bond. Max Rheinstein has referred to this as often "simply the feeling of no longer being tied to a partner who has come to be hated or despised or, perhaps, with lingering loyalty regarded as a psychological impediment to adventure."[67]

Over and above this sense of freedom, but integral to it, was the ability divorce gave to remarry. During the nineteenth century divorce laws shed most of the residual restrictions on remarriage by the guilty partner, so that all divorced people had the legal right to enter new marriages.[68] How often they did so in the late nineteenth century is not clear. Because divorces were still relatively rare, the number of divorced men and women in the population was small, and marriages involving divorcés and divorcées made only marginal contributions to the overall marriage rates. In 1900 only 3% of all brides in America had been previously married and divorced, and this percentage grew steadily during the twentieth century.[69] But the actual proportion of divorced men and women who remarried is not known for the period before World War

---

[66] The debates on divorce reform in England and France are discussed in Sections 11.3 and 11.4.

[67] Rheinstein, *Marriage Stability*, 282.

[68] During the short period when some divorce laws were reformed in a restrictive direction at the end of the nineteenth century, fifteen American states forbade remarriage within a year of divorce.

[69] Andrew J. Cherlin, *Marriage, Divorce, Remarriage* (Cambridge, Mass., 1981), 29.

I.[70] In the calculation of the attraction of divorce, however, it is the potential for remarriage that is important; it was central among the benefits divorce conferred.

That divorce was considered a more satisfactory response to marriage breakdown is shown by its increased popularity compared to the declining resort to alternative legal actions. As a general rule, judicial separations decreased as divorces rose, and the obvious conclusion is that spouses or couples who might have sought separations decided instead to dissolve their marriages. France is a good example of this tendency. As Figure 14.2 shows, separations increased steadily from the 1830s, although there was a period of decline during and immediately after the Franco-Prussian War (1870–1). Separations peaked in 1883 and fell in 1884, the year that divorce was legalized in France. Thereafter the number of divorces and the divorce rate rose steadily, and the number of separations and the separation rate stabilized. By 1910 the divorce rate in France was 0.21 per thousand population, the separation rate had settled at 0.06 per thousand, and the gap between these rates grew progressively wider. Looking ahead we can see that by 1925 the divorce rate had increased 150% (to 0.55 per thousand), and the separation rate had grown by only 33% (to 0.08 per thousand).[71]

A similar pattern was evident in England and Wales where, in addition to judicial separation, other forms of matrimonial relief were available. The most common was for many years a maintenance order issued by a magistrates' court that gave a married woman a claim to limited financial support from her absent husband if he were guilty of certain matrimonial offenses. Maintenance orders were not judicial separations, but simply arranged for the wife's support after a de facto separation;[72] although some of these separations were later subject to divorce petitions, others were not, the spouses continuing to be legally married. What is notable is that among the various legal options available in cases of separation or marriage breakdown in England – divorce, judicial separation, an order for restitution of conjugal rights, and maintenance orders – divorces gradually became the most popular. Before 1920, for example, divorces accounted for less than 10% of all matrimonial actions, but by the early 1930s they accounted for 24% of the total and by the early 1950s, 55%.[73] Again, as in France, the gap between the divorce rate and the rates of other actions

[70] Statistics for the postwar period are in Jacobson and Jacobson, *American Marriage and Divorce*, 69–70, but they were influenced by the war.
[71] Calculated from Camp, *Marriage and the Family in France*, 81, Table 24.
[72] In rare cases husbands obtained maintenance orders requiring their wives to support them.
[73] The proportions are as follows:

Period	Divorces	Other relief	Total	Divorces (%)
1910–13	919	10,947	11,866	7.7
1925–9	3,805	14,627	18,432	20.6
1930–4	4,578	14,551	19,129	23.9
1950–4	32,451	26,995	59,446	54.6

Source: Rowntree and Carrier, "Resort to Divorce," 190, Table 1.

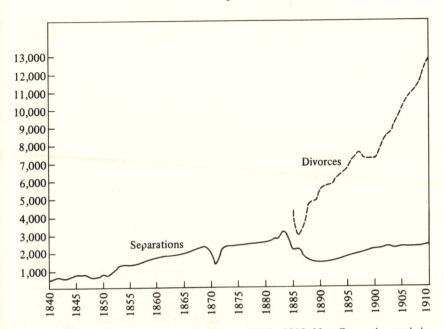

Figure 14.2 Separations and divorces in France, 1840–1910. *Note:* Separation statistics refer to 87 *départements* 1840–60, 1869–1910, and 90 *départements* 1861–9. Divorce statistics refer to divorces transcribed on the civil registers, not to the greater number of divorce judgments issued by the courts. *Source of statistics:* Wesley D. Camp, *Marriage and the Family in France since the Revolution* (New York, 1961), 78–80, Table 24.

widened: The number of applications for maintenance orders doubled from about 14,000 to 27,000 between the early 1920s and the 1950s, but in the same period the number of divorces increased more than eightfold, rising from fewer than 4,000 to more than 32,000 annually.[74] Over the long term, then, the increased divorce rate is partly explained by divorce's having become the most popular matrimonial remedy among those offered by various legal systems.

The implications and consequences of divorce were in many respects similar to those of widowhood in traditional society. Marriage was dissolved by divorce as it was by death; resources could be provided by property settlements and alimony as they were by inheritance;[75] children were secured by custody as they were by survivor's rights; and both divorced and widowed men and women were free to remarry. As we have seen, widowhood cast many women into poverty and hardship, and it could scarcely be thought of as a state to be envied.

[74] Ibid.
[75] The traditional "widow's third" (the widow's share of her dead husband's property) was echoed in the principle that a divorced wife should have one-third of her former husband's income as her maintenance. This principle was applied in England until the early twentieth century. Holcombe, *Wives and Property*, 100.

The crucial difference between divorce and widowhood, however, was that a woman who divorced chose her status after weighing the costs and benefits of her marriage against those she could expect when divorced. But this analogy of divorce with widowhood reminds us that although divorce was no doubt often the most attractive of the range of alternatives available to a woman or man who wanted to end a marriage, it was far from being an easy option. Up to and beyond World War I divorce everywhere was expensive and procedurally difficult to obtain, it was socially stigmatized, and most married people, women in particular, were in no financial position to contemplate life outside marriage. Women who worked were poorly paid, and men's incomes would rarely run to supporting two separate households.

The costs of divorce were an immediate deterrent to the poorer strata in all countries and states. In England the average cost of a divorce was about a hundred pounds in the early twentieth century,[76] and although that was substantially less than the hundreds of pounds that a divorce by private Act of Parliament or a separation by an ecclesiastical court could cost, it was still very high.[77] Rather than reduce the costs of divorce to make it more widely accessible, Parliament introduced cheaper alternative measures to help women who were deserted or brutally treated by their husbands. From 1878, as we have noted, magistrates could issue separation orders in circumstances such as aggravated assault and, later, desertion and the husband's refusal to maintain his wife, or habitual drunkenness, drug addiction, and venereal disease.[78] In issuing separation orders, magistrates could require husbands to make weekly payments to support their wives and children. The amount of this support was set, when maintenance orders were introduced in 1886,[79] at no more than two pounds a week for the wife and ten shillings for each child. At its maximum this was a generous enough sum at the time, but its value was steadily eroded and it was not increased until 1949, when the sums were set at five pounds and thirty shillings, respectively.

The relatively simple and inexpensive procedure for obtaining separation and maintenance orders from the magistrates' courts in England made them immensely popular. By the first decade of the twentieth century an average of about 7,500 married women obtained them each year.[80] At the same time, the annual average of divorces was a little under 800, of which about 300 were

---

[76] *Working Women and Divorce*, 9.
[77] An uncontested separation was estimated to cost between £300 and £500 in the 1850s. *British Parliamentary Papers*, "Marriage and Divorce," I, 29–31.
[78] These are summarized in O. M. McGregor, *Divorce in England* (London, 1957), 22–4.
[79] By the Maintenance of Wives (Desertion) Act, 1886.
[80] In the periods 1901–5 and 1906–10 the annual averages of maintenance orders were 7,595 and 7,309, respectively. McGregor, *Divorce in England*, 51, Table XIII. Applications for maintenance orders ran close to 11,000 annually in these periods. Rowntree and Carrier, "Resort to Divorce," 190, Table 1.

sought by women.[81] In short, the maintenance orders outranked divorces among women by more than twenty to one. This is not to say that all women who obtained maintenance orders would have petitioned for divorce if they could have afforded to. Some must have objected to divorce in principle, others wished to avoid the stigma of divorce, and still others – perhaps most – could not have satisfied the narrow requirements of prevailing English divorce law (that the husband be guilty of aggravated adultery) in any case. In general, however, costs must have prevented many women from having their marriages dissolved, and this situation persisted until effective legal aid for divorce actions was provided in 1949. Although there were provisions for women's legal costs to be paid by their husbands, there was no certainty that they would be enforced and, in any case, men were often in little better position to pay these costs than their wives were.

The expense of suing for divorce was also an important influence on the divorce rate elsewhere. Golder writes of nineteenth-century New South Wales that "the most obvious constraint on petitioners was the immediate problem of financing the suit."[82] Divorces in the Australian colonies could cost hundreds of pounds depending, as elsewhere, on their complexity, the number of witnesses called, and whether or not the action was contested. In the late 1880s divorces seem to have cost about a hundred pounds.[83] At the same time across the Tasman Sea, in New Zealand, some undefended divorces ran as high as £230, but most were cheaper. In Auckland in the 1880s and 1890s court costs ranged between £30 and £60, with lawyers' fees additional.[84] Divorces were also expensive in the United States, and in Canada, where in most provinces divorce could be obtained only by private Act of Parliament, the cost at the turn of the century was about $1,000.[85] In Nova Scotia, where judicial divorce was available, costs were much lower but still considerable, averaging more than $200 in the 1880s and 1890s.[86]

In what respects did the social profile of divorced men and women reflect the expense of divorce and other considerations such as the ability to live independently? Surprisingly, although the prevailing laws were often condemned as discriminatory against ordinary people, and as making divorce a privilege of the wealthy, the divorce lists spanned the social spectrum. In some nineteenth-century California divorces a high percentage of the couples were farmers

[81] In the periods 1901–5 and 1906–10 the annual averages of divorces were 787 and 779, respectively, of which women sought 297 and 339, respectively. *Royal Commission, Report 1951–1955*, 336, Table 1.
[82] Golder, *Divorce in 19th-Century N.S.W.*, 117.
[83] Ibid., 117–20.
[84] Phillips, *Divorce in New Zealand*, 18, 111.
[85] James G. Snell, "'The White Life for Two': The Defence of Marriage and Sexual Morality in Canada, 1890–1914," *Histoire Sociale – Social History* 16 (1983), 114.
[86] Smith, "Divorce in Nova Scotia."

14 Explaining the rise of divorce, 1870s–1980s

(14%), and cases in which the husband was in the skilled or unskilled trades or a manual laborer accounted collectively for 52% of the divorces. Couples in the upper and middle classes each contributed 17%. This profile is roughly congruent with the social distribution of the population at large and suggests not only that expectations of marriage were rising throughout society but that there were no obvious social or economic deterrents to divorce affecting one social class more than another.[87]

Other case studies of divorce, however, point to an overrepresentation of the better-off in divorce proceedings. In Los Angeles in the 1880s, as Table 14.1 indicates, there was a stronger representation of husbands from the upper social groups in divorce proceedings in comparison with the work force generally.[88] The implication of this distribution is that divorce was disproportionately weighted toward the better-off. Although the occupational profile of divorced men generally reflected the profile of men in the middle range (low white collar–high blue collar), the best-off were far more represented in divorce actions and the working classes much less represented.

The same was true of Canada. The expensive divorces by Act of Parliament were weighted toward the middle and upper classes,[89] and the great majority of the less costly divorces granted by the courts in Nova Scotia were sought by middle-class couples.[90] A similar pattern was found in Australian divorces. In New South Wales large landholders, professionals, and managers were disproportionately frequent petitioners for divorce in the 1870s, 1880s, and 1890s, and workers were underrepresented.[91] The same was true of New Zealand, where in Auckland divorces in the late nineteenth century almost one-third of the men in divorce actions derived from the professional, managerial, and proprietorial categories.[92] Still, in both Australia and New Zealand, as in the American studies, there was a significant, underrepresentative, presence of skilled and unskilled workers. In New South Wales one-third of the male petitioners fell into this category,[93] and in Auckland 39% of men in divorce proceedings were farmers and manual workers.[94]

Such proportions of working-class couples in the divorce lists were high compared to the English experience of the same period. More than half (59%) of the husbands involved in divorces in England in 1871, whose occupations are known, came from the highest strata of gentry, professionals, and managers; one-fifth (22%) came from the manual working class; and smaller contributions

---

[87] Griswold, *Family and Divorce*, 25–6.
[88] I have used husbands' occupations because more of these (358) are known than wives' (173).
[89] Backhouse, "'Pure Patriarchy'," 285n.72. Even so, there were some petitioners, such as a laborer and a railway conductor, whom one would expect to have had very modest means.
[90] Smith, "Divorce in Nova Scotia."
[91] Golder, *Divorce in 19th-Century N.S.W.*, 131, Table 4, and discussion, 128–36.
[92] Phillips, *Divorce in New Zealand*, 108.
[93] Skilled manual workers contributed 15%, unskilled and semiskilled manual workers 18%; Golder, *Divorce in 19th-Century N.S.W.*, 131, Table 4.
[94] Phillips, *Divorce in New Zealand*, 107–8.

608

14.3 Phase one: Up to World War I

Table 14.1 *Occupations of husbands in Los Angeles divorce sample (1880s) and Los Angeles work force (1890)*

	Divorces (%)	Work force (%)
High white collar		
Professional	7	6
Major proprietor	13	5
Subtotal	20	11
Low white collar		
Clerks, sales	8	15
Semiprofessional	< 1	1
Petty proprietor	28	17
Subtotal	36	33
High blue collar	23	20
Low blue collar		
Semiskilled worker	9	16
Unskilled	12	20
Subtotal	21	36
Totals	100	100

Source: Elaine Tyler May, *Great Expectations: Marriage and Divorce in Post-Victorian America* (Chicago, 1980), 176, Table 17.

were made by farmers and shopkeepers (16%) and clerical and retail workers (8%).[95]

Given the costs of divorce, the underrepresentation of couples from the lower social groups is hardly unexpected. What is surprising is their frequent high proportion. Somehow some manual workers, unskilled tradesmen and women, domestic servants, and others with apparently very modest incomes and little or no property were able to afford costs that should have been beyond their reach. In most cases we do not know how they managed this financial feat, but in some it is clear that it was the result of patient saving over many years. In one English case reported shortly before World War I, a woman had saved for twenty years to obtain a divorce.[96] A New Zealand woman, explaining why she had waited until 1894 to divorce her husband who had committed adultery with her sister in 1885, wrote that "I would have applied for this Decree of dissolution of marriage before this only that I was destitute of the necessary

---

[95] Recalculated from Rowntree and Carrier, "Resort to Divorce," 222, Table 11. Rowntree and Carrier include 23% of cases where the occupation is not known, but they suggest that most of these were from the higher social strata, thus reinforcing the profile derived from known occupations.

[96] Cited in Holcombe, *Wives and Property*, 105.

609

money."[97] Australian women borrowed and saved for their divorces,[98] and in Nova Scotia cases included male petitioners who waited nineteen years before they could save enough for a divorce.[99] It is clear that in some of these cases in which apparently poor men and women divorced, the costs of divorce had a delaying effect, rather than being the absolute deterrent it must have been in others. These cases also demonstrate the high priority some men and women gave to getting a divorce.

Yet another inhibition to divorce before World War I was the stigma attached to it, although it is difficult to recapture social attitudes in this period. The liberalization of divorce policies throughout Western society, notwithstanding the phase of conservatism around the turn of the century, attests to an increasing acceptance of the view that divorce was necessary in certain circumstances. But if its necessity was accepted, it was only as an evil, and divorce was widely regarded as a failure or weakness on the part of both spouses, not only the partner guilty of the matrimonial offenses. Even women who divorced in the most compelling circumstances could find themselves treated as social pariahs, as if they were responsible for the behavior that had led to the divorce. A submission to the 1909 royal commission on divorce in England noted that "public opinion generally condemns a divorced woman without regard to circumstances. . . . 'the disgrace' is dreaded and we are told that 'it would go against you at the works' and be a hindrance in looking for employment."[100] Moreover the stigma of divorce attached not only to the spouses involved but extended to their children and members of their wider families.

These are, however, impressionistic conclusions about attitudes to divorce in the period, and in the absence of opinion polls or other systematic evidence we have little more to go on. The treatment of divorce in literature might point us in the right direction but, as always, there is no way of knowing how reflective it is of prevailing social values. In some literary works, it is true, divorce was dealt with sympathetically. Thomas Hardy highlighted the unnecessary suffering that resulted from restrictive divorce laws, a perspective echoed by many other writers.[101] Yet others, however, pointed to the scandal and shame that divorce attracted, and these works, which focus on social attitudes, are perhaps more useful to us. An example is Arnold Bennett's *Whom God Hath Joined* (1906), which placed a fictional account of two divorces in an English Midlands town at the beginning of the twentieth century, in the context of contemporary law. One of the divorce petitioners in the novel (his wife is guilty of adultery),

[97] Quoted in Phillips, *Divorce in New Zealand*, 112.
[98] On women and divorce costs see Golder, *Divorce in 19th-Century N.S.W.*, 193–6.
[99] Smith, "Divorce in Nova Scotia."
[100] *Working Women and Divorce*, 39.
[101] Thomas Hardy, *Jude the Obscure* (1896). We might note that Hardy's own marriage went through a period of stress at the time he wrote this work: see biographical notes in ibid. (Harmondsworth, 1980), 9.

musing that there were only a few hundred divorces in England each year and that there had been none in his town, is horrified to realize that out of the quarter million people in the community "*he* had been chosen by destiny for this disgraceful renown."[102] This might well have been the gist of contemporary literary references to divorce. A study of divorce in American novels from the 1850s to World War I concluded that divorce was portrayed negatively and generally condemned as a moral and social evil.[103]

Divorce could present real problems to those in public life. One man who discovered this was John H. Sangster, a nineteenth-century Canadian educational reformer who was nominated in 1874 for membership in the Ontario Council of Public Instruction. Sangster had divorced his wife in the United States and later married one of his former students. This background overshadowed any qualifications he might have had for the position on the council, and Sangster was subjected to the full fury of Ontario's Victorian press. One newspaper declared, "applaud Sangster and you legalize prostitution, make marriage-rites hollow mockeries, rape the wife and mother of the most solemn pledges of her honour, and debase marriage from an honourable state into casual cohabitation." Sangster lost the election.[104]

In the first forty or fifty years of the modern period of divorce – up to World War I – divorce rates began to rise but rose slowly. The reasons that have been suggested are that economic changes and rising expectations of marriage led to a greater incidence of marriage breakdown, thus creating a wider constituency from which divorce might draw. At the same time, divorce and its attributes in terms of property, children, and remarriage became increasingly attractive among the various formal and informal responses to marriage breakdown. All of these factors, it is suggested, were especially important for women, whose status in marriage made them more likely than their husbands to want to divorce. Against these developments that militated in favor of divorce, others militated against it. Divorce was expensive and stigmatized and was effectively closed to couples in the lower social strata whose marriages had broken down. One way of understanding the overall effect of these changes is in terms of a balance of forces – social, economic, legal, and attitudinal – for and against divorce. Whereas the balance had been weighted against marriage breakdown and divorce until the nineteenth century, it shifted first in favor of marriage breakdown and then later, toward the end of the century, toward divorce.[105] In

---

[102] Arnold Bennett, *Whom God Hath Joined* (London, 1906), 50. Bennett himself separated in 1921.

[103] James Harwood Barnett, *Divorce and the American Divorce Novel, 1858–1937: A Study in Literary Reflections of Social Influences* (Philadelphia, 1939), 135–9. See also Ernest Earnest, *The American Eve in Fact and Fiction, 1775–1914* (Urbana, Ill., 1974), 151ff.

[104] Robert Pike, "Legal Access and the Incidence of Divorce in Canada: A Sociohistorical Analysis," *Canadian Review of Sociology and Anthropology* 12 (1975), 116.

[105] An implication of this is that in the first half of the nineteenth century there was a greater extent of marriage breakdown that did not take legal form. As we have noted, this does seem to have been a period of transition in marriage patterns and social concern about marriage (see Chapter 12).

this first phase, however, the deterrents to divorce were still strong counter-weights, so that although divorce rates began to rise, they did not do so rapidly or dramatically.

14.4 Phase two: 1918 to the 1960s

The second phase of modern divorce, the long period from World War I to about 1960, saw the rate of divorce increase more quickly, and divorce, a marginal phenomenon until 1914, become established as an integral part of the social and demographic system. It is possible that the war and its aftermath were partly responsible for the changes differentiating the two phases. As we have seen, in the late- and postwar periods there was a surge of divorces, and divorce rates throughout the West reached proportions that had hitherto been unimagined outside the minds of the most alarmist opponents of divorce. The likely reasons for the sudden rise of divorce rates have already been discussed in the previous chapter, but what must be considered is the likelihood that the divorce boom had the effect of undermining hostile attitudes toward divorce somewhat by showing that divorce was a reasonable response to marriage breakdown. The divorce boom fed a large cohort of divorced men and women into society generally and into the marriage market specifically, and increased social exposure to divorce at the personal level. Pike notes that in Canada before World War I, divorce was so rare "that most citizens had probably never seen, let alone been personally acquainted with, a divorced person."[106] That situation began to change during the war, and in such ways the postwar divorce surge could well have been the catalyst that led to changes in the way people thought and acted in respect to divorce.

It is difficult to discuss the specific effects of the war on attitudes and behavior because other factors coincided with the wartime and postwar increase in divorces. In various countries there were legal and procedural reforms that must also have contributed to the divorce rate. One of the important changes was a reduction of the costs of divorce in many places, either because greater prosperity lowered the costs relative to income or because legal aid schemes were put in place.

In England proceedings *in forma pauperis* (for poor persons) were extended in 1914 to include litigants with up to a hundred pounds in capital. Before 1914 the upper limit had been twenty-five pounds, which had effectively excluded regular wage earners. Because lawyers were expected to give their services free in these cases (though they could charge for expenses) means tests were rigorously applied, particularly from 1926 when poor persons' committees were set up by the various law societies. The impact of this reform, which should have made divorce more accessible further down the social scale, was obscured by the outbreak of World War I, but it might well have been responsible for the

---

[106] Pike, "Legal Access and the Incidence of Divorce," 125.

continued rise in the number of divorces during the early phases of conflict, when we might have expected a decline. Certainly, legal aid contributed to the surge of divorce petitioning from 1918 to 1920 in England, when more than half the divorces sought by men received financial assistance under the terms of the 1914 Poor Persons' Rules. Although a limitation was placed on financial aid in 1920 – in order to benefit, an applicant had to earn less than four pounds a week – the proportion of divorce petitions with assistance ranged between 30% and 40% during the late 1920s until World War II. With the implementation of the improved 1949 legal assistance plan in late 1950, not only did divorces increase in absolute numbers – from under 30,000 in 1950 to more than 38,000 in 1951 – but one-half and more of all petitions, and two-thirds of those filed by women, received aid.[107]

The reduction in the real financial costs of divorce, either by legal assistance, by increased prosperity, or by a greater willingness to pay the costs as divorce became more desirable, contributed to a marked shift in the social characteristics of the men and women who turned to divorce. Whereas they had tended to be overrepresentative of the upper social groups at the expense of the lower – a bias that could be explained solely in terms of costs but that was no doubt also the result of other factors – there was a growing representation of the working classes in the interwar years. In Los Angeles the overrepresentation of the high white-collar occupations and the underrepresentation of the low blue-collar occupations, which was a feature of the 1880s (see Table 14.1), had disappeared by 1920. In that year, 8% of men in divorce actions were from the highest social groups (compared to their 10% in the work force), 33% were low white-collar (27% in the work force), 26% were high blue-collar (33% in the work force), and 32% were low blue-collar (31% in the work force). Divorced men were thus closely representative of general social profile at the upper and lower levels, and the low white-collar workers (clerical, retail, and semiprofessionals) were a little overrepresented and the high blue-collar group (skilled foremen) somewhat underrepresented. In the space of thirty years, divorce had spread more or less evenly throughout the Los Angeles population.[108]

The same trend was noted elsewhere. In New Zealand by the 1920s men and women in salaried occupations, as distinct from professionals, employers, or the self-employed, were found in disproportionately high numbers in the divorce lists. In 1926, for example, self-employed men and employers accounted for 34% of the work force, but only 20% of divorced men.[109] In England the shift was also dramatic. Because the data are not accessible, little is known of the timing of change, but in the eighty years between 1871 and 1951 manual workers increased their presence among divorce petitioners from 22% to 69%.

[107] Rowntree and Carrier, "Resort to Divorce," 201–2, Table 2.
[108] May, *Great Expectations*, 176, Table 17. One problem with May's statistics is that the 1920 sample was part of the postwar phase, which might have skewed it for purposes of comparison with the nineteenth-century samples.
[109] 1926 New Zealand Census, in Phillips, *Divorce in New Zealand*, 94.

In the same period clerical workers held their own (8% in 1871, 9% in 1951), but the percentage of divorcing couples from the highest social strata dropped markedly; farmers and shopkeepers declined from 16% to 8%, and the combined gentry, professionals, and managers plummeted from 54% to 16% of the total.[110] In eighty years divorce in England was transformed from a predominantly élite recourse to one dominated by the working classes. This did not mean that working-class marriages were more prone to divorce, however; an analysis of 1951 English statistics showed that the social distribution of divorcing couples was almost exactly the same as the distribution within the continuing married population.[111]

Many modern studies have indicated a tendency for divorce rates to be higher among the lower socioeconomic strata. This is true of the United States, England, and many European countries. The reasons remain unclear, and there remain fundamental questions as to whether divorce might be a result of financial pressures associated with low incomes or whether other factors, such as low age at marriage, which generally correlate with divorce, are concentrated in these social groups. In the present context it is important that divorce has become widely accessible and is generally used by all social groups, and that this mass character of divorce developed during the interwar period. It resulted not least from the effective lowering of financial barriers to divorce, as incomes rose more rapidly than costs, financial assistance was made available, or as divorce was given a higher priority in the hierarchy of competing demands on incomes. Whatever the precise reasons in each case, the transformation of the social composition of divorcing couples was surely vital to the increase in divorce rates during the twentieth century. Had divorce retained the social bias it possessed in the late nineteenth century, its potential for growth would have been severely limited. By becoming instead a facility available for mass consumption, divorce took on a much greater potential for growth.

An important aspect of the social extension of divorce was the employment of women or their possibilities for employment. During the twentieth century there has been a general correlation between employed and divorced women, although, as we have seen, the direction of influence between the variables is not clear – whether employed women divorced or whether divorced women entered employment. In either case, if actual employment or potential employment is to be a factor in divorce decisions, there must be a labor market for women, and in this respect conditions during the twentieth century have generally favored divorce, for the proportion of women in the labor force outside the home has increased throughout Western society. In the United

[110] Recalculated from Rowntree and Carrier, "Resort to Divorce," 222, Table 11. Those whose occupations are unknown are excluded from this recalculation. Rowntree and Carrier suggest that they were predominantly manual workers, and this would serve only to sharpen the dramatic transformation of divorce in England over the eighty-year period.

[111] Manual workers made up 70% of both divorced and continuing married populations, whereas the two highest social categories contributed 22% to each. Ibid., 223, Table 12.

States, for example, labor force participation rates for all women doubled from 18% to 36% between 1890 and 1960. In the same period the percentage of married women in employment rose much faster, from 5% to 30%.[112] In England women accounted for 27% of the labor force in 1931, but 42% in 1966.[113] The examples may be multiplied, but they point to the same trend of increased participation rates by women in the labor force everywhere. Although women remained concentrated in certain areas of the work force, and although they continued to earn salaries that were inferior to men's, the increasing opportunities for employment bore directly on divorce. Either they provided an essential resource for employed married women who wanted to divorce or they constituted a labor market to which women could turn after divorce.[114]

In addition to these developments, changes in divorce law and policy themselves in this second phase made divorce more accessible. A prominent area of change was the liberalization of divorce law and judicial interpretation of it. There is no need to recapitulate the points made in Chapter 13 in these respects; the trend in Western society is clear enough, even though political developments in some countries in the 1930s, notably Germany and Austria, did produce exceptional effects. For the most part divorce laws were expanded to include more and more fault grounds or to add mutual consent and various forms of incompatibility. In almost every case of legal reform there was a subsequent rapid, if short-lived, increase in the number of divorces.

It is likely, too, that social attitudes toward divorce changed in a more positive direction between World War I and 1960. Again, it is impossible to gauge public opinion at any given time, and thus to estimate the timing and direction of change, but there are indicators that we can draw upon. One must be the very persistence and pace of legal reform in the period. Divorce laws were liberalized, the notion of fault was undermined definitively in many codes, and there is evidence of wider public pressure for even more liberal divorce laws. It might be, of course, simply that proponents of easier divorce were better organized or had more effective access to the mass media, but it is tempting to discern a general shift in attitudes in favor of divorce. The decline of press reporting of divorce cases, which was prohibited by law in many countries, also deprived divorce of some of its most sensational and scandalous connotations.

Public opinion polls in the United States indicate a shift in attitudes between 1936 and 1966. In 1936, 23% of Americans thought that divorce should be easier to obtain in their respective states, whereas 77% thought that it should be either kept as it was or made more difficult.[115] A 1945 survey of opinion on state divorce laws indicated that 9% of people wanted more liberal laws, 31% thought that their laws were "about right," and 35% thought that they should

[112] Jacob Mincer, "Labour Force Participation of Married Women: A Study of Labour Supply," in Alice H. Amsden, *The Economics of Women and Work* (Harmondsworth, 1980), 42.
[113] A. H. Halsey (ed.), *Trends in British Society Since 1900* (London, 1972), 43.
[114] Albrecht, Bahr, and Goodman, *Divorce and Remarriage*, 54, 106–7.
[115] William J. Goode, *World Revolution and Family Patterns* (New York, 1970), 84.

be made more strict. The remaining 25% were undecided.[116] This indicates a decline in the proportion in favor of more liberal divorce, and might well reflect either concern at the rising divorce rate at that time or a sense that, because so many divorces were being obtained, there was no need to relax the laws. Twenty years later, in 1966, 12% favored the liberalization of existing laws, 18% thought that they were satisfactory, and 34% wanted the laws made more restrictive. In this survey, 35% were undecided.[117] In simple statistical terms there was a marginal trend favoring the liberalization of divorce laws, but the surveys must be read in the context of increasingly liberal divorce policies. The letter and application of the divorce legislation of which Americans gave their opinions in 1966 was in general considerably more liberal than that which was in place in 1945. In both the 1945 and 1966 surveys the proportion wanting more restrictive laws was more or less balanced by those content with existing laws or in favor of liberalization, and this suggests that legislative changes in the period generally paralleled the movement of public opinion.

A similar shift in public opinion is evident in Canada, too. The percentage of respondents favoring easier divorce grew from 24% in 1943 to 50% in 1960 and to 60% in 1966.[118] There need not have been a unilinear trend in changes in attitudes toward divorce, however. The 1950s was a decade of political and social conservatism throughout Western society, and attitudes toward marriage and divorce might well have reflected it. Public opinion polls in Italy indicated the potential for volatility. Italians were surveyed at regular intervals on their attitudes toward the legalization of divorce from 1947 onward, and although those in favor of divorce rose from 28% in 1947 to 35% and 41% in 1953 and 1959, thus running against notions of conservatism in the period, they fell to 22% in 1962.[119]

As for other indices of attitudes toward divorce from the end of World War I, they are few and impressionistic. The survey of American divorce novels, which found literature in the nineteenth and early twentieth centuries to have portrayed divorce as a moral and social evil, detected a change after the war. The author concluded that postwar novelists rejected the notion that divorce was of vital concern to the public and instead stressed "the newer notion that marriage is a personal relation, especially where there are no children, and that divorce is an institutional device of great personal import, but one that concerns society very little."[120]

Shifts in public attitudes, easier and broad social access to divorce, and increasing employment opportunities for women must be ranked high in the explanations for the increase in divorce rates between 1918 and 1960. A further factor was very likely the increase in divorce itself, for although it may be

---

[116] "The Quarter's Polls," *Public Opinion Quarterly* 9 (1945), 233.
[117] Cherlin, *Marriage, Divorce, Remarriage*, 46–47.
[118] Pike, "Legal Access and the Incidence of Divorce," 120, Table 1.
[119] Narbona, *Divorcio*, 109; Memmi, "Le divorce et l'italienne," 501, Graphique 4.
[120] Barnett, *American Divorce Novel*, 138.

14.4 Phase two: 1918 to the 1960s

debated whether divorce breeds marriage breakdown, it seems probable that divorce does breed divorce. There is no explicit or unambiguous evidence on this point, but it is reasonable to assume that widespread divorce and the increased proportion of divorce and formerly divorced men and women in the population creates familiarity with the phenomenon. If this familiarity and personal contact undermined, rather than reinforced the notion that divorced men and women were depraved creatures devoid of morals and social decency, then the result would have been to raise tolerance of divorce. In this way the increased divorce rate had an effect on the normative context of divorce and contributed to its own increase by reducing the deterrent posed by social stigma. There is, however, no way to measure this hypothetical feedback effect of the divorce rate.[121]

A different version of this is to think of divorce as emulative behavior, men and women following the example of others in turning to the divorce courts. Although there are examples of this operating at the local level, it is hypothetical at the broad social level of analysis.[122] If there is a tendency for divorce rates to increase because of an internal growth dynamic of this sort, we should expect that the divorce booms that followed each of the world wars would have given successive boosts to the divorce rates. This might well have been the case after World War I; divorce rates in the 1920s were generally higher than a continuation of the prewar trend of increase would have produced.[123] But World War II did not have this effect on divorce rates. After the short period of very high rates in the immediate postwar years, peaking in most Western countries in 1946 or 1947, divorce rates either stabilized or declined somewhat during the 1950s. Certainly they were lower than we should have expected had the prewar trend been sustained. This was true in the United States, where rates did not begin to rise consistently until 1962. As Figure 14.1 shows, divorce rates fell between 1950 and 1960 in England, France, Switzerland, and Australia, while in Sweden they were stationary.

The reasons for the failure of the divorce rates to continue their rise during the 1950s are unclear. One area of explanation that has been advanced for the United States is that there was an attitudinal change favoring marriage, the family, home, and children. Some commentators have interpreted the adoption of these values as a reaction against the preceding two decades of economic hardship and war; they portray Americans, exhausted by the 1930s and 1940s,

---

[121] The notion of feedback of this kind is contested by some analysts of divorce.

[122] An excellent example of an "epidemic" of divorces emerged from eighteenth-century Connecticut. In one community there were five divorces from 1694 to 1729, eleven from 1736 to 1748, and two from 1749 until the end of the century. The bulge in the middle period resulted from couples emulating the divorce of a prominent couple. See Alison Duncan Hirsch, "The Thrall Divorce Case: A Family Crisis in Eighteenth-Century Connecticut," *Women and History* 4 (1982), 43–75. Another case, of several neighbors divorcing their wives in rapid succession, is noted in Roderick Phillips, *Family Breakdown in Late Eighteenth-Century France: Divorces in Rouen, 1792–1803* (Oxford 1980), 101–3.

[123] Rowntree and Carrier suggest that one-third of the increase in the divorce rate in England in the 1920s was due to the effects of the war; "Resort to Divorce," 203–5.

617

as retreating to their suburban homes and closing their doors on the world beyond the narrow confines of family, work, church, and school.[124] There is no doubt that during the 1950s social attitudes were generally conservative and family centered, notwithstanding apparent contradictions such as the increasing participation of married women in the labor force. But it is not clear how those attitudes relate precisely to the divorce rate. To attribute the decline in the divorce rate solely to attitudinal change places a great causal burden on a single factor.

Two other areas of explanation, related to attitudes, seem somewhat more promising. One is a cohort explanation, that is, one that draws on the life experiences of men and women married in a particular period, in this case those married in the five- or ten-year period after the end of World War II. These marriages, many of which would have been dissolved if the divorce trend had continued (but were not), consisted of men and women who had grown up during the economic depression of the 1930s and the economic and social dislocations of the war. It has been argued that such people were so touched by the effects of economic deprivation on their families that when they finally married, they felt stronger commitments to marriage and the family.[125] Many of them, in fact, must have despaired of ever marrying, so that they regarded their eventual marriages as an acquisition not to be squandered or easily tossed aside. This attitude alone might provide a partial explanation of lower divorce rates, but added to it was another factor, that these couples married into a strong economy, with good employment opportunities. The scenario for the 1950s, then, meant that men and women who had internalized strongly familial attitudes and modest material expectations from their experiences of the depression and war entered a postwar world of economic expansion where they could marry, have children, and enjoy a relatively high level of personal prosperity. This scenario goes a long way to explaining other contemporary demographic trends: earlier marriage and the baby boom. It also provides an explanation of changes in the divorce rate in terms of expectations of marriage and the likelihood of their fulfillment.[126]

Although these explanations might fit the United States well enough, they seem less applicable to Europe. While America enjoyed prosperity in the 1950s, much of Europe was still suffering the economic and social aftermath of the war well into that decade. Yet there, too, divorce rates failed to sustain their prewar trends of increase. Even in England, where changes to the legal assistance rules made divorce more accessible from late 1950, divorces surged in 1951 but quickly receded and then declined until the early 1960s. The precise reasons for these patterns of divorce remain unclear. Again, it is a pattern that was

---

[124] See John R. Seeley, R. Alexander Sim, and Elizabeth W. Loosley, *Crestwood Heights* (New York, 1956).
[125] Richard A. Easterlin, *Birth and Fortune: The Impact of Numbers on Personal Welfare* (New York, 1980).
[126] Ibid.

14.5 Phase three: Divorce since 1960

common to almost all Western states and countries, regardless of economic, social, and demographic structure. It is tempting to apply more generally the explanations suggested for the United States, that in the 1950s conditions favored marital stability and that the Western experience of the 1930s and 1940s produced a cultural reaction, one of whose manifestations was a higher degree of marital satisfaction. The material differences between the United States and many other Western countries make such a generalization hazardous, however.[127] Although trends in divorce during the 1950s were similar across Western society, as were other demographic tendencies, it seems more promising to seek an understanding of them in terms of the interplay of national and general Western experiences, rather than in terms of the latter alone.

14.5 Phase three: Divorce since 1960

The most recent phase of divorce, from the 1960s onward, has been characterized by a rapid and dramatic increase in divorce rates in every country, as Figure 14.1 indicates. The increase was accentuated by its following the stagnation or decline in divorce rates of the 1950s, but even without this contrast, the rates that prevailed from the early 1960s represented an acceleration over earlier trends. In the United States, for example, the annual changes in the divorce rate (that is, the extent to which the rate in a given year fell or rose compared to the rate in the preceding year) showed a decline from 1947 to 1958, a steady increase of between 4% and 5% annually from 1959, but increases of between 9% and 12% a year in the period 1968–72. After 1973 the rate of increase slowed, but the divorce rate still climbed, and only after 1982 did it fall slightly.[128]

Elsewhere in the 1960s divorce rates also accelerated in a manner that was unprecedented except for the postwar periods. The English divorce rate doubled between 1960 and 1970, then more than doubled again during the next decade. In France the phase of rapid increase began later but took a similar form, the rate more than doubling between 1970 and the early 1980s. In other countries increases have also been dramatic, some more, some less so. West Germany's divorce rate almost doubled between 1968 and 1983, for instance. Taking account of the variations in absolute rates, the magnitude of increase and the precise timing of change, we can conclude that from the 1960s divorce entered a new growth phase throughout Western society. It was not a return to "normal" trends after the declining rates of the 1950s, and cannot be explained as such.[129] In short, we must seek a particular set of explanations for the phase,

---

[127] On economic trends in Europe, see Walter Laqueur, *Europe since Hitler* (rev. edn., Harmondsworth, 1982), 179–276.

[128] *U.N. Demographic Yearbook*, various years. On changes in the divorce rate see Sar A. Levitan and Richard S. Belous, *What's Happening to the American Family?* (Baltimore, 1981), 31, Fig. 3.

[129] The notion of a return to the long-term pattern has been advanced to explain the decline of the birthrate in the 1960s and 1970s after the baby boom of the late 1940s to the early 1960s. See Cherlin, *Marriage, Divorce, Remarriage*, 45ff.

as well as for the fact that divorce rates began to decline in some countries in the early 1980s, although they continued to rise in others.

As we have already noted, divorce law reforms had little or nothing to do with setting off the most recent divorce rate increases. In almost all countries divorce rates had begun to rise before legal reforms were enacted or came into force, and the widespread introduction of no-fault divorce legislation during the 1970s was partly a response to increasing divorce, not a cause of it. This is not to say, however, that legal reforms might not have reinforced and given additional impetus to the trends that were already under way. In countries as diverse as Sweden, Australia, and England divorce law reform quite clearly gave a short-term boost to the national divorce rates (see Figure 13.2), and it is possible that this carried through over the longer term.

Legal change apart, various explanations of the latest phase of divorce have been advanced. They range from the breakdown of family life because of the increasing employment of women, to more liberal divorce policies, to changed individual attitudes toward marriage and divorce, to shifts in sexual morality, and to the effects of the women's liberation movement.[130] There is also the redistributive hypothesis, the notion that the rising divorce rate can largely be accounted for as the dissolution of a greater proportion of broken marriages than had previously been the case (see Chapter 10). This last explanation assumes that the rising divorce rate does not betoken a similar increase in marriage breakdown, whereas the other explanations imply that the divorce rate reflects the tendency for more marriages to break down. By and large, however, these explanations parallel the range of factors that have been proposed to explain the increasing popularity of divorce at most other periods in the past hundred years: easier access to divorce, married women's employment, and changes in social values. There was, in fact, an impressive conjunction of these factors during the 1960s and 1970s. Not only that, but where we are able to measure them, it appears there was a marked increase in their intensity.

Let us look first at the employment of women. We have noted the historical association between married women's employment and divorce, and the likelihood that employment or the possibility of employment, that is, the existence of a labor market for women to turn to, provides a vital potential resource for a woman contemplating separation. It might also facilitate a husband's decision to terminate his marriage, a point that is often overlooked; the relative financial independence of the wife would reduce the alimony he might be required to pay. It is also likely that a wife's employment reduces the disruption of separation to some extent by providing a source of continuity. To make these points is not to suggest that separation is undertaken lightly in marriages where the wife is employed, but it does mean that it can be undertaken more readily once the decision to separate has been made.

---

[130] Many polls suggest that a high percentage of people believe that the women's liberation movement has disrupted family life and marriage.

14.5 Phase three: Divorce since 1960

Rates of employment of married women have increased dramatically since the 1950s. Considering married women with children below school age, we find that in the United States 19% were employed in the labor force in 1959, 29% in 1969, and 43% in 1979. In other words, their employment rate more than doubled during the 1960s and 1970s.[131] In 1980, 50.2% of all married women in America, with a husband present, were employed.[132] In Canada in 1981 more than half of the women with a child under the age of three were in the work force, while for those with older children the rate of employment was 63%.[133] In Sweden the employment rate of married women was already high (46%) in the late 1960s, but it rose to 57% within a decade.[134] Again, the examples can be multiplied, but the general trend is clear enough from these. The link between separation and work, if not its causal direction, is also clear from the statistics. In the United States in 1980, as we have noted, 50% of married women with a husband present were employed, but this rate rose to 59% for married women with no husband present, that is, separated or deserted wives, and 75% for divorced women.[135]

The broader reasons for the increased employment of women need not be discussed here. What is important is the increase itself and its likely bearing on marital stability. Although it is possible that in many marriages the wife's employment eases financial pressures and can improve marital relationships by reducing the importance of marriage in the totality of sources from which personal satisfaction and fulfillment are derived, the association between women's employment and divorce emerges from too many studies for it to be dismissed. The minimal role it plays is in facilitating the decision to separate, but it may play a more active role in marriage breakdown. Marriages where the wife works out of financial necessity are likely to be subject to stress, and the fact that women who work outside the home tend to do the work inside the home as well adds to the pressure on them. It is not only the actual employment of women while living with their husbands that is important, but also the potential for employment. Separation might be facilitated when a woman is employed, but it is also facilitated – admittedly less so – when a married woman not in the work force has a reasonable expectation of being able to find employment. We should not underestimate the difficulties of transition, particularly for women who have been out of the work force for many years, but the potential for employment must be an important consideration for younger women who contemplate divorce. Separation preceding divorces tends to take place early in marriage, in any case.[136]

There are other dimensions linking women's employment and divorce. Some

[131] Cherlin, *Marriage, Divorce, Remarriage*, 50; 51, Fig. 2. 3.
[132] Waite, "U.S. Women at Work," 22, Table 6.
[133] Maureen Baker, *The Family: Changing Trends in Canada* (Toronto, 1984), 182.
[134] Trost, "Sweden," in Chester, *Divorce in Europe*, 39.
[135] Waite, "U.S. Women at Work," 22, Table 6.
[136] Albrecht, Bahr, and Goodman, *Divorce and Remarriage*, 63.

research has suggested that increased employment on the part of married women parallels a decline in their husbands' incomes. Again, this is a cohort explanation that places the increased divorce rates of the 1960s and 1970s in the context of the experiences of divorced men and women during their youth. It is suggested that those who married in the 1960s and 1970s grew up in the relative prosperity of the 1950s and acquired high material expectations. When they entered the labor market, however, they found themselves in competition with large numbers of peers – the result of the postwar baby boom – and were unable to achieve their expected standard of living as rapidly as they had planned. Women entered and stayed in the work force after marriage because couples could not achieve their material goals on a single income. The increased participation of married women in the work force was itself a factor in marriage breakdown, and in addition these marriages were under financial pressure.[137]

The rapid growth of women's, and especially married women's, employment throughout Western society is one of the most important associations with the rising divorce rate. Although the directions of influence or causality between the two trends must remain speculative at the social level, the suggested links are convincing enough. Some research studies have demonstrated that women perceived the lack of financial support as the main barrier to divorce. In one American study, for example, 36% of the women cited finances as a deterrent to their choosing to divorce, whereas only 10% of men did so.[138] We should assume that personal income from employment would lower the barriers and make divorce a more feasible option.

Married women often entered employment in this period, it is suggested, not because they wished to have a career or because they sought personal fulfillment from work, but because they had to, either through sheer necessity or because two incomes were needed for the couple to realize their expectations. To this extent the very conditions of financial pressure that lead to the wife's employment might be active in predisposing the couple toward marriage breakdown.[139] The situation is different where the wife undertakes employment for reasons other than simple economic necessity in the conventional sense. Material standards of living were one facet of the general expectations of marriage that had been rising from the late nineteenth century.

---

[137] Easterlin, *Birth and Fortune*. The role of expectations of material standards of living is suggested in research showing a proneness to divorce in marriages where the husband scored lower in socioeconomic terms than his wife's father. L. C. Coombs and Z. Zumeta, "Correlates of Marital Dissolution in a Prospective Fertility Study: A Research Note," *Social Problems* 18 (1970), 92–102.

[138] As barriers to divorce, women most commonly cited financial support (36%), religious beliefs (20%), and children (20%). Men cited children (27%), difficulty of divorce laws (17%), and personal religious beliefs (14%): Albrecht, Bahr, and Goodman, *Divorce and Remarriage*, 103, Table 34.

[139] Unemployment and financial problems are correlated with divorce in Kitson and Raschke, "Divorce Research," 8–11.

14.5 Phase three: Divorce since 1960

From the 1960s these expectations not only rose further, but their emphasis shifted toward the affective aspects of the conjugal relationship. Recent decades have seen an unprecedented emphasis on the emotional content of marriage and the desirability of deriving emotional fulfillment from it. Indeed, with the decline of the birthrate in Western society in this period and other changes in the character of the family life cycle, the conjugal relationship has come to dominate the family as the parent-child relationship has either disappeared or receded. Easier access to contraceptives and abortions have enabled many couples to have no children at all. Those couples who do have children tend to have fewer (the ideal family size having fallen), and the period during which children are present in the family has diminished as a proportion of the potential duration of marriage: With longer life expectancies, parents can expect to have thirty or more years of married life after their children have left home.

The increasing emphasis on the married couple's emotional relationship, rather than on their economic or parental roles, has produced intense demands on just that aspect of marriage which is arguably the most fragile. Evidence lies in the outpouring, during the 1960s and 1970s, of books and articles advising husbands and wives how to relate to each other, how to communicate, how to fulfill themselves within marriage, how to understand each other's needs and desires, how to maximize their emotional benefits and to enrich their spouses', and how to improve their sexual relationships.[140] One branch of this industry has focused on older men and women in recognition of the particular stresses that marriages are susceptible to after children have left home.

Widespread interest in marriage counseling and therapy is another facet of this new emphasis on emotional and sexual fulfillment. The proportion of couples who – individually or together – have attended counseling or been through therapy is probably small and concentrated in the middle classes. But the issues have been given mass circulation through articles and self-administered questionnaires in popular magazines, especially those targeted at a female readership. Examples include:

"Forever Single? What Women Really Feel, Fear and Hope For"
"Sexual Taboos: Why Breaking Them Keeps Couples Together"
"Same Lover, Sexier Sex: 5 Ways to Make Love Better"
"The Good News About Marrying Later" and
"Is He Marriage Material? 74 Sneaky Ways to Tell a Good Bet from a Deadbeat."[141]

Although it is difficult to describe the magnitude of such attitudinal changes, the changes themselves are undeniable. The same stress on romantic love, emotional intensity, and sexual satisfaction that has long been associated with premarital and extramarital relationships has spilled over into marriage. The

---

[140] On marriage manuals in the 1970s see Sheila M. Rothman, *Woman's Proper Place: A History of Changing Ideals and Practices, 1870 to the Present* (New York, 1978), 250–3.
[141] These examples are from *Glamour*, September 1986, October 1986, and February 1987.

decline of these qualities, the slide from intense passion to comfortable companionship after the initial years of married life has become less acceptable. As John Gillis writes in the conclusion of his history of British marriage, people "expect more of the conjugal relationship [since the 1960s]. It is made to bear the full weight of needs for intimacy, companionship, and love, needs which were previously met in other ways. Couples expect more of each other."[142] This conclusion applies far beyond Britain; it is a Western phenomenon. It must be added that the higher these emotional expectations rise, the less likely they are to be fulfilled.

Sharply rising expectations of marriage and improvements in women's employment potential go some way to explaining the increased incidence of marriage breakdown from the 1960s, but they do not explain the growth in the divorce rate. It is probably useful to make a distinction within the trend of increase itself, for divorce seems to have increased in two distinct stages. The first was a period of moderate increase that might have represented a return to the longer-term pattern. This would explain, for example, the phase from 1962 to 1969 when divorce rates in the United States increased moderately (by about 5% each year). It would also account for the gradual increases in the English and French divorce rates, as shown in Figure 14.1. The second phase, when the really impressive increase in the divorce rate took place, occurred at the end of the 1960s or were associated with legal reforms in the first half of the 1970s, or both.

The timing of this second stage, in the United States at least, coincided with an apparent change in attitudes toward the availability of divorce. Public opinion polls indicate that although attitudes toward divorce changed slowly between World War II and the mid-1960s, there was a substantial shift of opinion thereafter, as shown by the results of three successive surveys given in Table 14.2. The movement of opinion was in favor of more liberal divorce laws, and once again we must bear in mind that by 1978 almost all of the American states had liberalized their divorce laws, not least by introducing no-fault divorce. This means that although only 33% of Americans surveyed in 1968 were in favor of maintaining or liberalizing their divorce laws, by 1978 54% favored maintaining or liberalizing their already more liberal laws. In addition, instead of opposition to increasingly liberal divorce laws growing, as we should expect if public attitudes remained static while divorce was made easier, the extent of opposition actually fell. In other words, American attitudes toward divorce liberalized faster than the divorce laws. The main change in attitudes seems to have occurred between 1968 and 1974, just as laws began to be liberalized in America (beginning with the 1969 California act) and just as the divorce rate was in its phase of greatest increase. What we do not know, of

---

[142] Gillis, *For Better, For Worse*, 318. It is noteworthy that in a survey among divorced men and women, "emotional problems" and "no longer loving each other" were together cited more often than other perceived reasons for their marriage failures. Albrecht, Bahr, and Goodman, *Divorce and Remarriage*, 100, Table 33.

14.5 Phase three: Divorce since 1960

Table 14.2 *Public attitudes as to whether divorce in American states should be easier or more difficult*

	1968 (%)	1974 (%)	1978 (%)
"Easier"	18	32	27
"Stay as is"	15	21	27
"More difficult"	60	43	43
"No opinion/don't know"	7	4	3

Source: Andrew J. Cherlin, *Marriage, Divorce, Remarriage* (Cambridge, Mass., 1981), 48, Fig. 2–2.

Table 14.3 *French public opinion on divorce*

Those thinking marriage is:	1969 (%)		1972 (%)	
	Men	Women	Men	Women
Indissoluble	30–3	28–34	18	21
Dissoluble in serious cases	40–5	41–7	52	51
Dissoluble by mutual consent	22–8	24–7	30	28

Source: L. Roussel, "Attitudes de diverses générations à légard du mariage, de la famille et du divorce en France," *Population* 26 (1971), 114, Table XI; Anne Boigeol, et al., *Le divorce et les français* (2 vols. Paris, 1974), I, 25, Table B19; I, 26, Table B20.

course, is whether the change in attitudes was a factor in increasing the divorce rate or whether attitudes changed as a result of greater familiarity with divorce because of its greater incidence. It is most likely that the relationship was a reciprocal one, more liberal attitudes lowering inhibitions to divorce, leading more couples to terminate their broken marriages by divorce, with the resulting increase in divorces enhancing familiarity and reducing intolerance. It is pointless even to begin to speculate as to which was the primary influence.

A similar shift in attitudes toward divorce in this apparently important period in the late 1960s and early 1970s emerges from two surveys of opinion in France, one carried out in 1969, the other in 1972. As Table 14.3 shows, even in that short period there was a shift of opinion toward greater acceptance of divorce. It is interesting to note that the French divorce rate began to rise just at this period; having remained in the range 0.6–0.8 per thousand through the 1960s, it rose to 0.93 and 0.94 in 1971 and 1972, respectively, and continued to increase from then until the mid-1980s.

The familiarity with divorce that resulted from its increased incidence might well have made more people tolerant of it. This process has been reinforced by increasing references to divorce in the mass media and popular culture. Many more movies and television dramas focus on divorce, and American television situation comedies such as "Kate and Allie" and "Golden Girls," which portray divorced women (together with widows in the latter), contribute to a wider exposure to divorce. They contrast starkly with the television programs of earlier generations that stressed complete marriages and families. Marriage breakdown has long been a theme of movies, but only in recent years have films such as *Kramer vs. Kramer* and *The Good Father* focused so intensely on the social, legal, and personal aspects of divorce. Divorce has also become a minor theme in popular music. Accustomed to dealing with thwarted relationships and broken hearts, rock lyrics have taken a matrimonial turn. The theme of Elton John's "The Legal Boys" is the role of lawyers and professionals in divorce proceedings, while Billy Joel's reference to divorce in "Scenes from an Italian Restaurant" treated divorce as the routine matter it often seems to have become: a matter of course in which the spouses part the best of friends. Country and western music, which has a longer tradition than rock music of dealing with marriage, inevitably turned to divorce for inspiration; the best example is Tammy Wynette's "D-I-V-O-R-C-E," which deals with the effects of a divorce on a child. On television, divorce became a subject for mass entertainment. "Divorce Court" presents dramatized divorce actions in which petitioners and defendants plead their cases before a retired judge who brings down decisions according to general legal principles. The growth of divorce has also produced a consumer subculture of goods and services linked to divorce: divorce parties, divorce cakes, divorce rings, and divorce cards (sample text: "I've just heard...you're as free as a bird").[143]

In short, since the 1960s, but especially since the 1970s, divorce has lost much of its scandalous reputation, and is far less stigmatized as a result. The shift of legal principles away from fault and the need to prove adultery or other matrimonial offenses has undermined the association of divorce with scandalous and immoral behavior. Even though divorce is still often viewed negatively – by no means is it considered desirable for its own sake – it is treated more openly and not as something to be hidden from respectable society. Having been divorced did not prevent Ronald Reagan from being elected governor of California and later, in 1980, president of the United States, and the Canadian prime minister Pierre Trudeau separated from his wife for some years before their divorce in 1984. In 1978 divorce finally and unequivocally penetrated deeply into the British royal family, when the marriage between Princess Margaret, the sister of Queen Elizabeth, and Lord Snowdon was dissolved.

There is no doubt that since the 1960s attitudes toward divorce have been

---

[143] In the 1960s more fluid matrimonial patterns became associated with the world of entertainment on the west coast of the United States and more generally with California (even though the divorce rate there is by no means the highest among the American states). A fictional treatment of marriage and morals in this period is Cyra McFadden, *The Serial* (New York, 1977).

transformed, and this transformation has undermined yet another barrier to divorce: the scandal and shame it once brought in its wake. Like the other factors discussed in this section, such as the employment of women, reform of divorce laws, and the increasing expectations of marriage, the change in attitudes during the quarter century since 1960 has been unprecedented in its extent and intensity. If the rate of divorce is perceived as being influenced by the material, social, normative, and personal constraints on divorce, then it should not be surprising that the divorce rates rose so rapidly in this period; the various limitations, which had been slowly eroded during the previous three-quarters of a century, seemed to collapse within the space of a few years during the late 1960s and early 1970s.

Still, we should not present too stark a picture of cheap, procedurally easy, and casual divorces, of spouses separating without rancor and recriminations, and each living happily ever after, either alone or within a new marriage or relationship. The process of marriage breakdown and divorce is by definition an emotionally difficult one. It is a recognition that expectations cannot be fulfilled with a chosen partner, and there is almost necessarily a sense that one or both spouses has failed, in some way, to live up to the promises and hopes expressed at the time of marriage. It is questionable how far the no-fault principles of modern divorce laws have penetrated spouses' perceptions of marriage breakdown. They are still predominantly expressed in terms of fault, and in many cases, such as where there is violence and exploitation, quite rightly so, even if neither spouse can be exonerated entirely. The social implications of marriage breakdown have been mitigated as the social stigma attached to divorce has declined and as husbands and wives are no longer required to give details of their marriages in court. But within the private sphere of marriage, the pain and bitterness of marriage breakdown persists.

The divorce itself provokes various reactions. For some spouses, long-separated and with no outstanding disputes over property or children, divorce is nothing more than an administrative procedure certifying that their marriage is dead. For some, divorce comes as a relief, severing once and for all their ties with an abusive and alienated partner. For others, however, the very procedure of divorcing opens up a new set of trials as husbands and wives battle over property, alimony, and custody and access arrangements for their children.[144] These issues, which are the consequences of divorce, are the subjects of evolving legislation. The state of the law at any given time can deter men or

[144] One study indicates the worst periods or most difficult times in obtaining a divorce to be as follows:

	Men (%)	Women (%)	All (%)
Before decision to divorce	50	58	55
Between decision and divorce	25	20	22
Just after divorce	23	19	21
Now (at time of survey)	2	3	3

From Albrecht, Bahr, and Goodman, *Divorce and Remarriage*, 124, Table 43.

women from divorcing, and the practical effect of these laws on divorced spouses might well deter women in particular.

As we have seen, legal changes in the past hundred years have made divorce more feasible for women. Not only did divorce laws give property rights, but there were provisions for alimony, generally based on the court's assessment of the wife's need and the husband's ability to pay. Legal reforms in the 1960s and 1970s give the appearance of helping women even more by providing for an equal division of property after divorce.[145] These laws are based on the recognition that women make a vital contribution to the accumulation of matrimonial property and to the ability of their husbands to earn, by doing housework and by taking responsibility for looking after children. In practice, however, the introduction of the principle of equal division of property has often worked to the disadvantage of women. Under the former rules property had often been distributed between the spouses on the basis of fault, so that women, usually the petitioners and therefore recognized as the innocent partner, gained most of the property after divorce. In California, for example, women received most property in most settlements before 1970, but after the introduction of no-fault and equal division rules in that year, their share of property fell dramatically.[146] It might be argued that women had been given preferential treatment under the preexisting legislation and that they are now being treated no more and no less than fairly, but the fact remains that in terms of property, women have fared worse in recent times than they had before.

Property settlements are only one part of the more general economic readjustments that divorce requires. In two others, alimony and child-support payments, women also do better on paper than they do in practice. Although court orders for these payments have increased, they are often inadequate and, for the most part, the rate at which husbands comply with the orders is very low. Across the United States in 1981 fewer than half the women awarded child support received it as ordered in terms of amount and frequency. About 30% of women received some payments, and one-quarter of them received nothing at all.[147] A 1980 survey in Canada turned up similar findings; one-third of the women who were awarded support received it in full, one-third received it partially, and the remaining one-third received nothing whatsoever.[148]

In practice, then, as distinct from legal prescription, modern divorce results in hardships on many women and their children. Women have access to the work force, it is true, but in order to benefit from it many of them must make arrangements for child care, and even when employed, women earn considerably less than men. (In fact, women's wages have remained virtually unchanged at between one-half and two-thirds of men's wages since the seventeenth century.) Divorced women might be given an equal share of the matrimonial

[145] See Weitzman, *Divorce Reform*, 70–3.
[146] Ibid., 74, Table 9.
[147] Ibid., 283.
[148] Ibid.

property, but most of them are in the lower socioeconomic strata, so that the amount of property and money involved is generally small.[149] The courts are prepared to order former husbands to pay alimony and child support, but only a minority of these orders are complied with, and a substantial proportion of divorced women receive no payments whatsoever.

The overall effect of divorce on women varies from place to place and depends on the law, the effectiveness of its enforcement, and other provisions for social welfare, state-provided child care, equal-pay laws, and the like. In countries such as the United States and Canada, however, divorce has produced a new class of poor – divorced women and their dependent children. Lenore Weitzman's excellent study of the incomes of men and women after divorce showed that both underwent a decline, but that women's declined much more than men's. When the presence of children is taken into account – they are usually with their mother rather than with their father – and per capita household income is considered, the disparities are even greater, particularly in the middle and upper-middle classes. Most wives, Weitzman concluded, "experience rapid downward social mobility after divorce, while most husbands' economic status is substantially improved."[150] This assessment is borne out by the perceptions of men and women after divorce. One study found that 48% of divorced women reported their incomes to be "much lower" than that of their friends and associates, and only 7% of men did so; in contrast, 23% of divorced men reported that their incomes were higher than those of their friends, compared with only 7% of divorced women. The authors conclude that the downward economic mobility of women after divorce is stronger than any other variable in their analysis.[151]

It was suggested earlier that a married woman in traditional society might well be deterred from leaving her husband when she saw the effects of solitary life in the poverty of widows and deserted wives and their children. The same might be said of married women in relation to divorce in modern society, especially in the better-off social groups. The differences between the two periods and sets of situations are vast, however. For one thing, deprivation in traditional society could be absolute; in modern society it is relative. This is not to minimize the often appalling material consequences of modern divorce on women and children, but it might make them less effective as a deterrent. The other factor we might consider is how widely these negative consequences of divorce are known. The economic resources available to women after divorce look satisfactory: women might expect property and a regular income from alimony and child-support payments. The reality is quite different, however, and it seems that until recently it was a hidden consequence of divorce.

---

[149] In Weitzman's 1978 study, 60% of divorcing couples had less than $20,000 net worth. Ibid., 76.

[150] Ibid., 329.

[151] Albrecht, Bahr, and Goodman, *Divorce and Remarriage*, 134–6.

Domestic relative deprivation in modern Western society simply does not have the public character of poverty in traditional society.

These general economic considerations apart, there are particular groups of women for whom divorce is more inaccessible than others. Older women, especially those who have been out of the work force for many years, experience difficulty in obtaining employment. Many American studies point to the problems faced by such women, many of whom are not granted alimony or are awarded only limited-time maintenance to support them through the immediate postdivorce period. Finally, it is older women too – and men as well, though to a lesser extent – who are deterred from divorce because of its connotations and shame. Although social attitudes have shifted quite radically in the last decade or two, they have changed most rapidly among the younger generations. Older men and women retain the former, negative views of divorce, and have to confront their peers – friends and associates – who are likely to share their views.

14.6 Conclusion

The rise of divorce during the past hundred years defies precise and certain explanation in terms that can satisfactorily be applied across Western society generally. National and state legislation, different demographic and social structures, varying economic conditions and cultural climates all have their impact on divorce as they do on other aspects of personal and social behavior. Divorce is so intimately integrated into other demographic and social processes that it is impossible to isolate it clearly enough to be able to define all of the influences upon it, and a constant feedback effect makes it difficult to determine the directions of causality. Nevertheless, the rise of mass divorce during the twentieth century has been a sufficiently universal phenomenon throughout Western society to lead us to seek broadly applicable explanations. In the preceding pages they have been suggested for the different phases of growth of the divorce rates during the last century, and in these final pages we should draw attention to an explanatory framework.

Analysis of divorce rates at the broad level in terms of employment, economic conditions, nuptiality and fertility rates, and socioeconomic class frequently obscures the fact that each divorce involves the personal relationship of two married people. Perhaps we should more often begin our analysis at this end of the process rather than with the macrosocial factors associated with divorce as a demographic phenomenon. In essence, divorce and the divorce rate consist of the aggregate of decisions of men and women that their marriages have broken down and that they want them dissolved. Thus notions of marital expectations must be central to any explanation of either marriage breakdown or divorce. Rising expectations, together with the implicitly greater likelihood of failure to achieve them, are fundamental to the explanations offered in this chapter. Rising expectations are, in themselves, not the critical variable, for it is their relationship to the preceived quality of the marriage – and thus the realization or disappointment of the expectations – that determines whether or not the marriage has broken down. [It seems likely that the very elevation of expectations carries with it a correspondingly greater likelihood of disappointment. At certain periods, however, a particular conjunction of expectations and social conditions might relate in such a way as to reduce or enhance the risk of disappointment and marriage breakdown.] Richard Easterlin, for example, suggested that the low material expectations of those who grew up during the 1930s and 1940s, and who married into the prosperity of the 1950s, were so likely to achieve their expectations, that as a result their marriages were more stable than those of couples who married with high expectations in the 1960s but found themselves in a period of declining economic opportunities.[152] Elaine Tyler May proposed rising material expectations and their disappointment as central to an understanding of the rise of the divorce rate in late-nineteenth- and early-twentieth-century America.[153] The same point might be applied to Western society generally over the longer term, that with the rapid growth of mass production of consumer goods and their advertising in the mass media, material expectations have risen faster than the possibility of their being satisfied in the less well-off social strata. Expectations of marriage encompass much more than material goods, however, and we have noted the long-term increase and recent intense emphasis on emotional fulfillment as a prime expectation of modern marriages.

The broad socioeconomic context impinges on expectations of marriage, definitions of marriage breakdown, and on the decision to separate or divorce. The possibility of employment, calculations as to the relative advantages and disadvantages of remaining together or separating, all of these and other factors are weighed by couples unhappy in marriage. Their perceptions predispose them either to stay in the marriage, and thus to modify their expectations in order to accommodate themselves to its conditions, or to separate. It is suggested that factors such as women's employment and the reform of laws relating to women's property and children, made separation an increasingly viable alternative to marriage. In turn the access to this alternative enabled expectations of marriage to rise, and the rate of marriage breakdown to increase.

Finally we come to divorce. In spite of the many qualifications we must make, divorce has progressively been transformed from a last resort of the desperate few to being the most attractive and common response to marriage breakdown. It offers the complete dissolution of marriage, a distribution of property, arrangements for the custody of children, and, perhaps most importantly, the possibility of remarriage. Over time, the costs of divorce were reduced, the grounds expanded, and the stigma attached to it declined. Divorce spread

[152] Easterlin, *Birth and Fortune.*
[153] May, *Great Expectations.*

through all social classes and its rate increased. Most telling of all, divorce became a synonym for the termination of a marriage. In traditional society the evidence of a broken marriage was a deserted wife; in the nineteenth and for much of the twentieth centuries it was normal to speak of "getting a separation" when faced with marriage breakdown; today the first resort tends to be the last resort, divorce.

In short, the explanation of the rise of mass divorce suggested here rests on rising expectations of marriage; economic, social, legal, and cultural changes permitting more marriages to break down; and decreasingly problematic access to divorce. The various correlates or causes of divorce, which were discussed at the beginning of this chapter, can be encompassed within this framework. Youthfulness at marriage, for example, plays a role in the relationship of expectations and fulfillment. We should expect that expectations in these marriages are more volatile or less realistic than in marriages where the spouses were older at marriage. Marriages of young people also experience economic instability in the first critical years. Regional and urban–rural variations also fit within the framework; divorce rates can be understood as varying according to the economic conditions bearing on marriage breakdown. What is important is that instead of accumulating causes and correlates in no particular order or hierarchy of importance, we should attempt to fit them together coherently within a broad framework of explanation.

Throughout this discussion, however – and this is generally true of research on divorce – the feedback effect of divorce itself has been too often overlooked as a factor in the divorce rate. Too often the divorce rate is seen as passive, the result of socioeconomic and historical forces that push it up in this period and down in the next. Marriages are portrayed as fragile craft, rudderless and driven by the rising seas of expectations, their crew still arguing over which sail they should raise when the vessel of their dreams is dashed to pieces on the rocks of an economic downturn. Although it is true that social and economic conditions can favor the breakdown and dissolution of marriage, it should be clear that divorce itself has become part of the cultural climate within which marriages exist. To this extent there is a feedback effect, in which the existence of divorce as a viable alternative to marriage, together with the presence of an increasing number of divorces in society, contribute in turn to marriage breakdown and divorce.

The question of whether divorce causes marriage breakdown has long been debated. Opponents of divorce law liberalization have often argued that easy access to divorce encourages men and women to end their marriages. Although it is doubtful whether it actually encourages them to do so, access to divorce does enable them to consider alternatives to marriage. It is also likely that the liberalization of divorce laws has reinforced rising expectations of marriage. We have seen that more liberal laws and judicial interpretations were in part the result of pressure from divorce petitioners. It is logical to suppose that these more liberal policies themselves provided models and exemplars that were not lost on married couples. From these judicial decisions and new divorce laws they learned that they needed to tolerate a diminishing range of behavior and that the legal and judicial system endorsed expectations of marriage that included love, affection, and consideration. Although expectations of marriage are rarely explicit and documented, judicial decisions and more liberal divorce policies cannot but be considered one of the complex of influences that produced the rising expectations of marriage. Moreover, insofar as divorce was an alternative to marriage it was, like the other legal and economic conditions of any given time, a factor that made separation more feasible and lowered tolerance of objectionable behavior within marriage.

These hypotheses would lead us to expect higher rates of marriage breakdown where divorce policy is liberal than where divorce is either unobtainable or restrictive. Some studies have suggested such an association. There was a correlation between permissive divorce laws and the divorce rate in the United States before the major phase of liberalization in the 1970s.[154] A different study, focusing on marriage breakdown, compared the estimated rate of breakdown in two contiguous and socially, economically, and culturally similar regions of Italy and Switzerland between 1947 and 1956. The incidence of marriage breakdown (at 0.63 per thousand inhabitants) appeared to be more than four times greater in Switzerland, where divorce was easy, than in the Italian region (0.14 per thousand) where divorce was not possible.[155] Reporting these results, however, Max Rheinstein cast doubt on their value by suggesting that the incidence of de facto separation in the Italian survey had been underestimated. Not only is this a problem, but it is also impossible to assess the extent of "empty shell" marriages – marriages that have broken down but where the spouses continue to live together. The incidence of marriage breakdown must finally remain a dark figure, and any influences on it must remain hypothetical. Nonetheless it is unreasonable to suppose that divorce laws and the divorce rate, and the increasingly high profile of the divorced population, have had no impact on the perceptions and behavior of the married population.

A final issue we might consider in this chapter is the limits of growth of the divorce rate. Can it rise to the point that all marriages will be dissolved or are there limits to the extent that divorce can penetrate the married population? In theory there seems no reason why the divorce rate should not continue to rise indefinitely. By permitting remarriages it provides an ever-increasing stock of marriages on which to draw. But in practice it is clear that for a variety of reasons many marriages will never be dissolved except by death. The most important reason, easily overlooked by students of divorce, is that many couples do not want to divorce; they are happily married and they find their expectations fulfilled by their spouses. A recent study of marriages that had lasted fifteen or

---

[154] Kitson and Raschke, "Divorce Research," 15ff.
[155] These studies are discussed in Rheinstein, *Marriage Stability*, 305–6. Marriage breakdown was taken to include divorces, judicial separations, annulments, and informal separations as reported by researchers in Switzerland and by parish priests in Italy.

more years found that in 6% both spouses were unhappy with their marriage, in 10% one spouse was unhappy and the other happy, and in 83% both spouses considered themselves happily married.[156] In cases where marriages might be other than blissful and satisfying, divorce is ruled out for economic, religious, or other reasons.

It is hardly appropriate for a history of divorce to speculate about future trends in the divorce rate or in marriage patterns. There is a large body of literature to which the reader so inclined can turn. In the second half of the 1980s the divorce rates in some countries continue to climb, in others they have stagnated, and in still others show a tendency to decline. Whether this situation represents a diversification of trends or the varied timing of a generally shared trend, only time will tell and future historians will record.

[156] Robert H. Lauer and Jeanette C. Lauer, "Factors in Long-Term Marriages," *Journal of Family Issues* 7 (1986), 382–90.

Conclusion

The history of marriage breakdown and divorce is almost as long as the history of marriage itself. As Voltaire put it, "Divorce probably dates from the same time as marriage. I think, though, that marriage is a few weeks older, that is to say that a man fought with his wife after a fortnight, beat her after a month, and that they separated after living together for six weeks."[1] Of course, Voltaire confused divorce with marriage breakdown, but the gist of his comment is accurate enough, and it highlights the need to give historical depth to phenomena that are too often thought to be peculiar to very modern times.

This book has focused on the most recent thousand years of marriage breakdown and divorce and demonstrates not only that there is a history to be studied but also that it must be integrated carefully into much broader contexts. Even the most narrow analysis must relate divorce to wider considerations of marriage, sexuality, and the social relation between women and men, but a more satisfying account must go much further. The evolution of attitudes toward divorce can be understood only in relation to other sets of attitudes – toward marriage and the family in general, toward religion, social order, religion and morality. The formalization of attitudes into divorce policy and legislation reflected not only these attitudes but shifts in religious and political configurations, and the way in which legislators perceived general or specific marriage issues and their relationship to broader social and political policies. As for the incidence of divorce, it emerged from the accessibility of divorce in legal, economic, and social terms, and from the extent of marriage breakdown, which in turn was influenced by expectations of marriage and definitions of marriage breakdown. They, in their turn, resulted from such varying influences as the legal and social relation of wives and husbands, domestic and nondomestic economic conditions, and the feasibility of informal and formal means of separation.

The result is that although divorce and marriage breakdown can be isolated for study as a theme in the history of Western society, they do not have an autonomous history in any respect. They must be firmly anchored to their historical context in order to be understandable, and the breadth of these perspectives enables us to formulate a number of general conclusions from this

---

[1] Voltaire, *Oeuvres complètes de Voltaire* (35 vols., Paris, 1860), XIII, 140.

Conclusion

study of divorce. Within the many possible areas within which conclusions can be drawn, several are particularly interesting, and will be discussed here. They are the evolution of attitudes toward divorce, the relationship of divorce and marriage breakdown over time, and the insights that divorce can provide to the history of conjugal relationships.

It is difficult to pin down the chronology of changes in attitudes toward divorce, and that much more difficult to explain it. There is no doubt that social attitudes toward divorce are far less negative in the late twentieth century than they were a hundred years and more earlier, but with few exceptions we have little indication of general social attitudes before the advent of regular and systematic public opinion surveys after World War II. Before this time the attitudes and views of various members of the social and political élites – legislators, theologians, and intellectuals – can be determined, but they offer little guidance as to the direction of change. At any given period we can find some against divorce and others in favor, and within the latter group some advocated restrictive policies and others were more liberal. Not only is there no evidence of unanimity of attitude at any period, it is difficult to define anything resembling a consensus.

We should not look for a simple linear evolution of attitudes toward divorce in a positive direction, however, for shifts in opinion varied according to specific social and political contexts as well as according to class and gender. One insight into popular attitudes is provided by the experience of France during the revolution, when urban populations appear to have readily accepted divorce as a social practice. Not only were there many divorces in French cities such as Paris, Rouen, and Lyon at this time, but each divorce required the active participation of many citizens, women and men, as witnesses, arbiters, and supporters of the wives and husbands involved. In contrast, the rural populations retained their traditional opposition to divorce, thus reinforcing the distinction between town and country in eighteenth-century France. A further indication of varying attitudes emerged from England in the late nineteenth and early twentieth centuries. The opposition to divorce by the respectable middle classes, and particularly by middle-class women, is almost legendary, yet the survey of attitudes of working-class women presented to the 1909 royal commission on divorce reflected a general acceptance of the necessity of divorce in a wide range of domestic circumstances.

Although we can and must talk about changing attitudes toward divorce, then, we must not assume a steady change of opinion in a more positive direction. Any description of social attitudes must be carefully qualified in many respects, and the qualifications often overburden the limited evidence available to us. Even in recent times we must resist the temptation to over-estimate the extent to which divorce is considered acceptable. The rejection of the principle of divorce in the 1986 referendum in the Republic of Ireland should serve as a reminder that there remain extensive and influential bodies of opinion against divorce in any form.

Conclusion

Despite the impossibility of defining shifts in opinion very precisely, the broad movement away from negative attitudes is evident.[2] Two long-term series – national and state divorce laws and the doctrines of the major churches – have shown a clear, if uneven, trend of liberalization. What factors have influenced this trend?

Changes in secular and religious law and policy on divorce have frequently resulted from ideological or theological considerations. For instance, the often reluctant abandonment of the doctrine of marital indissolubility by the Protestant Reformers emerged from their biblical exegesis and from notions of justice, equity, and contract. There is no evidence that it was the result of economic or social changes within marriage and the family during the sixteenth century. Indeed, the same order of ideological considerations, including the application to family legislation of the principles of natural law and of contract, largely explain the development of divorce law and policy throughout Western society until the end of the eighteenth century. Only from this time might we also give social, economic, and demographic factors some weight in the formulation of divorce policies.

From the nineteenth century, for example, we must take into account what might be called popular pressure. This is not to suggest that there was a welling up of popular sentiment in favor of divorce, although the campaigns in favor of legalizing divorce in England from the 1830s and in France in the early 1880s might well have had an influence on legislators in those countries. In a more direct sense, however, petitioners for divorce were themselves influential in altering law and policy. One example is the way in which pressure of divorce petitions often forced procedural reform. Typically, the abandonment of legislative divorce, whether it was in England in 1857 or in the American states earlier and later in the nineteenth century, resulted from the sheer number of petitions that, even though negligible in modern terms, cut deeply into the time allotted for legislative business. Second, as noted earlier, petitioners and their lawyers pressed constantly at the bounds of divorce and gradually extended the definitions of such offenses as cruelty. A final example of the influence of divorce petitioners lies in their simple determination to divorce. In places as disparate as New York, Sweden, England, New Zealand, and Italy, legal reform in the twentieth century followed on evidence that citizens were not deterred by the restrictions of prevailing divorce legislation, and that widespread migration, connivance, collusion, and perjury had made a mockery of existing limitations.

---

[2] Although scarcely typical, British philosopher Bertrand Russell exemplified the shift in attitudes. Writing of Alys Pearsall Smith, who was to become his first wife, Russell noted that in about 1893 "we went on the river, and discussed divorce, to which she was more favourable than I was." Some years later, Russell agreed to a divorce because of his affair with Ottoline Morrell, and recorded that Pearsall Smith's "rage became unbearable. After she had stormed for some hours, I gave a lesson in Locke's philosophy to her niece. . . I then rode away on my bicycle, and with that my first marriage came to an end." Bertrand Russell, *The Autobiography of Bertrand Russell* (3 vols., London, 1967), I, 81, 204. Russell later wrote in favor of liberal divorce policies. See Bertrand Russell, et al., *Divorce* (New York, n.d. [?1930].

Conclusion

In these various ways, even before divorce reform pressure groups lobbied legislators for legal reform and before divorce reform figured on political agendas, there were popular influences on the shape of divorce law and policy.

What of underlying social, economic, and demographic changes that might have produced or been reflected in changes in attitudes toward divorce, and in divorce law and policy? Some historians, as we have noted, suggest that divorce is the modern substitute for spousal death in earlier generations, and this would lead them to explain the liberalization of divorce laws, in part at least, as a result of declining mortality rates. In analyses such as these, legal reform takes on a functional role within general social structures and can be explained independently of explicit or conscious human design.

It is tempting to ransack the various levels of social change in order to locate developments that appear to have an association with divorce, but we must treat any findings as speculative. One potentially fruitful area of investigation is the probability that marriage breakdown began to increase in the late eighteenth century, between fifty and a hundred years before divorce laws and policies began to be liberalized. The social and economic changes conducive to marriage breakdown began to make an impact in urbanizing and industrializing Western society from the late eighteenth century, and mortality rates also began their steady decline in this period. Various statistical series of divorce, separation, desertion, and marital conflict indicate an increase in marital stress and breakdown from the late eighteenth century, and the first half of the nineteenth century saw the beginnings of legal reforms dealing with related issues such as child custody and support for abandoned wives and children. It is probable that the period from the late eighteenth to the mid-nineteenth century saw a growing incidence of marriage breakdown, and the legal and policy reforms regarding not only divorce but also separation, child custody, desertion, domestic violence, and married women's property might thus be understood as responses to specific social changes, as well as reflecting the ideological influences of secularization and liberalism on legislation and policy.

The spread of marriage breakdown and divorce, and the easier accessibility of divorce must have been facilitated by fundamental economic changes that occurred in much of Western society from the late eighteenth century. With the development of a city-based working class and the shift of economic power from agriculture to industry, the character of personal property began to change dramatically. It was less and less likely to be in the form of real estate or other assets that were difficult to divide, and more and more likely to be movable property, investments, or simply skills and labor that had an increasingly marketable value. To this extent the unified economic base of traditional marriage was undermined and separation became that much less problematic. One recognition of this transformation was the married women's property legislation that was enacted throughout Western society in the second half of the nineteenth century.

The liberalization of divorce, it might be argued, also responded to such changes. The character of the traditional family economy, described in Chapter 10, was such as to make wife and husband mutually dependent, and thus effectively to exclude the viability of separation. With the increasing viability of separation – and, it is argued here, its increasing incidence – divorce became, over time, a more practicable alternative.

Such links between legal and social change, like the association of divorce and the decline of mortality, must remain at the level of hypotheses that will be judged to be more or less plausible on their individual merits. At the very least they are provocative areas for further research, for it is inconceivable, given our current understanding of the historical process, that changes in divorce policy and law have done no more than reflect changing attitudes toward religion, law, and society.

The suggestion that divorce law reform followed an increase in the incidence of marriage breakdown leads to one of the more important conclusions of this study, that concerning the historical relationship of divorce to marriage breakdown. Without recapitulating the evidence and the argument, we may simply reiterate the conclusion that, in general, marriages were stable in traditional Western society and that a significant extent of marriage breakdown is peculiar to modern times. This conclusion is at variance with the commonly expressed notion that marriage breakdown has historically been common and that rising divorce rates in recent times simply tend more accurately to reflect an essentially constant incidence of marriage breakdown. Although it is at odds with this redistributive hypothesis, the conclusion appears to be in accord with frequently made moral assessments of the state of modern marriage compared to marriage in earlier generations, and for this reason a number of qualifying statements need to be made.

The argument for marriage stability in the past made in this book rests not only on assessments of the quality of conjugal relationships in earlier times but also on the broad social, economic, and demographic contexts of marriage. Marriage in traditional society was culturally desirable and often essential in economic terms. The internal domestic imperatives of the family economy and the external constraints produced a flexible and potentially low level of marriage expectations and a high level of tolerance, both of which have changed over time. In more recent history, expectations of marriage have risen, tolerance of abusive and exploitative behavior has fallen, and the alternatives to married life that contributed to these changes have facilitated a greater incidence of marriage breakdown and separation. This emphasis on the wider social causes of marriage breakdown and divorce are a long way from the predominantly moral assessments that explain divorce rates in terms of character weakness, lack of commitment, and irresponsibility or in simply terms of an increasingly secular society.

One important implication of the conclusion reached in this book relates not to the character of marriage breakdown but to the conditions that led to the stability of marriage in traditional society – and, arguably, to the stability of some marriages in the modern world. On the general level, marriage stability in the past resulted not from the strength of affective or emotional bonds between wives and husbands. Although we would not want to go as far as some historians in arguing that affection was all but absent in marriages before the eighteenth century, the ties that bound men and women together in marriage were not principally of the emotional kind. Wives and husbands were, it seems principally bound by social and economic bonds of two sorts. The first was the condition of mutual dependence imposed by the traditional family economy; the second was the simple lack of viable alternatives to marriage, the relative absence of alternative resources in terms of dwelling, subsistance, and security. Even when affective criteria played an explicit role in the choice of spouse in traditional society, they were subordinate to the interest criteria that were often settled implicitly and first and that determined the marriage constituency from which an emotionally acceptable partner would be selected. Once the marriage had taken place, however, its stability depended not on its affective character but on its material content and context.

These conclusions would lead us to argue that if marriage has become less stable over time, it is not primarily because of changes in the emotional content of marriage but rather because the social context of marriage has been transformed.[3] It is true that these changes have had an effect on expectations of marriage and thus on the quality of affective relations between husbands and wives, but the underlying explanations of marriage stability on the one hand and instability on the other are social and economic, not affective and attitudinal.

The overall point of these various conclusions, which are expressed here in the most brief and general terms, is that marriage stability, marriage breakdown, and divorce cannot be understood in isolation from their social context. It is fundamentally misleading and pointless to interpret the increase in marriage breakdown and divorce as evidence of the decline of matrimonial commitment or domestic morality. Marriage is integral to broad social, economic, demographic, and cultural processes, and it is entirely futile to expect marriage to remain constant or to have a consistent social meaning while social structures, economic relationships, demographic patterns, and cultural configurations have undergone the massive changes of the past centuries. If this book has shown anything, it is that divorce and marriage breakdown have their place in the history of Western society. Yet although we can isolate them as themes for particular study, they cannot be analyzed or understood without reference to the many broader facets of historical change.

---

[3] This point was suggested by Engels in 1845: "If the family as it exists in our present-day society comes to an end then its disappearance will prove that the real bond holding the family together was not affection but merely self-interest engendered by the false concept of family property." Friedrich Engels, *The Condition of the Working Class in England* (Oxford, 1958), 165. Note that Engels is discussing not the disappearance of the family per se, but of its preindustrial form.

Select bibliography

This bibliography lists only those works and sources that bear most directly upon divorce, separation, marriage breakdown, and marriage and that have proved most useful in preparing the present study. It is therefore by no means a comprehensive bibliography of these subjects. For further references, readers should turn to guides such as the *International Bibliography of Research in Marriage and the Family* and Kenneth D. Sell and Betty H. Sell (eds.), *Divorce in the United States, Canada, and Great Britain: A Guide to Information Sources* (Detroit 1978), as well as to specialist journals such as (in English) the *Journal of Family History, Journal of Divorce, Journal of Family Issues,* and *Journal of Marriage and the Family*, all of which have broad international coverage.

The following bibliography is divided as follows:

A. Statistical, legal, judicial, and legislative sources, printed and unprinted.
B. Works dealing primarily with divorce, separation, and family breakdown:
    1. Primary works published before 1900;
    2. Secondary works, and primary works published from 1900.
C. Works dealing more generally with marriage and the family:
    1. Primary works published before 1900;
    2. Secondary works, and primary works published from 1900.

A. Statistical, legal, judicial, and legislative sources: Printed and unprinted

General

Breckinridge, Sophonisba P. (ed.), *The Family and the State: Select Documents* (Chicago, 1934). Collection of British and American statutes and judicial decisions.

Chester, Robert (ed.), *Divorce in Europe* (Leiden, 1977). Statutes and statistics by country.

Commaille, Jacques, et al., *Le divorce en Europe occidentale: La loi et le nombre* (Paris, 1983). Focus on post-1970 legal changes and divorce statistics.

United Nations Demographic Yearbook, 1951–   International divorce statistics by number and rate from 1930.

641

Select bibliography

Canada

Debates of the House of Commons of Canada.

England and Wales

British Parliamentary Papers: Reports of Commissioners on the Laws of Marriage and Divorce with Minutes of Evidence, Appendices and Indices (3 vols., Shannon, 1969).
Diocese of York: Bishop Redman's Visitation, 1597. Presentments in the Archdeaconries of Norwich, Norfolk and Suffolk (ed. J. F. Williams, Norwich, 1946).
Middlesex County Records (ed. John C. Jeaffreson, London, 1888).
Parliamentary Debates (Hansard).
Royal Commission on Marriage and Divorce: Report 1951–1955 (Cmd 9678, London, repr. 1966).
Statutes at Large of England and Great Britain.

France

Archives parlementaires 1st and 2nd series. Debates and statutes, 1789–1834.
Camp, Wesley D. Marriage and the Family in France since the Revolution (New York, 1961). Includes compilations of statistics.
Code Napoléon.
Journal officiel. Débats. Debates and statutes, 1879–1884.
Tribunaux de famille (family courts), Rouen: records of judgments, Archives départementales de la Seine-Maritime, Rouen.

Germany

Reichsgesetzblatt 106 (Berlin, July 8, 1938). Publication of Nazi divorce law.
Statistisches Jahrbuch für das Deutsche Reich, 1912–40. Annual marriage and divorce statistics.

New Zealand

New Zealand Official Yearbook. Annual divorce statistics.
New Zealand Parliamentary Debates.
Supreme Court, Auckland: divorces 1869–1900. New Zealand National Archives Records Centre, Auckland, J-AD, cartons 1–7.

Norway

Oslo Kapitels Kopibog, 1606–1618 (3 vols., ed. Oluf Kolsrad, Christiania [Oslo], 1913–49). Church court records.
Statistik Årbok and Historisk Statistik. Annual statistics.
Stavanger Domkapitels Protokol, 1571–1630 (3 vols., ed. Andreas Brandrud, Christiania [Oslo], 1897–1901). Church court records.

Select bibliography

Scotland

Reports of some recent decisions of the Consistorial Court of Scotland, in Actions of Divorce, concluding for Dissolution of Marriages celebrated under the England Law (ed. James Ferguson, Edinburgh, 1817).

Sweden

Statistik Årsbok för Sverige, 1919– . Annual statistics.
Uppsala Domkapitels Protokoll, Uppsala Landsarkiv, Uppsala. Church court records, seventeenth-century.

Switzerland

Registres de la Compagnie des Pasteurs de Genève au temps de Calvin (5 vols., ed. Robert M. Kingdon and J.-F. Bergier, Geneva, 1962). Judicial deliberations and judgments.

United States of America

Historical Statistics of the United States: Colonial Times to 1957 (Washington, D.C., 1957).
Marriage and Divorce, 1922–8 (Bureau of the Census, Washington, D.C., 1925–30). Annual and retrospective statistics at national, state, and regional levels.
Marriage and Divorce, 1867–1906 (ed. Dwight D. Carroll, Bureau of the Census, Washington, D.C., 1909). Compilation of statistics.
Records of the Court of Assistants of the Colony of Massachusetts Bay, 1630–1692 (3 vols., ed. John Noble, Boston, 1901). Church court records.
Records of the First Church in Boston, 1630–1868 (3 vols., ed. Richard D. Pierce, 1961). Church court records.
Records of the Suffolk County Court, 1671–1680 (2 vols., Boston, 1933). Court records.

Church law

Canons and Decrees of the Council of Trent (trans. J. Waterworth, London, 1848). Roman Catholic canon law of marriage and divorce.
English Church Canons of 1604 (ed. C. H. Davis, London, 1869).
Färnström, Emil, *Om Källorna till 1571 års Kyrkoordnung* (Stockholm, 1935). Sixteenth-century Swedish and German church laws.

B.1 Marriage breakdown, separation, and divorce: Primary works published before 1900

Adresse aux républicains sur le divorce, considéré dans ses rapports moraux et politiques (Paris, An IV [1795–6]).
L'ami des enfants: Motion en faveur du divorce (Paris, n.d. [?1789]).
An Answer to a Book, Intituled, The Doctrine and Discipline of Divorce (London, 1644).
Baylay, C. F. R., *Divorce: Considered with Respect to the Authority of the Gospels* (London, 1857).
Beza, Theodore, *Tractatio de Repudiis et Divortiis* (Geneva, 1573).

643

Select bibliography

Bonald, Louis Gabriel Ambroise de, *Du divorce* (Paris, 1800).

Bunny, Edmund, *Of Divorce for Adulterie, and Marrying Againe: that there is no warrant so to do* (Oxford, 1610).

Calvi, Carlo, *Ricerche sul Divorzio fra Christiani* (Pavia, 1790).

Cerfvol, de [pseud.], *Mémoire sur la population* (London [Paris], 1768).

Cri d'une honnête femme qui réclame le divorce conformément aux loix de la primitive Eglise, à l'usage actuel du Royaume catholique de Pologne, et à celui de tous les peuples de la terre qui existent ou qui ont existé, excepté nous (London, 1770).

A Clergyman [pseud.], *Why Should We Petition Against the New Divorce Bill?* (London, 1857).

"Concerning Divorce. A Swiss Brethren Tract on the Primacy of Loyalty to Christ and the Right to Divorce and Remarriage," [ca. 1533] *Mennonite Quarterly Review* 21 (1947), 114–9.

The Counsellor's Plea for the Divorce of Sir G. D. and Mrs. F. (London, 1715).

Demoustier, Charles Albert, *Le Divorce. Comédie en deux acts, en vers* (Paris, An III [1794–5]).

Desfontaines de la Vallée, Guillaume François, *Le Divorce: Comédie en un acte* (Paris, An II [1793–4]).

Deux projets de décret sur le divorce (Paris, n.d. [?1790]).

Divorce: Report as Received by the Lower House of the Convocation of York (London, 1894).

Divorce: A Sketch. Dedicated to the Matrons of England by An Old Bachelor (London, 1859).

Dove, John, *Of Divorcement: A Sermon preached at Paul's Cross the 10 of May 1601* (London, 1601).

Erasmus, Desiderius, *The Censure and Judgement of the Famous Clark Erasmus of Roterdam: whyther dyvorsement betwene man and wyfe stondeth with the lawe of God* (trans. Nicholas Lesse, London, 1550).

An Essay on Marriage: or, the Lawfulness of Divorce, in certain cases, considered. Adressed to the feelings of Mankind (Philadelphia, 1788).

Fatal Consequences of Domestick Divisions (London, 1737).

Fleming, Caleb, *The Oeconomy of the Sexes: Or the Doctrine of Divorce, the Plurality of Wives, and the Vow of Celibacy Freely Examined* (London, 1751).

A Hellish Murder Committed by a French Midwife, On the Body of her Husband, January 27. 1687/8 (London, 1688).

Hennet, Albert Joseph Ulpien, *Du divorce* (Paris, 1789).

Hervey, Arthur, *A Letter to the Rev. Christopher Wordsworth, D. D., Canon of Westminster, on the Declaration of the Clergy on Marriage and Divorce* (London, 1857).

Hill, George, *In the Case of Divorce, Should the guilty Party, as such, be refused Liberty to Marry again?* (London, 1857).

L'homme mal marié, ou questions à l'auteur de Du Divorce (Paris, n.d. [?1790]).

Howson, John, *Uxore dimissa propter fornicationem aliam non licet superinducere* (Oxford, 1602).

Hubert de Matigny, Hilaire Joseph, *Traité philosophique, théologique et politique de la loi du divorce, demandée aux Etats-Généraux par S.A.S. Mgr. Louis Philippe Joseph d'Orléans, premier Prince du Sang, où l'on traite la question du célibat des deux sexes, et des causes morales de l'adultère* (Paris, 1789).

Il est temps de donner aux époux qui ne peuvent vivre ensemble la faculté de former de nouveaux noeuds (Paris, 1791).

L'indissolubilité du mariage vengée, ou réfutation du livre intitulé Du Divorce (n.p., n.d.).

Lettre contenant la proposition d'un amendement à faire a la loi du divorce (n.p., n.d. [?Paris, 1793–]).

Linguet, Simon Nicolas Henri, *Légitimé du divorce, justifiée par les Saintes Ecritures, par les Pères, par les Conciles, etc., aux Etats-Généraux de 1789* (Brussels, 1789).

Loi du Divorce (n.p., n.d. [?Paris, 1789]).

Melanchthon, Philip, *De coniugio* in *Corpus Reformatorum* (eds. C. G. Bretschneider and H. E. Bindseil, Brunswick, 1847), XIV.

Member of the House of Lords [pseud.], *Remarks on some arguments against the Divorce Bill, 1857* (London, 1857).

Milton, John, *The Doctrine and Discipline of Divorce: restor'd to the good of both Sexes, From the bondage of Canon Law, and other mistakes, to the true meaning of Scripture, in the Law and Gospel compar'd* (2nd rev. edn., London, 1644).

The Judgement of Martin Bucer, concerning Divorce (London, 1644).

Colasterion (London, 1645).

Tetrachordon (London, 1645).

Morer, Thomas [attrib.], *A Treatise concerning Adultery and Divorce* (London, 1700).

Two Cases, the first of Adultery and Divorce (London, 1702).

Morris, J. W., *Observations on the Marriage Law* (London 1815).

Norton, Caroline, *A Letter to the Queen on Lord Chancellor Cranworth's Marriage and Divorce Bill* (London, 1856).

Plea for an Alteration of the Divorce Laws (London, 1831).

Presbyter Anglicanus [pseud.], *A Few Words Upon the Marriage and Divorce Question* (London, 1857).

Ramsey, William, *Conjugium Conjurgium: or, some Serious Considerations on Marriage. Wherein (by way of Caution and Advice to a Friend) its Nature, Ends, Events, Concomitant Accidents, etc., are Examined* (London, 1684).

Réflexions d'un bon citoyen en faveur du divorce (n.p., n.d. [?Paris, 1790]).

Remarks on the Law of Marriage and Divorce; suggested by the Hon. Mrs Norton's letter to the Queen (London, 1855).

A Review of the Divorce Bill of 1856, with propositions for an amendment of the laws affecting married persons (London, 1857).

Reynolds, H. W., *Origen and the York Report on Divorce* (Cambridge, 1895).

Selden, John, *Uxor Ebraica* in *Opera Omnia* (London, 1726).

The Speech of Baron von Gerlach, in the Prussian Chamber, on the Marriage Law (London, 1857).

A Treatise concerning Adultery and Divorce (London, 1700).

Trials for Adultery (7 vols., London, 1779–80).

A True Relation of the Most Horrible Murther, committed by Thomas White of Lane Green in the Parish of Auffley in the County of Salop, Gent, upon the Body of his Wife Mrs. Dorothy White (London, 1682).

Trumbull, Benjamin, *An Appeal to the Public, Especially to the Learned, with Respect to the Unlawfulness of Divorces* (New Haven, 1788).

Vauts, Moses à, *The Husband's Authority Unvail'd; wherein It is moderately discussed whether it be fit or lawfull for a good Man, to beat his bad Wife* (London, 1650).

A Warning for Bad Wives: or, the Manner of the Burning of Sarah Elston. Who was Burnt to death at a Stake on Kennington Common neer Southwark, on Wednesday the 24 of April 1678. For Murdering her husband Thomas Elston, the 25th of September last (London, 1678).

Select bibliography

A Wife and a Mother [pseud.], *What will the Commons do with the Divorce Bill?* (London, 1857).

Wolseley, Charles, *The Case of Divorce and Re-marriage thereupon Discussed...Occasioned by the late Act of Parliament for the Divorce of the Lord Rosse* (London, 1673).

B.2 Marriage breakdown, separation, and divorce: Secondary works, and primary works published from 1900

Adler, Felix, *Marriage and Divorce* (New York 1915).

Alarcon, M. Lopez, *El nuevo sistema matrimonial español* (Madrid, 1983).

Alberdi, Ines, *Historia y sociologia del divorcio en España* (Madrid, 1979).

Albrecht, Stan L., Howard M. Bahr, and Kristen L. Goodman, *Divorce and Remarriage: Problems, Adaptations and Adjustments* (Westport, Conn., 1983).

Allen, Nathan, "Divorces in New England," *North American Review* 130 (1880), 547–64.

Ambert, Anne-Marie, *Divorce in Canada* (Toronto, 1980).

Ames, Howard, *The Motives for, and a New System of Divorce founded on a comparative study of the history and development of Roman, Canonical, French and German divorce legislation* (Gottingen, 1891).

Amram, David Werner, *The Jewish Law of Divorce According to Bible and Talmud* (2nd edn., New York, 1968).

Anderson, Stuart, "Legislative Divorce – Law for the Aristocracy?" in G. R. Rubin and David Sugarman (eds.), *Law, Economy and Society: Essays in the History of English Law, 1750–1914* (London, 1984), 412–44.

Ariès, Philippe, "The Indissoluble Marriage," in Philippe Ariès and André Béjin (eds.), *Western Sexuality: Practice and Precept in Past and Present Times* (Oxford, 1985), 140–57.

Arrom, Silvia M., *La Mujer Mexicana ante el divorcio eclesiástico (1800–1857)* (Mexico City, 1976).

Barker, Arthur E., "Christian Liberty in Milton's Divorce Pamphlets," *Modern Languages Review* 35 (1940), 153–61.

Barnett, James Harwood, *Divorce and the American Divorce Novel, 1858–1937: A Study in Literary Reflections of Social Influences* (Philadelphia, 1939).

Bauer, Carol, and Laurence Ritt, "'A Husband is a beating animal' – Frances Power Cobbe Confronts the Wife-Abuse Problem in Victorian England," *International Journal of Women's Studies* 6 (1983), 99–118.

"Wife-Abuse, Late Victorian English Feminists, and the Legacy of Frances Power Cobbe," *International Journal of Women's Studies* 6 (1983), 195–207.

Bémont, Charles, *Le premier divorce de Henri VIII et le schisme d'Angleterre* (Paris, 1917).

Biggs, J. M., *The Concept of Matrimonial Cruelty* (London, 1962).

Bishop, Joel Prentiss, *Commentaries on the Law of Marriage and Divorce* (2 vols., 5th. edn., Boston, 1873).

Blake, Nelson, *The Road to Reno: A History of Divorce in the United States* (New York, 1962).

Bohanan, Paul (ed.), *Divorce and After* (New York, 1970).

Browne, G. F., *The Marriage of Divorced Persons in Church* (London, 1896).

Select bibliography

Bryce, James, "Marriage and Divorce under Roman and English Law," in *Select Essays in Anglo-American Legal History by Various Authors* (3 vols., Cambridge, 1909), III, 782–833.

Bull, Kirsti, *Skilsmisse* (Oslo, 1979).

Burns, Ailsa, *Breaking Up: Separation and Divorce in Australia* (Melbourne, 1980).

Byrne, James P., *The New Law of Divorce and Matrimonial Causes Applicable to Ireland* (Dublin, 1859).

Cable, Lana, "Coupling Logic and Milton's Doctrine of Divorce," *Milton Studies* 15 (1981), 143–59.

Cahen, Alfred, *Statistical Analysis of American Divorce* (New York, 1932).

Campos, Jose Guerra, *La ley de divorcio y el episcopado español (1976–1981)* (Madrid, 1981).

Carter, Hugh, and Paul C. Glick, *Marriage and Divorce: A Social and Economic Study* (rev. edn., Cambridge, Mass., 1976).

Censer, Jane Turner, " 'Smiling Through Her Tears': Ante-Bellum Southern Women and Divorce," *American Journal of Legal History* 25 (1981), 24–47.

Chapman, Cecil, *Marriage and Divorce* (London, 1911).

Chase, F. H., *What did Christ Teach about Divorce?* (London, 1921).

Cherlin, Andrew J., *Marriage, Divorce, Remarriage* (Cambridge, Mass., 1981).

Chester, Robert, "The Duration of Marriage to Divorce," *British Journal of Sociology* 22 (1971), 172–82.

"Is There a Relationship Between Childlessness and Marriage Breakdown?" in E. Pleck and J. Senderowitz (eds.), *Pronatalism: The Myth of Mom and Apple Pie* (New York, 1974), 114–26.

(ed.), *Divorce in Europe* (Leiden, 1977).

Cleveland, Arthur, "Indictments of Adultery and Incest before 1650," *Law Quarterly Review* 29 (1913), 57–60.

Cohen, Sheldon S., " 'To Parts of the World Unknown': The Circumstances of Divorce in Connecticut, 1750–1797," *Canadian Review of American Studies* 11 (1980), 275–93.

Cohn, Henry S., "Connecticut's Divorce Mechanism: 1636–1969," *American Journal of Legal History* 14 (1980), 35–54.

Coletti, Alessandro, *Storia del divorzio in Italia* (Rome, 1970).

Commaille, Jacques, and Yves Dezalay, "Les caractéristiques judiciaires du divorce en France," *Population* 26 (1971), 173–96.

Commaille, Jacques, et al., *Le divorce en Europe occidentale: La loi et le nombre* (Paris, 1983).

Coombs, L. C., and Z. Zumeta, "Correlates of Marital Dissolution in a Prospective Fertility Study: A Research Note," *Social Problems* 18 (1970), 92–102.

Cott, Nancy, "Divorce and the Changing Status of Women in Eighteenth-Century Massachusetts," *William and Mary Quarterly* 3rd. ser., 33 (1976), 586–614.

"Eighteenth-Century Family and Social Life Revealed in Massachusetts Divorce Records," *Journal of Social History* 10 (1976), 20–43.

Couch, Harvey, "Milton as Prophet: The Divorce Tracts and Contemporary Divorce Laws," *Journal of Family Law* 15 (1977), 569–81.

Cowley, Charles, *Our Divorce Courts* (2nd edn., Lowell, Mass., 1880).

Croce, Benedetto, "Il divorzio nelle provincie meridionali," in *Anedoti di varia litteratura* (Naples, 1942).

Select bibliography

Crouzel, Henri, *L'église primitive face au divorce: Du premier au cinquième siècle* (Paris, 1971).

Cruppi, Marcel, *Le divorce pendant la Révolution, 1792–1804* (Thèse de droit, Paris, 1909).

Damas, Pierre, *Les origines du divorce en France* (Bordeaux, 1897).

Darmon, Pierre, *Le tribunal de l'impuissance: Virilité et défaillances conjugales dans l'Ancienne France* (Paris, 1979).

Daudet, P., *L'établissement de la compétence de l'Eglise en matière de divorce et consanguinité* (Paris, 1941).

Dessertine, Dominique, *Divorcer à Lyon sous la Révolution et l'Empire* (Lyon, 1981).

Dewey, Frank L., "Thomas Jefferson's Notes on Divorce," *William and Mary Quarterly* 3rd. ser., 39 (1982), 212–23.

Dibdin, Lewis, and Charles E. H. Chadwyck Healey, *English Church Law and Divorce* (London, 1912).

Dietrich, Hans Christian, *Evangelisches Ehescheidungsrecht nach den Bestimmungen der deutschen Kirchenordnungen des 16. Jahrhunderts* (Erlangen, 1892).

Dike, Samuel W., *Some Fundamentals on the Divorce Question* (Boston, 1909).

Divorce in its Ecclesiastical Aspect by "Viator": A Rejoinder to the Bishop of Oxford's book "The Question of Divorce" (London, 1912).

Divorce Law of Sonora, Mexico (trans. and commentary by Antonio D. Melgarejo Randolph, New York, 1929).

Dominian, J., *Marital Breakdown* (Harmondsworth, 1974).

Ducrocq-Mathieu, Dominique, "Le divorce dans le district de Nancy de 1792 à l'an III," *Annales de l'Est* 5ᵉ série, 6 (1955), 213–27.

Dumas *fils*, Alexandre, *La question du divorce* (Paris, 1880).

Dumon, Wilfred A., "Divorce and the status of Women," in Marry Niphuis-Nell (ed.), *Demographic Aspects of the Changing Status of Women in Europe: Proceedings of the Second European Population Seminar, the Hague/Brussels, December 13–17, 1976* (Leiden, 1978), 33–47.

Duncan, William, *The Case for Divorce in the Irish Republic* (rev. edn., Dublin, 1982).

Dupont, J., *Mariage et divorce dans l'Evangile* (Bruges, 1909).

Eekelaar, John, *Family Security and Family Breakdown* (Harmondsworth, 1971).

Eekelaar, John, and Sanford N. Katz (eds.), *Family Violence: An International and Interdisciplinary Study* (Toronto, 1978).

Eells, Hastings, *The Attitude of Martin Bucer toward the Bigamy of Philip of Hesse* (New Haven, 1924).

Farge, Arlette, and Michel Foucault, *Le désordre des familles: lettres de cachet des Archives de la Bastille* (Paris, 1982).

Faulcon, Felix, *Précis historique de l'établissement du divorce en France* (Paris, 1800).

Fergusson, D. M. C., L. J. Horwood, and F. T. Shannon, "A Proportional Hazards Model of Family Breakdown," *Journal of Marriage and the Family* 46 (1984), 539–49.

Ferrell, Joseph S., "Early Statutory and Common Law of Divorce in North Carolina," *North Carolina Law Review* 41 (1963), 604–20.

Fitzpatrick, David, "Divorce and Separation in Modern Irish History," *Past and Present* 114 (1987), 172–96.

Forssius, Gustav, *La législation suédoise sur le mariage* (Stockholm, 1975).

Foster, Henry H., and Doris J. Freed, *Dissolution of the Family Unit* (New York, 1972).

Select bibliography

Freeman, Michael D., "The Phenomenon of Marital Violence and the Legal and Social Response in England," in Eekelaar and Katz, *Family Violence*.

Fried, Jacob (ed.), *Jews and Divorce* (New York, 1968).

Froude, J. A., *The Divorce of Catherine of Aragon* (London, 1891).

Furnivall, Frederick J., *Child-Marriages, Divorces and Ratifications, etc. in the Diocese of Chester, A.D. 1561–6* (London, 1897).

Galoppini, Annamaria, "Profilo storico del divorzio in Italia," *Il Diritto di Famiglia e delle Persone* 9 (1980), 594–666.

Gemmill, John A., *The Practice of the Parliament of Canada upon Bills of Divorce* (Toronto, 1889).

Glick, Paul C., and Arthur J. Norton, "Perspectives on the Recent Upturn in Marriage and Divorce," *Demography* 10 (1973), 301–14.

"Marrying, Divorcing and Living Together in the U.S. Today," *Population Bulletin 32* (Washington, D.C., 1979).

Golder, Hilary, *Divorce in 19th-Century New South Wales* (Kensington, N.S.W., 1985).

Goode, William J., *After Divorce* (Glencoe, Ill., 1956).

Gore, Charles, *The Question of Divorce* (London, 1911).

Goslière, Jean-Claude, *La réforme du divorce* (Paris, 1976).

Greenburg, E. F., and W. R. Nay, "Intergenerational transmission of marital instability reconsidered," *Journal of Marriage and the Family* 44 (1982), 335–47.

Griswold, Robert L., *Family and Divorce in California, 1850–1890* (Albany, N.Y., 1982).

"The Evolution of the Doctrine of Mental Cruelty in Victorian American Divorce, 1790–1900," *Journal of Social History* 19 (1986), 127–48.

Guibentif, Pierre, "L'évolution du droit du divorce de 1960 à 1981: Essai d'analyse des discours législatifs," in Commaille, *Divorce en Europe*.

Guthrie, Charles J., "The History of Divorce in Scotland," *Scottish Historical Review* 8 (1910), 39–52.

Halem, Lynne Carol, *Divorce Reform: Changing Legal and Social Perspectives* (New York, 1980).

Halkett, John, *Milton and the Idea of Matrimony: A Study of the Divorce Tracts and 'Paradise Lost'* (New Haven, 1970).

Harrell, Pat E., *Divorce and Remarriage in the Early Church* (Austin, Texas, 1967).

Hart, Hornell, and Henrietta Bowne, "Divorce, Depression, and War," *Social Forces* 22 (1944), 191–4.

Haskey, J., "Social Class and Socio-economic Differentials in Divorce in England and Wales," *Population Studies* 38 (1984), 419–38.

Hawser, William J., *Differences in Relative Resources, Familial Power and Spouse Abuse* (Palo Alto, 1982).

Haynes, E. S. P., *Divorce Problems of Today* (Cambridge, 1912).

Herbert, A. P., *The Ayes Have It: The Story of the Marriage Bill* (London, 1937).

Hindus, Michael S., and Lynne E. Witney, "The Law of Husband and Wife in Nineteenth-Century America: Changing Views of Divorce," in Weisberg, *Women and the Law* II, 133–54.

Hirsch, Alison Duncan, "The Thrall Divorce Case: A Family Crisis in Eighteenth-Century Connecticut," *Women and History* 4 (1982).

Hoffman, Saul, "Marital Instability and the Economic Status of Women," *Demography* 14 (1977), 67–76.

Hogg, Frederick Drummond, *Parliamentary Divorce Practice in Canada* (Toronto, 1925).

649

Select bibliography

Horstman, Allen, *Victorian Divorce* (London, 1985).

Howard, George E., *A History of Matrimonial Institutions* (3 vols., Chicago, 1904).

Hubrich, Eduard, *Das Recht der Ehescheidung in Deutschland* (Berlin, 1891).

Huguelet, Theodor L., "The Rule of Charity in Milton's Divorce Tracts," *Milton Studies* 6 (1974), 199–214.

Ireland, Ronald D., "Husband and Wife: Divorce, Nullity of Marriage and Separation," in *An Introduction to Scottish Legal History* (Edinburgh, 1958), 90–8.

Jacobson, Paul H., and Pauline F. Jacobson, *American Marriage and Divorce* (New York, 1959).

Jackson, Joseph, et al., (eds.), *Rayden's Law and Practice in Divorce and Family Matters* (11th. edn., London, 1971).

Jaulerry, Eliane, "Les dissolutions d'union en France, étudiées à partir des minutes de jugement," *Population* 26 (1971), 143–72.

Jensen, Jens, *Die Ehescheidung des Bischofs Hans von Lübeck von Prinzessin Julia Felicitas von Württemberg-Weiltingen, AD 1648–1653: Ein Beitrag zum protestantischen Ehescheidungsrecht im zeitalter des beginnenden Absolutismus* (Frankfurt am Main, 1984).

Johansen, Hanne Marie, "'At blive den tyran qvit': En studie av skilsmissesakene ved kapittelretten i Bergen, 1604–1708," *Bergens Historiske Forening Skrifter* 83–4 (1985), 7–43.

Johnson, Walter D., "Marital Dissolution and the Adoption of No-Fault Legislation," (Illinois Legislative Studies Center Paper 2, Springfield, Ill., 1975).

Joske, P. E., *The Law of Marriage and Divorce* (Sidney, 1925).

Kelly, Henry Ansgar, *The Matrimonial Trials of Henry VIII* (Stanford, 1976).

Kitchin, S. B., *A History of Divorce* (London, 1912).

Kitson, Gay C., and Helen J. Raschke, "Divorce Research: What We Know; What We Need to Know," *Journal of Divorce* 4 (1981), 1–37.

Koster, Donald N., *The Theme of Divorce in American Drama, 1871–1939* (Philadelphia, 1942).

Kristiansen, Jan Erik, *Skilsmisse i Norge* (Oslo, 1976).

Kuehn, Elaine, "Emancipation or survival? Parisian women and divorce: 1792–1804," (unpub. paper, Eighth Annual Conference, Western Society for French History, University of Oregon, Eugene, Oregon, 1980).

Kuiters, R., "Saint Augustin et l'indissolubilité du mariage," *Augustiniana* 9 (1959), 5–11.

Lantz, Herman R., *Marital Incompatibility and Social Change in Early America* (Beverly Hills, 1976).

Laqueur, Thomas W., "The Queen Caroline Affair: Politics as Art in the Reign of George IV," *Journal of Modern History* 54 (1982), 417–66.

Larsen, M. A., "The Influence of Milton's Divorce Tracts on Farquhar's *Beaux Stratagem*," *Proceedings of the Modern Languages Association* 39 (1924), 174–8.

Lasch, Christopher, "Divorce and the 'Decline of the Family'," in *The World of Nations* (New York, 1973).

Le Bras, Gabriel (ed.), *Divorce et séparation de corps dans le monde contemporaine* (Paris, 1952).

Ledermann, Sully, "Les divorces et les séparations de corps en France," *Population* 2 (1948), 313–44.

Levine, Mortimer, "Henry VIII's Use of the Spiritual and Temporal Jurisdictions in his

Select bibliography

Great Causes of Matrimony, Legitimacy, and Succession," *Historical Journal* 10 (1967), 3–10.

Levinger, G., "Sources of Marital Dissatisfaction among Applicants for Divorce," *American Journal of Orthopsychiatry* 36 (1966), 803–7.

Lezcarno, R., *El divorcio en la Segunda República* (Madrid, 1979).

Lhospice, Michel, *Divorce et dynastie* (Paris, 1960).

Lhote, Jean, "Le divorce à Metz sous la Révolution et l'Empire," *Annales de l'Est* 5e série, 3 (1952), 175–83.

Une anticipation sociale: le divorce à Metz et en Moselle sous la Révolution et l'Empire (Metz, 1981).

Lichtenberger, James P., *Divorce: A Study in Social Causation* (New York, 1909).

Lottin, Alain, "Vie et mort du couple. Difficultés conjugales et divorces dans le Nord de la France aux XVIIe et XVIIIe siècles," *XVIIe Siecle* 102–3 (1974), 59–78.

La désunion du couple sous l'Ancien Régime: l'exemple du Nord (Lille, Paris, 1975).

Luche, Paul, "La suppression du divorce," in *Le problème de population* (Lyon, 1923).

Lulli, Maria Graziella, "Il problema del divorzio in Italia dal sec. XVIII al codice de 1865," *Il Diritto di Famiglia e delle Persone* 3 (1974), 1230–47.

Maidment, Susan, "The Law's Response to Marital Violence: A Comparison Between England and the U.S.A.," in Eekelaar and Katz, *Family Violence*, 110–40.

Manneville, Philippe, "Les premiers divorces au Havre," (unpub. paper, Société d'Etudes Normandes, 1982).

Maraval, Simone, "L'introduction du divorce en Haute-Garonne (1792–1816): étude de moeurs révolutionnaires," (Mémoire de Diplôme d'Etudes Supérieures, Toulouse, 1951).

Markham, Thomas Hugh, *The Divorce and Matrimonial Causes Acts of 1857 and 1858, with all the decisions, new rules, orders, and tables of fees, etc.* (London, 1858).

Martin, Del, *Battered Wives* (San Francisco, 1976).

May, Elaine Tyler, "The Pressure to Provide: Class, Consumerism, and Divorce in Urban America, 1880–1920," *Journal of Social History* 12 (1978), 180–93.

Great Expectations: Marriage and Divorce in Post-Victorian America (Chicago, 1980).

May, Margaret, "Violence in the family: An Historical Perspective," in J. P. Martin (ed.), *Violence and the Family* (Chichester, 1978), 135–67.

McCurdy, William E., "Insanity as a Ground for Annulment or Divorce in English and American Law," *Virginia Law Review* 29 (1943), 771–810.

McKie, D. C., B. Prentice, and P. Reed, *Divorce: Law and the family in Canada* (Ottawa, 1983).

McGregor, O. M., *Divorce in England* (London, 1957).

Family Breakdown and Social Policy (London, 1973).

McNamara, Jo-Ann, and Suzanne F. Wemple, "Marriage and Divorce in the Frankish Kingdom" in Susan Mosher Stuard (ed.), *Women in Medieval Society* (Philadelphia, 1980), 95–124.

Meehan, Thomas, "'Not Made Out of Levity': Evolution of Divorce in Early Pennsylvania," *Pennsylvania Magazine of History and Biography* 92 (1968), 441–64.

Memmi, Dominique, "Le divorce et l'italienne: partis, opinion féminine et referendum du 12 mai 1974," *Revue d'histoire moderne et contemporaine* 30 (1983), 476–509.

Menefee, Samuel Pyeatt, *Wives for Sale* (Oxford, 1981).

Michael, Robert T., "The Rise in Divorce Rates, 1960–1974," *Demography* 15 (1978), 177–82.

Select bibliography

Michon, Lucien, "La famille et le mariage au temps de la Révolution," in Felix Senn (ed.), *Le maintien et la défense de la famille par le droit* (Paris, 1930).

Monahan, T. P., "Does Age Matter in Divorce?" *Social Forces* 32 (1953), 81–7.

Moor, K. A., and L. J. Waite, "Marital Dissolution, Early Motherhood and Early Marriage," *Social Forces* 60 (1981), 20–40.

Mueller, Gerhard O. W., "Inquiry into the State of a Divorceless Society: Domestic Relations, Law and Morals in England from 1660 to 1857," *University of Pittsburgh Law Review* 18 (1957), 545–78.

Næss, Hans Eyvind, "'Intet got oc roligt ecteskab at foruente': Var første skilmisselov, ekteskapsordinansen av 1582 og dens praktiske følger," *Historisk Tidsskrift* 1 (1982), 52–61.

Naquet, Alfred, *La loi du divorce* (Paris, 1903).

Narbona, Francisco, *El Divorcio Viaja a España* (Madrid, 1974).

Nash, Mary, *Mujer, Familia y Trabajo en España, 1875–1936* (Madrid, 1983).

Nolan, Val, Jr., "Indiana: Birthplace of Migratory Divorce," *Indiana Law Journal* 26 (1951).

Noonan, John T., *Power to Dissolve: Lawyers and Marriages in the Courts of the Roman Curia* (Cambridge, Mass., 1972).

Nörskov Olsen, Viggo, *The New Testament Logia on Divorce: A Study of their Interpretation from Erasmus to Milton* (Tübingen, 1971).

Norton, A. J., and Paul C. Glick, "Marital Instability in America: Past, Present and Future," in G. Levinger and D. C. Moles (eds.), *Divorce and Separation: Contexts, Causes and Consequences* (New York, 1979).

Nylander, Ivar, *Studier Rörande den Svenska Äktenskapsrättens Historia* (Uppsala, 1961).

O'Donnell, Carol, and Jan Craney (eds.), *Family Violence in Australia* (Melbourne, 1982).

Olivier-Martin, François, *La crise du mariage dans la législation intermédiaire (1789–1804)* (Thèse de droit, Paris, 1900).

O'Neill, William L., *Divorce in the Progressive Era* (New York, 1963).

"Divorce as a Moral Issue: A Hundred Years of Controversy," in Carol V. R. George (ed.), *"Remember the Ladies": New Perspectives on Women in American History* (Syracuse, N.Y., 1975), 127–43.

Owen, Eivion, "Milton and Selden on Divorce," *Studies in Philology* 43 (1946), 233–57.

Payne, Julian D., *The Law and Practice Relating to Divorce and Other Matrimonial Causes in Canada* (2nd edn., Calgary, 1964).

Perlette, John M., "Milton, Ascham, and the Rhetoric of the Divorce Controversy," *Milton Studies* 10 (1977), 195–215.

Phillips, Roderick, "Demographic Aspects of Divorce in Rouen, 1792–1816," *Annales de Démographie Historique* (1976), 429–41.

"Women and Family Breakdown in Eighteenth-Century France: Rouen 1780–1800," *Social History* 2 (1976), 197–218.

"Le divorce en France à la fin du XVIIIᵉ siècle," *Annales: Economies Sociétés Civilisations* 34 (1979), 385–98.

Family Breakdown in Late Eighteenth-Century France: Divorces in Rouen, 1792–1803 (Oxford, 1980).

"Gender Solidarities in Late Eighteenth-Century Urban France: The example of Rouen," *Histoire sociale-Social History* 13 (1980), 325–37.

"Tribunaux de famille et assemblées de famille à Rouen sous la Révolution," *Revue*

Select bibliography

historique de droit français et étranger 58 (1980), 69–79.

Divorce in New Zealand: A Social History (Auckland, 1981).

Pike, Robert, "Legal Access and the Incidence of Divorce in Canada: A Sociohistorical Analysis," *Canadian Review of Sociology and Anthropology* 12 (1975), 115–33.

Pinto, F. Brandão Ferreira, *Causas do Divórcio: Doutrina, Legislação, Jurisprudencia: Portugal e Brasil* (Coimbra, 1980).

Pizzey, Erin, *Scream Quietly or the Neighbours Will Hear* (Harmondsworth, 1973).

Pleck, Elizabeth, "The Whipping Post for Wife Beaters, 1876–1906," in David Levine et al., *Essays on the Family and Historical Change* (Arlington, 1983).

Preston, Samuel H., and John McDonald, "The Incidence of Divorce within Cohorts of American Marriages Contracted since the Civil War," *Demography* 16 (1979), 1–25.

Putting Asunder: A Divorce Law for Contemporary Society (London, 1964).

Rheinstein, Max, "Divorce Law in Sweden," in Bohanan (ed.), *Divorce and After*, 127–51.

Marriage Stability, Divorce and the Law (Chicago, 1972).

Riddell, William, "Legislative Divorce in Colonial Pennsylvania," *Pennsylvania Magazine of History and Biography* 57 (1933), 175–80.

Ringrose, Hyacinthe, *Marriage and Divorce Laws of the World* (New York, 1911).

Rockwell, William Walker, *Die Doppelehe des Landgrafen Philipp von Hessen* (Leipzig, 1903).

Roswell, Herbert, *Divorce and Remarriage* (London, 1914).

Rousseau, Oliver, "Divorce and Remarriage: East and West," *Concilium* 24 (1967), 57–69.

Roussel, Louis, "Les divorces et les séparations de corps en France (1936–1967)," *Population* XX (1936), 275–97.

"L'attitude des diverses générations à l'égard du mariage, de la famille et du divorce en France," *Population* 26 (1971), 101–42.

Roussel, Louis, et al., *Le divorce et les français* (2 vols., Paris, 1975).

Rowntree, Griselda, "Some Aspects of Marriage Breakdown in Britain during the Last Thirty Years," *Population Studies* 18 (1965), 147–63.

Rowntree, Griselda, and Norman H. Carrier, "The Resort to Divorce in England and Wales, 1858–1957," *Population Studies* 11 (1957), 188–233.

Russell, Bertrand, et al., *Divorce* [symposium of essays] (New York, n.d. [?1930]).

Safley, Thomas Max, "Marital Litigation in the Diocese of Constance, 1551–1620," *Sixteenth Century Journal* 12 (1981), 61–78.

"To Preserve the Marital State: the Basler Ehegericht, 1550–1592," *Journal of Family History* 7 (1982), 162–79.

Let No Man Put Asunder: The Control of Marriage in the German Southwest: A Comparative Study, 1500–1600 (Kirksville, 1984).

Savage, Gail L., "The Operation of the 1857 Divorce Act, 1860–1910. A Research Note," *Journal of Social History* 16 (1983), 103–10.

Schauer, Margery Stone, and Frederick Schauer, "Law as the Engine of State. The Trial of Anne Boleyn," *William and Mary Law Review* 22 (1980), 49–84.

Schmidt, Folke, "The 'leniency' of the Scandinavian Divorce Laws," *Scandinavian Studies in Law* 7 (1963), 107–21.

Schnapper, Bernard, "La séparation de corps de 1837 à 1914. Essai de sociologie juridique," *Revue historique* 259 (1978), 453–66.

Select bibliography

Schoen, R., and J. Baj, "Twentieth-Century Cohort Marriage and Divorce in England and Wales," *Population Studies* 38 (1984), 439–49.

Schoen, Robert, John Baj, and Karen Woodrow, "Marriage and Divorce in Twentieth-Century Belgian Cohorts," *Journal of Family History* 9 (1984).

Sellin, Johan Thorsten, *Marriage and Divorce Legislation in Sweden* (pub. Ph.D. diss., University of Pennsylvania, 1922).

Shanley, Mary Lyndon, "'One Must Ride Behind': Married Women's Rights and the Divorce Act of 1857," *Victorian Studies* 25 (1982), 355–76.

Sharpe, J. A., "Domestic Homicide in Early Modern England," *Historical Journal* 24 (1981), 29–48.

Smith, David Baird, "The Reformers and Divorce: A Study on Consistorial Jurisdiction," *Scottish Historical Review* 9 (1911), 10–36.

Smith, Kimberley, "Divorce in Nova Scotia, 1750–1890," in J. Phillips and P. Girard (eds.), *Essays in the History of Canadian Law, Volume 3: The Nova Scotian Experience* (Toronto, in press).

Smith, Preserved, "German Opinion of the Divorce of Henry VIII," *English Historical Review* 27 (1912), 678–81.

Spalletta, Matteo, "Divorce in Colonial New York," *New York Historical Society Quarterly* 39 (1955), 422–40.

Staves, Susan, "Money for Honor: Damages for Criminal Conversation," *Studies in Eighteenth-Century Culture* 11 (1982), 279–97.

Stone, Darwell, *Divorce and Re-Marriage* (London, 1913).

Studies on Divorce (Law Reform Commission of Canada, Ottawa, 1975).

Sumner, J. D., Jr., "The South Carolina Divorce Act of 1949," *South Carolina Law Quarterly* 3 (1951), 253–302.

Sundby, Olof, *Luthers Äktenskapsuppfattning: En Studie i den Kyrkdiga äktenskapsdebatten i Sverige efter 1900* (Stockholm, 1959).

Swisher, Peter Nash, "Foreign Migratory Divorces: A Reappraisal," *Journal of Family Law* 21 (1982–3), 9–52.

Tanner, Tony, *Adultery in the Novel: Contract and Transgression* (Baltimore, 1979).

Tebbs, H. V., *Essay on the "Scriptural Doctrines of Adultery and Divorce, and on the Criminal Character and Punishment of Adultery by the Ancient Laws of England and Other Countries"* (London, 1822).

Thibault-Laurent, Gérard, *La première introduction du divorce en France sous la Révolution et l'Empire* (Montpellier, 1938).

Thieme, Hans, *Die Ehescheidung Heinrichs VIII. und die europäischen Universitäten* (Karlsruhe, 1957).

Thornes, Barbara, and Jean Collard, *Who Divorces?* (London, 1979).

Tomass, J., "East German Law of Divorce," in E. J. Cohn (ed.), *Manual of German Law* (London, 1971).

Tomes, Nancy, "'A Torrent of Abuse': Crimes of Violence between Working-class Men and Women in London, 1840–1875," *Journal of Social History* 11 (1978), 328–45.

Traer, James F., "The French Family Court," *History* 196 (1974), 211–28.

Warner, Hugh C., *Divorce and Remarriage: What the Church Believes and Why* (London, 1954).

Weisberg, D. Kelly, "Under Great Temptations Here: Women and Divorce Law in Puritan Massachusetts," in Weisberg, *Women and the Law* II, 117–32.

Select bibliography

(ed.), *Women and the Law: A Social Historical Perspective* (2 vols., Cambridge, Mass., 1982).

Weitzman, Lenore J., *The Divorce Revolution: The Unexpected Social and Economic Consequences for Women and Children in America* (New York, 1985).

Whitney, Henry C., *Marriage and Divorce* (New York, 1894).

Willcox, Walter F., *The Divorce Problem: A Study in Statistics* (New York, 1897).

Winnett, A. R., *Divorce and Remarriage in Anglicanism* (London, 1958).

The Church and Divorce: A Factual Survey (London, 1968).

Wires, Richard, *The Divorce Issue and Reform in Nineteenth-Century Indiana* (Muncie, 1967).

Wolfram, Sybil, "Divorce in England, 1700–1857," *Oxford Journal of Legal Studies* 5 (1985), 155–86.

Woodhouse, Margaret K., "The Marriage and Divorce Bill of 1857," *American Journal of Legal History* 3 (1959), 260–75.

Woolsey, Timothy Dwight, *Essay on Divorce and Divorce Legislation, with Special Reference to the United States* (London, 1869).

Working Women and Divorce: An Account of Evidence Given on Behalf of the Women's Cooperative Guild before the Royal Commission on Divorce (London, 1911).

Wright, Carroll D., *A Report on Marriage and Divorce in the United States, 1867 to 1906* (Washington, D.C., 1909).

Yaron, Reuven, "On Divorce in Old Testament Times," *Revue internationale des droits de l'Antiquité* 3ᵉ série, 4 (1957), 117–28.

C.1 Marriage and the family:
Primary works first published before 1900

A. B., *A Letter of Advice concerning Marriage* (London, 1676).

Abbot, Robert, *A Wedding Sermon preached at Bentley in Darbyshire, upon Michaelmas day last past Anno Domini 1607* (London, 1608).

A Christian Family Builded by God, Directing all Governours of Families how to act (London, 1653).

Allestree, Richard, *The Ladies Calling* (Oxford, 1673).

Ames, William, *Conscience with the Power and Cases thereof* (n.p., 1639).

Astell, Mary, *Reflections upon Marriage* (London, 1700).

Augustine, *De bono conjugali* and *De incompetentibus nuptiis*, in *Treatises on Marriage and Other Subjects* (ed. R. J. Defferrari, New York, 1955).

Becon, Thomas, *The Catechism of Thomas Becon* (ed. John Ayre, Cambridge, 1884).

Bucer, Martin, *Martini Buceri Opera Latina* (ed. François Wendel, Paris, 1965).

Bullinger, Heinrich, *The Christen State of Matrimonye, wherein housbandes and wyfes lerne to kepe house together with loue* (n.p., 1543).

Fiftie Godlie and Learned Sermons, diuided into fiue Decades, conteyning the Chiefe and principall pointes of Christian Religion (London, 1577).

The Decades of Henry Bullinger (ed. Thomas Harding, Cambridge, 1852).

Bullinger, Heinrich, *The Golden Boke of Christen Matrimonye* (n.p., 1543).

Calvin, John, *The First Epistle of Paul the Apostle to the Corinthians* (Edinburgh, 1960).

Institutes of the Christian Religion (2 vols., Philadelphia, 1960).

Carter, Thomas, *Carters Christian Common Wealth; Or Domesticall Dutyes deciphered* (London, 1627).

655

Select bibliography

Cerfvol, de [pseud.], *La Gamologie, ou de l'éducation des filles destinées au mariage* (Paris, 1772).

Chudleigh, Mary ["Eugenia," psued.], *The Female Preacher. Being an Answer to a late Rude and Scandalous Wedding Sermon by Mr. John Sprint* (London, n.d.).

Crofts, Robert, *The Lover: or Nuptiall Love* (London, 1638).

Defoe, Daniel, *A Treatise Concerning the use and Abuse of the Marriage Bed* (London, 1727).

Dod, John, and Robert Cleaver, *A Godlie Forme of Householde Government* (London, 1612).

Dwight, Timothy, *Theology Explained and Defended in a Series of Sermons* (3 vols., London, 1827).

Gataker, Thomas, *Marriage Duties Briefly Couched Together; out of Colossians, 3.18,19* (London, 1620).

A Wife in Deed. A Sermon concerning the Matter of Marriage (London, 1624).

Hardy, Nathaniel, *Love and Fear: The Inseparable Twins of a Blest Matrimony* (London, 1658).

Hume, David, *Essays* (London, 1741).

Knox, John, *The Works of John Knox* (ed. David Laing, Edinburgh, 1848).

Lawes Resolutions of Women's Rights (London, 1639).

The Laws Respecting Women, As they regard their Natural Rights, or their Connections and Conduct (London, 1777).

A Letter to a Member of Parliament with Two Discourses enclosed in it. The one Shewing the Reason why a Law should pass to punish Adultery with Death (London, 1675).

Luther, Martin, *Luther's Works* (54 vols., Philadelphia, St. Louis, 1959–).

Montaigne, Michel de, *Essays* (2 vols., Oxford, 1927).

More, Thomas, *Utopia* in *Complete Works of St. Thomas More* (14 vols., New Haven, 1965).

Niccholes, Alexander, *A Discourse of Marriage and Wiving; and of the greatest Mystery therein contained: How to choose a good Wife* (London, 1615).

Ochino, Bernadino, *A Dialogue of Polygamy* (London, 1657).

Osborne, Francis, *Advice to a Son; or Directions for your better Conduct through the various and most important Encounters of this Life* (London, 1656).

Overbury, Thomas, *A Wife* (London, 1614).

Perkins, William, *Christian Oeconomie: or, a Short Survey of the Right Manner of erecting and Ordering a Familie, according to the Scriptures* in Perkins, *The Workes* (3 vols., Cambridge, 1608–9).

Rogers, Daniel, *Matrimoniall Honour, or, the Mutuall Crowne and comfort of godly, loyall, and Chaste Marriage* (London, 1642).

A Scourge for Poor Robin; or, The Exact Picture of a Bad Husband (London, 1678).

Smith, Henry, *The Sermons of Mr. Henry Smith* (2 vols., London, 1866).

Snawsell, Robert, *A Looking-Glasse for Married Folkes, wherein they may plainly see their Deformities; and also how to behave themselves one to another, and both of them towards God* (London, 1631).

Taylor, Thomas, *A Good Husband and a Good Wife* (London, 1625).

Whately, William, *A Bride-Bush; or, a Wedding Sermon: compendiously describing the duties of Married Persons: By performing whereof, Marriage shall be to them a great Helpe, which now finde it a little Hell* (London, 1617).

A Care-cloth: or a Treatise of the Cumbers and troubles of marriage: Intended to advise them

Select bibliography

that may, to shun them; that may not, well and patiently to bear them (London, 1624).

Wilkinson, Robert, *The Merchant Royall. A Sermon preached at White-Hall upon the sixth of Ianuarie 1607* (London, 1615).

Wing, John, *The Crowne Conjugall or, the Spouse Royall* (Middleburgh, 1620).

C.2 Marriage and the family:
Secondary works, and primary works published from 1900

Aers, David, and Bob Hodge, "'Rational Burning': Milton on Sex and Marriage," *Milton Studies* 13 (1979), 3–33.

Anderson, Michael, *Family Structure in Nineteenth-Century Lancashire* (Cambridge, 1971).

Approaches to the History of the Western Family, 1500–1914 (London, 1980).

Anderson, Olive, "The Incidence of Civil Marriage in Victorian England and Wales," *Past and Present* 69 (1975), 50–87.

Andrew, Donna, "Suicide and the Family in Eighteenth-Century English Periodicals," (unpub. paper, University of Guelph, Ontario).

Backhouse, Constance, "Shifting Patterns in Nineteenth-Century Canadian Custody Law," in David H. Flaherty (ed.), *Essays in the History of Canadian Law* (Toronto, 1981).

"'Pure Patriarchy': Nineteenth-Century Canadian Marriage," *McGill Law Journal* 13 (1986), 264–312.

Baker, Maureen, *The Family: Changing Trends in Canada* (Toronto, 1984).

Baulant, Micheline, "The Scattered Family: Another Aspect of Seventeenth-Century Demography," in Forster and Ranum (eds.), *Family and Society*, 104–16.

Bebel, August, *Women in the Past, Present, and Future* (London, 1885).

Bélier, André, *L'homme et la femme dans la morale calviniste* (Geneva, 1963).

Bels, Pierre, *Le mariage des Protestants français jusqu'en 1685* (Paris, 1968).

Bennett, Judith M., "Medieval Peasant Marriage: An Examination of Marriage Licence Fines in the Liber Gersumarum," in J. A. Raftis (ed.), *Pathways to Medieval Peasants* (Toronto, 1981).

Björnsson, Björn, *The Lutheran Doctrine of Marriage in Modern Icelandic Society* (Oslo, Reykjavik, 1971).

Blaisdell, Charmarie Jenkins, "Calvin's Letters to Women: the Courting of Ladies in High Places," *Sixteenth Century Journal* 13 (1982), 67–84.

Bonfield, Lloyd, Richard M. Smith, and Keith Wrightson (eds.), *The World We Have Gained: Histories of Population and Social Structure* (Oxford, 1986).

Bonnecase, Julien, *La philosophie du Code Napoléon appliquée au droit de la famille* (Paris, 1928).

Boyd, Kenneth M., *Scottish Church Attitudes to Sex, Marriage and the Family, 1850–1914* (Edinburgh, 1980).

Boyer, John W., "Freud, Marriage, and Late Viennese Liberalism: A Commentary from 1905," *Journal of Modern History* 50 (1978), 72–102.

Brand, Paul A., and Paul R. Hyams, "Seigneurial Control of Women's Marriage," *Past and Present* 99 (1983), 123–33.

Bridenthal, Renate, and Claudia Koontz (eds.), *Becoming Visible. Women in European History* (Boston, 1977).

Select bibliography

Brown, Roger Lee, "The Rise and Fall of Fleet Marriages," in Outhwaite, *Marriage and Society*, 117–36.

Brundage, James A., "Concubinage and Marriage in Medieval Canon Law," *Journal of Medieval History* 1 (1975), 1–17.

"Adultery and Fornication: A Study in Legal Theology," in Vern L. Bullough and James A. Brundage (eds.), *Sexual Practice and the Medieval Church* (Buffalo, N.Y., 1982), 129–34.

Bullough, Vern L., *Sexual Variance in Society and History* (Chicago, 1976).

Burguière, André, "Le rituel du mariage en France: pratiques ecclésiastiques et pratiques populaires (XVIe–XVIIIe siècle)," *Annales. Economies Sociétés Civilisations* 33 (1978), 637–49.

Cabourdin, Guy, "Le remariage," *Annales de Démographie Historique* 1978, 305–32.

Cairncross, John, *After Polygamy was Made a Sin* (London, 1974).

Calhoun, Arthur W., *A Social History of the American Family from Colonial Times to the Present* (3 vols., Cleveland, 1919).

Camp, Wesley D., *Marriage and the Family in France since the Revolution* (New York, 1961).

Carlsson, Lizzie, *"Jag giver dig min dotter." Trolovning och äktenskap i den svenska kvinnans äldre historia* (2 vols., Lund, 1965, 1972).

Clark, Homer H., Jr., *Cases and Problems in Domestic Relations* (2nd. edn., St. Paul, Minn., 1974).

Clinton, Catherine, *The Plantation Mistress. Woman's World in the Old South* (New York, 1982).

Corbett, P. E., *The Roman Law of Marriage* (Oxford, 1936).

Darrow, Margaret H., "Popular Concepts of Marital Choice in Eighteenth-Century France," *Journal of Social History* 18 (1985), 261–72.

Davidoff, Leonore, "Mastered for Life: Servant and Wife in Victorian and Edwardian England," *Journal of Social History* 7 (1974), 406–28.

Davies, Kathleen M., " 'The sacred condition of equality' – how original were Puritan doctrines of marriage?" *Social History* 5 (1977), 563–80.

"Continuity and Change in Literary Advice on Marriage," in Outhwaite (ed.), *Marriage and Society*, 58–80.

de Boer, Connie, "The Polls: Marriage – A Decaying Institution?" *Public Opinion Quarterly* 45 (1981), 265–75.

Degler, Carl, *At Odds: Women and the Family in America* (New York, 1980).

Demos, John, *A Little Commonwealth: Family Life in Plymouth Colony* (London, 1970).

"Demography and psychology in the historical study of family life: a personel report," in Laslett and Wall (eds.), *Household and Family in Past Time*, 561–70.

Deniel, Raymond, *Une image de la famille et de la société sous la Restauration* (Paris, 1965).

Dernburg, Heinrich, *Familienrecht und Erbrecht des Privatsrechts Preussens und des Reichs* (n.p., 1896).

Devance, Louis, "Les théories de la famille et de la population chez Fourier et Proudhon," (paper given at the Congrès des Sociétés Savantes, Besançon, 1974).

Dietz, G. W., "La nouvelle législation allemande sur le mariage," *Journal du Droit International* 66 (1939), 52–7.

Dolle, Hans, *Familienrecht: Darstellung des Deutschen Familienrechts mit Rechtsvergleichenden Hinweisen* (Karlsruhe, 1964).

Donahue, Charles, Jr., "The Policy of Alexander the Third's Consent Theory of

Marriage," in Stephen Kuttner (ed.), *Proceedings of the Fourth International Congress of Medieval Canon Law* (Vatican City, 1976).

Duby, Georges, *Medieval Marriage* (Baltimore, 1978).

The Knight, the Lady and the Priest: The Making of Modern Marriage in Medieval France (Cambridge, 1983).

Duby, Georges, and Jacques Le Goff (eds.), *Famille et parenté dans l'Occident médiéval* (Rome, 1977).

Dufour, Albert, *Le mariage dans l'école allemande du droit naturel moderne au XVIIIᵉ siècle* (Paris, 1972).

Dupâquier, Jacques, et al. (eds.), *Marriage and Remarriage in Populations of the Past* (London, 1981).

Dyvrik, Stale, "Gagne-pain ou sentiments? Trait du remariage en Norvège au dix-neuvième siècle," in Dupâquier et al. (eds.), *Marriage and Remarriage*.

Engels, Friedrich, *The Origin of the Family, Private Property and the State* (repr., New York, 1942).

Flandrin, Jean-Louis, *Les amours paysannes* (Paris, 1975).

Families in Former Times (Cambridge, 1979).

Le Sexe et l'Occident (Paris, 1981).

Forster, Robert, and Orest Ranum (eds.), *Family and Society* (Baltimore, 1976).

Frank, Roberta, "Marriage in the Middle Ages: Marriage in Twelfth- and Thirteenth-Century Iceland," *Viator*, 4 (1973), 473–84.

Fraser, Antonia, *The Weaker Vessel: Woman's Lot in Seventeenth-Century England* (London, 1984).

Freed, Doris Jonas, and Timothy B. Walker, "Family Law in the Fifty States: an Overview," *Family Law Quarterly* 18 (1985), 369–471.

Frye, R. M., "The Teachings of Classical Puritanism on Conjugal Love," *Studies in the Renaissance* 2 (1955), 148–59.

Garaud, Michel, *La Révolution française et la famille* (Paris, 1973).

Gaudemet, J., "Législation canonique et attitudes séculières à l'égard du lien matrimonial au XVIIᵉ siècle," *XVIIᵉ Siècle* 102–103 (1974), 15–30.

Gaunt, David, and Orvar Lofgren, "Remarriage in the Nordic Countries: the Cultural and Socio-economic Background," in Dupâquier et al. (eds.), *Marriage and Remarriage*.

Geiger, H. Kent, *The Family in Soviet Russia* (Cambridge, Mass., 1968).

Ghestin, Jacques, "L'action des parlements contre les 'mésalliances' aux XVIIᵉ et XVIIIᵉ siècles," *Revue historique de droit français et étranger* 4th sér., 34 (1956), 74–110, 196–224.

Gillis, John R., *For Better, For Worse: British Marriages, 1600 to the Present* (New York, 1985).

"Married but not Churched: Plebeian Sexual Relations and Marital Nonconformity in Eighteenth-Century Britain," *Eighteenth-Century Life* 9 (1985), 31–42.

Glendon, Mary Ann, *State, Law and Family: Family Law in Transition in the United States and Western Europe* (Amsterdam, 1977).

Goode, William J., *World Revolution and Family Patterns* (New York, 1970).

Goody, Jack, *The Development of the Family and Marriage in Europe* (Cambridge, 1983).

Gouesse, Jean-Marie, "Parenté, famille et mariage en Normandie aux XVIIᵉ et XVIIIᵉ siècles. Présentation d'une source et d'une enquête," *Annales. Economies Sociétés Civilisations* 27 (1972), 1139–54.

Select bibliography

Grimshaw, Patricia, Chris McCouville, and Ellen McEwen (eds.), *Families in Colonial Australia* (Sidney, 1985).

Grossberg, Michael, "Guarding the Altar. Physiological Restrictions and the Rise of State Intervention in Matrimony," *American Journal of Legal History* 26 (1982), 197–226.

Governing the Hearth: Law and the Family in Nineteenth-Century America (Chapel Hill, 1985).

Hafström, Gerhard, *Den svenska familjerättens historia* (Lund, 1975).

Hajnal, John, "European Marriage Patterns in Perspective," in D. V. Glass and D. E. C. Eversley (eds.), *Population in History* (London, 1965), 101–43.

Haller, W., and M. Haller, "The Puritan Art of Love," *Huntington Library Quarterly* 5 (1941–2), 235–72.

Hanawalt, Barbara, *The Ties That Bound: Peasant Families in Medieval England* (New York, 1986).

Hay, William, *William Hay's Lectures on Marriage* [1533–35] (ed. John C. Barry, Edinburgh, 1967).

Helmholz, R. H., *Marriage Litigation in Medieval England* (Cambridge, 1974).

Herlihy, David, "The Making of the Medieval Family: Symmetry, Structure and Sentiment," *Journal of Family History* 8 (1983), 116–30.

Hill, Christopher, *Milton and the English Revolution* (London, 1977).

Holcombe, Lee, *Wives and Property: Reform of the Married Women's Property Law in Nineteenth-Century England* (Toronto, 1983).

Houlbrooke, Ralph, *The English Family, 1450–1700* (London, 1984).

Hufton, Olwen, "Women and the Family Economy in Eighteenth-Century France," *French Historical Studies* 9 (1975), 1–22.

"Women Without Men. Widows and Spinsters in Britain and France in the Eighteenth Century," *Journal of Family History* 9 (1984), 355–76.

Ingram, Martin, "Ecclesiastical Justice in Wiltshire, 1600–1640, with Special Reference to Cases Concerning Sex and Marriage," (unpub. D.Phil. Thesis, University of Oxford, 1976).

Ireland, Ronald D., "Husband and Wife," in *An Introduction to Scottish Legal History* (Edinburgh, 1958), 82–9.

Irwin, Joyce L., *Womanhood in Radical Protestantism, 1525–1675* (New York, 1979).

Johnson, James T., "English Puritan Thought on the Ends of Marriage," *Church History* 38 (1969), 429–36.

A Society Ordained by God: English Puritan Marriage Doctrine in the First Half of the Seventeenth Century (Nashville, N.Y., 1970).

Joyce, George H., *Christian Marriage: An Historical and Doctrinal Study* (London, 1948).

Kanipe, Esther, "The Family, Private Property and the State in France, 1870–1914," (unpub. Ph.D. Dissertation, University of Wisconsin, Madison, 1976).

Karant-Nunn, Susan C., "Continuity and Change: Some Effects of the Reformation on the Women of Zwickau," *Sixteenth Century Journal* 13:2 (1982), 17–42.

Kirkpatrick, Clifford, *Nazi Germany: Its Women and Family Life* (Indianapolis, 1938).

Knodel, John, and Katherine A. Lynch, "The Decline of Remarriage: Evidence from German Village Populations in the Eighteenth and Nineteenth Centuries," *Journal of Family History* 10 (1985), 34–59.

Koehler, Lyle S., *A Search For Power: The "Weaker Sex" in Seventeenth-Century New England* (Urbana, Ill., 1980).

Select bibliography

Labarge, Margaret, *Women in Medieval Life. A Small Sound of the Trumpet* (London, 1986).

Lacey, T. A., *Marriage in Church and State* (London, 1947).

Lacey, W. K., *The Family in Classical Greece* (London, 1968).

Lantz, Herman R., "Romantic Love in the Pre-Modern Period: A Sociological Commentary," *Journal of Social History* 15 (1982), 349–70.

Lasch, Christopher, "The Suppression of Clandestine Marriage in England: the Marriage Act of 1753," *Salmagundi* 26 (1974), 90–109.

Laslett, Peter, "Philippe Ariès and 'la famille'," *Encounter* 66 (March 1976), 80–3.

Family Life and Illicit Love in Earlier Generations (Cambridge, 1977).

The World We Have Lost further explored (London, 1983).

Laslett, Peter, and Richard Wall (eds.), *Household and Family in Past Time* (Cambridge, 1972).

Lauer, Robert H., and Jeanette C. Lauer, "Factors in Long-Term Marriages," *Journal of Family Issues* 7 (1986), 382–90.

Le Bras, Gabriel, "Le mariage dans la théologie et dans le droit de l'Eglise du XIᵉ au XIIIᵉ siècle," *Cahiers de Civilisation Médiévale* 11 (1968), 191–202.

Lebrun, François, *La vie conjugale sous l'Ancien Régime* (Paris, 1975).

Le Roy Ladurie, Emmanuel, *Montaillou* (Harmondsworth, 1980).

Levasseur, Emile, *La population française* (Paris, 1891).

Levine, David, *Family Formation in an Age of Nascent Capitalism* (New York, 1977).

Levitan, Sar A., and Richard S. Belous, *What's Happening to the American Family?* (Baltimore, 1981).

Lévy, Jean-Philippe, "L'Officialité de Paris et les questions familiales à la fin du XIVᵉ siècle," *Etudes d'histoire du droit canonique, dediées à Gabriel Le Bras* (Paris, 1965, 1265–94.

Lucas, Angela, *Women in the Middle Ages: Religion, Marriage and Letters* (New York, 1983).

Macfarlane, Alan, *Marriage and Love in England, 1300–1840* (Oxford, 1986).

Miller, Leo, *John Milton Among the Polygamorphiles* (New York, 1974).

Mitterauer, Michael, and Reinhard Sieder, *The European Family* (Oxford, 1982).

Monter, E. William, "The Consistory of Geneva, 1559–1569," *Bibliothèque d'Humanisme et Renaissance* 38 (1976), 467–84.

"Women in Calvinist Geneva (1500–1800)," *Signs. Journal of Women in Culture and Society* 6 (1980), 189–209.

Morgan, Edmund S., *The Puritan Family: Religion and Domestic Relations in Seventeenth-Century New England* (Boston, 1944, repr. New York, 1966).

Muncy, Raymond Lee, *Sex and Marriage in Utopian Communities in Nineteenth-Century America* (Bloomington, 1973).

Naquet, Alfred, *Religion, Propriété, Famille* (Paris, 1869).

Nicholas, David, *The Domestic Life of a Medieval City: Women, Children, and the Family in Fourteenth-Century Ghent* (Lincoln, Neb., 1985).

Noonan, John T., *Contraception: A History of its Treatment by the Catholic Theologians and Canonists* (Cambridge, Mass., 1965).

Outhwaite, R. B. (ed.), *Marriage and Society: Studies in the Social History of Marriage* (London, 1981).

Ozment, Steven, *When Fathers Ruled: Family Life in Reformation Europe* (Cambridge, Mass., 1983).

Select bibliography

Pascu, St., and V. Pascu, "Le remariage chez les orthodoxes," in Dupâquier et al. (eds.), *Marriage and Remarriage*.

Piltz, Signe, *Luthers Lära om Äkenskapet* (Lund, 1952).

Plakans, Andrejs, *Kinship in the Past: An Anthropology of European Family Life, 1500–1900* (Oxford, 1984).

Powell, C. L., *English Domestic Relations, 1487–1653* (New York, 1917).

Quaife, G. R., *Wanton Wenches and Wayward Wives* (London, 1979).

Rawson, Beryl (ed.), *The Family in Ancient Rome* (London, 1986).

Rordorf, Willy, "Marriage in the New Testament and in the Early Church," *Journal of Ecclesiastical History* 20 (1969), 193–210.

Russell, Bertrand, *Marriage and Morals* (London, 1929).

Schlesinger, Rudolf (ed.), *The Family in the U.S.S.R.* (London, 1949).

Schücking, Levin L., *The Puritan Family: A Social Study from the Literary Sources* (London, 1969).

Searle, Eleanor, "Seigneurial Control of Women's Marriage: the Antecedents and Function of Merchet in England," *Past and Present* 82 (1979), 3–43.

Segalen, Martine, *Nuptialité et alliance: le choix de conjoint dans une commune de l'Eure* (Paris, 1972).

"Le mariage et la femme dans les proverbes du sud de la France," *Annales du Midi* 87 (1975), 265–88.

Amours et mariages de l'ancienne France (Paris, 1981).

Shanley, Mary Lyndon, "Marriage Contract and Social Contract in Seventeenth-Century English Political Thought," *Western Political Quarterly* 32 (1979), 79–91.

Sharpe, J. A., "Plebeian Marriage in Stuart England: Some Evidence from Popular Literature," *Transactions of the Royal Historical Society* 36 (1986), 69–90.

Sheehan, Michael M., "The Formation and Stability of Marriage in Fourteenth-Century England: Evidence of an Ely Register," *Medieval Studies* 33 (1971), 228–63.

Shorter, Edward, *The Making of the Modern Family* (New York, 1975).

Smith, Charles E., *Papal Enforcement of Some Medieval Marriage Laws* (Baton Rouge, 1940, repr. Port Washington, N.Y., 1972).

Smith, Norah, "Sexual Mores and Attitudes in Enlightenment Scotland," in Paul-Gabriel Boucé (ed.), *Sexuality in Eighteenth-Century Britain* (Manchester, 1982), 47–73.

Smout, T. C., "Scottish Marriage, Regular and Irregular, 1500–1940," in Outhwaite (ed.), *Marriage and Society*, 204–36.

Snell, James G., " 'The White Life for Two': The Defence of Marriage and Sexual Morality in Canada, 1890–1914," *Histoire sociale-Social History* 16 (1983), 111–28.

Spengler, Joseph J., *France Faces Depopulation: Postlude Edition, 1936–1976* (Durham, N.C., 1979).

Sponsler, Lucy A., "The Status of Married Women under the Legal System of Spain," *Journal of Legal History* 3 (1982), 125–52.

Stafford, Pauline, *Queens, Concubines and Dowagers: The King's Wife in the Early Middle Ages* (London, 1983).

Stauffeneger, R., "Le mariage à Genève vers 1600," *Société pour l'histoire du droit* 66, fasc. 27 (1966), 317–29.

Stone, Lawrence, *The Family, Sex and Marriage in England, 1500–1800* (London, 1977).

Select bibliography

Taylor, Barbara, *Eve and the New Jerusalem: Socialism and Feminism in the Nineteenth Century* (London, 1983).

Thomas, Keith, "Women and the Civil War Sects," *Past and Present* 13 (1958), 42–62.

"The Double Standard," *Journal of the History of Ideas* 20 (1959), 195–216.

"The Puritans and Adultery. The Act of 1650 Reconsidered," in Donald Pennington and Keith Thomas (eds.), *Puritans and Revolutionaries. Essays in Seventeenth-Century History Presented to Christopher Hill* (Oxford, 1978), 257–82.

Thompson, Roger, *Unfit for Modest Ears* (Totowa, N.J., 1979).

Traer, James F., *Marriage and the Family in Eighteenth-Century France* (Ithaca, N.Y., 1980).

Trumbach, Randolph, *The Rise of the Egalitarian Family* (New York, 1978).

Truxal, Andrew G., and Frances E. Merrill, *The Family in American Culture* (New York, 1947).

Ulrich, Laurel Thatcher, *Good Wives: Images and Reality in the Lives of Women in Northern New England, 1650–1750* (New York, 1982).

Vernier, Chester G., *American Family Laws* (5 vols., Stanford, 1932).

Wall, Richard, "Work, Welfare and the Family: An Illustration of the Adaptive Family Economy," in Bonfield, Smith, and Wrightson (eds.), *The World We Have Gained.*

Weiss, Ira L., *The Family System in America* (New York, 1971).

Wemple, Suzanne, *Women in Frankish Society: Marriage and the Cloister, 500–900* (Philadelphia, 1981).

Wendel, François, *Le mariage à Strasbourg à l'époque de la Réforme, 1520–1692* (Strasbourg, 1928).

Wilmott, P., and M. Young, *Family and Class in a London Suburb* (London, 1960).

Worsley-Bodin, J. F., *Mischiefs of the Marriage-Law: An Essay in Reform* (London, 1932).

Yost, John K., "The Value of Married Life for the Social Order of the Early English Renaissance," *Societas* 6 (1976), 25–39.

Index

665

Index

Church of England, *see* divorce, Church of
  England and
Clement VII, Pope, 73
Cocceji, Henri, 215
Cocceji, Samuel, 201, 215
Code Napoléon, *see* Napoleon I
cohabitation, mandatory, 283–5
concubinage, 18, 30
Connecticut, 139–40, 147, 150, 207, 251,
  315–16, 440–2, 509
consanguinity, *see* impediments to marriage
Constantine, Emperor, 18
contract theory, divorce and, 211–18
correction, moderate, 323–6
  see also cruelty; violence, marital
costs, *see* divorce, costs of
Cranmer, Thomas, 79–81
criminal conversation, 228–30, 294
  see also adultery
Cromwell, Oliver, 129–31
cruelty
  in divorce law, 247, 254, 263–4, 450–1,
    454–5
  in separations, 13, 53, 84, 89
  see also correction, moderate; violence,
    marital
Cuba, as divorce haven, 532

Delaware, 143, 497
Denmark, 51–2, 200, 512, 561–2
depression, economic, 552–5
desertion, 46–7, 48–9, 54–5, 56–8, 89,
  246–7, 252–3, 264–5, 285–9, 370–2,
  389, 434–5
Diderot, Denis, 166
dispensations for marriage, *see* impediments to
  marriage
divorce
  alimony and, 272, 600
  in Ancient Rome, 19
  attitudes toward, 105–16, 247–8, 524,
    610–11, 615–16, 624–6, 627–8, 636
  besom, 295
  Calvin and, 53–62
  children and, 214, 218–19, 270–1, 273–4,
    586, 600–2
  Church of England and, xv, 107–8, 113,
    131, 203–4, 419–20, 466, 467–8
  conservative reaction against, 461–3,
    489–93
  costs of, 228n, 418, 606–7, 612–13
  courts, 58, 60, 62–3, 194–202, 266–8

custody of children after, 273–4, 600–2
  as death substitute, 392–4
  definitions of, 3–5
  depression (economic) and, 552–5
  drunkenness as ground for, 495–7
  economic influences on, 552–5, 617–18
  emulation pattern in, 617
  in English Civil War, 116–19
  Enlightenment and, 163–75
  factors associated with, 584–9, 630–3
  fault/no fault, 90–2, 550, 561–72
  feedback effect, 632–3, 639
  French Revolution and, 175–85
  incompatibility as ground for, 120–2
  in international law, 438, 476–8
  liberalism and, 487–8
  Luther and, 45–52
  marriage breakdown, relationship to,
    316–21, 522–3, 633
  migratory, 473–8, 531–3
  mutual consent, by, 18, 260
  in New Testament, 2, 17–18
  no fault, *see* divorce, fault/no fault
  Orthodox church and, 22–3
  parliamentary, 132–3, 227–41
  Pauline Privilege and, 2, 17–18, 55–6,
    67–8, 70 .
  penitentials on, 21–2, 28–9
  policies, meaning of, 493–5
  and political ideologies, 116–19, 533–52
  popular rituals of, 31–4, 294–6
  population policies and, 168–71, 218–20,
    426
  Protestants and, 84–94, 201–2
  Puritans (English) and, 115–16, 131
  race and, 587
  radical Reformation and, 65–9
  Reformation and, 84–94, 163–4, 167
  research on, xii, 582–90
  Roman Catholic church on, 1–5, 15–30,
    34–6, 274–5, 466, 489–90; *see also*
    France, Roman Catholic church and
    divorce in
  secularization and, 194–202, 210–26
  sex ratio of petitioners for, 33–4, 230–1,
    238, 260–2, 275–6, 277
  social class and, 231–2, 268–70, 587–8,
    592–4
  socialism and, 481–8
  temperance movement and, 495–7
  war and, 458–60, 516–22, 544, 555–8
  women and, 122–3, 425, 484, 587, 592–4,

666

Index

Index

Index

Milton, John, 119–26, 128–9, 213, 216, 220
Minnesota, 509
Mississippi, 451
Missouri, 450
Montaigne, Michel de, 38–9, 163
Montana, 454
Montesquieu, Charles Louis Secondat, baron de, 171
More, Thomas, 1, 38
Morelly, 166
mortality, 392–4
Münster, 68–9
murder, spouse, 105, 281–2, 306–10, 345, 352, 427
Mussolini, Benito, 545, 546, 547
mutual consent, divorce by, 18, 260

Napoleon I, Emperor of France, 185–8
Napoleon III, Emperor of France, 422–3
Naquet, Alfred, 423–5, 486
national socialism, 547–51
natural law, divorce and, 210–18
Nazi divorce law, see national socialism
Netherlands, 134, 136, 206, 408–9, 517, 560
Nevada, 454, 475–6, 512, 531
New Brunswick, 434
New England, 134–5, 144–5, 241–56, 315–16, 351
New Hampshire, 138–9, 154, 155, 243, 443
New Haven, see Connecticut
New Jersey, 143, 152–3, 154, 509
New South Wales, 470
New Testament, divorce in, 2, 17–18
New York State, 141–2, 154, 157, 248–9, 443–5, 512, 531, 568–9
New Zealand, 435–6, 497, 510–1, 530, 558
Nicholas I, Pope, 25
Nietzsche, Friedrich, 492
no-fault divorce, see divorce, fault/no fault
Northampton, Marquis of, 79–81, 203
North Carolina, 154, 157, 445, 446–9
North Dakota, 454, 512
Norway, 51–2, 209, 277n118, 512
Nova Scotia, 150–1, 434
nullification of marriage, see annulment of marriage
Nuremberg, 195

Oecolampadius, Johannes, 64–5
Ohio, 452–3, 456, 509
Ontario, 530
Orthodox church, and divorce, 22–3

Owen, Robert, 481–2, 483–4, 484–6
Owen, Robert Dale, 457–8

parliamentary divorce, see England and Wales, parliamentary divorce
Pauline Privilege, 2, 17–18, 55–6, 67–8, 70
penitentials, 21–2, 28–9
Pennsylvania, 142–3, 148, 150, 151–2, 154, 155–7, 440, 510
Philip, landgrave of Hesse, 76
Pius VII, Pope, 188
Pius IX, Pope, 425, 465–6, 489
Plymouth Colony, 135–6, 147, 206–7, 243
politics, and divorce, 116–19, 258, 265–6, 533–52
polygamy, see bigamy
poor-relief, 383–4
Portugal, 432–3, 505–6, 541–3, 556, 577
poverty and marriage breakdown, 287, 371, 401–2, 383–4
prayer, 311–12
Prince Edward Island, 434
prostitution, 496, 499
Protestants
    and adultery, 43–4, 45–62, 77–8, 86–9
    and divorce, 84–94, 201–2
    and marriage, 41–4, 92–4
Prussia, 200–1, 215, 428–30
Pufendorf, Samuel, 212–13
Puritans (English)
    and divorce, 115–16, 131
    and marriage, 96n1, 329–30

Québec, 437, 439

race, and divorce, 587
Reformatio Legum Ecclesiasticarum, see divorce, Church of England
Reformation
    and divorce, 84–94, 163–4, 167
    radical, 65–9
remarriage, 3–4, 28–9, 47–8, 274, 367–9, 373, 380, 413–14, 467–8, 524, 603–4
Reno divorces, see Nevada
Rhode Island, 139, 154, 207, 243, 443
rituals, of divorce, 31–4, 294–6
Roman Catholic church
    on adultery, 13, 86
    councils, 21–4, 34–6
    on divorce, 1–5, 15–30, 34–6, 274–5, 466, 489–90
    and marriage, 15–17, 26–7, 27–8, 34–5

670

Index

Rome, Ancient, divorce in, 19
Roos, Lord, 132
Roosevelt, Theodore, 469
rough music, *see* charivaris
Russell, Bertrand, 537, 637n
Russian Revolution, *see* USSR

Salazar, Oliveira, 541–2, 577
Scotland, 60–2, 196, 204, 222–3, 239–40, 352, 497, 512, 530
secularization, 180, 191–226 passim
Selden, John, 125–6
separation
  in France, *see* France, separations
  informal, 283–5, 286
  judicial, 4, 13–15, 159–62, 229–30, 603–5
  seven-year absence rule, 298–9
sexuality, 15–17, 43–4, 46, 87–9, 384–5, 388–9, 498–500
  see also adultery; double standard of sexual morality
Shakers, 507
Shaw, George Bernard, 537
Simpson, Wallis, 527–9
social purity movement, 495–500
socialism and divorce, 481–8
solitary living, 283–5, 384–6
South Carolina, 158, 445
South Dakota, 454, 456, 475
Spain, 29, 34, 352, 433, 538–41, 577–8
Stanton, Elizabeth Cady, 501, 502
suicide, 310–11
Sweden, 50–1, 196–200, 209, 409–10, 511–12, 517, 556, 563, 571
Switzerland, 432, 463, 512, 556–7
Syllabus of Errors, see Pius IX, Pope

Taylor, Harriet, 488
temperance movement, 495–7, 503, 506–7
Tennessee, 154, 445
Tertullian, 28, 37
Texas, 445, 446
Trent, council of, 34–6
Trieste, 545
Tyndale, William, 77–9

Uncumber, St., 311–12
United States
  divorce laws, 439–61 passim, 468–70, 570
  divorces, 458–60, 462, 517, 531, 533, 553, 557, 558, 559, 619, 624
  marriage, 518

reputation of divorce laws, 465
  see also entries under individual colonies and states
urbanization, 271–2, 376–7
USSR, 523, 534–8
utopian socialists and divorce, 481–6, 490–1

venereal disease, 520
Vermont, 154, 443
violence, marital, 323–44 passim
  attitudes toward, 160, 262–3, 308–9, 323–30, 334–8, 339–41
  extent in past, 324, 333–4, 340–1, 342–3
  gender and, 328–9, 337–8
  law relative to, 14, 324–6, 329–34, 340–1
  marriage breakdown and, 342–4
  social class and, 341–2
  see also correction, moderate; cruelty; murder, spouse
Virginia, 145, 157, 207, 445, 446, 497
Visigoths, 23
visitations, 283–4, 297–8
Voltaire, 635

Wales, *see* divorce laws, England and Wales; divorce rates and numbers, England and Wales; England
war
  desertion and, 265
  see also American Civil War; English Civil War; World War I; World War II
Whately, William, 112–13, 213, 220
wife-beating, *see* correction, moderate; violence, marital
wife sale, 289–94, 388
  and adultery, 291–2, 294
witch-hunts, 384–5
Wolff, Christian, 217–18
women
  desertion and, 371–2, 383–4
  marriage breakdown and, 382–4
  property and, 374–5
  and solitary living, 384–6
  spouse murder and, 307–9
  and work, 271–2, 378–9, 379–80; *see also* family economy
  see also divorce, sex ratio of petitioners; divorce, women and; violence, marital
Women's Christian Temperance Union and divorce, 496, 503, 506–7
women's rights movement and divorce, 500–7, 514–15, 524

671